THOMSON

WADSWORTH

Publisher: Holly J. Allen
Religion Editor: Steve Wainwright
Assistant Editor: Kara Kindstrom
Editorial Assistant: Anna Lustig
Marketing Manager: Dave Garrison
Marketing Assistant: Justine Ferguson
Project Manager, Editorial Production: Mary Noel

Print/Media Buyer: Rebecca Cross
Permissions Editor: Stephanie Keough-Hedges
Production Service: Scott Rohr/Buuji, Inc.
Copy Editor: Heather McElwain
Cover Designer: Ross Carron Design
Cover Printer: Webcom, Ltd.
Compositor: Buuji, Inc.
Printer: Webcom, Ltd.

Printed in Canada
1 2 3 4 5 6 7 06 05 04 03 02

For more information about our products,
contact us at:
Thomson Learning Academic Resource Center
1-800-423-0563

For permission to use material from this text,
contact us by:
Phone: 1-800-730-2214   **Fax:** 1-800-730-2215
Web: http://www.thomsonrights.com

Library of Congress Cataloging-in-Publication Data
Theory and method in the study of religion :
a selection of critical readings/[edited by],
Carl Olson.
    p. cm.
    Includes biographical references and index.
    ISBN 0-534-53474-0 (alk. paper)
    1. Religion—Methodology. 2. Religion—
Study and teaching. I. Olson, Carl.

BL41 .T48 2002
200'.71—dc21   2001056838

Wadsworth/Thomson Learning
10 Davis Drive
Belmont, CA 94002-3098
USA

Asia
Thomson Learning
5 Shenton Way #01-01
UIC Building
Singapore 068808

Australia
Nelson Thomson Learning
102 Dodds Street
South Melbourne, Victoria 3205
Australia

Canada
Nelson Thomson Learning
1120 Birchmount Road
Toronto, Ontario M1K 5G4
Canada

Europe/Middle East/Africa
Thomson Learning
Berkshire House
168-173 High Holborn
London WC1 V7AA
United Kingdom

Latin America
Thomson Learning
Seneca, 53
Colonia Polanco
11560 Mexico D.F.
Mexico

Spain
Paraninfo Thomson Learning
Calle/Magallanes, 25
28015 Madrid, Spain

Theory and Method in the Study of Religion

A Selection of Critical Readings

Carl Olson
Allegheny College

THOMSON
™
WADSWORTH

Australia • Canada • Mexico • Singapore • Spain • United Kingdom • United States

This book is dedicated to all the past and future Allegheny College students who have endured and benefited from the junior seminar in Religious Studies on the topic of theory and method in the study of religion.

Contents

Chapter 5

Chapter 6

Chapter 7

Chapter 11

Preface

While teaching a required junior seminar for Religious Studies department majors and minors on the topic of method and theory in the study of religion, I noticed some years ago a lack of a good anthology of critical readings. Therefore, I resorted to course packs for selected readings to save students money because the authors that I wanted them to read were spread over several fields. Thus, this anthology was born in an undergraduate college course that wanted to explore the nature of religion as defined by different authors from diverse fields and to explore different methodological approaches to the subject of religion.

The overall purpose of this anthology is to provide students of religion with a useful collection of theoretical essays or statements about the nature of religion and different methodological ways of approaching a complex subject. In conjunction with each of the specific approaches, this anthology will include one or more critical essays or comments from scholars opposed to or critical of the specific position taken by a particular approach to the subject of religion. The purpose of this point/counterpoint approach is to enable students to grasp how someone might criticize a specific position, to discern its possible weak or problematic aspects, to sharpen the critical thinking skills of students, to stimulate classroom discussion, and to encourage students to develop their own positions by examining the advantages and disadvantages of particular theories.

The major issues upon which this anthology concentrates are the nature of religion and the variety of methods used to study religious phenomena. This approach will raise several related issues: What is the nature of religious studies? What is the origin of religion? What was the context in which different scholars studied religion and developed their theories? What preconceptions, biases, or beliefs did these scholars bring to the study of religion? Did some theorists have a philosophical, theological, political, or scientific agenda in addition to their intention to study religion? Did the theorists view religion in a negative or positive way? What was the purpose of a particular scholar? If scholars approached religion with certain preconceptions, how did these affect their theories of religion? To begin to answer such questions, it is wise to begin with theorists in the nineteenth century. This gives students of religion an opportunity to understand the definitions of religion and the methodological approaches against which twentieth-century scholars reacted.

Beside the theoretical and critical structure of this anthology, it is arranged to expose students to a wide variety of approaches to the study of religion such as the following: sociological, phenomenological, psychological, historical, anthropological, and structural. Because these scholarly disciplines often overlap with others for a specific theorist, the names of these various approaches to the subject of religion are to be conceived more as guides to understanding rather than as definite categories. This anthology also includes more recent approaches to the study of religion like ecological, feminist, and postmortem perspectives.

Even though there is a great deal of selectivity embodied in the editorial decision of what to include in the text, the text is designed, nonetheless, to offer college instructors enough material to allow them an opportunity to choose their own set of readings and to emphasize what they think is most important. Each section of the text includes an introduction by the editor to the issues raised by the theorists and their critics. The overall purpose of these introductions is to orientate students to the readings and to alert students to important issues and problems to be discussed in a particular section. These editorial introductions are not intended to enforce a particular approach as the best.

It is necessary to thank all the authors used in this anthology because without their contributions to the study of religion there would be no anthology in the first place. I also want to thank the folks at Wadsworth Publishing for their support, suggestions, and encouragement throughout this process, especially Justine Ferguson, Kara Kindstrom, and Worth Hawes. Although he has moved to another area of the company, I want to thank especially Peter Adams for his help, warm conversations, humor, and enthusiasm for this text from the start of the process. I would be remiss if I did not mention the many reviewers of my early proposal and text: Courtney Bender, Columbia University; Michel Desjardins, Wilfrid Laurier University; Tracy Fessenden, Arizona State University; Rosemary Drage Hale, Concordia University; John Kelsay, Florida State University; Mary N. MacDonald, Le Moyne College; Luther H. Martin, University of Vermont; and Brian Wilson, Western Michigan University. Their sagacious, critical, and constructive criticisms have improved the final product, a process that I intend to continue in the future with later editions. There were times when reviewers made conflicting suggestions. Thus I had to make some judgments about what to include or exclude based on the intended audience, the purpose of the text, and the difficulty of the readings. Special thanks go to Dean Lloyd Michaels, who will never be able to beat Andre Agassi in a tennis match even in his dreams, and President Richard Cook for making me the holder of the Teacher-Scholar Professorship in the Humanities at Allegheny College, which has provided me time to devote to this work. I will always be in the debt of my colleague Glenn Holland for his friendship over the years, his humor, and fortitude for enduring me. As for my colleague Helene Russell, I want to wish her all the best on her new adventures in seminary education and to let her know that we will miss her contributions to the welfare of the department. I want to offer thanks belatedly to my students in the junior seminars over the years for struggling with many of the theorists in this anthology. Allegheny students Christy Repep, Erin Barr, and wrong-way Tibor Solymosi helped with research chores in the library. Moreover, I want to thank the wonderful help that I received from the library personnel and computer service folks at the college on the hill, especially Jim Fadden and Karen Stone. And last, I want to thank my saintly wife Peggy. You are the best and most understanding wife that a writing hack like me could ever have or hope for in this life.

Chapter 1

Introduction

How is it possible to make sense of something that motivates people to love or hate, to save some and kill others, and to meet the needs of some but not others? How do you comprehend something that binds you or frees you? How can you understand something that unites people or separates them? How do you make sense of something that celebrates life or rejects it? How do you grasp something that requires a regimented and constrained lifestyle of an ascetic, while allowing the ecstatic dance of a mystic or shaman? How do you comprehend something that might encourage rational thinking or cause madness? This mysterious and fascinating something is religion.

When I teach an introduction to the study of religion to my college students, I often begin the course by asking students to define the nature of religion. After a student defines the subject, I write a shortened version of the definition on the blackboard until we have several definitions to dissect and discuss. This type of pedagogical exercise enables students to see that there are a variety of ways to define the nature of religion, that no single definition of religion is totally adequate when one views it, for instance, from a comparative perspective, and that the nature of religion is difficult to express in language. And yet, prior to the exercise, all students think they know what religion is in some general sense. When students are challenged to put the nature of religion into words, they struggle to define what seemed so obvious to them.

Students are not the only group to exhibit problems with defining religion. Scholars also hold wide varieties of opinion about the nature of religion. The Protestant theologian Paul Tillich (1886–1965) claims that religion is one's ultimate concern.[1] While it is necessarily true that human beings have many concerns, Tillich asserts that religion is a concern that is ultimate for humans, to the exclusion of conditional concerns. When a conditional or preliminary concern (for example, a person, nation, wealth, or thing) is turned into something ultimate, it becomes a form of idolatry.[2] Many scholars have adopted this definition because it holds an advantage over other definitions in the sense that it can be applied cross-culturally. For some scholars, Tillich's definition also offers what can be called a surplus of meaning that no one religious tradition can adequately capture because of the widespread diversity of religious beliefs, practices, institutions, and histories among the dead and living religious traditions of the world. Even though many scholars find Tillich's definition useful, other voices have investigated the term *religion* and concluded that it is not a very useful term.

Probably the best example of such a scholar is Wilfred Cantwell Smith. In his book *The Meaning and End of Religion,* he traces the evolution of the term *religion* (*religio*) in the West. Smith shows how the term changed meanings over time, how its origin is Western, how it becomes intellectualized over time, and how it becomes connected to polemics and apologetics. If this type of scenario is true, it is necessary to ask oneself the following question: Can the term *religion* be applied to non-Western traditions? The plural term *religions* represents the abstraction, depersonalization, and reification of the term. When it is applied to the religions of foreigners, the plural use of the term represents the tendency to stand outside of the religions of others with the intention most often of refuting them by a process of external classification. The result of such a development is that religion becomes something generic. Smith concludes that the term *religion* confuses us, distorts that to which we are referring, and is ultimately unnecessary. Part of the problem can be traced to the term itself because it lacks precision, utility, and legitimacy.

Due to the problematic nature of the terms *religion* and *religions,* Smith thinks that it is still important to embrace both the mundane and transcendent elements in the life of a person. He proposes a link between "cumulative tradition" on the one hand, and "faith" on the other. By the former, Smith means the objective data of a religious tradition (temples, scriptures, legal and social institutions, myths, and so forth). The link between the historical tradition and faith, which is a personal element, is the living person. If we follow Smith's suggestion and drop the term *religion* because of its many meanings, ambiguity, and confusing nature, we can substitute the terms *faith* or *faiths* to refer to our own personal religious position or that of others. Although there have been some scholars who followed Smith's suggestions, the majority have opted to retain the term *religion* even with its problematic and elusive nature.

One problem associated with adequately defining religion is the diversity of forms that it assumes around the world, contributing to widely different interpretations from many perspectives. With respect to the problematic nature of religion, John Hick concludes in his book, *An Interpretation of Religion,* that religion cannot be defined; it can only be described. As we have witnessed, the plural nature of religions lead inevitably to issues of precise terminology. Hick denies that the plural religions share a common essence. However, religions do share something in common. Citing the philosophy of Ludwig Wittgenstein and the discussion of family resemblance, Hick applies this concept to religion, and he argues that religions have no common essence. Religions are like members in a family, as they share many resemblances and differences. Each religious tradition is "similar in important respects to some others in the family, though not in all respects to any or in any respect to all."[3] Religions share in common a concern with the "real," a concept that Hick thinks fits better within a cross-cultural context. He gives his rationale:

> "The real" is then, I suggest, as good a generic name as we have for that which is affirmed in the varying forms of transcendent religious belief. For it is used within the major theistic and non-theistic traditions and yet is neutral between their very different ways of conceiving, experiencing and responding to that which they affirm in these diverse ways.[4]

Hick acknowledges that there are significant differences in the ways that diverse cultures conceive, experience, and respond to the so-called "real." Hick's position demonstrates, in part, a search for neutral language by scholars and an attempt to get an intellectual handle on the nature of a subject that is so difficult to grasp.

From a different perspective, Jonathan Z. Smith's view of problems associated with finding an adequate definition of religion turns away from the external world to the interior world of the scholar. Smith asserts that the scholar imagines religion because there is no real data for it. Smith does not mean that there are no data, expressions, phenomena, experiences, and so forth that are religious in some sense. What he means is that "there is no data for religion" itself. By means of the reflective imagination, a scholar creates religion itself. Smith explains the process that takes place in the following way:

> Religion is solely the creation of the scholar's study. It is created for the scholar's analytic purposes by his imaginative acts of comparison and generalization. Religion has no independent existence apart from the academy.[5]

Smith encourages the student and scholar of religion to become aware that religion itself is a construct of academic life.

From a different perspective, the postmodern thinker Mark C. Taylor captures the elusive nature of religion very nicely in his book entitled *About Religion*. In a sense, Taylor's remarks summarize the difficulty of coming to grips with religion:

> Religion is about a certain about. What religion is about, however, remains obscure for it is never quite there—nor is it exactly not there. Religion is about what is always slipping away. It is, therefore, impossible to grasp what religion is about—unless, perhaps, what we grasp is the impossibility of grasping. Even when we think we have it surrounded, religion eludes us. This strange slipping away is no mere disappearance but a withdrawal that allows appearances to appear. Though never here, what religion is about is not elsewhere.[6]

Besides revealing a philosophy of language in which terms like *religion* are mere signs that are supplements and do not signify anything permanent, this quotation indicates the slippery nature of the subject. It is thus not possible for us to be absolutely certain where to look for religion. In fact, we are often surprised by it. Taylor is especially interested in finding religion in the least expected places.

Overall, it is possible to classify the definition of religion into four general types: experiential, substantive, functionalist, and family resemblance. The experiential definition tries to identify a general religious experience and make it the primary characteristic feature of all religions (for example, the experience of the holy in the theory of Otto). The substantive definition examines the beliefs associated with various religions and seeks a common denominator (for example, Edward B. Tylor's definition of religion as belief in spiritual beings). Rather than what is believed, functionalist definitions focus on how people believe something and what role it plays in their everyday lives (Malinowski's theory, for example). This theory presupposes that everyone possesses certain individual and social needs that must be met, and religion becomes identified with a system of beliefs, practices, or symbols that serve to meet those needs. A family resemblance definition is evident in the work of John Hick and others that assert "religions are bound together in a family by a network of overlapping similarities and not by any strict identity; and that our conception of what counts as relevant similarities and a sufficient selection of religion-making characteristic can and must be extended in the actual survey and study of religions."[7] Using the family resemblance type of definition, it is possible to identity four major dimensions of religion: (1) theoretical (beliefs, myths, and doctrines, for example); (2) practical (rites and moral codes); (3) social (institutions and roles of laity and sacred personages); and (4) experiential (emotions, visions, attitudes). Religions can also be distinguished by characteristic kinds of objects (for example, gods, spirits, transcendent states), goals (salvation or liberation), and functions (issues of meaning and unity pertaining to social group or personal life).[8]

The experiential, substantive, and functionalist definitions of religion can be grouped together into what is called a monothetic definition. This type of definition is grounded on a set of sine qua non characteristics or a single sine qua non characteristic, whereas the family resemblance type of definition is a polythetic definition that is based on several characteristics. The monothetic type is based on a more absolute criteria or set of criteria, whereas the polythetic is based on a more relative identification. The polythetic is more flexible because not all characteristics or a single characteristic must be present for it to represent a religion, whereas the monothetic is more restrictive. This does not imply that the polythetic is without problems, because a scholar must ask oneself a number of questions: How many characteristics are sufficient to qualify as a religion? Will one's definition become ethnocentric if one chooses a particular religion as one's model?[9] In his book entitled *Dimensions of the Sacred,* Ninian Smart provides a good example of the polythetic approach and his use of what he calls dimensions.

With respect to the subject of religion and the readings in this anthology, it behooves students to ask themselves the following types of questions: Is my definition based on a distinction between what is sacred and profane? Does my definition of religion embody a rationalist insinuation that religion is a primitive way to explain occurrences in life? Does my definition of religion reflect primarily what people believe? Or is my definition of religion based according to what people do? Is my notion of religion a substantive definition? Does my attempt to describe religion depict it as a timeless essence? Is it possible that my definition of religion embodies a hidden metaphysical agenda? Depending on how one answers these types of questions, a definition may be either adequate or inadequate for one's purposes. Although it might seem difficult to believe because of the elusive nature of religion, the scholarly pursuit of its nature and the study of related aspects has led to what is called "Religious Studies" in many colleges and universities.

Religious Studies, Theology, and Disciplines

Religious studies is a field that German scholars have called *Religionswissenschaft* (science of religions), in contrast to *Naturwissenschaft* (natural science). The former field is part of what German scholars call *Geistewissenschaften*. Without being modeled necessarily on the natural sciences, the German term *Wissenschaft* (science) includes humanistic and social studies that are regarded as rigorous scholarly sciences, whereas the English usage tends to refer to the natural scientific model. Thus the German term *Wissenschaft* (science) is much wider in meaning and scope than the English term. Based on the German usage of the term, the study of religion must not be confused, however, with natural science, which concentrates on objects in the natural world, whereas the study of religion is concerned with data connected to persons. During the term's formative period of usage, *Religionswissenschaft* served as a synonym for comparative religion and a historical philological science. The use of the term *Religionswissenschaft* by a pioneering scholar like F. Max Müller, who is commonly given credit for initiating a call for a science of religion, influenced and shaped the field of religion, and Müller's ambiguous use of the term *science* continues to the present time. Nonetheless, to refer to religious studies as a field suggests that it encompasses a broad area that "includes all studies concerned with religious data, their observation, ascertainment, description, explanation, analysis, understanding, [and] interpretation."[10] This field is a product of Enlightenment thought, and it is especially a combination of Cartesian and Kantian perspectives.

Enlightenment thinkers viewed religion as eminently human. Their attempt to define religion was pursued within the context of an effort to discern the essential characteristics of human nature, which they tended to view as more complex than the old Aristotelian definition of a human being as a rational animal. They wanted to include thoughts, actions, and feelings as basic functions or capacities of human nature. The Enlightenment represented a resurgence of optimism in human capabilities guided by the light of reason, a stress upon living the good life on earth, freedom from the bonds of ignorance and superstition, emphasis on natural rights, a belief in the value of science and progress, and a conviction about the autonomy of humans. The Enlightenment stressed the importance of liberty, equality, tolerance, and common sense. There was a strong belief in the natural goodness and perfectibility of human nature, along with a conviction that a natural law prescribes the pursuit of pleasure, profit, and property. Moreover, the period exemplified a secularization of knowledge and thought.

Within the context of this intellectual and cultural mixture, René Descartes (1596–1650) contributed to the study of religion. He developed methods for the workings of critical intelligence by formalizing a central role for doubt in his relentless search for certainty. There are important tendencies in Descartes's philosophy that have implications for the later study of religion. Descartes looked for simple factors that served as the foundation for complex entities in his search for first principles. Along with the influence of Darwin's theory of evolution, Descartes's search for first principles is reflected in the quest for the origins of religion. This anthology begins with the quest for the origin of religion because of its importance in identifying the sine qua non of religion, that is, its basic and nonreducible core principle that differentiates it from everything else. The search for the essence of religion is a theme that runs through many of the writings contained in this anthology. The attempt to identify the essence of religion, or the single principle that could not be doubted, is connected to an assumption that one could prove the reality or validity of religion.

Like Descartes's search for certainty, Immanuel Kant (1724–1804) wanted to discern how and why we could be certain of something. Kant distinguished between theoretical reason and practical reason as part of his reexamination of the relationship of knowledge to reality. For Kant, knowledge was a unified process consisting of perception (intuition), imagination, and understanding functioning in a cooperative way. The human mind possesses the ability to experience sense impressions, unite them, and synthesize them. Within Kant's scheme of synthesis, sensations are transformed into perceptions within the forms of space and time. Perceptions are transformed into experiences by the concepts of our understanding. Finally, experience becomes systematic knowledge by means of general principles that Kant calls ideas, which are not given in experience (ideas like soul, the world, and God, for example). Although we can know nature or phenomena that appear in space and time, we are unable to know metaphysical reality. Fundamental to Kant's philosophy is this distinction between the phenomenal world (appearance) and reality (the thing-in-itself or the noumenal world). The latter is unknowable, whereas the former is knowable. However, Kant was not content to be limited to only empirical knowledge because he thought that there was also a synthetic a priori knowledge, which is unconditioned by experience. The primary example of such synthetic a priori knowledge is mathematics.

Kant's basic distinction between the phenomenal world and metaphysical reality also led him to make a fundamental distinction between natural religion and revealed religion. Natural religion represented common religious sensibilities shared by many people, whereas revealed religion was the religion of an institution like the church with its liturgy, theology, ritual, doctrine, creed, and dogma. The former type of religion was very accessible because it was not burdened by institutional requirements. It was part of the public domain, it was tolerant, and it lacked hierarchical control. The natural form of religion could be verified empirically. Moreover, Kant's insistence that reality cannot be known by human understanding because it is incapable of grasping religion as a thing-in-itself implied that any data or feature that one describes as religion can claim only a phenomenal status. Kant thought that people were moving toward natural religion, which would make them autonomous. If we take human nature into consideration, religion is grounded in ethics because of its association with human morality and ethical sensitivity.

The trend to explain religion on the basis of human nature continued with Friedrich Schleiermacher (1768–1834), who identified religion with feeling, the sine qua non of religion. This feeling of absolute dependence stressed the inwardness of religious sensibility and/or an interior self-consciousness that reminds us of our creatureliness and helplessness due to our finite and fragile condition. From Schleiermacher's perspective, religion became associated with a specific mode of consciousness that forms the basis for one's self-identity, and religion is grounded within the subject. This expansive and inclusive feeling of absolute dependence finds its highest expression for Schleiermacher in Christianity. Later, Rudolf Otto will reject Schleiermacher's treatment of feeling because of its narrow subjectivity and the limiting of aesthetics to the category of self-consciousness, and he will develop his own insights into the holy in a Kantian way as an a priori category.

Descartes, Kant, and Schleiermacher are good examples of three thinkers using the method of *reductio,* or, the first part, and *enumeratio,* the second step. For religion to be established on a natural basis, it is necessary for the religious factor to function as a complement and complete, for instance, ethical virtue by adding something to it which is missing. Without the occurrence of the second step, a human faculty that is devoid of religion is undeveloped and impoverished. In other words, by shifting religion from revelation to a natural foundation, something is lost, and needs to be recaptured by returning to the beginning. This recuperative process is made possible by the second step of the method called *enumeratio.* Walter H. Capps defines this second step in the following way: "*Enumeratio* is employed to help describe and defend the reasonableness of the details of revealed religion. That is, *enumeratio* certifies the contents of revealed religion but without certifying revelation."[11] Thus, the second step of the method recaptures what was lost in the initial step. This method illustrates the importance of method to the student of religion.

At the beginning of their study of religion, student novices often demonstrate certain presumptions, biases, and prejudices about what it is that they will be studying. Their expectations are unfilled when they discover that a course in the Hebrew or Christian scriptures is unlike a Sunday school class, or that a course in another religious tradition is unlike a course in theology. These unmet expectations often serve as an eye-opening experience, a broadening of one's intellectual horizons, and the beginning of a cross-cultural dialogue within one's own mind. From the perspective of some scholars, these types of healthy, maturing, and stimulating possibilities from the study of religion are enhanced by distinguishing religious studies from theology, although one could argue that similar types of positive experiences can be gained by studying the theologies of various religious traditions. However, if a scholar is to treat the subject of religion in a scientific manner, it is absolutely necessary to differentiate it from theology, according to some scholars.

Many scholars argue that religious studies, if it is to be truly a science, must distinguish itself from theology or even exclude theology. A particularly vociferous defender of this type of an approach is Donald Wiebe in his book, *The Politics of Religious Studies.* It is Wiebe's conviction that the study of religion has been shaped by theological assumptions and religious commitments. Why is this problematic for a scholar like Wiebe and others? Scholars with a theological agenda or a particular religious bias undermine any attempt to treat the study of religion in a scientific way. Moreover, according to its critics, theology is apologetic, partisan, embodies certain value judgments, is used to defend a particular religious position, and can be used to proselytize others. From the hindsight of a historical perspective, the assumptions and biases characteristic of a particular theological position have been used to uphold the truth of one's own religion against religions of others. These biases have tended to undervalue and even denigrate the religiosity of others, and have stood opposed to the natural sciences and philosophy. With respect to a person holding a particular theological position, there is an almost indistinguishable tendency to combine study with practice. Although it is possible for a person to practice a religion of one's choice, combining study and practice make the scientific study of religion impossible for scholars like Wiebe. Those seeing such dangers in the practice and study of a particular theological position want to exclude such subject areas as theology, philosophical theology, and philosophy of religion from the field called religious studies in order to make it into a science of religion. By reading the selections in this anthology, one will encounter authors with a theological agenda because it was common for scholars to compare Christianity with other religions to demonstrate the superiority of their own religious tradition. Of course, other thinkers compared science to religion to prove its superiority over religion or to demonstrate the infantile or unsophisticated nature of religious thinking. Due to some of the problems associated with theology, I have restricted selections from strictly theological thinkers, although I have compromised this restriction with feminist thinkers. This does not mean that theology does not have a place within the overall field of religious studies. Although I do not want to get sidetracked here, a case can be made to include theology among the various disciplines of religious studies because of its importance to understanding the development of religious traditions.

Delwin Brown addresses the possibility of embracing theology as a discipline within religious studies, arguing that a theologian is a person concerned with religious ideas similar to scholars who concentrate on other aspects of religious phenomena.[12] William F. May offers another perspective by pointing to the fact that many (although not all) religious traditions develop some kind of religious reflection or thought that emerges within the social context of specific religious communities or institutions.[13] Charles E. Winquist argues that to refuse a place for theology within religious studies implies a rejection of the "language of its own reflexivity."[14] In other words, to reject the language of theology is to lose the sensitivity necessary for a scholar to think about the thinking involved when another person thinks about something sacred. Theology can thus give us insight into how someone using such a thinking process decides to refer to something as sacred. Without theological sensitivity, a scholar runs the risk of lacking a critical self-consciousness. By lacking the insights provided by theology into religious thinking, the field of religious studies runs the risk of becoming blind in two senses: "It becomes blind to its own subjectivity and to theology as a possible object of its subjectivity."[15] Brown, May, and Winquist agree that theology possesses something worthwhile for the field of religious studies, and without a place for theology, the field is impoverished.

Within the encompassing embrace of the field of religious studies, there are many disciplines within which a person can stand when approaching the study of religion. As used in this context, a discipline serves as a guide to how one approaches one's subject matter within the field. Within the overall context of the field, the discipline of a researcher is the location where one begins one's inquiry and where one stands. Where a researcher stands often determines the kinds of questions that arise, the assumptions and intentions that are brought to one's work, the insights or discoveries to be gained, how one's understanding is shaped, and the results of one's research. The field of religious studies embodies many different disciplines. Among some of the major disciplines are the following: sociology, phenomenology, psychology, history of religions, anthropology, feminism, and postmodernism. The various disciplines are not isolated from each other because particular scholars often use a combination of these different disciplines. From a historical perspective, there is also some overlap between sociology and anthropology, and phenomenology and history of religions with respect to methods and subjects of study. These various disciplines also represent different methods of approaching the study of religion. It is common for a specific discipline to be connected usually to a particular method, although one will also discover differences among particular methodological approaches to the study of religion. The wide variety of methodological approaches to the study of religion reflects the complexity of the subject and its dimensions in different kinds of social, psychological, biological, historical, gender, and ecological contexts.

Because these various methods and approaches constitute the field of religious studies and are often used in combination with each other by a particular scholar, religious studies is a field that possesses a strong interdisciplinary character and is much less a field of a specific discipline with its own rules and guidelines. Religious studies also tends to be cross-cultural and comparative in character. Many scholars of religion use examples of particular religious phenomena or behavior from different cultures to compare and draw generalizations about their subject.

Besides disciplines or methods of approach to the study of religion, there are many subfields within religious studies. If you examine simply the annual convention program of the American Academy of Religion, it is possible to find subfields like the following: arts, literature, and religion; Buddhism; comparative studies; ethics; history of Christianity; philosophy of religion; religion and the social sciences; religion in South Asia; Islam; women and religion; black theology; lesbian–feminist issues in religion; mysticism; religion and ecology; religion and film; and religion, war, and peace. This is a mere sample of the many subfields of religious studies and does not even mention the area of biblical studies and its many subfields. It is important to note that not all of these subfields are differentiated by method because it is common for a variety of methods to be used in many of these subfields. Within the field of religious studies, there are many subjects, disciplines or methods, and subfields, which manifest a multitude of interests, intentions, sources, and perspectives. Thus, religious studies is a composite field constructed of many component and overlapping parts.

Some Basic Distinctions

Because this anthology focuses attention on method, it will prove helpful to make a distinction between it and theory and to also draw some other types of distinctions for the sake of clarity. Although it is absolutely necessary for the study of some aspect of religion, a method is not, however, normative in the sense of establishing a standard of correctness; it is rather instrumental in the sense that it performs a function that can be logical, conceptual, and logistical by bringing a subject into clearer focus, enabling one to construct paths of inquiry, and making analysis of one's findings possible.[16] A particular method is applied intentionally to the data being investigated, and it enables researchers to be systematic in their approach to the subject. Researchers establish methods to enable them to describe religious phenomena, to identify some phenomena as religious, to compare and contrast religious phenomena between cultures, to approach subjects in a systematic way, to synthesize findings, and to critically analyze what one encounters and finds. A method can also help one construct an integrated and coherent theory.

A theory is a construct from our experiences, encounters, and the application of methods. It enables us to unify our experiences into a coherent whole and to account for why something is the way that it is and not another way. By developing a theory, scholars argue for a particular position that they determine is valuable. Besides embodying positions and values, theories help us to construct an intellectual position from which we can argue for or against other theories. From a historical perspective, theories succeed each other, occurring when one theory demonstrates weaknesses or flaws in another theory. This suggests that theories have only a conditional validity because they will be abandoned most likely when they alter our originally accepted theory. With respect to the subject of religion, theories have two major possibilities: explanatory and interpretive.

A major difference between the interpretive and explanatory theories is that the former emphasizes the importance of human thought and feeling in religion, whereas the explanatory theory wants to peer beyond the religious mind and sensibilities to seek something deeper and hidden. The explanatory theory focuses on causation, and it treats religion as something problematic or something to be explained. In contrast, the interpretive theory accepts the given nature of religion as a way of life to be interpreted. Interpretive theory concentrates on configurations of meaning by reconstructing, for instance, the historical context of a religious phenomenon or occurrence. As this process develops, our understanding grows through our encounter with the subject. Another major difference between these types of theories is that the explanatory theory is expected to embody a high degree of predictability, whereas the interpretive theory is concerned with conditions of possibility.[17] In actual practice, there is often an overlapping of describing, explaining, and interpreting a religious phenomenon or practice by scholars.

Some theories of religion are inductive, whereas other theories are deductive in nature. The inductive theory is derived from historical knowledge that is discovered in time and place, and it argues from the specific to the general. The deductive theory represents knowledge gained from one's own philosophical position or previously accepted theory, and it works by arguing from the general to the specific. A theory based on a deductive argument has a conclusion that claims to follow from its premises with logical certainty. In this type of argument, it is impossible for premises to be true and its conclusion to be false. If a deductive argument possesses premises that necessarily lead to its conclusion, it is a valid argument. Otherwise, it is invalid. A theory based on an inductive argument has a conclusion that claims to be more or less probable but not certain. The conclusion of an inductive argument is likely to be probable but never logically certain. For instance, if one learns that all airplanes have been on time for a given day, one can conclude that one's airplane will be on time, but this conclusion is only probable because something could happen to interrupt the flight. Sometimes, deduction and induction are intimately joined. For example, if you know that there are 52 cards in a deck and that that there is a 50 percent chance of drawing a black card, you know this with logical certainty, although you cannot be certain of drawing a black card because of the odds. Thus, you know by means of deduction what your chances are by logical certainty, but you know through induction what the probability of your drawing a black card will be. It is important to become aware of how an author is arguing and whether or not the theory passes the test of reason and logical consistency.

Not all scholars of religion are enamoured of theory. As Eric J. Sharpe observes in his fine study of the history of comparative religion, theory dominates the early study of religion and much of this theory is shaped by the Darwinian–Spencerian evolutionary theory.[18] In more recent times, a general theory of religion has failed to take the place of earlier efforts. At the current time, there are both antitheory and protheory camps. For instance, among the former group, Wilfred Cantwell Smith emphasizes understanding religion rather than explaining it. By creating theories, we run the risks of depersonalizing religion and failing to see that meaning resides in persons.[19] Ninian Smart thinks that some degree of theory is inevitable because theoretical features are present with respect to decisions about the classification of phenomena, historical explanations, and the attempt to explain cross-cultural similarities and differences.[20] Hans Penner and Donald Wiebe are even stronger advocates for the necessity of theory than Smart. Penner uses microtheoretical studies to make his point.[21] Wiebe argues that theory must be "social scientific theory."[22] We can expect this argument about theory to continue into the foreseeable future.

Not only is the study of religion related to theory, it is intimately connected to the art of hermeneutics. Scholars of religion explain, describe, and interpret in the service of reaching understanding. Although explaining, describing, and interpreting can be distinguished as separate activities of a scholar, they are also interconnected. According to the hermeneutical theories of Hans-Georg Gadamer and Paul Ricoeur, explanation and understanding tend to overlap, even though the former is connected to the field of the natural sciences and the latter is related to the human sciences.[23] As explanations and descriptions make some aspect of religion, for instance, more intelligible, these actions are also offering interpretations. Not only are these three activities interconnected, they are also connected to understanding. Explaining, describing, and interpreting are all contained in the process of understanding a religious phenomenon, and they help to make understanding more explicit. Although Gadamer refers explicitly to interpretation, I think that a similar case can be made for explanation and description in the sense that each activity is not necessarily a means by which understanding is achieved; it is more that the three activities have "passed into the content of what is understood."[24] In the process of explaining and describing, scholars are selective about including some aspects and not others that they are studying. The choices made by scholars about what is significant and what is extraneous are part of the process of interpreting and understanding.

Even if there is a certain amount of guesswork in the beginning of the process because it is difficult to know for certain the intention of a writer or performer in a religious rite, understanding shares something with the three activities of explaining, describing, and interpreting in the sphere of meaning. The actualization of meaning by a scholar is an act of appropriation, an event in the present moment that reveals possible ways of viewing the object of study. This new way of perception is like the fusion of horizons between the researcher's world and the world of the religious other.[25] Researchers arrive at a moment when they come to understand not only something about the religion of another person, but also something more about themselves. Following Ninian Smart's call for methodological agnosticism, Clarke and Byrne suggest that scholars of religion keep separate activities like describing and explaining from judging the truth about the sacred in a particular religious culture.[26] Their point is that it is disingenuous and a misuse of one's position for a scholar to sit in judgment on another religious culture. The scholar's task is to strive for understanding and not spread dissension.

Preview of Coming Attractions

Not only does this anthology make it apparent that there are a wide variety of scholarly opinions about the nature of religion, it will also become evident that scholars interested in the nature of religion have approached the subject by using many different methods. Many scholars have used the comparative method with some success; others have used sociology, phenomenology, psychology, history, anthropology, or a combination of these methods. More recent approaches to religion are the ecological approach, feminist perspective, and various types of postmodern approaches. Although readers will be exposed to a variety of approaches to the study of religion, this anthology wants to concentrate on two fundamental questions: (1) What is religion? (2) What are some of the methods used to study it? An advantage of this type of focus will be an opportunity to witness the second-order tradition of the field of religious studies.

According to Walter H. Capps, an intellectual endeavor must manifest a second-order tradition to qualify as a field. He defines a second-order tradition as follows: "By second-order tradition we refer to a coordinated account of the primary schools of interpretation, methods of approach, traditions of scholarship, and, most significantly, a shared living memory of the ways in which all of these constitutive factors are related to each other."[27] What Capps implies is that an academic field cannot discern its way without being able to know its historical development in some kind of narrative way. In other words, it is impossible to know who or what we are, or where we are going, unless we know who or what we have been and how we got to the present point. To some extent, this anthology will fulfill Capps's observation about the necessity for a second-order tradition.

This anthology begins with theories of religion and approaches to the study of religion that originated in the nineteenth century. There are some critics who claim that these early approaches are outdated and misguided because the scholars were methodologically biased and were attempting to prove the superior nature of their own religion or Western culture. I think that it is important to include selections from the writings of such figures as Tylor, Frazer, Spencer, Lang, Lévy-Bruhl, and Müller to understand what later theorists were reacting against and to understand the nature of the tradition of scholarship that also influenced later scholars. Many of the earlier and later theorists were influenced by the theory of evolution and the search for the origins of religion. Many of them attempted to imitate the method of science to give their scholarship legitimacy in the eyes of scholars outside the study of religion and to give their work some measure of respectability. Because these concerns affected the scholarship about the nature of religion over an extended period of time, there is a certain amount of overlap between earlier and later thinkers. Thus, the arrangement of this anthology acknowledges a certain amount of overlap with respect to approaches to the study of religion. This means that the structure of this anthology is not intended to be rigid. Phenomenologists of religion, for instance, are not only interested in studying the phenomena of religion, but many are also concerned with its psychology, its place within society, its history, and other aspects.

The various definitions and approaches to the study of religion embodied within this anthology have been subjected to scholarly criticism by a wide variety of thinkers. This anthology thus includes a critical aspect that is intended to expose the reader to another perspective on a particular scholar's work. By reading essays that criticize a particular approach to the study of religion, readers will be able to consider both the advocate for a given position and the contrary criticism of the position, and they will be challenged to decide for themselves the strengths and weaknesses of a particular approach. The different perspectives of feminism and postmodernism challenge this tradition of scholarship within the field of religious studies. Generally speaking, feminists insist on a more inclusive gender paradigm for the study of religion, whereas postmodern thinkers tend to call the entire tradition of scholarship into question in their search for new paradigms of intelligibility. Because there will be no effort to enforce a particular approach as the best for the study of religion or to accept one definition of religion as the most satisfactory, readers will be encouraged to shape their own theory of religion and to see the advantages and disadvantages of certain methods while developing their own scholarly tools and methods for the study of religion.

NOTES

1. Paul Tillich, *Theology of Culture,* ed. Robert C. Kimball (New York: Oxford University Press, 1959), 7–8.

2. Idem, *Systematic Theology,* vol. 1 (Chicago: University of Chicago Press, 1966), 13.

3. John Hick, *An Interpretation of Religion: Human Responses to the Transcendent* (New Haven: Yale University Press, 1989), 4.

4. Ibid., 11.

5. Jonathan Z. Smith, *Imagining Religion: From Babylon to Jonestown* (Chicago: University of Chicago Press, 1982), xi.

6. Mark C. Taylor, *About Religion: Economies of Faith in Virtual Culture* (Chicago: University of Chicago Press, 1999), 1.

7. Pater B. Clarke and Peter Byrne, *Religion Defined and Explained* (Houndsmills and London: Macmillan, 1993), 6–7.

8. Ibid., 13.

9. Brian C. Wilson, "From the Lexical to the Polythetic: A Brief History of the Definition of Religion," In *What Is Religion?: Origins, Definitions, and Explanations,* ed. Thomas A. Idinopulos and Brian C. Wilson (Leiden: Brill, 1998), 158.

10. Jacques Waardenburg, "*Religionswissenschaft* New Style: Some Thoughts and Afterthoughts," *Annual Review of the Social Science of Religion* 2 (1978), 190.

11. Walter H. Capps, *Religious Studies: The Making of a Discipline* (Minneapolis: Fortress Press, 1995), 11.

12. Delwin Brown, "Believing Traditions and the Task of the Academic Theologian," *Journal of the American Academy of Religion* LXII/4 (1994), 1172.

13. William F. May, "Why Theology and Religious Studies Need Each Other," *Journal of the American Academy of Religion* LII/4 (1984), 749–50.

14. Charles E. Winquist, "Theology and the Pedagogy of the Sacred," In *The Sacred and Its Scholars: Comparative Methodologies for the Study of Primary Religious Data,* ed. Thomas A. Idinopulos and Edward A. Yonan (Leiden: E. J. Brill, 1996), 172.

15. Ibid., 173.

16. Capps, 344.

17. David S. Chidester, "Theory and Theology in the Study of Religion," *Religion in South Africa* 6/2 (1985), 82–83.

18. Eric J. Sharpe, *Comparative Religion: A History,* 2nd ed. (La Salle, IL: Open Court, 1986), xii.

19. Wilfred Cantwell Smith, "Methodology and the Study of Religion: Some Misgivings," In *Methodological Issues in Religious Studies,* ed. Robert Baird (Chico, CA: New Horizons Press, 1975), 105.

20. Ninian Smart, "Beyond Eliade: The Future of Theory in Religion," *Numen* 25 (1978), 172.

21. Hans Penner, "The Poverty of Functionalism," *History of Religions* 11 (1971), 91–97; "Creating a Brahman: A Structural Approach to Religion," In *Methodological Issues in Religious Studies,* ed. Robert Baird (Chico, CA: New Horizons Press, 1975).

22. Donald Wiebe, "Theory in the Study of Religion," *Religion* 13 (1984), 303.

23. Hans-Georg Gadamer, *Truth and Method,* trans. Garrett Barden and John Cumming (New York: Crossroad, 1982), 31; Paul Ricoeur, *Interpretation Theory: Discourse and the Surplus of Meaning* (Fort Worth, TX: Texas Christian University Press, 1976), 72.

24. Gadamer, 359.

25. Ibid., 273; Ricoeur, 93.

26. Clarke and Byrne, 74.

27. Capps, xvi.

Chapter 2

Religious Studies as an Academic Discipline

With its historical roots in the Enlightenment period in Western history and thought, the academic study of religion is nurtured in colleges and universities in the West where religion is examined, reflected upon, and interpreted. Within its academic setting, the study of religion is usually located in the curriculum of the humanities and social sciences. Due in part to the often rational and secular nature of the enterprise, the academic study of religion is not a subject that is studied in a religious way unless one wants to include approaches occurring in different kinds of seminaries where professional training takes place. Therefore, belief in the teachings of a particular religion is not necessary to study one's own religion or a religion that is foreign to one. Even though inherent personal interest or intellectual curiosity may motivate a person to study religion, it is studied within the academic world to make its complexity more intelligible to students of the subject. Students of religion find scholars arguing over the nature of religion and over methodological issues. However, it is not often clear where religion fits into the academic world. A brief review of its academic history in the West is a useful place to begin to comprehend where it fits into the academic world.

During the eighteenth century Enlightenment period of Western intellectual history, Immanuel Kant challenged others to know. This challenge involved the free quest for knowledge of all kinds. Kant and other thinkers of the time presupposed that there was nothing human understanding or reason could not grasp, even though there were some limits to these mental tools. Within the context of a tolerant attitude to seek knowledge, the possibility for the academic study of religion was created by the intellectual spirit of the Enlightenment. The possibility for the creation of the academic study of religion was accompanied by its departmentalization, growth of academic jargon, and narrow specialization.

In Europe and America, society was mainly dominated by a Christian orthodoxy, and religion tended to dominate the lives of college-aged students, although practical and theoretical perspectives might differ from one location to another. Within this predominate Christian context, liberal education was paramount to the training of future Christian leaders for a Christian culture. However, less sectarian voices could be found with figures like Benjamin Franklin and Thomas Jefferson in America.

When Franklin argued in the earlier part of the eighteenth century for a college in Pennsylvania, his conception was essentially secular and practical. If it was important to respond to the practical needs of an expanding population in a new land, Franklin's argument for such a college was devoid of any mention about church, ministry, or religion. Franklin's vision eventually resulted in his founding the University of Pennsylvania in Philadelphia. A similar model was advocated by Jefferson for the College of William and Mary in Virginia. Calling for high academic and professional standards of excellence, Jefferson's secular vision for the institution deliberately excluded the teaching of theology when it opened its doors in 1818. Not only did Jefferson's college lack a faculty of theology, it also did not have any provisions for campus religious activities. The secularizing spirit embodied in the visions of Franklin and Jefferson was to become even more prominent after World War II.

Unlike Franklin and Jefferson, many educators agreed that American colleges and universities must be nurtured by Christian values in the nineteenth century. Adapting the English college system to American needs, the typical American curriculum often centered on core subjects like Latin, Greek, mathematics, logic, and moral philosophy. These basic subjects were supplemented by such subjects as Hebrew, physics, and astronomy. Many early colleges, which had historical affiliations with some Protestant denominations and were often led by presidents who were former clergymen, were established as training grounds for prospective ministers. By providing training in mental discipline and supplying elements of truth to be discerned from Christian natural theology, these denominational colleges attempted to create educated gentlemen in order for them to become learned and cultured leaders of the country. The later nineteenth century witnessed a movement away from this Christian-centric type of education with the rise of the modern university, towards more specialization and the subsequent diversification of subjects into academic fields.

The modern university reflected Franklin's concern for a practical education to better serve the different classes of society and their pragmatic vocational needs. Along with this response to vocational demands by the public, some viewed the university as a place for pure research devoid of utilitarian ends. A third competing view of the university was offered by such educational leaders as Woodrow Wilson of Princeton University and A. Lawrence Lowell of Harvard University. Such leaders viewed the university as the cultivator, disseminator, and maintainer of liberal culture. Because these views are fundamentally competing and incompatible, the American university reflected a lack of unifying center or vision. The three competing and incompatible views were commonly found within the same institution.

This eclectic combination of incompatible visions of higher education was complicated by the influx of the spirit of science that contributed an even greater impetus toward a movement of specialization and compartmentalization of knowledge. This type of movement can be traced to borrowings from a German model of learning and the spirit of science characteristic of American universities. The German model advocated a science (*Wissenschaft*) for all branches of knowledge. What Americans understood by science differed from the German understanding that was grounded in philosophical presuppositions associated with German philosophical idealism. The German concept of *Wissenschaft* emphatically suggested a process of systematic scholarship devoid of the relativism and positivism characteristic of the American grasp of science. If American scholars understood science to be equivalent to natural science or empiricism, the highest form of science for the Germans was *Geisteswissenschaften* (humanistic disciplines), which was connected to *Weltanschauung* (world-view), a personal synthesis of observations and values, and *Bildung,* an education of cultivation that resulted in the development of the unique individualism of the scholar. Thus, the German ideal of science was opposed to the positivism and relativism characteristic of the American notion of science. The American grasp of science convinced scholars that nearly anything could be investigated by the sustained concentration of pure research and specialization. The movement toward specialization influenced the humanities curriculum and led to academic departments. This movement reflected an attitude that the various humanistic disciplines were independent fields of study. After the American Civil War, widening specialization increased the impetus toward professionalism within one's academic specialty. However, this specialization eventually hindered the integrated system of education.

The tendencies of specialization, secularization, consumer demands for new technical and professional programs, and widespread expansion of institutions of higher education had broad consequences for changes in Anglo-American education after World War II. During the rapid expansion of higher education in the period of the 1950s and 1960s, the academic study of religion began to prosper on a broader scale, and its nature and mission were altered in a way that helped it to begin to break free of the seminary curriculum model with its emphasis on the Bible, church history, theology, and ethics. The reduction or total elimination of religion courses or chapel attendance as requirements for graduation at many church-related institutions gave impetus to more imaginative approaches to the study of religion and the development of more pluralistic course offerings. College and university departments of religion began to offer courses in Eastern religions, Judaism, African religions, and courses on theory along with its former offerings. This tendency to broaden departmental offerings and the trend away from a seminary model continued into the 1970s. The transformation of religion as a subject of serious study was resisted by conservative protestant colleges that retained an exclusively Christian emphasis, but most institutions dropped the old approach of Christian nurturing and even loosened traditional historical connections to sponsoring religious bodies. Even though many private institutions experienced curricular changes in religion courses, the most dramatic changes occurred in public colleges and universities. During the 1960s and early 1970s, many state-supported institutions established programs of religion at the undergraduate level, while some of them added master's degree programs and a few added doctoral programs.

Although economic prosperity and general higher education growth fed the expansion of religion programs, the study of religion was also aided by the American federal courts. The courts drew an important distinction between religious indoctrination and teaching "about" religion. The courts ruled that teaching about religion was a legitimate course of study. Other voices argued that religion should not be a subject in a public institution that was supported by state and federal tax funds. These political voices stated that support for the study for religion violated the constitutional distinction between church and state.

The opportunity to teach about religion, which was provided by federal court decisions, was closely associated with the growth and development of the academic field of religious studies in colleges and universities throughout the country. A milestone in this development was reached in 1964 when the National Association of Biblical Instructors (NABI) agreed to change its name to the American Academy of Religion (AAR). This change in the professional organization was followed 2 years later by a change in its journal from *The Journal of Bible and Religion* to *The Journal of American Academy of Religion*. These changes on the national level reflected a continuing separation between teaching about religion and the professional training associated historically with ministerial education within the context of seminaries. These changes were also signs of the slow maturation of a new academic field within the context of undergraduate education.

A combination of a lack of financial support and a declining pool of high school students enrolling at colleges and universities caused a period of retrenchment in the 1980s. Departments of Religious Studies were forced to compete for scarce funds with both older established programs and new programs in subjects like women's studies, black studies, urban studies, and other disciplines. This period also witnessed an emphasis on career preparation, a decline in the appeal of liberal arts, and an emphasis on science and technology. Many Religious Studies departments responded to these new challenges by stressing multi-interdisciplinary approaches and the cross-cultural nature of the study of religion. And due to the pervasive nature of religion for much of human experience, it was to a student's advantage to study religion because it provided an understanding of different forms of human behavior and values to better comprehend peoples of foreign cultures encountered in a more closely interrelated world. In addition, a student was given intellectual tools to analyze and understand a changing world. These kinds of results prepared students for a variety of career possibilities. By demonstrating these kinds of practical career possibilities, this type of argument was a direct response to consumer demands for careerism, financial returns on an educational and monetary investment, and old fashioned American pragmatism that can be discerned with a cultural figure like Benjamin Franklin.

With the rapid expansion of the computer for education, business, and everyday use, religious studies encountered new challenges and opportunities in the 1990s. What will the future be for religious studies in the computer age? Even though it is difficult to predict the future with any great precision, it seems safe to affirm that the computer will greatly enhance opportunities for cross-cultural and interdisciplinary approaches to the subject.

Mark C. Taylor attempts to anticipate the future in an essay entitled "Unsettling Issues" that appeared in the *Journal of the American Academy of Religion* (LXII/4) in the mid-1990s. Besides warning about using the outdated divinity school model for a college religious studies curriculum, Taylor calls for a "transition from the modern to the postmodern 'university' by shifting from the paradigm of the factory to the paradigm of the network" (p. 957). The move to cyberspace demands a new paradigm in which disciplines are structured like a net in constant flux without being chaotic. Taylor envisions a more global classroom that uses computer technology that is interactive. He also sees the book, which represented the foundation of the modern university, giving way to hypertexts in the cyberspace university of the future. In this cyberspace university or college, word, image, and sound will be weaving together to create hypertexts. In conjunction with globalization that insists on elucidating similarities and differences of communities, such a scenario will necessarily force teaching and research to be more polymorphous in the future. Whether Taylor's vision becomes a historical actuality for religious studies remains to be seen, as does its consequences for the study of the subject. However, we can be assured that the study of religion will continue to face new challenges and will have to continue to adapt to future changes if it is to remain a viable academic subject worthy of serious study. The history of theories about the nature and methods of approaching religion can afford us guidelines as we proceed into a challenging and uncertain future.

The historical diversity of opinions about the nature of religion and methods adopted to study it will become evident as you proceed in this anthology. This scholarly diversity is indicative of a collective intellectual enterprise within higher education. It also reflects the plurality of ways to understand religion and its role in the world, in human lives, and in history. The essays that have been collected for this chapter reflect a discussion about the place of religious studies within the academic sphere of higher education.

The initial essay by Sam Gill, an expert on Native American Indian religion and professor at the University of Colorado in Boulder, Colorado, identifies some criteria by which the academic study of religion can be distinguished from other academic disciplines. Gill stresses its neutrality with respect to personal belief, race, culture, or gender. Although the academic study of religion is not unique in higher education, it is sensitive to multiculturalism, possesses historical and cultural importance, and is comparative in nature. Gill also indicates some of its problems.

From a different perspective, the essay by Jonathan Z. Smith, a professor of religion at the University of Chicago, raises a number of questions. Who or what invented religion? What kind of creation is religion? Is it some kind of Frankenstein monster? Is there a difference between the humanities and the social sciences? If religion is an abstraction of the scholar's mind, how can we speak about it in a meaningful way? Is the issue of reductionism important?

In response partly to the kinds of questions raised by Smith, Mary Gerhart, a professor at Hobart and William Smith Colleges located in Geneva, New York, calls on major changes in the field of religious studies that she envisions as including theology, art, literature, and philosophy. She looks closely at three fields: art, literature, and religion; women and religion; and science and religion. She addresses the direction she thinks that the field of religious studies must take and what theology must do to become more flexible.

In the fourth essay, Donald Wiebe, a professor of religion at Trinity College of the University of Toronto in Canada, raises several important questions for the student of religion. Can religion, for instance, have any social benefit without being true? On what should the study of religion be grounded? Is religious studies a vocation? Is the academic study of religion a science or a metaphysical exercise? Needless to say, these are not easy questions to answer. But it is important to raise such questions for the academic health of the field.

In her 1999 Presidential Address to the American Academy of Religion, Margaret R. Miles, Dean and Academic Vice President of the Graduate Theological Union in Berkeley, California, addresses concerns that are a bit different than those of Wiebe. Miles wants to overcome the differences between the study of religion and theological studies. After identifying the three public spheres of religious studies (public sphere, faith communities, and the university), she advocates understanding religious studies as a wide discursive field that is inherently interdisciplinary. Miles also raises the issue of difference and its application to gender, racial, ethnic, and sexual issues. After adopting a model for conceptualizing difference, she argues that it is possible to move toward a point where inclusiveness and separation oscillate.

The Academic Study of Religion

SAM GILL

THE EMERGENCE OF AN ACADEMIC STUDY of religion has been disappointing despite the boost it received thirty years ago when religion entered the curricula of state-supported American colleges and universities. The academic study of religion as envisioned here is distinguished by several bounding criteria:

1. The academic study of religion must not depend upon or require of its researchers, teachers, or students any specific religious belief or affiliation, race, culture, or gender.

2. The academic study of religion must be sensitive to multi-culturalism: the awareness that there are many peoples, cultures, and religions, none of which has any exclusive claims to be made with regard to religion as an academic subject.

3. The term "religion" must be understood as designating an academically constructed rubric that identifies the arena for common discourse inclusive of all religions as historically and culturally manifest. "Religion" cannot be considered as synonymous with Christianity or with the teaching of religion to members of specific traditions. "Religion" must not be thought of as the essence of the subject studied. "Religion" is not "the sacred," "ultimate concern," or belief in god (or some disguising euphemism). There is nothing religious about "religion." Religion is not *sui generis*. There are no uniquely religious data.

4. The methods of the academic study of religion are necessarily comparative. Religion is a category whose subdivisions are categories that demand comparison. Comparison must be understood as the play of fit and non-fit, of congruity and incongruity, rather than conformity with a pre-existing pattern.

Sam Gill, selections from "The Academic Study of Religion," The Journal of the American Academy of Religion *LXII/4 1994, 965–975. Reprinted by permission of Oxford University Press.*

5. Once it is comprehended that religion designates a significant aspect of a major portion of the human population throughout its history, dual motivations arise for the study of religion. On the one hand is the desire to appreciate, understand, and comprehend specific religions in their historical and cultural particularity. On the other hand is the opportunity afforded by the broadly comparative category, religion, to learn more about ourselves as human beings.

The academic study of religion, as distinguished by these criteria, has not enjoyed adequate development. As an academic discipline, distinct from the religious study of religion, it has failed to advance any sustainable body of theory, any cadre of religion theorists, any substantial body of literature. The inability to articulate the academic study of religion and the unsatisfactory defense of the place and role of religion studies in the modern academic environment have placed departments of religion at a low level of budgetary priority and at risk in many colleges and universities.

In contrast, what has thrived is the religious study of religion, that is studies in which the scholar is studying her or his own religion or a religion other than his or her own primarily for the purpose or purposes stipulated by the religion studied rather than the purpose or purposes stipulated by the academy. In other words, the study of any religion—whether one's own or another—in order to find God, to transcend desire, or any other reason that religious practitioners have for their religious practices, including study, is a religious, and not an academic, study. These religious studies have long American traditions and intellectual heritages spanning centuries. However, it will be contended that the success of these kinds of religious studies has likely contributed to the repressed and retarded development of the academic study of religion.

While there is a correlation of the academic study of religion with the university and the religious study of religion with seminaries and theological schools, both approaches occur in both kinds of institutions. These approaches are presented here as clearly distinctive, yet there is no intent that either has inherently greater value than the other. While these approaches have different bounding conditions it is possible that some scholarship may simultaneously adequately satisfy both sets of bounding conditions. This essay argues that it is important to make this distinction and it focuses on the approach labeled the academic study of religion, arguing that this approach should be the approach fostered by the American Academy of Religion. When the academic study of religion fails to understand and to accept the demands of being a member of the academic community, which it does routinely, it embraces vagueness; it invites its own dissolution. When the academic study of religion ignores the bounding conditions stated above, it abandons its own distinctiveness.

From the mid-nineteenth century the development of many academic fields—namely the social sciences and, to a lesser extent, the humanities—has emerged from and been motivated by boundary conditions similar to those listed above. Such boundaries are demanded of modern academic studies. Whereas such intellectual activities as Christian studies and Jewish studies precede and parallel the academic study of religion, there are no counterparts to these studies in the social sciences. The social scientific and humanistic academic enterprises often emerged by carefully and sometimes dramatically presenting positions in opposition to Western religious views and thereby, in contrast to the academic study of religion, won a measure of freedom and had to respond to the necessity to carefully distinguish and define themselves in terms of theory, method, and model. The academic study of religion, rather than arising as a field in its own right, has taken less inspired and productive paths. It has either simply extended to new culture areas the methods and theories of the pre-existing approaches—that is, of the religiously motivated studies of religion—or it has borrowed social scientific methods and theories by which to study religion. The former approach produces studies modeled largely on long heritages of the study of Western religious traditions in which history text, and thought are emphasized. The latter produces studies that are difficult to distinguish from the fields in which the theories and methods are borrowed. Neither approach has been much shaped by the boundary principles outlined above.

The academic study of religion has often failed to acknowledge what it is. It is academic; it is Western; it is intellectual. This identification does not mean the academic study of religion must be narrow-minded, insensitive, irresponsible, closed, or exclusive. It does mean that rational discourse is the basic mode of communication. It does mean that the boundary conditions stated above must be respected.

A brief critical discussion will illustrate the difficulties of the approaches taken.

Illustrative of the failure in developing the academic study of religion are the ways in which the question "what is religion?" has been approached. Often the question is approached by attempting to establish a mandate by setting forth an essentialist definition of religion prior to the study of the subject. This strategy correlates with the heritage of the religious study of religion where the limits of one's study are commonly distinguished by the nature of the data. To study Christianity, for example, is simply to study things Christian. Perhaps it seemed logical to extend this principle to the general academic study of religion by arguing that the academic study of religion is the study of data that are distinctively and uniquely religious. A definition of the essence of religion would function for the academic study of religion, it might be supposed, something like doctrine or a statement of faith. But this definitional approach requires that the religious distinctiveness of the subject be described and defended at the outset. The unreachable goal towards which the study is directed, that is to understand what religion is, is required as a precondition to the study.

Defending the *sui generis* character of religious data retards the academic study of religion. The effect is a degenerating discussion of definition while ignoring the specific historical and cultural subjects. Theory remains aloof or is the mere restatement or explication of the statement of essence. Founding the study of religion on essentialist definitions encourages discourse conducted on the authority of vision, insight, or experience rather than rational discourse, hypothetic inference, and the application of scientific method. Persuasion overshadows criticism. Academic freedom is replaced by the requirements of conformity. Inarguable results produced by relying on some religious givenness displaces academic responsibility. Comparative study becomes the instrument of academic proselytization, of exacting belonging. Diversity and difference are unwelcome.

The development of the study of religion that borrows its theories and methods from the social sciences (or other disciplines) faces the problem of distinguishing itself from the sources of borrowed theories. The problem has been tackled in several ways. One common defense has been to place the difference in the scholar, by holding that religion scholars are endowed with some special sensitivity that permits them to use scientific theories to the end of studying religion non-reductively, that is, studying religious data as religious in contrast to some reductive interest such as that of social scientists. Perhaps as newcomers to academia there has been a failure to recognize that all academic studies are reductive.

Reduction means to render data in terms of a chosen perspective, to look at a subject from one perspective or theory among many. This anti-reductive defense is based on an embarrassing mystification of the academic study of religion and an unfortunate misunderstanding of academic methods. Another defense has been to proclaim that the academic study of religion is distinguished as interdisciplinary or eclectic in its approach. This defense is a veil that attempts to conceal the dearth of religion theory.

Another way to show how the academic study of religion has failed to adequately develop is the treatment of comparison. The Christian missionary mandate has fostered much comparative study of religion as a method of expanding Christianity. Inevitably Christian terms, categories, and ideas have been fundamental to the comparative enterprise. The patternists' use of comparison was an extension of this Christian understanding of comparison, both in terms of the categories used and the attitude toward difference. For patternists the criteria for the religious are determined at the outset of the study. They use comparison as the method, the lens, by which to recognize or identify "the religious" in the history of religions. In the academic study of religion comparison has invariably meant fit or congruity to pre-exiting patterns or criteria. The academic study of religion has tended to restrict comparison primarily to finding similarity among different traditions, but this most often has meant concocting similarities and ignoring differences. Too much of the study of religion has been simply the extension of broadly accepted patterns and categories to data not yet rendered in terms of these patterns. This comparative approach diminishes both the broad advancement of an understanding of "religion" and the potential for seeing the distinctiveness of the specific.

To hold that the academic study of religion is necessarily comparative does not mean that every study must compare more than one religious tradition, a form now rather rare. Comparison is at the root of all learning, but knowledge is not advanced or of interest except where difference is discerned. Unfortunately differences and incongruities, if not simply ignored, have usually been explained away.

The comparative operations of the academic study of religion correlate with the broadly held essentialist view of religion—that is, that religion is "the sacred" or "ultimate concern" and that the attributes of "the sacred" and "ultimate concern" are goodness, purity, and unity, or of the center or origin. From this approach, to study religion means to discern and appreciate these desirable qualities in any culture. This is not only a weak form of comparison, it is also a form of imperialism because it reduces all cultures to reflections of these ideas. Furthermore, this comparative approach coupled with a vague and romanticized understanding of religion tends to be blind to any potentially negative (as evaluated in these same terms) aspects of religion, blind not only to the Jonestowns and the Wacos, but also to the poverty, suffering, oppression, and violence that are aspects of almost every religious tradition.

In light of these remarks I want to look at specific areas within the academic study of religion. The heritage for the academic study of small-scale exclusively-oral peoples is deeply rooted in the nineteenth century evolutionist studies in which the cultures then labeled "primitive" were sought for evidence of religion-in-the-making or the ur-religious or the original monotheism. The heritage for this study is the same as that for modern anthropology and the comparative study of religion. These particular cultures and traditions were the principal subjects for anthropological studies well into this century and remain highly important to that field.

There is significant potential—now more than ever—to the academic study of religion in the study of these cultures, a potential to move beyond the limitations set forth above. Nearly everything about these cultures and their religions questions the assumptions and approaches of the academic study of religion. For example, where the academic study of religion has depended almost exclusively on texts (scripture) and thought as reflected in writing (theology, doctrine, historical documents), none of these forms of data exists in exclusively-oral cultures. One finds instead dance, ritual, movement, objects. Such awareness of difference could lead to the development of techniques, methods, questions, and perspectives that are not only applicable to exclusively-oral cultures, but that also open new and important areas within the study of all religious cultures. The implications for the academic study of religion, for even this one issue, are enormous.

Courses on Native American religions are taught in colleges and universities throughout North America. The American Academy of Religion has recognized the area for the last twenty years. Still, during this period few scholars (certainly less than a dozen) within the academic study of religion have devoted the majority of their time to research and publication on the subject. Almost none of these scholars, few as they are, did their graduate schooling in the academic study of religion, but rather such fields as history and anthropology. Notably most of this group who did their graduate work in religion studied other traditions—Hinduism, Chinese religions, Christianity—rather than Native Americans. During most of this twenty-year period the only PhD program where one could study Native American religions was not even in North America, but in Sweden. Currently only a couple religion programs in North American support study of Native American religions at the PhD level.

The topics that have engendered lively discussion in recent years in the study of Native American religions are revealing. Discussion has frequently centered on whether or not active participation in the study of Native American religions should be restricted to those who speak Native American languages and have field experience. Another topic of recent interest is whether non-Native Americans should study and teach Native American religions. This discussion from start to finish has explored issues that divide along ethnic and racial lines (as even the question was formulated).

In terms of academic criteria both these issues are misplaced. The question of whether or not one ought to know one's subject in terms of the language and cultural setting seems to be the question of whether or not the area of study is an academic one. For there to be any discussion is evidence enough that it is not. Such a discussion could certainly not occur in other academic disciplines. If one wants to participate in the academic study of Judaism, it hardly needs to be stated that minimally one must know Hebrew. If one wants to contribute to the academic study of contemporary Hindu ritual practice, one must spend time in Hindu communities and know the relevant languages.

The issues of language and field study are linked to the second issue of whether or not non-Native Americans should teach (and it seems it would imply also to conduct research on) Native American religions. Here the matter has become almost purely political and has failed to raise any substantive academic issues. If the academic study of religion understood both what it means to be academic and how discussions permitted under the "religion" rubric are bounded, these topics would be irrelevant. There is no question that one must know languages and do field studies as appropriate to the methods and requirements of the larger academic community. Racial or cultural distinctions cannot possibly be relevant criteria by which to determine research or pedagogical competence in any sub-field. To hold that one race, ethnicity, or gender is somehow privileged in any area of academic study is racism and refutes important gains that have been made this century.

These discussions of academic qualifications are hopelessly sidetracking. Without the guiding academic context that should be provided by the broader academic study of religion, too often scholars in such small fields as the academic study of Native American religions simply talk about what seems personally most important. Native American members of the group often talk about their experiences, both in terms of their own tribal cultures and as Native Americans (oppressed minorities in academia as well as American culture). Non-Native Americans frequently talk about their attempts at academic studies of Native American religions, usually as tangential to a scholar's principal area of study, attempts that may be motivated by a romanticism of Native Americans or conducted without adequate language and field support.

The results of these discussions are usually not engaging or productive enough to support a vital academic field. The publications, few as they are, by members of this field tend to be as much discussions about what should or should not go on in the field, who should and should not contribute to the field, as they are productive studies of Native American religious topics. Discourse about the shape and nature of a field are important and inevitable to the health of a field, but it is a sure sign of the tenuousness and irrelevance of the field when this talk about the field becomes the principal topic of discussion, the main product of the field. . . .

Further evidence of the failure of the academic study of the religions of exclusively-oral small-scale cultures: within the academic study of religion, the study of Australian Aboriginal religions has been virtually abandoned, as have the small-scale cultures in Oceania and Indonesia. South and Central Americas and Africa fare little better. Around the world the religions of thousands of small-scale societies that are labeled peasant and folk receive almost no attention. The enormous potential of this area of study remains.

In most cultures around the world, save Western traditions especially Christianity, religion and dance are practically synonymous.

From the ancient Bharata natyam of South India to Hopi Kachina dances, from Jewish wedding dances to the Sufi whirling dervishes religion is not only expressed, but enacted, through dance. For many religious traditions, religion without dance is unimaginable. Yet, perhaps because of the paucity of dance in Christianity (and to a lesser extent other Western religions) and given the influence of Christian (and other Western religious) studies on the academic study of religion, dance, and to a somewhat lesser extent other forms of physical movement and ritual, have received almost no attention by students of religion. It is astonishing that the academic study of religion has been so little attentive to the religious forms by which most religious people identify their own religiousness.

Certainly in the academic study of religion there is a movement to be attentive to the study of ritual and more recently to the study of the body. Yet even these concerns suffer by being framed in the Cartesian and Western dualism—mind/body, spirit/body. For example, much of the present study of ritual is understood as the study of the non-textual in contrast with the textual, the study of nonverbal action as opposed to speech and writing. This bifurcation is at best misleading. . . .

Religion and Religious Studies: No Difference at All

JONATHAN Z. SMITH

FROM ONE PERSPECTIVE, if I take seriously the title for this session which has embedded within it the question we are to discuss, it will not take me very long to transact my part of the business. "What is the difference between religion and religious studies?" Either every difference

Jonathan Z. Smith, selections from "Religion and Religious Studies: No Difference at All," Soundings LXXI 2–3, 1988, 231–244.

or no difference at all. "What is the difference between religious studies and other humanistic and social scientific fields?" In principle, none.

I have given two opposing answers to the first question—that of the difference between religion and religious studies—because I know what is usually meant by such a question (for which, the approved answer would be, "every difference") and I know how I would like to take the question (under this guise, the answer I have proposed elsewhere would be, "no difference at all").

As usually understood, the distinction between religion and religious studies reduces to some version of the duality between "being religious" or "doing religion" and the study of the same. This sort of distinction is expressed in our conference document by the disclaimer, "the academic study of religion is clearly not itself religious." It is a preeminently political contrast, one of value in carving out a place for the study of religion within the university, but of dubious value beyond. It is, quite frankly, a ploy. We signal this political ancestry by using as contrast terms, "seminary," or "theological" or by adopting the valorizing terminology of the academy: first, *history (Geschichte)* or *science (Wissenschaft),* more recently, and happily free from Teutonic pedigree, studies. The elaboration of the distinction has set the political (and secondarily, the intellectual) agenda of religious studies in the last century as signaled in your conference document with the phrase, "it was clearly recognized at Santa Barbara that the task was to develop the academic study of religion in a manner appropriate to the letters and science mission of a modern, secular state university." Note which party conforms "in a manner appropriate" to whom. The political distinction was, at heart, a counsel to passivity and integration, not to interesting thought.

As a sheerly political move, analogous to other self-justifications from other fields who sought recognition and legitimation from centers of articulate power, the distinction can be applauded. Raised to the level of theory, it has

proved mischievous, especially when confused with other sorts of distinctions such as those between the "insider" and the "outsider"—the "emic" and the "etic" in contemporary jargon. Its most current formulation is that between the normative and the descriptive.

While I recognize the value of this distinction in some analytic contexts, as used in religious studies it appears all too often to be a continuation of the old political jargon (after many of the battles have been long settled). It does not yield the same sort of theoretical clarification that analogous distinctions provide: for example, as between the formal and the empirical, the monothetic and the polythetic, definition and classification. It continues to serve the old tactical ends of establishing legitimacy by lay, juridical language rather than theoretical discourse. It is but a more elegant form of the sort of language employed by the French Ministry of Education in 1885 (as Eric Sharpe reminds us) when it closed down the Catholic Theological Faculties and established the Fifth Section of Religious Sciences: "we do not wish to see the cultivation of polemics but of critical research, we wish to see the examination of texts and not the discussion of dogmas."[1] This language was continued by the United States Supreme Court in School District of Abington vs. Schempp, when Mr. Justice Goldberg declared, in what was to be the "Magna Carta" for religious studies within state universities: "It seems clear to me . . . that the Court would recognize the propriety of . . . the teaching about religion as distinguished from the teaching of religion in the public schools."[2]

Religion And Religious Studies

Not only is the putative distinction naive and political, it is also anachronistic. It speaks out of a period when the norms of theological inquiry (as experienced in the west) were largely governed by an intact canon, when the ideology of the human sciences were chiefly governed by the goal of achieving "objectivity" or "value-free" knowledge. The most superficial reading of much contemporary theological discourse will reveal that the notion of an intact canon has largely been abandoned or has been perceived as problematic. An equally superficial reading of the current literature of human sciences will reveal that the subjectivity of the individual researcher now stands at the very center of the critical enterprise. Kant, Marx, Freud, *et al.* have won over both sides. Within the academy, neither can escape the discourse of modernity.

Allow me to introduce a revision of the question by taking a bit of a detour, a set of reflections first stimulated by a project undertaken by Walter Capps at UCSB at least a decade ago. He convened a conference to study the "the undeniable fact that religious studies may have created a phenomenon against which it has been judiciously trying to distinguish itself. Religious studies, in effect, has stimulated religion." But, what a religion! For it has been, more often than not, one shorn of most if not all communal and consensual sanctions. We have seen the emergence, within the academy, of a highly personalist religiosity in which each individual constitutes his or her own ad hoc canon in the name of generic religion. (In Burkhardt's sense of the term, what we have seen is the emergence of a kind of religious "barbarism.") This generic term "religion" requires further attention.

I take it we can agree that the term "religion" is not an empirical category. It is a second-order abstraction. This changes our previous mode of discourse. While it is possible to speak of theorizing about religion in general, it is impossible to "do it" or "believe it" or be normative or descriptive with respect to it. Ways of meaningful speaking of first-order phenomena have become impossibly conjoined to a second-order abstraction resulting, at the very least, in misplaced concreteness. What meaning, then, can the word "religion" have in such a situation?

College catalogues and college-level textbooks display two chief understandings. The first employs the language of *religion* and postulates some essence of religion (usually vaguely defined in terms of ultimacy or transcendence) which becomes manifest in particular historical or geographical traditions or artifacts. However, the mechanism of the "manifestation" is rarely exhibited, and the ubiquity of the alleged essence is not much insisted on after the opening chapter or first lecture in the introductory course.

The second employs the language of the *religious*. It appears to make the claim that there is a religious aspect, approach, perspective, or dimension to some subject or area of human experience which has non-religious dimensions as well. As in the first case, the definition of the "religious" in such formulations is vague. The "religious" most frequently appears to function as a sort of extra-plus (the "most integrative" is quite common). Here the "religious" has come to mean some loosely characterized quality of life or experience.

It is we, that is to say, the academy, who fill these definitions with content or meaning, who give them status, who employ them as part of our language. It is we in the academy who imagine kingdoms, phyla, classes, orders, families and general life, after all, is lived only at the level of species or individuals. As Herb Fingarette wrote on another topic some years ago: "Home is always home for someone. . . . There is no absolute home in general." *Mutatis mutandis* religion in general.

This has led me to the relatively simple proposition that it is the study of religion that created the category, it is the study of religion that invented "religion." . . . This is to say, the concept "religion" functions as a category formation for religious studies as its close analogue "culture" functions for anthropology or "language" functions for general linguistics. Like them, it is to be judged solely by its theoretical utility.

As an aside I may add that there is no more pathetic spectacle in all of academia than the endless citation of the little list of fifty odd definitions of religion from James Leuba's

Psychology of Religion in introductory textbooks as proof that religion is beyond definition, that it is fundamentally a *mysterium*. Nonsense! We created it and, following the Frankenstein-ethos, we must take responsibility for it.[3]

I doubt, factually, that religious studies constitutes a "coherent disciplinary matrix in and of itself." I equally doubt that we should attempt to make the claim. It is, once again, an enterprise that served well the politics of establishing departments by some principle of intellectual economy. It is an enterprise that characterized nineteenth-century encyclopedia and philosophical classifications of the sciences, but I know of no other field preoccupied with making such claims at the present time. The question of distinction between fields of study in the academy has largely yielded to the complex question of the classification of objects of study within broad domains of inquiry. There is, most certainly, no "unique idiom or language of religious studies," . . . not even a dialect, at best, only a mongrel, polyglot jargon, again quite typical of the present academy. We are, at our firmest, what Steven Toulmin has termed a "would-be discipline," and we must be content, for the present, that that be the case. After all, the same characterization applies to the vast majority of our conversation partners within the academy in both the humanities and the social sciences. . . .

This last begins to hint at my reasons for responding to the second question before us, "What is the difference between religious studies and other humanistic and social scientific fields?" with the blunt answer: "In principle, none." That is to say, to the degree that we are citizens of the academy, sharing common presuppositions as to "what is the case" (e.g., the appeal in the conference document to the widely held notion of *homo symbolicus*), our commonalities, qua the academy, far outweigh what I would understand to be differences of economic efficiency that separate the currently mapped fields within the human sciences. From this point of view, I am more than content to

hold the position, critically described in Larson's paper that "the distinction between religious studies and other humanistic disciplines is largely heuristic" and that "religious studies is simply one more functional way of cutting up the pie in the modern university." Nor am I aware of other "would-be disciplines" making stronger claims. The internal differences within one field are often sharper than the extramural differences between one field and another, or, to personalize this, each of us frequently finds closer conversation partners with some representative of "other" fields than we do with the majority of members of our own putative area. What is more, Toulmin . . . gives us good reason why this is bound to be the case. . . .

For these and other reasons, I doubt the success of the fissive enterprise, let alone its legitimacy. However, there are other sorts of reasons for abstention from such differentiations which are for me far more provocative.

The first is the sense that we have reached a point in the academy where many of the fields within the human sciences are debating the same issues from quite similar perspectives. What appears to have emerged is a broad agreement upon a number of co-equal possibilities which, while surely characteristic of particular scholars or scholarly styles, cannot be used to identify one field over against another. Each alternative represents a potentially responsible choice for scholarship. Each has advantages and disadvantages, but in theoretical and methodological discourse, it is often the set of problems one is willing to live with that finally determines the stance. Students need to be exposed to exemplars of these wider universes of choice and to the consequences entailed by their acceptance—whether the examples be found within or without the area-code assigned to religious studies.

Time prevents more than a telegraphic citation of some of these issues. Each deserves long and careful study. To allude to just two: one of the issues that has exercised the AAR of late concerns the issues of privilege with respect to the interpretative enterprise. Is the interpreter privileged with respect to the native or to that which is being interpreted? Is the native, or the indigenous exegetical tradition, privileged with respect to the interpreter? Such issues are at least as old as Kant,[4] and while they have been raised recently within religious studies, they are also being hotly debated in most of the field within the human sciences—especially within literary studies and anthropology.[5] Is the controlling metaphor for relating and understanding an "other" that of photograph, text or dialogue? These questions are generic to the human sciences and encourage wide, corporate discussion and debate among our varied conversation partners.

Quite similar is that issue which is signaled by the shorthand term "reductionism," over which much ink has been spilled. On examination this turns out to be a pseudo-issue. It is not that there are reductive disciplines as opposed to non-reductive ones ("we're O.K. . . . but take care, the next tribe over is cannibalistic"), even supposing that we could agree on an adequate definition of "reductionism." A far broader issue appears to be at stake. For example, in *Ideology and Utopia*, Karl Mannheim distinguishes between "right wing" and "left wing" methodologies of the human sciences. . . . Redescribing the matter in this fashion, in terms of conservative and radical, eliminates the usual discourse in which the parties of the "right" tend to be all too readily identified with the non-reductive, and smokes out the other sorts of ideological assumption involved in this seemingly intuitively correct approach: no more good guys and bad guys. Parties of the "left" and "right," "jumpers" and "splinters," "hedgehogs" and "foxes," the "hermeneutics of recovery" and the "hermeneutics of suspicion"—these are coeval and coequal possibilities which can be entertained responsibly by scholars within each of the human sciences. I do not mean to suggest the absence of difference, only to insist that real intellectual differences may well need to be reconfigured in other than tra-

ditional disciplinary modes (*scilicet*, departments) around issues basic to all of the human sciences.

This leads to my final point. There is a growing recognition that there may no longer be a set of clear and interesting distinctions between the humanities (broadly conceived) and the social sciences (equally broadly understood). . . . From such a point of view, the second pedagogical and programmatic question "To what extent should graduate training in religious studies be intradepartmental and to what extent interdepartmental?" becomes moot. For education purposes (not to speak of intellectual ends), departments ought to be considered invisible.

To pick up an analogy from the conference document, our present, time-bound topography of fields of study may be seen, at best, as dialects within a far broader language system which has priority of claim upon both the students' and the scholars' attention. That old Latin tag from Terence, revived with such force in those Renaissance and Enlightenment academies that gave rise to the study of religion—"Nothing human is foreign to me" might now be revised: "Nothing in the human sciences is foreign to me."

NOTES

1. Quoted in Eric Sharpe, *Comparative Religion: A History* (London: Duckworth Press, 1975), 122.

2. It would be a worthwhile project to collect legal definitions of "religion." "Religion" was a juridical term long before it became an academic one.

3. See R. G. A. Dolby, "Classification of the Sciences: The Nineteenth Century Tradition," in Roy F. Ellen and David Reason, *Classification in their Social Context* (London: Academic Press, 1979), 167–93.

4. Immanuel Kant, *Critique of Pure Reason*, trans. Norman K. Smith (London: Macmillan & Company, 1956) 310 (B 370). See further discussion of Hans-Georg Gadamer, *Truth and Method* (New York: Crossroad Press, 1975), 170–71 for a brief history of the notion.

5. See among others, George E. Marcus and Michael M. J. Fischer, *Anthropology as Cultural Critique: An Experimental Moment in the Human Sciences* (Chicago: University of Chicago Press, 1986).

Dialogical Fields in Religious Studies

MARY GERHART

IN THE POPULAR PRESS, it sometimes appears as though religious wars continue not only in history and politics but also between the different specializations within the academic study of religion. In his article, "Why Catholics Stay in the Church" in a recent *New York Times* Magazine, for example, Andrew Greeley asserts that they stay because of the stories. This is an interesting argument both for what it claims and for the shock value of the title. Why do the stories upon which this religion reflects and interprets play such an essential role? Here is the way Greeley states the priority of story: ". . . while institutional authority, doctrinal propositions and ethical norms are components of a religious heritage—and important components—they do not exhaust the heritage. Religion is experience, image and story *before it is anything else and after it is everything else*" (40; emphasis mine).

Anyone who knows a religious tradition must have experienced its enviable strengths. Anyone raised in a religious tradition is likely to be steeped in stories which witness to a wide range of genre and gender differences. Anyone who reads religious scriptures is likely to be aware of the multiple ways these stories can go. Anyone who reads and hears the stories is also urged by their willing participation in a religious community to appropriate these texts into their present surroundings. These effects of live religious traditions can be vitiated by traditionalism. But traditions at their best allow themselves to be challenged by the contemporary situation and to be corrected when necessary.

The extent to which we may generalize this observation for religions other than Christianity is, of course, a further question. It does seem to be true for Judaism and Islam. Judaism had such good stories that Christianity bound its own stories to theirs very early on, with the result that Christianity has always been twice blessed with respect to written texts. Islam was also intrigued with some of the best stories from the Hebrew bible but it chose to retell the stories with differences instead of adopting them in context. Islam also has its own body of stories [*hadith* and *sunna*] about its founder and the early tradition.

Different traditions emphasize different stories, and unanimity on the issue of the role of stories is lacking within and across traditions. Nor is conflict on these issues of interpretation confined to the present. People have lost their jobs and lives as a result of internal territorial disputes. The death of Stephen (c36 C.E.), as recorded in Acts could be attributed to a dispute on the primacy of ritual over doctrine. The death of Al-Hallaj (922 C.E.) illustrates conflict between mystical experience and moral and doctrinal clarity. Wrestling with the experience of the ultimate inadequacy of reason in theology and philosophy, Blaise Pascal (1623–62) concluded that the god of the philosophers was inferior to the god of the prophets. . . .

What, then, are we to make of what will appear to many traditionalists as a proposal to reverse the priority of doctrine, institutional authority, and ethical norms over stories? Not that Greeley limits the meaning of story to texts. For him, the neighborhood parish is also "another story." Even so, the list appears to include primarily those elements which might seem, to despisers of religion, to be the childish elements—stories, rituals, and images. The issue

Mary Gerhart, selections from "Dialogical Fields in Religious Studies," Journal of the American Academy of Religion *LXII/4, 1994, 997–1011. Reprinted by permission of Oxford University Press.*

becomes academic—in the sense of disciplinary—however, when Greeley ratchets his argument up a notch with the following metaphysical claim: "In fact, it is in the poetic, the metaphorical, the experiential dimension of the personality that religion finds both its origins and raw power. Because we are reflective creatures we must also reflect on our religious experiences and stories; it is in the (lifelong) interlude of reflection that propositional religion and religious authority become important, indeed indispensable. But then the religiously mature person returns to the imagery, having criticized it, analyzed it, questioned it, to commit the self once more in sophisticated and reflective maturity to the story" (40).

In other words, human beings tell stories in order to represent their best interpretations. In this view truth is what they know through these interpretations.[1] Not that the stories are guarantors of truth or ethical living—or that the meanings of the stories are protected from abuse. Indeed, every generation must correct interpretations in the light of new exigencies, must imagine the structures that best allow the stories to take root in different soil and in lives different from the lives of those who heard the stories before. Nevertheless, the stories remain the prima facie evidence to be taken up as a solid core of empirical residue for a new generation to be fascinated with, perplexed by, charmed and challenged in turn.

I have introduced a scientific term into this last sentence because, in the past, consideration of the role of stories in religious understanding has often been kept within the confines of language studies, philosophy, theology and literary studies. However, I will argue later that a sea change is needed in the field of religious studies, one that must take place in the nexus of the field of theology, the field of art, literature and religion, and the field of science and religion. I perceive a persistent dichotomization between science and religion that continues to flaw both religious and scientific understanding. My wager is that productive work in this nexus requires not only expertise in the fields taken discretely but also scholarly and teacherly collaboration between and among these presently disparate fields.

Three Fields in the Study of Religion, 1968–1994

My scholarship and teaching has been in three fields in religious studies. The first field, called by various names that I will note below, not surprisingly stemmed from my graduate work and dominated my writing and classroom from 1972–1984. The second field, women and religion, began with my reading and reflection in the 1960s and developed as a complement to the first by writing and further reading. The third field, science and religion, from 1984 through the present, was the result not so much of a departure from the first as of a shift in attention to new questions, not all of which could be answered productively with resources from the fields in which I had been trained.

THE FIRST FIELD: ALR

Since the time of its formal inclusion in the university curriculum in the 1950s, the field has been known by several different names. For example, when I began my graduate study at the University of Chicago in the late '60s, the field was called "Theology and Literature." . . . In other words, theology and literature was originally conceived not as a sub-field but rather as an interdisciplinary field—one, it was presumed, that would be "mastered" by one scholar who took twice as long to train (in literary studies and in theology) as one who studied in either of the two fields taken alone. The first graduates of the Chicago program wrote dissertations that were interpretations of particular texts or of the corpus of particular authors. This fact may reflect the relative stability of the field of theology at the time. That is, the questions (other than those for clarification) which drove these inquiries were more likely to pertain to literature than to theological understandings.

Within one year of my arrival at the university, in 1969, the name of the field was changed from "Theology and Literature" to "Religion and Literature," reflecting a growing interest in the bridge between literature and the history of religions—a sense that the link between literature and Christian theology needed to be widened. My Master's degree was therefore in Theology and Literature and my doctorate (three years later) in Religion and Literature with the difference appearing primarily in the topics of dissertations done within the field: mine, I was told, was the first to be done on a theoretical topic. The further widening of the field in the next few years to include other than literary texts brought about another new name for the entire field: the American Academy of Religion reconstituted the field as "Arts, Literature, and Religion" to represent the diversification of what there was to be interpreted. . . .

From its beginnings, Arts, Literature, and Religion considered itself accountable to the methodological considerations of both literary/artistic criticism and theology. In its earliest days, however, the object of ALR was sometimes identified with that of apologetics. We now recognize that if appropriation is taken as the sole or even the major purpose, a distorted view of the task of the discipline can result: the task of ALR can begin to be thought of as superimposing explicitly religious meanings onto the meaning of texts and works of art. Did such distortions occur? Notwithstanding the probability that some examples of distortion could be found, the field was actually founded precisely to prevent too easy a transfer of meaning from doctrinal theology to literature and the arts. Moreover, if one closes one's eyes to issues of appropriation altogether, one foregoes the investigation of a vast amount of literature and art in which explicitly religious questions are at work. Regardless, modern literature increasingly was recognized as presenting a more complicated relationship with religious meaning than had been thought possible in the past. Today appropriation of texts and iconographic materials is recognized to be one of several important issues of interpretation.

THE SECOND FIELD: WOMEN AND RELIGION

I have drawn upon and developed ideas in the field of women and religion simultaneously with my work in the first and third fields. Many of the first questions in the second field came out of a liberal concern with equality. Val Saiving's groundbreaking essay, "The Human Situation: A Feminine Viewpoint" set the stage for a second resurgence of the question of gender equality. The first, a half century before, was Elizabeth Cady Stanton's collaborative project: *The Women's Bible* (1895–98). The basic question then was "Is the Bible itself sexist or did the translation insert sexism into the original texts?" Today it is widely accepted that both the original texts and their translations are likely to reflect gender bias. But the liberalist concern with equality of representation has been replaced by a more interesting and complex question—that of how elements designated as "feminine" are valued in relation to associated elements designated as "masculine." The point of this kind of inquiry is to recognize the positive and negative valences of typically female and male designations. The task goes beyond recognition to call into question and to "transvaluate" the valences so that they do not determine the status of or possibilities for persons of either gender. This question of valuation does not replace the question of equality so much as displace it temporarily: the wager is that equality will be achieved more effectively in the long run.

The question of valuation has been supplanted in turn by a third issue—that of personal gender identity in the light of both of the previous questions.[2] This issue can best be located at the site of personal choices newly informed by one's awareness of the historical inequality of the sexes and of the contemporary challenge to transform values traditionally associated with each. The public dimension of the third issue emerges as questions of strategy—

equivalent to questions of genre. What this third issue reveals is a need to correlate questions about gender with questions about genre (or strategy). In *Genre Choices; Gender Questions,* I suggest ways of formulating and ordering these questions: (1) Which genres (literary strategies) are typically read by or intended for the respective genders? (2) How do genres "redistribute" traditional characteristics defined by gender? (3) How do genres assist in the appreciation and acquisition of modes of speech and action inscribed in gender differences in a given culture at a particular time? There is ample evidence that the correlation of genre and gender makes possible a new method of inquiry. Once one is alert to the facets of both gender and genre it is possible to distinguish among inquiries according to the degree to which they are overgenred and overgendered or undergenred and undergendered.

THIRD FIELD:
SCIENCE AND RELIGION

I credit my opportunity to work in the field of science and religion to my institution's maintenance of a strong interdisciplinary program and to one colleague in particular with whom I have done bidisciplinary writing as well as teaching. Historically, the most important recent changes in the field of science can be said to have taken place after World War II when new technology employing detectors sensitive to radiation beyond visible light gave us new eyes in the development of new kinds of instrumentation.

These developments made it possible to see the Universe differently. The Universe appeared to be violent, for instance, instead of passive. In a similar way planet Earth was found to be more violent. In the science of plate tectonics, Earth scientists observed chunks of Earth colliding, building up mountains, and disappearing in subduction zones. Processes formerly thought by geologists to be more predictable because they were thought to be caused by water were now understood to be dynamic. In other words,

what had been discovered after World War II were new observational aspects of both Earth and Universe. The change also involved the applications of the second law of thermodynamics: we know that when things run alot, they also run down alot. That realization contributed to the understanding of ecological crisis, of the diminishing supply of natural resources, and of limits to growth. . . .

A shift in focus from Earth to Universe has raised old questions—such as that of the future of the human species—in a new context. How do new scientific technologies, e.g., the possibility of constructing colonies in space or of mapping the genes of the human body, challenge us to refigure the aspirations of the human species? The shift also changes the scale of some other traditional questions. This shift from Earth to Universe radically alters the sense of "ongoing" revelation in the three "religions of the book." To what extent may certain concepts, such as that of "covenant" and "Islam," need to be reinterpreted in the new scientific context? What aspects of the question of Christology are affected by the new cosmology in which Universe is the context rather than planet Earth?[3] How are the claims of ecological theology both supported and modified by the new scientific emphasis on the Universe as distinct from planet Earth?

Can the field of religion afford not to have an awareness of science as resource for theological inquiry? On the one hand, who else will respond to the confidence—perhaps overconfidence—of the new cosmologists that allows them to claim that ultimately there will be a scientific explanation for everything? Stephen Hawking, along with other cosmologists, has a vision of complete knowledge about the universe—a vision which excludes religious understanding as having no relevance for future states of affairs. . . .

Can the problem of metaphysical naivetÈ be addressed without trust built from frequent conversations and familiarity with one another's fields? Making more room for the relatively small but long-lived discipline of religion and science within the academy promises to contribute in both directions. Ultimately, we need to affirm both the importance of science's being informed by other disciplines, such as that of philosophical theology, and the importance of religious studies being informed by science. If confidence in the work of the intellect is to endure, we need mutually to inform and to contextualize that which otherwise, we know from the history of thought, will come to dominate and forget its limits.

Furthermore, the ambition which drives these new cosmologies suggests that work in the dialogical fields, such as that of religion and science, can best be carried out collaboratively rather than by one scholar attempting to merge perspectives that are remarkably divergent in many ways. Indeed, I don't think we can do it without being in dialogue. This is especially true since it is as hard to talk to cosmologists in their current state of self-confidence as it was earlier to talk with religious scholars in their earlier states of certitude.

We will also need new theoretical strategies for such collaboration. When fields are relatively close together, contiguities and similarities prevail in the extension of what is known. . . .

Bringing it All Together: Issues of Genre in Theological/ Religious and Secularist Studies

Most critical thinkers think that they recognize the difference between a fundamentalist position on the meaning of a scriptural text and a scholarly position or a secularist position. Critical scholars and secularists alike are likely to reject literal interpretations that jeopardize human rights and lives. These scholars could be expected to decry, for example, the laws that permit genocide in Bosnia as well as the threats on the life of the Islamic feminist, Taslima Nasrin, who was reported—falsely, she claimed—to have urged that a passage of the Quran be revised.

But although the secularist and the religious scholar may appear to be in agreement in their opposition to fundamentalism, their treatments of genric differences are widely divergent. Secularists tend to have a narrower capacity for differentiating among and interpreting adequately multiple genres. Often when secularist scholars begin to change their attitudes toward religion, they simultaneously begin to be curious about genres in which they previously had no interest. . . .

The use of the genre "argument" by religious scholars may also profit from closer study. Some theologians overestimate the sufficiency of the genre argument; some religious scholars use argument ahistorically to belittle arguments typical for other than their own favorite periods. Both foster habits of mind that too often become ideologies. Triumphalist thought in the guise of scholarship hinders, rather than furthers, progress in the field of Religious Studies. The field must become more aware of its own lack of neutrality in its own investigations and more tolerant of diversity within the genre "theology"; theology needs to become more flexible in its use of the genre "argument." Above all, theological and religious scholars could use a rigorous critique of their own use of classical logic. Logic is a grand editing program. It helps the thinker to select among those conundrums in thought that have been found to be worth holding in one's heart and mind and those which are best sacrificed to the clean sweep of a new broom—what Yeats called consignment to the "scrap heap of spent concepts." Logic assists in the process, but does not provide grounds for the selection.

I would agree that the strength of argument lies in its successful use of logic to uncover contradiction, to prioritize differences, and to mediate opposing positions. But the genre of argument best occurs after the fact. Argument presumes that something moving and important has already been expressed. In this sense, argument is more distanced from originating experience than many other genres although all are abstracted to some degree from lived experience. In another sense, of course, every story and poem has its own argument.

Originally I thought of the discipline of religion and literature as an addition to philosophical theology which has tended, according to Michael Buckley,[4] from the seventeenth century until recently, to prefer models patterned after those used in empirical proof (models which today even in science are in decline). Today I see ALR as an essential complement to other disciplines, one which shares equal space and engages in their mutual correction and enrichment. Situated at the juncture of several different approaches to interpretation, it provides a means for and a model of attending to facets of texts—such as genre and gender differences—that otherwise would be lost, subsumed into less discriminating interests, or explained away.

When interpretations go unchallenged in stable times, the genres of texts may appear to be transparent. Who has not confused or been confused by irony, assuming all the while that "getting it" was the resolution to the confusion? Swift's modest proposal regarding the beggary of Irish children turns out to be repulsively immodest, but we laugh nervously because the genre of satire prompts us to be not serious. Jokes, puzzles, koans all tease the limits of thought. Knowing the genre is a part of the skill of "making sense" of the text.

But in times of crisis, the interpretation of texts may be called into question, and to arrive at a new interpretation, the reader may have to try to interpret a text in the light of more than one genre—may indeed even have to invent new genres. To adopt a different or a new genre is to dramatize a new horizon of possibility. Indeed, what can be understood often depends on the availability of genre to the reader. It is sometimes tempting to think iconoclastically about particular genres which have been troublesome or have gone out of vogue. Since the seventeenth century, the resurrection texts of the Christian testament are no longer adequately understood only as miracle narratives—a loss which perhaps many secularists and religious scholars alike would celebrate. Nevertheless, we now know from the history of art,[5] this same preference resulted in the disappearance of Christ as magician (miracle-working images) in European sculpture: because they were not interpreted, they were not "seen," with the result that many of them deteriorated beyond repair.

If scholars of religion err by overlooking the configurational aspects of the basic texts of the traditions they study, they will overlook one major advantage they have over most scholars of secularity, i.e., those who ignore or oppose particular religions *qua* religious. Secularity glamorizes the enlightenment pretense of being able to ignore instances of such traditional genres as myth, by relegating them to the category of the "false." For its own reasons, secularity tends to curb the multiple effects of genre and to privilege a relatively small set of genres: for example, political addresses, irony, and satire. It also tends to identify gender issues exclusively with liberal politics and in so doing, to obscure or suppress some of the most interesting and often cunning aspects of gender—its capacity for singular as well as different relationships, its complicity with having and not having power, its ability to see the self as an other while it must assume the other as a kind of self. . . .

Conclusion

The editor of this journal has asked, What would it mean to make progress in the field of religious studies? Let me try a brief response in the light of the foregoing considerations.

The naive view thinks of progress in a linear mode. Moreover, that mode is overly opportunistic; it flourishes mostly by discrediting previous insights and by ignoring the ambiguity of its best achievements: its own hubris is hidden from itself. While there is no guaranteed strategy for overcoming this naive view, one might expect that collaboration in teaching and writing between scholars from different disciplines, instead of and in addition to their mastery of a single field, might go some distance in addressing the difficulty. This strategy is particularly true for the fields of science and religion because each is suspicious lest the other gain epistemological primacy.

If collaborative work can in fact be supported, we will see many changes in our ordinary ways of doing scholarship. It may no longer be—if it ever was—sufficient to know a text just a little better without any reference to what's happening on Earth and in the universe.

Then again, surely the universe of past and future holds surprises—surprises for which we will need both old and new stories to enable us to understand.

NOTES

1. David Tracy, *Plurality and Ambiguity: Hermeneutics, Religion, Hope* (Chicago: University of Chicago Press, 1994).

2. Julia Kristeva, "Women's Time," in *Feminist Theory: A Critique of Ideology,* Edited by Nannerl O. Keohane, Michelle Z. Rosaldo, and Barbara Gelpi (Chicago: University of Chicago Press, 1981).

3. Jack Hitt, "Would You Baptize an Extraterrestrial?" *New York Times Magazine* (May 29, 1994): 36–39.

4. Michael Buckley, *At the Origins of Modern Atheism* (New Haven: Yale University Press, 1987).

5. Thomas Mathews, *The Clash of the Gods: A Reinterpretation of Early Christian Art* (Princeton: Princeton University Press, 1993).

Why the Academic Study of Religion?

DONALD WIEBE

THE METHODOLOGICAL IMPLICATIONS of the motives that underlie the study of religion and, more particularly, the academic study of religion have not, I think, received the attention they deserve. They are of the utmost importance, however, for the differences of motivation between the study of religion legitimated by the modern university and the scholarly study of religion that antedates it, sponsor radically different, if not mutually exclusive, approaches to its study. In asking why the study of religion is undertaken as an *academic* exercise—which is, after all, a comparatively recent development— I shall be attempting to delineate, to some extent, the relation of motive to method in what has come to be called Religious Studies. In clarifying that relation I hope also to show that Religious Studies—that is, the academic study

of religion—must be a vocation in very much the same sense that Max Weber speaks of science as a vocation[1] and, therefore, that such study must take as merely preliminary a "religious studies" that is concerned only to "understand" rather than to explain the phenomenon of Religion.

The scholarly study of religion, as is well known, has a very long history. Much, if not all, of that study was religiously motivated; it was— and for many still is—a religious exercise designed for, or directed to, the betterment of the individual concerned and, ultimately, is concerned with "salvation." The ultimate goal of salvation is not, however, the only motivating factor to be found as justification of this enterprise. There were (are) other lesser, but in some sense contributory, goals that have implicitly

Donald Wiebe, selections from "Why the Academic Study of Religion? Motive and Method in the Study of Religion," Religious Studies 24, 1988, 403–413

grounded or been, consciously invoked as justi-fication for such study. Such motivations are not easily discerned, however, for they are not always consciously and explicitly espoused.

Recognition of the psychological, cultural and political roles religion has played in society and of its continuing importance in those respects in our own context seems for many to imply that the study of religion ought to be undertaken as support to religion in its mani-fold tasks—that is, that it ought to complement religion. Religion has been, and still is, absolutely necessary, it is argued, for personality integration and contributes significantly to human personal development. Not only has religion provided individual identity, it has been the "glue", so to speak, that has provided the cohesiveness necessary to social/societal exis-tence. And a study of religion that fails to rec-ognize these values and the truth of religion upon which they rest, it is then maintained, is obviously misdirected; it is at best but wasted effort if not, in fact, destructive. This implies, of course, that the study of religion is not under-stood as an exercise undertaken in and for itself but rather that it is to be seen as an instrument for the preservation of religion and its presumed beneficial effects. The purpose for the study, that is, lies outside itself, being found only in "the truth of religion," however that phrase is interpreted. And it should be noted that such aims for the study characterise not only the indi-vidual engaged in that work but also the insti-tutional structures that make the scholarly study of religion possible.

Such argument provides an answer to the question "Why the study of religion?" but not, I suggest, to the question why one might, more specifically, undertake the *academic* (or scien-tific) study of religion as established within the university curriculum. Neither is it the only answer possible, nor the most persuasive. Indeed, even though it gives some indication of the pragmatic value the study of religion might have, the argument does not really answer the question satisfactorily since it seems to involve a

non-sequitur of sorts. It is quite possible, that is, for religion to be of benefit to individual and society without being true; the benefits of reli-gion do not necessarily rest upon the cognitive truth of religion's claims even though they may depend upon the belief by the devotees that those claims are (cognitively) true. It is clear, that is, that the benefits religion has conferred, or now confers, upon individual and/or society may be achieved in other, and possibly better, ways. To assume that the study of religion ought to be the ally of religion is not immedi-ately obvious and therefore hardly the only grounds on which to base the study of religion. It must be recognized that knowledge of the falsity of religion—should that be the case—would also make the study of religion of prag-matic value since it would permit its manipulation for the benefit of individual and society, or its replacement for the benefit of individual and society, or its replacement with superior 'social mechanisms' for the fulfillment of such psychological or social needs. It seems that exactly that kind of argument is raised, for example, with regard to the study of magical and astrological systems of belief. The effects of such beliefs on numerous societies have not been invoked as indicative of the truth of the claims made, except by the faithful, nor that a study of those claims ought to be involved in promoting the results achieved through such systems of belief. There is no assumption here, that is, of the *sui generis* character of such sys-tems of experience and belief and consequently no argument for the recognition of, say, *Magiewissenschaft* as a new discipline or call for the establishment of departments of magic or astrology. (As I recall, Brian Magee once raised the question "If departments of religion why not departments of Magic?" on the BBC and, I think, quite rightly so.) The postulation of the *sui generis* character of religion but not of magic, it appears, rests on the uncritical assump-tion that religion, in some fundamental sense, is True while magic (astrology, etc.) is not. Indeed, if this is not the assumption that implicitly grounds that postulation, the explicitly acknowledged grounds for establishing departments of religion referred to above, namely religion's profound impact upon individuals and society, constitute adequate grounds for the creation of departments of magic that is, for academically legitimating what we might analogously refer to as "Magical Studies."

Concern for the practical value of religion, therefore, is not the same as the concern for the truth of religion in any cognitive sense. Indeed, understanding how religion has functioned in various societies constitutes knowledge about religion that is wholly independent of knowledge as to the truth or falsity of religious claims. Moreover, such mundane, objective knowledge is the only ground on which the pragmatic value of Religious Studies could be predicated short of presuming that the discipline can provide one with the insights of the religious experience itself. Furthermore, its pragmatic value would then be a matter of "political" action based on the knowledge gained and not intrinsic to the study itself. It may motivate the individual to undertake the study of religion but does not constitute the *raison d'etre* of the discipline itself. And it is the failure to recognize this that has been the bane of the *academic* study of religion which, like other academic enterprises, sees itself as a scientific and not a "political" vocation.

I have in the preceding discussion made reference to Religious Studies as a vocation. I have done so deliberately for it seems to me that much that Max Weber had to say of "science as a vocation" is applicable to the academic study of religion. Even his discussion of vocation in "the material sense of the term"—that is, to put it bluntly, with respect to the job prospects of the scholar—has a direct bearing on the religion graduate although I do not wish to focus attention on those matters here. What is pertinent, rather, is his discussion of "the inward calling for science" which is inextricably bound up with what Weber refers to as the disenchantment of the world—with a recognition that meaning is the product of human creativity. Weber maintains that discussion of "the *inward* calling for science" is of no assistance in answering the question as to the value or meaning of science within the total life of humanity, nor with ascertaining how one ought to live. Such questions are of a logically different order. Indeed, vocation in the sense of an inward calling for science presumes science is not directed toward answering such questions—that such questions, to rephrase the point, are not scientific questions. Rather, science "presupposes that what is yielded by scientific work is important in the sense that it is 'worth being known'", although Weber admits, that this presupposition itself cannot be proved by scientific means.[2] It is simply a matter of historical fact that aims such as these have emerged in the development of Western culture. The emergence of the desire for objective knowledge of "the world," that is, constitutes the introduction of a radically new value into human culture. Weber then proceeds to show, moreover, that where personal or societal value judgements are introduced into a scientific endeavour there full understanding of the facts ceases and the inward calling for science is dissipated and science destroyed. Science is a vocation, then, in the exclusive service of, as Weber puts it, self-clarification of ideas and knowledge of interrelated facts. "It is not," he writes, "the gift of grace of seers and prophets dispensing sacred values and revelations, nor does it partake of the contemplation of sages and philosophers about the meaning of the universe."[3] It is simply a human activity with a peculiar—recent—intentionality, so to speak. And what he has to say of the natural sciences applies, *mutatis mutandis,* to the social sciences including those focused on religious phenomena. . . .The academic or scientific study of religion is, I would argue, simply one of several special areas into which the scientific vocation of which Weber speaks is organized and that, like the others, it seeks self-clarification and knowledge of interrelated facts. What I shall attempt to do in the remainder of this essay, therefore, is to give a precise formulation of the aim of the study of religion *qua* study and to explicate the implications this has for the method of that study and how the subject ought to be taught in the academic/university setting.

To put the matter somewhat tautologically, the academic study of religion must be undertaken for academic—that is, purely intellectual/scientific—reasons and not as instrumental in the achievement of religious, cultural, political or other ends. This means, quite simply, that the academic/scientific study of religion must aim only at "understanding" religion where "understanding" is mediated through an intersubjectively testable set of statements about religious phenomena and religious traditions. As with any other scientific enterprise, therefore, the academic study of religion aims at public knowledge of public facts; and religions are important public facts. It is subject first and foremost to "the authority of the fact," although not thereby positivistically enslaved, so to speak, to "a cult of the fact" as my comments below on the role of theory in that study will clearly demonstrate. Religion, it must be recognized, is a form of human activity and therefore like any other form of human activity can become the object of human reflection.

This does not, of course, imply that persons who are religiously committed cannot be scientific students of religion or, for that matter, that Marxist atheists ought to be excluded from departments of Religious Studies. What it does imply, however, is that the value systems by which such individuals may be personally motivated to undertake the study of religion not be allowed to determine the results of their research. What is at issue here is the matter of what we might call "the institutional commitment" that characterises the academic study of religion—that is, the commitment to achieve intersubjectively testable knowledge about religions free of the influence of personal idiosyncratic bias or extraneous social/political aims. . . .

The goal of the academic study of religion, therefore, to reiterate, is an understanding of the phenomena/phenomenon of religion "con-tained in" scientifically warrantable claims about religion and religious traditions. Without intersubjectively testable statements about religions both at the level of particular descriptive accounts of the data *and* at the level of generalizations with respect to the data, no scientific understanding can be achieved.

At the simplest logical level the student of religion functions somewhat like the scientific naturalist with a concern "to collect," describe and classify the phenomena observed. (Being aware all the while, of course, that a mere accumulation of data does not in itself constitute a science.)[4] The range of data, obviously, is enormous, involving rites, rituals, beliefs, practices, art, architecture, music, and so on. Some depth of perspective in the descriptive accounts is provided in relating it to the field of events and structures of which it is a part; in comparing it to similar phenomena in other cultural and social contexts; and in providing at least a narrative account of its emergence and historical development. This work is carried out primarily within the framework of the positive historical and philological disciplines but does not exhaust the task of description.

The work of the phenomenologist, the hermeneut, and the "historian of religions" (in the broad sense of that phrase) in their concern for the *meaning* they think religious behaviour—beliefs, practice, rites, rituals, etc.—has *for the devotee* who participates in the tradition adds something new to the surface description of that tradition. Such "thick description" as it has been called,[5] increases understanding of overt actions seen without reference to how they are "taken" by the participant; ("seen" from the participant's point of view). The work of such students of religion is, as one might expect, much more of an imaginative activity than that of the positive historian or philologist. The results of their work is much less exact. The act of interpretation is in some sense the imposition of an external construction and therefore never likely to replicate exactly the participant's understanding of the phenomenon concerned.

It will, consequently, be intrinsically incomplete and open to debate, although not on that account totally without merit, for such "constructions" are not simply arbitrary but rather controlled by the context of information provided by the more positive sciences. That it does not allow the same degree of certitude that is to be found in the surface and depth descriptions of the other disciplines does not imply that that question of meaning can simply be ignored but rather that the student here will have to be satisfied with the more probable and plausible constructions and be willing to entertain alternatives to those constructions without overmuch fuss.

It needs to be emphasized here that this concern with meaning and "thick description" has nothing to do with speculative or intuitive insight as to the "real meaning" or truth of Religion—its ultimate meaning that comes from a knowledge of the ultimate ontological status of the "religious realities" as known by the participant within the tradition. Nor has it any kinship with direct, intuitive insight of the religiously perceptive student of religion. The meaning that holds the interest of the *academic* student of religion, rather, is a psychological matter; it involves overtones and undertones of actions, utterances, and events as well as an attempt to understand the psychological and emotional state or condition of the devotee who claims to know such ultimate mysteries. This kind of meaning, although not obvious at the surface level of religious phenomena, is not, as I have indicated, wholly beyond the reach of reason and scientific research.

Though knowledge of religion at the descriptive level is richly informative it is not primarily that for which the student of religion strives. Indeed, an increasing flow of such information soon inundates the individual for it is simply not possible for any one person to know all the particulars of the world's religious traditions. Like the other sciences, the study of religion seeks explanatory frameworks—theories—that account for the particulars; frameworks that

permit an understanding of the multiplicity of particulars in terms of relatively few axioms and principles that can easily be held in mind. That thrust towards explanation and theory is implicit already in the descriptive and taxonomic levels that reduce "individuals" to classes of things, persons, occurrences and events.

While explanations and theories transcend description they are nevertheless also dependent upon the descriptive level of activity of the student of religion. The data that accumulates as the result of the labours of the historian and phenomenologist are, in a sense, the substance for theoretical reflection in that they are what the theorist tries to provide a coherent account of. Moreover, the theories constructed to account for the data can only be properly adjudicated over against *new* observational data beyond that upon which theoretical reflection has been focused.

If these are the aims of the *academic* study of religion then that study is structurally indistinguishable from other scientific undertakings. The *academic* study of religion is, then, a positive science and not a religious or metaphysical enterprise in that it concerns itself with religion as a public fact and not a divine mystery. This does not mean that such a study must be limited to discussion of only the empirically observable behaviour of religious persons and communities—that it adopt, for example, the positivistic empiricism of a Skinnerian behaviourism. It merely implies that there not be "privileged access" for some to the "data"; that whatever does lie "beyond" the empirically observable whether that be the interior experience of the devotee or the "intentional object" of that experience—be somehow "intersubjectively available" for scrutiny and analysis. And that, it seems to me, presents no problems given that the empirically available religious traditions are considered by the devotees to be *expressions* of their faith, which faith is constituted by their religious experience and the truth of that "encounter" with "the ultimate," however it may be referred to in the various traditions.

Thorough scrutiny of all aspects of the tradition, therefore, cannot but provide us *some* understanding as to the nature of the "faith" although, quite obviously, not with the experiential quality and emotional forcefulness with which the devotee will claim to understand it. Thus, although there is an interior and esoteric aspect to religion, it is not wholly inaccessible to the "outsider" for it can be approached from "the outside in." Moreover, should the devotee claim a superior understanding where a conflict of claims arises and do so on the basis of her/his direct personal experience of "the Ultimate," the claim will be overruled on the grounds that it resorts to the use of "information" to which s/he has "privileged access." To allow such a claim to stand would be to place all understanding of religion in jeopardy (and not merely the scientific understanding of religion) since such grounds would then also be acceptable for the settling of intra-religious (and even intratraditional) conflict of claims as well. It is obvious, therefore, that the settlement of disputes would be achieved on highly idiosyncratic personal grounds that is, on the basis of private religious experience—in which each and every disputant would be wholly successful. It would, in the final analysis, then, commit us to a radical relativism that precludes all possibility of transpersonal truth-claims and with it, all possibility of a scientific (i.e., academic) study of religion. What one could then know of religion would be that which one could know of "faith" and that is only known *by* faith and the direct encounter of "the Ultimate." To know that the essence of religion is "faith" would be to know that it cannot be scientifically understood.

This, unfortunately, is too seldom noticed by students of religion. They fail to see that such reasoning makes the study of religion possible only from within the circle of the devotee/participant and therefore a religious rather than a scientific enterprise. The study of religion that appropriately finds its place within the university curriculum is rather that which I have sketched above. It is a critical study of a human cultural phenomenon and not a quest for some ultimate meaning or truth. It seeks "objective" knowledge of a particular aspect of human culture. It is, therefore, essentially a positive, (*not* positivistic) social scientific endeavour that, although not necessarily behaviouristic is nevertheless behaviouralist in its approach to religion in that it attempts to provide a public rather than a private knowledge.[6] . . .

To propagate one's faith is not the analysis of religious phenomena. The lecture-rooms of the university are wholly inappropriate for the propagation of either one's political or religious agendas. It is simply outrageous as Weber points out, to use the power of the lecture-room with its captive audience for such purposes. . . . Similarly, the student entering upon the academic study of religion ought not to seek from the professors what the professors ought not to give. They should not, that is, crave leaders, but rather teachers.

NOTES

1. Max Weber, "Science as a Vocation" in H. H. Gerth and C. Wright Mills (eds.), *From Max Weber: Essays in Sociology* (New York: Oxford University Press, 1946, pp. 129–156). It was originally published in *Gesammelte Aufsaetz zur Wissenschftslehre* (Tübingen, 1922, pp. 524–555). I use the notion of "vocation" not, obviously, in its religious sense but rather to emphasize the stark contrast in aims and intentions between a "religious calling" and a "scientific career."

2. Ibid., 143.

3. Ibid., 152.

4. See, for example, D. Sperber, *On Anthropological Knowledge* (Cambridge: Cambridge University Press, 1985, p. 11).

5. This notion is borrowed from C. Geertz's "Thick Description: Toward an Interpretive Theory of Culture," in his *The Interpretation of Cultures* (New York: Basic Books, 1973, pp. 3–30).

6. For possibilities of developing the argument in this direction see W. Richard Comstock, "A Behavioral Approach to the Sacred: Category Formation in Religious Studies," *The Journal of the American Academy of Religion*, XLIX (1981), 625–643.

Becoming Answerable for What We See

MARGARET R. MILES

WHILE A HISTORIAN can perhaps pretend to have watched too many centuries come and go to get very excited about the bald fact of the rapidly approaching twenty-first century, the moment nevertheless provides a convenient point at which to examine where we are as scholars of religion. In this address I will endeavor both to celebrate the academy and to propose a strenuous next task. . . .

You will notice in the remarks that follow that I do not distinguish between the "study of religion" and "theological studies." It is time, I believe, finally to lay to rest the debate over fundamental differences between "theological studies" and the "study of religion." The distinctions were usefully defined in 1991 in Ray Hart's JAAR article "Religious and Theological Studies in American Higher Education." But in 1999, these distinctions are without a difference. Theological studies, thought of as exploring a religious tradition from within, must also bring critical questions to the tradition studied. And the study of religion, often described as taking an "objective" or disengaged perspective, cannot be studied or taught without understanding the power and beauty, in particular historical situations, of the tradition or the author we study. Nor can religious studies avoid theology—the committed worldviews, beliefs, and practices of believers—by focusing on religious phenomenologies. Both "theological studies" and the "study of religion" must integrate critical and passionately engaged scholarship. I use, then, the providentially ambiguous term "religious studies" to integrate the falsely polarized terms, "theological studies" and "the study of religion."

The Context

Before we approach questions of where we are and how American religious studies might develop in the early years of the twenty-first century, a preliminary question must be considered. What is the present context, the historical and cultural moment in which American scholars of religion practice the craft of religious studies?

Diana Eck at Harvard University has recently published a CD-ROM entitled "On Common Ground: World Religions in America." She demonstrates that Americans are becoming increasingly religious, but not along the lines of the traditional mainstream of American religious life. The project offers a directory that includes listings of Hindu, Buddhist, Jain, and Baha'i temples, Islamic mosques, Sikh gurdwaras, neo-pagan groups, and Zoroastrian centers. These religious groups do not exist across vast geographical distances from one another as they did in the recent past; people of different religious orientations are now neighbors. The new diversity of American religious life is rapidly creating a stimulating and demanding situation in which the *study* of religion—as contrasted with *teaching* one's own religion—acquires increasing importance.

American religious pluralism creates an urgent need to respond to the question: Can religion serve the common good rather than dividing people and setting them in opposition to one another? If religion is to serve the common good, it will need to be studied, ardently and critically, for pitfalls as well as for insights. Most of the world's religions have a shameful past in that whenever a religion has had the

Margaret R. Miles, selections from "Becoming Answerable for What We See," Journal of the American Academy of Religion 68/3, 2000, 471–485. *Reprinted by permission of Oxford University Press and the author.*

power to compel adherence, it has almost always done so. Religious difference is apparently one of the most difficult kinds of difference for human beings to accept. The most blatant form of religious chauvinism, of course, is religious wars. But scholarship about religion has often exhibited a more subtle form. Theologian Paul Tillich pointed out that scholars tend to describe their own religion on its most profound level, while considering other religions on their most superficial levels as "futile human attempts to reach God." Yet, believing strongly in the divine revelation of one's own religion, one can still recognize that its beliefs and practices emerged in history as human efforts to give form and substance to that revelation. As human products, religious beliefs, practices, and institutions are always in need of critical scrutiny. Their effects, not merely their intentions, must be acknowledged and examined. In short, in a religiously plural society religious studies still bears the traditional responsibility of representing religion as providing accessible and fruitful proposals for living a richly human life. But it also has responsibility for critical scrutiny of the social effects of religious beliefs and practices.

The Three Publics

I have been speaking about one aspect of the role of religious studies in the public sphere. But religious studies has at least three publics: the public sphere, faith communities, and the university disciplines. And the public sphere is a far more complex arena than one in which Americans simply need to get along with people who have other religious loyalties than their own. Debates about reproductive technologies, about the role—if any—of religion in public schools, debates about national and global politics and policies: these issues and many more are presently engaging, and must continue to engage, religious studies scholars.

Consider the role of religious studies in relation to the second public, faith communities.

Should religious studies be thought of as primarily answerable to churches, synagogues, temples, or mosques? Within the American Academy of Religion some of us think of scholarship as responsible primarily to worshippers and others insist that scholarship is, or should be, independent of the scholar's own religious commitment and the faith communities of the tradition she studies. I believe that a fruitful tension, difficult to maintain, must be held between the two. Even the seminaries in which religious leaders are trained should not aim simply at pleasing the religious constituencies that support them with students and funding. In a consumer society it is tempting to commodify theological education. Yet scholarship has a prophetic imperative to challenge, unsettle, and discomfit religious people as well as to affirm and educate.

The third "public" of religious studies is the university. A recent book by Donald Wiebe, *The Politics of Religious Studies,* accuses the academy of compromising the scientific study of religion under the pressure of religious belief. He cites the AAR as a particular location where this occurs. Wiebe charges that religious studies has become a facade for promoting religion rather than for studying it. . . .

The academy includes, and must continue to include, within its ranks scholars who attend to all three of the "publics" of religious studies—those who consider their scholarship primarily answerable to religious bodies, those whose main discussion partners are in university departments, and those who address the pressing questions and problems of the public sphere. Let us not compete with one another to establish particular interests and foci at the expense of others. Let us relinquish partisan claims to represent the only "true" or "pure" religious studies. And let us not retain a distinction between theological studies and the study of religion whose usefulness is outlived, for there are several real and critical differences within the academy that need our attention. And it is to these that I now turn.

Differences in Religious Studies

I believe that the adequacy of our attention to several fundamental differences within the academy will determine the fruitfulness of religious studies into the twenty-first century. These critical points of difference within the AAR are: 1) disciplinary difference; 2) religious difference; and 3) gender, racial/ethnic, and sexual orientation difference. I will discuss each in turn and then propose a paradigm I find useful for thinking about differences within the academy.

DISCIPLINARY DIFFERENCE

One of the academy's most pressing present issues is how to keep the field of religious studies freshened by new content and methods from other fields without losing the integrity and distinctiveness of religious studies. In the 1999 AAR program book for the annual meeting, program units appear that represent disciplines new to religious studies in the last decade or so: Arts, Literature, and Religion; Critical Theory and Discourses on Religion; Feminist Theory and Religious Reflection; Men's Studies; Religion and Ecology; Ritual Studies; Rastafari in Global Contexts; Religion and Science; Religion and Popular Culture, to name a few of the relatively new topics. We must, I think, understand religious studies as a discursive field, a rich conversation, rather than as a single field with identifiable boundaries of content or method. Religious studies is *inherently* interdisciplinary.

Julie Thompson Klein's book, *Interdisciplinarity,* lists several objectives of interdisciplinary study that describe religious studies well. Interdisciplinary study, she writes, aims at answering complex questions, addressing broad issues, exploring disciplinary and professional relations, and solving problems that are beyond the scope of one discipline. Religious studies, like interdisciplinary studies, resists the fragmentation that can result from specialization. Religious studies endeavors to see features of religion and culture that are marginalized or

excluded by the foci of traditional disciplines. Even the field's traditional focus on language and texts is presently being challenged by growing interest in and attention to historical and contemporary images, film, and media culture. We must, I think, boldly maintain the AAR's commitment to interdisciplinarity.

RELIGIOUS DIFFERENCE

By this I mean not simply ecumenical difference or differences between religions but also the cultural differences that lie within and inform religious differences. What would it mean, in dominantly Christian educational institutions, to take religions other than Christianity and Judaism seriously?

Representatives of non-western religions have, for some time, been part of religious studies institutions. Many seminaries, religious studies departments, divinity schools, and doctoral programs even require coursework in a religion other than that of the student's primary focus. But non-western religions are still largely marginalized within curricula. The assumption is that a brief and limited acquaintance with a non-western religion will unproblematically enhance adherence to one's own religion. In other words, in order to make the study of religions other than one's own nonthreatening, scholars have tended to ignore other religions' truth claims. We reduce them to objects of study. When, however, we study other religions as we study our own, that is, in order to understand concretely and in detail each religion's intellectual and emotional power, we will need to acknowledge that it is threatening to study another religion in this way. I will describe a bit later the necessary ability to hold in permanent tension irreducible differences and similarities.

The rapidly expanding internationalization of religious studies both requires and stimulates encounters with religious others. Within the AAR, international conferences have been occurring for several years. A further step toward international dialogue was taken in September of this year when several AAR members participated in a panel at the Japanese Association of Religious Studies. Together with two Japanese scholars, Larry Sullivan, David Carrasco, and I explored "New Trends in Religious Studies" in our different contexts. This—and other—beginning international conversations will need to be deliberately cultivated, and appropriate ways of developing international connections will need to be explored.

GENDER, RACIAL/ETHNIC, AND SOCIAL ORIENTATION DIFFERENCE

The third form of difference addresses the academy at the beginning of the twenty-first century, namely, the participation of people new to religious studies. Scholars of religion have, until quite recently, worked within coteries of intellectual and social similarity, in institutions, fields, and religions. The institutionalization of these circles guaranteed their perpetuation. Their erosion has often been experienced as "the end of civilization as 'we' knew it." The problematic word here, and in the following sentences, is "we." "We" used to know what "theology" is. "We" used to be able to master the methods of a single discipline and use them in a way that was recognized and rewarded. "We" even used to be able to conduct faculty searches much more simply; we knew the leading scholars in our fields and we simply recruited one of their most promising students. "We" studied other religions by reading their classic texts and by meeting occasionally for interreligious dialogue with our educated counterparts in those religions.

But enclaves of similarity are presently dissolving, creating a situation of hermeneutical opportunity, a moment in which diverse religious and disciplinary perspectives, represented by scholars of various races, gender, sexual orientations, and ethnicities, freshen conversations within ancient disciplines. Important work has been done in the last twenty years to identify and challenge the complicity of conceptual schemes in creating and maintaining oppressive

and exclusive institutions and political and social arrangements. People new to the academy have moved, in bell hooks phrase, "from margin to center" as they bring mind-opening criticism to reigning scholarly assumptions. Feminists, African Americans, gay men and lesbian women, and Latino/Latina and Native American theologians meet together to discuss and discern their identities and their agenda. It is important for these groups to have institutional time and space for their conversations. Indeed, the new perspectives are of great importance to the health and vitality of academic institutions. We should notice, however, that there is a time-lag between the significance of their criticism and institutional change.

Moreover, the new theologians are now presenting theologies that incorporate, along with their most profound and trenchant criticism of mainstream academic work, constructive theological visions capable of attracting a broadly diverse audience. I think, for example, of books like Alejandro Garcia-Rivera's *The Community of the Beautiful.*

How are constructive theologies created that both incorporate cultural and textual criticism and attract broadly diverse adherents? The task, as I have already indicated, has two important overlapping moments: the critical moment and the constructive search in the vast material of our religious traditions for resources for construction. I will give examples of each in the time remaining.

The Critical Moment   Ray Hart's 1991 article, which I have already mentioned, footnotes several reasons for a perception among some people that seminary education is in decline. One of the reasons he gives is especially striking: "Most students [he writes] . . . are interested in 'truth.' But most professors do not think it is possible to gain knowledge of 'truth' from scripture or other religions. Therefore, potential seminary students will increasingly have less desire to attend seminaries, since the concept of truth has been lost to a great degree."

Has religious studies abandoned the concept of definable, non-negotiable, and universal truth? Certainly some scholars are less interested in the truth claims of the religion they study than in how it works in the cultural, social, and economic relationships of its environment. But rather than abandoning the concept of truth, are we not rather learning to say with humility and conviction, This is absolute truth for me, even while accepting and respecting another person who says, For me, this is absolute truth? It does not seem to me evident that claims to possession of a universal truth are as attractive as Hart assumed.

When we seek to stabilize rather than reform religious traditions, we tend to forget the widespread damages, personal and communal, that many people ascribe (perhaps reductionistically) to religion. One of the single most important realizations of my adult life was that the oppressive fundamentalism of my childhood could not simply be labeled "Christianity," much less "religion." But a great many Americans embrace secularity because they regard some undifferentiated entity called "religion" as unambiguously harmful. Thus, demonstrating the ability to be self-critical and to acknowledge the abuses perpetrated by some forms of religion could, I believe, attract as many thinking people as will be turned off and turned away by the decline of naive concepts of unassailable "truth." In short, it cannot be assumed that critical approaches to religion create "cultured despisers."

A Model for Conceptualizing Difference So much, for now, for the critical moment. What about the constructive moment? Where will we find models, paradigms, and tools for the present? Have western religious and philosophical traditions anything to offer with which to construct broadly attractive theologies? I will shortly give an example of one constructive moment. But before construction can occur, tools must be marshalled. One of my favorite stories, and a model of how tools can be found, occurs in the epic *Beowulf*. It goes like this: The camaraderie of the old mead hall is troubled by a local monster, Grendel, who habitually drops in while the troops are feasting and drinking to snatch one or two of them for his evening meal. Beowulf is called upon to deal with this rather unpleasant situation. He prepares to face the monster by polishing his trusty sword, a sword that has a genealogy of victories a page and a half long. Clearly, it has served him well in numerous circumstances. But when he descends to the monster's den and faces Grendel, to his consternation, his sword melts in his hand. Imagine his horror, a real male nightmare: a limp sword. Glancing desperately about, he seizes some pots and pans that are hanging on the wall, and with these he manages to slay the monster.

I will ignore for the moment some features of the story that may be problematic and/or provocative (for example, is the monster, as I suspect, an endangered species?!). Suffice it to say that it points out that one's tried and true weapons may not work in a new situation. But one may find effective tools on location if one glances around. I cite Beowulf's story to introduce a usable theory I found while glancing around. Please bear with me while I describe it; I think you will later see its usefulness for conceptualizing differences within religious studies.

Psychoanalyst Jessica Benjamin, in her book *Shadow of the Other*, proposes a theoretical model that acknowledges the complexity and sheer psychic work of dealing with difference. She refers to the two well publicized "stages" Freud identified as necessary for individual development, the preoedipal and the oedipal. In the preoedipal stage, the infant exists in what Freud describes as an "overinclusive" narcissism. In this stage the infant does not differentiate between her own sucking mouth and the mother's breast. By contrast, in the oedipal stage, the child's task is differentiation and separation from the (m)other, individuation, and the development of complementarity.

Benjamin argues persuasively that psychoanalysis since Freud has become so exclusively attentive to the oedipal task of separation and individuation that it has neglected to theorize any position beyond the oedipal. She proposes a third position, a postoedipal stage in which the task is to recuperate preoedipal "overinclusiveness" and to place it in continuing tension with oedipal differentiation. In the postoedipal stage identification and separation oscillate. Neither collapses into the other. Benjamin theorizes the postoedipal as a stage in which difference, modified by recognition and identification, is "exciting and pleasurable rather than merely threatening." The vehicle for this process, Benjamin says, is symbolization, which can reunite the antagonistic tendencies of identification and separation, thereby "expanding what we can own."

What Benjamin describes as an individual task, religions seek to accomplish on the cultural level. In Judaism and Christianity, for example, the call to a people to "come out from among them and be separate" exists in tension with the invitation to recognize consanguinity with the universe. Merging and distinguishing activities can be held in tension, Benjamin says, without splitting them into contradiction. And both in isolation carry potential dangers: overinclusiveness threatens homogenization in which the other's "irreducible alterity" is ignored, while separation threatens exclusion, repudiation, and aggression against difference. The great challenge, not only to religious studies but also to a racially, religiously, and ethnically diverse society, is to achieve the task of inclusion and recognition that nevertheless retains and honors difference.

Consider an application of Benjamin's proposal to the differences that face religious studies in the first decade of the third millennium. First, interdisciplinarity: Rather than jettisoning disciplines in favor of a vast amorphous undisciplined enterprise, each discipline can oscillate between the particularity of its own methods and content, and learning to use the content and methods of other disciplines as these become relevant to particular projects.

Similarly with religious difference: Benjamin's model pictures oscillation between awareness of fundamental and irreducible difference, and recognizing and identifying with the goals and values of a religion other than one's own. Finally, Benjamin's model can incorporate the critical perspectives of gender, race, ethnicity, and sexual orientation in constructive theologies attractive to a broadly diverse audience. Again, oscillation between particularity and identity, differentiation and unity, will preserve both.

My description of Benjamin's psychoanalytic theory is, I hope, an example of the usefulness to religious studies of theoretical work in another field. . . .

Conclusion

The temptation of a presidential address, one that I have not entirely resisted, is to attempt to say everything one thinks important. That temptation is reinforced this year by the imminence of a new millennium. An address to the twelfth largest professional society in the American Council of Learned Societies should be programmatic. It should identify problems and challenges and chart directions. It should address institutions and the broad field of religious studies, not merely scholars in one's own sub-field. Yet our best thinking is often informed by simple suggestions and humble sources, by the stories we collect, the books we chance to read, the people from whom we catch the love for a particular study.

Finally, it is not our problems and challenges, it is not our analyses or agenda that create the bond we share as religious studies scholars. Our primary bond is our commitment to our work—vivid and accountable intellectual work—and to a socially responsible life. Yet, no less serious an intellectual than the twentieth-century philosopher Suzanne Langer introduced her ground-breaking book, *Philosophy in a New Key,* with the following quotation from an obscure author, J. M. Thornburn: "All the genuine deep delight in life is in showing people the mud pies you have made, and life is at its best when we confidingly recommend our mud pies to each other's sympathetic consideration."

We must remind ourselves and each other, as this quotation does, that serious and important as our work is, it needs to be interlaced with moments of self-criticism, humor, and most importantly, delight. Augustine will have the final word: "Delight is, as it were, the weight of the soul. For delight orders the soul. Where the soul's delight is, there is its treasure" (*De musica VI.* 1 1.29). We are privileged to have the luxury of wonderful work. Let's get on with it.

Chapter 3

Quest for the Origins of Religion

In the nineteenth century, the study of religion was shaped by the theory of evolution advocated by Charles Darwin and Herbert Spencer. This pervasive influence set scholars on a quest for the origins of religion that they developed according to an evolutionary model. Although the selection of writings from figures included in this chapter could be classified as early attempts at anthropology or sociology, the single most important theme that united scholars like Tylor, Frazer, Spencer, and Lévy-Bruhl was the quest for the origins of religion. Needless to say, this group does not exhaust the list of scholars that could be included in this quest. Max Müller and Emile Durkheim, for example, could be included in such a list. In this anthology, we are confronted with a certain amount of overlap among the influences that shaped the work of scholars of religion and common interests among them. The overall structure of this anthology represents a series of judgment calls that are intended to be helpful to students and not to reflect precisely the particular discipline of each scholar.

Edward B. Tylor (1832–1917) was a pioneer in the field of anthropology, a profession that began by happenstance after he met the archaeologist Henry Christie in Cuba in 1856 and followed him on an expedition to Mexico. With his interest in human culture aroused, Tylor returned to England and eventually secured a position in the university museum at Oxford where he also lectured on anthropology. He held a newly established chair in anthropology from 1896 until his retirement in 1909. The influence of the theory of evolution was evident especially in the following published works: *Researches into the Early History of Mankind and the Development of Civilization* (1865) and *Primitive Culture: Researches into the Development of Mythology, Philosophy, Religion, Art, and Custom* (1871). Like other thinkers, Tylor presupposed that primitive (his term) human beings possessed chronological priority because they were closer on the scale of evolution to primeval beings. And like other scholars, Tylor wanted to reconstruct the development of civilization from the simplest to the more complex, which usually implied modern Western society. Tylor and others used myth, folklore, social customs, religious beliefs, practices, and attitudes to construct the evolutionary model of the development of human beings. He identified three fundamental stages of cultural evolution: hunter-gather or "savage" stage; "barbaric" stage that was characterized by the domestication of animals and plants; and the civilized stage that began with the art of writing. Tylor's work on religion was related to his attempt to outline a "science of culture" by writing a history of the human mind. He began with a question concerning whether or not religious conceptions exist in all cultures, even the most base of cultures. This question was motivated by a claim that there was no religion among some tribes. Tylor countered that natives of Australia, for instance, possessed beliefs in souls, demons, and deities, and accused Andrew Lang (1844–1912) and others of measuring primitive (Tylor's prejudicial, Western cultural term to refer to simple cultures) by higher Western religion. Using a comparative approach, Tylor based this method on objective observation and not speculation, an approach that led him to identify animism as the basis for the religion of lower tribes. Animism originated from the belief in the existence of the deceased souls of creatures and represented a deeper theory of the origin of spiritual beings. Tylor's theory embodied a twofold conviction: primitive religion was inferior and lower on the evolutionary scale than that of the civilized world. This type of cultural comparison was common for Tylor's historical period. He was interested in demonstrating that higher civilization currently showed survivals of animistic beliefs. A survival was any process, belief, or custom that had been maintained by force of habit, one that does not make sense or explain itself in the context of the world for the person or society being studied. Survivals were relics of a prior age and mental condition. Tylor referred to them as forms of superstition.

Beside Tylor, another candidate for founding father of anthropology and also a pioneer of comparative religion was Sir James George Frazer (1854–1941). Frazer was born in Glasgow, Scotland, and educated at Glasgow University and Trinity College of Cambridge University where he became a fellow in 1879. After a brief teaching appointment at the University of Liverpool (1907–1908), he worked the remainder of his career at Cambridge. In addition to giving the prestigious Gifford Lectures at St. Andrews in 1911 and 1912 and at Edinburgh in 1924, Frazer was a prolific writer. He was most famous for *The Golden Bough,* originally published in 1890 in two volumes, but growing to 12 volumes with the publication of the third edition by 1915. Other noteworthy publications included the following: *Psyche's Task* (1909); the four-volume work, *Totemism and Exogamy* (1910); the three-volume work, *The Belief in Immortality and the Worship of the Dead* (1913–1924); the three-volume work, *Folklore in the Old Testament* (1918); *The Worship of Nature* (1926); *Myths of the Origin of Fire* (1930); *The Fear of the Dead in Primitive Religion* (1933); *Creation and Evolution in Primitive Cosmogonies* (1935); *Aftermath* (1936); *Totemica* (1937); and the four-volume *Anthologia Anthropologica* (1938–1939). Frazer's approach to the study of religion can be characterized as encyclopedic because of the immense amount of materials that he gathered together to argue his case.

Without developing a final and conclusive theory of religion, Frazer developed some general theories on totemism and magic, and he discovered what he thought was an evolutionary sequence of human culture that began with magic, evolved into religion, and culminated with science. According to Frazer, religion, which represented a propitiation and conciliation of assumed superior powers by human beings, was fundamentally opposed to magic, a necessarily false discipline and basic mistaken application of the association of ideas and an erroneous system of natural law and science. In contrast to science, magic is more of an art to the "savage" and never a science, a notion that is lacking in the minds of "primitives" because they reason in ignorance of intellectual and physiological processes. Because homeopathic magic assumed that things that resemble each other are the same, and because contagious magic mistakenly assumed that things that were once in contact with other things continue to be in contact, Frazer wanted to expose these basic fallacies. He wanted to prove empirically that the "savage" did not think logically, was superstitious, and that magic was historically prior to religion. Frazer believed that magic would be replaced eventually by science as humankind matures and throws off the yoke of ignorance and superstition. Frazer thought that this mode of argument enabled him to expose the myth of the noble savage, which owed much to the philosophy of Jean-Jacques Rousseau and others less famous, and enabled Frazer to promote his own political agenda. There was no truth to the belief that the savage was the freest creature of humankind because the primitive was limited by custom and tradition. The basic problem with tribal societies can be traced to their political systems that tend to be democratic, whereas Frazer preferred a monarchical form of government because it represented symbolically and practically the emergence of humankind from the bondage of savagery with its prevalent ignorance and superstition. In fact, an absolute despotism is preferable to the alleged freedom of the "savage" from Frazer's perspective. The truth discovered by Frazer about the cultural and political status of the "primitive" can be enhanced by a comparative study of the beliefs and institutions of humankind. More than a way of simply satisfying the curiosity of scientifically enlightened and culturally sophisticated humans, the comparative approach can become a powerful tool to expedite progress by exposing weak points of modern society. Frazer wove together an evolutionary theory, an encyclopedic approach, a comparative method, and a political agenda.

In comparison to the long career of Frazer at the University of Cambridge, Friedrich Max Müller (1823–1900) was born in Dessau, Germany, and he received his advanced education at the University of Leipzig where he studied languages and Sanskrit along with psychology and anthropology. After securing his doctorate in 1843, he went to Berlin to study with Franz Bopp in comparative philology. He worked with the idealist philosopher Friedrich Wilhelm Joseph von Schelling (1775–1854) in philosophy, and studied Sanskrit and comparative religion with E. Burnouf. After a 2-year sojourn in London, he gravitated to Oxford in 1848 where he became a professor of modern European languages, and later in 1868, a professor of comparative philology. When he retired in 1875, he devoted all his attention to editing the famous *Sacred Books of the East* collection. Besides his published works on Sanskrit, Indian philosophy and religion, and several volumes in comparative mythology, Müller published a number of important works on religion that have important implications for method and the nature of religion. These works include the following: the four-volume *Chips from a German Workshop* (1867–1875); *Introduction to the Science of Religion* (1873); *Natural Religion* (1889); *Physical Religion* (1891); *Anthropological Religion* (1892); and *Theosophy or Psychological Religion* (1893).

By means of this body of literature, Müller called for a science of religion within the context of his vision of a human discovery of the underlying purpose of the religions of humankind and a reconstruction of a genuine *Civitas Dei* (City of God) that would encompass East and West. Müller's vision of this new science included changing the world, renewing Christianity, altering our views of others, seeking common ground between religious cultures, teaching useful lessons, and awakening us to the uniqueness of our own religion and the inevitable decay of religions. For this new science to be genuine, it was necessary for it to be comparative because the basis of all knowledge was comparison. This new science would also adhere to the laws of cause and effect and be inductive. The comparative method afforded a scholar an opportunity to gain a broader cultural perspective to reach a better understanding of common assumptions about the origin, character, and development of religion. Müller conceived of the method of comparison as a means of testing one's own faith and religion against others, and he was convinced that Christianity would win and demonstrate to everyone the unconscious progress that all faiths were making toward it. Overall, Müller grounded his theory in a finite perceptual epistemology that implied something greater than the finite entities that were connected with the primary data of religion. What Müller called "Natural Religion," a possession of all humankind, developed from the combining of moral sensibility with religion, which in turn had its roots in the perception of the infinite. These types of notions were to influence other scholars attempting to develop further a science of religion.

Before the trend for the quest for origins fell from scholarly fashion, Lucien Lévy-Bruhl (1857–1939) compared primitive mentality to modern Western modes of scientific thinking and found the former lacking in rigor and rationality. During his early education, Lévy-Bruhl concentrated on philosophy, and he taught at secondary schools. Receiving his doctorate in 1884, he took a couple of teaching posts until he arrived at the Sorbonne in 1896, where he served as professor of modern philosophy. Beside a 1-year visiting professorship at Harvard University, he was editor of the *Revue Philosophique* in 1917, and he cofounded the Institut d' Ethnologie with Paul Rivet and Marcel Mauss in 1925. In addition to works on modern French philosophy and ethics, Lévy-Bruhl's most important works with respect to the study of religion are the following: *Primitive Mentality* (1923); *How Natives Think* (1926); *The "Soul" of the Primitive* (1929); and *Primitives and the Supernatural* (1935).

Lévy-Bruhl called primitive or archaic mentality "prelogical reasoning," although he rejected the differences between modern and primitive mentality in his posthumously published work entitled *The Carnets* (1949). He argued that the mental differences were not matters of principle but more evidence of nuances of mentality. In his earlier works, however, he used comparison to measure modern Western modes of thinking with that of primitive thought. He focused primitive thought on collective representations, tended to ignore necessity, and identified the one and the many by means of the principle of participation. Lévy-Bruhl described this type of mentality as mystical, prelogical, and pervaded by a sense of affectional participation because some primitives think of themselves as animals or birds without thinking metaphorically or symbolically about this kind of identity. If the equation made between primitives and animal species suggested an actual participatory identity, if mystical mentality implied a connection to mysterious occult forces, and if we compared this type of primitive thinking with modern modes of thought, Lévy-Bruhl believed that we can conclude that the prelogical mode of thinking was indifferent to logical laws of contradiction, which necessarily meant that prelogical thinking was very different from his own type of thinking because it did not avoid contradictions. Unlike Tylor's emphasis on individual psychology to grasp the nature of religion, Lévy-Bruhl wanted to give priority to the sociocultural matrix that was imposed upon the individual, because the mind of the individual is shaped by the obligatory, collective representations of culture.

Besides the negative attitudes toward so-called primitives among these scholars, there was a tendency to insist on the universal applicability of the laws of cause and effect and to apply these laws to human behavior and belief. For a scientifically inclined person like Tylor, the human mind does not create, but rather it responds to the experiences of nature and life. Critics of these types of attitudes insist that there is no place for human creativity, a tendency to neglect the social component of religion, a manifestation of Western superiority versus the subjects of study, a negative and prejudicial attitude toward religion, and shortcomings with respect to method. From the perspective of historical hindsight, the quest for the origins of religion was a reaction in part by these scholars against the orthodox theological convictions of the cultural establishment of the late nineteenth century. The orthodox position suggested that modern civilization was a gift from God and that modern uncivilized behavior was the result of degeneration from a higher state. Most of these scholars also replaced the theological doctrine of human degeneration with that of the more scientific theory of evolution. Moreover, they rejected any notion that Western social institutions were products of divine origin, and insisted on their natural origins.

Guideline Questions

Why do these thinkers focus their attention on so-called primitive cultures and why not begin with Christianity?

What does this suggest about their use of language?

How do each of these scholars use the comparative method?

What does the emphasis on intelligence suggest about this type of scholarship?

From *Primitive Culture*

EDWARD B. TYLOR

The Science of Culture

Culture or Civilization, taken in its wide ethnographic sense, is that complex whole which includes knowledge, belief, art, morals, law, custom, and any other capabilities and habits acquired by man as a member of society. The condition of culture among the various societies of mankind, in so far as it is capable of being investigated on general principles, is a subject apt for the study of laws of human thought and action. On the one hand, the uniformity which so largely pervades civilization may be ascribed, in great measure, to the uniform action of uniform causes; while on the other hand its various grades may be regarded as stages of development or evolution, each the outcome of previous history, and about to do its proper part in shaping the history of the future. . . .

A first step in the study of civilization is to dissect it into details, and to classify these in their proper groups. Thus, in examining weapons, they are to be classed under spear, club, sling, bow and arrow, and so forth; . . . myths are divided under such headings as myths of sunrise and sunset, eclipse-myths, earthquake-myths, local myths which account for the names of places by some fanciful tale. . . . What this task is like, may be almost perfectly illustrated by comparing these details of culture with the species of plants and animals as studied by the naturalist. . . .

In studying both the recurrence of special habits or ideas in several districts, and their prevalence within each district, there come before us ever-reiterated proofs of regular causation producing the phenomena of human life, and of laws of maintenance and diffusion according to which these phenomena settle into permanent standard conditions of society, of definite stages of culture. . . .

Among evidence aiding us to trace the course which the civilization of the world has actually followed, is that great class of facts to denote in which I have found it convenient to introduce the term "survivals." These are processes, customs, opinions, and so forth, which have been carried on by force of habit into a new state of society different from that in which they had their original home, and they thus remain as proofs and examples of an older condition of culture out of which a newer has been evolved. . . .

Animism

Are there, or have there been, tribes of men so low in culture as to have no religious conceptions whatever? This is practically the question of the universality of religion, which for so many centuries has been affirmed and denied, with a confidence in striking contrast to the imperfect evidence on which both affirmation and denial have been based. Ethnographers, if looking to a theory of development to explain civilization, and regarding its successive stages as arising one from another, would receive with particular interest accounts of tribes devoid of all religion. Here, they would naturally say, are men who have no religion because their forefathers had none, men who represent a prae-religious condition of the human race, out of which in the course of time religious conditions have arisen. It does not, however, seem advisable to start from this ground in an investigation of religious development. Though the theoretical niche is ready and convenient, the actual statue to fill it

Edward B. Tylor, selections from Primitive Culture, *London: J. Murray, 1871.*

is not forthcoming. The case is in some degree similar to that of the tribes asserted to exit without language or without the use of fire; nothing in the nature of things seems to forbid the possibility of such existence, but as a matter of fact the tribes are not found. Thus the assertion that rude non-religious tribes have been known in actual existence, though in theory possibly, and perhaps in fact true, does not at present rest on that sufficient proof which, for an exceptional state of things, we are entitled to demand.

It is not unusual for the very writer who declares in general terms the absence of religious phenomena among some savage people, himself to give evidence that shows his expressions to be misleading. Thus Dr. Lang not only declares that the aborigines of Australia have no idea of a supreme divinity, creator, and judge, no object of worship, no idol, temple or sacrifice, but that "in short, they have nothing whatever of the character of religion, or of religious observance to distinguish them from the beasts that perish." More than one writer has since made use of this telling statement, but without referring to certain details which occur in the very same book. From these it appears that a disease like small-pox, which sometimes attacks the natives, is ascribed by them "to the influence of Budyah, an evil spirit who delights in mischief;" that when the natives rob a wild bees' hive, they generally leave a little of the honey for the Buddai; that at certain biennial gatherings of the Queensland tribes, young girls are slain in sacrifice to propitiate some evil divinity; and that, lastly, according to the evidence of Rev. W. Ridley, "whenever he has conversed with the aborigines, he found them to have definite traditions concerning supernatural beings—Baiame, whose voice they hear in thunder, and who made all things—Turramullun, the chief of demons, who is the author of disease, mischief, and wisdom, and appears in the form of a serpent at their great assemblies, etc."[1] By the concurring testimony of a crowd of observers, it is known that the natives of Australia were at their discovery, and have since remained, a race with

minds saturated with the most vivid belief in souls, demons, and deities. In Africa, Mr. Moffat's declaration as to the Bechaunas is scarcely less surprising—that "man's immortality was never heard of among that people," he having remarked in the sentence next before, that the word for the shades or manes of the dead is "liriti."[2] In South America, again, Don Felix de Azara comments on the positive falsity of the ecclesiastics' assertion that the native tribes have a religion. He simply declares that they have none; nevertheless in the course of his work he mentions such facts as that the Payagua bury arms and clothing with their dead and have some notions of a future life, and that the Guanas believe in a Being who rewards good and punishes evil. In fact, this author's reckless denial of religion and law to the lower races of this region justifies D' Orbigny's sharp criticism, that "this is indeed what he says of all the nations he describes, while actually proving the contrary of his thesis by the very facts he alleges in its support."[3]

Such cases show how deceptive are judgments to which breadth and generality are given by the use of wide words in narrow senses. Lang, Moffat and Azara are authors to whom ethnography owes much valuable knowledge of the tribes they visited, but they seem hardly to have recognized anything short of the organized and established theology of the higher races as being religions at all. They attribute irreligion to tribes whose doctrines are unlike theirs, in as much the same manner as theologians have so often attributed atheism to those whose deities differed from their own, from the time when the ancient invading Aryans described the aboriginal tribes of India as *adeva*, i.e. "godless," and the Greek fixed the corresponding term . . . on the early Christians as unbelievers in the classic gods, to the comparatively modern ages when disbelievers in witchcraft and apostolical succession were denounced as atheists; and down to our day, when controversialists are apt to infer, as in past centuries, that naturalists who support a theory of development of species therefore necessarily hold atheistic opinions.[4] These are in fact but examples of a general perversion of judgment in theological matters, among the results of which is a popular misconception of the religions of the lower races, simply amazing to students who have reached a higher point of view. Some missionaries, no doubt, thoroughly understand the minds of the savages they have to deal with, and indeed it is from men like Cranz, Dobrizhoffer, Charlevoix, Ellis, Hardy, Callaway, J. L. Wilson, T. Williams, that we have obtained our best knowledge of the lower phases of religious belief. But for the most part, the "religious world" is so occupied in hating and despising the beliefs of the heathen whose vast regions of the globe are painted black on the missionary maps, that they have little time or capacity left to understand them. It cannot be so with those who fairly seek to comprehend the nature and meaning of the lower phases of religions. These, while fully alive to the absurdities believed and the horrors perpetrated in its name, will yet regard with kindly interest all record of men's earnest seeking after truth with such light as they could find. Such students will look for meaning, however crude and childish, at the root of doctrines often most dark to the believers who accept them most zealously; they will search for the reasonable thought which once gave life to observances now become in seeming or reality the most abject and superstitious folly. The reward of these enquirers will be more rational comprehension of the faiths in whose midst they dwell, for no more can he who understands but one religion understand even that religion, than the man who knows but one language can understand that language. No religion of mankind lies in utter isolation from the rest, and the thoughts and principles of modern Christianity are attached to intellectual clues which run back through far prae-Christian ages to the very origin of human civilization, perhaps even of human existence.

While observers who have had fair opportunities of studying the religions of savages have thus sometimes done scant justice to the facts before their eyes, the hasty denials of others who have judged without even facts can carry no great weight. A 16th-century traveller gave an account of the natives of Florida which is typical of such: "Touching the religion of this people, which we have found, for want of their language we could not understand neither by signs nor gestures that they had any religion or law at all. . . We suppose that they have no religion at all, and that they live at their own libertie."[5] Better knowledge of these Floridans nevertheless showed that they had a religion, and better knowledge has reversed many another hasty assertion to the same effect; as when writers used to declare that the natives of Madagascar had no idea of a future state, and no word for soul or spirit;[6] or when Dampier enquired after the religion of the natives of Timor, and was told that they had none;[7] or when Sir Thomas Roe landed in Saldanha Bay on his way to the court of the Great Mogul, and remarked of the Hottentots that "they have left off their custom of stealing, but know no God or Religion."[8] Among the numerous accounts collected by Sir John Lubbock as evidence bearing on the absence or low development of religion among low races,[9] some may be selected as lying open to criticism from this point of view. Thus the statement that the Somoan Islanders had no religion cannot stand, in the face of the elaborate description by the Rev. G. Turner of the Samoan religion himself; and the assertion that the Tupinambas of Brazil had no religion is one not to be received on merely negative evidence, for the religious doctrines and practices of the Tupi race have been recorded by Lery, De Laet, and other writers. Even with much time and care and knowledge of language, it is not always easy to elicit from savages the details of their theology. They try to hide from the prying and contemptuous foreigner their worship of gods who seem to shrink, like their worshippers, before the white man and his mightier Deity. Mr. Sproat's experience in Vancouver's Island is an apt example of this state of things. He says:

"I was two years among the Ahts, with my mind constantly directed towards the subjects of their religious beliefs, before I could discover that they possessed any ideas as to an overruling power or a future state of existence. The traders on the coast, and other persons well acquainted with the people, told me that they had no such ideas, and this opinion was confirmed by conversation with many intelligent savages; but at last I succeeded in getting a satisfactory clue."[10] It then appeared that the Ahts had all the time been hiding a whole characteristics system of religious doctrines as to souls and their migrations, the spirits who do good and ill to men, and the great gods above all. Thus, even where there is no positive proof of religious ideas among any particular tribe had reached us, we should distrust its denial by observers whose acquaintance with the tribe in question has not been intimate as well as kindly. It is said of the Andaman Islanders that they have not the rudest elements of a religious faith; yet it appears that the natives did not even display to the foreigners the rude music which they actually possessed, so that they could scarcely have been expective to be communicative as to their theology, if they had any.[11] In our time the most striking negation of the religion of savage tribes is that published by Sir Samuel Baker, in a paper read in 1866 before the Ethnological Society of London, as follows: "The most northern tribes of the White Nile are the Dinkas, Shillooks, Nuehr, Kytch, Bohr, Aliab, and Shir. A general description will suffice for the whole, excepting the Kytch. Without any exception, they are without a belief in a Supreme Being, neither have they any form of worship or idolatry; nor is the darkness of their minds enlightened by even a ray of superstition." Had this distinguished explorer spoken only of the Latukas, or of other tribes hardly known to ethnographers except through his own intercourse with them, his denial of any religious consciousness to them would have been at least entitled to stand as the best procurable account, until more intimate communication should prove or disprove it. But

in speaking thus of comparatively well known tribes such as the Dinkas, Shilluks, and Nuehr, Sir S. Baker ignores the existence of published evidence, such as describes the sacrifices of the Dinkas, their belief in good and evil spirits (adjok and djyok), their good deity and heaven-dwelling creator, Dendid, as likewise Near the deity of the Nuehr, and the Shilluks' creator, who is described as visiting, like other spirits, a sacred wood or tree. Kaufmann, Brun Rollet, Lejean, and other observers, had thus placed on record details of the religion of these White Nile tribes, years before Sir S. Baker's rash denial that they had any religion at all.[12]

The first requisite in a systematic study of religions of the lower races, is to lay down a rudimentary definition of religion. By requiring in this definition the belief in a supreme deity or of a judgment after death, the adoration of idols or the practice of sacrifice, or other partially-diffused doctrines or rites, no doubt many tribes may be excluded from the category of religious. But such a narrow definition has the fault of identifying religion rather with particular developments than with the deeper motive which underlies them. It seems best to fall back at once on this essential source, and simply to claim, as a minimum definition of Religion, the belief in Spiritual Beings. If this standard be applied to the descriptions of low races as to religion, the following results will appear. It cannot be positively asserted that every existing tribe recognizes the belief in spiritual beings, for the native condition of a considerable number is obscure in this respect, and from the rapid change or extinction they are undergoing, may ever remain so. It would be yet more unwarranted to set down every tribe mentioned in history, or known to us by the discovery of antiquarian relics, as necessarily having possessed the defined minimum of religion. Greater still would be the unwisdom of declaring such a rudimentary belief natural or instinctive in all human tribes of all times; for no evidence justifies the opinion that man, known to be capable of so vast an intellectual development, cannot have emerged from a non-religious condition, previous to that religious condition in which he happens at present to come with sufficient clearness within our range of knowledge. It is desirable, however, to take our basis of enquiry in observation rather from speculation. Here, so far as I can judge from the immense mass of accessible evidence, we have to admit that the belief in spiritual beings appears among all low races with whom we have attained to thoroughly intimate acquaintance; whereas the assertion of absence of such belief must apply either to ancient tribes, or to more or less imperfectly described modern ones. The exact bearing of this state of things on the problem of the origin of religion may be thus briefly stated. Were it distinctly proved that non-religious savages exist or have existed, these might be at least plausibly claimed as representatives of the condition of Man before he arrived at the religious state of culture. It is not desirable, however, that this argument should be put forward, for the asserted existence of the non-religious tribes in question rests, as we have seen, on evidence, often mistaken and never conclusive. The argument for the natural evolution of religious ideas among mankind is not invalidated by the rejection of an ally too weak at present to give effectual help. Non-religious tribes may not exist in our day, but the fact bears no more decisively on the development of religion, than the impossibility of finding a modern English village without scissors or books or lucifer-matches bears on the fact that there was a time when no such things existed in the land.

I propose here, under the name of Animism, to investigate the deep-lying doctrine of Spiritual Beings, which embodies the very essence of Spiritualistic as opposed to Materialistic philosophy. Animism is not a new technical term, though now seldom used.[13] From its special relation to the doctrine of the soul, it will be seen to have a peculiar appropriateness to the view here taken of the mode in which theological ideas have been developed among mankind. The word Spiritualism,

though it may be, and sometimes is, used in a general sense, has this obvious defect to us, that it has become the designation of a particular modern sect, who indeed hold extreme spiritualistic views, but cannot be taken as typical representatives of these views in the world at large. The sense of Spiritualism in its wider acceptation, the general belief in spiritual beings, is here given to Animism.

Animism characterizes tribes very low in the scale of humanity, and thence ascends, deeply modified in its transmission, but from first to last preserving an unbroken continuity, into the midst of high modern culture. Doctrines adverse to it, so largely held by individuals or schools, are usually due not to early lowness of civilization, but to later changes in the intellectual course, to divergence from, or rejection of, ancestral faiths; and such newer developments do not affect the present enquiry as to the fundamental religious condition of mankind. Animism is, in fact, the groundwork of the Philosophy of Religion, from that of savages up to that of civilized men. And although it may at first seem to afford but a bare and meager definition of a minimum of religion, it will be found practically sufficient; for where the root is, the branches will generally be produced. It is habitually found that the theory of Animism divides into two great dogmas, forming parts of one consistent doctrine; first, concerning souls of individual creatures, capable of continued existence after the death or destruction of the body; second, concerning other spirits, upward to the rank of powerful deities. Spiritual beings are held to affect or control the events of the material world, and man's life here and hereafter; and it being considered that they hold intercourse with men, and receive pleasure or displeasure from human actions, the belief in their existence leads naturally, and it might almost be said inevitably, sooner or later to active reverence and propitiation. Thus, Animism, in its full development, includes the belief in souls and in a future state, in controlling deities and subordinate spirits, these doctrines practically resulting in some kind of active worship. One great element of religion, that moral element which among the higher nations forms its most vital part, is indeed little represented in the religion of the lower races. It is not that these races have no moral sense or no moral standard, for both are strongly marked among them, if not in formal precept, at least in that traditional consensus of society which we call public opinion, according to which certain actions are held to be good or bad, right or wrong. It is that the conjunction of ethics and Animistic philosophy, so intimate and powerful in the higher culture, seems scarcely yet to have begun in the lower. I propose here hardly to touch upon the purely moral aspects of religion, but rather to study the animism of the world so far as it constitutes, as unquestionably it does constitute, an ancient and world-wide philosophy, of which belief is the theory and worship is the practice. Endeavouring to shape the materials for an enquiry hitherto strangely undervalued and neglected, it will now be my task to bring as clearly as may be into view the fundamental animism of the lower races, and in some slight and broken outline to trace its course into higher regions of civilization. Here let me state once for all two principal conditions under which the present research is carried on. First, as to the religious doctrines and practices examined, these are treated as belonging to theological systems devised by human reason, without supernatural aid or revelation; in other words, as being developments of Natural Religion. Second, as to the connection between similar ideas and rites in the religions of the savage and the civilized world. While dwelling at some length on doctrines and ceremonies of the lower races, and sometimes particularizing for special reasons the related doctrines and ceremonies of the higher nations, it has not seemed my proper task to work out in detail the problems thus suggested among the philosophies and creeds of Christendom. Such applications, extending farthest from the direct scope of a work on primitive culture, are briefly stated in

general terms, or touched in slight allusion, or taken for granted without remark. Educated readers possess the information required to work out their general bearing on theology, while more technical discussion is left to philosophers and theologians specially occupied with such arguments. . . .

It remains to sum up in a few words the doctrine of souls, in the various phases it has assumed from the first to last among mankind. In the attempt to trace its main course through the successive grids on man's intellectual history, the evidence seems to accord best with a theory of its development, somewhat to the following effect. At the lowest levels of culture of which we have clear knowledge, the notion of a ghost-soul animating man while in the body, and appearing in dream and vision out of the body, is found deeply ingrained. There is no reason to think that this belief was learnt by savage tribes from contact with the higher races, nor that it is a relic of higher culture from which the savage tribes have denigrated; for what is here treated as the primitive animistic doctrine is thoroughly at home among savages, who appear to hold it on the very evidence of their senses, interpreted on the biological principle which seems to them most reasonable. We may now and then hear the savage doctrines and practices concerning souls claimed as relics of a high religious culture pervading the primaeval race of man. They are said to be traces of remote ancestral religion, kept up in scanty and perverted memory by tribes degraded from a nobler state. It is easy to see that such an explanation of some few facts, sundered from their connection with the general array, may seem plausible to certain minds. But a large view of the subject can hardly leave such argument in possession. The animism of savages stands for and by itself; it explains its own origin. The animism of civilized men, while more appropriate to advanced knowledge, is in great measure only explicable as a developed product of the older and ruder system. It is the doctrines and rites of the lower races which are, according to their philosophy, results of point-blank natural evidence and acts of straightforward practical purpose. It is the doctrines and rites of the higher races which show survival of the old in the midst of the new, modification of the old to bring it into conformity with the new, abandonment of the old because it is no longer compatible with the new. Let us see at a glance in what general relation the doctrine of souls among savage tribes stands to the doctrine of souls among barbaric and cultured nations. Among races within the limits of savagery, the general doctrine of souls is found worked out with remarkable breadth and consistency. The souls of animals are recognized by a natural extension from the theory of human souls; the souls of trees and plants follow in some vague partial way; and the souls of inanimate objects expand the general category to its extremist boundary. Thenceforth, as we explore human thought onward from the savage into barbarian and civilized life, we find a type of theory more conformed to positive science, but in itself less complete and consistent. Far on into civilization, men still act as though in some half-meant way they believed in souls or ghosts of objects, while nevertheless their knowledge of physical science is beyond so crude a philosophy. As to the doctrine of souls of plants, fragmentary evidence of the history of its breaking down in Asia has reached us. In our own day and country, the notion of souls of beasts is to be seen dying out. Animism, indeed, seems to be drawing in its outposts, and concentrating itself on its first and main position, the doctrine of the human soul. This doctrine has undergone extreme modification in the course of culture. It has outlived the almost total loss of one great argument attached to it—the objective reality of apparitional souls or ghosts seen in dreams and visions. The soul has given up its ethereal substance, and become an immaterial entity, "the shadow of a shade." Its theory is becoming separated from the investigations of biology and mental science, which now discuss the phenomena of the life and thought, the senses and the intellect, the emotions and the will, on a ground-work of pure experience. There has arisen an intellectual product whose very existence is of the deepest significance, a "psychology" which has no longer anything to do with "soul." The soul's place in modern thought is in the metaphysics of religion, and its especial office there is that of furnishing an intellectual side to the religious doctrine of the future life. Such are the alterations which have differenced the fundamental animistic belief in its course through successive periods of the world's culture. Yet it is evident that, notwithstanding all this profound change, the conception of the human soul is, as to its most essential nature, continuous from the philosophy of the savage thinker to that of the modern professor of theology. Its definition has remained from the first that of an animating, separable surviving entity, the vehicle of individual personal existence. The theory of the soul is one principal part of a system of religious philosophy, which unites, in an unbroken line of mental connection, the savage fetish-worshipper and the civilized Christian. The divisions which have separated the great religions of the world into intolerant and hostile sects are for the most part superficial in comparison with the deepest of all religious schisms, that which divides Animism from materialism.

NOTES

1. J. D. Lang, *Queensland,* pp. 340, 473, 380, 388, 444 (Buddai appears, p. 379, as causing a deluge; he is probably identical with Budyah).

2. Moffat, *South Africa,* p. 261.

3. Azara, *Voyage dans l'Amerique Meridionale* vol. II, pp. 3, 14, 25, 51, 60, 91, 119, etc.; d'Orbigny, *L'homme american* vol. 1, p. 318.

4. Muir, *Sanskrit Texts* part II, p. 435; Eusebius, *Historia Ecclesiastica,* IV, 15; Bingham, book I, ch. II; Vanini, *De Admirandis Naturae Arcanis,* dial. 37; Lecky, *History of Rationalism,* vol. I, p. 126; *Encyclopedia Britannica* (5th edition) s.v. 'Superstition'.

5. J. de Verrazano in *Hukluyt,* vol. III, p. 300.

6. See Ellis, *Madagascar,* vol. I, p. 429; Flacourt, *Historie de Madagascar,* p. 59.

7. Dampier, *Voyages,* vol. II, part II, p. 76.

8. Roe in *Pinkerton,* vol. VIII, p. 2.

9. Lubbock, *Prehistoric Times,* p. 564; see also *Origin of Civilization,* p. 138.

10. Sproat, *Scenes and Studies of Savage Life,* p. 205.

11. Mouat, *Andaman Islanders,* pp. 2, 279, 303. Since the above was written, the remarkable Andaman religion has been described by Mr. E. H. Man, in *Journal of the Anthropological Institute,* vol. Xii (1883), p. 156. [Note to 3rd edition.]

12. Baker, "Races of the Nile Basin," in *Transactions of the Ethnological Society,* vol. V, p. 231; "The Albert Nyanza," vol. I, p. 246. See Kaufmann, *Schilderungen uas Centralafrika,* p. 123; Brun-Rollet, *Le Nil Blanc et le Soudan,* pp. 100, 222, also pp. 164, 200, 234; G. Lejean in *Revue des Deux Mondes,* April 1, 1862, p. 760; Waitz,

Anthropologie, vol. II, pp. 72–75; Bastian, *Mensch,* vol. III, p. 208. Other recorded cases of denial of religion of savage tribes on narrow definition or inadequate evidence may be found in Meiners, *Geschichte der Religion,* vol. I, pp. 11–15 (Australians and Californians); Waitz, *Anthropologie,* vol. I, p. 323 (Aru Islanders, etc.); Farrar in *Anthropological Revue,* August 1864, p. CCXVII (Kafirs, etc.); Martius, *Ethnographica Americana,* vol. I, p. 583 (Manaos); J.G. Palfrey, *History of New England,* vol. I, p. 46 (New England tribes).

13. The term has been especially used to denote the doctrine of Stahl, the promulgator also of the phlogiston-theory. The Animism of Stahl is a revival and development in modern scientific shape of the classic theory identifying withal principle and soul. See his *Theoria Medica Vera,* Halle, 1737; and the critical dissertation on his views, Lemoine, *Le vitalisme et l'animisme de Stahl,* Paris, 1864.

From *The Golden Bough: A Study of Magic and Religion* and *Totemism and Exogamy*

JAMES GEORGE FRAZER

Preface to the Second Edition, September 1900

The kind reception accorded by critics and the public to the first edition of *The Golden Bough* has encouraged me to spare no pains to render the new one more worthy of their approbation. . . .

Thus on the whole I cannot but think that the course of subsequent investigation has tended to confirm the general principles followed and the particular conclusions reached in this book. At the same time I am as sensible as ever of the hypothetical nature of much that is advanced in it. It has been my wish and intention to draw as sharply as possible the line of demarcation between my facts and the hypotheses by which I have attempted to colligate them. Hypotheses are necessary but often temporary bridges built to connect isolated facts. If my light bridge should sooner or later break down or be superseded by more solid structures, I hope that my book may still have its interest as a repertory of facts.

But while my views, tentative and provisional as they probably are, thus remain much what they are, there is one subject on which they have undergone a certain amount of change, unless indeed it might be more exact to say that I seem to see clearly now what before was hazy. I mean the relation of magic to religion. When I first wrote this book, I failed, perhaps inexcusably, to

Reprinted from James George Frazer The Golden Bough: A Study of Magic and Religion, *2nd ed. (London: Macmillan & Company, 1900), and* Totemism and Exogamy *(London: Macmillan & Company, 1910).*

define even to myself my notion of religion, and hence was disposed to class magic loosely under it as one of its lower forms. I have now sought to remedy this defect by framing as clear a definition of religion as the difficult nature of the subject and my apprehension of it allowed. Hence I have come to agree with Sir A.C. Lyall and Mr. F.B. Jevons in recognising a fundamental distinction and even opposition of principle between magic and religion. More than that, I believe that in the evolution of thought, magic, as representing a lower intellectual stratum, has probably everywhere preceded religion. I do not claim any originality for this latter view. It has been already plainly suggested, if not definitely formulated by Professor H. Oldenberg in his able book *Die Religion des Veda,* and for aught I know it may have been explicitly stated by many others before and since him. I have not collected the opinions of the learned on the subject, but have striven to form my own directly from the facts. And the facts which bespeak the priority of magic over religion are many and weighty. Some of them the reader will find stated in the following pages; but the full force of the evidence can only be appreciated by those who have made a long and patient study of primitive superstition. I venture to think that those who submit to this drudgery will come more and more to the opinion I have indicated. That all my readers should agree either with my definition of religion or with the inferences I have drawn from it is not to be expected. But I would ask those who dissent from my conclusions to make sure they mean the same thing by religion that I do; for otherwise the difference between us may be more apparent than real. . . .

To us moderns a still wider vista is vouchsafed, a greater panorama is unrolled by the study which aims at bringing home to us the faith and the practice, the hopes and the ideals, not of two highly gifted races only, but of all mankind, and thus at enabling us to follow the long march, the slow and toilsome ascent, of humanity from savagery to civilisation. And the scholar of the Renaissance found not merely fresh food for thought but a new field of labour in the dusty and faded manuscripts of Greece and Rome, so in the mass of materials that is steadily pouring in from many sides—from buried cities of remotest antiquity as well as from the rudest savages of the desert and the jungle—we of today must recognise a new province of knowledge which will task the energies of generations of students to master. The study is still in its rudiments, and what we do now will have to be done over again and done better, with fuller knowledge and deeper insight, by those who come after us. To refer to a metaphor which I have already made use of, we of this age are only pioneers hewing lanes and clearings in the forest where others will hereafter sow and reap.

But the comparative study of the beliefs and institutions of mankind is fitted to be much more than a means of satisfying an enlightened curiosity and of furnishing materials for the researches of the learned. Well handled, it may become a powerful instrument to expedite progress if it lays bare certain weak spots in the foundations on which modern society is built—if it shows that much which we are wont to regard as solid rests on the sands of superstition rather than on the rock of nature. It is indeed a melancholy and in some respects thankless task to strike at the foundations of beliefs in which, as in a strong tower, the hopes and aspirations of humanity through long ages have sought a refuge from the storm and stress of life. Yet sooner or later it is inevitable that the battery of the comparative method should breach these venerable walls, mantled over with the ivy and mosses and wild flowers of a thousand tender and sacred associations. At present we are only dragging the guns into position: they have hardly yet begun to speak. The task of building up into fairer and more enduring forms the old structures so rudely shattered is reserved for other hands, perhaps for other and happier ages. We cannot foresee, we can hardly even guess, the new forms into which thought and society will run in the future. Yet this uncertainty ought not to induce us, from any consideration of expediency or regard for antiquity, to spare the ancient moulds, however beautiful, when these are proved to be out-worn. Whatever comes of it, wherever it leads us, we must follow truth alone. It is our only guiding star. . . .

Magic and Religion

Wherever sympathetic magic occurs in its unadulterated form, it assumes that in nature one event follows another necessarily and invariably without the intervention of any spiritual or personal agency. Thus its fundamental conception is identical with that of modern science; underlying the whole system is a faith, implicit but real and firm, in the order and uniformity of nature. The magician does not doubt that the same causes will always produce the same effects, that the performance of the proper ceremony, accompanied by the appropriate spell, will inevitably be attended by the desired results, unless, indeed, his incantations should chance to be thwarted and foiled by the more potent charms of another sorcerer. He supplicates no higher power: he sues the favour of no fickle and wayward being: he abases himself before no awful deity. Yet his power, great as he believes it to be, is by no means arbitrary and unlimited. He can wield it only so long as he strictly conforms to the rules of his art, or to what he called the laws of nature as conceived by him. . . . Thus the analogy between the magical and the scientific conceptions of the world is close. In both of them the succession of events is perfectly regular and certain, being determined by immutable laws, the operation of which can be foreseen and calculated precisely; the elements of caprice, of chance, and of accident are banished from the course of nature. Both of them open up a seemingly boundless vista of possibilities to him who knows the causes of things and can touch the secret springs that set in motion the vast and intricate mechanism of the world. Hence the strong attraction which magic and science alike have exercised on the human mind; hence the powerful stimulus that both have given to the pursuit of knowledge.

The fatal flaw of magic lies not in its general assumption of a sequence of events determined by law, but in its total misconception of the nature of the particular laws which govern that sequence. If we analyse the various cases of sympathetic magic, we shall find that they are all mistaken applications of one or other of two great fundamental laws of thought, namely, the association of ideas by similarity and the association of ideas by contiguity in space and time. A mistaken association of similar ideas produces homeopathic or imitative magic: a mistaken association of contiguous ideas produces contagious magic. . . . Legitimately applied they yield science; illegitimately applied they yield magic, the bastard sister of science. It is therefore a truism, almost a tautology, to say that all magic is necessarily false and barren; for were it ever to become true and fruitful, it would no longer be magic but science. . . .

There is probably no subject in the world about which opinions differ so much as the nature of religion, and to frame a definition of it which would satisfy every one must obviously be impossible. All that a writer can do is, first, to say clearly what he means by religion, and afterwards to employ the word consistently in that sense throughout his work. By religion, then, I understand a propitiation or conciliation of powers superior to man which are believed to direct and control the course of nature and of human life. Thus defined, religion consists of two elements, a theoretical and a practical, namely, a belief in powers higher than man and an attempt to propitiate or please them. Of the two, belief clearly comes first, since we must believe in the existence of a divine being before we can attempt to please him. But unless the belief leads to a corresponding practice, it is not a religion, but merely a theology. In other words, no man is religious who does not govern his conduct in some measure by the fear or love of God. On the other hand, mere practice, divested of all religious belief, is also not religion. . . . Hence belief and practice or, in theological language, faith and works are equally essential to religion, which cannot exist without both of them. . . .

We have seen that on the one hand magic is nothing but a mistaken application of the very simplest and most elementary processes of the mind, namely the association of ideas by virtue of resemblance or contiguity; and that on the other hand religion assumes the operation of conscious or personal agents, superior to man, behind the visible screen of nature. Obviously the conception of personal agents is more complex than a simple recognition of the similarity or contiguity of ideas; and a theory which assumes that the course of nature is determined by conscious agents is more abstruse and recondite, and requires for its apprehension a far higher degree of intelligence and reflection, than the view that things succeed each other simply by reason of their contiguity or resemblance. Thus, if magic be deduced immediately from elementary processes of reasoning, it becomes probable that magic arose before religion in the evolution of our race, and that man essayed to bend nature to his wishes by the sheer force of spells and enchantments before he strove to coax and mollify a coy, capricious, or irascible deity by the soft insinuation of prayer and sacrifice.

The conclusion which we have thus reached deductively from a consideration of the fundamental ideas of religion and magic is confirmed inductively by the observation that among the aborigines of Australia, the rudest savages as to whom we possess accurate information, magic is universally practised, whereas religion in the sense of a propitiation or conciliation of the higher powers seems to be nearly unknown. . . .

But if in the most backward state of human society now known to us we find magic thus conspicuously present and religion conspicuously absent, may we not reasonably conjecture that the civilised races of the world have also at some period of their history passed through a similar intellectual phase, that they attempted to force the great powers of nature to do their pleasure before they thought of courting their favour by offerings and prayer. . . .

If an Age of Religion has thus everywhere, as I venture to surmise, been preceded by an Age of Magic, it is natural that we should enquire what causes have led mankind, or rather a portion of them, to abandon magic as a principle of faith and practice and to betake themselves to religion instead. . . . With all due diffidence, then, I would suggest that a tardy recognition of the inherent falsehood and barrenness of magic set the more thoughtful part of mankind to cast about for a truer theory of nature and a more fruitful method of turning her resources to account. The shrewder intelligences must in time have come to perceive that magical ceremonies and incantations did not really affect the results which they were designed to produce, and which the majority of their simpler fellows still believed that they did actually produce. This great discovery of the inefficacy of magic must have wrought a radical though probably slow revolution in the minds of those who had the sagacity to make it. . . .

In this, or some such way as this, the deeper minds may be conceived to have made the great transition from magic to religion. But even in them the change can hardly ever have been sudden; probably it proceeded very slowly, and required long ages for its more or less perfect accomplishment. . . . Thus religion, beginning as a slight and partial acknowledgment of powers superior to man, tends with the growth of knowledge to deepen into a confession of man's entire and absolute dependence on the divine; his old free bearing is exchanged for an attitude of lowliest prostration before the mysterious powers of the unseen, and his highest virtue is to submit his will to theirs. . . .

Yet the history of thought should warn us against concluding that because the scientific theory of the world is the best that has yet been formulated, it is necessarily complete and final. We must remember that at bottom the generalization of science or, in common parlance, the laws of nature are merely hypotheses devised to explain that ever-shifting phantasmagoria of thought which we dignify with the high-sounding names of the world and the universe. In the last analysis magic, religion, and science are nothing but theories of thought; and as science has supplanted its predecessors, so it may hereafter be itself superseded by some more perfect hypothesis, perhaps by some totally different way of looking at the phenomena—of registering the shadows on the screen—of which we in this generation can form no idea. . . .

Totemism and Exogamy

A Totem is a class of material objects which a savage regards with superstitious respect, believing that there exists between him and every member of the class an intimate and altogether special relation. The name is derived from an Ojibway (Chippeway) word *totem,* the correct spelling of which is somewhat uncertain. It was first introduced into literature, so far as it appears, by J. Long, an Indian interpreter of last century, who spelt it *totam.*[1] The form *toodaim* is given by the Rev. Peter Jones, himself an Ojibway [2]; *dodaim* by Warren[3] and (*as* an alternative pronunciation to totem) by Morgan[4]; and *ododam* by Francis Assikinack, an Ottawa Indian[5]. According to the abbé Thavenet[6] the word is properly *ote,* in the sense of "family or tribe," possessive *otem,* and with the personal pronoun *nind otem* "my tribe," *kit otem* thy tribe." In English the spelling *totem* (Keating, James, Schoolcraft[7], etc.) has become estab-

lished by custom. The connection between a man and his totem is mutually beneficent; the totem protects the man, and the man shows his respect for the totem in various ways, by not killing it if it be an animal, and not cutting or gathering if it be a plant. As distinguished from a fetish, a totem is never an isolated individual, but always a class of objects, generally a species of animals or plants, more rarely a class of inanimate natural objects, very rarely a class of artificial objects.

Considered, in relation to men, totems are of at least three kinds: 1) the clan totem, common to a whole clan, and passing by inheritance from generation to generation; 2) the sex totem, common either to all males or to all females of a tribe, to the exclusion in either case of the other sex; 3) the individual totem, belonging to a single individual and not passing to his descendants. Other kinds of totems exist and will be noticed, but they may perhaps be regarded as varieties of the clan totem. The latter is by far the most important of all; and where we speak of totems or totemism without qualification, the reference is always to the clan totem.

. . . The clan totem is reverenced by a body of men and women who call themselves by the name of the totem, believe themselves to be of the blood, descendants of a common ancestor, and are bound together by common obligations to each other and by a common faith in the totem. Totemism is thus both a religious and a social system. In its religious aspect it consists of the relations of mutual respect and protection between a man and his totem; in its social aspect it consists of the relations of the clansmen to each other and to men of other clans. In the later history of totemism these two sides, the religious and the social, tend to part company; the social system sometimes survives the religious; and, on the other hand, religion sometimes bears traces of totemism in countries where the social system based on totemism has disappeared. How in the origin of totemism these two sides were related to each other it is, in our ignorance of that origin, impossible to say with certainty. But on the whole the evidence points strongly to the conclusion that the two sides were originally inseparable; that, in other words, the farther we go back, the more we should find that the clansman regards himself and his totem as beings of the same species, and the less he distinguishes between conduct towards his totem and towards his fellow clansmen.

The general explanation of totemism to which the *Intichiuma* ceremonies seem to point is that it is primarily an organised and cooperative system of magic designed to secure for the members of the community, on the one hand, a plentiful supply of all the commodities of which they stand in need, and, on the other hand, immunity from all the perils and dangers to which man is exposed in his struggle with nature. Each totem group, on this theory, was charged with the superintendence and control of some department of nature from which it took its name, and with which it sought, as far as possible, to identify itself. If the things which composed the department assigned to a particular group were beneficial to man, as in the case of edible animals and plants, it was the duty of the group to foster and multiply them; if, on the other hand, they were either noxious by nature, or might, under certain circumstances, become so, as in the case of ravenous beasts, poisonous serpents, rain, wind, snow, and so on, then it was the duty of the group to repress and counteract these harmful tendencies, to remedy any mischief they might have wrought, and perhaps to turn them as efficient engines of destruction against foes. This latter side of totemic magic, which may perhaps be described as the negative or remedial side, hardly appears in our accounts of Central Australian Totemism; but we shall meet with examples of it elsewhere.

In favour of this hypothetical explanation of totemism, I would urge that it is simple and natural, and in entire conformity with both the practical needs and the modes of thought of savage man. Nothing can be more natural than that man should wish to eat when hungry, to drink when he is thirsty, to have fire to warm him when he is cold, and fresh breezes to cool him when he is hot; and to the savage nothing seems simpler that to procure for himself these and all other necessaries and comforts by magic art. We need not, therefore, wonder that in very ancient times communities of men should have organised themselves more or less deliberately for the purpose of attaining objects so natural by means that seemed to them so simple and easy. The first necessity of savage, as of civilised, man is food, and with this it accords that wherever totemism exists the majority of the totems are invariably animals or plants—in other words, things which men can eat. The great significance of this fact has hitherto been concealed from us by the prohibition so commonly laid on members of a totem clan to eat their totem animal or plant. But the discovery of the *Intichiuma* ceremonies among the Central Australian tribes proves that in keeping our eye on the prohibition to eat the totem we have hitherto been looking at only one side of the medal, and that the less important of the two. For these ceremonies show—what no one had previously dreamed of—that the very man who himself abstains in general from eating his totem will, nevertheless, do all in his power to enable other people to eat it; nay, that this very business and function in life is to procure for his fellow tribesmen a supply of the animal or plant from which he takes his name, and to which he stands in so intimate a relation. With the new facts before us, we may safely conjecture that whatever the origin of the prohibition observed by each clan to eat its totem, the prohibition is essentially subordinate, and probably ancillary to the great end of enabling the community as a whole to eat of it—in other words, of contributing to the common food supply.

Viewed in this light, totemism is a thoroughly practical system designed to meet the everyday wants of the ordinary man in a clear and straightforward way. There is nothing vague or mystical about it, nothing of that metaphysical haze which some writers love to conjure up over the humble beginnings of human speculation, but which is utterly foreign to the simple, sensuous, and concrete modes of thought of the savage. Yet for all its simplicity and directness we cannot but feel that there is something impressive, and almost grandiose, in the comprehensiveness, the completeness, the vaulting ambition of this scheme, the creation of a crude and barbarous philosophy. All nature has been mapped out into departments; all men have been distributed into corresponding groups; and to each group of men has been assigned, with astounding audacity, the duty of controlling some one department of nature for the common good. Religion, it will be observed, has no place in the scheme. Man is still alone with nature, and fancies he can sway it at his will. Later on, when he discovers his mistake, he will bethink himself of gods, and beg them to pull for him the strings that hang beyond his reach.

A further recommendation of this way of regarding totemism is that it falls in with the traditions as well as with the practice of the Central Australian tribes. We have seen that, according to these traditions, people began by regularly eating their totems, and marrying women of the same totem group as themselves. To the ordinary view of totemism, which treats as fundamental the prohibitions to eat the totem animal or plant, and to marry women of the same totem group, these traditions present almost insuperable difficulties; the adherents of that view have, indeed, little choice but to reject the traditions as baseless, although strong grounds exist, as I have pointed out, for holding them to be authentic. But if we accept the theory that totemism is merely an organised system of magic intended to secure a supply, primarily of food, and secondarily of every thing else that a savage wants, the difficulties vanish. For, on this hypothesis, why should a man partake of the food which he is at so much pains to provide? And why should he not marry a woman whose function in life is the same as his own? Nay, we may go a step farther, and say that, according to a fundamental principle of totemism, there are good reasons why he should do both of these things. That principle, to which I would now direct the reader's attention, is the identification of a man with his totem.

Among the Central Australians, we are told, "the totem of any man is regarded, just as it is elsewhere, as the same thing as himself."[8] Thus a kangaroo man, discussing the matter with Messrs. Spencer and Gillen, pointed to a photograph of himself which had just been taken and remarked: "That one is just the same as me; so is a kangaroo." This incapacity to distinguish between a man and a beast, difficult as it is for us to realise, is common enough, even among savages who have not the totemic system. A Bushman, questioned by a missionary, "could not state any difference between a man and a brute—he did not know but a buffalo might shoot with bows and arrows as well as a man, if it had them."[9] (When the Russians first landed on one of the Alaskan Islands the natives took them for cuttle-fish, "on account of the buttons on their clothes."[10] The Bororos, a tribe of Brazilian Indians, calmly maintain that they are birds of a gorgeous red plumage, which live in their native forests. It is not merely that they will be changed into these birds at their death, but they actually are identical with them in their life, and they treat the birds accordingly, as they would their fellow tribesmen, keeping them in captivity, refusing to eat their flesh, and mourning for them when they die. However, they kill the wild birds for their feathers, and, though they will not kill, they pluck the tame ones to adorn their own naked brown bodies with the brilliant plumage of their feathered brethren.[11]

Now, it is by identifying himself with his totem that the Central Australian native produces the effects he aims at. If he desires to multiply grubs, he pretends to be a grub himself, emerging from the chrysalis state; if his wish is to ensure a plentiful supply of emus, he dresses himself up as an emu, and mimicks the bird; for by thus converting himself into a grub, or an emu, he thinks he can move the other grubs and emus to comply with his wishes. But it is not merely by disguising himself as an animal and copying its habits that the Central Australian savage seeks to identify himself with his totem. All over the world primitive man believes that by absorbing the flesh and blood of an animal he acquires the qualities of the creature, and so far identifies himself with it. Examples of the belief are too well known to be cited. The same idea forms the basis of the familiar blood-covenant practised by so many races: two men make themselves akin by each transfusing into the veins of the other a little of his own blood. From this point of view it is quite natural that the savage, desirous of uniting himself as closely as possible with his totem, should partake of its flesh and blood. And we have seen that according to the Central Australian traditions men did commonly eat their totems in days of old. In those early times the Kangaroo people may have lived chiefly on kangaroos, strengthening their kangaroo nature by constantly absorbing the flesh of the animal whose name they took and whose habits they copied. The Opossum men may have justified their name by consuming more opossum meat than anybody else; and so with the members of the other totem clans. With this it would agree that two clans of Western Australia, who are named after a small species of opossum and a little fish, believe themselves to be so called because they used to live chiefly on these creatures.[12] Even at present day in Central Australia, though men are in general nearly forbidden to partake of their totem animal or plant, they are still bound occasionally to eat a little of it as a solemn ceremony,

because it is believed that otherwise they could not successfully perform the *Intichiuma* ceremonies, and that the supply of the plant or animal would consequently fail. Clearly they think that, in order to multiply the members of their totem, they must identify themselves with it by taking into their bodies the flesh and blood of the animal or the fibre of the plant. Here, then, in the heart of Australia, among the most primitive savages known to us, we find the actual observance of that totem sacrament which Robertson Smith, with the intuition of genius, divined years ago,[13] but of which positive examples have hitherto been wanting.

The reason why men should in course of time deny themselves food on which they had formerly subsisted, and which they continued to provide for the use of others, is not obvious. We may conjecture that the change came about through an attempt to carry out more consistently than before that identification of a man with his totem, which seems to be of the essence of the system. Men may have remarked that animals as a rule, and plants universally, do not feed upon their own kind; and hence a certain inconsistency may have been perceived in the conduct of the Grub men who lived on grubs, of Grass-seed men who ate grass-seed, and so with other animal and vegetable totems. It might be argued that men who behaved so unlike the real animals and plants could not be true Grubs, Emus, Grass-seeds, and so on, and therefore could not effectively perform the all-important ceremonies for multiplying the beasts, birds, and vegetables on which the tribe depended for its subsistence. Further, a wish to conciliate and entice the creatures which it was desired to catch for food may have helped to establish the taboo on killing and eating the totem. This wish is widely prevalent among savages, and manifests itself in many quaint observances, which the hunter and his friends are bound to comply for the sake of alluring the game, and making death appear to them as painless and even attractive as may be. Among tribes which have the totemic system this need of adopting a conciliatory attitude towards any particular sort of animal would naturally be felt chiefly by that part of the community whose special business it was to breed and kill the animal in question; in other words, it would be felt chiefly by the group or clan which had the particular species of animal for its totem. For it is to be remembered that in early times the members of a clan appear to have been by profession the hunters or butchers as well as the breeders of their totem animal; this comes out in the legend of the Euro man who turned himself into a Kangaroo man in order to kill a kangaroo, and a trace of the same custom appears in the case of the other Euro man.

Now, if it came to be generally thought that a Kangaroo man, for example, would be more likely to entice kangaroos to their fate if he were, so to say, personally known to them as one who had no selfish ends to gain by cultivating their acquaintance, public opinion would gradually impress on the Kangaroo men the duty of abstaining in the interest of the majority from the slaughter and consumption of kangaroos, and they would be urged to confine themselves to their more important function of securing by magical means a plentiful supply of the animal for their fellows. If this explanation is right, the common practice of sparing the totem animal originated in anything but a superstitious reverence for the creature as a superior being endowed with marvelous attributes; it was more analogous to the blandishments with a shepherd or herdsman who will lavish on a sheep or a bullock for the purpose of catching the animal and handing it over to the butcher. Nor need we suppose that in abdicating their ancient right of eating kangaroo flesh the men of the Kangaroo totem were either coerced by their fellows or animated by a noble impulse of disinterested devotion to the common weal. A similar self-denying ordinance would be simultaneously imposed by common consent on all the other clans which had animals or plants for their totem; and thus each clan, in renouncing a single kind of food for the benefit of the community, would calculate on receiving in return a more abundant supply of all the rest, not so much because there would be fewer mouths to feed with each kind of viand, as because the abstinence practised by the several clans was expected to add to the efficacy of their charms for multiplying and attracting the game. For we must bear in mind that under the totemic system the various clans or stocks do not live isolated from each other, but are shuffled up together within a narrow area, and exert their magic powers for the common good.

NOTES

1. *Voyages and Travels of an Indian Interpreter,* p. 86, London, 1791.

2. *History of the Ojebway Indians,* London, 1861, p. 138.

3. "History of the Ojebways," in *Collections of the Minnesota Historical Society,* vol. V (St. Paul, Minn., 1885) p. 34.

4. *Ancient Society,* p. 165.

5. See *Academy,* 27th Sept. 1884, p. 203.

6. In J. A. Cuoq's *Lexique de la langue Algonquine* (Montreal, 1886), p. 312. Thavenet admits that the Indians use *ote* in the sense of "mark" (limited apparently to a family mark), but argues that the word must mean family or tribe.

7. *Expedition to Itasca Lake,* New York, 1834, p. 146, etc. Petitot spells it *todem* in his *Monographic des Dene-Dindjie,* p. 40; but he writes *otemisme* in his *Traditions Indiennes du Canada Nord-ouest,* p. 446.

8. *The Native Tribe of Central Australia,* p. 202, cf. p. 168.

9. J. Campbell, *Travels in South Africa, Being a Narrative of a Second Journey in that Country,* ii. p. 34.

10. I. Petroff, *Report on the Population, Industries, and Resources of Alaska,* p. 145.

11. K. von den Steinen, *Unter den Naturvolkern Zentral-Brasiliens,* pp. 352, 512.

12. Sir George Grey, *Vocabulary of the Dialects of South-Western Australia,* pp. 4, 95.

13. *Religion of the Semites,* p. 276 Edinburgh, 1889.

From *Chips from a German Workshop: Essays on the Science of Religion* and *Introduction to the Science of Religion*

F. MAX MÜLLER

A Science of Religion

I do not wish to disguise these difficulties which are inherent in a comparative study of the religions of the world. I rather dwell on them strongly, in order to show how much care and caution is required in so difficult a subject, and how much indulgence should be shown in judging of the shortcomings and errors that are unavoidable in so comprehensive a study. It was supposed at one time that a comparative analysis of the languages of mankind must transcend the powers of man: and yet by the combined and well directed efforts of many scholars, great results have here been obtained, and the principles that must guide the student of the Science of Language are now firmly established. It will be the same with the Science of Religion. By a proper division of labour, the materials that are still wanting, will be collected and published and translated, and when that is done, surely man will never rest till he has discovered the purpose that runs through the religions of mankind, and till he has reconstructed the true *Civitas Dei* on foundations as wide as the ends of the world. The Science of Religion may be the last of the sciences which man is destined to elaborate; but when it is elaborated, it will change the aspect of the world, and give a new life to Christianity itself.

The Fathers of the Church, though living in much more dangerous proximity to the ancient religions of the Gentiles, admitted freely that a comparison of Christianity and other religions was useful. "If there is any agreement," Basilius remarked, "between their [the Greeks] doctrines and our own, it may benefit us to know them: if not, then to compare them and to learn how they differ, will help not a little towards confirming that which is the better of the two."[1]

But this is not the only advantage of a comparative study of religions. The Science of Religion will for the first time assign to Christianity its right place among the religions of the world; it will show for the first time fully what was meant by the fullness of time; it will restore to the whole history of the world, in its unconscious progress towards Christianity, its true and sacred character.

Not many years ago great offense was given by an eminent writer who remarked that the time had come when the history of Christianity should be treated in a truly historical spirit, in the same spirit in which we treat the history of other religions, such as Brahmanism, Buddhism, or Mohammedanism. And yet what can be truer? He must be a man of little faith, who would fear to subject his own religion to the same critical tests to which the historian subjects all other religions. We need not surely crave a tender or merciful treatment for that faith which we hold to be the only true one. We should rather challenge for it the severest tests and trials, as the sailor would for the good ship

Reprinted from F. Max Müller Chips from a German Workshop: Essays on the Science of Religion, *vol. 1 (London: Longmans, Green & Company, 1867), and* Introduction to The Science of Religion *(London: Longmans, Green & Company, 1873).*

to which he entrusts his own life, and the lives of those who are most dear to him. In the Science of Religion, we can decline no comparisons, nor claim any immunities for Christianity, as little as the missionary can, when wrestling with the subtle Brahman, or the fanatical Mussulman, or the plain speaking Zulu. And if we send out our missionaries to every part of the world to face very kind of religion, to shrink from no contest, to be appalled by no objections, we must not give way at home or within our heart to any misgivings, that a comparative study of the religions of the world could shake the firm foundation on which we must stand or fall.

To the missionary more particularly a comparative study of the religions of mankind will be, I believe, of the greatest assistance. Missionaries are apt to look upon all other religions as something totally distinct from their own, as formerly they used to describe the languages of barbarous nations as something more like the twittering of birds than the articulate speech of men. The Science of Language has taught us that there is order and wisdom in all languages, and that even the most degraded jargons contain the ruins of former greatness and beauty. The Science of Religion, I hope, will produce a similar change in our views of barbarous forms of faith and worship; and missionaries, instead of looking only for points of difference, will look out more anxiously for any common ground, any spark of the true light that may still be revived, any altar that may be dedicated afresh to the true God.

And even to us at home, a wider view of the religious life of the world may teach many a useful lesson. Immense as is the difference between our own and all other religions of the world— and few can know that difference who have not honestly examined the foundations of their own as well as of other religions—the position which believers and unbelievers occupy with regard to their various forms of faith is very much the same all over the world. The difficulties which trouble us, have troubled the hearts and minds

of men as far back as we can trace the beginnings of religious life. The great problems touching the relation of the Finite to the Infinite, of the human mind as the recipient, and the Divine Spirit as the source of truth, are old problems indeed; and while watching their appearance in different countries, and their treatment under varying conditions, we shall be able, I believe, to profit ourselves, both by the errors which others committed before us, and by the truth which they discovered. We shall know that rocks that threaten every religion in this changing and shifting world of ours, and having watched many a storm of religious controversy and many a shipwreck in distant east, we shall face with greater calmness and prudence the troubled waters at home.

If there is one thing which a comparative study of religions places in the clearest light, it is the inevitable decay to which every religion is exposed. It may seem almost like a truism, that no religion can continue to be what it was during the lifetime of its founder and its first apostles. Yet it is but seldom borne in mind that without constant reformation, i.e., without a constant return to its fountainhead, every religion, even the most perfect, nay the most perfect on account of its very perfection, more even than others, suffers from its contact with the world, as the purest air suffers from the mere fact of its being breathed.

Whenever we trace back a religion to its first beginnings, we find it free from many of the blemishes that offend us in its later phases. The founders of the ancient religions of the world, as far as we can judge, were minds of a high stamp, full of noble aspirations, yearning for truth, devoted to the welfare of their neighbours, examples of purity and unselfishness. What they desired to found upon earth was but seldom realised, and their sayings, if preserved in their original form, offer often a strange contrast to the practice of those who profess to be their disciples. As soon as a religion is established, and more particularly when it has become the religion of a powerful state, the foreign and worldly elements encroach more and more on the original foundation, and human interests mar the simplicity and purity of the plan which the founder had conceived in his own heart, and matured in his communings with his God. Even those who lived with Buddha, misunderstood his words, and at the Great Council which had to settle the Buddhist canon, Asoka, the Indian Constantine, had to remind the assembled priests that "what had been said by Buddha, that alone was well said"; and that certain works ascribed to Buddha, as, for instance, the instruction given to his son, Rahula, were apocryphal, if not heretical.[2] With every century, Buddhism, when it was accepted by nations, differing as widely as Mongols and Hindus, when its sacred writings were translated into languages as wide apart as Sanskrit and Chinese, assumed widely different aspects, till at last the Buddhism of the Shamans in the steppes of Tatary is as different from the teaching of the original Samana, as the Christianity of the leader of the Chinese rebels is from the teaching of Christ. . . .

There is a strong feeling, I know, in the minds of all people against any attempt to treat their own religion as a member of a class, and, in one sense, that feeling is perfectly justified. To each individual, his own religion, if he really believes in it, is something quite inseparable from himself, something unique, that cannot be compared to anything else, or replaced by anything else. Our own religion is, in that respect, something like our own language. In its form it may be like other languages; in it essence and in its relation to ourselves, it stands alone and admits of no peer or rival.

But in the history of the world, our religion, like our own language, is but one out of many; and in order to understand fully the position of Christianity in the history of the world, and its true place among the religions of mankind, we must compare it, not with Judaism only, but with the religious aspirations of the whole world, with all, in fact, that Christianity came either to destroy or to fulfill. From this point of view Christianity forms part, no doubt, of

what people call profane history, but by that very fact, profane history ceases to be profane, and regains throughout that sacred character of which it had been deprived by a false distinction. . . . .

The Comparative Study of Religions

In beginning today a course of lectures on the *Science of Religion,*—or I should rather say on some preliminary points that have to be settled before we can enter upon a truly scientific study of the religions of the world,—I feel as I felt when first pleading in this very place for the Science of Language.

I know that I shall have to meet determined antagonists who will deny the possibility of a scientific treatment of religions as they denied the possibility of a scientific treatment of languages. I foresee even a far more serious conflict with familiar prejudices and deep-rooted convictions; but I feel at the same time that I am prepared to meet my antagonists, and have such faith in their honesty and love of truth, that I doubt not of a patient and impartial hearing on their part, and of a verdict influenced by nothing but by the evidence that I shall have to place before them.

In these our days it is almost impossible to speak of religion without giving offense either on the right or on the left. With some, religion seems too sacred a subject for scientific treatment; with others it stands on a level with alchemy and astrology, as a mere tissue of errors or hallucinations, far beneath the notice of the man of science.

In a certain sense, I accept both these views. Religion *is* a sacred subject, and whether in its most perfect or in its most imperfect form, it has a right to our highest reverence. . . .

No one—this I can promise—who attends these lectures, be he Christian or Jew, Hindu or Mohammedan, shall hear his own way of serving God spoken of irreverently. But true reverence does not consist in declaring a subject, because it is dear to us, to be unfit for free and honest inquiry: far from it! True reverence is shown in treating every subject, however sacred, however dear to ùs, with perfect confidence; without fear and without favour; with tenderness and love, by all means, but, before all, with an unflinching and uncompromising loyalty to truth.

On the other hand, I full admit that religion has stood in former ages, and stands also in our own age, if we look abroad, and if we look into some of the highest and some of the lowest places at home, on a level with alchemy and astrology. There exist superstitions, little short of fetishism; and, what is worse, there exists hypocrisy, as bad as that of the Roman augurs.

In practical life it would be wrong to assume a neutral position between such conflicting views. Where we see that the reverence due to religion is violated, we are bound to protest; where we see that superstition saps the roots of faith, and hypocrisy poisons the springs of morality, we must take sides. But as students of the Science of Religion we move in a higher and more serene atmosphere. We study error, as the physiologist studies a disease, looking for its cause, tracing its influences, speculating on possible remedies, but leaving the application of such remedies to a different class of men, to the surgeon and the practical physician. *Diversos diversa juvant* applies here as everywhere else, and a division of labour, according to the peculiar abilities and tastes of different individuals, promises always the best results. The student of the history of the physical sciences is not angry with the alchemists, nor does he argue with the astrologists; he rather tries to enter into their view of things, and to discover in the errors of alchemy and seeds of chemistry, and in the hallucinations of astronomy a yearning and groping after a true knowledge of the heavenly bodies. It is the same with the student of the Science of Religion. He wants to find out what Religion is, what foundation it has in the soul of man, and what laws it follows in its historical growth. For that purpose the study of errors is to him more instructive than the study of truth,

and the smiling augur as interesting a subject as the Roman suppliant who veiled his face in prayer, that he might be alone with his God.

The very title of the Science of Religion will jar, I know, on the ears of many persons, and a comparison of all the religions of the world, in which none can claim a privileged position, will no doubt seem to many dangerous and reprehensible, because ignoring that peculiar reverence which everybody, down to the mere fetish worshipper, feel for his own religion and for his own God. Let me say then at once that I myself have shared these misgivings, but that I have tried to overcome them, because I would not and could not allow myself to surrender either what I hold to be the truth, or what I hold still dearer than truth, the right of testing truth. Nor do I regret it. I do not say that the Science of Religion is all gain. No, it entails losses, and losses of many things which we hold dear. But this I will say, that, as far as my humble judgment goes, it does not entail the loss of anything that is essential to true religion, and that if we strike the balance honestly, the gain is immeasurably greater than the loss.

One of the first questions that was asked by classical scholars when invited to consider that value of the Science of Language, was, "What shall we gain by a comparative study of languages?" Languages, it was said, are wanted for practical purposes, for speaking and reading; and by studying too many languages at once, we run the risk of losing the firm grasp which we ought to have on the few that are really important. Our knowledge, by becoming wider, must needs, it was thought, become shallower, and the gain, if there is any, in knowing the structure of dialects which have never produced any literature at all, would certainly be outweighed by the loss in accurate and practical scholarship.

If this could be said of a comparative study of languages, with how much greater force will it be urged against a comparative study of religions! Though I do not expect that those who study the religious books of Brahmans and Buddhists, of Confucius and Laotse, of

Mahommed and Nanak, will be accused of cherishing in their secret heart the doctrines of those ancient masters, or of having lost the firm hold on their own religious convictions, yet I doubt whether the practical utility of wider studies in the vast field of the religions of the world will be admitted with greater readiness by professed theologians than the value of a knowledge of Sanskrit, Zend, Gothic, or Celtic for a thorough mastery of Greek and Latin, and for a real appreciation of the nature, the purpose, the laws, the growth and decay of language was admitted, or is even now admitted, by some of our most eminent professors and teachers.

People ask, What is gained by comparison?— Why, all higher knowledge is acquired by comparison, and rests on comparison. If it is said that the character of scientific research in our age is pre-eminently comparative, this really means that our researchers are now based on the widest evidence that can be obtained, on the broadest inductions that can be grasped by the human mind.

What can be gained by comparison? —Why, look at the study of languages. If you go back but a hundred years and examine the folios of the most learned writers on questions connected with language, and then open a book written by the merest trio in Comparative Philology, you will see what can be gained, what has been gained, by the comparative method. A few hundred years ago, the idea that Hebrew was the original language of mankind was accepted as a matter of course, even as a matter of faith, the only problem being to find out by what process Greek, or Latin, or any other language could have been developed out of Hebrew. The idea, too, that language was revealed, in the scholastic sense of the word, was generally accepted, although, as early as the fourth century, St. Gregory, the learned bishop of Nyssa, had strongly protested against it.[3] The grammatical framework of a language was either considered as the result of a conventional agreement, or the terminations of nouns and verbs were supposed to have sprouted forth like buds from the roots and stems of language; and the vaguest similarity in the sound and meaning of words was taken to be a sufficient criterion for testing their origin and their relationship. Of all this philological somnambulism we hardly find a trace in works published since the days of Humboldt, Bopp, and Grimm.

Has there been any loss here? Has it not been pure gain? Does language excite our admiration less, because we know that, though the faculty of speaking is the work of Him who works in all things, the invention of words for naming each object was left to man, and was achieved through the working of the human mind? Is Hebrew less carefully studied, because it is no longer believed to be a revealed language, sent down from heaven, but a language closely allied to Arabic, Syriac, and ancient Babylonian, and receiving light from these cognate, and in some respects more primitive, languages, for the explanation of many of its grammatical forms, and for the exact interpretation of many of its obscure and difficult words? Is the grammatical articulation of Greek and Latin less instructive because instead of seeing in their terminations of nouns and verbs merely arbitrary signs to distinguish the plural from the singular, or the future from the present, we can now perceive an intelligible principle in the gradual production of formal out of the material elements of language? And are our etymologies less important, because, instead of being suggested by superficial similarities, they are now based on honest historical and physiological research? Lastly, has our own language ceased to hold its own peculiar place? Is our love for our own native tongue at all impaired? Do men speak less boldly or pray less fervently in their own mother tongue, because they know its true origin and its unadorned history; because they know that everything in language that goes beyond the objects of sense, is and must be pure metaphor? Or does any one deplore the fact that there is in all languages, even in the jargons of the lowest savages, order and wisdom; nay, something that makes the world akin?

Why, then, should we hesitate to apply the comparative method, which has produced such great results in other spheres of knowledge, to a study of religion? That it will change many of the views commonly held about the origin, the character, the growth, and decay of the religions of the world, I do not deny; but unless we hold that fearless progression in new inquiries, which is our bounden duty and our honest pride in all other branches of knowledge, is dangerous in the study of religions, unless we allow ourselves to be frightened by the once famous dictum, that whatever is new in theology is false, this ought to be the very reason why a comparative study of religions should no longer be neglected or delayed.

When the students of Comparative Philology boldly adapted Goethe's paradox, *"He who knows one language, knows none,"* people were startled at first; but they soon began to feel the truth which was hidden beneath the paradox. Could Goethe have meant that Homer did not know Greek, or that Shakespeare did not know English, because neither of them knew more than their mother tongue? No! what was meant was that neither Homer nor Shakespeare knew what that language really was which he handled with so much power and cunning. Unfortunately, the old verb "to can," from which "canny" and "cunning," is lost in English, otherwise we should be able in two words to express our meaning, and to keep apart the two kinds of knowledge of which we are here speaking. As we say in German *konnen* is not *kennen,* we might say in English, *to can,* that is to be cunning, is not *to ken,* that is to know; and it would then become clear at once, that the most eloquent speaker and the most gifted poet, with all their cunning of words and skillful mastery of expression, would have but little to say if asked, what language really is? The same applies to religion. *He who knows one, knows none.* There are thousands of people whose faith is such that it could move mountains, and who yet, if they were asked what religion really is, would remain silent, or would speak of outward tokens rather than of the inward nature, or of the faculty of faith. . . .

Lastly, and this, I believe, is the most important advantage which we enjoy as students of the history of religion, we have been taught the rules of critical scholarship. No one would venture, now-a-days, to quote from any book, whether sacred or profane, without having asked these simple and yet momentous questions: When was it written? Where? and by whom? Was the author an eye-witness, or does he only relate what he has heard from others? And if the latter, were his authorities at least contemporaneous with the events which they relate, and were they under the sway of party feeling or any other disturbing influence? Was the whole book written at once, or does it contain portions of an earlier date; and if so, is it possible for us to separate these earlier documents from the body of the book?

A study of the original documents on which the principal religions of the world profess to be founded, carried on in this spirit, has enabled some of our best living scholars to distinguish in each religion between what is really ancient and what is comparatively modern; between what was the doctrine of the founders and their immediate disciples, and what were the afterthoughts and, generally, the corruptions, or, it may be, improvements, is not without its own peculiar charm, and full of practical lessons; yet, as it is essential that we should know the most ancient forms of every language, before we proceed to any comparisons, it is indispensable also that we should have a clear conception of the most primitive form of every religion, before we proceed to determine its own value, and to compare it with other forms of religious faith. Many an orthodox Mohammedan, for instance, will relate miracles wrought by Mohammed; but in the Koran, Mohammed says distinctly, that he is a man like other men. He disdains to work miracles, and appeals to the great works of Allah, the rising and setting of the sun, the rain that fructifies the earth, the plants that grow, and the living souls that are born into the world—who can tell whence? —as the real signs and wonders in the eyes of a true believer. . . .

It would be too much to say that the critical sitting of the authorities for a study of each religion has been already fully carried out. There is work enough still to be done. But a beginning, and a very successful beginning, has been made, and the results thus brought to light will serve as a wholesome caution to everybody who is engaged in religious researches. . . .

A Science of Religion, based on an impartial and truly scientific comparison of all, or at all, events, of the most important, religions of mankind, is now only a question of time. It is demanded by those whose voice cannot be disregarded. Its title, though implying as yet a promise rather than a fulfillment, has become more or less familiar in Germany, France, and America; its great problems have attracted the eyes of many inquirers, and its results have been anticipated either with fear or with delight. It becomes therefore the duty of those who have devoted their life to the study of the principal religions of the world in their original documents, and who value religion and reverence it in whatever form it may present itself, to take possession of this new territory in the name of true science, and thus to protect its sacred precincts from the inroads of those of the Jews and Christians, without ever having taken the trouble of learning the languages in which their sacred books are written. What should we think of philosophers writing on the religion of Homer, without knowing Greek, or on the religion of Moses, without knowing Hebrew? . . .

And let me remark this, in the very beginning, that no other religion, with the exception, perhaps, of early Buddhism, would have favored the idea of an impartial comparison of the principal religions of the world—would have tolerated our science. Nearly every religion seems to adopt the language of the Pharisee rather than of the publican. It is Christianity alone which, as the religion of humanity, as the religion of no caste, of no chosen people, has taught us to respect the history of humanity, as a whole, to discover the traces of a divine wisdom and love in the government of all the races of mankind, and to recognize, if possible, even in the lowest and crudest forms of religious belief, not the work of demoniacal agencies, but something that indicates a divine guidance, something that makes us perceive, with St. Peter, "that God is no respecter of persons, but that in every nation he that feareth Him and worketh righteousness is accepted with Him."

In no religion was there a soil so well prepared for the cultivation of Comparative theology as in our own. The position which Christianity from the very beginning took up with regard to Judaism, served as the first lesson in comparative theology, and directed the attention, even of the unlearned, to a comparison of two religions, differing in their conception of the Deity, in their estimate of humanity, in their motives of morality, and in their hope of immortality, yet sharing so much in common that there are but few of the psalms and prayers in the Old Testament in which a Christian cannot heartily join even now, and but few rules of morality which he ought not even now to obey. If we have once learned to see in the exclusive religion of the Jews a preparation of what was to be the all-embracing religion of humanity, we shall feel much less difficulty in recognizing in the mazes of other religions a hidden purpose; a wandering in the desert, it may be, but a preparation also for the land of promise. . . .

Religion and Language

Let us see now what religion is in those early ages of which we are here speaking; I do not mean religion as a silent power, working in the heart of man; I mean religion in its outward appearance, religion as something outspoken, tangible, and definite, that can be described and communicated to others. We shall find that in that sense religion lies within a very small compass. A few words, recognized as names of the deity; a few epithets that have been raised from their material meaning to a higher and more spiritual stage, I mean words which expressed originally bodily strength, or brightness, or purity, and which came gradually to mean greatness, goodness, and holiness; lastly, some more or less technical terms expressive of such ideas as *sacrifice, altar, prayer,* possibly *virtue* and *sin, body* and *spirit*—that is what constitutes the outward framework of the incipient religions of antiquity. If we look at this simple manifestation of religion we see at once why religion, during those early ages of which we are here speaking, may really and truly be called a sacred dialect of human speech; how at all events early religion and early language are most intimately connected, religion depending entirely for its outward expression on the more or less adequate resources of language.

If this dependence of early religion on language is once clearly understood, it follows, as a matter of course, that whatever classification has been found most useful in the science of language ought to prove equally useful in the science of religion. If there is a truly genetic relationship of languages, the same relationship ought to hold together the religions of the world, at least the most ancient religions. . . .

The intention of religion, wherever we meet it, is always holy. However imperfect, however childish a religion may be, it always places the human soul in the presence of God; and however imperfect and however childish the conception of God may be, it always represents the highest ideal of perfection which the human soul, for the time being, can reach and grasp. Religion therefore places the human soul in the presence of its highest ideal, it lifts it above the level of ordinary goodness, and produces at least a yearning after a higher and better life—a life in the light of God. . . .

There are two distinct tendencies to be observed in the growth of ancient religion. There is, on the one side, the struggle of the mind against the material character of language, a constant attempt to strip words of their coarse covering, and fit them, by main force, for the purposes of abstract thought. But there is, on the other side, a constant relapse from the spiritual into the material, and, strange to say, a predilection for the material sense instead of the spiritual. This action and reaction has been going on in the language of religion from the earliest times, and it is at work even now. . . .

I call this variety of acceptation, this misunderstanding, which is inevitable in ancient and also modern religion, the *dialectic growth and decay,* or, if you like, the *dialectic life of religion,* and we shall see again and again how important it is in enabling us to form a right estimate of religious language and thought. The dialectic shades in the language of religion are almost infinite; they explain the decay, but they also account for the life of religion. You may remember . . . from first to last religion is oscillating between these two opposite poles, and it is only if the attraction of one of the two poles becomes too strong, that the healthy movement ceases, and stagnation and decay set in. If religion cannot accommodate itself on the one side to the capacity of children, or if on the other side it fails to satisfy the requirements of men, it has lost its vitality, and it becomes either mere superstition or mere philosophy. . . .

But this is not all. The very imperfection of every name that had been chosen, their very inadequacy to express the fullness and infinity of the Divine, would keep up the search for new names till at last every part of nature in which an approach to the Divine could be discovered was chosen as a name of the Omnipresent. If the presence of the Divine was perceived in the strong wind, the strong wind became its name: if its presence was perceived in the earthquake and the fire, the earthquake and the fire became its names. Do you still wonder at polytheism or at mythology? Why, they are inevitable. They are, if you like, a *parler enfantin* of religion. But the world had its childhood, and when it was a child it spoke as a child, it understood as a child, it thought as a child; and, I say again, in that it spoke as a child its language was true, in that it believed as a child its religion was true. The fault rests with us, if we insist on taking the language of children for the language of men, if we attempt to translate literally ancient into modern language, oriental into occidental speech, poetry into prose. . . .

The *parler enfantin* in religion is not extinct; it never will be. Not only have some of the ancient childish religions been kept alive, as, for instance, the religion of India, which is to my mind like a half-fossilized megatherion walking about in the broad daylight of the nineteenth century; but in our own religion and in the language of the New Testament there are many things which disclose their true meaning to those who know what language is made of, who have not only ears to hear but a heart to understand the real meaning of parables. . . .

If we have once learnt to be charitable in the interpretation of the language of other religions, we shall more easily learn to be charitable in the interpretation of the language of our own; we shall no longer try to force a literal interpretation on words and sentences in our sacred books, which, if interpreted literally must lose their original purport and their spiritual truth. In this way, I believe that a comparative study of the religions of the world will teach us many a useful lesson in the study of our own: that it will teach us, at all events, to be charitable both abroad and at home.

NOTES

1. Basilius, *De legendis Graecorum libris*.

2. E. Burnouf, *Lotus de la bonne Loi*, Appendice, No. x, § 4.

3. Max Müller, *Lectures on the Science of Language*, Vol. I, p. 32.

Counterpoint:
From *In Search of Dreamtime:*
The Quest for the Origin of Religion

TOMOKO MASUZAWA

Tomoko Masuzawa is a professor of Religious Studies at the University of Michigan, Ann Arbor.

IT HAS BEEN SOME TIME since the question of the origin of religion was seriously entertained. Today, there is little sign of the matter being resuscitated and once again becoming the focus of the lively debate of old. Looking back upon the bold speculations of their forefathers, contemporary scholars of religion seem to consider themselves to be in a new phase of scholarship, having learned, above all, not to ask impossible questions. Reputedly, those grand old ideas—the so-called theories of the origin of religion—were conceived by the powerful Victorian imagination in the lacunae of concrete data, and it therefore should be hardly surprising that they turned out to be stillborn. Such is the present-day assessment of these "theories," and

Reprinted from Tomoko Masuzawa In Search of Dreamtime: The Quest for the Origin of Religion. *Copyright © 1993 The University of Chigaco Press. Reprinted by permission.*

if we still study these ideas today, it is supposed to be only in order to assist their more decorous—and more secure—second burial.

Still more serious than the paucity of factual grounding, however, it is the prerogative of origin itself that has come under suspicion in recent times, together with the assumption of the unity, simplicity, and self-identity of absolute beginning. In short, all of the pristine metaphysics of presence, permanence, and plenitude that the concept of origin is said to embody have been rendered problematic. In this connection, we have also come to see that the sovereignty of the author–originator over her text is as imaginary as any other assumption of a unitary origin.

In light of this overriding critique, it might seem a questionable endeavor to draw attention once again to the dubious exploits of those Great Books that so unambiguously set out in search of origins many decades ago, the books that are now laid to rest in the sepulchral category called "classics." While accounting for such venerable texts from time to time may be a respectful sort of activity, reading them is perhaps another matter. For, like an autopsy, reading can be an invasive procedure, which might, for that matter, induce some dead souls to a rude awakening. But if we are to encounter some unlaid ghost at the burial site of such "classics," there is a chance that the haunting spirit may tell us more than the dead author–master had intended or would have allowed.

What has prompted my return to some of those classic texts discussed in this book, however, is not simply a necromantic curiosity or, as it is usually and more respectably called, "historical interest." What first intrigued me, rather, was the incomplete state of their burial itself. And what strikes me as more peculiar still is the position of the contemporary scholar, who is perforce cast as a guardian of these tombs, obliged to stand at once venerating and condemning the dead. The singularity of this post seems to be in no small part due to the very construction—scaffolding? set-up?—of the contemporary study of religion.

This, in effect, is the disciplinary setup an aspiring student of religion is likely to find herself in at the threshold of a graduate school. First, presumably, there is something like an object called "religion," and this object, as it has been taught in the academy for the last half century or so, is intricately graced with an imposing network of rules and regulations. By and large these rules have to do with proper scholarly conduct. In addition to the usual litany of the general ethics of learning, which advises us to "approach" the subject matter gingerly and not to be too eager to "grasp" it, there is a remarkable profusion of warnings prohibiting violation and reduction. Concomitantly, there is an impression that this object which the scholar—or "Western man," as the position of the observer has been traditionally called[1]—seeks to examine, either historico-scientifically or hermeneutically, is something exquisitely "alive," or if not so at present, at least it was once alive. Be it a "religion," a "tradition," or a "primitive society," this type of object, which we as scholars of religion are duty-bound to understand, is said to possess integrity, a genius, and "organic wholeness" all its own. In today's harsh world of invasive sciences, it is felt, this precious object stands in imminent danger of being violated and reduced to a mere social fact, a mistake in grammar, a kind of collective neurosis, or perhaps even to nothing.

While this fear of sinning against the sanctity of "a living whole" would no doubt offer a fitting occasion for starting a general investigation into Western fantasies of global politics, I found one precept in particular more startling than any other. This is the dictum, "Thou shalt not quest for the origin of religion." It is as though our integrity as modern, factually responsible scholars of religion depended on our compliance with this fundamental vow, or rather, disavowal. This is striking especially in light of the fact that, together with this precept, we also learn that every one of the "founding fathers" of our discipline stunningly violated this rule and indulged and jubilated in the forbidden act. Hence, those great forefathers are to be at once denounced and admired; for, after all, we are told, they lived and wrote before there was any recognition of the prohibition. Apparently, they inhabited the prehistory of our discipline; indeed, they must be our own primal fathers, roaming the earth before the Fall or, at any rate, before reality set in, in such forms as the two world wars, the collapse of colonial regimes, and other unpleasant events of this century. Owing to these disappointments that irrevocably divided their era and ours, the patrimony due us turned out to be rather meager. Whatever the glorious exploits and putative discoveries of our forefathers may have been, their fantastic bounty followed them to their graves and expired, so it seems, leaving virtually nothing that we the epigones could invest in the future of our "discipline." In effect, their precious bequest to us amounts to just this prohibition, this piece of wisdom: Deny yourself the liberty your forefathers took unrestrained; renounce the desire for the origin, give up the desire for the ultimate naming of the source, the essence, the Reality, or anything with capital letters—abandon all this for the sake of *Wissenschaft*.

It seems uncertain if someone in this far end of the twentieth century would spontaneously think of launching on such a quest for an origin if left unchecked by this well-publicized interdiction. However that may be, a number of compelling reasons not to do so have been frequently presented to the students of religion, and many of these reasons are surely deserving of attention. But what is even more noteworthy is the voice, the gesture, the pathos of this prohibition itself. There is at once a humble pride and a special poignancy in this self-denial, or renunciation, on the part of the latter-day representative of "Western man"; in some other circumstances one might be tempted to call such a demeanor "religious." But if I were to give into the temptation here, it would not be in order to discredit or diminish the authority of

the voice of prohibition by calling it names. Rather, I am interested in raising another sort of question: Why should this particular renunciation of desire, this ascetic practice, be any less interesting, any less deserving of close analysis, than anything else in the world that is classified by "Western man" with the label "religion"?

Added to this singular practice of self-denial is another curious aspect of the modern study of religion: a sweeping assertion to the effect that religion itself, whether "primitive" or "highly developed," is preeminently concerned with origins. This notion can be elaborated in various ways. For instance, there is a recurrent claim among the scholars of religion that the quintessentially sacred myths are creation myths, and rituals are periodic recreation of those mythic times of beginning, or repetition of some "axial" event. This idea, which universally and uniformly valorizes the meaning of origins in religious beliefs and practices worldwide, first came into prominence with the myth-ritual school earlier in this century, and was immensely popularized by Mircea Eliade and others thereafter.

To be sure, there have been many strong cases made against this idea, and some of the most effective criticisms have come in the form of rigorous alternative interpretation of alleged creation myths and alleged reorigination rituals.[2] These criticisms notwithstanding, the fundamental "insight" of the myth-ritual school is still viable and continues to inform our sense of historicity, cultural diversity, and global plenitude—to the extent that we have not grown sufficiently suspicious of what is invested in these latter notions. This is another way of saying that, as post-structuralist criticism has put it most succinctly, the logic of origination animates and dominates much of our discursive practice, in religious studies as in many other fields. The preeminence of origin lives on and articulates itself in different transmutations, and, unless we find good reasons to dismiss the post-structuralist critique in toto, we would be hard pressed not to keep on insisting that the effect of the origin-logic operative in the study of religion is limited to its most frankly obvious form manifest in the particular brand of "history of religions." . . .

If this prevailing depiction of religion and religious peoples as origin oriented or origin obsessed is brought to bear upon the equally conspicuous matter of scholarly renunciation of origin quests mentioned earlier, this conjunction offers an interesting analytic situation. There is a curious configuration of agencies here: "Western man," who gives up the desire for origins for the sake of science but also imputes to the ones who are positioned to be the objects of "his" study the unrestrained indulgence in this desire. The opposition of renunciation versus gratification thus sharply demarcates and separates the modern scholar of religion from the primitive practitioner of religion, the studying subject from the studied object. As always, the declaration of difference is pronounced from the point of view of the subject, against the object. At the same time, it would seem, the configuration also allows a kind of vicarious participation in the forbidden. For, according to this delineation of difference, those "primitive," "archaic," or "religious" peoples conveniently play out the suppressed desire of the observing scientist without endangering the latter's authority invested in the asceticism of "objective observation."

Is this too good to be true? Do these other people—call them "primitive," "archaic," or simply "religious"—exist?

This question is not meant to be rhetorical, nor does it call for a merely empirical answer. Rather, it should call attention to itself, to its own grounds; for, the very question of the reality of the non-Western, nonmodern—in short, the other of "us"—arises from the prevailing discourse of "our science" itself, that is, from the grounds of the "Western" pursuit of knowledge, rather than from the incomplete state of this knowledge. But in addition to this recognition, of course, there are indeed many requisite questions to be asked if we hope to come to

terms critically with the present state of our "discipline." The principal desiderata, no doubt, would be comprehensive and specific analyses of the works of some key figures in the field today, as well as sustained investigations of institutional-particularly pedagogical—practices. This book, however, is at once more modest in its immediate aim and less frontal in its strategy.

The focal point of the present study is the ambiguity—or, perhaps more properly speaking, the ambivalence—permeating the scene of incomplete burial of the classical masters. First, there is the ambivalence of the contemporary appraisal and of the attitude toward the dead: admiration and virtual veneration for their daring on the one hand, and condemnation of their hubris and naiveté on the other. Second, there is the ambivalence of the position of the contemporary scholar, qua "Western man," that "he" both does and does not renounce the quest for origins. This second ambivalence is constitutional to the basis of scholarship as "he" understands it, and makes possible the whole enterprise of knowledge.

Thanks largely to psychoanalysis, we have learnt to expect the presence of a rather complicated process called repression whenever we encounter a highly charged ambivalence. This may indeed be a case in point. If repression is suspected in the contemporary study of religion and, in particular, in its self-understanding of the position vis-à-vis its own past, it may be strategically expedient to apply a method that is neither merely phenomenological/observational nor surgical/invasive, but perhaps a method akin to psychoanalysis. This alternative strategy is, in brief, to invert and to reverse the self-claimed positioning of the scholarship by deliberately turning out the "wrong" side, and thus casting the whole problematic in an entirely different light. In other words, if the ambivalence embodied by the subject-object demarcation is intended to justify the (ambivalent) silencing of the past masters and the disallowing of their direct "influence," we may now turn this situation around, inside out, and suggest that *there may be something in those now-discredited origin quests of yesteryear that can threaten the very configuration of positions that legitimate "Western man's" occupation in science/knowledge.* It may be that, despite their manifest intentions, those classical authors did not so much identify an origin, even erroneously, but rather they hit upon some monstrosity, a discovery which threatened to overpower the very basis of their origin quest; and it may be that those great forefathers, no less than their later critics and detractors, "failed to recognize" the import of their prodigious discovery and therefore did not account for the implications their own speculative adventures brought forth. . . .

This is perhaps as good a place as any to accede that each of my readings of the three authors may be termed, though perhaps in a rather loose sense, post-structuralist. I have no reason to object to this designation, assuming that by a post-structuralist reading we do not understand—as those who are hostile to post-structuralism sometimes do—a new, upgraded version of formalist exercise, or even more dismissively, an effete, formulaic reading that produces little else than torturously refined, but ultimately inconsequential results. . . .

The archaic, the other of the modern, is at once the other of us, the contemporary scholars of religion. But the other of oneself is always a double of oneself, a mirror image, a picture in reverse, a representation that doubles and couples the self and the other. This other—the archaic—is presented as peculiarly marked by a singular obsession with the moment of origin. What does this reflect vis-à-vis the modern scholarship on myth and ritual, the scholarship, that is, that rather emphatically denied itself the quest for the origin of religion some time ago? This scholarship is peculiarly marked by its obsession with cosmogony, paradigms, and archetypal narratives—in short, a preoccupation with the question of origin. Does this not signal a certain displacement, a certain shifting that

repeats and veils—which is a telltale sign of repressions displacement of that very desire which we once renounced and continue to deny ourselves?

Repetition veils. This tradition of scholarship caught up in the repetition compulsion of the originary economy is yet to be struck, yet to be disturbed from its own dreamtime, by the cacophony of postmodern debates. Or it is perhaps more accurate to say that the impact of such disturbances is at the present moment barely kept at bay, for there are indeed multiple voices hovering above our scholarly sanctuary. . . .

It is time to arrive finally at our post-. Time to gather our chips or, perhaps, time to recollect the movement of the hand that has just finished something.

What, then, are my results? Although I do want to claim that each reading brings into relief an aspect of Durkheim's, Müller's, or Freud's legacy that has been hitherto neglected or perhaps unsuspected, I do not envisage that the aspect thus "recovered" in my reading would somehow "fill a gap" in the existing scholarship and thus contribute toward its greater perfection—as if one should be expecting such a providential moment of completion sometime in the future. Nor is it my expectation that the "recovery" would occasion a wholesale transformation of the established intellectual legacy in such a way that it would be reorganized in accordance with a new pivot, new principle. I resist both these plot trajectories on account of their totalizing assumptions, be they completionist or transformationist. And I resist them because the nature of the recovery resulting from these readings is palpably incongruous with any such teleological scenarios. Least of all do I claim to have unearthed from these old texts some newfangled "tools" ready for immediate use by other research scholars in the field. I reject this utilitarian script because of its blatant positivism. What underlies such a script is a powerful, profoundly delusionary image of who we are as a student of religion, or rather, we as "Western man"; it deludes us to think as if so-called theory and methods were but a useful if also dangerous set of instruments mediating "the researcher/subject" on the one hand, and "the object" on the other, while remaining extrinsic to both; as if, by suspending and canceling this third thing, we could hope to deliver both "the subject" and "the object" in their virginal innocence. No matter how familiar and how compelling this picture may be, I should reiterate: this project begins precisely at the point of turning around and interrogating this compulsive image–idea itself, so as to render visible this very compelling power, which— according to some hermeneut's reckoning—has been propelling the "Western man's" will to knowledge ever further toward its world–historical destiny.

In brief, it is this image of "Western man" confronting "history" and "the world"—and not the "tools" allegedly in the hands of this imagined subject—that needs to be displaced if we are to arrive finally at our present, however belatedly, and to reconfigure the grounds where we stand. It is just this displacement, or a gradual disintegration of this image, that may be called the end result of this reading. Admittedly, the three authors I examine here did not address frontally issues such as the subject–object configuration operative in comparative religions or history of religions. *Nonetheless, a cumulative, and apparently unintended effect of their peculiar handling of time amounted to a quiet erosion of the fundament of this configuration.* Their individual quest for the origin of religion did not only result in discrediting itself, as later scholars like Eliade are eager to pronounce, but, far more radically, what they did in their quest gnawed at and steadily ate away the very backbone of our easy sense of history and time.

Historicity and temporality have been taken for granted for as long as we "moderns" can remember. Assuming all along the constancy, uniformity and utter objectivity of natural time, we qua "Western man" could feel assured that "history" as a truth narrative mapped onto such

a steady flow of time must be more real, more tangible and reliable than, say, speculations about a tenuous point of origination that those metaphysical questers went after. Moreover, the modern historian's time is not only empirical, uniform, and measurable, but time can be cut up into "periods," "eras," and "ages." Thus the two-fold function of time in our "historical sense," as Johannes Fabian suggested in *Time and The Other,* has allowed us to play some remarkable conceptual tricks. That is to say, on account of this double structure of time, certain of our contemporaries can be classified as, in some strange way, noncontemporaries, that is, as "archaic," "premodern," "primitive," or, lately, "preliterate," "primal." This deliberate anachronism has been a vital function in much of the modern historical discourse, and it has been too pervasive and too powerful for us to pretend that we had done away with it when we denounced some versions of evolutionism. (It must surely be significant that those various efforts to substitute new terms—such as *preliterate* and *primal*—for the purpose of avoiding the older ones that are now considered derogatory did not abolish the temporal sense inherent in those designations; and we continue to hear the anachronistic sense of "the originary" and "the anterior" in the newly chosen terms.)

Finally, the modern historicist crowning of its own age has moved us (qua "Western man") a step further, and most probably this was by far the most significant step. For now at this juncture, it is historical *consciousness* itself—or its alleged presence or absence—that has become the most powerful mark of difference between peoples, between the historically conscious subject ("Western man") and the historically unconscious or preconscious object (archaic, primitive, premodern), as we ascribe to one, and withhold from the other, a privileged relation to temporality.

All this, I now submit, is coming undone somewhere in the umbrageous folds of the textual legacy of these three figures. Above all, in their handling of time, temporality/historicity becomes something less than constant, it becomes intermittent, so to speak. This strangeness of time appears sometimes on the textual surface (that is, at the level of the progression of an argument), sometimes more explicitly as a theoretical articulation. At times this strange, antihistoricist sense of time shows up as a pure negativity of difference which interrupts, and at the same time sustains, a logical progression of the argument in search of the origin of religion, and, surprisingly, this pure negativity is directly equated with the very aim of the search, the essence/origin of religion (Durkheim). In another case, it shows up as a strongly antiteleological, nonorganic notion of history that cannot be contained and controlled by speech and thought; rather, human language itself turns out to be at once the culprit and the victim of the casuistic processes that masquerade as an organic history (Müller). Thirdly and most radically, positivity of time disappears altogether, while at the same time emerges a new, essentially negative sense of time—temporality as an effect of erasure, of forgetting (Freud).

It may seem paradoxical, if not to say perverse, that we should have to go back to those dusty old texts and to their exceedingly bizarre meditations on temporality in order for us to arrive at our own present. Although I would not insist that it had to be this way, the reward of this outrageous detour, perhaps, is that when we thus finally arrive at our time, we no longer seem to be standing at our post qua "Western man." Somehow, we are estranged from that picture, from the image of him standing, confronting the panorama of global history before his eyes, as if he alone were riding on the neck of Chronos. Perhaps we begin to imagine a new picture, just at the moment when we feel our own ground giving way, drifting irrevocably to time and to history.

NOTES

1. For a sustained articulation of this criticism based on shrewd interpretive alternatives, one can point to a number of works by Jonathan Z. Smith, for example. As one of the most concise examples of this criticism, see his "A Pearl of Great Price and a Cargo of Yams: A Study of Situational Incongruity," *Imagining Religion: From Babylon to Jonestown* (Chicago: University of Chicago Press, 1982).

2. Jonathan Z. Smith, "A Pearl of Great Price and a Cargo of Yams: A Study of Situational Incongruity," *Imagining Religion: From Babylon to Jonestown* (Chicago: University of Chicago Press, 1982), pp. 90–101.

From *How Natives Think*

LUCIEN LÉVY-BRUHL

Primitive Mentality And Religion

The representations which are termed collective, defined as a whole without entering into detail, may be recognized by the following signs. They are common to the members of a given social group; they are transmitted from one generation to another; they impress themselves upon its individual members, and awaken in them sentiments of respect, fear, adoration, and so on, according to the circumstances of the case. Their existence does not depend upon the individual; not that they imply a collective unity distinct from the individuals composing the social group, but because they present themselves in aspects which cannot be accounted for

Reprinted from Lucien Lévy-Bruhl, How Natives Think, *trans. Lilian A. Clare (New York: A. A. Knopf, 1925).*

by considering individuals merely as such. Thus it is that a language, although, properly speaking, it exists only in the minds of the individuals who speak it, is none the less an incontestable social reality, founded upon an ensemble of collective representations, for it imposes its claims on each one of these individuals; it is in existence before his day, and it survives him.

This fact leads at once to a very important result, one on which sociologists have rightly insisted, but had escaped the notice of anthropologists. To be able to understand the processes by which institutions have been established . . . we must first rid our minds of the prejudice which consists in believing that collective representations in general, and those of inferior races in particular, obey the laws of a psychology based upon the analysis of the individual subject. Collective representations have their own laws, and these . . . cannot be discovered by studying the "adult, civilized, white man." On the contrary, it is undoubtedly the study of the collective representations and their connections in uncivilized peoples that can throw some light upon the genesis of our categories and our logical principles. Durkheim and his collaborators have already given examples of what may be obtained by following this course, and it will doubtless lead to a theory of knowledge, both new and positive, founded upon the comparative method. . . .

In other words, the reality surrounding the primitives is itself mystical. Not a single being or object or natural phenomenon in their collective representations is what it appears to be to our minds. Almost everything that we perceive therein either escapes their attention or is a matter of indifference to them. . . .

Their mental activity is too little differentiated for it to be possible to consider ideas or images of objects by themselves apart from the emotions and passions which evoke these ideas or are evoked by them. Just because our mental activity is more differentiated, and we are more accustomed to analysing its functions, it is difficult for us to realize by any effort of imagination, more complex states in which emotional or motor elements are *integral parts* of the representation. It seems to us that these are not really representations, and if in fact we are to retain the term we must modify its meaning in someway. By this state of mental activity in primitives we must understand something which is not a purely or almost purely intellectual or cognitive phenomenon, but a more complex one, in which what is really "representation" to us is found blended with other elements of an emotional or motor character, coloured and imbued by them, and therefore implying a different attitude with regard to the objects represented. . . .

All such phenomena are to be expected if it be true that the perception of primitive is oriented differently from our own, and not preeminently concerned, as ours is, with the characteristics of the beings and manifestations which we call objective. To them the most important properties of the beings and objects they perceive, are their occult powers, their mystic qualities. Now one of these powers is that of appearing or not appearing in given circumstances. Either the power is inherent in the subject who perceives, who has been prepared for it by initiation, or else holds it by virtue of his participation in some superior being, and so on. In short, mystic relations may be established between certain persons and certain beings, on account of which these persons are exclusively privileged to perceive these beings. Such cases are analogous to the dream. The primitive, far from regarding the mystic perception in which he has no part, as suspect, sees in it, as in the dream, a more precious, and consequently more significant communication with invisible spirits and forces.

Conversely, when collective representations imply the presence of certain qualities in objects, nothing will persuade the primitives that they do not exist. To us, the fact that we do not perceive them there is decisive. It does not prove to them that they are not there, for possibly it is their nature not to reveal themselves to perception, or to manifest themselves in certain conditions only. Consequently, that which we call experience, and which decides, as far as we are concerned, what may be admitted or not admitted as real, has no effect upon collective representations. Primitives have no need of this experience to vouch for the mystic properties of being and objects: and for the same reason they are quite indifferent to the disappointments it may afford. Since experience is limited to what is stable, tangible, visible, and approachable in physical reality, it allows the most important of all, the occult powers, to escape. Hence we can find no example of the non-success of a magic practice discouraging those who believe in it. Livingstone gives an account of a prolonged discussion which he had with the rain-makers, and ends by saying: "I have never been able to convince a single one of them that their arguments are unsound. Their belief in these charms of theirs is unbounded."[1] In the Nicobar Islands, "the people in all the villages have now performed the ceremony called *tanangla,* signifying either 'support' or 'prevention.' Its object is to prevent illness caused by the northeast monsoon. Poor Nicobarese! They do the same thing year after year, but to no effect."[2]

Experience is particularly unavailing against the belief in the virtues of "fetishes" which secure invulnerability: a method of interpreting what happens in a sense which favours the belief is never lacking. In one case an Ashanti, having procured a fetish of this kind, hastened to put it to the proof, and received a gunshot wound which broke his arm. The "fetish man" explained the matter to the satisfaction of all, saying that the incensed fetish had that moment revealed the reason to him. It was because the young man had had sexual relations with his wife on a forbidden day. The wounded man confessed that this was true, and the Ashantis retained their convictions.[3] Du Chaillu tells us that when a native wears an iron chain around his neck he is proof against bullets. If the charm is not effectual, his faith in it remains unshaken, for then he believes that some maleficent won-

der-worker has produced a powerful "counter-spell," to which he falls a victim.[4] Elsewhere he says: "As I came from seeing the king, I shot at a bird sitting upon a tree, and missed it. I had been taking quinine, and I was nervous. But the negroes standing around at once proclaimed that this was a fetish-bird, and therefore I *could* not shoot it. I fired again, and missed again. Hereupon they grew triumphant in their declarations, well I . . . loaded again, took careful aim, and to my own satisfaction and their dismay, brought my bird down. Immediately they explained that I was a white man, and not entirely amenable to fetish laws; so I do not suppose my shot proved anything to them after all."[5] . . .

Primitive man, therefore, lives and acts in an environment of beings and objects, all of which, in addition to the properties that we recognize them to possess, are endued with mystic attributes. He perceives their objective reality mingled with another reality. He feels himself surrounded by an infinity of imperceptible entities, nearly always invisible to sight, and always redoubtable: ofttimes the souls of the dead are about him, and always he is encompassed my myriads of spirits of more or less defined personality. It is thus at least that the matter is explained by a large number of observers and anthropologists, and they make use of animistic terms to express this. Frazer has collected many instances which tend to show that this phenomenon obtains everywhere among undeveloped peoples.[6] . . .

Miss Kingsley lays great stress upon the homogeneity of the African native's representations of everything. "The African mind naturally approaches all things from a spiritual point of view . . . things happen because of the action of spirit upon spirit."[7] When the doctor applies a remedy "the spirit of the medicine works upon the spirit of the disease." The purely physical effect is beyond the power of conception unless it be allied with the mystic influence. Or rather, we may say that there is no really physical influence, there are only mystic ones. Accordingly it is almost impossible to get these primitives to differentiate, especially when it is a case of an accusation of murder through the practice of witchcraft, for instance. . . .

We thus have good authority for saying that this mentality differs from our own to a far greater extent that the language used by those who are partisans of animism would lead us to think. When they are describing to us a world peopled by ghosts and spirits and phantoms for primitives, we at once realize that beliefs of this kind have not wholly disappeared even in civilized countries. Without referring to spiritualism, we recall the ghost-stories which are so numerous in our folklore, and we are tempted to think that the difference is one degree only. Doubtless such beliefs may be regarded in our communities as a survival which testifies to an older mental condition, formerly much more general. But we must be careful not to see in them a faithful, though faintly outlined, reflection of the mentality of primitives. Even the most uneducated members of our societies regard stories of ghosts and spirits as belonging to the realm of the supernatural, between such apparitions and magical influences and the data furnished by ordinary perception and the experience of the broad light of day, the line of demarcation is clearly defined. Such a line, however, does not exist for the primitive. The one kind of perception and influence is quite as natural as the other, or rather, we may say that to him there are not two kinds. The superstitious man, and frequently also the religious man, among us, believes in a twofold order of reality, the one visible, palpable, and subordinate to the essential laws of motion; the other invisible, intangible, "spiritual," forming a mystic sphere which encompasses the first. But the primitive's mentality does not recognize two distinct worlds in contact with each other, and more or less interpenetrating. To him there is but one. Every reality, like every influence, is mystic, and consequently every perception is also mystic. . . .

In short, logical thought implies, more or less, consciously, a systematic unity which is best realizable in science and philosophy. And the fact that it can lead to this partially due to the peculiar nature of its concepts, to their homogeneity and ordered regularity. This is material which it has gradually created for itself, and without which it would not have been able to develop. . . .

Law of Participation

Now this material is not at the command of the primitive mind. Primitive mentality does indeed possess a language, but its structure, as a rule, differs from that of our languages. It actually does comprise abstract representations and general ideas; but neither this abstraction nor this generalization resembles that of our concepts. Instead of being surrounded by an atmosphere of logical potentiality, these representations welter, as it were, in an atmosphere of mystic possibilities. There is no homogeneity in the field of representation, and for this reason logical generalization, properly so called, and logical transactions with its concepts are impracticable. The element of generality consists in the possibility—already predetermined—of mystic action and reaction by entities upon each other, or of common mystic reaction in entities which differ from each other. Logical thought finds itself dealing with a scale of general concepts varying in degree, which it can analyse or synthesize at will. Prelogical thought busies itself with collective representations so interwoven as to give the impression of a community in which members would continually act and react upon each other by virtue of their mystic qualities, participating in, or excluding, each other.

Since abstraction and generalization mean this for prelogical mentality, and its preconnections of collective representations are such, it is not difficult to account for its classification of persons and things, strange as it frequently appears to us. Logical thought classifies by means of the very operations which form its concepts. Those sum up the work of analysis and synthesis which establishes species and genera, and thus arranges entities according to the increasing generality of the characteristics observed in them. In this sense classifications are not a process which differs from those which have preceded or will follow it. It takes place at the same time as abstraction and generalization: it registers their results, as it were, and its value is precisely what theirs has been. It is the expression of an order of interdependence, or hierarchy among the concepts, of reciprocal connection between persons and things, which endeavours to correspond as precisely as possible with the objective order in such a way that concepts thus arranged are equally valid for real objects, and real persons. It was the governing idea which directed Greek philosophical thought, and which inevitably appears as soon as the logical mind reflects upon itself and begins consciously to pursue the end to which it at first tended spontaneously.

But to the primitive mind this predominating concern for objective validity which can be verified is unknown. Characteristics which can be discerned by experience, in some sense in which we understand it, characteristics which we call objective, are of secondary importance in its eyes, or are important only as signs and vehicles of mystic qualities. Moreover, the primitive mind does not arrange its concepts in a regular order. It perceives preconnections, which it would never dream of changing, between the collective representations; and these are nearly always of greater complexity than concepts, properly so called. Therefore what can its classifications be? Perforce determined at the same time as the preconnections, they too are governed by the law of participation, and will present the same prelogical and mystic character. They will betoken the orientation peculiar to such a mind.

The facts already quoted are sufficient proof of this. When the Huichols, influenced by the law of participation, affirm the identity of corn, deer, hikuli and plumes, a kind of classification has been established between their representations, a classification the governing principle of

which is a common presence in these entities, or rather the circulation among these entities, of a mystic power which is of supreme importance to the tribe. The only thing is that this classification does not, as it should do in conformity with our mental processes, become compacted in a concept which is more comprehensive than that of the object it embraces. For them it suffices for the objects to be united, and felt as such, in a complexity of collective representation whose emotional force fully compensates, and even goes beyond, the authority which will be given to general concepts by their logical validity at a later stage.

In this way the classifications to which Durkheim and Mauss have called our attention, noting their very different characteristics from those which distinguish our logical classifications, may again be explained. In many undeveloped peoples—in Australia, in West Africa, according to Bennett's recent book,[8] among the North American Indians, in China and elsewhere—we find that all natural objects—animals, plants, stars, cardinal points, colours, inanimate nature in general—are arranged or have been originally arranged, in the same classes as the members of the social group, and if the latter are divided into so many totems, so, too, are the trees, rivers, stars, etc. A certain tree will belong to such and such a class, and will be used exclusively to manufacture the weapons, coffins, etc., of men who are members of it. The sun, according to the Aruntas, is a *Panunga* woman, that is, she forms part of the sub-group which can only intermarry with members of the *purula* sub-group. Here we have something analogous with that which we have already noticed about associated totems and local relationship, a mental habit quite different from our own, which consists in bringing together or uniting entities preferably by their mystic participations. This participation, which is very strongly felt between members of the same totem or the same group, between the ensemble of these members and the animal or plant species which is their totem, is also felt, though undoubtedly to a lesser degree, between the totemic group and those who have the same location in space. We have proofs of this in the Australian aborigines and in the North American Indians, where the place of each group in a common camping-ground is very precisely determined according to whether it comes from north or south or from some other direction. Thus it is felt once more between this totemic group and one of the cardinal points, and consequently between this group and all that participates in it, on the one hand, and this cardinal point and all that participates in it (its stars, rivers, trees, and so forth), on the other.

In this way is established a complexity of participations, the full explanation of which would demand exhaustive acquaintance with the beliefs and the collective representations of the group in all their details. They are the equivalent of, or at least they correspond with, what we know as classifications: the social participations being the most intensely felt by each individual consciousness and serving as a nucleus, as it were, around which other participations cluster. But in this there is nothing at all resembling, save in appearance, our logical classifications. These involve a series of concepts whose extent and connotation are definite, and they constitute an ascending scale the degrees of which reflection has tested. The prelogical mind does not objectify nature thus. It lives it rather, by feeling itself participate in it, and feeling these participations everywhere; and it interprets this complexity of participations by social forms. If the element of generality exists, it can only be sought for in the participation extending to, and the mystic qualities circulating among, certain entities, uniting them and identifying them in the collective representation.

In default of really general concepts, therefore, primitive mentality is conversant with collective representations which to a certain extent take their place. Although concrete, such representations are extremely comprehensive in this respect, that they are constantly employed, that they readily apply to an infinite number of cases, and that from this point of view they correspond, as we have said, with what categories are for logical thought. But their mystic and concrete nature has often puzzled investigators. These did indeed note its importance and could not fail to draw attention to it, though at the same time they realized that they were face to face with a method of thinking which was opposed to their own mental habits. Some examples in addition to those already quoted will help to make us realize these representations, which are general without however being at the same time abstract.

In the Yaos, Hetherwick notes[9] beliefs which appear incomprehensible to him. He cannot understand how it is that the *lisoka* (the soul, shade or spirit) can be at once personal and impersonal. In fact, after death the *lisoka* becomes *mulungu*. This word has two meanings: one, the soul of the dead, the other, "the spirit world in general, or more properly speaking the aggregate of the spirits of all the dead." This would be conceivable if *mulungu* meant a collective unity formed by the union of all the individual spirits; but this explanation is not permissible, for at the same time *mulungu* signifies "a state of property inhering in something, as life or health inheres in the body, and it is also regarded as the agent in anything that is beyond the range of his understanding." This is a characteristic trait which we shall find in all collective representations of this nature: they are used indifferently to indicate a person or persons, or a quality or property of a thing.

To get out of the difficulty, Hetherwick distinguishes between what he calls "three stages of animistic belief: (1) the human *lisoka* or shade, the agent in dreams, delirium, etc.; (2) this *lisoka* regarded as *mulungu,* and an object of worship and reverence, the controller of the affairs of this life, the active agent in the fortunes of the human race; (3) *mulungu* as expressing the great spirit agency, the creator of the world and all life, the source of all things animate or inanimate." It seems as if Hetherwick, like the French missionaries of old in New France, tends to interpret what he observes by the light of his own religious beliefs, but he adds, in good faith: "And yet between these three conceptions of the spirit nature no definite boundary line can be drawn. The distinction in the native mind is ever of the haziest. No one will give you a dogmatic statement of his belief on such points."

If Hetherwick did not get from the Yaos the answers he wanted, it may possibly have been because the Yaos did not understand his questions, but it was largely because he did not grasp their ideas. To the Yaos the transit from the personal soul, before or after death, to the impersonal soul or to the mystic quality which pervades every object in which there is something divine, sacred and mystic (not supernatural, for on the contrary nothing is more natural to primitive mentality than this kind of mystic power) is not felt. To tell the truth, there is not even such transit: there is "identity governed by the law of participation" such as we found in the case of the Huichols, entirely different from logical identity. And through the perpetual working of the law of participations, the mystic principle does not consider there is any difficulty about this.

It is the same with the North American Indians, about whom we have abundant and definite information. Miss Alice Fletcher,[10] in describing the mysterious power called *wakanda,* writes of their idea of the continuity of life, by which "a relation was maintained between the seen and the unseen, the dead and the living, and also between the fragment of anything and its entirety." Here continuity means what we call participation, since this continuity obtains between the living and the dead; between a man's nailparings, saliva, or hair and the man himself; between a certain bear or buffalo and the mystic ensemble of the bear or buffalo species.

Moreover, like the *mulungu* just spoken of, *wakanda* or *wakan* may signify not only a mystic reality, like that which Miss Fletcher calls "life," but a characteristic, a quality belonging to persons or things. Thus there are *wakan* men, who have gone through many previous existences. "They arise to conscious existence in the form of winged seeds, such as the thistle, . . . and pass through a series of inspirations, with different classes of divinities, till they are fully *wakanized* and prepared for human incarnation. They are invested with the invisible *wakan* powers of the gods. . . ." Similarly, day and night are *wakan.* The term is explained thus by an Indian: "While the day lasts a man is able to do many wonderful things, kill animals, men, etc. . . . But he does not fully understand why the day is, nor does he know who makes or causes the light. Therefore he believes that it was not made by hand, i.e., that no human being makes the day give light. Therefore the Indians say that the day is *wakan.* So is the sun. . . ." Here it is a property, a mystic quality inherent in things that is meant. And the Indian adds: "When it is night, there are ghosts and many fearful objects, so they regard the night as *wakan* . . .;"[11] A yet earlier investigator, quoted by Dorsey, had already remarked: "No one term can express the full meaning of the Dacota's *wakan.* It comprehends all mystery, secret power and divinity . . . All life is *wakan.* So also is everything which exhibits power, whether in action, as the winds and drifting clouds, or in passive endurance, as the boulder by the wayside. . . . It covers the whole field of fear and worship; but many things that are neither feared nor worshipped, but are simply wonderful, come under this designation."[12]

We may be inclined to ask, what, then, is *not wakan?* Such a question would in fact be urged by logical thought which demands the strict definition of its concepts, and a rigorously determined connotation and extent. But prelogical reasoning does not feel the need of this, especially when dealing with collective representations which are both concrete and very general. *Wakan* is something of a mystic nature in which any object whatever may or may not participate, according to circumstances. "Man himself may become mysterious by fasting, prayer, and vision."[13] A human being is not necessarily *wakan* or not *wakan*, therefore, and one of the duties of the medicine-man in this matter is to avoid errors which might have fatal results. *Wakan* might be compared with a fluid which courses through all existing things, and is the mystic principle of the life and virtue of all beings. "A young man's weapons are *wakan:* they must not be touched by a woman. They contain divine power. . . . A man prays to his weapons on the day of battle." . . .

Hubert and Mauss, in their acute analysis of the idea of the *mana* of the Melanesians, described by Codrington, and also that of the Huron *orenda,* have clearly brought out their relation to the idea of *wakan.*[14] What we have just said about the latter applies equally to these and to other similar conceptions of which it would be an easy matter to find examples elsewhere, also interpreted as animistic. Such an idea is that of *wong,* which we find in West Africa. "The Guinea Coast Negro's generic name for a fetish-spirit is *wong;* these aerial beings dwell in temple-huts and consume sacrifices, enter into and inspire their priests, cause health and sickness among men, and execute the behests of the mighty Heavengod. But part or all of them are connected with material objects and a native can say 'In this river, or tree or amulet, there is a *wong.*' . . . Thus among the *wongs* of the land are rivers, lakes and springs; districts of land, termite-hills, trees, crocodiles, apes, snakes, elephants, and birds."[15] It is from a missionary's report that Tylor has borrowed this account, and it is by no means difficult to find in it, not only, "the three stages of animistic belief" which Hetherwick noticed in the Yaos, but also a collective representation entirely similar to *wakan, mana, orenda,* and many others.

Collective representations of such a nature are to be found, more or less clearly indicated, in nearly all the primitive peoples who have been studied at all closely. They dominate, as Hubert and Mauss have well demonstrated, their religious beliefs and magic practices. It is possibly through them that the difference between prelogical mentality and logical thought can be best defined. When face to face with such representations the latter is always dubious. Are they realities which exist *per se,* or merely very general predicates? Are we dealing with one single and universal subject, with a kind of world-soul or spirit, or with a multiplicity of souls, spirits, divinities? Or again, do these representations imply, as many missionaries have believed, both a supreme divinity and an infinite number of lesser powers? It is the nature of logical thought to demand a reply to questions such as these. It cannot admit at one and the same time of alternatives which seem to be mutually exclusive. The nature of prelogical mentality, on the contrary, is to ignore the necessity. Essentially mystic as it is, it finds no difficulty in imagining, as well as feeling, the identity of the one and the many, the individual and the species, of entities however unlike they be, by means of *participation.* In this lies its guiding principle; this it is which accounts for the kind of abstraction and generalization peculiar to such a mentality, and to this, again, we must mainly refer the characteristic forms of activity we find in primitive peoples.

Transition to Higher Mental Types

. . . The participation or communion first realized by mystic symbioses and by the practices which affirmed it is obtained later by union with the object of the worship and belief called religious, with the ancestor, the god. The personalities of these objects comprises, as we know, an infinite variety of grades, from mystic forces of which we cannot say whether they are single or manifold, to divinities clearly defined by physical and moral attributes, such as those of the Melanesian or the Greek deities. It depends above all on the degree of development attained by the group studies, i.e., upon the type of its institutions as well as its mental type.

When we consider myths in their relation to the mentality of the social groups in which they originate, we are led to similar conclusions.

Where the participation of the individual in the social group is still directly felt, where the participation of the group with surrounding groups is actually lived—that is, as long as the period of mystic symbiosis lasts—myths are meager in number and of poor quality. This is the case with Australian aborigines and the Indians of Northern and Central Brazil, etc. Where the aggregates are of a more advanced type, as for instance, the Zunis, Iroquois, Melanesians, and others, there is, on the contrary, an increasingly luxuriant outgrowth of mythology. Can myths then likewise be the products of primitive mentality which appear when this mentality is endeavouring to realize a participation no longer directly felt—when it has recourse to intermediaries, and vehicles designed to secure a communion which has ceased to be a living reality? Such a hypothesis may seem to be a bold one, but we view myths with other eyes than those of the human beings whose mentality they reflect. We see them that which they do not perceive, and that which they imagine there we no longer realize. For example, when we read a Maori or Zuni or any other myth, we read it translated into our own language, and this very translation is a betrayal. To say nothing of the construction of the sentences, which is bound to be affected by our customary habits of thought, if only in the very order of the words, to primitives the words themselves have an atmosphere which is wholly mystic, whilst in our minds they chiefly evoke associations having their origin in experience. We speak, as we think, by means of concepts. Words, especially those expressive of group-ideas, portrayed in myths, are to the primitive mystic realities, each of which determines a *champ de force*. From the emotional point of view, the mere listening to the myth is to them something quite different from what it is to us. What they hear in it awakens a whole gamut of harmonics which do not exist for us.

Moreover, in a myth of which we take note, that which mainly interests us, that which we seek to understand and intercept, is the actual tenor of the recital, the linking-up of facts, the occurrence of episodes, the thread of the story, the adventures of the hero or mythical animal, and so forth. Hence the theories, momentarily regarded as classic, which see in myths a symbolic presentment of certain natural phenomena, or else the result of a "disease of language": hence the classifications (like that of Andrew Lang, for instance) which arrange myths in categories according to their context.[16] But this is overlooking the fact that the prelogical, mystic mentality is oriented differently from our own. It is undoubtedly not only indifferent to the doings and adventures and vicissitudes related in myths; it is even certain that these interest and intrigue the primitive's mind. But it is not the positive content of the myth that primarily appeals to him. He does not consider it as a thing apart; he undoubtedly sees it no more than we see the bony framework beneath the flesh of a living animal, although we know very well that it is there. That which appeals to him, arouses his attention and evokes his emotion, is the mystic element which surrounds the positive content of the story. This element alone gives myth and legend their value and social importance and, I might add, their power.

It is not easy to make such a trait felt nowadays, precisely because these mystic elements have disappeared as far as we are concerned, and what we call a myth is but the inanimate corpse which remains after the vital spark has fled. Yet if the perception of beings and objects in nature is wholly mystic to the mind of the primitive, would not the presentation of these same beings and objects in myths be so likewise? Is not the orientation in both cases necessarily the same? To make use of a comparison, though but an imperfect one, let us hark back to the time when in Europe, some centuries ago, the only history taught was sacred history. Whence came the supreme value and importance of that history, both to those who taught and those who learnt? Did it lie in the actual facts, in the knowledge of the sequence of judges, kings or prophets, of the misfortunes of the Israelites during their strife with the neighbouring tribes? Most certainly not. It is not from the historical, but from the sacred, point of view that the Biblical narrative was of incomparable interest. It is because the true God, perpetually intervening in the story, makes His presence manifest at all times, and to the Christian idea, causes the coming of His son to be anticipated. In short, it is the mystic atmosphere that surrounds the facts and prevents them from being ordinary battles, massacres or revolutions. Finally it is because Christendom finds in it a witness, itself divine, of its communion with its God.

Myths are, in due proportion, the Biblical narrative of primitive peoples. The preponderance of mystic elements, however, in the group ideas of myths, is even greater than in our sacred history. At the same time, since the law of participation still predominates in the primitive mind, the myth is accompanied by a very intense feeling of communion with the mystic reality it interprets. When the adventures, exploits, noble deeds, death and resurrection of a beneficent and civilizing hero are recounted in a myth, for instance, it is not the fact of his having given his tribe the idea of making a fire or of cultivating mealies that of itself interests and especially appeals to the listeners. It is here, as in the Biblical narrative, the participation of the social group in its own past, it is the feeling that the group is, as it were, actually living in that epoch, that there is a kind of mystic communion with that which has made it what it is. In short, to the mind of the primitive, myths are both an expression of the solidarity of the social group with itself in its own epoch and in the past and with the groups of beings surrounding it, and a means of maintaining and reviving this feeling of solidarity.

Such considerations, it may be urged, might apply to myths in which the human or semi-human ancestors of the social group, its civilizing or its protecting heroes, figure; but are they valid in the case of myths relating to sun, moon, stars, thunder, the sea, the rivers, winds, cardinal points, etc.? It is only to an intellect such as

ours that the objection appears a serious one. The primitive's mind works along the lines that are peculiar to it. The mystic elements in his ideas matter considerably more to him than the objective features which, in our view, determine and classify beings of all kinds, and as a consequence the classifications which we regard as most clearly evident escape his attention. Others, which to us are inconceivable, however, claim it. Thus the relationship and communion of the social group with certain animal and vegetable species, with natural phenomena like the wind or rain, with a constellation, appear quite as simple to him as his communion with an ancestor or legendary hero. To give but one instance, the aborigines studied by Spencer and Gillen regard the sun as a Panunga woman, belonging to a definite sub-class, and consequently bound by the ties of relationship to all the other clans of the tribe. Let us refer again to the analogy indicated above. In the sacred history of primitives natural history forms a part.

If this view of the chief significance of myths and of their characteristic function in aggregates of a certain mental type be correct, several consequences of some importance will ensue. This view does not render the careful and detailed study of myths superfluous. It provides neither a theory for classifying them in genera or species, nor an exact method of interpreting them, nor does it throw positive light upon their relations with religious observances. But it does enable us to avoid certain definite errors, and at any rate it permits of our stating the problem in terms which do not falsify the solution beforehand. It provides a general method of procedure, and this is to mistrust "explanatory" hypotheses which would account for the genesis of myths by a psychological and intellectual activity similar to our own, even while assuming it to be childish and unreflecting.

The myths which have long been considered the easiest to explain, for instance, those regarded as absolutely lucid, such as the Indian nature-myths, are on the contrary the most intriguing. As long as one could see in them the spontaneous product of a naive imagination impressed by the great natural phenomena, the interpretation of them was in fact self-evident. But if we have once granted that the mentality which generates myths is differently oriented from ours, and that its collective representations obey their own laws, the chief of which is the law of participation, the very intelligibility of these myths propounds a fresh problem. We are led to believe that, far from being primitive, these myths, in the form in which they have reached us, are something absolutely artificial, that they have been very highly and consciously elaborated, and this to such an extent that their original form is almost entirely lost. On the other hand, the myths which may possibly seem the easiest to explain are those which most directly express the sense of the social group's relationship, whether it be with its legendary members and those no longer living, or with the groups of beings which surround it. For such myths appear to be the most primitive in the sense that they are most readily allied with the peculiar prelogical, mystic mentality of the least civilized aggregates. Such, among others, are the totemic myths.

If, however, the aggregates belong to a type even slightly more advanced, the interpretation of their myths very soon becomes risky and perhaps impossible. In the first place, their increasing complexity diminishes our chances of correctly following up the successive operations of the mentality which produces these myths. This mentality not only refuses to be bound by the law of contradiction—a feature which most myths reveal at first sight, so to speak—but it neither abstracts nor associates, and accordingly it does not symbolize as our thought does. Our most ingenious conjectures, therefore, always risk going astray.

If Cushing had not obtained the interpretation of their myths from the Zunis themselves, would any modern intellect have ever succeeded in finding a clue to this prehistoric labyrinth? The true exposition of myths which are some-what complicated involves a reconstruction of the mentality which has produced them. This is a result which our habits of thought would scarcely allow us to hope for, unless, like Cushing, a savant were exceptionally capable of creating a "primitive" mentality for himself, and of faithfully transcribing the confidences of his adopted compatriots.

Moreover, even in the most favourable conditions, the state in which the myths are when we collect them may suffice to render them unintelligible and make any coherent interpretation impossible. Very frequently we have no means of knowing how far back they date. If they are not a recent product, who is our authority for assuming that some fragments at any rate have not disappeared, or, on the other hand, may not myths which were originally quite distinct, have been mingled in one incongruous whole? The mystic elements which were the predominant feature at the time when the myth originated may have lost some of their importance if the mentality of the social group has evolved at the same time as their institutions and their relations with neighbouring groups. May not the myth which has gradually come to be a mystery to this altered mentality have been mutilated, added to, transformed, to bring it into line with the new collective representations which dominate the group? May not this adaptation have been performed in a contrary sense, without regard to the participations which the myth originally expressed? Let us assume—an assumption by no means unreasonable—that it has undergone several successive transformations of this kind: by what analysis can we hope ever to retrace the evolution which has been accomplished, to find once more the elements which have disappeared, to correct the misconceptions grafted upon one another? The same problem occurs with respect to rites and customs which are often perpetuated throughout the ages, even while they are being distorted, completed in a contrary sense, or acquiring a new significance to replace that which is no longer understood.

NOTES

1. Livingstone, *Missionary Travels,* 1857, pp. 24–25.

2. Solomon, "Diaries Kept in Car Nicobar," *Journal of the Anthropological Institute,* vol. 32, p. 213.

3. Bowditch, *Mission to Ashanti,* p. 439.

4. Du Chaillu, *Explorations and Adventures in Equatorial Africa,* p. 338.

5. *Ibid.,* p. 179.

6. Frazer, *The Golden Bough,* 2nd edition., vol. II, pp. 41ff.

7. Miss Kingsley, *West African Studies,* p. 110.

8. Bennett, *At the Back of the Black Man's Mind,* London, 1906.

9. Hetherwick, "Some animistic beliefs among the Yaos of Central Africa", *J.A.I.,* vol. 32, pp. 89–95.

10. Alice Fletcher, "The signification of the Scalplock", *J.A.I.,* vol. 27, p. 437.

11. Dorsey, "Siouan Cults", *Report of the Bureau of the Smithsonian Institute* (Washington), vol. XI, p. 494.

12. *Ibid.,* p. 467.

13. *Ibid.,* pp. 432–433.

14. Hubert and Nauss, "Esquisse d'une theorie generale de la magie", *Annee Sociologique,* vol. VII (1904), pp. 108 *ff.*

15. E. B. Tylor, *Primitive Culture,* 4th edition, vol. II, p. 205

16. "Mythology", *Encyclopaedia Britannica,* 9th edition, vol. XVII, pp. 156–157.

Counterpoint:
I Am a Parrot (Red)

JONATHAN Z. SMITH

THERE ARE SOME ANIMALS which have played so decisive a role in the history of the history of religions that they may truly be seen as emblems (if not totems!) of our discipline. One might recall Saint Nilus and his camel which so animated discussions of sacrifice in the early quarter of this century . . . or, more recently, the pangolin in the important researches of Mary Douglas on taboo, dirt, and systems of order.[1] . . . However, the most notable creature of our time is, perhaps, the Brazilian parrot in the traditions of the Bororo tribe, which serves as the *"mythe de reference"* for the three published columes of Lévi-Strauss's *Mythologiques* despite formidable competition from jaguars, armadillos, and the like.[2] Perhaps this is due not only to the central role of the bird among the Bororo,[3] but also because the bird has a "prehistory"— historians of religion have met the Bororo and

their parrots before in an ethnographic report which has continued to fascinate scholars from its first mention in 1894 to the present. The report is given in the narrative of the second Brazilian expedition of Karl von den Steinen (1887–1888), *Unter den Naturvölkern Zentral-Brasiliens* (first edition, 1894; second edition, 1897).[4] Von den Steinen, after noting that in order to understand the native "we must put totally out of our minds the boundaries between man and the animal,"[5] goes on to report that "the Bororos boast of themselves that they are red parrots (Araras)." This, he insists, is not merely to claim that after death the Bororo become parrots or the parrots have been transformed into men. The Bororo conceive of themselves simultaneously as birds and men: "They think of themselves as parrots";[6] "the red parrots are Bororo, indeed the Bororo go even

Reprinted from Jonathan Z. Smith, "I Am a Parrot (Red)," History of Religion 11/4 (1972), pp. 391–413. Copyright © 1972 The University of Chicago Press. Reprinted by permission.

further as we have already noted and say 'we are parrots,' . . ."[7] On the other hand, von den Steinen does introduce metamorphic imagery: the Bororo call themselves parrots "as a caterpillar says that he is a butterfly";[8] and more explicitly (and in apparent contradiction to his previous remarks), "the Bororo are parrots because their dead transform themselves into parrots,"[9] "[their] belief is that the Bororo man or woman after death becomes a red parrot."[10]

. . . This paper will consider a number of representative examples of the use and interpretation of this particular utterance, "We are red parrots," in the history of the discussion of "primitive mentality." I intend by this study not only a chapter in the history of our discipline, but also a beginning attempt to clarify a thorny methodological question: How should the historian of religion interpret a religious statement which is apparently contrary to fact? The Bororo is not a parrot—as one psychiatrist noted, presumably applying the ultimate test of speciation, "he does not try to mate with other parakeets"—and any interpretation of von den Steinen's report must begin with this primary fact.

. . . The Bororo never said that they were red parrots in the sense that von den Steinen and the majority of his later commentators understood them. They declared several times, according to von den Steinen's own account, that when they are dead they will become red parrots, and thus they may speak of themselves as being red parrots in the present "as a caterpillar says that he is a butterfly." The identification is quite specific. Only the Bororo will become red parrots. When pressed, they speculated with von den Steinen that members of other tribes will become other species of birds, that Negroes will become black vultures and the white man would probably become a white heron.[11] This belief in the transformation of the Bororo after death into red parrots is well attested in the ethnographic literature. . . .

With one exception, no commentator on the Bororo tradition has noted that, following his report, von den Steinen speculated that the formula "we are birds" is a later, secondary form. The original formula, he suggested, was "I become a bird" or "I have a [soul] bird."[12] However, this history of the concept does not remove the difficulty of the saying, We are araras." This, von den Steinen continued to believe, rests on the inability of the Indian to distinguish animals from men.

On both internal and external grounds, we are justified in concluding that von den Steinen fundamentally misinterpreted the Bororo's intention. His own account predominantly witnesses to a postmorten belief in the transformation of the Bororo as not a parrot, and he offers a theory of the original form of the saying which requires this future understanding of the statement. The postmodern identification among the Bororo is independently confirmed by other ethnologists, the present identification of the Bororo as parrots is not. The theory which von den Steinen offers to account for the present identification, that the Bororo cannot distinguish between men and animals, is patently false even on the basis of von den Steinen's own report and owes more to his reading of contemporary anthropological theory than to field observation.

. . . it is possible to perform a "thought experiment." What if we did not have this apparent tension in von den Steinen between realized and futuristic parrothood and the supporting evidence of transmigration beliefs culled from later scholars? *What if we only knew that the Bororo insist that they are men and parrots at one and the same time?* The majority of scholars who have quoted von den Steinen have assumed that this was the case, and they have followed von den Steinen's mistaken lead in assuming that the key to exegesis lay in the fact that the Bororo cannot distinguish between animals and men or between different species of animals.

The earliest use of the Bororo tradition, and one that remains dominant in the literature, is an illustration of the alleged inability of primitive man to make distinctions. It is all but impossible to recover the origins of this regnant notion. Certainly its most sophisticated nineteenth-century form was represented by Tylor's argument that the origins of magic are to be found in a misapplication of the Laws of Association familiar from the writings of British and Scottish empiricists (especially Locke, Hume and Mill). This led Tylor to proclaim that "the sense of an absolute psychical distinction between man and beast, so prevalent in the civilised world, is hardly to be found among the lower races."[13] An early use of the Bororo material to illustrate this thesis is found in the works of Frazer. For Frazer, "haziness is the characteristic of the mental vision of the savage. Like the blind man at Bethsaida, he sees men like trees and animals walking in a thick intellectual fog."[14] Totemism was a central illustration of this "haziness," and it is in this connection that Frazer introduces the Bororo material, closely paraphrasing von den Steinen. Frazer notes, however, that "this curious identification of themselves with the birds does not of itself constitute totemism, though it may be said to be totemic in principle."[15] Although most scholars are certain that totemism is not present among the Bororo, the totemic interpretation of the identification has persisted, occurring most recently in Jensen's *Myth and Cult*.[16]

It was the publication, in 1910, of L. Lévy-Bruhl's *Les fonctions mentales dans les sociétés inférieures* which won for Bororo a secure place in literature. Lévy-Bruhl's most famous postulate was the *loi de participation* which he defined: "In the collective representations of primitive mentality object, being, phenomena can be, though in a way incomprehensible to us, both themselves and something other than themselves. . . ."[17] His first, and hence normative, example of this "law" was the Bororo. . . . Lévy-Bruhl introduces for the first time the term "prelogical," of which the Bororo are again to be seen as the normative example.

The citation in Lévy-Bruhl is quite close to von den Steinen's original. Lévy-Bruhl has added the detail that von den Steinen "could not before believe it" and has made one significant alteration in direct quotation. Von den Steinen has asserted that the Bororo understood themselves to be araras just as a caterpillar may speak of himself as a butterfly. Lévy-Bruhl's version omits the ambiguity between present and future (or the Aristotelian actuality and potentiality) in order to emphasize the element of participation. In his translation, the Bororos insist that "they are araras *at the present time*." . . . The mischief done by this cannot be overemphasized. It is Lévy-Bruhl and not von den Steinen's original report (no matter what the footnote may cite) which will be used by most subsequent writers as an illustration of primitive mentality. . . . Lévy-Bruhl's version and interpretation dominates the literature. It is only recently that books on "primitive mentality" have begun to dispense with the example of the Bororo.

Lévy-Bruhl's use of the Bororo identification of themselves with parrots had two crucial effects on all subsequent use of this tradition. First, it separated out the ambiguities of von den Steinen's original report and suppressed the transmigration-metamorphosis motif in favor of a totally present understanding of the identification. . . . Lévy-Buhl gloomily concludes his book by declaring that when the primitive collective breaks down in transition to "higher mental types" and "individualism" asserts itself, then "the Bororo tribesmen will no longer declare that they are araras. They will say that their ancestors were araras, that they are of the same substance, as araras, that they will become araras after death."[18] From this point on, those who cite the Bororo-*are*-parrots tradition omit the metamorphosis; those who cite the Bororo-*will-become*-parrots tradition omit the identification. It is the present rather than the futuristic understanding of the identification that will preoccupy scholars. That a man should think of himself as simultaneously a man and a bird seems absurd, primitive, and hence worthy of comment. That a man should think of himself as becoming a bird after death seems "normal" by comparison. . . . The present identification is exotic and thereby revelatory of primitive mentality; the future is not. Second, by driving an absolute wedge between "primitive" and "civilized" thought and by insisting that each had its own laws, Lévy-Bruhl set the stage for the consideration of the Bororo as profoundly alien, so different that they made no sense. . . .

Beyond this question, the interpretation of Lévy-Bruhl and his successors was based on a literal understanding of the sentence. The identification made sense, even though it is false, because the Bororo lack a logic of distinction. I may note, parenthetically, that the futuristic interpretation is equally literal, although it assumes that the Bororo do possess distinctions between actuality and potentiality and that this "Aristotelianism" is the key to exegesis. Whether this implicitly invokes the argument about the characteristic lack of distinction among primitives remains a question. Men do not, in fact, become birds in strict analogy to the acorn becoming an oak or the caterpillar a butterfly. . . . Either one must assume that the Bororo ignore or are ignorant of the fact that men and birds are not the same species (in contradistinction to the acorn and oak and the caterpillar and the butterfly which are) or one must assume that for the Bororo man, bird, oak, acorn, butterfly, caterpillar, each constitutes a separate species which can transfer itself into another species at will. In either case, the von den Steinen–Lévy-Bruhl interpretation appears to be maintained.

It is now time to withdraw our experiment and reflect on its results. We have been engaged in tracing the history of an error—no less revealing for being a mistake. In the history of interpretation of the Bororo, there has been a noticeable shift from *surface* to *depth,* from the placing of the Bororo within a contextless catalogue of illustrations of a general theory of primitive mentality to a depth analysis of the underlying principles of a *particular* culture.[19] In this process, the statement, "I am a parrot,"

has shifted from being an absurdity to be explained away or a puzzle to a serious statement, the truth of which might be empathetically entertained by a non-Bororo. . . . The statement, "I am a parrot," has come to be seen as revealing a truth rather than being the result of a peculiar process of thought. By utilizing terminology such as "mode" or "symbolic," it has been possible to affirm the humanness and the parrotness of the Bororo without allowing one to subsume the other. Historians of religion will presumably be attracted by this anthropological approach which bears so close a resemblance to Eliade's well-known paradox of sacrality: "By manifesting the sacred, any object becomes *something else,* yet it continues to remain itself."[20] Yet we must be cautious at this point, for the relativism of the anthropologist is not shared by Eliade. . . . For the one, a functionalist criterion of truth is employed; for the other, an ontological. Both possess problems in yielding specific explanations and interpretations. . . .

Thus in the case of the Bororo identification, one approach has been to take the statement literally, judge it by our standards, and conclude that it is false, an error or a misapplication of our normal, rational procedures. This is the approach of Tylor and Frazer. The question of the meaning of the assertion, "I am a parrot," is not nearly as important to this view as an account of its genesis. The second approach, represented by Lévy-Bruhl, takes the statement literally but holds that our standards do not apply. It contravenes our laws of logic but follows intelligible rules of its own. The statement, "I am a parrot," is a different statement than it appears to us to be. What appear to function as the subject, copulative, and predicate noun in this sentence are none of these in our understanding of the terms. The question of meaning, in such a view, is likewise held in suspense, despite the many specific interpretations offered. If a characteristic of the "logic" of "primitive mentality" is that it is not constrained to avoid contradictions, how may we interpret the statement by involving a logic of identification which, for us, is but the concomitant of noncontradiction? If the statement is really different than it appears to be and if our standards do not apply, how can we ever hope to understand it? . . . A literal understanding of "I am a parrot" has led to two consequences: they mean it and they are wrong, or they mean it, but we can never understand what they mean. . . .

The history of the exegesis of the Bororo statement has driven us to raise the question of truth from which, as historians of religion, we have largely abstained. When confronted with experiences and statements which appear contrary to fact, we have most usually bracketed the question of veracity prompting acidulous criticisms from our more historically minded colleagues; while, at the same time, making grandiose, metaphysical claims, such as "myth is true," which have irritated our philosophical colleagues.[21] In other instances, we have simply repeated or paraphrased a tradition as if this offers self-evident truth (Professor van Baaren's witty title is apropos: "Are the Bororos Parrots or Are We?"). . . .

NOTES

1. Mary Douglas, "Animals in Lele Religious Thought," *Africa*, I (1957), 46–58 (reprinted in J. Middleton, ed., *Myth and Cosmos* [Garden City, L.I., 1967], pp. 213–247); M. Douglas, *Purity and Danger: An Analysis of Concepts of Pollution and Taboo* (New York:, 1966), *passim*.

2. C. Lévi-Strauss, *The Raw and the Cooked* (New York, 1969), pp. 35–37 *et passim*.

3. C. Albisetti, A. J. Venturelli, *Enciclopédia Bororo* (Campo Grande, 1962), Vol. I, pp. 725–730; Lévi-Strauss, *The Raw and the Cooked,* esp. p. 47.

4. K. von den Steinen, *Unter den Naturvölkern Zentral-Brasiliens* (Berlin, 1894), esp. pp. 352f.

5. Ibid., p. 351.

6. Ibid., p. 352f.

7. Ibid., p. 512.

8. Ibid., p. 353.

9. Ibid., p. 353.

10. Ibid., p. 511.

11. Ibid., p. 512.

12. Ibid., p. 512f.

13. E. B. Tylor, *Primitive Culture,* 3d ed. (London, 1891: rp. New York, 1958), Vol. II, p. 53.

14. J. G. Frazer, *Totemism and Exogamy* (London, 1910), Vol. IV, p. 61.

15. Ibid., Vol. III, p. 576.

16. A. Jensen, *Myth and Cult among Primitive Peoples* (Chicago, 1963), p. 148.

17. L. Lévy-Bruhl, *Les fonctions mentales dans les sociétés inférieures,* 6th ed. (Paris, 1922), p. 77.

18. Lévy-Bruhl, *How Natives Think,* p. 328.

19. Lienhardt, p. 98.

20. M. Eliade, *The Sacred and the Profane* (New York, 1959), p. 12.

21. See H. Penner and E. Yonan, "Is a Science of Religion Possible?" *Journal of Religion,* LI (1972), 107–133.

Chapter 4

Phenomenology and the Science of Religion

The possibility of a science of religion was answered positively by the scholars of religion in this chapter. Freidrich Max Müller was among an earlier group of scholars seeking to approach religion in a scientific way. It is also possible to add the names of Cornelis Petrus Tiele and Pierre D. Chantepie de la Saussaye among pioneers in the scientific study of religion. The scientific developments and breakthroughs made during their historical periods influenced such scholars, and motivated them to imititate the precision and certainty promised by the scientific method. Even though this chapter will not include selections from Tiele and Chantepie de la Saussaye, it is important to review their contributions to the phenomenological approach for the sake of a proper historical context for the other scholars included in this chapter.

Tiele (1830–1902) was born in Leiden, Holland, studied theology at the University of Amsterdam, served as a Remonstrant minister for 20 years, and became a professor at the Remonstrants' Seminary. After the seminary was absorbed by the University of Leiden, Tiele taught in a new chair covering the subjects of the history of religions and the philosophy of religion until his retirement in 1900. Much of his work focused on Egyptian, Assyrian, and Mesopotamian religions. His major English publications that pertained to religion were the following: *Outlines of the History of Religion, to the Spread of the Universal Religions* (1877), *History of Egyptian Religion* (1882), the two-volume *Elements of the Science of Religion, Morphological and Ontological* (1897–1899), and *The Religion of the Iranian People* (1912).

In these various works, Tiele wanted to extricate the scholarship of religion from the hermeneutical circle (a context from which a scholar works to interpret religious phenomena) by avoiding formulating an ideal of the nature of religion, even though he was convinced that it was grounded in human nature and originated from the human soul. Rather than proceed from an ideal of religion, which was neither an entirely natural nor artificial product of human beings, he conceived of the science of religion as a universal investigation that involved a multiplicity of facts and invited a scholar of religion to classify them and to draw inferences. The multiplicity of religious facts was united by the human mind within the context of an objective stance by scholars that enabled them to distinguish the forms of religion itself. Tiele cautioned the scholar not to champion one form of religion over another, although a practical result was to allow one to demonstrate the superiority of one form over another. It was not, however, the objective of the scientist to advocate one form of religion as the best, which was a more apologetic task. The historical nature of this new science implied that its initial task was to trace the evolution of religion, although the exact method of the natural science could not be applied to the science of religion. Tiele's vision for this new science included the use of a deductive method that was neither a totally empirical approach, resulting in a positivistic position unable to explain the facts encountered, nor was it a strictly historical method able only to yield historical results. Tiele's deductive approach utilized reason to unlock results that were given by induction, empirical analysis, historical research, and comparison. His phenomenological method involved a two-stage approach: morphological (classificatory) description, which was antecedent to any attempt to identify a religion's essence or source, and the ontological, which represented a study of the permanent elements in religion amidst all the changes. These immutable forms represented the core and the source of religion. While also being cognizant of the psychological, social, and human dimensions of religion, Tiele's vision for a science of religion also embodied a method that was empirical, historical, and comparative.

Another Dutch scholar named Pierre D. Chantepie de la Saussaye (1848–1920) called for a science of religion. By his study of theology at the University of Utrecht, he was awarded the doctorate in 1871 on a dissertation focusing on methods connected to the quest for the origin of religion. He served as a minister for the Dutch Reformed Church for several years while pursuing his intellectual interests. In 1878, he was appointed to a new chair of the History of Religions department at the University of Amsterdam. He later held a chair at the University of Leiden. Chantepie de la Saussaye published two major works that were translated into English: *Manual of the Science of Religion* (1891) and *The Religion of the Teutons* (1902).

In the former book, Chantepie de la Saussaye suggested that a basic presupposition of this science of religion was that a unity existed among all religions. To develop a science of religion, it was necessary to establish two conditions: a general philosophy of history and religion as an object of philosophical knowledge. The latter condition referred to a philosophy of religion with its foundation already in the works of Kant and Schleiermacher, although Hegel was the genuine founder of this science because he gave it a direction and objective. With a firm foundation in these disciplines, a scholar of religion was prepared by studying the philosophy of religion to find the manifestations of religion, and by also using the history of religions, which included not only historical development but also ethnography, to determine the essence of religion. Like Max Müller and Tiele, Chantepie de la Saussaye conceived of this science of religion as having a comparative component that would function to sharpen the focus of the scholar. Chantepie de la Saussaye was opposed to comparing Christianity to tribal forms of religion. The scientific spirit of his project was emphasized by his introduction of the notion of a phenomenology of religion. Even though Chantepie de la Saussaye envisioned a close connection between phenomenology and psychology, he argued that phenomenology received its material from religious acts, cults, and customs. More precisely, phenomenology was a method for describing, sorting, and classifying the perceptually manifest components of religion, even though he wanted to stress that it was impossible to use phenomenology with a prior understanding of the nature of religion. Even if a scholar discovered the origin of religion, this discovery would not elucidate its meaning, and any attempt to discern its essence would not completely explain it.

Among the majority of thinkers attempting to study religion in a scientific manner, Edmund Husserl profoundly influenced scholars, because his philosophy provided a methodology for approaching religion in a scientific manner, although the term *phenomenology* historically gained a well-defined technical meaning in the philosophy of Hegel, where it referred to knowledge as it appears to consciousness. Hegel intended to investigate and describe phenomenal knowing as it progressed toward knowledge of the Absolute. In contrast to Hegel, Husserl, who was previously a mathematician and physicist, viewed his own philosophy as a radicalization of Descartes's philosophy, and as based on an absolute certainty that was beyond the ability to doubt. Moreover, Husserl wanted to develop philosophy as a rigorous science. To develop philosophy in this way, Husserl called for a return to the immediate, original data of our consciousness that is incontestably evident. Husserl was convinced that there was not a single principal that philosophy could use as a starting point. Its point of beginning was rather an entire field of original experiences.

For Husserl, phenomenology was a new way of looking at things, which was difficult to reach for an ordinary person because one was submerged naturally in a shadowy morass that he referred to as our natural way or attitude of experiencing and thinking. It was possible to ascend from this natural attitude and its limitations by means of the method of phenomenological reduction. There were two stages: eidetic reduction and phenomenological reduction proper. The first stage began with the act of perceiving a thing, investigating it, and intuiting the invariant that arises in the form of the immutable and unique *eidos* (essence) before our consciousness. By essence, Husserl understood "pure generalities" that manifest before our mind, pure possibilities whose validity is independent of our experience. This eidetic vision gave the observer the ability to see the essence of the phenomenon in an objective way. Husserl did not claim that essences were real, eternal, or superior to particulars. The essence of a particular phenomenon can be understood as a pure generality or structure. Thus, eidetic reduction moved from a particular phenomenon to general essences, whereas phenomenological reduction proper was connected to leading us from the phenomenal world to our immediate world of experience (*Lebenswelt*), or from the phenomenal ego to transcendental subjectivity. This initial stage demonstrates that Husserl wanted to rid philosophy of abstractions and secondary qualities. He wanted to get to the world of primary experience, the life world (*Lebenswelt*), because this is the world that is present before one begins to reflect upon it.

This second stage represented the famous *epoché* or bracketing of our natural beliefs about objects of experience in order to strip perceived foreign appearances and allow the essences to be found. For the scholar, a major advantage of bracketing was avoiding questions about objective truth. In other words, the scholar suspended judgments about the objective existence or nonexistence of the objects of consciousness. This enabled scholars to explore more carefully that which was given to consciousness. Without getting into great detail, the process of reduction enabled scholars to question what they took for granted, encouraged them to change their attitudes, gave them the opportunity to look at the world anew, enabled phenomenologists to become disinterested spectators, caused previously experienced reality to become mere phenomenon, and allowed discovery of a transcendental ego. Moreover, the method of reduction enabled them to return to the experienced world, to break the natural attitude, to consider the phenomena as they are, and uncover intentionality.

Husserl referred to the intentionality of consciousness, and he called it the main theme of phenomenology in his work entitled *Ideas: General Introduction to Pure Phenomenology*. Husserl meant that consciousness was always conscious of something, which implied that things are constituted through consciousness and are relative to a knower. More specifically, intentionality takes the raw data of sensations and creates a synthetic unity, and gives shape to the essences of things. Husserl was not, for instance, interested in the red, white, and blue ball, but he was concerned with such a ball as a typification because he wanted to define ultimately the structural types of thought itself. If one breaks down the different cognitive elements, fundamental sensations, formal characteristics, and the essence of the multicolored ball, this all becomes open to phenomenological analysis. Husserl wanted to make clear that intentionality bestowed real identity on data and provided a continuous identity to the varying modifications of the data within the stream of consciousness. For instance, intentionality with respect to internal time awareness connected past, present, and future. Therefore, every act of consciousness required a certain object, and this object was codetermined by the character of the conscious act in which it manifested itself. The intentionality of consciousness integrated the raw materials into a whole object, identified particular perceptions from others, synthesized stages of intuitive fulfillment, and constituted the object meant. Within the field of the phenomenology of religion and its overlapping approach to the study of religion with the history of religions, it is possible to identify Husserl's eidetic reduction with the creation of various kinds of typologies, the classifying of religions, and arranging of religious phenomena into patterns of coherence. Although this very brief introduction to the philosophy of Husserl hardly does justice to the complexities of his thought, his notions of reduction and bracketing of beliefs and prejudices, eidetic vision and essences, the primacy of perception, emphasis on a scientific method, and the importance of intentionality are all elements from his philosophy that will resound with scholars of religion following a phenomenological approach.

It was with a certain amount of trepidation that I placed Rudolf Otto (1869–1937) within the discipline of phenomenology because his understanding of religion was not shaped by the method of Husserl. In fact, Otto's approach more closely resembles the phenomenology of psychology developed by Karl Jaspers. Otto's approach to religion was influenced in a negative way by the approach of Schleiermacher because of his treatment of feeling in a manner that limited it to subjectivity. His understanding of religion was shaped in a positive way by Kant via Jakob Fries (1773–1843), who did not adhere to Kant's treatment of a priori categories (valid independent of empirical observation) as ideal and devoid of cognitive content until shaped by sensory experience. After Fries reworked Kant's philosophy, Otto wanted to treat a priori categories like space, time, and causality as cognitive categories that provide genuine knowledge, although subject to the limits of sensory experience. Thus we find Otto depicting the holy as a solely a priori category. I have included Otto in this part of the anthology because of his influence on many phenomenologists and their endorsement of his substantive definition of religion as the *numinous,* his concern for issues like the essence of religion, meaning, use of the comparative method, and his insistence that religion be understood as a sui generis reality, a position that manifests the influence of Ernst Troeltsch (1865–1923) and his insistence that religion was a unique and valid category. In short, Otto's position was adopted, augmented, amended, misunderstood, and misappropriated by many scholars. Otto was a student of theology, and his work also demonstrates the influence of the protestant reformer Martin Luther and his doctrine of justification by faith alone. Otto obtained the *Lizentiat* from the University of Göttingen in 1898 where he also taught systematic theology. In 1907, he earned his doctoral degree from the University of Tübingen. He taught at the University of Breslau and the University of Marburg until his retirement in 1929. A number of Otto's books were translated into English: *Naturalism and Religion* (1907), *The Idea of the Holy: An Inquiry into the Non-Rational Factor in the Idea of the Divine and its Relation to the Rational* (1923), *India's Religion of Grace and Christianity Compared and Contrasted* (1930), *The Philosophy of Religion* (1931), *Mysticism East and West: A Comparative Analysis of the Nature of Mysticism* (1932), and *The Kingdom of God and the Son of Man: A Study in the History of Religion* (1938).

Otto thought that prior scholarship tended to stress the rational elements of religion to the neglect of the irrational, resulting in an unbalanced and inaccurate account of its nature. For Otto, religion was unique and irreducible or sui generis and an a priori category. This position invested religion or the holy with a certain privilege over other cultural phenomena. Although it was not completely like aesthetics, religion shared with it a surplus of meaning that went beyond the ethical and rational aspects of it. Due to the excessive nature of the meaning of religion, it is only possible for metaphors, analogies, and symbols that he called "ideograms" to approach it. In his theory of religion, Otto wanted to identify its essence, which he isolated as the numinous, and incorporate a discussion of the reaction that people feel as they encounter the numinous. Much in the spirit of the phenomenological method, Otto was concerned with the object of religion and the reaction to it by the experiencing subject. The result of Otto's efforts was an influential work that can justifiably be called a classic text of religious studies.

Gerardus van der Leeuw (1890–1950), received his doctoral degree from the University of Leiden in 1916 with a dissertation on ancient Egyptian deities. After serving as a minister for a couple of years in the Dutch Reform Church, he was appointed to a chair at the University of Groningen. His three most significant books in English were *Religion in Essence and Manifestation: A Study in Phenomenology* (1938), *Virginibus Puerisque: A Study on the Service of Children in Worship* (1939), and *Sacred and Profane Beauty: The Holy in Art* (1963). The title of van der Leeuw's book on phenomenology demonstrated Hegel's influence on his work. By investigating the appearances and manifestations of things, Hegel thought that it was possible to grasp the essence (*Wesen*) of something. Ultimately, it was possible to show how to understand all phenomena in their diversity, as based in an underlying essence or unity that Hegel called *Geist* (spirit).

A glance at the outline of van der Leeuw's phenomenology also enables us to witness the influence of Husserl because he divided his work into the following five parts: the object of religion, the subject of religion, the object and subject in their reciprocal relationship (inward and outward action), the world, and forms (religions). This structure focused on what appeared without neglecting the subject that perceived the phenomena. If we considered both the objective and subjective aspects of religion and their interrelationship, it was possible to discover that power belongs to both aspects. For van der Leeuw, power became the central aspect of religion that was intimately interwoven with sacredness. He stressed the impersonal, potent, and dangerous nature of power that inspired awe manifested as both fear and attraction, which was similar to Otto's discussion of the numinous. The tool for grasping power was phenomenology, which was an approach that used *epoché* (bracketing) and sought understanding of what appeared. Van der Leeuw thought that the goal of the study of religion should be understanding rather than explanation. By means of empathy, the object of study passed into the subject by transposing oneself into the phenomenon and reexperiencing it, reaching a psychological reality that is not spatiotemporal. Becoming familiar with this lifestream, one contemplated its essence, and one intuitively analyzed it. Sameness was accounted for by the stream of consciousness, and difference was identified by the act of perception. The experiences of individuals of similar phenomena were connected to "ideal types," which van der Leeuw understood as structural connections among similar phenomena and instruments of understanding, but these "ideal types" lacked spatiotemporal reality, although they did manifest another kind of reality connected to meaning.

The many contributions of Ninian Smart (1927–2001) offered a bit different program to the study of religion. Besides his texts on various world religions and philosophies, Smart, who was educated at Oxford University, published the following works that pertain to this anthology: *Reasons and Faiths* (1958), *The Religious Experience* (1969), *The Concept of Worship* (1972), *The Phenomenon of Religion* (1973), *The Science of Religion and the Sociology of Knowledge* (1973), *Worldviews* (1983), and *The Dimensions of the Sacred* (1996). After teaching for many years at the University of Lancaster, Smart was invited to hold a joint appointment at the University of California at Santa Barbara. Smart focused his attention upon the organic development of religion within history. By using terms like *organism* to refer to religion, Smart stressed its interrelatedness and interpenetration, and the way that orthodoxy and heterodoxy interact as a religious tradition. Besides the influence of Husserl upon his work, Smart's thought was also influenced by an influential Austrian philosopher of language, Ludwig Wittgenstein (1889–1951), and his notion of family resemblance as it applies to religious phenomena. By using this notion from Wittgenstein, Smart avoided looking for the essence of a phenomenon.

To organize his material, Smart referred to "dimensions" or "strands" (doctrine, mythology, ethics, ritual, social institutions, and religious experience, for example) in his attempt to identify that which is constant and invariable in religion, although this does not imply that each dimension is equally present to the same extent in all religious traditions. Not only do these dimensions belong to a unified organism and provide it with its internal dynamism, but they are reciprocally related to each other in such a way that doctrine is connected, for instance, to myth and both are related to ethics. Due to these various dimensions and their complexity, it behooves the scholar to approach religion in a multidimensional way. Furthermore, Smart proposed that the scholar must also consider both the external and internal aspects of religious phenomena. A good example of an internal explanation of a phenomenon is the six-dimensional account that considers the interactions of the components. However, the external explanation is a much broader perspective that attempts to grasp how the outside environment has shaped a religion during its development.

Guideline Questions:

Why does Otto concentrate his focus on religious experience, and what are the advantages and disadvantages of this kind of approach?

What is power for van der Leeuw and why is it so central to this theory of religion?

What are the consequences and advantages of discussing the various dimensions of religion for Smart?

From *The Idea of the Holy*

RUDOLF OTTO

The Rational and the Non-rational

It is essential to every theistic conception of God, most of all to the Christian, that it designates and precisely characterizes deity by the attributes spirit, reason, purpose, good will, supreme power, unity, selfhood. The nature of God is thus thought of by analogy with our human nature of reason and personality; only, whereas in ourselves we are aware of this as qualified by restriction and limitation, as applied to God the attributes we use are "completed," i.e. thought as absolute and unqualified. Now all these attributes constitute clear and definite concepts: they can be grasped by the intellect; they can be analysed by thought; they even admit of definition. An object that can be thought conceptually may be termed *rational*. The nature of deity described in the attributes above mentioned is, then a rational nature; and a religion which recognizes and maintains such a view of God is in so far a "rational" religion. Only on such terms is *belief* possible in contrast to mere *feeling*. And of Christianity at least it is false that "feeling is all, the name but sound and smoke";—where "name" stands for conception or thought. Rather we count this the very mark and criterion of a religion's high rank and superior value—that it should have no lack of *conceptions* about God; that it should admit knowledge—the knowledge that comes by faith—of the transcendent in terms of conceptual thought, whether those already mentioned or others which continue and develop them. Christianity not only possesses such conceptions but possesses them in unique clarity and abundance, and this, thought not the sole or even the chief, yet a very real sign of its superiority over religions of other forms and at other levels. This must be asserted at the outset and with the most positive emphasis.

But, when this is granted, we have to be on our guard against an error which would lead to a wrong and one-sided interpretation of religion. This is the view that the essence of deity can be given completely and exhaustively in such "rational" attributions as have been referred to above and in others like them. It is not an unnatural misconception. We are prompted to it by the traditional language of edification, with its characteristic phraseology and ideas; by the learned treatment of religious themes in sermon and theological instruction; and further even by our Holy Scriptures themselves. In all these cases the "rational" element occupies the foreground, and often nothing else seems to be present at all. But this is after all to be expected. All language, in so far as it consists of words, purports to convey ideas or concepts—that is what language means—and the more clearly and unequivocally it does so, the better the language. And hence expositions of religious truth in language inevitably tend to stress the "rational" attributes of God.

But though the above mistake is thus a natural one enough, it is none the less seriously misleading. For so far are these "reational" attributes from exhausting the idea of deity, that they in fact imply a non-rational or suprarational Subject of which they are predicates. They are "essential" (and not merely "accidental") attributes of that subject, but they are also,

Reprinted from Rudolf Otto, The Idea of the Holy, trans. John W. Harvey. London: Oxford University Press, 1923, 2nd ed., 1950. Reprinted by permission of Oxford University Press.

it is important to notice, synthetic essential attributes. That is to say, we have to predicate them of a subject which they qualify, but which in its deeper essence is not, nor indeed can be, comprehended in them, which rather requires comprehension of a quite different kind. Yet, though it eludes the conceptual way of understanding, it must be in some way or other within our grasp, else absolutely nothing could be asserted of it. . . .

Here for the first time we come up against the contrast between rationalism and profounder religion, and with this contrast and its signs we shall be repeatly concerned in what follows. . . . The difference between rationalism and its opposite is to be found elsewhere. It resolves itself rather into a peculiar difference of *quality* in the mental attitude and emotional content of the religious life itself. All depends upon this: in our idea of God is the non-rational overborne, even perhaps wholly excluded, by the rational? Or conversely, does the non-rational itself preponderate over the rational? Looking at the matter thus, we see that the common dictum, that orthodoxy itself has been the mother of rationalism, is in some measure well founded. . . . So far from keeping the non-rational element in religion alive in the heart of the religious experience, orthodox Christianity manifestly failed to recognize its value, and by this failure gave to the idea of God a one-sidedly intellectualistic and rationalistic interpretation. . . .

And so it is salutary that we should be incited to notice that religion is not exclusively contained and exhaustively comprised in any series of "rational" assertions; and it is well worth while to attempt to bring the relation of the different "moments" of religion to one another clearly before the mind, so that its nature may become more manifest. . . .

"Numen" and the "Numinous"

"Holiness"—"the holy"—is a category of interpretation and valuation peculiar to the sphere of religion. . . . While it is complex, it contains a quite specific element or "moment," which sets it apart from "the rational" in the meaning we gave to that work above, and which remains inexpressible. . . .

The fact is we have come to use the words "holy," "sacred" (*heilig*) in an entirely derivative sense, quite different from that which they originally bore. We generally take "holy" as meaning "completely good"; it is the absolute moral attribute, denoting the consummation of moral goodness. . . .

But this common usage of the term is inaccurate. It is true that all this moral significance is contained in the word "holy," but it includes in addition—as even we cannot but feel—a clear overplus of meaning, and this is now our task is to isolate. . . . It will be useful, at least for the temporary purpose of the investigation, to invent a special term to stand for "the holy" *minus* its moral factor or "moment," and, as we can now add, minus its "rational" aspect altogether.

It will be our endeavour to suggest this unnamed Something to the reader as far as we may, so that he may himself feel it. There is no religion in which it does not live as the real innermost core, and without it no religion would be worthy of the name. . . . And we then use the word "holy" to translate them. But this "holy" then represents the gradual shaping and filling in with ethical meaning, or what we shall call the "schematization," of what was a unique original feeling-response, which can be in itself ethically neutral and claims consideration in its own right. . . .

Accordingly, it is worth while, as we have said, to find a word to stand for this element in isolation, this "extra" in the meaning of "holy" above and beyond the meaning of goodness. By means of a special term we shall the better be able, first, to keep the meaning clearly apart and distinct, and second, to apprehend and classify correctly whatever subordinate forms or stages of development it may show. For this purpose I adopt a word coined from the Latin *numen*. . . . I shall speak, then, of a unique "numinous" category of value and of a definitely "numinous" state of mind, which is always found wherever the category is applied. This mental state is perfectly *sui generis* and irreducible to any other; and therefore, like every absolutely primary and elementary datum, while it admits of being discussed, it cannot be strictly defined. . . .

The Elements of the "Numinous"

. . . Schleiermacher has the credit of isolating a very important element in such an experience. This is the "feeling of dependence." But this important discovery of Schleiermacher is open to criticism in more than one respect. . . . Desiring to give it a name of its own, I propose to call it "creature-consciousness" or creature-feeling. It is the emotion of a creature, submerged and overwhelmed by its own nothingness in contrast to that which is supreme above all creatures. . . .

"MYSTERIUM TREMENDUM"

. . . Let us consider the deepest and most fundamental element in all strong and sincerely felt religious emotion. Faith unto salvation, trust, love—all these are there. But over and above these is an element which may also on occasion, quite apart from them, profoundly affect us and occupy the mind with a wellnigh bewildering strength. Let us follow it up with every effort of sympathy and imaginative intuition wherever it is to be found, in the lives of those around us, in sudden, strong ebullitions of personal piety and the frames of mind such ebullitions evince. . . . If we do so we shall find we are dealing with something for which there is only one appropriate expression, "*mysterium tremendum*." . . . Conceptually mysterium denotes merely that which is hidden and esoteric, that which is beyond conception or understanding, extraordinary and unfamiliar. The term does not define the object more positively in its qualitative character. But though what is enunciated in the word is negative, what is meant is something absolutely and intensely positive. This pure positive we can

experience in feelings, feelings which our discussion can help to make clear to us, in so far as it arouses them actually in our hearts. . . .

Tremor is in itself merely the perfectly familiar and "natural" emotion of *fear*. But here the term is taken, aptly enough but still only by analogy, to denote a quite specific kind of emotional response, wholly distinct from that of being afraid, though it so far resembles it that the analogy of fear may be used to throw light upon its nature. There are in some languages special expressions which denote, either exclusively or in the first instance, this "fear" that is more than fear proper. The Hebrew *hiqdîsh* (hallow) is an example. To "keep a thing holy in the heart" means to mark it off by a feeling of peculiar dread, not to be mistaken for any ordinary dread, that is, to appraise it by the category of the numinous. . . .

The awe or "dread" *may* indeed be so overwhelmingly great that it seems to penetrate to the very marrow, making the man's hair bristle and his limbs quake. But it may also steal upon him almost unobserved as the gentlest of agitations, a mere fleeting shadow passing across his mood. It has therefore nothing to do with intensity, and no natural fear passes over into it merely by being intensified. I may be beyond all measure afraid and terrified without there being even a trace of the feeling of uncanniness in my emotion. . . .

Though the numinous emotion in its completest development shows a world of difference from the mere "daemonic dread," yet not even at the highest level does it belie its pedigree or kindred. Even when the worship of "daemons" has long since reached the higher level of worship of "gods," these gods still retain as *numina* something of the "ghost" in the impress they make on the feelings of the worshipper, viz. The peculiar quality of the "uncanny" and "aweful," which survives with the quality of exaltedness and sublimity or is symbolized by means of it. And this element, softened though it is, does not disappear even on the highest level of all, where the worship of God is at its purest. Its disappearance would be indeed an essential loss. The "shudder" reappears in a form ennobled beyond measure where the soul, held speechless, trembles inwardly to the farthest fibre of its being. It invades the mind mightily in Christian worship with the words: "Holy, holy, holy." . . .

We have been attempting to unfold the implications of that aspect of the *mysterium tremendum* indicated by the adjective, and the result so far may be summarized in two words, constituting, as before, what may be called an "ideogram," rather than a concept proper, viz "absolute unapproachability."

It will be felt at once that there is yet a further element which must be added, that, namely of "might," "power," "absolute overpoweringness." We will take to represent this the term *majestas,* majesty—the more readily because anyone with a feeling for language must detect a last faint trace of the numinous still clinging to the word. The *tremendum* may then be rendered more adequately *tremenda majestas,* or "aweful majesty." This second element of majesty may continue to be vividly preserved, where the first, that of unapproachability, recedes and dies away, as may be seen, for example, in mysticism. It is especially in relation to this element of majesty or absolute overpoweringness that the creature-consciousness, of which we have already spoken comes upon the scene, as a sort of shadow or subjective reflection of it. Thus, in contrast to "the overpowering" of which we are conscious as an object over against the self, there is the feeling of one's own submergence, of being but "dust and ashes" and nothingness. . . .

We come upon the ideas, first, of the annihilation of self, and then, as its complement, of the transcendent as the sole and entire reality. . . . The point from which speculation starts is not a "consciousness of absolute dependence"—of myself as result and effect of a divine cause—for that would in point of fact lead to insistence upon the reality of the self; it starts from a consciousness of the absolute superiority or supremacy of a power other than myself, and

it is only as it falls back upon ontological terms to achieve its end—terms generally borrowed from natural science—that that element of the *tremendum,* originally apprehended as "plenitude of power," becomes transmuted into "plenitude of being." . . .

There is, finally, a third element comprised in those of *tremendum* and *majestas,* awefulness and majesty, and this I venture to call the "urgency" or "energy" of the numinous object. It is particularly vividly perceptible in the . . . "wrath"; and it everywhere clothes itself in symbolical expressions—vitality, passion, emotional temper, will, force, movement, excitement, activity, impetus. These features are typical and recur again and again from the daemonic level up to the idea of the "living" God. . . .

THE ANALYSIS OF "MYSTERIUM"

We gave to the object to which the numinous consciousness is directed the name *mysterium tremendum,* and we then set ourselves first to determine the meaning of the adjective *tremendum*—which we found to be itself only justified by analogy—because it is more easily analysed than the substantive idea *mysterium.* We have now to turn to this, and try as best we may, by hint and suggestion, to get to a clearer apprehension of what it implies.

It might be thought that the adjective itself gives an explanation of the substantive; but this is not so. It is not merely analytical; it is a synthetic attribute to it; i.e., *tremendum* adds something not necessarily inherent in *mysterium.* It is true that the reactions in consciousness that correspond to the one readily and spontaneously overflow into those that correspond to the other; in fact, anyone sensitive to the use of words would commonly feel that the idea of "mystery" (*mysterium*) is so closely bound up with its synthetic qualifying attribute "aweful" (*tremendum*) that one can hardly say the former without catching an echo of the latter, "mystery" almost of itself becoming "aweful mystery" to us. But the passage from the one idea to the other need not by any means be always so easy. The elements of meaning implied in "awefulness" and "mysteriousness" are in themselves definitely different. The latter may so far preponderate in the religious consciousness, may stand out so vividly, that in comparison with it the former almost sinks out of sight; a case which again could be clearly exemplified from some forms of mysticism. Occasionally, on the other hand, the reverse happens, and the *tremendum* may in turn occupy the mind without the *mysterium.*

This latter, then, needs special consideration on its own account. We need an expression for the mental reaction peculiar to it; and here, too, only one word seems appropriate, though, as it is strictly applicable only to a "natural" state of mind, it has here meaning only by analogy: it is the word "stupor." *Stupor* is plainly a different thing from *tremor;* it signifies blank wonder, an astonishment that strikes us dumb, amazement absolute. Taken, indeed, in its purely natural sense, *mysterium* would first mean merely a secret or a mystery in the sense of that which is alien to us, uncomprehended and unexplained; and so far *mysterium* is itself merely an ideogram, an analogical notion taken from the natural sphere, illustrating, but incapable of exhaustively rendering, our real meaning. Taken in the religious sense, that which is "mysterious" is—to give it perhaps the most striking expression—the "wholly other" (θάμερου, *anyad, alienum*), that which is quite beyond the sphere of the usual, the intelligible, and the familiar, which therefore falls quite outside the limits of the "canny," and is contrasted with it, filling the mind with blank wonder and astonishment. . . .

In accordance with laws of which we shall have to speak again later, this feeling or consciousness of the "wholly other" will attach itself to, or sometimes be indirectly aroused by means of, objects which are already puzzling upon the "natural" plane, or are of a surprising or astounding character, such as extraordinary phenomena or astonishing occurrences or things in inanimate nature, in the animal world, or among men. But there once more we are

dealing with a case of association between things specifically different—the "numinous" and the "natural" moments of consciousness—and not merely with the gradual enhancement of one of them—the "natural"—till it becomes the other. As in the case of "natural fear" and "daemonic dread" already considered, so here the transition from natural to daemonic amazement is not a mere matter of degree. But it is only with the latter that the complementary expression *mysterium* perfectly harmonizes, as will be felt perhaps more clearly in the case of the adjectival form "mysterious." . . .

The truly "mysterious" object is beyond our apprehension and comprehension, not only because our knowledge has certain irremovable limits, but because in it we come upon something inherently "wholly other," whose kind and character are incommensurable with our own, and before which we therefore recoil in a wonder that strikes us chill and numb, . . . the "wholly other," something which has no place in our scheme of reality but belongs to an absolutely different one, and which at the same time arouses an irrepressible interest in the mind. . . .

THE ELEMENT OF FASCINATION

The qualitative content of the numinous experience, to which "the mysterious" stands as *form,* is in one of its aspects the element of daunting "awefulness" and "majesty," which has already been dealt with in detail; but it is clear that it has at the same time another aspect, in which it shows itself as something uniquely attractive and *fascinating.*

These two qualities, the daunting and the fascinating, now combine in a strange harmony of contrasts, and the resultant dual character of the numinous consciousness, to which the entire religious development bears witness, at any rate from the level of the "daemonic dread" onwards, is at once the strangest and most noteworthy phenomenon in the whole history of religion. The daemonic-divine object may appear to the mind an object of horror and dread, but at the same time it is no less something that allures with a potent charm, and the creature, who trembles before it, utterly cowed and cast down, has always at the same time the impulse to turn to it, nay even to make it somehow his own. The "mystery" is for him not merely something to be wondered at but something that entrances him; and beside that in it which bewilders and confounds, he feels a something that captivates and transports him with a strange ravishment, rising often enough to the pitch of dizzy intoxication; it is the Dionysiac-element in the numen.

The ideas and concepts which are the parallels or "schemata" on the rational side of this non-rational element of "fascination" are love, mercy, pity, comfort; these are all "natural" elements of the common psychical life, only they are here thought as absolute and in completeness. But important as these are for the experience of religious bliss or felicity, they do not by any means exhaust it. . . .

It may well be possible, it is even probable, that in the first stage of its development the religious consciousness started with only one of its poles—the "daunting" aspect of the numen—and so at first took shape only as "daemonic dread." But if this did not point to something beyond itself, if it were not but one "moment" of a completer experience, pressing up gradually into consciousness, then no transition would be possible to the feelings of positive self-surrender to the numen. . . .

Possession of and by the numen becomes an end in itself; it begins to be sought for its own sake; and the wildest and most artificial methods of asceticism are put into practice to attain it. In a word, the *vita religiosa* begins; and to remain in these strange and bizarre states of numinous possession becomes a good in itself, even a way of salvation, wholly different from the profane goods pursued by means of magic. Here, too, commences the process of development by which the experience is matured and purified, till finally it reaches its consummation in the sublimest and purest states of the "life within the Spirit" and in the noblest mysticism. Widely

various as these states are in themselves, yet they have this element in common, that in them the mysterium is experienced in its essential, positive, and specific character, as something that bestows upon man a beatitude beyond compare, but one whose real nature he can neither proclaim in speech nor conceive in thought, but may know only by a direct and living experience. It is a bliss which embraces all those blessings that are indicated or suggested in positive fashion by any "doctrine of salvation," and it quickens all of them through and through; but these do not exhaust it. Rather by its all-pervading, penetrating glow it makes of these very blessings more than the intellect can conceive in them or affirm of them. It gives the peace that passes understanding, and of which the tongue can only stammer brokenly. Only from afar, by metaphors and analogies, do we come to apprehend what it is in itself, and even so our notion is but inadequate and confused. . . .

Everywhere salvation is something whose meaning is often very little apparent, is even wholly obscure, to the "natural" man; on the contrary, *so far as he understands it,* he tends to find it highly tedious and uninteresting, sometimes downright distasteful and repugnant to his nature, as he would, for instance, find the beatific vision of God in our own doctrine of salvation, or the *henōsis* of "God all in all" among the mystics. . . .

It is not only in the religious feeling of longing that the moment of fascination is a living factor. It is already alive and present in the moment of "solemnity," both in the gathered concentration and humble submergence of private devotion, when the mind is exalted to the holy, and in the common worship of the congregation, where this is practised with earnestness and deep sincerity, as, it is to be feared, is with us a thing rather desired than realized. It is this and nothing else that in the solemn moment can fill the soul so full and keep it so inexpressibly tranquil. . . . And this shows that above and beyond our rational being lies hidden the ultimate and highest part of our nature, which can find no satisfaction in the mere allaying of the needs of our sensuous, psychical, or intellectual impulses and cravings. The mystics called it the basis or ground of the soul.

We saw that in the case of the element of the mysterious the "wholly other" led on to the supernatural and transcendent and that above these appeared the "beyond" (επέκεινα) of mysticism, through the non-rational side of religion being raised to its highest power and stressed to excess. It is the same in the case of the element of "fascination"; here, too, is possible a transition into mysticism. At its highest point of stress the fascinating becomes the "overabounding," "exuberant." . . .

Means of Expression of the Numinous

It may serve to make the essential nature of the numinous consciousness clearer if we call to mind the manner in which it expresses itself outwardly, and how it spreads and is transmitted from mind to mind. There is, of course, no "transmission" of it in the proper sense of the word; it cannot be "taught," it must be "awakened" from the spirit. And this could not justifyingly be asserted, as it often is, of religion as a whole and in general, for in religion there is very much that can be taught—that is, handed down in concepts and passed on in school instruction. What is incapable of being so handed down is this numinous basis and background to religion, which can only be induced, incited, and aroused. This is least of all possible by mere verbal phrase or external symbol; rather we must have recourse to the way all other moods and feelings are transmitted, to a penetrative imaginative sympathy with what passes in the other person's mind. More of the experience lives in reverent attitude and gesture, in tone and voice and demeanour, expressing its momentousness, and in the solemn devotional assembly of a congregation at prayer, than in all the phrases and negative nomenclature which

we have found to designate it. . . . If a man does not *feel* what the numinous is, when he reads the sixth chapter of Isaiah, then no "preaching, singing, telling," in Luther's phrase, can avail him. Little of it can usually be noticed in theory and dogma, or even in exhortation, unless it is actually *heard.* Indeed no element in religion needs so much as this the *viva vox,* transmission by living fellowship inspiration of personal contact.

But the mere word, even when it comes as a living voice, is powerless without the "spirit in the heart" of the hearer to move him to apprehension. And this spirit, this inborn capacity to receive and understand, is the essential thing. If that is there, very often only a very small incitement, a very remote stimulus, is needed to arouse the numinous consciousness. It is indeed astonishing to see how small a stimulus suffices—and that too coming sometimes only in clumsy and bewildered guise—to raise the spirit of itself to the strongest pitch of the most definitely religious excitement. But where the wind of the spirit blows, there the mere "rational" terms themselves are indued with power to arouse the feeling of the "non-rational," and become adequate to tune the mood at once to the right tone. Here "schematization" starts at once and needs no prompting. He who "in spirit" reads the written word lives in the numinous, though he may have neither notion of it nor name for it, nay, though he may be unable to analyse any feeling of his own and so make explicit to himself the nature of that numinous strand running through the religious experience.

For the rest, the methods by which the numinous feeling is presented and evoked are indirect; i.e., they consist in those means by which we express kindred and similar feelings belonging to the "natural" sphere. We have already become acquainted with these feelings, and we shall recognize them at once if we consider what are the means of expression which religion has employed in all ages and in every land.

One of the most primitive of these—which is later more and more felt to be inadequate, until it is finally altogether discarded as "unworthy"—is quite naturally the "fearful" and horrible, and even at times the revolting and the loathsome. Inasmuch as the corresponding feelings are closely analogous to that of the *tremendum*, their outlets and means of expression may become indirect modes of expressing the specific "numinous awe" that cannot be expressed directly. . . .

So far we have been concerned with that element or factor of the numinous which was the first our analysis noted and which we proposed to name symbolically "the aweful" (*tremendum*). We pass now to consider the means by which the second—the element of "the mysterious" (*mysterium*)—is expressed. Here we light upon the analogical mode of manifestation that in every religion occupies a foremost and extraordinary place, and the theory of which we are now in a position to give. I refer to *miracle*. "Miracle is the dearest child of Faith"; if the history of religions had not already taught us the truth of Schiller's saying, we might have reached it by anticipation *a priori* from the element of "the mysterious," as already shown. Nothing can be found in all the world of "natural" feelings bearing so immediate an analogy—*mutatis mutandis*—to the religious consciousness of ineffable, unutterable mystery, the "absolute other," as the incomprehensible, unwonted, enigmatic thing, in whatever place or guise it may confront us. This will be all the more true if the uncomprehended thing is something at once *mighty* and *fearful,* for then there is a twofold analogy with the numinous—that is to say, an analogy not only with the *mysterium* aspect of it, but with the *tremendum* aspect, and the latter again in the two directions already suggested of *fearfulness* proper and *sublimity.* This exemplifies the general truth already considered that any form of the numinous consciousness may be stirred by means of feelings analogous to it of a "natural" kind, and then itself pass over into these, or, more properly, be replaced and figurative ways of expressing feeling with rational concepts, it then systematizes them, and out of them spins, like a monstrous web, a "science of God," which is and remains something monstrous. . . .

Two Processes of Development

This permeation of the rational with the non-rational is to lead, then, to the deepening of our rational conception of God; it must not be the means of blurring or diminishing it. . . . We must no longer understand by "the holy" or "sacred" the merely numinous in general, nor even the numinous at its own highest development; we must always understand by it the numinous completely permeated and saturated with elements signifying rationality, purpose, personality, morality. . . .

That which the primitive religious consciousness first apprehends in the form of "daemonic dread," and which, as it further unfolds, becomes more elevated and ennobled, is in origin not something rational or moral, but something distinct, non-rational, an object to which the mind responds in a unique way with the special feeling-reflexes that have been described. And this element or "moment" passes in itself through a process of development of its own, quite apart from the other process—which begins at an early stage—by which it is "rationalized" and "moralized," i.e., filled with rational and ethical meaning. Taking this non-rational process of development first, we have seen how the "daemonic dread," after itself passing through various gradations, rises to the level of "fear of the gods," and thence to "fear of God." . . . The feelings of dependence upon and beatitude in the numen, from being relative, become absolute. The false analogies and fortuitous associations are gradually dispelled or frankly rejected. The numen becomes God and Deity. It is then to God and Deity, as "numen" rendered absolute, that the attribute denoted by the terms qādôsh, sanctus, ἅγιος, holy, pertains, in the first and directest sense of the words. It is the culmination of a development which works itself out purely in the sphere of the non-rational. This development constitutes the first central fact of religious study, and it is the task of religious history and psychology to trace its course.

Next, secondary and subsidiary to this, is the task of tracing the course of the process of rationalization and moralization on the basis of the numinous consciousness. It nearly, if not quite, synchronizes and keeps pace with the stages of the purely numinous development, and, like that, it can be traced in its different gradations in the most widely different regions of religious history. Almost everywhere we find the numinous attracting and appropriating meanings derived from social and individual ideals of obligation, justice, and goodness. These become the "will" of the numen, and the numen their guardian, ordainer, and author. More and more these ideas come to enter into the very essence of the numen and charge the term with ethical content. "Holy" becomes "good," and "good" from that very fact in turn becomes "holy," "sacrosanct"; until there results a thenceforth indissoluble synthesis of the two elements, and the final outcome is thus the fuller, more complex sense of "holy," in which it is at once *good and sacrosanct.* . . .

And this process of rationalization and moralization of the numinous, as it grows ever more clear and more potent, is in fact the most essential part of what we call "the History of Salvation" and prize as the ever-growing self-revelation of the divine. But at the same it should be clear to us that this process of the "moralization of the idea of God," often enough represented to us as a principal problem, setting the main line for inquiry into the history of religion, is in no wise a suppression of the numinous or its supersession by something else—which would result not in a God, but a God-substitute—but rather the completion and charging of it with a new content. That is to say, the "moralization" process assumes the numinous and is only completed upon this as basis.

The Holy as an A Priori Category

It follows from what has been said that the "holy" in the fullest sense of the word is a combined, complex category, the combining elements being its rational and non-rational components. But in *both*—and the assertion must be strictly maintained against all sensationalism and naturalism—it is a *purely a priori* category.

The rational ideas of absoluteness, completion, necessity, and substantiality, and no less so those of the good as an objective value, objectively binding and valid, are not to be "evolved" from any sort of sense-perception. And the notions of "epigenesis," "heterogony," or whatever other expression we may choose to denote our compromise and perplexity, only serve to conceal the problem, the tendency to take refuge in a Greek terminology being here, as so often, nothing but an avowal of one's own insufficiency. Rather, seeking to account for the ideas in question, we are referred away from all sense-experience back to an original and underivable capacity of the mind implanted in the "pure reason" independently of all perception.

But in the case of the non-rational elements of our category of the Holy we are referred back to something still deeper than the "pure reason." At least as this is usually understood, namely, to that which mysticism has rightly named the *fundus animae*, the "bottom" or "ground of the soul" (*Seelengrund*). The ideas of the numinous and the feelings that correspond to them are, quite as much as the rational ideas and feelings, absolutely "pure," and the criteria which Kant suggests for the "pure" concept and the "pure" feeling of respect are most precisely applicable to them. . . .

The numinous . . . issues from the deepest foundation of cognitive apprehension that the soul possesses, and, though it of course comes into being in and amid the sensory data and empirical material of the natural world and cannot anticipate or dispense with those, yet it does not arise *out of* them, but only *by their means.*

They are the incitement, the stimulus, and the "occasion" for the numinous experience to become astir, and, in so doing, to begin—at first with a naïve immediacy of reaction—to be interfused and interwoven with the present world of sensuous experience, until, becoming gradually purer, it disengages itself from this and takes its stand in absolute contrast to it. The proof that in the numinous we have to deal with purely *a priori* cognitive elements is to be reached by introspection and a critical examination of reason such as Kant instituted. We find, that is, involved in the numinous experience, beliefs and feelings qualitatively different from anything that "natural" sense-perception is capable of giving us. They are themselves not perceptions at all, but peculiar interpretations and valuations, at first of perceptual data, and then—at a higher level—of posited objects and entities, which themselves no longer belong to the perceptual world, but are thought of as supplementing and transcending it. And as they are not themselves sense-perceptions, so neither are they any sort of "transmutation" of sense-perceptions. The only "transmutation" possible in respect to sense-perception is the transformation of the intuitively given concrete percept, of whatever sort, into the corresponding concept; there is never any question of the transformation of *one* class of percepts into a class of entities qualitatively *other*. The facts of the numinous consciousness point therefore—as likewise do also the "pure concepts of the understanding" of Kant and the ideas and value-judgements of ethics or aesthetics—to a hidden substantive source, from which the religious ideas and feelings are formed, which lies in the mind independently of sense-perception; a "pure reason" in the profoundest sense, which, because of the "surpassingness" of its content, must be distinguished from both the pure theoretical and the pure practical reason of Kant, as something yet higher or deeper than they. . . .

We call the source of growth a hidden "predisposition" of the human spirit, which awakens when aroused by diverse excitations. That there are "predispositions" of this sort in individuals no one can deny who has given serious study to the history of religion. They are seen as propensities, "predestining" the individual to religion, and they may grow spontaneously to quasi-instinctive presentiments, uneasy seeking and groping, yearning and longing, and become a religious *impulse,* that only finds peace when it has become clear to itself and attained its goal. . . .

These are manifestations of a *predisposition* becoming a search and a driving *impulsion.* But here, if nowhere else, the "fundamental biogentic law" really does hold good, which uses the stages and phases in the growth of the individual to throw light upon the corresponding stages in the growth of his species. The *predisposition* which the human reason brought with it when the species Man entered history became long ago, not merely for individuals but for the species as a whole, a *religious impulsion,* to which incitements from without and pressure from within the mind both contributed. It begins in undirected, groping emotion, a seeking and shaping of representations, and goes on, by a continual onward striving, to generate ideas, till its nature is self-illumined and made clear by an explication of the obscure *a priori* foundation of thought itself, out of which it originated. And this emotion, this searching, this generation and explication of ideas, give the warp of the fabric of religious evolution, whose woof we are to discuss later. . . .

We conclude, then, that not only the rational but also the non-rational elements of the complex category of "holiness" are *a priori* elements and each in the same degree. Religion is not in vassalage either to morality or teleology, *ethos* or *telos,* and does not draw its life from postulates; and its non-rational content has, no less than its rational, its own independent roots in the hidden depths of the spirit itself.

But the same *a priori* character belongs, in the third place, to the *connexion* of the rational and the non-rational elements in religion, their inward and necessary union. The histories of religion recount indeed, as though it were something axiomatic, the gradual interpenetration of the two, the process by which "the divine" is charged and filled out with ethical meaning. And this process is, in fact, *felt* as something axiomatic, something whose inner necessity we feel to be self-evident. But then this inward self-evidence is a problem in itself; we are forced to assume an obscure, *a priori* knowledge of the necessity of this synthesis, combining rational and non-rational. For it is not only by means a *logical* necessity. . . .

As the rational elements, following a priori principles, come together in the historical evolution of religions with the non-rational, they serve to "schematize" these. This is true, not only in general of the relation of the rational aspect of "the holy," taken as a whole, to its non-rational, taken as a whole, but also in detail of the several constituent elements of the two aspects. The *tremendum,* the daunting and repelling moment of the numinous, is schematized by means of the rational ideas of justice, moral will, and the exclusion of what is opposed to morality; and schematized thus, it becomes the holy "wrath of God," which Scripture and Christian preaching alike proclaim. The *fascinans,* the attracting and alluring moment of the numinous, is schematized by means of the ideas of goodness, mercy, love, and, so schematized, becomes all that we mean by Grace, that term so rich in import, which unites with the holy wrath in a single "harmony of contrasts," and like it is, from the numinous strain in it, tinged with mysticism. The "moment" *mysteriosum* is schematized by the absoluteness of all rational attributes applied to the Deity. Probably the correspondence here implied—between "the mysterious" and the *absoluteness* of all rational attributes—will not appear at first sight so immediately evident as in the two foregoing cases, wrath and grace. None the less it is a very exact correspondence. God's rational attributes can be distinguished from like attributes applied to the created spirit by being not relative, as those

are, but absolute. Human love is relative, admitting of degrees, and it is the same with human knowledge and human goodness. God's love and knowledge and goodness, on the other hand, and all else that can be asserted of Him in conceptual terms, are formally absolute. The *content* of the attributes is the same; it is an *element of form* which marks them apart as attributes of God. . . . The absolute exceeds our power to comprehend; the mysterious wholly eludes it. The absolute is that which surpasses the limits of our understanding, not through its actual qualitative character, for that is familiar to us, but through its formal character. The mysterious, on the other hand, is that which lies altogether outside what can be thought, and is, alike in form, quality, and essence, the utterly and "wholly other." We see, then, that in the case of the moment of "mystery," as well as those of "awefulness" and "fascination," there is an exact correspondence between the non-rational element and its rational *schema,* and one that admits of development.

By the continual living activity of its non-rational elements a religion is guarded from passing into "rationalism." By being steeped in and saturated with rational elements it is guarded from sinking into fanaticism or mere mysticality, or at least from persisting in these, and is qualified to become a religion for all civilized humaniity. The degree in which both rational and non-rational elements are jointly present, united in healthy and lovely harmony affords a criterion to measure the relative rank of religions—and one, too, that is specifically religious. Applying this criterion, we find that Christianity, in this as in other respects, stands out in complete superiority over all its sister religions. The lucid edifice of its clear and pure conceptions, feelings, and experiences is built up on a foundation that goes far deeper than the rational. Yet the non-rational is only the basis, the setting, the woof in the fabric, ever preserving for Christianity its mystical depth, giving religion thereby the deep undertones and heavy shadows of mysticism, without letting it develop into a mere rank growth of mysticality. . . .

History and the A Priori in Religion: Summary and Conclusion

We have considered "the holy" on the one hand as an *a priori* category of mind, and on the other as manifesting itself in outward appearance. The contrast here intended is exactly the same as the common contrast of inner and outer, general and special revelation. And if we take "reason" (*ratio*) as an inclusive term for all cognition which arises in the mind from principles native to it, in contrast to those based upon facts of history, then we may say that the distinction between holiness as an *a priori* category and holiness as revealed in outward appearance is much the same as that between "reason" (in this wide sense) and history.

Every religion which, so far from being a mere faith in traditional authority, springs from personal assurance and inward convincement (i.e. from an inward first-hand cognition of its truth)—as Christianity does in a unique degree—must presuppose principles in the mind enabling it to be independently recognized as true. But these principles must be *a priori* ones, not to be derived from "experience" or "history." It has little meaning, however edifying it may sound, to say that they are inscribed upon the heart by the pencil of the Holy Spirit "in history." . . . Such an assertion is itself a presumption that it is possible to distinguish the signature of the Spirit from others, and thus that we have an *a priori* notion of what is of the Spirit independently of history.

And there is a further consideration. There is something presupposed by history as such—not only the history of mind or spirit, with which we are here concerned—which alone makes it history, and that is the existence of a *quale*, something with a potentiality of its own, capable of *becoming*, in the special sense of coming to be that to which it was predisposed and predeter-

mined. An oak tree can *become*, and thus have a sort of "history," whereas a heap of stones cannot. The random addition and subtraction, displacement and rearrangement, of elements in a mere aggregation can certainly be followed in narrative form, but this is not in the deeper sense an historical narrative. We only have the history of a people in proportion as it enters upon its course equipped with an endowment of talents and tendencies; it must already *be something* if it is really to *become* anything. And biography is a lamentable and unreal business in the case of a man who has no real unique potentiality of his own, no special idiosyncrasy, and is therefore a mere point of intersection for various fortuitous causal series, acted upon, as it were, from without. Biography is only a real narration of a real life where, by the interplay of stimulus and experience on the one side and predisposition and natural endowment on the other, something individual and unique comes into being, which is therefore neither the result of a "mere self-unfolding" nor yet the sum of mere traces and impressions, written from without from moment to moment upon a *tabulsa rasa*. In short, to propose a history of mind is to presuppose a mind or spirit determinately qualified; to profess to give a history of religion is to presuppose a spirit specifically qualified for religion.

There are, then, three factors in the process by which religion comes into being in history. First, the interplay of predisposition and stimulus, which in the historical development of man's mind actualizes the potentiality in the former, and at the same time helps to determine its form. Second, the groping recognition, by virtue of this very disposition, of specific portions of history as the manifestation of "the holy," with consequent modification of the religious experience already attained both in its quality and degree. And third, on the basis of the other two, the achieved fellowship with "the holy" in knowing, feeling, and willing. Plainly, then, religion is only the offspring of history in so far as history on the one hand develops our disposition for knowing the holy, and on the other is itself repeatedly the manifestation of the holy. "Natural" religion, in contrast to historical, does not exist, and still less does "innate" religion.

A priori cognitions are not such as every one does have—such would be *innate* cognitions—but such as every one is *capable* of having. The loftier *a priori* cognitions are such as—while every one is indeed capable of having them—do not, as experience teaches us, occur spontaneously, but rather are "awakened" through the instrumentality of other more highly endowed natures. In relation to these the universal "predisposition" is merely a faculty of *receptivity* and a *principle of judgement and acknowledgement,* not a capacity to produce the cognitions in question for oneself independently. This latter capacity is confined to those specially "endowed." And this "endowment" is the universal disposition on a higher level and at a higher power, differing from it in quality as well as in degree. . . .

Counterpoint:
Understanding and Teaching Rudolph Otto's
The Idea of the Holy

THOMAS A. IDINOPULOS

Thomas A. Idinopulos teaches at Miami University in Oxford, Ohio. Among his published books are the following: *Jerusalem, Weathered by Miracles,* and *The Erosion of Faith.*

. . . OTTO'S DESCRIPTIVE ACCOUNT of the unique experience of religious feeling as *mysterium tremendum et fascinans,* is the simpler, more vivid, and perhaps more convincing part of his book. The complexity begins when Otto moves from a description of religious feeling to an analysis of the idea of the holy, the origins and essence of religion, and finally of religion's historical development and fulfillment. This account which mixes phenomenology, epistemology, and theology in bewildering amounts, seems at times to confuse rather than to clarify the nature of religious feeling. Yet it is a necessary part of Otto's account of religion, as we shall see.

However complex Otto's argument is about religion, his genius as a writer was to give his readers the confidence that religious experience has a unique content and a distinct meaning. . . . In this respect Otto continued the task begun earlier by Friedrich Schleiermacher in 1799 with the publication of his *Speeches on Religion To Its Culture Despisers,* which was to defend the uniqueness of religion against the

Reprinted from Thomas A. Idinopulos, "Understanding and Teaching Rudolph Otto's The Idea of the Holy *in* The Sacred and Its Scholars: Comparative Methodologies for the Study of Primary Religious Data, *ed. Thomas A. Idinopulos and Edward A. Yonan (Leiden: E. J. Brill, 1996) pp. 139–155.*

naturalists who would equate religion with ethics or reduce it to psychological and social reactions to life's situations.

The dominant theological influence on Otto's idea of the holy was Luther's doctrine of justification by faith alone. The main philosophical influence was Immanuel Kant's notion of the *a priori*. Otto was also influenced by the interpretation given to Kant's epistemology by Jakob Fries and by the argument of Ernst Troeltsch that religion was a unique and valid category of meaning.

Kant spoke of the *a priori* as a predisposition of the human mind to knowledge of the sensory world. Utilizing the *a priori* Otto argued there is a religious *a priori* or predisposition of mind to religious knowledge. That *a priori*, he named the holy (*Das Heilige*), and identified it as "a category of interpretation and valuation peculiar to the sphere of religion." [5] We should understand Otto here to mean that the holy, which is part and parcel of our mind's working, makes it possible for us to recognize and appropriately respond to religious experience as religious. This recognition occurs in the experience of certain numinous feelings such as creatureliness, dread, awe, and wonder. . . .

Adapting Kant's proposition about knowledge to religion, Otto wanted to argue that religion comes into being as the result of numinous feeling that is the experience of both an objective numinous reality (which seems to occasion religion) and an inner numinous, *a priori* mind (which causes religion). The connections here between experience, mind, and object as affecting religion, so far as I can judge, is not made clear in Otto's major book on the holy or any of the other books which deal with the holy. In supposing that there is a connection between the experience of numinous feeling to the religiously cognitive and *a priori* capacity of mind, without actually explaining that connection, much of the confusion in Otto's account of religion occurs. The confusion becomes acute when one asks about the numinous object which Otto acknowledges [10–11] as necessary to religious knowledge but never explains in its relation to the *a priori* working of the religious mind. Confusion might have been avoided had Otto made a clear distinction between what in religion is a matter of *a priori* knowledge and what is apprehended *a posteriori*, through experience. That he did not do. Repeatedly what we find in Otto's book is a hazing over of the difference of subject and object, experience and mind, numinous feeling and the *a priori* idea of the holy. The end result is that at the end of Otto's book we are in no doubt as to what religion means (the holy) but we are still left wondering as to what exactly caused religion and how it developed.

The failure to clarify the connections between experience and mind, the *a posteriori* and *a priori* in religion does not diminish Otto's achievement. His book on the holy contains a profound and penetrating analysis of religion by giving us a language to refer to and make some sense of a central but not very well understood dimension of human experience. Otto accomplishes this initially by distinguishing the numinous or non-rational aspect of the holy from the rational or ethical aspect. The word numinous comes from the Latin word for deity, *numen*. What is the numinous? Otto answers by referring to an "overplus of meaning," to "a unique original feeling response," something "above and beyond the meaning of goodness." [5–6] The numinous is experienced as "creature-feeling" or "creature-consciousness." . . .

In "creature-feeling" we are made aware through awe and wonder of the *Tremendum*. *Tremendum* is the self-awareness of being mere nothing, of being reduced to dust and ashes as Patriach Abraham was before the august presence of the Lord. If *tremendum* is the feeling of being judged and full of fright in the presence of the holy, then *fascinans* is the polar opposite feeling of being drawn to and attracted by the holy, as witnessed in those sacramental acts in which the religious person puts on, partakes of, and "consumes" the divine. Also the feeling of *mysterium* pervades our experiences of *tremendum* and *fascinans*. The mysterium is the "wholly other," a reference to the transcendent numinous reality which is unknowable by thought and inexpressible by any expression of human religion.

It is striking that Otto issues a warning against any presumption to understand the holy without having had experiences of the numinous. He writes that "whoever knows no such moments in his experience, is requested to read no further." Why? Because, he answers, one should be able to recall "instrinsically religious feelings." [8] "This [numinous] mental state," Otto tell us, "is perfectly sui generis and irreducible to any other." . . .

On Otto's account the holy is a potency in us aroused and fulfilled by certain qualities of our experience, giving us the sense of something immensely significant in our lives and yet something "wholly other."

Further, Otto's account gives me a way of thinking about the holy which does not fall prey to psychological reductionism or to metaphysical speculations about the nature of the Other. Through Otto's ideas I am able to acknowledge the external reality of the holy, the Other, without having to demonstrate philosophically that this reality exists in the way that cows, clouds, and dreams exist. In religious experience I am made aware of a distinct quality of meaning—holiness, transcendent mystery, Otherness—which I could not reduce to or equate with any other type of meaning. Further in religious experience I am aware through feeling of a mysterious *something,* external to the self, yet intimately connected to me, something extraordinary, and demanding recognition of its own distinctness. . . .

Consistent with his Kantianism, Otto thinks that we cannot go beyond our religious experience, beyond our numinous consciousness to gain certain knowledge of God-in-himself, that he is and who he is. The essential reality of God is a mystery to us. The God we know is the God who has entered our consciousnes through the *a priori* function of numinous experience. This unseen and mysterious God who is known only

in and through the religious consciousness—is the God of our faith.

Here additional questions arise for students of Otto's thought: What is the connection between the God-of-faith and God-himself? What, as asked earlier, is the connection between numinous feeling and the *a priori* category of the holy? If religious meaning is expressed to us through the *a priori* category of the holy, which interprets and evaluates this meaning, what is the meaning of the holy itself? If the experience of the holy is not exclusively and merely psychological experience, then the holy must have an object outside the human mind. If so, then what is the object—content or referent of the holy? Since the word numinous is drawn from numen, then is numen or deity the referent of the holy? Clearly Otto means the holy to have objective meaning and validity but he also believes that the objective referent of religion cannot be rationally demonstrated or empirically inferred. This being so what then prevents the conclusion that religion, despite Otto's best efforts to argue otherwise, is about nothing more than our own feelings, our own psychologically self-induced states of mind? . . .

Here we should consider what Otto called the rational-moral component of the holy. Otto asserted that the non-rational experience of religion through a distinct feeling, the numinous, is of the essence of religion. It was also his view that religious consciousness develops and "matures" through the addition of the rational-ethical component. The rational component of religion works to "schematize," the non-rational component by providing a framework for its systematic expression. . . .

Just what Otto means by "schematization" is not easy to determine, as Otto-scholars have admitted. What is clear is that Otto recognizes in religious ideas and in religiously motivated morality a criterion for identifying and evaluating the historical development of religions. For Otto the rational-ethical component gives monotheistic religions their superiority over earlier animistic and polytheistic religions. And it is the combining of non-rational and rational, emotional and ethical factors which, Otto believed, gives Christianity in particular its own perfection.

In Otto's mind the rational or ethical component of the holy is so closely linked to the historical development of religion that his discussion of one necessarily entails the other. . . . Otto asserts that the rational or ethical component of the holy is part of the *a priori* structure of the religious consciousness, and even further that the combining or synthesis of non-rational (emotional) with rational (ethical) factors is also part of the *a priori* religious consciousness. Now this "synthesis" is not easy to grasp. . . .

Otto's answer is that there is no logical or necessary evolution of empirically understood religious history. In other words there is no logical or rational necessity that spirits should historically evolve into gods and they into the One God. Rather, what has taken place is an evolution of the religious consciousness, which is the working out through history of the *a priori* conditions of that consciousness. In relation to the *a priori* conditions of the religious consciousness, which "synthesizes" non-rational and rational factors, religion has evolved, matured, progressed by the evolvement of moral-rational values through non-rational, emotional energies. . . .

So far as I can see Otto provides no argument as to why the evolvement of rational values should be regarded as qualitatively superior to non-rational energies of mind. The superiority of the rational seems to be "given," a working of the *a priori* religious consciousness which requires no demonstration of defence. . . .

If we assent to Otto's argument that the experience of the holy is shaped by an *a priori* religious consciousness, must we also agree that this *a priori* consciousness extends to the evolution of religion, which is now said to produce ever higher or more perfect values? I don't think so. The two arguments can be separated. We can describe the universal structure of human consciousness without having to com-

mit ourselves to the proposition that consciousness evolves in a certain way and perfects itself. This must be so since we can never know with certainty, given the absence of reliable information, as to what was the "consciousness" of ancient peoples.

Clearly the science of biological evolution had a decisive influence on Otto's theory of religious evolution. This is obvious in his book, *Naturalism and Religion* (English edition, 1907), where whole chapters are devoted to a detailed explication of Darwin's thought and to the Darwinian philosophies that arose from it. Otto saw in Darwin's ideas a picture of the rich, variegated, evolving character of the world of organisms, and he seems to think that religions, ritual practices, and the human religious consciousness had to be part of that evolving world. Otto assumed that religion was integral to human organic evolution, an assumption which allowed him to contest the naturalistic methods of the anthropologists, who tended to view religion as a mechanical response to external psychological and social forces.

The feeling of the numinous, not the belief in the One God, links, monotheists to animists and polytheists. Otto writes that "in our own awakening and growth to mental and spiritual maturity we trace in ourselves in some sort the evolution by which the seed develops into the tree . . ." Thus in the rudimentary experience of the holy as the "other," "creatureliness," "the tremendum," Otto recognized the continuity of experience and meaning working through all the world's religions at all times, from animism to monotheism. But Otto, following Schleiermacher also wanted to assert an evolutionary development of religious consciousness, which works to "purify" the religious consciousness of inferior, profane elements. . . .

In explaining this purification we confront his notion of the relation between rational and non-rational factors of the holy. It was Otto's idea that the animistic religion of ancient peoples was overly emotional, sensuous, superstitious, crude, a widely numinous or non-rational evocation of the holy. The evolution of religion through time parallels the evolution of culture from profane to spiritual forms of meaning. The evolution of religion and culture is distinguished by the synthesizing of non-rational or numinous with rational and ethical meaning. Otto recognized an advanced stage of religion in monotheism, specifically in Hebraic religion, and most particularly in Christianity, which, he thought, synthesizes the rational and non-rational perfectly. . . .

In using this expression "healthy and lovely harmony" Otto, it seems to me, betrays the normative judgement by which he has assessed the qualitative worth of religions and thereby arrived at the "perfection" of Christianity. For what Otto truly admires in religion is not its emotional or mystical elements, which can lead to fanaticism, nor its rational and moral values, which if stripped of feeling and mystical depth can appear to be arid and empty. What he truly admires in religion is balance. And this balance seems to suggest something of the Greek golden mean, which allows for nothing in excess. German intellectuals of Otto's generation of the nineteenth and early twentieth centuries had enormous affection for Greek classical wisdom. Otto seems to think of the synthesis of rational and non-rational factors, the emotional and the ethical, the mystical and the moderate, as a superior religious wisdom. Employing that "wisdom" normatively he is able to his own satisfaction to arrange a qualitative hierarchy of religion, beginning with the primitives and ending with Judaism and Christianity. Further, Christianity's superiority over Judaism is partly shown in a unique divine revelation which is directed beyond one nation to all nations. . . .

Just as water and oil do not mix so phenomenology and theology do not mix. The problem of Otto's book here was that he tried to provide a phenomenological account of the holy while committed theologically to what he believed to be the true content of the holy. . . .

It is in the summary conclusions of his book that Otto makes clear the important relation between religion and history, and between reli-

gion and art. Religion appears in history but it does not originate in history. . . .

The cause of religion is the *a priori* condition of the human mind, which admits of both non-rational and rational factors. Thus the evolution of religions is an historical evolution not because of history but because of the very structure of the consciousness wherein that which was potential has become realized. Need it become realized?

Otto answered negatively. The religious predisposition present in every human being need not become fulfilled. A person possesses spirit but may choose to lead a secular life. The capacity for religion is not in itself the experienced reality of religion. This means for Otto that religion is not, strictly speaking, natural or innate in human beings. Religion is not something that flows naturally out of a person or makes its appearance mechanically because of genetic coding. Rather religion is aroused in one to the degree that a person is open to it or does not resist it. Religion comes to expression, appears in history, when and only when human beings achieve "fellowship with 'the holy' in knowing, feeling, and willing." [176]

Here Otto drew an analogy between the prophet and the artist, both of whom are skilled in what he calls, "the Spirit." "The prophet corresponds in the religious sphere to the creative artist in that of art: he is the man in whom the Spirit shows itself alike as the power to hear the "voice within." . . . [178]

I believe Otto was right to regard the holy as that value common to all authentic religions; and further right to recognize analogies of the holy in the experiences of art, architecture, music, friendship, romance, sexuality, and silence. In this he followed Schleiermacher. . . . Thus it makes sense of Otto to say that the experience of the sublime in the realm of aesthetics bears a close resemblance ("analogy") to that of the holy in the realm of the religious. For a sense of the sublime in art cannot be taught, anymore than a sense of the holy in religion can be taught; both can only be awakened, evoked, brought to human consciousness by experiences of religion and art.

Surely it is true that works of art possess a mystery and power that evoke in us the sense of the sublime. I know it was true of me that my own first conscious sense of the sublime was evoked in hearing one of Beethoven's last quartets, the C-Sharp Minor—an experience that left me wondering how anything so mysterious and moving could find its way to musical notes and the playing of stringed instruments.

It was years of listening to the Beethoven's C-Sharp Minor that I began to feel that the genius of the composition lay as much in the skill with which silence was employed as in the pattern of sounded notes. Here, as much as in anything else, is the analogy between the sublime and the holy. Both radically depend on silence or on empty space to suggest the infinite, the eternal, in the midst of the sensuous forms displayed. For is it not in the silence that attends the consecration of the host, after the choir is stilled, when the priest invokes the mystery of earthly elements transformed into the body and blood of Christ—is it not precisely in those hushed moments that the sacred mystery weighs heaviest on the communicant, that the *numen praesens* is perceived through feeling.

It would be wrong to say that what is felt is some sort of sacred object or objectified numen. Over and over again what is described by the religious person and what I tried to describe in my own experiences is the quality of a felt relationship. The sense of the holy is always the sense of a relationship, even if the relationship is one of the fear of God or dread of the mysterious sacred power exercised over one's life.

Within the religious relationship the subject is drawn to the holy, to unite with it, to become a part of it, to consume it and be consumed by it. Thus Otto, in describing the experience of *fascinans*, speaks of "those queer sacramental observances and rituals and procedures of communion in which the human being seeks to get the numen into his possession." [32] And so the "shamanistic ways of procedure, possession, indwelling, self-fulfillment in exaltation and ecstasy." [33]

Eastern Orthdox theology speaks of *theosis*, that divination accomplished through Christ whereby God became human so that the human could become God. This theosis or becoming God, Gregory of Palamas understood as an ongoing mystical process, which can take myriad creative forms from religion and art to sexuality and science. Otto would have approved.

From *Religion in Essence and Manifestation*

GERADUS VAN DER LEEUW

Phenomenon and Phenomenology

1. Phenomenology seeks the *phenomena*, as such; the phenomena, again, is *what "appears."* This principle has a threefold implication:

(1) Something exists; (2) This something "appears;" (3) Precisely because it "appears" it is a "phenomenon." But "appearance" refers equally to what appears and to the person to whom it appears; the phenomenon, therefore,

Reprinted from Religion in Essence and Manifestation, *2 Volumes, Peter Smith Publisher, Inc., Gloucester, MA, 1967.*

is neither pure object, nor *the* object, that is to say, the actual reality, whose essential being is merely concealed by the "appearing" of the appearances; with this a specific metaphysics deals. The term "phenomenon," still further, does not imply something purely subjective, not a "life" of the subject[1]; so far as is at all possible, a definite branch of psychology is concerned with this. The "phenomenon" as such, therefore, is an object related to a subject, and a subject related to an object; although this does not imply that the subject deals with or modifies the object in any way whatever, nor (conversely) that the object is somehow or other affected by the subject. The phenomenon, still further, is not produced by the subject, and still less substantiated or demonstrated to "someone." If (finally) this "someone" begins to discuss what "appears," then phenomenology arises.

In its relation to the "someone" to whom the phenomenon appears, accordingly, it has three levels of phenomenality: (1) its (relative) *concealment;* (2) its *gradually becoming revealed;* (3) its (relative) *transparency.* These levels, again, are not equivalent to, but are correlated with, the three levels of life: (1) Experience, (2) Comprehension, and (3) Testimony; and the last two attitudes, when systematically or scientifically employed, constitute the procedure of phenomenology.

By "experience" is implied an actually subsisting life which, with respect to its meaning, constitutes a unity.[2] Experience, therefore, is not pure "life," since in the first place it is objectively conditioned and, secondly, it is inseparably connected with its interpretation as experience. "Life" itself is incomprehensible: "What the disciple of Sais unveils is form, not life."[3] For the "primal experience," upon which our experiences are grounded, has always passed irrevocably away by the time our attention is directed to it. My own life, for example, which I experienced while writing the few lines of the preceding sentence, is just as remote from me as is the "life" associated with the lines I wrote thirty years ago in a school essay. I cannot call it

back again: it is completely past. In fact, the experience of the lines of a moment ago is no nearer to me than is the experience of the Egyptian scribe who wrote his note on papyrus four thousand years ago. That he was "another" than myself makes no difference whatever, since the boy who prepared the school work thirty years ago is also, to my contemplation, "another," and I must objectify myself in my experience of those bygone days. The immediate, therefore, is never and nowhere "given"; it must always be reconstructed[4]; and to "ourselves," that is to our most intimate life, we have no access. For our "life" is not the house wherein we reside, nor again the body, with which we can at least do something: on the contrary, confronted with this "life" we stand helpless. What appears to us as the greatest difference and the most extreme contrast possible—the difference, namely, between ourselves and the "other," our neighbour, whether close by or in distant China, of yesterday or of four thousand years ago—all that is a mere triviality when measured against the colossal *aporia*, the insoluble dilemma, in which we find ourselves as soon as we wish to approach life itself. Even when we reduce life to its appearance in history, we remain perplexed: the gate remains closed, that to yesterday just as that to olden times; and every historian knows that he may commence anywhere at all, but in any case he ends with himself; in other words, he *reconstructs.*[5] What, then, does this reconstruction imply?

It may be described, to begin with, as the sketching of an outline within the chaotic maze of so-called "reality," this outline being called *structure.* Structure is a connection which is neither merely experienced directly, nor abstracted either logically or causally, but which is *understood.* It is an organic whole which cannot be analyzed into its own constituents, but which can from these be comprehended; or in other terms, a fabric of particulars, not to be compounded by the addition of these, nor the deduction of one from the others, but again only *understood* as a whole.[6] In other words: structure is certainly experienced, but not immediately; it is indeed constructed, but not logically, causally, and abstractly. Structure is reality significantly organized. But the significance, in its own turn, belongs in part to reality itself, and in part to the "someone" who attempts to understand it. It is always, therefore, both comprehension and comprehensibility: and this, indeed, in an unanalyzable, experience connection. For it can never be asserted with any certainty what is my own comprehension, and what is the intelligibility of what is comprehended; and this is the purport of the statement that the understanding of a connection, or of a person or event, *dawns upon us.*[7] Thus the sphere of meaning is a third realm, subsisting above mere subjectivity and mere objectivity.[8] The entrance gate to the reality of primal experience, itself wholly inaccessible, is *meaning: my* meaning and *its* meaning, which have become irrevocably one in the act of comprehension.

Still further, the interconnection of meaning—structure—is experienced by understanding, first of all at some given moment; the meaning dawns upon me. But this is not the whole truth, since comprehension is never restricted to the momentary experience. It extends over several experiential unities simultaneously, as indeed it also originates from the comprehension of these unities of experience. But these other experiences, which are at the same time comprehended in combination, and which cooperate in understanding, of course present a similarity to what has been instantaneously understood which, precisely in and through comprehension itself, manifests itself as community of essential nature. The comprehended experience thus becomes coordinated, in and by understanding, within experience of some yet wider objective connection. *Every individual experience, therefore, is already connection;* and every connection remains always experience; this is what we mean by speaking of *types,* together with structures.[9]

The appearance, to continue, subsists as an image. It possesses backgrounds and associated planes; it is "related" to other entities that appear, either by similarity, by contrast, or by a hundred *nuances* that can arise here: conditions, peripheral or central position, competition, distance, etc. These relationships, however, are always *perceptible* relationships, "*structural connections*"[10]: they are never factual relationships nor causal connections. They do not, of course, exclude the latter, but neither do they enunciate anything about them; they are valid only within the structure relations. Such a relation, finally, whether it concerns a person, a historical situation or a religion, is called a *type,* or an *ideal type.*[11]

"Type" in itself, however, has no reality; nor is it a photograph of reality. Like structure, it is timeless and need not actually occur in history.[12] But it possesses life, its own significance, its own law. The "soul," again, as such, never and nowhere "appears"; there is always and only some definite kind of soul which is believed in, and is in this definiteness unique. It may even be said that the ideas of the soul are formed by any two persons, it may be in the same cultural and religious circle, are never wholly the same. Still there is a *type* of soul, a structural relation of distinctive soul-structures. The type itself (to repeat) is timeless: nor is it real. Nevertheless it is alive and appears to us; what then are we to do in order actually to observe it.

2. We resort to phenomenology: that is to say, we must discuss whatever has "appeared" to us—in this sense the term itself is quite clear.[13] This discussion, still further, involves the following stages, which I enumerate in succession although, in practice, they arise never successively but always simultaneously, and in their mutual relations far more frequently than in series:

A. What has become manifest, in the first place, receives a *name.* All speech consists first of all in *assigning names:* "the simple use of names constitutes a form of thinking intermediate between perceiving and imagining."[14] In giving names we separate phenomena and also associate them; in other words, we classify. We include or reject: this we call a "sacrifice" and that a "purification"; since Adam named the animals, speakers have always done this. In this assignment of names, however, we expose ourselves to the peril of becoming intoxicated, or at least satisfied, with the name—the danger which Goethe represented as "transforming observations into mere concepts, and concepts into words," and then treating these words "as if they were objects."[15] We attempt to avoid this danger by

B. The interpolation of the phenomenon into our own lives.[16] This introduction, however, is no capricious act; we can do no otherwise. "Reality" is always *my* reality, history *my* history, "The retrogressive prolongation of man now living."[17] We must, however, realize what we are doing when we commence to speak about what has appeared to us and which we are naming. Further, we must recall that everything that appears to us does not submit itself to us directly and immediately, but only as a symbol of some meaning to be interpreted by us, as something which offers itself to us for interpretation. And this interpretation is impossible unless we experience the appearance, and this, indeed, not involuntarily and semiconsciously, but intentionally and methodically. Here I cite the impressive statement of Usener who, although he knew nothing of phenomenology, was fully aware of what it implies: "Only by surrendering oneself, and by submersion in these spiritual traces of vanished time[18] . . . can we train ourselves to recall their feeling; then chords within ourselves, gradually becoming sympathetic, can harmoniously vibrate and resound, and we discover in our own consciousness the strands linking together old and new."[19] This too is what Dilthey describes as the "experience of a structural connection," such experience, it is true, being more an art than a science.[20] It is in fact the primal and primitively human art of the actor which is indispensable to all arts, but to the sciences of mind also—to sympathize keenly and closely with experience other than one's own, but also with one's own experience of

yesterday, already become strange! To this sympathetic experience, of course, there are limits; but these are also set to our understanding of ourselves, it may be to an even greater degree; *homo sum, humani nil a me alienum puto:* this is no key to the deepest comprehension of the remotest experience, but is nevertheless the triumphant assertion that the essentially human always remains essentially human, and is, as such, comprehensible—unless indeed he who comprehends has acquired too much of the professor and retained too little of the man! . . . Only the persistent and strenuous application of this intense sympathy, only the uninterrupted learning of his role, qualifies the phenomenologist to interpret appearances. In Jaspers' pertinent words: "Thus every psychologist experiences the increasing clarity of his mental life for himself; he becomes aware of what has hitherto remained unnoticed, although he never reaches the ultimate limit."[21]

C. Not only is the "ultimate limit" never attainable in the sense referred to by Jaspers: it implies, still further, the unattainability of existence. Phenomenology, therefore, is neither metaphysics, nor the comprehension of empirical reality. It observes *restraint* (the *epoche*), and its understanding of events depends on its employing "brackets."[22] Phenomenology is concerned only with "phenomena," that is with "appearance"; for it, there is nothing whatever "behind" the phenomenon. This restraint, still further, implies no mere methodological device, no cautious procedure, but the distinctive characteristic of man's whole attitude to reality. Scheler has very well expressed this situation: "to be human means to hurl a forcible 'No!' at this sort of reality. Buddha realized this when he said how magnificent it is to *contemplate* everything, and how terrible it is to *be:* Plato, too, in connecting the contemplation of ideas to a diverting of the soul from the sensuous content of objects, and to the diving at the soul into its own depths, in order to find the origins; of things. Husserl, also, implies nothing different than this when he links the knowledge of ideas with 'phenomenological reduction'—that is a 'crossing through' or 'bracketing' of (the accidental) coefficients of the existence of objects in the world in order to obtain their *essentia*."[23] This of course involves no preference of some "idealism" or other to some kind of "realism." On the contrary: it is simply maintained that man can be positive only in turning away from things, as they are given to him chaotically and formlessly, and by first assigning them form and meaning. Phenomenology, therefore, is not a method that has been reflectively elaborated, but is man's true vital activity, consisting in losing himself neither in things nor in the *ego*, neither in hovering above objects like a god nor dealing with them like an animal, but in doing what is given to neither animal nor god: comprehendingly standing aside and contemplating what appears.

D. Contemplation of appearances implies a *clarification* of what has been observed: all that belongs to the same order must be united, while what is different in type must be separated. These distinctions, however, should certainly not be decided by appealing to causal connections in the sense that A arises from B, while C has its own origin uniting it to D—but solely and simply by employing structural relations somewhat as the landscape painter combines his groups of objects, or separates them from one another. The juxtaposition, in other words, must not become externalization, but structural association;[24] and this means that we seek the ideal typical interrelation, and then attempt to arrange this within some yet wider whole of significance, etc.[25]

E. All these activities, undertaken together and simultaneously, constitute genuine *comprehension:* the chaotic and obstinate "reality" thus becomes a manifestation, a revelation. The empirical, ontal or metaphysical *fact* becomes a *datum;* the object, living speech; rigidity, expression.[26] "The sciences of mind are based on the relations between experience, expression and comprehension":[27] I understand this to mean that the intangible experience in itself cannot be apprehended nor mastered, but that it manifests something to us, an appearance: says something, an utterance. The aim of science, therefore is to understand this *logos;* essentially, science is hermeneutics.[28]

Now when we are concerned, as in our own case, with the domain of historical research, this would appear to be the stage at which historical scepticism threateningly intrudes into our investigations, and renders all comprehension of remote times and regions impossible to us. We might then reply that we are quite ready to acknowledge that we can *know* nothing, and that we admit, further, that perhaps we understand very little; but that, on the other hand, to understand the Egyptian of the first dynasty is, in itself, no more difficult than to understand my nearest neighbour. Certainly the monuments of the first dynasty are intelligible only with great difficulty, but as an expression, as a human statement, they are no harder than my colleague's letters. In this respect, indeed, the historian can learn from the psychiatrist: "If we are astonished by an ancient myth or an Egyptian head, and confront it with the conviction that there is something that is intelligible in accord with our own experience, although it is infinitely remote from us and unattainable, just as we are amazed by a psycho-pathological process or an abnormal character, we have at least the possibility of a more deeply comprehending glance, and perhaps of achieving a living representation. . . ."[29]

F. But if phenomenology is to complete its own task, it imperatively requires perpetual correction by the most conscientious philological and archaeological research. It must therefore always be prepared for confrontation with material facts, although the actual manipulation of these facts themselves cannot proceed without interpretation—that is without phenomenology; and every exegesis, every translation, indeed every reading, is already hermeneutics. But this purely philological hermeneutics has a more restricted purpose than the purely phenomenological. For it is concerned in the first place with the Text, and then with the fact in the sense of what is concretely implied, of what can be translated in other words. This of course necessitates meaning, only it is a shallower and broader meaning than phenomenological comprehension.[30] But as soon as the latter withdraws itself from control by philological and archaeological interpretation, it becomes pure art or empty fantasy.[31]

G.   This entire and apparently complicated procedure, in conclusion, has ultimately no other goal than pure objectivity. Phenomenology aims not at things, still less at their mutual relations, and least of all at the "thing in itself." It desires to gain access to the facts themselves;[32] and for this it requires a meaning, because it cannot experience the facts just as it pleases. This meaning, however, is purely objective: all violence, either empirical, logical, or metaphysical, is excluded. Phenomenology regards every event in the same way that Ranke looked on each epoche as "in an immediate and direct relation to God," so that "its value depends in no degree on whatever results from it, but on its existence as such, on its own self."[33] It holds itself quite apart from modern thought, which would teach us "to contemplate the world as unformed material, which we must first of all form, and conduct ourselves as the lords of the world."[34] It has, in fact, one sole desire: *to testify* to what has been manifested to it.[35] This it can do only by indirect methods, by a second experience of the event, by a thorough reconstruction; and from this road it must remove many obstacles. To see face to face is denied to us. But much can be observed even in a mirror; and it is possible to speak about things seen.

Religion

1. We can try to comprehend religion from a flat plain, from ourselves as the centre; and we can also understand how the essence of religion is to be grasped only from above, beginning with God. In other words: we can—in the matter already indicated—contemplate religion as intelligible experience; or we can concede to it the status of incomprehensible revelation. For in its "reconstruction," experience is a phenomenon. Revelation is not; but man's reply to revelation, his assertion about what was been revealed, is also a phenomenon from which, indirectly, conclusions concerning the revelation itself can be derived (*per viam negationis*).

Considered in the light of both of these methods, religion implies that man does not simply accept the life that is given to him. In life he seeks *power;* and he does not find this, or not to an extent that satisfies him, then he attempts to draw the power, in which he believes, into his own life. He tries to elevate life, to enhance its value, to gain for it some deeper and wider meaning. In this way, however, we find ourselves on the horizontal line: religion is the extension of life to its uttermost limit. The religious man desires richer, deeper, wider life: he desires power for himself. In other terms: in and about his own life man seeks something that is superior, whether he wishes merely to make use of this or to worship it.

He who does not merely accept life, then, but demands something from it—that is, power—endeavours to find some meaning in life. He arranges life into a significant whole: and thus culture arises. Over the variety of the given he throws his systematically fashioned net, on which various designs appear: a work of art, a custom, an economy. From the stone he makes himself an image, from the instinct a commandment, from the wilderness a tilled field; and thus he develops power. But he never halts; he seeks ever further for constantly deeper and wider *meaning*. When he realizes that a flower is beautiful and bears fruit, he enquires for its ampler, ultimate significance; when he knows that his wife is beautiful, that she can work and bear children, when he perceives that he must respect another man's wife, just as he would have his own respected, he seeks still further and asks for her final meaning. Thus he finds the secret of the flower and of woman; and so he discovers their religious significance.

The religious significance of things, therefore, is that on which no wider nor deeper meaning whatever can follow. It is the meaning of the whole: it is the last word. But this meaning is never understood, this last word is never spoken; always they remain superior, the ultimate meaning being a secret which reveals itself repeatedly, only nevertheless to remain eternally concealed. It implies an advance to the farthest boundary, where only one sole fact is understood—that all comprehension is "beyond"; and thus the ultimate meaning is at the same moment the limit of meaning.[36]

Homo religiosus thus betakes himself to the road to omnipotence, to complete understanding, to ultimate meaning. He would fain comprehend life, in order to dominate it. As he understands soil so as to make it fruitful, as he learns how to follow animals' ways, so as to subject them to himself—so too he resolves to comprehend the world, in order to subjugate it to himself. Therefore he perpetually seeks new superiorities: until at last he stands at the very frontier and perceives that the ultimate superiority he will never attain, but that it reaches him in an incomprehensible and mysterious way. Thus the horizontal line of religion resembles the way of St. Christopher, who seeks his master and at last finds him too.

2. But there is also a vertical way: from below upwards, and from above downwards. This way however is not, like the former, an experience that passed through before a frontier. It is a revelation, coming from beyond that frontier. The horizontal path, again, is an experience which certainly has an inkling or presage of revelation, but which cannot attain to it. The vertical way, on the other hand, is a revelation, which never becomes completely experienced, though it participates in experience. The first road is certainly not a tangible, but is all the more an intelligible, phenomenon. The second is not a phenomenon at all, and is neither attainable nor comprehensible; what we obtain from it phenomenologi-

cally, therefore, is merely its reflection in experience. We can never comprehend God's utterance by means of any purely intellectual capacity: what we can understand is only our own answer; and in this sense, too, it is true that we have the treasure only in an earthen vessel.

Man, seeking power in life, does not reach the frontier; but he realizes that he has been removed to some foreign region. Thus he not only reaches the place from which a prospect of infinite distance is disclosed to him, but he knows too that, while he is still on the way, he is at every moment surrounded by marvellous and far-off things. He has not only a firm assurance (*Ahnung*) of the superior, but is also directly seized by it. He has not merely descried the throne of the Lord *from afar,* and fain would have sent on his heart in advance, but he realizes too that *this* place itself is dreadful, because it is a "house of God" and a "gate of heaven." Perhaps angels descend to his resting place: perhaps demons press upon his path. But he knows quite definitely that *something meets him on the road*. It may be the angel who goes before him and will lead him safely: it may be the angel with the flashing sword who forbids him the road. But it is quite certain that something foreign has traversed the way of his own powerfulness.

And just because it is not to be found in the prolongation of man's own path, this strange element has no name whatever. Otto has suggested "the numinous," probably because this expression says nothing at all! This foreign element, again, can be approached only *per viam negationis;* and here again it is Otto who has found the correct term in his designation "the Wholly Other." For this, however, religions themselves have coined the word "holy." The German term is derived from Heil, "powerfulness"; the Semitic and Latin, *sanctus,* and the primitive expression, *tabu,* have the fundamental meaning of "separated," "set aside by itself." Taken all together, they provide the description of what occurs in all religious experience: *a strange, "Wholly Other," Power obtrudes into life.*

Man's attitude to it is first of all *astonishment,* and ultimately *faith.*

3. The limit of human powerfulness, in conclusion, and the commencement of the divine, together constitute the goal which has been sought and found in the religion of all time—*salvation.* It may be the enhancing of life, improvement, beautifying, widening, deepening; but by "salvation" there may also be meant completely new life, a devaluation of all that has preceded, a new creation of the life that has been received "from elsewhere." But in any case, religion is always directed towards salvation, never towards life itself as it is given; and in this respect all religion, with no exception, is the religion of deliverance.[37]

The Phenomenology of Religion

1. Phenomenology is the systematic discussion of what appears. Religion, however, is an ultimate experience that evades our observation, a revelation which in its very essence is, and remains, concealed. But how shall I deal with what is thus ever elusive and hidden? How can I pursue phenomenology when there is no phenomenon? How can I refer to "phenomenology of religion" at all?

Here there clearly exists an antinomy that is certainly essential to all religions, but also to all understanding; it is indeed precisely because it holds good for *both,* for religion and understanding alike, that our own science becomes possible. It is unquestionably quite correct to say that faith and intellectual suspense (the *epoche*) do not exclude each other. It may further be urged that the Catholic Church, too, recognizes a *duplex ordo* of contemplation, on the one hand purely rational, and on the other wholly in accord with faith; while such a Catholic as Przywara also wishes to exclude every apologetic subsidiary aim from philosophy, and strenuously maintains the *epoche.* But at the same time one cannot but recognize that all these reflections are the result of embarrassment. For it is at bottom utterly impossible contemplatively to confront an event which, on the one hand, is an ultimate experience, and on the other manifests itself in profound emotional agitation, in the attitude of such pure intellectual restraint. Apart from the existential attitude that is concerned with reality, we could never know anything of either religion or faith. It may certainly be advisable and useful methodically to presuppose this intellectual suspense; it is also expedient, since crude prejudice can so readily force its way into situations where only such an existential attitude would be justifiable. But, once again, how shall we comprehend the life of religion merely by contemplative observation from a distance? How indeed can we understand what, in principle, wholly eludes our understanding?

Now we have already found that not the comprehension of religion alone, but *all* comprehension without exception, ultimately reaches the limit where it loses its own proper name and can only be called "becoming understood." In other words: the more deeply comprehension penetrates any event, the better it "understands" it, the clearer it becomes to the understanding mind that the ultimate ground of comprehension lies not within itself, but in some "other" by which it is comprehended from beyond the frontier. Without this absolutely valid and decisive comprehension, indeed, there would be no understanding whatever. For all comprehension that extends "to the ground" ceases to be comprehension before it reaches the ground, and recognizes itself as a "becoming understood." In other terms: all comprehension, irrespective of whatever object it refers to, is ultimately religious: all significance sooner or later leads to ultimate significance. . . .

Understanding, in fact, itself presupposes intellectual restraint. But this is never the attitude of the cold-blooded spectator: it is, on the contrary, the loving gaze of the lover on the beloved object. For all understanding rests upon self-surrendering love. Were that not the case, then not only all discussion of what appears in religion, but all discussion of appearance in general, would be quite impossible; since to him who does not love, nothing whatever is manifested; this is the Platonic, as well as the Christian, experience.

I shall therefore not anticipate fruitlessly, and convert phenomenology into theology. Nor do I wish to assert that the faith upon which all comprehension is grounded, and religion as itself faith, are without further ado identical. But "it is plainly insufficient to permit theology to follow on philosophy (for my purpose, read 'phenomenology') purely in virtue of its content, since the fundamental problem is one of method, and concerns the claim of philosophy (again, here, phenomenology) to justification in view of the obvious data, and also the impossibility of referring back faith as the methodical basis of theology, to these data. In other terms: the problem becomes that of what is obviously evidence."[38] And I am prepared, with Przywara, to seek the intimate relationship that nevertheless exists between faith and the obvious data, in the fact that the evidence they provide is essentially a "preparedness for revelation."[39]

2. The use of the expression: history of religion, science of religion, comparative history of religion, psychology of religion, philosophy of religion: and others similar to these, is still very loose and inexact; and this is not merely a formal defect, but is practical also.[40] It is true that the different subdivisions of the sciences concerned with religion (the expression here is employed in its widest possible sense), cannot subsist independently of each other; they require, indeed, incessant mutual assistance. But much that is essential is forfeited as soon as the limits of the investigation are lost to sight. The history of religion, the philosophy and psychology of religion, and alas! theology also, are each and all harsh mistresses, who would fain compel their servants to pass beneath the yoke which they hold ready for them; and the phenomenology of religion desires not only to distinguish itself from them, but also, if possible, to teach them to restrain themselves! I shall therefore

first of all indicate what the phenomenology of religion is not, and what fails to correspond to its own essential character in the character or usage of the other disciplines.

The phenomenology of religion, then, is not the poetry of religion; and to say this is not at all superfluous, since I have myself expressly referred to the poetic character of the structural experience of ideal types. In this sense, too, we may understand Aristotle's assertion that the historian relates what has happened, while the poet recounts what might have occurred under any given circumstances; and that poetry is therefore a philosophical affair and of more serious import than history; as against all bare historicism and all mere chronicle, this should always be remembered. Nor should it be forgotten that art is just as much investigation as is science, which forces itself into notice in the procedure of both from beginning to end: in his own work, then, the phenomenologist is bound up with the object; he cannot proceed without repeatedly confronting the chaos of the given, and without submitting again and again to correction by the facts; while although the artist certainly sets out from the object, he is not inseparably linked with this. In other words: the poet need know no particular language, nor study the history of times; even the poet of so-called historical novel need not do this. In order to interpret a myth he may completely remodel it, as for example Wagner treated the German and Celtic heroic sagas. Here the phenomenologist experiences his own limit, since the path lies always between the unformed chaos of the historical world and its structural endowment with form. All his life he oscillates hither and thither. But the poet advances.

Secondly, the phenomenology of religion is not the history of religion. History, certainly, cannot utter one word without adopting some phenomonological viewpoint; even a translation, or the editing of a Text, cannot be completed without hermeneutics. On the other hand, the phenomenologist can only work with historical material, since he must know what documents are available and what their character is, before he can undertake their interpretation. The historian and the phenomenologist, therefore, work in the closest possible association; they are indeed in the majority of cases combined in the person of a *single* investigator. Nevertheless the historian's task is essentially different from the phenomenologist's, and pursues other aims.[41] For the historian, everything is directed first of all to establishing what has actually happened; and in this he can never succeed unless he understands. But also, when he fails to understand, he must describe what he has found, even if he remains at the stage of mere cataloguing. But when the phenomenologist ceases to comprehend, he can have no more to say. He strides here and there; the historian of course does the same, but more frequently he stands still, and often he does not stir at all. If he is a poor historian, this will be due only to idleness or incapacity; but if he is a sound historian, then his halts imply a very necessary and admirable resignation.

Thirdly, the phenomenology of religion is not a psychology of religion. Modern psychology, certainly, appears in so many forms that it becomes difficult to define its limits with respect to other subjects.[42] But that phenomenology is not identical with experimental psychology should be sufficiently obvious, though it is harder to separate it from the psychology of form and structure. Nevertheless it is probably the common feature of all psychologies that they are concerned only with the psychical. The psychology of religion, accordingly, attempts to comprehend the psychical aspects of religion. In so far therefore as the psychical is expressed and involved in all that is religious, phenomenology and psychology have a common task. But in religion far more appears than the merely psychical: the whole man participates in it, is active within it and is affected by it. In this sphere, then, psychology would enjoy competence only if it rose to the level of the science of Spirit—of course in its philosophic sense—in general which, it must be said, is not seldom the case.

But if we are to restrict psychology to its own proper object, it may be said that the phenomenologist of religion strides backwards and forwards over the whole field of religious life, but the psychologist of religion over only a part of this.

Fourthly, the phenomenology of religion is not a philosophy of religion, although it may be regarded as a preparation therefore. For it is systematic, and constitutes the bridge between the special sciences concerned with the history of religion and philosophical contemplation.[43] Of course phenomenology leads to problems of a philosophic and metaphysical character, "which it is itself not empowered to submit";[44] and the philosophy of religion can never dispense with its phenomenology. Too often already has that philosophy of religion been elaborated which naively set out from "Christianity"—that is, from the Western European standpoint of the nineteenth century, or even from the humanistic deism of the close of the eighteenth century. But whoever wishes to philosophize about religion must know what it is concerned with; he should not presuppose this as self-evident. Nevertheless the aim of the philosopher of religion is quite different; and while he must certainly know what the religious issues are, still he has something other in view; he wishes to move what he has discovered by means of the dialectical motion of Spirit. His progress, too, is hither and thither: only not in the sense of phenomenology; rather is it immanent in the Spirit. Every philosopher, indeed, has somewhat of God within him: it is quite seemly that he should stir the world in his inner life. But the phenomenologist should not become merely frightened by the idea of any similarity to God: he must shun it as the sin against the very spirit of his science.

Finally, phenomenology of religion is not theology. For theology shares with philosophy the claim to search for truth, while phenomenology, in this respect, exercises the intellectual suspense of the epoche. But the contrast lies even deeper than this. Theology discusses not merely a horizontal line leading, it may be, to God, nor only a vertical, descending from God and ascending from Him. Theology speaks about God Himself. For phenomenology, however, God is neither subject nor object; to be either of these He would have to be a phenomenon—that is, He would have to appear. But He does not appear: at least not so that we can comprehend and speak about Him. If He does appear He does so in a totally different manner, which results not in intelligible utterance, but in proclamation; and it is with this that theology has to deal. It too has a path "hither and thither"; but the "hither" and the "thither" are not the given and its interpretation, but concealment and revelation, heaven and earth, perhaps heaven, earth and hell. Of heaven and hell, however, phenomenology knows nothing at all; it is at home on earth, although it is at the same time sustained by love of the beyond.

3. In accordance with what has been remarked . . . the phenomenology of religion must in the first place assign names—sacrifice, prayer, saviour, myth, etc. In this way it appeals to appearances. Secondly, it must interpolate these appearances within its own life and experience them systematically. And in the third place, it must withdraw to one side, and endeavour to observe what appears while adopting the attitude of intellectual suspense. Fourthly, it attempts to clarify what it has seen, and again (combining all its previous activities) try to comprehend what has appeared. Finally, it must confront chaotic "reality," and its still uninterpreted signs, and ultimately testify to what it has understood. Nevertheless all sorts of problems that may be highly interesting in themselves must thereby be excluded. Thus phenomenology knows nothing of any historical "development" of religion. Its perpetual task is to free itself from every non- phenomenological standpoint and to retain its own liberty, while it conserves the inestimable value of this position always anew.[45]

Power

1. That which those sciences concerned with Religion regard as the *Object* of Religion is, for Religion itself, the active and primary Agent in the situation or, in this sense of the term, the *Subject*. In other words, the religious man perceives that with which his religion deals as primal, as originative or causal; and only to reflective thought does this become the Object of the experience that is contemplated. For Religion, then, God is the active Agent in relation to man, while the sciences in question can concern themselves only with the activity of man in his relation to God; of acts of God Himself they can give no account whatever.

2. But when we say that *God* is the Object or religious experience, we must realize that "God" is frequently an extremely indefinite concept which does not completely coincide with what we ourselves usually understand by it. Religious experience, in other terms, is concerned with a "Somewhat." But this assertion often means no more than that this "Somewhat" is merely a vague "something"; and in order that man may be able to make more significant statements about this "Somewhat," it must force itself upon him, must oppose itself to him as being Something *Other*. Thus the first affirmation we can make about the Object of Religion is that it is a *highly exceptional* and *extremely impressive* "Other." Subjectively, again, the initial state of man's mind is amazement; and as Soderblom has remarked, this is true not only for philosophy but equally for religion. As yet, it must further be observed, we are in no way concerned with the supernatural or the transcendent: we can speak of "God" in a merely figurative sense; but there arises and persists an experience which connects or unites itself to the "Other" that thus obtrudes. Theory, and even the slightest degree of generalization, are still far remote; man remains quite content with the purely practical recognition that this Object is a departure from all that is usual and familiar; and this again

is the consequence of the *Power* it generates. The most primitive religious experience, therefore, and even a large proportion of that of antiquity, we must in this respect accustom ourselves to interpret the supernatural element in the conception of God by the simple notion of an "Other," of something foreign and highly unusual, and at the same time the consciousness of absolute dependence, so well known to ourselves, by an indefinite and generalized feeling of remoteness.

3. In a letter written by the missionary R. H. Codrington, and published by Max Müller in 1878, the idea of *mana* was referred to for the first time, and naturally in the style of those days, as a "Melanesian name for the Infinite," this description of course being due to Müller.[46] . . . In the South Sea Islands *mana* always means a Power; but the islanders include in this term, together with its derivatives and compounds, such various substantival, adjectival and verbal ideas as Influence, Strength, Fame, Majesty, Intelligence, Authority, Deity, Capability, extraordinary Power: whatever is successful, strong, plenteous: to reverence, be capable, to adore and to prophesy. It is quite obvious, however, that the supernatural, in our sense of this term, cannot here be intended. . . . Now *mana* actually has this significance; the warrior's *mana*, for instance, is demonstrated by his continuous success in combat, while repeated defeat shows that his *mana* has deserted him. . . . Power may be employed in magic, while the magical character pertains to every unusual action; yet it would be quite erroneous to designate potency in general as magical power, and Dynamism as the theory of magic. Magic is certainly manifested by power; to employ power, however, is not in itself to act magically, although every extraordinary action of primitive man possesses a tinge of the magical.[47] The creation of the earth is the effect of the divine *mana*, but so is all capacity; the chief's power, the happiness of the country, depend on *mana*: similarly the beam of the latrine has its own mode, probably because excreta, like all parts of the body, function as receptacles of power. . . .

It is inevitable, still further, that since Power is in no degree systematically understood, it is never homogeneous nor uniform. One may possess either great or limited *mana;* two magicians may attack each other by employing two sorts of *mana*. Power enjoys no moral value whatever. *Mana* resides alike in the poisoned arrow and in European remedies, while with the Iroquois *orenda*[48] one both blesses and curses. It is simply a matter of Power, alike for good or evil.

4. Codrington's discovery was followed by others in the most diverse parts of the world. The *orenda* of the Iroquois has just been referred to; "it appears that they interpreted the activities of Nature as the ceaseless strife between one *orenda* and another."[49] The Sioux Indians, again, believe in *wakanda,* at one time a god of the type of originator, at another an impersonal Power which acquires empirical verification whenever something extraordinary is manifested. Sun and moon, a horse (a *wakanda*-dog!), cult implements, places with striking features: all alike are regarded as *wakan* or *wakanda,* and once again its significance must be expressed by widely different terms— powerful, holy, ancient, great, etc. In this instance also the theoretical problem of the universality of *wakanda* is not raised; the mind still remains at the standpoint of empirically substantiating the manifestation of Power.

In contrast with *mana,* however, and together with some other ideas of Power, *wakanda* represents one specific type, since it is capable of transformation into the conception of a more or less personal god. This is also the case with the *manitu* of the Algonquins of North-West America, which is a power that confers their capacity on either harmful or beneficent objects, and gives to European missionaries their superiority over native medicine-men. Animals are *manido* whenever they possess supernatural power; but *manitu* is also employed in a personal sense for spirit, and *kitshi manitu* is the Great Spirit, the Originator. . . .

Finally, Power may be assigned to some definite bearer or possessor from whom it emanates. Such a power is the Arabian *baraka*, which is regarded as an emanation from holy men and closely connected with their graves; it is acquired by pilgrimage, and to be cured of some disease a king's wife seeks the *baraka* of a saint. This beneficent power also is confined to specific localities; thus the place in which to study is not indifferent so far as its results are concerned, and in Mecca "the attainment of knowledge is facilitated by the *baraka* of the spot."[50]

5. But even when Power is not expressly assigned a name the idea of Power often forms the basis of religion, as we shall be able to observe almost continually in the sequel. Among extensive divisions of primitive peoples, as also those of antiquity, the Power in the Universe was almost invariably an impersonal Power. Thus we may speak of Dynamism—of the interpretation of the Universe in terms of Power; I prefer this expression to both Animism and Pre-Animism—to the former because "Universal Animism" smacks too much of theory. The primitive mind never halts before the distinction between inorganic, and organic, Nature; what it is always concerned with is not Life, which appears to explain itself, but Power, authenticated purely empirically by one occurrence after another; thus the Winnebago (Sioux) offers tobacco to any unusual object because it is *wakan*. From the term "Pre-Animism," however, it would be inferred that, chronologically, priority is due to the idea of Power as contrasted with other conceptions such as the animistic. But here there can be no question whatever as to earlier or later stages in development, but quite simply of the texture or constitution of the religious spirit, as this predominated in other and earlier cultures than our own, but also as it lives and flourishes even in our own day.

6. To recapitulate: I have dealt with the idea of Power which empirically, and within some form of experience, becomes authenticated in things and persons, and by virtue of which these are influential and effective. This potency is of different types: it is attributed to what we regard as sublime, such as Creation, exactly as it is to pure capacity or "luck." It remains merely dynamic, and not in the slightest degree ethical or "spiritual." Nor can we speak of any "primitive Monism," since to do so presupposes theory that does not as yet exist. Power is thought of only when it manifests itself in some very striking way; with what confronts efficiency on objects and persons in ordinary circumstances, on the other hand, man does not concern himself. At the same time it is quite true that the idea of Power, as soon as it becomes incorporated within other cultural conditions, expands and deepens into the concept of a Universal Power.

To this Power, in conclusion, man's reaction is amazement (*Scheu*), and in extreme cases fear. Marett employs the fine term "awe"; and this attitude is characterized by Power being regarded, not indeed as supernatural, but as extraordinary, of some markedly unusual type, while objects and persons endowed with this potency have that essential nature of their own which we call "sacred."

Potency, Awe, Tabu

1. The experience of the potency of things or persons may occur at any time; it is by no means confined to specific seasons and occasions. Powerfulness always reveals itself in some wholly unexpected manner; and life is therefore a dangerous affair, full of critical moments. If then one examines them more closely, even the most ordinary events, the customary associations with one's neighbours, or similarly one's long familiar tasks, prove to be replete with "mystic" interconnections. . . .

Objects, persons, times, places or actions charged with Power are called *tabu (tapu)*, a word from the same cultural domain as *mana*. It indicated "what is expressly named," "exceptional," while the verb *tapui* means "to make holy."[51] Tabu is thus a sort of warning:

"Danger! High Voltage!" Power has been stored up, and we must be on our guard. The *tabu* is the expressly authenticated condition of being replete with power, and man's reaction to it should rest on a clear recognition of this potent fullness, should maintain the proper distance and secure protection.

The *tabu* is observed in different ways and with regard to highly contrasted objects. To the Greek the *king* and the *foreigner* or *stranger* appeared as objects of *aidos,* of awe, to be duly respected by keeping one's distance.[52] Almost everywhere the king is looked upon as powerful, so that he should be approached only with the greatest caution, while the foreigner, bearer of a power unknown and therefore to be doubly feared, stands on an equal footing with an enemy; *hostis* is both stranger or foreigner, and enemy. . . .

2. We characterize the distance between the potent and the relatively powerless as the relationship between *sacred* and *profane,* or secular. The "sacred" is what has been placed within boundaries, the exceptional (Latin *sanctus*); its powerfulness creates for it a place of its own. "Sacred" therefore means neither completely moral nor, without further qualification, even desirable or praiseworthy. On the contrary, sacredness and even impurity may be identical: in any event the potent is dangerous. The Roman *tribunus plebis,* just referred to, was so sacred, *sacrosanctus,* that merely to meet him on the street made one impure.[53] Among the Maori also *tapu* means "polluted" just as much as "holy"; but in any case it carries a prohibition with it, and therefore prescribes keeping one's proper distance. It is, then, scarcely correct to regard the contrast between sacred and secular as developing out of the distinction between threatening danger and what is not perilous.[54] Power has its own specific quality which forcibly impresses men as dangerous. Yet the perilous is not the sacred, but rather the sacred dangerous. In a quite classical way Soderblom has presented the contrast between holy and profane as the primal, and governing antithesis in all religion, and has shown how the old viewpoint, that Wonder . . . is the beginning of Philosophy, can be applied with yet greater justice to Religion. For whoever is confronted with potency clearly realizes that he is in the presence of some quality with which in his previous experience he was never familiar, and which cannot be evoked from something else but which, *sui generis* and *sui juris,* can be designated only by religious terms such as "sacred" and "numinous." All these terms have a common factor in that they indicate a firm conviction, but at the same time no definite conception, of the completely different, the absolutely distinct. The first impulse aroused by all this is avoidance, but also seeking: man should avoid Power, but he should also seek it. No longer can there be a "why" or "wherefore" here; and Soderblom is undeniably correct when, in this connection, he defines the essence of all religion by saying that it is mystery.[55] Of that aspect there was already a deep subjective assurance even when no god was invoked. For to religion "god" is a late comer.

3. In the human soul, then, Power awakens a profound feeling of awe which manifests itself both as fear and as being attracted. There is no religion whatever without terror, but equally none without love, or that *nuance* of being attracted which corresponds to the prevailing ethical level. For the simplest form of religious feeling Marett has suggested the fine word *Awe,* and Otto the term *Scheu,* which is somewhat less comprehensive; the Greek *aidos* too is most impertinent.[56] The expression adopted must be a very general one, since it is a question of establishing an attitude which includes the whole personality at all its levels and in countless *nuances.* Physical shuddering, ghostly horror, fear, sudden terror, reverence, humility, adoration, profound apprehension, enthusiasm—all these lie *in nuce* within the awe experienced in the presence of Power. And because these attitudes show two main tendencies, one away from Power and the other towards it, we speak of the *ambivalent* nature of awe.

Of course *tabu* means a prohibition, and Power reveals itself first of all always as something to be avoided. Everywhere, too, the prohibition announces itself earlier than the command; but Freud has very ably shown how the former always implies the latter.[57] Man is fully conscious only of the prohibition, while the command usually remains unrecognized. What we hate we love, and what we truly love we could at the same time hate. "For each man kills the thing he loves," said Oscar Wilde, and this is far more than a brilliant phrase. In the presence of the something different which we recognize as "Wholly Other," our conduct is always ambivalent. Love may be described as an attempt to force oneself into the place of the other; hate, as the fear of love.

NOTES

1. The term "experience" (*erlebnis*) is itself objectively oriented (we always experience something) and designates a "structure"; cf. Note, p. 461.

2. Dilthey, *Gesammelte Schiften*, VII, 194.

3. *Ibid.*, 195.

4. cf. E. Spranger, *Die Einheit der Psychologie, Sitzbar. d. Preuss, Akad. d. Wiss.* 24, 1926, 188, 191. F. Kruger, Ber. *uber den* Viii. *Kongress fur experim.* Psych., 33.

5. cf. on a different field of research, P. Bekker, *Musikgeschichte*, 1926, 2.

6. The so-called hermeneutic circle, to which G. Wobbermin particularly drew attention; cf. Wach, *Religionswissenchaft*, 49.

7. cf. A.A. Grunbaum, *Herrscen und Lieben*, 1925, 17. Spranger, *Lebensformen*, 6 *ff.*

8. Spranger, *Ibid.*, 436.

9. Spranger, *Einheit der Psychologie*, 177; cf. Wach's observation that the close connection between the theory of types and that of hermeneutics has not yet been adequately emphasized; *Religionswissenchaft*, 149.

10. This term was introduced by Karl Jaspers: *verstandliche Beziehungen.*

11. On the history of the idea cf. B. Pfister, *Die Entfuhrung in die Probleme der allgemeinen Psychologi*, 206; van der Leeuw, *Uber gischen Forschung und irhe Anwendung auf die Geschichte, insonderheit die Religionsgeschichte*, SM. II, 1926, *passim; cf.* further P. Hofmann, *Das religiose Erlebnis*, 1925, 8.

12. Spranger, *Lebensformen*, 115; Binswanger, *Einführung in die Probleme der allgemeinen Psychologic*, 296.

13. What I myself understand by the phenomenology of religion is called by Hackmann "The General Science of Religion"; other terms for this type of research that have appeared (once more to disappear, however) are "Transcendental Psychology," "Eidology," and *Formenlehre der religiosen Vorstellungen* (Usener).

14. McDougall, *An Outline of Psychology*, 284.

15. *Farbenlehre* in Binswanger, *op. cit.*, 31.

16. The expression usually employed, "Empathy" (*Einfuhllung*) overstresses the feeling aspect of the process, although not without some justification.

17. Spranger, op. cit. 430.

18. This applies equally to the so-called "present."

19. *Gotternamen*, 1896, VII.

20. Binswanger, op. cit., 246; van der Leeuw, op. cit., 14f.

21. Chesterton, *The Everlasting Man, 111; cf.* Hofmann, *Religioses Erlebnis*, 4f.

22. K. Jaspers, *Allgemeine Psychopathologie*, 1923, 204.

23. Max Scheler, *Die Stellung des Menschen im Kosmos*, 1928, 63; cf. Heidegger, *Sein und Zeit*, 38.

24. Binswanger, op. cit., 302; cf. Jaspers, *Psychopathologie*, 18, 35.

25. Spranger, *Lebensformen*, II.

26. Heidegger, op. cit., 37; Dilthey, op. cit., VII, 71, 86.

27. Dilthey, *Ibid.*, 131.

28. Binswanger, *op. cit.*, 244, 288.

29. Jaspers, *Psychopathologie*, 404; cf. Usener, *Gotternamen*, 62.

30. Spranger gives an excellent example in his comparison of the ever more deeply penetrating meanings of a biblical text; *Einheit der Psychologie*, 180 ff.

31. Wach, *Religionswissenchaft*, 117; van der Leeuw, op. cit., *passim.*

32. Heidegger, op. cit., 34.

33. L. von Ranke, *Weltgeschichte*, VIII, 1921, 177.

34. E. Brunner, *Gott und Mensch*, 1930, 40.

35. cf. W.J. Aalders, *Wetenschap als Getuigenis*, 1930.

36. Spranger, op. cit., *passim.*

37. Hofmann, *Das religiose Erlebnis*, 12 ff.

38. Przywara, *Ibid.*, 92.

39. *Ibid.*, 95.

40. Wach, *Religionswissenchaft,* 12.

41. Wach, *Ibid.,* 56.

42. cf. Spranger, *Einheit der Psychologie.*

43. Wach, *Rel. wiss.* 131.

44. Wach, *Rel. wiss.* 82.

45. Th. de Laguna, "The Sociological Method of Durkheim," *Phil. Rev.* 29, 1920, 224. E. Troeltsche, *Gesammelte Schriften,* II, 1913, 490.

46. Jaspers, *Allgemeine Psychopathologie,* 36.

47. *Begrebet Angest (The Concept of Dread), Saml. Vaerker,* IV, 1923, 360; cf. the entire fine passage.

48. "To seek to derive numinous power for, magical is altogether to invert the situation, since long before the magician could appropriate and manipulate it, it had been 'apperceived as numinous' in plant and animal, in natural processes and objects, in the horror of the skeleton, and also independently of all these." Otto, *Gefuhl des Uberweltlichen,* 56.

49. Hewitt, "Orenda and a Definition of Religion," *Amer. Anthropologist,* N.S. IV, 1902.

50. O. Rescher, *Studien uber den Inhalt von 1001 Nacht, Islam* 9, 1918, 24 f.

51. Soderblom, *Das Werden des Gottesglaubens,* 31 f.

52. cf. Theol. *Worterbuch zum N.T.*

53. Plutarch, *Queaestiones romanae,* 81. This passage seems not quite clear, but in any case impurity, involved by the sacredness of the tribune, is implied.

54. As B. Anlermann does in Chantepie, 152; cf. General Literature, p.19 *ante.*

55. Very well expressed in the essay: "Points of Contact for Missionary Work," *Int. Review of Missions,* 1919.

56. cf. Murray, *The Rise of the Greek Epic.*

57. *Totem and Taboo,* 31 f., 41 f,

Counterpoint:
An Ambivalent Relationship to the Holy:
Gerardus van der Leeuw on Religion

RICHARD J. PLANTINGA

. . . I WOULD LIKE TO TAKE this opportunity to present the view of religion of a major representative of one important tradition within Religionswissenschaft, namely, that of the Dutch scholar Gerardus van der Leeuw (1890–1950). Van der Leeuw is an interesting case study, it seems to me, because as a twentieth-century historian and phenomenologist of religion, he had a good overview of the world of religion, ranging from so-called primitive religion to Christianity, from Indian religion to ancient Greek religion, from ancient Egyptian religion to German Romanticism.

I will thus sketch van der Leeuw's view of religion in this essay. I will not, however, discuss his view of method in the study of religion: this would go beyond the necessary limitations of space imposed upon the present study. Nor will I attempt to draw large and systematic conclusions about religion in Western history. . . .

Van der Leeuw's Conception of Religion

Before turning to van der Leeuw's view of religion, a word about his view of the business of

Reprinted from Richard J. Plantinga, "An Ambivalent Relationship to the Holy: Gerardus van derLeeuw on Religion" in Religion in History: The Word, the Idea, the Reality, *ed. Michel Despland and Gérard Vallée (Waterloo, Ontario: Wilfrid Laurier University Press, 1992), pp. 93–100. Copyright © 1992.*

offering definitions of religion is in order. One can, he notes, adopt the view of religion found in any one religion—most often one's own—and allow this to stand for religion in general, explaining other religions as falsehoods. A much better approach, van der Leeuw says, is to attempt the very difficult task of seeking what is common in the many different conceptions of the object of religion. One then seeks a term that is as "colourless" as possible, a term that will do justice to all the forms of religion which it is intended to summarize. However, this approach, too, is riddled with difficulties. Van der Leeuw points out that such definitions of religion often tell us more about the intentions and opinions of the person doing the defining and the period in which they were written than they tell us about the phenomenon of religion itself. For, as Schleiermacher argued in *Über die Religion,* one finds religion only in religions—and thus by implication not in definitions of religion.

Having thus drawn attention to the precarious character of that which he was about to undertake, van der Leeuw sought to characterize religion—a phenomenon rooted in human experience—by preliminarily defining it as a relationship of a person to something or someone "other." The world of religion displays a variety of ways of conceiving this "other" by which one is touched, which one encounters in experience, which intrudes into one's life. Because of this intrusive nature of the other, van der Leeuw notes, life is a dangerous affair filled with critical moments. In thus stressing the experiential character of the human encounter with the other, van der Leeuw writes: "The essence of all religions . . . is a relation to a power or to powers—a real relation and real powers, a relation which is felt to be stronger, more real and more living than the relation we have with our fellow human beings." The power (*Macht*—one of the central notions in van der Leeuw's Phenomenologie) referred to here may be impersonal. It may also be personal; that is, it may be combined with will and

form. In fact, van der Leeuw says, in "the three words power, will and form is contained almost the entire concept of the object of religion."[1] In discussing the concept of religion, van der Leeuw called for circumspection with respect to the term "God."

While many people are prone to think of religion in terms of belief in and worship of God, such a view of religion is problematic for more than one reason. First of all, van der Leeuw notes, if one chooses to think about religion in terms of God, the term must be so carefully circumscribed as to die the death of a thousand qualifications and so cease to say anything significant. In the second place, in thinking about religion in terms of God, one often does so with a particular conception of God in mind. Naturally, doing so has great potential for distortion where one's own conception of God does not obtain or where God is not a part of religion. God is, if not a Christian, then at least a Greek representation of the object of religion which is not applicable everywhere in the world of religion. Instead of this Graeco-Christian conception, one ought to think of God as the indication of that to which human religious striving directs itself. Notions of God thus arise out of the experience of power encountered in life to which one seeks a relation. In this connection, van der Leeuw speaks of the "double experience of form": numinous experience (experience with power and encounter with will) is formless and without structure; the double experience of form produces representations—power and will acquire name and form as demons, gods, or God. In this way, humanity overcomes its painful solitude. Van der Leeuw hastens to add that this is no Feuerbachian or Freudian process: what one sees here is not projection, theorizing, or abstraction but rather something concrete and empirical—giving name and form to the experience of power and will. It is in light of this that one should understand van der Leeuw's prima facie strange remark that "God" is a latecomer to the history of religion.

Thus, instead of God, one would do better to speak of *numen,* which is a less personal designation for half-formed power with an element of will. Likewise, the Dutch term *religie,* derived from the Latin religion is a less precise and hence more desirable term than the Dutch term *godsdienst,* which is widely used in the Dutch language as a synonym for *religie.* The former indicates only a relation while the latter rather narrowly fixes the object of the relation and focusses on only one religious form.

The encounter with the object of the relation constitutive of religion is characterized by van der Leeuw as wholly other, different, out of the ordinary, strange, marked off, *tabu, mana*-like, greater than oneself, superior, powerful, numinous, sacred. All of these terms can be summed up in the terms "holy," "holiness," and "the Holy," which van der Leeuw borrowed from two scholars for whom he had very high regard: Nathan Söderblom and Rudolf Otto. In summarizing this impressive encounter with the other, van der Leeuw expresses himself in rather pregnant fashion by saying that "in religion one interprets one's experience as revelation."[2] Thus, religion is a relationship to the Holy. . . .

The human reaction to this encounter is one of awe, amazement, wonder. This the most basic of religious feelings, is not at all straightforward. That is, one's relationship to the other can take various forms. One may seek to dominate the other, or serve it, or love it, or fear it, or seek unity with it. Whatever the form, one's relation to the other or the Holy is two-sided. In the presence of this uncanny other, one has feelings of fear, dread, repulsion, terror, horror, apprehension, *tremendum*—as well as love, longing, attraction, surrender, adoration, reverence, *fascinans.* Thus van der Leeuw writes: "Religion is an ambivalent relationship to the Holy."[3] Why this is so one cannot say: the essence of religion is a mystery. However, one can say that the person seeks a relationship to the Holy because he or she is impelled by it.

An encounter with the Holy does not leave one unchanged; after this experience, the religious person feels a demand and the necessity of fulfilling a task. In other words, awe develops into observance. This, according to van der Leeuw, is the significance of the Latin religion which may mean the bond of a person to something or the fact that a person pays attention to something. In fact, both meanings are possible: "Religion is the phenomenon whereby one binds oneself or knows oneself to be bound to something or someone; one pays attention to something, one reckons with something."[4] Thus, the opposite of *homo religiosus* is *homo neglegens* (and the modern feeling is one in which awe has become formalized and hence meaningless).

Life is thus a given and a possibility. That is to say, one does not accept life the way it is— one is concerned with one's world and one's relationship to the Holy. One is thus on the alert; one seeks to flee the Holy, or to dominate it, or to form habits in regard to it (rites and customs)—or one adopts a posture of faith. In other words, existential concern develops into a certain type of conduct, which often has a celebratory character. Thus it is that one observes various religious expressions, the chief of which are cult, myth, doctrine, and inner religious life.[5]

With such a conception of religion, it is not difficult to see why van der Leeuw was uncomfortable with Schleiermacher's famous definition of religion (shared by van der Leeuw's teacher, W. B. Kristensen) as "das schlechthinnige Abhangigkeitsgefühl." On the one hand, this definition says too much: fear, terror, and rebellion against the Holy, which one finds in the history of religion, are screened by the notion of dependence. On the other hand, this definition does not say enough: the feelings of surrender, devotion, and love, which one also finds in the history of religion, are not properly expressed.

Finally, van der Leeuw notes the limitations of conceiving religion as a human phenomenon.

That is to say, religion is not merely human experience, feeling, action, and so forth. For the religious person (as opposed to the scholarly investigator of religion), religion is something quite different. "To the person who experiences, religious experience is precisely not experience in the first place, but an act of God."[6] As he notes time and again in the *Phänomenologie*, the object of the science of religion is the subject, the primary agent for religion itself. . . .

Thus, it is necessary to speak, not of religion, but of faith. Faith, however, is hidden from historical conception. The task of its investigation belongs to philosophy of religion and theology. The historian of religion must thus bear in mind that the truly religious person conceives his or her religion in such a way that history can only speak of the human and least important part of it. . . .

Conclusion

Ever since I read Professor Smith's *The Meaning and End of Religion* several years ago, I have been somewhat queasy about the use of the term "religion." Is it a useful concept? To focus this question a little more to suit the present investigation and apply it to van der Leeuw's conception of religion: does the notion of an ambivalent relationship to the Holy help one understand Buddhist meditation, *The Bhagavad-Gita*, or Azande witchcraft? It seems to me that it does. In Gadamerian terms, one might say that van der Leeuw's conception of religion is a useful prejudgement, one that fosters understanding and hence one that has a rightful place in an operational definition of religion. Others have concurred with this view: van der Leeuw was a highly influential figure in the study of religion between roughly 1925 and 1950, and his influence can be seen beyond the middle point of

this century in, among others, the work of Mircea Eliade, who in turn has had a sizeable influence on the study of religion in the latter half of this century.[7]

But certainly not everyone has found the van der Leeuw approach to religion congenial. There is also a counter-tradition within *Religionswissenschaft* that seeks to adopt a rather "scientific" attitude to religion. To this tradition, terms such as "holy," "sacred," "transcendence," and the like are too theological and hence not useful for objectively and empirically studying and explaining the cultural phenomenon of religion. . . .

NOTES

1. Gerardus van der Leeuw, *Phänomenologie der Religion*, 2nd revised edition (Tübingen: J. C. B. Mohr, 1956), p. 83.

2. See Nathan Söderbloom, "Holiness, General and Primitive," In *Encyclopedia of Religion and Ethics*, Edited by James Hastings (Edinburgh: T. & T. Clark, 1913), Volume 6, pp. 731–41; Rudolf Otto, *Das Heilige*, 2nd Edition (Munich: C. H. Beck'sche Verlagsbuchhandlung, 1932).

3. Gerardus van der Leeuw, "Inleiding," In *De godsdiensten der wereld*, Edited by Gerardus van der Leeuw (Amsterdam: H. Meulenhoff, 1941), Volume 1, p. 4.

4. Ibid., p. 2.

5. Idem, "Religion: I. Erscheinungs- und Ideenwelt," In *Die Religion in Geschichte und Gegenwart*, Edited by Herman Gunkel and Leopold Zscharnack (Tübingen: J. C. B. Mohr, 1930), Vol. 4, pp. 1862–63; "Godsdienst, 1," In *Winkler Prins Algemeene Encyclopaedie*, Edited by J. De Vries 5th Edition (Amsterdam: N. V. Utigevers-Maatschappij, 1935), Volume 8, pp. 346–47; "Inleiding," p. 5; *Phänomenologie der Religion*, pp. 533–37.

6. Idem, "Erlebnis, religiöses," In *Die Religion in Geschichte und Gegenwart*, Edited by Hermann Gunkel and Leopold Zscharnack, 2nd Edition (Tübingen: J. C. B. Mohr, 1928), Volume 2, p. 256.

7. Mircea Eliade, *Traité d'histoire des religions* (Paris: Payot, 1987).

From *Dimensions of the Sacred: An Anatomy of the World's Beliefs*

NINIAN SMART

THIS BOOK RANGES WIDELY over the religions and ideologies of this world. I believe that by seeing the patterns in the way religion manifests itself, we can learn to understand how it functions and vivifies the human spirit in history. In this book I consciously try to classify the elements of worldviews, both in their beliefs and in their practices. These classifications come from reflections about the varying cultures of humankind. Though I sometimes simplify, this is in the hope of clarifying perceptions. . . .

In providing a kind of physiology of spirituality and of worldviews, I hope to advance religious studies' theoretical grasp of its subject matter, namely that aspect of human life, experience and institutions in which we as human beings interact thoughtfully with the cosmos and express the exigencies of our own nature and existence. I do not here take any faith to be true or false. Judgment on such matters can come later. But I do take all views and practices seriously.

This book is in some sense a phenomenology of religion. That is, it belongs in the same genre as Gerardus van der Leeuw's famous *Religion in Essence and Manifestation*. But my book, and indeed van der Leeuw's, could also be called a morphology of religion, incorporating a theory. It explores and articulates the "grammar of symbols"—the modes and forms in which religion manifests itself.

The word "phenomenology" derives from the philosophical tradition of Husserl. But comparative religionists (henceforth I shall simply call them religionists) use it in a differ-ent way from philosophers. Among religionists it means the use of *epoché* or suspension of belief, together with the use of empathy, in entering into the experiences and intentions of religious participants. This implies that, in describing the way people behave, we do not use, so far as we can avoid them, alien categories to evoke the nature of their acts and to understand those acts. In this sense phenomenology is the attitude of informed empathy. It tries to bring out what religious acts mean to the actors.

But this book is something else: it is intended to delineate the various manifestations of religion in complex ways. It discusses a number of theories—about myths, doctrines, art, rituals, experience, organizations, ethics, law—and a certain amount of religion, politics and economics. So it is an ambitious enterprise.

Gerardus van der Leeuw used the term "essence," which implies a definition of religion. I do not here wish to affirm a definition in the strict sense. Moreover, I believe that there are sufficient affinities between religious and secular worldviews (such as applied Marxism and nationalisms) to include the secular in the scope of this work. I hope this will make the book comprehensive. To split a category can be dangerous if it is taken too far. Because religion is separated from secular worldviews, for instance, it is assumed that East Germany was a secular state; in fact Marxism functioned in that country much as a state religion, as Lutheranism once had. If you did not adhere to the state religion you were denied opportunities in education and employment.

Reprinted from Ninian Smart, Dimensions of the Sacred: An Anatomy of the World's Beliefs
(Berkeley: University of California Press, 1996), pp. 1–14. Copyright © 1996 Ninian Smart.

So my enterprise here, though largely concerned with religion, can also be categorized as a version of worldview analysis.

The term "worldview" is not the best. It suggests something too cerebral. But religions and comparable worldviews should be studied at least as much through their practices as through their beliefs. Likewise nationalism involves more than a set of myths or stories about "our" country: it involves practical actions and acknowledgments of loyalty; it involves joy when "we" win (at soccer or at war), the speaking of "our" language, appreciation of the monuments and beauties of "our" country. So when I use "worldview" I mean incarnated worldview, where the values and beliefs are embedded in a practice. That is, they are expressed in action, laws, symbols, organizations. . . .

Cross-Cultural Phenomenology of Religion

The phenomenology (that is, the theory and morphology) of religion has usually been conducted in European languages, notably English, French, German and Italian. . . . But it is important to make use of terms drawn from non-European traditions. Shaman, mana, totem, tabu/tapu, yoga and karma have all entered the English language, but there are other vital terms which have not and which might be most useful in cross-cultural comparisons.

The dominance of the English tongue in cross-cultural comparisons is no accident. It is largely a product of colonialism and therefore of unequal cultural power relationships. Moreover, British and American scholars played an important role in developing the subject. There was often the tacit assumption that Christianity was normal religion, and that it was against this norm that the primary comparisons were to be launched. English is fast becoming the major global tongue and is therefore a proper vehicle for such explorations, but there is no reason why we should not employ a range of cross-cultural terms to further comparisons. I shall in this book make use of a number of crucial expressions, including *bhakti* (devotion), *dhyana* (meditation) and *li* (appropriate behaviour). Sometimes distinctions and nuances are clearer and richer in other languages than English. There may be differing ways of carving up the territory. Sometimes this may justify us in creating neologisms. In the West it has often been assumed that God and gods are normal: a system is either theistic or polytheistic. But what about the Theravada? Its Ultimate is not God or the gods, but nirvana. Should we then see Christianity and Judaism as major non-nirvanistic religions?

In affirming that phenomenology should be conducted on a cross-cultural basis, I am saying two things: that its findings should make use of cross-cultural terminology and sensitivity; and that there should be no assumption of the priority of one tradition as the norm. This is where informed empathy has another role, in creating the sensitivity to allow me (a Westerner, a Scot, a male, an Episcopalian, albeit with Buddhist leanings) to enter into other cultures' attitudes. But in thinking about the cross-cultural we need to reflect on what the boundaries of cultures are.

The Boundaries of Traditions, Religions, Cultures

The word "cross-cultural" may be understood to refer to items belonging to broad cultural areas, such as China, South Asia and Europe. But there can of course be many traditions within areas: thus Jaina, Buddhist and Hindu traditions are important in classical India. But even here there are vital sub-traditions within each, while some scholars rightly question whether we can really treat Hinduism as a single tradition. In modern times perhaps we can, because that is how to a great degree it is perceiving itself. But what about in classical times? We have to be realistic in the study of religion and take the richness and variegations seriously.

That is often why the insider can be wrong about her tradition. When Kristensen said that the insider is always right, he meant that she is right about herself. That is, she has certain feelings and beliefs and they are an important part of the data we as religionists are set to explore. *But an* insider can be terribly wrong about her tradition, ignorant about or insensitive to the variety of her religious heritage. I once heard a Baptist minister give a lecture on Christianity which was, phenomenologically speaking, absurd. What he identified as true Christianity would not be accepted by great swathes of Catholicism, Orthodoxy, Episcopalianism, Methodism and so on. Indeed, one major use of the word "phenomenology" is to mark off what we as religionists are trying to do from those committed interpretations which essentially are part of preaching.

Thus we must distinguish between descriptive and normative uses of such terms as "Buddhism" and "Christianity." But the most important point here is that traditions are plural. Moreover, they may vary regionally as well as by lineage or tradition. The Episcopal church in Fiji may vary greatly from its counterpart in Scotland; Theravada Buddhism may differ markedly in Thailand and Burma; the Unification Church in Korea and England may have great differences.

While the comparative study of religion is usually conceived in macro terms, it could equally well be construed as dealing with micro or intra-tradition comparisons.

Questions of Comparison: Platform and Context

The expression "comparative religion" or "comparative study of religion" (I would prefer "comparative study of worldviews") has met with some disfavour in differing eras. In a backlash against missionary colonialism the word "comparative" has been taken to express a certain arrogance—comparisons, as the saying goes, being odious. It has sometimes been under suspicion for an opposed reason, it being thought that comparativists love likenesses excessively, thus blurring the uniqueness of the preferred religion (some form of Christianity).[1] But there is no need at all, for comparison to stand on a superior platform, and comparing traditions, sub-traditions or whatever involves the discerning not only of likenesses but of differences.

It might be thought that my present ambitious project has its own platform, maybe not that of the certain and confident missionary, but that of the Western "scientist" who wishes to look at religions and worldviews from a platform of analysis and superior understanding. It is true that in a sense I do start from a platform of "science." I believe that religious studies can be, within the limits of recognition that it is a human enterprise (being by and about human beings) scientific.[2] But I cannot believe that by itself this claim is arrogant. Arrogance arises rather from the manner in which a method is pursued. If the anthropologist visits a village simply to get material for a doctorate, without consideration for the villagers as fellow human beings with their own sensitivities and concerns, that is arrogant and heartless. But the enterprise of advancing knowledge by itself is not arrogant. Yet what of knowledge and power relations? What if the whole structure of knowledge displays a certain arrogance?

I would defend the comparative study of religion on a number of grounds. First, it has often acted as counterpoise to cultural tribalism, such as often prevails in Western universities and, especially, in theological schools. Second, it often raises fruitful questions for contemplation by religions and more generally worldviews: any real similarity between the piety of one tradition and that of another poses obvious questions for each. Third, because of ideological prejudices, religious studies is too often neglected among the social sciences, where projection theories seem to be fashionable: the comparative study of worldviews can be a source of insights, as Weber well knew.

The deeper challenge to cross-cultural studies concerns context. The point was most incisively made by Hendrik Kraemer.[3] Even if we think that we have made a valid comparison, for instance between Luther's and Shinran's account of "grace," the divergence of context between the two may invalidate the comparison, in the sense of alike-claiming. The details of context give quite diverse flavours to the two phenomena.

The problem with this thesis is that everything becomes so particularized as to be incommensurable with anything else. This is self-defeating in a number of ways. It means that there is no vocabulary which can properly describe the offerings of different cultures. Besides, while we know that each individual human being is unique, implying that each person has a divergent set of flavours drenching her experience, it does not follow that we have no common feelings and perspectives. It does not follow that we cannot study medicine, which depends upon a range of alike-claims. We all have noses, even if each one is subtly different from all others. Anyway the proof is in the actualities: and we shall see how well the theoretical and descriptive similarities laid forth in this book stand up to the necessary contextualities. Part of my way of dealing with the problem is the use of dynamic and dialectical phenomenology.

Dynamic Patterns and Dialectical Relations in Phenomenology

Because of essentialism (the view that a given type of phenomenon has a common essence) and other factors, earlier phenomenology tends to be synchronic and static. There is no harm in this within certain limits. Alike-claims and unalike-claims can be of this character. But we may also want to see if there are patterns of change. Do new religions tend to get institutionalized in certain ways? And, if so, what other effects does this have? Do certain forms of religious experience release creative or organizational behaviour in their recipients? And so on. *If we can discern patterns,* that is what I call dynamic phenomenology. Now obviously patterns of change in human history tend to be synergistic, so that they combine. Alternatively, a pattern of change in one context leads to different results in another context.

By dialectical phenomenology I mean more particularly the relationship between *different dimensions* of religion and worldviews. In general we can say about any system or scheme that one element in it is in principle affected by all others. An organism functions as a whole, so that an injury to one part affects the whole to a greater or lesser degree. A set of religious doctrines, for instance the teachings of Eastern Orthodoxy, is a sort of loose organism. It is not necessarily a consistent whole, but one doctrine, such as the creation, is affected by others, such as the incarnation of Christ (so Christ becomes Creator) or the definition of the sacraments (so the created world is viewed as sacramental). We can therefore see items in this field in the context of the scheme in which they are embedded. But more than this, we can view the items in one dimension (in this case the doctrinal dimension) in their interaction with items in other dimensions, for instance the practical (or ritual) dimension. The idea that the world is created out of nothing should be seen in the light of the intensity of Christian worship: no limitation should be set on the glory of God. The idea that there is an ineffable aspect of God or Brahman should be related to the mystical path, as well as to other factors, such as the performative analysis of indescribability in the context of supreme praise (in other words, seeing how the language of ineffability actually performs the act of praising: you get something like this in "I cannot say how grateful I am" which conveys how grateful I am).

Again we can see dialectical phenomenology at work in relation to a secular worldview. It is part of the doctrine of the United States that it favours and incarnates democratic values: this in turn has effects on the style of the Presidency. Its rituals include the practice of the President's going out and about among the people and being populist in his actions (displaying himself as a "man of the people").

The Dimensional Analysis of Worldviews

To flesh all this out I need to give a more detailed account of what I mean by the dimensions of religion.[4] The pattern which I put forward is primarily directed towards what traditionally in English are called religions (I will not at this juncture go into a comparison of other concepts such as *dharma, magga, tao, chiao, din and religio*). But the schema also applies to worldviews other than religious ones.

The schema has a double purpose. One is to provide a realistic checklist of aspects of a religion so that a description of that religion or a theory about it is not lopsided. There is a tendency in older histories of Christianity for instance to emphasize the history of doctrines and organizational matters: you can pick up church histories (so called, for the title already makes some assumptions) which say very little about the spiritual and practical life, or about ethical and legal matters, or about the social dimension on the ground, other than the organizational side. Some treatments of the Hindu tradition concentrate on myth and social organization, and say very little about the philosophical side or about patterns of experience and feeling.

So one purpose is to achieve balance. The other is to give a kind of functional delineation of religions in lieu of a strict definition. I also

avoid defining religion in terms of its foci or content. That is, I am not saying that religion involves some belief, such as belief in God or gods, because in some religions, notably in Theravada Buddhism and Jainism and in phases of the Confucian tradition, such beliefs are secondary, to say the least. As we shall see, two of my dimensions can concern the gods most lavishly—namely, the doctrinal and mythic dimensions—so it seems better not to try to define religion by content. The best we could do is use a phrase like "ultimate concern,"[5] yet this is rather empty and too wide-ranging. Or we could trot out the "transcendent": a useful place-holder, open to as many ambiguities as "religion" itself.

I do not deny that there is a role for place-holders. We need a term to stand for the phenomenological object of religious practice and experience. I prefer "focus," in part because it has a plural ("foci"), whereas "the ultimate" cannot be very naturally plural and in part because it does not carry any ontological baggage.[6] It does not matter whether Vishnu exists or not—that is, it does not matter for our purposes, though for the faithful of course it matters—or whether there is a transcendent ultimate; but we can still recognize that Vishnu is the focus of the Vaishnava's dreams and worship, as Christ is the focus of the Eucharist. But it does not define religion to say that it has a focus.

The notion of a focus enables us to talk about worship and other activities in meaningful ways without having to comment on whether there is a Vishnu or a Christ. But it does enable us to think of Vishnu as focus entering into the believer's life, dynamizing his feelings, commanding his loyalty and so on. This is an advantage in discussing a controversial subject like religion. For a believer the focus is real, and we can accept this even if we do not want to say that it (or she or he) exists. I thus distinguish between "real" and "existent" as adjectives. The former I use, in this context, to refer to what is phenomenologically real in the experience of the believer. Whether the real in this sense exists is an altogether different question.

To return to the dimensions: in each case I give them a double name, which helps to elucidate them and sometimes to widen them. . . . The seven are as follows (the order is rather random).

1. The ritual or practical dimension. This is the aspect of religion which involves such activities as worship, meditation, pilgrimage, sacrifice, sacramental rites and healing activities. We may note that meditation is often not regarded as a ritual, though it is often strictly patterned. This is partly why I also call this dimension the practical.[7]

2. The doctrinal or philosophical dimension. For different reasons religions evolve doctrines and philosophies. Thus the doctrine of impermanence is central to Buddhism. It also interacts dialectically with the ritual or practical dimension, since philosophical reflection of a certain kind aids meditation, and meditation in turn helps the individual to see existentially the force of the doctrine. Some traditions are keener on doctrinal rectitude than others: Catholicism more than Quakerism, Buddhism more than traditional African religions, Theravada more than Zen. We may note that diverse traditions put differing weights on the differing dimensions. Religions are by no means equidimensional.

3. The mythic or narrative dimension. Every religion has its stories. The story of Christ's life, death and resurrection is clearly central to the Christian faith. The story of the Buddha's life, though somewhat less central to Buddhism, is still vital to Buddhist piety. In the case of secular worldviews and to an important degree in modernizing traditions, history is the narrative which takes the place of myth elsewhere. So the version of history taught in a nation's schools is not only a major ingredient in the national sense of identity, but enhances pride in "our" ancestors, "our" national heroes and heroines.

4. The experiential or emotional dimension. It is obvious that certain experiences can be important in religious history—the enlightenment of the Buddha, the prophetic visions of Muhammad, the conversion of Paul and so on. Again there are variations in the importance attached to visionary and meditative experiences: they are obviously vital to Zen and Native American classical religion (the vision quest); they are less important in Scottish Calvinism. But they or associated emotional reactions to the world and to ritual are everywhere more or less dynamic, and have been studied extensively.

5. The ethical or legal dimensions. A religious tradition or subtradition affirms not only a number of doctrines and myths but some ethical and often legal imperatives. The Torah as a set of injunctions is central to orthodox Judaism; the Shari'a is integral to Islam; Buddhism affirms the four great virtues (*brahmavihâras*); Confucianism lays down the desired attitudes of the gentleman; and so on. Again, the degree of investment in ideal human behaviour varies: it is central to Quakerism, less important in the Shinto tradition (though Shinto ritual was tied to the notion of the *kokutai* or national essence during the Meiji era and into the between-wars period). In modern national states certain norms of civil behaviour tend to be prescribed in schools.

6. The organizational or social component. Any tradition will manifest itself in society, either as a separate organization with priests or other religious specialists (gurus, lawyers, pastors, rabbis, imams, shamans and so on), or as coterminous with society. Embedded in a social context, a tradition will take on aspects of that context (thus the Church of England cleric begins to play a part in the English class system).

7. The material or artistic dimension. A religion or worldview will express itself typically in material creations, from chapels to cathedrals to temples to mosques, from icons and divine statuary to books and pulpits. Such concrete expressions are impor-

tant in varying ways. If you only have to carry around a book (like an evangelical preacher in Communist Eastern Europe) you are freer than if you have a great monastery or convent to occupy. Let me sketch out, for a couple of worldviews, how these dimensions operate. I shall take classical Christianity first (namely Catholic and Orthodox Christianity in the centuries not long after Constantine).

1. Ritually the Church had evolved more or less elaborate patterns for celebrating the mass, liturgy or eucharist. It had various other sacramental rites, ranging from baptism to marriage to consigning the dead to the next world. It was also evolving the cult of saints, pilgrimages and so on. In practical terms there was a growing emphasis on the life of meditation. This helped to enhance doctrines relating to the ineffability of the Divine Being (especially the assumption in the liturgy and myths that God was male).

2. The religion had succeeded in fusing together motifs from the Jewish tradition and from Neo-Platonism (that is, the worldview of Plotinus and other religious followers of Plato during the 3rd and 4th centuries C.E.). Those charged with settling its doctrines tackled many current intellectual problems (assisted by thinkers such as Augustine and the Eastern Fathers) and grappled with matters arising from the narrative dimension. If, as the Biblical stories affirmed, God was successively creator, incarnate Jesus and mysterious inspirer, how could all this be reconciled with monotheistic Judaism? The answer was the Trinity doctrine, generator of heresies but gradually settling down as the norm within the two great churches.

3. The main narratives came to derive from the Old and New Testaments, though the church had to explain itself historically from those times up to the present—hence that great interpretation of history in Augustine's *The City of God*. The myths were wedded to ritual: for instance, in the eucharist's re-enactment of the story of the Last Supper, or in the evolution of a church calendar that re-enacted other parts of the story through the year and celebrated the saints, the heroines and heroes of the salvation history.

4. The creation of networks of monasticism favoured the cultivation of mysticism, which was reinforced by the absorption of NeoPlatonist ideals. In addition, the development of colourful, even glorious ritual enhanced the more ordinary emotions of the devotional life.

5. The settling of the church into more defined ecclesiastical organizations helped the formation of a legal system, while Christian ethics was already well established through the Ten Commandments and the definitions of Paul and others in the epistles.

6. Organizationally, the two halves of the church eventually drifted apart, though each retained a fairly well-defined structure in alliance with the secular power. Most notable was the growth of monasteries, reflecting new ways of being Christian after the religion became fashionable, which in turn gave rise to a need to strengthen the spiritual life.

7. Meanwhile the churches had taken over many of the glorious buildings of the old Roman Empire and went on to construct new ones, giving Christianity a formidable material dimension reinforced by techniques of painting which encouraged the decoration of churches. Icons in the East performed an important ritual function, despite the largely aniconic traditions of Judaism, out of which Christianity had evolved.

NOTES

1. Louis Henry Jordan, *Comparative Religion: Its Genesis and Growth* (Edinburgh, 1905).

2. *Ninian Smart,* The Science of Religion and the Sociology of Knowledge (Princeton, 1973).

3. Hendrik Kraemer, *The Christian Message in a Non-Christian World* (New York, 1938).

4. Ninian Smart, *The World's Religions* (Cambridge, 1989).

5. Paul Tillich, *What Is Religion?* (New York, 1969).

6. Smart, *Science of Religion.*

7. E. E. Evans-Pritchard, *Theories of Primitive Religion* (Oxford, 1965).

Counterpoint:
From *The Politics of Religious Studies*

DONALD WIEBE

Donald Wiebe teaches at the University of Toronto where he also serves as Dean of the faculty of Divinity at Trinity College. Besides publishing many articles in scholarly journals, he is also the author of the following books: *Religion and Truth: Towards an Alternative Paradigm for the Study of Religion* and *The Irony of Theology and the Nature of Religious Thought.*

SMART'S CONCERN in *The Phenomenon of Religion* is to try to establish what is entailed in coming to a scientific understanding of religion. In contrast to his analysis in *The Science of Religion and the Sociology of Knowledge,* he does not in the former work explicitly distinguish a scientific study of religion from a more general study of religion. This does not mean, however, that such a distinction is missing altogether or plays no significant role in the methodology he elaborates here for the academic study of religion. At first glance Smart's argument in *The Phenomenon of Religion* appears straightforwardly scientific. As in *The Science of Religion and the Sociology of Knowledge* Smart sees a notable contrast between theology as a scholarly Discipline and the scientific study of religion. The contrast derives from a difference of intellectual approach by the practitioners of the respective disciplines. Theology, claims Smart, involves what he refers to as "Expression," by which he means a response of commitment, on the part of the scholar, to the "object" under investigation culminating in testimony to that experience. The approach of the scientific student of religion to the object of inquiry, on the other hand, precludes such "involvement" and is therefore more objective. . . .

Smart knows that it is exceedingly rare, if not impossible, to maintain a wholly objective position from which to undertake the study of religion. Nevertheless he maintains that the study of religion need not on that account proceed as though any degree of bias were admissible for students in this field. There are different degrees of bias, with different degrees of significance. . . . Indeed, if it did, one would have to conclude unhappily that to understand a religion would require endorsement of it. On the contrary: Smart insists that recognition of some omnipresent bias "by no means entails that it is necessary to Express [that is, to endorse religion] in order to do Religion [that is, to study religion]" (28).

The "anatomy of the study of religion" also provided by Smart in the opening chapter of *The Phenomenon of Religion* supports such an interpretation of his analysis of Religious Studies. It is clear from this discussion that, for Smart, the "understanding" of religion that should be the concern of the scholar in this field is scientific rather than hermeneutical. He expands upon the tasks of description and explanation: description always precedes explanation, uncovering the content, so to speak, of the religious phenomenon under scrutiny; whereas explanation clears up any puzzles presented by that content.

Given this understanding of the nature of the scientific study of religion it is not surprising that Smart should see himself as providing a neutral framework for the discipline. What must be noted here, however, is Smart's rejection of what he refers to as "flat neutralism." Neutralism, to be sure, requires a "bracketing" of Expression, (a refusal to adopt the religious attitude of the persons or community being studied), but "bracketing Expression," he insists, is not the same as ignoring Expression altogether; to do that would simply be to take up the old-style empiricist study of religious phenomena restricted to a discussion of the external characteristics of religion only. That type of analysis, he argues, "flattened out" description and made it impossible to capture the "fine grain," which led to a distortion of the phenomenon's true character. Consequently, according to Smart, the student of religion must always take seriously the Expression characterizing the lives of the devotees in the tradition being studied. Of course, for Smart, "taking seriously" does not mean an endorsement of the faith, but rather a willingness of the scholar "to enter into engagement with those who carry on the Expression of the faith . . ." (31). He continues: "[This does not] entail that [the scholar] is thereby chiefly

concerned with Expression" (31). The engagement merely helps avoid description of the religious phenomenon that does not do it justice. However, to insure that the Expression of the devotee is properly understood, while not allowing that element of Expression to dominate in an apologetic thrust, Smart suggests that the Expression of the devotee always appear in brackets; bracketed Expression simply being a faithful "re-presentation" of another's commitments without either endorsement or rejection.

It is clear that given Smart's notion of neutralism in the study of religion and its differences from a straightforwardly empirical approach to that study (that is, to a flat neutralism), he is entertaining a notion of a study of religion broader than the scientific (that is, an approach permitting questions that even though not outrightly theological are more than merely scientific). Indeed, Smart sees in the work of Mircea Eliade—and in particular in Eliade's notion of a creative hermeneutic approach to the study of religions—an example of the kind of study that is "more" than science but "less" than theology. . . . Thus, on the problem of objectivity Smart concludes: "Religion [the study of religion] incorporates, by bracketing, Expression into its descriptions, and that there is no strong reason to hold that particular commitment is necessary to the practice of [the study of] Religion" (34).

Close scrutiny of this conclusion reveals a lack of precision regarding the task of the academic student of religion; nor is it clear whether the study of religion in fact implies endorsement, if not of a particular religion then of religion in general. Smart's conclusion to the argument of the book as a whole exposes that ambiguity even more pointedly. Acknowledging that the task of theology is to Express a worldview and to Express commitment to it, he writes: "If Religion [that is, the study of religion] has any share in this activity, it is at one remove. It cannot easily affirm, out of its own substance, that men are sinful or that the Creator is good. What it can do is to show that the understanding of religion and even of ideology, is a necessary and indeed illuminating part of the human enterprise of accounting for the world in which we live" (148). If the academic or scientific study of religion, however, is directed toward gaining knowledge about religions rather than toward testifying to religious values, then it must be said that the latter, if not a specifically theological task, is nevertheless a metaphysical one and should therefore be left to philosophers and metaphysicians.

It is not difficult to understand Smart's reasoning and the source of its ambiguity, for a description of a religious phenomenon must include reference to the object of worship—to what Smart calls the Focus of religion. And since the Focus of a religion transcends human boundaries, it might appear as though the student of religion, like the devotee, assumes religion to be more than simply a human phenomenon. Consequently Smart is right to insist that the student ask the question "Is the Focus . . . part of the phenomenon which the observers witness?" He also rightly maintains that the student cannot answer this in the same realist fashion as the devotee. Consequently, the principle of "bracketing" is once again invoked in relation to questions about the existence of the Focus of religion that allow the student to acknowledge the reality—but not the truth or falsity—of the Focus in the life of the devotee. Smart refers to this approach as "bracketed realism" that does not so much leave the question of the existence of the Focus unanswered as unasked (62).

From Smart's analysis it might appear that the student of religion must treat religion as a merely human phenomenon. Yet no such conclusion is actually drawn. Having rejected Peter Berger's methodological atheism because it requires a priori reductionistic explanations of religion—making his methodological atheism indistinguishable from atheism *tout court*—

Smart maintains that only a phenomenological description of religion recognizing the reality of the Focus is acceptable. Unlike the a priori reductionism of Berger's methodology (which assumes a projected character for the Focus of religion), the phenomenological description eschews ontological assumptions. . . . Ultimately Smart asserts: "Now if we have rejected projectionism within phenomenology, we cannot hold that phenomenology simply deals with human events and products, though it certainly does at least this" (68). . . . He seems to contravene the very essence of the phenomenological approach to the study of religion, because he suggests that the question of the existence of the Focus is left unanswered, whereas, as he himself has already acknowledged, the phenomenologist is one who ought not to pose the question in the first place. . . .

As Smart points out, religions themselves explain the world—or attempt to explain the world. Such explanations, of course, involve supernatural causes and therefore clash with the naturalistic explanations sought by scientific students of religion. As an illustration Smart contrasts a religious ("internal") explanation of the conversion of Saul of Tarsus (later Saint Paul) with the scientific ("external") explanation of the experience; but he asks in the process whether the latter's reductionistic assumption—that is, that Paul's religious experience could be solely explained in psychohistorical terms—is any less metaphysical than Paul's "explanation" of the experience in terms of an encounter with the transcendent (the supernatural). Ultimately Smart urges the student of religion, even though he or she is in search of natural explanations for religious phenomena, to leave open the possibility of alternative explanations going beyond the scientific; for Smart at least, these would be based on a phenomenological description of the Focus of the devotee's experience and would not conflict with the scientific explanation. The student of religion would apparently remain agnostic with respect to the role of the supernatural in human affairs while paradoxically recognizing the power of the supernatural. . . . The significance of this . . . is that it uses what Smart refers to as phenomenological explanation—that is, explanation that invokes the supernatural without assumption as to its ontological status. A precise elaboration of this is not provided by Smart; no detailed account of "phenomenological explanation" is given beyond the examples employed that illustrate its character. And for this reason I find Smart's argument too thin to be persuasive.

Many students of religion see a "new era of promise" for the field of Religious Studies in its identification with the sciences and its concomitant legitimation as an independent entity within the modern university; Smart, however, quite clearly does not. He acknowledges that the study of religion needed emancipation, so to speak, from theology, but he denies that such emancipation is only possible by total identification of the academic study religion with the naturalism implicit in a scientific methodology. The alternative methodology he attempts to elaborate in *The Phenomenon of Religion,* however—one permitting objective learning about religion without decrying the feeling of its living power—is not without flaws that ultimately keep it from being distinguished from theology. There is an indication of this early on in Smart's analysis when he borrows from Eliade's notion of "creative hermeneutics" in his new ("phenomenological"?) approach to the study of religion. For Smart, of course, the notion allows the student to say something about the value and significance of religion for human beings. The flaw, however, lies in there being no ground on which that value can be established and means by which it can be delimited. Smart does claim to be aware that such an approach might incur a sliding into an (implicit) theology, but I do not think he adequately perceives the seriousness of this situation. . . .

The foundation upon which Smart attempts to establish his distinction between the study of religion (Religious Studies) and the scientific study of religion is the principle of phenomenological bracketing. In this Smart is influenced by the work of Gerardus van der Leeuw, making explicit many of the implications of phenomenological bracketing left implicit by the latter. Smart's argument, however, is not persuasive. There is no doubt that van der Leeuw, like Eliade, wished to use the scientific study of religion for nonscientific ends. For van der Leeuw, the (phenomenological) study of religion was a religious exercise to which the scientific study should contribute. But, as I have shown elsewhere, to require the scientific study of religion to make such a contribution would rob it of its scientific character—and I am not sure that van der Leeuw addresses this problem any more successfully than Smart.

The primary issue at stake in Smart's bracketing methodology involves the philosophical problem of the nature of the religious phenomenon; that is, should the student of religion treat religion as a purely human phenomenon? As I have already pointed out above, Smart raises this question in chapter 2 of *The Phenomenon of Religion.* . . . And although the point of "bracketing," according to Smart, is to keep such philosophical issues from intruding upon the scientific study of religion, a simple substitution of "yes" for "no" to the question equally constitutes an ontological judgment without the benefit of philosophical argument. If following Smart's argument, the Focus is to be a part of the phenomenon witnessed by the scientific observers, then it can be neither the "Focus-as-it-is-in-it-self" (if it exists, that is) nor the "Focus-as-projection," but rather the "Focus-as-it-is-in-the-mind-of-the-devotee." This Smart refers to as Bracketed Realism (61). Further difficulties exist with such a position, however, for it assumes that the Focus is real for the devotee because the devotee believes the Focus to exist. But the assumption that this holds true for all devotees is obviously problematic, especially with respect to those who have reinterpreted the tradition in liberal, post-Enlightenment terms. It is not at all clear, then, whether the notion of bracketed realism resolves the critical problem about the value of the religious phenomenon.

Bracketed Realism, in Smart's view, avoids both the reductionism of projectionist, social-science theories of religion as well as the realism implied by the devotee's commitment. But lest Bracketed Realism be allowed to evolve into a form of nefarious methodological atheism repugnant to a proper understanding of society, Smart backs up his proposed approach with reference to Peter Berger's work in which the latter unacceptably forces treatment of religious phenomena as entirely human in character. . . . Smart does not entirely reject Berger's analysis, but he counters that a methodological agnosticism can retain what it has to offer while yet adhering to the principle of the bracket. Although methodological agnosticism should by definition differ from methodological atheism, in what way this is so is not made clear. In fact the argument could be made that the two are not different at all. And Smart draws more from this analysis of bracketed realism than is warranted in his insistence that phenomenology does not deal simply with human events and products. His earlier rejection of "projectionist" had been the rejection of an a priori theoretical stance and not a falsification of all projection theories, actual and possible. His claim here seems to rule out, in an a priori manner, all possible protectionist accounts of religion; this is tantamount to asserting the actual Existence of the Focus, in so doing runs afoul of the requirement of bracketing. The most Smart ought to claim here is that phenomenology may in some sense "be in touch with" more than simply human events and products. . . .

In fact, much of Smart's argument actually seems to support my critique of his position.

The "analogies" he uses to explicate the meaning of his Existence-Reality distinction do not always carry the force he thinks they do. The "pen-friend" and "Father Christmas" scenarios, for example, have more to say about the Reality of "transcendent" Foci in the minds of their devotees than they do about their objective existence, and therefore they support reductionist rather than nonreductionist interpretations of religion. A closer look at the Father Christmas analogy will help clarify this point. A phenomenological description of the "Father Christmas Event" must make clear that the character is "real" in the lives of the children. However, the description also must make clear that this "reality" is only created by the fact that the children believe him to exist. (The reason for the "reality" of Father Christmas in the lives of adults who do not believe that he exists will, of course, find a different kind of explanation.) The description of the childrens' relationship to Father Christmas, therefore, is no more than a description of a human condition. And if so here, then one may ask why not so in the case of religious "realities." The phenomenological description, to be sure, must involve a description of the "existence-belief" of the devotee, but it does not require acceptance of that belief. The latter would, in fact, define a philosophical or religious undertaking that the bracketing is designed to avoid.

Nor is the fact that the devotee finds reductionistic accounts of religion unacceptable a sufficient reason for the student of religion to adopt a metaphysical position assuming the existence of the Focus. Smart's account of the conversion of Saul of Tarsus to Christianity, to which I have made reference once already, seems to illustrate this, but he does not draw from the account conclusions I think inescapable. That is, he underestimates the potential for a phenomenological description to undermine the metaphysical in the context of "explaining" the world. For such a phenomenological description is superior to one that excludes the reasons devotees provide for the metaphysical claims they espouse. Of course, a nonreductionistic description of the reality claim, which attempts an understanding of why the claim is made, is a fuller description of the religious phenomenon—and therefore a better description. . . .

Yet Smart cannot bolster the distinction with any argument that is not circular—other than the thin claim that methodological agnosticism allows the student of religion to draw certain kinds of conclusions about the meaning of religion not permitted by scientific study. It would appear, therefore, that the more general study of religion is close to the religio-theological study of religion that does not operate within such an agnostic framework. The principle of bracketing, then, is a kind of crypto-theological enterprise, predisposing the student of religion to assume the "truth" of religion (that is, to assume that the Focus of religion exists).

The religious nature of such a phenomenological approach becomes even clearer once one recognizes that the principle of bracketing taints the search for explanations of religious events. For all his talk of explanation in *The Phenomenon of Religion* (and elsewhere Smart ultimately restricts the study of religion to providing descriptions of the phenomenon. This follows from the fact that explaining any phenomenon, in violation of the methodological rule of bracketing, depends upon whether one assumes the "truth" to be illusory or veridical. Admittedly the descriptions Smart seeks are far more complex than those usually provided by the kind of empiricistic students he criticizes. But it is precisely because of the complexity that Smart's restriction of the study of religion to description takes on an apologetic tone. Bracketing, it will be remembered, requires the student of religion to assume, even if only for the sake of accurate description, that the devotee is always right. Thus, thorough description will include accounts of the devotees' own explanations for their religious affiliation.

Although such accounts are provided within brackets, so to speak, so that the question of their truth or falsity is not at issue, they nevertheless lend more coherence to the phenomenon. Yet Smart gives no consideration here to the fact that such supernatural explanations as the student of religion is required to include in describing the phenomenon may stand in outright conflict with naturalistic explanations that constitute the acknowledged findings of the academic student of religion. . . . For to ask the scientific student of religion to give up the cognitive framework that diverges from that of the religious devotee is tantamount to asking the researcher to give up the scientific project pure and simple. To take the scientist seriously in this regard would amount to according privilege to the scientist's worldview over that of the religious person—and this Smart finds objectionable. What Smart fails to recognize here, however, is that this privilege only operates within the framework of the academy. In fact, it is difficult to see how it could be otherwise, just as it would be inconceivable for the devotee to give up the worldview that gives meaning to existence. Even if religion holds the truth, and science is incapable of seeing it because of a restrictive methodology, that does not constitute grounds for arguing that the academic study of religion ought to be anything other than scientific. And if "the more general student of religion" seeks "explanatory" accounts of religion outside the cognitive universe of the scientific student of religion, then such a student stands in conflict with the scientific approach and has no greater right within that setting than the devotee or the theologian. At best, one could concede Smart's claims that religion cannot be studied within a scientific setting. That "something more" than the scientific should be sought obviously involves a recognition of at least the plausibility of religions truth; and such recognition could only be due either to religious experience of some kind or to metaphysical or theological argument, neither of which is appropriate to the activity of academic departments set aside for the scientific study of religious phenomena.

Though this critique of Smart's understanding of phenomenology of religion and his "bracketed realism" cannot claim to have falsified his methodological proposal for Religious Studies as distinct from the scientific study of religion, it does, I hope, call it into question.

For it points out that Smart has not been successful in arguing for a distinction between a scientific study of religion and a more general study of religion that is nonscientific but also simultaneously a nonreligious, nontheological study of religion. The claim on behalf of a "New Era of Promise" in the study of religion is illusory and therefore a disservice to science.

Chapter 5

History of Religions

In his momentous work on Christian church history entitled *The City of God,* Augustine, who was bishop of the north African city of Hippo in the fourth century and one of the most influential thinkers of Christian history, did not compose a true philosophy of history, a view based on inductions from observable trends in history. His work was rather similar to a theology of history. This implies that Augustine was not concerned with world history or with finding patterns in history to discern general laws. For Augustine, history was not a scientific discipline; it was rather providential, a play written by God. According to Augustine, time and history were redeemed because of the Christ-event that gave history its meaning. An important implication was that time was no longer cyclical and reversible because Christ lived, died, and was resurrected only once.

In contrast to Augustine's conception of history, Hegel conceived of what he called the World-Spirit (*Weltgeist*) as the operative force in world history, a process whereby Spirit comes to actual consciousness of itself as freedom. This consciousness is attained in and through the human mind. To attain its end, the Spirit worked through world-historical individuals. Such individuals were bearers of the World-Spirit by means of participating in the more limited totality referred to as *Volksgeist* (spirit of a people or state), a cultural complex integrating the art, religion, politics, and technology of a people into a unified self-consciousness. Therefore, the state or culture was the ultimate bearer of history for Hegel, and the individual was significant only as a moment in the movement of universal freedom. The meaning and progress of history perceived by Hegel and Augustine was not shared by the four historians of religions of this chapter, although they shared with Hegel and Augustine a keen interest in history.

For the sake of accuracy, this chapter overlaps with the previous chapter on the phenomenology of religion because numerous phenomenologists also viewed themselves as historians of religions. What especially distinguishes the three figures covered in this chapter from those in the previous chapter is that they all share an emphasis on the importance of history as a methodological tool for the study of religion. These three figures are Mircea Eliade, Jonathan Z. Smith, and Wendy Doniger. All of these scholars have held teaching positions at the University of Chicago.

From his scholarly perch at the University of Chicago, Eliade dominated the overlapping fields of phenomenology of religion and the history of religions. Born in Bucharest, Romania, in 1907, Eliade became a salaried writer as a young man for the newspaper *Cuvântul* (The Word), through the help of his mentor Nae Ionescu. After completing his philosophy degree with a thesis on Pico della Mirandola, Campanella, and Giordana Bruno, Eliade traveled to India in 1928 to study with Surendranath Dasgupta, a renowned scholar of Indian philosophy, at the University of Calcutta. After a falling out with his mentor, he resided in an ashram at Rishikesh and practiced yoga for 6 months with Swami Shivananda. After completing his doctoral thesis on yogic techniques, he returned to Romania to serve in the military to satisfy his mandatory 1-year commitment. In 1933, he won critical and popular success with the publication of *Maitreya,* a literary reworking of his romantic involvement in India. Other novels were to follow, but he published his doctoral dissertation in French in 1936 under the title *Yoga: Essai sur les origines de la mystique indienne.*

He began his teaching career as an assistant to his Romanian mentor, and he became associated with the right-wing political organization called the Legion of the Archangel Michael (popularly known as the Iron Guard), although he considered himself a nonpolitical person. In 1938, the Romanian authorities incarcerated him in a concentration camp, but he refused to recant his association with the group or its members. During the Second World War, he served his country as a cultural adviser to the Romanian legation in England and Lisbon. After a teaching position at the École des Hautes Études in Paris, participating in the Eranos Conference in Switzerland, and receiving a research stipend from the Bollingen Foundation of New York for 3 years, Eliade was invited to give the Haskell Lectures at the University of Chicago. This led to a visiting academic appointment at the university and finally an offer for a permanent position. While at the University of Chicago, he published a number of works: *Shamanism, Images and Symbols, Yoga: Immortality and Freedom, The Forge and the Crucible,* and *The Sacred and the Profane.* His career reached a milestone when he was awarded the title of Sewell L. Avery Distinguished Service Professor by his institution in 1962. Although he suffered from acute rheumatoid arthritis after 1960, until his death of a stroke in 1986, he continued to produce scholarly works like the three-volume *A History of Religious Ideas* and served as chief editor of the multi-volume *Encyclopedia of Religion.* Overall, his life was dedicated to various scholarly and literary pursuits.

Religionswissenschaft or the history of religions, as Eliade referred to it, uses an empirical method of approach. Aware of the importance of both history and the meaning of religious phenomena, historians of religions try to systematize the results of their findings and reflect on the structures revealed by the phenomena. Phenomenology or philosophy of religion completed this aspect of the work of historians of religions. From Eliade's perspective, the historian of religions must also be concerned with the structure of religious phenomena because such structures are nontemporal. In this sense, the historian of religions must go beyond the ordinary historian. Rather than simply reconstructing an event, historians of religions must discern the history of a particular manifestation of the sacred, but they must also explain the modality of the sacred that the manifestation reveals. Before historians of religions can isolate and comprehend the structure of a religious form, they must examine all the historical examples possible. This suggests that the history of religions is by nature an encyclopedic approach to its subject. Thus, Eliade understands the science of religion in a very broad sense of the term because it embraces phenomenology and philosophy of religion without neglecting the historically concrete.

Besides his encyclopedic approach, Eliade envisions his discipline as holding out the hope for a new form of humanism, which is also connected to his call for a creative hermeneutics that will stimulate philosophical thought, lead to a change in human beings, form a source for new cultural values, and enable one to discover one's place in the world. These various benefits are not, however, without risks, because there is the danger of becoming obsessed or trapped by the subject of study and the difficulty of finding the sacred camouflaged within the ordinary. These dangers suggest that a quest for a creative hermeneutics and a new humanism are akin to successfully traversing a wasteland. Eliade's encyclopedic approach to his subject, his grand vision, the inclusion of philosophical and theological dimensions to his work, and the synthesis of religious knowledge have given way, at least for a time, to more modest endeavors.

A consistent long-time critic of Eliade has been Jonathan Z. Smith, who did his graduate work at Yale University. Smith holds an endowed chair, Robert O. Anderson Distinguished Professor of the Humanities, at the University of Chicago. Besides numerous articles in scholarly journals, Smith has published the following books: *Map is Not Territory* (1978), *Imaging Religion* (1982), *To Take Place* (1987), and *Drudgery Divine* (1990) He also has served as the general editor of *The Harper-Collins Dictionary of Religion*. In some of these works, Smith criticizes Eliade for his use of comparison and morphological classification that Smith argues tends to be impressionistic and not a method for serious inquiry. Smith also criticizes Eliade for using an unhistorical method that ignores linear development and does not give us new knowledge. Smith affirms an interest in difference between religious phenomena, whereas Eliade is blind to differences, according to Smith, because he concentrates on sameness. Smith's approach to comparison is shaped by the analytical, philosophical insights of Ludwig Wittgenstein (1889–1951), who reminds us that comparison is not about identity because it requires difference.

Occupying an endowed chair named for Eliade at the University of Chicago, Wendy Doniger has devoted much of her career to the study of myth, much like her Romanian predecessor. Doniger was born in New York City in 1940, and she did her undergraduate work at Radcliffe College before receiving a master's and doctoral degrees from Harvard University with a dissertation under the direction of Daniel H. Ingalls, a renowned Sanskrit scholar. After doing a year of research in Moscow and Leningrad at the Institut Vostokovedeniia from 1970–1971, she received a Ph.D. Degree from Oxford University under the supervision of R. C. Zaehner. Her professional teaching career included appointments at the Oriental Institute at Oxford University, School of Oriental and African Studies at the University of London, University of California at Berkeley, and the Graduate Theological Union in Berkeley before the University of Chicago employed her in 1978. During her career, she has received several honorary degrees, and been awarded the Medal of the Collège de France in 1992. In addition to countless articles in books and journals, several translations and edited anthologies, Doniger has published the following books in English that pertain to the topic of this anthology: *Asceticism and Eroticism in the Mythology of Śiva* (1973), *The Origins of Evil in Hindu Mythology* (1976), *Women, Androgynes, and Other Mythical Beasts* (1980), *Dreams, Illusion, and Other Realities* (1984), *Other Peoples' Myths: The Cave of Echoes* (1988), *The Implied Spider: Politics and Theology in Myth* (1998), *Splitting the Difference: Gender and Myth in Ancient Greece and India* (1996), and *The Bedtrick: Tales of Sex and Masquerade* (2000). These works enable us to witness her transition from a practitioner of the method of structuralism in her first published book to her call for a "tool box" approach to the study of myth and religion.

Doniger admits that her so-called "tool box" approach is eclectic, but it possesses the advantage of enabling a scholar to select an appropriate method for a specific mode of interpretation. It is possible to fill one's tool box with methods such as psychoanalysis, literary criticism, history, ethnology, structuralism, philosophy, sociology, zoology, feminist theory, legal theory, and homosexual theory. By selecting an appropriate methodological tool, it is possible to discern patterns within myths or any other religious phenomenon. It is the data under study that dictate which method is the most appropriate for a particular topic. Doniger disagrees with scholars calling for falsifiable theories because she is convinced that unfalsifiable theories are difficult to avoid. An important aspect of her method is the use of comparison that is suggested by the nature of myth itself, because it is an inherently comparative form of narrative.

Guideline Questions

Is there evidence for a theological perspective in the work of Eliade? If so, what would such a perspective compromise?

From the perspective of Smith, what is it that we study when we inquire into the subject of religion? And does the answer to this question compromise the comparative method?

Why does Doniger think a "tool box" approach to the study of religion is necessary? And what are the implications of this approach for the study of myth?

From *The Sacred and the Profane: The Nature of Religion*

MIRCEA ELIADE

When the Sacred Manifests Itself

Man becomes aware of the sacred because it manifests itself, shows itself, as something wholly different from the profane. To designate the *act of manifestation* of the sacred, we have proposed the term *hierophany*. It is a fitting term, because it does not imply anything further; it expresses no more than is implicit in its etymological content, i.e., that *something sacred shows itself to us*. It could be said that the history of religions—from the most primitive to the most highly developed—is constituted by a great number of hierophanies, by manifestations of sacred realities. From the most elementary hierophany—e.g., manifestation of the sacred in some ordinary object, a stone or a tree—to the supreme hierophany (which, for a Christian, is the incarnation of God in Jesus Christ) there is no solution of continuity. In each case we are confronted by the same mysterious act—the manifestation of something of a wholly different order, a reality that does not belong to our world, in objects that are an integral part of our natural "profane" world.

The modern Occidental experiences a certain uneasiness before many manifestations of the sacred. He finds it difficult to accept the fact that, for many human beings, the sacred can be manifested in stones or trees, for example. But as we shall soon see, what is involved is not a veneration of the stone in itself, a cult of the tree in itself. The sacred tree, the sacred stone are not adored as stone or tree; they are worshipped precisely because they are *hierophanies*, because they show something that is no longer stone or tree but the *sacred,* the *ganz andere.*

It is impossible to overemphasize the paradox represented by every hierophany, even the most elementary. By manifesting the sacred, any object becomes *something else,* yet it continues to remain itself, for it continues to participate in its surrounding cosmic milieu. A *sacred* stone remains a *stone;* apparently (or, more precisely, from the profane point of view), nothing distinguishes it from all other stones. But for those to whom a stone reveals itself as sacred, its immediate reality is transmuted into a supernatural reality. In other words, for those who have a religious experience all nature is capable of revealing itself as cosmic sacrality. The cosmos in its entirety can become a hierophany.

The man of the archaic societies tends to live as much as possible *in* the sacred or in close proximity to consecrated objects. The tendency is perfectly understandable, because, for primitives as for the man of all premodern societies, the *sacred* is equivalent to a *power,* and, in the last analysis, to *reality.* The sacred is saturated with *being.* Sacred power means reality and at the same time enduringness and efficacity. The polarity sacred-profane is often expressed as an opposition between *real* and *unreal* or pseudo-real. (Naturally, we must not expect to find the archaic languages in possession of this philosophical terminology, *real-unreal,* etc.; but we find the *thing.*) . . .

Two Modes of Being in the World

The reader will very soon realize that *sacred* and *profane* are two modes of being in the world, two existential situations assumed by man in the course of his history. These modes of being in

Reprinted from The Sacred and the Profane: The Nature of Religion, *trans. Willard R. Trask (New York: Harcourt, Brace and Company, 1959).*

the world are not of concern only to the history of religions or to sociology; they are not the object only of historical, sociological, or ethnological study. In the last analysis, the *sacred* and *profane* modes of being depend upon the different positions that man has conquered in the cosmos; hence they are of concern both to the philosopher and to anyone seeking to discover the possible dimensions of human existence.

It is for this reason that, though he is a historian of religions, the author of this book proposes not to confine himself only to the perspective of his particular science. The man of the traditional societies is admittedly a *homo religiosus,* but his behavior forms part of the general behavior of mankind and hence is of concern to philosophical anthropology, to phenomenology, to psychology. . . .

The Sacred and History

Our primary concern is to present the specific dimensions of religious experience, to bring out the differences between it and profane experience of the world. I shall not dwell on the variations that religious experience of the world has undergone in the course of time. It is obvious, for example, that the symbolisms and cults of Mother Earth, of human and agricultural fertility, of the sacrality of woman, and the like, could not develop and constitute a complex religious system except through the discovery of agriculture; it is equally obvious that a preagricultural society, devoted to hunting, could not feel the sacrality of Mother Earth in the same way or with the same intensity. Hence there are differences in religious experience explained by differences in economy, culture, and social organization—in short, by history. Nevertheless, between the nomadic hunters and the sedentary cultivators there is a similarity in behavior that seems to us infinitely more important than their differences: *both live in a sacralized cosmos,* both share in a cosmic sacrality manifested equally in the animal world and in the vegetable world. We need only compare their existential situations with that of

a man of the modern societies, *living in a desacralized cosmos,* and we shall immediately be aware of all that separates him from them. At the same time we realize the validity of comparisons between religious facts pertaining to different cultures; all these facts arise from a single type of behavior, that of *homo religiosus. . . .*

Homogeneity of Space and Hierophany

For religious man space is not homogeneous; he experiences interruptions, breaks in it; some parts of space are qualitatively different from others. "Draw not nigh hither," says the Lord to Moses; "put off thy shoes from off thy feet, for the place whereon thou standest is holy ground" (Exodus, 3, 5). There is, then, a sacred space, and hence a strong, significant space; there are other spaces that are not sacred and so are without structure or consistency, amorphous. Nor is this all. For religious man, this spatial nonhomogeneity finds expression in the experience of an opposition between space that is sacred— the only *real* and *real-ly* existing space—and all other space, the formless expanse surrounding it.

It must be said at once that the religious experience of the nonhomogeneity of space is a primordial experience, homologizable to a founding of the world. It is not a matter of theoretical speculation, but of a primary religious experience that precedes all reflection on the world. For it is the break affected in space that allows the world to be constituted, because it reveals the fixed point, the central axis for all future orientation. When the sacred manifests itself in any hierophany, there is not only a break in the homogeneity of space; there is also revelation of an absolute reality, opposed to the nonreality of the vast surrounding expanse. The manifestation of the sacred ontologically founds the world. In the homogeneous and infinite expanse, in which no point of reference is possible and hence no orientation can be established, the hierophany reveals an absolute fixed point, a center.

So it is clear to what a degree the discovery—that is, the revelation—of a sacred space possesses existential value for religious man; for nothing can begin, nothing can be *done*, without a previous orientation—and any orientation implies acquiring a fixed point. It is for this reason that religious man has always sought to fix his abode at the "center of the world." *If the world is to be lived in,* it must be founded—and no world can come to birth in the chaos of the homogeneity and relativity of profane space. The discovery or projection of a fixed point—the center—is equivalent to the creation of the world; and we shall soon give some examples that will unmistakably show the cosmogonic value of the ritual orientation and construction of sacred space.

For profane experience, on the contrary, space is homogeneous and neutral; no break qualitatively differentiates the various parts of its mass. Geometrical space can be cut and delimited in any direction; but no qualitative differentiation and, hence, no orientation are given by virtue of its inherent structure. We need only remember how a classical geometrician defines space. Naturally, we must not confuse the *concept* of homogeneous and neutral geometrical space with the *experience* of profane space, which is in direct contrast to the experience of sacred space and which alone concerns our investigation. The *concept* of homogeneous space and the history of the concept (for it has been part of the common stock of philosophical and scientific thought since antiquity) are a wholly different problem, upon which we shall not enter here. What matters for our purpose is the *experience* of space known to nonreligious man—that is, to a man who rejects the sacrality of the world, who accepts only a profane existence, divested of all religious presuppositions.

It must be added at once that such a profane existence is never found in the pure state. To whatever degree he may have desacralized the world, the man who has made his choice in favor of a profane life never succeeds in completely doing away with religious behavior. This will become clearer as we proceed; it will appear that even the most desacralized existence still preserves traces of a religious valorization of the world.

But for the moment we will set aside this aspect of the problem and confine ourselves to comparing the two experiences in question—that of sacred space and that of profane space. The implications of the former experience have already been pointed out. Revelation of a sacred space makes it possible to obtain a fixed point and hence to acquire orientation in the chaos of homogeneity, to "found the world" and to live in a real sense. The profane experience, on the contrary, maintains the homogeneity and hence the relativity of space. No *true* orientation is now possible, for the fixed point no longer enjoys a unique ontological status; it appears and disappears in accordance with the needs of the day. Properly speaking, there is no longer any world, there are only fragments of a shattered universe, an amorphous mass consisting of an infinite number of more or less neutral places in which man moves, governed and driven by the obligations of an existence incorporated into an industrial society.

Yet this experience of profane space still includes values that to some extent recall the nonhomogeneity peculiar to the religious experience of space. There are, for example, privileged places, qualitatively different from all others—a man's birthplace, or the scenes of his first love, or certain places in the first foreign city he visited in youth. Even for the most frankly nonreligious man, all these places still retain an exceptional, a unique quality; they are the "holy places" of his private universe, as if it were in such spots that he had received the revelation of a reality *other* than that in which he participates through his ordinary daily life. . . .

Theophanies and Signs

To exemplify the nonhomogeneity of space as experienced by nonreligious man, we may turn to any religion. We will choose an example that is accessible to everyone—a church in a modern city. For a believer, the church shares in a different space from the street in which it stands. The door that opens on the interior of the church actually signifies a solution of continuity. The threshold that separates the two spaces also indicates the distance between two modes of being, the profane and the religious. The threshold is the limit, the boundary, the frontier that distinguishes and opposes two worlds—and at the same time the paradoxical place where those worlds communicate, where passage from the profane to the sacred world becomes possible.

A similar ritual function falls to the threshold of the human habitation, and it is for this reason that the threshold is an object of great importance. Numerous rites accompany passing the domestic thresholds—bow, a prostration, a pious touch of the hand, and so on. The threshold has its guardians—gods and spirits who forbid entrance both to human enemies and to demons and the powers of pestilence. It is on the threshold that sacrifices to the guardian divinities are offered. Here too certain palaeo-oriental cultures (Babylon, Egypt, Israel) situated the judgment place. The threshold, the door *show* the solution of continuity in space immediately and concretely; hence their great religious importance, for they are symbols and at the same time vehicles of *passage* from the one space to the other.

What has been said will make it clear why the church shares in an entirely different space from the buildings that surround it. Within the sacred precincts the profane world is transcended. On the most archaic levels of culture this possibility of transcendence is expressed by various *images of an opening;* here, in the sacred enclosure, communication with the gods is made possible; hence there must be a door to the world above, by which the gods can descend to earth and man can symbolically ascend to heaven. We shall soon see that this was the case in many religions; properly speaking, the temple constitutes an opening in the upward direction and ensures communication with the world of the gods.

Every sacred space implies a hierophany, an irruption of the sacred that results in detaching a territory from the surrounding cosmic milieu and making it qualitatively different. . . .

Often there is no need for a theophany or hierophany properly speaking; some sign suffices to indicate the sacredness of a place. "According to the legend, the *marabout* who founded El-Hamel at the end of the sixteenth century stopped to spend the night near a spring and planted his stick in the ground. The next morning, when he went for it to resume his journey, he found that it had taken root and that buds had sprouted on it. He considered this a sign of God's will and settled in that place."[1] In such cases the sign, fraught with religious meaning, introduces an absolute element and puts an end to relativity and confusion. Something that does not belong to this world has manifested itself apodictically and in so doing has indicated an orientation or determined a course of conduct.

When no sign manifests itself, it is provoked. For example, a sort of *evocation* is performed with the help of animals; it is they who show what place is fit to receive the sanctuary or the village. This amounts to an evocation of sacred forms or figures for the immediate purpose of establishing an orientation in the homogeneity of space. A sign is asked, to put an end to the tension and anxiety caused by relativity and disorientaion—in short, to reveal an absolute point of support. For example, a wild animal is hunted, and the sanctuary is built at the place where it is killed. Or a domestic animal—such as a bull—is turned loose; some days later it is searched for and sacrificed at the place where it is found. Later the altar will be raised there and the village will be built around the altar. In all these cases, the sacrality of a place is revealed by animals. This is as much as to say that men are not free to choose the sacred site, that they only seek for it and find it by the help of mysterious signs.

These few examples have shown the different means by which religious man receives the revelation of a sacred place. In each case the hierophany has annulled the homogeneity of space and revealed a fixed point. But since religious man cannot live except in an atmosphere impregnated with the sacred, we must expect to find a large number of techniques for consecrating space. As we saw, the sacred is pre-eminently the *real*, at once power, efficacity, the source of life and fecundity. Religious man's desire to live in the sacred is in fact equivalent to his desire to take up his abode in objective reality, not to let himself be paralyzed by the never-ceasing relativity of purely subjective experiences, to live in a real and effective world, and not in an illusion. This behavior is documented on every plane of religious man's existence, but it is particularly evident in his desire to move about only in a sanctified world, that is, in a sacred space. This is the reason for the elaboration of techniques of *orientation* which, properly speaking, are techniques for the *construction* of sacred space. But we must not suppose that *human* work is in question here, that it is through his own efforts that man can consecrate a space. In reality the ritual by which he constructs a sacred space is efficacious in the measure in which it *reproduces the work of the gods.* But the better to understand the need for ritual construction of a sacred space, we must dwell a little on the traditional concept of the "world"; it will then be apparent that for religious man every world is a sacred world.

Chaos And Cosmos

One of the outstanding characteristics of traditional societies is the opposition that they assume between their inhabited territory and the unknown and indeterminate space that surrounds it. The former is the world (more precisely, our world), the cosmos; everything outside it is no longer a cosmos but a sort of "other world," a foreign, chaotic space, peopled by ghosts, demons, "foreigners" (who are assimilated to demons and the souls of the dead). At first sight this cleavage in space appears to be due to the opposition between an inhabited and organized—hence cosmicized—territory and the unknown space that extends beyond its frontiers; on one side there is a cosmos, on the other a chaos. But we shall see that if every inhabited territory is a cosmos, this is precisely because it was first consecrated, because, in one way or another, it is the work of the gods or is in communication with the world of the gods. The world (that is, our world) is a universe within which the sacred has already manifested itself, in which, consequently, the break-through from plane to plane has become possible and repeatable. It is not difficult to see why the religious moment implies the cosmogonic moment. The sacred reveals absolute reality and at the same time makes orientation possible; hence it *founds the world* in the sense that it fixes the limits and establishes the order of the world. . . .

An unknown, foreign, and unoccupied territory (which often means, "unoccupied by our people") still shares in the fluid and larval modality of chaos. By occupying it and, above all, by settling in it, man symbolically transforms it into a cosmos through a ritual repetition of the cosmogony. What is to become "our world" must first be "created," and every creation has a paradigmatic model—the creation of the universe by the gods. When the Scandinavian colonists took possession of Iceland (*landnáma*) and cleared it, they regarded the enterprise neither as an original undertaking nor as human and profane work. For them, their labor was only repetition of a primordial act, the transformation of chaos into cosmos by the divine act of creation. When they tilled the desert soil, they were in fact repeating the act of the gods who had organized chaos by giving it a structure, forms, and norms.[2]

Whether it is a case of clearing uncultivated ground or of conquering and occupying a territory already inhabited by "other" human beings, ritual taking possession must always repeat the cosmogony. For in the view of archaic societies everything that is not "our world" is not yet a world. A territory can be made ours only by creating it anew, that is, by consecrating it. . . .

Consecration of a Place—Repetition of the Cosmogony

It must be understood that the cosmicization of unknown territories is always a consecration; to organize a space is to repeat the paradigmatic work of the gods. . . .

Life is not possible without an opening toward the transcendent; in other words, human beings cannot live in chaos. Once contact with the transcendent is lost, existence in the world ceases to be possible. . . .

To settle in a territory is, in the last analysis, equivalent to consecrating it. When settlement is not temporary, as among the nomads, but permanent as among sedentary peoples, it implies a vital decision that involves the existence of the entire community. Establishment in a particular place, organizing it, inhabiting it, are acts that presuppose an existential choice—the choice of the universe that one is prepared to assume by "creating" it. Now, this universe is always the replica of the paradigmatic universe created and inhabited by the gods; hence it shares in the sanctity of the gods' work. . . .

The Center of the World

The cry of the Kwakiutl neophyte, "I am at the Center of the World!" at once reveals one of the deepest meanings of sacred space. Where the break-through from plane to plane has been affected by a hierophany, there too an opening has been made, either upward (the divine world) or downward (the underworld, the world of the dead). The three cosmic levels—earth, heaven, underworld—have been put in communication. As we just saw, this communication is sometimes expressed through the image of a universal pillar, *axis mundi,* which at once connects and supports heaven and earth and whose base is fixed in the world below (the infernal regions). Such a cosmic pillar can be only at the very center of the universe, for the whole of the habitable world extends around it. Here, then, we have a sequence of religious conceptions and cosmological images that are inseparably connected and form a system that may be called the "system of the world" prevalent in traditional societies: (a) a sacred place constitutes a break in the homogeneity of space; (b) this break is symbolized by an opening by which passage from one cosmic region to another is made possible (from heaven to earth and vice versa; from earth to the underworld); (c) communication with heaven is expressed by one or another of certain images, all of which refer to the *axis mundi:* pillar (cf. the *universalis columna*), ladder (cf. Jacob's ladder), mountain, tree, vine, etc.; (d) around this cosmic axis lies the world (= our world), hence the axis is located "in the middle," at the "navel of the earth"; it is the Center of the World. . . .

We shall begin with an example that has the advantage of immediately showing not only the consistency but also the complexity of this type of symbolism—the cosmic mountain. . . . According to Islamic tradition, the highest place on earth is the *ka'aba,* because "the Pole Star bears witness that it faces the center of Heaven." For Christians, it is Golgotha that is on the summit of the cosmic mountain. All these beliefs express the same feeling, which is profoundly religious: "our world" is holy ground *because it is the place nearest to heaven,* because from here, from our abode, it is possible to reach heaven; hence our world is a high place. In cosmological terms, this religious conception is expressed by the projection of the favored territory which is "ours" onto the summit of the cosmic mountain. . . .

This same symbolism of the center explains other series of cosmological images and religious beliefs. Among these the most important are: (a) holy sites and sanctuaries are believed to be situated at the center of the world; (b) temples are replicas of the cosmic mountain and hence constitute the pre-eminent "link" between earth and heaven; (c) the foundations of temples descend deep into the lower regions. . . .

"Our World" is Always Situated at the Center

From all that has been said it follows that the true world is always in the middle, at the Center, for it is here that there is a break in plane and hence communication among the three cosmic zones. Whatever the extent of the territory involved, the cosmos that it represents is always perfect. An entire country (e.g., Palestine), a city (Jerusalem), a sanctuary (the Temple in Jerusalem), all equally well present an *imago mundi*. Treating of the symbolism of the Temple, Flavius Josephus wrote that the court represented the sea (i.e., the lower regions), the Holy Place represented earth, and the Holy of Holies heaven (*Ant. Jud.*, III, 7, 7). It is clear, then, that both the *imago mundi* and the Center are repeated in the inhabited world. Palestine, Jerusalem, and the Temple severally and concurrently represent the image of the universe and the Center of the World. This multiplicity of centers and this reiteration of the image of the world on smaller and smaller scales constitute one of the specific characteristics of traditional societies.

To us, it seems an inescapable conclusion that the *religious man sought to live as near as possible to the Center of the World.* He knew that his country lay at the midpoint of the earth; he knew too that his city constituted the navel of the universe, and, above all, that the temple or the palace were veritably Centers of the World. But he also wanted his own house to be at the Center and to be an *imago mundi*. . . .

In short, whatever the dimensions of the space with which he is familiar and in which he regards himself as situated—his country, his city, his village, his house—religious man feels the need always to exist in a total and organized world, in a cosmos.

A universe comes to birth from its center; it spreads out from a central point that is, as it were, its navel. It is in this way that, according to the *Rig Veda* (X, 149), the universe was born and developed—from a core, a central point. . . .

It follows that *every construction or fabrication has the cosmogony as paradigmatic model.* The creation of the world becomes the archetype of every creative human gesture, whatever its plane of reference may be. . . .

City-Cosmos

Since "our world" is a cosmos, any attack from without threatens to turn it into chaos. And as "our world" was founded by imitating the paradigmatic work of the gods, the cosmogony, so the enemies who attack it are assimilated to the enemies of the gods, the demons, and especially to the archdemon, the primordial dragon conquered by the gods at the beginning of time. An attack on "our world" is equivalent to an act of revenge by the mythical dragon, who rebels against the work of the gods, the cosmos, and struggles to annihilate it. "Our" enemies belong to the powers of chaos. *Any destruction of a city is equivalent to a retrogression to chaos. Any victory over the attackers reiterates the paradigmatic victory of the gods over the dragon (that is, over chaos).* . . .

Some Conclusions

. . . There is no need to dwell on the truism that, since the religious life of humanity is realized in history, its expressions are inevitably conditioned by the variety of historical moments and cultural styles. But for our purpose it is not the infinite variety of the religious experiences of space that concerns us but, on the contrary, their elements of unity. Pointing out the contrast between the behavior of nonreligious man with respect to the space in which he lives and the behavior of religious man in respect to sacred space is enough to make the difference in structure between the two attitudes clearly apparent.

If we should attempt to summarize the result of the descriptions that have been presented in this chapter, we could say that the experience of sacred space makes possible the "founding of the world": where the sacred manifests itself in space, *the real unveils itself,* the world comes into existence. But the irruption of the sacred does not only project a fixed point into the formless fluidity of profane space, a center into chaos; it also effects a break in plane, that is, it opens communication between the cosmic planes (between earth and heaven) and makes possible ontological passage from one mode of being to another. It is such a break in the heterogeneity of profane space that creates the center through which communication with the transmundane is established, that, consequently, founds the world, for the center renders *orientation* possible. Hence the manifestation of the sacred in space has a cosmological valence; every spatial hierophany or consecration of a space is equivalent to a cosmogony. The first conclusion we might draw would be: *the world becomes apprehensible as world, as cosmos, in the measure in which it reveals itself as a sacred world.*

Every world is the work of the gods, for it was either created directly by the gods or was consecrated, hence cosmicized, by men ritually reactualizing the paradigmatic act of Creation. This is as much as to say that religious man can live only in a sacred world, because it is only in such a world that he participates in being, that he has a real existence. This religious need expresses an unquenchable ontological thirst. Religious man thirsts for being. His terror of the chaos that surrounds his inhabited world corresponds to his terror of nothingness. The unknown space that extends beyond his world—an uncosmicized because unconsecrated space, a mere amorphous extent into which no orientation has yet been projected, and hence in which no structure has yet arisen—for religious man, this profane space represents absolute nonbeing. If, by some evil chance, he strays into it, he feels emptied of his ontic substance, as if he were dissolving in Chaos, and he finally dies.

This ontological thirst is manifested in many ways. In the realm of sacred space which we are now considering, its most striking manifestation is religious man's will to take his stand at the very heart of the real, at the Center of the World—that is, exactly where the cosmos came into existence and began to spread out toward the four horizons, and where, too, there is the possibility of communication with the gods; in short, precisely where he is *closest to the gods.* We have seen that the symbolism of the center is the formative principle not only of countries, cities, temples, and palaces but also of the humblest human dwelling, be it the tent of a nomad hunter, the shepherd's yurt, or the house of the sedentary cultivator. This is as much as to say that every religious man places himself at the Center of the World and by the same token at the very source of absolute reality, as close as possible to the opening that ensures him communication with the gods.

But since to settle somewhere, to inhabit a space, is equivalent to repeating the cosmogony and hence to imitating the work of the gods, it follows that, for religious man, every existential decision to situate himself in space in fact constitutes a religious decision. By assuming the responsibility of creating the world that he has chosen to inhabit, he not only cosmicizes chaos but also sanctifies his little cosmos by making it like the world of the gods. Religious man's profound nostalgia is to inhabit a "divine world," is his desire that his house shall be like the house of the gods, as it was later represented in temples and sanctuaries. In short, this religious nostalgia expresses *the desire to live in a pure and holy cosmos, as it was in the beginning, when it came fresh from the Creator's hands.*

The experience of sacred time will make it possible for religious man periodically to experience the cosmos as it was *in principio,* that is, at the mythical moment of Creation.

From *The Quest: History and Meaning in Religion*

MIRCEA ELIADE

A New Humanism

. . . Hermeneutics is of preponderant interest to us because, inevitably, it is the least-developed aspect of our discipline. Preoccupied, and indeed often completely taken up, by their admittedly urgent and indispensable work of collecting, publishing, and analyzing religious data, scholars have sometimes neglected to study their meaning. Now, these data represent the expression of various religious experiences; in the last analysis they represent positions and situations assumed by men in the course of history. Like it or not, the scholar has not finished his work when he has reconstructed the history of a religious form or brought out its sociological, economic, or political contexts. In addition, he must understand its meaning—that is, identify and elucidate the situations and positions that have induced or made possible its appearance or its triumph at a particular historical moment.

It is solely insofar as it will perform this task—particularly by making the meanings of religious documents intelligible to the mind of modern man—that the science of religions will fulfill its true cultural function. For whatever its role has been in the past, the comparative study of religions is destined to assume a cultural role of the first importance in the near future. As we have said on several occasions, our historical moment forces us into confrontations that could not even have been imagined fifty years ago. On the one hand, the peoples of Asia have recently reentered history; on the other, the so-called primitive peoples are preparing to make their appearance on the horizon of greater history (that is, they are seeking to become *active subjects* of history instead of its *passive objects,* as they have been hitherto). But if the peoples of the West are no longer the only ones to "make" history, their spiritual and cultural values will no longer enjoy the privileged place, to say nothing of the unquestioned authority, that they enjoyed some generations ago. These values are now being analyzed, compared, and judged by non-Westerners. On their side, Westerners are being increasingly led to study, reflect on, and understand the spiritualities of Asia and the archaic world. These discoveries and contacts must be extended through dialogues. But to be genuine and fruitful, a dialogue cannot be limited to empirical and utilitarian language. A true dialogue must deal with the central values in the cultures of the participants. Now, to understand these values rightly, it is necessary to know their religious sources. For, as we know, non-European cultures, both oriental and primitive, are still nourished by a rich religious soil.

This is why we believe that the history of religions is destined to play an important role in contemporary cultural life. This is not only because an understanding of exotic and archaic religions will significantly assist in a cultural dialogue with the representatives of such religions. It is more especially because, by attempting to understand the existential situations expressed by the documents he is studying, the historian of religions will inevitably attain to a deeper knowledge of man. It is on the basis of such a knowledge that a new humanism, on a worldwide scale, could develop. We may even ask if the history of religions cannot make a contribution of prime importance to its formation. For, on the one hand, the historical and comparative study of religions embraces all the cultural forms so far known, both the ethnological cultures and those that have played a major role in history; on the other hand, by studying the religious expressions of a culture, the scholar approaches it from within, and not merely in its sociological, economic, and political contexts. In the last analysis, the historian of religions is destined to elucidate a large number of situations unfamiliar to the man of the West. It is through an understanding of such unfamiliar, "exotic" situations that cultural provincialism is transcended.

But more is involved than a widening of the horizon, a quantitative, static increase in our "knowledge of man." It is the meeting with the "others"—with human beings belonging to various types of archaic and exotic societies—that is culturally stimulating and fertile. It is the personal experience of this unique hermeneutics that is creative. It is not beyond possibility that the discoveries and "encounters" made possible by the progress of the history of religions may have repercussions comparable to those of certain famous discoveries in the past of Western culture. We have in mind the discovery of the exotic and primitive arts, which revivified modern Western aesthetics. We have in mind especially the discovery of the unconscious by psychoanalysis, which opened new perspectives for our understanding of man. In both cases alike, there was a meeting with the "foreign," the unknown, with what cannot be reduced to familiar categories—in short, with the "wholly other." Certainly this contact with the "other" is not without its dangers. . . .

Obviously such "encounters" will become culturally creative only when the scholar has passed beyond the stage of pure erudition in other words, when, after having collected, described, and classified his documents, he has also made an effort to understand them on their own plane of reference. This implies no depreciation of erudition. . . . Like every human phenomenon, the religious phenomenon is extremely complex. To grasp all its valences and all its meanings, it must be approached from several points of view.

. . . We will add but one observation: A work of art reveals its meaning only insofar as it is regarded as an autonomous creation; that is, insofar as we accept its mode of being—*that of an artistic creation*—and do not reduce it to one of its constituent elements (in the case of a poem, sound, vocabulary, linguistic structure, etc.) or to one of its subsequent uses (a poem which carries a political message or which can serve as a document for sociology, ethnography, etc.).

In the same way, it seems to us that a religious datum reveals its deeper meaning when it is considered on its plane of reference, and not when it is reduced to one of its secondary aspects or its contexts. To give but one example: Few religious phenomena are more directly and more obviously connected with sociopolitical circumstances than the modem messianic and millenarian movements among colonial peoples (cargo-cults, etc.). Yet identifying and analyzing the conditions that prepared and made possible such messianic movements form only a part of the work of the historian of religions. For these movements are equally creations of the human spirit, in the sense that they have become what they are—*religious movements,* and not merely gestures of protest and revolt—through a creative act of the spirit. In short, a religious phenomenon such as primitive messianism must be studied just as the *Divina Commedia* is studied, that is, by using all the possible tools of scholarship (and not, to return to what we said above in connection with Dante, merely his vocabulary or his syntax, or simply his theological and political ideas, etc.). For, if the history of religions is destined to further the rise of a new humanism, it is incumbent on the historian of religions to bring out the autonomous value—the value as *spiritual creation*—of all these primitive religious movements. To reduce them to sociopolitical contexts is, in the last analysis, to admit that they are not sufficiently "elevated," sufficiently "noble." . . .

This does not mean, of course, that a religious phenomenon can be understood outside of its "history," that is, outside of its cultural and socioeconomic contexts. There is no such thing as a "pure" religious datum, outside of history, for there is no such thing as a human datum that is not at the same time a historical datum. Every religious experience is expressed and transmitted in a particular historical context. But admitting the historicity of religious experiences does not imply that they are reducible to non-religious forms of behavior. Stating that a religious datum is always a historical datum does not mean that it is reducible to a non-religious history—for example, to an economic, social, or political history. We must never lose sight of one of the fundamental principles of modern science: *the scale creates the phenomenon*. . . .

We have no intention of developing a methodology of the science of religions here. The problem is far too complex to be treated in a few pages. But we think it useful to repeat that the *homo religiosus* represents the "total man"; hence, the science of religions must become a total discipline in the sense that it must use, integrate, and articulate the results obtained by the various methods of approaching a religious phenomenon. It is not enough to grasp the meaning of a religious phenomenon in a certain culture and, consequently, to decipher its "message" (for every religious phenomenon constitutes a "cipher"); it is also necessary to study and understand its "history," that is, to unravel its changes and modifications and, ultimately, to elucidate its contribution to the entire culture. In the past few years a number of scholars have felt the need to transcend the alternative religious phenomenology or history of religion and to reach a broader perspective in which these two intellectual operations can be applied together. It is toward the integral conception of the science of religions that the efforts of scholars seem to be orienting themselves today. To be sure, these two approaches correspond in

some degree to different philosophical temperaments. And it would be naive to suppose that the tension between those who try to understand the *essence* and the *structures* and those whose only concern is the history of religious phenomena will one day be completely done away with. But such a tension is creative. It is by virtue of it that the science of religions will escape dogmatism and stagnation.

The results of these two intellectual operations are equally valuable for a more adequate knowledge of *homo religiosus*. For, if the "phenomenologists" are interested in the meanings of religious data, the "historians," on their side, attempt to show how these meanings have been experienced and lived in the various cultures and historical moments, how they have been transformed, enriched, or impoverished in the course of history. But if we are to avoid sinking back into an obsolete "reductionism," this history of religious meanings must always be regarded as forming part of the history of the human spirit.

More than any other humanistic discipline (i.e., psychology, anthropology, sociology, etc.), history of religions can open the way to a philosophical anthropology. For the sacred is a universal dimension and . . . the beginnings of culture are rooted in religious experiences and beliefs. Furthermore, even after they are radically secularized, such cultural creations as social institutions, technology, moral ideas, arts, etc., cannot be correctly understood if one does not know their original religious matrix, which they tacitly criticized, modified, or rejected in becoming what they are now: secular cultural values. Thus, the historian of religions is in a position to grasp the permanence of what has been called man's specific existential situation of "being in the world," for the experience of the sacred is its correlate. In fact, man's becoming aware of his own mode of being and assuming his presence in the world together constitute a "religious" experience.

Ultimately, the historian of religions is forced by his hermeneutical endeavor to "relive" a multitude of existential situations and to unravel a number of presystematic ontologies. A historian of religions cannot say, for example, that he has understood the Australian religions if he has not understood the Australians' *mode of being in the world*. . . . Even at that stage of culture we find the notion of a plurality of modes of being as well as the awareness that the singularity of the human condition is the result of a primordial "sacred history." . . .

NOTES

1. René Basset, *Revue des Traditions Populaires*, XXII, 1907, p. 287.

2. Cf. Mircea Eliade, *The Myth of the Eternal Return* (New York: Pantheon Books, 1954), pp. 11ff.

Counterpoint: Feminist Anthropology and the Gendering of Religious Studies

ROSALIND SHAW

Rosalind Shaw teaches at Tufts University. She has published *Dreaming, Religion and Society in Africa* and *Syncretism/Anti-Syncretism*.

FEMINIST PROJECTS of disciplinary transformation may be caught up in contradictions arising from the histories of the disciplines in which change is sought. In the history and phenomenology of religions, problems of disciplinary transformation appear to extend far beyond the difficulties of eradicating "male bias" or of including women's standpoints. Such transformation may entail nothing less than the dissolution and reconstruction of the discipline itself. In anthropology, attempts to effect a feminist metamorphosis in the 1970s and early 1980s were subject to contradictions whose identification and critique by Strathern assisted scholars in rethinking the relationship between feminism and anthropology.[1] Strathern's characterization of the "awkward relationship" between anthropology and feminism finds important parallels in

the history of religions, and her critiques may usefully be applied to certain forms of feminist religious studies today.

Strathern characterizes feminism and anthropology as close neighbors, enmeshed in a relationship of mutual mockery. They do not so much contradict as "mock" each other, she argues, because each so nearly attains the ideal which eludes the other. On the one hand, anthropologists have a comparative perspective which can give them a critical distance from dominant Euro-American understandings of gender and women's power—a distance which is highly valued in much of feminist thought. On the other hand, anthropologists are striving to reform anthropology from the conditions of its production, in which knowledge has been constituted within unequal power relationships

Reprinted from Rosalind Shaw, "Feminist Anthropology and the Gendering of Religious Studies," in Religion and Gender, *ed. Ursula King (London: Blackwell Publishers, 1994).*

between white Western anthropologists and colonized peoples of the Third World, among whom most anthropologists have worked. Anthropologists' struggles to effect a shift from a "view from above" in order to reinvent anthropology contrast sharply with the apparent ease with which feminist scholars have assumed a "view from below," in which relations of domination are analyzed from a subordinate standpoint.

While anthropology "mocks" feminism from its advantaged position for cultural critiques of Western social forms, then, feminism—from its own assumed standpoint of the subordinate's perspective—mocks anthropology. Anthropology can never really achieve its desired perspective of the "view from below" until non-Western anthropologists have a stronger voice in its reinvention. Because of this mutual mockery, "feminist anthropology" is, for Strathern, not quite an oxymoron, but a hybrid beast. The awkwardness between feminism and anthropology thus involves disjunctions which extend beyond the problems of introducing women's perspectives into a discipline with a history of "male bias." This is because other forms of domination—in particular those of colonialism and racism—are just as central as that of gender inequality to the relationship between feminist thought and anthropology.

The same could be said of those forms of domination implicit in the relationship between feminism and the history of religions, but the mockery here is one-sided. Like anthropology, the history of religions has a long tradition of a perspective which is valued highly in feminist scholarship. A hermeneutic approach which makes empathy with lived religious experience central to interpretation and comparison was developed in the history and phenomenology of religions when other disciplines were working through their positivist phases. Since critiques of positivism have been prominent in many strands of feminist epistemology, the history of religions could be said to have had at its core an interpretive standpoint which many have seen as central to feminist scholarship.

But in practice, the history/phenomenology of religions is an apt illustration that a hermeneutic of empathy and experience is far from being automatically feminist. The question of whose subjective experience is being empathized with is crucial. All too typically, it is not that of real persons but of a "collective subject" whose supposedly authoritative experience is either undifferentiated by gender, race, class or age, or defined explicitly as male. In particular, the writings of Eliade and his followers are premised upon this collective subject, usually known as "*Homo religiosus.*" . . .

What does "lived religious experience" mean when it is located in a purportedly universal subject? And how universal can this impersonal subject be when represented through such unabashedly gender-specific depiction? In this totalizing but exclusionary empathy for a reified *Homo religiosus,* the mockery of feminism by the history of religions—like the mockery of feminism by anthropology—falls flat.

This mockery, moreover, is not reciprocated. Those in mainstream history of religions have not typically striven for ideals represented by feminist scholarship. . . . But to argue that the standpoint of mainstream history and phenomenology of religions and the standpoint of feminist critiques are merely two perspectives among many misses the point of such critiques: it is not just that all knowledge is partial, but that some perspectives represent a "view from above." In the history of religion, a "view from above" is entrenched through, first, the overwhelming emphasis given to religious texts and, second, the concept of the *sui generis* nature of religion, in which religion is treated as a discrete and irreducible phenomenon which exists "in and of itself." Feminist scholarship can only collide with, rather than mock, mainstream history of religions: not only has the latter had a very poor record of overhauling itself in terms of critiques "from below," but its central *sui generis* argument is incompatible with the very basis of such critiques.

The "Distinctively Religious" and the Distinctly Apolitical

Both the textual and the *sui generis* definitions emphasized in religious studies scholarship are, in practice, "bracketing" devices which support each other in representing religion as socially decontextualized and ungendered. Understandings of "religion as scripture" tend, for example, to privilege (a) religions with texts, and (b) scholarly elites within scriptural religious traditions who claim the authority to interpret texts (and from whom women are usually debarred). The religious understandings of those excluded from authorizing discourses of textual interpretation are implicitly discounted and relegated to a "lower" level. . . .

Like the understanding of "religion as text," the concept of the *sui generis* nature of religion also entails the decontextualization of religion. In mainstream history of religions, understandings of "the uniquely religious" are usually constituted by excluding or peripheralizing social and political content in defining what really counts as "religion." Historians of religion who make the *sui generis* claim do not suggest that "pure religious" phenomena can exist empirically, but that "certain experiences or phenomena exhibit a fundamental religious character and that our method must be commensurate with the nature of our subject-matter. From the perspective of the History of Religions, the sociological, economic, or anthropological dimensions of the phenomena are secondary."[2]

Thus desocialized, "the uniquely religious" is deemed interpretable only "on its own terms": studies of religion which entail social or political analysis are typically dismissed as reductionist. . . . Since "religion" as a category is not indigenous to most parts of the world, moreover, the *sui generis* concept often involves the imposition of "the irreducibly religious" upon a landscape of human practices and understandings which do not divide up into the categories cherished by Western scholars.

As part of its discouragement of debates about "the nature of religion," the discourse of irreducibility also deflects questions of power and inequality: the "distinctively religious" is constituted as distinctly apolitical. . . . Eliade leaves us in no doubt that for him "mere gestures of protest and revolt" are not part of the creative repertoire of "the human spirit." But for those within millenarian movements, politics and protest are implicated in the very constitution of their religious practice. Their experience of colonial power is "interior" to—not somehow detachable from—their lived religious experience. Power, then, cannot simply be bracketed off as a "dimension" or "aspect" of religion.

To take another example, attempting to understand a woman's experience of religion in terms of (not just "in the context of") her position within a male-dominated religious tradition is reductionist only if we have severed "religion" from "power" in the first place. On the contrary, it would be a "reduction"—in the rather different sense of a diminished and distorted representation of her experience—to bracket off "male dominance" and "gender asymmetry" as a mere biographical backdrop to, but not really part of, experiences which she calls "religious." With power and social organization detached from the analysis of gender and religion, we are left either with meaningless accounts of "religious gender roles" ("the men do this; the women do that"), or with disconnected descriptions of female deities ("add goddesses and stir").

The *sui generis* concept thus stands in a contradictory relationship to the premises of feminist scholarship. By making power irrelevant to "the nature of religion," it denies the scholar of religion a language with which to make a critique "from below," relegating the very basis of a distinction between a "view from above" and a "view from below" to the realm of crass reductionism. By making it central to their discourse, scholars in the history of religions are effectively insulated from uncomfortable questions about standpoint and privilege—questions upon which feminist scholarship is based. The relationship between feminism and mainstream history of religions is not merely awkward; it is mutually toxic.

Institutional Embattlement and the Politics of Interpretation

The concept of the irreducibility of religion was not, of course, intentionally formulated as a bulwark against feminist critiques (even if this is, in fact, a consequence). Its hegemony has to be understood within the politics of disciplinary identity, in the embattled institutional position of the history of religions within the academy. Like feminist scholarship and women's studies, religious studies is ambiguously situated as both a distinct discipline and a multidisciplinary field analogous to American studies or science studies. As such, in many universities it has been in constant danger of being demoted from a department to a sub-department or an interdisciplinary program. In other institutions it is perceived to be subsumed by—and hence institutionally indistinct from—theology: in British universities in particular, the era of cuts euphemistically described as "rationalization" in the late 1970s and throughout the 1980s saw the closure of most departments of religious studies which were not sheltered within departments of theology. In public, secular American universities, on the other hand, religious studies is often attacked as an apparent anomaly. . . .

In addition to this institutional embattlement, mainstream history of religions has for several decades been intellectually marginalized, consistently out of phase with broader debates and paradigm-shifts which cut across disciplines, such as feminism, structuralism, postmodernism, reflexivity, and cultural critique. It has been so ignored by scholars in other disciplines who are concerned with religion that any attention from the latter tends to bring forth a spate of published reactions. . . . Up to the 1960s, the strong phenomenological strand of the history

of religions placed it, in many ways, ahead of its time. This also placed it beyond the pale, however, during the positivist and scientistic phase of anthropology and other social sciences during their structural-functionalist and structuralist eras. In the 1960s and 1970s, however, anthropological interests shifted towards a concern with meaning and interpretation which took the form of symbolic anthropology in the USA (e.g., Geertz) and semantic anthropology in the UK (e.g., Crick). These shifts entailed a reawakening of interest in religion and in phenomenology, but this took place for the most part as if the phenomenology of religion had never existed.

It has been in response to the double threat of institutional embattlement and intellectual marginalization that the boundary-defending argument of the *sui generis* nature of religion—and accompanying claims for the unique interpretive privilege of the history of religions—have been developed into a kind of disciplinary creed. "Antireductionist" arguments, usually reiterated as a counter-critique of a structural-functionalist anthropology which has not existed for thirty years, are still part of the prevailing discourse of the history of religions today (when many anthropologists, ironically, can scarcely remember what structural-functionalism was).

The "straw discipline" argument of antireductionism may sometimes be tactically useful in institutional battles over departmental autonomy and resources, but at the ultimately self-defeating cost of continued intellectual marginalization. "By imagining a continuing struggle between religious studies and the social sciences," one scholar of religion observes sadly, "we can be encouraged that someone is taking us seriously, even if that someone is mostly only we ourselves."[3] The high disciplinary walls which scholars of religion have created have cut them off from many new intellectual directions, debates and discourses, thereby transforming mainstream history of religions from an exciting approach ahead of its time in the 1950s and

1960s to a broken record endlessly rehearsing thirty-year-old debates in the 1990s. . . .

The Gendering of Religious Studies

By reconceptualizing power as integral to—as opposed to a detachable "dimension" of—religion, feminist religious studies has the potential to generate conceptual change and renewal. Yet its capacity for disciplinary transformation is currently cramped by hangovers from mainstream religious studies which some forms of feminist religious studies have carried with them. In this way, these (fairly dominant) strands of feminist religious studies are in a position analogous to that of feminist anthropology in the 1970s, which responded to the marginalizing of women in the discipline's mainstream by an essentializing discourse which placed it securely in a feminist "ghetto." . . .

Particularly important here was Strathern's critique of the assumption of a unitary and essentialized category of "woman" which unites the female researcher with the women in the (different) social and cultural context she is researching. Strathern's scepticism helped to sensitize white feminist anthropologists to criticisms of Western feminism by non-Western women and women of color, who pointed out that their race and their history of colonization make a difference which makes it impossible to talk of a universal "women's nature." Currently, few feminist scholars in any discipline assume a universal "female reality." That many scholars in feminist religious studies are an exception to this derives, I believe, from the universalizing and essentializing tendencies of the discipline's mainstream. . . .

Through such appropriation of the experience of women in other times and places, a feminized *Homo religiosus* lives on. A feminist religious studies which does not incorporate differences between women—in particular between the researcher and the women she writes about—will merely invoke the concept of power without applying it to its own colonizing discourse. That sensitivity to these differences does not, of course, mean "objectivity" is clear in examples of feminist studies of women's religion which demonstrate such sensitivity.[4] Quite the reverse: it requires more reflexivity rather than less; more attention to intersubjectivity; more attention to the voices of other women as personal actors that one cannot speak for; and more attention to the web of social relationships and cultural practices through which their power and experience are constituted.

NOTES

1. Marilyn Strathern, "Culture in a Netbag: On the Manufacture of a Subdiscipline in Anthropology," *Man* 16 (1981): 665–688; "An Awkward Relationship: The Case of Feminism and Anthropology," *Signs* 12 (1987): 276–292.

2. Douglas Allen, *Structure and Creativity in Religion: Hermeneutics in Mircea Eliade's Phenomenology and New Directions* (The Hague: Mouton, 1978), pp. 83–84.

3. Wayne Elzey, "Mircea Eliade and the Battle Against Reductionism," *Religion and Reductionism*, ed. Thomas Idinopulos and Edward Yonan (Leiden: E. J. Brill, 1994), p. 94.

4. Janice Boddy, *Wombs and Alien Spirits: Women, Men and the Zar Cult in Northern Sudan* (Madison: University of Wisconsin Press, 1989) and Karen McCarthy Brown, *Mama Lola: A Vodou Priestess in Brooklyn* (Berkeley: University of California Press, 1991).

From *Map Is Not Territory: Studies in the History of Religions*

JONATHAN Z. SMITH

Map Is Not Territory

. . . I take the terms "Human Sciences," "Humanities" and "History" to function synonymously and to serve as limiting perspectives on my understanding of religion. They play the same role as that stubborn stone in Doctor Johnson's fabled retort to Bishop Berkeley, that is, as boundaries of concreteness over against which to judge more speculative and normative inquiries in religious studies. As I have written in another context, the philosopher or the theologian has the possibility of exclaiming with Archimedes: "Give me a place to stand on and I will move the world." There is, for such a thinker, the possibility of a real beginning, even of achieving The Beginning, a standpoint from which all things flow, a standpoint from which he may gain clear vision. The historian has no such possibility. There are no places on which he might stand apart from the messiness of the given world. There is, for him, no real beginning, but only the plunge which he takes at some arbitrary point to avoid the unhappy alternatives of infinite regress or silence. His standpoint is not discovered, rather it is fabricated with no claim beyond that of sheer survival. The historian's point of view cannot sustain clear vision.

The historian's task is to complicate not to clarify. He strives to celebrate the diversity of manners, the variety of species, the opacity of things. He is therefore barred from making a frontal assault on his topic. Like the pilgrim, the historian is obliged to approach his subject obliquely. He must circumambulate the spot several times before making even the most fleeting contact. His method, like that of Tristram Shandy, Gentleman, is that of the digression. . . .

The historian provides us with hints that remain too fragile to bear the burden of being solutions. He is a man of insights: not, preeminently, a man of vision.

The second implication that I derive from the limiting effect of these conjunctions is that religion is an inextricably human phenomenon. In the West, we live in a post-Kantian world in which man is defined as a world-creating being and culture is understood as a symbolic process of world-construction. It is only, I believe, from this humane, post-Enlightenment perspective that the academic interpretation of religion becomes possible. Religious studies are most appropriately described in relation to the Humanities and the Human Sciences, in relation to Anthropology rather than Theology.

What we study when we study religion is one mode of constructing worlds of meaning, worlds within which men find themselves and in which they choose to dwell. What we study is the passion and drama of man discovering the truth of what it is to be human. History is the framework within whose perimeter those human expressions, activities and intentionalities that we call "religious" occur. Religion is the quest, within the bounds of the human, historical condition, for the power to manipulate and negotiate one's "situation" so as to have "space" in which to meaningfully dwell. It is the power to relate one's domain to the plurality of environmental and social spheres in such a way as to guarantee the conviction that one's existence "matters."

Reprinted from Map Is Not Territory: Studies in the History of Religions *(Leiden: E. J. Brill, 1978).*

Religion is a distinctive mode of human creativity, a creativity which both discovers limits and creates limits for humane existence. What we study when we study religion is the variety of attempts to map, construct and inhabit such positions of power through the use of myths, rituals and experiences of transformation.

Allow me to illustrate these reflections with a story. A number of years ago, in preparation for entering an agricultural school, I worked on a dairy farm in upstate New York. I would have to rise at about a quarter to four and fire up the wood burning stove, heat a pan of water and lay out the soap and towels so that my boss could wash when he awoke half an hour later. Each morning, to my growing puzzlement, when the boss would step outside after completing his ablutions, he would pick up a handful of soil and rub it over his hands. After several weeks of watching this activity, I finally, somewhat testily, asked for an explanation: "Why do you start each morning by cleaning yourself and then step outside and immediately make yourself dirty?" "Don't you city boys understand anything?" was the scornful reply. "Inside the house it's dirt; outside, it's earth. You must take it off inside to eat and be with your family. You must put it on outside to work and be with the animals." What my boss instinctively knew is what we have only recently discovered through reading books such as Mary Douglas', *Purity and Danger,* that there is nothing that is inherently or essentially clean or unclean, sacred or profane. There are situational or relational categories, mobile boundaries which shift according to the map being employed. . . .

I would term this cosmology a locative map of the world and the organizer of such a world, an imperial figure. It is a map of the world which guarantees meaning and value through structures of congruity and conformity.

Students of religion have been most successful in describing and interpreting this locative, imperial map of the world—especially within archaic, urban cultures. . . .

The most persuasive witnesses to a locative, imperial world-view are the production of well organized, self-conscious scribal elites who had a deep vested interest in restricting mobility and valuing place. The texts are, by and large, the production of temples and royal courts and provide their raison d'être—the temple, upon which the priest's and scribe's income rested, as "Center" and microcosm; the requirements of exact repetition in ritual and the concomitant notion of ritual as a reenactment of divine activities, both of which are dependent upon written texts which only the elite could read; and propaganda for their chief patron, the king, as guardian of cosmic and social order. In most cases one cannot escape the suspicion that, in the locative map of the world, we are encountering a self-serving ideology which ought not to be generalized into the universal pattern of religious experience and expression.

I find the same conservative, ideological element strongly to the fore in a variety of approaches to religion which lay prime emphasis upon congruency and conformity, whether it be expressed through phenomenological descriptions of repetition, functionalist descriptions of feedback mechanisms or structuralist descriptions of mediation. Therefore it has seemed to me of some value, in my own work, to explore the dimensions of incongruity that exist in religious materials. For I do believe that religion is, among other things, an intellectual activity—and, to play upon Paul Ricoeur's well-known phrase, it is the perception of incongruity that gives rise to thought.

In our quest to distinguish cultural man from natural man, emphasis has rightly been laid on those activities of man which are unique, especially language and historical consciousness. But it has been one of the ironies of our intellectual history that we also use these faculties and this vision of human culture and creativity to dichotomize the world into human beings (who are generally like-us) and non-human beings (who are generally not-like-us), into the "we" and the "them" which are the boundaries of any ethnic map.

In classical Greek anthropology, this distinction was made on the basis of language. To be human was to be a Hellene, to speak intelligible, non-stuttering speech (that is to say, Greek). To be, in a cultural sense, non-human was to be a barbarian, to speak unintelligible, stuttering, animal or child-like speech (*bar, bar, bar* from which the word "barbarian" is derived). In the nineteenth and twentieth centuries, growing out of Western imperialist and colonialist experience and ideology, we have distinguished between those who have history and those who have no history—or, to put it more accurately, between those who make history whom we call human or visible beings and those who undergo history whom we call non-human or invisible beings. . . .

The West is active, it makes history, it is visible, it is human. The non-Western world is static, it undergoes history, it is invisible, it is non-human. At times, this contrast is revealed in telling semantic shifts, for example, the Classical Greeks are "Western"; the Byzantine Greeks are "Eastern."

The same sort of mapping occurs within the field of religious studies, especially with respect to the dubious category of "World Religions." A World Religion is a religion like ours; but it is, above all, a tradition which has achieved sufficient power and numbers to enter our history, either to form it, interact with it, or to thwart it. All other religions are invisible. We recognize both the unity within and the diversity between the "great" World Religions because they correspond to important geopolitical entities with which we must deal. All "primitives," by way of contrast, may be simply lumped together as may be so-called "minor religions" because they do not confront our history in any direct fashion. They are invisible. . . .

What troubles me is that these two portraits of the primitive—the nineteenth century negative evaluation and the twentieth century positive (even nostalgic) appreciation—are but the two sides of the same coin. They are but variations on the even older ambivalence: the Wild Man and the Noble Savage. Both see the primitive as essentially not-like-us. To the degree that we identify change, historical consciousness and critical reason with being human (and we do), the nineteenth century interpretation maintained that the savage was non-human; the twentieth century interpretation suggests, at best, that the primitive is another kind of human. Both interpretations take the primitive's myths literally, and believe him to do the same, the nineteenth century holding that anyone who believes such stuff is a fool, a child or subhuman; the twentieth century arguing that the myths are true, although possessing another kind of truth than that which we usually recognize.

Such interpretations have severely limited our capacity for understanding the worlds of other men. On the conceptual level it robs them of their humanity, of those perceptions of discrepancy and discord which give rise to the symbolic project that we identify as the very essence of being human. It reduces the primitive to the level of fantasy where experience plays no role in challenging belief . . ., where discrepancy does not give rise to thought but rather is thought away. . . .

My model of application has been much influenced by recent studies of African divination. The diviner, by manipulating a limited number of objects which have an assigned, though broad, field of meaning and by the rigorous interrogation of his client in order to determine his situation, arrives at a description of a possible world of meaning which confers significance on his client's question or distress. The diviner offers a "plausibility structure"; he suggests a possible "fit" between the structure he offers and the client's situation and both the diviner and client delight in exploring the adequacy and inadequacy, the implications and applicability of the diviner's proposal.

Myth, as narrative, is the analogue to the limited number of culturally determined objects manipulated by the diviner. Myth, as application, represents the complex interaction between diviner, client and situation.

There is something funny, there is something crazy about myth for it shares with the comic and the insane the quality of obsessiveness. Nothing, in principle, is allowed to elude its grasp. The myth, like the diviner's objects, is a code capable, in theory, of universal application. But this obsessiveness, this claim to universality is relativized by the situation. There is delight and there is play in both the fit and the incongruity of the fit between an element in the myth and this or that segment of the world or of experience which is encountered. It is this oscillation between "fit" and "no fit" which gives rise to thought. Myth shares with other forms of human speech such as the joke or riddle, a perception of a possible relationship between different "things." It delights, it gains its power, knowledge and value from the play between. . . .

In my most recent work, I am attempting to develop this understanding of myth in two quite different groups of materials. I am working with a variety of Mediterranean religious texts from late antiquity in which incongruity is expressed through motifs of transcendence, rebellion and paradox. I am also attempting to study a diverse collection of primitive materials—a set of traditions which are usually labeled "hunting magic" in which a discrepancy exists between what the hunters say they do when they hunt and what they actually do, a discrepancy that is raised to thought in rituals which enact a perfect hunt; a group of cargo cult materials in which the indigenous situation is rendered problematic by the incongruous presence of the white man; and a group of archaic myths which share the theme of a fundamental rupture between the world of the ancestors and the present human conditions. While it would be of some importance to indicate how these different sets of studies have reenforced each other as an indication of my commitment to the comparative enterprise, I shall obey the strictures of space and confine myself to one example drawn from the final group.

Perhaps the best known example of the mythologem of rupture is the story of Hainuwele, a tale that was first collected from the Wemale tribe of Ceram (one of the Moluccan islands, immediately west of New Guinea) in 1927. As this myth has been a favorite text for those who have insisted upon a radical separation of the primal myth from its application, its reconsideration will provide a test case for the adequacy of my proposal.

The text is too long to quote, so I shall offer only a brief summary. It begins "Nine families of mankind came forth in the beginning from Mount Nunusaku where the people had emerged from clusters of bananas" and goes on to narrate how an ancestor named Ameta found a coconut speared on a boar's tusk and, in a dream, was instructed to plant it. In six days a palm had sprung from the nut and flowered. Ameta cut his finger and his blood dripped on the blossom. Nine days later a girl grew from the blossom and in three more days she became adolescent. Ameta cut her from the tree and named her Hainuwele, "coconut girl." "But she was not like an ordinary person, for when she would answer the call of nature, her excrement consisted of all sorts of valuable articles, such as Chinese dishes and gongs, so that Ameta became very rich." During a major religious festival, Hainuwele stood in the middle of the dance grounds and excreted a whole series of valuable articles (Chinese porcelain dishes, metal knives, copper boxes, golden earrings and great brass gongs). After nine days of this activity, "the people thought this thing mysterious . . . they were jealous that Hainuwele could distribute such wealth and decided to kill her." The ancestors dug a hole in the middle of the dance ground, threw Hainuwele in and danced the ground firm on top of her. Ameta dug up her corpse, dismembered it and buried the cut pieces. These pieces gave rise to previously unknown plant species, especially tuberous plants which have been, ever since, the principal form of food on Ceram.[1]

The chief interpreter of this myth, Adolf Jensen, has understood the tale to describe the origins of death, sexuality and cultivated food plants—that is to say, as a description of human existence as distinct from ancestral times. While I cannot within the scope of this lecture treat each detail, I find no hint in the text that sexuality or death is the result of Hainuwele's murder nor that the cultivation of plants are solely the consequence of her death.

Death and sexuality are already constitutive of human existence in the very first line of the text with its mention of the emergence of man from clusters of bananas. It is a widely spread Oceanic tale of the origin of death—found as well among the Wemale, that human finitude is the result of a choice or conflict between a stone and a banana. Bananas are large, perennial herbs which put forth tall, vigorous shoots which die after producing fruit. The choice, the conflict in these tales is between progeny followed by death (the banana) and eternal but sterile life (the stone). The banana always wins. Thus Jensen's interpretation collapses with the very first line. Man as mortal and sexual, indeed the correlation of death and sexuality, is the presupposition of the myth of Hainuwele, not its result. Ameta's dream, before the birth of Hainuwele, indicates that the cultivation of plants is likewise present. Jensen's interpretation rests on only a few details: that Hainuwele was killed, buried, dismembered and that from pieces of her body tuberous plants grew. This is a widespread motif, rendered more "plausible" by the fact that this is the way in which tubers such as yams are actually cultivated. The yam is stored in the ground, dug up and divided into pieces and these are then planted and result in new yams. That tropical yams can grow to a length of several feet and weigh a hundred pounds only furthers the analogy with the human body.

If Jensen's exegesis must be set aside, what then is the myth about? Our sense of incongruity is clearly seized by her curious mode of production—the excretion of valuable objects—and it is this act which clearly provides the motivation for the central act in the story, her murder. We share our sense of incongruity with the Wemale, for "they thought this thing mysterious . . . and plotted to kill her."

There is, in fact, a double incongruity for the objects Hainuwele excretes are all manufactured trade goods—indeed they are all goods which are used on Ceram as money. Using the phrase literally, the myth of Hainuwele is a story of the origin of "filthy lucre," of "dirty money."

The text is not an origin of death or an origin of tubers tale. It is not primarily concerned with the discrepancy between the world of the ancestors and the world of men. It is, I would suggest, a witness to the confrontation between native and European economic systems. The text is important not because it opens a vista to an archaic tuber-cultivator culture but because it reflects what I would term a "cargo situation" without a cargo cult. It reflects a native strategy for dealing with a new, incongruous situation, a strategy that thinks with indigenous elements (the diviner's pot). The myth of Hainuwele is not a primal myth (as Jensen insists), it is rather a stunning example of application.

In Oceanic exchange systems, the central ideology is one of "equivalence, neither more nor less, neither 'one up' nor 'one down'" to quote a recent field report.[2] Foodstuffs are stored, not as capital assets, but in order to be given away in feasts and ceremonies that restore equilibrium. Wealth and prestige is not measured by either resourceful thrift or conspicuous consumption, but by one's skill in achieving reciprocity. Exchange goods are familiar. They are local objects which a man grows or manufactures. Theoretically everyone could grow or make the same things in the same quantity. The difference is a matter of "accident" and therefore must be "averaged out" through exchange.

Foreign trade goods and money function in quite a different way and their introduction into Oceania created a social and moral crisis that we may term the "cargo situation." How could one enter into reciprocal relations with the white man who possesses and hoardes all this "stuff"; whose manufacture took place in some distant land which the native has never seen? How does one achieve equilibrium with the white man who does not appear to have "made" his money? If the white man was merely a stranger, the problem would be serious but might not threaten every dimension of Oceanic life. But in Oceanic traditions, the ancestors are white and, therefore, the native cannot simply ignore the white man (even if this was a pragmatic possibility) —he is one of their own, but he refuses to play according to the rules or is ignorant of them. The problem of reciprocity cannot be avoided. What can the native do to make the white man (his ancestor who has returned) admit to his reciprocal obligations? His ignorance and refusal to recognize the rules and his obligations is a problem for native theodicy. The strategies for gaining his recognition of reciprocity is a question for native soteriology.

A variety of means have been employed to meet this "cargo situation." In explicit cargo cults, it is asserted that a ship or airplane will arrive from the ancestors carrying an equal amount of goods for the natives. Or that the European's goods were originally intended for the natives, but that someone has readdressed their labels. A native savior will journey to the land of the ancestors, correct the labels or bring a new shipment, or the ancestors will redress the injury on their own initiative.

In other more desperate cults, the natives destroy everything that they own as if by this dramatic gesture to awaken the white man's moral sense of reciprocity. "See, we have now given away everything. What will you give in return?" Both of these solutions assume the validity of exchange and reciprocity and appeal to it.

Other solutions, not part of cargo cults, but part of what I have termed the cargo situation appeal to mythic resources which underlie the exchange system rather than to the system itself.

Kenelm Burridge, in his classic studies *Mambu* and *Tangu Traditions,* has shown how, among the Tangu in the Australian Trust Territory of New Guinea, a traditional pedagogic tale concerning the social relations between older and younger brother has been reworked to reveal that the difference in status between the white man (younger brother) and the native (older brother) is the result of an accident and is therefore, in native terms, a situation of disequilibrium which requires exchange.[3]

I should like to make a similar claim for Hainuwele. That a "cargo situation" existed in the Moluccas is beyond dispute. After a period of "benign neglect," the Dutch embarked on a policy of intensive colonialist and missionary activities during the years 1902–1910 which included the suppression on ancestral and head-hunting cults and (important for my interpretation) the imposition of a tax which had to be paid in cash rather than labor exchange. A number of nativistic, rebellious cults arose, known collectively as the Mejapi movements (i.e., "the ones who hide").

In traditional Moluccan society this term had applied to the gesture of a disaffected villager who would withdraw from his community and live alone in the forest in protest against a village chief. Such a gesture shamed the chief and upset the equilibrium of the village. A complex series of exchanges was required in order to restore harmony.

In their cargo form, the Mejapi movements constructed separate villages which sought to achieve direct contact with the ancestors and which would be fed by a "ship from heaven."

The Mejapi cults represent an attempt to appeal to a traditional pattern of socio-political relations applied to a new, non-traditional situation. But the white man failed to receive the "signal." He was not shamed and did not enter into exchange.

I would date the present version of the Hainuwele tale from the same period. Hainuwele disrupts a major ceremony which celebrates traditional values and exchange and produces imported objects, produces cash, in an abnormal way, objects which have so great a value that no exchange is possible.

But the Ceramese have a mythic precedent for this situation. "In the beginning," when Yam Woman, Sago Woman or some other similar figure, mysteriously produced a previously unknown form of food, the figure was killed, the food consumed and thereby acculturated. The same model, in the Hainuwele myth, is daringly applied to the white man and his goods.

I am suggesting that Jensen and others were essentially correct in calling attention to the theme of creative murder in these societies, but that their lack of sensitivity to incongruity and application has led them to ignore what is most creative in Hainuwele. They have been also led astray by Judaeo-Christian presuppositions. The murder of Hainuwele does not result in a loss of Paradise where food was spontaneously at hand (as in our Western Fall story)—spontaneity and endless productivity are not virtues in an exchange economy. The deed does not result in mortality, sexuality and agricultural labor (again as in the Fall story)—I have argued that these elements are presupposed by the myth. Rather murder and eating is a means of making something "ours," is a means of acculturation.

The myth of Hainuwele is an application of this archaic mythologem to a new "cargo" situation. The killing of Hainuwele does not represent a rupture with an ancestral age; rather her presence among men disrupts traditional, native society. The setting of the myth is not in the "once upon a time" but in the painful post-European "here and now."

The Ceramese myth of Hainuwele or the Tangu tale of the Two Brothers does not solve the dilemma, overcome the incongruity or resolve the tension. Rather it provides the native with an occasion for thought. It is a testing of the adequacy and applicability of native categories to new situations and data. As such, it is preeminently a rational and rationalizing enterprise, an instance of an experimental method. The experiment was a failure. The white man was not brought into conformity with native categories, he still fails to recognize a moral claim of reciprocity. But this is not how we judge the success of a science. We judge harshly those who have abandoned the novel and the incongruous to a realm outside of the confines of understanding and we value those who (even though failing) stubbornly make the attempt at achieving intelligibility, who have chosen the long, hard road of understandings.

The position I have sketched in this lecture was an attempt to achieve what one of my old professors used to term "an exaggeration in the direction of the truth." It seemed worth undertaking at this juncture as there is no description about which so many different schools agree as the congruency of native thought and religion. I believe that this assumption has prevented us from seeing the craft, the capacity of thought and imagination, the impulse towards experimentation that is awakened only at the point where congruency fails.

I have suggested that myth is best conceived not as a primordium, but rather as a limited collection of elements with a fixed range of cultural meanings which are applied, thought with, worked with, experimented with in particular situations. That the power of myth depends upon the play between the applicability and inapplicability of a given element in the myth to a given experiential situation. That some rituals rely for their power upon a confrontation between expectation and reality and use of perception of that discrepancy as an occasion for thought.

All of this is to say that the usual portrait of the primitive (the non-human "them" of our cultural map) —whether in the nineteenth century negative form or our more recent positive evaluation—has prevented us from realizing what is human and humane in the worlds of other men. We have not been attendant to the ordinary, recognizable features of religion as negotiation and application but have rather perceived it to be an extraordinary, exotic category of experience which escapes everyday modes of thought. But human life—or, perhaps more pointedly, humane life—is not a series of burning bushes. The categories of holism, of congruity, suggest a static perfection to primitive life which I, for one, find inhuman.

To return to my starting point. Those myths and rituals which belong to a locative map of the cosmos labor to overcome all incongruity by assuming the interconnectedness of all things, the adequacy of symbolization (usually expressed as a belief in the correspondence between macro- and microcosm) and the power and possibility of repetition. They allow for moments of ritualized disjunction, but these are part of a highly structured scenario (initiation, New Year) in which the disjunctive (identified with the liminal or chaotic) will be overcome through recreation. These values, within the great, urban, imperial cultures will frequently become reversed. What I have termed a utopian map of the cosmos is developed which perceives terror and confinement in interconnection, correspondence and repetition. The moments of disjunction become coextensive with finite existence and the world is perceived to be chaotic, reversed, liminal. Rather than celebration, affirmation and repetition, man turns in rebellion and flight to a new world and a new mode of creation. (The gnostic revaluation of ancient Near Eastern mythology, the yogic reversal of Brahmanic traditions would be good examples of such utopian cosmologies.)

The dimensions of incongruity which I have been describing in this paper, appear to belong to yet another map of the cosmos. These traditions are more closely akin to the joke in that they neither deny nor flee from disjunction, but allow the incongruous elements to stand. They suggest that symbolism, myth, ritual, repetition, transcendence are all incapable of overcoming disjunction. They seek, rather, to play between the incongruities and to provide an occasion for thought.

Such are three maps of the worlds of other men. They are not to be identified with any particular culture at any particular time. They remain coeval possibilities which may be appropriated whenever and wherever they correspond to man's experience of the world. Other maps will be drawn as the scholar of religions continues his task. The materials described in this paper suggest that we may have to relax some of our cherished notions of significance and seriousness. We may have to become initiated by the other whom we study and undergo the ordeal of incongruity. For we have often missed what is humane in the other by the very seriousness of our quest. We need to reflect on and play with the necessary incongruity of our maps before we set out on a voyage of discovery to chart the worlds of other men. For the dictum of Alfred Korzybski is inescapable: "Map is not territory"—but maps are all we possess.

NOTES

1. See A. E. Jensen, *Hainuwele: Volkserzählungen von der Molukkeninsel Ceram* (Frankfurt, 1939); *Das religiöse Weltbild einer fruben Kultur* (Stuttgart, 1938) and, in English translation, *Myth and Cult among Primitive Peoples* (Chicago, 1963), esp. 83–115, 162–190.

2. K. Burridge, *Mambu* (New York, 1970), pp. 82–85.

3. Ibid., pp. 154–176 and *Tangu Traditions* (Oxford, 1969), pp. 113ff., 229f., 330, 400–411.

Counterpoint:
No Place to Stand: Jonathan Z. Smith
as *Homo Ludens,* The Academic Study of Religion
Sub Specie Ludi

SAM GILL

Sam Gill is Professor of religious studies at the University of Colorado at Boulder, Colorado. He has published essays on Native American Indian religions and the following books: *Native American Religions: An Introduction, Mother Earth: An American Story, Sacred Words, Songs of Life: An Introduction, Story Tracking, Beyond the Primitive: The Religions of Nonliterate Peoples, Native American Religious Action: A Performance Approach to Religion.*

RAISING QUESTIONS, demolishing unquestioned categories and patterns, insisting that discerning difference is fundamental to comparison, these are the trademarks of Jonathan Z. Smith's scholarship. His perspective and the accompanying academic operations foster studies that produce theory in religion, theory that I will argue might well be understood in terms of play.

Juxtaposition is Smith's initiating operation. He sets two or more "things" side by side— texts, interpretations, quotations and their sources, ideas, and approaches. Juxtaposition is more than placing two things in adjacent spaces. Juxtaposition is a placement that implies relationship. Juxtaposition is the necessary precondition to comparison. It demands comparison. An effective juxtaposition engages a tension among the items juxtaposed, a tension that raises questions not easily answered. In an engaging juxtaposition there is movement back and forth among the elements. An interplay.

In comparison the acceptance of difference is the grounds of its being interesting, creative, and important. Difference drives the interplay.

Smith conceives this difference most commonly in such terms as incongruity, lack of fit, and incredulity. He frequently invokes Paul Ricoeur's axiom "incongruity gives rise to thought," or as he has stated more formally: there is through comparison "a methodical manipulation of that difference to achieve some stated cognitive end."[1]

Juxtaposition frames the comparative enterprise. Difference fuels comparison. To initiate and maintain the playful process is as important as forcing it to precipitate some unwarranted conclusion. The thoughtful process generates theory and insight.

Smith does not limit this dynamic process to the technical academic methods of a student of religion and culture. He recognizes that they are present as well in the structures of religious experience. His analyses tend to move easily between the study of some aspect of a specific religious tradition and the study of religion itself and, even more broadly, the whole educational process.

Smith also shifts back and forth between the study of religion and academic self-criticism. But the method is constant: juxtaposition

Reprinted from Sam Gill, "No Place to Stand: Jonathan Z. Smith as Homo Ludens, *The Academic Study of Religion* Sub Specie Ludi," *Journal of the American Academy of Religion 66/2 (1998): 283–312.*

(comparison), difference (incongruity or incredulity), thought (reflection).

Numerous pairs are played against each other: 1) the entities juxtaposed for comparison, 2) the deconstructive and reconstructive phases (that is, difference and thought or incongruity and reflection), 3) the study of religious phenomena and the self-conscious analysis of academic method, and 4) the subject and the object of the enterprise. Smith's approach depends in the most basic way upon juxtaposition, upon the holding together of two things that cannot easily subsume one another. He does not seek some final resolution but rather an occasional clarification, even the revelation of more interesting juxtapositions.

Religion And The Study Of Religion

Smith's approach to religion can be considered *sub specie ludi*. Play is an important element running through Jonathan Smith's study of religion; key both to appreciating and critically evaluating his work. Furthermore, understanding Smith's notion of play has implications for other recitings of religion. . . . Religion, as Smith understands it, is a mode of human creativity. . . .

With respect to religion Smith shows us that the playful character of being human is exemplified as an oscillation among an array of active and passive, willful and receptive attributes: activities and intentionalities, invention and participation, creation and discovery, quest and location, manipulate and negotiate, construct and map, analysis and reflective imagination. The activities, expressions, and intentionalities that are considered to be religious take such forms as myths, rituals, and experiences of transformation. These actions are not distinguished by any unique religiousness, they are open to analysis as religious in terms of their characterization of worlds, situations, spaces, domains, spheres, powers, and positions. The study of religion parallels its practice and experience. As religion is an "attempt to map, construct and inhabit . . . positions of power," the study of

religion is an attempt to map those data that are chosen to exemplify religion. Whereas religion maps, constructs, and inhabits "through the use of myths, rituals and experiences of transformation," the study of religion maps through the "imaginative acts of comparison and generalization." Myths, rituals, and experiences of transformation are structurally parallel to academic theories and methods. It is not the religiousness of the data that directs the study of religion, it is the imaginative and self-conscious selection of theory.

Throughout his work, Smith's concern, given his view of religion, is where the academic stands in her or his endeavor. Hence, it is no surprise that the issue of "place" is a persistent topic.

Place

Smith's critical examination of Mircea Eliade's most basic and universal pattern and symbolism—the "center"—began as early as 1971 in a lecture entitled "The Wobbling Pivot," in which he suggested that Eliade overemphasized the center to the exclusion of other place categories. He presented a series of queries and applications intended to complement and extend Eliade's conception. Smith attributes to Eliade a generative theory of religion: "The question of the character of the place on which one stands is the fundamental question as Eliade has taught us."[2] Perhaps Smith learned this from Eliade, but his various analyses of Eliade's studies of religion show that, for Eliade, it was a question not so much posed as it was a question to which he provided what he and many others have considered the definitive answer.

A statement made by Claude Levi-Strauss is likely the more important and persistent inspiration for the formation and development of Smith's concerns with the interconnection of "place" and the analysis of religious experience. As early as 1968 in a lecture entitled "Birth Upside Down or Right Side Up?" and as recently as the preface to *To Take Place,* and several times in between, Smith quotes the following passage from Levi-Strauss' *The Savage Mind:* "A native thinker makes the penetrating comment that 'All sacred things must have their place.' It could even be said that being in their place is what makes them sacred for if they were taken out of their place, even in thought, the entire order of the universe would be destroyed. Sacred objects therefore contribute to the maintenance of order in the universe by occupying the places allocated to them. Examined superficially and from the outside, the refinements of ritual can appear pointless. They are explicable by a concern for what one might call 'micro-adjustment'—the concern to assign every single creature, object or feature to a place within a class."[3]

There is for Smith a high potential for insight when students of religion attend to categories of place. The designation of meaning, sometimes referred to as "sacrality," is related to place. The language of symbol and social structure expresses an individual's or a culture's vision of its place. Place is articulated in the act of creating and discovering worlds of meaning. Whereas Mircea Eliade equates the "sacred" with the place category of the center, Smith enriches and even confounds this simple identity. Whereas Levi-Strauss equates the "sacred" with "being in place," this is but the beginning for Smith.

Smith articulates a notion of place in the terms of two categories he labels "locative" and "utopian." A *locative* vision of the world emphasizes place. A *utopian* vision of the world emphasizes the value of being in no place. . . .

Although Smith emphasizes that taken together these maps present the basic dichotomy among religions (and he exemplifies them with specific religious traditions), one cannot simply classify religions in terms of these maps. The locative map has been by far the more familiar. But, as Smith notes, this reflects the way in which the study of religion has been approached.

The locative map is necessarily a centered map. It depends upon some order or set of organizing principles, that is, some center whether or not it is spatially marked. Eliade proclaimed an identity between the "sacred" and this locative, centered, map of the world. He contrasted all other maps as "profane" or non-religious. In "The Wobbling Pivot" Smith suggests that the elements of chaos, which Eliade identified as profane, can be more effectively comprehended in the context of a religious worldview. Chaos, Smith says, "is a sacred power; but it is frequently perceived as being sacred 'in the wrong way.'" He cites the myth of the charioteer in Plato's Phaedrus (253–254) to illustrate his argument: "If one had only the white horse of decorum, temperance, and restraint, he would never reach heaven and the gods. If one had only the lawless black horse, he would rape the gods when he appeared before them. Without the black horse there would be neither motion nor life; without the white horse there would be no limits."[5]

Smith holds that there is an interdependence between the locative center-oriented map and the utopian chaos-generating map. He links the sacred and the chaotic (rather than the profane), and thus shows that there is a religiousness to being out of place as well as to being in place. Still, partly because the locative map has been so successfully and extensively documented by students of religion, but also because of the nature of maps, the utopian map tends to be seen as at most a subtle development upon, enrichment of, the old model; that is, a momentary phase in the reformulation of new locative orders. In "The Influence of Symbols on Social Change" Smith shows that social change is often motivated when a culture experiences chaos. He follows Suzanne Langer's view that man "can adapt himself somehow to anything his imagination can cope with; but he cannot deal with Chaos."[6] And this seems especially true for students of religion.

The utopian map cannot stand as a structural equivalent and parallel to the locative map; it can scarcely be conceived at all except in terms of the rejection of or rebellion against a locative map. Although Smith cites examples of the utopian map, it does not seem that he is actually interested in establishing it as a separate map. Rather, it seems he wants to show how these two maps are interdependent, how they stand together in complex relationships that are fundamental to religion.

Incongruity, issues of fit, constitute another relational factor that Smith develops. In his "Map Is Not Territory" incongruity is focal. In the penultimate paragraph of this essay Smith summarizes his concern with incongruity in what he describes as a third map of the world. . . . According to Smith none of the three maps can "be identified with any particular cultures at any particular time. They remain coeval possibilities which may be appropriated whenever and wherever they correspond to man's experience of the world."[7] This view follows upon Smith's earlier observation in "The Influence of Symbols on Social Change": "Each society has moments of ritualized disjunction, moments of 'descent into chaos,' of ritual reversal, of liminality, of collective anomie. But these are part of a highly structured scenario in which these moments will be overcome through the creation of a new world, the raising of an individual to a new status, or the strengthening of community."[8]

Smith's concern is more with fit than with pattern, and this constitutes his more fundamental revision. Smith views humans as both creators and discoverers of their place in the world (with the corresponding notion that their view of their world can be articulated in terms of place). This means that human religious and social actions are generated by and given meaning in the terms of fit, the relationship between map and territory.

Smith's discussion, developed in the terms of three maps, would be clearer (at least to me) if understood as attitudes toward maps or mapping strategies. Religions take shape in the process of juxtaposing experience with structuring maps. What Smith describes as a locative map is an attitude that seeks congruence of map (worldview) and territory (experience). It stretches the map to encompass all aspects of the territory, even apparent disjunctions like initiation and the New Year. The locative attitude would seek an expansion of the map to approach the scale of one to one. The motivation is to find the meaning of experience in the corresponding perfect and complete fit of the map. In contrast, what Smith describes as a utopian map is an anti-map attitude. The utopian attitude finds maps artificial, constraining, threatening. The utopian motivation is to shrink the scale and inclusiveness of maps, to diminish their influence, to find meaning in experience itself rather than any map correspondences.

These two attitudes toward maps are mirror images. Neither is achievable in its pure form except in the most special and momentary of circumstances. When a map achieves full scale it is experienced either as suffocating or as indistinguishable from the territory it charts. When all designations and categorizations of place are eliminated in the utopian moment of "being in no place," there can be no vision of the world at all. The utopian, like the locative, attitude is a process forever seeking fulfillment and a process always defined in terms of a rejected map (Smith uses the terms "rebellion" and "flight" and the examples "gnostic revaluation" and "yogic reversal").

In this place-founded imagination of religion, map, whatever its kind, is indispensable. What Smith shows is that there is a range of attitudes about the relationship between map and territory spanning a domain defined by ideals at the opposing extremes which he terms "locative" and "utopian." Smith's insight has been to shift the study of religion from a classification of map types, of the identification of religion with one map coordinate, to an examination of the dynamics of the relationships between maps (worldviews) and territories (human experiences). It is to see that religiousness occurs in the play between map and territory, worldview and experience. Juxtaposition, comparison, difference, thought.

The third, yet unnamed, map that Smith describes is not so much a third ideal, though technically Smith presents it as such, as it is a necessary product of Smith's analytical scheme. This position, as Smith envisions this religious map, allows "that symbolism, myth, ritual, repetition, transcendence are all incapable of overcoming disjunction." However, following my argument, in the face of the impossible (or at best rare and momentary) achievement of either the locative or utopian ideals, the only positive alternative is to "allow the incongruous elements to stand." Here the incongruity is not only that between map and territory but between either ideal goal and its respective accomplishment.

One may choose to limit religion to those rare moments of achieving the locative or utopian goals (as in happily accepted complete dogmatism or rarefied mystical moments) and to the more or less tragic strivings toward these ideals. This has been a common choice of students of religion and it remains a popular notion. Smith shows students of religion the double-face, the holding together of tragedy and comedy. Without rejecting a basically tragic view, one may complement it with a comic and playful view allowing religion the mode of experience "to play between the incongruities and to provide an occasion for thought." Rather than some third unnamed seemingly exceptional subdivision, all religion occurs as the inevitable play between map and territory. It is the play of fit. To return to Smith's analogy of the charioteer, all cultures must drive chariots reined at once to the desire to have a place for everything with everything in its place and the desire to be free of all constraints, or, put negatively, reined to the boredom with and oppression of a static and dogmatic order as well as to the terror and anxiety of chaos.

Smith's accomplishment here may be described as enriching the categories and char-

acterizations of place that distinguish religion. Because he presents his discussion of place in terms of different kinds of maps, I fear many may limit his accomplishment to this. His more important accomplishment is in giving the play to place, that is, in showing us that religions may be engagingly understood by considering the way they think about and act toward the relationship between maps (worldviews) and territories (experience). And extending that, Smith shows us that religion arises in and exists because of the play of difference.

Homo Ludens: Smith as Play

Smith's standard method of source criticism would seem to belie his statement that map is not territory and that we have only maps. Smith clearly holds the cited sources as territory at least in the sense of having priority or primacy over the presentations made of them. But what I think he means when he says that maps are all we have is that he understands the academic study of religion to be confined to the analysis of texts. He recognizes that the most primary sources are still texts that purport to map some text-independent reality or territory. Smith confines his work to texts, to maps. This is consistent with the range of Smith's source criticism. He compares Frazer's presentation to the sources he cites, but he does not attempt to compare those primary textual sources with any text-independent human reality. It appears that Smith sees this "reflecting on and playing with the necessary incongruity of our own maps" as preliminary or preparatory to charting "the worlds of other men," but he does not, or at least rarely does he, go on to do so, and it would appear either he is not interested or feels it premature.

Thus, in this widely cited and highly important statement it appears Smith both embraces and denies the map-territory distinction. He confines academic work to the comparative study of maps without regard to territories, all the while admitting that such territories at least exist. It is that we do not have these territories; we cannot have other than textual records of them. This confinement of the academic study of religion to text is particularly interesting since Smith's understanding of religion is elaborated through his carefully self-conscious development of theories of place, myth, and ritual that emphasize mapping, application, human experience, history, and society. . . .

There is a major advantage in Smith's restricting the work of scholars to texts. It enables a comparative task that leads to a measure of objective accomplishment, that is, conclusiveness. In the frame of comparing map with map, text with text, while excluding consideration of the map and text independent realities, the results are conclusive and seemingly inarguable. In this relative domain Smith can be certain of the territory. Interestingly, in contrast to his own dictum, he has a very firm place on which to stand. So, for example, in his study of Frazer's presentation of the Balder myth Smith's comparison supports the frank and unqualified conclusion that Frazer's presentation is loaded with "errors of fact and interpretation." This stance is taken in many of Smith's studies. He reveals the incongruities through comparison. And in these comparative operations Smith is unhesitating and forthright in declaring presentation of fact and interpretation as either accurate or in error.

But why does Smith go to such lengths to compare presentations with source texts? The case of Frazer is especially revealing. Smith reports that Frazer's earliest critics recognized his failure and that Frazer himself acknowledged his failure as deliberate. So what could possibly motivate Smith's exhaustive comparative analysis? That is, if it is a foregone conclusion that Frazer at least acknowledged his failure, it would not seem worth the enormous effort of Smith's analysis simply to verify Frazer's statement. Thus, it would seem that Smith was principally interested in *how* Frazer failed. This, indeed, is what his analysis shows, that is, that Frazer is *homo ludens*. According to Smith,

Frazer knowingly and deliberately construed his sources to deal with issues other than those he stated as his purpose. He was perpetrating a joke and therein, in Smith's view, lies the glory of the work. Smith praises Frazer finally for his approach and style which Smith identifies as "a comic playful stance."

In this study I believe that Smith forges his understanding of the role of the religion scholar. Though Smith is able to cite Frazer (in the preface to the tenth volume!) to show that his intention was other than what he had stated, it is actually Smith's study that reveals the humor of Frazer's work and illuminates the distinctiveness of its character as a riddle and joke. Smith does not do this by an interpretation of Frazer's work alone but only through the exhaustive, tedious, but ultimately exciting examination of how Frazer creatively used his sources. This revelation, or I would suggest construction, is apparently worth the extent of Smith's effort, and we must attempt to understand why. I do not believe that Frazer's work can be interesting on the terms Smith states apart from Smith's study of it. Whereas Smith calls Frazer a poor comic, having produced a bad joke, apart from Smith's analysis I don't think any reader would find Frazer a comic at all. We would no more see the bad joke than we would recognize the many errors in his presentation of Balder.

Smith is perpetrating a joke himself. He, much more than Frazer, is the player, the trickster. As Frazer did with Balder, Smith does with Frazer, but much more ingeniously and self-consciously. He reworks his source maps in order to deal with issues other than those explicitly stated. Religion, for Smith, is the invention of scholars, a product of scholarly maps and mappings. While the maps appear to be about "the worlds of other men," the joke is that they are only about the worlds of the scholars who must "reflect and play on" them to work out their own issues. It is, as shown above, surprising to Smith when our work actually has any effect on the real world of men. Smith, like

Frazer, is interested in the priesthood of Nemi or the Scandinavian myth of Balder (indeed, he is interested in Frazer and his work) primarily because these subjects provide the symbols by which academic maps are drawn. They were both interested only in the texts, the maps, that are articulated in the terms "of other men." Smith is showing that this territorial analogy reveals what distinguishes the academic enterprise. Religion, as a modern western academic invention, is comprised of only what we write about it.

Through the detailed objective comparison of map (e.g., Frazer's *Golden Bough* or Eliade's report on the Arrernte) with territory (the ethnographic and literary sources) Smith is able to demonstrate that scholars do not simply objectively present their subjects; indeed, they often do not even present a legitimate face of their subjects. What they do is to recreate their subjects in terms that meet their own needs, both personal and academic. Smith shows that Frazer actually recreates Balder for his own purposes, the attempt to transcend death, and that the loads of facts Balder, as stalking-horse, is made to carry are concocted by none other than Frazer himself.

Shockingly, Smith shows that what we have thought to be the territory of religion—the substance and subjects of the works of scholars like Frazer and Eliade who seem to inundate us with factual information about scholarly-independent realities—is actually comprised of projections of scholarly maps. The joke, it would seem, is that there are no territories, or that real territories are inaccessible to the scholar. The joke is that for the study of religion there is no territory, only maps made to resemble it. Recognizing the joke illuminates Smith's view of the map-territory distinction as the metaphor by which to distinguish scholarship. In Jean Baudrillard's terms, what scholars have presented us has been a "precession of simulacra" rather than reality. And this work is what, as scholars, we are in the business to do. It would seem clarifying to me now to rephrase

Korzybski's statement as "Map is *now* territory," which renders the rest, that is any play between map and territory, completely absurd. Smith's conclusions are the same as Frazer's, the holding at once of the comic and tragic views, the double-face.

I believe that Smith is fully aware of this absurdity and that his work finally does not embrace playing this absurdity endlessly as in a sandbox. Our only choice, as he puts it, is "the plunge" that avoids "the unhappy alternatives of infinite regress or silence." It is, as Smith states, a standpoint "fabricated with no claim beyond that of sheer survival." This is the full force of play in Smith's approach—the choosing, the assumption of a standpoint, however temporarily, and while fully acknowledging its absurdity.

To take a stance, in this complex multi-cultural world, without recognizing its absurdity is either religious, narrow-minded, or naive. To refuse to take any stance at all is either to indulge infinite regress, a favorite of many postmodernists, or silence. The alternative, which is at least more interesting, is the perspective of play: seriously taking a stance while acknowledging its absurdity. Scholarship, as Frazer found, is like life in that it must go on despite its absurdity.

NOTES

1. Paul Ricoeur, *The Symbolism of Evil* (New York: Harper & Row, 1987). p. 14.

2. Jonathan Z. Smith, "The Wobbling Pivot," In *Map Is Not Territory: Studies in the History of Religions* (Leiden: E. J. Brill, 1978), p.103.

3. Ibid., p. 10.

4. Ibid., p. 97.

5. Ibid.

6. Idem, "The Influence of Symbols on Social Change," In *Map Is Not Territory.*

7. Idem, "Map Is Not Territory," In *Map Is Not Territory,* p. 309.

8. Idem, "The Influence of Symbols," p. 145.

From *Women, Adrogynes, and Other Mythical Beasts*

WENDY DONIGER

The Toolbox of Pluralism

When one is confronting a body of raw material (and this is the first step in any original analysis), it is good to have tucked away somewhere in one's mind all the patterns that other scholars have seen in other materials, all the ways in which they have tried to solve analogous problems. In this way one develops a vocabulary in which to recognize and express the patterns that appear in the new corpus and to formulate new patterns as the need arises. The material itself will usually suggest what is the most appropriate pattern to look for at each point. Often the explicit content of a myth will give a broad hint as to how it might be interpreted: if it is about castration, try Freud; if it is about heresy, try theology. In the first analysis, it pays to be literal-minded; after that (and particularly if the head-on approach fails to bear fruit), one can indulge in the search for more arcane meanings. As we shall see, such meanings are usually there, and one learns to suspect their presence by becoming familiar with the systems of clues that various forms of analysis have built up and by noting these things: certain configurations of the text, such as lack of apparent meaning on the overt level; problems of interpretation in the native tradition; and multiple variations, at certain crucial points in the myth, among the different recensions.

This is the toolbox approach to the study of myth: carry about with you as wide a range of tools as possible, and reach for the right one at the right time. . . . Problem-solving techniques that are logically incompatible may be used in tandem as long as one is willing to make one's own diagnosis, to take the responsibility for choosing the "right one," on each separate occasion, rather than choosing a single one, once and for all, as a matter of principle.

Carstairs noted a similar medical eclecticism twenty years ago, directly linked with an eclectic attitude to mythology: "In the village, no statement, and no narrative, was ever felt to be entirely right or wrong, and so none was discarded. Contradictory, incompatible explanations were allowed to co-exist, as in the case of illnesses, which might be attributed to three different sorts of agency, and treated in three ways at once."[1] Carstairs points out that Hindus not only were not bothered by this pluralism but were bothered by any attempt to eliminate alternative views: "For them, it was no less provocative of anxiety to be asked to choose between two incompatible alternatives than it is for us to tolerate our own inconsistency."[2] Yet he notes in passing that we, too, are in certain circumstances inclined to recognize contradictory aspects of human experience, and the examples that he cites are again directly relevant to the analysis of mythology: the Freudian concept of ambivalence and the Jungian concept of the interplay of opposite tendencies in the personality.

There is an old pedigree for Indian eclecticism. The Vedic Indians worshiped several different gods as the supreme god, one at a time; this serial monogamy in theism inspired Max Müller to coin the term "Henotheism" (or "Kathenotheism"), "one god at a time." . . . Indians carry off this sort of thing better than we do, but we do it too. The Hindu acceptance of contradiction may be facilitated by the fact

Reprinted from Wendy Doniger Women, Adrogynes, and Other Mythical Beasts *(Chicago: University of Chicago Press, 1980).*

that Hinduism is orthoprax rather than ortho-dox: if one behaves correctly, it does not matter what one believes.

The evidence that the Hindus use toolbox approaches themselves—and that they use them in the construction of their mythologies—raises several interesting possibilities of validation. Does the fact that the Hindus behave in this way validate the toolbox method as applied to Hindus? Does it validate it for cultures in which the informants do not themselves use it? Does it invalidate it for such people? Or does it make no difference at all? One may feel oneself to be on firmer ground knowing that one is doing some-thing at least similar to what one's informants habitually do, but this is not essential, and one need not accept the corollary that one is on shaky ground if the informant does not endorse the methodology or that, on the other hand, a method that mirrors a native technique is justi-fied if it is otherwise unheuristic. Moreover, in a broader sense, all mythologies reflect an eclectic method of construction; for Claude Lévi-Strauss[3] has demonstrated that myth-makers, like *bricoleurs*, piece their cosmologies together with the cultural scraps that are at hand, and Edmund Leach maintains that in combining various versions of a myth the structuralist is merely piecing back together what the culture as a whole has fragmented from an originally multivalent message.

NOTES

1. G. Morris Carstairs, *The Twice-Born* (London: 1958), 91.

2. Ibid., p. 53.

3. Claude Lévi-Strauss, *The Savage Mind* (Chicago: University of Chicago Press, 1966), pp. 16—22.

From *The Implied Spider: Politics & Theology in Myth*

WENDY DONIGER

The Context

Attention to cultural specificity is part of the Hippocratic oath of historians of religions, including mythologists. The need for historical, in addition to cultural, specificity demands even more rigor, for it requires that the phenomenon (in my case, the myth) be contextualized not only in space (the bounds of the culture) but also in time (the particular moment in that cul-ture when the myth was told). This demand is one that many historians of religions regard as even more essential to their work than the demand for cultural specificity.

Texts have contexts, are determined by their contexts; the context in which "the same" story is told may totally transform its meaning, like the glass of water in the old toast to the exiled kings: when James II and James III were in exile in France, their supporters in England, forced to toast the reigning kings whom they did not recognize, would raise their wine glasses and say, "To the king"—but they would hold their wine glasses over their water glasses, so that they were in fact toasting "the king over the water." Exponents of the myth-and-ritual school argue that the ritual (the equivalent of the gesture

---

Reprinted from Wendy Doniger, The Implied Spider: Politics & Theology in Myth *(New York: Columbia University Press, 1998).*

with the wine glass) holds the key to the meaning of the myth (the equivalent of the words of the toast). With myths such as the story of Eden . . . the particular point in time and space in which the myth is told may serve, like the glass of water in the toast, to turn the meaning on its head. Even if we acknowledge that the myth in all of its widely distributed forms carries some cross-cultural human meaning, what it says about this basic meaning differs not only from culture to culture but within individual cultures. And when one culture borrows a plot or a theme from another, it becomes a different plot; it is not "the same" story anymore. . . .

Wherever possible, it is important to note the context: who is telling the story and why. Even when we do not know the answers to these questions (as is usually the case, especially with ancient texts), it is still useful at least to hazard an educated guess (a guess I will try to make about women's voices). Even though we cannot know the context of the readers (let alone the authors) of many of our ancient texts, we ourselves, as readers, are a context, sometimes the only one to which we have access: we can always know (and sometimes only know) what the texts mean to us. And when we do not know the true voice of the tellers, the original authors and audiences, we must, *faute de mieux,* listen to the voices in the text.

But even when we do know the author, the text's embeddedness in its culture makes it extend beyond its "author." Texts may be not only androgynous but also, ultimately, nonsectarian. Their authors may not be anonymous, but they are collective. And that collectivity extends beyond the bounds of culture to other cultures that may share many of the same plots and agendas, despite their different historical experiences. Moreover, the contexts themselves are embedded in the texts if we know how to look for them, in the unique details that each text takes from its context.

Clearly we lose a great deal when we lose context. But comparative work need not be contextualized to be rigorous, and concern for

context can become hypertrophied. Of course, it is essential for the comparatist to know the general context in order to have data against which to test any interpretation (this means learning languages, reading commentaries, and so forth). But it is not essential for this thick cultural description to be a part of the interpretation ultimately presented to the reader as a basis of comparison. Though something precious is lost when context is lost, something else, also precious, is gained. The argument for comparison must justify taking myths out of their historical context and supplying instead the context of other myths, other related ideas, as Lévi-Strauss argued long ago. And, as he has not explicitly argued but as his own writings seem to imply, these other myths may be taken from other cultures. Often the best way to understand a myth is by understanding how it differs from other myths in the same culture as well as from variants in other cultures.

We might also compare the contexts themselves, and some people do. We can, for instance, compare performative contexts, asking in each case, What makes a teller choose to tell that story then? What else is going on? We can also compare the relations between text and context in two parallel situations. . . .

Comparing contexts—more precisely, comparing the relations of texts to their contexts—might allow us to advance the comparative enterprise without lapsing into the follies of universalism, by taking a kind of middle ground. If we construct another continuum, this time one of the individual, the group/culture, and the human race, we might focus on one relatively solid intermediary path between the two extremes: cultural morphology, or the morphology of cultural types. For groups or societies that have the same sorts of structures and practices may tell the same sorts of myths. Perhaps it is best to look for parallels not within a single culture (treating men and women, rich and poor, as the same, overlooking the differences between kings and peasants, men and women), let alone across cultures, but between the same sorts of people in different cultures (Chinese peasant women and Indian peasant women). This project would take account of differences between men and women as storytellers, and also between rich and poor, dominant and oppressed, through the comparison of contexts. . . .

The morphological approach also allows us to acknowledge what the historicizing approach often obscures, that the negative aspects of other peoples' prejudices (such as their attitudes to women) are also shared (a sexist stance that might be called politically erect). When cultural studies silences the cross-cultural critique, as it sometimes does, it may back into another political problem by implicitly validating injustices committed within another culture—just as cultural relativism often does, though coming from another direction. Cultural morphology could tackle these injustices in a new way. But comparing the contexts threatens to take them out of context, and thus to land us in an infinite regress (are all peasants alike? all women?). Moreover, a telling embedded in its context requires a lot of space, and thus limits the comparison. . . .

Cross-Cultural Solutions

Demonstrating that a particular myth does in fact occur in every known culture is theoretically impossible, since stories are being forgotten and cultures created all the time. Moreover, this task is, in practice, unlikely to be achieved even in approximation. But even if we were able to prove that a certain myth was universal, we would have to explain its universality in terms of some universalist theory (Jungian, Freudian, Eliadean, or at least diffusionist), a daunting proposition. On the other hand, to assert that a myth occurs cross-culturally is merely to show that its meanings are not bounded by any one particular culture, a far less ambitious task (though no sinecure, either).

The universalism of most systems of comparison can, I think, be avoided. The great universalist theories were constructed from the top

down: that is, they assumed certain continuities about broad concepts such as sacrifice, or a High God, or an Oedipal complex; but these continuities necessarily involved cognitive and cultural factors that, it seems to me, are the least likely places in which to look for cross-cultural continuities. The method that I am advocating is, by contrast, constructed from the bottom up. It assumes certain continuities not about over-arching human universals but about particular narrative details concerning the body, sexual desire, procreation, parenting, pain, and death, details which, though unable to avoid mediation by culture entirely, are at least less culturally mediated than the broader conceptual categories of the universalists. . . .

A scholar working from the bottom up leans more heavily on data, informed, even inspired, though she may be by theory; she begins with a thorough historical study and then goes on to make it comparative. A scholar's experiences of real life and texts form her tastes and interests, the ingredients of the third side, the motivating idea; but that idea then leads her back to her texts, where she may find unexpected details that will in turn modify the idea of what she is looking for. Working from the bottom up forces a scholar to take into consideration many variants, many examples to induce a generalization, for the bottom-up argument is more numerological than logical, more inductive than deductive: it seeks to persuade by the sheer volume of its data rather than by the inevitability (or falsifiability) of the sequence of its assertions.[1] Induction, which is always a bootstraps operation, must be at the very least bolstered by meticulous, painstaking, fastidious scholarship.

Working from the bottom up also encourages a scholar to build an argument like an Irish wall: a good Irish wall needs no mortar, for if the stones are selected carefully and arranged so that they fit together tightly, they will hold one another up and the wall will stand. So too, if a scholar selects her texts carefully and places them in a sequence that tells the story she wants to tell, she will need relatively little theory to explain why they belong together and what sort of an argument they imply together.

The Implied Spider

Geertz is wary of certain assumptions about the nature of what is "the same" in different cultures: "When ingeniously juxtaposed, these fields can shed a certain amount of light on one another; but they are neither variants of one another nor expressions of some superfield that transcends them both."[2] Instead of a "superfield that transcends them," I would suggest that they are expressions of an experience that precedes them, without which one would not "ingeniously juxtapose" them at all, or come into the light that such a juxtaposition can shed. In another famous essay, Geertz speaks of humans as animals suspended in webs of significance that they themselves have spun, webs of culture. Obeyesekere goes on to cite the Upanishadic metaphor of God as a spider emitting the world inside himself . . .

This is a useful metaphor for the comparatist if we take the spider to be, not as in Obeyesekere's usage the maker of culture (or the anthropologist) who spins the web of the myth (or the ethnography), but the shared humanity, the shared life experience, that supplies the web-building material, the raw material of narrative to countless human webmakers, authors, including human anthropologists and human comparatists. These human storytellers gather up the strands that the spider emits, like silk workers harvesting the cocoons of silkworms, to weave their own individual cultural artifacts, their own Venn-diagram webs of shared themes all newly and differently interconnected. My image of what I want to call the implied spider draws upon Wayne Booth's useful concept of the "implied author" (which itself builds upon Wolfgang Iser's concept of the "implied reader"),[3] the author implied by the individual passions revealed in his writing.[4] The implied spider generates, and is therefore implied by, the stuff that myths are made on;

this is my answer to Obeyesekere's question, "out of what?" I argue that we must believe in the existence of the spider, the experience behind the myth, though it is indeed true that we can never see this sort of spider at work; we can only find the webs, the myths that human authors weave. . . .

The fact that we cannot recover the experience, or the implied spider, does not mean that they do not exist. We cannot see the wind either, but we can watch it move, carving a path in a field of long grass. Where Geertz and Obeyesekere were talking about the elusiveness of culture, theologians apply the spider to proofs of the existence of God. . . .

The Postcolonial and Postmodern Critique of Comparison

I have been arguing for the uses of comparison despite the problems that it poses. But in the discipline of the history of religions, scholars have, by and large, abandoned universalist comparative studies of the sort that Mircea Eliade made so popular, as had the triumvirate of Frazer, Freud, and Jung before him. Many people think that such studies cannot be done at all, while others think that they should not be done at all. So far in this chapter, I have tried to tackle the question of whether they can be done; now let us consider whether they should be done. . . .

The most common arguments against extant works of comparison are that they lack rigor; that they advance unfalsifiable universalist hypotheses; and that they are politically unhealthy. I will take up these three challenges one by one.

As for the lack of rigor, it is certainly true that there is a great deal of shoddy and superficial comparative work flying about; the less talented acolytes of the great comparatists of the early twentieth century have fallen into many of the pits I have described above as well as others that we will consider below, and given comparison a bad name. One of the reasons I lost my temper with Joseph Campbell was because he did it wrong and made it harder for me to persuade people that it was possible to do it right; his static monomyth is the very antithesis of the ceaselessly engaged and always subject-filled approach that I argue for here. Many comparatists suffer from what has been called "Fluellenism," after Captain Fluellen, Shakespeare's Welshman who insisted on comparing Alexander the Great and the young Henry V; when others tried to point out the differences between the two men . . . Fluellens are always seduced by superficial convergences, which may be coincidental or otherwise meaningless. What does it mean, for instance, that the same sentence "The train has arrived," in Finnish and in Hungarian, but the part of the sentence that means "the train" in Finnish means "has arrived" in Hungarian, and vice versa? When confronted by such data, the responsible comparatist must cry out, "Get thee behind me, Satan." . . .

Clearly I am calling for a comparison that relates, that frames, that clarifies. I would also insist that the comparatist have a knowledge of the language of the primary texts of at least one of the traditions in question, which would then inspire a proper sense of caution and limited ambitions in the inevitable dealings with translations of texts from other traditions, an understanding of what one can and cannot do with translations. And the comparatist must know the context—at the very least, have read a good book by someone who really knows the context—in order to know the meaning of the text, even though she may not use the context in the comparison. I hesitate to say any more in the abstract about rigor other than that, like pornography, lack of rigor is something I always know when I see it. Rigor for me comes out of practice, out of being aware of the sorts of problems and assumptions that are addressed in this book; and out of adhering carefully to a step-by-step method like the one that I am about to describe. So much for rigor.

As for unfalsifiable theories, few conceptually bold studies in any field can avoid them entirely, but their harm can be minimized if they are not

followed unconsciously or reductionistically but are invoked explicitly and in groups; in this way the comparatist drawing upon more than one theory might allow their shortcomings to hold one another up like two drunks, or cancel one another out, if not kill one another off like the cats of Kilkenny in the limerick ("and instead of two cats, there weren't any"). (This means eclecticism.) And hypotheses about patterns of meaning in any group of stories may be, if not falsified, at least tried in the field of many, many stories from many, many cultures, retold with attention to many, many details, or tested for anachronism, incoherence of explanation, and so forth.

The question of the politics of myth is more complex. There is, I think, some irony in the fact that the modern comparative study of religion was in large part designed in the pious hope of teaching our own people that "alien" religions were like "ours" in many ways. (By "ours" we usually meant Protestantism, as do scholars who mean, but never say, what is said by Mr. Thwackum in Fielding's *Tom Jones:* "When I mention religion, I mean the Christian religion; and not only the Christian religion, but the Protestant religion; and not only the Protestant religion, but the Church of England.") The hope was that if we learned about other religions, we would no longer hate and kill their followers; that "to know them is to love them." Emmanuel Levinas argues that the face of the other says, "Don't kill me";[5] this is the face that the comparative enterprise strives to illuminate. A glance at any newspaper should tell us that this goal has yet to be fulfilled in the world at large.

But the academic world, having gone beyond this simplistic paradigm, now suffers from a post-postcolonial backlash. In this age of multinationalism and the politics of individual ethnic and religious groups, of identity politics and minority politics, to assume that two phenomena from different cultures are "the same" in any significant way is regarded as demeaning to the individualism of each, a reflection of the old racist attitude that "all wogs look alike." In our day too, and at the other end of the anticolonial continuum, seeing correspondences between cultures has come to be regarded as politically retrograde for different reasons. . . .

Moreover, in the present climate of anti-Orientalism, it is regarded as imperialist of a scholar who studies India, for instance, to stand outside (presumably, above) phenomena from different cultures and to equate them. Merely by emphasizing their commonalities, we are implicated in what Rolena Adorno has called "the process of fixing 'otherness' by grasping onto similarities." Other evil effects of simplistic comparison have already taken their toll in some of the social sciences today (particularly political science and economics), where dominant theories like that of "rational choice," supposedly the same for everyone, have driven out the more particularized disciplines of area studies. Psychologists also have, until quite recently, too often assumed a universal biological, cognitive, and affective base for human behavior, neglecting cultural factors.

But we must beware of leaping from the frying pan of universalism into the fire of another sort of essentialism that can result from contextualizing a myth in one cultural group. In this Kali Yuga of cultural essentialism, we must search for something that is essential but not essentialist. Indeed, I might formulate the basic problem addressed in this chapter as the problem of competing essentialisms. And by essentialism I mean hypotheses about the unity of a group that a scholar holds on to even when they have destructive results, like a monkey who traps himself by refusing to let go of a banana in his fist inside a cage whose opening is big enough for his fist but not for the banana. I mean a priori prejudices (and, as I have argued, any scholarly hypothesis must begin with something like such a prejudice) that are not dropped or modified when members of the target groups turn out to be different. I want to say to all the reductionists I know: "Let go of the banana." Paul Feyerabend once wrote a book entitled

Against Method; my method could be called, "Against Reductionism."

The emphasis on individual cultures, when reduced to the absurd (as it too often is), may lead to problems of infinite regress, first, as we have just seen, in the ever-broadening comparisons of contexts and ultimately, in the ever-narrowing contexts themselves. This emphasis tends to generate a smaller and smaller focus until it is impossible to generalize even from one moment to the next: nothing has enough in common with anything else to be compared with it even for the purpose of illuminating its distinctiveness; each event is unique, like William James's crab, himself alone, not just a crustacean.[6] The radical particularizing of much recent theory in cultural anthropology, for instance, seems to deny any shared base to members of the same culture, much less to humanity as a whole. But any discussion of difference must begin from an assumption of sameness; Wilhelm Dilthey has said that "Interpretation would be impossible if expressions of life were completely strange. It would be unnecessary if nothing strange were in them."[7] If we start with the assumption of absolute difference there can be no conversation, and we find ourselves trapped in the self-reflexive garden of a Looking-Glass ghetto, forever meeting ourselves walking back in through the cultural door through which we were trying to escape. . . .

But similarity and difference are not equal, not comparable; they have different uses. We look to similarity for stability, to build political bridges, to anchor our own society, while we spin narratives to deal with our uneasiness at the threat of difference. Either similarity or difference may lead to a form of paralyzing reductionism and demeaning essentialism, and thence into an area where "difference" itself can be politically harmful. For where extreme universalism means that the other is exactly like you, extreme nominalism means that the other may not be human at all. Many of the people who argued (and continue to argue) that Jews or blacks or any other group defined as "wogs" were all alike (that is, like one another) went on to argue (or, more often, to assume) that they were all different (that is, different from us white people, us Protestants), and this latter argument easily led to the assertion that such people did not deserve certain rights like the rest of us. Essentialized difference can become an instrument of dominance; European colonialism was supported by a discourse of difference.

I have argued that the members of a single cultural "group" may be very different, and it is just as insulting to say that all Japanese are alike as to say that the Japanese are just like the French. (The same goes for *fin de siècle* types: the essentialism of time can be just as harmful as the essentialism of place.) I applaud the art historian Sir Ernst Gombrich, who resists categories like "Renaissance man" or "Romantic psychology" as one would resist claims for "Aryan man" or "German physics."[8] The culturally essentialized position is in itself both indefensible and politically dangerous. Yet it is often assumed in "culturally contextualized" and historically specific studies: "Let me tell you how everyone felt at the *fin de siècle* in Europe and America." The focus on the class or ethnic group, if monolithic, can become not only boring but also racist.

My aim is an expansive, humanistic outlook on inquiry that enhances our humanity in both its peculiarity and its commonality. I am unwilling to close the comparatist shop just because it is being picketed by people whose views I happen, by and large, to share. I have become sensitized to the political issues, but I do not think that they ultimately damn the comparative enterprise. I want to salvage the broad comparative agenda even if I acquiesce, or even participate, in the savaging of certain of its elements. I refuse to submit to what Umberto Eco has nicely termed "textual harrassment" and Velcheru Narayana Rao calls (in Sanskrit) *bhava-hatya*, literally "ideacide" but in actuality a good translation for "ideology": murder by idea, as well as the murder of ideas (Sanskrit

compounds, like myths, can swing both ways like that). I am not now, and have never been, a card-carrying member of the British Raj. But I refuse to stop reading and translating texts edited by people who were. There is much in the colonial scholarship on India that is worth keeping. . . .

But there is also much in the postcolonial critique that is worth keeping; indeed, we can no longer think without it. We are aware, willy-nilly, of how our texts have come to us; they now say to us, like third-world immigrants in England, "We're here because you were there." Colonialism is no longer the political force it once was, but it is still there, especially if we use a word like imperialism instead of colonialism and bear in mind the aspects of our scholarship that still invade the countries we study, like the Coke bottle that intrudes into the lives of The Natives in the (racist) film *The Gods Must Be Crazy*. In particular, the postcolonial critique has made us aware of how deeply evolutionist ideas are embedded in the history of comparison, and how hard we must work to overcome them. The joke about the caveperson and the tiger rests upon evolutionist ideas, as does, ultimately, the idea of a common humanity.

But we can overcome the negative fallout from evolutionism; we don't have to go on doing it like that. The very fact that we have been made aware of these problems should make it possible for us to avoid them, at least to some extent. There are sharks in the waters of comparison, but now that we know they're there we can still swim—a bit more cautiously, perhaps. We now realize, for instance, that the cultures we are comparing have compared, too; that they are subjects, like us, as well as the objects of our study. Herodotus compared his ancient Greeks with the Egyptians; a number of recent studies have documented the attitudes of the ancient Chinese, Hindus, and others toward the Others on their borders.[9] In this way we can switch focus: the text you look at becomes a text you look through; the mirror becomes a window. . . .

In pursuing the multivocal, multicultural agenda, we must face the implications of the fact that we use other peoples' stories for our purposes. The political problem inheres in the asymmetry of power between the appropriating culture and the appropriated. Thus, if Europe has dominated India, it is deemed wrong for a European to make use of an Indian myth. But it seems to me that there are very different ways of using other peoples' myths, some of them fairly innocuous, and that the usual alternative to appropriating a foreign text (however inadequate or exploitative or protective that appropriation may be) can be even worse: ignoring it or scorning it. Moreover, the European appropriation need not supplant the Indian version; the native voice can be heard even above the academic clamor of the foreign voice.

The gift that the postcolonial critique has given us is a heightened awareness of what we are doing, why, and the dangers involved. But the gift sours when the giver takes it back by arguing that these dangers are so great that we cannot do it at all. We should use the postcolonial consciousness not to exclude Western scholars from the study of non-Western myths, which merely contributes to the ghettoization of the Western world of ideas, but to show how myths (and the comparative study of myths) can be used as ghetto-blasters in our own society as well as in the world at large—that is, to blast apart the ghettoes of ideology. Surely it is possible to bring into a single (if not necessarily harmonious) conversation the genuinely different approaches that several cultures have made to similar (if not the same) human problems. To return to the image of the lens, we must supplement the tunnel vision of identity politics with the wide screen of cross-cultural studies.

The postcolonial agenda is compatible with some agendas of postmodernism, the age that rejects metanarratives and argues for the infinite proliferation of images. For postmodernism, sameness is the devil, difference the angel; the mere addition of an accent *aigu* transforms the modest English word into the magic buzzword

for everything that right-thinking (or, as the case may be, left-thinking) men and women care about: *différence* (or, buzzler yet, *différance*). From Paris the new battle cry rings out: *Vive la différance!* . . .

But the postmodern critique has not solved the problem of cultural difference. . . . Yet there is a crucial difference between premodern constructions of difference and postmodern *différance*. Deconstructionism, in particular, has promoted the concepts of multivocality and multiple interpretations that are essential to the method for which I will argue. . . . And it has sharpened our awareness of our unexamined assumptions about individual authors, a subject to which I wish now to turn.

The Problem of Individualism

. . . The postmodern critique thus helps us to avoid some of the distortions that result from a certain kind of concentration on individual authors. . . . There is a danger of losing human meaning if you select only what is in the common core. To avoid this universalizing trap, we might try to move in the other direction, to take explicit account of the "personal predilections" of many different individuals.

For each telling adds something unique, sometimes transformingly unique, to the shared base, and we must ask of each telling the Passover question: Why is this variant different from all other variants? What particular contribution does this retelling make? We might do better, therefore, to anchor our cross-cultural paradigms in the unique insights of particular tellings of our cross-cultural themes. This is one way of steering between the Scylla of universalism and the Charybdis of cultural essentialism: by concentrating on the insights from individual myths, we need not assume that all Hindus are alike, or all Jews. A telling of a myth from one country is as likely to share some things with a telling from another as with a telling from elsewhere in the same country. Just as our awareness of the individual scholar making the analysis, the third side of the triangle, provides an anti-essentialist anchor, so too does our awareness of the individual contribution of the text's author. This focus takes the call for difference very seriously indeed and follows it to the ultimate case, that of the individual whose insights transcend her particular moment and speak to us across time and space. The emphasis on the individual balances the move outward, from culture to cross-culture, with a move inward, from culture to the individual author. It balances the focus on the individual with a focus on the human on the other end of the continuum—the microscope and then the telescope, thus opening up a second front in the battle against the constricting category of culture.

This method argues that *All's Well That Ends Well* must be read not merely as a typical (or even atypical) story of a man who rejects his wife, nor merely in the context of Elizabethan England (an approach that assumes that Shakespeare can be "explained" by nothing but the same influences that formed all other Elizabethans—an extension of the statement by Laura Bohannan's British challenger that Shakespeare is a "very English poet"). Instead, this method would treat that text as the peculiar insight of one Elizabethan Englishman who was in many ways different from all others. The focus on individual insight leads us to a variety of what Paul Ricoeur called a second naïveté, positing a "sameness" that only superficially resembles a quasi-Jungian universalism but is actually based on a *pointillism* formed from the individual points of individual authors. . . .

My emphasis upon the individual at all levels of society, from high culture to popular culture, is designed to address this question as well as the deconstructionist objection to universalism and to the sort of humanism I am advocating: the objection that humanism falsely universalizes an ideological fiction based on the interests of the privileged. This position also argues ultimately for that particular flash of difference that is best illuminated by the context of sameness. And where the emphasis on the characteristics of a whole class or culture falls to take into account not only parallels in other cultures but originality in any culture, the emphasis on one individual (in comparison with other, less inspired individual tellers) can at least pinpoint the moment of inspiration, if not account for it. The arguments that I have made for *pointillism* and will make for *bricolage* are designed to counter naïve claims about novelty and to stress the creative dimension of thinking.

The individual spark of originality should be sought in other cultures as well as in our own. In his discussion of the analogical imagination, David Tracy sounds a note of warning: analogical concepts must never lose what he calls "the tensive power of the negative. If that power is lost, analogical concepts become mere categories of easy likenesses slipping quietly from their status as similarities-in-difference to mere likenesses, falling finally into the sterility of a relaxed univocality and a facilely affirmative harmony." In my own rather similar-and-different context, mythological rather than theological, the role of "the tensive power of the negative" is played by what some might call "the tensive power of historical specificity" and I would call "the tensive power of the individual." To lose awareness of this power is to fall into the "facilely affirmative harmony" of reductionist schools of comparative mythology. Yet to lose awareness of the "similarity-in-difference" is also fatal to our enterprise. We must strike a balance between centripetal and centrifugal forces in a myth.

NOTES

1. G. Morris Carstairs, *The Twice-Born* (London: 1958), 91.

2. Ibid., p. 53

3. Claude Lévi-Strauss, *The Savage Mind* (London, 1966), pp. 16-22.

4. For a devastating critique of this "encyclopedic" approach, see Jonathan Z. Smith, "Adde Parvum Parvo Magnus Acervus Erit," 249-53.

5. Geertz, *After the Fact*, 28.

6. Wolfgang Iser, *The Implied Reader.*

7. Wayne Booth, *The Rhetoric of Fiction,* 70-77.

8. Emmanuel Levinas, *Totality and Infinity,* 198-99.

9. William James, *The Varieties of Religious Experience* (New York: Modern Library Edition, 1929), 10.

10. Wilhelm Dilthey, *Pattern and Meaning in History,* 77.

11. Sir Ernst Gombrich, *The Essential Gombrich.*

12. See, for instance, David Gordon White, *Myths of the Dog-Man.*

Counterpoint:
The Clinging Spider Web of Context:
A Review of *The Implied Spider* by Wendy Doniger

J. E. LLEWELLYN

J. E. Llewellyn teaches at Southwest Missouri State University in Springfield, Missouri. He has published *Arya Samaj as a Fundamentalist Movement: A Study in Comparative Fundamentalism* and *The Legacy of Women's Uplift in India: Contemporary Women Leaders in the Arya Samaj.*

. . . DESPITE HER OWN MISGIVINGS about theory and method, Doniger, in *The Implied Spider,* forges an apology for the comparative study of myth, because this practice is under attack from the two-headed monster of postmodernism and postcolonialism. . . . Even in the history of religions, Doniger notes with dismay, "scholars have, by and large, abandoned universalist comparative studies of the sort that Mircea Eliade made so popular, as had the triumvirate of Frazer, Freud, and Jung before him. Many people think that such studies cannot be done at all, while others think that they should not be done at all" (64). In The *Implied Spider,* Doniger clings doggedly to the old-fashioned notion that "the cross-cultural comparison of myths is pragmatically possible, intellectually plausible, and politically productive" (4–5).

The occasionally argumentative tone of *The Implied Spider* notwithstanding, the author admits that her defense of comparative mythol-ogy proceeds largely on the back of metaphor. . . . My review is composed of a close reading of two passages from *The Implied Spider,* followed by some critical comments on the thesis of the book. I begin with a critique of the image of the spider itself. Such rhetorical nit-picking is justi-fied by Doniger's own admission about the importance of metaphor in this book. In fact, I would argue that this framework is a character-istic strategy in all of Doniger's monographs, which are held together in part by recurring metaphorical images.

"The Implied Spider"

A number of images appear early in *The Implied Spider,* are repeated occasionally, and serve to knit the book into one whole. I have chosen to focus here on the spider and her web because this metaphor was assigned particular impor-tance by the author, in her choice of the title of

Reprinted from J. E. Llewellyn, "The Clinging Spider Web of Context: A Review of The Implied Spider by Wendy Doniger," Religious Studies Review 26/1 (2000): 42–49.

the book, and also by the designer. The jacket cover features a large image of a spider in gradations of red and yellow on a white web against a dark background. Then the first page of each chapter is ornamented by not one, but two spiders, one a small dark drawing at the top of the page and the other a larger halftone image almost filling the page behind the printed text. Altogether I counted an impressive thirty pictures of spiders in this book, which is clearly not intended for the arachnaphobic reader.

In the text, we first meet the spider and her web in a section headed "The Implied Spider." This opens with Doniger noting that Clifford Geertz has spoken of "humans as animals suspended in webs of significance that they themselves have spun, webs of culture" (61). Doniger goes on to write that Gananath Obeyesekere has commented on Geertz's use of this image, contrasting it with passages from the Upanishads, in which God creates the world by drawing it out of himself, as a spider draws out its web. In Geertz's work, Obeyesekere finds no *deus ex machina,* no God spinning the webs of human meaning. . . . Apparently Obeyesekere judges this to be a problem in Geertz, a gap in his metaphysics. . . .

Having entangled the spider webs of Geertz, the Upanishads, and Obeyesekere, Doniger increases the confusion by investing the metaphor of webs and spiders with yet another, and quite different, meaning. . . . Doniger here is essentially equating the spiders and webs of Geertz and Obeyesekere, both of whom use the web as a metaphor for culture, for the world of meaning that humans construct for themselves. For Geertz and Obeyesekere, the human beings who are making that meaningful world (including anthropologists who study the meaning-making of others) are the spiders. Doniger wants to make something new out of these spiders and their webs, so she adds another level to the metaphor. The spiders become "the shared humanity, the shared life experience," which ultimately is the basis of myth. Adding a new level, we find culture constructed by "human storytellers," who use the "web-building material, the raw material of narrative" to weave their stories, "like silk workers harvesting the cocoons of silkworms" (61). This analysis would lead me to conclude that the web itself, in Doniger's use of this metaphor, must be the stuff that the shared-life-experience/spider produces and that the storyteller/silk-worker then harvests. But the specific language that Doniger uses undercuts my analysis since she calls the stuff emitted by the experience/spider "web-building material," not the web itself. . . . Here we have a simple pair of double correspondences: spider : web = experience : myth. But I must insist that this conclusion seems to eliminate a couple of other levels that are operative earlier in Doniger's explication. What happened to the "web-building material" and to the "silk workers"?

Now that Doniger has introduced us to the spider, she goes on to explain why she has labeled it "implied." As the quotation in the preceding paragraph indicates, the spider, which is the "life experience" out of which myths are constructed, is never directly open to view. This is not because experience is "just given" and not subject to analysis; rather the problem is that we are dealing with "shared" life experience. Elsewhere in *The Implied Spider* Doniger argues that it is possible to compare myths across cultures because human beings even from different cultures have some common concerns. . . . Doniger goes on to detail some of the experiences she has in mind in a list that extends from the existential to the bathetic. . . . These great common human experiences are the stuff of which myth is made (although we cannot get behind any particular myth to attain direct access to the experience); they are Doniger's hidden spiders.

But in what sense are these spiders "implied"? Doniger says that she is using this term in the same way that Wayne Booth does when he discusses the "implied" author in *The Art of Rhetoric.* Booth notes the extraordinary emphasis placed on objectivity in the work of many great authors. Yet Booth insists that no novel is free of all values and norms. Rather, the reader divines a set of commitments in a work of fiction, which are then presumed to be those of the author. The history of literature has seen many moralizing tomes written by reprobates, which demonstrates that the values of a book are not necessarily those of its creator. The implied author is a kind of "second self" constructed by the author as she writes. Booth is not entirely clear on who is doing the implying in all of this. The problem would be less acute if he spoke of the inferred author. Then we could say that it is the reader who infers an author with a certain set of values; I do not think it makes sense to say that the reader implies an author. This question became acute for me when I read the following two sentences, which follow a discussion of the proper term for this authorial second self: "We can be satisfied only with a term that is as broad as the work itself but still capable of calling attention to that work as the product of a choosing, evaluating person rather than as a self-existing thing. The 'implied author' chooses, consciously or unconsciously, what we read: we infer him as an ideal, literary, created version of the real man; he is the sum of his own choices." In the first sentence, Booth appeared to be arguing that the author creates her Doppelgänger, but in the second sentence it is the Doppelgänger itself who is doing the creating. Since the Doppelgänger does not actually exist outside the work of fiction, then Booth may mean that the novel itself "implies" its author. It is critical to consider this problem because of its applicability to the lowly arachnid in Doniger's book. Spiders, of course, make not only the "web-building material" but also the webs themselves. The silk-worker may take that web and make it into something else, but the web itself was made by the spider. Yet, if the spider in Doniger's argument is experience, then I do not think we can say that it creates the web of myth. The implied spider of shared human experience is inferred by a listener to a myth. It may be implied by the myth itself, but

that seems to assign an agency to myths that properly belongs only to persons. To return to Booth, even if the "implied author" is implied by the novel itself in some kind of indirect sense, as a kind of rhetorical effect, nevertheless the novel also has an actual author. In Doniger's system, authors are not as important. In that sense her implied spider seems rather unlike Booth's implied author. . . .

Not only are the uses to which Doniger puts her sources confusing, so too are the implications of the metaphor of the spider. Over the course of just four pages, the spider goes from being the human who spins a web of meaning (Geertz and Obeyesekere), to God who produces the world from himself like a spider (in Obeyesekere's reading of the Upanishads and in the *Zohar*), to the shared human experience from which myths are made (in Doniger's own usage), to the transmigrating soul (in Doniger's reading of the Upanishads), to the self searching for meaning (in Whitman and Kierkegaard), to myths that contain meaning (again a suggestion by Doniger herself), to texts that contain myths, such as the *Iliad* and *Hamlet* (Doniger yet again), and finally to humans as creators of language (from Aitchison). . . .

A little later, Doniger contrasts the comparativist with the painter, since the former must work with materials that are given rather than creating something new. . . . I think that my objections to the section headed "The Implied Spider" are, to a certain extent, a reaction to a *bricolage*. When Picasso painted "Still Life with Chair Caning," there must have been critics who said, "That is the cane seat from a chair. What's it doing in a painting?" But that was, of course, the point. Similarly, the spiders that Doniger has pulled from the Upanishads and other sources are still trailing the webs that bound them into other arguments in their original sources. That Doniger was able to find so many interesting spiders is at the very least a testament to the range of her scholarly interests. That these spiders are assembled here into an argument with so much built-in tension may only heighten the aesthetic pleasure of some readers. Yet in the end, I am not sure that there is an argument in "The Implied Spider." In the beginning, this section of Doniger's book appears to be about myth and meaning, but in the end it proves to be about the uses to which the spider has been put in metaphor. Although the latter topic is interesting, it is not nearly as interesting as the former. To the extent that this section lacks an argument, it cannot add much to the argument of the book as a whole.

"Inverted Political Versions"

At the beginning of this section of *The Implied Spider,* Doniger takes on an influential critical student of myth when she quotes (101) Roland Barthes's *Mythologies.* . . . Doniger takes issue with Barthes as she goes on to write, "Barthes is speaking here of right-wing myths that pretend to be depoliticized, neutralized, but his remarks apply, I think, only to the neutral nonexistent micromyth" (101). It is important to realize that Barthes is not writing about oppressive right-wing myths, as opposed to liberating left-wing myths. Rather, according to Barthes, there are only right-wing myths. . . .

The only truly leftist act for Barthes is revolution, and this always involves the activist in the messy business of confrontation with reality. For the revolutionary, there is no flight from history into the abstractions of mythology. Hiding from history is what every myth is all about as far as Barthes is concerned, and to that extent all myths are a part of the problem.

To this claim, Doniger replies that the only politically neutral myth is the micromyth. Earlier in *The Implied Spider,* Doniger recommends analyzing myths into their component parts. Beneath the myth are the elements of which it is composed: bits of narrative devoid of editorial content, a "neutral structure," "a non-existent story with no point of view" (88). These are the micromyths. As an instance of this, Doniger offers "A woman and a serpent in a tree gave a man a fruit . . ." (88). This is not quite the Adam and Eve story that we know, because every time that story is told it has a point ("It was all Eve's fault," or "Blame it on the serpent," or what have you), but the micromyth has no point. Now, if we take the elevator of mythical analysis up from the basement, where the micromyths are found, to the penthouse, bypassing the level of myths themselves, then we come to the macromyths. A macromyth is what the comparativist constructs by bringing together many myths with common elements. It is a "multinational multimyth," to use Doniger's language (93). It is important to realize that neither the micromyth nor the macromyth are given in experience; rather both are artifacts of the comparative study of myth. It may seem that the micromyth is rather like the shared life experiences of the previous section of this review, since these are the elements of which myths are composed but which are never purely given in any myth. Yet there are passages in *The Implied Spider* in which those shared experiences are described as peak experiences, such as love and death, and so they sound rather unlike the bland "A woman and a serpent in a tree gave a man fruit. . . ." The micromyth is not an element of experience, I would argue, but is a byproduct of the comparative analysis of myth, where some narrative details must be pared away in order to identify what similar myths have in common.

Doniger argues against Barthes that it is only the micromyths that are "neutralized" by being "depoliticized" (101). All myths are editorials, or so it would seem. None are straight news stories. No myth just reports events; rather each myth recounts events in order to make some point. In that sense all myths are political. Doniger goes even further, arguing that any given myth may be used to make diametrically opposed political points. This is one of the important "claims for myth" that Doniger spells out in the introduction to *The Implied Spider:* "it expresses both an idea and its opposite, reveals—or sometimes conceals—certain basic cultural attitudes to important (usually insoluble) questions, and is transparent to a variety of constructions of meaning" (3). In the introduction, Doniger indicates that this claim will be substantiated in the fourth chapter of *The Implied Spider*, of which "Inverted Political Versions" is a part. Here Doniger illustrates the "protean political nature of myths" by looking at examples of "polarized retellings" from popular culture. She admits from the outset that she will not be dealing here with myths in the strict sense. For instance, most of the materials in this section lack "any explicit religious content" (101).

This is one of the problems with "Inverted Political Versions," in my reading of it. I am not sure that the analysis there can serve in any argument about how myths work, because it is really not about myth in the sense that this term is used elsewhere in *The Implied Spider*. Another problem with the section, which becomes apparent only on closer analysis of the material, is that at least some of the examples are not about conflicting political arguments. Take the first story that Doniger tells about a Russian T-shirt. Apparently riders in Moscow subways are subjected to a recording of a droning voice as trains are preparing to depart, "Warning, the doors are closing." In 1991, "the moment of glasnost," T-shirts began to appear on the streets in the Russian capital depicting subway doors made of prison bars with the legend "Warning, the doors are opening" (101–102). Despite the fact that this is an interesting tale, it is hardly an instance of the political reversal of a myth, or even of a story. We might take the T-shirt as having a political point certainly, but not the droning voice in the Moscow subway. This is a compelling case of an image from popular culture being invested with a surprising new meaning, but the image itself was no argument in its first incarnation.

The second example that Doniger gives of a politically inverted retelling may seem more relevant. It is the story of the French King Louis XIV and his secret twin. When this tale was first told in film in 1929 (*The Iron Mask*), the brave d'Artagnan has to protect the virtuous Sun King from the machinations of ambitious courtiers and his evil twin. Yet by the 1939 remake (*The Man in the Iron Mask*), and also in the 1998 film of the same name, it is the good brother who has to be saved from the base Louis (102). Here we have an obvious reversal of the story, but it is unclear to me that we have a reversal of the political point. By the time that *The Iron Mask* was made in 1929, Louis XIV had been dead for more than two hundred years. Surely the political point of the film could not have been that he was a great king, especially in contrast with a base brother who only existed in fiction. In the politics of Hollywood in 1939, who could the evil Louis have been a stand-in for? Perhaps Adolf Hitler or even Franklin Delano Roosevelt. While these are interesting conjectures, I must underline that Doniger does not even entertain them. For her the political inversion of the story stops when Louis and his brother trade moral masks.

It should be noted that there are other examples of political retrofitting in "Inverted Political Versions" that are more convincing, such as competing versions of battles between "cowboys and Injuns" and the conflicting uses to which the myth of the Valkyries is put in Wagner's Ring cycle and Francis Ford Coppola's *Apocalypse Now* (103–104). Yet, overall, I think that Doniger might be accused of the same crime for which Barthes convicts myths, i.e., that she tells stories in which the historical actors and their interests are obscured. When it comes to the political inversion of myth, I am not even sure that it is the historical actors who are the agents. Barthes argues that mythology is a peculiar system of signs because it takes images that already mean something and makes them mean something else. On this point mythology is to be distinguished from language, a system in which the signs that are used, the phonemes, for instance, mean nothing in and of themselves prior to their incorporation into language. Yet in mythology the original meaning of the signs is covered over by the meaning with which they are invested by the myth (121–27). My reading of Barthes is that there is generally some connection between what an image originally meant and what it comes to mean in a myth, but there is a fairly heavy emphasis on the latter at the expense of the former, so that it is almost possible to say that a mythology can take any image to mean anything. Myths are not quite as plastic in *The Implied Spider;* at least this is my understanding of Doniger's argument. A myth can be used to make certain political points but not every imaginable political point, which is why myths may tend to be given diametrically opposed political readings, and not just any old reading. In that sense, any given myth is like a hammer. It can be used to drive in a nail, and it can be used to pull one out, but it cannot be used to screw in a screw. By the same token, the story of Louis XIV and his twin can be used to comment about good kings or bad kings but not about the price of eggs in Denmark. Before she gets to "Inverted Political Versions," Doniger writes: "This quality of myth, its ability to contain in latent form several different attitudes to the events that it depicts, allows each different telling to draw out, as it were, the attitude that it finds compatible" (84). Here myths seem to come with interpretations built in, although those interpretations may be various and conflicting. The storyteller (note that she is only implied) may choose to unpack one of those interpretations rather than another, based on her attitude, but she may not make up any imaginable interpretation. . . .

As I have already explained, the problem with mythology, as Barthes sees it, is not that it is reactionary in a narrow sense (supporting the capitalists against the workers, for example). Rather, mythology is deployed to hide the historical and contingent behind a facade of the naturally given. In that context, I think that Barthes would find Teilhard's Edenic future just as problematic as Eliade's golden past, since both represent a flight from the here and now. The same criticism could be leveled at *The Implied Spider* as a whole, not just to "Inverted Political Versions," and to other books by Doniger as well. Against the charge that the comparative study of mythology is politically suspect, Doniger does not do enough to analyze the politics of myths, to conjecture by whom they were crafted, in what contexts, and to what ends.

For classical myths, unlike some of the products of contemporary culture, it is often impossible to come to any definite conclusion about the historical circumstances of the authors. This may be a practical problem that is an accident of history: an author's biography may be shrouded in the distant past. Yet Doniger's very definition of myth points in the direction of another problem when she writes that, among other things, a myth "is a story believed to have been composed in the past about an event in the past, or, more rarely, in the future" (2). I take this to mean that a myth is generally presented as a very old story, even when it is first composed, a rhetorical strategy that would necessitate some dissembling about the story's author. It is significant that perhaps the classical culture that has been least effective in preserving the biographies of its authors is the very culture that is Doniger's specialty, South Asia. . . .

Conclusion

There is a sense in which my criticism of "The Implied Spider" section is the same as my criticism of "Inverted Political Versions." In the former, Doniger piles up examples of metaphorical spiders but without pausing for long to consider the significance of each of these metaphors in the original from which it has been borrowed. Then in "Inverted Political Versions" she tells stories of myths that have been stood on their heads to serve diametrically opposed political ends but does not always spell out very clearly what she takes those ends to be. In both cases, I would have been more convinced had she had been more patient (or perhaps plodding) in elaborating the context of the stories that she tells.

I hope the reader will forgive me for introducing one more multistory metaphor from *The Implied Spider* to underline the centrality of my criticism. At the very beginning of the book, Doniger introduces optical aids as a metaphor for myths and other narratives. Narratives that are entirely personal (such as "a realistic novel, or even a diary") are microscopes, while those that are entirely impersonal and abstract (such as "a theoretical treatise, or even a mathematical formula") are telescopes (7–8). Myths fall somewhere in the middle of the spectrum between diaries and formulae and thus are narratives that look at experience without optical aids. Optical technology is pressed into service once again in the study of myth, where telescopes are used by the grand theorists (such as Freud, Jung, and Eliade), while microscopes are focused on the level of "individual insight." In this early reprise of the visual metaphor, the unaided-eye view means looking at myths within "contextualized cultural studies" (10). In the first use of the optical metaphor, the "normal view" is privileged, with myths giving access to meaning in a way that diaries or formulae cannot. In the second use of the metaphor, however, telescopes and microscopes are celebrated over the naked eye. Doniger acknowledges that in her work, she has chosen "to focus on the individual and the human race in general, at the cost of the focus on any ethnic group or historical moment or cultural milieu" (11).

This provides the material to frame my criticism of *The Implied Spider*. As Doniger herself insists, an analysis of the universal meaning of a myth and its individual message must include an appreciation for the historical contexts in which that myth is articulated. "Attention to cultural specificity is part of the Hippocratic oath of historians of religions, including mythologists," she writes (43). In *The Implied Spider*, we are offered broad scholarship, entertaining stories, and even passionate political arguments, yet there remain many spiders—and other metaphors, myths and political investments—whose cultural contexts are obscure.

Chapter 6

Sociology of Religion

The sociological approach to the study of religion tends to focus its attention on the interaction between religion and society. Generally, sociologists view religion as socially constructed because human experience and religion are shaped by various kinds of social forces. Because of his work entitled *Cours de Philosophie Positive* that appeared in its full form by 1842, Auguste Comte, a lapsed Catholic, is often given credit as the founder of the discipline along with Henri Saint-Simon because he modeled his new discipline on the natural sciences, which gave an early positivistic shape to sociology. These early roots of sociology embodied a conviction that religion and theology would eventually disappear, as societies became more modern, rational, scientific, and sophisticated.

If Comte and Saint-Simon are given credit for founding a new discipline, scholars give Emile Durkheim (1858–1917) credit for being the most significant figure in the era of modern sociology. Educated at the École Normale Supérieure, Durkheim worked as a secondary school teacher at Sens, taught social sciences at the University of Bordeaux, and eventually became professor of philosophy at the Sorbonne in 1902. Earlier in 1897, Durkheim founded the influential publication *Année Sociologique,* in which the science of sociology was developed and introduced to a wider audience. Durkheim published several books reflecting his theory of religion that were translated into English: *The Elementary Forms of the Religious Life: A Study in Religious Sociology* (1912), *The Rise of Sociological Method* (1938), *Sociology and Philosophy* (1953), *Incest, The Nature and Origin of the Taboo* (1963), and with his nephew Hubert Mauss, *Primitive Classification* (1963). These various works emphasize Durkheim's attention to issues of methodology, use of morphological classification and description, acceptance of the theory of evolution, and his own attempt to offer an evolutionary account of the development of elementary societies to contemporary forms of society and religious life that he viewed as a movement from magic to rationality. His case studies tended to focus on Australian aboriginal tribes, and he attempted to draw universal claims from them about the relation between religion and society. Like many scholars before him, Durkheim was interested in the origin of religion for what it might reveal about the beginnings of human thought. He was convinced that he discovered this origin in totemism, a sacred symbol that represents an impersonal force supporting a tribe's beliefs, rituals, and way of life. The totem served simultaneously as a symbol of the clan and god.

Breaking with a common assumption at the historical time that belief was central to religion, Durkheim grounded his definition of religion in the distinction between sacred and profane, and he stressed community. He also gave equal significance to practices in his definition. Religion possessed a binding force for all societies because it united members around common shared values and social goals by providing them with narratives about their place within the cosmos, their common historical heritage, and purpose of life. The cohesive power of religion manifested the patterns that social groups use to form common identities as a group, versus other groups that allow a given group to express its common destiny. Religion can also sanction the governing structure of a society and the exercise of its political power. With its collective conscience grounded in its religion and shared solidarity, a social group can unite for action such as wars or other kinds of peaceful cooperative endeavors, because individuals have internalized patterns of acceptable social behavior. Moreover, religion continued to exist because society cannot maintain its existence without ceremony.

From Durkheim's sociological perspective, religion represented a projection of society in a symbolized form. Therefore, religion symbolized a social reality. To grasp the nature of religion, it was necessary to investigate the social needs to which religion is a response. From a methodological perspective, Durkheim wanted to identify and describe social facts without bias, classify his findings, analyze them, and finally be able to verify them in a scientific manner. He followed this approach because he was convinced that social facts are as real as anything else in the world. By social facts, he understood shared phenomena like language, laws, customs, ideas, values, traditions, techniques, and products within a particular society.

If Durkheim dominated the field of sociology in France, it was Max Weber (1864–1920) who served as the major figure in Germany. After law school and a brief stint in the military, Weber pursued post-graduate work in Berlin while he simultaneously practiced law. He received his doctorate with a dissertation on commercial groups during the medieval period, and passed a second examination in law 2 years later in 1891. He continued to practice law in Berlin while also becoming a professor of commercial and German law. His teaching career took him to positions at the University of Freiburg, University of Heidelberg, University of Vienna, and finally at the University of Munich where he died. In the fall of 1904, he visited the United States to attend the Congress of Arts and Science held in St. Louis, Missouri. Several of his works were posthumously published in English that reflect his interest in religion: *The Protestant Ethic and the Spirit of Capitalism* (1930), *Essays in Sociology* (1946), *On the Methodology of the Social Sciences* (1949), *The Religion of China* (1951), *Ancient Judaism* (1952), *The Religion of India* (1958), *The Sociology of Religion* (1963), and *On Charisma and Institution Building* (1968). Unlike Durkheim, Weber was opposed to the theory of evolution.

Weber took the new discipline of sociology in a different direction than Durkheim and his school. He moved away from the positivist position and its assimilation of sociology to the natural sciences shaped by the influence of Auguste Comte. In contrast to the holistic and functional approach of Durkheim to society, Weber shifted analysis away from society as a unitary whole to the individual in studies, for instance, of subjects like charisma. This led Weber to stress social action over social structure to discern a causal explanation of the causes and effects of social action without neglecting the subjective aspects of the person. Weber was interested in the inter-relationship between human motives and intentions. Weber did not reject the ideal-istic philosophical tradition out of which he came, and remained at the same time a historical thinker concerned with meaning. Thereby, he developed a historical soci-ology of religion. Weber attempted to weave together the antagonistic positions of idealists with the neo-Kantians by considering not only the phenomenal but also the noumenal world formed by human dispositions that one can gain access by means of analysis, experimentation, and interpretation of the spatiotemporal world. Weber's key notion was *Verstehen* (understanding), which is an extra-empirical and supra-analytical attitude that possessed the ability to give one access to the noumenal world formed by motives and intentions.

Besides making use of comparison in his methodology, Weber wanted to stress the gradual evolution of rationalization within Western society. The comparative aspects of his work are evident in his analytical construct called the "ideal-type," which rep-resented a rational construction of given elements of social reality into a compre-hensible conception. Such "ideal-types," or configurations of meaning for Weber, were found among the priest, prophet, magician, and shaman. Such ideal-types were configurations of meaning, functioning as abstractions to assist sociological analysis and ultimately enhance understanding. These ideal-types were compared with each other, and actions of various religious figures were examined and compared to deter-mine into which type it fit best. The ideal-types gave history a pattern to enhance understanding, enabled one to compare historical data, allowed one to compare among types, and motivated one to compare between ideal-types and historical data.

By focusing on the connection between motives and intentions (noumenal realm) with acts and events (phenomenal realm), Weber argued that religion was more than simply a social construct or a function of human tendencies to develop societies. Because religion served as a source for ideas and practices that transcended the phe-nomenal world of society, it was able to act upon this realm in independent and unpredictable ways. Therefore, religion worked to not only challenge the established order but also created social change. Besides its potential to transform society, reli-gion also played a more conservative role to maintain the existing social structure and to legitimate the status quo. Weber's classic example of the dynamic nature of reli-gion was the interdependence of Protestantism (motive) and Capitalism (action). For Weber, Protestantism worked as a source of motivation from which the action of Capitalism followed. This type of an example also suggested that religious ideas (noumenal aspect) possessed a potential independent causal importance in any instance of social change (action).

Guideline Questions

What are the methodological implications for Durkheim's position that no religions are false?

How does charisma function in religion for Weber, and how does it affect his ideal-types?

From *Elementary Forms of the Religious Life*

EMILE DURKHEIM

Religious Sociology and the Theory of Knowledge

In this book we propose to study the most primitive and simple religion which is actually known, to make an analysis of it, and to attempt an explanation of it. A religious system may be said to be the most primitive which we can observe when it fulfills the two following conditions: in the first place, when it is found in a society whose organization is surpassed by no others in simplicity; and secondly, when it is possible to explain it without making use of any element borrowed from a previous religion.

We shall set ourselves to describe the organization of this system with all the exactness and fidelity that an ethnographer or an historian could give it. But our task will not be limited to that: sociology raises other problems than history or ethnography. It does not seek to know the passed forms of civilization with the sole end of knowing them and reconstructing them. But rather, like every positive science, it has as its object the explanation of some actual reality which is near to us, and which consequently is capable of affecting our ideas and our acts: This reality is man, and more precisely, the man of today, for there is nothing which we are more interested in knowing. Then we are not going to study a very archaic religion simply for the pleasure of telling its peculiarities and its singularities, if we have better adapted than any other to lead to an understanding of the religious nature of man, that is to say, to show us an essential and permanent aspect of humanity.

But this proposition is not accepted before the raising of strong objections. It seems very strange that one must turn back, and be transported to the very beginning of history, in order to arrive at an understanding of humanity as it is at present. This manner of procedure seems particularly paradoxical in the question which concerns us. In fact, the various religions generally pass as being quite unequal in value and dignity; it is said that they do not all contain the same quota of truth. Then it seems as though one could not compare the highest forms of religious thought with the lowest, without reducing the first to the level of the second. If we admit that the crude cults of the Australian tribes can help us to understand Christianity, for example, is that not supposing that this latter religion proceeds from the same mentality as the former, that it is made up of the same superstitions and rests upon the same errors? This is how the theoretical importance which has sometimes been attributed to primitive religions has come to pass as a sign of a systematic hostility to all religion, which, by prejudging the results of the study, vitiates them in advance.

There is no occasion for asking here whether or not there are scholars who have merited this reproach, and who have made religious history and ethnology a weapon against religion. In any case, a sociologist cannot hold such a point of view. In fact, it is an essential postulate of sociology that a human institution cannot rest upon an error and a lie, without it could not exist. If it were not founded in the nature of things, it would have encountered in the facts a resistance over which it could never have triumphed. So

Reprinted from Emile Durkheim Elementary Forms of the Religious Life, *trans. Joseph Ward Swain (London: George Allen & Unwin Ltd., 1915.)*

when we commence the study of primitive religions, it is with the assurance that they hold to reality and express it; this principle will be seen to re-enter again and again in the course of the analyses and discussions which follow, and the reproach which we make against the schools from which we have separated ourselves is that they have ignored it. When only the letter of the formulae is considered, these religious beliefs and practices undoubtedly seem disconcerting at times, and one is tempted to attribute them to some sort of deep-rooted error. But one must know how to go underneath the symbol to the reality which it represents and which gives it its meaning. The most barbarous and the most fantastic rites and the strangest myths translate some human need, some aspect of life, either individual or social. The reasons with which the faithful justify them may be, and generally are, erroneous; but the true reasons do not cease to exist, and it is the duty of science to discover them.

In reality, then, there are no religions which are false. All are true in their own fashion; all answer, though in different ways, to the given conditions of human existence. It is undeniably possible to arrange them in a hierarchy. Some can be called superior to others, in the sense that they call into play higher mental functions, that they are richer in ideas and sentiments, that they contain more concepts with fewer sensations and images, and that their arrangement is wiser. But howsoever real this greater complexity and this higher ideality may be, they are not sufficient to place the corresponding religions in different classes. All are religious equally, just as all living beings are equally alive, from the most humble plastids up to man. So when we turn to primitive religions it is not with the idea of depreciating religion in general, for these religions are no less respectable than the others. They respond to the same needs, they play the same role, they depend upon the same causes; they can also well serve to show the nature of the religious life, and consequently to resolve the problem which we wish to study.

But why give them a sort of prerogative? Why choose them in preference to all others as the subject of our study? It is merely for reasons of method.

In the first place, we cannot arrive at an understanding of the most recent religions except by following the manner in which they have been progressively composed in history. In fact, historical analysis is the only means of explanation which it is possible to apply to them. It alone enables us to resolve an institution into its constituent elements, for it shows them to us as they are born in time, one after another. On the other hand, by placing every one of them in the condition where it was born, it puts into our hands the only means we have of determining the causes which gave rise to it. Every time that we undertake to explain something human, taken at a given moment in history—be it a religious belief, a moral precept, a legal principle, an aesthetic style or an economic system—it is necessary to commence by going back to its most primitive and simple form, to try to account for the characteristics by which it was marked at that time, and then to show how it developed and became complicated little by little, and how it became that which it is at the moment in question. One readily understands the importance which the determination of the point of departure has for this series of progressive explanations, for all the others are attached to it. It was one of Descartes' principles that the first ring has a predominating place in the chain of scientific truths. But there is no question of placing at the foundation of the science of religions an idea elaborated after the Cartesian manner, that is to say, a logical concept, a pure possibility, constructed simply by force of thought. What we must find is a concrete reality, and historical and ethnological observation alone can reveal that to us. But even if this cardinal conception is obtained by a different process than that of Descartes, it remains true that it is destined to have a considerable influence on the whole series of propositions which the science establishes. Biological evolution has been conceived quite differently ever since it has been known that monocellular beings do exist. In the same way, the arrangement of religious facts is explained quite differently, according as we put naturism, animism or some other religious forms at the beginning of the evolution. Even the most specialized scholars, if they are unwilling to confine themselves to a task of pure erudition, and if they desire to interpret the facts which they analyse, are obliged to choose one of these hypotheses, and make it their starting point. Whether they desire or not, the questions which they raise necessarily take the following form: how has naturism or animism been led to take this particular form, here or there, or to enrich itself or impoverish itself in such and such a fashion? Since it is impossible to avoid taking sides on this initial problem, and since the solution given is destined to affect the whole science, it must be attacked at the outset: that is what we propose to do.

Besides this, outside of these indirect reactions, the study of primitive religions has of itself an immediate interest which is of primary importance.

If it is useful to know what a certain particular religion consists in, it is still more important to know what religion in general is. This is the problem which has aroused the interest of philosophers in all times; and not without reason, for it is of interest to all humanity. Unfortunately, the method which they generally employ is purely dialectic: they confine themselves to analysing the idea which they make for themselves of religion, except as they illustrate the results of this mental analysis by examples borrowed from the religions which best realize their ideal. But even if this method ought to be abandoned, the problem remains intact, and the great service of philosophy is to have prevented its being suppressed by the disdain of scholars. Now it is possible to attack it in a different way. Since all religions can be compared to each other, and since all are species of the same class, there are necessarily many elements which are common to all. We do not mean to speak simply of the outward and visible characteristics which

they all have equally, and which make it possible to give them a provisional definition from the very outset of our researches; the discovery of these apparent signs is relatively easy, for the observation which it demands does not go beneath the surface of things. But these external resemblances suppose others which are profound. At the foundation of all systems of beliefs and of all cults there ought necessarily to be a certain number of fundamental representations or conceptions and of ritual attitudes which, in spite of the diversity of forms which they have taken, have the same objective significance and fulfill the same functions everywhere. There are the permanent elements which constitute that which is permanent and human in religion; they form all the objective contents of the idea which is expressed when one speaks of *religion* in general. How is it possible to pick them out?

Surely it is not by observing the complex religions which appear in the course of history. Every one of these is made up of such a variety of elements that it is very difficult to distinguish what is secondary from what is principal, the essential from the accessory. Suppose that the religion considered is like that of Egypt, India or the classical antiquity. It is a confused mass of many cults, varying according to the locality, the temples, the generations, the dynasties, the invasions, etc. Popular superstitions are there confused with the purest dogmas. Neither the thought nor the activity of the religion is evenly distributed among the believers; according to the men, the environment and the circumstances, the beliefs as well as the rites are thought of in different ways. Here they are priests, there they are monks, elsewhere they are laymen; there are mystics and rationalists, theologians and prophets, etc. In these conditions it is difficult to see what is common to all. In one or another of these systems it is quite possible to find the means of making a profitable study of some particular fact which is specially developed there, such as sacrifice or prophecy, monasticism or the mysteries; but how is it possible to find the common foundation of the religious life underneath the luxuriant vegetation which covers it? How is it possible to find, underneath the disputes of theology, the variations of ritual, the multiplicity of groups and the diversity of individuals, the fundamental states characteristic of religious mentality in general?

Things are quite different in the lower societies. The slighter development of individuality, the small extension of the group, the homogeneity of external circumstances, all contribute to reducing the differences and variations to a minimum. The group has an intellectual and moral conformity of which we find but rare examples in the more advanced societies. Everything is common to all. Movements are stereotyped; everybody performs the same ones in the same circumstances, and this conformity of conduct only translates the conformity of thought. Every mind being drawn into the same eddy, the individual type nearly confounds itself with that of the race. And while all is uniform, all is simple as well. Nothing is deformed like these myths, all composed of one and the same theme which is endlessly repeated again and again. Neither the popular imagination nor that of the priests has had either the time or the means of refining and transforming the original substance of the religious ideas and practices; these are shown in all their nudity, and offer themselves to an examination, it requiring only the slightest effort to lay them open. That which is accessory or secondary, the development of luxury, has not yet come to hide the principal elements. All is reduced to that which is indispensable, to that without which there could be no religion. But that which is indispensable is also that which is essential, that is to say, that which we must know before all else.

Primitive civilizations offer privileged cases, then, because they are simple cases. That is why, in all fields of human activity, the observations of ethnologists have frequently been veritable revelations, which have renewed the study of human institutions. For example, before the middle of the nineteenth century, everybody was convinced that the father was the essential element of the family; no one has dreamed that there could be a family organization of which the paternal authority was not the keystone. But the discovery of Bachofen came and upset this old conception. Up to very recent times it was regarded as evident that the moral and legal relations of kindred were only another aspect of the psychological relations which result from a common descent; Bachofen and his successors, MacLennan, Morgan and many others still laboured under this misunderstanding. But since we have become acquainted with the nature of the primitive clan, we know that, on the contrary, relationships cannot by explained by consanguinity. To return to religions, the study of only the most familiar ones had led men to believe for a long time that the idea of god was characteristic of everything that is religious. Now the religion which we are going to study presently is, in a large part, foreign to all idea of divinity; the forces to which the rites are there addressed are very different from those which occupy the leading place in our modern religions, yet they aid us in understanding these latter forces. So nothing is more unjust than the disdain with which too many historians still regard the work of ethnographers. Indeed, it is certain that ethnology has frequently brought about the most fruitful revolutions in the different branches of sociology. It is for this same reason that the discovery of unicellular beings, of which we just spoke, has transformed the current idea of life. Since in these very simple beings, life is reduced to its essential traits, these are less easily misunderstood.

But primitive religions do not merely aid us in disengaging the constituent elements of religion; they also have a great advantage that they facilitate the explanation of it. Since the facts there are simpler, the relations between them are more apparent. The reasons with which men account for their acts have not yet been elaborated and denatured by studied reflection; they are nearer and more closely related to the motives which have really determined these acts. In order to understand a hallucination perfectly, and give it its most appropriate treatment, a physician must know its original point of departure. Now this event is proportionately easier to find if he can observe it near its beginnings. The longer the disease is allowed to develop, the more it evades observation; that is because all sorts of interpretations have intervened as it advanced, which tend to force the original state into the background, and across which it is frequently difficult to find the initial one. Between a systematized hallucination and the first impressions which give it birth, the distance is often considerable. It is the same thing with religious thought. In proportion as it progresses in history, the causes which called it into existence, though remaining active, are no longer perceived, except across a vast scheme of interpretations which quite transform them. Popular mythologies and subtle theologies have done their work: they have superimposed upon the primitive sentiments others which are quite different, and which, though holding to the first, of which they are an elaborated form, only allow their true nature to appear very imperfectly. The psychological gap between the cause and the effect, between the apparent cause and the effective cause, has become more considerable and more difficult for the mind to leap. The remainder of this book will be an illustration and a verification of this remark on method. It will be seen how, in the primitive religions, the religious fact still visibly carries the mark of its origins; it would have been well-nigh impossible to infer them merely from the study of the more developed religions.

The study which we are undertaking is therefore a way of taking up again, *but under new conditions,* the old problem of the origin of religion. To be sure, if by origin we are to understand the very first beginning, the question has nothing scientific about it, and should be resolutely discarded. There was no given moment when religion began to exist, and there is consequently no need of finding a means of transporting ourselves thither in thought. Like every human institution, religion did not commence anywhere. Therefore, all speculations of this sort are justly discredited; they can only consist in subjective and arbitrary constructions which are subject to no sort of control. But the problem which we raise is quite another one. What we want to do is to find a means of discerning the ever-present causes upon which the most essential forms of religious thought and practice depend. Now for the reasons which were just set forth, these causes are proportionately more easily observable as the societies where they are observed are less complicated. That is why we try to get as near as possible to the origins. It is not that we ascribe particular virtues to the lower religions. On the contrary, they are rudimentary and gross; we cannot make of them a sort of model which later religions only have to reproduce. But even their grossness makes them instructive, for they thus become convenient for experiments, as in them, the facts and their relations are easily seen. In order to discover the laws of the phenomena which he studies, the physicist tries to simplify these latter and rid them of the secondary characteristics. For that which concerns institutions, nature spontaneously makes the same sort of simplifications at the beginning of history. We merely wish to put these to profit. Undoubtedly we can only touch very elementary facts by this method. When we shall have accounted for them as far as possible, the novelties of every sort which have been produced in the course of evolution will not yet be explained. But while we do not dream of denying the importance of the problems thus raised, we think that they will profit by being treated in their turn, and that it is important to take them up only after those of which we are going to undertake the study at present. . . .

Definition of Religious Phenomena and of Religion

If we are going to look for the most primitive and simple religion which we can observe, it is necessary to begin defining what is meant by a religion; for without this, we would run the risk of giving the name to a system of ideas and practices which has nothing at all religious about it, or else of leaving to one side many religious facts, without perceiving their true nature. That this is not an imaginary danger, and that nothing is thus sacrificed to a vain formalism of method, is well shown by the fact that owing to his not having taken this precaution, a certain scholar to whom the science of comparative religions owes a great deal, Professor Frazer, has not been able to recognize the profoundly religious character of the beliefs and rites which will be studied below, where, according to our view, the initial germ of the religious life of humanity is to be found. So this is a prejudicial question, which must be treated before all others. It is not that we dream of arriving at once at the profound characteristics which really explain religion: these can be determined only at the end of our study. But that which is necessary and possible, is to indicate a certain number of external and easily recognizable signs, which will enable us to recognize religious phenomena wherever they are met with and which will deter us from confounding them with others. We shall proceed to this preliminary operation at once.

But to attain the desired results, it is necessary to begin by freeing the mind of every preconceived idea. Men have been obliged to make for themselves a notion of what religion is, long before the science of religions starts its methodical comparisons. The necessities of existence force all of us, believers and non-believers, to represent in some way these things in the midst of which we live, upon which we must pass judgment constantly, and which we must take into account in all our conduct. However, since these preconceived ideas are formed without any method, according to the circumstances and chances of life, they have no right to any credit whatsoever, and must be rigorously set aside in the examination which is to follow. It is not our prejudices, passions or habits that we should demand the elements of the definition which we must have; it is from the reality itself which we are going to define.

Let us set ourselves before this reality. Leaving aside all conceptions of religion in general, let us consider the various religions in their concrete reality, and attempt to disengage that which they have in common; for religion cannot be defined except by the characteristics which are found wherever religion itself is found. In this comparison, then, we shall make use of all the religious systems which we can know, those of the present and those of the past, the most primitive and simple as well as the most recent and refined: for we have neither the right nor the logical means of excluding some and retaining others. For those who regard religion as only a natural manifestation of human activity, all religions, without any exception whatsoever, are instructive; for all, after their manner, express man, and thus can aid us in better understanding this aspect of our nature. Also, we have seen how far it is from being the best way of studying religion to consider by preference the forms which it presents among the most civilized peoples.

But to aid the mind in freeing itself from these usual conceptions which, owing to their prestige, might prevent it from seeing things as they really are, it is fitting to examine some of the most current of the definitions in which these prejudices are commonly expressed, before taking up the question on our own account.

One idea which generally passes as characteristic of all that is religious, is that of the supernatural. By this is understood all sorts of things which surpass the limits of our knowledge; the supernatural is the world of the mysterious, of the unknowable, of the un-understandable. Thus religion would be a sort of speculation upon all that which evades science or distinct thought in general. "Religions diametrically opposed in their overt dogmas," said Spencer, "are perfectly at one in the tacit conviction that the existence of the world, with all it contains and all which surrounds it, is a mystery calling for an explanation"; he thus makes them consist essentially in "the belief in the omnipresence of something which is inscrutable."[1] In the same manner, Max Müller sees in religion "a struggle to conceive the inconceivable, to utter the unutterable, a longing after the Infinite."[2]

It is certain that the sentiment of mystery has not been without a considerable importance in certain religions, notably in Christianity. It must also be said that the importance of this sentiment has varied remarkably at different moments in the history of Christianity. There are periods when this notion passes to an inferior place, and is even effaced. For example, for the Christians of the seventeenth century, dogma had nothing disturbing for the reason; faith reconciled itself easily with science and philosophy, and the thinkers, such as Pascal, who really felt that there is something profoundly obscure in things, were so little in harmony with their age that they remained misunderstood by their contemporaries. It would appear somewhat hasty, therefore, to make an idea subject to parallel eclipses, the essential element of even the Christian religion.

In all events, it is certain that this idea does not appear until late in the history of religions; it is completely foreign, not only to those peoples who are called primitive, but also to all others who have not attained a considerable degree of intellectual culture. . . . These definitions set aside, let us set ourselves before the problem.

First of all, let us remark that in all these formulae it is the nature of religion as a whole that they seek to express. They proceed as if it were a sort of indivisible entity, while, as a matter of fact, it is made up of parts; it is a more or less complex system of myths, dogmas, rites and ceremonies. Now a whole cannot be defined except in relation to its parts. It will be more methodical, then, to try to characterize the various elementary phenomena of which all religions are made up, before we attack the system produced by their union. This method is imposed still more forcibly by the fact that there are religious phenomena which belong to no determined religion. Such are those phenomena which constitute the matter of folklore. In general, they are debris of passed religions, in organized survivals; but there are some which have been formed spontaneously under the influence of local causes. In our European countries Christianity has forced itself to absorb and assimilate them; it has given them a Christian colouring. Nevertheless, there are many which have persisted up until a recent date, or which still exist with a relative autonomy: celebrations of May Day, the summer solstice or the carnival, beliefs relative to genii, local demons, etc., are cases in point. If the religious character of these facts is now diminishing, their religious importance is nevertheless so great that they have enabled Mannhardt and his school to revive the science of religions. A definition which did not take account of them would not cover all that is religious.

Religious phenomena are naturally arranged in two fundamental categories: beliefs and rites. The first are states of opinion, and consist in representations; the second are determined modes of action. Between these two classes of facts there is all the difference which separates thought from action.

The rites can be defined and distinguished from other human practices, moral practices, for example, only by the special nature of their object. A moral rule prescribes certain manners of acting to us, just as a rite does, but which are addressed to a different class of objects. So it is the object of the rite which must be characterized, if we are to characterize the rite itself. Now it is in the beliefs that the special nature of this object is expressed. It is possible to define the rite only after we have defined the belief.

All known religious beliefs, whether simple or complex, present one common characteristic: they presuppose a classification of all the things, real and ideal, of which men think, into two classes or opposed groups, generally designated by two distinct terms which are translated well enough by the words *profane* and *sacred* (*Profane, sacre*). This division of the world into two domains, the one containing all that is sacred, the other all that is profane, is the distinctive trait of religious thought; the beliefs, myths, dogmas, and legends are either representations or systems of representations which express the nature of sacred things, the virtues and powers which are attributed to them, or their relations with each other and with profane things. But by sacred things one must not understand simply those personal beings which are called gods or spirits; a rock, a tree, a spring, a pebble, a piece of wood, a house, in a word, anything can be sacred. A rite can have this character; in fact, the rite does not exist which does not have it to a certain degree. There are words, expressions and formulae which can be pronounced only by the mouths of consecrated persons; there are gestures and movements which everybody cannot perform. If the Vedic sacrifice has had such an efficacy that, according to mythology, it was the creator of the gods, and not merely a means of winning their favour, it is because it possessed a virtue comparable to that of the most sacred beings. The circle of sacred objects cannot be determined, then, once for all. Its extent varies infinitely, according to the different religions. That is how Buddhism is a religion: in default of gods, it admits the existence of sacred things, namely, the four noble truths and the practices derived from them.

Up to the present we have confined ourselves to enumerating a certain number of sacred things as examples: we must now show by what general characteristics they are to be distinguished from profane things.

One might be tempted, first of all, to define them by the place they are generally assigned in the hierarchy of things. They are naturally considered superior in dignity and power to profane things, and particularly to man, when he is only a man and has nothing sacred about him. One thinks of himself as occupying an inferior and dependent position in relation to them; and surely this conception is not without some truth. Only there is nothing in it which is really characteristic of the sacred. It is not enough that one thing be subordinated to another for the second to be sacred in regard to the first. Slaves are inferior to their masters, subjects to their king, soldiers to their leaders, the miser to his gold, the man ambitious for power to the hands

which keep it from him; but if it is sometimes said of a man that he makes a religion of those beings or things whose eminent value and superiority to himself he thus recognizes, it is clear that in any case the word is taken in a metaphorical sense, and that there is nothing in these relations which is really religious.

On the other hand, it must not be lost to view that there are sacred things of every degree, and that there are some in relation to which a man feels himself relatively at his ease. An amulet has a sacred character, yet the respect which it inspires is nothing exceptional. Even before his gods, a man is not always in such a marked state of inferiority; for it very frequently happens that he exercises a veritable physical constraint upon them to obtain what he desires. He beats the fetish with which he is not contended, but only to reconcile himself with it again, if in the end it shows itself more docile to the wishes of its adorer.[3] To have rain, he throws stones into the spring or sacred lake where the god of rain is thought to reside; he believes that by this means he forces him to come out and show himself.[4] Moreover, if it is true that man depends upon his gods, this dependence is reciprocal. The gods also have need of man; without offerings and sacrifices they would die. We shall even have occasion to show that this dependence of the gods upon their worshippers is maintained even in the most idealistic religions.

But if a purely hierarchic distinction is a criterium at once too general and too imprecise, there is nothing left with which to characterize the sacred in its relation to the profane except the heterogeneity. However, this heterogeneity is sufficient to characterize this classification of things and to distinguish it from all others, because it is very particular: *it is absolute.* In all the history of human thought there exists no other example of two categories of things so profoundly differentiated or so radically opposed to one another. The traditional opposition of good and bad is nothing beside this; for the good and the bad are only two opposed species of the same class, namely morals, just as sickness and health are two different aspects of the same order of facts, life, while the sacred and the profane have always and everywhere been conceived by the human mind as two distinct classes, as two worlds between which there is nothing in common. The forces which play in one are not simply those which are met with in the other, but a little stronger; they are of a different sort. In different religions, this opposition has been conceived in different ways. Here, to separate these two sorts of things, it has seemed sufficient to localize them in different parts of the physical universe; there, the first have been put into an ideal and transcendental world, while the material world is left in full possession of the others. But howsoever much the forms of the contrast may vary,[5] the fact of the contrast is universal.

This is not equivalent to saying that a being can never pass from one of these worlds into the other: but the manner in which this passage is effected, when it does take place, puts into relief the essential duality of the two kingdoms. In fact, it implies a veritable metamorphosis. This is notable demonstrated by the initiation rites, such as they are practiced by a multitude of peoples. This initiation is a long series of ceremonies with the object of introducing the young man into the religious life: for the first time, he leaves the purely profane world where he passed his first infancy, and enters into the world of sacred things. Now this change of state is thought of, not as simple and regular development of pre-existent germs, but as a transformation *totius substantiae*—of the whole being. It is said that at this moment the young man dies, that the person that he was ceases to exist, and that another is instantly substituted for it. He is re-born under a new form. Appropriate ceremonies are felt to bring about this death and re-birth, which are not understood in a merely symbolic sense, but are taken literally.[6] Does this not prove that between the profane being which he was and the religious being which he becomes, there is a break of continuity?

This heterogeneity is even so complete that it frequently degenerates into a veritable antagonism. The two worlds are not only conceived as separate, but as even hostile and jealous rivals of each other. Since men cannot fully belong to one except on condition of leaving the other completely, they are exhorted to withdraw themselves completely from the profane world, in order to lead an exclusively religious life. Hence comes the monasticism which is artificially organized outside of and apart from the natural environment in which the ordinary man leads the life of this world, in a different one, closed to the first, and nearly its contrary. Hence comes the mystic asceticism whose object is to root out from man all the attachment for the profane world that remains in him. From that come all the forms of religious suicide, the logical working-out of this asceticism; for only the manner of fully escaping the profane life is, after all, to forsake all life.

The opposition of these two classes manifests itself outwardly with a visible sign by which we can easily recognize this very special classification, wherever it exists. Since the idea of the sacred is always and everywhere separated from the idea of the profane in the thought of men, and since we picture a sort of logical chasm between the two, the mind irresistibly refuses to allow the two corresponding things to be confounded, or even to be merely put in contact with each other; for such a promiscuity, or even too direct a contiguity, would contradict too violently the dissociation of these ideas in mind. The sacred thing is *par excellence* that which the profane should not touch, and cannot touch with impunity. To be sure, this interdiction cannot go so far as to make all communication between the two worlds impossible; for if the profane could in no way enter into relations with the sacred, this latter could be good for nothing. But, in addition to the fact that this establishment of relations is always a delicate operation in itself, demanding great precautions and a more or less complicated initiation, it is quite impossible, unless the profane is to lose its specific characteristics and become sacred after a fashion and to a certain degree itself. The two classes cannot even approach each other and keep their own nature at the same time.

Thus we arrive at the first criterium of religious beliefs. Undoubtedly there are secondary species within these two fundamental classes which, in their turn, are more or less incompatible with each other. But the real characteristic of religious phenomena is that they always suppose a bipartite division of the whole universe, known and knowable, into two classes which embrace all that exists, but which radically exclude each other. Sacred things are those which the interdictions protect and isolate; profane things, those to which these interdictions are applied and which must remain at a distance from the first. Religious beliefs are the representations which express the nature of sacred things and the relations which they sustain, either with each other or with profane things. Finally, rites are the rules of conduct which prescribe how a man should comport himself in the presence of these sacred objects.

When a certain number of sacred things sustain relations of coordination or subordination with each other in such a way as to form a system having a certain unity, but which is not comprised within any other system of the same sort, the totality of these beliefs and their corresponding rites constitutes a religion. From this definition it is seen that a religion is not necessarily contained within one sole and single idea, and does not proceed from one unique principle which, though varying according to the circumstances under which it is applied, is nevertheless at bottom always the same: it is rather a whole made up of distinct and relatively individualized parts. Each homogeneous group of sacred things, or even each sacred thing of some importance, constitutes a centre of organization about which gravitate a group of beliefs and rites, or a particular cult; there is no religion; howsoever unified it may be, which does not recognize a plurality of sacred things. Even Christianity, at least in its Catholic form, admits, in addition to the divine personality which, incidentally, is triple as well as one, the Virgin, angels, saints,

souls of the dead, etc. Thus a religion cannot be reduced to one single cult generally, but rather consists in a system of cults, each endowed with a certain autonomy. Also, this autonomy is variable. Sometimes they are arranged in a hierarchy, and subordinated to some predominating cult, into which they are finally absorbed; but sometimes, also, they are merely rearranged and united. The religion which we are going to study will furnish us with an example of just this latter sort of organization.

At the same time we find the explanation of how there can be groups of religious phenomena which do not belong to any special religion; it is because they have not been, or are no longer, a part of any religious system. If, for some special reason, one of the cults of which we just spoke happens to be maintained while the group of which it was a part disappears, it survives only in a disintegrated condition. That is what has happened to many agrarian cults which have survived themselves as folklore. In certain cases, it is not even a cult, but a simple ceremony or particular rite which persists in this way.

Although this definition is only preliminary, it permits us to see in what terms the problem which necessarily dominates the science of religions should be stated. When we believed that sacred beings could be distinguished from others merely by the greater intensity of the powers attributed to them, the question of how men came to imagine them was sufficiently simple: it was enough to demand which forces had, because of their exceptional energy, been able to strike the human imagination forcefully enough to inspire religious sentiments. But if, as we have sought to establish, sacred things differ in nature from profane things, if they have a wholly different essence, then the problem is more complex. For we must first of all ask what has been able to lead men to see in the world two heterogeneous and incompatible worlds, though nothing is sensible experience seems able to suggest the idea of so radically a duality to them. . . .

There still remain those contemporary aspirations towards a religion which would consist entirely in internal and subjective states, and which would be constructed freely by each of us. But howsoever real these aspirations may be, they cannot affect our definition, for this is to be applied only to facts already realized, and not to uncertain possibilities. One can define religions such as they are, or such as they have been, but not such as they more or less vaguely tend to become. It is possible that this religious individualism is destined to be realized in facts; but before we can say just how far this may be the case, we must first know what religion is, of what elements it is made up, from what causes it results, and what function it fulfills—all questions whose solution cannot be foreseen before the threshold of our study has been passed. It is only at the close of this study that we can attempt to anticipate the future.

Thus we arrive at the following definition: *A religion is a unified system of beliefs and practices relative to sacred things, that is to say, things set apart and forbidden—beliefs and practices which unite into one single moral community called a Church, all those who adhere to them.* The second element which thus finds a place in our definition is no less essential than the first; for by showing that the idea of religion is inseparable from that of the Church, it makes it clear that religion should be an eminently collective thing.

Naturism and Animism

Armed with this definition we are now able to set out in search of this elementary religion which we propose to study.

Even the crudest religions with which history and ethnology make us acquainted are already of a complexity which corresponds badly with the idea sometimes held of primitive mentality. One finds there not only a confused system of beliefs and rites, but also such a plurality of different principles, and such a richness of essential notions, that it seems impossible to see in them anything but the late product of a rather long evolution. Hence it has been concluded that to discover the truly original form of the religious

life, it is necessary to descend by analysis beyond these observable religions, to resolve them into their common and fundamental elements, and then to seek among these latter some one from which the others were derived.

To the problem thus stated, two contrary solutions have been given.

There is no religious system, ancient or recent, where one does not meet, under different forms, two religions, as it were, side by side, which, though being united closely and mutually penetrating each other, do not cease, nevertheless, to be distinct. The one addresses itself to the phenomena of nature, either the great cosmic forces, such as winds, rivers, stars or the sky, etc., or else the objects of various sorts which cover the surface of the earth, such as plants, animals, rock, etc.; for this reason it has been given the name of *naturism*. The other has spiritual beings as its object, spirits, souls, geniuses, demons, divinities properly so-called, animated and conscious agents like man, but distinguished from him, nevertheless, by the nature of their powers and especially by the peculiar characteristic that they do not affect the senses in the same way: ordinarily they are not visible to human eyes. This religion of spirit is called *animism*. Now, to explain the universal coexistence of these two sorts of cults, two contradictory theories have been proposed. For some, animism is the primitive religion, of which naturism is only a secondary and derived form. For the others, on the contrary, it is the nature cult which was the point of departure for religious evolution; the cult of spirits is only a peculiar case of that.

These two theories are, up to the present, the only ones by which the attempt has been made to explain rationally the origins of religious thought. Thus the capital problem raised by the history of religions is generally reduced to asking which of these two solutions should be chosen, or whether it is not better to combine them, and in that case, what place must be given to each of the two elements. Even those scholars who do not admit either of these hypotheses in their systematic form, do not refuse to retain certain propositions upon which they rest. Thus we have a certain number of theories already made, which must be submitted to criticism before we take up the study of the facts for ourselves. It will be better understood how indispensable it is to attempt a new one, when we have seen the insufficiency of these traditional conceptions. . . .

Totemism as an Elementary Religion

Howsoever opposed their conclusions may seem to be, the two systems which we have just studied agree upon one essential point: they state the problem in identical terms. Both undertake to construct the idea of the divine out of the sensations aroused in us by certain natural phenomena, either physical or biological. For the animists it is dreams, for the naturists, certain cosmic phenomena, which served as the point of departure for religious evolution. But for both, it is in the nature, either of man or of the universe, that we must look for the germ of the grand opposition which separates the profane from the sacred.

But such an enterprise is impossible: it supposes a veritable creation *ex nihilo*. A fact of common experience cannot give us the idea of something whose characteristic is to be outside the world of common experience. A man, as he appears to himself in his dreams, is only a man. Natural forces, as our senses perceive them, are only natural forces, howsoever great their intensity may be. Hence comes the common criticism which we address to both doctrines. In order to explain how these pretended data of religious thought have been able to take a sacred character which has no objective foundation, it would be necessary to admit that a whole world of delusive representations has superimposed itself upon the other, denatured it to the point of making it unrecognizable, and substituted a pure hallucination for reality. Here, it is the illusions of the dream which brought about this transfiguration; there, it is the brilliant and vain company of images evoked by the word. But in one case as in the other, it is necessary to regard religion as the product of a delirious imagination.

Thus one positive conclusion is arrived at as the result of this critical examination. Since neither man nor nature have of themselves a sacred character, they must get it from another source. Aside from the human individual and the physical world, there should be some other reality, in relation to which this variety of delirium which all religion is in a sense, has a significance and an objective value. In other words, beyond those which we have called animistic and naturistic, there should be another sort of cult, more fundamental and more primitive, of which the first are only derived forms of particular aspects.

In fact, this cult does exist: it is the one to which ethnologists have given the name of totemism. . . .

From this historical resume it is clear that Australia is the most favourable field for the study of totemism, and therefore we shall make it the principal area of our observations.

In his *Totemism*, Frazer sought especially to collect all the traces of totemism which could be found in history or ethnology. He was thus led to include in his study societies, the nature and degree of whose culture differs most widely: ancient Egypt,[7] Arabia and Greece,[8] and the southern Slavs[9] are found there, side by side with the tribes of Australia and America. This manner of procedure is not at all surprising for a disciple of the anthropological school. For this school does not seek to locate religions in the social environments of which they are a part, and to differentiate them according to the different environments to which they are thus connected. But rather, as is indicated by the name which it has taken to itself, its purpose is to go beyond the national and historical differences to the universal and really human bases of the religious life. It is supposed that man has a religious nature of himself, in virtue of his own constitution, and independently of all social conditions, and they propose to study this. For researchers of this sort, all peoples can be called upon equally well. It is true that they prefer the more primitive peoples, because this fundamental nature is more apt to be unaltered here; but since it is found equally well among the most civilized peoples, it is but natural that they too should be called as witnesses. Consequently, all those who pass as being not too far removed from the origins, and who are confusedly lumped together under the rather imprecise rubric of *savages,* are put on the same plane and consulted indifferently. Since from this point of view, facts have an interest only in proportion to their generality, they consider themselves obliged to collect as large a number as possible of them; the circle of comparisons could not become too large.

Our method will not be such a one, for several reasons.

In the first place, for the sociologist as for the historian, social facts vary with the social system of which they form a part; they cannot be understood when detached from it. This is why two facts which come from two different societies cannot be profitably compared merely because they seem to resemble each other; it is necessary that these societies themselves resemble each other, that is to say, that they be only varieties of the same species. The comparative method would be impossible, if social types did not exist, and it cannot be usefully applied except within a single type. What errors have not been committed for having neglected this precept! It is thus that facts have been unduly connected with each other which, in spite of exterior resemblances, really have neither the same sense nor the same importance: the primitive democracy and that of today, the collectivism of inferior societies and actual socialistic tendencies, the monogamy which is frequent in Australian tribes and that sanctioned by our laws, etc. Even in the work of Frazer such confusions are found. It frequently happens that he assimilates simple rites of wild-animal-worship to practices that are really totemic, though the distance, sometimes very great, which separates the two social systems would exclude all idea of assimilation. Then if we do not wish to fall into these same errors, instead of scattering our researches over all the societies possible, we must concentrate them upon one clearly determined type.

It is even necessary that this concentration be as close as possible. One cannot usefully compare facts with which he is not perfectly well acquainted. But when he undertakes to include all sorts of societies and civilizations, one cannot know any of them with the necessary thoroughness; when he assembles facts from every country in order to compare them, he is obliged to take them hastily, without having either the means or the time to carefully criticize them. Tumultuous and summary comparisons result, which discredit the comparative method with many intelligent persons. It can give serious results only when it is applied to so limited a number of societies that each of them can be studied with sufficient precision. The essential thing is to choose those where investigations have the greatest chance to be fruitful.

Also, the value of the facts is much more important than their number. In our eyes, the question whether totemism has been more or less universal or not, is quite secondary. If it interests us, it does so before all because in studying it we hope to discover relations of a nature to make us understand better what religion is. Now to establish these relations it is neither necessary nor always useful to heap up numerous experiences upon each other; it is much more important to have a few that are well studied and really significant. One single fact may make a law appear, where a multitude of imprecise and vague observations would only produce confusion. In every science, the scholar would be overwhelmed by the facts which present themselves to him, if he did not make a choice among them. It is necessary that he distinguish those which promise to be most instructive, that he concentrate his attention upon these, and that he temporarily leave the others to one side.

That is why, with one reservation which will be indicated below, we propose to limit our research to Australian societies. They fulfil all the conditions which were just enumerated. They are perfectly homogeneous, for though it is possible to distinguish varieties among them, they all belong to a common type. This homogeneity is even so great that the forms of social organization are not only the same, but that they are even designated by identical or equivalent names in a multitude of tribes, sometimes very distant from each other.[10] Also, Australian totemism is the variety for which our documents are the most complete. Finally, that which we propose to study in this work is the most primitive and simple religion which it is possible to find. It is therefore natural that to discover it, we address ourselves to societies as slightly evolved as possible, for it is evidently there that we have the greatest chance of finding it and studying it well. Now there are no societies which present this characteristic to a higher degree than the Australian ones. Not only is their civilization most rudimentary—the house and even the hut are still unknown—but also their organization is the most primitive and simple which is actually known; it is that which we have elsewhere called *organization on a basis of clans.* . . .

NOTES

1. *First Principles,* p. 37.

2. *Introduction to the Science of Religions,* p. 18 Cf. *Origin and Development of Religion,* p. 23.

3. Schultze, *Fetischismus,* p. 129.

4. Examples of these usages will be found in Frazer, *Golden Bough,* 2nd ed. I, pp. 81 ff.

5. The conception according to which the profane is opposed to the sacred, just as the irrational is to the rational, or the intelligible is to the mysterious, is only one of the forms under which this opposition is expressed. Science being once constituted, it has taken a profane character, especially in the eyes of the Christian religions; from that it appears as though it could not be applied to sacred things.

6. See Frazer, "On some ceremonies of the Central Australian tribes" in *Australian Association for the Advancement of Science,* 1901, pp. 313 ff. This conception is also of an extreme generality. In India, the simple participation in the sacrificial act has the same effects; the sacrificer, by the mere act of entering within the circle of sacred things, changes his personality. (See Hubert and Mauss, *Essai sur le Sacrifice* in the *Annee Sociologique,* II, p. 101).

7. *Totemism,* p. 12.

8. *Ibid.,* p. 15.

9. *Ibid.,* p. 32.

10. This is the case with the phratries and matrimonial classes; on this point, see Spencer and Gillen, *Northern Tribes,* ch. III; Howitt, *Native Tribes,* pp. 109 and 137–142; Thomas, *Kinship and Marriage in Australia,* ch. VI and VII.

Counterpoint:
From *Religion Defined and Explained*

PETER B. CLARKE AND PETER BYRNE

Peter B. Clarke and Peter Byrne teach at King's College, University of London. Besides several editing projects, Clarke has published the following books: *Mahdism in West Africa: The Ijebu Mahdiyya Movement, New Trends and Developments in African Religions, New Trends and Developments in the World of Islam, Black Paradise: The Rastafarian Movement, Islam in Modern Nigeria,* and *West Africa and Islam.* Byrne has also edited several books, and he is the author of the following works: *The Moral Interpretation of Religion, Philosophical and Ethical Problems in Mental Handicap, The Philosophical and Theological Foundations of Ethics, Prolegomena to Religious Pluralism,* and *Natural Religion and the Nature of Religion.*

Reprinted from Peter B. Clarke and Peter Byrne Religion Defined and Explained, *pp. 165–8, 169–172. Copyright © 1993 St. Martin's Press. Reprinted by permission of Macmillan Ltd.*

A Critique of Durkheim's Theory of Religion

Many scholars have pointed out the ethnographic failings of Durkheim's account of Australian aboriginal society and these have been summarised by Evans-Pritchard[1] and Lukes,[2] among others. One of the strongest criticisms made against Durkheim's theory on ethnographic grounds is that much of what he took to be characteristic of totemism—ceremonies, sacred objects and so on, the basis of his entire study of primitive religion—is in fact atypical. Moreover, totemism cannot always be associated with clans, nor is it a religion or even a form of religion but a mode of social organisation, a theory of human descent from a plant or animal or some other natural object which can vary from one tribe to another. Furthermore, it is not the clan but the horde or tribe which is the corporate group and this mistake renders so much of the evidence on which Durkheim bases his theory of religion unusable.

Clearly, these assumptions about totemism greatly weaken Durkheim's position, as do others including his idea of Australian totemism as the first form of totemism and his belief that the most simple forms of social organisation were to be found among Australian aboriginals. Other assumptions also have to be treated with great caution for lack of evidence, including the idea that the gods of Aboriginal Australians are derived from ideas related to totems and the notion that *mana/wakan* comes from the totemic principle.

Some of his ideas about primitive peoples, such as their supposedly undifferentiated, uniform way of perceiving and interpreting the world, also damage Durkheim's theory. In primitive society there are often numerous rival gods competing for the attention and loyalty of followers by offering their divergent paths to health and success. Moreover, the notion that in so-called primitive society the world is divided into two diametrically opposed camps of the sacred and profane . . . does nothing to help Durkheim's case. But it is worth pointing out once again that these ethnographic weaknesses do not mean that there is nothing of value in Durkheim's account of Aboriginal life; a number of anthropologists, including Malinowski, though highly critical of it on many points, have found it illuminating, especially from a methodological point of view.[3]

But there are many criticisms of Durkheim's methodology also. For example, as Lukes points out, *petitio principii*, or begging the question, is a feature from the start to the finish of *The Elementary Forms*. . . . As was previously noted, Durkheim's definition singles out the sacred as forming the content of religion, as its distinguishing feature. There is also a strong emphasis on religion's communal character through the use of the term "church"; it is this group or community aspect of religion that divides it off from magic. But the appropriateness of these precise terms of definition seems to depend on the theory of religion that follows. Durkheim then proceeds to demonstrate this theory by recourse to one test case—Australian totemism—that is deemed to support the thesis, although where his evidence does not come up to scratch other evidence from American Indian society is arbitrarily drawn upon to bolster the case. Experimenting in this way is not only unscientific but also—because done on such a small case—severely limits one's understanding of the phenomenon under review.

Durkheim provides a real or essentialist definition, one that seeks to identify what constituted the causally necessary elements of religion. His definition is hardly a neutral operational one. The extent to which the definition relies on the theory that comes later may be seen when we reflect on the inadequacy of the sacred/profane dichotomy. The sacred . . . is presented in *The Elementary Forms* as the polar opposite of the profane, a dichotomy which some scholars, among them Malinowski, found useful, while others have attacked it on philosophical and empirical grounds. A rigid dichotomy of this kind, it has been argued, cannot exist where one of the categories, in this case the profane, is no more than a residual category.[4] And at the empirical level it has been shown by Evans-Pritchard among others that far from being opposites the two notions are often found to be inseparable.[5]

If, as Evans-Pritchard and others maintain, sacred (that is religiously important) objects in many communities are not consistently set apart and forbidden, then this is not a good way of getting at their character as religious. Moreover, the general category of that which is set apart and forbidden would appear to include all that a society regards as taboo, frightening or unclean, and thus many things that have no particular connection with religion. Being set apart and forbidden thus appears to be neither a necessary nor a sufficient condition of being sacred. This way of getting at a common denominator in religion is no doubt present in Durkheim because he wishes to avoid getting entangled in any substantive definition of religion. He does not wish to make "sacred" a shorthand for "that which is connected with the gods," for this would be to exclude non-theistic religion at the outset. But "being set apart and forbidden" does not help as an alternative to the alleged failings of a substantive definition of the sacred and so Durkheim is left to fall back on the socially unifying function of sacred things to do the real work. Hence, his definition has almost immediately to rely on his theory that the nature of social and moral ties is the source and meaning of the sacred.

The definition of religion that Durkheim provides not only singles out the sacred as the content of religion—it is the symbol of the collective entity which, in practice, is the object of worship—but also informs us of the nature of the relationship—a functional one . . . between the essential elements of religion and of their principal effect, the integration of society. This, however, is to assume what has to be proved: that beliefs and practices do in reality unite all who adhere to them into one moral community called a church. Indeed, Durkheim appears to have been so obsessed with the idea of religion

as the principal means of integrating society that he failed to consider the possibility of it being a disruptive, destabilising force.

By assuming in these and other ways what has to be proved Durkheim turns his definition into a theory and when he does attempt to substantiate his theory of religion and show its worth in relation to other theories, he does so by turning to society and society only for his explanation. This not surprisingly has given rise to the charge of unilateralism. His discovery in society of a comprehensive, total explanation for religion has led some observers to speak of his "sociocentric fixation.". . . Mary Douglas, however, maintains that in certain respects Durkheim was not sufficiently "sociocentric." She believes, for instance, that "Durkheim did not push his thoughts on the social determination of knowledge to their full and radical conclusion."[6] Douglas suggests that Durkheim in a sense placed scientific truth above society and that this was due in large measure to certain assumptions he made, among them the existence of objective, non-socially determined scientific knowledge. . . .

Whatever the merits of Douglas's criticism, a strong case can be made for saying that Durkheim's social explanation of religion is inconsistent with his own stated aims and massively under-argued.

We have documented already Durkheim's claim that his theory, in contrast to those of others, accounts for religion by showing how it latches onto something real and is non-illusory. However, since he makes society both the cause and symbolic referent of religious beliefs it is questionable how far he succeeds in this. . . . But what is this but the assertion that the manifest content of religious ideas is false, albeit they metaphorically refer to something true? And if the manifest content of religion is false, this implies that the participants in it are under an illusion, and not merely ignorant of the ultimate origins of their beliefs. It is arguable that the entire shape of Durkheim's discussion of religious beliefs in Book II of *The Elementary Forms* is directed toward explaining how an illusion arises and is maintained. Sacredness is perceived in the Aboriginal communities under discussion as a peculiar force which resides in selected external objects, animate and inanimate. The task is to explain what this sacred force might consist in. Such sacred forces have a crucial "ambiguity" (225): they are felt as external to the individual, are attached to external things, yet are not physical and not perceptible as physical things are. The ambiguity is resolved by diagnosing religious forces as nothing other than the collective, anonymous force of the clan projected onto external objects (223). It is because the force of the clan, excited in collective effervescence, does transcend and sustain the individual that sacredness has these attributes. What is explained is how a force comes to be projected onto external things by the human mind. Religious forces represent the way in which collective consciousness acts upon individual consciousness. This is saved from being pure illusion by the facts that: the social forces behind the process possess many of the formal qualities which sacred things appear to have, the projection is social in nature and not an individual illusion, and the social forces and their projection have real and necessary consequences for the maintenance of society.

To be set against these last-mentioned facts is the point that the manifest content of religious ideas is mistaken, a point brought home when Durkheim tells us that ". . . the god is only the figurative expression of society" (227) and when he affirms as a consequence of his account of ritual in Part III of *The Elementary Forms* that sacred beings can live only in human consciousness (347) and that "sacred beings exist only when they are represented as such in the mind" (345). A number of points need to be stressed here. We need to remind ourselves that no theorist can long pretend that there is no truth or insight at all in religion. Even Feuerbach claims that suitably reinterpreted religious ideas contain references to what is real. It matters, then, not so much whether a theory allows religion to refer to some real things as to which real things it allows it to refer successfully. On this will depend what

we say about religion's content. If in a state of high drunkenness someone sees and describes his car as a battleship, he refers to something real but is under an illusion about its nature.

Durkheim clearly is offering the thought that the religious believers are mistaken (grossly so) about the nature of the sacred, even though there is something real behind their ideas of the sacred. In this light his assertions about religion having a future are to be taken with caution. Would it survive acceptance that the "god is only the figurative expression of society"? A determined methodological atheism seems to underlie the choices Durkheim leaves himself with. Faced with the ambiguity of the sacred he can allow only two options: it has either physical reality or the reality of projected moral force. It does not have the former, so it must have the latter. That he excludes a third possibility (there actually is a non-mundane reality which is manifested through ordinary things) represents a *metaphysical* choice Durkheim makes in advance. There is no argument for it: its alleged necessity is hidden behind the presumption that we must have a "scientific" approach to religion. . . .

The illusory character of the projected sacred is perhaps mitigated by one additional factor in Durkheim's theory of society. There is a hint in *The Elementary Forms* that he holds that all realities are shaped by collective, social representations. Through "collective representation" the human mind in society shapes the world in which it lives (435–41). . . .

There is also the frequently expressed criticism that Durkheim totally neglected the subjective element in his account of religion, that Douglas herself and other contemporary cultural theorists, including Habermas and Foucault, have no difficulty leaving out this dimension altogether from their work. This they do on the grounds that for purposes of analysis a distinction can be made between the individuals who create culture and the cultural objects and artifacts themselves, and that the cultural theorist's concern is with the relations between the latter and not with purely subjective intentions or meanings. However, it remains one of the most common criticisms of Durkheim, and one which will be briefly examined here by way of conclusion to this chapter and as lead-on to the next, that he systematically ignored the individual, subjective dimension in his treatment of religion, and by way of corollary he is criticised for not allowing any room for the mystic, the prophet, the shaman and so on.

There can be little doubt about the fact that Durkheim saw religion as pre-eminently social. And, as we have seen, he regarded it as a "social fact" and saw it as the "foundation of collective life" (419ff). However, he did not dismiss the individual as irrelevant to the course of a religion's development. As Pickering points out, Durkheim readily accepted the importance of prophets and religious leaders although he did not examine this aspect of religion in any detail due, he explains, to the complex nature of the subject. Moreover, he did accept the reality of individual religious and moral experiences and wrote of the enabling effect that communicating with one's god could have on the individual.

It is, nevertheless, the case that Durkheim spent little time on the individual element in religion. This, however, was not because he regarded it as *per se* unimportant but rather because from the point of view of the social scientist it was largely unmanageable. For Durkheim the subject matter of sociology was,

and indeed had to be, the irreducible reality of social life which was located in the moral force of collective ideas or representations. And although these ideas were generated by individuals in community, they became trans-subjective, taking on a "real" life of their own. None of this, however, was a criticism of studying the individual, as opposed, that is, to the social. There was certainly room for research of the kind that Freud and Jung would engage in, research that would scientifically examine those deeper recesses of the individual inaccessible to ordinary perception, in the way Durkheim believed he had scientifically examined what had been the hidden, social foundations and the latent social consequences of religion.

NOTES

1. E. Evans-Pritchard, *Theories of Primitive Religion* (Oxford: Clarendon Press, 1965).

2. S. Lujes, *Emile Durkheim: His Life and Work* (Harmondsworth: Penguin, 1973).

3. B. Malinowski, *Magic, Science and Religion* (London, 1925).

4. W. Pickering, *Durkheim's Sociology of Religion: Themes and Theories* (London: Routledge & Kegan Paul, 1984), p. 140ff.

5. Evans-Pritchard, p. 65.

6. M. Douglas, *Implicit Meanings: Essays in Anthropology* (London: Routledge & Kegan Paul, 1978), p. xi.

From *The Sociology of Religion*

MAX WEBER

The Rise of Religions

To define "religion," to say what it is, is not possible at the start of a presentation such as this. Definition can be attempted, if at all, only at the conclusion of the study. The essence of religion is not even our concern, as we make it

Reprinted from The Sociology of Religion *by Max Weber. Copyright © 1956 by J. C. B. Mohr (Paul Siebeck). English translation by Ephraim Fischoff © 1963, 1991 by Beacon Press. Reprinted by permission of Beacon Press, Boston.*

our task to study the conditions and effects of a particular type of social behavior.

The external courses of religious behavior are so diverse that an understanding of this behavior can only be achieved from the viewpoint of the subjective experiences, ideas, and purposes of the individuals concerned—in short, from the viewpoint of the religious behavior's "meaning" (*Sinn*). . . .

A process of abstraction, which only appears to be simple, has usually already been carried out in the most primitive instances of religious behavior which we examine. Already crystallized is the notion that certain beings are concealed "behind" and responsible for the activity of the charismatically endowed natural objects, artifacts, animals, or persons. This is the belief in spirits. At the outset, "spirit" is neither soul, demon, nor god, but something indeterminate, material, yet invisible, nonpersonal and yet somehow endowed with volition. By entering into a concrete object, spirit endows the latter with its distinctive power. The spirit may depart from its host or vessel, leaving the latter inoperative and causing the magician's charisma to fail. In other cases, the spirit may diminish into nothingness, or it may enter into another person or thing.

That any particular economic conditions are prerequisites for the emergence of a belief in spirits does not appear to be demonstrable. But belief in spirits, like all abstraction, is most advanced in those societies within which certain persons possess charismatic magical powers that inhere only in those with special qualifications. Indeed it is this circumstance that lays the foundation for the oldest of all "vocations," that of the professional necromancer. In contrast to the ordinary layman, the magician is the person who is permanently endowed with charisma. Furthermore, he has taken a lease on, or has at least made a unique object of his cultivation, the distinctive subjective condition that notably represents or mediates charisma, namely ecstasy. For the layman, this psychological state is accessible only in occasional actions. . . .

Because of the routine demands of living, the layman may experience ecstasy only occasionally, as intoxication. To induce ecstasy, he may employ any type of alcoholic beverage, tobacco, or similar narcotics—and especially music—all of which originally served orgiastic purposes. In addition to the rational manipulation of spirits in accordance with economic interests, the manner in which ecstasy was employed constituted another important concern of the magician's art, which, naturally enough, developed almost everywhere into a secret lore. On the basis of the magician's experience with the conditions of orgies, and in all likelihood under the influence of his professional practice, there evolved the concept of "soul" as a separate entity present in, behind or near natural objects, even as the human body contains something that leaves it in dream, syncope, ecstasy, or death. . . .

Various consequences of significance to magical art emerged from the development of a realm of souls, demons, and gods. These beings cannot be grasped or perceived in any concrete sense but manifest a type of transcendental being which normally is accessible only through the mediation of symbols and significances, and which consequently is represented as shadowy and even unreal. Since it is assumed that behind real things and events there is something else, distinctive and spiritual, of which real events are only the symptoms or indeed the symbols, an effort must be made to influence, not the concrete things, but the spiritual powers that express themselves through concrete things. This is done through actions that address themselves to a spirit or soul, hence done by instrumentalities that "mean" something, i.e., symbols. Thereafter, naturalism may be swept away by a flood of symbolic actions. The occurrence of this displacement of naturalism depends on the success with which the professional masters of the symbolism use their status of power within the community to impart vigor and intellectual elaboration to their beliefs. The displacement of naturalism will also depend upon the significance of magic for the distinctive character of the economy and upon the power of the organization the necromancers succeed in creating. . . .

For our purposes here, the examination of particular varieties of gods and demons would be of only slight interest, although gods and demons, like vocabularies of languages, have been directly influenced primarily by the economic situations and the historic destinies of different peoples. Since these developments are concealed from us by the mists of time, it is frequently no longer possible to determine why some particular type of deity achieved superiority over others. A certain god may have achieved eminence because he was originally a natural object of importance for economic life; such was the case with gods derived from the stellar bodies. Or he may have originated from some organic process which the gods and demons possess or influence, evoke or impede: disease, death, birth, fire, drought, rainstorm, and harvest failure. The outstanding economic importance of certain events may enable a particular god to achieve primacy within the pantheon, as for example the primacy of the god of heaven. He may be conceived of primarily as the master of light and warmth, but among groups that raise cattle he is most frequently conceived of as the lord of reproduction. . . .

Gods, Magicians, and Priests

. . . The possible combinations of the various principles involved in the construction of a pantheon or in the achievement of a position of primacy by one or another god are almost infinite in number. Indeed, the jurisdictions of the divine figures are as fluid as those of the officials of patrimonial regimes. Moreover, the differentiation between jurisdictions of the various gods is intersected by the practice of religious attachment or courtesy to a particular god who is especially cultivated or directly invoked and who is treated as functionally universal. Thus all possible functions are attributed to the universal god, even functions which have been assigned

previously to other deities. This is the "henotheism" which Max Müller erroneously assumed to constitute a special stage of evolution. In the attainment of primacy by a particular god, purely rational factors have often played an important concomitant role. Wherever a considerable measure of constancy in regard to certain prescriptions became clearly evident—most often in the case of stereotyped and fixed religious rites—and where this was recognized by rationalized religious thought, then those deities that evinced the greatest regularity in their behavior, namely the gods of heaven and the stars, had a chance to achieve primacy. . . .

A power conceived by analogy to living persons may be coerced into the service of man, just as the naturalistic power of a spirit could be coerced. Whoever possesses the requisite charisma for employing the proper means is stronger even than the god, whom he can compel to do his will. In these cases, religious behavior is not worship of the god but rather coercion of the god, and invocation is not prayer but rather the exercise of magical formulae. Such is one ineradicable basis of popular religion, particularly in India. Indeed, such coercive religion is universally diffused, and even the Catholic priest continues to practice something of this magical power in executing the miracle of the mass and in exercising the power of the keys. By and large this is the original, though not exclusive, origin of the orgiastic and mimetic components of the religious cult—especially of song, dance, drama, and the typical fixed formulae of prayer.

The process of anthropomorphization may take the form of attributing to the gods the human behavior patterns appropriate to a mighty terrestrial potentate, whose freely disposed favor can be obtained by entreaty, gifts, service, tributes, cajolery, and bribes. On the other hand, his favor may be earned as a consequence of the devotee's own faithfulness and good conduct in conformity with the divine will. In these ways, the gods are conceived by analogy to earthly rulers: mighty beings whose power differs only in degree, at least at first. As gods of this type evolve, worship of divinity comes to be regarded as a necessity.

The two characteristic elements of "divine worship," prayer and sacrifice, have their origin in magic. In prayer, the boundary between magical formula and supplication remains fluid. The technically rationalized enterprise of prayer (in the form of prayer wheels and similar devices, or of prayer strips hung in the wind or attached to icons of gods or saints, or of carefully measured wreaths of roses—virtually all of which are products of the methodical compulsion of the gods by the Hindus) everywhere stands far closer to magic than to entreaty. Individual prayer as real supplication is found in religions that are otherwise undifferentiated, but in most cases such prayer has a purely business-like, rationalized form that sets forth the achievements of the supplicant in behalf of the god and then claims adequate recompense therefor.

Sacrifice, at its first appearance, is a magical instrumentality that in part stands at the immediate service of the coercion of the gods. For the gods also need the soma juice of the sorcerer-priests, the substance which engenders their ecstasy and enables them to perform their deeds. This is the ancient notion of the Aryans as to why it is possible to coerce the gods by sacrifice. It may even be held that a pact can be concluded with the gods which imposes obligations on both parties; this was the fateful conception of the Israelites in particular. Still another view of sacrifice holds that it is a means of deflecting, through magical media, the wrath of the god upon another object, a scapegoat or above all a human sacrifice.

But another motive for sacrifice may be of greater importance, and it is probably older too: the sacrifice, especially of animals, is intended as a *communio,* a ceremony of eating together which serves to produce a fraternal community between the sacrificers and the god. This represents a transformation in the significance of the even older notion that to rend and consume a strong (and later a sacred) animal enables the eaters to absorb its potencies. Some such older magical meaning—and there are various other possibilities—may still provide the act of sacrifice with its essential form, even after genuine cultic views have come to exert considerable influence. Indeed, such a magical significance may even regain dominance over the cultic meaning. The sacrificial rituals of the Brahmanas, and even of the Atharva Veda, were almost purely sorcery, in contrast to the cultic sacrifices of the ancient Nordics. On the other hand, there are many departures from magic, as when sacrifices are interpreted as tribute. First fruits may be sacrificed in order that the god may not deprive man of the enjoyment of the remaining fruits; and sacrifice is often interpreted as a self-imposed punishment or sacrificial sin-offering that averts the wrath of the gods before it falls upon the sacrificer. To be sure, this does not yet involve any awareness of sin, and it initially takes place in a mood of cool and calculated trading, as for example in India.

The relationships of men to supernatural forces which take the forms of prayer, sacrifice and worship may be termed "cult" and "religion," as distinguished from "sorcery," which is magical coercion. Correspondingly, those beings that are worshipped and entreated religiously may be termed "gods," in contrast to "demons," which are magically coerced and charmed. There may be no instance in which it is possible to apply this differentiation absolutely, since the cults we have just called "religious" practically everywhere contain numerous magical components. The historical development of the aforementioned differentiation frequently came about in a very simple fashion when a secular or priestly power suppressed a cult in favor of a new religion, with the older gods continuing to live on as demons.

The sociological aspect of this differentiation is the rise of the "priesthood" as something distinct from "practitioners of magic." Applied to reality, this contrast is fluid, as are all sociological phenomena. Even the theoretical differentiae of these types are not unequivocally determinable. Following the distinction between "cult" and "sorcery," one may contrast those professional functionaries who influence the gods by means of worship with those magicians who coerce demons by magical means; but in many great religions, including Christianity, the concept of the priest includes such a magical qualification.

Or the term "priest" may be applied to the functionaries of a regularly organized and permanent enterprise concerned with influencing the gods, in contrast with the individual and occasional efforts of magicians. Even this contrast is bridged over by a sliding scale of transitions, but as pure type the priesthood is unequivocal and can be said to be characterized by the presence of certain fixed cultic centers associated with some actual cultic apparatus.

Or it may be thought that what is decisive for the concept of priesthood is that the functionaries, regardless of whether their office is hereditary or personal, be actively associated with some type of social organization, of which they are employees or organs operating in the interests of the organization's members, in contrast with magicians, who are self-employed. Yet even this distinction, which is clear enough conceptually, is fluid in actuality. The sorcerer is not infrequently a member of an organized guild, and is occasionally the member of a hereditary caste which may hold a monopoly of magic within the particular community. Even the Catholic priest is not always the occupant of an official post. In Rome he is occasionally a poor mendicant who lives a hand-to-mouth existence from the proceeds of single masses, the acquisition of which he solicits.

Yet another distinguishing quality of the priest, it is asserted, is his professional equipment of special knowledge, fixed doctrine, and vocational qualifications, which brings him into contrast with sorcerers, prophets, and other types of religious functionaries who exert their influence by virtue of personal gifts (charisma) made manifest in miracle and revelation. But this again is no simple and absolute distinction, since the sor-

cerer may sometimes be very learned, while deep learning need not always characterize working priests. Rather, the distinction between priest and magician must be established qualitatively with reference to the different nature of the learning in the two cases. As a matter of fact we must later, in our exposition of the forms of domination, distinguish the rational training and discipline of priests from the different preparation of charismatic magicians. The latter preparation proceeds in part as an "awakening education" using irrational means and aiming at rebirth, and proceeds in part as a training in purely empirical lore. But in this case also, the two contrasted types flow into one another. . . .

The Prophet

We shall understand "prophet" to mean a purely individual bearer of charisma, who by virtue of his mission proclaims a religious doctrine or divine commandment. No radical distinction will be drawn between a "renewer of religion" who preaches an older revelation, actual or supposititious, and a "founder of religion" who claims to bring completely new deliverances. The two types merge into one another. In any case, the formation of a new religious community need not be the result of doctrinal preaching by prophets, since it may be produced by the activities of non-prophetic reformers. Nor shall we be concerned in this context with the question whether the followers of a prophet are more attracted to his person, as in the cases of Zoroaster, Jesus, and Muhammad, or to his doctrine, as in the cases of Buddha and the prophets of Israel.

For our purposes here, the personal call is the decisive element distinguishing the prophet from the priest. The latter lays claim to authority by virtue of his service in a sacred tradition, while the prophet's claim is based on personal revelation and charisma. It is no accident that almost no prophets have emerged from the priestly class. As a rule, the Indian teachers of salvation were not Brahmins, nor were the

Israelite prophets priests. Zoroaster's case is exceptional in that there exists a possibility that he may have descended from the hieratic nobility. The priest, in clear contrast, dispenses salvation by virtue of his office. Even in cases in which personal charisma may be involved, it is the hierarchical office that confers legitimate authority upon the priest as a member of a corporate enterprise of salvation.

But the prophet, like the magician, exerts his power simply by virtue of his personal gifts. Unlike the magician, however, the prophet claims definite revelations, and the core of his mission is doctrine or commandment, not magic. Outwardly, at least, the distinction is fluid, for the magician is frequently a knowledgeable expert in divination, and sometimes in this alone. At this stage, revelation functions continuously as oracle or dream interpretation. Without prior consultation with the magician, no innovations in communal relations could be adopted in primitive times. To this day, in certain parts of Australia, it is the dream revelations of magicians that are set before the councils of clan heads for adoption, and it is a mark of secularization that this practice is receding.

On the other hand, it was only under very unusual circumstances that a prophet succeeded in establishing his authority without charismatic authentication, which in practice meant magic. At least the bearers of new doctrine practically always needed such validation. It must not be forgotten for an instant that the entire basis of Jesus' own legitimation, as well as his claim that he and only he knew the Father and that the way to God led through faith in him alone, was the magical charisma he felt within himself. It was doubtless this consciousness of power, more than anything else, that enabled him to traverse the road of the prophets. During the apostolic period of early Christianity and thereafter the figure of the wandering prophet was a constant phenomenon. There was always required of such prophets a proof of their possession of particular gifts of the spirit, of special magical or ecstatic abilities. . . .

It is characteristic of the prophets that they do not receive their mission from any human agency, but seize it, as it were. To be sure, usurpation also characterized the assumption of power by tyrants in the Greek *polis*. These Greek tyrants remind one of the legal *aisymnetes* in their general functioning, and they frequently pursued their own characteristic religious policies, e.g., supporting the emotional cult of Dionysos, which was popular with the masses rather than with the nobility. But the aforementioned assumption of power by the prophets came about as a consequence of divine revelation, essentially for religious purposes. Furthermore, their characteristic religious message and their struggle against ecstatic cults tended to move in an opposite direction from that taken by the typical religious policy of the Greek tyrants. The religion of Muhammad, which is fundamentally political in its orientation, and his position in Medina, which was in between that of an Italian *podesta* and that of Calvin at Geneva, grew primarily out of his purely prophetic mission. A merchant, he was first a leader of pietistic conventicles in Mecca, until he realized more and more clearly that the organization of the interests of warrior clans in the acquisition of booty was the external basis provided for his missionizing.

On the other hand, there are various transitional phases linking the prophet to the teacher of ethics, especially the teacher of social ethics. Such a teacher, full of a new or recovered understanding of ancient wisdom, gathers disciples about him, counsels private individuals in personal matters and nobles in questions relating to public affairs, and purports to mold ethical ways of life, with the ultimate goal of influencing the crystallization of ethical regulations. The bond between the teacher of religious or philosophical wisdom and his disciple is uncommonly strong and is regulated in an authoritarian fashion, particularly in the sacred laws of Asia. Everywhere the disciple-master relationship is classified among those involving reverence. . . .

Thus, the distinctive character of the earliest prophecy, in both its dualistic and monotheistic forms, seems to have been determined decisively—aside from the operation of certain other concrete historical influences—by the pressure of relatively contiguous great centers of rigid social organization upon less developed neighboring peoples. The latter tended to see in their own continuous peril from the pitiless bellicosity of terrible nations the anger and grace of a heavenly king.

Regardless of whether a particular religious prophet is predominantly of the ethical or predominantly of the exemplary type, prophetic revelation involves for both the prophet himself and for his followers—and this is the element common to both varieties—a unified view of the world derived from a consciously integrated and meaningful attitude toward life. To the prophet, both the life of man and the world, both social and cosmic events, have a certain systematic and coherent meaning. To this meaning the conduct of mankind must be oriented if it is to bring salvation, for only in relation to this meaning does life obtain a unified and significant pattern. Now the structure of this meaning may take varied forms, and it may weld together into a unity motives that are logically quite heterogeneous. The whole conception is dominated, not by logical consistency, but by practical valuations. Yet it always denotes, regardless of any variations in scope and in measure of success, an effort to systematize all the manifestations of life; that is, to organize practical behavior into a direction of life, regardless of the form it may assume in any individual case. Moreover, it always contains the important religious conception of the world as a cosmos which is challenged to produce somehow a "meaningful," ordered totality, the particular manifestations of which are to be measured and evaluated according to this requirement. . . .

Counterpoint:
From *Max Weber's Vision of History: Ethics and Methods*

GUENTHER ROTH

Guenther Roth has edited works about Weber and translated some of his writings. He has also published *The Social Democrats in Imperial Germany.*

Levels of Historical Analysis: Sociological, Historical, Situational

Weber's levels of historical analysis resulted from his perception of the purpose of historiography, its contemporary possibilities and limitations, and this perception was influenced by the intellectual situation in which he found himself. He came to stand at a crucial juncture in modern historiography, the point at which

Reprinted from Guenther Roth & Wolfgang Schluchter, Max Weber's Vision of History: Ethics and Methods. *University of California Press. Copyright © 1979 The Regents of the University of California.*

disillusionment with the evolutionary views of the preceding three generations (whether Deist or naturalist) made a methodological reorientation strongly desirable. This disillusionment came about partly because of changes in intellectual climate—ongoing secularization, but also the incipient skepticism toward scientific laws as all-explanatory devices; partly it was the result of rapidly accumulating research that did not seem to support the various evolutionary-stage theories. If there was no deterministic scheme of evolutionary development, the only empirical alternative seemed to be the construction of "type concepts" or socio-historical models and of secular theories of long-range historical transformation. . . .

The three levels are all historical in a general sense, but in Weber's terminology the first is that of sociology—of type or model construction and of rules of experience—whereas the second level, the causal explanation of past events, is labeled by him "historical" in quotation marks, or sometimes "developmental." Here we find his secular theories. . . .

Mommsen is right in saying that Weber became a sociologist by retreating from "history," the level of causal analysis. But this was only a strategic retreat. Although *Economy and Society* was not meant to explain the uniqueness of Western rationalism, it offers a typological framework for its study; thus it is sociology strictly as a "preliminary" and "preparatory" exercise. Its typology consists of models such as bureaucracy, patrimonialism, charismatic rulership and community, hierocracy, church, sect, and others that are constructed from different times and places. But even in *Economy and Society* there are many historical explanations that amount to sketches of secular theories about the genesis and consequences of particular historical phenomena, from the Protestant ethic to the modern state.[1]

The socio-historical models as well as the secular theories are not intended to explain what is happening in a given situation. One model alone cannot adequately describe a given case; a battery of models or hyphenated types, such as patrimonial bureaucracy, can provide a better approximation. Their utility lies in serving as base lines for identifying the distinctiveness of a case. While secular theories attempt to trace a long line of causation, they too have limited usefulness with regard to a given situation. Theories such as those of democratization and industrialization diminish in explanatory value when we look at the relatively short time span of a few years or even two or three decades, because they are concerned with long-range structural changes. Phenomena like the charismatic eruption of an ethic of conviction during the 1960s cannot be sufficiently explained by recourse to the secular theory of corporate capitalism, since that theory covers the time span of "the silent fifties" as well as the waning of charismatic mass excitement in the early seventies. Hence the need for situational analysis, which probes into the contemporary play of forces—apart from the necessary recourse to models such as the charismatic community.

The construction of models and secular theories can have ideological overtones, just as situational analysis can be relatively neutral in partisan struggles. However, situational analysis is also the vehicle for political analysis proper, which is concerned with the assessment of a given distribution of power with a view toward changing or preserving it, not with secular change or differences between civilizations. In his voluminous writings on agrarian and industrial capitalism and constitutional reform, Weber dealt explicitly with questions of how to bring about change—just as Marx did. When David Beetham synthesized Weber's secular theory of modern politics from his more political rather than his more academic writings, he also showed that the two kinds of writing differ in their analytical emphasis, not just their manifest intent. Much more is involved here than the difference between political evaluation and scholarly "freedom from value judgment." It is true that "the point of [Weber's] political writings is to be sought in the political context, and that of his sociology, in the first instance at least, within a particular scientific tradition."[2] However, because the focus of political analysis is on how to bring about (or prevent) change, "it is possible to find in Weber's political writings a sense of the interrelationship of forces in society which is frequently lacking in his academic work."[3] In his political writings, then, the crucial issue is the relationship between a given state and society, the clash of the major social groupings in the political arena—in other words, for him, too, political analysis must be class analysis in one way or another.

When Beetham claims that in *Economy and Society* "there is little politics as Weber himself defined it,"[4] he seems to mean that the overall frame of analysis is not the struggle for power among the social classes. This would be true especially of the sociology of domination, which, after all, was an attempt to extend Georg Jellinek's social theory of the state. It was an undertaking within the "particular scientific tradition" of comparative constitutional theory, which is not directly concerned with class struggles. Yet part of Weber's achievement lies in the fact that he treated empirically the "validity" of modes of legitimation in relation to the perennial power struggles between rulers and staffs (and partly also the subjects). . . .

To sum up: In Weber's practiced methodology "sociology" is the generalized aspect of the study of history and contrasts with the causal analysis of individual phenomena—the task of "history." Both sociology and historiography proceed from the causality inherent in social action. When Weber defined sociology as "a science concerning itself with the interpretive understanding of social action and thereby with the causal explanation of its course and consequences," he meant to affirm that in history only men act, not social organisms or reified collectivities. The construction of socio-historical models, such as patrimonialism or rule by notables, is possible because, in principle, we can understand the intentions of men and causally explain the course and consequences of their actions. Of course, such structural types transcend the task of "history" to explain causally a given event; model construction synthesizes the historical observation of many individual actors. The main point about interpretive sociology was that we should try to understand the ideas and intentions of historical actors rather than search for "scientific" laws of social evolution, as Marx and other evolutionists had done. However, on the levels of both model and secular theory, history provided many lessons in unintended consequences. Revolutionary charisma tends toward routinization; rule-oriented bureaucracy tends toward becoming a vested interest; and political patrimonialism, an effort at centralized control, tends toward decentralization. The paradoxes and ironies are built right into the models. The same is true of Weber's most famous secular theory, "The Protestant Ethic and the Spirit of Capitalism": the transition from the Protestant ethic to the spirit of capitalism and in turn to the "iron cage" of advanced capitalism was one of the secular developments, fateful for Western history, which poignantly demonstrated the "heterogony of purposes."

Weber's philosophy of history was pragmatic rather than pessimistic. Unless we save ourselves, nothing and nobody will save us. Historical knowledge, which comprises the levels of analysis discussed here, is necessary for self-clarification, for deciding what we want and where we want to go. But that knowledge cannot lead to the kind of science of society that would unlock the secrets of history and provide a master key to the future.

NOTES

1. Wolfgang J. Mommsen, "Gesellschaftliche Bedingtheit und gesellschaftliche Relevanz historischer Aussagen," *Die Funcktion der Geschichte in unserer Zeit,* ed. Ernst Weymar and Eberhard Jäckel (Stuttgart: Klett, 1975), p. 218.

2. David Beethan, *Max Weber and the Theory of Modern Politics* (London: Allen & Unwin, 1974), p. 30.

3. Ibid., p. 252.

4. Ibid., p. 15.

Chapter 7

Anthropology

Anthropology can be simply defined as the study of human beings in all their diversity as members of the animal species and as both creators and products of culture. The terms *anthropology* and *ethnology* began to appear around the end of the eighteenth century, although the genuine form of anthropology began to take shape during the nineteenth century. The history of anthropology is rather complex and beyond the scope of this introduction to develop at any great length. Its historical development included several elements. Taxonomists of nature and science like Linnaeus and Comte de Buffon imagined that the physical and cultural varieties of humans were somehow analogous to differences among plants and zoological species. French and Scottish Enlightenment thinkers like Rousseau, Voltaire, and Hume criticized their own societies with evidence from other cultures when developing their social philosophies. The spread of Christian missions to many parts of the world, along with the connection to European colonial power, shaped attitudes toward other cultures to the detriment of these foreign cultures with simple technology. European governments financed voyages looking for political and economic advantages that often led to colonial annexation and exploitation of foreign lands. With the influence of Darwin's theory of evolution, scholars began to question and doubt the biblical account of history. Early anthropologists like Tylor, Frazer, Robertson Smith, and others were typical representatives of white, European culture, nurtured in a Christian environment, often agnostic and rationalistic, and influenced by the theory of evolution and belief in universal progress. These events, cultural identity, and sources of influence shaped early attempts at practicing anthropology. Understood from within this framework, early European anthropologists were convinced of their innate social and cultural superiority in contrast to the tribal societies that they studied and about which they wrote. These kinds of arrogant attitudes began, however, to change as anthropology developed more sophistication and improved its methods.

The work of Bronislaw Kaspar Malinowski (1884–1942) is an excellent example of such a change. Born and educated in Krakow, Poland, Malinowski obtained his doctorate in physics and mathematics. After working for a couple of years as a physical chemist in Leipzig, he decided to become an anthropologist, and he traveled to England to study at the London School of Economics, where he got his degree in 1916. Before he received his doctorate in anthropology, he went to Australia; however, he was incarcerated as a foreign enemy due to his Austrian nationality, although he was granted permission to conduct a few field trips to such locations as New Guinea and the Trobriand Islands for his research. During these trips he lived among the natives. The University of London employed him from 1923 to 1938, when he assumed a position at Yale University. From 1940 to 1941, he performed fieldwork in Mexico. He died in New Haven, Connecticut in 1942. During his distinguished career, Malinowski published important works that pertain to the subject of religion: *Argonauts of the Western Pacific* (1922), *Coral Gardens and Their Magic* (2 volumes, 1935), *The Foundations of Faith and Morals* (1936), *A Scientific Theory of Culture and Other Essays* (1944), *Magic, Science and Religion, and Other Essays* (1954), and *Sex, Culture and Myth* (1962). These works reflected Malinowski's conviction that an anthropologist must be a participant observer in the culture being studied.

Malinowski's innovative approach for his time period was to live among the people being studied, participating in their daily activities, learning and speaking their language, and recording observations. The participant observer method led to more accurate accounts of the studied religion. Malinowski's name became synonymous with functionalism, which attempted to view a society as a functioning whole. Not only must the anthropologist study customs and practices of a society in their complete context, the scholar must explain discoveries in terms of the functions that they fulfilled for a given people. Thus it was unnecessary to explain religion by invoking the theory of evolution. Malinowski's notion of function was connected to his theory of human needs that any society must meet (metabolism, reproduction, bodily comforts, safety, movement, growth, and health, for example).

Malinowski distinguished religion from magic. Not only did they have different purposes, although equally functional in a society, magic was intended, moreover, to cause a specific effect (such as recovery from sickness, abundant crops, children), whereas religion did not strive for a precise goal. Religious practices were performed because this was the traditional way of doing things, or because it was appropriate to perform them on certain occasions.

If Malinowski focused his primary attention on the biological needs of individuals, Alfred R. Radcliffe-Brown (1881–1955) concentrated on the needs of society, which he viewed as an organism analogous to the structure of the human body. His theory became known as structural functionalism, in contrast to the functionalism of Malinowski. Born and educated in Wales, Radcliffe-Brown did his advanced work at Trinity College of the University of Cambridge. After fieldwork on the Andaman Islands for 2 years, he became a fellow of Trinity College where he taught comparative sociology. He also taught ethnology at the London School of Economics and became an honorary professor at the University of Liverpool. From 1910 until 1912, he conducted fieldwork in western Australia. He spent time in Sydney during World

War I until he became Director of Education in the kingdom of Tonga on the Friendship Islands. After teaching in a few different parts of South Africa, he returned to Sydney and its university to assume a teaching position and established the journal *Oceania in* 1930. Other teaching assignments took him to the University of Chicago, University of Yenching in China, and Oxford University. The following titles were among his published books with implications for religion: *Three Tribes of Western Australia* (1913), *The Andaman Islanders Study in Social Anthropology* (1922), *The Social Organization of Australian Tribes* (1931), *Structure and Function in Primitives Society: Essays and Addresses* (1952), *A Natural Science of Society* (1957), and *Method in Social Anthropology: Selected Essays* (1958). Throughout his career, Radcliffe-Brown was concerned about methodological issues.

Radcliffe-Brown's rejection of an evolutionary type of approach to religion was evidence of his emphasis upon context and process. He wanted to treat a particular social system as a process instead of an entity because he wanted to stress the dynamic aspect of a social system and not view it as something static. He also wanted to reject the view that religion represented erroneous and illusory beliefs. It makes better sense to view religion as a complex system by which humans live together in an orderly way. By following this path, it was possible to better understand the function of religion to form, symbolize, and maintain social order. Traditional ancestral cults were often, for instance, associated with lineage structures, whereas Australian totemic religion represented a cosmological system in which natural categories were adopted into the kinship system. Religion also functioned to articulate the sense of dependence of a society, which is expressed in the sense of obligation of a society and its sanctioning of rules of behavior. Radcliffe-Brown was also interested in why people adopt a ritual attitude toward animals or other things. He connected this phenomenon to the ability of a thing or event to produce social well-being.

The dynamic nature of religion and the human context was stressed in more recent times by Victor Turner (1920–1983), who was born in Glasgow, Scotland, received his undergraduate education at University College in London, and obtained his doctorate from Victoria University of Manchester. His teaching career took him from Victoria University of Manchester to the United States, with teaching stints at Cornell University (1968–77), University of Chicago (1968–77) where he held a chair named for William R. Kenan, Professor of Anthropology and Social Thought, and the University of Virginia (1977–83). Turner published many influential works: *Ndembu Divination: Its Symbolism and Techniques* (1961), *Chihamba the White Spirit* (1962), *Essays in the Ritual of Social Relations* (1963), *The Drums of Affliction* (1968), *The Forest of Symbols: Essays in African Religion* (1967), *The Ritual Process* (1969), *Dramas, Fields, and Metaphors* (1974), *Revelation and Divination in Ndembu Ritual* (1975), *Image and Pilgrimage in Christian Culture: Anthropological Perspectives* (with Edith Turner, 1978), *Process, Performance, and Pilgrimage* (1979), and *From Ritual to Theatre* (1982). These works reflected the influence of the Belgian anthropologist Arnold van Gennep and his book entitled *Rites of Passage,* and the philosophy of the Jewish thinker Martin Buber and his theory of community.

Turner focused considerable attention on liminality, an indefinite or in-between period of uncertainty, ambiguity, and lack of status, to stress the fluctuating nature of social order and cultural patterns that are constantly experiencing an often orderly transformation akin to the crossing of a liminal threshold. Turner used the images of the theater like drama and performance to emphasize the dynamic nature of society, ritual actions, and culture. In fact, action was performative in the sense that it caused changes in the environment and with the collective and personal identities of active participants. The most important form of action for religious people was ritual, which worked to explain and justify a person's plight and make it more tolerable. This suggested to Turner that religion was an imaginative search for truth about the human condition and a quest for meaning that connects a person to everything surrounding the person. In the final analysis, Turner wanted to stress that society was a dialectical process and not a static thing.

In contrast to Turner, Clifford Geertz (born 1926) received his undergraduate education at Antioch College in Ohio and completed his doctoral work at Harvard University. He did fieldwork in both Java and Bali. After occupying teaching positions at the University of California and the University of Chicago (1960–1970), Geertz assumed his long association with the Institute for Advanced Study at Princeton University. His major publications include the following: *The Religion of Java* (1960), *Islam Observed: Religious Development in Morocco and Indonesia* (1968), *The Interpretation of Cultures: Selected Essays* (1973), *Negra: The Theatre State in Nineteenth Century Bali* (1980), *Local Knowledge: Further Essays in Interpretive Anthropology* (1983), *Works and Lives: The Anthropologist as Author* (1988), *After the Fact* (1995), and *Available Light: Anthropological Reflections on Philosophical Topics* (2000). Geertz has been the recipient of several honorary degrees, book prizes, and other academic honors. These various works reflected a perspective in anthropology called interpretive and demonstrated a concentration on cultures and not simply societies because society was one segment of a wider system of ideas, customs, attitudes, symbols, and institutions.

Geertz's interpretive approach to the study of religion did not involve sharing the lives of the people studied and thus was not dependent upon empathy with the life situation of others. By examining what was publicly accessible to the scholar, it was possible to comprehend the function of religious symbols that were integral to the way of life of the people within the culture being studied. This approach suggests that Geertz's position represented a revised form of the *Verstehen* approach of Weber, but it was devoid of empathetic feeling. Overall, Geertz was influenced more by Talcott Parsons with whom he studied at Harvard University. This did not mean that he wanted to look at a religious culture from the outside. He wanted rather to examine religions from the inside according to its own categories. Borrowing a notion from the philosopher Gilbert Ryle, Geertz advocated "thick description," which involved describing what people are doing and grasping what they think that they are doing. In other words, one had to examine the intentions of the others or, in general, their ethos. Like Ninian Smart, Geertz demonstrated that religion, culture, and symbols are organically interconnected because they represent the interdependent components of a single organism. Because religion is a way of approaching the world,

Geertz tended to view it in terms of a worldview. This tendency did not imply that Geertz neglected the individual because he thought that religion served society by serving the individual.

Geertz affirmed that religion served as a source of meaning and ultimate explanations for people, although there were other sources of meaning like common sense, ideology, and aesthetics. Any culture system of which religion was a part provided meaning because it was comprehensive in the sense of providing a conception of reality and a way of life. Furthermore, religion provided a worldview and ethos, a model of behavior and conceptual ideas. Religion included a wide range of meaningful experiences that included intellectual, emotional, and moral experiences. Thus there is a distinctive and identifiable religious perspective on the world along with other perspectives.

Mary Douglas (born 1921) was another anthropologist associated with Princeton University, although for a much briefer time than Geertz. Douglas also taught at University College in London (1951–1977), Northwestern University, and other institutions in the United States. She was educated at St. Anne's College, Oxford University where she did her undergraduate and graduate work. She published two books that were especially significant for the study of religion: *Purity and Danger* (1966) and *Natural Symbols* (1970). For these books, Douglas did fieldwork in the Belgian Congo and studied the Lele tribe. Based on her fieldwork, she viewed the origin and function of religion as a need to fulfill an intellectual order. The fundamental intention of her work was to connect symbolic systems with behavioral modes, and she accomplished this task by linking social and symbolic structures. Among her other works in anthropology are the following: *Essays in the Sociology of Perception* (1982), *Risk and Culture* (with Aaron Wildaysky, 1982), *Risk Acceptability* (1985), *How Institutions Think* (1986), *Risk and Blame* (1922), and *In the Wilderness: The Doctrine of Defilement in the Book of Numbers* (1993).

Douglas desired to develop a model of social anthropology that could be used comparatively to interpret widely divergent societies and symbol systems. This implied finding principles of social organization abstract enough to be applied cross-culturally, while maintaining contact with concrete human experience. She found her abstract principles with the distinction between group and grid. The notion of group referred to the external boundaries of a society and its sense of itself as a group. Within the context of the notion of group, social pressure is important and suggests the extent to which one is constrained and controlled by others. If there was a strong group for instance, this indicated that a person is tightly controlled by social pressure, which often became a demand for conformity to social norms. Grid referred to the internal order or system of classification that was shared by members of the group. It referred to rules that related one person to others. The grid enabled one to bring order and intelligibility to one's experience. Its effectiveness depended on its scope and coherence. A narrow scope might cause difficulty, for instance, ordering the broader dimensions of experience. The strength or weakness of the grid was relative to the society, and it depended on the goodness of fit between classification and the range of experience to be ordered. Douglas proceeded to apply this distinction between group and grid to different societies according to the relative strengths of its senses of this basic distinction. If grid and group were high, there were, for instance, strong concerns for piety, appropriate roles, controlled bodily behavior, and concern for pollution of the individual and social bodies. To illustrate her abstract principles of group and grid, Douglas stressed the human body and its symbolism because bodily symbolism expressed different social experiences, governed basic social attitudes toward spirit and matter, and received its power from social life. From Douglas's perspective, the social and physical bodies are interrelated because the former contains the way the physical body is perceived and the latter sustains a particular view of society. Due to their interconnectedness and interreaction, bodily control expressed social control. This is why Douglas is interested in such issues as pollution, purity, and danger.

In contrast to Douglas, the impressive corpus of work by Claude Lévi-Strauss (born 1908 in Brussels, Belgium) was inspired by the method of structural linguistics and its perceived scientific approach to the study of language. Unlike some prior approaches to the study of religion, a structural approach was not concerned with the quest for origins or causes of religion. Because the world, personal cognition, and knowledge of the world are structured, the structuralist approach was better prepared to interpret a subject like religion. Furthermore, because humans possessed a tendency to create ordered symbolic and social worlds, their cultural products are structured as human creations. It was unnecessary to look behind the phenomena of language to grasp the notion that structure is a precondition for order within human culture. Even though structures are abstract, they did not embody meaning in themselves. This was typical of the structuralist position that nothing possessed meaning in itself. It was more accurate to assert that a structure acquired meaning by means of its relations to other meanings.

The movement associated with Lévi-Strauss called Structuralism owed its inspiration to Ferdinand de Saussure (1857–1913), author of *Memoire sur le système primitif des voyelles dans les langues Indo-européennes* (1878). De Saussure's students reconstructed another influential work, *Course de linguistique générale* (1906–1911), from his lecture notes. This work approached language as a system of signs and gave birth to the new science of semiology. Other important figures in Structuralism influenced Lévi-Strauss: Roman Jakobson (1896–1982) authored *Slavic Languages* (1955) and *Phonological Studies* (1962), which created a methodological bridge between linguistics and literary criticism, and Nikolai Trubetzkoy, was another important figure from the so-called Prague school of linguistics. The structural approach allowed Lévi-Strauss to trace rules of binary opposition to cultural artifacts like myths and other phenomena. Lévi-Strauss thought that these fundamental oppositions (male and female, raw and cooked, nature and culture, for example) reflected the workings of the human mind and the internal logic of social systems. These ideas and approaches were elaborated in the following published books: *Tristes Tropiques* (1961), *Totemism* (1963), *The Savage Mind* (1966), *Structural Anthropology* (1968), *The Elementary Structures of Kinship* (1969), *The Raw and the Cooked* (1969), *Myth and Meaning* (1978), *From Honey to Ashes* (1973), *The Origin of Table Manners* (1978), *The Naked Man* (1981), *The Way of Masks* (1982), and *The*

Jealous Potter (1988). These published works reflected his interest in kinship theory, the logic of myth, the human mind, and the theory of totemic classification. They also demonstrated a rationalistic and holistic approach to the study of society. Even though he called himself a disciple of Durkheim, he searched for the basic structures of the mind by uniting psychology with ethnology, being convinced that such mental structures were immanent within cultural data, like myth and symbols. According to Lévi-Strauss, anthropology was a semiological science that adopted meaning as its guiding principle. And based on his early experiences as an anthropologist in Brazil, he concluded that an underlying unity that he identified with the human mind existed behind the diversity of societies. Lévi-Strauss shared such notions and methodological approach with students through his teaching and fieldwork stints at such places as the University of São Paulo, Brazil, New School for Social Research in New York City where he spent the years of World War II, Musée de l'Homme, École Pratique des Hautes Études, and the College de France. He has received numerous academic honors for his scholarship.

Lévi-Strauss viewed religion in relationship to magic. In his book entitled *The Savage Mind,* he writes "There is no religion without magic any more than there is magic without at least a trace of religion" (p. 221). This quotation manifests a rejection of the evolutionary approach of many of his successors. Lévi-Strauss also distinguished religion from totemism because he saw the relationship between the clan and animal as homologous and metaphorical rather than as represented by an institution. Totemism should be understood as a classificatory mode of thought that mediates between natural and social forms of classification. In contrast to the nature of religion and its relationship to other phenomena, Lévi-Strauss demonstrated much more interest in myth. He methodologically wanted to break it down into its shortest possible parts and to examine how these parts related to other aspects of the narrative. It was necessary to approach myth globally because a myth consisted of variants and tended to be repetitive. This approach to myth is grounded in the structuralist conviction that structure represented a network of relations. Even though myth continued to grow over time, its structure remained constant. It was this structure that Lévi-Strauss wanted to examine for what it informed us about the human mind.

Guideline Questions

If the study of so-called primitive religions raised issues of relativism and truth value, what were the consequences of raising such issues for the rationality and validity of the Judeo-Christian myths and practices?

How do the methodological approaches of these anthropologists affect their understanding of religion?

Do any of these anthropologists suggest that it is possible to develop a general theory of religion?

If rationality is a feature of modern industrial society, if it is connected to the methods of experimental science, and if it becomes the benchmark for the evolution of a civilization, what implications do these attitudes have for those studying primitive civilizations?

From *Magic, Science and Religion and Other Essays*

BRONISLAW MALINOWSKI

Primitive Man and His Religion

There are no peoples however primitive without religion and magic. Nor are there, it must be added at once, any savage races lacking either in the scientific attitude or in science, though this lack has been frequently attributed to them. In every primitive community, studied by trustworthy and competent observers, there have been found two clearly distinguishable domains, the Sacred and the Profane; in other words, the domain of Magic and Religion and that of Science.

On the one hand there are the traditional acts and observances, regarded by the natives as sacred, carried out with reverence and awe, hedged around with prohibitions and special rules of behavior. Such acts and observances are always associated with beliefs in supernatural forces, especially those of magic, or with ideas about beings, spirits, ghosts, dead ancestors, or gods. On the other hand, a moment's reflection is sufficient to show that no art or craft however primitive could have been invented or maintained, no organized form of hunting, fishing, tilling, or search for food could be carried out without the careful observation of natural process and a firm belief in its regularity, without the power of reasoning and without confidence in the power of reason; that is, without the rudiments of science. . . .

One achievement of modern anthropology we shall not question: the recognition that magic and religion are not merely a doctrine or a philosophy, not merely an intellectual body of opinion, but a special mode of behavior, a prag-matic attitude built up of reason, feeling, and will alike. It is a mode of action as well as a system of belief, and a sociological phenomenon as well as a personal experience. But with all this, the exact relation between the social and the individual contributions to religion is not clear, as we have seen from the exaggerations committed on either side. Nor is it clear what are the respective shares of emotion and reason. All these questions will have to be dealt with by future anthropology, and it will be possible only to suggest solutions and indicate lines of argument in this short essay.

Rational Mastery by Man of His Surroundings

The problem of primitive knowledge has been singularly neglected by anthropology. Studies on savage psychology were exclusively confined to early religion, magic and mythology. Only recently the work of several English, German, and French writers, notably the daring and brilliant speculations of Professor Lévy-Bruhl, gave an impetus to the student's interest in what the savage does in his more sober moods. The results were startling indeed: Professor Lévy-Bruhl tells us, to put it in a nutshell, that primitive man has no sober moods at all, that he is hopelessly and completely immersed in a mystical frame of mind. . . .

First, has the savage any rational outlook, any rational mastery of his surroundings, or is he, as M. Lévy-Bruhl and his school maintain, entirely "mystical"? The answer will be that every prim-

Reprinted from Magic, Science and Religion and Other Essays *(Westport, CT: Greenwood Press, Publishers, 1984.)*

itive community is in possession of a considerable store of knowledge, based on experience and fashioned by reason.

The second question then opens: Can this primitive knowledge be regarded as a rudimentary form of science or is it, on the contrary, radically different, a crude empiry, a body of practical and technical abilities, rules of thumb and rules of art having no theoretical value? This second question, epistemological rather than belonging to the study of man, will be barely touched upon at the end of this section and a tentative answer only will be given. . . .

Since in the matter under discussion there is an appalling lack of relevant and reliable observations, I shall have largely to draw upon my own material, mostly unpublished, collected during a few years field work among the Melanesian and Papuo-Melanesian tribes of Eastern New Guinea and the surrounding archipelagoes. As the Melanesians are reputed, however, to be specially magic-ridden, they will furnish an acid test of the existence of empirical and rational knowledge among savages living in the age of polished stone. . . .

Magic is undoubtedly regarded by the natives as absolutely indispensable to the welfare of the gardens. What would happen without it no one can exactly tell, for no native garden has ever been made without its ritual, in spite of some thirty years of European rule and missionary influence and well over a century's contact with white traders. But certainly various kinds of disaster, blight, unseasonable droughts, rains, bush-pigs and locusts, would destroy the unhallowed garden made without magic.

Does this mean, however, that the natives attribute all the good results to magic? Certainly not. If you were to suggest to a native that he should make his garden mainly by magic and scamp his work, he would simply smile on your simplicity. He knows as well as you do that there are natural conditions and causes, and by his observations he knows also that he is able to control these natural forces by mental and physical effort. His knowledge is limited, no doubt, but as far as it goes it is sound and proof against mysticism. If the fences are broken down, if the seed is destroyed or has been dried or washed away, he will have recourse not to magic, but to work, guided by knowledge and reason. His experience has taught him also, on the other hand, that in spite of all his forethought and beyond all his efforts there are agencies and forces which one year bestow unwonted and unearned benefits of fertility, making everything run smooth and well, rain and sun appear at the right moment, noxious insects remain in abeyance, the harvest yields a superabundant crop; and another year again the same agencies bring ill luck and bad chance, pursue him from beginning till end and thwart all his most strenuous efforts and his best-founded knowledge. To control these influences and these only he employs magic.

Thus there is a clear-cut division: there is first the well-known set of conditions, the natural course of growth, as well as the ordinary pests and dangers to be warded off by fencing and weeding. On the other hand there is the domain of the unaccountable and adverse influences, as well as the great unearned increment of fortunate coincidence. The first conditions are coped with by knowledge and work, the second by magic.

This line of division can also be traced in the social setting of work and ritual respectively. Though the garden magician is, as a rule, also the leader in practical activities, these two functions are kept strictly apart. Every magical ceremony has its distinctive name, its appropriate time and its place in the scheme of work, and it stands out of the ordinary course of activities completely. Some of them are ceremonial and have to be attended by the whole community, all are public in that it is known when they are going to happen and anyone can attend them. They are performed on selected plots within the gardens and on a special corner of this plot. Work is always tabooed on such occasions, sometimes only while the ceremony lasts, sometimes for a day or two. In his lay character the leader and magician directs the work, fixes the dates for starting, harangues and exhorts slack or careless gardeners. But the two roles never overlap or interfere: they are always clear, and any native will inform you without hesitation whether the man acts as magician or as leader in garden work. . . .

Most epistemologists would not, however, be satisfied with such a "minimum definition" of science, for it might apply to the rules of an art or craft as well. They would maintain that the rules of science must be laid down explicitly, open to control by experiment and critique by reason. They must not only be rules of practical behavior, but theoretical laws of knowledge. Even accepting this stricture, however, there is hardly any doubt that many of the principles of savage knowledge are scientific in this sense. The native shipwright knows not only practicality of buoyancy, leverage, equilibrium, he has to obey these laws not only on water, but while making the canoe he must have the principles in his mind. He instructs his helpers in them. He gives them the traditional rules, and in a crude and simple manner, using his hands, pieces of wood, and a limited technical vocabulary, he explains some general laws of hydrodynamics and equilibrium. Science is not detached from the craft, that is certainly true, it is only a means to an end, it is crude, rudimentary, and inchoate, but with all that it is the matrix from which the higher developments must have sprung. . . .

Science, of course, does not exist in any uncivilized community as a driving power, criticizing, renewing, constructing. Science is never consciously made. But on this criterion, neither is there law, nor religion, nor government among savages.

The question, however, whether we should call it *science* or only *empirical* and *rational knowledge* is not of primary importance in this context. We have tried to gain a clear idea as to whether the savage has only one domain of reality or two, and we found that he has his profane world of practical activities and rational outlook besides the sacred region of cult and belief. We have been able to map out the two domains and to give a more detailed description of the one. We must now pass to the second.

Life, Death and Destiny in Early Faith and Cult

We pass now to the domain of the sacred, to religious and magical creeds and rites. . . . While it was difficult not to admit into the enclosure of religion one after the other, spirits and ghosts, totems and social events, death and life, yet in the process religion seemed to become a thing more and more confused, both an all and a nothing. It certainly cannot be defined by its subject matter in a narrow sense, as "spirit worship," or as "ancestor cult," or as the "cult of nature." It includes animism, animalism, totemism, and fetishism, but it is not any one of them exclusively. The *ism* definition of religion in its origins must be given up, for religion does not cling to any one object or class of objects, though incidentally it can touch and hallow all. Nor, as we have seen, is religion identical with Society or the Social, nor can we remain satisfied by a vague hint that it clings to life only, for death opens perhaps the vastest view on to the other world. As an "appeal to higher powers," religion can only be distinguished from magic and not defined in general, but even this view will have to be slightly modified and supplemented.

The problem before us is, then, to try to put some order into the facts. This will allow us to determine somewhat more precisely the character of the domain of the Sacred and mark it off from that of the Profane. It will also give us an opportunity to state the relation, between magic and religion.

1. The Creative Acts of Religion It will be best to face the facts first and, in order not to narrow down the scope of the survey, to take as our watchword the vaguest and most general of indices: "Life." As a matter of fact, even a slight acquaintance with ethnological literature is enough to convince anyone that in reality the physiological phases of human life, and, above all, its crises, such as conception, pregnancy, birth, puberty, marriage, and death, form the nuclei of numerous rites and beliefs. Thus beliefs about conception, such as that in reincarnation, spirit-entry, magical impregnation, exist in one form or another in almost every tribe, and they are often associated with rites and observances. During pregnancy the expectant mother has to keep certain taboos and undergo ceremonies, and her husband shares at times in both. At birth, before and after, there are various magical rites to prevent dangers and undo sorcery, ceremonies of purification, communal rejoicings and acts of presentation of the newborn to higher powers or to the community. Later on in life the boys and, much less frequently, the girls have to undergo the often protracted rites of initiation, as a rule shrouded in mystery and marred by cruel and obscene ordeals.

Without going any further, we can see that even the very beginnings of human life are surrounded by an inextricably mixed-up medley of beliefs and rites. They seem to be strongly attracted by any important event in life, to crystallize around it, surround it with a rigid crust of formalism and ritualism—but to what purpose? Since we cannot define cult and creed by their objects, perhaps it will be possible to perceive their function.

A closer scrutiny of the facts allows us to make from the outset a preliminary classification into two main groups. Compare a rite carried out to prevent death in childbed with another typical custom, a ceremony in celebration of a birth. The first rite is carried out as a means to an end, it has a definite practical purpose which is known to all who practice it and can be easily elicited from any native informant. The postnatal ceremony, say a presentation of a newborn or a feast of rejoicing in the event, has no purpose: it is not a means to an end but an end in itself. It expresses the feelings of the mother, the father, the relatives, the whole community, but

there is no future event which this ceremony foreshadows, which it is meant to bring about or to prevent. This difference will serve us as a *prima facie* distinction between magic and religion. While in the magical act the underlying idea and aim is always clear, straightforward, and definite, in the religious ceremony there is no purpose directed toward a subsequent event. It is only possible for the sociologist to establish the function, the sociological *raison d'être* of the act. The native can always state the end of the magical rite, but he will say of a religious ceremony that it is done because such is the usage, or because it has been ordained, or he will narrate an explanatory myth. . . .

Let us realize that in primitive conditions tradition is of supreme value for the community and nothing matters as much as the conformity and conservatism of its members. Order and civilization can be maintained only by strict adhesion to the lore and knowledge received from previous generations. Any laxity in this weakens the cohesion of the group and imperils its cultural outfit to the point of threatening its very existence. Man has not yet devised the extremely complex apparatus of modern science which enables him nowadays to fix the results of experience into imperishable molds, to test it ever anew, gradually to shape it into more adequate forms and enrich it constantly by new additions. The primitive man's share of knowledge, his social fabric, his customs and beliefs, are the invaluable yield of devious experience of his forefathers, bought at an extravagant price and to be maintained at any cost. Thus, of all his qualities, truth to tradition is the most important and a society which makes its tradition sacred has gained by it an inestimable advantage of power and permanence. Such beliefs and practices, therefore, which put a halo of sanctity round tradition and a supernatural stamp upon it, will have a "survival value" for the type of civilization in which they have been evolved.

We may, therefore, lay down the main function of initiation ceremonies: they are a ritual and dramatic expression of the supreme power and value of tradition in primitive societies; they also serve to impress this power and value upon the minds of each generation, and they are at the same time an extremely efficient means of transmitting tribal lore, of insuring continuity in tradition and of maintaining tribal cohesion.

We still have to ask: What is the relation between the purely physiological fact of bodily maturity which these ceremonies mark, and their social and religious aspect? We see at once that religion does something more, infinitely more, than the mere "sacralizing of a crisis of life." From a natural event it makes a social transition, to the fact of bodily maturity it adds the vast conception of entry into manhood with its duties, privileges, responsibilities, above all with its knowledge of tradition and the communion with sacred things and beings. There is thus a creative element in the rites of religious nature. The act establishes not only a social event in the life of the individual but also a spiritual metamorphosis, both associated with the biological event but transcending it in importance and significance. . . .

2. Providence in Primitive Life Propagation and nutrition stand first and foremost among the vital concerns of man. Their relation to religious belief and practice has been often recognized and even overemphasized. Especially sex has been, from some older writers up to the psychoanalytic school, frequently regarded as the main source of religion. In fact, however, it plays an astonishingly insignificant part in religion, considering its force and insidiousness in human life in general. Besides love magic and the use of sex in certain magical performances—phenomena not belonging to the domain of religion—there remain to be mentioned here only acts of licence at harvest festivities or other public gatherings, the facts of temple prostitution and, at the level of barbarism and lower civilization, the worship of phallic divinities. Contrary to what one would expect, in savagery sexual cults play an insignificant role. It must also be remembered that acts of ceremonial

licence are not mere indulgence, but that they express a reverent attitude towards the forces of generation and fertility in man and nature, forces on which the very existence of society and culture depends. Religion, the permanent source of moral control, which changes its incidence but remains eternally vigilant, has to turn its attention to these forces, at first drawing them merely into its sphere, later on submitting them to repression, finally establishing the ideal of chastity and the sanctification of askesis.

When we pass to nutrition, the first thing to be noted is that eating is for primitive man an act surrounded by etiquette, special prescriptions and prohibitions, and a general emotional tension to a degree unknown to us. Besides the magic of food, designed to make it go a long way, or to prevent its scarcity in general—and we do not speak here at all of the innumerable forms of magic associated with the procuring of food—food has also a conspicuous role in ceremonies of a distinctly religious character. First-fruit offerings of a ritual nature, harvest ceremonies, big seasonal feasts in which crops are accumulated, displayed, and, in one way or another, sacralized, play an important part among agricultural people. Hunters, again, or fishers celebrate a big catch or the opening of the season of their pursuit by feasts and ceremonies at which food is ritually handled, the animals propitiated or worshipped. All such acts express the joy of the community, their sense of the great value of food, and religion through them consecrates the reverent attitude of man towards his daily bread.

To primitive man, never, even under the best conditions, quite free from the threat of starvation, abundance of food is a primary condition of normal life. It means the possibility of looking beyond the daily worries, of paying more attention to the remoter, spiritual aspects of civilization. If we thus consider that food is the main link between man and his surroundings, that by receiving it he feels the forces of destiny and providence, we can see the cultural, nay, biological importance of primitive religion in the sacralization of food. We can see in it the germs of what in higher types of religion will develop into the feeling of dependence upon Providence, of gratitude, and of confidence in it. . . .

3. Man's Selective Interest in Nature This brings us to the subject of totemism . . . the following questions have to be asked about totemism. First, why does a primitive tribe select for its totems a limited number of species, primarily animals and plants; and on what principles is this selection made? Secondly, why is this selective attitude expressed in beliefs of affinity, in cults of multiplication, above all in the negative injunctions of totemic taboos, and again in injunctions of ritual eating, as in the Australian "totemic sacrament"? Thirdly and finally, why with the subdivision of nature into a limited number of selected species does there run parallel a subdivision of the tribe into clans correlated with the species?

. . . We have seen that food is the primary link between the primitive and providence. And the need of it and the desire for its abundance have led man to economic pursuits, collecting, hunting, fishing, and they endow these pursuits with varied and tense emotions. A number of animal and vegetable species, those which form the staple food of the tribe, dominate the interests of the tribesmen. To primitive man nature is his living larder, to which—especially at the lowest stages of culture—he has to repair directly in order to gather, cook, and eat when hungry. The road from the wilderness to the savage's belly and consequently to his mind is very short, and for him the world is an indiscriminate background against which there stand out the useful, primarily the edible, species of animals or plants. Those who have lived in the jungle with savages, taking part in collecting or hunting expeditions, or who have sailed with them over the lagoons, or spent moonlit nights on sandbanks waiting for the shoals of fish or for the appearance of turtle, know how keen and selective is the savage's interest, how it clings to the

indications, trails, and to the habits and peculiarities of his quarry, while it yet remains quite indifferent to any other stimuli. Every such species which is habitually pursued forms a nucleus round which all the interests, the impulses, the emotions of a tribe tend to crystallize. A sentiment of social nature is built round each species, a sentiment which naturally finds its expression in folklore, belief, and ritual. . . .

The primitive is deeply interested in the appearance and properties of beasts; he desires to have them and, therefore, to control them as useful and edible things; sometimes he admires and fears them. All these interests meet and, strengthening each other, produce the same effect: the selection, in man's principal preoccupations, of a limited number of species, animal first, vegetable in the second place, while inanimate or man-made things are unquestionably but a secondary formation, an introduction by analogy, of objects which have nothing to do with the substance of totemism.

The nature of man's interest in the totemic species indicates also clearly the type of belief and cult to be there expected. Since it is the desire to control the species, dangerous, useful, or edible, this desire must lead to a belief in special power over the species, affinity with it, a common essence between man and beast or plant. Such a belief implies, on the one hand, certain considerations and restraints—the most obvious being a prohibition to kill and to eat; on the other hand, it endows man with the supernatural faculty of contributing ritually to the abundance of the species, to its increase and vitality.

This ritual leads to acts of magical nature, by which plenty is brought about. Magic, as we shall see presently, tends in all its manifestations to become specialized, exclusive and departmental and hereditary within a family or clan. In totemism the magical multiplication of each species would naturally become the duty and privilege of a specialist, assisted by his family. The families in course of time become clans, each having its headman as the chief magician of its totem. . . .

Thus we find our questions answered: man's selective interest in a limited number of animals and plants and the way in which this interest is ritually expressed and socially conditioned appear as the natural result of primitive existence, of the savage's spontaneous attitudes towards natural objects and of his prevalent occupations. From the survival point of view, it is vital that man's interest in the practically indispensable species should never abate, that his belief in his capacity to control them should give him strength and endurance in his pursuits and stimulate his observation and knowledge of the habits and natures of animals and plants. Totemism appears thus as a blessing bestowed by religion on primitive man's efforts in dealing with his useful surroundings, upon his "struggle for existence." At the same time it develops his reverence for those animals and plants on which he depends, to which he feels in a way grateful, and yet the destruction of which is a necessity to him. And all this springs from the belief of man's affinity with those forces of nature upon which he mainly depends. Thus we find a moral value and a biological significance in totemism, in a system of beliefs, practices, and social arrangements which at first sight appears but a childish, irrelevant, and degrading fancy of the savage.

4. Death and the Reintegration of the Group
Of all sources of religion, the supreme and final crisis of life—death—is of the greatest importance. Death is the gateway to the other world in more than the literal sense. According to most theories of early religion, a great deal, if not all, of religious inspiration has been derived from it—and in this orthodox views are on the whole correct. Man has to live his life in the shadow of death, and he who clings to life and enjoys its fullness must dread the menace of its end. And he who is faced by death turns to the promise of life. Death and its denial—Immortality—have always formed, as they form

today, the most poignant theme of man's forebodings. The extreme complexity of man's emotional reactions to life finds necessarily its counterpart in his attitude to death. Only what in life has been spread over a long space and manifested in a succession of experiences and events is here at its end condensed into one crisis which provokes a violent and complex outburst of religious manifestations.

Even among the most primitive peoples, the attitude towards death is infinitely more complex and, I may add, more akin to our own, than is usually assumed. It is often stated by anthropologists that the dominant feeling of the survivors is that of horror at the corpse and of fear of the ghost. This twin attitude is even made by no less an authority than Wilhelm Wundt the very nucleus of all religious belief and practice. Yet this assertion is only a halftruth, which means no truth at all. The emotions are extremely complex and even contradictory; the dominant elements, love of the dead and loathing of the corpse, passionate attachment to the personality still lingering about the body and a shattering fear of the gruesome thing that has been left over, these two elements seem to mingle and play into each other. This is reflected in the spontaneous behavior and in the ritual proceedings at death. In the tending of the corpse, in the modes of its disposal, in the post-funerary and commemorative ceremonies, the nearest relatives, the mother mourning for her son, the widow for her husband, the child for the parent, always show some horror and fear mingled with pious love, but never do the negative elements appear alone or even dominant. . . .

The savage is intensely afraid of death, probably as the result of some deep-seated instincts common to man and animals. He does not want to realize it as an end, he cannot face the idea of complete cessation, of annihilation. The idea of spirit and of spiritual existence is near at hand, furnished by such experiences as are discovered and described by Tylor. Grasping at it, man reaches the comforting belief in spiritual continuity and in the life after death. Yet this belief does not remain unchallenged in the complex, double-edged play of hope and fear which sets in always in the face of death. To the comforting voice of hope, to the intense desire of immortality, to the difficulty, in one's own case, almost the impossibility, of facing annihilation there are opposed powerful and terrible forebodings. The testimony of the senses, the gruesome decomposition of the corpse, the visible disappearance of the personality—certain apparently instinctive suggestions of fear and horror seem to threaten man at all stages of culture with some idea of annihilation, with some hidden fears and forebodings. And here into this play of emotional forces, into this supreme dilemma of life and final death, religion steps in, selecting the positive creed, the comforting view, the culturally valuable belief in immortality, in the spirit independent of the body, and in the continuance of life after death. In the various ceremonies at death, in commemoration and communion with the departed, and worship of ancestral ghosts, religion gives body and form to the saving beliefs.

Thus the belief in immortality is the result of a deep emotional revelation, standardized by religion, rather than a primitive philosophic doctrine. Man's conviction of continued life is one of the supreme gifts of religion, which judges and selects the better of the two alternatives suggested by self-preservation—the hope of continued life and the fear of annihilation. The belief in spirits is the result of the belief in immortality. The substance of which the spirits are made is the full-blooded passion and desire for life, rather than the shadowy stuff which haunts his dreams and illusions. Religion saves man from a surrender to death and destruction, and in doing this it merely makes use of the observations of dreams, shadows, and visions. The real nucleus of animism lies in the deepest emotional fact of human nature, the desire for life.

Thus the rites of mourning, the ritual behavior immediately after death, can be taken as pattern of the religious act, while the belief in immortality, in the continuity of life and in the nether world, can be taken as the prototype of an act of faith. Here, as in the religious ceremonies previously described, we find self-contained acts, the aim of which is achieved in their very performance. The ritual despair, the obsequies, the acts of mourning, express the emotion of the bereaved and the loss of the whole group. They endorse and they duplicate the natural feelings of the survivors; they create a social event out of a natural fact. Yet, though in the acts of mourning, in the mimic despair of wailing, in the treatment of the corpse and in its disposal, nothing ulterior is achieved, these acts fulfill an important function and possess a considerable value for primitive culture.

What is this function? The initiation ceremonies we have found fulfill theirs in sacralizing tradition; the food cults, sacrament and sacrifice bring man into communion with providence, with the beneficent forces of plenty; totemism standardizes man's practical, useful attitude of selective interest towards his surroundings. If the view here taken of the biological function of religion is true, some such similar role must also be played by the whole mortuary ritual.

The death of a man or woman in a primitive group, consisting of a limited number of individuals, is an event of no mean importance. The nearest relatives and friends are disturbed to the depth of their emotional life. A small community bereft of a member, especially if he be important, is severely mutilated. The whole event breaks the normal course of life and shakes the moral foundations of society. The strong tendency on which we have insisted in the above description: to give way to fear and horror, to abandon the corpse, to run away from the village, to destroy all the belongings of the dead one—all these impulses exist, and if given way to would be extremely dangerous, disintegrating the group, destroying the material foundations of primitive culture. Death in a primitive society is, therefore, much more than the removal of a member. By setting in motion one part of the deep forces of the instinct of self-preservation, it threatens the very cohesion and solidarity of the group, and upon this depends the organization of that society, its tradition, and finally the whole culture. For if primitive man yielded always to the disintegrating impulses of his reaction to death, the continuity of tradition and the existence of material civilization would be made impossible.

We have seen already how religion, by sacralizing and thus standardizing the other set of impulses, bestows on man the gift of mental integrity. Exactly the same function it fulfills also with regard to the whole group. The ceremonial of death which ties the survivors to the body and rivets them to the place of death, the beliefs in the existence of the spirit, in its beneficent influences or malevolent intentions, in the duties of a series of commemorative or sacrificial ceremonies—in all this religion counteracts the centrifugal forces of fear, dismay, demoralization, and provides the most powerful means of reintegration of the group's shaken solidarity and of the re-establishment of its morale.

In short, religion here assures the victory of tradition and culture over the mere negative response of thwarted instinct. . . .

The Public and Tribal Character of Primitive Cults

The festive and public character of the ceremonies of cult is a conspicuous feature of religion in general. Most sacred acts happen in a congregation; indeed, the solemn conclave of the faithful united in prayer, sacrifice, supplication, or thanksgiving is the very prototype of a religious ceremony. Religion needs the community as a whole so that its members may worship in common its sacred things and its divinities, and society needs religion for the maintenance of moral law and order.

In primitive societies the public character of worship, the give-and-take between religious faith and social organization, is at least as pronounced as in higher cultures. It is sufficient to glance over our previous inventory of religious phenomena to see that ceremonies at birth, rites of initiation, mortuary attentions to the dead, burial, the acts of mourning and commemoration, sacrifice and totemic ritual are one and all public and collective, frequently affecting the tribe as a whole and absorbing all its energies for the time being. This public character, the gathering together of big numbers, is especially pronounced in the annual or periodical feasts held at times of plenty, at harvest or at the height of the hunting or fishing season. Such feasts allow the people to indulge in their gay mood, to enjoy the abundance of crops and quarry, to meet their friends and relatives, to muster the whole community in full force, and to do all this in a mood of happiness and harmony. At times during such festivals visits of the departed take place: the spirits of ancestors and dead relatives return and receive offerings and sacrificial libations, mingle with the survivors in the acts of cult and in the rejoicings of the feast. Or the dead, even if they do not actually revisit the survivors, are commemorated by them, usually in the form of ancestor cult. Again, such festivities being frequently held, embody the ritual of garnered crops and other cults of vegetation. But whatever the other issues of such festivities, there can be no doubt that religion demands the existence of seasonal, periodical feasts with a big concourse of people, with rejoicings and festive apparel, with an abundance of food, and with relaxation of rules and taboos. The members of the tribe come together, and they relax the usual restrictions, especially the barriers of conventional reserve in social and in sexual intercourse. The appetites are provided for, indeed pandered to, and there is a common participation in the pleasures, a display to everyone of all that is good, the sharing of it in a universal mood of generosity. To the interest in plenty of material goods there is joined the interest in the multitude of people, in the congregation, in the tribe as a body. . . .

In fact, instead of going concretely into all the types of religious ceremony, we might have established our thesis by an abstract argument: since religion centers round vital acts, and since all these command public interest of joint co-operative groups, every religious ceremony must be public and carried out by groups. All crises of life, all important enterprises, arouse the public interest of primitive communities, and they have all their ceremonies, magical or religious. The same social body of men which unites for the enterprise or is brought together by the critical event performs also the ceremonial act. Such an abstract argument, however, correct though it be, would not have allowed us to get a real insight into the mechanism of public enactment of religious acts such as we have gained by our concrete description.

Social and Individual Contributions in Primitive Religion

We are forced therefore to the conclusion that publicity is the indispensable technique of religious revelation in primitive communities, but that society is neither the author of religious truths, nor still less its self-revealed subject. The necessity of the public *mise en scène* of dogma and collective enunciation of moral truths is due to several causes. Let us sum them up.

First of all, social co-operation is needed to surround the unveiling of things sacred and of supernatural beings with solemn grandeur. The community wholeheartedly engaged in performing the forms of the ritual creates the atmosphere of homogeneous belief. In this collective action, those who at the moment least need the comfort of belief, the affirmation of the truth, help along those who are in need of it. The evil, disintegrating forces of destiny are thus distributed by a system of mutual insurance in spiritual misfortune and stress. In bereavement, at the crisis of puberty, during impending danger and evil, at times when prosperity might be used well or badly—religion standardizes the right way of thinking and acting and society takes up the verdict and repeats it in unison.

In the second place, public performance of religious dogma is indispensable for the maintenance of morals in primitive communities. Every article of faith, as we have seen, wields a moral influence. Now morals, in order to be active at all, must be universal. The endurance of social ties, the mutuality of services and obligations, the possibility of co-operation, are based in any society on the fact that every member knows what is expected of him; that, in short, there is a universal standard of conduct. No rule of morals can work unless it is anticipated and unless it can be counted upon. In primitive societies, where law, as enforced by judgments and penalties, is almost completely absent, the automatic, self-acting moral rule is of the greatest importance for forming the very foundations of primitive organization and culture. This is possible only in a society where there is no private teaching of morals, no personal codes of conduct and honor, no ethical schools, no differences of moral opinion. The teaching of morals must be open, public, and universal.

Thirdly and finally, the transmission and the conservation of sacred tradition entails publicity, or at least collectiveness of performance. It is essential to every religion that its dogma should be considered and treated as absolutely inalterable and inviolable. The believer must be firmly convinced that what he is led to accept as truth is held in safekeeping, handed on exactly as it has been received, placed above any possibility of falsification or alteration. Every religion must have its tangible, reliable safeguards by which the authenticity of its tradition is guaranteed. In higher religions, we know the extreme importance of the authenticity of holy writings, the supreme concern about the purity of the text and the truth of interpretation. The native races have to rely on human memory. Yet, without books or inscriptions, without bodies of theologians, they are not less concerned about the purity of their texts, not less well safeguarded against alteration and misstatement. There is only one factor which can prevent the constant breaking of the sacred thread: the participation of a number of people in the safe-keeping of tradition. The public enactment of myth among certain tribes, the official recitals of sacred stories on certain occasions, the embodiment of parts of belief in sacred ceremonies, the guardianship of parts of tradition given to special bodies of men: secret societies, totemic clans, highest-age grades—all these are means of safeguarding the doctrine of primitive religions. We see that wherever this doctrine is not quite public in the tribe there is a special type of social organization serving the purpose of its keeping.

These considerations explain also the orthodoxy of primitive religions, and excuse their intolerance. In a primitive community, not only the morals but also the dogmas have to be identical for all members. As long as savage creeds have been regarded as idle superstitions, as make-believe, as childish or diseased fancies, or at best crude philosophic speculations, it was difficult to understand why the savage clung to them so obstinately, so faithfully. But once we see that every canon of the savage's belief is a live force to him, that his doctrine is the very cement of social fabric—for all his morality is derived from it, all his social cohesion and his mental composure—it is easy to understand that he cannot afford to be tolerant. And it is clear also that once you begin to play ducks and drakes with his "superstitions," you destroy all his morality, without much chance of giving him another instead.

We see thus clearly the need for the prominently overt and collective nature of religious acts and for the universality of moral principles, and we also realize clearly why this is much more prominent in primitive religions than in civilized ones. Public participation and social interest in matters religious are thus explicable by clear, concrete, empirical reasons, and there is no room for an entity, revealing itself in artful disguise to its worshippers, mystified and misled in the very act of revelation. The fact is that the social share in religious enactment is a condition necessary but not sufficient, and that without the analysis of the individual mind, we cannot take one step in the understanding of religion. . . .

Magic and Religion

Both magic and religion arise and function in situations of emotional stress: crises of life, lacunae in important pursuits, death and initiation into tribal mysteries, unhappy love and unsatisfied hate. Both magic and religion open up escapes from such situations and such impasses as offer no empirical way out except by ritual and belief into the domain of the supernatural. This domain embraces, in religion, beliefs in ghosts, spirits, the primitive forebodings of providence, the guardians of tribal mysteries; in magic, the primeval force and virtue of magic. Both magic and religion are based strictly on mythological tradition, and they also both exist in the atmosphere of the miraculous, in a constant revelation of their wonder-working power. They both are surrounded by taboos and observances which mark off their acts from those of the profane world.

Now what distinguishes magic from religion? We have taken for our starting-point a most definite and tangible distinction: we have defined, within the domain of the sacred, magic as a practical art consisting of acts which are only means to a definite end expected to follow later on; religion as a body of self-contained acts being themselves the fulfillment of their purpose. We can now follow up this difference into its deeper layers. The practical art of magic has its limited, circumscribed technique: spell, rite, and the condition of the performer form always its trite trinity. Religion, with its complex aspects and purposes, has no such simple technique, and its unity can be seen neither in the form of its acts nor even in the uniformity of its subject matter, but rather in the function which it fulfills and in the value of its belief and ritual. Again, the belief in magic, corresponding to its plain practical nature, is extremely simple. It is always the affirmation of man's power to cause certain definite effects by a definite spell and rite. In religion, on the other hand, we have a whole supernatural world of faith: the pantheon of spirits and demons, the benevolent powers of totem, guardian spirit, tribal all-father, the vision of the future life, create a second supernatural reality for primitive man. The mythology of religion is also more varied and complex as well as more creative. It usually centers round the various tenets of belief, and it develops them into cosmogonies, tales of culture heroes, accounts of the doings of gods and demigods. In magic, important as it is, mythology is an ever-recurrent boasting about man's primeval achievements.

Magic, the specific art for specific ends, has in every one of its forms come once into the possession of man, and it had to be handed over in direct filiation from generation to generation. Hence it remains from the earliest times in the hands of specialists, and the first profession of mankind is that of a wizard or witch. Religion, on the other hand, in primitive conditions is an affair of all, in which everyone takes an active and equivalent part. Every member of the tribe has to go through initiation, and then himself initiates others. Everyone wails, mourns, digs the grave and commemorates, and in due time everyone has his turn in being mourned and commemorated. Spirits are for all, and everyone becomes a spirit. The only specialization in religion that is, early spiritualistic mediumism—is not a profession but a personal gift. One more difference between magic and religion is the play of black and white in witchcraft, while religion in its primitive stages has but little of the contrast between good and evil, between the beneficent and malevolent powers. This is due also to the practical character of magic, which aims at direct quantitative results, while early religion, though essentially moral, has to deal with fateful, irremediable happenings and supernatural forces and beings, so that the undoing of things done by man does not enter into it. The maxim that fear first made gods in the universe is certainly not true in the light of anthropology.

In order to grasp the difference between religion and magic and to gain a clear vision of the three-cornered constellation of magic, religion, and science, let us briefly realize the cultural function of each. The function of primitive knowledge and its value have been assessed already and indeed are not difficult to grasp. By acquainting man with his surroundings, by allowing him to use the forces of nature, science, primitive knowledge, bestows on man an immense biological advantage, setting him far above all the rest of creation. The function of religion and its value we have learned to understand in the survey of savage creeds and cults given above. We have shown there that religious faith establishes, fixes, and enhances all valuable mental attitudes, such as reverence for tradition, harmony with environment, courage and confidence in the struggle with difficulties and at the prospect of death. This belief, embodied and maintained by cult and ceremonial, has an immense biological value, and so reveals to primitive man truth in the wider, pragmatic sense of the word.

What is the cultural function of magic? We have seen that all the instincts and emotions, all practical activities, lead man into impasses where gaps in his knowledge and the limitations of his early power of observation and reason betray him at a crucial moment. Human organism reacts to this in spontaneous outbursts, in which rudimentary modes of behavior and rudimentary beliefs in their efficiency are engendered. Magic fixes upon these beliefs and rudimentary rites and standardizes them into permanent traditional forms. Thus magic supplies primitive man with a number of ready-made ritual acts and beliefs, with a definite mental and practical technique which serves to bridge over the dangerous gaps in every important pursuit or critical situation. It enables man to carry out with confidence his important tasks, to maintain his poise and his mental integrity in fits of anger, in the throes of hate, of unrequited love, of despair and anxiety. The function of magic is to ritualize man's optimism, to enhance his faith in the victory of hope over fear. Magic expresses the greater value for man of confidence over doubt, of steadfastness over vacillation, of optimism over pessimism.

Looking from far and above, from our high places of safety in developed civilization, it is easy to see all the crudity and irrelevance of magic. But without its power and guidance early man could not have mastered his practical difficulties as he has done, nor could man have advanced to the higher stages of culture. Hence the universal occurrence of magic in primitive societies and its enormous sway. Hence do we find magic an invariable adjunct of all important activities. I think we must see in it the embodiment of the sublime folly of hope, which has yet been the best school of man's character.

From *Structure and Function in Primitive Society: Essays and Addresses*

A. R. RADCLIFFE-BROWN

History and Theory

The difference between the historical study of social institutions and the theoretical study can be easily seen by comparing economic history and theoretical economics, or by comparing the history of law with theoretical jurisprudence. In anthropology, however, there has been and still is a great deal of confusion which is maintained by discussions in which terms such as "history" and "science" or "theory" are used by disputants in very different meanings. These confusions could be to a considerable extent avoided by using the recognised terms of logic and methodology and distinguishing between idiographic and nomothetic enquiries.

In an idiographic enquiry the purpose is to establish as acceptable certain particular or factual propositions or statements. A nomothetic enquiry, on the contrary, has for its purpose to arrive at acceptable general propositions. We define the nature of an enquiry by the kind of conclusions that are aimed at.

History, as usually understood, is the study of records and monuments for the purpose of providing knowledge about conditions and events of the past, including those investigations that are concerned with the quite recent past. It is clear that history consists primarily of idiographic enquiries. In the last century there was a dispute, the famous *Methodenstreit,* as to whether historians should admit theoretical considerations in their work or deal in generalisations. A great many historians have taken the view that nomothetic enquiries should not be included in historical studies, which should be confined to telling us what happened and how it happened. Theoretical or nomothetic enquiries should be left to sociology. But there are some writers who think that a historian may, or even should, include theoretical interpretations in his account of the past. . . .

In anthropology, meaning by that the study of what are called the primitive or backward peoples, the term ethnography applies to what is specifically a mode of idiographic enquiry, the aim of which is to give acceptable accounts of such peoples and their social life. Ethnography differs from history in that the ethnographer derives his knowledge, or some major part of it, from direct observation of or contact with the people about whom he writes, and not, like the historian, from written records. Prehistoric archaeology, which is another branch of anthropology, is clearly an idiographic study, aimed at giving us factual knowledge about the prehistoric past.

The theoretical study of social institutions in general is usually referred to as sociology, but as this name can be loosely used for many different kinds of writings about society we can speak more specifically of theoretical or comparative sociology. . . .

Certain confusions amongst anthropologists result from the failure to distinguish between historical explanation of institutions and theoretical understanding. If we ask why it is that a certain institution exists in a particular society the appropriate answer is a historical statement as to its origin. To explain why the United States has a political constitution with a President, two Houses of Congress, a Cabinet, a Supreme Court, we refer to the history of North America. This is historical explanation in the proper sense of the term. The existence of an institution is explained by reference to a complex sequence of events forming a causal chain of which it is a result.

The acceptability of a historical explanation depends on the fullness and reliability of the historical record. In the primitive societies that are studied by social anthropology there are no historical records. We have no knowledge of the development of social institutions among the Australian aborigines for example. Anthropologists, thinking of their study as a kind of historical study, fall back on conjecture and imagination, and invent "pseudo-historical" or "pseudo-causal" explanations. . . . The view taken here is that such speculations are not merely useless but are worse than useless. This does not in any way imply the rejection of historical explanation but quite the contrary.

Comparative sociology, of which social anthropology is a branch, is here conceived as a theoretical or nomothetic study of which the aim is to provide acceptable generalisations. The theoretical understanding of a particular institution is its interpretation in the light of such generalisations.

Social Process

A first question that must be asked if we are to formulate a systematic theory of comparative sociology is: What is the concrete, observable, phenomenal reality with which the theory is to be concerned? Some anthropologists would say that the reality consists of "societies" conceived as being in some sense or other discrete real entities. Others, however, describe the reality that has to be studied as consisting of "cultures," each of which is again conceived as some kind of discrete entity. Still others seem to think of the subject as concerned with both kinds of entities, "societies" and "cultures," so that the relation of these then presents a problem.

My own view is that the concrete reality with which the social anthropologist is concerned in observation, description, comparison and classification, is not any sort of entity but a process, the process of social life. The unit of investigation is the social life of some particular region of the earth during a certain period of time. The process itself consists of an immense multitude of actions and interactions of human beings, acting as individuals or in combinations or groups. Amidst the diversity of the particular events there are discoverable regularities, so that it is possible to give statements or descriptions of certain *general features* of the social life of a selected region. A statement of such significant general features of the process of social life constitutes a description of what may be called a *form of social life*. My conception of social anthropology is as the comparative theoretical study of forms of social life amongst primitive peoples.

A form of social life amongst a certain collection of human beings may remain approximately the same over a certain period. But over a sufficient length of time the form of social life itself undergoes change or modification. Therefore, while we can regard the events of social life as constituting a process, there is over and above this the process of change in the form of social life. In a synchronic description we give an account of a form of social life as it exists at a certain time, abstracting as far as possible from changes that may be taking place in its features. A diachronic account, on the other hand, is an account of such changes over a period. In comparative sociology we have to deal theoretically with the continuity of, and with changes in, forms of social life.

Culture

Anthropologists use the word "culture" in a number of different senses. It seems to me that some of them use it as equivalent to what I call a form of social life. In its ordinary use in English "culture," which is much the same idea as cultivation, refers to a process, and we can define it as the process by which a person acquires, from contact with other persons or from such things as books or works of art, knowledge, skill, ideas, beliefs, tastes, sentiments. In a particular society we can discover certain processes of *cultural tradition,* using the word tradition in its literal meaning of handing on or handing down. The understanding and use of a language is passed on by a process of cultural tradition in this sense. An Englishman learns by such a process to understand and use the English language, but in some sections of the society he may also learn Latin, or Greek, or French, or Welsh. In complex modern societies there are a great number of separate cultural traditions. By one a person may learn to be a doctor or surgeon, by another he may learn to be an engineer or an architect. In the simplest forms of social life the number of separate cultural traditions may be reduced to two, one for men and the other for women.

If we treat the social reality that we are investigating as being not an entity but a process, then culture and cultural tradition are names for certain recognisable aspects of that process, but not, of course, the whole process. The terms are convenient ways of referring to certain aspects of human social life. It is by reason of the existence of culture and cultural traditions that human social life differs very markedly from the social life of other animal species. The transmission of learnt ways of thinking, feeling and acting constitutes the cultural process, which is a specific feature of human social life. It is, of course, part of that process of interaction amongst persons which is here defined as the social process thought of as the social reality. Continuity and change in the forms of social life being the subjects of investigation of comparative sociology, the continuity of cultural traditions and changes in those traditions are amongst the things that have to be taken into account. . . .

Statics and Dynamics

Comte pointed out that in sociology, as in other kinds of science, there are two sets of problems, which he called problems of statics and problems of dynamics. In statics we attempt to discover and define conditions of existence or of co-existence; in dynamics we try to discover conditions of change. The conditions of existence of molecules or of organisms are matters of statics, and similarly the conditions of existence of societies, social systems, or forms of social life are matters for social statics. Whereas the problems of social dynamics deal with the conditions of change of forms of social life.

The basis of science is systematic classification. It is the first task of social statics to make some attempt to compare forms of social life in order to arrive at classifications. But forms of social life cannot be classified into species and genera in the way we classify forms of organic life; the classification has to be not specific but typological, and this is a more complicated kind of investigation. It can only be reached by means of the establishing of typologies for features of social life or the complexes of features that are given in partial social systems. Not only is the task complex but it has been neglected in view of the idea that the method of anthropology should be a historical method.

But though the typological studies are one important part of social statics, there is another task, that of formulating generalisations about the conditions of existence of social systems, or of forms of social life. The so-called first law of social statics is a generalisation affirming that for any form of social life to persist or continue the various features must exhibit some kind and measure of coherence or consistence, but this only defines the problem of social statics, which is to investigate the nature of this coherence.

The study of social dynamics is concerned with establishing generalisations about how social systems change. It is a corollary of the hypothesis of the systematic connection of features of social life that changes in some features are likely to produce changes in other features.

Social Evolution

The theory of social evolution was formulated by Herbert Spencer as part of his formulation of the general theory of evolution. According to that theory the development of life on the earth constitutes a single process to which Spencer applied the term "evolution." The theory of organic and super-organic (social) evolution can be reduced to two essential propositions: (1) That both in the development of forms of organic life and in the development of forms of human social life there has been a process of diversification by which many different forms of organic life or of social life have been developed out of a very much smaller number of original forms; (2) That there has been a general trend of development by which more complex forms of structure and organisation (organic or social) have arisen from simpler forms. The acceptance of the theory of evolution only requires the

acceptance of these propositions as giving us a scheme of interpretation to apply to the study of organic and social life. But it must be remembered that some anthropologists reject the hypothesis of evolution. We can give provisional acceptance to Spencer's fundamental theory, while rejecting the various pseudo-historical speculations which he added to it, and that acceptance gives us certain concepts which may be useful as analytical tools.

Adaptation

This is a key concept of the theory of evolution. It is, or can be, applied both to the study of the forms of organic life and to the forms of social life amongst human beings. A living organism exists and continues in existence only if it is both internally and externally adapted. The internal adaptation depends on the adjustment of the various organs and their activities, so that the various physiological processes constitute a continuing functioning system by which the life of the organism is maintained. The external adaptation is that of the organism to the environment within which it lives. The distinction of external and internal adaptation is merely a way of distinguishing two aspects of the *adaptational system* which is the same for organisms of a single species.

When we come to the social life of animals another feature of adaptation makes its appearance. The existence of a colony of bees depends on a combination of the activities of the individual worker bees in the collection of honey and pollen, the manufacture of wax, the building of the cells, the tending of eggs and larvae and the feeding of the latter, the protection of the store of honey from robbers, the ventilation of the hive by fanning with their wings, the maintenance of temperature in the winter by clustering together. Spencer uses the term "co-operation" to refer to this feature of social life. Social life and social adaptation therefore involve the adjustment of the behaviour of individual organisms to the requirements of the process by which the social life continues.

When we examine a form of social life amongst human beings as an adaptational system it is useful to distinguish three aspects of the total system. There is the way in which the social life is adjusted to the physical environment, and we can, if we wish, speak of this as the ecological adaptation. Secondly, there are the institutional arrangements by which an orderly social life is maintained, so that what Spencer calls co-operation is provided for and conflict is restrained or regulated. This we might call, if we wished, the institutional aspect of social adaptation. Thirdly, there is the social process by which an individual acquires habits and mental characteristics that fit him for a place in the social life and enable him to participate in its activities. This, if we wish, could be called cultural adaptation, in accordance with the earlier definition of cultural tradition as process. What must be emphasised is that these modes of adaptation are only different aspects from which the total adaptational system can be looked at for convenience of analysis and comparison.

The theory of social evolution therefore makes it a part of our scheme of interpretation of social systems to examine any given system as an adaptational system. The stability of the system, and therefore its continuance over a certain period, depends on the effectiveness of the adaptation.

Social Function

The term function has a very great number of different meanings in different contexts. In mathematics the word, as introduced by Euler in the eighteenth century, refers to an expression or symbol which can be written on paper, such as "log. X," and has no relation whatever to the same word as used in such a science as physiology. In physiology the concept of function is of fundamental importance as enabling us to deal with the continuing relation of structure and process in organic life. A complex organism, such as a human body, has a structure as an arrangement of organs and tissues and flu-

ids. Even an organism that consists of a single cell has a structure as an arrangement of molecules. An organism also has a life, and by this we refer to a process. The concept of organic function is one that is used to refer to the connection between the structure of an organism and the life process of that organism. The processes that go on within a human body while it is living are dependent on the organic structure. It is the function of the heart to pump blood through the body. The organic structure, as a living structure, depends for its continued existence on the processes that make up the total life processes. If the heart ceases to perform its function the life process comes to an end and the structure as a living structure also comes to an end. Thus process is dependent on structure and continuity of structure is dependent on process.

In reference to social systems and their theoretical understanding one way of using the concept of function is the same as its scientific use in physiology. It can be used to refer to the interconnection between the social structure and the process of social life. It is this use of the word function that seems to me to make it a useful term in comparative sociology. The three concepts of process, structure and function are thus components of a single theory as a scheme of interpretation of human social systems. The three concepts are logically interconnected, since "function" is used to refer to the relations of process and structure. The theory is one that we can apply to the study both of continuity in forms of social life and also to processes of change in those forms. . . .

Religion and Society

When we regard the religions of other peoples, or at least those of what are called primitive peoples, as systems of erroneous and illusory beliefs, we are confronted with the problem of how these beliefs came to be formulated and accepted. It is to this problem that anthropologists have given most attention. My personal opinion is that this method of approach, even though it may seem the most direct, is not the one most likely to lead to a real understanding of the nature of religions.

There is another way in which we may approach the study of religions. We may entertain as at least a possibility the theory that any religion is an important or even essential part of the social machinery, as are morality and law, part of the complex system by which human beings are enabled to live together in an orderly arrangement of social relations. From this point of view we deal not with the origins but with the social functions of religions, i.e. the contribution that they make to the formation and maintenance of a social order. There are many persons who would say that it is only true religion (i.e. one's own) that can provide the foundation of an orderly social life. The hypothesis we are considering is that the social function of a religion is independent of its truth or falsity, that religions which we think to be erroneous or even absurd and repulsive, such as those of some savage tribes, may be important and effective parts of the social machinery, and that without these "false" religions social evolution and the development of modern civilisation would have been impossible.

The hypothesis, therefore, is that in what we regard as false religions, though the performance of religious rites does not actually produce the effects that are expected or hoped for by those who perform or take part in them, they have other effects, some at least of which may be socially valuable.

How are we to set to work to test this hypothesis? It is of no use thinking in terms of religion in general, in the abstract, and society in the abstract. Nor is it adequate to consider some one religion, particularly if it is the one in which we have been brought up and about which we are likely to be prejudiced one way or another. The only method is the experimental method of social anthropology, and that means that we must study in the light of our hypothesis a sufficient number of diverse particular religions or religious cults in their relation to the particular societies in which they are found. This is a task not for one person but for a number.

Anthropologists and others have discussed at length the question of the proper definition of religion. I do not intend to deal with that controversial subject on this occasion. But there are some points that must be considered. I shall assume that any religion or any religious cult normally involves certain ideas or beliefs on the one hand, and on the other certain observances. These observances, positive and negative, i.e. actions and abstentions, I shall speak of as rites. . . .

My suggestion is that in attempting to understand a religion it is on the rites rather than on the beliefs that we should first concentrate our attention. Much the same view is taken by Loisy, who justifies his selection of sacrificial rites as the subject of his analysis of religion by saying that rites are in all religions the most stable and lasting element, and consequently that in which we can best discover the spirit of ancient cults. . . .

Thirty-seven years ago (1908), in a fellowship thesis on the Andaman Islanders (which did not appear in print till 1922), I formulated briefly a general theory of the social function of rites and ceremonies. It is the same theory that underlies the remarks I shall offer on this occasion. Stated in the simplest possible terms the theory is that an orderly social life amongst human beings depends upon the presence in the minds of the members of a society of certain sentiments, which control the behaviour of the individual in his relation to others. Rites can be seen to be the regulated symbolic expressions of certain sentiments. Rites can therefore be shown to have a specific social function when, and to the extent that, they have for their effect to regulate, maintain and transmit from one generation to another sentiments on which the constitution of the society depends. I ventured to suggest as a general formula that religion is everywhere an expression in one form or another of a sense of dependence on a power outside ourselves, a power which we may speak of as a spiritual or moral power. . . .

The rites performed at the totem centre by the members of the local group to which it belongs, or under their leadership and direction, are thought to renew the vitality of this life-spirit of the species. In eastern Australia the totem centre is spoken of as the "home" or "dwelling-place" of the species, and the rites are called "stirring up." Thus, the rite at a rain totem centre brings the rain in its due season, that at a kangaroo totem centre ensures the supply of kangaroos, and that at the baby totem centre provides for the birth of children in the tribe.

These rites imply a certain conception, which I think we can call specifically a religious conception, of the place of man in the universe. Man is dependent upon what we call nature: on the regular successions of the seasons, on the rain falling when it should, on the growth of plants and the continuance of animal life. But, as I have already said, while for us the order of nature is one thing and the social order another, for the Australian they are two parts of a single order. Well-being, for the individual or for the society, depends on the continuance of this order free from serious disturbance. The Australians believe that they can ensure this continuance, or at least contribute to it, by their actions, including the regular performance of the totemic rites. . . .

I have dwelt, if only cursorily, with two types of religion: ancestor-worship and Australian totemism. In both of them it is possible to demonstrate the close correspondence of the form of religion and the form of the social structure. In both it is possible to see how the religious rites reaffirm and strengthen the sentiments on which the social order depends. Here then are results of some significance for our problem. They point to a certain line of investigation. We can and should examine other religions in the light of the results already reached. But to do this we must study religions in action;

we must try to discover the effects of active participation in a particular cult, first the direct effects on the individual and then the further effects on the society of which these individuals are members. When we have a sufficient number of such studies, it will be possible to establish a general theory of the nature of religions and their role in social development. . . .

At a somewhat higher stage of development, "when the social organism has been perfected, when the tribe has become a people, and this people has its gods, its religion, it is by this religion itself that the strength of the national conscience is measured, and it is in the service of national gods that men find a pledge of security in the present, of prosperity in the future. The gods are as it were the expression of the confidence that the people has in itself; but it is in the cult of the gods that this confidence is nourished." At a still higher stage of social development, the religions which give men a promise of immortality give him thereby an assurance which permits him to bear courageously the burdens of his present life and face the most onerous obligations. . . .

To me this formula seems unsatisfactory in that it lays stress on what is only one side of the religious (or magical) attitude. I offer as an alternative the formula that religion develops in mankind what may be called a sense of dependence. What I mean by this can best be explained by an example. In an ancestor-worshipping tribe of South Africa, a man feels that he is dependent on his ancestors. From them he has received his life and the cattle that are his inheritance. To them he looks to send him children and to multiply his cattle and in other ways to care for his wellbeing. This is one side of the matter; on his ancestors he can depend. The other side is the belief that the ancestors watch over his conduct, and that if he fails in his duties they will not only cease to send him blessings, but will visit him with sickness or some other misfortune. He cannot stand alone and depend only on his own efforts; on his ancestors he must depend. . . .

I suggest to you that what makes and keeps a man a social animal is not some herd instinct, but the sense of dependence in the innumerable forms that it takes. The process of socialisation begins on the first day of an infant's life and it has to learn that it both *can* and *must* depend on its parents. From them it has comfort and succour; but it must submit also to their control. What I am calling the sense of dependence always has these two sides. We can face life and its chances and difficulties with confidence when we know that there are powers, forces and events on which we can rely, but we must submit to the control of our conduct by rules which are imposed. The entirely asocial individual would be one who thought that he could be completely independent, relying only on himself, asking for no help and recognising no duties. . . .

Like any other scientific theory it is provisional, subject to revision and modification in the light of future research. It is offered as providing what seems likely to be a profitable method of investigation. What is needed to test and further elaborate the theory is a number of systematic studies of various types of religion in relation to social systems in which they occur.

I will summarise the suggestions I have made:

1. To understand a particular religion we must study its effects. The religion must therefore be studied in action.

2. Since human conduct is in large part controlled or directed by what have been called sentiments, conceived as mental dispositions, it is necessary to discover as far as possible what are the sentiments that are developed in the individual as the result of his participation in a particular religious cult.

3. In the study of any religion we must first of all examine the specifically religious actions, the ceremonies and the collective or individual rites.

4. The emphasis on belief in specific doctrines which characterises some modern religions seems to be the result of certain social developments in societies of complex structure.

5. In some societies there is a direct and immediate relation between the religion and the social structure. This has been illustrated by ancestor-worship and Australian totemism. It is also true of what we may call national religions, such as that of the Hebrews or those of the city states of Greece and Rome. But where there comes into existence a separate independent religious structure by the formation of different churches or sects or cult-groups within a people, the relation of religion to the total social structure is in many respects indirect and not always easy to trace.

6. As a general formula (for whatever such a formula may be worth) it is suggested that what is expressed in all religions is what I have called the sense of dependence in its double aspect, and that it is by constantly maintaining this sense of dependence that religions perform their social function.

Counterpoint:
The Poverty of Functionalism

HANS H. PENNER

Hans H. Penner was a professor of Religious Studies at Dartmouth College in Hanover, New Hampshire for many years. He published the following books: *Teaching Lévi-Strauss* and *Impasse and Resolution: A Critique of the Study of Religion*.

THE STUDY OF RELIGION, Religionswissenschaft in the broadest sense, does not lack evidence or new discoveries. The past few decades alone have provided a tremendous increase in religious data and information concerning religious traditions. What is lacking are adequate theories which will enlighten us with regard to the wealth of material at our disposal.

Despite the increase in data, three general theories of religion seem to remain constant in most texts. The first claims autonomy for both the method and the phenomena. The second strives for some kind of integration of methods and phenomena, while the third claims some form of functionalism as the basic method for the study of religion. . . .

I cannot enter into the problems and controversies raised by the first two approaches except for a few brief comments. The first claim has yet to show that there is anything explicitly distinctive in the method it uses or the content which is the result. It misconceives both "reduction," which it opposes, and "understanding," which it claims as a special method. The second approach, although striving for an integration, usually posits a metamethod similar to the first, or results in placing methods together which are theoretically in conflict, if not incommensurable with each other.

Functionalism as a third approach for studying religion has remained both influential and controversial. The influence of the approach by well-known scholars does not need to be argued. However, the controversy among most historians of religions about functionalism is concerned with its so-called reductionistic results. As I have already pointed out, most, if not all, of these controversies concerning reduction are misconceived. In very simple terms, reduction is taken to mean a "reduction of phenomena" instead of "reduction of theories." Once we learn that reducibility involves theories, not data, this controversy should cease to have the illusory effect it has on our reflections concerning method. As far as I know, few if any historians of religions have seen this issue and the consequence it involves for our development.

Now the problem with functionalism is not that it is reductive; all theories are reductions. Since most criticisms have missed this, much of our debate over functionalism in the history of religions has missed the crucial point. We have either remained threatened by functionalism or we have accepted it as valid in itself or as an auxiliary approach to religion.

The main issue at stake is whether functionalism is an explanation or an adequate theory of religion. The argument which follows is

From Hans H. Penner, *"The Poverty of Functionalism,"* History of Religions *11* (1972): *91–97.*
Copyright © 1972 *The University of Chicago Press. Reprinted by permission.*

certainly not new. It has spread into all of the major disciplines in the social sciences. The only reason for this brief essay, therefore, is to present the problem of functionalism in order that we may see that functionalism is not a threat or an aid because it is not an explanation of religion. And once this is clearly grasped it becomes meaningless to debate the old issues concerning functionalism and religion. In fact, it releases us to work out new approaches to religion, since the door remains wide open for theoretical reflection.

The argument can be stated in two parts: first, from within functionalism as presented primarily by anthropology, and second, from a criticism of functionalism itself.

The definition that "religion is what religion does" is well known. Functionalism claims to be a theory which explains religion in terms of what it does. Both Malinowski and Evans-Pritchard have written essays which have become classic representations of this theory. In recent years, however, this theory has become the subject of severe criticism.

Melford Spiro is certainly one of the outstanding anthropologists in the United States who disagrees with the central thesis of this position, that it explains religion. He is not only sensitive to the historical traditions of a religion, but remains one of very few contemporary anthropologists with an adequate grasp of the logic of definition and theories. It is refreshing to read his various essays and books in which he confronts the problems of religion as an anthropologist. It is unfortunate that a recent review of *Burmese Supernaturalism* did not enter into a discussion of the methodological chapters of this book.[1] A careful examination of his study of *Burmese Supernaturalism* reveals a penetrating analysis of functionalism. If we take Spiro seriously, it becomes clear that in at least one instance functionalism is not an explanation of religion.

Spiro begins with what I believe is an accurate evaluation of functionalism. He equates functional explanation with "causal explanation" in that it is concerned with "antecedent-consequent" relationships. As we shall see later on in this essay, this means that functional explanations are concerned with "if-then" explanations. He goes on to say, quite accurately, that functionalism takes religion as an antecedent which is to be explained by reference to its consequence, for example, maintenance of the society, or personal integration. Spiro then argues that functionalism can only explain religion if it can be shown that the relation between religion (the antecedent) and the social or personality maintenance (consequent) is "intended," and adds that this intention may be either conscious or unconscious. Without entering into the problems of the meaning of an "intention," which is either conscious or unconscious, it is clear that Spiro is saying that we can speak of a functional explanation only if the individual "intends" the antecedent condition (religious belief) to be a causal variable for maintenance or integration.

I must admit that there are serious difficulties in Spiro's use of "intention" and "motivational variables" as "causal variables." Perhaps at some future date he will clarify the use of such terms since they involve enormous complexities. For the present, let us grant him the argument that motivational variables are "one kind of causal explanation." Let us also agree, for the sake of the argument, that intentions can be conscious or unconscious, and that they create "expectations" of a causal kind.

What Spiro has made explicitly clear is that most functional anthropologists "explain" religion as an "unintended" consequence; that is maintenance of society or the like. At this point, and disregarding the problems in the term "unintended," I am in complete agreement with his analysis. Surely, Spiro is correct in concluding that it is inadmissable "to argue that [an] unintended consequence of religion is the cause of religion."

The results of such an analysis show that if functionalism explains anything at all, it explains society by reference to religion. Reflection upon this argument will help us clarify the point that if this is indeed what anthropologists are doing (intentionally or unintentionally) then there is no conflict between anthropology and the discipline called "history of religions." For, according to Spiro, when functional methods are used, it is society, or social solidarity, that is explained, not religion.

Spiro's position, of course, cannot be equated with the complexity and development of anthropology itself. However, it is refreshing to read this clarification, despite the fact that such well-known anthropologists as E. Leach continue to insist that myths are "nothing more than ways of describing the formal relationships that exist between real persons and real groups in ordinary society."[2] This is an excellent example of the persistence of the functional fallacy which Spiro has attempted to clarify. . . . It will indeed be a difficult task to convince a Shaivite that his belief in Shiva is nothing more than a way of describing the formal relations that exist between persons or groups in his society. Such "explanations" of religion could lead one to believe that what is really desired is a reformation in other cultures rather than a science of culture, religion, or society.

Viewing functionalism from this point it should be clear that the problem is not that it "reduces" religion, or explains religion away, but that it does not explain religion at all. This in itself should be sufficient for releasing the historian of religions to advance his research without worrying about whether he should or should not include functionalism in his approach to the study of religion.

Given this clarification, functionalism remains a theory which must be dealt with. Despite Spiro's rejection of functionalism as an explanation of religion, he does maintain that it is a causal explanation or else not explanatory. What we must do, in other words, is translate functional propositions of explanation into causal propositions of explanation. Unless I misunderstand him, Spiro does not deny that we can indeed explain societies (at least in part) by reference to religion as a functional variable. Without going into the problems, let us beware of yielding to the temptation of reversing the usual methods of functionalism in order to explain religion by reference to social facts as variables! That is to say, let us not turn Spiro and others upside down.

Knowing that the functional analysis of religion in the social sciences does not explain religion is very helpful. To be able to show that functionalism does not explain anything as a "kind of causal explanation" should put this whole issue to rest once and for all. It is at this point that historians of religions may help anthropologists in the clarification of theory. I am assuming that although we are not explaining the same data the one thing we have in common is the clarification of our theories, which are essential to explanation and interpretation.

Twelve years ago, Carl Hempel wrote an essay in which he concluded that functionalism was at best a heuristic device, not a causal explanations.[3] This essay should become required reading for every student of religion who has confronted functionalism, claims functionalism as a method of explanation, or thinks it necessary to include it as a valid method beside others.

Although the essay has been given its deserved attention in the past few years, it seems to have escaped the eyes of most historians of religions. Since this is the case, a brief summary of Hempel's argument is necessary.

Using such well-known scholars as Malinowski, Radcliffe-Brown, Parsons, and Merton, Hempel convincingly argues that functionalism is both a logical fallacy and unempirical. Since functionalism as a theory has maintained that it is both logical and empirical as an explanation, the burden of proof now rests upon functionalists.

Hempel's main argument is that functionalists argue for the following theory of explanation:

a) At a certain time a society functions adequately in a certain setting.

b) A society functions adequately in a certain setting only if a certain necessary condition (social maintenance) is satisfied.

c)   If religion (myth, ritual, belief) were present in the society, then as an effect the necessary condition (social maintenance) would be satisfied.

d)   Therefore, at a certain time religion is present in the society.

Notice that Hempel has translated functional terms into statements that agree with what Spiro has called "causal explanations." The statements are concerned with "antecedent-consequent" (if-then) relations. He also agrees with Spiro that functionalism takes religion as the antecedent condition and explains it by reference to its consequence. But the conclusion, which Spiro has not emphasized, is false. The conclusion does not follow simply because it involves the fallacy of affirming the consequent. This would be like arguing that, if I miss my plane I will be late for my appointment. I was late for my appointment. Therefore I missed my plane.

The argument could hold only if (c) were a necessary and sufficient condition for society. However, no functional study of religion has come close to maintaining this without involving itself in a tautology, contradicting its claim to empirical observation.

Furthermore, Hempel has pointed out that the claim of empiricism falls apart when such terms as "need," "functional requirement,"

"adaptation," and "maintenance" are used as key terms in the explanation. In brief, functionalism is neither a causal explanation nor empirical.

What we should learn from all this is that the problem with functionalism is not that it explains religion away, reduces religion, or translates religion. The fact of the matter is that functionalism does not explain religion at all. Together with "understanding," it is at best a heuristic device which may lead us to clarity and rigor as we begin to create our own theories concerning religion. Once again, the final problem in the study of religion is not the paucity of data, but the poverty of theories which are necessary for an adequate description and explanation of religion. Whatever the future development of "Religionswissenschaft," one thing is certain: it will only be as sound as the validity of the theories it uses.

NOTES

1. Melford E. Spiro, *Burmese Supernaturalism* (Englewood Cliffs, NJ, 1967), esp. chap. 5.

2. E. R. Leach, *Political Systems of Highland Burma* (London, 1954), p. 182.

3. C. G. Hempel, "The Logic of Functional Analysis," in *Symposium on Sociological Theory*, ed. L. Gross (Evanston, IL, 1959).

From *The Ritual Process: Structure and Anti-Structure*

VICTOR TURNER

VAN GENNEP HIMSELF defined *rites de passage* as "rites which accompany every change of place, state, social position and age." To point up the contrast between "state" and "transition," I employ "state" to include all his other terms. It is a more inclusive concept than "status" or

Reprinted from Victor Turner, The Ritual Process: Structure and Anti-Structure *(New York: Aldine de Gruyter). Copyright © 1969 by Victor W. Turner. Renewed 1997 by Edith Turner.*

"office," and refers to any type of stable or recurrent condition that is culturally recognized. Van Gennep has shown that all rites of passage or "transition" are marked by three phases: separation, margin (or *limen,* signifying "threshold" in Latin), and aggregation. The first phase (of separation) comprises symbolic behavior signifying the detachment of the individual or group either from an earlier fixed point in the social structure, from a set of cultural conditions (a "state"), or from both. During the intervening "liminal" period, the characteristics of the ritual subject (the "passenger") are ambiguous; he passes through a cultural realm that has few or none of the attributes of the past or coming state. In the third phase (reaggregation or reincorporation), the passage is consummated. The ritual subject, individual or corporate, is in a relatively stable state once more and, by virtue of this, has rights and obligations vis-à-vis others of a clearly defined and "structural" type; he is expected to behave in accordance with certain customary norms and ethical standards binding on incumbents of social position in a system of such positions.

Liminality

The attributes of liminality or of liminal *personae* ("threshold people") are necessarily ambiguous, since this condition and these persons elude or slip through the network of classifications that normally locate states and positions in cultural space. Liminal entities are neither here nor there; they are betwixt and between the positions assigned and arrayed by law, custom, convention, and ceremonial. As such, their ambiguous and indeterminate attributes are expressed by a rich variety of symbols in the many societies that ritualize social and cultural transitions. Thus, liminality is frequently likened to death, to being in the womb, to invisibility, to darkness, to bisexuality, to the wilderness, and to an eclipse of the sun or moon.

Liminal entities, such as neophytes in initiation or puberty rites, may be represented as possessing nothing. They may be disguised as monsters, wear only a strip of clothing, or even go naked, to demonstrate that as liminal beings they have no status, property, insignia, secular clothing indicating rank or role, position in a kinship system—in short, nothing that may distinguish them from their fellow neophytes or initiands. Their behavior is normally passive or humble; they must obey their instructors implicitly, and accept arbitrary punishment without complaint. It is as though they are being reduced or ground down to a uniform condition to be fashioned anew and endowed with additional powers to enable them to cope with their new station in life. Among themselves, neophytes tend to develop an intense comradeship and egalitarianism. Secular distinctions of rank and status disappear or are homogenized. The condition of the patient and her husband in Isoma had some of these attributes—passivity, humility, near-nakedness—in a symbolic milieu that represented both a grave and a womb. In initiations with a long period of seclusion, such as the circumcision rites of many tribal societies or induction into secret societies, there is often a rich proliferation of liminal symbols.

Communitas

What is interesting about liminal phenomena for our present purposes is the blend they offer of lowliness and sacredness, of homogeneity and comradeship. We are presented, in such rites, with a "moment in and out of time," and in and out of secular social structure, which reveals, however fleetingly, some recognition (in symbol if not always in language) of a generalized social bond that has ceased to be and has simultaneously yet to be fragmented into a multiplicity of structural ties. These are the ties organized in terms either of caste, class, or rank hierarchies or of segmentary oppositions in the stateless societies beloved of political anthropologists. It is as though there are here two major "models" for human interrelatedness, juxtaposed and alternating. The first is of society as a structured, differentiated, and often hierarchical system of politico-legal-economic positions with many types of evaluation, separating men in terms of "more" or "less." The second, which emerges recognizably in the liminal period, is of society as an unstructured or rudimentarily structured and relatively undifferentiated *comitatus*, community, or even communion of equal individuals who submit together to the general authority of the ritual elders.

I prefer the Latin term "communitas" to "community," to distinguish this modality of social relationship from an "area of common living." The distinction between structure and communitas is not simply the familiar one between "secular" and "sacred," or that, for example, between politics and religion. Certain fixed offices in tribal societies have *many* sacred attributes; indeed, every social position has *some* sacred characteristics. But this "sacred" component is acquired by the incumbents of positions during the *rites de passage*, through which they changed positions. Something of the sacredness of that transient humility and modelessness goes over, and tempers the pride of the incumbent of a higher position or office. . . . Liminality implies that the high could not be high unless the low existed, and he who is high must experience what it is like to be low. . . .

Dialectic of the Development Cycle

From all this I infer that, for individuals and groups, social life is a type of dialectical process that involves successive experience of high and low, communitas and structure, homogeneity and differentiation, equality and inequality. The passage from lower to higher status is through a limbo of statuslessness. In such a process, the opposites, as it were, constitute one another and are mutually indispensable. Furthermore, since any concrete tribal society is made up of multiple personae, groups, and categories, each of which has its own developmental cycle, at a given moment many incumbencies of fixed positions coexist with many passages between positions. In other words, each individual's life experience contains alternating exposure to structure and communitas, and to states and transitions.

Attributes of Liminal Entities

The phase of reaggregation in this case comprises the public installation of the Kanongesha with all pomp and ceremony. While this would be of the utmost interest in study of Ndembu chieftainship, and to an important trend in current British social anthropology, it does not concern us here. Our present focus is upon liminality and the ritual powers of the weak. These are shown under two aspects. First, Kafwana and the other Ndembu commoners are revealed as privileged to exert authority over the supreme authority figure of the tribe. In liminality, the underling comes uppermost. Second, the supreme political authority is portrayed "as a slave," recalling that aspect of the coronation of a pope in western Christendom when he is called upon to be the "*servus servorum Dei.*" Part of the rite has, of course, what Monica Wilson has called a "prophylactic function."[1] The chief has to exert self-control in the rites that he may be able to have self-mastery thereafter in face of the temptations of power. But the role of the humbled chief is only an extreme example of a recurrent theme of liminal situations. This theme is the stripping off of preliminal and postliminal attributes.

Let us look at the main ingredients of the Kumukindyila rites. The chief and his wife are dressed identically in a ragged waist-cloth and share the same name—mwadyi. This term is also applied to boys undergoing initiation and to a man's first wife in chronological order of marriage. It is an index of the anonymous state of "initiand." These attributes of sexlessness and anonymity are highly characteristic of liminality. In many kinds of initiation where the neophytes are of both sexes, males and females are dressed alike and referred to by the same term. This is true, for example, of many baptismal ceremonies in Christian or syncretist sects in Africa: for example, those of the *Bwiti* cult in the Gabon (James Fernandez; personal communication). It is also true of initiation into the Ndembu funerary association of Chiwila. Symbolically, all attributes that distinguish categories and groups in the structured social order are here in abeyance; the neophytes are merely entities in transition, as yet without place or position.

Other characteristics are submissiveness and silence. Not only the chief in the rites under discussion, but also neophytes in many *rites de passage* have to submit to an authority that is nothing less than that of the total community. This community is the repository of the whole gamut of the culture's values, norms, attitudes, sentiments, and relationships. Its representatives in the specific rites—and these may vary from ritual to ritual—represent the generic authority of tradition. In tribal societies, too, speech is not merely communication but also power and wisdom. The wisdom (*mana*) that is imparted in sacred liminality is not just an aggregation of words and sentences; it has ontological value, it refashions the very being of the neophyte. That is why, in the *Chisungu* rites of the Bemba, so well described by Audrey Richards, the secluded girl is said to be "grown into a woman" by the female elders—and she is so grown by the verbal and nonverbal instruction she receives in precept and symbol, especially by the revelation to her of tribal sacra in the form of pottery images.[2]

The neophyte in liminality must be a *tabula rasa*, a blank slate, on which is inscribed the knowledge and wisdom of the group, in those respects that pertain to the new status. The ordeals and humiliations, often of a grossly physiological character, to which neophytes are submitted represent partly a destruction of the previous status and partly a tempering of their essence in order to prepare them to cope with their new responsibilities and restrain them in advance from abusing their new privileges. They have to be shown that in themselves they are clay or dust, mere matter, whose form is impressed upon them by society.

Another liminal theme exemplified in the Ndembu installation rites is sexual continence. This is a pervasive theme of Ndembu ritual. Indeed, the resumption of sexual relations is usually a ceremonial mark of the return to society as a structure of statuses. While this is a feature of certain types of religious behavior in almost all societies, in preindustrial society, with its strong stress on kinship as the basis of many types of group affiliation, sexual continence has additional religious force. For kinship, or relations shaped by the idiom of kinship, is one of the main factors in structural differentiation. The undifferentiated character of liminality is reflected by the discontinuance of sexual relations and the absence of marked sexual polarity.

It is instructive to analyze the homiletic of Kafwana, in seeking to grasp the meaning of liminality. The reader will remember that he chided the chief-elect for his selfishness, meanness, theft, anger, witchcraft, and greed. All these vices represent the desire to possess for oneself what ought to be shared for the common good. An incumbent of high status is peculiarly tempted to use the authority vested in him by society to satisfy these private and privative wishes. But he should regard his privileges as gifts of the whole community, which in the final issue has an overright over all his actions. Structure and the high offices provided by structure are thus seen as instrumentalities of the commonweal, not as means of personal aggrandizement. The chief must not "keep his chieftainship to himself." He "must laugh with the people," and laughter (*ku-seha*) is for the Ndembu a "white" quality, and enters into the definition of "whiteness" or "white things." Whiteness represents the seamless web of connection that ideally ought to include both the living and the dead. It is right relation between, people, merely as human beings, and its fruits are health, strength, and all good things.

"White" laughter, for example, which is visibly manifested in the flashing of teeth, represents fellowship and good company. It is the reverse of pride (*winyi*), and the secret envies, lusts, and grudges that result behaviorally in witchcraft (*wuloji*), theft (*wukombi*), adultery (*kushimbana*), meanness (*chifwa*), and homicide (*wubanji*). Even when a man has become a chief, he must still be a member of the whole community of persons (*antu*), and show this by "laughing with them," respecting their rights, "welcoming everyone," and sharing food with them. The chastening function of liminality is not confined to this type of initiation but forms a component of many other types in many cultures. A well-known example is the medieval knight's vigil, during the night before he receives the accolade, when he has to pledge himself to serve the weak and the distressed and to meditate on his own unworthiness. His subsequent power is thought partially to spring from this profound immersion in humility.

The pedagogics of liminality, therefore, represent a condemnation of two kinds of separation from the generic bond of communitas. The first kind is to act only in terms of the rights conferred on one by the incumbency of office in the social structure. The second is to follow one's psychobiological urges at the expense of one's fellows. A mystical character is assigned to the sentiment of humankindness in most types of liminality, and in most cultures this stage of transition is brought closely in touch with beliefs in the protective and punitive powers of divine or preterhuman beings or powers. . . .

Millenarian Movements

Among the more striking manifestations of communitas are to be found the so-called millenarian religious movements. . . . The attributes of such movements will be well known to most of my readers. Here I would merely recall some of the properties of liminality in tribal rituals that I mentioned earlier. Many of these correspond pretty closely with those of millenarian

movements: homogeneity, equality, anonymity, absence of property (many movements actually enjoin on their members the destruction of what property they possess to bring nearer the coming of the perfect state of unison and communion they desire, for property rights are linked with structural distinctions both vertical and horizontal), reduction of all to the same status level, the wearing of uniform apparel (sometimes for both sexes), sexual continence (or its antithesis, sexual community, both continence and sexual community liquidate marriage and the family, which legitimate structural status), minimization of sex distinctions (all are "equal in the sight of God" or the ancestors), abolition of rank, humility, disregard for personal appearance, unselfishness, total obedience to the prophet or leader, sacred instruction, the maximization of religious, as opposed to secular, attitudes and behavior, suspension of kinship rights and obligations (all are siblings or comrades of one another regardless of previous secular ties), simplicity of speech and manners, sacred folly, acceptance of pain and suffering (even to the point of undergoing martyrdom), and so forth.

It is noteworthy that many of these movements cut right across tribal and national divisions during their initial momentum. Communitas, or the "open society," differs in this from structure, or the "closed society," in that it is potentially or ideally extensible to the limits of humanity. In practice, of course, the impetus soon becomes exhausted, and the "movement" becomes itself an institution among other institutions—often one more fanatical and militant than the rest, for the reason that it feels itself to be the unique bearer of universal-human truths. Mostly, such movements occur during phases of history that are in many respects "homologous" to the liminal periods of important rituals in stable and repetitive societies, when major groups or social categories in those societies are passing from one cultural state to another. They are essentially phenomena of transition. This is perhaps why in so many of these movements much of their mythology and symbolism is borrowed from those of traditional rites de passage, either in the cultures in which they originate or in the cultures with which they are in dramatic contact.

Hippies, Communitas, and the Powers of the Weak

In modern Western society, the values of communitas are strikingly present in the literature and behavior of what came to be known as the "beat generation," who were succeeded by the "hippies," who, in turn, have a junior division known as the "teeny-boppers." These are the "cool" members of the adolescent and young-adult categories—which do not have the advantages of national *rites de passage*—who "opt out" of the status-bound social order and acquire the stigmata of the lowly, dressing like "bums," itinerant in their habits, "folk" in their musical tastes, and menial in the casual employment they undertake. They stress personal relationships rather than social obligations, and regard sexuality as a polymorphic instrument of immediate communitas rather than as the basis for an enduring structured social tie. The poet Allen Ginsberg is particularly eloquent about the function of sexual freedom. The "sacred" properties often assigned to communitas are not lacking here, either: this can be seen in their frequent use of religious terms, such as "saint" and "angel," to describe their congeners and in their interest in Zen Buddhism. The Zen formulation "all is one, one is none, none is all" well expresses the global, unstructured character earlier applied to communitas. The hippie emphasis on spontaneity, immediacy, and "existence" throws into relief one of the senses in which communitas contrasts with structure. Communitas is of the now; structure is rooted in the past and extends into the future through language, law, and custom. While our focus here is on traditional preindustrial societies it becomes clear that the collective dimensions,

communitas and structure, are to be found at all stages and levels of culture and society.

Liminality, Low Status, and Communitas

The time has now come to make a careful review of a hypothesis that seeks to account for the attributes of such seemingly diverse phenomena as neophytes in the liminal phase of ritual, subjugated autochthones, small nations, court jesters, holy mendicants, good Samaritans, millenarian movements, "dharma bums," matrilaterality in patrilineal systems, patrilaterality in matrilineal systems, and monastic orders. Surely an ill-assorted bunch of social phenomena! Yet all have this common characteristic: they are persons or principles that (1) fall in the interstices of social structure, (2) are on its margins, or (3) occupy its lowest rungs. . . .

For me, communitas emerges where social structure is not. Perhaps the best way of putting this difficult concept into words is Martin Buber's—though I feel that perhaps he should be regarded as a gifted native informant rather than as a social scientist! Buber uses the term "community" for "communitas": "Community is the being no longer side by side (and, one might add, above and below) but with one another of a multitude of persons. And this multitude, though it moves towards one goal, yet experiences everywhere a turning to, a dynamic facing of, the others, a flowing from I to *Thou*. Community is where community happens."

Buber lays his finger on the spontaneous, immediate, concrete nature of communitas, as opposed to the norm-governed, institutionalized, abstract nature of social structure. Yet, communitas is made evident or accessible, so to speak, only through its juxtaposition to, or hybridization with, aspects of social structure. Just as in Gestalt psychology, figure and ground are mutually determinative, or, as some rare elements are never found in nature in their purity but only as components of chemical compounds, so communitas can be grasped only in some relation to structure. Just because the communitas component is elusive, hard to pin down, it is not unimportant. . . . Communitas, with its unstructured character, representing the "quick" of human interrelatedness, what Buber has called *das Zwischenmenschliche,* might well be represented by the "emptiness at the center," which is nevertheless indispensable to the functioning of the structure of the wheel. . . .

Communitas breaks in through the interstices of structure, in liminality; at the edges of structure, in marginality; and from beneath structure, in inferiority. It is almost everywhere held to be sacred or "holy," possibly because it transgresses or dissolves the norms that govern structured and institutionalized relationships and is accompanied by experiences of unprecedented potency. The processes of "leveling" and "stripping," to which Goffman has drawn our attention, often appear to flood their subjects with affect. Instinctual energies are surely liberated by these processes, but I am now inclined to think that communitas is not solely the product of biologically inherited drives released from cultural constraints. Rather is it the product of peculiarly human faculties, which include rationality, volition, and memory, and which develop with experience of life in society—just as among the Tallensi it is only mature men who undergo the experiences that induce them to receive *bakologo* shrines.

The notion that there is a generic bond between men, and its related sentiment of "humankindness," are not epiphenomena of some kind of herd instinct but are products of "men in their wholeness wholly attending." Liminality, marginality, and structural inferiority are conditions in which are frequently generated myths, symbols, rituals, philosophical systems, and works of art. These cultural forms provide men with a set of templates or models which are, at one level, periodical reclassifications of reality and man's relationship to society, nature, and culture. But they are more than classifications, since they incite men to action as well as

to thought. Each of these productions has a multivocal character, having many meanings, and each is capable of moving people at many psycho-biological levels simultaneously.

There is a dialectic here, for the immediacy of communitas gives way to the mediacy of structure, while, in *rites de passage,* men are released from structure into communitas only to return to structure revitalized by their experience of communitas. What is certain is that no society can function adequately without this dialectic. Exaggeration of structure may well lead to pathological manifestations of communitas outside or against "the law." Exaggeration of communitas, in certain religious or political movements of the leveling type, may be speedily followed by despotism, overbureaucratization, or other modes of structural rigidification. For, like the neophytes in the African circumcision lodge, or the Benedictine monks, or the members of a millenarian movement, those living in community seem to require, sooner or later, an absolute authority, whether this be a religious commandment, a divinely inspired leader, or a dictator. Communitas cannot stand alone if the material and organizational needs of human beings are to be adequately met. Maximization of communitas provokes maximization of structure, which in its turn produces revolutionary strivings for renewed communitas. The history of any great society provides evidence at the political level for this oscillation. . . .

Modalities of Communitas

. . . Essentially, communitas is a relationship between concrete, historical, idiosyncratic individuals. These individuals are not segmentalized into roles and statuses but confront one another rather in the manner of Martin Buber's "I and Thou." Along with this direct, immediate, and total confrontation of human identities, there tends to go a model of society as a homogeneous, unstructured communitas, whose boundaries are ideally coterminous with those of the human species. Communitas is in this respect strikingly different from Durkheimian "solidarity," the force of which depends upon an in-group/out-group contrast. . . . But the spontaneity and immediacy of communitas—as opposed to the jural-political character of structure—can seldom be maintained for very long. Communitas itself soon develops a structure, in which free relationships between individuals become converted into norm-governed relationships between social personae. Thus, it is necessary to distinguish between: (1) *existential* or *spontaneous* communitas approximately what the hippies today would call "a happening,". . . (2) *normative* communitas, where, under the influence of time, the need to mobilize and organize resources, and the necessity for social control among the members of the group in pursuance of these goals, the existential communitas is organised into a perduring social system; and (3) *ideological* communitas, which is a label one can apply to a variety of utopian models of societies based on existential communitas.

Ideological communitas is at once an attempt to describe the external and visible effects—the outward form, it might be said—of an inward experience of existential communitas, and to spell out the optimal social conditions under which such experiences might be expected to flourish and multiply. Both normative and ideological communitas are already within the domain of structure, and it is the fate of all spontaneous communitas in history to undergo what most people see as a "decline and fall" into structure and law. In religious movements of the communitas type, it is not only the charisma of the leaders that is "routinized" but also the communitas of their first disciples and followers. . . .

Furthermore, structure tends to be pragmatic and this-worldly; while communitas is often speculative and generates imagery and philosophical ideas. One example of this contrast, to which our seminar gave a great deal of attention, is that kind of normative communitas that characterizes the liminal phase of tribal initiation rites. . . .

In our seminar, also, we frequently came across instances, in religion and literature, in which normative and ideological communitas are symbolized by structurally inferior categories, groups, types, or individuals, ranging from the mother's brother in patrilineal societies, to conquered autochthonous peoples, Tolstoy's peasants, Gandhi's *harijans,* and the "holy poor" or "God's poor" of medieval Europe. For example, today's hippies, like yesterday's Franciscans, assume the attributes of the structurally inferior in order to achieve communitas.

Ideological and Spontaneous Communitas

The scattered clues and indications we have encountered in preliterate and preindustrial societies of the existence in their cultures, notably in liminality and structural inferiority, of the egalitarian model we have called normative communitas, become in complex and literate societies, both ancient and modern, a positive torrent of explicitly formulated views on how men may best live together in comradely harmony. Such views may be called, as we have just noted, ideological communitas. In order to convey the wide generality of these formulations of the ideal structureless domain, I would like to adduce, almost at random, evidence from sources far removed from one another in space and time. In these sources, both religious and secular, a fairly regular connection is maintained between liminality, structural inferiority, lowermost status, and structural outsiderhood on the one hand, and, on the other, such universal human values as peace and harmony between all men, fertility, health of mind and body, universal justice, comradeship and brotherhood between all men, the equality before God, the law or the life force of men and women, young and old, and persons of all races and ethnic groups. And of especial importance in all these utopian formulations is the persisting adhesion between equality and absence of property. . . .

To my mind, the "essential We" has a liminal character, since perdurance implies institutionalization and repetition, while community (which roughly equals spontaneous communitas) is always completely unique, and hence socially transient. At times Buber appears to be misled about the feasibility of converting this experience of mutuality into structural forms. Spontaneous communitas can never be adequately expressed in a structural form, but it may arise unpredictably at any time between human beings who are institutionally reckoned or defined as members of any or all kinds of social groupings, or of none. Just as in preliterate society the social and individual developmental cycles are punctuated by more or less prolonged instants of ritually guarded and stimulated liminality, each with its core of potential communitas, so the phase structure of social life in complex societies is also punctuated, but without institutionalized provocations and safeguards, by innumerable instants of spontaneous communitas.

In preindustrial and early industrial societies with multiplex social relations, spontaneous communitas appears to be very frequently associated with mystical power and to be regarded as a charism or grace sent by the deities or ancestors. Nevertheless, by impetrative ritual means, attempts are made, mostly in the phases of liminal seclusion, to cause the deities or ancestors to bring this charism of communitas among men. But there is no specific social form that is held to express spontaneous communitas. Rather is it expected best to arise in the intervals between incumbencies of social positions and statuses, in what used to be known as "the interstices of the social structure." In complex industrialized societies, we still find traces in the liturgies of churches and other religious organizations of institutionalized attempts to prepare for the coming of spontaneous communitas.

This modality of relationship, however, appears to flourish best in spontaneously liminal situations—phases betwixt and between states where social-structural role-playing is dominant, and especially between status equals. . . .

Once more we come back to the necessity of seeing man's social life as a process, or rather as a multiplicity of processes, in which the character of one type of phase—where communitas is paramount—differs deeply, even abysmally, from that of all others. The great human temptation, found most prominently among utopians, is to resist giving up the good and pleasurable qualities of that one phase to make way for what may be the necessary hardships and dangers of the next. Spontaneous communitas is richly charged with affects, mainly pleasurable ones. Life in "structure" is filled with objective difficulties: decisions have to be made, inclinations sacrificed to the wishes and needs of the group, and physical and social obstacles overcome at some personal cost. Spontaneous communitas has something "magical" about it. Subjectively there is in it the feeling of endless power. But this power untransformed cannot readily be applied to the organizational details of social existence. It is no substitute for lucid thought and sustained will. On the other hand, structural action swiftly becomes arid and mechanical if those involved in it are not periodically immersed in the regenerative abyss of communitas. Wisdom is always to find the appropriate relationship between structure and communitas under the given circumstances of time and place, to accept each modality when it is paramount without rejecting the other, and not to cling to one when its present impetus is spent.

NOTES

1. Monica Wilson, *Rituals of Kinship among the Nyakyusa* (London: Oxford University Press, 1957), pp. 46–54.

2. Audrey Richards, *Chisungu* (London: Faber and Faber, 1956).

Counterpoint:
From *Fragmentation and Redemption:*
Essays on Gender and the Human Body in Medieval Religion

CAROLINE WALKER BYNUM

Caroline Walker Bynum teaches at Columbia University where she is now a dean. Besides some edited works, she has published the following books: *Holy Feast and Holy Fast: The Religious Significance of Food to Medieval Women; Jesus as Mother: Studies in the Spirituality of the High Middle Ages; Resurrection of the Body in Western Christianity 200–1336; Docere verbo et exemplo: An Aspect of Twelfth-Century Spirituality;* and *Metamorphosis and Identity.*

. . . AND IT SEEMS CLEAR to me that Victor Turner's own sense of what he is up to, taken very broadly, is appealing to any historian of religion. Turner's notion of the fundamental units of social reality as dramas builds temporality and change into all analysis; Turner's sense of dominant symbols as multivocal requires that symbols and ritual be understood in their social context; Turner's emphasis on the "orectic" (sensory) pole of meaning enables students of religion to talk of emotional, psychological and spiritual elements that psychohistory has tried, woefully unsuccessfully, I fear, to introduce into historical analysis. Therefore, in concluding that certain of Turner's theories seriously misrepresent the complexity of religious experience, I shall not be suggesting that anthropology and history are incompatible. Rather, I shall be arguing both that some of Turner's generalizations violate the subtlety of his own methodological commitments and that Turner's theory of religion is inadequate because it is based implicitly on the Christianity of a particular class, gender and historical period.

Second, I do not intend to provide a critique of Turner's own application of his theory to the European Middle Ages, particularly in his well-known essays on Thomas Becket and Francis of Assisi. It would be easy to show that, compared to the richness of Turner's analysis of Ndembu ritual, his sense of twelfth- and thirteenth-century symbols is thin. "Poverty" to Francis, the *imitatio Christi* or *via crucis* to Becket, become in Turner's own hands almost "signs" rather than "symbols"; they lose much of the multivocality they unquestionably have in their own historical context. For all Turner's effort to use a social drama analysis, his history of the Franciscan order sounds remarkably like the history of the institutionalization and, therefore, corruption of a dream that was the standard interpretation of Francis until recently. His discussion of Becket does not advance much beyond the picture of radical conversion from one ideal to another, which has always been seen as the crux of the matter—in legend and literature as well as in the work of historians. It is not surprising that Turner uses Turner's model best when he knows the society under study most deeply. And indeed, one is struck by the fact that even in his most recent writings, the Ndembu examples are the most powerful—the clearest, most precise, most analytical and cogent—whereas the modern examples are

From *Caroline Walker Bynum,* Fragmentation and Redemption *(New York: Zone Books, 1991).*

often tossed in without the care or the elaboration necessary to make the analysis convincing. But for me to suggest simply that Turner could sometimes do a Turnerian analysis better than he does would contribute nothing to a study of Turner's model.

What I want to do, therefore, is to apply to my own research in the later Middle Ages Turner's notion of social drama as underlying both narrative and ritual. I want to focus especially on two aspects of Turner's notion of social drama, namely his understanding of "dominant symbols" (particularly as elaborated in the *Forest of Symbols* [1967]) and his notion of the central place in what he calls "liminality" of images of status reversal or status elevation (particularly as elaborated in *The Ritual Process* [1969] and in subsequent works). I understand Turner to be arguing at his most general (and he is frequently quite general) that human experience, at least a great part of the time, occurs in units Turner calls "social dramas" (a subset of what he calls "processual units") namely, that it takes a four-stage form: breach between social elements, crisis, adjustment or redress, and, finally, either reintegration of the group or person or "element" into the social structure or recognition of irreparable breach. This social drama, to Turner, underlies both narrative (that is, the way we tell our important stories) and ritual (that is, the way we behave when we perform or enact certain formal, prescribed patterns that not only express but also move us into and elaborate our shared values). It is in the third stage that we find what Turner calls, borrowing the idea from van Gennep, "liminality"—a moment of suspension of normal rules and roles, a crossing of boundaries and violating of norms, that enables us to understand those norms, even (or perhaps especially) where they conflict, and move on either to incorporate or reject them.[1] In the specific form of social drama called ritual, we find that rituals of life-crisis (that is, change in life-status: for example, puberty or election as chief) often use images of inversion in the liminal stage (for example, the initiate becomes a

"fool" or a "woman"). Calendrical rituals (that is, those that celebrate the recurring pattern of the year: for example, harvest rituals) often use images of status elevation (for example, children wear masks of adults or of monsters at Halloween). Especially central in the liminal stage of ritual are what Turner calls "dominant symbols"—symbols that "condense" and "unify" into a moment disparate *significata* and bring together two poles of meaning: normative and emotional. A dominant symbol (for example, the Ndembu milk tree) can, therefore, only be understood in the context in which it is experienced. There it has meaning that includes as much the sensory, natural and physiological facts to which it refers (for example, milk, food, nurture, nursing, breasts, etc.) as the disparate social values for which it may stand (for example—in the case of the milk tree—both tribal custom and matriliny, on the one hand, and, on the other, conflict between mother and daughter, men and women). From such fine and multitextured analysis of symbol and story, Turner sometimes moves on—quite a bit less successfully—to general cultural critique, calling for the liminoid (that is, the liminal-like) in modern life and cautiously praising *communitas,* his term for that feeling of union with one's fellow human beings which in preindustrial societies was released in the liminal phase of ritual.

There are some obvious problems with applying Turner's writings to historical research, not least among them the fact that Turner does not have a complete and coherent theory to the extent that Geertz and Lévi-Strauss do. As I indicated above, all Turner's ideas involve in some way the insight that, in explaining human experience, one is explaining process or drama rather than structure, and that liminality or suspension of social and normative structures is a crucial moment in the process. But the very fact that periods of liminality provide escape from roles and critiques of structures (in a functionalist sense of "structure") indicates that Turner has in certain ways never left the functionalist anthropology in which he was trained. And

Turner himself, however quick he may have been to provide commentary on modernity, has said repeatedly that for the industrialized world "liminality" is only a metaphor. It is, therefore, not certain either how far Turner's insights fit together into a system or how many of Turner's own insights Turner himself thinks applicable to the European Middle Ages, a society between "primitive" and industrial. I do not, however, want either to create a single "Turner theory" or to criticize such a theory by doing an exegesis of Turner. Others can do that better than I— Turner himself among them. Rather, I want to apply what clearly are some of Turner's insights—his notions of narrative, of dominant symbol and of the imagery of reversal and elevation—to my work on later medieval piety. Since Turner himself has extrapolated from analysis of ritual in "primitive" societies to more general theories about symbols and stories, I feel free to test his ideas against the religious texts that are the major source for historians of the Middle Ages. I want to show how certain of Turner's ideas, especially his sensitive and subtle notion of dominant symbols, enable me to describe aspects of European religiosity for which scholars have long needed terms. But I also want to argue that there are places where Turner's notions fail to describe what I find in my research, that those places fit into a pattern, and that this pattern suggests a fundamental limitation in the Turnerian idea of liminality, at least in the extended or metaphorical sense of Turner's later writings.

In evaluating Turner's social drama model and his theory of symbol, I want to concentrate on a major form of medieval narrative, the saint's life, and on a major Christian ritual or dominant symbol, the eucharist. I chose these initially because they seem to be the most obvious illustrations of Turner's ideas. . . . But as I have explored more closely the relationship of Turner's models to these medieval stories and symbols, a curious fact has emerged. Turner's ideas describe the stories and symbols of men better than those of women. Women's stories insofar as they can be discerned behind the tales told by male biographers are in fact less processual than men's; they don't have turning points. And when women recount their own lives, the themes are less climax, conversion, reintegration and triumph, the liminality of reversal or elevation, than continuity. Moreover, women's images and symbols—which, according to Turner's model, should reflect either inversion (for example, poverty) insofar as women are superior (for example, of aristocratic status), or elevation (for example, maleness, military prowess) insofar as women *qua* women are inferior—do not quite do either. Rather, they continue or enhance in image (for example, bride, sick person) what the woman's ordinary experience is, so that one either has to see the woman's religious stance as permanently liminal or as never quite becoming so.

These observations suggest to me that Turner's theory of religion may be based, more than he is aware, on the particular form of Christianity (with its strong emphasis on world denial and inversion of images) that has characterized elites in the Western tradition—educated elites, aristocratic elites and male elites. We will, however, understand this only if we use the category of gender very carefully. For my examination of Turner in no way implies that he fails to look at women either in his theory or in his fieldwork (where surely his analysis of women's rituals has been both extensive and subtle). In many places he suggests that women are liminal or that women, as marginals, generate communitas. What I am suggesting is exactly that Turner looks at women; he stands with the dominant group (males) and sees women (both as symbol and as fact) as liminal to men. In this he is quite correct, of course, and the insight is a powerful one. But it is not the whole story. The historian or anthropologist needs to stand with women as well. And when Turner attempts to stand with the inferior, he assumes symmetry—that is, he assumes that the inferior are exactly the reverse of the superior. If the superior in society generate images of lowliness in liminality, the inferior will generate images of power. To use Turner's own example, ghetto teenagers in Chicago have first and second vice presidents in their street gangs. My research indicates that such things are very rare and that the images generated by the inferior are usually not reversals or elevations at all. Thus, liminality itself—as fully elaborated by Turner—may be less a universal moment of meaning needed by human beings as they move through social dramas than an escape for those who bear the burdens and reap the benefits of a high place in the social structure. As recent liberation theologians have pointed out, it is the powerful who express imitation of Christ as (voluntary) poverty, (voluntary) nudity and (voluntary) weakness. But the involuntary poor usually express their *imitatio Christi* not as wealth and exploitation but as struggle.[2]

Male and Female Stories

Let me now turn to the later Middle Ages to illustrate the strengths and limitations of Turner's notion of liminality. First, then, the stories and symbols of men.

Male lives from the twelfth to the fifteenth centuries—both as lived and as told—may be nicely explicated as social dramas. As one would expect for religious virtuosi, charismatic figures and saints, the liminal phase usually issues in breach with previous role and previous group—that is, in conversion. Images of reversal and inversion are dominant in the converted life, particularly at moments of transition. If we take as an example one of the most famous of all medieval biographies, Bonaventure's life of Francis, we find that the story is not only told as a series of successful crises, breaches with former status and life, but also that Francis, the wealthy merchant's son, adopts images of poverty, nudity, weakness, even of femaleness, at key moments. At the two most decisive breaches of a life filled with crisis—that is, when he renounces his earthly father and when he dies—

Francis takes off all his clothes.[3] These two moments are each accompanied by adoption of disease and suffering (in the first case, dwelling among lepers; in the second, union with the crucifix in stigmata).[4] And the moment of conversion is a moment of womanly fertility: Bonaventure tells us that Francis took off his clothes and his shoes, renounced his father, threw away his money, prayed to Mary, and like her gave birth to his first child (his first disciple).[5] When the pope first rejects and later accepts Francis, Francis tells the story of a poor woman (by implication himself) who bears children of the Holy Spirit;[6] three women meet Francis and address him as "Lady Poverty";[7] Bonaventure suggests that ministers are fathers and preachers, but Francis, who insisted on remaining layman rather than cleric, is a mother, laboring for her children by example—that is, by suffering birth pangs.[8] Francis is described as cradling all creation—from a rabbit to the baby Jesus—in his arms as a mother.[9] But Francis's renunciation of his earthly father is decisive; real change occurs. And, in Bonaventure's prose, the Francis who returns from being crucified in the stigmata is now a "knight," a captain of Christ's army, sealed (for all his lay status) by the seal of Christ the High Priest.[10] In death Francis is described as founder and leader, model and exemplar, and father of his friars.[11] The life is a drama. The story told of it is a drama. From the liminality of weakness, nudity and womanliness comes the leader and model who changes the religious life of the thirteenth century.

Not only are male lives social dramas; men themselves use images of reversal to express liminality. And chief among these images is woman—as fact and as symbol . . . Men frequently describe not only themselves but even Christ and God as female and, as I have argued in *Jesus as Mother*, such descriptions are frequently part of their anxiety over administrative responsibilities. Abbots and novice masters in the throes of self-doubt about their leadership talk of themselves and their God as tender and maternal. "Woman" was clearly outside medieval European notions of social structure, as Georges Duby repeatedly emphasizes in his study of the "three orders" of society;[12] and male writers clearly saw the image of the "female" (virgin, bride or mother) as an image for the male self when it escaped those three orders. . . .

To the well-known fact that men described themselves as women in moments or statuses of liminality, we can add the less commonly observed fact that men had recourse to actual women as liminal. Hildegard of Bingen, Birgitta of Sweden, Catherine of Siena and Joan of Arc are only the most obvious examples of women whose visions, attained while they were in a state of radical apartness (underlined by virginity or illness or low social status), were for men a means of escape from and reintegration into status and power. Two important biographers of the early thirteenth century, Thomas of Cantimpré and James of Vitry, created, through a number of lives, the image of the holy woman as critique of, reproach to, and solution for male pride, ambition and irreligiosity. The biographers of two Franciscan ternaries, Angela of Foligno and Margaret of Cortona, see these women as "mothers" who have only "sons"— that is, the local friars for whom they provide healing, visions, advice, rebuke and comfort.[13] . . .

Although a powerful and sometimes threatening image to the men who encountered it, so much so that they perhaps saw female cross-dressing where none existed, to women it was a means to change roles. In the later Middle Ages, it is male biographers who describe women as "virile" when they make religious progress. To men, women reverse images and "become men" in renouncing the world. But medieval women do not describe themselves as men as a way of asserting either humility or spiritual prowess. Women either describe themselves as truly androgynous (that is, they use male and female images without a strong sense of a given set of personality characteristics going

with the one or the other gender) or as female (bride, lover, mother). . . .

The point I am making here is an obvious one. Women could not take off all their clothes and walk away from their fathers or husbands, as did Francis. Simple social facts meant that most women's dramas were incomplete. And there may be psychological reasons for women's images as well as social ones. Ramanujan, who has found a similar pattern in the lives of female Indian saints, has argued, using Nancy Chodorow's psychological research, that women are in general less likely to use images of gender reversal or to experience life-decisions as sharp ruptures because women, raised by women, mature into a continuous self whereas boys, also raised by women, must undergo one basic reversal (i.e., from wanting to "be" their mothers to acceptance of being fathers).[14]

The Eucharist as Symbol to Men and Women

If we turn from women's stories to women's symbols, we find that certain aspects of Turner's approach are extremely helpful. Although Western Christianity had few women's rituals, certain key Christian rituals and symbols were especially important in women's spirituality in the later Middle Ages. One of these was the eucharist. And if one applies to late medieval eucharistic devotion Turner's notion of "dominant symbol," much that was before neglected or obscure becomes clear. Turner's idea of symbols as polysemic or multivocal, as including in some real sense the physiological and natural processes to which they refer as well as normative and social structural abstractions, provides a welcome escape from the way in which the eucharist and its related devotions have usually been treated by liturgists, historians of theology and literary historians.

Such historians have frequently assumed that a devotion or an experience is "explained" once its literary ancestors or theological content are found: thus, Dorothy of Montau's quite physical pregnancy (swelling) with Christ before receiving the eucharist is explained by the biblical metaphor of the good soul as Christ's mother (Mark 3.35); Margery Kempe's cuddling with Christ in bed is simply a case of an uneducated woman taking literally metaphors from the Song of Songs. Turners sense of ritual as process or drama moves us beyond this old-style history of theology or literature with its search for sources toward the new "history of spirituality"—where "spirituality" really means "lived religion." . . .

When we turn to the eucharist in particular, Turner's notion of symbol as involving in some deep way a "likeness" between the orectic (the sensory) and the abstract or normative poles of meaning redirects our attention to the fact that the communion was food. People were eating God. The eucharist, albeit a recapitulation of Christ's execution, was not therefore a symbol of death but of life, birth and nursing. As I have argued elsewhere, it stood for Christ's humanness and therefore for ours. By eating it and, in that eating, fusing with Christ's hideous physical suffering, the Christian not so much escaped as became the human. By "saturating," as Turner puts it, the fact of eating, the eucharist itself summed up the asceticism (denial of the body, especially through fasting) and the antidualism (joy in creation and in physicality), which were part of medieval Catholicism. Not merely a mechanism of social control, a way of requiring yearly confession and therefore submission to the supervision of local clergy, the eucharist was itself both intensely feared and intensely desired. As symbol, it encapsulated two themes in late medieval devotion: an audacious sense of closeness to the divine (Christians ate Jesus!) and a deep fear of the awfulness of God (if one ate without being worthy, one ate one's own destruction!). Moreover, processual analysis helps us to see that the liturgy surrounding the eucharist was a drama. Thus, we understand that when, in the thirteenth century, elevation of the host came to replace either consecration

or reception of the elements as the climax of the ritual, the entire meaning was changed. God came to be taken in through the eyes rather than the mouth; he was thus taken in most fully where ecstatic, out-of-body experiences added a deeper level of "seeing" to bodily seeing.[15]

But if Turner's notion of dominant symbol is useful in deepening any historian's understanding of this central Christian ritual, certain problems arise in seeing women's relationship to the eucharist in particular as processual. Turner's model would predict that, for women (excluded in theory from Church office because of social and ontological inferiority), the eucharist would express status elevations. To a limited extent, this is what we find. Women occasionally—although only very occasionally—feel empowered to act in a priestly capacity by their reception of the eucharist, or see themselves (or other women) in vision as priests. Gertrude of Helfta, Angela of Foligno, and Lukardis of Oberweimar, among others, receive from Christ in the eucharist the power to preach, teach and criticize, to hear confessions and pronounce absolution, to administer the eucharist to others. More frequently, women's visions criticize clerical incompetence or immorality. But the women, released into another role in vision and image, never, of course, actually become priests. And such visions, exactly as Turner's model would predict, serve as much to integrate the female ecstatic into basic Christian structures as to liberate her from them when they fail her. In some visions, recipient is elevated above celebrant, as when the host flies away from the corrupt priest into the mouth of the deserving nun or when Christ himself brings the cup to a woman who has been forbidden to receive it exactly because of her ecstatic possession. But the very fact that the majority of visions that project women into power through reversed images actually occur in the context of the eucharist ultimately only integrates the woman more fully into clerically controlled structures.

In order to have visions, she must attend the liturgy, controlled by exactly that clergy which her visions might seem to bypass or criticize. . . .

Of course, if one starts by assuming Turner's notion of "antistructure," one may describe this "structureless" aspect of woman's religious life by Turner's term *communitas*. But Turner's *communitas* is the antithesis to structure: the source for it, the release from it, the critique of it. What I am describing here is not something that "breaks into society through the interstices of structure" but something both simpler and more central: a normal aspect of women's lives. If one looks with women rather than at women, women's lives are not liminal to women—but neither, except in a very partial way, are male roles or male experiences.

Medieval women, like men, chose to speak of themselves as brides, mothers and sisters of Christ. But to women this was an accepting and continuing of what they were; to men, it was reversal. Indeed, all women's central images turn out to be continuities. Equally important for women, in eucharist and in ecstasy, were images of eating and images of illness—and both eating and illness were fundamentally expressions of the woman's physicality. Told by the theological and exegetical tradition that they represented the material, the physical, the appetitive and lustful whereas men represented soul or mind, women elaborated images of self that underlined natural processes. And in these images, the woman's physical "humanness" was "saved," given meaning by joining with the human-divine Christ. Illness, self-induced or God-given, was identification with the Crucifixion; eating was consuming and being consumed by the human body that was also God. We should not be misled by modern notions of illness or of brides as images of passivity. When the woman saw herself as bride or lover, the image was deeply active and fully sensual; when the woman sought illness as fact and as metaphor, it was a fully active fusing with the death agonies of Christ. Although each of these women's symbols is complex in ways I cannot

elaborate here, none is in any obvious sense either elevation or reversal. . . .

My work on late medieval religiosity thus indicates that Turner's notion of liminality, in the expanded, "metaphorical" sense which he has used for nonprimitive societies, is applicable only to men. Only men's stories are full social dramas; only men's symbols are full reversals. Women are fully liminal only to men. I do not think the problem lies in the fact that later medieval Europe is a society that presented a far greater variety of roles and possibility of choice than the society of the Ndembu, for which Turner first began to formulate his processual anthropology. If this were so, I would not find both his specific and his general insights so useful for understanding male stories. Bonaventure's view of Francis and James of Vitry's view of Mary of Oignies seem well described and deeply penetrated when scrutinized through the lens of "liminality." The problem seems rather to be that the dichotomy of structure and chaos, from which liminality or *communitas* is a release, is a special issue for elites, for those who in a special sense are the structures. A model that focuses on this need for release as the ultimate sociopsychological need may best fit the experience of elites. Indeed, in the Western tradition, such a model may, however unwittingly, arise from a particular form of Christianity that has been that of the elites. The model of Jesus as poor, naked, defenseless, suffering, tender and womanly—which was particularly popular in the later Middle Ages—was an idea that especially appealed to the lower aristocracy and the new urban, merchant class.[16] . . . What women's images and stories expressed most fundamentally was neither reversal nor elevation but continuity.

I would object to any effort to make my description of women's images at a particular moment in the Western tradition either universalist or prescriptive. A good deal of what seems to me irresponsible theologizing about women has been done recently, based on a superficial understanding of the history of Christianity; and certain claims about women's need for female symbols or for affectivity or for the unstructured are among the most empty and ill-informed. Indeed, they may succumb to something of the same stereotype of "the female" that is built into Turner's notion of women as liminal for men. But my description of how actual women's stories and symbols function in the later Middle Ages does raise doubts about Turner's notion of liminality as universalist and prescriptive. Perhaps, after all, "social drama" and van Gennep's concept of liminality are less generalizable than Turner supposed and speak less fully to the complexity of human experience.

These doubts, however, throw us back exactly to the implications of the very best of the work of the early Victor Turner. Insofar as I am arguing that we must, at least some of the time, stand with those whom we study, Turner has already said it. If symbols are, in fact, multivocal, condensing and lived, we will understand them only when we look with as well as over and beyond the participants who use them, feeling as well as knowing their dramas in their own context. My critique of Turner's theory of liminality is thus one he might have given himself.

NOTES

1. See Arnold van Gennep, *The Rites of Passage,* trans. M. B. Vizedom and G. L. Caffee (1908; reprint, London: Routledge & Kegan Paul, 1960).

2. Gustavo Gutierrez, *A Theology of Liberation: History, Politics and Salvation,* trans. Caridad Inda and John Eagleson (Maryknoll, NY: Orbis Books, 1973), especially ch. 3, pp. 287–306.

3. Bonaventure, *The Life of St. Francis,* in *Bonaventure: The Soul's Journey into God* . . . , trans. E. Cousins (New York: Paulist Press, 1978), pp. 193–94, 317.

4. Bonaventure, *Life of Francis,* pp. 195, 303–07.

5. Ibid., pp. 199–200.

6. Ibid., pp. 204–06.

7. Ibid., p. 243.

8. Ibid., pp. 251–52.

9. Ibid., pp. 257, 278.

10. Ibid., pp. 311–13.

11. Ibid., p. 321.

12. Georges Duby, *The Three Orders: Feudal Society Imagined,* trans. Arthur Goldhammer (Chicago: University of Chicago Press, 1980), pp. 89, 95, 131–33.

13. *The Book of Divine Consolation of the Blessed Angela of Foligno,* trans. M. G. Steegmann (Reprint New York: Cooper Square, 1966); "The Life of Margaret of Cortona," in J. Bollandus and G. Henschius (eds.) *Acta sanctorum* . . . *editio novissima,* ed. J. Carnandet et. al. (Paris: Palmé, etc. 1863).

14. A. K. Ramanujan, "On Women Saints," in J. Hawley and D. M. Wulff (eds.) *The Divine Consort: Radha and the Goddesses of India* (Berkeley: Berkeley Religious Studies Series, 1982), pp. 316–24; and Nancy Chodorow, *The Reproduction of Mothering: Psychoanalysis and the Sociology of Gender* (Berkeley: University of California Press, 1978).

15. See Jungmann, *Mass,* vol. 2, pp. 120–22, 206ff; Peter Browne, *Die Verehrung der Eucharistie im Mittelalter* (Munich: Hueber, 1933); and Edouard Dumoutet, *Corpus Domini: Aux sources de la piété eucharistique médiévale* (Paris: Beauchesne, 1942).

16. Grundmann, *Religiöse Bewegungen.*

From *The Interpretation of Cultures*

CLIFFORD GEERTZ

CULTURE, this acted document, thus is public, like a burlesqued wink or a mock sheep raid. Though ideational, it does not exist in someone's head; though unphysical, it is not an occult entity. The interminable, because unterminable, debate within anthropology as to whether culture is "subjective" or "objective," together with the mutual exchange of intellectual insults ("idealist!"—"materialist!"; "mentalist!"—"behaviorist!"; "impressionist!"—"positivist!") which accompanies it, is wholly misconceived. Once human behavior is seen as (most of the time; there *are* true twitches) symbolic action—action which, like phonation in speech, pigment in painting, line in writing, or sonance in music, signifies—the question as to whether culture is patterned conduct or a frame of mind, or even the two somehow mixed together, loses sense. The thing to ask about a burlesqued wink or a mock sheep raid is not what their ontological status is. It is the same as that of rocks on the one hand and dreams on the other—they are things of this world. The thing to ask is what their import is: what it is, ridicule or challenge, irony or anger, snobbery or pride, that, in their occurrence and through their agency, is getting said.

This may seem like an obvious truth, but there are a number of ways to obscure it. One is to imagine that culture is a self-contained "superorganic" reality with forces and purposes of its own; that is, to reify it. Another is to claim that it consists in the brute pattern of behavioral events we observe in fact to occur in some identifiable community or other; that is, to reduce it. But though both these confusions still exist, and doubtless will be always with us, the main source of theoretical muddlement in contemporary anthropology is a view which developed in reaction to them and is right now very widely held—namely, that, to quote Ward Goodenough, perhaps its leading proponent, "culture [is located] in the minds and hearts of men."

Variously called ethnoscience, componential analysis, or cognitive anthropology (a terminological wavering which reflects a deeper uncertainty), this school of thought holds that culture is composed of psychological structures by means of which individuals or groups of individuals guide their behavior. "A society's culture," to quote Goodenough again, this time in a passage which has become the *locus classicus* of the whole movement, "consists of whatever it is one has to know or believe in order to operate in a manner acceptable to its members." And from this view of what culture is follows a view, equally assured, of what describing it is—the writing out of systematic rules, an ethnographic algorithm, which, if followed, would make it possible so to operate, to pass (physical appearance aside) for a native. In such a way, extreme subjectivism is married to extreme formalism, with the expected result: an explosion of debate as to whether particular analyses (which come in the form of taxonomies, paradigms, tables, trees, and other ingenuities) reflect what the natives "really" think or are merely clever simulations, logically equivalent but substantively different, of what they think.

As, on first glance, this approach may look close enough to the one being developed here to be mistaken for it, it is useful to be explicit as to what divides them. If, leaving our winks and sheep behind for the moment, we take, say, a

Reprinted from Clifford Geertz, The Interpretation of Cultures *(New York: Basic Books, 1973).*

Beethoven quartet as an, admittedly rather special but, for these purposes, nicely illustrative, sample of culture, no one would, I think, identify it with its score, with the skills and knowledge needed to play it, with the understanding of it possessed by its performers or auditors, nor, to take care, *en passant,* of the reductionists and reifiers, with a particular performance of it or with some mysterious entity transcending material existence. The "no one" is perhaps too strong here, for there are always incorrigibles. But that a Beethoven quartet is a temporally developed tonal structure, a coherent sequence of modeled sound—in a word, music—and not anybody's knowledge of or belief about anything, including how to play it, is a proposition to which most people are, upon reflection, likely to assent. . . .

Culture is public because meaning is. You can't wink (or burlesque one) without knowing what counts as winking or how, physically, to contract your eyelids, and you can't conduct a sheep raid (or mimic one) without knowing what it is to steal a sheep and how practically to go about it. But to draw from such truths the conclusion that knowing how to wink is winking and knowing how to steal a sheep is sheep raiding is to betray as deep a confusion as, taking thin descriptions for thick, to identify winking with eyelid contractions or sheep raiding with chasing woolly animals out of pastures. The cognitivist fallacy—that culture consists (to quote another spokesman for the movement, Stephen Tyler) of "mental phenomena which can [he means "should"] be analyzed by formal methods similar to those of mathematics and logic"—is as destructive of an effective use of the concept as are the behaviorist and idealist fallacies to which it is a misdrawn correction. Perhaps, as its errors are more sophisticated and its distortions subtler, it is even more so. . . .

In short, anthropological writings are themselves interpretations, and second and third order ones to boot. (By definition, only a "native" makes first order ones: it's *his* culture.) They are, thus, fictions; fictions, in the sense that they are "something made," "something fashioned"—the original meaning of *fictiō*—not that they are false, unfactual, or merely "as if" thought experiments. To construct actor-oriented descriptions of the involvements of a Berber chieftain, a Jewish merchant, and a French soldier with one another in 1912 Morocco is clearly an imaginative act, not all that different from constructing similar descriptions of, say, the involvements with one another of a provincial French doctor, his silly, adulterous wife, and her feckless lover in nineteenth century France. In the latter case, the actors are represented as not having existed and the events as not having happened, while in the former they are represented as actual, or as having been so. This is a difference of no mean importance; indeed, precisely the one Madame Bovary had difficulty grasping. But the importance does not lie in the fact that her story was created while Cohen's was only noted. The conditions of their creation, and the point of it (to say nothing of the manner and the quality) differ. But the one is as much a *fictiō*—"a making"—as the other.

Anthropologists have not always been as aware as they might be of this fact: that although culture exists in the trading post, the hill fort, or the sheep run, anthropology exists in the book, the article, the lecture, the museum display, or, sometimes nowadays, the film. To become aware of it is to realize that the line between mode of representation and substantive content is as undrawable in cultural analysis as it is in painting; and that fact in turn seems to threaten the objective status of anthropological knowledge by suggesting that its source is not social reality but scholarly artifice.

It does threaten it, but the threat is hollow. The claim to attention of an ethnographic account does not rest on its author's ability to capture primitive facts in faraway places and carry them home like a mask or a carving, but on the degree to which he is able to clarify what goes on in such places, to reduce the puzzlement—what manner of men are these?—to which unfamiliar acts emerging out of unknown backgrounds naturally give rise. This raises some serious problems of verification, all right or, if "verification" is too strong a word for so soft a science (I, myself, would prefer "appraisal"), of how you can tell a better account from a worse one. But that is precisely the virtue of it. If ethnography is thick description and ethnographers those who are doing the describing, then the determining question for any given example of it, whether a field journal squib or a Malinowski-sized monograph, is whether it sorts winks from twitches and real winks from mimicked ones. It is not against a body of uninterpreted data, radically thinned descriptions, that we must measure the cogency of our explications, but against the power of the scientific imagination to bring us into touch with the lives of strangers. It is not worth it, as Thoreau said, to go round the world to count the cats in Zanzibar. . . .

Anthropologists don't study villages (tribes, towns, neighborhoods . . .); they study in villages. You can study different things in different places, and some things—for example, what colonial domination does to established frames of moral expectation—you can best study in confined localities. But that doesn't make the place what it is you are studying. In the remoter provinces of Morocco and Indonesia I have wrestled with the same questions other social scientists have wrestled with in more central locations—for example, how comes it that men's most importunate claims to humanity are cast in the accents of group pride?—and with about the same conclusiveness. One can add a dimension—one much needed in the present climate of size-up-and-solve social science; but that is all. There is a certain value, if you are going to run on about the exploitation of the masses in having seen a Javanese sharecropper, turning earth in a tropical downpour or a Moroccan tailor embroidering kaftans by the light of a twenty-watt bulb. But the notion that this gives you the thing entire (and elevates you to some moral vantage ground from which you can look down upon the ethically less privileged) is an idea which only someone too long in the bush could possibly entertain.

The "natural laboratory" notion has been equally pernicious, not only because the analogy is false—what kind of a laboratory is it where none of the parameters are manipulable?—but because it leads to a notion that the data derived from ethnographic studies are purer, or more fundamental, or more solid, or less conditioned (the most favored word is "elementary") than those derived from other sorts of social inquiry. The great natural variation of cultural forms is, of course, not only anthropology's great (and wasting) resource, but the ground of its deepest theoretical dilemma: how is such variation to be squared with the biological unity of the human species? But it is not, even metaphorically, experimental variation, because the context in which it occurs varies along with it, and it is not possible (though there are those who try) to isolate the y's from x's to write a proper function.

The famous studies purporting to show that the Oedipus complex was backwards in the Trobriands, sex roles were upside down in Tchambuli, and the Pueblo Indians lacked aggression (it is characteristic that they were all negative—"but not in the South"), are, whatever their empirical validity may or may not be, not "scientifically tested and approved" hypotheses. They are interpretations, or misinterpretations, like any others, arrived at in the same way as any others, and as inherently inconclusive as any others, and the attempt to invest them with the authority of physical experimentation is but methodological sleight of hand. Ethnographic findings are not privileged, just particular: another country heard from. To regard them as anything more (or *anything less*) than that distorts both them and their implications, which are far profounder than mere primitivity, for social theory.

Another country heard from: the reason that protracted descriptions of distant sheep raids (and a really good ethnographer would have gone into what kind of sheep they were) have general relevance is that they present the sociological mind with bodied stuff on which to feed. The important thing about the anthropologist's findings is their complex specificness, their circumstantiality. It is with the kind of material produced by long-term, mainly (though not exclusively) qualitative, highly participative, and almost obsessively fine-comb field study in confined contexts that the mega-concepts with which contemporary social science is afflicted— legitimacy, modernization, integration, conflict, charisma, structure, . . . meaning—can be given the sort of sensible actuality that makes it possible to think not only realistically and concretely about them, but, what is more important, creatively and imaginatively with them.

The methodological problem which the microscopic nature of ethnography presents is both real and critical. But it is not to be resolved by regarding a remote locality as the world in a teacup or as the sociological equivalent of a cloud chamber. It is to be resolved—or, anyway, decently kept at bay—by realizing that social actions are comments on more than themselves; that where an interpretation comes from does not determine where it can be impelled to go. Small facts speak to large issues, winks to epistemology, or sheep raids to revolution, because they are made to.

Which brings us, finally, to theory. The besetting sin of interpretive approaches to anything—literature, dreams, symptoms, culture— is that they tend to resist, or to be permitted to resist, conceptual articulation and thus to escape systematic modes of assessment. You either grasp an interpretation or you do not, see the point of it or you do not, accept it or you do not. Imprisoned in the immediacy of its own detail, it is presented as self-validating, or, worse, as validated by the supposedly developed sensitivities of the person who presents it; any attempt to cast what it says in terms other than its own is regarded as a travesty—as, the anthropologist's severest term of moral abuse, ethnocentric.

For a field of study which, however timidly (though I, myself, am not timid about the matter at all), asserts itself to be a science, this just will not do. There is no reason why the conceptual structure of a cultural interpretation should be any less formulable, and thus less susceptible to explicit canons of appraisal, than that of, say, a biological observation or a physical experiment—no reason except that the terms in which such formulations can be cast are, if not wholly nonexistent, very nearly so. We are reduced to insinuating theories because we lack the power to state them.

At the same time, it must be admitted that there are a number of characteristics of cultural interpretation which make the theoretical development of it more than usually difficult. The first is the need for theory to stay rather closer to the ground than tends to be the case in sciences more able to give themselves over to imaginative abstraction. Only short flights of ratiocination tend to be effective in anthropology; longer ones tend to drift off into logical dreams, academic bemusements with formal symmetry. The whole point of a semiotic approach to culture is, as I have said, to aid us in gaining access to the conceptual world in which our subjects live so that we can, in some extended sense of the term, converse with them. The tension between the pull of this need to penetrate an unfamiliar universe of symbolic action and the requirements of technical advance in the theory of culture, between the need to grasp and the need to analyze, is, as a result, both necessarily great and essentially irremovable. Indeed, the further theoretical development goes, the deeper the tension gets. This is the first condition for cultural theory: it is not its own master. As it is unseverable from the immediacies thick description presents, its freedom to shape itself in terms of its internal logic is rather limited. What generality it contrives to achieve grows out of the delicacy of its distinctions, not the sweep of its abstractions.

And from this follows a peculiarity in the way, as a simple matter of empirical fact, our knowledge of culture . . . cultures . . . a culture . . . grows: in spurts. Rather than following a rising curve of cumulative findings, cultural analysis breaks up into a disconnected yet coherent sequence of bolder and bolder sorties. Studies do build on other studies, not in the sense that they take up where the others leave off, but in the sense that, better informed and better conceptualized, they plunge more deeply into the same things. Every serious cultural analysis starts from a sheer beginning and ends where it manages to get before exhausting its intellectual impulse. Previously discovered facts are mobilized, previously developed concepts used, previously formulated hypotheses tried out; but the movement is not from already proven theorems to newly proven ones, it is from an awkward fumbling for the most elementary understanding to a supported claim that one has achieved that and surpassed it. A study is an advance if it is more incisive—whatever that may mean—than those that preceded it; but it less stands on their shoulders than, challenged and challenging, runs by their side.

It is for this reason, among others, that the essay, whether of thirty pages or three hundred, has seemed the natural genre in which to present cultural interpretations and the theories sustaining them, and why, if one looks for systematic treatises in the field, one is so soon disappointed, the more so if one finds any. Even inventory articles are rare here, and anyway of hardly more than bibliographical interest. The major theoretical contributions not only lie in specific studies—that is true in almost any field—but they are very difficult to abstract from such studies and integrate into anything one might call "culture theory" as such. Theoretical formulations hover so low over the interpretations they govern that they don't make much sense or hold much interest apart from them. This is so, not because they are not general (if they are not general, they are not theoretical), but because, stated independently of their applications, they seem either commonplace or vacant. One can, and this in fact is how

the field progresses conceptually, take a line of theoretical attack developed in connection with one exercise in ethnographic interpretation and employ it in another, pushing it forward to greater precision and broader relevance; but one cannot write a "General Theory of Cultural Interpretation." Or, rather, one can, but there appears to be little profit in it, because the essential task of theory building here is not to codify abstract regularities but to make thick description possible, not to generalize across cases but to generalize within them. . . .

Such a view of how theory functions in an interpretive science suggests that the distinction, relative in any case, that appears in the experimental or observational sciences between "description" and "explanation" appears here as one, even more relative, between "inscription" ("thick description") and "specification" ("diagnosis")—between setting down the meaning particular social actions have for the actors whose actions they are, and stating, as explicitly as we can manage, what the knowledge thus attained demonstrates about the society in which it is found and, beyond that, about social life as such. Our double task is to uncover the conceptual structures that inform our subjects' acts, the "said" of social discourse, and to construct a system of analysis in whose terms what is generic to those structures, what belongs to them because they are what they are, will stand out against the other determinants of human behavior. In ethnography, the office of theory is to provide a vocabulary in which what symbolic action has to say about itself—that is, about the role of culture in human life—can be expressed. . . .

Religion as a Cultural System

As we are to deal with meaning, let us begin with a paradigm: viz., that sacred symbols function to synthesize a peoples ethos—the tone, character, and quality of their life, its moral and aesthetic style and mood—and their world view—the picture they have of the way things in sheer actuality are, their most comprehensive ideas of order. In religious belief and practice a group's ethos is rendered intellectually reasonable by being shown to represent a way of life ideally adapted to the actual state of affairs the world view describes, while the world view is rendered emotionally convincing by being presented as an image of an actual state of affairs peculiarly well-arranged to accommodate such a way of life. This confrontation and mutual confirmation has two fundamental effects. On the one hand, it objectivizes moral and aesthetic preferences by depicting them as the imposed conditions of life implicit in a world with a particular structure, as mere common sense given the unalterable shape of reality. On the other, it supports these received beliefs about the world's body by invoking deeply felt moral and aesthetic sentiments as experiential evidence for their truth. Religious symbols formulate a basic congruence between a particular style of life and a specific (if, most often, implicit) metaphysics and in so doing sustain each with the borrowed authority of the other.

Phrasing aside, this much may perhaps be granted. The notion that religion tunes human actions to an envisaged cosmic order and projects images of cosmic order onto the plane of human experience is hardly novel. But it is hardly investigated either, so that we have very little idea of how, in empirical terms, this particular miracle is accomplished. We just know that it is done, annually, weekly, daily, for some people almost hourly; and we have an enormous ethnographic literature to demonstrate it. But the theoretical framework which would enable us to provide an analytic account of it, an account of the sort we can provide for lineage segmentation, political succession, labor exchange, or the socialization of the child, does not exist.

Let us, therefore, reduce our paradigm to a definition, for, although it is notorious that definitions establish nothing, in themselves they do, if they are carefully enough constructed, provide a useful orientation, or reorientation, of thought, such that an extended unpacking of them can be an effective way of developing and controlling a novel line of inquiry. They have the useful virtue of explicitness: they commit themselves in a way discursive prose, which, in this field especially, is always liable to substitute rhetoric for argument, does not. Without further ado, then, a religion is: (1) *a system of symbols which acts to* (2) *establish powerful, pervasive, and long-lasting moods and motivations in men by* (3) *formulating conceptions of a general order of existence and* (4) *clothing these conceptions with such an aura of factuality that* (5) *the moods and motivations seem uniquely realistic.*

A SYSTEM OF SYMBOLS
WHICH ACTS TO . . .

Such a tremendous weight is being put on the term "symbol" here that our first move must be to decide with some precision what we are going to mean by it. This is no easy task, for, rather like "culture," "symbol" has been used to refer to a great variety of things, often a number of them at the same time.

In some hands it is used for anything which signifies something else to someone: dark clouds are the symbolic precursors of an oncoming rain. In others it is used only for explicitly conventional signs of one sort or another: a red flag is a symbol of danger, a white of surrender. In others it is confined to something which expresses in an oblique and figurative manner that which cannot be stated in a direct and literal one, so that there are symbols in poetry but not in science, and symbolic logic is misnamed. In yet others, however, it is used for any object, act, event, quality, or relation which serves as a vehicle for a conception—the conception is the symbol's "meaning"—and that is the approach I shall follow here.[1] The number 6, written, imagined, laid out as a row of stones, or even punched into the program tapes of a computer, is a symbol. But so also is the Cross, talked about, visualized, shaped worriedly in air or fondly fingered at the neck, the expanse of painted canvas called "Guernica" or the bit of painted stone called a churinga, the word "reality," or even the morpheme "-ing." They are all symbols, or at least symbolic elements, because they are tangible formulations of notions, abstractions from experience fixed in perceptible forms, concrete embodiments of ideas, attitudes, judgments, longings, or beliefs. To undertake the study of cultural activity—activity in which symbolism forms the positive content—is thus not to abandon social analysis for a Platonic cave of shadows, to enter into a mentalistic world of introspective psychology or, worse, speculative philosophy, and wander there forever in a haze of "Cognitions," "Affections," "Conations," and other elusive entities. Cultural acts, the construction, apprehension, and utilization of symbolic forms, are social events like any other; they are as public as marriage and as observable as agriculture. . . .

So far as culture patterns, that is, systems or complexes of symbols, are concerned, the generic trait which is of first importance for us here is that they are extrinsic sources of information. By "extrinsic," I mean only that—unlike genes, for example—they lie outside the boundaries of the individual organism as such in that intersubjective world of common understandings into which all human individuals are born, in which they pursue their separate careers, and which they leave persisting behind them after they die. By "sources of information," I mean only that—like genes—they provide a blueprint or template in terms of which processes external to themselves can be given a definite form. As the order of bases in a strand of DNA forms a coded program, a set of instructions, or a recipe, for the synthesis of the structurally complex proteins which shape organic functioning, so culture patterns provide such programs for the institution of the social and psychological processes which shape public behavior. Though the sort of information and the mode of its transmission are vastly different in the two cases, this comparison of gene and symbol is more than a strained analogy of the familiar "social heredity" sort. It is actually a substantial relationship, for it is precisely because of the fact that genetically programmed processes are so highly generalized in men, as compared with lower animals, that culturally programmed ones are so important; only because human behavior is so loosely determined by intrinsic sources of information that extrinsic sources are so vital. To build a dam a beaver needs only an appropriate site and the proper materials—his mode of procedure is shaped by his physiology. But man, whose genes are silent on the building trades, needs also a conception of what it is to build a dam, a conception he can get only from some symbolic source—a blueprint, a textbook, or a string of speech by someone who already knows how dams are built—or, of course, from manipulating graphic or linguistic elements in such a way as to attain for himself a conception of what dams are and how they are built. . . .

Unlike genes, and other nonsymbolic information sources, which are only models for, not models of, culture patterns have an intrinsic double aspect: they give meaning, that is, objective conceptual form, to social and psychological reality both by shaping themselves to it and by shaping it to themselves.

It is, in fact, this double aspect which sets true symbols off from other sorts of significative forms. Models *for* are found, as the gene example suggests, through the whole order of nature; for wherever there is a communication of pattern, such programs are, in simple logic, required. Among animals, imprint learning is perhaps the most striking example, because what such learning involves is the automatic presentation of an appropriate sequence of behavior by a model animal in the presence of a learning animal which serves, equally automatically, to call out and stabilize a certain set of responses genetically built into the learning animal.[2] The communicative dance of two bees, one of which has found nectar and the other of which seeks it, is another, somewhat different, more complexly coded, example.[3] Craik has even suggested that the thin trickle of water which first finds its way down from a mountain spring to the sea and smooths a little channel for the greater volume of water that follows after it plays a sort of model *for* function.[4] But models of—linguistic, graphic, mechanical, natural, etc., processes which function not to provide sources of information in terms of which other processes can be patterned, but to represent those patterned processes as such, to express their structure in an alternative medium—are much rarer and may perhaps be confined, among living animals, to man. The perception of the structural congruence between one set of processes, activities, relations, entities, and so on, and another set for which it acts as a program, so that the program can be taken as a representation, or conception—a symbol—of the programmed, is the essence of human thought. The intertransposability of models for and models of which symbolic formulation makes possible is the distinctive characteristic of our mentality.

. . . TO ESTABLISH POWERFUL, PERVASIVE, AND LONG-LASTING MOODS AND MOTIVATIONS IN MEN. . .

They shape it by inducing in the worshipper a certain distinctive set of dispositions (tendencies, capacities, propensities, skills, habits, liabilities, pronenesses) which lend a chronic character to the flow of his activity and the quality of his experience. A disposition describes not an activity or an occurrence but a probability of an activity being performed or an occurrence occurring in certain circumstances. . . .

Another part of what we mean is that he has, when properly stimulated, a susceptibility to fall into certain moods, moods we sometimes jump together under such covering terms as "reverential," "solemn," or "worshipful." Such generalized rubrics actually conceal, however, the enormous empirical variousness of the dispositions involved, and, in fact, tend to assimilate them to the unusually grave tone of most of our own religious life. The moods that sacred symbols induce, at different times and in different places, range from exultation to melancholy, from self-confidence to self-pity, from an incorrigible playfulness to a bland listlessness—to say nothing of the erogenous power of so many of the world's myths and rituals. No more than there is a single sort of motivation one can call piety is there a single sort of mood one can call worshipful.

The major difference between moods and motivations is that where the latter are, so to speak, vectorial qualities, the former are merely scalar. Motives have a directional cast, they describe a certain overall course, gravitate toward certain, usually temporary, consummations. But moods vary only as to intensity: they go nowhere. They spring from certain circumstances but they are responsive to no ends. Like fogs, they just settle and lift; like scents, suffuse and evaporate. When present they are totalistic: if one is sad everything and everybody seems dreary; if one is gay, everything and everybody seems splendid. Thus, though a man can be vain, brave, willful, and independent at the same time, he can't very well be playful and listless, or exultant and melancholy, at the same time.[5] Further, where motives persist for more or less extended periods of time, moods merely recur with greater or lesser frequency, coming and going for what are often quite unfathomable reasons. But perhaps the most important difference, so far as we are concerned, between moods and motivations is that motivations are "made meaningful" with reference to the ends toward which they are conceived to conduce, whereas moods are "made meaningful" with reference to the conditions from which they are conceived to spring. We interpret motives in terms of their consummations, but we interpret moods in terms of their sources. . . .

. . . BY FORMULATING CONCEPTIONS OF A GENERAL ORDER OF EXISTENCE AND . . .

That the symbols or symbol systems which induce and define dispositions we set off as religious and those which place those dispositions in a cosmic framework are the same symbols ought to occasion no surprise. . . . If sacred symbols did not at one and the same time induce dispositions in human beings and formulate, however obliquely, inarticulately, or unsystematically, general ideas of order, then the empirical differentia of religious activity or religious experience would not exist. A man can indeed be said to be "religious" about golf, but not merely if he pursues it with passion and plays it on Sundays: he must also see it as symbolic of some transcendent truths. . . .

. . . AND CLOTHING THOSE CONCEPTIONS WITH SUCH AN AURA OF FACTUALITY . . .

There arises here, however, a more profound question: how is it that this denial comes to be believed? How is it that the religious man moves from a troubled perception of experienced disorder to a more or less settled conviction of fundamental order? Just what does "belief" mean in a religious context? . . .

It seems to me that it is best to begin any approach to this issue with frank recognition that religious belief involves not a Baconian induction from everyday experience—for then we should all be agnostics—but rather a prior acceptance of authority which transforms that experience. The existence of bafflement, pain, and moral paradox—of The Problem of Meaning—is one of the things that drives men toward belief in gods, devils, spirits, totemic principles, or the spiritual efficacy of cannibalism (an enfolding sense of beauty or a dazzling perception of power are others), but it is not the basis upon which those beliefs rest, but rather their most important field of application. . . .

If we place the religious perspective against the background of three of the other major perspectives in terms of which men construe the world—the common-sensical, the scientific, and the aesthetic—its special character emerges more sharply. What distinguishes common sense as a mode of "seeing" is, as Schutz has pointed out, a simple acceptance of the world, its

objects, and its processes as being just what they seem to be—what is sometimes called naive realism—and the pragmatic motive, the wish to act upon that world so as to bend it to one's practical purposes, to master it, or so far as that proves impossible, to adjust to it.[6] The world of everyday life, itself, of course, a cultural product, for it is framed in terms of the symbolic conceptions of "stubborn fact" handed down from generation to generation, is the established scene and given object of our actions. . . .

The religious perspective differs from the common-sensical in that, as already pointed out, it moves beyond the realities of everyday life to wider ones which correct and complete them, and its defining concern is not action upon those wider realities but acceptance of them, faith in them. It differs from the scientific perspective in that it questions the realities of everyday life not out of an institutionalized scepticism which dissolves the world's givenness into a swirl of probabilistic hypotheses, but in terms of what it takes to be wider, nonhypothetical truths. Rather than detachment, its watchword is commitment; rather than analysis, encounter. And it differs from art in that instead of effecting a disengagement from the whole question of factuality, deliberately manufacturing an air of semblance and illusion, it deepens the concern with fact and seeks to create an aura of utter actuality. It is this sense of the "really real" upon which the religious perspective rests and which the symbolic activities of religion as a cultural system are devoted to producing, intensifying, and, so far as possible, rendering inviolable by the discordant revelations of secular experience. It is, again, the imbuing of a certain specific complex of symbols—of the metaphysic they formulate and the style of life they recommend—with a persuasive authority which, from an analytic point of view, is the essence of religious action.

Which brings us, at length, to ritual. For it is in ritual—that is, consecrated behavior—that this conviction that religious conceptions are veridical and that religious directives are sound is somehow generated. It is in some sort of ceremonial form—even if that form be hardly more than the recitation of a myth, the consultation of an oracle, or the decoration of a grave—that the moods and motivations which sacred symbols induce in men and the general conceptions of the order of existence which they formulate for men meet and reinforce one another. In a ritual, the world as lived and the world as imagined, fused under the agency of a single set of symbolic forms, turn out to be the same world, producing thus that idiosyncratic transformation in one's sense of reality to which Santayana refers in my epigraph. Whatever role divine intervention may or may not play in the creation of faith—and it is not the business of the scientist to pronounce upon such matters one way or the other—it is, primarily at least, out of the context of concrete acts of religious observance that religious conviction emerges on the human plane. . . .

. . . THAT THE MOODS
AND MOTIVATIONS SEEM UNIQUELY
REALISTIC

But no one, not even a saint, lives in the world religious symbols formulate all of the time, and the majority of men live in it only at moments. . . . Religion is sociologically interesting not because, as vulgar positivism would have it, it describes the social order (which, in so far as it does, it does not only very obliquely but very incompletely), but because, like environment, political power, wealth, jural obligation, personal affection, and a sense of beauty, it shapes it.

The movement back and forth between the religious perspective and the common-sense perspective is actually one of the more obvious empirical occurrences on the social scene, though, again, one of the most neglected by social anthropologists, virtually all of whom have seen it happen countless times. Religious belief has usually been presented as a homogeneous characteristic of an individual, like his place of residence, his occupational role, his kinship position, and so on. But religious belief in the midst of ritual, where it engulfs the total person, transporting him, so far as he is concerned, into another mode of existence, and religious belief as the pale, remembered reflection of that experience in the midst of everyday life are not precisely the same thing, and the failure to realize this has led to some confusion, most especially in connection with the so-called primitive-mentality problem. . . .

For an anthropologist, the importance of religion lies in its capacity to serve, for an individual or for a group, as a source of general, yet distinctive, conceptions of the world, the self, and the relations between them, on the one hand—its model *of* aspect—and of rooted, no less distinctive "mental" dispositions—its model *for* aspect—on the other. From these cultural functions flow, in turn, its social and psychological ones.

Religious concepts spread beyond their specifically metaphysical contexts to provide a framework of general ideas in terms of which a wide range of experience—intellectual, emotional, moral—can be given meaningful form. . . .

The anthropological study of religion is therefore a two-stage operation: first, an analysis of the system of meanings embodied in the symbols which make up the religion proper, and, second, the relating of these systems to social-structural and psychological processes. My dissatisfaction with so much of contemporary social anthropological work in religion is not that it concerns itself with the second stage, but that it neglects the first, and in so doing takes for granted what most needs to be elucidated. To discuss the role of ancestor worship in regulating political succession, of sacrificial feasts in defining kinship obligations, of spirit worship in scheduling agricultural practices, of divination in reinforcing social control, or of initiation rites in propelling personality maturation, are in no sense unimportant endeavors, and I am not recommending they be abandoned for the kind of jejune cabalism into which symbolic analysis of exotic faiths can so easily fall. But to attempt them with but the most general, common-sense view of what ancestor worship, animal sacrifice, spirit worship, divination, or initiation rites are as religious patterns seems to me not particularly promising. Only when we have a theoretical analysis of symbolic action comparable in sophistication to what we now have for social and psychological action, will we be able to cope effectively with those aspects of social and psychological life in which religion (or art, or science, or ideology) plays a determinant role.

Ethos, World View, and the Analysis of Sacred Symbols

Religion is never merely metaphysics. For all peoples the forms, vehicles, and objects of worship are suffused with an aura of deep moral seriousness. The holy bears within it everywhere a sense of intrinsic obligation: it not only encourages devotion, it demands it; it not only induces intellectual assent, it enforces emotional commitment. Whether it be formulated as *mana,* as *Brahma,* or as the Holy Trinity, that which is set apart as more than mundane is inevitably considered to have far-reaching implications for the direction of human conduct. Never merely metaphysics, religion is never merely ethics either. The source of its moral vitality is conceived to lie in the fidelity with which it expresses the fundamental nature of reality. The powerfully coercive "ought" is felt to grow out of a comprehensive factual "is," and in such a way religion grounds the most specific requirements of human action in the most general contexts of human existence.

In recent anthropological discussion, the moral (and aesthetic) aspects of a given culture, the evaluative elements, have commonly been summed up in the term "ethos," while the cognitive, existential aspects have been designated by the term "world view." A people's ethos is the tone, character, and quality of their life, its moral and aesthetic style and mood; it is the underlying attitude toward themselves and their world that life reflects. Their world view is their picture of the way things in sheer actuality are, their concept of nature, of self, of society. It contains their most comprehensive ideas of order. Religious belief and ritual confront and mutually confirm one another; the ethos is made intellectually reasonable by being shown to represent a way of life implied by the actual state of affairs which the world view describes, and the world view is made emotionally acceptable by being presented as an image of an actual state of affairs of which such a way of life is an authentic expression. This demonstration of a meaningful relation between the values a people holds and the general order of existence within which it finds itself is an essential element in all religions, however those values or that order be conceived. Whatever else religion may be, it is in part an attempt (of an implicit and directly felt rather than explicit and consciously thought-about sort) to conserve the fund of general meanings in terms of which each individual interprets his experience and organizes his conduct.

But meanings can only be "stored" in symbols: a cross, a crescent, or a feathered serpent. Such religious symbols, dramatized in rituals or related in myths, are felt somehow to sum up, for those for whom they are resonant, what is known about the way the world is, the quality of the emotional life it supports, and the way one ought to behave while in it. Sacred symbols thus relate an ontology and a cosmology to an aesthetics and a morality: their peculiar power comes from their presumed ability to identify fact with value at the most fundamental level, to give to what is otherwise merely actual, a comprehensive normative import. The number of such synthesizing symbols is limited in any culture, and though in theory we might think that a people could construct a wholly autonomous value system independent of any metaphysical referent, an ethics without ontology, we do not in fact seem to have found such a people. The tendency to synthesize world view and ethos at some level, if not logically necessary, is at least empirically coercive; if it is not philosophically justified, it is at least pragmatically universal. . . .

It is a cluster of sacred symbols, woven into some sort of ordered whole, which makes up a religious system. For those who are committed to it, such a religious system seems to mediate genuine knowledge, knowledge of the essential conditions in terms of which life must, of necessity, be lived. Particularly where these symbols are uncriticized, historically or philosophically, as they are in most of the world's cultures, individuals who ignore the moral-aesthetic norms the symbols formulate, who follow a discordant style of life, are regarded not so much as evil as stupid, insensitive, unlearned, or in the case of extreme dereliction, mad. In Java, where I have done field work, small children, simpletons, boors, the insane, and the flagrantly immoral are all said to be "not yet Javanese," and, not yet Javanese, not yet human. Unethical behavior is referred to as "uncustomary," the more serious crimes (incest, sorcery, murder) are commonly accounted for by an assumed lapse of reason, the less serious ones by a comment that the culprit "does not know order," and the word for "religion" and that for "science" are the same. Morality has thus the air of simple realism, of practical wisdom; religion supports proper conduct by picturing a world in which such conduct is only common sense.

It is only common sense because between ethos and world view, between the approved style of life and the assumed structure of reality, there is conceived to be a simple and fundamental congruence such that they complete one another and lend one another meaning. . . . What all sacred symbols assert is that the good for man is to live realistically; where they differ is in the vision of reality they construct.

However, it is not only positive values that sacred symbols dramatize, but negative ones as well. They point not only toward the existence of good but also of evil, and toward the conflict between them. The so-called problem of evil is a matter of formulating in world-view terms the actual nature of the destructive forces within the self and outside of it, of interpreting murder, crop failure, sickness, earthquakes, poverty, and oppression in such a way that it is possible to come to some sort of terms with them. . . .

The force of a religion in supporting social values rests, then, on the ability of its symbols to formulate a world in which those values, as well as the forces opposing their realization, are fundamental ingredients. It represents the power of the human imagination to construct an image of reality in which, to quote Max Weber, "events are not just there and happen, but they have a meaning and happen because of that meaning." The need for such a metaphysical grounding for values seems to vary quite widely in intensity from culture to culture and from individual to individual, but the tendency to desire some sort of factual basis for one's commitments seems practically universal; mere conventionalism satisfies few people in any culture. However its role may differ at various times, for various individuals, and in various cultures, religion, by fusing ethos and world view, gives to a set of social values what they perhaps most need to be coercive: an appearance of objectivity. In sacred rituals and myths values are portrayed not as subjective human preferences but as the imposed conditions for life implicit in a world with a particular structure.

The view of man as a symbolizing, conceptualizing, meaning-seeking animal, which has become increasingly popular both in the social sciences and in philosophy over the past several years, opens up a whole new approach not only to the analysis of religion as such, but to the understanding of the relations between religion and values. The drive to make sense out of experience, to give it form and order, is evidently as real and as pressing as the more familiar biological needs. And, this being so, it seems unnecessary to continue to interpret symbolic activities—religion, art, ideology—as nothing but thinly disguised expressions of something other than what they seem to be: attempts to provide orientation for an organism which cannot live in a world it is unable to understand. If symbols, to adapt a phrase of Kenneth Burke's, are strategies for encompassing situations, then we need to give more attention to how people define situations and how they go about coming to terms with them. Such a stress does not imply a removal of beliefs and values from their psychobiological and social contexts into a realm of "pure meaning," but it does imply a greater emphasis on the analysis of such beliefs and values in terms of concepts explicitly designed to deal with symbolic material.

The concepts used here, ethos and world view, are vague and imprecise; they are a kind of prototheory, forerunners, it is to be hoped, of a more adequate analytical framework. But even with them, anthropologists are beginning to develop an approach to the study of values which can clarify rather than obscure the essential processes involved in the normative regulation of behavior. One almost certain result of such an empirically oriented, theoretically sophisticated, symbol-stressing approach to the study of values is the decline of analyses which attempt to describe moral, aesthetic, and other normative activities in terms of theories based not on the observation of such activities but on logical considerations alone. Like bees who fly despite theories of aeronautics which deny them the right to do so, probably the overwhelming majority of mankind are continually drawing normative conclusions from factual premises (and factual conclusions from normative premises, for the relation between ethos and world view is circular) despite refined, and in their own terms impeccable, reflections by professional philosophers on the "naturalistic fallacy." An approach to a theory of value which looks toward the behavior of actual people in actual societies living in terms of actual cultures for both its stimulus and its validation will turn us away from abstract and rather scholastic arguments in which a limited number of classical positions are stated again and again with little that is new to recommend them, to a process of ever-increasing insight into both what values are and how they work. Once this enterprise in the scientific analysis of values is well launched, the philosophical discussions of ethics are likely to take on more point. The process is not that of replacing moral philosophy by descriptive ethics, but of providing moral philosophy with an empirical base and a conceptual framework which is somewhat advanced over that available to Aristotle, Spinoza, or G. E. Moore. The role of such a special science as anthropology in the analysis of values is not to replace philosophical investigation, but to make it relevant.

NOTES

1. S. Langer, *Philosophy in a New Key,* 4th ed. (Cambridge, MA, Harvard University Press, 1960).

2. K. Lorenz, *King Solomon's Ring* (London, Crowell, 1952).

3. K. von Frisch, "Dialects in the Language of the Bees," *Scientific American,* August 1962.

4. Kenneth Craik, *The Nature of Explanation,* (Cambridge: Cambridge University Press, 1967).

5. G. Ryle, *The Concept of Mind* (London and New York, Hutchinson, 1949), p. 99.

6. A. Schutz, *The Problem of Social Reality.*

Counterpoint:
From *Genealogies of Religion: Discipline and Reasons of Power in Christianity and Islam*

TALAL ASAD

Talal Asad teaches at Johns Hopkins University. He has authored the following books: *The Sociology of Developing Societies: The Middle East* and *The Kababish Arabs: Power, Authority, and Consent in a Nomadic Tribe*.

The Construction of Religion as an Anthropological Category

. . . In what follows I want to examine the ways in which the theoretical search for an essence of religion invites us to separate it conceptually from the domain of power. I shall do this by exploring a universalist definition of religion offered by an eminent anthropologist: Clifford Geertz's "Religion as a Cultural System." I stress that this is not primarily a critical review of Geertz's ideas on religion—if that had been my aim I would have addressed myself to the entire corpus of his writings on religion in Indonesia and Morocco. My intention . . . is to try to identify some of the historical shifts that have produced our concept of religion as the concept of a transhistorical essence—and Geertz's article is merely my starting point.

It is part of my basic argument that socially identifiable forms, preconditions, and effects of what was regarded as religion in the medieval Christian epoch were quite different from those so considered in modern society. I want to get at this well-known fact while trying to avoid a simple nominalism. What we call religious power was differently distributed and had a different thrust. There were different ways in which it created and worked through legal insti-

tutions, different selves that it shaped and responded to, and different categories of knowledge which it authorized and made available. Nevertheless, what the anthropologist is confronted with, as a consequence, is not merely an arbitrary collection of elements and processes that we happen to call "religion." For the entire phenomenon is to be seen in large measure in the context of Christian attempts to achieve a coherence in doctrines and practices, rules and regulations, even if that was a state never fully attained. My argument is that there cannot be a universal definition of religion, not only because its constituent elements and relationships are historically specific, but because that definition is itself the historical product of discursive processes.

A universal (i.e., anthropological) definition is, however, precisely what Geertz aims at: A *religion*, he proposes, is "(1) a system of symbols which act to (2) establish powerful, pervasive, and long-lasting moods and motivations in men by (3) formulating conceptions of a general order of existence and (4) clothing these conceptions with such an aura of factuality that (5) the moods and motivations seem uniquely realistic." In what follows I shall examine this definition, not only in order to test its interlinked assertions, but also to flesh out the counterclaim that a transhistorical definition of religion is not viable.

The Concept of Symbol as a Clue to the Essence of Religion

Geertz sees his first task as the definition of symbol: "any object, act, event, quality, or relation which serves as a vehicle for a conception—the conception is the symbol's meaning." But this simple, clear statement—in which symbol (any object, etc.) is differentiated from but linked to conception (its meaning)—is later supplemented by others not entirely consistent with it, for it turns out that the symbol is not an object that serves as a vehicle for a conception, *it is itself the conception.* Thus, in the statement "The number 6, written, imagined, laid out as a row of stones, or even punched into the program tapes of a computer, is a symbol," what constitutes all these diverse representations as versions of the same symbol ("the number 6") is of course *a conception.* Furthermore, Geertz sometimes seems to suggest that even as a conception a symbol has an intrinsic connection with empirical events from which it is merely "theoretically" separable: "the symbolic dimension of social events is, like the psychological, itself theoretically abstractable from these events as empirical totalities." At other times, however, he stresses the importance of keeping symbols and empirical objects quite separate: "there is something to be said for not confusing our traffic with symbols with our traffic with objects or human beings, for these latter are not in themselves symbols, however often they may function as such." Thus, "symbol" is sometimes an aspect of reality, sometimes of its representation.

These divergencies are symptoms of the fact that cognitive questions are mixed up in this account with communicative ones, and this makes it difficult to inquire into the ways in which discourse and understanding are connected in social practice. To begin with we

might say, as a number of writers have done, that a symbol is not an object or event that serves to carry a meaning but a set of relationships between objects or events uniquely brought together as complexes or as concepts, having at once an intellectual, instrumental, and emotional significance. If we define symbol along these lines, a number of questions can be raised about the conditions that explain how such complexes and concepts come to be formed, and in particular how their formation is related to varieties of practice. Half a century ago, Vygotsky was able to show how the development of children's intellect is dependent on the internalization of social speech. This means that the formation of what we have here called "symbols" (complexes, concepts) is conditioned by the social relations in which the growing child is involved—by the social activities that he or she is permitted or encouraged or obliged to undertake—in which other symbols (speech and significant movements) are crucial. The conditions (discursive and nondiscursive) that explain how symbols come to be constructed, and how some of them are established as natural or authoritative as opposed to others, then become an important object of anthropological inquiry. It must be stressed that this is not a matter of urging the study of the origin and function of symbols in addition to their meaning—such a distinction is not relevant here. What is being argued is that the authoritative status of representations/discourses is dependent on the appropriate production of other representations/discourses; the two are intrinsically and not just temporally connected.

Systems of symbols, says Geertz, are also *culture patterns,* and they constitute "extrinsic sources of information." Extrinsic, because "they lie outside the boundaries of the individual organism as such in that inter-subjective world of common understandings into which all human individuals are born." And sources of information in the sense that "they provide a blueprint or template in terms of which processes external to themselves can be given a definite form." Thus, culture patterns, we are told, may be thought of as "models *for* reality" as well as "models *of* reality."

This part of the discussion does open up possibilities by speaking of modeling: that is, it allows for the possibility of conceptualizing discourses in the process of elaboration, modification, testing, and so forth. Unfortunately, Geertz quickly regresses to his earlier position: "culture patterns have an intrinsic double aspect," he writes; "they give meaning, that is objective conceptual form, to social and psychological reality both by shaping themselves to it and by shaping it to themselves." This alleged dialectical tendency toward isomorphism, incidentally, makes it difficult to understand how social change can ever occur. The basic problem, however, is not with the idea of mirror images as such but with the assumption that there are two separate levels—the cultural, on the one side (consisting of symbols) and the social and psychological, on the other—which interact. This resort to Parsonian theory creates a logical space for defining the essence of religion. By adopting it, Geertz moves away from a notion of symbols that are intrinsic to signifying and organizing practices, and back to a notion of symbols as meaning-carrying objects external to social conditions and states of the self ("social and psychological reality").

This is not to say that Geertz doesn't think of symbols as "doing" something. In a way that recalls older anthropological approaches to ritual, he states that religious symbols act "by inducing in the worshipper a certain distinctive set of dispositions (tendencies, capacities, propensities, skills, habits, liabilities, proneness) which lend a chronic character to the flow of his activity and the quality of his experience." And here again, symbols are set apart from mental states. But how plausible are these propositions? Can we, for example, predict the "distinctive" set of dispositions for a Christian worshipper in modern, industrial society? Alternatively, can we say of someone with a "distinctive" set of dispositions that he is or is not a Christian? The

answer to both questions must surely be no. The reason, of course, is that it is not simply worship but social, political, and economic institutions in general, within which individual biographies are lived out, that lend a stable character to the flow of a Christian's activity and to the quality of her experience.

Religious symbols, Geertz elaborates, produce two kinds of dispositions, moods and *motivations.* . . . Now, a Christian might say that this is not their essence, because religious symbols, even when failing to produce moods and motivations, are still religious (i.e., true) symbols—that religious symbols possess a truth independent of their effectiveness. Yet surely even a committed Christian cannot be unconcerned at the existence of truthful symbols that appear to be largely powerless in modern society. He will rightly want to ask: What are the conditions in which religious symbols can actually produce religious dispositions? Or, as a nonbeliever would put it: How does (religious) power create (religious) truth? . . .

Isn't Geertz's formula too simple to accommodate the force of this religious symbolism? Note that here it is not mere symbols that implant true Christian dispositions, but power—ranging all the way from laws (imperial and ecclesiastical) and other sanctions (hellfire, death, salvation, good repute, peace) to the disciplinary activities of social institutions (family, school, city, church) and of human bodies (fasting, prayer, obedience, penance). Augustine was quite clear that power, the effect of an entire network of motivated practices, assumes a religious form because of the end to which it is directed, for human events are the instruments of God. It was not the mind that moved spontaneously to religious truth, but power that created the conditions for experiencing that truth. Particular discourses and practices were to be systematically excluded, forbidden, denounced —made as much as possible unthinkable; others were to be included, allowed, praised, and drawn into the narrative of sacred truth. The configurations of power in this sense have, of course, varied profoundly in Christendom from one epoch to another—from Augustine's time, through the Middle Ages, to the industrial capitalist West of today. The patterns of religious moods and motivations, the possibilities for religious knowledge and truth, have all varied with them and been conditioned by them. Even Augustine held that although religious truth was eternal, the means for securing human access to it were not.

From Reading Symbols to Analyzing Practices

One consequence of assuming a symbolic system separate from practices is that important distinctions are sometimes obscured, or even explicitly denied. "That the symbols or symbol systems which induce and define dispositions we set off as religious and those which place these dispositions in a cosmic framework are the same symbols ought to occasion no surprise." But it does surprise! Let us grant that religious dispositions are crucially dependent on certain religious symbols, that such symbols operate in a way integral to religious motivation and religious mood. Even so, the symbolic process by which the concepts of religious motivation and mood are placed within "a cosmic framework" is surely quite a different operation, and therefore the signs involved are quite different. Put another way, theological discourse is not identical with either moral attitudes or liturgical discourses—of which, among other things, theology speaks. Thoughtful Christians will concede that, although theology has an essential function, theological discourse does not necessarily induce religious dispositions, and that, conversely, having religious dispositions does not necessarily depend on a clear-cut conception of the cosmic framework on the part of a religious actor. Discourse involved in practice is not the same as that involved in speaking about practice. It is a modern idea that a practitioner cannot know how to live religiously without being able to articulate that knowledge.

Geertz's reason for merging the two kinds of discursive process seems to spring from a wish to distinguish in general between religious and secular dispositions. . . . The argument that a particular disposition is religious partly because it occupies a conceptual place within a cosmic framework appears plausible, but only because it presupposes a question that must be made explicit: how do authorizing processes represent practices, utterances, or dispositions so that they can be discursively related to general (cosmic) ideas of order? In short, the question pertains to the authorizing process by which "religion" is created. . . .

The Constructution of Religion in Early Modern Europe

In this way, Natural Religion not only became a universal phenomenon but began to be demarcated from, and was also supportive of, a newly emerging domain of natural science. I want to emphasize that the idea of Natural Religion was a crucial step in the formation of the modern concept of religious belief, experience, and practice, and that it was an idea developed in response to problems specific to Christian theology at a particular historical juncture.

By 1795, Kant was able to produce a fully essentialized idea of religion which could be counterposed to its phenomenal forms. . . . From here, the classification of historical confessions into lower and higher religions became an increasingly popular option for philosophers, theologians, missionaries, and anthropologists in the nineteenth and twentieth centuries. As to whether any particular tribe has existed without any form of religion whatever was often raised as a question, but this was recognized as an empirical matter not affecting the essence of religion itself.

Thus, what appears to anthropologists today to be self-evident, namely that religion is essentially a matter of symbolic meanings linked to ideas of general order (expressed through either or both rite and doctrine), that it has generic functions/features, and that it must not be confused with any of its particular historical or cultural forms, is in fact a view that has a specific Christian history. From being a concrete set of practical rules attached to specific processes of power and knowledge, religion has come to be abstracted and universalized. In this movement we have not merely an increase in religious toleration, certainly not merely a new scientific discovery, but the mutation of a concept and a range of social practices which is itself part of a wider change in the modern landscape of power and knowledge. That change included a new kind of state, a new kind of science, a new kind of legal and moral subject. To understand this mutation it is essential to keep clearly distinct that which theology tends to obscure: the occurrence of events (utterances, practices, dispositions) and the authorizing processes that give those events meaning and embody that meaning in concrete institutions.

Religion as Meaning and Religious Meanings

The equation between two levels of discourse (symbols that induce dispositions and those that place the idea of those dispositions discursively in a cosmic framework) is not the only problematic thing in this part of Geertz's discussion. He also appears, inadvertently, to be taking up the standpoint of theology. This happens when he insists on the primacy of meaning without regard to the processes by which meanings are constructed. . . .

The requirement of affirmation is apparently innocent and local, but through it the entire field of evangelism was historically opened up, in particular the work of European missionaries in Asia, Africa, and Latin America. The demand that the received practices must *affirm something about the fundamental nature of reality,* that it should therefore always be possible to state meanings for them which are not plain nonsense, is the first condition for determining whether they belong to "religion." The unevangelized come to be seen typically either as those who have practices but affirm nothing, in which case meaning can be attributed to their practices (thus making them vulnerable), or as those who do affirm something (probably "obscure, shallow, or perverse"), an affirmation that can therefore be dismissed. In the one case, religious theory becomes necessary for a correct reading of the mute ritual hieroglyphics of others, for reducing their practices to texts; in the other, it is essential for judging the validity of their cosmological utterances. But always, there must be something that exists   beyond   the observed practices, the heard utterances, the written words, and it is the function of religious theory to reach into, and to bring out, that background by giving them meaning.

Geertz is thus right to make a connection between religious theory and practice, but wrong to see it as essentially cognitive, as a means by which a disembodied mind can identify religion from an Archimedean point. The connection between religious theory and practice is fundamentally a matter of intervention—of constructing religion in the world (not in the mind) through definitional discourses, interpreting true meanings, excluding some utterances and practices and including others. Hence my repeated question: how does theoretical discourse actually define religion? What are the historical conditions in which it can act effectively as a demand for the imitation, or the prohibition, or the authentication of truthful utterances and practices? How does power create religion?

What kinds of affirmation, of meaning, must be identified with practice in order for it to qualify as religion? According to Geertz, it is because all human beings have a profound need for a general order of existence that religious symbols function to fulfill that need. It follows that human beings have a deep dread of disorder. . . . It is the function of religious symbols to meet perceived threats to order at each of these points (intellectual, physical, and moral). . . .

Notice how the reasoning seems now to have shifted its ground from the claim that religion must affirm something specific about the nature of reality (however obscure, shallow, or perverse) to the bland suggestion that religion is ultimately a matter of having a positive attitude toward the problem of disorder, of affirming simply that in some sense or other the world as a whole is explicable, justifiable, bearable. This modest view of religion (which would have horrified the early Christian Fathers or medieval churchmen) is a product of the only legitimate space allowed to Christianity by post-Enlightenment society, the right to individual *belief:* the human condition is full of ignorance, pain, and injustice, and religious symbols are a means of coming positively to terms with that condition. One consequence is that this view would in principle render any philosophy that performs such a function into religion (to the annoyance of the nineteenth-century rationalist), or alternatively, make it possible to think of religion as a more primitive, a less adult mode of coming to terms with the human condition (to the annoyance of the modern Christian). In either case, the suggestion that religion has a universal function in belief is one indication of how marginal religion has become in modern industrial society as the site for producing disciplined knowledge and personal discipline. As such it comes to resemble the conception Marx had of religion as ideology—that is, as a mode of consciousness which is other than consciousness of reality, external to the relations of production, producing no knowledge, but expressing at once the anguish of the oppressed and a spurious consolation.

Geertz has much more to say, however, on the elusive question of religious meaning: not only do religious symbols formulate conceptions of a general order of existence, they also clothe those conceptions with an aura of factuality. This, we are told, is "the problem of belief." *Religious belief* always involves "the prior acceptance of authority," which transforms experience. . . . This seems to imply that

religious belief stands independently of the worldly conditions that produce bafflement, pain, and moral paradox, although that belief is primarily a way of coming to terms with them. But surely this is mistaken, on logical grounds as well as historical, for changes in the object of belief change that belief; and as the world changes, so do the objects of belief and the specific forms of bafflement and moral paradox that are a part of that world. What the Christian believes today about God, life after death, the universe, is not what he believed a millennium ago—nor is the way he responds to ignorance, pain, and injustice the same now as it was then. The medieval valorization of pain as the mode of participating in Christ's suffering contrasts sharply with the modern Catholic perception of pain as an evil to be fought against and overcome as Christ the Healer did. That difference is clearly related to the post-Enlightenment secularization of Western society and to the moral language which that society now authorizes.

Geertz's treatment of religious belief, which lies at the core of his conception of religion, is a modern, privatized Christian one because and to the extent that it emphasizes the priority of belief as a state of mind rather than as constituting activity in the world. . . . In modern society, where knowledge is rooted either in an a Christian everyday life or in an a religious science, the Christian apologist tends not to regard belief as the conclusion to a knowledge process but as its precondition. However, the knowledge that he promises will not pass (nor, in fairness, does he claim that it will pass) for knowledge of social life, still less for the systematic knowledge of objects that natural science provides. Her claim is to a particular state of mind, a sense of conviction, not to a corpus of practical knowledge. But the reversal of belief and knowledge she demands was not a basic axiom to, say, pious learned Christians of the twelfth century, for whom knowledge and belief were not so clearly at odds. On the contrary, Christian belief would then have been built on knowledge—knowledge of theological doctrine, of canon law and Church courts, of the details of clerical liberties, of the powers of ecclesiastical office (over souls, bodies, properties), of the preconditions and effects of confession, of the rules of religious orders, of the locations and virtues of shrines, of the lives of the saints, and so forth. Familiarity with all such (religious) knowledge was a precondition for normal social life, and belief (embodied in practice and discourse) an orientation for effective activity in it—whether on the part of the religious clergy, the secular clergy, or the laity. Because of this, the form and texture and function of their beliefs would have been different from the form and texture and function of contemporary belief—and so too of their doubts and their disbelief. . . .

At any rate, I think it is not too unreasonable to maintain that "the basic axiom" underlying what Geertz calls "the religious perspective" is not everywhere the same. It is preeminently the Christian church that has occupied itself with identifying, cultivating, and testing belief as a verbalizable inner condition of true religion.

Religion as a Perspective

The phenomenological vocabulary that Geertz employs raises two interesting questions, one regarding its coherence and the other concerning its adequacy to a modern cognitivist notion of religion. I want to suggest that although this vocabulary is theoretically incoherent, it is socially quite compatible with the privatized idea of religion in modern society.

Thus, "the religious perspective," we are told, is one among several—common-sense, scientific, aesthetic—and it differs from these as follows. It differs from the common-sense perspective, because it "moves beyond the realities of everyday life to wider ones which correct and complete them, and [because] its defining concern is not action upon those wider realities but acceptance of them, faith in them." It is unlike the scientific perspective, because "it questions the realities of everyday life not out of an institutionalized scepticism which dissolves the

world's givenness into a swirl of probabilistic hypotheses, but in terms of what it takes to be wider, nonhypothetical truths." And it is distinguished from the aesthetic perspective, because "instead of effecting a disengagement from the whole question of factuality, deliberately manufacturing an air of semblance and illusion, it deepens the concern with fact and seeks to create an aura of utter actuality." In other words, although the religious perspective is not exactly rational, it is not irrational either.

It would not be difficult to state one's disagreement with this summary of what common sense, science, and aesthetics are about. But my point is that the optional flavor conveyed by the term perspective is surely misleading when it is applied equally to science and to religion in modern society: religion is indeed now optional in a way that science is not. Scientific practices, techniques, knowledges, permeate and create the very fibers of social life in ways that religion no longer does. In that sense, religion today is a perspective (or an "attitude," as Geertz sometimes calls it), but science is not. In that sense, too, science is not to be found in every society, past and present. We shall see in a moment the difficulties that Geertz's perspectivism gets him into, but before that I need to examine his analysis of the mechanics of reality maintenance at work in religion.

Consistent with previous arguments about the functions of religious symbols is Geertz's remark that "it is in ritual—that is, consecrated behavior—that this conviction that religious conceptions are veridical and that religious directives are sound is somehow generated." The long passage from which this is taken swings back and forth between arbitrary speculations about what goes on in the consciousness of officiants and unfounded assertions about ritual as imprinting. At first sight, this seems a curious combination of introspectionist psychology with a behaviorist one—but as Vygotsky argued long ago, the two are by no means inconsistent, insofar as both assume that psychological phenomena consist essentially in the consequence of various stimulating environments.

Geertz postulates the function of rituals in generating religious conviction ("In these plastic dramas men attain their faith as they portray it"), but how or why this happens is nowhere explained. Indeed, he concedes that such a religious state is not always achieved in religious ritual. . . . But the question remains: What is it that ensures the participant's taking the symbolic forms in the way that leads to faith if the line between religious and nonreligious perspectives is not so easy to draw? Mustn't the ability and the will to adopt a religious standpoint be present prior to the ritual performance? That is precisely why a simple stimulus-response model of how ritual works will not do. And if that is the case, then ritual in the sense of a sacred performance cannot be the place where religious faith is attained, but the manner in which it is (literally) played out. If we are to understand how this happens, we must examine not only the sacred performance itself but also the entire range of available disciplinary activities, of institutional forms of knowledge and practice, within which dispositions are formed and sustained and through which the possibilities of attaining the truth are marked out—as Augustine clearly saw.

I have noted more than once Geertz's concern to define religious symbols according to universal, cognitive criteria, to distinguish the religious perspective clearly from nonreligious ones. The separation of religion from science, common sense, aesthetics, politics, and so on, allows him to defend it against charges of irrationality. If religion has a distinctive perspective (its own truth, as Durkheim would have said) and performs an indispensable function, it does not in essence compete with others and cannot, therefore, be accused of generating false consciousness. Yet in a way this defense is equivocal. Religious symbols create dispositions, Geertz observes, which seem uniquely realistic. Is this the point of view of a reasonably confident agent (who must always operate within the denseness of historically given probabilities) or that of a skeptical observer (who can see through the representa-

tions of reality to the reality itself)? It is never clear. And it is never clear because this kind of phenomenological approach doesn't make it easy to examine whether, and if so to what extent and in what ways, religious experience relates to something in the real world that believers inhabit. This is partly because religious symbols are treated, in circular fashion, as the precondition for religious experience (which, like any experience, must, by definition, be genuine), rather than as one condition for engaging with life.

Toward the end of his essay, Geertz attempts to connect, instead of separating, the religious perspective and the common-sense one—and the result reveals an ambiguity basic to his entire approach. First, invoking Schutz, Geertz states that the everyday world of common-sense objects and practical acts is common to all human beings because their survival depends on it. . . . Next, he informs us that individuals move "back and forth between the religious perspective and the common-sense perspective." These perspectives are so utterly different, he declares, that only "Kierkegaardian leaps" can cover the cultural gaps that separate them. Then, the phenomenological conclusion: "Having ritually 'leapt' into the framework of meaning which religious conceptions define, and the ritual ended, returned again to the common-sense world, a man is—unless, as sometimes happens, the experience fails to register—changed. *And as he is changed, so also is the common-sense world,* for it is now seen as but the partial form of a wider reality which corrects and completes it." (emphasis added).

This curious account of shifting perspectives and changing worlds is puzzling—as indeed it is in Schutz himself. It is not clear, for example, whether the religious framework and the common-sense world, between which the individual moves, are independent of him or not. Most of what Geertz has said at the beginning of his essay would imply that they are independent, and his remark about common sense being vital to every man's survival also enforces this reading. Yet it is also suggested that as the believer changes his perspective, so he himself changes; and that as he changes, so too is his common-sense world changed and corrected. So the latter, at any rate, is not independent of his moves. But it would appear from the account that the religious world is independent, since it is the source of distinctive experience for the believer, and through that experience, a source of change in the common-sense world: there is no suggestion anywhere that the religious world (or perspective) is ever affected by experience in the common-sense world.

This last point is consistent with the phenomenological approach in which religious symbols are sui generis, marking out an independent religious domain. But in the present context it presents the reader with a paradox: the world of common sense is always common to all human beings, and quite distinct from the religious world, which in turn differs from one group to another, as one culture differs from another; but experience of the religious world affects the common-sense world, and so the distinctiveness of the two kinds of world is modified, and the common-sense world comes to differ, from one group to another, as one culture differs from another. The paradox results from an ambiguous phenomenology in which reality is at once the distance of an agent's social perspective from the truth, measurable only by the privileged observer, and also the substantive knowledge of a socially constructed world available to both agent and observer, but to the latter only through the former.

Conclusion

Perhaps we can learn something from this paradox which will help us evaluate Geertz's confident conclusion: "The anthropological study of religion is therefore a two-stage operation: first, an analysis of the system of meanings embodied in the symbols which make up *the religion proper,* and, second, the relating of these systems to social-structural and psychological processes" (emphasis added). How sensible this sounds, yet how mistaken, surely, it is. If religious symbols are understood, on the analogy with words, as vehicles for meaning, can such meanings be established independently of the form of life in which they are used? If religious symbols are to be taken as the signatures of a sacred text, can we know what they mean without regard to the social disciplines by which their correct reading is secured? If religious symbols are to be thought of as the concepts by which experiences are organized, can we say much about them without considering how they come to be authorized? Even if it be claimed that what is experienced through religious symbols is not, in essence, the social world but the spiritual, is it possible to assert that conditions in the social world have nothing to do with making that kind of experience accessible? Is the concept of religious training entirely vacuous?

The two stages that Geertz proposes are, I would suggest, one. Religious symbols—whether one thinks of them in terms of communication or of cognition, of guiding action or of expressing emotion—cannot be understood independently of their historical relations with nonreligious symbols or of their articulations in and of social life, in which work and power are always crucial. My argument, I must stress, is not just that religious symbols are intimately linked to social life (and so change with it), or that they usually support dominant political power (and occasionally oppose it). It is that different kinds of practice and discourse are intrinsic to the field in which religious representations (like any representation) acquire their identity and their truthfulness. From this it does not follow that the meanings of religious practices and utterances are to be sought in social phenomena, but only that their possibility and their authoritative status are to be explained as products of historically distinctive disciplines and forces. The anthropological student of particular religions should therefore begin from this point, in a sense unpacking the comprehensive concept which he or she translates as "religion" into heterogeneous elements according to its historical character.

. . . My aim has been to problematize the idea of an anthropological definition of religion by assigning that endeavor to a particular his-tory of knowledge and power (including a par-ticular understanding of our legitimate past and future) out of which the modern world has been constructed.

From *Purity and Danger: An Analysis of Concepts of Pollution and Taboo*

MARY DOUGLAS

. . . As we know it, dirt is essentially disorder. There is no such thing as absolute dirt: it exists in the eye of the beholder. If we shun dirt, it is not because of craven fear, still less dread or holy terror. Nor do our ideas about disease account for the range of our behaviour in clean-ing or avoiding dirt. Dirt offends against order. Eliminating it is not a negative movement, but a positive effort to organise the environment. . . .

Pollution ideas work in the life of society at two levels, one largely instrumental, one expres-sive. At the first level, the more obvious one, we find people trying to influence one another's behaviour. Beliefs reinforce social pressures: all the powers of the universe are called in to guar-antee an old man's dying wish, a mother's dig-nity, the rights of the weak and innocent. Political power is usually held precariously and primitive rulers are no exception. So we find their legitimate pretensions backed by beliefs in extraordinary powers emanating from their per-sons, from the insignia of their office or from words they can utter. Similarly the ideal order of society is guarded by dangers which threaten transgressors. These danger-beliefs are as much threats which one man uses to coerce another as dangers which he himself fears to incur by his own lapses from righteousness. They are a strong language of mutual exhortation. At this level the laws of nature are dragged in to sanc-tion the moral code: this kind of disease is caused by adultery, that by incest; this meteoro-logical disaster is the effect of political disloyalty, that the effect of impiety. The whole universe is harnessed to men's attempts to, force one another into good citizenship. Thus we find that certain moral values are upheld and certain social rules defined by beliefs in dangerous con-tagion, as when the glance or touch of an adul-terer is held to bring illness to his neighbours or his children.

It is not difficult to see how pollution beliefs can be used in a dialogue of claims and counter-claims to status. But as we examine pollution beliefs we find that the kind of contacts which are thought dangerous also carry a symbolic load. This is a more interesting level at which pollution ideas relate to social life. I believe that some pollutions are used as analogies for expressing a general view of the social order. For example, there are beliefs that each sex is a dan-ger to the other through contact with sexual fluids. According to other beliefs only one sex is endangered by contact with the other, usually

Reprinted from Mary Douglas, Purity and Danger: An Analysis of Concepts of Pollution and Taboo *(New York: Routledge, 1966).*

males from females, but sometimes the reverse. Such patterns of sexual danger can be seen to express symmetry or hierarchy. It is implausible to interpret them as expressing something about the actual relation of the sexes. I suggest that many ideas about sexual dangers are better interpreted as symbols of the relation between parts of society, as mirroring designs of hierarchy or symmetry which apply in the larger social system. What goes for sex pollution also goes for bodily pollution. The two sexes can serve as a model for the collaboration and distinctiveness of social units. So also can the processes of ingestion portray political absorption. Sometimes bodily orifices seem to represent points of entry or exit to social units, or bodily perfection can symbolise an ideal theocracy. . . .

The native of any culture naturally thinks of himself as receiving passively his ideas of power and danger in the universe, discounting any minor modifications he himself may have contributed. In the same way we think of ourselves as passively receiving our native language and discount our responsibility for shifts it undergoes in our life time. The anthropologist falls into the same trap if he thinks of a culture he is studying as a long established pattern of values. In this sense I emphatically deny that a proliferation of ideas about purity and contagion implies a rigid mental outlook or rigid social institutions. The contrary may be true. . . .

In all the cosmologies . . . the lot of individual humans is thought to be affected by power inhering in themselves or in other humans. The cosmos is turned in, as it were, on man. Its transforming energy is threaded on to the lives of individuals so that nothing happens in the way of storms, sickness, blights or droughts except in virtue of these personal links. So the universe is man-centred in the sense that it must be interpreted by reference to humans.

But there is a quite other sense in which the primitive undifferentiated world view may be described as personal. Persons are essentially not things. They have wills and intelligence. With their wills they love, hate and respond emotion-

ally. With their intelligence they interpret signs. But in the kind of universe I am contrasting with our own world view, things are not clearly distinct from persons. Certain kinds of behaviour characterise person to person relations. First, persons communicate with one another by symbols in speech, gesture, rite, gift and so on. Second, they react to moral situations. However impersonally the cosmic forces may be defined, if they seem to respond to a person-to-person style of address their quality of thing is not fully differentiated from their personality. They may not be persons but nor are they entirely things. . . .

So here is another way in which the primitive, undifferentiated universe is personal. It is expected to behave as if it was intelligent, responsive to signs, symbols, gestures, gifts, and as if it could discern between social relationships.

The most obvious example of impersonal powers being thought responsive to symbolic communication is the belief in sorcery. The sorcerer is the magician who tries to transform the path of events by symbolic enactment. He may use gestures or plain words in spells or incantations. Now words are the proper mode of communication between persons. If there is an idea that words correctly said are essential to the efficacy of an action, then, although the thing spoken to cannot answer back, there is a belief in a limited kind of one-way verbal communication. And this belief obscures the clear thing-status of the thing being addressed. A good example is the poison used for the oracular detection of witches in Zandeland.[1] The Azande themselves brew their poison from bark. It is not said to be a person but a thing. They do not suppose there is a little man inside which works the oracle. Yet for the oracle to work the poison must be addressed aloud, the address must convey the question unequivocally and, to eliminate error of interpretation, the same question must be put in reverse form in the second round of consultation. In this case not only does the poison hear and understand the words, but it has limited powers of reply. Either it kills the chicken or it does not. It can only give yes and no answers. It cannot initiate a conversation or conduct an unstructured interview. Yet this limited response to questioning radically modifies its thing-status in the Azande universe. It is not an ordinary poison, but more like a captive interviewee filling in a survey questionnaire with crosses and ticks. . . .

Finally there are the beliefs which imply that the impersonal universe has discernment. It may discern between fine nuances in social relations such as whether the partners in sexual intercourse are related within prohibited degrees, or between less fine ones such as whether a murder has been committed on a fellow-tribesman or on a stranger, or whether a woman is married or not. Or it may discern secret emotions hidden in men's breasts. There are many examples of implied discernment of social status. The hunting Cheyenne thought that the buffaloes who provide their main livelihood were affected by the rotten smell of a man who had murdered a fellow-tribesman and they moved away, thus endangering the survival of the tribe. The buffalo were not supposed to react to the smell of murder of a foreigner. . . .

To sum up, a primitive world view looks out on a universe which is personal in several different senses. Physical forces are thought of as interwoven with the lives of persons. Things are not completely distinguished from persons and persons are not completely distinguished from their external environment. The universe responds to speech and mime. It discerns the social order and intervenes to uphold it. . . .

So the primitive world view which I have defined above is rarely itself an object of contemplation and speculation in the primitive culture. It has evolved as the appanage of other social institutions. To this extent it is produced indirectly, and to this extent the primitive culture must be taken to be unaware of itself, unconscious of its own conditions.

In the course of social evolution institutions proliferate and specialise. The movement is a double one in which increased social control makes possible greater technical developments and the latter opens the way to increased social control again. Finally we find ourselves in the modern world where economic interdependence is carried to the highest pitch reached by mankind so far. One inevitable by-product of social differentiation is social awareness, self-consciousness about the processes of communal life. And with differentiation go special forms of social coercion, special monetary incentives to conform, special types of punitive sanctions, specialised police and overseers and progress men scanning our performance, and so on, a whole paraphernalia of social control which would never be conceivable in small-scale undifferentiated economic conditions. This is the experience of organic solidarity which makes it so hard for us to interpret the efforts of men in primitive society to overcome the weakness of their social organisation. . . .

Powers And Dangers

Granted that disorder spoils pattern; it also provides the materials of pattern. Order implies restriction; from all possible materials, a limited selection has been made and from all possible relations a limited set has been used. So disorder by implication is unlimited, no pattern has been realised in it, but its potential for patterning is indefinite. This is why, though we seek to create order, we do not simply condemn disorder. We recognise that it is destructive to existing patterns; also that it has potentiality. It symbolises both danger and power.

Ritual recognises the potency of disorder. In the disorder of the mind, in dreams, faints and frenzies, ritual expects to find powers and truths which cannot be reached by conscious effort. Energy to command and special powers of healing come to those who can abandon rational control for a time. . . .

In these beliefs there is a double play on inarticulateness. First there is a venture into the disordered regions of the mind. Second there is the venture beyond the confines of society. The man who comes back from these inaccessible regions brings with him a power not available to those who have stayed in the control of themselves and of society.

This ritual play on articulate and inarticulate forms is crucial to understanding pollution. In ritual form it is treated as if it were quick with power to maintain itself in being, yet always liable to attack. Formlessness is also credited with powers, some dangerous, some good. . . .

Danger lies in transitional states, simply because transition is neither one state nor the next, it is undefinable. The person who must pass from one to another is himself in danger and emanates danger to others. The danger is controlled by ritual which precisely separates him from his old status, segregates him for a time and then publicly declares his entry to his new status. Not only is transition itself dangerous, but also the rituals of segregation are the most dangerous phase of the rites. . . . The theme of death and rebirth, of course, has other symbolic functions: the initiates die to their old life and are reborn to the new. The whole repertoire of ideas concerning pollution and purification are used to mark the gravity of the event and the power of ritual to remake a man—this is straightforward.

During the marginal period which separates ritual dying and ritual rebirth, the novices in initiation are temporarily outcast. For the duration of the rite they have no place in society. Sometimes they actually go to live far away outside it. Sometimes they live near enough for unplanned contacts to take place between full social beings and the outcasts. Then we find them behaving like dangerous criminal characters. They are licensed to waylay, steal, rape. This behaviour is even enjoined on them. To behave anti-social is the proper expression of their marginal condition. To have been in the margins is to have been in contact with danger, to have been at a source of power. It is consistent with the ideas about form and formlessness to treat initiands coming out of seclusion as if they were themselves charged with power, hot, dangerous, requiring insulation and a time for

cooling down. Dirt, obscenity and lawlessness are as relevant symbolically to the rites of seclusion as other ritual expressions of their condition. They are not to be blamed for misconduct any more than the foetus in the womb for its spite and greed.

It seems that if a person has no place in the social system and is therefore a marginal being, all precaution against danger must come from others. He cannot help his abnormal situation. This is roughly how we ourselves regard marginal people in a secular, not a ritual context. . . .

To plot a map of the powers and dangers in a primitive universe, we need to underline the interplay of ideas of form and formlessness. So ideas about power are based on an idea of society as a series of forms contrasted with surrounding non-form. There is power in the forms and other power in the inarticulate area, margins, confused lines, and beyond the external boundaries. If pollution is a particular class of danger, to see where it belongs in the universe of dangers we need an inventory of all the possible sources of power. In a primitive culture the physical agency of misfortune is not so significant as the personal intervention to which it can be traced. The effects are the same the world over: drought is drought, hunger is hunger; epidemic, child labour, infirmity—most of the experiences are held in common. But each culture knows a distinctive set of laws governing the way these disasters fall. The main links between persons and misfortunes are personal links. So our inventory of powers must proceed by classifying all kinds of personal intervention in the fortunes of others.

The spiritual powers which human action can unleash can roughly be divided into two classes—internal and external. The first reside within the psyche of the agent—such as evil eye, witchcraft, gifts of vision or prophecy. The second are external symbols on which the agent must consciously work: spells, blessings, curses, charms and formulas and invocations. These powers require actions by which spiritual power is discharged.

This distinction between internal and external sources of power is often correlated with another distinction, between uncontrolled and controlled power. According to widespread beliefs, the internal psychic powers are not necessarily triggered off by the intention of the agent. He may be quite unaware that he possesses them or that they are active. These beliefs vary from place to place. For example, Joan of Arc did not know when her voices would speak to her, could not summon them at will, was often startled by what they said and by the train of events which her obedience to them started. The Azande believe that a witch does not necessarily know that his witchcraft is at work, yet if he is warned, he can exert some control to check its action.

By contrast, the magician cannot utter a spell by mistake; specific intention is a condition of the result. A father's curse usually needs to be pronounced to have effect.

Where does pollution come in the contrast between uncontrolled and controlled power, between psyche and symbol? As I see it, pollution is a source of danger altogether in a different class: the distinctions of voluntary, involuntary, internal, external, are not relevant. It must be identified in a different way.

First to continue with the inventory of spiritual powers, there is another classification according to the social position of those endangering and endangered. Some powers are exerted on behalf of the social structure; they protect society from malefactors against whom their danger is directed. Their use must be approved by all good men. Other powers are supposed to be a danger to society and their use is disapproved; those who use them are malefactors, their victims are innocent and all good men would try to hound them down—these are witches and sorcerers. This is the old distinction between white and black magic.

Are these two classifications completely unconnected? Here I tentatively suggest a correlation: where the social system explicitly recognises positions of authority, those holding such positions are endowed with explicit spiritual power, controlled, conscious, external and approved—powers to bless or curse.

When the system requires people to hold dangerously ambiguous roles, these persons are credited with uncontrolled, unconscious, dangerous, disapproved powers—such as witchcraft and evil eye.

In other words, where the social system is well articulated, I look for articulate powers vested in the points of authority; where the social system is ill-articulated, I look for inarticulate powers vested in those who are a source of disorder. I am suggesting that the contrast between form and surrounding non-form accounts for the distribution of symbolic and psychic powers: external symbolism upholds the explicit social structure and internal, unformed psychic powers threaten it from the non-structure. . . .

There are probably many more variant types of socially ambiguous or weakly defined statuses to which involuntary witchcraft is attributed. It would be easy to go on piling up examples. Needless to say, I am not concerned with beliefs of a secondary kind or with short-lived ideas which flourish briefly and die away. If the correlation were generally to hold good for the distribution of dominant, persistent forms of spiritual power, it would clarify the nature of pollution. For, as I see it, ritual pollution also arises from the inter play of form and surrounding formlessness. Pollution dangers strike when form has been attacked. Thus we would have a triad of powers controlling fortune and misfortune: first, formal powers wielded by persons representing the formal structure and exercised on behalf of the formal structure: second, formless powers wielded by interstitial persons: third, powers not wielded by any person, but inhering in the structure, which strike against any infraction of form. This three-fold scheme for investigating primitive cosmologies unfortunately comes to grief over exceptions which are too important to brush aside. . . .

To sum up, beliefs which attribute spiritual power to individuals are never neutral or free of the dominant patterns of social structure. If some beliefs seem to attribute free-floating spiritual powers in a haphazard manner, closer inspection shows consistency. The only circumstances in which spiritual powers seem to flourish independently of the formal social system are when the system itself is exceptionally devoid of formal structure, when legitimate authority is always under challenge or when the rival segments of an acephalous political system resort to mediation. Then the main contenders for political power have to court for their side the holders of free-floating spiritual power. Thus it is beyond doubt that the social system is thought of as quick with creative and sustaining powers.

Now is the time to identify pollution. Granted that all spiritual powers are part of the social system. They express it and provide institutions for manipulating it. This means that the power in the universe is ultimately hitched to society, since so many changes of fortune are set off by persons in one kind of social position or another. But there are other dangers to be reckoned with, which persons may set off knowingly or unknowingly, which are not part of the psyche and which are not to be bought or learned by initiation and training. These are pollution powers which inhere in the structure of ideas itself and which punish a symbolic breaking of that which should be joined or joining of that which should be separate. It follows from this that pollution is a type of danger which is not likely to occur except, where the lines of structure, cosmic or social, are clearly defined.

A polluting person is always in the wrong. He has developed some wrong condition or simply crossed some line which should not have been crossed and this displacement unleashes danger for someone. Bringing pollution, unlike sorcery and witchcraft, is a capacity which men share with animals, for pollution is not always set off by humans. Pollution can be committed intentionally, but intention is irrelevant to its effect—it is more likely to happen inadvertently.
. . .

External Boundaries

The idea of society is a powerful image. It is potent in its own right to control or to stir men to action. This image has form; it has external boundaries, margins, internal structure. Its outlines contain power to reward conformity and repulse attack. There is energy in its margins and unstructured areas. For symbols of society any human experience of structures, margins or boundaries is ready to hand.

Van Gennep shows how thresholds symbolise beginnings of new statuses. Why does the bridegroom carry his bride over the lintel? Because the step, the beam and the door posts make a frame which is the necessary everyday condition of entering a house. The homely experience of going through a door is able to express so many kinds of entrance. So also are cross roads and arches, new seasons, new clothes and the rest. No experience is too lowly to be taken up in ritual and given a lofty meaning. The more personal and intimate the source of ritual symbolism, the more telling its message. The more the symbol is drawn from the common fund of human experience, the more wide and certain its reception.

The structure of living organisms is better able to reflect complex social forms than door posts and lintels. So we find that the rituals of sacrifice specify what kind of animal shall be used, young or old, male, female or neutered, and that these rules signify various aspects of the situation which calls for sacrifice. The way the animal is to be slaughtered is also laid down. The Dinka cut the beast longitudinally through the sexual organs if the sacrifice is intended to undo an incest; in half across the middle for celebrating a truce; they suffocate it for some occasions and trample it to death for others. Even more direct is the symbolism worked upon the human body. The body is a model which can stand for any bounded system. Its boundaries can represent boundaries which are threatened or precarious. The body is a complex structure. The functions of its different parts and their relation afford a source of symbols for other complex structures. We cannot possibly interpret rituals concerning excreta, breast milk, saliva and the rest unless we are prepared to see in the body a symbol of society, and to see the powers and dangers credited to social structure reproduced in small on the human body. . . .

These are obviously technical questions in which the anthropologist cannot engage. But on two points the anthropologist has something to say. One is the question of whether primitive cultures really can be said to revel in excremental magic. The answer to this is surely No. The other is whether primitive cultures seem to be seeking an escape from reality. Do they really use their magic, excremental or other, to compensate for loss of success in external fields of endeavour? Again the answer is No.

To take the matter of excremental magic first. The information is distorted, first as to the relative emphasis on bodily as distinct from other symbolic themes, and second as to the positive or negative attitudes to bodily refuse seen in primitive ritual.

To take up the latter point first: the use of excrement and other bodily exuviae in primitive cultures is usually inconsistent with the themes of infantile erotic fantasy. So far from excrement, etc., being treated as a source of gratification, its use tends to be condemned. So far from being thought of as an instrument of desire, the power residing in the margins of the body is more often to be avoided. . . .

So far from using bodily magic as an escape, cultures which frankly develop bodily symbolism may be seen to use it to confront experience with its inevitable pains and losses. By such themes they face the great paradoxes of existence . . . insofar as ethnography supports the idea that primitive cultural themes can be compared with the fantasies of infantile sexuality.

To correct the two distortions of evidence to which this subject is prone we should classify carefully the contexts in which body dirt is thought of as powerful. It may be used ritually for good, in the hands of those vested with power to bless. Blood, in Hebrew religion, was regarded as the source of life, and not to be touched except in the sacred conditions of sacrifice. Sometimes the spittle of persons in key positions is thought effective to bless. . . . The same goes for body dirt as ritual instrument of harm. It may be credited to the incumbents of key positions for defending the structure, or to sorcerers abusing their positions in the structure, or to outsiders hurling bits of bone and other stuff at weak points in the structure.

But now we are ready to broach the central question. Why should bodily refuse be a symbol of danger and of power? Why should sorcerers be thought to qualify for initiation by shedding blood or committing incest or anthropophagy? Why, when initiated, should their art consist largely of manipulating powers thought to inhere in the margins of the human body? Why should bodily margins be thought to be specially invested with power and danger?

First, we can rule out the idea that public rituals express common infantile fantasies. These erotic desires which it is said to be the infant's dream to satisfy within the body's bounds are presumably common to the human race. Consequently body symbolism is part of the common stock of symbols, deeply emotive because of the individual's experience. But rituals draw on this common stock of symbols selectively. Some develop here, others there. Psychological explanations cannot of their nature account for what is culturally distinctive.

Second, all margins are dangerous. If they are pulled this way or that the shape of fundamental experience is altered. Any structure of ideas is vulnerable at its margins. We should expect the orifices of the body to symbolise its specially vulnerable points. Matter issuing from them is marginal stuff of the most obvious kind. Spittle, blood, milk, urine, faeces or tears by simply issuing forth have traversed the boundary of the body. So also have bodily parings, skin, nail, hair clippings and sweat. The mistake is to treat bodily margins in isolation from all other margins. There is no reason to assume any primacy for the individual's attitude to his own bodily and emotional experience, any more than for his cultural and social experience. This is the clue which explains the unevenness with which different aspects of the body are treated in the rituals of the world. . . .

Four kinds of social pollution seem worth distinguishing. The first is danger pressing on external boundaries; the second, danger from transgressing the internal lines of the system; the third, danger in the margins of the lines. The fourth is danger from internal contradiction, when some of the basic postulates are denied by other basic postulates, so that at certain points the system seems to be at war with itself. . . .

To sum up. There is unquestionably a relation between individual preoccupations and primitive ritual. But the relation is not the simple one which some psychoanalysts have assumed. Primitive ritual draws upon individual experience, of course. This is a truism. But it draws upon it so selectively that it cannot be said to be primarily inspired by the need to solve individual problems common to the human race, still less explained by clinical research. Primitives are not trying to cure or prevent personal neuroses by their public rituals. Psychologists can tell us whether the public expression of individual anxieties is likely to solve personal problems or not. Certainly we must suppose that some interaction of the kind is probable. But that is not at issue. The analysis of ritual symbolism cannot begin until we recognise ritual as an attempt to create and maintain a particular culture, a particular set of assumptions by which experience is controlled.

Any culture is a series of related structures which comprise social forms, values, cosmology, the whole of knowledge and through which all experience is mediated. Certain cultural themes are expressed by rites of bodily manipulation. In this very general sense primitive culture can be said to be autoplastic. But the objective of these rituals is not negative withdrawal from reality. The assertions they make are not usefully to be compared to, the withdrawal of the infant into thumb-sucking and masturbation. The rituals enact the form of social relations and in giving these relations visible expression they enable people to know their own society. The rituals work upon the body politic through the symbolic medium of the physical body.

The System at War with Itself

When the community is attacked from outside at least the external danger fosters solidarity within. When it is attacked from within by wanton individuals, they can be punished and the structure publicly reaffirmed. But it is possible for the structure to be self-defeating. . . . Perhaps all social systems are built on contradiction, in some sense at war with themselves. But in some cases the various ends which individuals are encouraged to pursue are more harmoniously related than in others.

Sexual collaboration is by nature fertile, constructive, the common basis of social life, but sometimes we find that instead of dependence and harmony, sexual institutions express rigid separation and violent antagonism. So far we have noted a kind of sex pollution which expresses a desire to keep the body (physical and social) intact. Its rules are phrased to control entrances and exits. Another kind of sex pollution arises from the desire to keep straight the internal lines of the social system. . . . A third type may arise from the conflict in the aims which can be proposed in the same culture.

In primitive cultures, almost by definition, the distinction of the sexes is the primary social distinction. This means that some important institutions always rest on the difference of sex. If the social structure were weakly organised, then men and women might still hope to follow their own fancies in choosing and discarding sexual partners, with no grievous consequences for society at large. But if the primitive social structure is strictly articulated, it is almost bound to impinge heavily on the relation between men and women. Then we find pollution ideas enlisted to bind men and women to their allotted roles. . . .

There is one exception we should note at once. Sex is likely to be pollution-free in a society where sexual roles are enforced. In such a case anyone who threatened to deviate would be promptly punished with physical force. . . .

It is important to recognise that male dominance does not always flourish with such ruthless simplicity. . . . We saw that when moral rules are obscure or contradictory there is a tendency for pollution beliefs to simplify or clarify the point at issue. . . . When male dominance is accepted as a central principle of social organisation and applied without inhibition and with full rights of physical coercion, beliefs in sex pollution are not likely to be highly developed. On the other hand, when the principle of male dominance is applied to the ordering of social life but is contradicted by other principles such as that of female independence, or the inherent right of women as the weaker sex to be more protected from violence than men, then sex pollution is likely to flourish. Before we take up this case there is another kind of exception to consider.

We find many societies in which individuals are not coerced or otherwise held strictly to their allotted sexual roles and yet the social structure is based upon the association of the sexes. In these cases a subtle, legalistic development of special institutions provides relief. Individuals can to some extent follow their personal whims, because the social structure is cushioned by fictions of one kind or another. . . .

The System Shattered and Renewed

Now to confront our opening question. Can there be any people who confound sacredness with uncleanness? We have seen how the idea of contagion is at work in religion and society. We have seen that powers are attributed to any structure of ideas and that rules of avoidance make a visible public recognition of its boundaries. But this is not to say that the sacred is unclean. Each culture must have its own notions of dirt and defilement which are contrasted with its notions of the positive structure which must not be negated. To talk about a confused blending of the Sacred and the Unclean is outright nonsense. But it still remains true that religions often sacralise the very unclean things which have been rejected with abhorrence. We must, therefore, ask how dirt, which is normally destructive, sometimes becomes creative.

First, we note that not all unclean things are used constructively in ritual. It does not suffice for something to be unclean for it to be treated as potent for good. In Israel it was unthinkable that unclear things, such as corpses and excreta could be incorporated into the Temple ritual, but only blood, and only blood shed in sacrifice. Among the Oyo Yoruba where the left hand is used for unclean work and it is deeply insulting to proffer the left hand, normal rituals sacralise the precedence of the right side, especially dancing to the right. . . .

One answer lies in the nature of dirt itself. The other lies in the nature of metaphysical problems and of particular in reflections which call for expression.

To deal with dirt first. In the course of any imposing of order, whether in the mind or in the external world, the attitude to rejected bits and pieces goes through two stages. First they are recognisably out of place, a threat to good order, and so are regarded as objectionable and vigorously brushed away. At this stage they have some identity: they can be seen to be unwanted bits of whatever it was they came from, hair or food or wrappings. This is the stage at which they are dangerous; their half-identity still clings to them and the clarity of the scene in which they obtrude is impaired by their presence. But a long process of pulverizing, dissolving and rotting awaits any physical things that have been recognised as dirt. In the end, all identity is gone. The origin of the various bits and pieces is lost and they have entered into the mass of common rubbish. It is unpleasant to poke about in the refuse to try to recover anything, for this revives identity. So long as identity is absent, rubbish is not dangerous. It does not even create ambiguous perceptions since it clearly belongs in a defined place, a rubbish heap of one kind or another. Even the bones of buried kings rouse little awe and the thought that the air is full of the dust of corpses of bygone races has no power to move. Where there is no differentiation there is no defilement. . . .

In this final stage of total disintegration, dirt is utterly undifferentiated. Thus a cycle has been completed. Dirt was created by the differentiating activity of mind, it was a by-product of the creation of order. So it started from a state of non-differentiation; all through the process of differentiating its role was to threaten the distinctions made: finally it returns to its true indiscriminable character. Formlessness is therefore an apt symbol of beginning and of growth as it is of decay. . . .

In its last phase then, dirt shows itself as an apt symbol of creative formlessness. But it is from its first phase that it derives its force. The danger which is risked by boundary transgression is power. Those vulnerable margins and those attacking forces which threaten to destroy good order represent the powers inhering in the cosmos. Ritual which can harness these for good is harnessing power indeed.

So much for the aptness of the symbol itself. Now for the living situations to which it applies, and which are irremediably subject to paradox. The quest for purity is pursued by rejection. It follows that when purity is not a symbol but something lived, it must be poor and barren. It is part of our condition that the purity for which we strive and sacrifice so much turns out to be hard and dead as a stone when we get it. . . . It is another thing to try and make over our existence into an unchanging lapidary form. Purity is the enemy of change, of ambiguity and compromise. . . .

The final paradox of the search for purity is that it is an attempt to force experience into logical categories of non-contradiction. But experience is not amenable and those who make the attempt find themselves led into contradiction. . . .

NOTES

1. E. E. Evans-Pritchard, *Witchcraft, Oracles and Magic among the Azande* (Oxford: Oxford Univeristy Press, 1937).

Counterpoint:
Bodies, Natural and Contrived:
The Work of Mary Douglas

SHELDON R. ISENBERG AND DENNIS E. OWEN

Both Isenberg and Owen teach at the University of Florida in Gainesville, Florida.

. . . ONE OF THE MOST SERIOUS problems for the anthropologist and religionist . . . has been to find a methodology which can simultaneously handle a set of interlocking problems. (1) It must be a methodology able to deal with religious experiences of individuals as well as com-

Reprinted from Sheldon R. Isenberg and Dennis E. Owen, "Bodies, Natural and Contrived: The Work of Mary Douglas," Religious Studies Review 3/1 *(1977): 1–17.*

munal religious phenomena, i.e., it must be able to bridge the psychology and the sociology of religion. (2) An adequate methodology must use classification which do not in themselves carry judgments of value, no matter how subtle, e.g., that it is "better" or "worse" to be primitive or modern. (3) It should allow meaningful comparison and differentiation across the whole realm of human religious behavior, e.g., comparisons from different geographical areas and different timespans. (4) It should not *a priori* be reductionist. A Freudian analysis, for instance, presumes all religious behavior to involve escape from the reality principle, while a Marxist analysis presumes the primacy of economic relationships. In both cases religion is taken to be a reflex of deeper psychosocial structures. (5) Such a methodology must be able to deal with simple and complex social settings, a small unified tribe as well as a huge, differentiated industrialized society. (6) It should be able to understand dynamic situations, conversions, schisms, revolutions—all sorts of social and personal changes. (7) Then, a technical requirement: the method should entail a theory which can generate empirically disconfirmable hypotheses, a notorious failing of "deprivation theory." (8) Finally, a requirement that is perhaps the most difficult to achieve, namely, that the methodology should be utilizable by the personally religious as well as the authentically secular person. It should not require heroic measures, such as the sociologically and psychologically improbable *epoché* of the phenomenologist, to insulate the analysis of data from the personal stance of the investigator. It is our conviction that the methodology now being worked out by Mary Douglas approaches the fulfillment of the desiderata listed above, and it is further our belief that students of all aspects of religion might derive benefits from knowing her work. What follows, then, is an examination of her published corpus by reference to her methodology and two of her own applications in areas particularly familiar to the authors, namely, the study of Jewish purity rules and the

study of witchcraft; this is followed by some examples of our own applications of her methodology with references to some attempts by others to do the game. Finally, we offer some speculations about where her methods might take religious studies.

Purity

A key element in Douglas' system is her treatment of purity and defilement or pollution. She sees purity rules operating at many social levels: at the personal level—what you can eat, whom you can touch, how to handle bodily wastes; at the social level—who can marry whom, under what conditions participation in various activities is allowed or not; at the cultic level—who can enter the sacred precincts; and even at the cosmic level—for Daniel, the defilement of the sanctuary defiled the cosmos as a whole. To understand the system of purity rules, their logic and function, is to understand much about a society. Instead of following along venerable tracks of inquiry which seek to identify a "sacred" which requires protection from pollution through purity regulations, she seeks a broader sense of the meaning of purity for any given culture by considering the relativity of dirt. . . . Another way of putting it, a way crucial to understanding her other key analytical concepts, group and grid, is that the distinction of pure from non-pure involves a classification system, an ordering system the internalization of which is a vital part of the socialization process.

The system of pollution rules, then, implies a classification system which correlates with the patterns of all other classification systems in a given society. It is so basic because it is fundamentally concerned with the body. . . . Through pollution rules a social value or classification system is socialized into the individual's body. The individual's body is presented to him, taught to him by society, usually in the manifestation of parents, and then by peers, perhaps also by schools. Our attitudes about our bodies arise from society's image of itself. So if we can learn how a person understands the workings of that complex system called the body, its organization, its spatial arrangement, and its priorities of needs, then we can guess much about the total pattern of self-understanding of the society, such as its perception of its own workings, its organization, its power structure, and its cosmology. The human body, then, is a universal symbol system: every society attempts in some way to socialize its members, to educate its bodies. Thus, Douglas' book title, *Natural Symbols*, is ironic, for the body is the natural symbol system, but the body is never experienced naturally, for it is always socially mediated.

Granted that the individual's body is patterned in a way analogous to the patterning of the social body, how do we make meaningful cross-cultural comparisons of the patterns? To put it another way, Douglas is hypothesizing that a certain understanding of the body accompanies certain social structures, an hypothesis that may be empirically tested. If the social structure is changed, for whatever reason, the body understanding will change in analogous ways. Further, the ideology (or cosmology) that validates or supports (or rejects!) the social structure will change analogously. Society appears somewhat like a symphony, with harmonious lines of sound always trying to play the same melody line. . . . We communicate in various ways, verbally and non-verbally. When we communicate verbally, we use styles appropriate to the message and to the social situation. We communicate with body movement, with the clothes we wear or don't wear. All of the various media enhance and reinforce the message. The ways in which we are taught to control our bodies also reflect the general cultural style. At different times we are more or less aware of the appropriateness of our behavior. On the other hand, we often do not behave in socially approved ways, so that our bodies can also be set against the rules of the social body. . . . Douglas' implication is that the intensity of social controls will be experienced as demands

for strong bodily controls. (Think [of] the West Point cadet standing at attention.) So far in her argument, bodily control directly correlates with social control. But demands for control and the will and capacity to control the self are not the same. . . .

We now begin to see the particular place the purity rule takes in Douglas' system. Strong concern for purity implies one sort of social structure, less concern implies another. . . . Measuring the concern for purity then becomes one way of categorizing different social structures. Concerns for purity are expressed in ritual demands, the violation of which is held to have consequences in the personal and social order. The demands have to do with the internal ordering of the society, its internal system of classification (its grid), and they also have to do with the external boundaries of the society (its sense of itself group). Different societies may be categorized, as we shall see, according to relative strengths of the senses of grid and group. Where the sense of both grid and group are high, there we find strong concerns for piety, appropriate roles, controlled bodily behavior, and concern for pollution of the individual and the social bodies. In such a society, a group that works for or desires change, for whatever reasons, will reject the formalism, the ritual, the purity rules, or, comprehensively, the whole system of social controls that enforce the classification system that is being rejected. Individuals who live in tension with the establishment value system (e.g., many involved in the arts, numerous political revolutionaries, many in the academy) will often express their rejection by adopting informal dress styles, shaggy hair, etc. Prophets in the Bible are often described as wearing outlandish dress, engaging in unusual behavior including bodily ecstasy, and are often reputed to come from the desert areas, the non-civilized spaces of the cosmos. The behavior and adornment of the personal body express in all kinds of ways the tension with social body.

One of the most significant methodological claims made by Douglas involves the application of such concepts as purity and ritual to all human behavior without worrying about its primitive or modern setting, or the religious or secular nature of the event. Formality and informality become the criteria. To talk about ritual we do not have to come to some prior definition of "the sacred" for the society, for ritual and purity express the intensity of society's differentiation of itself from what it conceives to be "nature." . . .

Group and Grid

The equation of God with society is certainly not new. Most of us probably met it during the course of an undergraduate discussion of Feuerbach and only later were we treated to Karl Barth's warning that our inverter of Hegel was a "non-knower of evil." More complex versions of the same equation were offered by Durkheim and Freud who, by reducing society to patriarchy, created some of the most powerful myths of our time. An interesting sidelight in all of this was the question of the truth of religious beliefs, a confusion made possible by overlooking the fact that the origin of beliefs is no determinant of truth, and a mistake remarkably similar to the claim that the meaning of a proposition is the same as its method of verification. Still, the issue of the relation of religion, or more generally, cosmology or symbol systems, to society has been pursued with mixed results. We have already alluded to the ultimate failing of deprivation theory—it simply does not work in too many instances. Similar problems arise with legitimation theory. Where the former would have us see religion as compensation for want, the latter suggests justification for plenty. No doubt there are cases where one or the other of these models will have real explanatory power. The problem is that they tell us little about the relations of cosmologies to societies, and are rendered rather impotent by the vast array of religious and social types which meet any student of the field. Two things become necessary: a method for correlating particular cosmologies with particular social organizations and a means for being responsive to change at both the social and symbolic levels.

Natural Symbols, which represents a coalescence of Douglas' work, meets both requirements. Although Douglas should probably not be considered a structuralist, her writing is definitely informed by the insights of structural anthropology. A significant portion of the attractiveness of structuralism lies in its promise of unfolding universal patterns within human activity. Herein too lies much of our apprehension, for that which explains everything in general too often illuminates nothing in particular. Methodologies which treat myths and other symbol systems as if they had existed eternally, or as if historical development and contingencies were of little note, are guilty at the very least of alienating spirit from flesh, myth from mythmaker. Interpretive schemes failing to coordinate symbol systems with behavioral systems neglect the obvious—that symbolizing, whatever else it may be, is fundamentally a form of human activity. If a structuralist approach is to tell more about life without telling us less about mentalistic structures, it must, as Douglas suggests, develop models which are capable of linking symbol systems to behavioral modes.[1] The solution to this problem offered in *Natural Symbols* is to link social and symbolic structures instead of reducing the latter to the dual organization of the human mind. Such a task, however, is basically comparative, for it requires the development of a model which can interpret widely divergent societies and symbol systems without doing undue violence to their individual integrity. The trick, of course, is to find principles of social organization which are abstract enough to be applied cross-culturally while still maintaining contact with concrete human experience.

Relying primarily on the work of psycho-linguist Basil Bernstein, Douglas suggests that there are two key elements of social and cultural organization which need to be taken into account. As we noted above, she terms these "group" and "grid." Group designates social pressure and is intended to indicate the extent to which an individual finds himself constrained and controlled by others. "Strong group" indicates a social situation in which the individual is tightly controlled by social pressure; "weak group" indicates the reverse. Douglas' use of group to refer to social pressure is itself significant. Strong social pressure is experienced as a demand for conformity to social norms. The more pressure of this sort, the more individual identity will be located within a narrow range of approved alternatives. Furthermore, strong pressure for conformity usually raises the price for non-conformity to that of exclusion from the social group. Consequently, it is possible as well as desirable to correlate pressure with group identity. High-pressure situations will also be situations in which one is very likely to find oneself either within the group or beyond the pale.[2] It seems clear that in order for a society to function even at a minimal level, it will need more than the mere experience of group identity and pressure. Such identity and pressure get the limits of one's living space, but do little in terms of organizing that space so that those who share it can structure their relationships into manageable patterns.

There can be no pressure for conformity unless there is also something to which one can conform, no group identity without symbolic representation. The internal order of society and its shared understanding fall under Douglas' concept of grid. She describes grid as a system of shared classifications or symbols by which one brings order and intelligibility to one's experience. The effectiveness with which any system of classifications can order experience, in Douglas' terms its weakness or strength, depends upon its scope and coherence.[3] A classification system which is narrow in scope may encounter difficulty in ordering the broader dimensions of experience. Likewise, a classification system fraught with contradictions or lacking in coherence may also be incapable of experiential organization. The same will again hold true in a situation where one has competing classification

systems. Here the competition lessens the effectiveness of each of the systems. Each of these instances counts as weak grid. The contrast between weak and strong grid itself raises some interesting questions, but for the moment let us assume that strong grid entails a classification system which is coherent, consistent, and broad in scope. We now have a device which allows us to rank social systems against each other—presuming, of course, success in our fieldwork.

It would be somewhat misleading to suggest that group and grid, pressure and classification, are independent variables, since it seems unlikely that we could have pressure without some degree of classification. The model, it seems to us, needs some refinement at this point. One possibility is to look for a kind of dual aspect to systems of classification, an approach which appears to be strongly implied in Douglas' use of Basil Bernstein.[4] Bernstein sees societies developing two kinds of speech codes. One he calls "restricted code," the other "elaborated code." Restricted code is basically a symbol system which expresses and supports the social structure. It tends to be somewhat limited in scope, narrow in its range of expression and heavily dependent upon context (unspoken shared assumptions). Restricted code is used in positional social structures which allocate power and status to roles rather than to persons, e.g., a social structure whose motto is "salute the uniform and not the man." In terms of Douglas' model, restricted code, an implicitly shared classification system, seems to be the symbolic expression of group identity and pressure. Here we might expect to find sets of condensed symbols the violation of which will very likely constitute a violation of group boundaries. Hence a Jew eating pork, a Bog Irish man eating meat on Friday, and a flagburner all violate the condensed symbols of their communities and may face discipline or even expulsion. The symbols of restricted code provide a society with its self-representation and consequently will themselves establish symbolic boundaries between the inside of the group and everything else. Elaborated code is less contextually dependent. It will attempt to make verbally explicit those meanings which restricted code leaves implicit. Here speech and thought tend toward independence from group identity and pressure. Elaborated code will be broader in scope, allow a wider range of expression, and be rather neutral on the question of social identity. The primary function of elaborated code, Douglas writes, will be "to organize thought processes, distinguish and combine ideas."[5] Here we have classification systems working free of the social order although they could be used to support a social organization—a philosophical justification of a particular organization, for example. An attack upon such a philosophical justification would not necessarily constitute an attack upon the social form.

What we see emerging from Douglas' use of Bernstein is a dualism of classification systems. One side of such systems is to be associated with group identity and pressure, and functions as restricted code. The other side is concerned with a more neutral analysis and corresponds to elaborated code. Our problem here becomes clear when we consider the task of determining whether a society is to be categorized as having strong or weak grid. Suppose our society has a clearly articulated set of symbols which is very narrow in scope and highly intolerant of deviations from the norm. Will we consider this an instance of weak grid? Not necessarily; for if the society is insulated, and the range of experience is narrow, it is entirely possible for the classification system to organize experience without much disturbing the remainder. If the insulation should break down and the society be exposed to a wider range of experience, the result is likely to be a weakening of the effectiveness of the classification system. . . .

The strength or weakness of grid, then, is relative to the society in question. It depends upon the "goodness of fit" between the classification system and the range of experience to be ordered. Our concepts of group and grid therefore must take into account the overlap of the terms. Strong group will indicate the following: high pressure to conform to social norms, a strong sense of group identity including clear distinctions between inside and outside and a clear set of boundaries separating the two, and a restricted set of condensed symbols expressing and reinforcing group identity. Weak group will indicate little pressure, porous boundaries, few and fuzzy symbols. Strong grid will usually entail the existence of a classification system in the sense of elaborated code, but in some instances may indicate primarily restricted code. In weak grid we should expect the elaborated code to be absent. The restricted code will be present, but is likely to be rather narrow and easily threatened by social conflict.

The most interesting aspect of Douglas' model for the religionist is its ability to correlate particular social organizations with cosmological structures. It should be possible to move back and forth between social organizations and cosmologies, deriving the structure of one from the structure of the other. The claim upon which this crucial aspect of the model is based is that there is a human "drive to achieve consonance in all levels of experience" which "produces concordance among the means of expression."[6] . . . Here Douglas appears to be unpacking some of the mechanisms through which the equation of God with society can be sustained. In addition, Douglas is inviting us to discover particular parallels between social structure and all means of expression, verbal and non-verbal. The physical body in this view becomes a microcosm of the social body.[7] Knowledge about one can yield knowledge about the other. . . . Douglas here points directly to the consonance of experience and expression. It is the case that human beings inhabit numerous bodies simultaneously—physical bodies, social bodies, religious bodies, and bodies of thought. Consonance of experience and expression means that one may expect to find parallel structures in all of these bodies, and, further, at symbolic bodies, particularly in cosmology, can be seen as an expression of social experience. For example, let us return to the issue of bodily control. Interest in the openings of the physical body will be a function of social control measured in terms of group in the model. The more the social group is interested in preserving its identity and purity, the more the physical body will be subjected to tight restrictions as to what can pass through its boundaries. Hence a society classified as strong group will view trance as dangerous, for trance states involve the invasion of bodily boundaries by external forces and, in many cases, the relinquishing of intentional control over one's person, posing a threat to strong normative social control. When social conditions are changed, one finds parallel changes occurring at other levels. Weak group fails to produce interest in defining and maintaining the boundaries of both social and physical bodies. There will be less concern with entrances and exits, less fear, perhaps no fear of trance states. . . .

Here we have one example of how we can go about deriving cosmology from social structure. There are many more possibilities, but let us outline the four extreme types, the combinations of group and of their accompanying cosmologies.

Strong Group and Grid

Purity: strong concern for purity; well-defined purification rituals; purity rules define and maintain social structure

Ritual: a ritualistic society; ritual expresses the internal classification system

Magic: belief in the efficacy of symbolic behavior

Personal Identity: a matter of internalizing clearly articulated social roles; individual subservient to but not in conflict with society

Body: tightly controlled but a symbol of life

Trance: dangerous; either not allowed or tightly controlled and limited to a group of experts

Sin: the violation of formal rules; focus upon behavior instead of internal state of being; ritual (magic) efficacious in counteracting sin

Cosmology: anthropomorphic; non-dualistic; the universe is just and non-capricious

Suffering and Misfortune: the result of automatic punishment for the violation of formal rules; part of the divine economy

Strong Group, Weak Grid

Purity: strong concern for purity but the inside of the social and physical bodies are under attack; pollution present and purification ritual ineffective

Ritual: ritualistic; ritual focused upon group boundaries, concerned with expelling pollutants (witches) from social body

Magic: ineffective in protecting individual and social bodies; a source of danger and pollution

Personal Identity: located in group membership, not in the internalization of roles, which are confused; distinction between appearance and internal state

Body: social and physical bodies tightly controlled but under attack; invaders have broken through bodily boundaries; not a symbol of life

Trance: dangerous; a matter of demonic possession; evil

Sin: a matter of pollution; evil lodged within person and society; sin much like a disease; internal state of being more important than adherence to formal rules, but the latter still valued

Cosmology: anthropomorphic; dualistic; warring forces of good and evil; universe is not just and may be whimsical

Suffering and Misfortune: unjust; not automatic punishment; attributed to malevolent forces

Weak Group, Strong Grid

Purity: pragmatic attitude; pollution not automatic; bodily waste not threatening, may be recycled

Ritual: will be used for private ends if present; ego remains superior; condensed symbols do not delimit reality

Magic: private; may be a strategy for success

Personal Identity: pragmatic and adaptable

Body: instrumental; self-controlled; pragmatic attitude

Trance: not dangerous

Sin: failure; loss of face; stupidity

Cosmology: geared to individual success and initiative; cosmos is benignly amoral; God as junior partner

Suffering and Misfortune: an intelligent person ought to be able to avoid them

Weak Group, Weak Grid

Purity: rejected; anti-purity

Ritual: rejected; anti-ritual; effervescent; spontaneity valued

Magic: none; magic rejected

Personal Identity: no antagonism between society and self but old society may be seen as oppressive; roles rejected, self-control and social control low

Body: irrelevant; life is spiritual; purity concerns absent but body may be rejected; may be used freely or asceticism may prevail

Trance: approved, even welcomed; no fear of loss of self-control

Sin: a matter of ethics and interiority

Cosmology: likely to be impersonal; individual access, usually direct; no mediation; benign

Suffering and Misfortune: love conquers all

Douglas offers various examples of these social types and we need not repeat them here. We should, however, at least point out some of the difficulties one is likely to meet in an application of her model, and suggest some avenues for further reflection. How, for example, may we use Douglas in an analysis of a complex modern society? Would a corporation count as strong group? No doubt Exxon has a strong sense of corporate identity, but as a social group it would seem to be constituted almost entirely by what Douglas is calling grid. The model, in other words, seems to assume organic societies; its relevance for the mechanical or instrumental is not so immediately obvious. In complex societies where isolation becomes increasingly less possible, Douglas' social types would seem to be more difficult to find in anything resembling a pure form. . . .

Ritual Speculation

Natural Symbols is presented as a book about ritual. The issue frames the book and provides Douglas with her entree into the relationship of cosmology to social structure. She begins by redeeming ritual from the dustbin of immature activity, astonishing us with the obvious—some people and cultures are genuinely ritualistic. They are not going through mere motions which could better be reduced to ethical motivation. The attitude which would relegate ritual to a primitive past, happily behind those of us who inhabit the civilized world, is born at best from naivete and at worst from western arrogance eager to view ethical monotheism as the crowning jewel of world religions. Douglas does not deny that ritual can and does become empty, but she would have us see this process as a function of particular kinds of social experience. Ritual, in her view, is preeminently a form of communication, a form which can be highly efficient and condensed. . . .

Let us take the matter of sensitivity to condensed symbols. The strong group/strong grid society, as we have indicated, is one in which individuals attain identity through the internalization of clearly articulated roles. Society assumes priority over the self, which is under great pressure to conform to public demands. Indeed humanness and role are one. . . . Since humanness and its possible behavioral actualizations are explicitly presented to the individual in strong grid/strong group, and since individuals are under heavy pressure to conform to a particular set of approved actualizations, the boundaries of "reality" are not likely to be porous. It seems likely to be the case that the internalization of a system of public, socially generated symbols makes possible the experience of a high degree of intersubjectivity such that communication can be implicit, contextual, wordless. This would seem to be one of the rewards of strong grid/strong group. Individuals would be justified through their participation in the grid (roles, the classification system). Ritual, then, becomes an expression of and a reinforcement for the view and experience of reality, a thick exchange of meanings.

Anti-ritualism, which Douglas rightly questions regarding its claim to moral superiority, involves a loss of sensitivity to condensed symbols. It also involves a sense of oppression since it is possible to distinguish between anti-ritualism and non-ritualism. The anti-ritualist and the non-ritualist are generated by weak group. They will be products of what Bernstein calls the personal control system while the ritualist will probably be a product of a positional system. Released from strong pressure to conform to the public reality, the individual is free to develop worlds of private meaning. He has learned to differentiate person from role and finds the latter limiting if not oppressive. Condensed symbols cannot encapsulate an opening reality. Roles become facades under which the real self waits to be discovered. Communication strives to become explicit, finding that old symbols constrain the self in someone else's meaning. . . .

At the risk of trying to stretch a bit too far we would suggest that some of the recent fascination with Eastern religions lies here. As symbol systems appear increasingly oppressive, the self finds its alienation deepening. A solution to this problem is the elimination of the ego. When symbols lose their effectiveness, one option is silence. If we are reading Douglas correctly, there are some lessons to be found here. Douglas assumes that we have a desire for intimacy—we want to communicate fully, to penetrate the barriers between self and self, to overcome our isolation. We wish to speak without words freeing ourselves finally from the limitations of language. . . . When we see ourselves from this perspective the need of women to find new language is to be taken seriously. However, the search for a language with which to speak and share our being, endemic to users of the elaborated code (ourselves included), may ultimately deepen its own alienation. We find ourselves seeking relationships unmediated by roles what Victor Turner calls "communitas." At some level language itself implies separation and publicly approved categories imply chasms. Intimacy here cannot be mediated, but information cannot be communicated without a shared classification system. Communication requires structure. There may be a catch in the endeavor for as we spurn all forms of roles and convention we may be eliminating our experience of intersubjectivity. If the self is a social construct will we wind up with no language to speak and nothing with which to speak it? . . .

Douglas reminds us that attempts to understand the nature of, and relationships between, all phenomena presume an implicit or explicit cosmology. She invites us to explore the boundaries of such cosmologies, to make those that are implicit explicit, to correlate them with social experience, and to follow out the implications of the central classification system for the ways human beings make choices at all levels of their experience. For instance, Freud understood his therapy to be successful if his patient became more socially viable; success or health was measured by the ability to function successfully within the public classification system. His analysis, however, took the form of making explicit the personally implicit, relating all human choices to experiences remarkably capable of description in a language of theatre; though confused, we could at least be tragic. Choosing to see myth as the expression of personal experience, as opposed to social, Freud reduces cosmology to family squabbles. However, the explanation of behavior by reference to private past experiences itself encourages reliance upon private classification systems. According to Douglas, successful analysands should be profoundly unsuited for that social existence toward which Freud aims them, for sanity depends upon the plausibility of an unverifiable classification system.

What is impressive about Douglas' work is its claim to such wide applicability; all media of communication come under her purview. Those of her questions which are valuable are so in an astonishing variety of areas. The breadth of her publication attests to that. We have suggested before some difficulties with her models. Her own extraordinarily sensitive and constructive response to criticism is in full display in her second edition of *Natural Symbols*. It is clear that the system is not intended to be static. Its wider application results in appropriate modifications. Its claim to generating hypotheses which are refutable needs further extensive testing, particularly in relationship to complex cultures with groups within groups. What we have discovered in attempting our own explorations is that her questions, whether we can answer them or not given our information and insight, are always informative and never boring.

NOTES

1. Mary Douglas, *Natural Symbols: Explorations in Cosmology* (London: Barrie and Jenkins, 1970), pp. 94–95.

2. Ibid., p. 83.

3. Ibid., p. 82.

4. Ibid., pp. 77–81.

5. Ibid., p. 44.

6. Ibid., p. 95.

7. Ibid., p. 101.

From *Structural Anthropology*

CLAUDE LÉVI-STRAUSS

DESPITE SOME RECENT ATTEMPTS to renew them, it seems that during the past twenty years anthropology has increasingly turned from studies in the field of religion. At the same time, and precisely because the interest of professional anthropologists has withdrawn from primitive religion, all kinds of amateurs who claim to belong to other disciplines have seized this opportunity to move in, thereby turning into their private playground what we had left as a wasteland. The prospects for the scientific study of religion have thus been undermined in two ways.

The explanation for this situation lies to some extent in the fact that the anthropological study of religion was started by men like Tylor, Frazer, and Durkheim, who were psychologically oriented although not in a position to keep up with the progress of psychological research and theory. Their interpretations, therefore, soon became vitiated by the outmoded psychological approach which they used as their basis. Although they were undoubtedly right in giving their attention to intellectual processes, the way they handled these remained so crude that it

discredited them altogether. . . . Instead of trying to enlarge the framework of our logic to include processes which, whatever their apparent differences, belong to the same kind of intellectual operation, a naïve attempt was made to reduce them to inarticulate emotional drives, which resulted only in hampering our studies.

Of all the chapters of religious anthropology probably none has tarried to the same extent as studies in the field of mythology. From a theoretical point of view the situation remains very much the same as it was fifty years ago, namely, chaotic. Myths are still widely interpreted in conflicting ways: as collective dreams, as the outcome of a kind of esthetic play, or as the basis of ritual. Mythological figures are considered as personified abstractions, divinized heroes, or fallen gods. Whatever the hypothesis, the choice amounts to reducing mythology either to idle play or to a crude kind of philosophic speculation.

In order to understand what a myth really is, must we choose between platitude and sophism? Some claim that human societies merely express, through their mythology,

Reprinted from Claude Lévi-Strauss, Structural Anthropology, *trans. Claire Jacobson and Brooke Grundfest Schoef (New York: Basic Books, 1963).*

fundamental feelings common to the whole of mankind, such as love, hate, or revenge or that they try to provide some kind of explanations for phenomena which they cannot otherwise understand—astronomical, meteorological, and the like. But why should these societies do it in such elaborate and devious ways, when all of them are also acquainted with empirical explanations? On the other hand, psychoanalysts and many anthropologists have shifted the problems away from the natural or cosmological toward the sociological and psychological fields. But then the interpretation becomes too easy: If a given mythology confers prominence on a certain figure, let us say an evil grandmother, it will be claimed that in such a society grandmothers are actually evil and that mythology reflects the social structure and the social relations; but should the actual data be conflicting, it would be as readily claimed that the purpose of mythology is to provide an outlet for repressed feelings. Whatever the situation, a clever dialectic will always find a way to pretend that a meaning has been found.

Mythology confronts the student with a situation which at first sight appears contradictory. On the one hand it would seem that in the course of a myth anything is likely to happen. There is no logic, no continuity. Any characteristic can be attributed to any subject; every conceivable relation can be found. With myth, everything becomes possible. But on the other hand, this apparent arbitrariness is belied by the astounding similarity between myths collected in widely different regions. Therefore the problem: If the content of a myth is contingent, how are we going to explain the fact that myths throughout the world are so similar?

It is precisely this awareness of a basic antinomy pertaining to the nature of myth that may lead us toward its solution. For the contradiction which we face is very similar to that which in earlier times brought considerable worry to the first philosophers concerned with linguistic problems; linguistics could only begin to evolve as a science after this contradiction had been overcome. Ancient philosophers reasoned about

language the way we do about mythology. On the one hand, they did notice that in a given language certain sequences of sounds were associated with definite meanings, and they earnestly aimed at discovering a reason for the linkage between those sounds and that meaning. Their attempt, however, was thwarted from the very beginning by the fact that the same sounds were equally present in other languages although the meaning they conveyed was entirely different. The contradiction was surmounted only by the discovery that it is the combination of sounds, not the sounds themselves, which provides the significant data.

It is easy to see, moreover, that some of the more recent interpretations of mythological thought originated from the same kind of misconception under which those early linguists were laboring. Let us consider, for instance, Jung's idea that a given mythological pattern—the so-called archetype—possesses a certain meaning. This is comparable to the long-supported error that a sound may possess a certain affinity with a meaning: for instance, the "liquid" semi-vowels with water, the open vowels with things that are big, large, loud, or heavy, etc., a theory which still has its supporters.[1] Whatever emendations the original formulation may now call for,[2] everybody will agree that the Saussurean principle of the arbitrary character of linguistic signs was a prerequisite for the accession of linguistics to the scientific level.

To invite the mythologist to compare his precarious situation with that of the linguist in the prescientific stage is not enough. As a matter of fact we may thus be led only from one difficulty to another. There is a very good reason why myth cannot simply be treated as language if its specific problems are to be solved; myth is language: to be known, myth has to be told; it is a part of human speech. In order to preserve its specificity we must be able to show that it is both the same thing as language, and also something different from it. Here, too, the past experience of linguists may help us. For language itself can be analyzed into things which are at the same time similar and yet different. This is precisely what is expressed in Saussure's distinction between *langue* and *parole,* one being the structural side of language, the other the statistical aspect of it, *langue* belonging to a reversible time, *parole* being nonreversible. If those two levels already exist in language, then a third one can conceivably be isolated.

We have distinguished *langue* and *parole* by the different time referents which they use. Keeping this in mind, we may notice that myth uses a third referent which combines the properties of the first two. On the one hand, a myth always refers to events alleged to have taken place long ago. But what gives the myth an operational value is that the specific pattern described is timeless; it explains the present and the past as well as the future. This can be made clear through a comparison between myth and what appears to have largely replaced it in modern societies, namely, politics. When the historian refers to the French Revolution, it is always as a sequence of past happenings, a nonreversible series of events the remote consequences of which may still be felt at present. But to the French politician, as well as to his followers, the French Revolution is both a sequence belonging to the past—as to the historian—and a timeless pattern which can be detected in the contemporary French social structure and which provides a clue for its interpretation, a lead from which to infer future developments. . . . It is that double structure, altogether historical and ahistorical, which explains how myth, while pertaining to the realm of *parole* and calling for an explanation as such, as well as to that of *langue* in which it is expressed, can also be an absolute entity on a third level which, though it remains linguistic by nature, is nevertheless distinct from the other two.

A remark can be introduced at this point which will help to show the originality of myth in relation to other linguistic phenomena. Myth is the part of language where the formula *traduttore, traditore* reaches its lowest truth value. From that point of view it should be placed in the gamut of linguistic expressions at the end opposite to that of poetry, in spite of all the claims which have been made to prove the contrary. Poetry is a kind of speech which cannot be translated except at the cost of serious distortions; whereas the mythical value of the myth is preserved even through the worst translation. Whatever our ignorance of the language and the culture of the people where it originated, a myth is still felt as a myth by any reader anywhere in the world. Its substance does not lie in its style, its original music, or its syntax, but in the *story* which it tells. Myth is language, functioning on an especially high level where meaning succeeds practically at "taking off" from the linguistic ground on which it keeps on rolling.

To sum up the discussion at this point, we have so far made the following claims: (1) If there is a meaning to be found in mythology, it cannot reside in the isolated elements which enter into the composition of a myth, but only in the way those elements are combined. (2) Although myth belongs to the same category as language, being, as a matter of fact, only part of it, language in myth exhibits specific properties. (3) Those properties are only to be found *above* the ordinary linguistic level, that is, they exhibit more complex features than those which are to be found in any other kind of linguistic expression.

If the above three points are granted, at least as a working hypothesis, two consequences will follow: (1) Myth, like the rest of language, is made up of constituent units. (2) These constituent units presuppose the constituent units present in language when analyzed on other levels—namely, phonemes, morphemes, and sememes—but they, nevertheless, differ from the latter in the same way as the latter differ among themselves; they belong to a higher and more complex order. For this reason, we shall call them *gross constituent units.*

How shall we proceed in order to identify and isolate these gross constituent units or mythemes? We know that they cannot be found among phonemes, morphemes, or sememes, but only on a higher level; otherwise myth would become confused with any other kind of speech.

Therefore, we should look for them on the sentence level. The only method we can suggest at this stage is to proceed tentatively, by trial and error, using as a check the principles which serve as a basis for any kind of structural analysis: economy of explanation; unity of solution; and ability to reconstruct the whole from a fragment, as well as later stages from previous ones.

The technique which has been applied so far by this writer consists in analyzing each myth individually, breaking down its story into the shortest possible sentences, and writing each sentence on an index card bearing a number corresponding to the unfolding of the story.

Practically each card will thus show that a certain function is, at a given time, linked to a given subject. Or, to put it otherwise, each gross constituent unit will consist of a *relation*.

However, the above definition remains highly unsatisfactory for two different reasons. First, it is well known to structural linguists that constituent units on all levels are made up of relations, and the true difference between our *gross* units and the others remains unexplained; second, we still find ourselves in the realm of a non-reversible-time, since the numbers of the cards, correspond to the unfolding of the narrative. Thus the specific character of mythological time, which as we have seen is both reversible and nonreversible, synchronic and diachronic, remains unaccounted for. From this springs a new hypothesis, which constitutes the very core of our argument: The true constituent units of a myth are not the isolated relations but *bundles of such relations,* and it is only as bundles that these relations can be put to use and combined so as to produce a meaning. Relations pertaining to the same bundle may appear diachronically at remote intervals, but when we have succeeded in grouping them together we have reorganized our myth according to a time referent of a new nature, corresponding to the prerequisite of the initial hypothesis, namely a two-dimensional time referent which is simultaneously diachronic and synchronic, and which accordingly integrates the characteristics of *langue* on the one hand, and those of *parole* on the other. To put it

in even more linguistic terms, it is as though a phoneme were always made up of all its variants.

Two comparisons may help to explain what we have in mind.

Let us first suppose that archaeologists of the future coming from another planet would one day, when all human life had disappeared from the earth, excavate one of our libraries. Even if they were at first ignorant of our writing, they might succeed in deciphering it—an undertaking which would require, at some early stage, the discovery that the alphabet, as we are in the habit of printing it, should be read from left to right and from top to bottom. However, they would soon discover that a whole category of books did not fit the usual pattern—these would be the orchestra scores on the shelves of the music division. But after trying, without success, to decipher staffs one after the other, from the upper down to the lower, they would probably notice that the same patterns of notes recurred at intervals, either in full or in part, or that some patterns were strongly reminiscent of earlier ones. Hence the hypothesis: What if patterns showing affinity, instead of being considered in succession, were to be treated as one complex pattern and read as a whole? By getting at what we call harmony, they would then see that an orchestra score, to be meaningful, must be read diachronically along one axis—that is, page after page, and from left to right—and synchronically along the other axis, all the notes written vertically making up one gross constituent unit, that is, one bundle of relations.

The other comparison is somewhat different. Let us take an observer ignorant of our playing cards, sitting for a long time with a fortune-teller. He would know something of the visitors: sex, age, physical appearance, social situation, etc., in the same way as we know something of the different cultures whose myths we try to study. He would also listen to the seances and record them so as to be able to go over them and make comparisons—as we do when we listen to myth-telling and record it. Mathematicians to whom I have put the problem agree that if the man is bright and if the material available to him is sufficient, he may be able to reconstruct the nature of the deck of cards being used, that is, fifty-two or thirty-two cards according to the case, made up of four homologous sets consisting of the same units (the individual cards) with only one varying feature, the suit.

Now for a concrete example of the method we propose. We shall use the Oedipus myth, which is well known to everyone. I am well aware that the Oedipus myth has only reached us under late forms and through literary transmutations concerned more with esthetic and moral preoccupations than with religious or ritual ones, whatever these may have been. But we shall not interpret the Oedipus myth in literal terms, much less offer an explanation acceptable to the specialist. We simply wish to illustrate—and without reaching any conclusions with respect to it—a certain technique, whose use is probably not legitimate in this particular instance, owing to the problematic elements indicated above. The "demonstration" should therefore be conceived, not in terms of what the scientist means by this term, but at best in terms of what is meant by the street peddler, whose aim is not to achieve a concrete result, but to explain, as succinctly as possible, the functioning of the mechanical toy which he is trying to sell to the onlookers.

The myth will be treated as an orchestra score would be if it were unwittingly considered as a unilinear series; our task is to reestablish the correct arrangement. Say, for instance, we were confronted with a sequence of the type: 1, 2, 4, 7, 8, 2, 3, 4, 6, 8, 1, 4, 5, 7, 8, 1, 2, 5, 7, 3, 4, 5, 6, 8 . . . , the assignment being to put all the 1's together, all the 2's, the 3's, etc.; the result is a chart:

1	2		4			7	8
	2	3	4		6		8
1			4	5		7	8
1	2			5		7	
		3	4	5	6		8

We shall attempt to perform the same kind of operation on the Oedipus myth, trying out several arrangements of the mythemes until we find one which is in harmony with the principles

enumerated above. Let us suppose, for the sake of argument, that the best arrangement is the following (although it might certainly be improved with the help of a specialist in Greek mythology, see [p. 332])

We thus find ourselves confronted with four vertical columns, each of which includes several relations belonging to the same bundle. Were we to *tell* the myth, we would disregard the columns and read the rows from left to right and from top to bottom. But if we want to *understand* the myth, then we will have to disregard one half of the diachronic dimension (top to bottom) and read from left to right, column after column, each one being considered as a unit.

All the relations belonging to the same column exhibit one common feature which it is our task to discover. For instance, all the events grouped in the first column on the left have something to do with blood relations which are overemphasized, that is, are more intimate than they should be. Let us say, then, that the first column has as its common feature the *overrating of blood relations*. It is obvious that the second column expresses the same thing, but inverted: *underrating of blood relations*. The third column refers to monsters being slain. As to the fourth, a few words of clarification are needed. The remarkable connotation of the surnames in Oedipus' father-line has often been noticed. However, linguists usually disregard it, since to them the only way to define the meaning of a term is to investigate all the contexts in which it appears, and personal names, precisely because they are used as such, are not accompanied by any context. With the method we propose to follow the objection disappears, since the myth itself provides its own context. The significance is no longer to be sought in the eventual meaning of each name, but in the fact that all the names have a common feature: All the hypothetical meanings (which may well remain hypothetical) refer to *difficulties in walking straight and standing upright*.

What then is the relationship between the two columns on the right? Column three refers to monsters. The dragon is a chthonian being

Cadmos sees his sister Europa ravished by Zeus		Cadmos kills the dragon	
	The Spartoi kill one another		
	Oedipus kills his father, Laios		Labdacos (Laios' father) = *lame* (?) Laios (Oedipus' father) = *left-sided* (?)
		Oedipus kills the Sphinx	
			Oedipus = *swollen foot* (?)
Oedipus marries his mother, Jocasta			
	Eteocles kills his brother, Polynices		
Antigone buries her brother, Polynices despite prohibition			

which has to be killed in order that mankind be born from the Earth; the Sphinx is a monster unwilling to permit men to live. The last unit reproduces the first one, which has to do with the *autochthonous origin* of mankind. Since the monsters are overcome by men, we may thus say that the common feature of the third column is *denial of the autochthonous origin of man*.

This immediately helps us to understand the meaning of the fourth column. In mythology it is a universal characteristic of men born from the Earth that at the moment they emerge from the depth they either cannot walk or they walk clumsily. This is the case of the chthonian beings in the mythology of the Pueblo: Muyingwu, who leads the emergence, and the chthonian Shumaikoli are lame ("bleeding-foot," "sore-foot"). The same happens to the Koskimo of the Kwakiutl after they have been swallowed by the chthonian monster, Tsiakish: When they returned to the surface of the earth "they limped forward or tripped sideways." Thus the common feature of the fourth column is the *persistence of the autochthonous origin of man*. It follows that column four is to column three as column one is to column two. The

inability to connect two kinds of relationships is overcome (or rather replaced) by the assertion that contradictory relationships are identical inasmuch as they are both self-contradictory in a similar way. Although this is still a provisional formulation of the structure of mythical thought, it is sufficient at this stage.

Turning back to the Oedipus myth, we may now see what it means. The myth has to do with the inability, for a culture which holds the belief that mankind is autochthonous . . . to find a satisfactory transition between this theory and the knowledge that human beings are actually born from the union of man and woman. Although the problem obviously cannot be solved, the Oedipus myth provides a kind of logical tool which relates the original problem—born from one or born from two? —to the derivative problem: born from different or born from same? By a correlation of this type, the overrating of blood relations is to the underrating of blood relations as the attempt to escape autochthony is to the impossibility to succeed in it. Although experience contradicts theory, social life validates cosmology by its similarity of structure. Hence cosmology is true.

Two remarks should be made at this stage.

In order to interpret the myth, we left aside a point which has worried the specialists until now, namely, that in the earlier (Homeric) versions of the Oedipus myth, some basic elements are lacking, such as Jocasta killing herself and Oedipus piercing his own eyes. These events do not alter the substance of the myth although they can easily be integrated, the first one as a new case of auto-destruction (column three) and the second as another case of crippledness (column four). At the same time there is something significant in these additions, since the shift from foot to head is to be correlated with the shift from autochthonous origin to self-destruction.

Our method thus eliminates a problem which has, so far, been one of the main obstacles to the progress of mythological studies, namely, the quest for the *true* version, or the *earlier* one. On the contrary, we define the myth as consisting of all its versions; or to put it otherwise, a myth remains the same as long as it is felt as such. A striking example is offered by the fact that our interpretation may take into account the Freudian use of the Oedipus myth and is certainly applicable to it. Although the Freudian problem has ceased to be that of autochthony versus bisexual reproduction, it is still the problem of understanding how one can be born from two: How is it that we do not have only one procreator, but a mother plus a father? Therefore, not only Sophocles, but Freud himself, should be included among the recorded versions of the Oedipus myth on a par with earlier or seemingly more "authentic" versions.

An important consequence follows. If a myth is made up of all its variants, structural analysis should take all of them into account. After analyzing all the known variants of the Theban version, we should thus treat the others in the same way: first, the tales about Labdacos' collateral line including Agave, Pentheus, and Jocasta herself; the Theban variant about Lycos with Amphion and Zetos as the city founders; more remote variants concerning Dionysus (Oedipus' matrilateral cousin); and Athenian legends where Cecrops takes the place of Cadmos, etc. For each of them

a similar chart should be drawn and then compared and reorganized according to the findings: Cecrops killing the serpent with the parallel episode of Cadmos; abandonment of Dionysus with abandonment of Oedipus; "Swollen Foot" with Dionysus' *loxias,* that is, walking obliquely; Europa's quest with Antiope's; the founding of Thebes by the Spartoi or by the brothers Amphion and Zetos; Zeus kidnapping Europa and Antiope and the same with Semele; the Theban Oedipus and the Argian Perseus, etc. We shall then have several two-dimensional charts, each dealing with a variant, to be organized in a three-dimensional order . . . so that three different readings become possible: left to right, top to bottom, front to back (or vice versa). All of these charts cannot be expected to be identical; but experience shows that any difference to be observed may be correlated with other differences, so that a logical treatment of the whole will allow simplifications, the final outcome being the structural law of the myth. . . .

Our method not only has the advantage of bringing some kind of order to what was previously chaos; it also enables us to perceive some basic logical processes which are at the root of mythical thought. Three main processes should be distinguished. . . .

Three final remarks may serve as conclusion.

First, the question has often been raised why myths, and more generally oral literature, are so much addicted to duplication, triplication, or quadruplication of the same sequence. If our hypotheses are accepted, the answer is obvious: The function of repetition is to render the structure of the myth apparent. For we have seen that the synchronic-diachronic structure of the myth permits us to organize it into diachronic sequences . . . which should be read synchronically (the columns). Thus, a myth exhibits a "slated" structure, which comes to the surface, so to speak, through the process of repetition.

However, the slates are not absolutely identical. And since the purpose of myth is to provide a logical model capable of overcoming a contradiction (an impossible achievement if, as it happens, the contradiction is real), a theoretically infinite number of slates will be generated, each one slightly different from the others. Thus, myth grows spiral-wise until the intellectual impulse which has produced it is exhausted. Its *growth* is a continuous process, whereas its *structure* remains discontinuous. If this is the case, we should assume that it closely corresponds, in the realm of the spoken word, to a crystal in the realm of physical matter. This analogy may help us to better understand the relationship of myth to both *langue* on the one hand and *parole* on the other. Myth is an intermediary entity between a statistical aggregate of molecules and the molecular structure itself.

Prevalent attempts to explain alleged differences between the so-called primitive mind and scientific thought have resorted to qualitative differences between the working processes of the mind in both cases, while assuming that the entities which they were studying remained very much the same. If our interpretation is correct, we are led toward a completely different view—namely, that the kind of logic in mythical thought is as rigorous as that of modern science, and that the difference lies, not in the quality of the intellectual process, but in the nature of the things to which it is applied. This is well in agreement with the situation known to prevail in the field of technology: What makes a steel ax superior to a stone ax is not that the first one is better made than the second. They are equally well made, but steel is quite different from stone. In the same way we may be able to show that the same logical processes operate in myth as in science, and that man has always been thinking equally well; the improvement lies, not in an alleged progress of man's mind, but in the discovery of new areas to which it may apply its unchanged and unchanging powers.

NOTES

1. See, for instance, Si R. A. Paget, "The Origin of Language," *Journal of World History*, I, No. 2 (UNESCO, 1953).

2. See Émile Benveniste, "Nature du signe linguistique," *Acta Linguistica*, I, No. 1 (1939).

Counterpoint:
From *Religion in Relation: Method, Application and Moral Location*

IVAN STRENSKI

Ivan Strenski teaches at the University of California, Santa Barbara. He has published the following books: *Durkheim and the Jews of France, Malinowski and the Work of Myth,* and *Four Theories of Myth in Twenetieth-Century History: Cassirer, Eliade, Lévi-Strauss and Malinowski.*

STRUCTURAL ANTHROPOLOGY puzzles even the most persistent reader. Despite Lévi-Strauss's regular explications, fundamental questions remain unanswered. In response, an exegetical industry has grown up around Lévi-Strauss, partly to aid the clarification of obscure areas in

Reprinted from Ivan Strenski, Religion in Relation: Method, Application and Moral Location *(Columbia: University of South Carolina Press, 1993).*

his thought, partly to situate structural anthropology within a familiar context. This chapter is concerned with the scientific status of structural anthropology, especially as such a question bears on the issue of falsifiability: are structural claims falsifiable? And in what way?

Falsifiability and Science

With some qualifications I follow Popper[1] in holding that falsifiability is a suitable criterion for marking scientific theories. For Popper, scientific theories are not distinguished primarily by their success in achieving confirmation. Indeed, almost any type of viewpoint may in some way claim cases of confirmation; yet, we rightly avoid calling any viewpoint scientific. If mere confirmability were the principal criterion of a scientific theory, then we should have to include neurology and physics in the same class as astrology and flat-earthism. Popper argues that a theory is scientific to the degree it lays itself open in principle to tests, to falsification or refutation.

As a criterion of science, however, falsifiability strikes a negative chord. Thus, Popper says, "A theory which is not refutable by any conceivable event is non-scientific."[2] For Popper, scientific activity involves "learning from our mistakes."[3] Some have argued against Popper that falsificationism gives us little insight into the creative activities of analogical reasoning and model-building which lie at the centre of science.[4] On this view, Popper proposes, at best, a strategy for eliminating non-scientific theories, not a method for constructing scientific ones.

One can, however, concur with this criticism of Popper without denying that falsifiability still remains useful in screening out non-scientific theories or models. Part of this use lies in its ability to provide a broad criterion for marking scientific theories. Although one talks of "empirical falsification," the term "empirical" can range from values as narrow as sense-data observation to those as broad as the notion of "experience." I do not think empiricism reduces to positivism or sensationalism, although Lévi-

Strauss seems to take empiricism to be an epistemology based on mere "sense-perception."[5] Empiricism has grown beyond such structures. Along with such an enlightened empiricist as Popper, one can affirm that central to the scientific attitude is the willingness to make claims which risk refutation. It is not then so much the method of falsification that matters, although "experience" probably comes about as close to a method as we shall get. Even if experience constitutes a restriction, then it is at least an extraordinarily broad one. Although I shall advocate a brand of empiricism, it is also an equally broad kind of empiricism.

Falsifiability and Structural Anthropology in General

Now, Lévi-Strauss never raises the subject of falsification. This is not because the concept does not apply to structural anthropology; it is merely because Lévi-Strauss does not himself apply it. But this requires some explaining. Let me lay out three reasons why this subject is avoided by Lévi-Strauss.

First, I would suggest that Lévi-Strauss believes he has no need of a negative criterion of science like falsifiability because he already has a positive criterion in the notions of the bifurcation of nature and model-building. For Lévi-Strauss, scientific activity consists in explaining empirical reality in terms of non-empirical mechanisms. . . . In so far as this amounts to the rejection of experience in a broad sense, Lévi-Strauss rejects falsifiability.

The second reason Lévi-Strauss avoids falsifiability is symptomatic of the first. In accepting a positive criterion of science, he is led to concentrate on establishing the initial plausibility of his anthropology by accumulating confirmations of the structuralist approach. This accounts in some way for the fact that the bulk of Lévi-Strauss's mature work consists of the *Mythologiques,* an undertaking devoted to amassing evidence of the practical fruitfulness of structural anthropology. In this light, the negative question of what might constitute refutation of structural claims would not seem to arise naturally as first matter of business.

The third reason behind Lévi-Strauss's avoidance of the problem of falsifiability is his belief in the objectivity of structural claims. Structural anthropology seeks to be "objective"[6] to "understand Being in relation to itself and not in relation to oneself."[7] Although one may admire this kind of ambition, one also must mistrust it at least if Popper's vision of scientific humility has merit.

I shall return to these particular approaches to avoiding falsifiability in the course of this chapter. Let me just state at this point that I do not think Lévi-Strauss's reasons for leaving aside the matter of falsification are good enough. Indeed, I want to show how his belief in the objectivity of structural explanations grows naturally out of his belief in the validity of the repudiation of experience in the human sciences. In this way, I want to show how structuralism soon becomes ideology as it leaves aside experiential falsification in its rush to establish the plausibility of its programme. Even though it may not fit naturally into Lévi-Strauss's paradigm of science, I want to show how a focus on falsification can illuminate and challenge the very nature of structural anthropology.

Structuralist Practice and Promise: The Case of Myth

Let me begin by focusing on the problem of falsifying an elementary structural analysis of a myth set within a particular society. Lévi Strauss's structural analysis of Oedipus or Asdiwal would serve as examples. How can one avoid impressionism and arbitrary analyses here? As a first approximation, I should say that it would seem reasonable [for] anthropological practice to reject a candidate structural analysis of a story if its society of currency in good faith also disavows it. At first sight, the structure of a story depends on what the story is taken to mean by its society of currency. The meaning of a story, in turn, depends on the context of situ-

ation in which the story occurs, and the details of the history and culture of a particular society. Falsifying a particular structural claim would first involve refuting a certain semantic claim since, as Lévi-Strauss suggests, the establishment of the "syntax"[8] of a set of myths only occurs after the "semantic field surrounding a given myth"[9] has been mapped.

The seeds of this contextual method of falsifying or testing structural analyses of myths can thus be found in Lévi-Strauss's actual procedures. One can find elements of this approach in any work he has done on myths. Briefly, let us consider some of the features of his analysis of the myth of Oedipus. In this case, obvious pains are taken to assure plausibility by setting elements of that analysis within a certain period of Greek prehistory. How else can Oedipus's difficulty in walking be linked with autochthonic beliefs unless we have some reasons to suspect that such a belief held sway in ancient Greece? By implication, should not evidence denying such beliefs begin the process of falsifying the kind of meaning and structure Lévi-Strauss builds up in the case of the Oedipus story? In this way, Lévi-Strauss would demonstrate loyalty not only to primitive societies as "their pupil, their witness,"[10] but also to his "teachers" Durkheim and Mauss, whom he credits with having "always taken care to substitute, as a starting point . . . the conscious representations prevailing among the natives themselves. . . ."[11] Things do not go as smoothly, however, as these words suggest. . . .

I am arguing that Lévi-Strauss's performances in the *Mythologiques* and earlier analyses of myth are quite "scientific" enough. Indeed, these studies give us an example of the only way structural analyses could be scientific. Nutini calls the *Mythologiques* a "magnificent failure as a scientific enterprise," because Lévi-Strauss is "unwilling to leave the realm of social relations," because he attempts an "empirical construction of a theory of myth without the notion of structure as a supra-empirical entity. . . ."[12] Turning Nutini on his head, I am arguing that willingness to submit structural analyses for broad empirical falsification to the societies to which they apply is precisely the reason for calling such analyses "scientific." In this sense, the implicit principles actually guiding Lévi-Strauss's structural analysis of myth are better criteria of science than those with which he and Nutini might replace them.

I do not for a moment think that the empirical falsification of structural analyses of myths will be easy. No one expects tribesmen either spontaneously to volunteer the interpretation the structuralist has in mind, or spontaneously to try to refute such analyses. Yet, if they reject a structural analysis in good faith and offer a plausible counter-analysis, I think one should at least admit the provisional falsification of that analysis. No one should underestimate the awkwardness of empirical falsification on the social level. Individuals as well as groups may, among other things, systematically and unconsciously deceive themselves. All I suggest is that if structural analysis at this level is scientific at all, then it must be falsifiable in principle in some empirical way, in this case by reference to the avowals of the people involved. In this sense, spontaneity or consciousness at a particular moment matters less than what would happen if the people involved were pressed on the matter. If they assent to the claims of the structural anthropologist, and if their assent rested on sound bases, we would have all the confirmation we perhaps could ever have; if they reject our claims and provide us with a plausible counter-explanation, we would correspondingly have to accept falsification and revise our explanation. This conviction is all the more poignant because, for the most part, Lévi-Strauss himself seems to agree with it, if we are to judge by the way he seems to analyse myths.

The practice of structuralism, then, lags behind its promise. If we believe Nutini, structural analysis of a plenary sort has not yet been attempted. For all its grandeur, even the *Mythologiques* has not cast its net deeply or widely enough to get beyond the particularities of empirical cultures. It has not really repudi-ated experience: structural anthropology ultimately seeks true human universals, which are the "stable . . . elements that will make possible comparison. . . ." Lévi Strauss's long-range goal is to transcend the world of experience. . . .

In other places Lévi-Strauss describes these structures as "profound" "general" and as having an "objective ground."[13] Other critics of Lévi-Strauss, notably James Boon[14] and Jean Piaget,[15] have termed such structures "deep" to signify their remoteness from experience and their prestige. I shall adopt this terminology in order to raise the question of how deep structural claims resist falsification. In particular, what is it about deep structures that makes it unlikely that they ever could be falsified? In what does their non-empirical nature consist?

Deep Structures as Concrete

For Lévi-Strauss, deep structures are unfalsifiable because they possess three theoretically interdependent, yet seemingly inconsistent properties. Deep structures are (1) concrete properties of the human brain (and matter),[16] (2) abstract macrosociological models and (3) general prescriptions, paradigms or "programmes."[17] To different degrees and in different ways, deep structures are opaque to experience.

As concrete properties of the human brain, deep structures are absolutely unconscious. They transcend experience because they cannot be introspected. In some mysterious way, social anthropology and neurology seem bent on the same course—the discovery of deep neural structures, "constraints specific to the human mind."[18] But, if this identity of aim holds, deep structural claims would seem as easily falsifiable as neurological claims. Indeed, deep structural claims would be identical to neurological claims and falsifiable by looking into brains. In contrast to his earlier criticism of Radcliffe-Brown,[19] Lévi-Strauss thus embraces the biological sciences, seeking to integrate them with the social and cultural sciences into a global anthropology. . . .

Lévi-Strauss never spells out, to my satisfaction at least, what such a harmonious "reintegration" might involve. While one awaits the next installment in the clarification of this matter, Lévi-Strauss's association of categorically distinct objects in the example below seems to implicate structural anthropology in a serious logical blunder. To the extent that I am correct in this judgement, and in so far as Lévi-Strauss assumes the neurological locus of deep structures, structural anthropology rests on a logical mistake. . . . Now whatever else may be true, it is at least logically mistaken to say that "physicochemical processes" are "not substantially different" from "analytical procedures." Nor for Lévi-Strauss is such a claim a mere picturesque image, not to be taken literally by the reader. In recent writings, Lévi-Strauss has made a special point of the efforts structural anthropology makes to overcome metaphysical dualism without at the same time relapsing into a crude materialism: "By reconciling soul and body, mind and ecology, thought and word, structuralism tends towards the only kind of materialism consistent with the ways in which science is developing." This perspective might explain why Lévi-Strauss believes physical and logical "processes" are processes in the same sense, or why he talks of "mind" and "brain" in the same ways: although "physico-chemical processes" are sequences of causes, and "analytical procedures" sequences of meanings, meaning and cause may well lose their logical differences within the framework of the new materialism Lévi-Strauss advocates.

Yet, if one is to judge by this and other examples, Lévi-Strauss really only achieves a groping sense of what such a new materialism might actually be. In its present nascent state, the language of new materialism seems rather more like a "pidgin" or "mixed" anthropological language, than a proper anthropological form of speech. If I am right, Lévi-Strauss does no more than confuse categorical differences between the language of physical objects and languages of a mental, psychological or logical nature. No new level of discourse has been achieved; it is merely our old crudely pluralistic way of speaking which Lévi-Strauss has misused. . . .

The main problem, however, with the repudiation of experience and the postulation of absolutely opaque unconscious structures in the human sciences is that there seems no compelling reason to do so. Although this may sanction Lévi-Strauss's claim to intellectual kinship with Freud and the life sciences, it is disproportionate to the requirements of anthropology. The success of that supposed "failure," the *Mythologiques,* gives perhaps the best answer one can give to the need of absolute unconscious structures in the human sciences. . . .

Deep Structures as Abstract

With deep structures as abstract macrosociological models, we put aside the mare's nest of conceptual problems arising in interpreting deep structures in both a logical and neurological way. One discovers, on the other hand, that the question of falsification is far more vexing here. Deep structures are unfalsifiable because their high abstraction takes them out of reach of possible experience. One is reminded of Gellner's quip about his Marxist philosopher friends who "expound the following device for avoiding clashes between the faith and possible evidence: Marxism presents a general picture too abstract to be empirically tested, and therefore it is permissible to hold it."[20]

I am not sure about the Marxist background to Lévi-Strauss's thinking in this context. One is certain, however, about the similar influence of demographic methodology on macrosociological structural anthropology: structural anthropology is a kind of "socio-demography."[21]

If abstraction were the only reason deep structures were thought to avoid empirical testing, things would not be quite so serious. Even highly abstract models of social relations, like demographic ones, for example, do not ultimately transcend empirical falsification. Demographic generalizations can be falsified empirically because they are at least patchworks of empirical facts. Vast demographic generalizations like the national birth-rate are, after all, at least averaged sums of local birth-rates and individual births. Structural macrosociological models are not simply inductive generalizations and accumulations of such empirical facts. Further, unlike demographic models, they are not "true" because of their correspondence with empirical social relations, norms, beliefs[22] or even indigenous native explanations of their own society. Therefore, it is hard indeed to see how one could ever refute or test such structures empirically. The world of social relations, norms, beliefs and indigenous explanations are the "facts." But in Lévi-Strauss's view, the "facts" need further explanation in terms of deep trans-empirical structures. He believes the vocation of the structuralist is to bifurcate nature and get beyond the "facts"—not to allow phenomena to misrepresent themselves as the deep reality of social life.

From the perspective of the concrete structures of the brain, one sees these abstract macrosociological structures of society as kinds of projections or utterly unconscious products of the brain. On top of these, in turn, one finds the empirical level of social life. The job is to explain this level of social life in terms of its deeper levels. Lévi-Strauss tries to do this much as one explains a jig-saw puzzle in terms of the cams of a jig-saw;[23] society is explained ultimately in terms of the brain. Thus, one can agree with Murphy[24] and others who interpret Lévi-Strauss's position as one between Hegel's mentalism and Marx's materialism. For Lévi-Strauss both mental and social aspects of the world are mediated by the brain, which is to say that the brain structures are psychological, as well as our social and cultural make-up. One might add that our logic is also governed by the brain in the same way, if one brings in Lévi-Strauss's association of neurological and logical processes noted above.

I believe that the macrosociological aspect comes closest to the core of structural anthropology. It is a quest for principles which (logically) constitute social totalities. The vision of this end has been clouded by Lévi-Strauss's desire to repudiate experience and to give these logical principles a *locus*—in the "mind" (wherever or whatever this might be) or brain. But this kind of talk is not only incoherent, it is irrelevant as well: principles or structures do not need a locus. Nor do they need to be absolutely unconscious. Structures are simply the principles that there are for illuminating self-regulating social wholes. No more, no less.

Deep Structures as "Programmes"

From the very start, structures, "programmes"[25] paradigms, or frameworks are involved in the human sciences. At first this happens in two ways: first, Lévi-Strauss believes the data one gathers are already unconsciously "structured" beforehand by the men one studies. Second, one "structures" these data further by assimilating and interpreting them. At each stage, we are insulated from brute neural "facts" by layers of prescriptions—by theory-laden framework. This encourages healthy scepticism of native reports and explanations of their own social situation. It also makes the anthropologist himself properly wary of his own presuppositions. No longer can one say with the fieldworker, "You will believe me, I was there." Not only are the fieldworker's approach and experience theory-laden, but so are the data gathered from his informants and their experience. Therefore, to the extent one accepts this picture of experience defined and limited by frameworks or structures, empirical falsification of frameworks seems ruled out. All this may be to the good. Empiricists can afford to have their confidence shaken from time to time. Lévi-Strauss has, however, gone rather too far in rejecting the core truth of empiricism: it is clearly no more than Freudian dogma to write off the "conscious models" of natives as "by definition very poor ones, since they are not intended to explain the phenomena but to perpetuate them."[26] It may well be that utterances and social relations conceal their deep structural grounds, and the deepest levels of a person's being are opaque to them. But this would involve taking "bad faith" or ignorance as normative of human behaviour—which ironically puts any view claiming to know the deep truth about humans in the same light. In the field as well as in ordinary life, one needs surely to be critical of what people say, without committing the opposite fallacy of believing nothing they say. Lévi-Strauss's suggestions seem to transcend anything one can fairly assert about people today. It seems certainly premature to reject in principle the notion that structural claims are experientially falsifiable by the people one studies, no matter how much experience is structured beforehand. Otherwise, what is such an anthropology but an ideology in Popper's sense, like Freudianism?[27]

. . . Lévi-Strauss is at least proposing that we look on persons and society from the standpoint of formal and systematic features of their action. What is more, one knows Lévi-Strauss believes deep structures also exist concretely in the brain, and thus behind the proposal to look on persons in a structural way lies the deeper belief that persons are essentially formal and systematic animals. In apprehending deep structures, we would thus get down to the most general logical (neurological) preconditions of humanity and sociability. . . .

Ordinary Experience and the Human Sciences

We have seen that from the beginning Lévi-Strauss's conception of science turns on the view that the truth about social life is opaque to ordinary experience. Although I have argued against general bifurcation of nature in the human sciences, I do not doubt that in some degree it may be quite appropriate at times. If one accepts, for example, Lévi-Strauss's ideas about the brain and society, one would at least be justified in drawing a sharp boundary between the deep reality of social life as constituted by brain structures and our ordinary experience of social life. Yet, of course, no absolute boundary exists even here, since one may include experiences aided by microscopes, for example.

It seems absurd, however, to generalize from the neurological and macrosociological features of people to a paradigm for the whole of human life. Much of the reality of human life lies closer to the level of ordinary experience than Lévi-Strauss's neurological and macrosociological frameworks admit. Since ordinary experience seems so important a part of what it means to be a man, one should resist the repudiation of ordinary experience unless pressed to do so. We undertake a needless and expensive task if we sever the natural connections between ordinary experience and theory in the social sciences. Indeed, if I am right about the indispensability of ordinary experience to a definition of human nature, the general bifurcation of nature in this context makes social science impossible. In its place one either has natural science, like neurology, or one has ideology, like Freudianism. Although it is clearly legitimate and desirable to see how far one can go with Lévi-Strauss to "dissolve man" at least in the interests of parsimony, one should confront persons as they experience themselves and others. I want to argue that "scientific" anthropology is only possible if we retain the links between ordinary experience and deep structural claims.

This position should not be confused with dogmatic humanism; I do not believe one has the right to dismiss the bifurcation of nature entirely from the human sciences—any more than one has the general right to embrace it without question. In this connection it is well to remember that the study of humanity and society encompasses widely divergent activities. Neurophysiology, for example, takes the human person as "thing," as a straightforward physical organism, without giving social nature any standing. Demography also considers persons as "things" in the related, but distinct, sense that questions of meaning and consciousness are taken for granted or as subsidiary to questions of structural or formal relationships with other men. On the other hand, ethnology and history, for instance, concern themselves with the human person as a participant in a community of shared meanings and values. Society is here looked on as a "representation" in Durkheim's sense. Given our present knowledge, it is hard to see how one could do justice to the ways men act, if we abandoned one of these approaches. In so far as various human sciences array themselves along the continuum between society as "thing" or "representation," they would seem to complement each other in important ways.[28]

Since Lévi-Strauss's "new anthropology" assumes society to be a "thing," it seems best-suited for those areas and levels of social life where society really does have the nature of "thing." For example, in so far as communication may be concerned, the "new anthropology" would seem to be most at home where "communication" had the broad formal sense developed in system theory, rather than its linguistic sense—its having to do with meaning. . . .

Meaning and Structure: The Case of Myth

To the extent that one cannot study the "rules" of society independently of their use, the "new anthropology" would seem to impoverish our understanding of social life. Myth, it seems, is one of these areas—especially as one is concerned about questions of meaning. By analogy, my remarks will try to extend John Searle's recent criticism of Chomsky's syntactic approach to language to Lévi-Strauss's structural approach to myth. . . . I do not, however, accuse Lévi-Strauss of the unqualified formalism against which he has tried to defend himself.[29] Structures are indeed abstracted from meaningful data of social life in some way. Yet they are structures precisely because they are more formal than the data which they are said to explain. I do argue, however, that to the degree one is concerned about the meaning of things in culture,

and in so far as meaning depends on context and use, an exclusively structural, formal or "syntactic" approach would seem unable to help us.

This is why Lévi-Strauss's uncritical association of economic and kinship systems with systems of myth or symbol seems to me misleading. Lévi-Strauss seems bent either on playing down semantic questions or on assimilating them to syntactic or formal ones. It is, for example, misleading for Lévi-Strauss to suggest that women communicate in a kinship system in the same way as words in a language or mythical oppositions in a story. In the kinship system, women communicate as things in a system of exchange or as elements in a formal organization of relations spelt out by systems theory. (All this, it is true, can be said of language and myth as well.) Yet, unless women are included in the linguistic or mythical system of a society, they do not communicate in the sense that words of a language or elements of a story communicate or signify. Women do not have meaning at all as part of a system of economic exchange or for-mal relations, but only as part of the linguistic or mythical system. Thus language and myth communicate in the non-linguistic senses women usually do, with the addition of the symbolic or semantic sense, which women take on only to the extent they are recognized by myth or language. . . .

As a systems or "syntactical"[30] approach to myth, Lévi-Strauss suggests that we might better understand myths if we left aside the question of their meaning and use, and concentrated on their formal structure. The significance as well as the oddity of this view consists in the fact that myth, like language, is an element of culture with high semantic value. One does not expect to eschew questions of meaning precisely where they typically arise. Nor, when they arise, does one expect to have these questions of meaning answered by reference to the syntax of myth. Still less does one expect Lévi-Strauss to disclaim interest in "how men think in myths, but how myths operate in men's minds without their being aware of the fact."[31] Yet these things are exactly what one should have expected in the light of Lévi-Strauss's repudiation of experience and his conviction that society is a "thing."

The real question is, of course, to what degree structural anthropology is right in treating what seems like an element of society naturally suited for treatment as "representation," namely myth, as if it were a "thing." To what degree might it be fruitful to treat myth as a form of communication in the systems sense alone? Specifically, can this approach answer questions about myth as a form of communication in the semantic or linguistic sense? Granted there is something unfair in these question—as if they could be answered *a priori*. Yet one can begin to examine the question of the scientific status of this approach to meaning by raising the question of falsifiability.

In what way does one falsify claims about the meaning of myth, especially in light of Lévi-Strauss's view that "myths operate in men's minds without their being aware of the fact"? How do we test whether the "final meaning" of a body of myths is that they "signify the mind that evolves them"? Does "meaning" here make any sense at all, since Lévi-Strauss does not intend a linguistic or semantic sense of the ability of myth to "signify"?

A glimmer of the relation of these deep operations to our question seems to centre on the notion of oppositions. For Lévi-Strauss, myths at least reflect the mind's tendency to generate oppositions in thinking. A purely structural property, the notion of formal opposition, seems to provide Lévi-Strauss with sufficient evidence to justify claims about meaning. In his analysis of the Oedipus myth, for example, Lévi-Strauss believes he is justified in saying that this myth means something about ideological contradictions, because the myth, in his view, can be analyzed for oppositions. Similarly, in the analysis of the myth of Asdiwal, that he discerns oppositions implies for Lévi-Strauss that the story wants to tell us something about irreconcilable conflicts in society, or even deeper, in human thinking itself. But such interpretations seem sheer ideology dressed up in scientific clothing unless one can falsify these claims experientially. For whom do myths mean what Lévi-Strauss says they do? Unless he wants us to repeat all the fallacies of Freud's theory of the Unconscious,[32] one cannot merely stipulate that such and such is the real unconscious meaning which people helplessly disavow and conceal from themselves and the anthropologist. Although Nutini (and Lévi-Strauss in some of his moods) does not seem to find the earlier mode of relating myths to their society of currency for falsification, a "scientific" approach to myth, I think we can here begin to see why it is—especially as the question of meaning is involved. Otherwise we are left with two unhappy choices: to the extent these meanings are "deep," ordinary empirical falsification seems ruled out. To the extent we are concerned with meaning, the empirical examination of the brain seems to be of no use. Whatever else "meaning" might be, it is certainly not illuminated by the Freudian doctrine of absolute unconscious structures. Nor is it coherent to identify meaning with some neurological structure. Thus when it comes to explaining levels of culture like myth, where meaning is a necessary element, a purely structural approach breaks down. Such an approach needs to be supplemented by disciplines which treat society as "representation" rather than "thing."

NOTES

1. Karl Popper, *Conjectures and Refutations,* 3rd ed. (London: Routledge & Kegan Paul, 1969), 33–41.

2. Ibid., p. 36.

3. Karl Popper, *Objective Knowledge* (London: Oxford University Press, 1972), 360.

4. Ron Harré, *The Principles of Scientific Thinking* (Chicago: University of Chicago Press, 1970).

5. Claude Lévi-Strauss, *Tristes Tropiques* (New York: Atheneum, 1961), 60f.

6. Idem, *The Raw and the Cooked* (New York: Harper and Row, 1970), 26f.

7. Idem, *Tristes Tropiques,* 62f.

8. Idem, *The Raw and the Cooked,* 7.

9. Ibid., 4.

10. Idem, *The Scope of Anthropology* (London: Cape, 1967), 3.

11. Idem, *Structural Anthropology* (Garden City: Doubleday, 1967), 274.

12. Hugo Nutini, "The Ideological Bases of Lévi-Strauss's Structuralism," *American Anthropology* 73 (1971), 542.

13. Lévi-Strauss, *The Raw and the Cooked,* 26.

14. James Boon, *From Symbolism to Structuralism* (Oxford: Blackwell, 1972), 220.

15. Jean Piaget, *Structuralism* (New York: Harper, 1970), 98.

16. Claude Lévi-Strauss, "Structuralism and Ecology," *Barnard Alumnae* (Spring, 1972), 14.

17. Idem, "Structuralism and Ecology," 7.

18. Ibid.

19. Idem, *The Savage Mind* (London: Weidenfeld & Nicolson, 1966), 247.

20. Ernest Gellner, *Thought and Change* (London: Weidenfeld & Nicolson, 1964), 123–4n.

21. Lévi-Strauss, "Structuralism and Ecology," 14.

22. Idem, *Structural Anthropology,* 297; Piaget, *Structuralism,* 108.

23. Claude Lévi-Strauss, "On Manipulated Sociological Model," *Bijdragen Tod de Taal-Land-en Volkenkunde* 116 (1960), 52.

24. Robert Murphy, *The Dialectics of Social Life* (London: Allen & Unwin, 1972), 18.

25. Ardener, "The New Anthropology and its Critics," 542

26. Lévi-Strauss, *The Scope of Anthropology,* 273.

27. Ardener, "The New Anthropology and its Critics," 460.

28. Alan Ryan, *The Philosophy of the Social Sciences* (London: Macmillan, 1970), 149–58.

29. Claude Lévi-Strauss, "A Conversation with Claude Lévi-Strauss," by A. Akoun, J. Mousseau & F. Morin, *Psychology Today* 5 (1972), 76.

30. Lévi-Strauss, *The Raw and the Cooked,* 5.

31. Ibid., 5.

32. Alasdair MacIntyre, *The Unconscious* (London: Routledge & Kegan Paul, 1958).

Chapter 8

Psychology of Religion

It has been typical of the social sciences to make a distinction between hard and soft approaches to their subject matter. A hard approach has been associated with the rigor of the natural sciences with respect to theory formation and the ability to test resulting theories. This type of approach placed great importance upon experimentation and mathematical analysis. A soft approach stressed observing individuals in social settings, joining them in various social actions, simply talking to people under study, or usually a combination of all three options. These basic differences between hard and soft approaches were at times distinguished as quantitative and qualitative. Within the discipline of psychology, a quantitative approach was associated with physiological psychology, behaviorism, or cognitive psychology, whereas a qualitative approach was connected with psychodynamic schools of psychology like the psychoanalysis of Freud or the analytical psychology of Jung.

An excellent example of the quantitative approach was the experimental analysis of the influential B. F. Skinner, a Harvard University psychologist, who argued that a subject's environment controls its behavior. This implied that the existence of an autonomous individual was impossible. Through the use of complex apparatus and automatic recording devices, Skinner manipulated the environment of animals like mice and pigeons, which share similar kinds of nervous systems, and that of more complex types compared to human beings to discern general principles that demonstrate precisely any connection between behavior and any consequences that follow from that connection. From his behaviorist perspective, Skinner argued that there was a high probability that a result will recur in the future, if an effect was reinforced by some kind of reinforcing stimuli (for example, some food or satisfaction). Of course, without the reinforcing stimuli, the resultant behavior or response rate will slowly decline and eventually cease. A religious phenomenon like faith was a result of certain kinds of behavior that were rewarded over time or will be in the future. Some scholars questioned Skinner's basic methodological assumption—principles discovered with simpler species were applicable to more complex human beings. Moreover, because religious behavior is beyond the scope of scientific analysis, Skinner never really attempted a systematic study of it except to claim that religion was used by others to control human behavior. And because of his lack of a serious attempt to investigate religion and the limits of his methodological approach to the subject of religion, the behavioral approach of Skinner will not be included in this anthology.

Currently it is common for those working in psychology of religion to dismiss the approaches of Freud and Jung as being too speculative and not scientific enough to emulate the natural sciences. Nonetheless, Freud and Jung were pioneers in the psychology of religion with many interesting and provocative thoughts on the subject of religion. Because of their historical importance and broad influence on later scholars, it is important to include them in any collection of writings concerning the psychology of religion.

Sigmund Freud (1856–1939) was a major intellectual figure and force in the twentieth century. His influence continues to this day, for instance, with respect to the terminology that he introduced into the language of the world, with such terms as *id, superego, Oedipus complex,* and so forth. Freud was the first child born to his father's younger second wife in Freiberg in Moravia, a part of the Austro-Hungarian Empire at that time. The family moved to Vienna in 1860 where Freud spent much of his life until his death in London after fleeing Nazi persecution. Freud trained as a medical student at the University of Vienna and passed his final medical examination in 1881. After deciding to become a clinical neurologist, he worked at the Institute of Cerebral Anatomy until 1885 and later with J. M. Charcot, in Paris, where he turned his focus toward psychopathology. Along with J. Breuer in Vienna, Freud focused on clinical psychology, and they collaborated on studies of hysteria. During this period of time, Freud developed his so-called "talking method" of free association in psychotherapy that superceded the prior method of hypnotism. He founded the Vienna Psycho-Analytical Society in 1908, whereas the International Psycho-Analytical Association was founded in 1910. In 1909, Freud and Jung traveled to America to lecture at Clark University in Worcester, Massachusetts. Freud became a full professor at the University of Vienna in 1920, and he maintained an active private practice along with an active writing schedule. The English translation of his collected works embodies 24 volumes. For the subject of religion, his most important works are the following: *Totem and Taboo* (1913), *The Future of an Illusion* (1927), *Civilization and Its Discontents* (1930), and *Moses and Monotheism* (1939). Within these works, Freud connected the actions of religious people and neurotics, and he argued that both groups preferred to act in a patterned or ceremonial way. If they deviated from the rules and procedures, they tended to feel guilty. Because religion often demands repression of our basic selfishness, and psychological neuroses originate from repressed fundamental instincts, religious behavior resembled mental illness by manifesting a universal obsessional neurosis of our frustrated instincts. Moreover, Freud connected religion to a projection of infantile dependencies onto external reality. Because such a projection originated within the inner recesses of human psychological processes, all religious claims were erroneous. If this was the case, Freud thought that it was merely necessary to explain how religion originated and why it continued to exist among people. Before sketching Freud's view of the development of religion in his three major works devoted to the subject, it seems wise to review briefly some of his major notions that form the background to his overall approach and attitude toward religion.

From the perspective of Freud's theory of human development, an infant began its existence as a bundle of instinctual desires that he called the id (Latin for "it"), which was unconscious and unaware of itself and represented the location of instincts and original reservoir of psychic energy. This fundamental and earliest part of the human personality was the location of wishes for food, violence, and sexuality, which were basic bodily drives. The id experienced a gradual change along an identifiably marked path, although it was always possible to regress to an earlier stage of development. Freud connected the tendency of humans to regress to religion, which he argued was an infantile response and a defense mechanism to the dangers presented by our encounter with an alien and hostile world. The other major aspects of the human psyche were the ego (derived from Latin for "I"), which was devoid of its own energy, and the superego (a derivative). For Freud, the ego represented the reality principle where a person made decisions. Such decisions were made within the context of balancing between satisfying the desire of the id and being prepared to curb or deny them satisfaction when they conflicted with the demands of civilization. As a person developed, the ego might grow in strength, while the id lost power. The ego can divert the energy of the id, forming accurate mental representations of the real world that replaced illogical wish fulfillment. From birth, we were shaped and influenced by social, family, national, and cultural pressures that Freud called the superego, an intersection of psychology and exterior influences that contributed to the development of the human personality. Because superego originated when a child identified with the parents, superego was based on the child's idealized and omnipotent parents. The superego possessed the power to reward or punish, which was carried out respectively by the ego and conscience. When the conscience, which opposed both the id and ego, worked to block the discharge of instinctual energy, it accomplished such action directly by inhibiting impulsive behavior and wish-fulfillment and indirectly by way of the ego mechanisms. The superego was also the agent of the death instinct, representing its attempt to destroy the ego, whereas the ego was an agent of life instincts that included the sexual instincts with their own sources in erogenous zones like the mouth, anus, and genital organs of a human being. There was, moreover, a connection between the superego and the so-called Oedipus complex, which Freud borrowed from the Greek play by Sophocles that told the tale of King Oedipus who unwittingly killed his father and married his mother.

The Oedipus complex must be understood within the context of infantile sexual development, which began with the oral phase during the initial 18 months of an infant's life, when pleasure derived along with nourishment from sucking at a mother's breast. From the eighteenth month of life to age 3, Freud identified the anal phase at which time pleasure derived from control of excretion; age 3 and onward marked the phallic stage of development at which time the genital organs assumed importance. During this stage, pleasure was derived from masturbation and sexual fantasies until a stage of latency at around age 6 that lasted until the early teenage years. A child experienced the desire to displace one of their parents and become the lover of the other, during the phallic stage of development. This was called the Oedipus complex. This complex ended when the son stopped fearing the loss of his penis, what Freud called the castration complex. This complex resulted from the threat of the parents or someone else cutting the son's penis off to discourage him from touching and manipulating his sexual organ. The son was forced to submit to his father, gave up hopes of possessing his mother, and settled for satisfaction provided by his sexual fantasies. For young girls, the lack of a penis led them into their Oedipus complex, which found expression in penis envy; girls found satisfaction for their penis envy by extending their longing for it to the bearer of such an organ. By imagining that they had a penis, young girls sought an amorous encounter with their father and identified with the mother by imaging the gift of a baby. After girls abandoned such a fruitless wish, they retained a feeling of inferiority and jealousy because their explicit penis envy, a female equivalent of castration anxiety in males, became more broadly displaced with maturity. The Oedipus complex played an important role in Freud's theory of religion, beginning with his book *Totem and Taboo*.

In his argument, Freud painted a picture of the earliest human beings living as extended families of women and children dominated by a single powerful male figure. Although the groups offered safety, loyalty, and affection, the young males experienced frustration and envy because they were unable to satisfy their sexual instincts because the father dominated all the females. The males were unable to control their sexual urges, and they banded together to murder their father and consume his body to possess the females. After murdering their father, the males were joyful and felt liberated at first. But this initial euphoria gave way to guilt and remorse for their action. Desiring to restore the dominated figure that they had killed, the sons found a substitute and symbol of the father in the totem animal, and they agreed to worship it and not kill it. As time passed, the taboo against killing the totem became a universal commandment against all killing. With feelings of remorse and guilt over the murder of their father, the sons established a second taboo against incest, with the sons agreeing to find new wives external to the clan. Moreover, the sons reenacted the primeval murder of the first father and thereby reaffirmed their love for him in the totem sacrifice. Although the primordial father was dead, the guilty sons now projected this figure onto God. By confessing their family allegiance to the father, eating the flesh of the totem animal identified with the father figure, and controlling their sexual desire, the sons hid their unconscious emotions because the totem sacrifice recreated their original murder, rebellion, and cannibalizing of the father and released their accumulated frustration and hate from continuing to deny their instinctual, Oedipal urges.

Twelve years after the publication of *Totem and Taboo*, Freud published *Future of an Illusion* in 1927, a work that tended to focus on the present state of religion and its future possibilities more than the previous book. According to Freud, religious teachings were not revealed by God, could not be verified by scientific method, and were not logical conclusions based on solid scientific evidence. Nonetheless, people wanted or wished them ardently to be true. It was in this sense that religious beliefs were illusions. Freud did not identify illusion with delusion, which was also something that people wanted to be true, although it can never become true. In contrast to a delusion, an illusion was not necessarily an error, false, or contradictory to reality. An illusion cannot be proven or refuted. Freud thought that we should not be satisfied with deceiving ourselves, and we should strive to correct our thinking. Although Freud made clear in this work that religion had made important contributions to civilization by taming our asocial instincts, we needed to get rid of and replace it with greater knowledge to be gained through science. Why was this scenario desirable from Freud's perspective? Freud presupposed that we were ill and benighted. He wanted to restore people to health and help them to gain knowledge that would free them from the chains of religion. Thus the themes of illness and health ran throughout this work.

Freud's final major work devoted to religion was *Moses and Monotheism,* which was based on a series of essays composed from 1934–1938 and published in the year of his death. This book concentrated on Judaism and its monotheistic faith. Freud began by rewriting the story of Moses, who was depicted as an Egyptian prince and adherent of the religion of the radical Pharaoh Akhennaton. It was this pharaoh who taught the exclusive worship of the god Aten, an imageless deity, law protector, and god of love. Moses adopted Hebrew slaves as his people, led them from captivity, and united them around this new religion. According to Freud's revision of Jewish history, the Jews rebelled against Moses, killed him, and rejected his god, whom they replaced with Yahweh, a more stern and violent deity. The later prophets of the Jewish faith attempted to recover and revive the faith of Moses. This prophetic enterprise led to a revival of Jewish monotheism and gave birth to Christianity. The religion of Moses reflected the Jewish nostalgia for a divine father figure. From Freud's perspective, Moses corresponded to the primordial father killed by the horde of sons suffering from frustrated sexual urges, whose death reenacted the original murderous action of the sons. The communal guilt was repressed by erasing the memory of Moses. Thus the genuine Mosaic religion experienced a period of latency until the Hebrew prophets, restoring an original and pure monotheism, revived it. Freud drew a lesson about neurosis from this narrative: whatever was repressed would return eventually. If Freud thought that religion was a manifestation of a mental illness and that we could recover our health by overcoming religion, we find a much different attitude toward religion in the depth psychology of Jung.

Carl Gustav Jung, who was born in 1875 in Kesswil, Switzerland, shared with Freud the conviction that religion originated in the unconscious, although Jung also stated that the same was true of art, music, literature, and other elements of culture. Jung and Freud conceived of the unconscious differently in the sense that the former conceived of it as more positive and not as infantile and bestial. Other differences will be evident as we proceed with a discussion of Jung's theory. Jung's studies at the University of Basel began in the natural sciences and later concentrated on medicine. After his studies were completed, he accepted a position in psychiatry at the Burghölzli Hospital of the University of Zürich and worked under the guidance of Eugen Bleuler. He earned his doctorate in 1902 with a dissertation on occult phenomena. Three years later Jung obtained dual positions at the University of Zürich and as chief medical doctor at its hospital. After a joint trip to America in 1909 to lecture at Clark University in Massachusetts, Jung and Freud split in 1913 over intellectual differences. Jung also retired from his teaching position, although he continued his psychiatric practice and published the results of his research. After trips to

Africa and America to study tribal peoples, Jung returned to teaching in 1933 at the Federal Higher Technical School in Zürich, only to retire in 1942 due to health problems. He did hold a position at the University of Basel for a brief time before retiring due to recurring health problems. Much like Eliade, Jung often presented papers at the annual Eranos gatherings at Ascona. Jung died in 1961 in Küsnacht, Switzerland, but he lived to witness the establishment of an institute named after him to carry on his work in Zürich. A number of important works on religion were published by Jung, and were gathered into his *Collected Works* (18 volumes) that were translated into English. For Jung's interpretation of subjects related to religion, attention should be given to the following works: *The Secret of the Golden Flower* (1931), *Psychology of Religion* (1938), *Introduction to a Science of Mythology* (with Karl Kerényi, 1951), *Psychology and Alchemy* (1953), *Answer to Job* (1956), and *Psychology and Religion: West and East* (1958).

In contrast to Freud, Jung disagreed that the libido was exclusively sexual because he conceived of it as a nonspecific psychic energy. Jung disagreed with Freud about the Oedipus complex, which he did not grasp as a stage of development. Jung denied the inevitably of a sexual conflict between the father and son, and he rejected the mother as an object of incestuous desire because he stressed her protective and nurturing roles. A son's longing for his mother was spiritual rather than incestuous, reflecting a symbolic return to the womb to be reborn in a process of self-realization. Jung agreed with Freud that everyone possessed a personal unconscious that contained repressed wishes and suppressed subliminal perceptions of long-forgotten experiences. Moreover, Jung also envisioned a collective unconscious that was located at a deeper level than the ordinary unconscious. The collective unconscious, which was defined as impulses to action devoid of conscious motivation, could be inferred, however, from empirical observation of instinctual action, although there was a limit on such actions that were universal for Jung. Within the collective unconscious, Jung located the archetypes that were the product of recurring experiences of life like the cycle of the seasons, experiences of birth, death, danger, and attempts to satisfy one's desire for sex and food. Jung's conceptualization of the psyche was also very different from that of Freud.

The innermost center of the human psyche was the self, which was invisible and unconscious. This psychic totality was the result of the unification of the conscious and unconscious, and it functioned to guide the other parts of the psychic structures by implementing a roadmap for the stages of life. With its teleological function and innate tendency to seek fulfillment in its life, the self possessed access to a much broader realm of experience than the more limited conscious ego. Not only did the self assist us in adapting to our environment; it also helped us to relate to God and the life of the spirit. Situated at the conjunction of the exterior or spatial world and the interior or psychic realm was the conscious ego, which bore our personality, our awareness of our own existence and personal identity, organized our thoughts, intuitions, feelings and sensations, and possessed access to unrepressed memories. Moreover, the ego grasped meaning and value, necessary ingredients for a worthwhile life. In contrast to the ego, personas were the façades or social masks that people presented to the external world; they represented the totality of conventional attitudes that were adopted because people belonged to certain occupations, social classes, political parties, or nations. There was a danger of losing contact with the personality if people identified too strongly with one social mask, or when they could not maintain the social persona that they had created for themselves. If the personas were what they presented to the external world, the shadow represented a totality of personal characteristics that people wished to hide from both others and themselves. This negative aspect of a person could be projected onto another individual, which allowed a person to perceive one's own dark features reflected in another person. Even though the shadow and persona were opposites, they complemented and counterbalanced each other by compensating for each other. A split between the persona and shadow resulted in neuroses.

In addition to these features of the human psyche, a crucial archetypal system was the anima and animus for Jung. The former is the female complex in a male, and the latter is the male complex in a woman. Within their unconscious, men and women retained an ideal representation of the other, which suggested that each gender was attracted to complementary traits that they found in each other. In a negative way, it was possible to account for such human behavior as love at first sight or infatuation. A danger of such behavior was that one failed to see people as they really were in everyday life. From a more positive perspective, it was also possible to grasp a projection of wisdom, inspiration, or creativity. The anima and animus provided a potential way for internal and external adaptation of the psyche by functioning as mediators of the unconscious to the ego in dream states and in the imagination.

As suggested by the archetypal natures of the anima and animus, archetypes were engraved on the psyche and represented the possibility for certain kinds of perception or action. Jung made a distinction between archetypal images and unconscious archetypes as such, which were centers of psychic energy that represented a predisposition to have a certain inherited experience. Because the archetypal patterns were already established in the psyche, they predisposed us to approach and experience life in particular ways. Jung conceived of archetypes as biological entities that had evolved by means of the process of natural selection, and were universal and not a result of individual experience. Not only were archetypes likely to manifest themselves in critical situations, they also appeared in dreams, which tended to compensate for the one-sided limitations of consciousness. In this way dreams helped to promote a fuller adaptation to life by supporting and strengthening the ego and enhancing the development of one's personality. Within our dream states, it was possible to experience archetypal figures like the mother, child, father, and wise man; archetypal events like birth, death, separation from parents, and marriage; or archetypal objects like water, sun, moon, fish, snakes, and dangerous predators. Jung connected the archetypes to the process of individual maturation that proceeded through a series of innate archetypal expectations like that of warmth and nourishment. Jung also conceived this process as what he called the individuation principle that represented an awakening of the self or becoming more fully conscious of itself and its possibilities for growth. The entire process included self-realization and a self-differentiation that involved choosing one's own uniqueness. Within the context of this process, religion played an important role by providing a context for its unfolding. Thus religion represented an archetypal requirement for human nature and manifested a consciousness altered by the experience of the numinous. Jung argued that an experience of the archetype of God was synonymous with the archetype of the self, although Jung did not intend to imply that one could prove the existence of God.

A much different type of spirit was evident in the scholarship of William James (1842–1910), who abandoned a career in art to pursue medicine. After eventually earning his M.D. from Harvard University, he decided not to enter the medical profession for health reasons. After teaching in the area of natural history and creating the first American laboratory of psychology, he was appointed to a teaching position in philosophy at Harvard, from which he also taught physiology and psychology. During 1901–1902, James delivered the prestigious Gifford Lectures at Edinburgh University in Scotland,which were published as *The Varieties of Religious Experience: A Study in Human Nature*. James's most significant work in the field of psychology was a two-volume classic entitled *The Principles of Psychology* (1890), which was followed by *The Will to Believe and Other Essays in Popular Philosophy* (1897). The later works of James concentrated mostly on philosophy, with the publication of the following books: *Pragmatism* (1907), *The Meaning of Truth* (1909), *A Pluralistic Universe* (1909), *Some Problems of Philosophy* (1911), *Essays in Radical Empiricism* (1912), and a couple of books based on his memories and collected scholarly essays.

These works reflected James's interest in the psychological treatment of consciousness rather than stressing the subconscious or unconscious, because he was convinced that consciousness was much vaster than we previously realized. The expansion of consciousness occurred beyond the threshold of the ego, with such psychological phenomena as mind-curing healing, conversion, and mysticism. James identified religion with what he called "the genuinely strenuous life," and he stressed its feelings, acts, intuitive experiences, and its solitary nature. In fact, religion was the most strenuous mode of life possible because it involved the radical transformation of one's existence, a breaking of old habitual ways, concentration on broader meanings, and the creation of a totally new way of life. To live this new mode of life, one must be willing to exert an enormous effort, perform self-sacrifice, possess courage, and overcome hardships and obstacles. The religious life manifested freedom and a sense of the presence of a transcendent power beyond oneself. The various facts of religious life supported what James referred to as a piecemeal supernaturalism that was based upon the convictions that the visible realm is connected to a spiritual world, our genuine end is this transcendent world, and harmony with this higher world produces a spiritual energy that affects the mundane world.

To understand James's approach to religion, it is necessary to call attention to three major distinctions that he made in his study of the subject. The first distinction was based on the difference between primary and secondary modes of experience. James argued that individual experiences and ideas were the primary sources for religion, social change, and development. Secondary features like theology, dogma, and philosophy tended to degenerate and decline over time as they circulated to a broader social sphere. James also drew a distinction between original founders of world religions and later developments like churches, which represented a supplementary tradition. The original founders of world religions like Jesus, Buddha, or Muhammad owed their authority and power to original, direct, and personal contact with the divine. This second distinction suggests that James stressed conscious experience of central religious figures or those who have advanced far on the spiritual path, like mystics, over the experience of ordinary people. These initial two distinctions are grounded in his distinction between knowledge by acquaintance and knowledge about something. The former type of knowledge is a preverbal, unmediated kind of knowledge that gains awareness of the simple presence of something, whereas knowledge about something is interconnected with a person's cultural influences and personal psychology. With this kind of distinction in mind, James used an introspective approach that suggested genuine observation of real events to the subject of religion. In addition, James developed the method of serial study to enhance interpretation. His method of serial study placed phenomena within a series from their origins to their decay or degeneration. He also stressed the need to use, for instance, personal documents composed by such figures as mystics and religious leaders. The third distinction drawn by James was the difference between healthy-minded and unhealthy-minded individuals or sick souls. The first distinction represented the "once-born," which was characterized by optimism, whereas the pessimistic unhealthy-minded were called the "twice-born," because such people experienced a second birth by dying from their unreal life. In contrast to the unhealthy-minded, the healthy-minded person was apparently happy and opposed to change because such a person thought that life was a continuous development devoid of crisis or disruptive discontinuities and that evil could be overcome by technical means. But evidence suggested that change was necessary to achieve one's greatest spiritual potential. Nonetheless, the goal of both figures was essentially the same inner unification. Having drawn these basic distinctions, James proceeded to approach the subject of religious experience in an empirical fashion and was able to draw some philosophical conclusions based on his findings.

In a way similar to William James's focus on the experience of religious leaders, Erick H. Erikson (1902–1994) concentrated on major religious figures by publishing his insights using a psychoanalytic and psychohistorical approach to his subjects, although he shared a radical empirical approach to the subject of religion with James. Erikson's most important contributions to the subject of religion are the following two works: *Young Man Luther* (1958) and *Gandhi's Truth: On the Origins of Militant Nonviolence* (1969). Important theoretical works include the following: *Childhood and Society* (1950), *Identity and the Life Cycle* (1959), *Insight and Responsibility* (1964), *History and the Historical Moment* (1975), *Toys and Reasons* (1977), *The Life Cycle Completed* (1982). Born in Frankfurt-am-Mein and educated at a humanistic Gymnasium, Erikson studied art and wandered around Europe as a young man until he joined a friend to teach children in Vienna. There, he was drawn into the circle of Freud's immediate associates. Erikson graduated from both the Vienna Montessari Teacher's Association and the Vienna Psychoanalytic Society before he moved to America in 1933 due to the rise of fascism. He joined the Harvard Psychological Clinic, although he did not have a university degree. He received an M.A. from Harvard University and later taught there after teaching at the University of California, Berkeley, for nearly 10 years. He also held positions at Yale University and the residential Austin Riggs center in Massachusetts. With trained anthropologists, he spent time observing American Indian tribes in South Dakota and the Yurok on the Pacific Coast. For his book on Gandhi, he was honored with the Pulitzer Prize and the National Book Award in 1970. His various published works reflected a concern for the human life cycle and religion, which he understood as playing a major role in the development of the individual.

Two major principles supported Erikson's psychological theory of the human life cycle. They were the epigenetic principle, which suggested the influence of scholars like Konrad Lorenz and Julian Huxley, and the principle of relativity, reflecting indebtedness to Albert Einstein. As a result of the evolutionary process, the epigenetic principle suggested that the human organism possessed an inherent plan that tends to unfold as it progresses through life in a pattern analogous to the development of fetal organ systems. Thus the life cycle process was systematic, sequential, orderly, and interconnected with the prior stages. Erikson identified eight stages of the life cycle that were accompanied by corresponding virtues: infancy and childhood were connected with hope, will, purpose, and competence; the adolescent virtue was fidelity; and the adult virtues were love, care, and wisdom. By virtue, Erikson envisioned something active that possessed inherent strength. In his later work, he expanded his theory to include negative counterparts to the virtues that he referred to as "basic antipathies," which are the following: withdrawal, compulsion, inhibition, inertia, repudiation, exclusivity, rejectivity, and disdain. These various virtuous counterparts functioned to paralyze development of the life cycle and thus should be understood as basic pathologies. Therefore, at each stage of development, individuals were challenged to resolve psychosocial crises if they were to advance. Each stage of ego development was accompanied by a psychosocial crisis that represented a counterpart to ego growth and was summarized in the following way: trust/basic mistrust (infancy); autonomy/shame and doubt (early childhood); initiative/guilt (play age); industry/inferiority (school age); identity/identity confusion (adolescence); intimacy/isolation (young adult); generativity/stagnation (adulthood); and integrity/despair and disgust (old age). What fascinated Erikson was the way a human organism functioned when adapting to its broader environment and how it developed. Within the context of the development of the self, which Erikson differentiated from the ego, God played an important role with the unfolding of self-awareness. In his book on Martin Luther, Erikson argued that the reformer transcended his ego and arrived at self-awareness in relationship to God, who played a role in the formation of Luther's identity, along with social and historical factors. This entire process of development represented the acquisition of a coherent sense of self from the numerous self-images that have accrued since one's childhood. By aiming at self-identity, a person gains a sense of who one truly is. The growth of the ego was fostered by what Erikson called ritualization, a meaningful and recurring interplay between individuals that was attentive to ceremony and connected to a higher symbolic meaning, Ritualization enabled one to avoid the behavioral extremes of excessive self-control and unrestrained intemperance. Erikson's remarks about religion reveal that he was mostly concerned with how it functioned rather than its true nature. He was also concerned with how individuals developed toward growth and maturity. He thought that the key to a person's goal was based on acquiring adaptive skills, and he was concerned with the causal role of a person's social and cultural environment, whereas Freud stressed instinctual drives of the individual. These tendencies of Erikson made his grasp of religion less reductive than that of Freud.

In contrast to Erikson, a more comparatively Freudian approach to religion was adopted by René Girard (b. 1923). Girard was born in Avignon, France. He later studied at the École des Chartes in Paris and received his doctorate from Indiana

University in America. Girard has taught at the Institut d'Études Françaises d'Avignon since 1962 and concurrently at Stanford University since 1981. His major contributions to the subject of religion are the following works translated into English: *Violence and the Sacred* (1977), *The Scapegoat* (1986), and *Job: The Victim of His People* (1987). These works reflect his focus on the origins of violence and religion and how they are interwoven with what he calls mimetic desire, which suggests desiring the same thing as someone else. Girard also used these works to agree with Freud and to criticize him for failing to understand mimetic desire, which directly challenged Freud's theories of the Oedipus complex and sexual rivalry in narcissism.

For instance, in the Greek myth of Dionysus and Euripides's play *The Bacchae*, Girard found a spontaneous and senseless form of violence. Within these sources and others, Girard found elements to support his theory of a sacrificial crisis that embodied elements of group violence, revenge, dismemberment of victims, and the performance of violence to eliminate violence. He argued that violence functioned to eliminate differences, an essential part of the sacrificial crisis. In the play of Euripides, there was a loss of distinction, for instance, between a human and a beast, and there was equally a loss of distinction between a human and god. In part, Girard's theory presupposed a negative view of human nature as driven by desire and violence. The destructive nature of people found religion useful because it protected people from their own violence by humanizing and transforming violence into a transcendent and ever-present danger. Like the numinous defined by Otto, the violence of Girard's conception strikes people as both seductive and terrifying, causing them to be both attracted and repelled. Mimetic desire caused by rivalry and its resulting violence for the object of desire was contagious, causing a crisis with no apparent solution. A solution arose spontaneously by the collective murder of a scapegoat, which ended the violence by channeling it toward the victim, away from society, and symbolically uniting society.

Although Girard was influenced by Freud, he also attempted to differentiate aspects of his theory from the latter. Girard challenged, for instance, Freud's theory of the Oedipus complex with his notion of mimetic desire. He also argued that Freud misunderstood desire and sexual rivalry. And contrary to the Freudian theory of narcissism, Girard argued that desire was never directed toward the person that the subject resembled; desire was directed rather to the other's desires as imagined by the subject. Overall, Girard's theory demonstrated the resurfacing of the old quest for origins, evident in the work of scholars like Frazer and many others.

In contrast to the psychological positions of previous male scholars, Naomi R. Goldenberg offers a feminist perspective and critical critique of some of the male figures. After completing her undergraduate studies at Douglas College, she earned a master's degree at the C. G. Jung Institute in Zurich, Switzerland, in 1973 and completed her doctoral work at Yale University in 1976. She accepted a position at the University of Ottawa in Ontario, Canada, where she has taught throughout her career in the areas of psychology of religion and women and religion. Her major publications include the following books: *Changing the Gods* (1980), *End of God* (1982), *Returning Words to Flesh* (1990), and *Resurrecting the Body* (1993). Goldenberg admits in her published works to being influenced by the feminist philosopher Judith Butler and the psychologist Melanie Klein.

According to Goldenberg, Butler influenced her to view religion as repeated social performances that gain their power from the authority associated with texts, rituals, and institutions. From a different perspective, Melanie Klein, who has argued that each sex envies the other and desires the attributes of the opposite sex, leads Goldenberg to think that religion is also connected to the male imitation of women in part. Due to the contingent nature of masculinity, Goldenberg argues that religion is a male form of ideation and practice that enables men to transform themselves into the opposite sex and escape their basic limited natures. Nonetheless, she thinks that psychoanalysis and feminism share more than the subject of sexuality does because they also have in common similar ways of approaching human salvation in the sense of being messianic. They also share methods for transforming the self and world. What she wants to examine is how psychoanalysis can be enriched by feminist insights.

Guideline Questions

How and why did Freud and Jung arrive at very different assessments of the value of religion for human well-being?

What advantages or disadvantages result from James's theory of religious experience that focuses on the psychology of major religious figures?

How can religion play a role in the development of one's identity in the theory of Erikson?

In the theory of Girard, what is the exact relationship between the sacred and violence?

According to Goldenberg, why is the shift to thealogy significant?

From *The Standard Edition of the Complete Psychological Works of Sigmund Freud* and *Future of an Illusion*

SIGMUND FREUD

The Technique of Psycho-Analysis

Our plan of cure is based on these discoveries. The ego is weakened by the internal conflict and we must go to its help. The position is like that in a civil war which has to be decided by the assistance of an ally from outside. The

Reprinted from The Standard Edition of the Complete Psychological Works of Sigmund Freud, *vol. XXIII, (London: The Hogarth Press and the Institute of Psychoanalysis, 1964); and* Future of an Illusion, *vol. XXI (London: The Hogarth Press and the Institute of Psychoanalysis, 1961).*

analytic physician and the patient's weakened ego, basing themselves on the real external world, have to band themselves together into a party against the enemies, the instinctual demands of the id and the conscientious demands of the super-ego. We form a pact with each other. The sick ego promises us the most complete candour—promises, that is, to put at our disposal all the material which its self-perception yields it; we assure the patient of the strictest discretion and place at his service our experience in interpreting material that has been influenced by the unconscious. Our knowledge is to make up for his ignorance and to give his ego back its mastery over lost provinces of his mental life. This pact constitutes the analytic situation.

No sooner have we taken this step than a first disappointment awaits us, a first warning against over-confidence. If the patient's ego is to be a useful ally in our common work, it must, however hard it may be pressed by the hostile powers, have retained a certain amount of coherence and some fragment of understanding for the demands of reality. But this is not to be expected of the ego of a psychotic; it cannot observe a pact of this kind, indeed it can scarcely enter into one. It will very soon have tossed us away and the help we offer it and sent us to join the portions of the external world which no longer mean anything to it. Thus we discover that we must renounce the idea of trying our plan of cure upon psychotics—renounce it perhaps for ever or perhaps only for the time being, till we have found some other plan better adapted for them.

There is, however, another class of psychical patients who clearly resemble the psychotics very closely—the vast number of people suffering severely from neuroses. The determinants of their illness as well as its pathogenic mechanisms must be the same or at least very similar. But their ego has proved more resistant and has become less disorganized. Many of them, in spite of their maladies and the inadequacies resulting from them, have been able to maintain themselves in real life. These neurotics may show themselves ready to accept our help. We will confine our interest to them and see how far and by what methods we are able to "cure" them.

With the neurotics, then, we make our pact: complete candour on one side and strict discretion on the other. This looks as though we were only aiming at the post of a secular father confessor. But there is a great difference, for what we want to hear from our patient is not only what he knows and conceals from other people; he is to tell us too what he does not know. With this end in view we give him a more detailed definition of what we mean by candour. We pledge him to obey the fundamental rule of analysis, which is henceforward to govern his behaviour towards us. He is to tell us not only what he can say intentionally and willingly, what will give him relief like a confession, but everything else as well that his self-observation yields him, everything that comes into his head, even if it is disagreeable for him to say it, even if it seems to him unimportant or actually nonsensical. If he can succeed after this injunction in putting his self-criticism out of action, he will present us with a mass of material—thoughts, ideas, recollections—which are already subject to the influence of the unconscious, which are often its direct derivatives, and which thus put us in a position to conjecture his repressed unconscious material and to extend, by the information we give him, his ego's knowledge of his unconscious.

But it is far from being the case that his ego is content to play the part of passively and obediently bringing us the material we require and of believing and accepting our translation of it. A number of other things happen, a few of which we might have foreseen but others of which are bound to surprise us. The most remarkable thing is this. The patient is not satisfied with regarding the analyst in the light of reality as a helper and adviser who, moreover, is remunerated for the trouble he takes and who would himself be content with some such role as that of a guide on a difficult mountain climb. On the contrary, the patient sees in him the return, the reincarnation, of some important figure out of his childhood or past, and consequently transfers on to him feelings and reactions which undoubtedly applied to this prototype. This fact of transference soon proves to be a factor of undreamt of importance, on the one hand an instrument of irreplaceable value and on the other hand a source of serious dangers. This transference is ambivalent: it comprises positive (affectionate) as well as negative (hostile) attitudes towards the analyst, who as a rule is put in the place of one or other of the patient's parents, his father or mother. So long as it is positive it serves us admirably. It alters the whole analytic situation; it pushes to one side the patient's rational aim of becoming healthy and free from his ailments. Instead of it there emerges the aim of pleasing the analyst and of winning his applause and love. It becomes the true motive force of the patient's collaboration; his weak ego becomes strong; under its influence he achieves things that would ordinarily be beyond his power; he leaves off his symptoms and seems apparently to have recovered merely for the sake of the analyst. The analyst may shamefacedly admit to himself that he set out on a difficult undertaking without any suspicion of the extraordinary powers that would be at his command.

Moreover, the relation of transference brings with it two further advantages. If the patient puts the analyst in the place of his father (or mother), he is also giving him the power which his super-ego exercises over his ego, since his parents were, as we know, the origin of his super-ego. The new super-ego now has an opportunity for a sort of after-education of the neurotic; it can correct mistakes for which his parents were responsible in educating him. But at this point a warning must be given against misusing this new influence. However much the analyst may be tempted to become a teacher, model and ideal for other people and to create men in his own image, he should not forget that that is not his task in the analytic relationship, and indeed that he will be disloyal to his task if he allows himself to be led on by his inclinations. If he does, he will only be repeating a mistake of the parents who crushed their child's independence by their influence, and he will only be replacing the patient's earlier dependence by a new one. In all his attempts at improving and educating the patient the analyst should respect his individuality. The amount of influence which he may legitimately allow himself will be determined by the degree of developmental inhibition present in the patient. Some neurotics have remained so infantile that in analysis too they can only be treated as children.

. . . It is the analyst's task constantly to tear the patient out of his menacing illusion and to show him again and again that what he takes to be new real life is a reflection of the past. And lest he should fall into a state in which he is inaccessible to all evidence, the analyst takes care that neither the love nor the hostility reach an extreme height. This is effected by preparing him in good time for these possibilities and by not overlooking the first signs of them. Careful handling of the transference on these lines is as a rule richly rewarded. If we succeed, as we usually can, in enlightening the patient on the true nature of the phenomena of transference, we shall have struck a powerful weapon out of the hand of his resistance and shall have converted dangers into gains. For a patient never forgets again what he has experienced in the form of transference; it carries a greater force of conviction than anything he can acquire in other ways.

We think it most undesirable if the patient acts outside the transference instead of remembering. The ideal conduct for our purposes would be that he should behave as normally as possible outside the treatment and express his abnormal reactions only in the transference.

The method by which we strengthen the weakened ego has as a starting-point an extending of its self-knowledge. That is not, of course, the whole story but it is a first step. The loss of such knowledge signifies for the ego a surrender of power and influence; it is the first tangible sign that it is being hemmed in and hampered by the demands of the id and the super-ego. Accordingly, the first part of the help we have to offer is intellectual work on our side and encouragement to the patient to collaborate in it. This first kind of activity, as we know, is intended to pave the way to another, more difficult, task. We shall not lose sight of the dynamic element in this task, even during its preliminary stage. We gather the material for our work from a variety of sources—from what is conveyed to us by the information given us by the patient and by his free associations, from what he shows us in his transferences, from what we arrive at by interpreting his dreams and from what he betrays by his slips or *parapraxes.* All this material helps us to make constructions about what happened to him and has been forgotten as well as about what is happening in him now without his understanding it. But in all this we never fail to make a strict distinction between our knowledge and his knowledge. We avoid telling him at once things that we have often discovered at an early stage, and we avoid telling him the whole of what we think we have discovered. We reflect carefully over when we shall impart the knowledge of one of our constructions to him and we wait for what seems to us the suitable moment—which it is not always easy to decide. As a rule we put off telling him of a construction or explanation till he himself has so nearly arrived at it that only a single step remains to be taken, though that step is in fact the decisive synthesis. If we proceeded in another way and overwhelmed him with our interpretations before he was prepared for them, our information would either produce no effect or it would provoke a violent outbreak of resistance which would make the progress of our work more difficult or might even threaten to stop it altogether. But if we have prepared everything properly, it often happens that the patient will at once confirm our construction

and himself recollect the internal or external event which he had forgotten. The more exactly the construction coincides with the details of what has been forgotten the easier will it be for him to assent. On that particular matter *our* knowledge will then have become *his* knowledge as well. . . .

Let us once more glance over the situation which we have reached in our attempt at bringing help to the patient's neurotic ego. That ego is no longer able to fulfill the task set it by the external world (including human society). Not all of its experiences are at its disposal, a large proportion of its store of memories have escaped it. Its activity is inhibited by strict prohibitions from the super-ego, its energy is consumed in vain attempts at fending off the demands of the id. Beyond this, as a result of continuous irruptions by the id, its organization is impaired, it is no longer capable of any proper synthesis, it is torn by mutually opposed urges, by unsettled conflicts and by unsolved doubts. To start with, we get the patient's thus weakened ego to take part in the purely intellectual work of interpretation, which aims at provisionally filling the gaps in his mental assets, and to transfer to us the authority of his super-ego; we encourage it to take up the struggle over each individual demand made by the id and to conquer the resistances which arise in connection with it. At the same time we restore order in the ego by detecting the material and urges which have forced their way in from the unconscious, and expose them to criticism by tracing them back to their origin. We serve the patient in various functions, as an authority and a substitute for his parents, as a teacher and educator; and we have done the best for him if, as analysts, we raise the mental processes in his ego to a normal level, transform what has become unconscious and repressed into preconscious material and thus return it once more to the possession of his ego. On the patient's side a few rational factors work in our favour, such as the need for recovery which has its motive in his sufferings, and the intellectual interest that we may awaken in him in the theories and revelations of psychoanalysis; but of far greater force is the positive transference with which he meets us. Fighting against us, on the other hand, are the negative transference, the ego's resistance due to repression (that is, its unpleasure at having to lay itself open to the hard work imposed on it), the sense of guilt arising from its relation to the superego and the need to be ill due to deepgoing changes in the economics of his instincts. The share taken by the last two factors decides whether the case is to be regarded as slight or severe. Apart from these, a few other factors may be discerned as having a favourable or unfavourable bearing. A certain psychical inertia, a sluggishness of the libido, which is unwilling to abandon its fixations, cannot be welcome to us; the patient's capacity for sublimating his instincts plays a large part and so does his capacity for rising above the crude life of the instincts; so, too, does the relative power of his intellectual functions. . . .

The Future of an Illusion

When one has lived for quite a long time in a particular civilization and has often tried to discover what its origins were and along what path it has developed, one sometimes also feels tempted to take a glance in the other direction and to ask what further fate lies before it and what transformations it is destined to undergo. But one soon finds that the value of such an enquiry is diminished from the outset by several factors. Above all, because there are only a few people who can survey human activity in its full compass. Most people have been obliged to restrict themselves to a single, or a few, fields of it. But the less a man knows about the past and the present the more insecure must prove to be his judgement of the future. And there is the further difficulty that precisely in a judgement of this kind the subjective expectations of the individual play a part which it is difficult to assess; and these turn out to be dependent on purely personal factors in his own experience, on the greater or lesser optimism of his attitude to life, as it has been dictated for him by his temperament or by his success or failure. Finally, the curious fact makes itself felt that in general people experience their present naïvely, as it were, without being able to form an estimate of its contents: they have first to put themselves at a distance from it—the present, that is to say, must have become the past—before it can yield points of vantage from which to judge the future. . . .

Human civilization, by which I mean all those respects in which human life has raised itself above its animal status and differs from the life of beasts—and I scorn to distinguish culture and civilization—, presents, as we know, two aspects to the observer. It includes on the one hand all the knowledge and capacity that men have acquired in order to control the forces of nature and extract its wealth for the satisfaction of human needs, and, on the other hand, all the regulations necessary in order to adjust the relations of men to one another and especially the distribution of the available wealth. The two trends of civilization are not independent of each other: firstly, because the mutual relations of men are profoundly influenced by the amount of instinctual satisfaction which the existing wealth makes possible; secondly, because an individual man can himself come to function as wealth in relation to another one, in so far as the other person makes use of his capacity for work, or chooses him as a sexual object; and thirdly, moreover, because every individual is virtually an enemy of civilization, though civilization is supposed to be an object of universal human interest. It is remarkable that, little as men are able to exist in isolation, they should nevertheless feel as a heavy burden the sacrifices which civilization expects of them in order to make a communal life possible. Thus civilization has to be defended against the individual, and its regulations, institutions and commands are directed to that task. They aim not only at effecting a certain distribution of wealth but at maintaining that distribution; indeed, they have to protect everything that contributes to the conquest of nature and the production of wealth against men's hostile impulses. Human creations are easily-destroyed, and science and technology, which have built them up, can also be used for their annihilation. . . .

It is just as impossible to do without control of the mass by a minority as it is to dispense with coercion in the work of civilization. For masses are lazy and unintelligent; they have no love for instinctual renunciation, and they are not to be convinced by argument of its inevitability; and the individuals composing them support one another in giving free rein to their indiscipline. It is only through the influence of individuals who can set an example and whom masses recognize as their leaders that they can be induced to perform work and undergo the renunciations on which the existence of civilization depends. All is well if these leaders are persons who possess superior insight into the necessities of life and who have risen to the height of mastering their own instinctual wishes. But there is a danger that in order not to lose their influence they may give way to the mass more than it gives way to them, and it therefore seems necessary that they shall be independent of the mass by having means to power at their disposal. To put it briefly, there are two widespread human characteristics which are responsible for the fact that the regulations of civilization can only be maintained by a certain degree of coercion—namely, that men are not spontaneously fond of work and that arguments are of no avail against their passions. . . .

But with the recognition that every civilization rests on a compulsion to work and a renunciation of instinct and therefore inevitably provokes opposition from those affected by these demands, it has become clear that civilization cannot consist principally or solely in wealth itself and the means of acquiring it and the arrangements for its distribution; for these things are threatened by the rebelliousness and destructive mania of the participants in civiliza-

tion. Alongside of wealth we now come upon the means by which civilization can be defended—measures of coercion and other measures that are intended to reconcile men to it and to recompense them for their sacrifices. These latter may be described as the mental assets of civilization.

For the sake of a uniform terminology we will describe the fact that an instinct cannot be satisfied as a "frustration," the regulation by which this frustration is established as a "prohibition" and the condition which is produced by the prohibition as a "privation." The first step is to distinguish between privations which affect everyone and privations which do not affect everyone but only groups, classes or even single individuals. The former are the earliest; with the prohibitions that established them, civilization—who knows how many thousands of years ago?—began to detach man from his primordial animal condition. We have found to our surprise that these privations are still operative and still form the kernel of hostility to civilization. The instinctual wishes that suffer under them are born afresh with every child; there is a class of people, the neurotics, who already react to these frustrations with asocial behaviour. Among these instinctual wishes are those of incest, cannibalism, and lust for killing. . . .

Every child presents this process of transformation to us; only by that means does it become a moral and social being. Such a strengthening of the super-ego is a most precious cultural asset in the psychological field. Those in whom it has taken place are turned from being opponents of civilization into being its vehicles. The greater their number is in a cultural unit the more secure is its culture and the more it can dispense with external measures of coercion. Now the degree of this internalization differs greatly between the various instinctual prohibitions. As regards the earliest cultural demands, which I have mentioned, the internalization seems to have been very extensively achieved, if we leave out of account the unwelcome exception of the neurotics. But the case is altered when we turn to the other instinctual claims. Here we observe with surprise and concern that a majority of people obey the cultural prohibitions on these points only under the pressure of external coercion—that is, only where that coercion can make itself effective and so long as it is to be feared. This is also true of what are known as the *moral* demands of civilization, which likewise apply to everyone. Most of one's experiences of man's moral untrustworthiness fall into this category. There are countless civilized people who would shrink from murder or incest but who do not deny themselves the satisfaction of their avarice, their aggressive urges or their sexual lusts, and who do not hesitate to injure other people by lies, fraud and calumny, so long as they can remain unpunished for it; and this, no doubt, has always been so through many ages of civilization.

If we turn to those restrictions that apply only to certain classes of society, we meet with a state of things which is flagrant and which has always been recognized. It is to be expected that these under-privileged classes will envy the favoured ones their privileges and will do all they can to free themselves from their own surplus of privation. Where this is not possible, a permanent measure of discontent will persist within the culture concerned and this can lead to dangerous revolts. If, however, a culture has not got beyond a point at which the satisfaction of one portion of its participants depends upon the suppression of another, and perhaps larger, portion—and this is the case in all present day cultures—it is understandable that the suppressed people should develop an intense hostility towards a culture whose existence they make possible by their work, but in whose wealth they have too small a share. In such conditions an internalization of the cultural prohibitions among the suppressed people is not to be expected. On the contrary, they are not prepared to acknowledge the prohibitions, they are intent on destroying the culture itself, and possibly even on doing away with the postulates on which it is based. The hostility of these classes to civilization is so obvious that it has caused the more latent hostility of the social strata that are better provided for to be overlooked. It goes without solving that a civilization which leaves so large a number of its participants unsatisfied and drives them into revolt neither has nor deserves the prospect of a lasting existence. . . .

In what does the peculiar value of religious ideas lie?

We have spoken of the hostility to civilization which is produced by the pressure that civilization exercises, the renunciations of instinct which it demands. If one imagines its prohibitions lifted—if, then, one may take any woman one pleases as a sexual object, if one may without hesitation kill one's rival for her love or anyone else who stands in one's way, if, too, one can carry off any of the other man's belongings without asking leave—how splendid, what a string of satisfactions one's life would be! True, one soon comes across the first difficulty: everyone else has exactly the same wishes as I have and will treat me with no more consideration than I treat him. And so in reality only one person could be made unrestrictedly happy by such a removal of the restrictions of civilization, and he would be a tyrant, a dictator, who had seized all the means to power. And even he would have every reason to wish that the others would observe at least one cultural commandment: "thou shalt not kill."

But how ungrateful, how short-sighted after all, to strive for the abolition of civilization! What would then remain would be a state of nature, and that would be far harder to bear. It is true that nature would not demand any restrictions of instinct from us, she would let us do as we liked; but she has her own particularly effective method of restricting us. She destroys us—coldly, cruelly, relentlessly, as it seems to us, and possibly through the very things that occasioned our satisfaction. It was precisely because of these dangers with which nature threatens us that we came together and created civilization, which is also, among other things, intended to make our communal life possible. For the principal task of civilization, its actual raison d'être, is to defend us against nature. . . .

For this situation is nothing new. It has an infantile prototype, of which it is in fact only the continuation. For once before one has found oneself in a similar state of helplessness: as a small child, in relation to one's parents. One had reason to fear them, and especially one's father; and yet one was sure of his protection against the dangers one knew. Thus it was natural to assimilate the two situations. Here, too, wishing played its part, as it does in dream-life. The sleeper may be seized with a presentiment of death, which threatens to place him in the grave. But the dream-work knows how to select a condition that will turn even that dreaded event into a wish-fulfilment: the dreamer sees himself in an ancient Etruscan grave which he has climbed down into, happy to find his archaeological interests satisfied. In the same way, a man makes the forces of nature not simply into persons with whom he can associate as he would with his equals—that would not do justice to the overpowering impression which those forces make on him—but he gives them the character of a father. He turns them into gods, following in this, as I have tried to show, not only an infantile prototype but a phylogenetic one.

In the course of time the first observations were made of regularity and conformity to law in natural phenomena, and with this the forces of nature lost their human traits. But man's helplessness remains and along with it his longing for his father, and the gods. The gods retain their threefold task: they must exorcize the terrors of nature, they must reconcile men to the cruelty of Fate, particularly as it is shown in death, and they must compensate them for the sufferings and privations which a civilized life in common has imposed on them. . . .

As regards the apportioning of destinies, an unpleasant suspicion persisted that the perplexity and helplessness of the human race could not be remedied. It was here that the gods were most apt to fail. If they themselves created Fate, then their counsels must be deemed inscrutable. The notion dawned on the most gifted people of antiquity that Moira [Fate] stood above the gods and that the gods themselves had their own destinies. And the more autonomous nature became and the more the gods withdrew from it, the more earnestly were all expectations directed to the third function of the gods—the more did morality become their true domain. It now became the task of the gods to even out the defects and evils of civilization, to attend to the sufferings which men inflict on one another in their life together and to watch over the fulfilment of the precepts of civilization, which men obey so imperfectly. Those precepts themselves were credited with a divine origin; they were elevated beyond human society and were extended to nature and the universe.

And thus a store of ideas is created from man's need to make his helplessness tolerable and built up from the material of memories of the helplessness of his own childhood and the childhood of the human race. It can clearly be seen that the possession of these ideas protects him in two directions—against the dangers of nature and Fate, and against the injuries that threaten him from human society itself. Here is the gist of the matter. Life in this world serves a higher purpose; no doubt it is not easy to guess what that man, the soul, which in the course of time has so slowly and unwillingly detached itself from the body, that is the object of this elevation and exaltation. . . .

I have tried to show that religious ideas have arisen from the same need as have all the other achievements of civilization: from the necessity of defending oneself against the crushingly superior force of nature. To this a second motive was added—the urge to rectify the shortcomings of civilization which made themselves painfully felt. Moreover, it is apposite to say that civilization gives the individual these ideas, for he finds them there already; they are presented to him ready-made, and he would not be able to discover them for himself. . . .

It is, of course, my duty to point out the connecting links between what I said earlier and what I put forward now, between the deeper and the manifest motives, between the father-complex and man's helplessness and need for protection.

These connections are not hard to find. They consist in the relation of the child's helplessness to the helplessness of the adult which continues it. So that, as was to be expected, the motives for the formation of religion which psycho-analysis revealed now turn out to be the same as the infantile contribution to the *manifest* motives. Let us transport ourselves into the mental life of a child. You remember the choice of object according to the anaclitic [attachment] type, which psycho-analysis talks of? The libido there follows the paths of narcissistic needs and attaches itself to the objects which ensure the satisfaction of those needs. In this way the mother, who satisfies the child's hunger, becomes its first love-object and certainly also its first protection against all the undefined dangers which threaten it in the external world—its first protection against anxiety, we may say.

In this function [of protection] the mother is soon replaced by the stronger father, who retains that position for the rest of childhood. But the child's attitude to its father is coloured by a peculiar ambivalence. The father himself constitutes a danger for the child, perhaps because of its earlier relation to its mother. Thus it fears him no less than it longs for him and admires him. The indications of this ambivalence in the attitude to the father are deeply imprinted in every religion, as was shown in *Totem and Taboo.* When the growing individual finds that he is destined to remain a child forever, that he can never do without protection against strange superior powers, he lends those powers the features belonging to the figure of his father; he creates for himself the gods whom he dreads, whom he seeks to propitiate, and

whom he nevertheless entrusts with his own projection. Thus his longing for a father is a motive identical with his need for protection against the consequences of his human weakness. The defence against childish helplessness is what lends its characteristic features to the adult's reaction to the helplessness which he has to acknowledge—a reaction which is precisely the formation of religion. . . .

Let us now take up the thread of our enquiry. What, then, is the psychological significance of religious ideas and under what heading are we to classify them? The question is not at all easy to answer immediately. After rejecting a number of formulations, we will take our stand on the following one. Religious ideas are teachings and assertions about facts and conditions of external (or internal) reality which tell one something one has not discovered for oneself and which lay claim to one's belief. Since they give us information about what is most important and interesting to us in life, they are particularly highly prized. Anyone who knows nothing of them is very ignorant; and anyone who has added them to his knowledge may consider himself much the richer. . . .

Let us try to apply the same test to the teachings of religion. When we ask on what their claim to be believed is founded, we are met with three answers, which harmonize remarkably badly with one another. Firstly, these teachings deserve to be believed because they were already believed by our primal ancestors; secondly, we possess proofs which have been handed down to us from those same primaeval times; and thirdly, it is forbidden to raise the question of their authentication at all. In former days anything so presumptuous was visited with the severest penalties, and even today society looks askance at any attempt to raise the question again. . . .

If all the evidence put forward for the authenticity of religious teachings originates in the past, it is natural to look round and see whether the present, about which it is easier to form judgements, may not also be able to furnish evidence of the sort. If by this means we could succeed in clearing even a single portion of the religious system from doubt, the whole of it gains enormously in credibility. . . .

I think I have prepared the way sufficiently for an answer to both these questions. It will be found if we turn our attention to the psychical origin of religious ideas. These, which are given out as teachings, are not precipitates of experience or end-results of thinking: they are illusions, fulfilments of the oldest, strongest and most urgent wishes of mankind. The secret of their strength lies in the strength of those wishes. As we already know, the terrifying impression of helplessness in childhood aroused the need for protection—for protection through love—which was provided by the father; and the recognition that this helplessness lasts throughout life made it necessary to cling to the existence of a father, but this time a more powerful one. Thus the benevolent rule of a divine Providence allays our fear of the dangers of life; the establishment of a moral world-order ensures the fulfilment of the demands of justice, which have so often remained unfulfilled in human civilization; and the prolongation of earthly existence in a future life, provides the local and temporal framework in which these wish-fulfilments shall take place. Answers to the riddles that tempt the curiosity of man, such as how the universe began or what the relation is between body and mind, are developed in conformity with the underlying assumptions of this system. It is an enormous relief to the individual psyche if the conflicts of its childhood arising from the father—complex-conflicts which it has never wholly overcome—are removed from it and brought to a solution which is universally accepted.

When I say that these things are all illusions, I must define the meaning of the word. An illusion is not the same thing as an error; nor is it necessarily an error. . . . What is characteristic of illusions is that they are derived from human wishes. In this respect they come near to psychiatric delusions. But they differ from them,

too, apart from the more complicated structure of delusions. In the case of delusions, we emphasize as essential their being in contradiction with reality. Illusions need not necessarily be false—that is to say, unrealizable or in contradiction to reality. . . . Thus we call a belief an illusion when a wish-fulfilment is a prominent factor in its motivation, and in doing so we disregard its relations to reality, just as the illusion itself sets no store by verification. . . .

If men are taught that there is no almighty and all-just God, no divine world-order and no future life, they will feel exempt from all obligation to obey the precepts of civilization. Everyone will, without inhibition or fear, follow his asocial, egoistic instincts and seek to exercise his power; Chaos, which we have banished through thousands of years of the work of civilization, will come again. . . .

Religion has clearly performed great services for human civilization. It has contributed much towards the taming of the asocial instincts. But not enough. It has ruled human society for many thousands of years and has had time to show what it can achieve. If it had succeeded in making the majority of mankind happy, in comforting them, in reconciling them to life and in making them into vehicles of civilization, no one would dream of attempting to alter the existing conditions. But what do we see instead? We see that an appallingly large number of people are dissatisfied with civilization and unhappy in it, and feel it as a yoke which must be shaken off; and that these people either do everything in their power to change that civilization, or else go so far in their hostility to it that they will have nothing to do with civilization or with a restriction of instinct. . . .

Civilization has little to fear from educated people and brain-workers. In them the replacement of religious motives for civilized behaviour by other, secular motives would proceed unobtrusively; moreover, such people are to a large extent themselves vehicles of civilization. But it is another matter with the great mass of the uneducated and oppressed, who have every reason for being enemies of civilization. So long as they do not discover that people no longer believe in God, all is well. But they will discover it, infallibly, even if this piece of writing of mine is not published. And they are ready to accept the results of scientific thinking, but without the change having taken place in them which scientific thinking brings about in people. . . .

We now observe that the store of religious ideas includes not only wish-fulfilments but important historical recollections. This concurrent influence of past and present must give religion a truly incomparable wealth of power. But perhaps with the help of an analogy yet another discovery may begin to dawn on us. Though it is not a good plan to transplant ideas far from the soil in which they grew up, yet here is a conformity which we cannot avoid pointing out. We know that a human child cannot successfully complete its development to the civilized stage without passing through a phase of neurosis sometimes of greater and sometimes of less distinctness. This is because so many instinctual demands which will later be unserviceable cannot be suppressed by the rational operation of the child's intellect but have to be tamed by acts of repression, behind which, as a rule, lies the motive of anxiety. Most of these infantile neuroses are overcome spontaneously in the course of growing up, and this is especially true of the obsessional neuroses of childhood. The remainder can be cleared up later still by psychoanalytic treatment. In just the same way, one might assume, humanity as a whole, in its development through the ages, fell into states analogous to the neuroses, and for the same reasons—namely because in the times of its ignorance and intellectual weakness the instinctual renunciations indispensable for man's communal existence had only been achieved by it by means of purely affective forces. The precipitates of these processes resembling repression which took place in prehistoric times still remained attached to civilization for long periods. Religion would thus be the universal obsessional neurosis of humanity; like the obsessional neurosis of children, it arose out of the Oedipus complex, out of the relation to the father. If this view is right, it is to be supposed that a turning-away from religion is bound to occur with the fatal inevitability of a process of growth, and that we find ourselves at this very juncture in the middle of that phase of development. . . .

I know how difficult it is to avoid illusions; perhaps the hopes I have confessed to are of an illusory nature, too. But I hold fast to one distinction. Apart from the fact that no penalty is imposed for not sharing them, my illusions are not, like religious ones, incapable of correction. They have not the character of a delusion. If experience should show—not to me, but to others after me, who think as I do—that we have been mistaken, we will give up our expectations. Take my attempt for what it is. A psychologist who does not deceive himself about the difficulty of finding one's bearings in this world, makes an endeavour to assess the development of man, in the light of the small portion of knowledge he has gained through a study of the mental processes of individuals during their development from child to adult. In so doing, the idea forces itself upon him that religion is comparable to a childhood neurosis, and he is optimistic enough to suppose that mankind will surmount this neurotic phase, just as so many children grow out of their similar neurosis. . . .

We believe that it is possible for scientific work to gain some knowledge about the reality of the world, by means of which we can increase our power and in accordance with which we can arrange our life. If this belief is an illusion, then we are in the same position as you. But science has given us evidence by its numerous and important successes that it is no illusion. . . .

No, our science is no illusion. But an illusion it would be to suppose that what science cannot give us we can get elsewhere.

Counterpoint:
From *Gone Primitive:*
Savage Intellects, Modern Lives

MARIANA TORGOVNICK

Mariana Torgovnick teaches at Duke University. Among her major publications are the following books: *Closure in the Novel, Primitive Passions: Men, Women, and the Quest for Ecstasy, The Visual Arts, Pictorialism, and the Novel: James, Lawrence, and Woolf,* and *Eloquent Obsessions: Writing Cultural Criticism.*

Entering Freud's Study

. . . Freud conceived of himself as an imaginary citizen of Rome; the Nazis conceived of him as a prize Jew whom they reluctantly spared the death camp. By 1938, when the photographs of Freud's study and consulting room in *Bergasse 19* were taken, the disjunction between these perceptions had become painfully clear. That year saw Austria annexed by Germany, Jews vilified and beaten in the streets of Vienna, Anna and Martin Freud brought in for questioning by the Gestapo (an event for which they prepared by acquiring a powerful poison), long lines of desperate Austrian Jews at visa offices, the excesses of Die Kristallnacht. In June of 1938 Freud and his family went into exile in England, after the Nazis yielded to international pressure that they be allowed to leave the country of their birth. In fact, we have the archive of Freud's personal space in *Bergasse 19* because his Viennese followers correctly perceived that Freud's apartment was a doomed place, and that theirs was a subculture on the eve of extinction.

All of these terrible things could happen in Freud's beloved Vienna in part because of the Nazis' processing of Jews as primitives. As we have seen, the arrangement of objects in Freud's consulting room and study made distinctions between Freud as the civilized man and the animal-like primitive. Anti-Jewish propaganda portrayed Jews in the same terms Freud and his culture routinely used for primitives. Although he rarely acknowledged its existence, this kind of propaganda, which the Nazis manipulated so skillfully and brought to a new level of explicitness, may have motivated Freud's insistent need to see himself and Jews who were like him as civilized beings antithetical to the primitive, even as it heightened his suspiciousness about the benefits of civilization itself.

A persistent Western fantasy saw the Jews as needing to drink Christian blood, much as primitives were conceived, frequently, as cannibals. Jews from Eastern Europe were frequently represented (by assimilated Jews as well as gentiles) as "primitive"—ritualistic, collective, superstitious, alien, and distasteful. Their odd dress and odd language (Yiddish) reinforced the impression of their Otherness. In infamous propaganda films, shots of *shtetl* Jews would be intercut with cartoonlike caricatures of Jewish features or with shots of swarming insects and rats, and hence Jews were perceived as an undifferentiated mass liable to extermination.

To prepare occupied populations for anti-Jewish measures, the Nazis frequently mounted exhibitions in which Jewish "Otherness" would be displayed visually and palpably; they resembled European expositions and circuses that displayed primitive peoples and their objects as freaks and curiosities. The Nazi exhibitions often included posters and photographs denouncing Jews prominent in European intellectual life, including Freud himself, whose books were burned by the Nazis as early as 1933. Freud arranged the objects in his study and consulting room to suggest an alliance between himself and civilization; Nazi propaganda used visual display to make opposite suggestions, aligning Freud, by virtue of his Jewishness, with the expendable primitive.

Sander Gilman has shown, in a study of Jewish "self-hatred," that Freud was, like many assimilated Germanic Jews, fundamentally secular. He shared the sense of superiority, and even "vehement contempt," many Germanic Jews felt toward provincial Jews from Eastern Europe. He felt he had "excelled" (his word) his Hasidic father. He changed his name from the Jewish Sigusmund (used in anti-Semitic jokes) to the Germanic Sigmund. He repressed Yiddish as a spoken language in his own life and repressed its importance in early cases, like Anna O.'s, which produced his theories of hysteria. If Gilman is right that Freud repressed certain aspects of the category "Jewishness," the repressed had begun a forced return by the late twenties and early thirties. During these decades, Freud defiantly emphasized more and more the fact that he was Jewish, though he repeatedly treated the question of what it meant to be Jewish. His definitions intersect with the dialectic of the civilized and the primitive and reflect his increasing and yet ambivalent need to identify himself as a civilized man, a claim that rested on his status as a man of science.

By 1930 it was abundantly clear to Freud that worsening economic conditions had revived the most violent forms of anti-Semitism. He could no longer gaze on the processes of history as a distressed but clearly "civilized" man; he was now put in the position of the threatened Other,

declared "inferior and degenerate." In that year, *Civilization and Its Discontents* alludes quite directly to Freud's concern over increased persecution of the Jews as scapegoats during the Great Depression. . . . Also in 1930, in a preface he added to a new edition of *Totem and Taboo*, Freud both hints and denies that Jewishness colors his renewed interest in the transition between primitive and civilized social life. He declares in the preface that his "essence" is Jewish, despite his nonbelief in Jewish lore, and that he "has no desire to alter" that essence. But he does make a few suggestions for updating Judaism—and not necessarily in minor ways.

In this preface, Freud describes his own work as "unprejudiced science" which "adopts no Jewish standpoint." He urges what he calls the "new Jewry" to follow his example and to embrace "unprejudiced science." Freud thus distinguishes between an "old" (unassimilated, religious) Jewry and a "new" (assimilated, secular) Jewry to which he himself belongs. Under the impact of Aryan rhetoric, Freud fights against the identification of the Jew with the primitive by expressly redefining the Jew as a being who conforms to the secular, scientific spirit of the modern age—in his own case, typifies it. He evades the question of what a Jewish "essence" consists of, stripped of any religious sense; in fact, he proposes that science may one day illuminate this vexing question. He similarly evades the question of whether distinctions like that he suggests between an "old" and "new" Jewry play the Nazis' own damnable game of self and Other.

Freud once felt sure that Europeans like the Germans and Austrians were civilized and that primitive life belonged to the past. But by Freud's last years in Vienna, the categories of the "primitive" and the "civilized"—once, for Freud, so clearly separate in time and so arranged in hierarchical order—had become fundamentally more unstable under the pressure of Nazism. Political events made Freud more and more willing to reckon civilization's costs as well as benefits and to entertain the idea that Western civilization had gone, inexorably, wrong—that is the burden of *Civilization and Its Discontents*. But Freud still ultimately saw himself as an apologist for civilization.

Given the material he had to work with, Freud might have arrived at a radical critique of the very ideas of "hierarchy" and "mastery" in the political contexts of the late twenties and the thirties: the Nazis had, after all, given both concepts a bad name. Instead Freud continued to lay siege to the top level of power. Freud's picture of himself as a man of science (and the gender is important) allowed him to believe that he wrote from within the system of European civilization; it sustained his sense of himself as European (Roman) citizen rather than Jewish Other. Ironically, like many in his day, Freud was unable to perceive how science itself could be perverted into a pseudoscience that served the Nazis' genocidal ends through a rhetoric of "race" and "eugenics," and through the safeguarding of Aryan stock at death camps manned by honored doctors. . . .

As Freud's collection of statues suggests, he possessed an intense visual imagination, and he dramatizes his ideas about the primitive by writing a scene (a "spectacle" he calls it) from human "prehistory." That "spectacle" encodes some of the same ideas and hierarchies we have seen embodied in Freud's consulting room and study. The setting is a primeval landscape. A large rock looms in the background; a primeval horde cowers in the foreground before the entrance to its cave, from which comes the reassuring brightness and warmth of fire. The leader of the horde is the father, who mates indiscriminately with all the women of the horde, his wives and daughters. The other, younger, men are excluded from mating and fiercely jealous. They remain at the mercy of the tyrant until they decide one day to band together and kill the father. They do kill him, instituting, as penance, law, exogamous sexual relations, and religions in which the slain father becomes first the totem animal and then the Father god among gods, and finally the God of monotheism among the Jews.

From this imagined scene of primal Oedipal murder in *Totem and Taboo* would come Freud's explanation for Western anti-Semitism in *Moses and Monotheism* (1939): Christians, Freud believed, acknowledged guilt for the murder of the primal father by accepting Christ the son's sacrifice as atonement; by refusing to acknowledge Christ as Lord, Jews fueled Christian resentment by declining to share mankind's guilt for the murder of the father. This connection between the murder of the father and anti-Semitism is not yet present in *Totem and Taboo*. But *Totem and Taboo* makes utterly clear how Freud's version of the primitive both depends on and supports a traditional, patriarchal model of culture, with Oedipal patterns concerning the father as the central psychological mainspring.

In *Civilization and Its Discontents*, Freud writes a sequel to the story he told in *Totem and Taboo* about the transition between the primitive and the civilized. Like the original, the sequel tells the story of a primeval society ruled by men which became a civilized society, also ruled by men. *Civilization and Its Discontents* revisits the primal rock of *Totem and Taboo*, with primal fire and primal horde, to imagine a different scene than the murder of the father. This time, men and women hover around the comforting fire. Suddenly, the men begin to urinate on the fire, something the women are physiologically prevented from doing. One man, destined to become a man of power, refrains from urinating and commands the others to do so as well. He henceforth controls the fire and becomes the horde's leader and guardian.

This scene—as silly in the original as in the retelling—is a bizarre fantasy which typifies how Freud's theories of the development of individuals and cultures are parallel and male-based. Freud imagines (and is comfortable with) a version of the primitive in which women are excluded from primal moments and unable to seize power; he evolves his script of prehistory in accord with his culture's gender assumptions. He divides history into the categories female/male and primitive/civilized. He then allies himself with the "triumphant" categories—civilized male.

Magically, and at odds with his social realities, Freud becomes one of "us," not one of "them." It was a comforting pattern which reproduced the arrangement of objects we have seen in Freud's study, with Freud rigidly aligned with the head of the Roman citizen atop a classical column. It was the same pattern of mastery and control that Freud, sitting at his desk or in "Freud's corner," communicated to his patients and to the viewers of photographs like that on the title page of *Totem and Taboo*. Freud's control over his environment—his ownership and mastery of statues and paintings, his ability to make them tell the stories he wants to hear—echoes and reinforces his control over his patients and over the psychoanalytic process, especially as recorded in Freud's case histories. Ultimately, it prefigures his ideals of self-control and self-mastery, ideals he has bequeathed to us in his influential theories. It is surely significant that Freud's model of the mind depends on rooting out portions of the psyche that frustrate our lives as good citizens—depends, indeed, on a life of fragmentation, conflict, and exile from wholeness, which it is then the goal of psychoanalysis to make liveable. These are the prerogatives available to men of science.

But Freud's version of the primitive was something less than purely scientific—as he himself was aware when he called it a "scientific myth." It was, in fact, produced more by personal and professional needs than by the ideal of scientific observation. From *Totem and Taboo* through *Civilization and Its Discontents*, Freud imagines primitive prehistory in terms of his own psychological theories. He concludes, for example, that "obsessional neurotics behave exactly like savages" on the basis of "submit[ting] the recorded facts [about primitive taboos] to analysis, as though they formed part of the symptoms presented by neurosis."[1] The procedure is entirely circular and self-generating, yielding not "results" based on observation, but axioms based on metaphors.

Freud relies absolutely on the imaginary union of children, primitives, and neurotics in developing his crucial parallel between the origins of civilized institutions and of individual neuroses. He does this despite repeated notations in his footnotes that should have prevented metaphor from slipping into fact. Freud says, for example, that primitives have an unknown past of their own which makes their present state an uncertain parallel to our own (the West's) past, only metaphorically analogous to what is usually called the "childhood of man."[2] He also says, quite clearly, that primitive customs are collective, while neuroses are individual. Strictly speaking, it should thus have been impossible for Freud to compare the traditions and institutions of primitive societies with the beliefs of children or the oddities of the individual neurotic. Indeed, primitive societies might have provided Freud with examples of collective forms of social existence to serve as radical alternatives to Western individualism. But Freud could not stop his powerful analogy-making machine: it was too slickly oiled by his need to be the Roman citizen, a modern man among modern civilized men.

Critics often identify Freud's primitive with the masculine—as when Ransohoff, in her captions to Engelman's *Bergasse 19*, alludes to the "phallic primitive." But this identification of masculinity with the "primitive" id misses a crucial point: for Freud, when societies evolved from the primitive to the civilized after the primal murder of the father, individual men did too. "The primitive" was something left behind, residual, like the "id" within the mature ego. Often (though not exclusively) for Freud, residual "primitive" feelings were associated with the mother and, hence, with femininity. In this sense, it is not surprising that Freud turned, after *Civilization and Its Discontents*, quite explicitly to the questions addressed in "Female Sexuality" (1931) and "Femininity" (1933): the nature of feminine sexual development and the reasons why women (Freud believed) lack a strong ethical sense. In fact, it is possible to read the opening of *Civilization and Its Discontents* as the prelude to the themes developed in these two essays.

In Freud's work, the feminine often functions as the primitive does and as religious Judaism does—as something "the Roman citizen" rejects and controls in his march toward civilization. Sometimes the connection between the female and the primitive in Freud's mind is hard to miss, as when he compares the female psyche to a "dark continent," with himself as the intrepid explorer Stanley. "Female Sexuality" (1931) is equally clear in aligning the female with the primitive: the period when infants are attached to their mothers (a period Freud believed of paramount importance for women) is described there as like the Minoan past of Greek civilization, "grey with age, and shadowy and almost impossible to revivify."[3]

Sometimes, especially in earlier work, the connection between women and "the primitive" is subtler, though it predicts the associations that we have already seen. In *Beyond the Pleasure Principle* (1920) Freud describes how a little boy's game of "Fort/Da" prepared him for his mother's intermittent departures. He tells how the boy learned to cope with his mother's absences and then, several years later (during which another child had been born into the family), "showed no signs of grief" when his mother died. Freud applauds the child's ability to separate from the mother as a "great cultural achievement."[4] His language implicitly makes the child's withdrawal from the mother analogous to society's transition from the primitive to the civilized. He makes no comment about the boy's lack of grief: female presence is elided in favor of male development.

In *Civilization and Its Discontents,* Freud addresses the question of the female role in human development in a crucial way, though the book's reference to the female is not immediately apparent. In this work, the female enters the discussion indirectly, through the issue of the infant's attachment to the mother as undifferentiated from the self. Freud's discussion of this phenomenon follows more general attention to a category of experiences in which the individual undergoes "a feeling as of something limitless, unbounded—as it were, 'oceanic.'"[5]

The prototype of such experiences of boundlessness, Freud will ultimately suggest, is the infant's feeling of oneness with the mother—hence the link between "the oceanic" and the female. Freud treats the "oceanic" in a way that reveals how it was for him like religious Jewishness and the primitive, a category he wished to suppress and leave behind because it was at odds with the modern city-state and the sense of consummate individualism upon which it depends. But there is something fearful and even erratic about Freud's handling of the "oceanic"; in fact, until he is able to connect it to an infantile state, and hence to associate it with women, he feels distinctly threatened by it.

Freud's discussion of the "oceanic" seems to come out of nowhere at the beginning of *Civilization and Its Discontents.* As the book begins, Freud considers the idea (urged upon him by his friend Romain Rolland) that the "oceanic feeling" of being "unlimited, boundless"—a feeling not, at this point, connected to infants and mothers—is the origin of the religious sense. Freud is intent on refuting this thesis since it discredits the theories elaborated in *Totem and Taboo* and *The Future of an Illusion,* which trace the religious feeling to guilt over the primal horde's patricidal act. Since the "oceanic" stresses feelings of connection and oneness rather than Oedipal rivalry with the father, it cannot be allowed to stand as an important factor in human and cultural evolution. . . .

Freud is in some ways surprisingly candid about his need to dismiss the oceanic. Although his friend reports having had this oceanic feeling and claims that "millions of people" do as well, Freud himself claims never to have experienced it. Based simply on his own sensations, Freud decides to remove the "oceanic" from "the foreground" of attention. He admits that being able to summarily dismiss the "oceanic" is strategic. For the idea of the "oceanic"—with its emphasis on a "permeable" ego and feelings of collectivity as something desirable—threatens the very foundations of psychoanalysis as a discipline. . . . Freud proceeds to tell the following story to justify the efforts of his lifetime and glorify the emergence of the sense of self. Although Freud would say that his story includes both males and females, he was really thinking about males; though I use neuter nouns, Freud's story demands a male protagonist for its pattern of heroic exile to be especially clear.

The archetypal moment when the ego fails to perceive its difference from the outside world is that of "an infant at the breast"[6]: this subsequently becomes our culture's dominant image of the "oceanic" in human experience and portrays the "oceanic" as an obvious—and "regressive"—extension of the feelings of the child in the womb. The need to restore the pleasures of the breast and opposite needs to escape pain gradually cause the individual "to learn a procedure by which, through a deliberate direction of one's sensory activities and through suitable muscular action, one can differentiate between what is internal—what belongs to the ego—and what is external—what emanates from the outside world."[7] The "oceanic" feeling thus eases into the perception of self and other under what Freud calls the "reality principle." The very phrases capture Freud's sense of hierarchy: the oceanic is a "sense," a "feeling"; reality is a "principle."

If the "oceanic" survives this process, it does so, Freud claims, in the way that "Rome" contains past civilizations "buried in the soil of the city or beneath its modern buildings."[8] . . . Freud's insistence that the oceanic (like all that existed before Rome) is "in no sense still preserved" but rather "absorbed into the later phases" seems peculiar and overstated. The overstatement denies the continued existence of the "oceanic," yet seems to protest too much. Indeed, Freud's statements in *Civilization and Its Discontents* deny his earlier formulations about the reaccessibility of "primitive" mental formations.

The analogy between the mature ego (below which lie the scattered remains of the id) and the Roman city occupies four of the ten pages Freud devotes to the "oceanic." The analogy is not a casual gesture. In fact, it recapitulates the ideology already encoded in the visual displays we

have seen in Freud's study and consulting room. The "oceanic" is identified with the infant at the breast, with "the primitive pleasure principle," and with id forces: the "oceanic" is the primitive and the conjunction of the infantile and the female, none of which conform to "the reality principle." The mature ego is identified with the imperial city-state, which will colonize primitives quite literally and colonize (in the figurative sense) many feelings, including feelings of free sexuality and oceanic oneness. The "oceanic" must be "ousted from a place in the foreground" because it would displace the individualistic paternal line (the Roman line) to which Freud wishes to trace civilization, its benefits, and its discontents. The "oceanic," with its absence of boundaries and divisions, is something we need to be protected from if we are to take our places in the "mature" culture of the West: we must fear it as we fear the primitive and separate from it as we separate from "primitive" sexual or aggressive urges and from the bodies of our mothers. That separation has fearful consequences Freud does not pause for long to examine: an alienation from one's past and from one's environment, the establishment and perpetuation of relations of mastery rather than reciprocity, the repudiation of "the feminine" as a source of "primary narcissism" and loss of self. It is a fateful separation, and fateful in the context of Freud's thinking.

It is, in fact, another version of the fall into transcendental homelessness, another form of exile. In "The 'Uncanny,'" Freud refers to the mother's body as "the place where each of us lived once upon a time and in the beginning" and attributes to everyone the utterance "this place is familiar to me, I've been here before."[9] In his repudiation of the "oceanic" sense in *Civilization and Its Discontents,* Freud denies the mother's body, brands it as something that the mature ego must leave behind, as primitive freedom must be left behind by a civilized person. Freud misses here an important, alternative direction. He never fully considers the questions invited by his opening meditation on the oceanic. If there is a state of mind, and potentially a state of culture, that could be derived from the original relationship of our bodies to the bodies of our mothers, what differences in father-centered psychoanalytic theories would follow? What differences in the relation of men and women to the physical world would follow? . . .

NOTES

1. Sigmund Freud, *Totem and Taboo,* trans. James Strachey (New York: Norton, 1950), pp. 56, 46.

2. Ibid., p. 4.

3. Idem, "Female Sexuality," *Standard Edition,* vol. 2, p. 225.

4. Idem, *Beyond the Pleasure Principle,* trans. James Strachery (New York: Norton, 1961).

5. Idem, *Civilization and Its Discontents,* trans. James Strachery (New York: Norton, 1961), p. 11.

6. Idem, *The Future of an Illusion,* trans. James Strachery (New York: Norton, 1961), p. 14.

7. Ibid., p. 15.

8. Ibid., p. 18.

9. Idem, "The Uncanny," *Standard Edition,* vol 17, p. 245.

From *Psychology and Religion: West and East*

CARL G. JUNG

The Autonomy of the Unconscious

Although I have often been called a philosopher, I am an empiricist and adhere as such to the phenomenological standpoint. I trust that it does not conflict with the principles of scientific empiricism if one occasionally makes certain reflections which go beyond a mere accumulation and classification of experience. As a matter of fact I believe that experience is not even possible without rejection, because "experience" is a process of assimilation without which there could be no understanding. As this statement indicates, I approach psychological matters from a scientific and not from a philosophical standpoint. Inasmuch as religion has a very important psychological aspect, I deal with it from a purely empirical point of view, that is, I restrict myself to the observation of phenomena and I eschew any metaphysical or philosophical considerations. I do not deny the validity of these other considerations, but I cannot claim to be competent to apply them correctly. . . .

Since I am going to present a rather unusual argument, I cannot assume that my audience will be fully acquainted with the methodological standpoint of the branch of psychology I represent. This standpoint is exclusively phenomenological, that is, it is concerned with occurrences, events, experiences—in a word, with facts. Its truth is a fact and not a judgment. When psychology speaks, for instance, of the motif of the virgin birth, it is only concerned with the fact that there is such an idea, but it is not concerned with the question whether such an idea is true or false in any other sense. The idea is psychologically true inasmuch as it exists. Psychological existence is subjective in so far as an idea occurs in only one individual. But it is objective in so far as that idea is shared by a society—by a *consensus gentium.*

This point of view is the same as that of natural science. Psychology deals with ideas and

Reprinted from Carl Jung, Psychology and Religion: West and East, *trans. R. F. C. Hull,* Bollingen Series XX. The Collected Works of C. G. Jung *vol. 11 (New York: Pantheon Books, 1958).*

other mental contents as zoology, for instance, deals with the different species of animals. An elephant is "true" because it exists. The elephant is neither an inference nor a statement nor the subjective judgment of a creator. It is a phenomenon. But we are so used to the idea that psychic events are willful and arbitrary products, or even the inventions of a human creator, that we can hardly rid ourselves of the prejudiced view that the psyche and its contents are nothing but our own arbitrary invention or the more or less illusory product of supposition and judgment. The fact is that certain ideas exist almost everywhere and at all times and can even spontaneously create themselves quite independently of migration and tradition. They are not made by the individual, they just happen to him—they even force themselves on his consciousness. This is not Platonic philosophy but empirical psychology.

In speaking of religion I must make clear from the start what I mean by that term. Religion, as the Latin word denotes, is a careful and scrupulous observation of what Rudolf Otto aptly termed the *numinosum,* that is, a dynamic agency or effect not caused by an arbitrary act of will. On the contrary, it seizes and controls the human subject, who is always rather its victim than its creator. The *numinosum*—whatever its cause may be—is an experience of the subject independent of his will. At all events, religious teaching as well as the *consensus gentium* always and everywhere explain this experience as being due to a cause external to the individual. The *numinosum* is either a quality belonging to a visible object or the influence of an invisible presence that causes a peculiar alteration of consciousness. This is, at any rate, the general rule.

There are, however, certain exceptions when it comes to the question of religious practice or ritual. A great many ritualistic performances are carried out for the sole purpose of producing at will the effect of the *numinosum* by means of certain devices of a magical nature, such as invocation, incantation, sacrifice, meditation and other yoga practices, self-inflicted tortures of various descriptions, and so forth. But a religious belief in an external and objective divine cause is always prior to any such performance. The Catholic Church, for instance, administers the sacraments for the purpose of bestowing their spiritual blessings upon the believer; but since this act would amount to enforcing the presence of divine grace by an indubitably magical procedure, it is logically argued that nobody can compel divine grace to be present in the sacramental act, but that it is nevertheless inevitably present since the sacrament is a divine institution which God would not have caused to be if he had not intended to lend it his support.

Religion appears to me to be a peculiar attitude of mind which could be formulated in accordance with the original use of the word *religio,* which means a careful consideration and observation of certain dynamic factors that are conceived as "powers": spirits, daemons, gods, laws, ideas, ideals, or whatever name man has given to such factors in his world as he has found powerful, dangerous, or helpful enough to be taken into careful consideration, or grand, beautiful, and meaningful enough to be devoutly worshipped and loved. In colloquial speech one often says of somebody who is enthusiastically interested in a certain pursuit that he is almost "religiously devoted" to his cause. . . .

I want to make clear that by the term "religion" I do not mean a creed. It is, however, true that every creed is originally based on the one hand upon the experience of the *numinosum* and on the other hand upon . . . trust or loyalty, faith and confidence in a certain experience of a numinous nature and in the change of consciousness that ensues. The conversion of Paul is a striking example of this. We might say, then, that the term "religion" designates the attitude peculiar to a consciousness which has been changed by experience of the *numinosum.* . . .

A Psychological Approach to the Trinity

There can be no doubt that the doctrine of the Trinity originally corresponded with a patriarchal order of society. But we cannot tell whether social conditions produced the idea or, conversely, the idea revolutionized the existing social order. The phenomenon of early Christianity and the rise of Islam, to take only these two examples, show what ideas can do. The layman, having no opportunity to observe the behaviour of autonomous complexes, is usually inclined, in conformity with the general trend, to trace the origin of psychic contents back to the environment. This expectation is certainly justified so far as the ideational contents of consciousness are concerned. In addition to these, however, there are irrational, affective reactions and impulses, emanating from the unconscious, which organize the conscious material in an archetypal way. The more clearly the archetype is constellated, the more powerful will be its fascination, and the resultant religious statements will formulate it accordingly, as something "daemonic" or "divine." Such statements indicate possession by an archetype. The ideas underlying them are necessarily anthropomorphic and are thereby distinguished from the organizing archetype, which in itself is irrepresentable because unconscious. They prove, however, that an archetype has been activated.

Thus the history of the Trinity presents itself as the gradual crystallization of an archetype that moulds the anthropomorphic conceptions of father and son, of life, and of different persons into an archetypal and numinous figure, the "Most Holy Three-in-One." The contemporary witnesses of these events apprehended it as something that modern psychology would call a psychic presence outside consciousness. If there is a consensus of opinion in respect of an idea, as there is here and always has been, then we are entitled to speak of a collective presence. Similar "presences" today are the Fascist and Communist ideologies, the one emphasizing the power of the chief, a communal ownership of goods in a primitive society.

"Holiness" means that an idea or thing possesses the highest value, and that in the presence of this value men are, so to speak, struck dumb.

Holiness is also revelatory: it is the illuminative power emanating from an archetypal figure. Nobody ever feels himself as the subject of such a process, but always as its object. He does not perceive holiness, it takes him captive and overwhelms him; nor does he behold it in a revelation, it reveals itself to him, and he cannot even boast that he has understood it properly. Everything happens apparently outside the sphere of his will, and these happenings are contents of the unconscious. Science is unable to say anything more than this, for it cannot, by an act of faith, overstep the limits appropriate to its nature.

Christ As Archetype

The Trinity and its inner life process appear as a closed circle, a self-contained divine drama in which man plays, at most, a passive part. It seizes on him and, for a period of several centuries, forced him to occupy his mind passionately with all sorts of queer problems which today seem incredibly abstruse, if not downright absurd. It is, in the first place, difficult to see what the Trinity could possibly mean for us, either practically, morally, or symbolically. Even theologians often feel that speculation on this subject is a more or less otiose juggling with ideas, and there are not a few who could get along quite comfortably without the divinity of Christ, and for whom the role of the Holy Ghost, both inside and outside the Trinity, is an embarrassment of the first order. . . .

If we are to answer this psychological question, we must first of all examine the Christ-symbolism contained in the New Testament, together with the patristic allegories and medieval iconography, and compare this material with the archetypal content of the unconscious psyche in order to find out what archetypes have been constellated. The most important of the symbolical statements about Christ are those which reveal the attributes of the hero's life: improbable origin, divine father, hazardous birth, rescue in the nick of time, precocious development, conquest of the mother and of death, miraculous deeds, a tragic, early end, symbolically significant manner of death, post-mortem effects (reappearances, signs and marvels, etc.). As the Logos, Son of the Father, *Rex gloriae, Judex mundi,* Redeemer, and Saviour; Christ is himself God, an all-embracing totality, which, like the definition of Godhead, is expressed iconographically by the circle or mandala. Here I would mention only the traditional representation of the *Rex gloriae* in a mandala, accompanied by a quaternity composed of the four symbols of the evangelists (including the four seasons, four winds, four rivers, and so on). Another symbolism of the same kind is the choir of saints, angels, and elders grouped round Christ (or God) in the centre. Here Christ symbolizes the integration of the kings and prophets of the Old Testament. As a shepherd he is the leader and centre of the flock. He is the vine, and those that hang on him are the branches. His body is bread to be eaten, and his blood wine to be drunk; he is also the mystical body formed by the congregation. In his human manifestation he is the hero and God-man, born without sin, more complete and more perfect than the natural man, who is to him what a child is to an adult, or an animal (sheep) to a human being.

These mythological statements, coming from within the Christian sphere as well as from outside it, adumbrate an archetype that expresses itself in essentially the same symbolism and also occurs in individual dreams or in fantasy-like projections upon living people (transference phenomena, hero-worship, etc.). The content of all such symbolic products is the idea of an overpowering, all-embracing, complete or perfect being, represented either by a man of heroic proportions, or by an animal with magical attributes, or by a magical vessel or some other "treasure hard to attain," such as a jewel, ring, crown, or, geometrically, by a mandala. This archetypal idea is a reflection of the individual's wholeness, i.e., of the self, which is present in him as an unconscious image. The conscious mind can form absolutely no conception of this totality, because it includes not only the conscious but also the unconscious psyche, which is, as such, inconceivable and irrepresentable.

It was this archetype of the self in the soul of every man that responded to the Christian message, with the result that the concrete Rabbi Jesus was rapidly assimilated by the constellated archetype. In this way Christ realized the idea of the Self. But as one can never distinguish empirically between a symbol of the self and a God-image, the two ideas, however much we try to differentiate them, always appear blended together, so that the self appears synonymous with the inner Christ of the Johannine and Pauline writings, and Christ with God ("of one substance with the Father"), just as the atman appears as the individualized self and at the same time as the animating principle of the cosmos, and Tao as a condition of mind and at the same time as the correct behaviour of cosmic events. Psychologically speaking, the domain of "gods" begins where consciousness leaves off, for at that point man is already at the mercy of the natural order, whether he thrive or perish. To the symbols of wholeness that come to him from there he attaches names which vary according to time and place.

The self is defined psychologically as the psychic totality of the individual. Anything that a man postulates as being a greater totality than himself can become a symbol of the self. For this reason the symbol of the self is not always as total as the definition would require. Even the Christ-figure is not a totality, for it lacks the nocturnal side of the psyche's nature, the darkness of the spirit, and is also without sin. Without the integration of evil there is no totality, nor can evil be "added to the mixture by force." One could compare Christ as a symbol to the mean of the first mixture: he would then be the middle term of a triad, in which the One and Indivisible is represented by the Father, and the Divisible by the Holy Ghost, who, as we know, can divide himself into tongues of fire. But this triad, according to the *Timaeus,* is not yet a reality. Consequently a second mixture is needed.

The goal of psychological, as of biological, development is self-realization, or individuation. But since man knows himself only as an ego, and the self, as a totality, is indescribable and indistinguishable from a God-image, self-realization—to put it in religious or metaphysical terms—amounts to God's incarnation. That is already expressed in the fact that Christ is the son of God. And because individuation is an heroic and often tragic task, the most difficult of all, it involves suffering, a passion of the ego: the ordinary, empirical man we once were is burdened with the fate of losing himself in a greater dimension and being robbed of his fancied freedom of will. He suffers, so to speak, from the violence done to him by the self. The analogous passion of Christ signifies God's suffering on account of the injustice of the world and the darkness of man. The human and the divine suffering set up a relationship of complementarity with compensating effects. Through the Christ-symbol, man can get to know the real meaning of his suffering: he is on the way towards realizing his wholeness. As a result of the integration of conscious and unconscious, his ego enters the "divine" realm, where it participates in "God's suffering." The cause of the suffering is in both cases the same, namely "incarnation," which on the human level appears as "individuation." The divine hero born of man is already threatened with murder; he has nowhere to lay his head, and his death is a gruesome tragedy. The self is no mere concept or logical postulate; it is a psychic reality, only part of it conscious, while for the rest it embraces the life of the unconscious and is therefore inconceivable except in the form of symbols. The drama of the archetypal life of Christ describes in symbolic images the events in the conscious life—as well as in the life that transcends consciousness—of a man who has been transformed by his higher destiny.

Counterpoint:
From *Resurrecting the Body:*
Feminism, Religion, and Psychotherapy

NAOMI R. GOLDENBERG

Naomi R. Goldenberg teaches psychology of religion at the University of Ottawa in Ontario, Canada. Among her published books are the following: *Changing of the Gods* and *Returning Words to Flesh: Feminism, Religion and Psychotherapy.*

A Critical View of Archetypal Thinking

Jung says many different things about archetypes. Sometimes he talks about them in a low-key manner as portraits of typical Ways of thinking and acting. At other times, he speaks about them in scientific terms as the images of the instincts or as invisible patterns like the electromagnetic axial systems of a crystal. Often he

Reprinted from Naomi R. Goldenberg, Resurrecting the Body: Feminism, Religion, and Psychotherapy *(Crossroad Publishing Company, 1993).*

links his notion of archetype to Plato's theory of forms.

To make matters even more complicated, Jung's followers talk about archetypes in several other ways.[1] Some try to clarify Jung's ideas by settling on deceptively simple definitions of the term "archetype." Others focus on studies of specific images which they identify as archetypes. Still others, following the lead of James Hillman, develop an "archetypal psychology" in which images are explored and elaborated for therapeutic purposes. The archetypal psychologists sometimes prefer to use the word "image" instead of archetype. However, I would argue that they often tend to think of images in the same ways that more traditional Jungians think about archetypes.

With all these ideas about archetypes inhabiting the texts of both Jung and Jungians, it is impossible to settle on limits to the term which will do justice to every Jungian reflection on it. Further, with myriad sources available to quote, it is possible to make the word "archetype" mean just about anything you would like.[2] Nevertheless, while I cannot give you the definition of archetype, I can identify a specific quality of the term which pervades Jungian thought. It is a characteristic I find problematic. For me, the objectionable quality of archetypal thinking is the idea that archetypes are transcendent to the physical human world and that they are, in part at least, not dependent on human or material contingency. Instead of directing our attention to the web of past and present social contexts which give rise to psychological phenomena, archetypal thinking draws us away from exploring our human circumstances. It leads us to imagine the influence of god-like entities such as the "Self," the "Psyche," "Eros," "Logos," "anima," and "animus." This direction in archetypal theory hampers our ability to think clearly and effectively about psychological and social problems. I'll discuss the problematic ideas I see archetypal theory producing with regard to three themes: personal therapy, empathy among social groups, and moral agency.

First, I find that in personal therapy, the idea that archetypes, images, or ancient mythologems are at work in a life instead of parents, grandparents, siblings, friends, and neighbors turns attention away from the intricate and profound ways in which we human beings structure each other's lives. Understanding your cycles of depression and anxiety as caused by biblical forces or by Greek divinities can romanticize psychological suffering but cannot unearth the roots of that suffering in your own life. The exploration of images in art and literature must be accompanied by a thoroughgoing reflection on personal history in order to be effective therapeutically. If inquiry into the details of a life is neglected in favor of discussion of parallels in myths, the actual causes of psychological problems will be disguised and mystified in therapy.

Jung himself is an example of someone whose understanding of his life is hampered by archetypal thinking. I have written about how Jung mystifies his psychological difficulties in his autobiography.[3] He writes about his life in terms of encounters with theistic forces such as the dark side of God, the anima, of personalities number one and two. Instead of thinking very carefully about how he was influenced by a depressed, moody, irritable father and by an undependable mother who, he says, often lied to him and spoke "to the surrounding air," Jung attributes his deep unhappiness to impersonal forces such as a "fatal resistance to life in this world." He never seems to think about how his feelings are contingent on his particular family situation.

Because Jung could not bear to face the degree to which he was frightened and rejected by real people in his life, he developed a psychology which downplays the significance of human relationships. Jungian therapy generally places no great stress on the complexities of human emotional growth in infancy and childhood. The painful psychological wounds within a personal history often go unnoticed and unnamed. They are rendered invisible and thus left to fester. Although the system he developed accorded Jung some emotional satisfaction and much professional success, those of us who need to understand our suffering psychologically should be wary of following his methods.

Second, I see archetypal thinking as a hindrance to empathy among social groups. This is clear from what Jung had to say about three groups of people to whom he did not belong: women, blacks, and Jews. These statements may be very difficult for those who have gained much from Jung to accept. As much as I enjoy stirring things up, I do not mean to slander Jung. My purpose here is to encourage us all to consider how archetypal thinking makes the following statements possible and insulates them from effective challenge.

About women, Jung writes:

> No one can get around the fact that by taking up a masculine profession, studying and working like a man, woman is doing something not wholly in accord with, if not directly injurious to, her feminine nature. She is doing something that would scarcely be possible for a man to do, unless he were a Chinese. Could he, for instance, be a nursemaid or run a kindergarten? When I speak of injury, I do not mean merely physiological injury, but above all psychic injury. It is a woman's outstanding characteristic that she can do anything for the love of a man. But those women who can achieve something important for the love of a thing are most exceptional, because this does not agree with their nature. Love for a thing is a man's prerogative.[4]

About blacks, Jung writes:

> Another thing that struck me about America was the great influence of the Negro, a psychological influence naturally, not due to the mixing of blood. . . . American music draws its main inspiration from the Negro, and so does the dance. The expression of religious feeling, the revival meetings, the Holy Rollers, and the other abnormalities are strongly influenced by the Negro, and the famous American naiveté, in its charming as well as its more unpleasant form, invites comparison with the child-likeness of the Negro. . . .[5]

This infection by the primitive can . . . be observed just as well in other countries, though not to the same degree and in this form. In Africa, for example, the white man is a diminishing minority and must therefore protect himself from the Negro by observing the most rigorous social forms, otherwise he risks "going black." If he succumbs to the primitive influence he is lost. But in America the Negro, just because he is a minority, is not a degenerative influence, but rather one which, peculiar though it is, cannot be termed unfavorable—unless one happens to have a jazz phobia.

About Jews, Jung writes:

> The Jew, as relatively a nomad, never has produced and presumably never will produce a culture of his own, since all his instincts and gifts require a more or less civilized host-people for their development. . . . The Aryan unconscious has a higher potential than the Jewish; that is the advantage and disadvantage of a youthfulness not yet fully estranged from barbarisms.[6]

In contrast to his remarks about women and blacks, these statements about Jews did get Jung into trouble in his lifetime. He was accused of being anti-Semitic by Robert Hillyer in the *Saturday Review of Literature*. Carol Baumann, an American student of Jung's, living in Switzerland, interviewed Jung about the controversy. Jung defends himself with particular reference to the two remarks quoted above:

> Since this article was to be printed in Germany (in 1934) I had to write in a somewhat veiled manner, but to anyone in his senses the meaning should be clear I had to help these people. It had to be made clear that I, an Aryan outside Germany, stood for a scientific approach to psychotherapy. That was the point! I cannot see anything in the least anti-Semitic in this statement It is simply an appraisal of certain psychological differences in background, and in point of fact it is complimentary to the Jews to point out that they are in general more conscious and differentiated than the average Aryan, who has remained close to barbarism!

And it is an historical fact that the Jews have shown a remarkable ability to become carriers of the cultures in all lands wherever they have spread. This shows a high degree of civilization, and such adaptability is a matter for admiration. Some people show a funny kind of resentment when one speaks of differences in psychology—but one must admit that different nationalities and different races have different outlooks and different psychologies.[7] . . .

Am I hypersensitive about such things? Being both a Jew and a woman, I do take offense at Jung's descriptions of what he terms my basic nature. I am appalled at what he says about blacks. These ideas about women, blacks, and Jews are important because instead of being peripheral to the theory Jung developed, they are, in fact, fostered by it.

I have heard Jungians argue that Jung's racist and sexist remarks are typical of the prejudices of his culture and thus should not be taken too seriously. I think this defense warrants careful attention. If we contextualize these statements in terms of the historical influences on Jung as a theorist, we begin to pull the rug out from under the notion of archetypes. By saying that Jung's thinking about blacks, Jews, and women reflects the conditions in which he lived, we recognize that what he claims to be the basic nature of women, blacks, and Jews is contingent on his own position in the world. And if we excuse Jung in this case by saying that his ideas about race and sex are the products of his times, we raise the possibility that his other ideas are also the products of his times. This line of thought can lead us to realize how all human ideas are subject to conditions. We, like Jung, are thinking with the tools of our histories.

It is important to acknowledge that when Jung tells us about his vision of women, blacks, and Jews, he does not say that this is his vision. He seems to feel he can talk about "women's nature," "Jewish potential," or a white's fear of "going black," as if these things are facts apparent to everyone.

Because Jung treats his own ideas as objective truths without wondering about his position as a subject, his theories do not encourage such reflection in us. Jungian theory does not lead us to investigate the webs of culture, language, and history which constructed Jung's white, male, bourgeois, Swiss Protestant vision of women, blacks, and Jews. Instead of heightening our curiosity about both the conditions which support varieties of human experience and about the conditions which structure our perceptions of human difference, instead of challenging our propensity to impute fixed natures to ourselves and to others, Jungian archetypal theory encourages closure. Archetypal thinking, at its worst, champions a language of pronouncement and decree—"women are essentially this, blacks are basically that, and Jews are what I say they are." . . .

Jung writes that "there are present in every psyche forms which are unconscious but nonetheless active—living dispositions, ideas in the Platonic sense, that preform and continually influence our thoughts and feelings and actions."[8] These archetypes, he thinks, "are not disseminated only by tradition, language, and migration, but . . . can rearise spontaneously, at any time, at any place, and without any outside influence."[9]

We should be critical of such a statement. If we believe that ideas can rearise spontaneously, without any outside influence, our awareness of our own responsibility is diminished. This is my third objection to archetypal thinking: it disguises human agency.

We live in a time when our collective capacity for destruction is threatening all life. The malfunctioning of the insecticide plant in Bhopal, India, in 1986 is but one tragedy exemplifying our grave problems. . . .

Issues such as poverty, world hunger, the arms race, and pollution of the environment should influence the way we evaluate our thinking. Comprehending the dangers we pose to both human and non-human life on the planet should be a central goal of the theories we build. Our situation demands that we be wary of our time-honored forms of thought and reflection because these ways of thinking might now be contributing to our problems. We need to search the inventory of philosophy, psychology, and religion to find those concepts which will let us learn more about how we have built the deep structures of our culture. We need to learn how things connect—how one part of the globe affects another part. We need to see how human presence, human action, and human behavior construct the world. We need to see these often unseen things so that we can try to change ourselves.

The notion of archetypes does not help us to see the complicated ways in which we humans affect one another. Instead of encouraging us to understand how circumstances of infancy, or of biology, or of economics, or of politics, give rise to human conditions, the theory of archetypes encourages us to settle for mystification. . . . I object to such excessive reverence because it simplifies and stupefies. To refuse to search for the material complexities, the human complexities, which produce our ideas, our visions, and our behavior is a form of reductionism which

we can no longer afford. Our archetypes, our myths, our "gods" must be approached. . . .

NOTES

1. For a more detailed account of the development of archetypal theory, see my article, "Archetypal Theory after Jung," *Spring* 1975 (Zürich: Spring Publications, 1975), pp. 199–220.

2. In her essay, "The Common language of Women's Dreams: Colloquy of Mind and Body," in *Feminist Archetypal Theory,* pp. 187–219.

3. See "Looking at Jung Looking at Himself: A Psychoanalytic Rereading of *Memories, Dreams, Reflections,*" chapter 8 in *Resurrecting the Body.*

4. C. G. Jung, *The Collected Works of C. G. Jung,* ed. William McGuire et al., trans. R. F. C. Hull, Bollingen Series 20, 20 vols (Princeton: Princeton University Press, 1954-79), 10: 117–18.

5. Ibid., pp. 46–47.

6. See "On the Attack in Saturday Review of Literature," in *C. G. Jung Speaking: Interviews and Encounters,* ed. William McGuire and R. F. C. Hull (Princeton: Princeton University Press, 1977), pp. 194–95.

7. Ibid., pp. 194–95.

8. Jung, *Collected Works,* 9 (1): 79.

9. Ibid.

From *The Varieties of Religious Experience*

WILLIAM JAMES

RELIGION . . . shall mean for us the feelings, acts, and experiences of individual men in their solitude, so far as they apprehend themselves to stand in relation to whatever they may consider the divine. Since the relation may be either moral, physical, or ritual, it is evident that out of religion in the sense in which we take it, the-

ologies, philosophies, and ecclesiastical organizations may secondarily grow. In these lectures, however, as I have already said, the immediate personal experiences will amply fill our time, and we shall hardly consider theology or ecclesiasticism at all. . . .

Reprinted from William James, The Varieties of Religious Experience *(Cambridge: Harvard University Press, 1985).*

As regards the origin of the Greek gods, we need not at present seek an opinion. But the whole array of our instances leads to a conclusion something like this: It is as if there were in the human consciousness *a sense of reality, a feeling of objective presence, a perception* of what we may call "*something there*" more deep and more general than any of the special and particular "sense" by which the current psychology supposes existent realities to be originally revealed. If this were so, we might suppose the senses to waken our attitudes and conduct as they so habitually do, by first exciting this sense of reality; but anything else, any idea, for example, that might similarly excite it, would have that same prerogative of appearing real which objects of sense normally possess. So far as religious conceptions were able to touch this reality-feeling, they would be believed in spite of criticism, even though they might be so vague and remote as to be almost unimaginable, even though they might be such non-entities in point of *whatness* as Kant makes the objects of his moral theology to be.

The most curious proofs of the existence of such an undifferentiated sense of reality as this are found in experiences of hallucination. It often happens that an hallucination is imperfectly developed: the person affected will feel a "presence" in the room, definitely localized, facing in one particular way, real in the most emphatic sense of the word, often coming suddenly, and as suddenly gone; and yet neither seen, heard, touched, nor cognized in any of the usual "sensible" ways. . . .

I spoke of the convincingness of these feelings of reality, and I must dwell a moment longer on that point. They are as convincing to those who have them as any direct sensible experiences can be, and they are, as a rule, much more convincing than results established by mere logic ever are. One may indeed be entirely without them; probably more than one of you here present is without them in any marked degree; but if you do have them, and have them at all strongly, the probability is that you cannot help regarding them as genuine perceptions of truth, as revelations of a kind of reality which no adverse argument, however unanswerable by you in words, can expel from your belief. The opinion opposed to mysticism in philosophy is sometimes spoken of as rationalism. Rationalism insists that all our beliefs ought ultimately to find for themselves articulate grounds. Such grounds, for rationalism, must consist of four things: (1) definitely statable abstract principles; (2) definite facts of sensation; (3) definite hypotheses based on such facts; and (4) definite inferences logically drawn. Vague impressions of something indefinable have no place in the rationalistic system, which on its positive side is surely a splendid intellectual tendency, for not only are all our philosophies fruits of it, but physical science (amongst other good things) is its result. . . .

The Sick Soul

At our last meeting, we considered the healthy-minded temperament, the temperament which has a constitutional incapacity for prolonged suffering, and in which the tendency to see things optimistically is like a water of crystallization in which the individual's character is set. We saw how this temperament may become the basis for a peculiar type of religion, a religion in which good, even the good of this world's life, is regarded as the essential thing for a rational being to attend to. This religion directs him to settle his scores with the more evil aspects of the universe by systematically declining to lay them to heart or make much of them, by ignoring them in his reflective calculations, or even, on occasion, by denying outright that they exist. Evil is a disease; and worry over disease is itself an additional form of disease, which only adds to the original complaint. Even repentance and remorse, affections which come in the character of ministers of good, may be but sickly and relaxing impulses. The best repentance is to stand up and act for righteousness, and forget that you ever had relations with sin. . . .

Within the Christian body, for which repentance of sins has from the beginning been the critical religious act, healthy-mindedness has always come forward with its milder interpretation. Repentance according to such healthy-minded Christians means *getting away from* the sin, not groaning and writhing over its commission. The Catholic practice of confession and absolution is in one of its aspects little more than a systematic method of keeping healthy-mindedness on top. By it a man's accounts with evil are periodically squared and audited, so that he may start the clean page with no old debts inscribed. Any Catholic will tell us how clean and fresh and free he feels after the purging operation. Martin Luther by no means belonged to the healthy-minded type in the radical sense in which we have discussed it, and he repudiated priestly absolution for sin. Yet in this matter of repentance he had some very healthy-minded ideas, due in the main to the largeness of his conception of God. . . .

Now in contrast with such healthy-minded views as these, if we treat them as a way of deliberately minimizing evil, stands a radically opposite view, a way of maximizing evil, if you please so to call it, based on the persuasion that the evil aspects of our life are of its very essence, and that the world's meaning most comes home to us when we lay them most to heart. We have now to address ourselves to this more morbid way of looking at the situation. But as I closed our last hour with a general philosophical reflection on the healthy-minded way of taking life, I should like at this point to make another philosophical reflection upon it before turning to that heavier task. You will excuse the brief delay.

If we admit that evil is an essential part of our being and the key to the interpretation of our life we load ourselves down with a difficulty that has always proved burdensome in philosophies of religion. Theism, whenever it has erected itself into a systematic philosophy of the universe, has shown a reluctance to let God be anything less than All-in-All. In other words, philosophic theism has always shown a tendency to become pantheistic and monistic, and to consider the world as one unit of absolute fact; and this has been at variance with popular or practical theism, which latter has ever been more or less frankly pluralistic, not to say polytheistic, and shown itself perfectly well satisfied with a universe composed of many original principles, provided we be only allowed to believe that the divine principle remains supreme, and that the others are subordinate. In this latter case God is not necessarily responsible for the existence of evil; he would only be responsible if it were not finally overcome. But on the monistic or pantheistic view, evil, like everything else, must have its foundation in God; and the difficulty is to see how this can possibly be the case if God be absolutely good. This difficulty faces us in every form of philosophy in which the world appears as one flawless unit of fact. Such a unit is an *Individual,* and in it the worst parts must be as essential as the best, must be as necessary to make the individual what he is; since if any part whatever in an individual were to vanish or alter, it would no longer be that individual at all. The philosophy of absolute idealism, so vigorously represented both in Scotland and America today, has to struggle with this difficulty quite as much as scholastic theism struggled in its time; and although it would be premature to say that there is no speculative issue whatever from the puzzle, it is perfectly fair to say that there is no clear or easy issue, and that the only obvious escape from paradox here is to cut loose from the monistic assumption altogether, and to allow the world to have existed from its origin in pluralistic form, as an aggregate or collection of higher and lower things and principles, rather than an absolutely unitary fact. For then evil would not need to be essential; it might be, and may always have been, an independent portion that had no rational or absolute right to live with the rest, and which we might conceivably hope to see got rid of at last.

Now the gospel of healthy-mindedness, as we have described it, casts its vote distinctly for this pluralistic view. Whereas the monistic philosopher finds himself more or less bound to say, as Hegel said, that everything actual is rational, and that evil, as an element dialectically required, must be pinned in and kept and consecrated and have a function awarded to it in the final system of truth, healthy-mindedness refuses to say anything of the sort. Evil, it says, is emphatically irrational, and not to be pinned in, or preserved, or consecrated in any final system of truth. It is a pure abomination to the Lord, an alien unreality, a waste element, to be sloughed off and negated, and the very memory of it, if possible, wiped out and forgotten. The ideal, so far from being co-extensive with the whole actual, is a mere extract from the actual, marked by its deliverance from all contact with this diseased, inferior, and excrementitious stuff.

Here we have the interesting notion fairly and squarely presented to us, of there being elements of the universe which may make no rational whole in conjunction with the other elements, and which, from the point of view of any system which those other elements make up, can only be considered so much irrelevance and accident—so much "dirt," as it were, and matter out of place. I ask you now not to forget this notion; for although most philosophers seem either to forget it or to disdain it too much ever to mention it, I believe that we shall have to admit it ourselves in the end as containing an element of truth. The mind-cure gospel thus once more appears to us as having dignity and importance. We have seen it to be a genuine religion, and no mere silly appeal to imagination to cure disease; we have seen its method of experimental verification to be not unlike the method of all science; and now here we find mind-cure as the champion of a perfectly definite conception of the metaphysical structure of the world. I hope that, in view of all this, you will not regret my having pressed it upon your attention at such length.

Let us now say good-by for a while to all this way of thinking, and turn towards those persons who cannot so swiftly throw off the burden of the consciousness of evil, but are congenitally fated to suffer from its presence. Just as we saw that in healthy-mindedness there are shallower and profounder levels, happiness like that of the mere animal, and more regenerate sorts of happiness, so also are there different levels of the morbid mind, and the one is much more formidable than the other. There are people for whom evil means only a mal-adjustment with *things,* a wrong correspondence of one's life with the environment. Such evil as this is curable, in principle at least, upon the natural plane, for merely by modifying either the self or the things, or both at once, the two terms may be made to fit, and all go merry as a marriage bell again. But there are others for whom evil is no mere relation of the subject to particular outer things, but something more radical and general, a wrongness or vice in his essential nature, which no alteration of the environment, or any superficial rearrangement of the inner self, can cure, and which requires a supernatural remedy. . . .

The securest way to the rapturous sorts of happiness of which the twice-born make report has as an historic matter of fact been through a more radical pessimism than anything that we have yet considered. We have seen how the lustre and enchantment may be rubbed off from the goods of nature. But there is a pitch of unhappiness so great that the goods of nature may be entirely forgotten, and all sentiment of their existence vanish from the mental field. For this extremity of pessimism to be reached, something more is needed than observation of life and reflection upon death. The individual must in his own person become the prey of a pathological melancholy. As the healthy-minded enthusiast succeeds in ignoring evil's very existence, so the subject of melancholy is forced in spite of himself to ignore that of all good whatever: for him it may no longer have the least reality. Such sensitiveness and susceptibility to mental pain is a rare occurrence where the nervous constitution is entirely normal; one seldom finds it in a healthy subject even where he is the victim of the most atrocious cruelties of outward fortune. So we note here the neurotic constitution, of which I said so much in my first lecture, making its active entrance on our scene, and destined to play a part in much that follows. Since these experiences of melancholy are in the first instance absolutely private and individual, I can now help myself out with personal documents. Painful indeed they will be to listen to, and there is almost an indecency in handling them in public. . . .

Arrived at this point, we can see how great an antagonism may naturally arise between the healthy-minded way of viewing life and the way that takes all this experience of evil as something essential. To this latter way, the morbid-minded way, as we might call it, healthy-mindedness pure and simple seems unspeakably blind and shallow. To the healthy-minded way, on the other hand, the way of the sick soul seems unmanly and diseased. With their grubbing in rat-holes instead of living in the light, with their manufacture of fears, and preoccupation with every unwholesome kind of misery, there is something almost obscene about these children of wrath and cravers of a second birth. If religious intolerance and hanging and burning could again become the order of the day, there is little doubt that, however it may have been in the past, the healthy-minded would at present show themselves the less indulgent party of the two.

In our own attitude, not yet abandoned, of impartial onlookers, what are we to say of this quarrel? It seems to me that we are bound to say that morbid-mindedness ranges over the wider scale of experience, and that its survey is the one that overlaps. The method of averting one's attention from evil, and living simply in the light of good is splendid as long as it will work. It will work with many persons; it will work far more generally than most of us are ready to suppose; and within the sphere of its successful operation there is nothing to be said against it as a religious solution. But it breaks down impotently as soon as melancholy comes; and even though one [can] be quite free from melancholy one's self, there is no doubt that healthy-mindedness is inadequate as a philosophical doctrine, because the evil facts which it refuses positively to account for are a genuine portion of reality; and they may after all be the best key to life's significance, and possibly the only openers of our eyes to the deepest levels of truth. . . .

The completest religions would therefore seem to be those in which the pessimistic elements are best developed. Buddhism, of course, and Christianity are the best known to us of these. They are essentially religions of deliverance: the man must die to an unreal life before he can be born into the real life. . . .

Conversion

To be converted, to be regenerated, to receive grace, to experience in an assurance, are so many phrases which denote religion, the process, gradual or sudden, by which a self hitherto divided, and consciously wrong inferior and unhappy, becomes unified and of its firmer hold upon religious realities. This at least is what conversion signifies in general terms, whether or not we believe that a direct divine operation is needed to bring such a moral change about. . . .

Some persons, for instance, never are, and possibly never under any circumstances could be, converted. Religious ideas cannot become the centre of their spiritual energy. They may be excellent persons, servants of God in practical ways, but they are not children of his kingdom. They are either incapable of imagining the invisible; or else, in the language of devotion, they are life-long subjects of "barrenness" and "dryness." Such inaptitude for religious faith may in some cases be intellectual in its origin. Their religious faculties may be checked in their natural tendency to expand, by beliefs about the world that are inhibitive, the pessimistic and materialistic beliefs, for example, within which so many good souls, who in former times would have freely indulged their religious propensities, find themselves nowadays, as it were, frozen; or the agnostic vetoes upon faith as something weak and shameful, under which so many of us to-day lie cowering, afraid to use our instincts. In many persons such inhibitions are never overcome. To the end of their days they refuse to believe, their personal energy never gets to its religious centre, and the latter remains inactive in perpetuity.

In other persons the trouble is profounder. There are men anaesthetic on the religious side, deficient in that category of sensibility. Just as a bloodless organism can never, in spite of all its goodwill, attain to the reckless "animal spirit" enjoyed by those of sanguine temperament; so the nature which is spiritually barren may admire and envy faith in others, but can never compass the enthusiasm and peace which those who are temperamentally qualified for faith enjoy. All this may, however, turn out eventually to have been a matter of temporary inhibition. Even late in life some thaw, some release may take place, some bolt be shot back in the barrennest breast, and the man's hard heart may soften and break into religious feeling. Such cases more than any others suggest the idea that sudden conversion is by miracle. So long as they exist, we must not imagine ourselves to deal with irretrievably fixed classes. . . .

If, abstracting altogether from the question of their value for the future spiritual life of the individual, we take them on their psychological side exclusively, so many peculiarities in them remind us of what we find outside of conversion that we are tempted to class them along with other automatisms, and to suspect that what makes the difference between a sudden and a gradual convert is not necessarily the presence of divine miracle in the case of one and of something less divine in that of the other, but rather a simple psychological peculiarity, the fact, namely, that in the recipient of the more instantaneous grace we have one of those subjects who are in possession of a large region in which mental work can go on subliminally, and from which invasive experiences, abruptly upsetting the equilibrium of the primary consciousness, may come. . . .

Converted men as a class are indistinguishable from natural men; some natural men even excel some converted men in their fruits; and no one ignorant of doctrinal theology could guess by mere every-day inspection of the "accident" of the two groups of persons before him, that their substance differed as much as divine differs from human substance.

The believers in the non-natural character of sudden conversion have had practically to admit that there is no unmistakable class-mark distinctive of all true converts. The super-normal incidents, such as voices and visions and overpowering impressions of the meaning of suddenly presented scripture texts, the melting emotions and tumultuous affections connected with the crisis of change, may all come by way of nature, or worse still, be counterfeited by Satan. The real witness of the spirit to the second birth is to be found only in the disposition of the genuine child of God, the permanently patient heart, the love of self eradicated. And this, it has to be admitted, is also found in those who pass no crisis, and may even be found outside of Christianity altogether. . . .

Saintliness

The collective name for the ripe fruits of religion in a character is Saintliness. The saintly character is the character for which spiritual emotions are the habitual centre of the personal energy; and there is a certain composite photograph of universal saintliness, the same in all religions, of which the features can easily be traced.

They are these:

1. A feeling of being in a wider life than that of this world's selfish little interests; and a conviction, not merely intellectual, but as it were sensible, of the existence of an Ideal Power. In Christian saintliness this power is always personified as God; but abstract moral ideals, civic or patriotic utopias, or

inner visions of holiness or right may also be felt as the true lords and enlargers of our life, in ways which I described in the lecture on the Reality of the Unseen.

2. A sense of the friendly continuity of the ideal power with our own life, and a willing self-surrender to its control.

3. An immense elation and freedom, as the outlines of the confining selfhood melt down.

4. A shifting of the emotional centre towards loving and harmonious affections, towards "yes, yes," and away from "no," where the claims of the non-ego are concerned.

These fundamental inner conditions have characteristic practical consequences, as follows:

a. *Asceticism*—The self-surrender may become so passionate as to turn into self-immolation. It may then so overrule the ordinary inhibitions of the flesh that the saint finds positive pleasure in sacrifice and asceticism, measuring and expressing as they do the degree of his loyalty to the higher power.

b. *Strength of Soul*—The sense of enlargement of life may be so uplifting that personal motives and inhibitions, commonly Omnipotent, become too insignificant for notice, and new reaches of patience and fortitude open out. Fears and anxieties go, and blissful equanimity takes their place. Come heaven, come hell, it makes no difference now!

c. *Purity*—The shifting of the emotional centre brings with it, first, increase of purity. The sensitiveness to spiritual discords is enhanced, and the cleansing of existence from brutal and sensual elements becomes imperative. Occasions of contact with such elements are avoided: the saintly life must deepen its spiritual consistency and keep unspotted from the world. In some temperaments this need of purity of spirit takes an ascetic turn, and weaknesses of the flesh are treated with relentless severity.

d. *Charity*—The shifting of the emotional centre brings, secondly, increase of charity, tenderness for fellow-creatures. The ordinary motives to antipathy, which usually set such close bounds to tenderness among human beings, are inhibited. The saint loves his enemies, and treats loathsome beggars as his brothers.

Mysticism

First of all, then, I ask, What does the expression "mystical states of consciousness" mean? How do we part off mystical states from other states?

The words "mysticism" and "mystical" are often used as terms of mere reproach, to throw at any opinion which we regard as vague and vast and sentimental, and without a base in either facts or logic, for some transference, or spirit-return. Employed in this way the word has little value: there are too many less ambiguous synonyms. So, to keep it useful by restricting it, I will do what I did in the case of the word "religion," and simply propose to you four marks which, when an experience has them, may justify us in calling it mystical for the purpose of the present lectures. In this way we shall save verbal disputation, and the recriminations that generally go therewith.

1. *Ineffability*—The handiest of the marks by which I classify a state of mind as mystical is negative. The subject of it immediately says that it defies expression, that no adequate report of its contents can be given in words. It follows from this that its quality must be directly experienced; it cannot be imparted or transferred to others. In this peculiarity mystical states are more like states of feeling than like states of intellect. No one can make clear to another who has never had a certain feeling, in what the quality or worth of it consists. One must have musical ears to know the value of a symphony; one must have been in love one's self to understand a lover's state of mind. Lacking the heart or ear, we cannot interpret the musician or the lover justly, and are even likely to consider him weak-minded or absurd. The mystic finds that most of us accord to his experiences an equally incompetent treatment.

2. *Noetic quality*—Although so similar to states of feeling, mystical states seem to those who experience them to be also states of knowledge. They are states of insight into depths of truth unplumbed by the discursive intellect. They are illuminations, revelations, full of significance and importance, all inarticulate though they remain; and as a rule they carry with them a curious sense of authority for after-time.

These two characters will entitle any state to be called mystical, in the sense in which I use the word. Two other qualities are less sharply marked, but are usually found. These are:

3. *Transiency*—Mystical states cannot be sustained for long. Except in rare instances, half an hour, or at most an hour or two, seems to be the limit beyond which they fade into the light of common day. Often, when faded, their quality can but imperfectly be reproduced in memory; but when they recur it is recognized; and from one recurrence to another it is susceptible of continuous development in what is felt as inner richness and importance.

4. *Passivity*—Although the oncoming of mystical states may be facilitated by preliminary voluntary operations, as by fixing the attention, or going through certain bodily performances, or in other ways which manuals of mysticism prescribe; yet when the characteristic sort of consciousness once has set in, the mystic feels as if his own will were in abeyance, and indeed sometimes as if as he were grasped and held by a superior power. This latter peculiarity connects mystical states with certain definite phenomena of secondary or alternative personality, such as prophetic speech, automatic writing, or the mediumistic trance. When these latter conditions are well pronounced, however, there may be no recollection whatever of the phenomenon, and it may have no significance for the subject's usual inner life, to which, as it were, it makes a mere interruption. Mystical states, strictly so called, are never merely interruptive. Some memory of their content always remains, and a profound sense of their importance. They modify the inner life of the subject between the times of their recurrence. Sharp divisions in this region are, however, difficult to make, and we find all sorts of gradations and mixtures.

These four characteristics are sufficient to mark out a group of states of consciousness peculiar enough to deserve a special name and to call for careful study. Let it then be called the mystical group. . . .

This incommunicableness of the transport is the keynote of all mysticism. Mystical truth exists for the individual who has the transport, but for no one else. In this, as I have said, it resembles the knowledge given to us in sensations more than that given by conceptual thought. Thought, with its remoteness and abstractness, has often enough in the history of philosophy been contrasted unfavorably with sensation. It is a commonplace of metaphysics that God's knowledge cannot be discursive but must be intuitive, that is, must be constructed more after the pattern of what in ourselves is called immediate feeling, than after that of proposition and judgment. But our immediate feelings have no content but what the five senses supply; and we have seen and shall see again that mystics may emphatically deny that the senses play any part in the very highest type of knowledge which their transports yield. . . .

My next task is to inquire whether we can invoke it as authoritative. Does it furnish any *warrant for the truth* of the twice-bornness and supernaturality and pantheism which it favors? I must give my answer to this question as concisely as I can.

In brief my answer is this—and I will divide it into three parts:

1. Mystical states, when well developed, usually are, and have the right to be, absolutely authoritative over the individuals to whom they come.

2. No authority emanates from them which should make it a duty for those who stand outside of them to accept their revelations uncritically.

3. They break down the authority of the non-mystical or rationalistic consciousness, based upon the understanding and the senses alone. They show it to be only one kind of consciousness. They open out the possibility of other orders of truth, in which, so far as anything in us vitally responds to them, we may freely continue to have faith. . . .

Conclusions

The material of our study of human nature is now spread before us; and . . . set free from the duty of description, we can draw our theoretical and practical conclusions. . . . Defending the empirical method, I foretold that whatever conclusions we might come to could be reached by spiritual judgments only, appreciations of the significance for life of religion, taken "on the whole." Our conclusions cannot be as sharp as dogmatic conclusions would be, but I will formulate them, when the time comes, as sharply as I can.

Summing up in the broadest possible way the characteristics of the religious life, as we have found them, it includes the following beliefs:

1. That the visible world is part of a more spiritual universe from which it draws its chief significance;

2. That union or harmonious relation with that higher universe is our true end;

3. That prayer or inner communion with the spirit thereof—be that spirit "God" or "law"—is a process wherein work is really done, and spiritual energy flows in and produces effects, either psychological or material, within the phenomenal world.

Religion includes also the following psychological characteristics:

4. A new zest which adds itself like a gift to life, and takes the form either of lyrical enchantment or of appeal to earnestness and heroism;

5. An assurance of safety and a temper of peace, and, in relation to others, a preponderance of loving affections.

In illustrating these characteristics by documents, we have been literally bathed in sentiment. In re-reading my manuscript, I am almost appalled at the amount of emotionality which I find in it. After so much of this, we can afford to be dryer and less sympathetic in the rest of the work that lies before us. The sentimentality of many of my documents is a consequence of the fact that I sought them among the extravagances of the subject. If any of you are enemies of what our ancestors used to brand as enthusiasm, and are, nevertheless, still listening to me now, you have probably felt my selection to have been sometimes almost perverse, and have wished I might have stuck to soberer examples. I reply that I took these extremer examples as yielding the profounder information. To learn the secrets of any science, we go to expert specialists, even though they may be excentric persons, and not to commonplace pupils. We combine what they tell us with the rest of our wisdom, and form our final judgment independently. Even so with religion. We who have pursued such radical expressions of it may now be sure that we know its secrets as authentically as anyone can know them who learns them from another; and we have next to answer, each of us for himself, the practical question: what are the dangers in this element of life? And in what proportion may it need to be restrained by other elements, to give the proper balance?

And the first thing that strikes us is that the religious man in the sense used in these lectures is only one type of man. Round about him are other men who say they cannot realize this experimental commerce with the divine; and taken collectively there is no flagrant difference of worth in the two classes of persons. Each set contains mean specimens and noble specimens, and looked at in the world's practical light they might well seem co-ordinate types. In general we may count it a fact that to no one type of man whatsoever is the total fullness of truth immediately revealed. Each of us has to borrow from the other parts of truth seen better from the other's point of view. So that our question now is this—Is the religious man's experience of intercourse fit to be taken as evidence? Is he like the traveller, whose testimony about foreign countries we should be foolish not to believe? May he instruct us as to the actual existence of a higher world with which our world is in relation, even though personally he be in other respects no better than ourselves. To say yes to this question is to side with supernaturalism taken in a wide sense, in its world-old quarrel with naturalism.

. . . I mean to side thus with supernaturalism, and to give you, in the almost absurdly brief compass allotted, the chief reasons for my faith.

First, though, let me answer one question, and get it out of the way, for it has more than once already vexed us. Ought it to be assumed that in all men the mixture of religion with other elements should be identical? Ought it, indeed, to be assumed that the lives of all men should show identical religious elements? In other words, is the existence of so many religious types and sects and creeds regrettable?

To these questions I answer "No" emphatically. And my reason is that I do not see how it is possible that creatures in such different positions and with such different powers as human individuals are, should have exactly the same functions and the same duties. No two of us have identical difficulties, nor should we be expected to work out identical solutions. Each, from his peculiar angle of observation, takes in a certain sphere of fact and trouble, which each must deal with in a unique manner. One of us must soften himself, another must harden himself; one must yield a point, another must stand firm—in order the better to defend the position assigned him. If an Emerson were forced to be a Wesley, or a Moody forced to be a Whitman, the total human consciousness of the divine would suffer. The divine can mean no single quality, it must mean a group of qualities, by being champions of which in alternation, different men may all find worthy missions. Each attitude being a syllable in human nature's total message, it takes the whole of us to spell the meaning out completely. So a "god of battles" must be allowed to be the god for one kind of person, a god of peace and heaven and home, the god for another. We must frankly recognize the fact that we live in partial systems, and that parts are not interchangeable in the spiritual life. . . .

In spite of the appeal which this impersonality of the scientific attitude makes to a certain magnanimity of temper, I believe it to be shallow, and I can now state my reason in comparatively few words. That reason is that, so long as we deal with the cosmic and the general, we deal only with the symbols of reality, but *as soon as we deal with private and personal phenomena as such, we deal with realities in the completest sense of the term.* I think I can easily make clear what I mean by these words.

The world of our experience consists at all times of two parts, an objective and a subjective part, of which the former may be incalculably more extensive than the latter, and yet the latter can never be omitted or suppressed. The objective part is the sum total of whatsoever at any given time we may be thinking of, the subjective part is the inner "state" in which the thinking comes to pass. What we think of may be enormous—the cosmic times and spaces, for example—whereas the inner state may be the most fugitive and paltry activity of mind. Yet the cosmic objects, so far as the experience yields them, are but ideal pictures of something whose existence we do not inwardly possess but only point at outwardly, while the inner state is our very experience itself; its reality and that of our experience are one. A conscious field *plus* its object as felt or thought of *plus* an attitude towards the object *plus* the sense of a self to whom the attitude belongs—such a concrete bit of personal experience may be a small bit, but it is a solid bit as long as it lasts; not hollow, not a mere abstract element of experience, such as the "object" is when taken all alone. It is a *full* fact, even though it be an insignificant fact; it is of the *kind* to which all realities whatsoever must belong; the motor currents of the world run through the like of it; it is on the line connecting real events with real events. That unshareable feeling which each one of us has of the pinch of his individual destiny as he privately feels it rolling out on fortune's wheel may be disparaged for its egotism, may be sneered at as unscientific, but it is the one thing that fills up the measure of our concrete actuality, and any would-be existent that should lack such a feeling, or its analogue, would be a piece of reality only half made up.

If this be true, it is absurd for Science to say that the egotistic elements of experience should be suppressed. The axis of reality runs solely through the egotistic places—they are strung upon it like so many beads. To describe the world with all the various feelings of the individual pinch of destiny, all the various spiritual attitudes, left out from the description—they being as describable as anything else-would be something like offering a printed bill of fare as the equivalent for a solid meal. Religion makes no such blunder. The individual's religion may be egotistic, and those private realities which it keeps in touch with may be narrow enough; but at any rate it always remains infinitely less hollow and abstract, as far as it goes, than a Science which prides itself on taking no account of anything private at all. . . .

Let us agree, then, that Religion, occupying herself with personal destinies and keeping thus in contact with the only absolute realities which we know, must necessarily play an eternal part in human history. The next thing to decide is what she reveals about those destinies, or whether indeed she reveals anything distinct enough to be considered a general message to mankind. We have done as you see, with our preliminaries, and our final summing up can now begin. . . .

Let me then propose, as an hypothesis, that whatever it may be on its *farther* side, the "more" with which in religious experience we feel ourselves connected is on its *hither* side the subconscious continuation of our conscious life. Starting thus with a recognized psychological fact as our basis, we seem to preserve a contact with "science" which the ordinary theologian lacks. At the same time the theologian's contention that the religious man is moved by an external power is vindicated, for one of the peculiarities of invasions from the subconscious region is that they take on objective appearances, and suggest to the subject an external control. In the religious life the control is felt as "higher"; but since on our hypothesis it is primarily the higher faculties of our own hidden mind which are controlling, the sense of union with the power beyond us is a sense of something, not merely apparently, but literally true. . . .

Disregarding the over-beliefs, and confining ourselves to what is common and generic, we have in *the fact that the conscious person is continuous with a wider self through which saving experiences come,* a positive content of religious experience which, it seems to me, *is literally and objectively true as far as it goes.* If I now proceed to state my own hypothesis about the farther limits of this extension of our personality, I shall be offering my own over-belief—though I know it will appear a sorry under-belief to some of you—for which I can only bespeak the same indulgence which in a converse case I should accord to yours.

The farther limits of our being plunge, it seems to me, into an altogether other dimension of existence from the sensible and merely "understandable" world. Name it the mystical region, or the supernatural region, whichever you choose. So far as our ideal impulses originate in this region (and most of them do originate in it, for we find them possessing us in a way for which we cannot articulately account), we belong to it in a more intimate sense than that in which we belong to the visible world, for we belong in the most intimate sense wherever our ideals belong. Yet the unseen region in question is not merely ideal, for it produces effects in this world. When we commune with it, work is actually done upon our finite personality, for we are turned into new men, and consequences in the way of conduct follow in the natural world upon our regenerative change.

But that which produces effects within another reality must be termed a reality itself, so I feel as if we had no philosophic excuse for calling the unseen or mystical world unreal.

God is the natural appellation, for us Christians at least, for the supreme reality, so I will call this higher part of the universe by the name of God. We and God have business with each other; and in opening ourselves to his influence our deepest destiny is fulfilled. The universe, at those parts of it which our personal being constitutes, takes a turn genuinely for the worse or for the better in proportion as each one of us fulfills or evades God's demands. As far as this goes I probably have you with me, for I only translate into schematic language what I may call the instinctive belief of mankind: God is real since he produces real effects.

The real effects in question, so far as I have as yet admitted them, are exerted on the personal centres of energy of the various subjects, but the spontaneous faith of most of the subjects is that they embrace a wider sphere than this. Most religious men believe (or "know," if they be mystical) that not only they themselves, but the whole universe of beings to whom the God is present, are secure in his parental hands. There is a sense, a dimension, they are sure, in which we are all saved, in spite of the gates of hell and all adverse terrestrial appearances. God's existence is the guarantee of an ideal order that shall be permanently preserved. This world may indeed, as science assures us, some day burn up or freeze; but if it is part of his order, the old ideals are sure to be brought elsewhere to fruition, so that where God is, tragedy is only provisional and partial, and shipwreck and dissolution are not the absolutely final things. Only when this farther step of faith concerning God is taken, and remote objective consequences are predicted, does religion, as it seems to me, get wholly free from the first immediate subjective experience, and bring a *real hypothesis* into play. A good hypothesis in science must have other properties than those of the phenomenon it is immediately invoked to explain, otherwise it is not prolific enough. God, meaning only what enters into the religious man's experience of union, falls short of being an hypothesis of this more useful order. He needs to enter into wider cosmic relations in order to justify the subject's absolute confidence and peace.

That the God with whom, starting from the hither side of our own extra-marginal self, we come at its remoter margin into commerce should be the absolute world-ruler, is of course a very considerable over-belief. Over-belief as it is, though, it is an article of almost everyone's religion. Most of us pretend in some way to prop it upon our philosophy, but the philosophy itself is really propped upon this faith. What is this but to say that Religion, in her fullest exercise of function, is not a mere illumination of facts already elsewhere given, not a mere passion, like love, which views things in a rosier light. It is indeed that, as we have seen abundantly. But it is something more, namely, a postulator of new *facts* as well. The world interpreted religiously is not the materialistic world over again, with an altered expression; it must have, over and above the altered expression, a *natural constitution* different at some point from that which a materialistic world would have. It must be such that different events can be expected in it, different conduct must be required.

This thoroughly "pragmatic" view of religion has usually been taken as a matter of course by common men. They have interpolated divine miracles into the field of nature, they have built a heaven out beyond the grave. It is only transcendentalist metaphysicians who think that, without adding any concrete details to Nature, or subtracting any, but by simply calling it the expression of absolute spirit, you make it more divine just as it stands. I believe the pragmatic way of taking religion to be the deeper way. It gives it body as well as soul, it makes it claim, as everything real must claim, some characteristic realm of fact as its very own. What the more characteristically divine facts are, apart from the actual inflow of energy in the faith-state and the prayer-state, I know not. But the over-belief on which I am ready to make my personal venture is that they exist. The whole drift of my education goes to persuade me that the world of our present consciousness is only one out of many worlds of consciousness that exist, and that those other worlds must contain experiences which have a meaning for our life also; and that although in the main their experiences and those of this world keep discrete, yet the two become continuous at certain points, and higher energies filter in. By being faithful in my poor measure to this over-belief, I seem to myself to keep more sane and true. I can, of course, put myself into the sectarian scientist's attitude, and imagine vividly that the world of

sensations and of scientific laws and objects may be all. But whenever I do this, I hear that inward monitor of which W. K. Clifford once wrote, whispering the word "bosh!" Humbug is humbug, even though it bear the scientific name, and the total expression of human experience, as I view it objectively, invincibly urges me beyond the narrow "scientific" bounds. Assuredly, the real world is of a different temperament-more intricately built than physical science allows. So my objective and my subjective conscience both hold me to the over-belief which I express. Who knows whether the faithfulness of individuals here below to their own poor over-beliefs may not actually help God in turn to be more effectively faithful to his own greater tasks?

Counterpoint:
Settled Issues and Neglected Questions: How Is Religion to be Studied?

SUSAN THISTLETHWAITE

Susan Thistlethwaite teaches at the Chicago Theological Seminary in Chicago, Illinois, where she is a professor of theology. Besides a few edited volumes, she has published the following books: *Sex, Race, and God: Christian Feminism in Black and White* and *Metaphors for the Contemporary Church*.

ONE RELIGION SCHOLAR'S settled issue is another one's neglected question. I take this to be axiomatic even within, or perhaps especially within, my sub-discipline of Christian theology. The declining years of the twentieth century are especially rife with this perspectival difference of opinion all across the field of religion.

From the perspective of the field as a whole, one question that has been widely considered settled is being questioned both within our major professional organization, the American Academy of Religion, and throughout the world. That question is, "How is religion to be studied?"

Reprinted from Susan Thistlethwaite, "Settled Issues and Neglected Questions: How Is Religion to be Studied?" Journal of the American Academy of Religion, LXII/4 (1994): 1037–1045. Reprinted by permission.

For many in the American Academy of Religion, religion is to be studied by professional scholars who are trained in the academic disciplines and who do their research and teaching in an atmosphere of disciplined reflection. For many around the world, however, and for increasing numbers of members of the AAR, the ideal of scholarly reflection on religion is suspect in a number of different ways.

There are some who are suspicious of the ideal of scholarship and argue that commitment and practice (to say nothing of praxis) are the only acceptable way to pursue the study of religion. It is scarcely unusual, in many places in the world, for academic meetings in religion to begin with prayer. This has not been the practice of the American Academy of Religion, though it may surprise many members to find out that in some sections and small groups, seminars and the like, prayer has not been unknown, especially in the recent annual meetings.

It has also happened that the American Academy of Religion, by a vote of the membership, protested to the U.S. government the slaughter of seminary faculty and staff in El Salvador. Not all members present at that meeting agreed with the organization writing a formal protest (while they, of course, also deplored the slaughter of religious teachers and workers). They asked, "Is such a political act part of the study of religion?"

And there are those who would argue that their particular faith is being subjected to heretical attack when scholarly methods are applied and feel themselves justified in disallowing such methods, sometimes even with physical force.

How is religion to be studied?

The Study of Religion

The mission statement of the American Academy of Religion reflects the sum of what has been widely considered "settled" by people who profess to study religion in the United States and Canada (by far the largest number of AAR members). This statement is enormously instructive and probably, except by those of us who had the unenviable task recently of contributing to its execution, unread.

> The American Academy of Religion is a learned society and professional association of teachers and scholars in the field of religion. Through academic conferences and meetings, publications, and a variety of programs and membership services, the Academy fosters excellence in scholarship and teaching. Within a context of free inquiry and critical examination, the Academy welcomes all disciplined reflection on religion and seeks to enhance its broad public understanding.

The American Academy of Religion is the product of the efforts of members of the Society of Biblical Literature who, in 1909, broke off from that organization in order to found the National Association of Biblical Instructors. The latter association was to be distinguished from the SBL by more attention to pedagogy and professional issues.

By 1963, however, the name had become an anachronism since NABI had among its membership numerous scholars whose field was not the bible, but the then rapidly growing areas of religion, both Christian and non-Christian. After a self-study, the American Academy of Religion was incorporated in 1964. That is, a scant 30 years ago.

The history of the AAR is not just a history of institutional development: it is an intellectual history as well. To be able to regard religion as a phenomenon to which the intellectual tools of linguistic analysis, comparative study, historical critique and the like could be applied was the contribution of the nineteenth century. Like the nascent fields of psychology and sociology, religion as a phenomenon, like the human mind or human society, came to be seen not as a given, but as an object of study. William James, in his landmark work *The Varieties of Religious Experience*, published in the same year the National Association of Biblical Teachers was founded, defines religion as "the sense of life by virtue of which man does not destroy himself, but lives on. It is the force by which he lives."[1] James himself plainly believed that "critical examination" of the phenomena of religion was not only possible, but desirable, and that a context of "free inquiry" would afford excellent insight into the experience deemed religious.

The Critics

The whole notion particularly of "free inquiry" is under attack from so many different directions it is difficult to list them all, let alone summarize the various views. The critics of "free inquiry" do not all agree with one another; in fact, the debate among critics is likely to be far more acrimonious than with the over-arching object of critique.

For a brief overview of the critics, I will use William James' *The Varieties of Religious Experience* as a foil. The feminist critique of James would be that his vaunted objectivity in the study of religious phenomena, eschewing the "God's eye view" of an older orthodoxy, has substituted a "male's eye view." The reference to women's religious experience, infrequent in the book, increases in the chapter on "saintliness." The following paragraph is illustrative:

> Take a self-indulgent woman's life in general. She will yield to every inhibition set by her disagreeable sensations, lie late in bed, live upon tea or bromides, keep indoors from the cold. Every difficulty finds her obedient to its "no." But make a mother of her, and what have you? Possessed by maternal excitement, she now confronts wakefulness, weariness, and toil without an instant of hesitation or word of complaint.[2]

This sentimental, Victorian paternalism in the distinguished pragmatist gets no brake from the "great minds" he cites: Voltaire, Whitman, Emerson, Luther, Tolstoy, John Bunyan, or Jonathan Edwards (though Mrs. Edwards gets a word under "saintliness"). Feminist critique of the study of religion has been to dispute the validity of the "critical examination" criterion when it has been applied to women's experience and to note that inquiry has been anything but "free."

The post-structuralist critique would take this argument a step further (and it has been a critique widely used by feminists and racial/ethnic minorities) and dispute the very possibility on which the James' argument rests, namely that inquiry can be "free" and examination "critical." The texts and codes of our own social situation will inevitably color our reading of any "experience" and indeed the "theory of the subject" is intellectually bankrupt.

An even more profound critique of James' work in religion could be had by applying the insights of Toni Morrison's splendid essay *Playing in the Dark: Whiteness and the Literary Imagination*. There is no work penned in America, Morrison argues, "free of what Herman Melville called 'the power of blackness,' especially not in a country in which there was a resident population, already black, upon which the imagination could play; through which historical, moral, metaphysical, and social fears, problems, and dichotomies could be articulated."[3]

James makes no explicit reference to African-American religion, an omission significant in itself since he considers Buddhism, Hinduism, and Islam frequently. Yet, race is present as a powerful backdrop to his contrast of the religion of "healthy-mindedness" and the "sick soul" of a religion dominated by emotion and a consciousness of sin and evil. James writes, "The sanguine and healthy-minded live habitually on the sunny side of their misery-line, the depressed and melancholy live beyond it, in darkness and apprehension."[4] In fact, in the chapter on "The Sick Soul" the metaphor of darkness as descriptive of the "sick soul" appears frequently. Morrison observes, "Race has become metaphorical—a way of referring to and disguising forces, events, classes, and expressions of social decay and economic division far more threatening to the body politic than biological 'race' ever was."[5] Can we study religion "freely" without such metaphorical interpretations? Is not the whole notion of "critical examination" renovated by Morrison's insights?

The religion of "healthy-mindedness," the phenomenon in which James is most interested, would leave out virtually all that those in the liberation movements of the two-thirds world find indispensable as critiques: the social consciousness of sin and the awareness of the depth of human evil. The "victory of healthy-mindedness . . ." must be attributed to "preachers [who], far from magnifying our consciousness of sin, seem devoted rather to making little of it."[6] To the exponents of liberation movements, dispassion and a lack of commitment in the study of religion leave out of examination everything that makes religion a force for good in the world. In this latter sense "free" is a code word for maintaining the status quo.

And, there is the inability of even a dedication to objective description of religion on the part of a writer in the Christian West to overcome stereotypes of world religions and their practitioners: James writes of the "hot and rigid monotheism of the Arab mind."[7] What has

been the track record of Western scholars in their analysis of world religions? Have world religions been treated with respect?

James arguably made a great advance in the study of religion. We must not be sanguine that the same flaws that appear in his purportedly disinterested and objective study are absent from our own efforts at free inquiry and disciplined scholarship. Yet, this does not mean that the effort to study religion achieved over the last century is without merit. But it is not without flaw. . . .

NOTES

1. William James, *The Varieties of Religious Experience: A Study in Human Nature* (New York: Collier Books, 1902), p. 15.

2. Ibid., p. 213.

3. Ibid., p. 36.

4. Ibid., p. 120.

5. Ibid., p. 63.

6. Ibid., p. 87.

7. Ibid., p. 316.

From *Young Man Luther: A Study in Psychoanalysis and History*

ERIK H. ERIKSON

As to the dichotomy of psychoanalysis and religion, I will not approach it like a man with a chip on each shoulder. Psychology endeavors to establish what is demonstrably true in human behavior, including such behavior as expresses what to human beings seems true and feels true. I will interpret in psychological terms whatever phenomena clinical experience and psychoanalytic thought have made me recognize are dependent on man's demonstrable psychic structure. This is my job, as a clinician and as a teacher—a job which (as I have pointed out) includes the awareness that psychoanalysis for historical reasons often occupies a position on the borderline of what is demonstrably true and of what demonstrably feels true. The fact that

Reprinted from Erik H. Erikson, Young Man Luther: A Study in Psychoanalysis and History *(New York: W. W. Norton & Company, Inc., 1958).*

each new vital focus of psychoanalytic research inadvertently leads to a new implied value system obliges us to ask ourselves whether or not we mean what we seem to be saying. It obligates us, as well as our critics, to differentiate psychoanalysism from psychoanalysis, and to realize that ours is not only a profession recognized among professions, but also a system of thought subject to fashionable manipulation by molders of public opinion. Our very success suggests that our partisanship be judicial.

Religion, on the other hand, elaborates on what feels profoundly true even though it is not demonstrable: it translates into significant words, images, and codes the exceeding darkness which surrounds man's existence, and the light which pervades it beyond all desert or comprehension. This being a historical book, however, religion will occupy our attention primarily as a source of ideologies for those who seek identities. In depicting the identity struggle of a young great man I am not as concerned with the validity of the dogmas which laid claim to him, or of the philosophies which influenced his systematic thought, as I am with the spiritual and intellectual milieu which the isms of his time—and these isms had to be religious—offered to his passionate search.

My focus, then, is on the "ideological." In modern history, this word has assumed a specifically political connotation, referring to totalitarian systems of thought which distort historical truth by methods ranging from fanatic self-deception to shrewd falsification and cold propaganda. Karl Mannheim has analyzed this word and the processes for which it stands from the sociological point of view.[1] In this book, *ideology* will mean an unconscious tendency underlying religious and scientific as well as political thought: the tendency at a given time to make facts amenable to ideas, and ideas to facts, in order to create a world image convincing enough to support the collective and the individual sense of identity. Far from being arbitrary or consciously manageable (although it is as exploitable as all of man's unconscious strivings), the total perspective created by ideological simplification reveals its strength by the dominance it exerts on the seeming logic of historical events, and by its influence on the identity formation of individuals (and thus, on their "ego-strength"). In this sense, this is a book on identity and ideology. . . .

The limitations of my knowledge and of the space at my disposal for this inquiry preclude any attempt to present a new Luther or to remodel an old one. I can only bring some newer psychological considerations to bear on the existing material pertaining to one period of Luther's life. . . . The young monk interests me particularly as a young man in the process of becoming a great one.

It must have occurred to the reader that the story of the fit in the choir attracted me originally because I suspected that the words "I am not!" revealed the fit to be part of a most severe identity crisis—a crisis in which the young monk felt obliged to protest what he was not (possessed, sick, sinful) perhaps in order to break through to what he was or was to be. I will now state what remains of my suspicion, and what I intend to make of it.

Judging from an undisputed series of extreme mental states which attacked Luther throughout his life, leading to weeping, sweating, and fainting, the fit in the choir could well have happened; and it could have happened in the specific form reported, under the specific conditions of Martin's monastery years. If some of it is legend, so be it; the making of legend is as much part of the scholarly rewriting of history as it is part of the original facts used in the work of scholars. We are thus obliged to accept half-legend as half-history, provided only that a reported episode does not contradict other well-established facts; persists in having a ring of truth; and yields a meaning consistent with psychological theory.

Luther himself never mentioned this episode, although in his voluble later years he was extraordinarily free with references to physical and mental suffering. It seems that he always remembered most vividly those states in which he struggled through to an insight, but not those in which he was knocked out. Thus, in his old age, he remembers well having been seized at the age of thirty-five by terror, sweat, and the fear of fainting when he marched in the Corpus Christi procession behind his superior, Dr. Staupitz, who carried the holy of holies. (This Dr. Staupitz, as we will see, was the best father figure Luther ever encountered and acknowledged, he was a man who recognized a true *homo religiosus* in his subaltern and treated him with therapeutic wisdom.) But Staupitz did not let Luther get away with his assertion that it was Christ who had frightened him. He said, "*Non est Christus, quia Christus non terret, sed consolatur.*" (It couldn't have been Christ who terrified you, for Christ consoles.) This was a therapeutic as well as a theological revelation to Luther, and he remembered it. However, for the fit in the choir, he may well have had an amnesia.

Assuming then that something like this episode happened, it could be considered as one of a series of seemingly senseless pathological explosions; as a meaningful symptom in a psychiatric case-history; or as one of a series of religiously relevant experiences. It certainly has, as even Scheel suggests, *some* marks of a "religious attack," such as St. Paul, St. Augustine, and many lesser aspirants to saintliness have had. However, the inventory of a total revelation always includes an overwhelming illumination and a sudden insight. The fit in the choir presents only the symptomatic, the more pathological and defensive, aspects of a total revelation: partial loss of consciousness, loss of motor coordination, and automatic exclamations which the afflicted does not know he utters.

In a truly religious experience such automatic exclamations would sound as if they were dictated by divine inspiration; they would be positively illuminating and luminous, and be intensely remembered. In Luther's fit, his words obviously expressed an overwhelming inner need to deny an accusation. In a full religious attack the positive conscience of faith would reign and determine the words uttered; here negation and rebellion reign: "I am *not* what my father said I was and what my conscience, in bad moments, tends to confirm I am." The raving

and roaring suggest a strong element of otherwise suppressed rage. And, indeed, this young man, who later became a voice heard around the world, lived under monastic conditions of silence and meditation; at this time he was submissively subdued, painfully sad, and compulsively self-inspective—too much so even for his stern superiors' religious taste. All in all, however, the paroxysm occurred in a holy spot and was suggested by a biblical story, which places the whole matter at least on the borderline between psychiatry and religion.

If we approach the episode from the psychiatric viewpoint, we can recognize in the described attack (and also in a variety of symptomatic scruples and anxieties to which Martin was subject at the time) an intrinsic ambivalence, an inner two-facedness, such as we find in all neurotic symptoms. The attack could be said to deny in its verbal part ("I am not") what Martin's father had said, namely, that his son was perhaps possessed rather than holy; but it also proves the father's point by its very occurrence in front of the same congregation who had previously heard the father express his anger and apprehension. The fit, then, is both unconscious obedience to the father and implied rebellion against the monastery; the words uttered both deny the father's assertion, and confirm the vow which Martin had made in that first known anxiety attack during a thunderstorm at the age of twenty-one, when he had exclaimed, "I want to be a monk." We find the young monk, then, at the crossroads of obedience to his father—an obedience of extraordinary tenacity and deviousness—and to the monastic vows which at the time he was straining to obey almost to the point of absurdity.

We may also view his position as being at the crossroads of mental disease and religious creativity and we could speculate that perhaps Luther received in three (or more) distinct and fragmentary experiences those elements of a total revelation which other men are said to have acquired in one explosive event. Let me list the elements again: physical paroxysm; a degree of unconsciousness; an automatic verbal utterance; a command to change the over-all direction of effort and aspiration; and a spiritual revelation, a flash of enlightenment, decisive and pervasive as a rebirth. The thunderstorm had provided him with a change in the over-all direction of his life, a change toward the anonymous, the silent, and the obedient. In fits such as the one in the choir, he experienced the epileptoid paroxysm of ego-loss, the rage of denial of the identity which was to be discarded. And later in the experience in the tower . . . he perceived the light of a new spiritual formula.

The fact that Luther experienced these clearly separate stages of religious revelation might make it possible to establish a psychological rationale for the conversion of other outstanding religionists, where tradition has come to insist on the transmission of a total event appealing to popular faith. Nothing, to my mind, makes Luther more a man of the future—the future which is our psychological present—than his utter integrity in reporting the steps which marked the emergence of his identity as a genuine *homo religiosus*. I emphasize this by no means only because it makes him a better case (although I admit it helps), but because it makes his total experience a historical event far beyond its immediate sectarian significance, namely, a decisive step in human awareness and responsibility. To indicate this step in its psychological coordinates is the burden of this book.

Martin's general mood just before he became a monk, a mood into which he was again sliding at the time of the fit in the choir, has been characterized by him and others as a state of *tristitia*, of excessive sadness. Before the thunderstorm, he had rapidly been freezing into a melancholy paralysis which made it impossible for him to continue his studies and to contemplate marriage as his father urged him to do. In the thunderstorm, he had felt immense anxiety. Anxiety comes from *angustus*, meaning to feel hemmed in and choked up; Martin's use of *circumvallatus*—all walled in—to describe his experience in the thunderstorm indicates he felt a sudden constriction of his whole life space, and could see only one way out: the abandonment of all of his previous life and the earthly future it implied for the sake of total dedication to a new life. This new life, however, was one which made an institution out of the very configuration of being walled in. Architecturally, ceremonially, and in its total world-mood, it symbolized life on this earth as a self-imposed and self-conscious prison with only one exit, and that one, to eternity. The acceptance of this new frame of life had made him, for a while, peaceful and "godly"; at the time of his fit, however, his sadness was deepening again.

As to this general veil of sadness which covered the conflicts revealed so explosively in the choir, one could say (and the psychiatrist has said it) that Martin was sad because he was a melancholic; and there is no doubt that in his depressed moods he displayed at times what we would call the clinical picture of a melancholia. But Luther was a man who tried to distinguish very clearly between what came from God as the crowning of a worthwhile conflict, and what came from defeat; the fact that he called defeat the devil only meant he was applying a diagnostic label which was handy. He once wrote to Melanchthon that he considered him the weaker one in public controversy, and himself the weaker in private struggles—"if I may thus call what goes on between me and Satan." One could also say (and the professor has said it) that Martin's sadness was the traditional *tristitia*, the melancholy world mood of the *homo religiosus*; from this point of view, it is a "natural" mood, and could even be called the truest adaptation to the human condition. This view, too, we must accept to a point—the point where it becomes clear that Martin was not able in the long run to embrace the monastic life so natural to the traditional *tristitia*; that he mistrusted his sadness himself; and that he later abandoned this melancholic mood altogether for occasional violent mood swings between depression and elation, between self-accusation and the abuse of others. Sadness, then, was primarily the overall symptom of his youth, and was a symptom couched in a traditional attitude provided by his time.

Youth can be the most exuberant, the most careless, the most self-sure, and the most unself-consciously productive stage of life, the individual's insight from authoritarian conscience; his wholeness is that of the individual ego, but the question is whether collective man will create a world worth being whole for.

We will call what young people in their teens and early twenties look for in religion and in other dogmatic systems an *ideology*. At the most it is a militant system with uniformed members and uniform goals; at the least it is a "way of life," or what the Germans call a *Weltanschauung,* a world-view which is consonant with existing theory, available knowledge, and common sense, and yet is significantly more: an utopian outlook, a cosmic mood, or a doctrinal logic, all shared as self-evident beyond any need for demonstration. What is to be relinquished as "old" may be the individual's previous life; this usually means the perspectives intrinsic to the life-style of the parents, who are thus discarded contrary to all traditional safeguards of filial devotion. The "old" may be a part of himself, which must henceforth be subdued by some rigorous self-denial in a private life-style or through membership in a militant or military organization; or, it may be the world-view of other castes and classes, races and peoples: in this case, these people become not only expendable, but the appointed victims of the most righteous annihilation.

The need for devotion, then, is one aspect of the identity crisis which we, as psychologists, make responsible for all these tendencies and susceptibilities. The need for repudiation is another aspect. In their late teens and early twenties, even when there is no explicit ideological commitment or even interest, young people offer devotion to individual leaders and to teams, to strenuous activities, and to difficult techniques; at the same time they show a sharp and intolerant readiness to discard and disavow people (including, at times, themselves). This repudiation is often snobbish, fitful, perverted, or simply thoughtless.

These constructive and destructive aspects of youthful energy have been and are employed in making and remaking tradition in many diverse areas. Youth stands between the past and the future, both in individual life and in society; it also stands between alternate ways of life. As I pointed out in "The Problem of Ego-Identity," ideologies offer to the members of this age-group overly simplified and yet determined answers to exactly those vague inner states and those urgent questions which arise in consequence of identity conflict. Ideologies serve to channel youth's forceful earnestness and sincere asceticism, as well as its search for excitement and its eager indignation, toward that social frontier where the struggle between conservatism and radicalism is most alive. On that frontier, fanatic ideologists do their busy work and psychopathic leaders their dirty work; but there, also, true leaders create significant solidarities. . . .

Luther accepted man's distance from God as existential and absolute, and refused any traffic with the profanity of a God of deals; Freud suggests that we steadfastly study our unconscious deals with morality and reality before we haughtily claim free will, or righteously good intentions in dealings with our fellowmen.

Luther limited our knowledge of God to our individual experience of temptation and our identification in prayer with the passion of God's son. In this, all men are free and equal. Freud made it clear that the structure of inner *Konflict,* made conscious by psychoanalysis and recognized as universal for any and all, is all we can know of ourselves—yet it is a knowledge inescapable and indispensable. The devoutly sceptical Freud proclaimed that man's uppermost duty (no matter what his introspective reason would make him see, or his fate suffer) was *das Leben auszuhalten:* to stand life, to hold out.

In this book I have described how Luther, once a sorely frightened child, recovered through the study of Christ's Passion the central meaning of the Nativity; and I have indicated in what way Freud's method of introspection brought human conflict under a potentially more secure control by revealing the boundness of man in the loves and rages of his childhood. Thus both Luther and Freud came to acknowledge that "the child is in the midst." Both men perfected introspective techniques permitting isolated man to recognize his individual patienthood. They also reasserted the other pole of existence, man's involvement in generations: for only in facing the helplessness and the hope newly born in every child does mature man (and this does include woman) recognize the irrevocable responsibility of being alive and about.

Let us consider, then, what we may call the metabolism of generations.

Each human life begins at a given evolutionary stage and level of tradition, bringing to its environment a capital of patterns and energies; these are used to grow on, and to grow into the social process with, and also as contributions to this process. Each new being is received into a style of life prepared by tradition and held together by tradition, and at the same time disintegrating because of the very nature of tradition. We say that tradition "molds" the individual, "channels" his drives. But the social process does not mold a new being merely to housebreak him; it molds generations in order to be remolded, to be reinvigorated, by them. Therefore, society can never afford merely to suppress drives or to guide their sublimation. It must also support the primary function of every individual ego, which is to transform instinctual energy into patterns of action, into character, into style—in short, into an identity with a core of integrity which is to be derived from and also contributed to the tradition. There is an optimum ego synthesis to which the individual aspires; and there is an optimum societal metabolism for which societies and cultures strive. In describing the interdependence of individual aspiration and of societal striving, we describe something indispensable to human life. . . .

In discussing the identity crisis, we have, at least implicitly, presented some of the attributes of any psychosocial crisis. At a given age, a human being, by dint of his physical, intellectual and emotional growth, becomes ready and eager to face a new life task, that is, a set of choices and tests which are in some traditional way prescribed and prepared for him by his society's structure. A new life task presents a crisis whose outcome can be a successful graduation, or alternatively, an impairment of the life cycle which will aggravate future crises. Each crisis prepares the next, as one step leads to another; and each crisis also lays one more cornerstone for the adult personality. I will enumerate all these crises (more thoroughly treated elsewhere) to remind us, in summary, of certain issues in Luther's life; and also to suggest a developmental root for the basic human values of faith, will, conscience, and reason—all necessary in rudimentary form for the identity which crowns childhood.

The first crisis is the one of early infancy. How this crisis is met decides whether a man's innermost mood will be determined more by basic trust or by basic mistrust. The outcome of this crisis—apart from accidents of heredity, gestation, and birth—depends largely on the quality of maternal care, that is, on the consistency and mutuality which guide the mother's ministrations and give a certain predictability and hopefulness to the baby's original cosmos of urgent and bewildering body feelings. The ratio and relation of basic trust to basic mistrust established during early infancy determines much of the individual's capacity for simple faith, and consequently also determines his future contribution to his society's store of faith—which, in turn, will feed into a future mother's ability to trust the world in which she teaches trust to newcomers. In this first stage we can assume that a historical process is already at work; history writing should therefore chart the influence of historical events on growing generations to be able to judge the quality of their future contribution to history. As for little Martin, I have drawn conclusions about that earliest time when his mother could still claim the baby, and when he was still all hers, inferring that she must have provided him with a font of basic trust on which he was able to draw in his fight for a primary faith present before all will, conscience, and reason, a faith which is "the soul's virginity."

The first crisis corresponds roughly to what Freud has described as orality; the second corresponds to anality. An awareness of these correspondences is essential for a true understanding of the dynamics involved.

The second crisis, that of infancy, develops the infantile sources of what later becomes a human being's will, in its variations of willpower and wilfulness. The resolution of this crisis will determine whether an individual is apt to be dominated by a sense of autonomy, or by a sense of shame and doubt. The social limitations imposed on intensified wilfulness inevitably create doubt about the justice governing the relations of grown and growing people. The way this doubt is met by the grown-ups determines much of a man's future ability to combine an unimpaired will with ready self-discipline, rebellion with responsibility.

The interpretation is plausible that Martin was driven early out of the trust stage, out from "under his mother's skirts," by a jealously ambitious father who tried to make him precociously independent from women, and sober and reliable in his work. Hans succeeded, but not without storing in the boy violent doubts of the father's justification and sincerity; a lifelong shame over the persisting gap between his own precocious conscience and his actual inner state; and a deep nostalgia for a situation of infantile trust. His theological solution—spiritual return to a faith which is there before all doubt, combined with a political submission to those who by necessity must wield the sword of secular law—seems to fit perfectly his personal need for compromise. While this analysis does not explain either the ideological power or the theological consistency of his solution, it does illustrate that ontogenetic experience is an indispensable link and transformer between one stage of history and the next. This link is a psychological one, and the energy transformed and the process of transformation are both charted by the psychoanalytic method. . . .

Luther was a man who would not settle for an easy appeasement of these feelings on any level, from childhood through youth to his manhood, or in any segment of life. His often impulsive and intuitive formulations transparently display the infantile struggle at the bottom of the lifelong emotional issue.

His basic contribution was a living reformulation of faith. This marks him as a theologian of the first order; it also indicates his struggle with the ontogenetically earliest and most basic problems of life. He saw as his life's work a new delineation of faith and will, of religion and the law: for it is clear that organized religiosity, in circumstances where faith in a world order is monopolized by religion, is the institution which tries to give dogmatic permanence to a reaffirmation of that basic trust—and a renewed victory over that basic mistrust—with which each human being emerges from early infancy. In this way organized religion cements the faith which will support future generations. Established law tries to formulate obligations and privileges, restraints and freedoms, in such a way that man can submit to law and order with a minimum of doubt and with little loss of face, and as an autonomous agent of order can teach the rudiments of discipline to his young. The relation of faith and law, of course, is an eternal human problem, whether it appears in questions of church and state, mysticism and daily morality, or existential aloneness and political commitment.

The third crisis, that of initiative versus guilt, is part of what Freud described as the central complex of the family, namely, the Oedipus complex. It involves a lasting unconscious association of sensual freedom with the body of the mother and the administrations received from her hand; a lasting association of cruel prohibition with the interference of the dangerous father; and the consequences of these associations for love and hate in reality and in phantasy. . . . We have reviewed the strong indications of an especially heavy interference by Hans Luder with Martin's attachment to his mother, who, it is suggested, secretly provided for him what Goethe openly acknowledged as his mother's gift . . . gaiety and the pleasure of confabulation. We have indicated how this gift, which later emerged in Luther's poetry, became guilt-laden and was broken to harness by an education designed to make a precocious student of the boy. We have also traced its relationship to Luther's lifelong burden of excessive guilt. . . .

The stage of initiative, associated with Freud's phallic stage of psycho-sexuality, ties man's budding will to phantasy, play, games, and early work, and thus to the mutual delineation of unlimited imagination and aspiration and limiting, threatening conscience. As far as society is concerned, this is vitally related to the occupational and technological ideals perceived by the child; for the child can manage the fact that there is no return to the mother as a mother and no competition with the father as a father only to the degree to which a future career outside of the narrower family can at least be envisaged in ideal future occupations: these he learns to imitate in play, and to anticipate in school. We can surmise that for little Martin the father's own occupation was early precluded from anticipatory phantasy, and that a life of scholarly duty was obediently and sadly envisaged instead. This precocious severity of obedience later made it impossible for young Martin to anticipate any career but that of unlimited study for its own sake, as we have seen in following his path of obedience—in disobedience.

In the fourth stage, the child becomes able and eager to learn systematically, and to collaborate with others. The resolution of this stage decides much of the ratio between a sense of industry or work completion, and a sense of tool-inferiority, and prepares a man for the essential ingredients of the ethos as well as the rationale of his technology. He wants to know the *reason* for things, and is provided, at least, with rationalizations. He learns to use whatever simplest techniques and tools will prepare him most generally for the tasks of his culture. In Martin's case, the tool was literacy, Latin literacy, and we saw how he was molded by it—and how later he remolded, with the help of printing, his nation's literary habits. With a vengeance he could claim to have taught German even to his enemies.

But he achieved this only after a protracted identity crisis which is the main subject of this book. Whoever is hard put to feel identical with one set of people and ideas must that much more violently repudiate another set; and whenever an identity, once established, meets further crises, the danger of irrational repudiation of otherness and temporarily even of one's own identity increases.

I have already briefly mentioned the three crises which follow the crisis of identity; they concern problems of intimacy, generativity, and integrity. The crisis of intimacy in a monk is naturally distorted in its heterosexual core. What identity diffusion is to identity—its alternative and danger—isolation is to intimacy. In a monk this too is subject to particular rules, since a monk seeks intentional and organized isolation, and submits all intimacy to prayer and confession.

Luther's intimacy crisis seems to have been fully experienced and resolved only on the Wartburg; that is, after his lectures had established him as a lecturer, and his speech at Worms as an orator of universal stamp. On the Wartburg he wrote *De Votis Monasticis,* obviously determined to take care of his sexual needs as soon as a dignified solution could be found. But the intimacy crisis is by no means only a sexual, or for that matter, a heterosexual, one: Luther, once free, wrote to men friends about his emotional life, including his sexuality, with a frankness clearly denoting a need to share intimacies with them. The most famous example, perhaps, is a letter written at a time when the tragicomedy of these priests' belated marriages to runaway nuns was in full swing. Luther had made a match between Spalatin and an ex-nun, a relative of Staupitz. In the letter, he wished Spalatin luck for the wedding night, and promised to think of him during a parallel performance to be arranged in his own marital bed.

Also on the Wartburg, Luther developed, with his translation of the Bible, a supreme ability to reach into the homes of his nation; as a preacher and a table talker he demonstrated his ability and his need to be intimate for the rest of his life. One could write a book about Luther on this theme alone; and perhaps in such a book all but the most wrathful utterances would be found to be communications exquisitely tuned to the recipient.

Owing to his prolonged identity crisis, and also to delayed sexual intimacy, intimacy and generativity were fused in Luther's life. We have given an account of the time when his generativity reached its crisis, namely, when within a short period he became both a father, and a leader of a wide following which began to disperse his teachings in any number of avaricious, rebellious, and mystical directions. Luther then tasted fully the danger of this stage, which paradoxically is felt by creative people more deeply than by others, namely, a sense of stagnation, experienced by him in manic-depressive form. As he recovered, he proceeded with the building of the edifice of his theology; yet he responded to the needs of his parishioners and students, including his princes, to the very end. Only his occasional outbursts expressed that fury of repudiation which was mental hygiene to him, but which set a lasting bad example to his people.

We now come to the last, the integrity crisis which again leads man to the portals of nothingness, or at any rate to the station of having been. I have described it thus:

> Only he who in some way has taken care of things and people and has adapted himself to the triumphs and disappointments adherent to being, by necessity, the originator of others and the generator of things and ideas—only he may gradually grow the fruit of these seven stages. I know no better word for it than ego integrity. Lacking a clear definition, I shall point to a few constituents of this state of mind. It is the ego's accrued assurance of its proclivity for order and meaning. It is a post-narcissistic love of the human ego—not of the self—as an experience which conveys some world order and some spiritual sense, no matter how dearly paid for. It is the acceptance of one's one and only life cycle as something that had to be and that, by necessity, permitted of no substitutions: it thus means a new, a different, love of one's parents. It is a comradeship with the ordering ways of distant times and different pursuits, as expressed in the simple products and sayings of such times and pursuits. Although aware of the relativity of all

the various life styles which have given meaning to human striving, the possessor of integrity is ready to defend the dignity of his own life style against all physical and economic threats. For he knows that an individual life is the accidental coincidence of but one life cycle with but one segment of history; and that for him all human integrity stands or falls with the one style of integrity of which he partakes. The style of integrity developed by his culture or civilization thus becomes the "patrimony of his soul," the seal of his moral paternity of himself. . . . Before this final solution, death loses its sting.

This integrity crisis, last in the lives of ordinary men, is a life-long and chronic crisis in a *homo religiosus*. He is always older, or in early years suddenly becomes older, than his playmates or even his parents and teachers, and focuses in a precocious way on what it takes others a lifetime to gain a mere inkling of: the questions of how to escape corruption in living and how in death to give meaning to life. Because he experiences a breakthrough to the last problems so early in his life maybe such a man had better become a martyr and seal his message with an early death; or else become a hermit in a solitude which anticipates the Beyond. We know little of Jesus of Nazareth as a young man, but we certainly cannot even begin to imagine him as middle-aged.

This short cut between the youthful crisis of identity and the mature one of integrity makes the religionist's problem of individual identity the same as the problem of existential identity. To some extent this problem is only an exaggeration of an abortive trait not uncommon in late adolescence. One may say that the religious leader becomes a professional in dealing with the kind of scruples which prove transitory in many all-too-serious postadolescents who later grow out of it, go to pieces over it, or find an intellectual or artistic medium which can stand between them and nothingness.

The late adolescent crisis, in addition to anticipating the more mature crises, can at the same time hark back to the very earliest crisis of life—trust or mistrust toward existence as such. This concentration in the cataclysm of the adolescent identity crisis of both first and last crises in the human life may well explain why religiously and artistically creative men often seem to be suffering from a barely compensated psychosis, and yet later prove superhumanly gifted in conveying a total meaning for man's life; while malignant disturbances in late adolescence often display precocious wisdom and usurped integrity. The chosen young man extends the problem of his identity to the borders of existence in the known universe; other human beings bend all their efforts to adopt and fulfill the departmentalized identities which they find prepared in their communities. He can permit himself to face as permanent the trust problem which drives others in whom it remains or becomes dominant into denial, despair, and psychosis. He acts as if mankind were starting all over with his own beginning as an individual, conscious of his singularity as well as his humanity; others hide in the folds of whatever tradition they are part of because of membership, occupation, or special interests. To him, history ends as well as starts with him; others must look to their memories, to legends, or to books to find models for the present and the future in what their predecessors have said and done. No wonder that he is something of an old man (a *philosophus,* and a sad one) when his agemates are young, or that he remains something of a child when they age with finality. . . .

The danger of a reformer of the first order, however, lies in the nature of his influence on the masses. In our own day we have seen this in the life and influence of Gandhi. He, too, believed in the power of prayer; when he fasted and prayed, the masses and even the English held their breath. Because prayer gave them the power to say what would be heard by the lowliest and the highest, both Gandhi and Luther believed that they could count on the restraining as well as the arousing power of the Word. In such hope great religionists are supported—one could say they are seduced—by the fact that all people, because of their common undercurrent of existential anxiety, at cyclic intervals and during crises feel an intense need for a rejuvenation of trust which will give new meaning to their limited and perverted exercise of will, conscience, reason, and identity. But the best of them will fall asleep at Gethsemane; and the worst will accept the new faith only as a sanction for anarchic destructiveness or political guile. If faith can move mountains, let it move obstacles out of their way. But maybe the masses also sense that he who aspires to spiritual power, even though he speaks of renunciation, has an account to settle with an inner authority. He may disavow their rebellion, but he is a rebel. He may say in the deepest humility, as Luther said, that "his mouth is Christ's mouth"; his nerve is still the nerve of a usurper. So for a while the world may be worse for having had a vision of being better. From the oldest Zen poem to the most recent psychological formulation it is clear that "the conflict between right and wrong is the sickness of the mind."

The great human question is to what extent early child training must or must not exploit man's early helplessness and moral sensitivity to the degree that a deep sense of evil and of guilt become unavoidable; for such a sense in the end can only result in clandestine commitment to evil in the name of higher values. Religionists, of course, assume that because a sense of evil dominated them even as they combated it, it belongs not only to man's "nature," but is God's Plan, even God's gift to him. The answer to this assumption is that not only do child training systems differ in their exploitation of basic mistrust, shame, doubt, and guilt—so do religions. The trouble comes, first, from the mortal fear that instinctual forces would run wild if they were not dominated by a negative conscience; and second, from trying to formulate man's optimum as negative morality, to be reinforced by rigid institutions. In this formulation all man's erstwhile fears of the forces and demons of nature are reprojected onto his inner forces, and onto the child, whose dormant energies are alternatively vilified as potentially criminal, or romanticized as altogether angelic. Because man needs a disciplined conscience, he thinks he must have a bad one; and he assumes that he has a good conscience when, at times, he has an easy one. The answer to all this does not lie in attempts to avoid or to deny one or the other sense of badness in children altogether; the denial of the unavoidable can only deepen a sense of secret, unmanageable evil. The answer lies in man's capacity to create order which will give his children a disciplined as well as a tolerant conscience, and a world within which to act affirmatively.

In this book we are dealing with a Western religious movement which grew out of and subsequently perpetuated an extreme emphasis on the interplay of initiative and guilt, and an exclusive emphasis on the divine Father-Son. Even in this scheme, the mother remains a counterplayer however shadowy. Father religions have mother churches.

One may say that man, when looking through a glass darkly, finds himself in an inner cosmos in which the outlines of three objects awaken dim nostalgias. One of these is the simple and fervent wish for a hallucinatory sense of unity with a maternal matrix, and a supply of benevolently powerful substances; it is symbolized by the affirmative face of charity, graciously inclined, reassuring the faithful of the unconditional acceptance of those who will return to the bosom. In this symbol the split of autonomy is forever repaired: shame is healed by unconditional approval, doubt by the eternal presence of generous provision.

In the center of the second nostalgia is the paternal voice of guiding conscience, which puts an end to the simple paradise of childhood and provides a sanction for energetic action. It also warns of the inevitability of guilty entanglement, and threatens with the lightning of wrath. To change the threatening sound of this voice, if need be by means of partial surrender and manifold self-castration, is the second imperative demand which enters religious endeavor. At all cost, the Godhead must be forced to indicate that He Himself mercifully planned crime and punishment in order to assure salvation.

Finally, the glass shows the pure self itself, the unborn core of creation, the—as it were, preparental—center where God is pure nothing: *ein lauter Nichts,* in the words of Angelus

Silesius. God is so designated in many ways in Eastern mysticism. This pure self is the self no longer sick with a conflict between right and wrong, not dependent on providers, and not dependent on guides to reason and reality.

These three images are the main religious objects. Naturally, they often fuse in a variety of ways and are joined by hosts of secondary deities. But must we call it regression if man thus seeks again the earliest encounters of his trustful past in his efforts to reach a hoped for and eternal future? Or do religions partake of man's ability, even as he regresses, to recover creatively? At their creative best, religions retrace our earliest inner experiences, giving tangible form to vague evils, and reaching back to the earliest individual sources of trust; at the same time, they keep alive the common symbols of integrity distilled by the generations. If this is partial regression, it is a regression which, in retracing firmly established pathways, returns to the present amplified and clarified. Here, of course, much depends on whether or not the son of a given era approaches the glass in good faith: whether he seeks to find again on a higher level a treasure of basic trust safely possessed from the beginning, or tries to find a birthright denied him in the first place, in his childhood. It is clear that each generation (whatever its ideological heaven) owes to the next a safe treasure of basic trust; Luther was psychologically and ideologically right when he said in theological terms that the infant has faith if his community means his baptism. Creative moments, however, and creative periods are rare. The process here described may remain abortive or outlive itself in stagnant institutions in which case it can and must be associated with neurosis and psychosis, with self-restriction and self-delusion, with hypocrisy and stupid moralism.

Freud has convincingly demonstrated the affinity of some religious ways of thought with those of neurosis.[2] But we regress in our dreams, too, and the inner structures of many dreams correspond to neurotic symptoms. Yet dreaming itself is a healthy activity, and a necessary one. And here too, the success of a dream depends on the faith one has, not on that which one seeks: a good conscience provides that proverbially good sleep which knits up the raveled sleeve of care. All the things that made man feel guilty, ashamed, doubtful, and mistrustful during the daytime are woven into a mysterious yet meaningful set of dream images, so arranged as to direct the recuperative powers of sleep toward a constructive waking state. The dreamwork fails and the dream turns into a nightmare when there is an intrusion of a sense of foreign reality into the dreamer's make-believe, and a subsequent disturbance in returning from that superimposed sense of reality into real reality.

Religions try to use mechanisms analogous to dreamlife, reinforced at times by a collective genius of poetry and artistry, to offer ceremonial dreams of great recuperative value. It is possible, however, that the medieval Church, the past master of ceremonial hallucination, by promoting the reality of hell too efficiently, and by tampering too successfully with man's sense of reality in this world, eventually created, instead of a belief in the greater reality of a more desirable world, only a sense of nightmare in this one.

I have implied that the original faith which Luther tried to restore goes back to the basic trust of early infancy. In doing so I have not, I believe, diminished the wonder of what Luther calls God's disguise. If I assume that it is the smiling face and the guiding voice of infantile parent images which religion projects onto the benevolent sky, I have no apologies to render to an age which thinks of painting the moon red. Peace comes from the inner space.

NOTES

1. Karl Mannheim, *Utopia and Ideology* (New York: Harcourt Brace, 1949).

2. Sigmund Freud, *The Future of an Illusion*, trans. W. D. Robson-Scott (New York: Liveright Publishing Corp., 1949).

Counterpoint:
The Significance of Erikson's Psychology for Modern Understandings of Religion

PETER HOMANS

Peter Homans teaches at the University of Chicago in Chicago, Illinois. Besides edited volumes, he has published the following works: *The Ability to Mourn: Disillusionment and the Social Origins of Psychoanalysis, Jung in Context: Modernity and the Making of a Psychology, Theology After Freud: An Interpretive Inquiry* and *The Dialogue between Theology and Psychology*.

ONE OF THE PARADOXES of the psychoanalytic study of religion lies in the fact that it has combined vigorous interest in the nature of religion with an equally vigorous critical attitude toward it. On the one hand, religion has occupied a position of prominence in psychoanalytic stud-

Reprinted from Peter Homans, "The Significance of Erikson's Psychology for Modern Understandings of Religion," Childhood and Selfhood: Essays on Tradition, Religion, and Modernity in the Psychology of Erik H. Erikson, *ed. Peter Homans (Lewisburg: Bucknell University Press, 1978, pp. 231–263).*

ies of culture or, as they are sometimes referred to, "applications" of psychoanalysis. In fact, of the various cultural phenomena to which this psychology has been applied, religion has received as much or more attention than any other. On the other hand, this psychology has been as critical of religion as it has been persistent in discussing it.

A second paradox characterizes the psychoanalytic study of religion. This vigorous though critical work on the nature of religion has not been combined with approaches to religion in the social sciences generally, particularly those approaches that have examined Western religious traditions, in both past and contemporary forms. While much work has been done in relating psychoanalytic theorizing to the social sciences generally, and while these sciences have made very definite commitments to the study of religion, there has been little integrative effort between psychoanalytic work on religion and social scientific studies of it. A lack of reciprocal discussion between psychoanalytic writers on religion and scholars in religious studies constitutes a third paradox. These two groups of workers have made little effort to utilize the ideas and findings of the other in order to broaden or unify their own paradigms.

The customary way of accounting for this state of affairs consists of offering the now-commonplace observation that writers on religion in the psychoanalytic tradition have not, for the most part, studied religion as a discrete and particular human experience. Psychoanalytic studies of religion have instead dwelt upon broad generalizations about the nature of religion on the whole, and when these studies have taken it upon themselves to examine concrete and particular manifestations of religion, they have done so largely for the purposes of illustrating an already-formed theory. Such a pattern is unlikely to attract either social scientists who study religion or scholars of religion, both of whom actively strive for a far more flexible and reciprocal relation between interpretive frameworks and specific, historical data. But in all fairness to the psychoanalytic approach, it must be noted that nonpsychoanalytic psychologists of religion display the same weakness. Neither sociologists of religion nor theologians and philosophers of religion have been attracted, for example, to the psychological writings of either James, Allport, or Maslow.

The purpose of this paper is to explore two of these paradoxes—the persistence of psychoanalytic interest in religion despite a wholly critical tone and the lack of interchange between psychoanalytic psychology and religious studies despite a common subject matter—through the writings of one of the most articulate and innovative of contemporary psychoanalytic writers, Erik Erikson. Erikson's work is deeply indebted to classic, psychoanalytic theory; when he recurs to authority in psychological matters, it is always first of all to the Freudian legacy. On the other hand, his work does not simply repeat the psychoanalytic approach to religion, but instead represents a considerable departure from it. Like the classic writers, he too has chosen religion as one of the most suitable objects for the "application" of psychoanalysis. However, unlike his forebears, Erikson has studied specific religious phenomena such as Luther's writings and their commentaries, and the religious and political circumstances surrounding Gandhi's life work—in considerable detail. But surely the most noticeable feature of Erikson's psychological writings on religion is the positive valuation he accords to it and, in particular, to Protestantism. It is this aspect of his thought that constitutes the particular focus of this paper—namely, how does Erikson transform Freudianism, which is so critical of religion, into a more complex and more generous estimate of it?

Erikson's Understanding of Religion

Erikson has not written a systematic statement of his psychological theory of religion. Instead, the theory emerges from psychohistorical observations on religious figures and from comments tangential to these observations. This is true even in the case of *Young Man Luther,* which is subtitled *A Study in Psychoanalysis and History,* but which nonetheless contains a great deal of psychological commentary on religion. This commentary is, however, both here and in other works, sufficiently sustained to make possible the construction of a coherent theory or understanding of religion.

Erikson makes three different types of reference to religion—that is, his many observations and comments fall into three different groupings. The most important of these is the epigenetic type of reference, already touched on above: religion is defined in terms of its effects upon the growth process. A second reference, one less frequently made and far more difficult to comprehend, but one that is easily as important as the first, is to "religious actuality." Religion is associated with the achievement by individuals of historical actuality, which Erikson sets at the opposite pole from psychological reality. A third reference, also infrequently made but also quite easy to grasp, describes religion as a form of nostalgia.

Of the three types of reference, the epigenetic definition of religion receives the most attention in Erikson's thought, and within this developmental framework religion is spoken of most of all in terms of the first stage of life, as trust, hope, and faith. Religion is experienced with great intensity during the earliest phase of growth, and it is mediated by the infant's mother in a form that enables him to adopt an attitude of trust in life.[1] Religion in this case is not of necessity regressive in a negative sense. It is, rather, a means of reaffirming, from time to time, resources derived from the earliest phase of life.

The second epigenetic reference to religion is made in the context of ideology and the associated developmental task of identity formation. At this point religion appears in a very different form and serves a very different function, although it is, finally, an elaboration of the first allusion. Religion as ideology refers, not to a global affective state, but to a system of discrete ideas about the nature and meaning of the con-temporary world-ideas that serve to relate the individual in a positive way to the historical order, to the social and political institutions of history. Ideology is the institutional support for the formation of identity. . . . Because of its rational and conceptual character, ideology is quite different from the predominantly emotional experience of trust. But the former is finally a continuation of the latter. Ideology provides a system of "good reasons" why the world should be invested with a positive attitude of trust rather than with suspicion and alienation. Thus it is simply the conceptual dimension of basic trust; or, to reverse the relation, basic trust is the affective dimension of ideology. Trust and ideology are the psychological infrastructures of faith and doctrine, respectively.

The epigenetic basis of religion is surprisingly symmetrical. Religion appears at the beginning of life, again midway through life, and at the last stage of life as well, where it appears in relation to the task of integrity. In this instance it provides the context for an experience of self-transcendence. Religion discloses to the finite ego-identity the existence of an ultimate reality that derives from beyond finite, conscious experience. The religious support for integrity engages a realm of knowledge and experience that lies beyond the immediacies of either primitive trust or more discerning ideology. Religion is a form of transcendence that is "existential" rather than social. . . .

Belief in the existence of a "super-I" is surely a matter very different from both trust and ideology. Yet just as ideology was an elaboration of trust, this "existential" dimension is successor to both. For through the affirmation of a "super-I"—a commitment that requires both affective and cognitive assets—the individual becomes "trustworthy." That is to say, he becomes deserving of the trust of the young. And with this act the individual life cycle not only completes itself but also articulates the cycle of generations, completing it as well.

The life cycle is made up at every point of a double movement: there is a thrust outward into society and history, and then a movement backward—into selfhood, singularity, and separateness. The two movements achieve a special kind of balance in the stage of identity formation, and religion supports the life cycle, not only at this crucial stage or turning point, but also at the points that precede it and succeed it. But this epigenetic reference to religion, if left to itself, renders all understanding of the life process excessively abstract. Erikson has accordingly adopted an alternate way of describing the relation between the ego and history, especially at the stage of identity formation, which brings to the discussion a more subjective and experiential tone. He distinguishes between "psychological reality" and "historical actuality," and then concludes that there is something religious about historical actuality. Religious actuality thus constitutes his second major reference to religion.[2]

Psychological reality refers to an orientation of the mind that under any given set of circumstances searches for causes and effects. It is synonymous with Freud's conception of the reality principle and of reality testing, and with Heinz Hartmann's redefinition of the former as the capacity to take into account the real features of an object or a situation.[3] It is the instrumental attitude adopted by the ego in order to cope with the "here and now" of the everyday world. *Psychological reality* refers to what common sense has come to call "adjusting to reality." As such, it is the therapeutic goal and epistemological basis of classic psychoanalysis.

Erikson finds this view of reality narrow, constraining, and inaccurate, for it cannot account for the process of mutual activation whereby one person evokes in another through intuition and active participation—that combination of autonomy and self-recognition that is the mark of a genuine sense of identity. Mutual activation is as much "a fact" as psychological reality, but it is also a process dependent upon a sense of self that is in turn rooted in the historical cycle of generations. Therefore Erikson juxtaposes to psychological reality the notion of historical actuality: to be real is also to be actual. Reality

denotes perception based upon the discernment of causes; actuality connotes "the world verified in immediate immersion and interaction." . . .

The distinction between psychological reality and historical actuality is neither merely a psychological distinction, nor is it restricted to the sphere of ethics alone; actuality is also a religious phenomenon. In *Gandhi's Truth*[4] Erikson describes Gandhi as a "religious actualist," and this discussion makes clear the bond that exists in Erikson's mind between religion and actuality. . . . Gandhi . . . "absorbed from Indian culture a conception of truth (*sat*) which he attempted to make actual in all compartments of human life." In other words, Gandhi's religion provided him with the knowledge and ability to produce the "mutual maximization of a greater and higher unity among men," such that "each must begin to become actual by combining what is given in his individual development and in his historical time." This capacity to communicate a "sense of the actual" inevitably leads the creative individual into the role of religious innovation, because "his very passion and power will make him want to make actual for others what actualizes him. This means to create or recreate institutions."

Erikson does not address his psychological questions to the essential core of religious tradition, but instead reflects upon the psychological effects of religion. These reflections lead him to the conclusion that religion creates actuality, so described, or rather that religion produces actuality in the face of a situation that would otherwise be comprised entirely of "mere reality." Just as, in the case of Luther, Erikson sought the psychological infrastructure of identity and ideology beneath Luther's personal faith and his doctrine of justification by faith, so here Erikson seeks and finds actuality beneath the religious leadership and innovation of Gandhi.

It should be clear from this linkage between religion and actuality that the latter includes elements of trust, ideology, and transcendence, that it, in effect, welds these together. And it should be equally clear that actualism is inseparable from the formation, maintenance, and continuation of institutions. Here is further evidence of the centrality of institutions in Erikson's view of life and religion. Actualism, as the essence of human interaction, cannot take place outside of an institutional process, for it constitutes the need for institutions, just as institutions make it possible. The point raises once again the question of the necessity of religion for psychosocial health (actuality). Erikson is clearly ambiguous on this issue. On the one hand, he is taken by the power of religious images (such as those provided by the Hindu life cycle) to construct actuality: . . .Yet at the same time he insists that, while religions have in the past been the most reliable sources of trust, ideology, and integrity, the modern person may well choose a different mode of access to these processes, so necessary for effective and relatively stress free living.

The epigenetic principle and the distinction between reality and actuality provide the major references for Erikson's psychological interpretation of religion. However, there is a third approach to religion that, although extremely important, lucid, and informative, is often overlooked because it is so infrequently mentioned. This is the "definition" of religion as nostalgia, a hearkening back, on the part of the individual, to the earliest, most powerful, and impressive experiences in the life cycle. . . .

Conclusion: The Persistence of the Problem of Projection in Erikson's Thought

. . . The most fundamental division in contemporary thought about religion lies between the view of religion as a sui generis phenomenon given to men from beyond their existing knowledge and the view of religion as the projection of some infrastructure. From this more fundamental, presuppositional point of view religion as order and religion as spontaneity—that is, the sociological and psychological approaches to religion—are both based upon the assumption of projection, whereas the view of religion as transcendence completely disavows the projective hypothesis.

This hypothesis stipulates that religious phenomena are experienced by the believer "as if" they were completely real and completely independent of him, although from the interpreter's point of view their meaning lies as much in their origin as in their experiential convincingness. . . .

Erikson speaks of religion as transcendence, and in doing so he joins the theologians in emphasizing the sui generis nature of religious reality. And his discussions of ideology also emphasize its sui generis nature and are remarkably free from sociological reductionism. But beneath these trends lies a more fundamental commitment to the view of religion as projection. . . . It should be noted that, in viewing religion as a projection of a developmental infrastructure, Erikson is assigning to it a positive, not a negative significance. To put the matter bluntly, religion is a "good projection." But this valuation of religion does not cancel out its fundamentally projective character, nor does it obviate the problems that ensue whenever the projective view is employed. For Erikson only stipulates its positive nature.

In this omission, Erikson jeopardizes his entire psychological theory of religion. All that he says—in terms of transcendence and integrity and in terms of order and ideology—rests upon the projective hypothesis. The view of religion as transcendence is an expression of the question of whether the projection is real and true. Erikson stipulates that this is so, but offers no discussion or evidence. The view of religion as order is the question of the nature of the structure of the projection. Erikson offers ideology as an answer, but tells us only that ideology is developmentally necessary and leaves open such questions as what in an ideology is convincing and plausible and whether some ideologies are truer than others, or, if truth is no criterion, then whether some ideologies are better others. These questions of transcendence and order related to the problem of spontaneity, the problem of origin of the projection—how it was created. Erikson does little more than identify its epigenetic rootage, stipulating its moral rightness and epistemological validity. . . .

NOTES

1. Erikson, see esp. *Identity and the Life Cycle* (New York: W. W. Norton & Co., 1980), p. 65; *Childhood and Society*, (New York: W. W. Norton & Co., 1950) p. 250; *Identity: Youth and Crisis*, (New York: W. W. Norton & Co., 1968) p. 83.

2. The following discussion is drawn from Erikson, "Psychological Reality and Historical Actuality," in *Insight and Responsibility*, pp. 162–66.

3. Erikson briefly summarizes Hartmann's views and criticizes them for being "Cartesian," Erikson, *Insight and Responsibility*, p. 163.

4. Erik Erikson, *Gandhi's Truth: On the Origins of Militant Nonviolence* (New York: W. W. Norton & Co., 1969). This discussion of religious actuality is drawn from pp. 396–400.

From *Violence and the Sacred*

RENE GIRARD

VIOLENCE IS NOT TO BE DENIED, but it can be diverted to another object, something it can sink its teeth into. Such, perhaps, is one of the meanings of the story of Cain and Abel. The Bible offers us no background on the two brothers except the bare fact that Cain is a tiller of the soil who gives the fruits of his labor to God, whereas Abel is a shepherd who regularly sacrifices the first-born of his herds. One of the brothers kills the other, and the murderer is the one who does not have the violence-outlet of animal sacrifice at his disposal. This difference between sacrificial and nonsacrificial cults determines, in effect, God's judgement in favor of Abel. To say that God accedes to Abel's sacrificial offerings but rejects the offerings of Cain is simply another way of saying—from the viewpoint of the divinity—that Cain is a murderer, whereas his brother is not.

A frequent motif in the Old Testament, as well as in Greek myth, is that of brothers at odds with one another. Their fatal penchant for violence can only be diverted by the intervention of a third party, the sacrificial victim or victims. Cain's "jealousy" of his brother is only another term for his one characteristic trait: his lack of a sacrificial outlet.

According to Moslem tradition, God delivered to Abraham the ram previously sacrificed by Abel. This ram was to take the place of Abraham's son Isaac; having already saved one human life, the same animal would now save another. What we have here is no mystical hocus-pocus, but an intuitive insight into the essential function of sacrifice, gleaned exclusively from the scant references in the Bible.

Another familiar biblical scene takes on new meaning in the light of our theory of sacrificial substitution, and it can serve in turn to illuminate some aspects of the theory. The scene is that in which Jacob receives the blessing of his father Isaac.

Isaac is an old man. He senses the approach of death and summons his eldest son, Esau, on whom he intends to bestow his final blessing. First, however, he instructs Esau to bring back

Reprinted from Rene Girard, Violence and the Sacred, *trans. Patrick Gregory (Baltimore: Johns Hopkins University Press, 1989).*

some venison from the hunt, so as to make a "savory meat." This request is overheard by the younger brother, Jacob, who hastens to report it to his mother, Rebekah. Rebekah takes two kids from the family flock, slaughters them, and prepares the savory meat dish, which Jacob, in the guise of his elder brother, then presents to his father.

Isaac is blind. Nevertheless Jacob fears he will be recognized, for he is a "smooth man," while his brother Esau is a "hairy man." "My father peradventure will feel me, and I shall seem to him as a deceiver; and I shall bring a curse upon me, not a blessing." Rebekah has the idea of covering Jacob's hands and the back of his neck with the skins of the slaughtered goats, and when the old man runs his hands over his younger son, he is completely taken in by the imposture. Jacob receives the blessing that Isaac had intended for Esau.

The kids serve in two different ways to dupe the father—or, in other terms, to divert from the son the violence directed toward him. In order to receive his father's blessing rather than his curse, Jacob must present to Isaac the freshly slaughtered kids made into a "savory meat." Then the son must seek refuge, literally, in the skins of the sacrificed animals. The animals thus interpose themselves between father and son. They serve as a sort of insulation, preventing the direct contact that could lead only to violence. Two sorts of substitution are telescoped here: that of one brother for another, and that of an animal for a man. Only the first receives explicit recognition in the text; however, this first one serves as the screen upon which the shadow of the second is projected.

Once we have focused attention on the sacrificial victim, the object originally singled out for violence fades from view. Sacrificial substitution implies a degree of misunderstanding. Its vitality as an institution depends on its ability to conceal the displacement upon which the rite is based. It must never lose sight entirely, however, of the original object, or cease to be aware of the act of transference from that object to the

surrogate victim; without that awareness no substitution can take place and the sacrifice loses all efficacy. The biblical passage discussed above meets both requirements. The narrative does not refer directly to the strange deception underlying the sacrificial substitution, nor does it allow this deception to pass entirely unnoticed. Rather, it mixes the act of substitution with another act of substitution, permitting us a fleeting, sidelong glimpse of the process. The narrative itself, then, might be said to partake of a sacrificial quality; it claims to reveal one act of substitution while employing this first substitution to half-conceal another. There is reason to believe that the narrative touches upon the mythic origins of the sacrificial system.

The figure of Jacob has long been linked with the devious character of sacrificial violence. In Greek culture Odysseus plays a similar role. The story of Jacob's benediction can be compared to the episode of the Cyclops in the *Odyssey*, where a splendidly executed ruse enables the hero to escape the clutches of a monster.

Odysseus and his shipmates are shut up in the Cyclops' cave. Every day the giant devours one of the crew; the survivors finally manage to blind their tormentor with a flaming stake. Mad with pain and anger, the Cyclops bars the entrance of the cave to prevent the men from escaping. However, he lets pass his flock of sheep, which go out daily to pasture. In a gesture reminiscent of the blind Isaac, the Cyclops runs his hands over the back of each sheep as it leaves the cave to make sure that it carries no passenger. Odysseus, however, has outwitted his captor, and he rides to freedom by clinging to the thick wool on the underside of one of the rams.

A comparison of the two scenes, one from Genesis and the other from the *Odyssey*, lends credence to the theory of their sacrificial origins. In each case an animal intervenes at the crucial moment to prevent violence from attaining its designated victim. The two texts are mutually revealing: the Cyclops of the *Odyssey* underlines the fearful menace that hangs over the hero (and that remains obscure in the Genesis story); and the slaughter of the kids in Genesis, along with the offering of the "savory meat," clearly implies the sacrificial character of the flock, an aspect that might go unnoticed in the *Odyssey*. . . .

Sacrifice plays a very real role in these societies, and the problem of substitution concerns the entire community. The victim is not a substitute for some particularly endangered individual, nor is it offered up to some individual of particularly bloodthirsty temperament. Rather, it is a substitute for all the members of the community, offered up by the members themselves. The sacrifice serves to protect the entire community from its own violence; it prompts the entire community to choose victims outside itself. The elements of dissension scattered throughout the community are drawn to the person of the sacrificial victim and eliminated, at least temporarily, by its sacrifice. . . .

It is easy to ridicule a religion by concentrating on its more eccentric rites, rites such as the sacrifices performed to induce rain or bring fine weather. There is in fact no object or endeavor in whose name a sacrifice cannot be made, especially when the social basis of the act has begun to blur. Nevertheless, there is a common denominator that determines the efficacy of all sacrifices and that becomes increasingly apparent as the institution grows in vigor. This common denominator is internal violence—all the dissensions, rivalries, jealousies, and quarrels within the community that the sacrifices are designed to suppress. The purpose of the sacrifice is to restore harmony to the community, to reinforce the social. In a general study of sacrifice there is little reason to differentiate between human and animal victims. . . .

In order for a species or category of living creature, human or animal, to appear suitable for sacrifice, it must bear a sharp resemblance to the *human* categories excluded from the ranks of the "sacrificeable," while still maintaining a degree of difference that forbids all possible confusion. As I have said, no mistake is possible in the case of animal sacrifice. But it is quite another case with human victims. If we look at the extremely wide spectrum of human victims sacrificed by various societies, the list seems heterogeneous, to say the least. It includes prisoners of war, slaves, small children, unmarried adolescents, and the handicapped; it ranges from the very dregs of society, such as the Greek pharmakos, to the king himself. . . .

All our sacrificial victims, whether chosen from one of the human categories enumerated above or, *a fortiori,* from the animal realm, are invariably distinguishable from the nonsacrificeable beings by one essential characteristic: between these victims and the community a crucial social link is missing, so they can be exposed to violence without fear of reprisal. Their death does not automatically entail an act of vengeance.

The considerable importance this freedom from reprisal has for the sacrificial process makes us understand that sacrifice is primarily an act of violence without risk of vengeance. . . . The desire to commit an act of violence on those near us cannot be suppressed without a conflict; we must divert that impulse, therefore, toward the sacrificial victim, the creature we can strike down without fear of reprisal, since he lacks a champion. . . .

The function of sacrifice is to quell violence within the community and to prevent conflicts from erupting. Yet societies like our own, which do not, strictly speaking, practice sacrificial rites, seem to get along without them. Violence undoubtedly exists within our society, but not to such an extent that the society itself is threatened with extinction. The simple fact that sacrificial practices, and other rites as well, can disappear without catastrophic results should in part explain the failure of ethnology and theology to come to grips with these cultural phenomena, and explain as well our modern reluctance to attribute a real function to them. After all, it is hard to maintain that institutions for which, as it seems, we have no need are actually indispensable. . . .

Why does the spirit of revenge, wherever it breaks out, constitute such an intolerable menace? Perhaps because the only satisfactory revenge for spilt blood is spilling the blood of the killer; and in the blood feud there is no clear distinction between the act for which the killer is being punished and the punishment itself. Vengeance professes to be an act of reprisal, and every reprisal calls for another reprisal. The crime to which the act of vengeance addresses itself is almost never an unprecedented offense; in almost every case it has been committed in revenge for some prior crime.

Vengeance, then, is an interminable, infinitely repetitive process. Every time it turns up in some part of the community, it threatens to involve the whole social body. There is the risk that the act of vengeance will initiate a chain reaction whose consequences will quickly prove fatal to any society of modest size. The multiplication of reprisals instantaneously puts the very existence of a society in jeopardy, and that is why it is universally proscribed. . . .

Vengeance is a vicious circle whose effect on primitive societies can only be surmised. For us the circle has been broken. We owe our good fortune to one of our social institutions above all: our judicial system, which serves to deflect the menace of vengeance. The system does not suppress vengeance; rather, it effectively limits it to a single act of reprisal, enacted by a sovereign authority specializing in this particular function. The decisions of the judiciary are invariably presented as the final word on vengeance.

Vocabulary is perhaps more revealing here than judicial theories. Once the concept of interminable revenge has been formally rejected, it is referred to as private vengeance. The term implies the existence of a *public* vengeance, a counterpart never made explicit. By definition, primitive societies have only *private* vengeance. Thus, public vengeance is the exclusive property of well-policed societies, and our society calls it the judicial system. . . .

In a universe where the slightest dispute can lead to disaster—just as a slight cut can prove fatal to a hemophiliac—the rites of sacrifice serve to polarize the community's aggressive impulses and redirect them toward victims that may be actual or figurative, animate or inanimate, but that are always incapable of propagating further vengeance. The sacrificial process furnishes an outlet for those violent impulses that cannot be mastered by self-restraint; a partial outlet, to be sure, but always renewable, and one whose efficacy has been attested by an impressive number of reliable witnesses. The sacrificial process prevents the spread of violence by keeping vengeance in check. . . .

In primitive societies the risk of unleashed violence is so great and the cure so problematic that the emphasis naturally falls on prevention. The preventive measures naturally fall within the domain of religion, where they can on occasion assume a violent character. Violence and the sacred are inseparable. But the covert appropriation by sacrifice of certain properties of violence—particularly the ability of violence to move from one object to another—is hidden from sight by the awesome machinery of ritual. . . .

Religion invariably strives to subdue violence, to keep it from running wild. Paradoxically, the religious and moral authorities in a community attempt to instill nonviolence, as an active force into daily life and as a mediating force into ritual life, through the application of violence. Sacrificial rites serve to connect the moral and religious aspects of daily life, but only by means of a lengthy and hazardous detour. Moreover, it must be kept in mind that the efficacy of the rites depends on their being performed in the spirit of *pietas,* which marks all aspects of religious life. We are beginning to understand why the sacrificial act appears as both sinful and saintly and illegal as well as a legitimate exercise of violence. However, we are still far from a full understanding of the act itself. . . .

Primitive religion tames, trains, arms, and directs violent impulses as a defensive force against those forms of violence that society regards as inadmissible. It postulates a strange mixture of violence and nonviolence. The same can perhaps be said of our own judicial system of control.

There may be a certain connection between all the various methods employed by man since the beginning of time to avoid being caught up in an interminable round of revenge. They can be grouped into three general categories: (1) preventive measures in which sacrificial rites divert the spirit of revenge into other channels; (2) the harnessing or hobbling of vengeance by means of compensatory measures, trials by combat, etc., whose curative effects remain precarious; (3) the establishment of a judicial system—the most efficient of all curative procedures. . . .

The procedures that keep men's violence in bounds have one thing in common: they are no strangers to the ways of violence. There is reason to believe that they are all rooted in religion. As we have seen, the various forms of prevention go hand in hand with religious practices. The curative procedures are also imbued with religious concepts—both the rudimentary sacrificial rites and the more advanced judicial forms. *Religion* in its broadest sense, then, must be another term for that obscurity that surrounds man's efforts to defend himself by curative or preventative means against his own violence. It is that enigmatic quality that pervades the judicial system when that system replaces sacrifice. This obscurity coincides with the transcendental effectiveness of a violence that is holy, legal, and legitimate successfully opposed to a violence that is unjust, illegal, and illegitimate. . . .

A unique generative force exists that we can only qualify as religious in a sense deeper than the theological one. It remains concealed and draws its strength from this concealment, even as its self-created shelter begins to crumble. The acknowledgment of such a force allows us to assess our modern ignorance—ignorance in regard to violence as well as religion. Religion shelters us from violence just as violence seeks shelter in religion. If we fail to understand certain religious practices it is not because we are

outside their sphere of influence but because we are still to a very real extent enclosed within them. . . .

To make a victim out of the guilty party is to play vengeance's role, to submit to the demands of violence. By killing, not the murderer himself, but someone close to him, an act of perfect reciprocity is avoided and the necessity for revenge by-passed. If the counterviolence were inflicted on the aggressor himself, it would by this very act participate in, and become indistinguishable from, the original act of violence. In short, it would become an act of pure vengeance, requiring yet another act of vengeance and transforming itself into the very thing it was designed to prevent.

Only violence can put an end to violence, and that is why violence is self-propagating. Everyone wants to strike the last blow, and reprisal can thus follow reprisal without any true conclusion ever being reached. . . .

The mechanism of reciprocal violence can be described as a vicious circle. Once a community enters the circle, it is unable to extricate itself. We can define this circle in terms of vengeance and reprisals, and we can offer diverse psychological descriptions of these reactions. As long as a working capital of accumulated hatred and suspicion exists at the center of the community, it will continue to increase no matter what men do. Each person prepares himself for the probable aggression of his neighbors and interprets his neighbor's preparations as confirmation of the latter's aggressiveness. In more general terms, the mimetic character of violence is so intense that once violence is installed in a community, it cannot burn itself out.

To escape from the circle it is first necessary to remove from the scene all those forms of violence that tend to become self-propagating and to spawn new, imitative forms.

When a community succeeds in convincing itself that one alone of its number is responsible for the violent mimesis besetting it; when it is able to view this member as the single "polluted" enemy who is contaminating the rest;

and when the citizens are truly unanimous in this conviction—then the belief becomes a reality, for there will no longer exist elsewhere in the community a form of violence to be followed or opposed, which is to say, imitated and propagated. In destroying the surrogate victim, men believe that they are ridding themselves of some present ill. And indeed they are, for they are effectively doing away with those forms of violence that beguile the imagination and provoke emulation. . . .

Men cannot confront the naked truth of their own violence without the risk of abandoning themselves to it entirely. They have never had a very clear idea of this violence, and it is possible that the survival of all human societies of the past was dependent on this fundamental lack of understanding.

The Oedipus myth, as we have attempted to explain it in the preceding pages, follows a structural pattern that conforms to that of the surrogate victim. Let us now try to determine whether the pattern recurs in other myths. From what we have seen, it seems likely that the process of finding a surrogate victim constitutes a major means, perhaps the sole means, by which men expel from their consciousness the truth about their violent nature—that knowledge of past violence which, if not shifted to a single "guilty" figure, would poison both the present and the future. . . .

The complete explanation of the Oedipus myth—that is, the determining of the precise function of the surrogate victim—permits us to understand the aim of the sacrificers. They are striving to produce a replica, as faithful as possible in every detail, of a previous crisis that was resolved by means of a spontaneously unanimous victimization. All the dangers, real and imaginary, that threaten the community are subsumed in the most terrible danger that can confront a society: the sacrificial crisis. The rite is therefore a repetition of the original, spontaneous "lynching" that restored order in the community by reestablishing, around the figure of the surrogate victim, that sentiment of social accord that had been destroyed in the onslaught of reciprocal violence. Like Oedipus, the victim is considered a polluted object, whose living presence contaminates everything that comes in contact with it and whose death purges the community of its ills—as the subsequent restoration of public tranquillity clearly testifies. That is the pharmakos [that] was paraded about the city. He was used as a kind of sponge to sop up impurities, and [that] afterward he was expelled from the community or killed in a ceremony that involved the entire populace. . . .

In ritual sacrifice the victim, when actually put to death, diverts violence from its forbidden objectives within the community. But for whom, precisely, is this victim substituted? Heretofore we could only conceive of this substitution in terms of individual psychological mechanisms, which clearly do not provide an adequate picture of the process. If there were no surrogate victim to transform the sacrifice from an essentially private concern into one involving the whole community, we would be obliged to regard the victim as a substitute for particular individuals who have somehow provoked the sacrificer's anger. If the transfer is purely personal, as it is in psychoanalysis, then sacrifice cannot be a true social institution involving the entire community. But sacrifice, as we know, is essentially a communal institution. "Individualization" marks a later, decadent stage in its evolution, a development contrary to its original spirit.

To understand how and why sacrifice functions as it does, we should consider the proposition that the ritual victim is never substituted for some particular member of the community or even for the community as a whole: *it is always substituted for the surrogate victim.* As this victim itself serves as a substitute for all the members of the community, the sacrificial substitution does indeed play the role that we have attributed to it, protecting all the members of the community from their respective violence—but always through the intermediary of the surrogate victim. . . .

The original act of violence is unique and spontaneous. Ritual sacrifices, however, are multiple, endlessly repeated. All those aspects of the original act that had escaped man's control—the choice of time and place, the selection of the victim—are now premeditated and fixed by custom. The ritual process aims at removing all element of chance and seeks to extract from the original violence some technique of cathartic appeasement. The diluted force of the sacrificial ritual cannot be attributed to imperfections in its imitative technique. After all, the rite is designed to function during periods of relative calm; as we have seen, its role is not curative, but preventive. If it were more "effective" than it in fact is—if it did not limit itself to appropriate sacrificial victims but instead, like the original act of violence, vented its force on a participating member of the community—then it would lose all effectiveness, for it would bring to pass the very thing it was supposed to prevent: a relapse into the sacrificial crisis. The sacrificial process is as fully adapted to its normal function as collective murder is to its abnormal and normative function. There is every reason to believe that the minor catharsis of the sacrificial act is derived from that major catharsis circumscribed by collective murder.

Ritual sacrifice is founded on a double substitution. The first, which passes unperceived, is the substitution of one member of the community for all, brought about through the operation of the surrogate victim. The second, the only truly "ritualistic" substitution, is superimposed on the first. It is the substitution of a victim belonging to a predetermined sacrificial category for the original victim. The surrogate victim comes from inside the community, and the ritual victim must come from outside; otherwise the community might find it difficult to unite against it. . . .

It goes without saying that the rite has its violent aspects, but these always involve a lesser violence, proffered as a bulwark against a far more virulent violence. Moreover, the rite aims at the most profound state of peace known to any community: the peace that follows the sacrificial crisis and results from the unanimous accord venerated by the surrogate victim. To banish the evil emanations that accumulate within the community and to recapture the freshness of this original experience are one and the same task. Whether order reigns supreme or whether its reign is already challenged, the same model, the same plan of action is invariably proposed. It is the plan, associated with the victorious resolution of all communal crises, that involves violence against the surrogate victim. . . .

Greek legends often contain vague reference to a sacrifice—a human sacrifice—offered by a community, city, or army to some god. The persons involved agree on the need for such a sacrifice but disagree on the choice of victim. To understand the situation the investigator must reverse the order of events. First comes the violence, spontaneous and senseless; then comes the sacrificial explanation, genuinely sacrificial in that it conceals the senseless and basically intolerable aspect of the violence. The sacrificial explanation is rooted in an act of terminal violence, violence that can only be labeled sacrificial retrospectively, because it brought all hostilities to an end. These stories may represent the minimal form of mythological fabrication. A collective murder that brings about the restoration of order imposes a kind of ritualistic framework on the savage fury of the group, all of whose members are out for one another's blood. Murder becomes sacrifice; the angry free-for-all that preceded it is transformed into a ritual dispute over the choice of the most suitable victim, one that satisfies the piety of the faithful or has been selected by the god. In effect, the real question behind these preliminaries is, Who will kill whom? . . .

Religion, then, is far from "useless." It humanizes violence; it protects man from his own violence by taking it out of his hands, transforming it into a transcendent and ever-present danger to be kept in check by the appropriate rites appropriately observed and by a modest and prudent demeanor. Religious misinterpretation is a truly constructive force, for it purges man of the suspicions that would poison his existence if he were to remain conscious of the crisis as it actually took place. . . .

Men would not be able to shake loose the violence between them, to make of it a separate entity both sovereign and redemptory, without the surrogate victim. Also, violence itself offers a sort of respite, the fresh beginning of a cycle of ritual after a cycle of violence. Violence will come to an end only after it has had the last word and that word has been accepted as divine. The meaning of this word must remain hidden, the mechanism of unanimity remain concealed. For religion protects man as long as its ultimate foundations are not revealed. To drive the monster from its secret lair is to risk loosing it on mankind. To remove men's ignorance is only to risk exposing them to an even greater peril. The only barrier against human violence is raised on misconception. In fact, the sacrificial crisis is simply another form of that knowledge which grows greater as the reciprocal violence grows more intense but which never leads to the whole truth. It is the knowledge of violence, along with the violence itself, that the act of expulsion succeeds in shunting outside the realm of consciousness. . . .

Desire, as we have seen, is attracted to violence triumphant and strives desperately to incarnate this "irresistible" force. Desire clings to violence and stalks it like a shadow because violence is the signifier of the cherished being, the signifier of divinity. . . .

Violence strikes men as at once seductive and terrifying; never as a simple means to an end, but as an epiphany. Violence tends to generate unanimity, either in its favor or against it. And violence promotes imbalance, tipping the scales of Destiny in one direction or another. . . .

I have used the phrase "violence and the sacred"; I might as well have said "violence or the sacred." For the operations of violence and the sacred are ultimately the same process. . . . Violence is venerated insofar as it offers men what little peace they can ever expect. Non-

violence appears as the gratuitous gift of violence; and there is some truth in this equation, for men are only capable of reconciling their differences at the expense of a third party. The best men can hope for in their quest for nonviolence is the unanimity-minus-one of the surrogate victim. . . .

Polarized by the sacrificial killing, violence is appeased. It subsides. We might say that it is expelled from the community and becomes part of the divine substance, from which it is completely indistinguishable, for each successive sacrifice evokes in diminishing degree the immense calm produced by the act of generative unanimity, by the initial appearance of the god. . . .

If it is true that the community has everything to fear from the sacred, it is equally true that the community owes its every existence to the sacred. For in perceiving itself as uniquely situated outside the sphere of the sacred, the community assumes that it has been engendered by it; the act of generative violence that created the community is attributed not to men, but to the sacred itself. Having brought the community into existence, the sacred brings about its own expulsion and withdraws from the scene, thereby releasing the community from its direct contact. . . .

The outcome of this relationship is as follows: although men cannot live in the midst of violence, neither can they survive very long by ignoring its existence or by deluding themselves into the belief that violence, despite the ritual prohibitions attendant on it, can somehow be put to work as the mere tool or servant of mankind. The complex and delicate nature of the community's dealings with the sacred, the ceaseless effort to arrive at the ordered and uninterrupted accord essential to the well-being of the community, can only be expressed, for want of the naked truth, in terms of optimum *distance*. If the community comes too near the sacred it risks being devoured by it; if, on the other hand, the community drifts too far away, out of range of the sacred's therapeutic threats and warnings, the effects of its fecund presence are lost. . . .

All sacrificial rites are based on two substitutions. The first is provided by generative violence, which substitutes a single victim for all the members of the community. The second, the only strictly ritualistic substitution, is that of a victim for the surrogate victim. As we know, it is essential that the victim be drawn from outside the community. The surrogate victim, by contrast, is a member of the community. Ritual sacrifice is defined as an inexact imitation of the generative act. Why, we may ask, does sacrifice systematically exclude those who seem the most appropriate victims, who bear the closest resemblance to the original: the members of the community?

The need for some distinction between the original victim and the ritual victims can readily be explained. If the sacrificial victim belonged to the community (as does the surrogate victim), then his death would promote further violence instead of dispelling it. Far from reiterating the effects of generative violence, the sacrifice would inaugurate a new crisis. But because certain conditions must be met, an organization capable of meeting them does not inevitably have to come into being. If we think it does, we succumb to the functionalist illusion. The second sacrificial substitution still poses a problem that must be resolved. . . .

If the sole fact of being selected as a future victim is sufficient to metamorphose the chosen object, to make a sacred personage out of him, then it is not hard to uncover the reasoning behind the different choices of original victim and ritual victims. When a victim has been killed he belongs to the sacred; it is the sacred itself that permits its own expulsion or is expelled in the victim's person. The surrogate victim thus appears as a monster. He is no longer regarded in the same way as the other members of the community.

If the sacrificeable categories are generally made up of creatures who do not and have never belonged to the community, that is

because the surrogate victim belongs first and foremost to the sacred. The community, by contrast, has emerged from the sacred and separated itself from it. Members of the community, then, are less suitable as ritual victims than are nonmembers. That is why ritual victims are chosen from outside the community, from creatures (like animals and strangers) that normally dwell amidst sacred things and are themselves imbued with sacredness.

From our vantage point as objective observers the other members of the community seem closer to the original victim and consequently far more suitable, in accordance with the theory of imitation, as sacrificial objects. But the viewpoint of the primordial religious experience is determined by the generative violence. From that perspective the surrogate victim is completely transformed. It is this transformation that serves to protect the community from violence, that prevents the faithful from choosing one of their own number as a replacement for the original victim, and that consequently helps prevent any new outbreak of reciprocal violence. If the ritual victim is drawn from outside the community—if the very fact of choosing a victim bestows on him an aura of exteriority—the reason is that the surrogate victim is not perceived as he really was—namely, as a member of the community like all the others. . . .

We should not conclude, however, that the surrogate victim is simply foreign to the community. Rather, he is seen as a "monstrous double." He partakes of all possible differences within the community, particularly the difference between within and without; for he passes freely from the interior to the exterior and back again. Thus, the surrogate victim constitutes both a link and a barrier between the community and the sacred. To even so much as represent this extraordinary victim the ritual victim must belong both to the community and to the sacred.

It should now be clear why ritual victims tend to be drawn from categories that are neither outside nor inside the community, but marginal to it: slaves, children, livestock. This marginal quality is crucial to the proper functioning of the sacrifice.

If the victim is to polarize the aggressive tendencies of the community and effect their transfer to himself, continuity must be maintained. There must be a "metonymic" relationship between members of the community and ritual victims. There must also be discontinuity. The victim must be neither too familiar to the community nor too foreign to it. . . .

The mechanism of the surrogate victim is redemptive twice over: by promoting unanimity it quells violence on all fronts, and by preventing an outbreak of bloodshed within the community it keeps the truth about men from becoming known. The mechanism transposes this truth to the realm of the divine, in the form of an inscrutable god. . . .

In the evolution from ritual to secular institutions men gradually draw away from violence and eventually lose sight of it; but an actual break with violence never takes place. That is why violence can always stage a stunning, catastrophic comeback. The possibility of such an occurrence conforms to the dire predictions of divine vengeance that are to be found in every religious system.

Counterpoint:
The Festival in Light of the Theory
of the Three Milieus: A Critique
# of Girard's Theory of Ritual Scapegoating

RICHARD STIVERS

Richard Stivers teaches sociology at Illinois State University in Normal, Illinois. He has published the following works: *Evil in Modern Myth and Ritual, Hair of the Dog: Irish Drinking and American Stereotype, The Culture of Cynicism: American Morality in Decline,* and *Technology as Magic: The Triumph of the Irrational.*

RENE GIRARD has challenged his critics to accept his hypothesis about mimetic desire and violent scapegoating as the origin of ritual and of culture itself or to propose an alternative explanation. This challenge is to be understood in the spirit of humility about his theory, for he is willing to enter into genuine dialogue about his seminal idea. I accept his challenge, not by rejecting his idea, but by modifying his hypothesis in light of an equally startling one—Ellul's theory of the three milieus.

Girard's hypothesis, that ritual scapegoating is a cultural solution to the contagious conflict engendered by mimetic desire, purports to be universal in regard to history and human nature, at least until the advent of an irreversible event. It is a solution that defies conscious criticism until the texts of the Old and New Testament

Reprinted from Richard Stivers, "The Festival in Light of the Theory of the Three Milieus: A Critique of Girard's Theory of Ritual Scapegoating," Journal of the American Academy of Religion, *LXI/3 (1991): 505–538.*

expose ritual killing as scapegoating. Until that time human nature appears to be cast adrift in a torrent of mimetic desire only to be saved from universal spiraling violence through ritual acts of scapegoating. With the revelation of ritual killing as scapegoating, there is the opportunity for humans to confront both their violence and the violent solution to their violence.

I maintain that Girard's theory fits only part of history and that the realization of ritual killing as scapegoating is due less to Biblical revelation than to radical changes in history. In order to support my thesis I draw upon Jacques Ellul's theory of the three milieus.[1] Ellul's is a theory of history, but one that is *not* finalistic; it is dialectical at the level of existence. Unlike Girard, who posits a universal human nature, Ellul assumes one that changes as its life-milieu changes. The milieu, in part a human creation, becomes an objective the origin of the force with which humans interact. This, I take it, is sacred, the original act of reification.

I propose, then, to accept Girard's hypothesis in its entirety for the milieu of society but to reject it in respect to the earlier milieu of nature and the later milieu of technology. I argue that both desire and the sacred are experienced in relation to their various milieus and are best understood in the context of the ritualized festival, the meaning of which, in turn, changes according to its milieu. I begin with a summary of Girard's theory of mimetic desire and ritual scapegoating, proceed to a presentation of Ellul's theory of history, and ultimately place the two theories in juxtaposition to yield a theory of the sacred and of the ritualized festival.

Girard's Theory of Mimetic Desire and Ritual Scapegoating

Girard discovered mimetic desire, at least the tacit conception such, in certain great works of literature—Shakespeare, Cervantes, Dostoevsky. Later he examined sacrificial rites in the context of religious myths and brilliantly articulated a theory of the relationship between mimetic desire and ritual sacrifice.

Mimetic desire is desire complicated by competition for the object of desire. Desire becomes mimetic when one desires what someone else desires; the other becomes a model for me: I desire to be like the person who desires what I now desire. I am thus attracted to this other person. Concurrently, however, this other is a rival: we both desire the same object. The object of desire grows in importance as the competition for it intensifies.

My rival gives two messages: be like me; do not be like me. The rival is flattered at first by imitation, for everyone wants to be admired; the initial feeling of pride is quickly countered by the fear of losing the object of common desire. As a rival, the other is an obstacle to the realization of desire. Hence, I am repelled by my rival. Attraction and repulsion.

Mimetic rivalry is contagious, as is the violence it engenders.[2] Violence is itself mimetic. I respond to your violent act with a similar act of my own. We become like each other in our violence. Still others enter the fray, for each momentary victory attracts new opponents. This is the mimetic crisis: the certain prospect of widespread violence with no apparent solution.

A solution emerges spontaneously, one that is the originary act from which ritual, religion, and society itself spring forth. The solution is a collective murder that both ends the violence and symbolically unites the remaining competitors—the killing of a common enemy, *a scapegoat*.[3] What may appear as an arbitrary act is not recognized as such by the collaborators; the scapegoat is not recognized as scapegoat. For the act of ritual killing to be effective as an agent of unification, it must not be recognized as an act of scapegoating. The scapegoat will be viewed as the source of all evil and thus as one who deserves to be killed.

In *The Scapegoat,* Girard explains the stereotypes of persecution by which a scapegoat is selected. The first stereotype is that of the crisis. Some event perceived as momentous, externally or internally provoked, causes people to act increasingly similarly, such as hoarding food in time of famine. Social order is invariably based upon structural and cultural differences that translate into different but complementary actions. Consequently, a great similarity in action is tantamount to social disorder. The second stereotype is about the "crime" that precipitated the homogeneity of behavior, the loss of social differences. The crime has a trail that leads to the perpetrator(s). The third stereotype concerns universal signs for the choice of the scapegoat. The victims are always those who are different, whether ethnically, culturally, or physically; the differences must be readily observable. The scapegoat is not consciously accused of being different but rather of "crimes that eliminate distinction." The eliminated distinctions are those between good and evil and between social ranks. The victim is ultimately condemned for not being different in a manner appropriate to cultural assumptions.

Here is the crux of the matter. As Girard explains, there are two kinds of differences—within and without the system. Diversity is a necessary component of social life: everyone has the need to appear different from others in some respects. Concurrently there must be a larger unity that envelops the various diversities and makes sense of them.[4]

By identifying a victim as the cause of the cause of disorder in society, as responsible for the original crisis (famine, plague, poisoning) that in turn leads to the crisis of contagious violent behavior, the scapegoaters are simultaneously establishing boundaries between the system and what lies outside and reestablishing diversity of action within the system. The scapegoat belongs outside the system because he caused the individuals within the system to shed their diversity and become dangerously alike.

Girard argues that ritual scapegoating, sacrifice, and rites of all sorts have their origin in an act of killing. The murder of the scapegoat unites the members of the society by permitting evil to be expelled. Society cannot confront the arbitrary nature of its violence and of its own complicity in the contagious violence preceding the original act of scapegoating. Hence religious myths conceal the act of murder as scapegoating; instead they represent the murdered as fully deserving to be killed. Simultaneously, however, the ritual victim is sacralized, transformed into a deity who now can be made to work for the benefit of society. For instance, in the Seneca myth of creation, after the good twin (the Creator) defeats his brother the evil twin (the Great World Rim Dweller), a pact is made between the evil twin and the Seneca. In return for food and supplications, the evil twin would "cure incurable disease, avert deadly tornadoes, cast out malevolent witches, and bring order to a whole community."[5]

The originary act of murder is not just kept alive in myth; it is systematically repeated in ritual. The reenactment is often a dramatic enactment rather than an actual repetition of the originary act of killing. There may likewise be a substitution for the ritual victim—animals, even crops, may become symbolic surrogates. In Girard's view, then, the ambiguity of sacred value resides in this fundamental contradiction: violence (evil) is the origin of order (good). If violence is sacred, it is so only because it is the source of unity, the order of all against one.[6]

Ritual scapegoating in the modern era, however, does not deify the victim. . . . The farther away from its violent origins a community and its religion get, the more ritual scapegoating loses its meaning and purpose. Eventually the point is reached where rituals that celebrate order and incorporation take precedence over rituals of disorder—those of transgression and those of sacrifice.[7] The time comes when scapegoating will be justified for political reasons.

Yet it is not the passage of time alone that desacralizes ritual scapegoating; rather it is the New Testament, the story of Christ, Girard argues.[8] In this nonsacrificial rendering of the New Testament, Girard attempts to demonstrate that Christ's purpose was not to become the perfect sacrificial victim, to atone for human sin, to make reparation to the Father, instead it was to overcome violence and to establish an existential paradigm of Christian love: to love one's enemy, even one's scapegoaters. In so doing, Christ exposed scapegoating as scapegoating, as an act of total duplicity. Whether the scapegoat was guilty of his purported crime is irrelevant—in Christ's case there was no crime of any kind—for the scapegoat has heaped upon his head the problems and sins of everyone. In the logic of scapegoating the crime of the one is the cause of the misery of the multitude. The New Testament (and the Old Testament to a lesser extent) permits us to establish the concept of the scapegoat. As Girard maintains, from this moment on, scapegoating can readily be understood for what it is. Its efficacy is now only transitory. Yet the violence is not abated because of this knowledge about the inner workings of scapegoating; it only becomes more diffuse. As Girard says at the close of *The Scapegoat,* to this knowledge must be added the will to forgive.[9]

Ellul's Theory of the Three Milieus

In order to lay a historical foundation for examining Girard's theory, which is essentially metahistorical, we need to consider French historian and sociologist Jacques Ellul's theory of the three milieus. Ellul's concept of milieu is as precise as permitted by such a broad phenomenon.[10] A milieu is an environment, at once both material and symbolic, in which humans face their most formidable problems and from which they derive the means of survival and the meaning of life. A milieu has three basic characteristics: immediacy, sustenance and peril, and mediation. We are in immediate and direct relationship with our milieu; it forces us to adapt, to conform, just as surely as we manipulate it. From the milieu we derive all that we need to live—sustenance for the body and the spirit: food, clothing, shelter, order, and meaning. Concurrently, however, the milieu is the greatest threat to human existence, as in pestilence, famine, poisons, wild animals, political strife,

war, pollution. The milieu, then, is *ambiguous* in value and produces an *ambivalent* reaction on our part—attraction and revulsion, desire and fear. This, I think, is the fundamental reason for the ambiguity of the sacred, which will be discussed in greater detail later.

A milieu is composed of two basic ingredients: meaning and power. Insofar as it is symbolic, a milieu is a human creation. The power of the milieu is harnessed for human ends; still, as an objective power it is not fully or even largely under conscious control. The dominant power of a milieu assumes one of three forms: nature, society, or technology. In the first instance, the power is a given. We exist in relation to the power of nature, and about this relationship symbolization first occurs. The power of society and that of technology (as a system) are human creations, but they are experienced in holistic fashion as objective forces; they are reified. In Ellul's theory, then, humans have lived in three milieus—nature, society, and technology. Yet this is no finalist theory of history in which the third stage represents the culmination of history; moreover, there is no deterministic principle that underlays the process.

Each subsequent milieu, e.g., society in relation to nature, mediates the preceding one, rendering it an indirect force. The preceding milieu becomes an ideological *model* for the subsequent milieu, thereby providing an illusion of where power resides. In dialectical fashion, however, it is actually the subsequent milieu that is used to interpret the preceding one. For example, in the milieu of society, nature is actually read through society; it is anthropomorphized. Therefore, nature as a model for society is to a great extent a nature that is already a reflection of society.

To these three characteristics of a milieu we can add one that is implicit in Ellul's formulation: regeneration or renewal. Each milieu has a different principle by which it is regenerated. For nature the principle of regeneration is the feast; for society, it is sacrifice; for technology, it is consumption. . . .

The Festival: The Sacred, Regeneration, and Desire

In the previous section I unequivocally accept Girard's thesis of ritual scapegoating as the origin of society. Furthermore, I agree with his theory of mimetic desire and the nexus between the two. I do not, however, think that the theory of mimetic desire and ritual scapegoating applies either to the milieu of nature or to that of technology. This in no way takes away from Girard's achievement; rather it establishes its temporal boundaries. I have already made a step in this direction by arguing that the feast is the principle of regeneration in the milieu of nature, just as sacrifice is in the milieu of society. Let us now examine the sacred, desire, and the principle of regeneration in each of the three milieus as a way of developing a theory of the festival.

The sacred is in the most general sense the life-milieu. What better fits Eliade's definition of the sacred as power and reality than the milieu? That the milieu places us in an unresolvable situation of nurture and danger is the source of the ambiguity of the sacred. Caillois' theory of the sacred explores this basic ambiguity: the sacred is both that which is holy and unsullied and that which is evil and defiling; likewise the profane is that which is evil and defiling and the neutral. His deft linguistic analysis reveals that rather than two terms—sacred and profane—there are actually three terms—sacred of respect, sacred of transgression, and profane. The term sacred of transgression is implicit in the natural languages he examined; hence it existed without conceptualization. The idea of a sacred of transgression is embedded in the meaning common to the ambiguous terms sacred and profane—defilement.[11] The fundamental tension a milieu creates is responsible for the ambivalence toward the sacred: attraction and repulsion, fascination and fear.

Both Caillois and Eliade understood the ambiguity of the sacred as being both chaos and creation, with the latter emerging from the former and requiring periodic renewal. Nature was their model of the sacred because they assumed that it was the model of the people they studied. Moreover, they understood that nature and secondarily society consist of two opposing forces so linked that the renewal of the milieu involved the movement from the one pole (chaos, evil, death) to the other pole (creation, good, life). What is revealed here is the experience of a milieu as a dynamic rather than a static phenomenon. The milieu exists and renews itself by virtue of the passage from one pole to its opposite.

In the prehistoric period, nature is experienced as sacred, manifested in specific hierophanies. The two cosmic poles that organize the milieu of nature are life and death. The principle of regeneration is the feast, the ritualized meal. Food (especially meat when available) and eating symbolize the movement from death to life and permit a certain communion with what is eaten. The more deeply immersed humans are in the milieu of nature, the more important the ritual meal is over against the act of killing. The festival, *which is the ritualization of the experience of regeneration,* is, in this instance, the feast.

In the historic period, both nature and society are experienced as sacred, but nature has the face of society. Nature is read through society but concomitantly nature is the ideological arena onto which social conflicts are projected. The deities in nature face the same moral and political tensions and conflicts that humans do. Sacred history, the history of the ancestors, becomes more important than the cosmogony. Eventually the earthly king becomes sacred and may even be seen to be the ruler of nature. The aristocratic class may be viewed as quasi-sacred, as descendants of the ancestors. Finally, the church as a religious society may unwittingly be regarded as sacred.

Politics and morality arise in the milieu of society to the extent that the most pressing problems become moral. In this milieu the polar tension is between good and evil. Strictly speaking the terms sacred and profane only arise in this milieu and have a decidedly ethical cast. Eliade observes that, until the undesired parts of life were regarded as *evil,* they were "accepted as constitutive and unexceptionable moments of the cosmic totality."[12] The idea of retribution is seen to be universal, encompassing both nature and society. Natural disasters and failures become a punishment for transgressions. Girard's theory accounts for the principle of regeneration in the milieu of society—human sacrifice. Sacrifice as scapegoating represents the expulsion of evil. Caillois implicitly understood this when he said that a theory of the festival would have to be "correlated with a theory of sacrifice." Sacrifice, he observed, "is akin to the inner mechanism that sums it up and gives it meaning."[13]

The festival is enlarged now to include, in addition to the feast and the hunt, scapegoating and every form of transgression—the violation of taboo, role-reversal, and so forth. To chaos, suffering, and death is now added moral chaos or evil. We may even speculate that the taboos surrounding the hunted as embodied in the "master of the animals" are the imposition of moral norms within the milieu of society on a much earlier and essentially amoral activity. The taboo is itself an artifact of the milieu of society.

Insofar as food, animals, and survival remain a central and immediate concern, society has to be accounted for mythologically from nature, e.g., out of the body of the slain demi-deity, and the form time assumes continues to be that of nature, even though the content is the sacred history of the tribe. Nature is reduced to the distant origin of society and, like the high god, its paramount symbol, it recedes into the background as the more immediate and serious political and moral issues occupy the foreground.

In the post-historic period both society and technology are experienced as sacred, but now society is read through technology. The paramount political and moral problems are being transformed into technological problems to be solved by technical experts, e.g., the medicalization of moral issues.[14] Technology is both power and reality today. Although at one level technology (as rational, efficient, objectified

method) is abstract, at another level it is concrete-technological objects, consumer goods. These act as hierophanies.

A technological society is one whose chief value, purpose, or goal is efficiency, maximum production and maximum consumption. Over against rational technique stands inefficiency as instinct, the will to power, eros. These opposite poles of a technological milieu are, however, at a deeper level related. First, as Ellul notes,[15] technology and instinctual desire form a dialectic: desire today can only be satisfied by technology, and technology can only advance by the constant stimulation of appetite. Jean Brun first called attention to the paradox that the cold, impersonal, abstract force of technology does not finally appeal to reason and moderation but to our desire for power and possessions. Technology as a system is the "head of Apollo" superimposed upon instinct, the will to power, the "body of Dionysius."[16]

The more reason becomes objectified and collectivized in the technological system, the smaller the role for subjective reason based on symbolically meaningful experiences becomes. This tends to enlarge the play of irrational or instinctual forces. Moreover, the cumulative impact of technology acts as a repressive force; the more technology demands of us in terms of regulations, schedules, and coordination, the more we apparently need to escape this kind of rationality by plunging into the irrational, into random sensations.[17] The result is a society that is at once both extraordinarily rational and irrational.

The instincts most associated with the will to power are sexuality and aggression. Indeed sex and violence can be interpreted as an ersatz sacred of transgression over against the technological system.[18] As forms of inefficiency they are the negative to the positive pole of efficiency (technology). If a milieu is comprised of two poles in tension, and the principle of regeneration involves the movement from the negative to the positive, then here that principle is *experimental consumption.*

The sacred power of technology becomes manifest in technological objects (consumer goods). These hierophanies of consumption become differentially sacred depending upon individual circumstances. We have already seen, however, that technology, while manifestly opposed to instinct, is perfectly suited to it at a deeper level because both represent the will to power. Moreover, advertising uses sex and violence to sell these consumer goods, for instance, the eroticizing of the automobile. Even more important than advertising's direct use of sex and violence is its indirect use: the consumer goods of advertising are placed in spatial relationship to the sex and violence saturated programs of the mass media. In this sense programs are an ad for advertisements. In consuming the technological object we are indirectly consuming the instinctual power of sex and violence. Enlarge the sphere of the instinctual, and the desire to possess and use technological objects increases. The motto is: the more we consume (if only vicariously) sex and violence, the more technological objects we will consume; the more objects we consume, the more instinctual power we possess.

Caillois[19] observes that excess is at the "heart of the festival." The more one pushes the negative pole, the greater the abundance at the positive pole. In the milieu of technology the festival is primarily centered in the excess of sex and violence in the mass media. As the ritualization of the principle of regeneration, the festival always begins with the negative pole—death, evil, the instinctual (sex and violence)—in the movement to the positive pole—life, good, efficiency (abundance of technological objects).

In the milieu of technology, society is still sacred but in a secondary way. Societal power remains formidable and is organized around the poles of the nation-state and revolution.[20] The technologization of society aggravates political problems by reducing politics purely to a matter of power. With the disappearance of hierarchy (in Dumont's sense), there is nothing left but competition for power among special interest groups only partially controlled by the political state. As de Jouvenal has clearly shown, political revolutions in the past several centuries have only led to an increase in state power. Just as technology *effectively* operates outside the moral domain, so does politics today.

Scapegoating continues in the post-historic period (the milieu of technology), but in greatly diffused and secularized forms. Most of the conflicts over gender, ethnicity, and race, for instance, have gone beyond the point of legitimate grievances to that of scapegoating. With the serious decline of a common morality in the milieu of technology, all struggles tend to be conflicts over power. The only serious issue today for any group that has been previously disadvantaged is the achievement of an equality of power. A full equality of power, of course, cannot be achieved without complete homogeneity—the standardization Kierkegaard and Tocqueville feared.

Girard notes the decline of effective scapegoating in the modern era but attributes it largely to a gradual desacralization of the scapegoating mechanism.[21] This does not suggest a decline in the amount of scapegoating, which may actually increase, but rather points to its transitory character. I concur but have arrived at a different reason for this desacralization. While I agree that scripture exposes scapegoating for what it is and that scapegoating is only effective when it remains unconscious, I think that the primary reason is to be found in the gradual transition to the milieu of technology, beginning in the nineteenth century, which replaced scapegoating with another principle as the foundation of order. As society becomes subordinate to technology, scapegoating has less to do with order and consensus and more to do with the endless group competition for the power that actually resides in the technological system and the political state (in a secondary way).

Yet politics (morality) remains on an illusory ideological level, an arena in which we attempt to resolve problems that are almost exclusively technological. As we have seen, nature once provided the ideological and idealistic backdrop for society; now society does the same for technology.

At this point we must confront Girard's concept of mimetic desire. This, too, I find to be peculiar to the milieu of society. My argument is that imitation and desire, like ritual and the sacred, exist in relation to the dominant life-milieu. Moreover, it is only in the milieu of society that imitation and desire initially have different objects.

In the milieu of nature, humans were so immersed in and dependent upon nature that there was little if any awareness of the distinction between animal and human. As previously mentioned, the earliest cave art has animals almost exclusively as its subjects. When humans first enter the artistic scene in the Upper Paleolithic period it is in ceremonial relationship with animals, on an equal footing with them.[22] There is even some evidence that humans imitated the appearance of animal by wearing animal skins and so forth. My conjecture is that both imitation and desire were affixed to nature. Desire that has not been so decisively influenced by a social milieu that it becomes the desire to be like someone else centers on the possession and consumption of those natural objects that insure survival and bring pleasure. Natural desire and imitation are channeled into the feast: I become what I eat.

In the milieu of society, imitation and desire are both separate and united. Girard has described the process by which the initial object of desire and the rival for this object become conflated. My desire is now the desire to imitate my rival, the obstacle to the initial object of desire. Or better yet, I desire the object of my rival's desire because I desire to be like him. The initial separation of object of desire and imitation is finally overcome. Girard's great insight reinterpreted is that desire finally comes to reflect the milieu of society. Were it not for objects of desire that are distinct from the rival to begin with, there would be no imitation nor social desire. Only in the milieu of society does the individual

perceive a clear distinction between nature and society, on the one hand, and society and technology, on the other hand. One can readily understand how social or mimetic desire and the rivalry for status is a deadly problem. Someone must be eliminated—the scapegoat. Mimetic desire is channeled into ritual scapegoating: I become and do not become (the ambivalence toward the scapegoat who performs the "service" of restoring order) what I sacrifice.

In the milieu of technology desire and imitation are united as they were in the milieu of nature; there is no separation even initially, between the two. The technological milieu consists both of a system of rationalized methods and technological objects and the universe of visual images (especially in the media). Desire and imitation exist in relation to these, so in this milieu only technological objects and the material visual images that "represent" them are permitted.[23]

No one has understood this better than Guy Debord in Society of the Spectacle.[24] The spectacle as the "image-object," the visual image of a commodity, is the main product today. The spectacle is the "catalogue of commodities" intended for both real vicarious and consumption (through visualization). The spectacle includes both commodities as visual images and material visual images of commodities. Reality is experienced in and through the spectacle. Two aspects of this require further clarification: How have humans come to regard themselves and others as commodities, consumer goods, and technological objects, and why have the material visual images of the mass media become more real than reality itself? . . .

Technology's mediation of human relationships makes life more abstract and impersonal. The visual images of the mass media, however, provide an ersatz reality often more emotionally satisfying than the reality of our own lives. Reality is on television and in the movies. As I argued earlier, the visual images of the media have deconstructed symbolic language so that the images ultimately are only images of possessions (objects) or images of power, objects (human or otherwise) acting in relation to other objects—acts of possession, consumption, control, or violence. We become spectators of life, visually consuming the exciting actions of objects. These image objects that comprise the spectacle are the stuff of both desire and imitation. . . .

Not just imitation but desire as well is unleashed by technology and visual images. Marx observed that desire increases with the growth in technology. The more technological objects we see, the more our desire is titillated. Ellul observes that the enormous proliferation of visual images results in our "demand for everything immediately."25 . . .

Mimetic desire and rivalry are an artifact of the milieu of society. Competition for survival in the milieu of nature was competition with nature itself. Because of the anticipated abundance of resources and the small size of and dispersion of human groups, conflict between humans was controlled in part by the redistribution of food. In the milieu of technology, where desire is unleashed in full force along with the imitation that accompanies it, there is savage competition for consumer goods and services, but the object of imitation is far removed in these object-images of the media. The violence that ensues is not mimetic, but only a competition for scarce resources. Technology and the political state have only been partially successful in controlling this competition.

The festival is the occasion for fulfillment of desire and the regeneration of the milieu. It is sacred time, and as such it produces what Victor Turner calls *communitas,* the sense of being all in one and one in all that comes from excess and renewal, that which is out of the ordinary. There is no single act or principle of origin that can explain the festival, for it is relative to the human life-milieu.

NOTES

1. Jacqques Ellul, *What I Believe,* trans. Geoffrey Bromiley (Grand Rapids, MI: Eerdmans, 1989), pp. 89–140.

2. Paul Dumochel, "Introduction," in *Violence and Truth,* ed. Paul Dumochel (Stanford: Stanford University Press, 1985), pp. 11–17.

3. Rene Girard, *The Scapegoat,* trans. Yvonne Freccero (Baltimore: Johns Hopkins University Press, 1986).

4. Willem Vanderburg, *The Growth of Minds and Cultures* (Toronto: University of Toronto Press, 1985), pp. 27–29.

5. Anthony Wallace, *The Death and Rebirth of the Seneca* (New York: Vintage Books, 1969), p. 92.

6. Rene Girard, *Things Hidden Since the Foundation of the World,* trans. Stephen Bann and Michael Metteer (Stanford: Stanford University Press, 1987), p. 32.

7. Idem, *The Scapegoat,* p. 79.

8. Idem, *Things Hidden,* Book II, chapter 1.

9. Idem, *The Scapegoat,* chap. 15.

10. Ellul, pp. 99–103.

11. Roger Caillois, *Man and the Sacred,* trans. Meyer Barash (New York: Free Press, 1959), chap. 1.

12. Mircea Eliade, *The Quest* (Chicago: University of Chicago Press, 1969), p. 174.

13. Caillois, p. 185.

14. Jacques Ellul, *The Political Illusion,* trans. Konard Kellen (New York: Knopf, 1967).

15. Idem, *The Technological System,* trans. Joachim Neugroschel (New York: Continuum, 1980), pp. 316–18.

16. Idem, *The Betrayal of the West,* trans. Matthew O'Connell (New York: Seabury, 1978), p. 166.

17. Idem, *The Technological Society,* trans. John Wilkinson (New York: Knopf, 1964), pp. 387–427.

18. Idem, *The New Demons,* trans. C. Edward Hopkin (New York: Seabury, 1975); Richard Stivers, *Evil in Modern Myth and Ritual* (Athens: University of Georgia Press, 1982).

19. Caillois, p. 98.

20. Ellul, *The New Demons,* pp. 82–87.

21. Girard, *Things Hidden,* p. 126.

22. Alexander Marshack, *The Roots of Civilization* (New York: McGraw-Hill, 1972), p. 272.

23. Ellul, *The Technological System,* p. 47.

24. Guy Debord, *Society of the Spectacle* (Detroit: Black and Red, 1983), paragraph 15.

25. Jacques Ellul, *The Humiliation of the Word,* trans. Joyce Hanks (Grand Rapids, MI: Eerdmans, 1985), p. 209.

From *Resurrecting the Body: Feminism, Religion, and Psychotheraphy*

NAOMI R. GOLDENBERG

WE HAVE BEEN PROGRESSIVELY dehumanizing ourselves by taking our human senses, human functions, human parts and abstracting them from our human bodies. We then create machines to do our seeing, listening, touching, talking, or thinking for us in a more perfect form. I see nothing wrong with this when we use machines to support and enhance life—as in the case of artificial limbs or with the use of labor-saving technology. The problem arises when we begin to envy the machines—when we try to imitate them and thus model our selves on inanimate objects. We then lose touch with what it is to be human.

But it isn't just with machines that we dissociate ourselves from our humanness. I think there are certain habits deep in Western thought that we must examine. There are customary ways of thinking that encourage us to flee from what is human and to despise ourselves. I think that we fall into these habits—these flights from people—whenever we imagine ourselves in any fashion as controlled or influenced by purposeful entities outside ourselves. Religions usually call these things gods; in philosophy, Plato calls them forms; and in psychology, Jung calls them archetypes. By treating these things as real, we distort our world and dehumanize ourselves.

I think that we need to shrink from theories that foster contempt for physical life. At present, our human race is threatening the entire world with both nuclear holocaust and chemical pollution. We have become a species which spends approximately half of our collective energy and resources in devising our own destruction. I am not at all sure that intellectual practice can do much to assuage such danger. But we have to try. We must immerse ourselves in theories that support life.

I suggest that many of our Western religious traditions can now offer little help in formulating strategies for living. The concept of a God who is outside the context of human contingency is itself a machine fantasy. *Deus est machina.* By imagining any rules or laws, any propensity toward good or evil, any knowledge or wisdom, as coming from outside a human sphere, we fuel the modern contempt for what is human. A transcendent godhead is an idea we can no longer afford.

But what then? What sort of theory can now carry a salvific message? I suggest that such theory lies in a place theology has shunned—the human body. Instead of theology, I recommend two bodies of theory that appreciate human physicality: psychoanalysis and feminism.

Theology Versus Psychoanalysis

The idea of finding grounds for an optimistic view of human possibility within the corpus of psychoanalytic theory is ridiculous from the standpoint of traditional theology. It is generally concluded among theologians who discuss Freud that if one stays with the psychoanalytic perspective the world looks quite bleak and life is emptied of hope. . . .

I suggest that the conflict between psychoanalysis and religion can be usefully seen as a conflict about the body and what the body

Reprinted from Naomi R. Goldenberg, Resurrecting the Body: Feminism, Religion, and Psychotheraphy *(New York: Crossroads Publishing Company, 1993).*

knows. Religion, on the one hand, sees the source of some kinds of knowledge—namely, "religious" knowledge—as lying outside the body. It maintains that there is a purposeful reality external to human beings which can afflict, direct, or instruct human existence. Psychoanalysis, on the other hand, refuses to accept an external source for any human knowledge. Psychoanalysis sees human knowledge as growing out of wholly human experience. For psychoanalysis, the word "knowledge" is similar to the word "thought" or "idea." All knowledge, all thought, all ideas come from somatic sources. To put it very simply, and I think, not too simply, in psychoanalysis all knowledge is carnal knowledge. . . .

"Body" in Religion and Psychoanalysis

Body certainly is hopeless if we conceive it in terms of the major traditions of Western philosophy. The dominant theme in Western thought since Plato has been that the body is a vehicle for a higher entity—mind or soul. The body is thought of as being a temporary place where mind, soul or psyche resides. General knowledge, it is believed, develops in the mind. Religious knowledge, however, is thought of as emanating from something even higher than mind or soul. Various terms—gods, forms, archetypes—are used to refer to the thing outside of mind, the thing which informs the mind.

I am simplifying the differences among these terms in order to point out a basic difference between a religious notion of the person and a psychoanalytic one. There is always a duality about the human being in religions such as Christianity, Islam, and Judaism; in philosophies that are religious, such as Platonism; and in psychologies that are religious, such as Jungian psychology. Something—usually mind or soul—is contrasted with body, and is then seen as better, nobler, cleaner, and ultimately of a different character or substance than the body. In such religious views of the person, the higher part is

seen as being closer to whatever is accorded divine, directive status. The soul is closer to the forms. The psyche is linked with the archetypes. And mind or reason is joined with God.

If we accept this familiar dualistic view of the person, the body becomes unimportant. This happens because all the truly fine things about human beings are seen as coming from the mind or soul which in turn is believed to have obtained the good things from something wholly transcendent to anything physical. I would argue that this view of the person as having two parts, one of which is "better" in the sense of being closer to God, holds true in general terms for both Christianity and Judaism. In both religions, the flesh is seen as needing salvation. In Christianity, the flesh is redeemed by Jesus' sacrifice; in Judaism, it is saved by adherence to God's rules for living. In both religions, the body is slighted because something other than body—indeed, something other than human—is placed in charge. . . .

In contrast to this religious conception of body, there is the psychoanalytic view. In psychoanalysis, the body becomes more complex because the mind is never separated from it. All of the fine things about human beings—their intellects, their morality, their aesthetic sensibilities—arise from bodily sources. Many have seen this analytic view as reductive because mind and soul are reduced to body. I would put it another way. Instead of reducing the mind, psychoanalysis elevates the body by granting it all the qualities which most of Western philosophy reserves for the mind.

The respect of psychoanalysis for the complexity of body lies in its origins as a mode of treatment for the bodily ailments of women in the nineteenth century. . . .

No matter how complex Freud's later theory became, it never lost this original focus. It never departed from the notion that the flesh is cognizant of its history. In his later works, Freud expressed the hope that scientific progress would one day enable psychoanalysis to formulate psychological statements in physiological terms. . . . Later, in 1939, he explained that psychoanalysis identifies "what is truly psychical" with somatic phenomena. The concept of the unconscious, he suggested, is how analysis refers to somatic processes which future research might name more precisely.[1]

The early discovery that memory resides in the body means that, in psychoanalysis, every physical experience is metaphoric. For example, in psychoanalysis, sex can never be a simple activity of the genitals. Instead, analysis sees sex as involved with earlier experiences of nutrition, excretion, muscular excitation, and sensory activity. Genital sexuality, just as other physical experiences, reverberates with echoes of childhood and infancy. For psychoanalysis, the flesh can never be literal since, as long as it lives, it teems with past memories and wishes for the future. Body is forever imaging its desires and forever elaborating its past.

Thus, in a Freudian perspective, the body becomes the complex context of all experience. The body is seen as charged with an intellect or, more accurately, with an energy that is constantly expressing somatic history. Thought is one form of this expression; action is another. For psychoanalysis, thought, like action, is itself an activity of the body. It is this notion of body as the matrix of human cognition that, I suggest, must animate modern philosophy, if that philosophy is to foster respect for life.

Thoughts, Words, and Physical History

The relationship between thought as expressed in words and bodily life is necessarily stressed in psychoanalysis since treatment aims to alter physical conditions via language. . . . For analysis, then, mental phenomena such as words, thoughts, or ideas are never disembodied. Rather, they are conditioned both by somatic drives and by the past physical and social context in which those drives were experienced.

Freud believes that for thought to be healthy, it must always connect with the experiential context from which it arises. For example, he describes schizophrenia as a condition in which the link between words and what they represent is severed. "When we think in abstractions," he writes, "there is a danger that we may neglect the relations of words to unconscious thing-presentations, and it must be confessed that the expression and content of our philosophizing then begins to acquire an unwelcome resemblance to the mode of operation of schizophrenics."[2] This stress on seeking the origin of thought in past somatic experience explains Freud's attitude toward words as phenomena which lead backwards and which carry meaning because they are conditioned by memories, by sense perceptions, and by bodily history. . . .

Feminism, Psychoanalysis, and the Body

The movement which has a greater chance of bringing Western thought back to the body is feminism. Feminism can pervade society more than can psychoanalysis. The women's movement can reach beyond therapeutic consulting rooms and academic journals into the fabric of daily life. Although psychoanalysis can become part of feminism and thus share its impact, it has little chance of having significant influence on its own.

As I have said before, feminism can become a vehicle for psychoanalytic insight because psychoanalysis and feminism share the theme of sexuality.[3] Feminists uncover issues relating to sexuality and physicality in respected philosophical moral and religious systems, just as Freudians reveal physical and emotional motives behind the rational structures of culture. Both theories continually remind us of the bodily ideas concealed in the products and behavior of "higher" civilization.

Both psychoanalytic theory and feminist theory lead back to the body through their insistence on the importance and complexity of sexuality. Certainly, there are important differences between the two outlooks. Psychoanalysis predates feminism and has so far failed to examine itself in the light of feminist argument. Reading Freud and many other psychoanalytic thinkers from a feminist perspective is as disturbing as it is revealing. Psychoanalytic literature is rife with male bias: bias toward male anatomy, traditional male roles, and ubiquitous male privilege. Sometimes Freud's sexism is merely funny, such as his warning to Wilhelm Fliess to keep the early drafts about the sexual etiology of the neuroses away from Fliess's "young wife."[4] But sometimes, Freud's sexism is maddening, such as his insistence on the moral inferiority of women.[5] These sexist origins make it imperative for psychoanalysis to reconsider its appraisal of the female body and, concomitantly, to reevaluate its view of the female psyche.

By combining the perspectives of feminism and psychoanalysis on the topic of sexuality, gaps in the outlooks of both can be filled in. . . .

The deep psychic association of women with body could bring the consciousness of body to much scholarship in the decades ahead, if feminist theory becomes more a part of academic disciplines. In a sense, attending to women's writing is listening to the body talk. What will the body say that is new?[6] It is most likely that women will actually write things that are very old. One of the most valuable contributions feminism can make to discourse is that of fostering writing and speaking styles that reveal their subjective origins in the personal and collective past. Feminist writing at its best, I think, can shatter the illusion of objectivity which turns so much modern scholarship into mechanized jargon. It can return rationality to its roots in emotion and body.

I visualize this goal for feminism through an image from Greek history. At certain times in the long history of the Delphic oracle, the female priestess known as the Pythia would prophesize in ecstatic gibberish. A male priest would then interpret her utterances and give the petitioner the oracles reply. It was the priest's job to make sense of the priestess's babble.

This relationship between pythia and priest typifies the stereotyped roles played by men and women throughout much of history. Women play the role of the fecund yet inarticulate body—full of magic and mysterious wisdom. Men, in contrast, play the role of the "Word"—full of meaning and objective definitions. One could say that women, forced to play the pythias of civilization, have spoken in the language of primary process—immediate, emotional and physical. Men, in contrast, have spoken in the language of secondary process with a style more distant, cool and detached. It occurs to me that the role of the Pythia was played by all the female hysterics whose ramblings and bodily postures were then interpreted by Freud and Breuer, who became the high priests of psychoanalysis. Analysis itself thus became an activity which interprets primary process thinking in terms of secondary process language. Its power derives from a melding of gender-specific modes of expression.

The widespread illusion that primary and secondary process thought are separate—or, to put it another way, the perception that fantasy is separate from objective thought—is sustained by the separation of men and women into rigid roles such as priest and pythia. Women are seen as the inarticulate body because women form the human universe when babbling is the only human speech possible. The gibberish of primary process and the overwhelming physical desires of infancy are, at present, almost exclusively linked with women. When men share in the care of infants, the symbols of this early time will change. It will be possible to imagine men as body as well.

It is even just possible that shared childcare will not be necessary to alter our imagination. The symbolism of body and mind might well change from the direction of adulthood as women become more articulate, more obvious in every aspect of public culture.

In any case, the possibility of imagining body as male is not the most significant change that feminism could effect. As women speak more and are heard more in public settings, the human body could become increasingly coherent and increasingly influential. It could become more difficult to advocate philosophical systems in which words are far abstracted from their relationships to the somatic world. Hermeneutics might then discover the original text, that is, the human body. In the beginning was definitely not the Word. The biblical statement reverses the order. It is flesh that makes the words.

A new hermeneutics will have to recognize the perpetual subversion of the body. All our systems of thought, all our disciplines of knowledge, are perpetually, continually changing and thus perpetually and continually inaccurate. Our systems can only be approximations of our always desiring, always alive, very human bodies. Thus, paradoxically, when our systems become more approximate, and less sacred, they become truer and closer to life. . . .

The Return of the Goddess

. . . In addition to explaining how analytic thought can be used to understand the Goddess, I also intend to show how the Goddess movement can illuminate certain trends within psychoanalysis. To accomplish this dual purpose, I will concentrate first on four tendencies that I see as common to both ways of thinking. I suggest that anyone who thinks in the terms of either contemporary psychoanalytic theory or of the Goddess movement is urged (1) to focus on the past as a central source of meaning; (2) to focus on female images of power and desire and therefore to deconstruct central images of patriarchal authority; (3) to describe the individual as formed within the context of a community; and (4) to recognize fantasy as a key structure of "rational" thought. . . .

The branch of psychoanalytic theory which is most relevant to feminist theology is object relations theory. This highly influential offshoot of earlier Freudian theory developed in Britain out of the work of analysts such as Melanie Klein,

W. R. D. Fairbairn, D. W. Winnicott, and Michael Bahnt.[7] Object relations theory is usually contrasted to the classical approach to psychoanalysis, which is often termed "instinct theory" or "drive theory." Instinct theory depicts the person as an individual, a separate being who is motivated by the vicissitudes of certain basic "drives" which are believed to be inherent in the human organism. In contrast, object relations theory stresses the interconnectedness of people. To an object relations analyst, a person is always seeking relationships with "objects"—that is, with people—with whom a shared world of feelings and activities can be constructed. In general, then, object relations theory focuses more on the human being in relationship to others, while instinct theory is more concerned with the psychodynamics of human subjects thought of as more or less discrete entities.[8]

Another difference between the approach of object relations and that of instinct theory, is that object relations tends to reach further back into childhood. Classical Freudian analysis had been chiefly interested in the human being after the age of five. In contrast, object relations theory began to stress the developmental significance of infancy and very early childhood. Contemporary object relations theorists conceptualize nearly every aspect of a person's behavior and character against the background of the earliest beginnings of her or his life. . . .

Female Prehistory and the Deconstruction of the Phallus

Even more significant than their shared reverence for the deep past is the fact that both thealogy and object relations theory agree on what, or rather who, is the most important part of the past. Object relations theory departs from classical analytic theory by replacing Freud's keen interest in the father with an intense preoccupation with the mother. Like the Goddess movement in religion, object relations theory places a woman at the beginning of the universe and thus champions a shift from an interest in male symbols to a focus on female ones. Both ways of thinking pose a challenge to the importance of the father. . . .

According to hypotheses framed by researchers into Goddess religion, Yahweh grew to power as a jealous God whose followers smashed the icons of those who worshiped female divinities tied to nature. Gradually, holidays which were once understood as marking the seasonal cycles of "mother earth" became joined to accounts of male triumphs. The Exodus story obscured tales of the goddesses and their festivals of spring. The winter solstice became identified with a military victory instead of with the birth of the child of the Goddess. A harvest celebration thanking the mother deities for food became an occasion to read a male God's commandments. As Christian symbolism became popular, Jesus replaced all the sons and lovers of the goddesses. He urged his followers to place more value on male words than on those "paps which gave thee suck." In later centuries, a male clergy nearly succeeded in erasing the contribution of Christian women from recorded history.[9] Complete submission to male authority became the only appropriate role for women. All the deities that represented the great Goddess—the independent, often dangerous virgins and the lusty, powerful mothers—were reduced to one Virgin Mother, whose most celebrated utterance is "Let it be done to me according to thy Will."

The Goddess movement proposes that sexual politics have formed the traditional religious myths of Western culture. Because Goddess sympathizers suspect that patriarchal symbols rest on a stratum that both suppresses and appropriates a female prehistory, they are led to question all the important rites and images of the dominant faiths. They wonder if the bar mitzvah might not be the glorified male counterpart of a ceremony marking the onset of menstruation.[10] They feel empathy and curiosity toward denigrated graven images such as the golden calf. They dare to ask just what was so awful about Jezebel, Vashti, and Lilith?[11] They

look at the Father, Son, and Holy Ghost and see another trinity—Diana, Luna, and Hecate.

This awareness of a possible female background to the symbols and customs of male power creates psychological distance from those symbols and customs. By raising the suspicion that solid male institutions are not all they have seemed or, rather, are more than they have seemed, Goddess ideology loosens the grip of masculine symbols upon the contemporary imagination. Both the facts and the fantasies of the Goddess movement function to crack the edifice of patriarchy by encouraging the emergence of suppressed patterns of language, visions, dreams, and theories.

I find a similar subversion of male discourse and symbols in the work of certain female theorists of psychoanalysis. Melanie Klein writes that the male fear of castration is actually derived from earlier anxiety about the disappearance of the mother's breast. Klein thinks that each infant sees the breast as a part of his or her own body— a part that sometimes vanishes to cause great discomfort. The male child transfers this early experience of bodily loss to his feelings about another physical protrusion, his penis.[12] Similarly, Klein believes that when penis-envy occurs in women, it leads back to a desire to possess the mother's breast. Thus, for her, the power behind the symbol of the penis in adulthood is explained by the earlier importance of the breast.[13]

More recently, Luce Irigaray presents another theory to account for the intense male fear of castration.[14] She suggests that the idea that a part of the body might be lost forever has its origin in the severing of the umbilical cord. Since a connection to the mother is lost when the umbilicus is snipped off, the cutting of the cord at the beginning of every life is traumatic. This event might well underlie all fears about the loss of pieces of the body. Irigaray's theory implies, I think, that for men, the penis may be the only way back to the umbilical cord [that] has been cut. While women have the option of closely identifying with their mothers, men's only hope of return lies in the penis. Since patriarchal culture restricts the ways in which men may be like their mothers, the penis becomes overvalued as the sole masculine tie to femininity. . . .

By pointing to a female background behind the prominent male icons of both religion and psychology, the Goddess movement and object relations theory work to displace the father from his domination of the symbolic order. Both bodies of theory express and accelerate the slow erosion of male authoritarianism in Western culture.

A Shared Vision of the Human Being in Community

Another similarity between Goddess religion and object relations theory is that both stress the dependence of human beings on their communities. Unlike much patriarchal philosophy, which emphasizes individualism and self-determination, Goddess religion and object relations theory teaches that people are created in large part by their relationships.

For object relations analysts, the focus on human life in community derives from the significance which the theory places on infancy and early childhood. Babies or young children simply cannot exist without the constant care and supervision of at least one adult, who is usually a woman. A baby is thus never a solitary being. . . .

The Goddess movement, like object relations theory in particular and feminist theory in general, is concerned with expanding awareness of the conditions which make lives what they are. Thealogy, however, focuses on some other, nonhuman aspects of the context of life. The Goddess movement takes seriously the ancient pagan perception that human life is part of a larger web of life which includes all of nature. Like the ecology movement, thealogy sees human life in a dynamic planetary context which is determined by the state of the water, the soil, and the air. The entire earth is conceptualized as the body of the Goddess and thus is sacred. No part of the ecosystem is separate from her, and thus no part of the material world is considered secular or profane. . . .

I suggest that the mutual concern of psychoanalysis and thealogy with articulating the context of human life arises because both philosophies center around the map of a powerful woman in the past. Since every human life begins in the body of a woman, the image of a woman, whether thought of as mother or as Goddess always points to an early history of connectedness: Mother-*mater*-matter-matrix. "Woman" is the stuff out of which all people are made. In the beginning was her flesh, and, after the beginning, she continues to suggest human historicity, to suggest human connection to and dependence upon the outside world. It is this deep memory of birth union, I think, which turns any serious reflection on women into a reflection on the interconnection of human beings with each other and with all the things which make up the body of the world. It is pre-birth experience and post-birth mothering which destine feminist theory to expand awareness of the context which supports everything human.

At a basic level, the image of woman is the image of human context—the image of human connection to the world. Object relations theory limits the image to mother and thus theorizes context somewhat narrowly as the mother-infant relationship. Thealogy extends the image to deity and thus envisions context more grandly as the planet as a whole. Both derive their insights into the matrices that support human life from an image of a woman-in-the-past. Classical Freudian psychoanalysis with its focus on an often absent *paterfamilias* and traditional religion with its focus on a father in heaven could never inspire similar reflection about the complex contingency of human existence.

Agreement that the Basis of Thought Lies in Fantasy

One aspect of the human context upon which both thealogians and analysts agree is fantasy. Both groups understand fantasy, or wish, as constituting the primary matrix for all mental processes.

In witchcraft, the cultivation of wishing pervades almost every practice. Goddess religion can often appear as "wishcraft" because it teaches women to use spells and rituals to express their hopes, ambitions, and desires. Much of the effectiveness of those "magical" practices can be explained by their ability to focus the mind and to mobilize willpower. Witches feel that a goal which can be visualized in detail is more likely to be a goal which can be reached. Thus they concentrate on representing wishes symbolically either in the form of physical objects such as amulets and talismans or in the choreography and incantations of ceremonies and rituals.

In addition to employing fantasy in religious practice, thealogians also use it to "do thealogy," that is, to theorize about the Goddess. Sometimes the idea of a matriarchy in the past is put forward as a wish about history—a desire to be realized in the present and future. . . .

Unlike the witches, object relations analysts do not believe that willpower can control fantasy. To the object relations analyst, the structure of a person's fantasy life is laid down in infancy and early childhood. . . . In object relations theory, a person's general attitude expresses the parameters of fantasies which have been sketched from the time of earliest infancy—a time when satisfaction depended on forces entirely outside each baby's control. Thus, to psychoanalysts, a person's attitude, inner world, and fantasy life are greatly influenced by her or his early environment and by the caregivers who shaped that environment. Analysts believe that a basic change in fantasy expression occurs only if something, such as analysis, effects a change in psychic dynamics. To them fantasy is too much a product of personal history to be seriously influenced by the rituals and spells employed by the Goddess worshipers.

Even though the analysts and the witches disagree about the malleability of fantasy, attitude, and expectation, they both maintain that the inner world of anticipation and wish is the basis of all human thought and action. Consciousness and directed rational thought are considered to be relatively superficial phenomena which derive from older, more encompassing unconscious structures. . . .

That which has been repressed is now returning. The contemporary focus on women in all areas of creative thought in all domains of the Muses—means that the sources of thought itself will become clearer. This is the real significance of the return of the Goddess. When theology becomes thealogy, the metaphysical comes home to the physical.

NOTES

1. Sigmund Freud, *The Standard Edition of the Complete Psychological Works of Sigmund Freud,* ed. James Strachery, 24 vols. (London: Hogarth Press, 1953–74), 23:158.

2. Ibid., 14:204.

3. Shulamith Firestone, *The Dialectic of Sex: The Case for Feminist Revolution* (New York: Bantam Books, 1971), p. 44.

4. Freud, 1: 179.

5. Ibid., 19: 257–58.

6. Julia Kristeva, "Women's Time," trans. Alice Jardine and Harry Blake, in *Signs* 7, no. 1 (Autumn 1981): 32.

7. Melanie Klein, *Love, Guilt, and Reparation and Other Works,* 1921–1945 (New York: Delacorte Press, 1975), and *Envy and Gratitude and Other Works,* 1946–1963 (New York: Delacorte Press, 1975).

8. Jay R. Greenburg and Stephen A. Mitchell, *Object Relations in Psychoanalytic Theory* (Boston: Harvard University Press, 1983).

9. Elisabeth Schüssler-Fiorenza, *In Memory of Her: A Feminist Theological Reconstruction of Christian Origins* (New York: Crossroad, 1983).

10. Bruno Bettelheim, *Symbolic Wounds, Puberty Rites, and Envious Male* (New York: Collier Books, 1962).

11. Mary Gendler, "The Restoration of Vashti," in *The Jewish Women,* ed. Elizabeth Koltun (New York: Schocken Books, 1976), pp. 241–47.

12. Klein, *Love, Guilt, Reparation,* p. 48.

13. Idem, *Envy and Gratitude,* p. 199.

14. Luce Irigaray, *The Speculum of the Other Woman,* trans. Gillian Gill (Ithaca: Cornell University Press, 1985), and *This Sex Which Is Not One,* trans. Catherine Porter (Ithaca: Cornell University Press, 1985).

Counterpoint:
Woman, Nature and Power:
Emancipatory Themes in Critical Theory and Feminist Theology

MARSHA HEWITT

CRITICAL THOUGHT must make the real world, including its politics, the object of its critique, if it has any interest in being relevant to and articulating the struggles and wishes of its age. Critical thought seeks to expose the possibilities for emancipation inherent in a particular historical context in the name of what society might look like under the reasonable conditions of life. Critical theory, then, is not sharply a theory of emancipation, it is the "practice of it as well."[1] In the 20th century two such critical theories have developed that each have the goal of the liberation of human beings from all forms of oppression and alienation in both thought and action. On the one hand, there is the tradition of "critical social theory" represented in the work of writers such as Max Horkheimer, Theodor Adorno and Herbert Marcuse, who are often referred to as belonging to the "Frankfurt School." On the other, there is feminist theory which, while not a monolithic theory and political practice, is all immanent critique of domination and alienation from women's perspective. Feminist critical theology is a form of feminist theory that seeks to mount a critique of women's oppression within the theological traditions of Christianity and its corresponding institutional structures. As such, feminist critical theology contributes toward a more universal understanding of the dynamics of the power that renders women as its objects.

My purpose in this essay is to generate a dialectical encounter between critical social the-

ory and feminist theology in order to discover what themes they share in common and how they may be understood as mutually clarifying theories of oppression that contribute to the transformation and completion of each others' emancipatory project. One of the most promising contributions of critical theory for feminist theory/theology lies in its analysis of the domination of nature as a central feature of the history of Western civilization, and its integral connection with the striving for mastery over human beings. Feminism extends the critique of the domination of nature by probing its connections with the domination of women, a key element in the civilizing process of the West. In this way feminism is able to cast further light, possible only from women's perspective, on the dialectic of reason and nature. . . .

Critical theory's reified, abstract concept of "woman" undermines its emancipatory intent, and results in the inner subversion of its utopian and transformative potential. I will suggest later that some forms of feminist theology demonstrate a similar tendency insofar as they produce new reifications of "woman" that work against the historical possibility of women's liberation.

The emancipatory potential of critical theory is located in its conscious effort to "mediate between this limited particular experience and the comprehensive universal experience of humankind."[2] This formulation of the theory/praxis relation is promising for the construction of an emancipatory feminist critical theory and theology because the focus on the particular neither disappears into empty abstraction nor dissolves into meaningless relativity. Every effort, however, to mount such a critical theory and to appropriate it from a particular perspective (in this case feminism) must reflect critically upon its own intellectual roots if it is to understand not only its own emancipatory potential, but also those inner tendencies that may cause the theory to drift into ideology and regressive reification that endanger any liberatory project. A further task of feminist critical theory and theology must be to show how the liberatory potential of philosophic and theological thought is limited by casting male experience as the universal human experience. Although the main philosophic and theological traditions of the West are profoundly androcentric, this androcentrism exists more by contingency than by necessity. Practical philosophic traditions whose main preoccupation is with the realization of reason and freedom are in need of an immanent critique from the perspective of women's experience, if they are to be faithful to their emancipatory integrity.

Part of the task of this essay is to contribute toward such a critique, which is in fact a meta-critique insofar as it is a *critique of the critique* of the domination of women and nature in both critical theory and feminist theology. I will attempt to expose those "blind spots" in both critical theory and feminist theology which, against their own intentions, tend toward views of "woman" as an idealized, hypostatized "female," "feminine principle" or category that denies women's historical agency and concrete subjectivity. An analysis of the "woman" question in critical theory exposes an ideological moment that prevents the possibility of the liberation of women, and forecloses on the emancipatory potential of the theory itself. In order to restore critical theory to its own emancipatory intent it is necessary to address both the subjective experience of women as historical and social beings and the actual forms of domination that oppress them.

There are theoretical dimensions within feminist theology that ideologize women in a fashion similar to critical theory by representing "woman" in abstract terms and concentrating on what "she" symbolizes rather than presenting women as historically and socially mediated beings. In this respect, critical theory and similar forms of feminist theology elevate the ontological at the expense of the existential, producing ideologies and reifications that leave the social status quo undisturbed. Hopefully, a critique of these tendencies will restore the emancipatory potential of both critical theory and feminist theology.

Despite critical theory's difficulties in articulating women's experience, it was consistent in understanding its task as both practical and theoretical. . . . Feminist critical theory/theology shares in the task of negative critique, whose goal is future transformation. In this sense feminism, like critical theory, is an "explanatory-diagnostic" and "anticipatory-diagnostic" and "anticipatory-utopian"[3] social theory oriented toward the ingression of future possibility into the present reality through the negation of existent forms of alienation and oppression. Integral to the negative critique of both is the articulation of the domination of nature and "woman" that underlies most Western intellectual and theological traditions, resonating in a fourfold domination of men over women, men over other men, men over nature, and the domination of the "natural" in oneself. . . .

I agree with Ruether's view that, while there is much evidence to suggest that our most ancient religious consciousness imagined the cosmos as a primal womb, the existence of matriarchial social and political formations does not inevitably follow, nor does it follow that societies which included the Mother Goddess in their polytheistic pantheons enjoyed peaceful and egalitarian social relations, nor that they were dominated by women. Even on the mythological level the Goddess did not rule alone but always had a male companion and consort. The elimination of the Goddess in the ancient near East occurred partially as a result of the monotheistic process, which culminated in the hegemony of Yahwism, and even there the memory of the Goddess has not been completely eradicated. The presence of the Goddess in world religions, however, does not mean that a golden age of matriarchy ever existed, nor that women ever enjoyed the revered status of the Goddess in their daily lives.

One must proceed with caution in making claims about the Goddess and mother-right to ensure that women do not become reified in new images of the divine that renders their concrete, historical existence invisible. Horkheimer and Marcuse did just this in their glorifications of the "feminine," which functioned for Horkheimer as the only humanizing force left to an otherwise alienated world of instrumentalized relations under capitalism,[4] and for Marcuse as "the return of the repressed" in the guise of Female-Eros in whom the memory of total gratification and pleasure was preserved.[5] Marcuse even postulated the existence of a revolutionary "female counter-force" that threatened the hegemony of the male-associated Performance Principle, promising the transformation of the individual and society into a new culture of "receptivity" and "sensuousness."[6] Women become hypostatized into "feminine essence" whose transformative power is perceived to be derived from female bodily specificity and its corresponding psychic attributes. For living, historical women this becomes another element of oppression, regulating their behaviour and restricting their opportunities, forcing women to bear the "preposterous contradiction of love in a loveless world. . . ."[7] Horkheimer's identification of women with humanizing influences in the influences in the family and Marcuse's "female counter-force" both undermine the historical project of emancipation, collapsing it into a private experience of moments of freedom found within the reassuring warmth of material love. The retreat of revolutionary praxis into esoteric realms of interiority supports the atomizing and alienating power of capitalism that pervades most aspects of life in increasingly intangible forms of domination.

I suggest that the turn to the Goddess in contemporary feminist theology results as well in the production of new reifications of "woman" that likewise undermine women's struggles for liberation. Goddess spirituality contains a tendency to elevate female biology as fecundity and perpetual renewal to the level of ontology, generating world views and ethical approaches centred around female bodily experience. This approach to feminist theology is part of what may be called "gynocentric feminism," that takes women's bodily experience and traditional feminine activities as the source of positive and creative practices that, if no longer devalued and marginalized, promise to bring about the transformation of society. The problem with any feminist theory derived from women's bodily experience and sexuality is that it traps women once more within the parameters of their physicality, reinstating all the old stereotypes that have contributed to the oppression of women. The current theological shift to the Goddess has the same effect, reducing femaleness to biological functioning and its corresponding attributes of mothering, nurturing, care and so on.

The idealization of woman in terms of female physiology can have a legitimating, ideological function for authoritarian political forces whose implicit aim is to reinforce domination over women, such as can be seen, for example, in the anti-abortion movement. The reification of female biology and its social expressions cannot provide an adequate basis for a feminist movement, in that glorified images of "the feminine" are counterfactual to the lived experiences of most women who may well perceive their biological functions with some ambivalence. For example, however much the baby may be wanted pregnancy cannot be experienced as an unalloyed pleasure, either psychologically or physically. The focus on female specificity grounded exclusively in anatomy fails to grasp those social mediations which reflect our self-consciousness in harmful and distorted ways, including our awareness of our "natural" selves. Furthermore, such a feminist perspective assumes that there is a "stable subject" of feminism that exists behind the socio-cultural category, of gender specificity.[8] The "stable subject," "woman," is divinized in the image of the goddess, and further presupposes an identitary logic between abstract "woman" and concrete *women,* thereby undermining a more promising trend in contemporary feminist theory/theology that seeks to embrace difference and diversity between women as a new basis of solidarity. . . .

The underlying logic of Goddess spirituality and gynocentric feminist theories/theologies is identitary in that it assumes the correspondence between a distinctly female "essence" and characteristics, attributes and values out of which alternative practices, lifestyle and even politics may arise. The troubling question is, what of those women who struggle against oppression but do not find themselves reflected in gynocentric images and cannot derive from them concrete political solutions for their specific problems? A feminist critical theory/theology that aspires to articulate the sufferings and struggles of individual women with a view to their liberation can only do so out of a "consistent sense of nonidentity." . . .

NOTES

1. Max Horkheimer, "Traditional and Critical Theory," *Critical Theory: Selected Essays* (New York: Continuum, 1972), p. 233.

2. This description of the task of theory, and the relationship between theory and action, is developed in Mihailo Markovic's essay, "Reason and Historical Praxis," *Marxist Humanism and Praxis.*

3. Seyla Benhabib, *Critique, Norm and Utopia: A Study of the Foundations of Critical Theory* (New York: Columbia University Press, 1986), p. 226.

4. Horkheimer, p. 118.

5. See Herbert Marcuse, *Eros and Civilization: A Philosophical Inquiry into Freud* (New York: Vintage Books, 1962).

6. See Herbert Marcuse, *Counterrevolution Revolt* (Boston: Beacon, 1972), and "Marxism and Feminism," *Women's Studies* 2 (1974): 279–88.

7. Sheila Rowbotham, *Woman's Consciousness, Man's World* (Harmondsworth: Penguin, 1974), p. 77.

8. See, for example, Judith Butler's critique in *Gender Trouble: Feminism and the Subversion of Identity* (New York: Routledge, 1990).

Chapter 9

Ecological/Biological Approaches

A German disciple of the evolutionary theorist Charles Darwin named Ernst Haeckel coined the term *ecology* in 1866 to suggest a pattern of interaction between organisms and their environments. The so-called ecology of religion is a more recent development that originated in American research work known as cultural ecology, which is concerned with how natural environment is affected by culture. Issues like the interrelationship between an ecosystem and culture and how the environment is mediated by culture are also germane to cultural ecology. Cultural ecology tends to emphasize the investigation of the interaction between nature and culture, whereas the ecology of religion is more concerned with a group's adaptation to a particular kind of natural environment and the kind of religion that is produced by certain kinds of environment. Ecologists of religion tend to share a conviction that religion, for instance, in tribal cultures is anything but accidental; it is rather dependent upon natural environmental factors like modes of adaptation and sociology. Once investigators identify a case, they compare that particular case to other religions to discern what parallel cases might reveal about another religion's mode of adaptation to its natural environment. It is possible to compare, for instance, hunting peoples of the Arctic region of the globe, tribes inhabiting tropical rain forests like the pygmies of the Itori forest, Native American Indians living on the great plains, or the bushmen of the Kalahari desert. This approach suggests that such scholars are concerned with types of religion and their relationship to their natural environments. It also suggests that ecology of religion is methodologically cross-cultural.

It is important to distinguish the ecology of religion from a historically earlier theory called Naturism that was associated with the work of Max Müller and Wilhelm Schmidt. Müller's theory stressed that strong feeling and emotions are evoked by peoples in response to the terrifying nature of natural phenomena. According to Müller, the sense of terror and wonder inspired by nature in primitive people caused them to personify nature by means of a misuse of language. Schmidt wanted to trace theories about the origin of the idea of God to establish and prove the notion of a primitive monotheism. After encountering the majesty and overwhelming power of nature, the primitive responded by attributing the powers of nature to spiritual beings. These kinds of approaches to nature and religion are far removed from those that ecology of religion is primarily concerned with studying and understanding. Ecologists of religion begin with humans in their natural environment. They want to examine how people relate to other animal species and plant life with respect to their responsibilities and to what extent human destiny is intertwined with other species. The ecology of religion is concerned with issues about either accepting or conforming to the natural environment, or whether it is best to attempt to improve it by taking a more active approach by altering, shaping, and developing it with the long-term hope of perfecting it.

Some theorists think that world religions encourage an ecological approach because ecological themes are common within them. Buddhists, for instance, stress nonviolence to all living creatures because unnecessary violence leads in part to increased suffering. The Buddhist and Hindu notion of rebirth suggests that human life is connected with nonhuman life. There is evidence in early Hinduism of the deification of natural forces and objects as evident, for example, by the identification of the earth with the goddess Prithivi and the creation stories of Purusha, a cosmic human from which all things originated, or the cosmic egg creation story in the ancient Vedic texts. There is a tendency in India to regard nature as something sacred. The country of India itself is considered a holy place that is interconnected by its holy cities and sites. Within the Shinto religion of Japan, nature is conceived as sacred and the source of spiritual fulfillment. A Japanese Buddhist monk named Saigyo (1118–1190) argued that humans can learn much from plants and trees about the Buddha-nature. The Japanese Zen master named Dogen (1200–1253) took this type of thinking even further by experiencing nature itself as Buddha-nature.

In Chinese religions there is a tendency to view everything as part of the same whole because nothing exists outside of the world. If all things are interrelated and continuous with each other, reality possesses a relational character. The Chinese conceived of the cosmos as something dynamic and not static because it is pervaded by *ch'i,* vital energy. Therefore, everything in the cosmos changes and is transformed. And despite conflict, tension, and violence the deeper nature of the cosmos is always tranquil. This organic cosmos and its ever-changing patterns are subject to the alternation of two major principles, *yin* and *yang,* which represent the polarities of female and male elements that allow nature to express itself in the harmonious interplay of the two polar principles. If the feminine *yin* is associated with the moon, cold, water, earth, nourishment, sustainment, recessiveness, autumn, and winter, the masculine *yang* represents the opposites of sun, fire, heat, heaven, creation, dominance, spring, and summer. The Chinese consider these polar principles complementary. Rather than attempting to control or dominate these powerful forces, the Chinese are more concerned with adjusting to or conforming to these forces to move with them more harmoniously. Such an attitude and approach is evident in the Chinese Taoism notion of nonaction (*wu-wei*), which is an effortless and uncontrived mode of acting that lets things be and flow in harmony with the natural rhythms of nature.

A different type of ecological spirit is discovered among Native American Indian tribes. At the time of origin, people appeared in animal form, according to the mythology of the Kwakiutl of the Pacific Northwest coast, making people and animals identical during the period of origin. After creation, some of these beings removed their animal forms to become the ancestors of people, while others kept their animal shapes and became ancestors of animal species. A summer hunting season of killing and eating animals enables them to become united to humans in human form. This creation myth plays an important role within Kwakiutl culture during the course of the year because the relationship between animals and humans is reversed during the winter ritual to restore the primordial identity between animals and humans in animal form. This is manifested by humans donning masks of animals during ceremonial dances and thereby becoming the animals. The origin myth and ritual suggests the interdependence and reciprocal nature of the relationship between the two parties. The Mistassini Cree, a hunting, trapping, and gathering tribe located around James Bay in northern Canada, draw the analogy from human life that animals also live as social beings. The Cree religion involves establishing rapport with the animals and their spirit masters. Hunting among this tribe is both something material and spiritual. People must demonstrate respect for the animals that are asked to give themselves to the hunter. The same kind of respect for animals is found among the Northern Saulteaux people when they hunt for bears. They address the animal by using specific names or kinship designation, apologize for killing it, provide reasons why the killing is necessary, plead with the animals to remain calm and not to get angry, and respect the animal after its death by dressing it, hanging its parts on a pole, and making offerings to it. Another type of honoring is evident among the Alaskan Eskimos as expressed in their bladder festival. The bladders of game animals, which symbolize their souls, are inflated, painted, and hung in the men's society house to honor the animals slain during the course of the year.

A leading international expert on the subject of religions of Native American Indians was the Swedish scholar Åke Hultkrantz, who served as professor of comparative religion and head of the Institute of Comparative Religion at the University of Stockholm for many years. Hultkrantz has done field work among the Scandinavian Lapps in 1944 and 1946, Wind River Shoshoni and Arapaho Indians of Wyoming between 1948 and 1958, and the Northern Plains Indians in 1977. He was born in Kalmar, Sweden in 1920, and earned his degrees and completed his doctoral dissertation at the University of Stockholm in 1953. His lifelong fascination with Native American Indians began as a young boy when he read many romanticized accounts of their lifestyle. Among his many essays and books on the subject of Native American Indians, the following books have appeared in English: *Conceptions of the Soul among North American Indians* (1953), *Prairie and Plains Indians* (1973), *The Religions of the American Indians* (1979), *Belief and Worship in Native North America* (1981), *The Study of American Indian Religions* (1983), *Shamanic Healing and Ritual Drama* (1992), *Native Religions of North America: The Power of Visions and Fertility* (1997), *The Soul and Native Americans* (1997), and *The Attraction of Peyote* (1997). Hultkrantz's methodological stance was grounded in phenomenology and the history of religions type of approach to the subject until he supplemented it with the ecology of religion, which implied for him the study of environmental integration of religion and its implications. The major advantage of using this type of approach is that it pragmatically offers more solutions.

Hultkrantz envisions an ecological reawakening with which the ecology of religion should actively participate. Hultkrantz understands the ecology of religion as devoted to examining the experiences of peoples within their environments and conceptions of nature. Ecologists of religion also want to look at the relationship between religion and environment, how the religion and environment might be integrated, and how the environment shaped the religion. The ecology of religion possesses importance for cross-cultural comparisons, typology, change, and religious dynamics. Hultkrantz does not, however, want to include an examination of theological issues with this new approach.

If Hultkrantz's advocacy of ecology of religion crosses boundaries between cultures and disciplines, a similar type of approach is offered by the classical scholar and student of ancient religions named Walter Burkert (b. 1931). He is a professor of classical philology at the University of Zurich. Among his many works appearing in English, the following are especially significant: *Structure and History in Greek Mythology and Ritual* (1979), *Homo Necans: The Anthropology of Ancient Greek Sacrificial Ritual and Myth* (1983), *Greek Religion* (1985), *Ancient Mystery Cults* (1987), *The Orientalizing Revolution* (1992), and *Creation of the Sacred: Tracks of Biology in Early Religions* (1998). Instead of the discipline of ecology, Burkert uses sociobiology to throw new light on the subject of religion.

According to Burkert, if we consider religion in the widest possible perspective, it is necessary to acknowledge that it is both a ubiquitous cross-cultural phenomena and persistent over the course of time. Burkert asks himself: How can we account for the ubiquity and persistence of religion? To answer this question and many others, he proposes a new thesis. Burkert argues that religion is common to all human cultures, which interact with each other and change over time. Religion is concerned with the invisible, which necessarily implies that it cannot be empirically verified. Religion is manifested by human interaction and communication. It is, moreover, serious. To understand the universal nature of religion, Burkert wants to search for its origins beyond particular cultures by considering the process of human evolution. Even though he acknowledges the importance of culture and language in shaping religion, Burkert wants to also consider our biological development that precedes recorded history, shapes our brain and patterns of behavior, and continues to influence the way we live. Thus, Burkert wants to look for the traces left by biology upon us during the process of human evolution. This suggests that Burkert is concerned with issues like biological imprinting upon a person, the transmission of fear and anxiety, and human ritual action compared to the actions of animals in their natural habitat.

Another type of approach to the issues of ecology and biology and their relation to religion is offered by ecofeminism. This approach is part of Mary Radford Ruether's and Delores Williams's critique of dualistic and hierarchical types of thinking because they enable the domination of nature by human beings. It is exactly this attempt to dominate and master nature that produced the ecological crisis. Feminists respond to this crisis by calling attention to what they perceive to be a connection between the hatred, exploitation, and oppression of women, with attitudes to do the same thing to nature. Feminists call attention to the long historical association between women and nature in many cultures. The so-called ecofeminists favor a biocentric paradigm that embodies the interconnected nature of natural things and their preservation. It is possible to get a better perspective on ecofeminism by examining its problems historically.

If we focus on the example of the philosopher-scientist named Francis Bacon from the seventeenth century, we discover a good example of the type of attitudes against which ecofeminists are fighting. Bacon argued, for instance, that humans have been mandated by God to master and dominate the natural world, with the purpose of achieving ascendancy over nature to tame, control, and harness its awesome power. From Bacon's biblical and scientific view, it was the destiny of humans to restore the rule of Adam over nature as preordained by God. Such a project would require a religious elite whose duty it would be to discover nature's secrets by means of scientific investigation and to control nature by means of technology. Bacon viewed nature as both mechanistic and female. From this type of perspective, science is a masculine enterprise and involves the constraining and controlling of something that is equated with the female gender. By applying the masculine, scientific method to nature, it is possible to become the master and exploiter of nature. By applying feminist's analysis, methods, and concepts to nature, ecofeminists seek to replace the ecologically destructive male ethic of science and objectivity with a feminine ethic of interdependence, interconnectedness, and wholeness. This approach stands in sharp contrast to the distance from nature demanded by the so-called scientific, masculine approach. Ecofeminists strive to develop a "deep" empathy or rapport with nature. They seek to respect nature rather than exploit it, to communicate with it rather than dominate it, and to participate in it rather than being isolated from it. They tend to perceive nature as something sacred rather than profane. Although Williams and their feminist approaches to religion will be introduced in the next chapter, it is appropriate to review the career of Ruether before moving to the next chapter.

Rosemary Radford Ruether was born on November 2, 1936 in St. Paul, Minnesota. Ruether is the author or editor of more than 27 books on feminism, theology, and social justice issues. Among her many important contributions to religion are some of the following works: *The Radical Kingdom: The Western Experience of Messianic Hope* (1970), *Liberation Theology: Human Hope Confronts Christian History and American Power* (1972), *Faith and Fratricide: The Theological Roots of Anti-Semitism* (1974), *New Woman New Earth: Sexist Ideologies and Human Liberation* (1975), *Mary, The Feminine Face of the Church* (1977), *Sexism and God-Talk: Toward a Feminist Theology* (1983), and *Women-Church: Theology and Practice of Feminist Liturgical Communities* (1985). Ruether holds a chair, the Georgia Harkness Professor of Applied Theology, at Garrett-Evangelical Theological Seminary, and serves as a member of the graduate faculty of Northwestern University in Evanston, Illinois. Her various published works reflect Ruether's concern with issues of social, political, and racial injustice, as well as issues pertaining to women's liberation and religion.

Guideline Questions

What are the advantages of approaching the study of religion from Hultkrantz's ecological approach in contrast to simply a phenomenological, historical, sociological, or psychological approach?

What does a scholar gain or lose by assuming Burkert's biological approach to the study of religion in comparison to other possible methods?

What kinds of solutions does Ruether propose for the ecological crisis?

What connections does Williams draw between sin, nature, and the bodies of black women?

Ecology of Religion:
Its Scope and Methodology

ÅKE HULTKRANTZ

1. TO THE STUDENT OF RELIGION, in particular the historian of religion, the mere hint of a religio-ecological approach may be challenging and provocative in a negative sense. Is there not sufficient testimony that religions, more than any other segments of culture, are part of the traditional heritage of mankind and as such can only be understood against their historical background? Moreover, are not religious data too subtle to be dealt with from ecological points of view? Indeed, what has ecology as a whole to do with religion?

Criticism of this sort that has crept up now and then following the publication of my first articles in the subject is understandable. A research program like ecology of religion undoubtedly sounds like a *contradictio in adiecto*. Still, properly seen it is not unrealistic. The critics omit the fact that religions, in their formal manifestations, make use of environment and adapt themselves to it. This is exactly what ecology of religion is about: the study of the environmental integration of a religion and its implications. Superficially, this aspect of religion has little importance, touching only the peripheral stones of the religious edifice. If we look closer into the issue however we soon become aware that new forms of access offer themselves to the understanding of religion. Ecology of religion is, as I see it, not the alternative to the historical or phenomenological approaches, but a way of securing new information for these approaches.

At this point we may return to the critical views, presented above. The objection that religious data should only be handled in their historical framing can easily be dismissed. The historical nature of religions is a matter of course. However, this in itself does not rule out other lines of inquiry than those of history. There is as we know the psychology of religion, and the systematic comparison of religious elements that we call phenomenology of religion; and there is the anthropology of religion with its efforts to apply functional and structural points of view to religious data. Similarly we now have the ecological approach, which, as was just pointed out, may enrich our historical understanding. . . .

Ecology of religion is concerned with forms of religious expression, and specific religious contents motivated by these forms, but not with the communication of ultimate meaning and value. In my understanding, at least, conclusions as to the latter are not allowed by the ecological approach.

Ecology is today a theme of paramount importance not only in contemporary science but also in the practical outlook on life, in planning for the future and in the struggle for the conservation of natural resources, a meaningful milieu for mankind and, indeed, the survival of man. It seems to be part of the ecological reawakening that man's religions should also be fitted into this total scheme. Two approaches offer themselves here to the student of religion: one is, research on man's experience of his environment, and his ideas of Nature; the other is, the analysis of the environmental integration of man's religions.

Reprinted from Åke Hultkrantz, "Ecology of Religion: Its Scope and Methodology," Science of Religion Studies in Methodology, *ed. Lauri Honko. Berlin: Mouton Publishers, 1979, pp. 221–236.*
Reprinted by permission of Mouton de Gruyter, a division of Walter de Gruyter Grublt & Co.

The former approach presents us with a world view which may be religious in certain instances, but not always, and definitely not in our modern society.[1] It is a kind of investigation that is not ecological *stricto sensu*, since the concern is not with the relations between religion and environment, but with man's opinion about these relations. Much work remains to be done in this field. One problem is, for instance, to what extent human beings outside our western civilization, and inside it in the pre-Rousseau days, have paid attention to the beauty of Nature as an expression of divine order. It seems certain, anyhow, that even the most impressive phenomena of Nature fail to leave a lasting stamp on the imagination of primitive peoples if they belong to the regular pattern of events.[2] On the other hand, natural actions that disrupt the ordinary pattern, or seem to do so, fire the imagination of man, and may actually change the religious order.[3]

It is the other approach, which is more truly an ecological approach, which will concern us here. Briefly, it is moderately environmentalistic in the sense that it attributes a decisive influence to environment in the organization and development of religious forms. In this context environment means the natural surroundings, topography, biotope, climate, as well as the demography and the natural resources which may be measured quantitatively in a culture. It is too often the case in ecological debates that only the latter, economic aspect is observed. Even analysts of religion have interpreted environment in such narrow terms.[4] However, an accurate application of ecology in the study of culture and religion should imply the whole range of ecological phenomena. The religio-ecological approach investigates religion in its general environmental framing and should not be evaluated as a tool for economic determinism. The question may then be asked what gain we have from an approach so all-embracing and vaguely defined. More specifically, in what way may such a complex as the Protestant creed in Northern Europe be illuminated by the ecology of religion? The answer is of course, very slightly indeed, if at all. The religio-ecological approach is primarily a key to the study of those religions whose cultures are dependent on the natural environment, that is, the so-called primitive religions. As human culture has evolved, its dependency on nature has successively diminished. Religion, being tied up with the cultural development, has, in its process of evolutionary growth, increasingly become independent of the ecological factors that once held it in their grip. If we turn to those religions that have not been affected by urbanization and industrialization they evince both directly and indirectly a remarkable impact by the environment. This is why we may talk of hunting religions, agricultural religions, pastoral or herding religions, etc. Since religion has a conservative tendency, religious features that were adjusted to earlier ecological patterns often remain in later religious constellations. For instance, in agrarian cultures the spirits of the field appear in animal disguise, most certainly a left-over from the hunting cultures.

Fundamental to the religio-ecological approach is the insight that nature not only restricts and impedes, but also stimulates cultural processes. The early anthropogeographers and students of human ecology took the positive, change-promoting power of environmental influence for granted. . . .

The ecological approach to religion is not new. It was part of the older procedures in human ecology, it was practiced in the religio-historical analyses of Near Eastern religions,[5] and it was implied in the doctrine of the older evolutionists that experiences of Nature provided man with gods and myths. We do not say today that volcanoes gave birth to gods, but we recognize that they formed, or contributed to form, the expressions for the beliefs in gods attached to such mountains. Today the ecological ideas of the past reappear refined and modified, at the same time as we have become conscious of them and their methodological importance. In this sense the religio-ecological approach is new in the study of religions.

We shall now see how it may be used, and to what conclusions it may lead us.

2. First of all, new insights into a particular religion, its pattern and functioning may be gained by an ecological analysis. It is very common today that religions are interpreted via an investigation of the social system. However, the social system is in a high degree dependent on, yes, even an outgrowth of, the ecological system. For instance, a vegetational area is the natural habitat of an agricultural people, the woman, once a collector of plants, is the cultivator of the soil (the man being the hunter, a heritage from a preceding hunting culture), matrilocality and uxorilocality becomes the convenient rule, and, as Murdock and others have proved, a matrilinear social organization is built up on this foundation. This may seem to be a very simplified scheme, but it indicates how the process mechanism in social evolution has a primal driving force that, in this case, is ecology.

Now, the observation that a religion, or part of it, may be described in ecological terms does not involve any "reductionistic" attitude. We do not touch the religious values as such—they have their anchorage in the psychic equipment of man. We find, however, that the forms of a tribal religion may be meaningfully described in their interactions with the ecological adaptation of the culture as a whole, and, as a matter of fact, that they are partly produced by this process. . . .

Religion is in most respects a creation of man's psychic experience and cultural tradition. In particular this is the case with mythology and other epical religious traditions, although their setting may be colored by the physical environment. Also more abstract notions, like soul and beliefs, are usually part of a traditional pattern that is validated by individual psychic experiences. In some important aspects however religion is tied up with the cultural structure and thereby, in some religions, with the ecological foundations of culture. In other aspects it reflects the environment more directly. We can

say that ecology acts creatively on these religions—the "primitive" religions—by enforcing or stimulating cultural and religious adaptation through a filter of technological possibilities, value patterns and belief traditions. It is possible to arrange the levels of religio-ecological integration according to the following scale, which is purely functional and should not be mistaken for an evolutionary diagram:

a) Primary integration: environmental adaptation of basic cultural features, such as subsistence and productive arrangements, technology etc. and behavior patterns associated with these features, such as certain social and religious attitudes. Steward calls this constellation of features a "cultural core," an appellation that may be accepted here. To the cultural core belong such religious beliefs and rituals that are, as it were, part of the subsistence activities. So-called animal ceremonialism, or rituals around the slain animal in a hunting culture, and the calendar cycle of rites around the crops in an agricultural milieu, belong to these "subsistence rituals." In their exact appearance they are influenced by historical factors, such as diffusion and inheritance of specific forms; in their general pattern they reflect ecological adaptational processes.

An important instance of primary integration exists in those cases where the religious value system is structured to correspond with subsistence needs. Thus, the Naskapi of Labrador have developed a complex divination system in order to be able to locate the game in times of severe cold and scarcity of food. Indeed, their whole religion can be defined as one of divination.[6]

b) Secondary integration: the indirect adaptation of religious beliefs and rituals. The latter are organized into a framework that takes its forms from the social structure, which is, in its turn, a model suggested by the economic and technological adaptation to environment. It is a well-known fact that a complicated, stratified pantheon only occurs where there is a stratified social structure that owes its existence to a rich agricultural environment, an environment that allows a surplus economy, a dense population, and professional specialization. Again we are talking about patterns and structures, not about specific beliefs and specific rites that have historical accidental circumstances as their cause.

c) Morphological integration: the covering of religious features with forms taken from the physical and biological environment. Religious concepts and rites are by their very nature traditional but borrow their formal appearance from phenomena within the actual biotope. Thus, the hunter's spirits show themselves in animal disguise, the shaman dresses himself in deer attire, the offerings are performed in sacred groves, etc. The choice of forms is not arbitrary but is related to the symbolism that is inherent in them. For instance, the bird dress of a shaman tells us of the bird-like supernatural powers of the shaman or his assistant spirits. It has already been pointed out that myths often depict the natural environment in the area where they are narrated.

It should be obvious that the interaction between environment, cultural core and traditional factors gives us a most useful key to the understanding of religious forms and religious process. We realize that it is not enough to analyze an exotic religion by referring to cultural index, cultural history and social structure; environment is also a factor to be taken into account. In particular we can assess those religions in ecological terms whose cultures are most exposed to the forces of environment. In technically more advanced civilizations the ecological factor is negligible, but some of the religious symbols that have been transmitted historically still reveal an origin dependent on ecological adaptation. In Christianity, for example, the good shepherd and the lamb of God are symbols taken from a pastoral environment. . . .

3. A second target for the religio-ecological approach is the phenomenological comparison between religions and religious traits. As we know, phenomenology of religion tries to identify types which have a universal or regional representation. The scientific control of the investigated materials for the establishment of such types is of course more rigid and reliable in restricted regional areas where the researcher is a specialist. Such areas are usually defined as historical-geographical units, the ethnologist's "culture" or "culture area." In principle, at least, such cultures represent a certain degree of enviromental adaptation; the culture-area designation is however more inclusive (cf. for instance the Southwest of North America). Cultural ecology and ecology of religion provide us with a new operative concept that allows bolder comparisons, a type concept relating to whole cultures and religions.

Again we turn back to Steward and his concept of the "cultural core." As we remember, the cultural core is the constellation of basic features in a culture. If, now, we find similar cultural cores in other cultures, and they have "similar functional interrelationships resulting from local ecological adaptations and similar levels of sociocultural integration," we arrive at a "culture type."[7] "Level of sociocultural integration" means here the form of society involved in the ecological process, such as the family unit, or band, or village, or nation, etc.; different cultures are organized on different social levels. The cultural-type concept thus transcends the culture-area concept with its continuous and limited extent. . . .

Just as we may identify a cultural type cross-culturally we may, I think, identify its religious correlate, the "type of religion," in the same perspective. Of course, there is a major difference between the two type concepts: one refers to the cultural core as a whole, the other to the religious and magic behavior associated with the main features of the cultural core (or primary integration, as it has been called above). Furthermore, where Steward talks of levels of sociocultural integration I should like to emphasize subsistence activities as the most important means for identifying a cross-cultural type of religion. . . .

4. A third goal for the ecology of religion is to arrange the types of religion into historical strata. The gain of this procedure would be that religious traits that can be interpreted ecologically will be referred to particular historical configurations. The historian of religion will be aware of the fact that theriomorphic spirits have their natural beginnings in hunting religions of a very early date, or that priests attending to idols and sacred bundles make their first appearance in agricultural religions of a later date. I am here referring to a relative chronological order, to the general succession of forms, not to specific cases; for in the actual cases some hunting cultures may be younger than agrarian cultures, or they may have adopted a hunting existence after having been agriculturists, as the Cheyenne Indians did in the 18th century. In other words, our perspective is here "evolutionistic." . . .

Anyhow, the ecologically motivated coupling of particular idea or rite complexes to particular religious types enables us to relate them to the succession of cultural stages as defined by prehistorians and ethnologists. In particular that will be possible when the cultures that are discussed are independent, that is, not organized within the wider framework of a technically and socially more complex culture.

Here we can proceed one step further. Provided that religious patterns and their cultural setting constitute a holistic unity, or nearly so (there is no such thing as a complete integrative culture with all parts functioning positively), we may establish credible hypotheses concerning prehistoric religions. I say hypotheses, for what is not revealed to us by documents cannot be empirically verified. Most hypotheses on prehistoric religions proceed from the concept of analogy: one reconstructs a possible religious situation by adducing religious facts from contemporary primitive societies. By anchoring the interpretation in a religio-ecological approach we may restrict the selection of analogies to those which conform with the cultural type of the prehistoric remains. The method

presupposes that we know the cultural type, including the probable pattern of social organization, from the analysis of settlements, graves, temples, rock-drawings, etc. As we know, modern archaeology is striving to reach results in these complicated matters.

The procedure chosen by the ecologist of religion may take the following course. First, he tries to identify the cultural type, and the social organization as revealed by archaeological facts. Next, he associates the cultural core and social organization with a specific kind or type of religion, and perhaps a segment within this type of religion. The type of religion must have been defined before, as an outcome of comparative religio-ecological research on religions in contemporary primitive societies. It is therefore a necessary task for ecologists of religion to contribute to an index of religious types.[8] By relating archaeological data to an appropriate type of religion the researcher will be able to disclose the general nature of religious ideas at a certain site. Specific archaeological traits—a bear grave, a rock-drawing—may communicate direct evidence for the general religious interpretation, and corroborate the religio-ecological operation.

Ecology of religion thus introduces a new way of dealing with the difficult subject of prehistoric religions. It cannot as such illuminate single beliefs and ideas, but it equips us with credible hypotheses concerning religious structures and patterns.[9]

5. The fourth and last contribution that the religio-ecological approach can achieve for us is to indicate an imminent process of religious change. If the holistic thesis holds good that phases of religious expression belong to the primary ecological integration of culture, then changes in the basic structure of the cultural core should be expected to affect the structure of religion. Here again we must return to Steward's culture-ecological theory.

It is Steward's conviction that modifications in ecological integration are the most powerful factor in bringing about the evolution of culture, or, as he also calls it, cultural process or cultural change. He states: "Over the millenia cultures in different environments have changed tremendously, and these changes are basically traceable to new adaptations required by changing technology and productive arrangements."[10] This opinion seems to be justified as far as it concerns the primitive cultures, the cultures of the foragers, hunters, hoe-cultivators, nomads, etc., but has also some bearing on modern civilization. Its implication is that in the long run the organization of religious features will conform to the new state of environmental adaptation. In other words, once we know the changes in the basic features of the cultural core we realize that changes will take place in the religious structure. In some cases the direction of these changes can be anticipated.

6. It should have emerged from the foregoing how many new vistas will be opened by the application of a religio-ecological perspective. Such topics are illuminated as the interaction between nature and religion more important than was recently assumed—, ecological integration or convergence as an alternative to historical diffusion in the explanation of similar religious forms in different places, the interpretation of prehistoric religions, and religious change. It is important to remember that ecology of religion never supplants other methods, but offers more solutions.

Above all, ecology of religion helps us to achieve a deeper perspective on religious dynamics. We perceive that the forms and patterns of religion often depend on exterior conditions and that much of what we usually conceive to be genuine expressions of religious content are actually fortuitous manifestations. For instance, in the belief in an afterlife the realms of the dead mirror the environment of living man; the central idea is the faith in the next existence, whereas its forms are casual. It is often nowadays considered that some elementary religious symbols convey a universal import. Without denying this possibility I should like to point out that many symbols are in

reality determined by social milieu or natural environment. It is therefore important to analyze the outworks of religion before interpreting its meaning.

Ecology of religion thus diverts religion of its fortuitous forms; it shows what is the casual expression and the genuine belief. By removing the external attributes of a religion, suggested by environmental adaptation and historical process, we may arrive at the basic ideas and values of that religion. A more profound view of the intrinsic values of so-called primitive religions will, I think, provide us with a key to the understanding of those great religious traditions that are dominant today.

NOTES

1. Mircea Eliade, *The Sacred and the Profane* (New York, 1959), p. 179.

2. Cf. E. E. Evans-Pritchard, *Theories of Primitive Religion* (Oxford, 1965), p. 54.

3. Hultkrantz, "The Indians and the Wonders of Yellowstone: A Study of the Interrelations of Religion, Nature and Culture," *Ethnos* 19 (1954), pp. 34–68.

4. See e.g. C. Meinhof, *Die Religionen der Afrikaner in Ihrem Zusammenhang mit dem Wirtschtsleben* (Oslo, 1926).

5. Cf. H. and H. A. Frankfort, "The Emancipation of Thought from Myth," in H. Frankfort et al. eds. *The Intellectual Adventure of Ancient Man* (Chicago, 1946), pp. 363–73.

6. Hultkrantz, "La divination en Amérique du Nord," in A. Caquot and M. Leibovici, eds. *La divination,* Vol. II (Paris, 1968), p. 75.

7. J. H. Steward, *The Theory of Culture Change: The Methodology of Multilinear Evolution* (Urbana, IL, 1955), pp. 5–6.

8. An effort to create an acceptable index of culture types has been made by J. J. Hester, "A Comparative Typology of New World Cultures," *American Anthropologist* 64–5 (1962), pp. 1001–15.

9. Hultkrantz, "The Religio-Ecological Method in the Research on Prehistoric Religion," *Actes du 1er symposium international sur les religions de la préhistoire* (Valca Monica, 1975).

10. Steward, op. cit. in n. 11, p. 37.

From *Creation of the Sacred: Tracks of Biology in Early Religions*

WALTER BURKERT

"NEITHER HISTORY nor anthropology knows of societies from which religion has been totally absent."[1] The observation that practically all tribes, states, and cities have some form of religion has been made repeatedly, ever since Herodotus. Ancient philosophers made this "consensus of nations" proof for the existence of the gods. The question is not whether ethnographers may still find a few exceptions to that consensus; it is the universality of the consensus that has to be explained. To be sure, differences in belief and practice are dramatic; indeed, religion can be a most serious obstacle for communication between different groups, producing "pseudo-species" which exclude and may try to exterminate each other; but even this divisive tendency is a common feature.

The ubiquity of religion is matched by its persistence through the millennia. It evidently has survived most drastic social and economic changes: the neolithic revolution, the urban revolution, and even the industrial revolution. If religion ever was invented, it has managed to infiltrate practically all varieties of human cultures; in the course of history, however, religion has never been demonstrably reinvented but has always been there, carried on from generation to generation since time immemorial. As for the founders of new religions, such as Zarathustra, Jesus, or Mohammed, their creative achievement consisted in transforming, reversing, or rearranging existing patterns and elements, which continue to carry an undeniable family resemblance to older forms. . . .

The first principal characteristic of religion is negative: that is, religion deals with the nonob-vious, the unseen, that "which cannot be verified empirically." Protagoras the sophist spoke of the *adelótes*, the "unclearness" or "nonevidence" of the gods.[2] Religion is manifest in actions and attitudes that do not fulfill immediate practical functions. What is intended and dealt with cannot be seen, or touched, or worked upon in the usual fashion of everyday life. This is why strangers are usually puzzled by religious practice. Conversely, we are tempted to suppose that anything puzzling and not immediately apparent may be religious—a problem often met in prehistoric archaeology; drastic misunderstandings may of course occur. It is difficult to "get" what is meant in religious behavior, but some common basis for empathy, interpretation, and translation evidently does exist. The criterion of *adelótes* is insufficient, yet it remains basic.

It is true that this unclearness is often emphatically denied by the insiders. . . . *Adelótes* can neither be abolished nor denied; it can be given a positive twist, however, by proclaiming it a secret.

To get beyond the barrier of unclearness, special forms of experience—meditation, vision, and ecstasy—are commonly invoked; thus the paranormal range of feelings is called upon to establish a direct encounter with the supernatural. Yet the remarkable fact is not the existence of ecstasy and other forms of altered consciousness; it is their acceptance and interpretation by the majority of normal people. The ecstatic phenomena are integrated into religion and confirm existing belief, and these manifestations are themselves shaped by cultural training and practice insofar as they become communicable and accessible to others. In fact, they are judged and selected by an existing religion's own categories: "test the spirits."

The second principal characteristic of religion stands in antithesis to the ineffable: religion manifests itself through interaction and communication. It is thus a relevant factor in the systems of civilization. Even the lonely ascetic communicates, as he becomes the object of admiration, propaganda, and pilgrimage. In fact, religious communication always focuses in two directions, toward the unseen and toward the contemporary social situation. Through attitudes, acts, and language certain non-obvious entities or partners with special characteristics and interests are introduced, recognized, and tended. Distinct from humans and still analogous in many respects, they are deemed superior specifically because of their invisibility, the supernatural as such. People give them various names, class them as spirits, demons, gods, or equate them with long-dead ancestors. Religion thus becomes a "culturally patterned interaction with culturally postulated superhuman beings."[3] Communication with these entities interferes with normal relations within society and thus often turns out to be a special form of indirect communication, using the supernatural to strengthen the effect of intended conventional communication. In this sense one might even say the divine is a social tool to manipulate communication. At any rate, it is the practice of interaction, together with its consequences, that makes religion "uniquely realistic."

Implicit in the first two is the third characteristic of religion: its claim for priority and seriousness, for which Paul Tillich used the term "ultimate concern." Religion is thus set apart from other forms of symbolic communication, from play and from art. Although in play as in ritual there is an element that transcends reality, an "as if" structure which creates unseen partners with whom to interact, these playmates can be dismissed at will. In religion there is a postu-

late of priority and necessity, of certainty that given thoughts and actions are essential and unavoidable. All other plans, projects, predilections, or desires are downgraded, foregone, or at least postponed. . . . Religion is serious; hence it is vulnerable to laughter and derision. But the unseen, in the form of personal partners, calls for submission and veneration, and the ego has to take second rank. As supernatural power spreads to objects, these acquire limits of access or use, whether as taboo or just sacredness. Religion can be deadly serious in the most direct way, sanctioning violence in a terrifying spectrum, ranging from human sacrifice to internecine wars, from witch-burning to an Ayatollah's *fatwa*—and no less shocking acts of self-sacrifice, down to mass suicide . This absolute seriousness, derived from dealing with unseen superiors, is the prerogative of the sacred that characterizes religion.

Religions, both past and present, appear in special cultural, social, and historical settings; they can be elaborated as symbolic systems and interpreted in fascinating ways. Yet this universal and prehistoric phenomenon cannot be explained by or derived from any single cultural system. The search for the source of religion calls for a more general perspective, beyond individual civilizations, which must take account of the vast process of human evolution within the more general evolutionary process of life. This process was once hypostasized as Nature; we may still use it as a metaphor. In this sense the history of religions implies the problem of "natural" religion. Cultural studies must merge with general anthropology, which is ultimately integrated into biology.

Sociobiology?

To introduce biology into cultural studies is to enter a battlefield. . . . With the refinement of evolution theory, sociobiology was proclaimed as "the new synthesis" by E. O. Wilson. This has not silenced criticism at all; controversies are bound to continue. . . .

The basic hypothesis of sociobiology is the "coevolution of genes and culture," with constant feedback between the two. From its Darwinian inheritance sociobiology takes the concept of survival fitness, related to the chances of procreation, and tries to correlate certain institutions or ideas with such fitness. . . . Misfits will diminish in number and gradually disappear. Cultural progress and modification of genes go together.

Sociobiology could be called the computerized version of social Darwinism. Whereas Lorenz had still largely relied on observation and empathy, evolution theory now moves along the lines of game theory, models of which can be tested by computer programs. In this context one basic idea of social Darwinism, the principle of group selection, was exploded immediately, by disproving the claim that group solidarity would naturally win in the struggle for survival. It is the genes, not the individuals, that get passed on; hence it is the cheater within a group who enjoys the greatest advantage and by this very fitness will multiply his genes. . . . It remains true, however, that certain strategies of behavior within a group will prove to be more successful than others and thus make a difference even in gene selection. . . .

The most complicated issue is still how to verify the connection between cultural phenomena and biological preconditions. Even primitive functions of life and simple processes of growth depend upon the interaction of many genes and numerous intermediate stages and agents that make up the phenotype. Behavior is hopelessly complex already at the level of primates. In response to ever changing situations, behavior will always present a mixture of innate responses and learned programs. Even in the realm of animals it is very difficult to isolate one from the other by experiments; at the human level experimentation is not possible.

In addition, in human social life quite different levels and criteria of success come to the fore; these cannot be represented by a single set of numbers in computer games. There is always variety, and seldom extinction. No doubt dominant members of a society have more chances to raise their children successfully; but it appears that again and again special elites rose to power who produced fewer children but, through an elaborate culture, kept control over their inferiors who produced more children. Should this be called a lack of fitness of the ruling class? . . .

The fitness of religion in the sense of procreation and survival value is not at all agreed upon. Many religions call for renunciation of worldly goods and retreat from competitive struggle, as Buddhism and Christianity notably do. Christianity has extolled martyrs and altruistic self-sacrifice. Drastic examples of self-destroying religious behavior include saints starving themselves to death and sectarian groups committing collective suicide. Still—the very propaganda effect of martyrdom proves that, on balance, even these may be strategies of success. The loss is matched by an increase in acceptance. Propaganda, by its very name, is a form of procreation. "The blood of the martyrs is the seed of the church"[4]—a striking metaphor of biological growth. Self-denial is to result in multiplication; the grain of wheat dies to bring forth a rich harvest.[5] Cases of self-sacrifice occur even lower on the evolutionary scale: some mate spiders lose their life at copulation, bees work to exhaustion to feed the queen's offspring. In fact, the individual's sacrifice for the benefit of his or her genetic relatives can be seen as a strategy to multiply the genes shared by the family. This is "inclusive fitness," a concept developed by William Hamilton.[6] In an analogous way, even religions that proclaim self-sacrifice may be basically adaptive. Because on the whole the history of religions has been a story of success, a good strategy for survival in the long run must have been at work. In other words, a certain survival fitness of religion has to be granted.

In contrast to the foregoing, another school of thought imputes to religion the very opposite of survival fitness; we may call it the opium thesis.[7] Religious ideas and practices are accused of fulfilling human wishes in a fantastic, unrealistic, and possibly detrimental way, just as drugs do when they provide the illusion of happiness while misusing and overriding the normal cerebral functions. Not that this would make religion exempt from biology: even the spread of malfunctions is a biological fact. But is illusion dysfunctional? The discovery of endorphins, natural pain relievers in the brain, rather points to the positive biological function of illusive happiness to overcome dramatic crises of stress and pain. A case could be made even for the sociobiological advantage of religious illusions.

Ancient religions normally gravitate to the dominating classes and the representatives of power. After the triumph of Christianity, for many centuries of European history that has also been the situation of the Christian churches. Islam expressly claims to direct law, social order, and political authority. Successful religions tend to use power and even violence to suppress dissident groups or rival religions, both within and beyond their territory. Christianity as well as Islam have become world religions by ousting the more ancient forms of religious polytheism, and they remain adamant in fighting atheism. The same militancy occurs on the individual level: within strictly religious societies a non-religious child, rebellious in feeling and behavior, will hardly have a chance of survival. Yet if the dominant majorities are stabilized by religion, there are also minorities that persist through their religion, some of them retaining special influence just by remaining a religious minority. Some disadvantaged minorities survive in a kind of niche existence for millennia, held together by their religion. The dominant religions of course present advantages to their adherents and disadvantages to their opponents, so they are bound to have momentous effects on selection. Nonetheless, minority groups still survived, centuries of Christian and Islamic rule.

It is notable that many religions urgently advocate procreation within the group. Isolation and procreation became the Jewish strategies for surviving the historical catastrophe of the Babylonian exile; in reinforcement, Mosaic law forbade the use of established forms of birth control such as homosexuality, prostitution, abortion, and exposure of children. In effect, a Jewish population explosion occurred in Hellenistic times. A similar sexual morality caused Christian groups to grow beyond proportion within the Roman empire. Until the present day Catholicism and Islam both passionately opposed birth control. Is it a biological instinct, the thrust of selfish genes, that works behind the laws of Moses or Allah? . . .

It is tempting to assume that the very advantage secured by religion is stability and thus continuity of culture. As the "software" of civilization became too precious and too complicated to leave its preservation to individual choice or chance, new institutions had to arise to guarantee social cohesion across long spans of time. Incipient forms of culture observed in other primates, such as washing grain in water or transporting stones to crush nuts, can be lost again without endangering the species. For *homo sapiens,* the technique to preserve fire did need continuous care. But this may be just an instance of the necessity of culture: it cannot be lost without catastrophe; it cannot be put at stake by experiments. The permanent authority of ancestors or immortal gods provides the needed stability.

Yet as provider of continuity, religion remains paradoxical from the sociobiological perspective. Survival fitness, in the long run, means adaptability to changing conditions; in the cultural systems the key to success is the ability to learn fast and to keep learning in a changing world. Religion, however, strives to teach the unchanging "eternal truths," and to make sure that beliefs and attitudes remain unchanged. What kind of fitness is it that renders people unfit for change, and how can we say that it has been successful?

A final surmise is that the success of religion may be attributed to its providing a heightened endurance in the face of catastrophe, encouraging procreation even in desperate circumstances.

This comes close to the "endorphin" hypothesis. We humans are capable of experiencing states described as "loss of reality"—chimpanzees are apparently immune to this—in such diverse manifestations as extreme Patriotism, the fascination of games and sports, the scientist's or artist's proverbial distraction or rather concentration, and, not least, the fervor of religious behavior. In such cases the mental system overrides reality, and the invisible gets the better of the obvious. Although religious obsession could be called a form of paranoia, it does offer a chance of survival in extreme and hopeless situations, when others, possibly the nonreligious individuals, would break down and give up. Mankind, in its long past, will have gone through many a desperate situation, with an ensuing breakthrough of *homines religiosi*.

These positive or self-stabilizing functions of religion seem more or less plausible and are not mutually exclusive; it is difficult, however, to find concrete evidence for them, especially since the ubiquity of religion means that neutral test groups are not available. But even if accepted, these functions do not in fact prove any correlation between religion and gene selection. Religions are established by learning, they are propagated both through imitation and through explicit verbal teaching. Traditions developed in this way can evidence a kind of cultural fitness for survival without any genetic basis. . . .

What remains is an intercultural family resemblance of religious phenomena throughout the world and over the ages. Likewise, the emotional aura encircling religion cannot be easily dismissed. Biologists hold that each of our spontaneous feelings can be qualified as the reflection of some biological function. . . . Konrad Lorenz has drawn attention to the shudders of anxiety or even of elation that we still experience, shivers running down our backs and arms in appropriate situations, which are nervous reactions intended to raise the mane at the back and head, as they still do among gorillas and chimpanzees. For us, "hair-raising" sur-

vives mainly as a metaphor, but once it was part of the aggressive behavioral program.[8] Today, when we speak of the sacred shivers of awe that characterize religion in particular, we may be forgetting that origin. Yet anxiety linked to aggression through biological inheritance manifests itself in our emotions, including patriotic and religious enthusiasm.

In this context, it may help to take into consideration more closely the most important universal of humans: language. Language is learned in childhood in every society, together with the various special phonologies and semantics that make crosscultural understanding so difficult. Language is linked to an uninterrupted chain of historical tradition; it has never—in tens of thousands of years—been reinvented. Language is exclusively human, even if chimpanzees can be taught its rudiments to a surprising degree. But it is no less true that language has a biological foundation, most evident in the development of a vocal apparatus which is missing in chimpanzees and whose presence in Neanderthal man is doubtful. A genetic alteration was critical to its development. Language also has a clear sociobiological function. In fact it has become one of the most important conditions for survival in our social systems: an individual incapable of speech usually drops out. Thus gene selection has been associated with social functions within the evolution of culture. If language is a phenomenon of culture, culture has determined and continues to control the genes in this case, while language still remains to be taught afresh to every generation. Human language thus may be called a hybrid of culture and biology. . . .

Parallel to language, religion too, as an effective means of most serious communication, can be hypothesized to have arisen at a certain stage in prehistory as a competitive act, a way of gaining an advantage over those who did not take part in it. Religion may well be older than the kind of language we know, insofar as it is bound to ritual, which entails fixed behavioral patterns marked by exaggeration and repetition and often characterized by obsessive seriousness—patterns which are prominent even in most modern varieties of religious communication. In principle, ritual reflects a preverbal state of communication, to be learned by imitation and to be understood by its function. It seems to be more primitive and may be more ancient than speech; it clearly has analogies in the behavior of animals. Although rituals do not necessarily leave archaeological traces, yet funeral practice is well attested for Neanderthal man, while his ability to speak is in doubt.[9] We are free to imagine that a richer palette of rituals existed among hominids at an early stage, such as dances in the context of hunting, warfare, or mating display, but also veneration, even worship, of the unseen. This could be called a complex of prereligion, perpetuated to a large extent in the rituals of religions we know. But it must remain a guess.

The possibility of a sociobiological derivation of religion thus remains shrouded in prehistory. The idea is attractive. There is a vast expanse of time available for the evolutionary process, with tens of thousands, or even hundreds of thousands of generations to fill the hiatus between chimpanzee and *homo sapiens,* whereas in other cases studied by sociobiology the problem of the time span involved seemed insurmountable. Religion, stemming from time immemorial and often characterized by the principle of unchangeable continuity, might well provide a model case for the "coevolution of genes and culture." . . . We can only vaguely reconstruct the decisive cultural conditions. While uncertainties multiply with time, the evidence evaporates. Sociobiology, insisting as it does on precise parameters in mathematical models, cannot find appropriate applications in these realms. Probabilities, selective observations, and hunches will have to take its place.

The biological organization of the brain and other cybernetic systems of living beings existed long before verbalized culture; that it continues to influence our behavior and communication cannot be denied. Aboriginal programs of action, sequences, sentiments, expectations, notions, and values are inherited from the most distant past. Some of the most obvious are the search for food, fear, flight and aggression, and of course sex. Even meanings have their prehistory. It is notoriously difficult to construe semantics from pure logic, but quite easy to recognize certain reactions that have adaptive or communicative functions: a leopard, a snake, "fight or flight"—these are meanings which antedate language by far. The chicken knows the flying hawk before it has any experience of it; the cock knows the weasel;[10] certain monkeys have distinct signs for leopard, eagle, and snake.[11] The process of *semeiosis,* the use of signs and symbols, operates within the whole sphere of living organisms and was evidently invented long before the advent of man.

This does not mean that genes prescribe culture—clearly, they do not. But it could be said that they give recommendations that become manifest in the repetition of like patterns, "the kinds of memories most easily recalled, the emotions they are most likely to evoke." The biological makeup forms preconditions or "attractors" to produce phenomena in a consistent fashion, even if these patterns are created and recreated afresh in each case. Scientific proof of such connections by means of statistics or experience remain impossible; what can be shown is the near-universality and persistence of patterns through place and time, and the existence of certain analogies or even homologies in structure and function in animal behavior. This suggests that details and sequences in rituals, tales, works of art, and fantasies hark back to more original processes in the evolution of life; they become understandable not in isolation nor within their different cultural contexts, but in relation to this background. . . .

To sum up: the thesis of sociobiology in the strong sense of "coevolution of genes and culture" cannot be verified in the case of religion, as such evolution antedates observable periods and remains too complex to establish unequivocal relations between the two. The absence of evidence is still not a license to separate culture from biology or religion from substructures formed within the evolution of life. Religion's hybrid character—between biology and culture—calls for an interdisciplinary meeting of methods: derivation should go together with interpretation. In this sense, an analysis of religious worlds in view of the underlying landscape may be attempted.

A Common World: Reduction and Validation

In human history language has been the decisive phenomenon, analogous to religion and related to it. Ever since the Greeks, language, *logos,* has been judged the crucial difference between us and other species: man is the "animal endowed with language," *zoon logikon.* The course of evolution has been one of growing success in obtaining and processing information, in continuous feedback between the environment and living organism. The nervous system gave rise to the possibilities of learning, that is, of storing information and modifying programs in the course of the individual's life. "Software" of this kind, however, remains inseparable from the "hardware" and is destroyed with it. The effects of learning cannot persist; only the genes preserve information. The cycle of birth and death can be breached to some extent through sharing and passing on information. Incipient cultural tradition of this kind remained rudimentary, even if the distance from amoeba to ape was immense, until the momentous advent of language. Through language information can not only be acquired, processed, and stored individually, but fully transferred to others, to be processed and recalled in parallel efforts. Corresponding to the neural functions of sensation and of motion are two main forms of verbal interaction: to state the facts and to command action, which means sharing the sources of information on the one hand, and partaking in the results of information processing on the other. Through copying and exchange, programs and information have become largely independent from the hardware and from the accidents of individual death. Information survival asserts itself side by side with and even instead of genetic survival.

Language development means nothing less than the advent of a common mental world, allowing not only for common actions and common feelings but for common thoughts and plans, concepts and values. All humans henceforth are linked to an uninterrupted chain of tradition, taking over the mental worlds of their elders, working on them and passing them on.

Religion, defined at the level of communication, belongs to this mental world, and by virtue of its seriousness it claims preeminence. The problem of religion, in consequence, may be restated in the form of a question. How and why, within this common mental world shaped by language tradition, have certain realms been established for which no evidence exists, and for which we claim dominion over communication and action by virtue of seriousness? Is this a by-product, a degeneration, an "opium effect," or on the contrary some kind of *a priori* condition for a common world? If we adopt the Durkheimian concept of "collective representations," we might ask, why do people accept them, and why certain ones among them? . . .

The point is that the common world of language characteristically produces contents beyond any immediate evidence. Communication works via signs, and what they refer to must be guesswork at first, to be confirmed by repetition, by context, previous knowledge, or additional information and experience. Some signs will remain opaque and yet are stored in expectation of later clarification. As learning takes precedence over experience, a personal encounter with what has been learned and known in advance may or may not follow in the span of a lifetime. Language refers to objects far away as well as to the past and to the future, segments of reality inaccessible to verification.[12] Fiction, dreaming, and the workings of imagination evidently have some function for the individual, preparing or rehearsing human activities or helping with solving problems while avoiding direct confrontations. Thoughts or plans can be expressed or manipulated collectively through speech. Worlds beyond experience, or at least some misty provinces or blind spots, thus grow out of the process of linguistic communication. They may be reshaped by misunderstanding. This even happens within religious tradition, producing strange and fascinating items. Elysium, a name for a blissful spot in the beyond, seems to have emerged in such a way. An accumulation of preformed, verbalized traditions will always transcend individual experience. Nobody has seen the phoenix, but all know about him.

Such a process of accumulated verbal tradition can be anticipated by ritual, which refers through formulaic acts to nonpresent partners, and is strongly reinforced by art. Ever since the Upper Paleolithic people have drawn pictures of well-known objects, bisons, horses, or mammoths, as well as of baffling, enigmatic icons that demand special interpretation. . . .

If a body of supernatural entities, communicable through language and pictures, comes to occupy a certain space in our common mental world, it is subject to the controlling functions of reduction and simplification. In the face of the constantly growing accumulation of data infiltrating personal experience, the common world must be simplified. Sheer addition of individual knowledge would soon surpass the capacity of any available system for recording it, even within a small group and within a few generations. Tradition consists of condensed, systematized information. Language continually operates in this way through two of its main functions, generalization and metaphor; these are strategies to keep the sign system finite. Logical functions too work to that end, through negation, class-inclusion, the constitution of patterns and analogies. . . .

Within the process of religious transmission, a strictly biological hypothesis would assume that some form of "imprinting" happens.

Biological imprinting is restricted to certain conditions, to special functions, times, and situations; in other words, it is totally dependent upon the "landscape" of a well-programmed species; it has unchangeable consequences. A newborn duckling, after leaving its egg, takes for its parent whatever creature makes the first contact; later experience cannot change this. . . .

The observable forms of religious transmission are learning processes effected through ritual and language. The most salient features in this process are repetition plus more or less harsh forms of intimidation. Repetition is a major factor in learning, and it is critical in ritual. There is no transmission of religion without ritual. A primary function of ritual is to initiate the young into the customs of their elders—the very epitome of cultural learning, which relies upon memory.[13] In the same spirit, it is for the sake of the whole community that "collective representations" are inculcated by ceremonies repeated at regular intervals.[14] Celebrations of festivals have become central manifestations of religion. People perform prescribed acts, learning that these have always been done in that way; in this context, they are also told their collective lore, their myths. Two sign systems, ritual and language, come together to reinforce each other, to form the mental structures that determine the categories and the rules of life. The most effective elements are dance and song, in which repetitive rhythms and sounds combine to create the great collective experience. . . .

There is no denying that anxiety is often evoked to validate religious messages, and that it has its repercussions upon the substance of religion. To transmit religion is to transmit fear. . . . Shudders of awe are central for the experience of the sacred. The very means of indelible transmission, threat and terror, are correlated with the contents of the religious part of the mental world: the prerogative of the sacred requires the fear of god.

Yet anxiety, fear, and terror are not just free-floating emotions brought on by psychological fantasy. They have clear biological functions in protecting life. Seriousness means giving priority to certain vitally important programs.[15] The utmost seriousness of religion is linked to the great overriding fear of death. The value of religion, manifest in the forms of religion's cultural transmission and in the insiders' confessions, is that it deals with the "ultimate concern" and thus fits the biological landscape. The drama of religion's interaction with the unseen by manipulating and displacing anxiety takes place with death as the backdrop. Man knows about death, and that death cannot be abolished, but this knowledge develops in a peculiar way. Personal death is a reality beyond imagination, an x, an unknown, inaccessible to experience; the experience of other people's deaths, however, prompts imaginative dealings with the unknown within the common mental world, with displacement, disclaimers, shifting substitutes, and continuing indelible shock, assuaged or rekindled in turn.

Anxiety was bound to multiply at the human level, the level of a conscious representation of the world both near and far, of past and future. We may wonder how herds of African zebras and gnus are able to graze in the presence of lions. The lions will attack at some point, but only at the moment of immediate danger does an animal take flight; the others save their energy and go on grazing, and before long so will the animal that escaped the predator this time—what else can they do? But humans, as they consciously seek to control their environment, storing recollections and anticipating the future, cannot forget the presence of lingering lions. They can try to attack and to kill the predators in turn; they may succeed in creating a peaceable environment: this is one reason why many primitive cultures enjoy the symbols of killing. Yet man will fall in his attempts to remove all anxiety-arousing dangers from the world, especially as his violence meets with the violence of other men. Death remains the constant.

To shield mental life from despair and depression, which are factually lethal, there must be counterforces, optimism, faith, or "opium." This may be the final necessity for sharing fictitious worlds which employ seriousness, nay terror, to counter worldly fears by fear in a hierarchy that reaches toward the absolute. "The highest fear is the fear of god,"[16] Aeschylus stated, and he was not alone in offering this message. "The fear of god drives out the fear of men." As religious reality claims precedence over mundane reality, frightful dealings with death and killing gain overwhelming importance in the form of funerary and sacrificial rituals.

This apparently negative preoccupation of religion is just a foil for what is really at stake. A resounding voice in the self-interpretation of most religions, diverse as they may be in other respects, is the longing for life.[17] . . . Gods grant life, gods protect life, just as their wrath can destroy life. The impetus of biological survival appears internalized in the codes of religion. Following this impetus, there is the postulate of immortality or eternal life, the most powerful idea of many religions. Even self-sacrifice is for the sake of eternal life. The negation of death presupposes the fact of death. The idea of the supernatural emerges within the landscape of nature. Religion's seriousness, so manifest in our feelings, reflects the hard rocks of the biological landscape, the dangers, limits, and the drive for the preservation of life. Religion keeps to the tracks of biology. Some extremists may happen to get off the tracks, but they will disappear unless they somehow make their way back.

Life's achievement is self-replication, self-regulation, and homeostasis. Hence the gods are the most persistent guarantors of order, the forceful regulators. Life needs seclusion for its own protection, building up cells to separate what is inside from the outside; the religious worldview usually adopts some privileged center to keep in touch with the divine despite chaotic or diabolical surroundings. If reality appears dangerous or downright hostile to life, religion calls for something beyond experience to restore the balance. Catastrophes do happen; but in the widespread myths of the flood the endings always tell of the survivors preparing to offer sacrifice. Religion is basically optimistic.

NOTES

1. R. A. Rappaport, "The Sacred in Human Evolution," *Annual Review of Ecology and Systematics* 2 (1971), p. 23.

2. Diels-Kranz, 80 B 6.

3. Spiro, quoted in C. Renfrew, *The Archaeology of Cult* (London, 1985), p. 12.

4. Tert. *Apol.* 50, 13.

5. John 12.24.

6. Cf. W. D. Hamilton, "The Genetic Evolution of Social Behavior," *Journal of Theoretical Biology* 7 (1964), p. 1.

7. K. Marx, "Einleitung zur Kritik der Hegelschen Rechsphilosophie," *Deutsch-französische Jahrbücher* 1844, Marx-Engels-Werke I, 378.

8. K. Lorenz, *On Aggression* (New York, 1963), pp. 259–264.

9. See L. B. Slobodkin, *Simplicity and Complexity in the Games of the Intellect* (Cambridge, MA, 1992, p. 35).

10. H. von Ditfurth, *Der Geist fiel nicht vom Himmel: Der Evolution unseres Bewusstseins* (Hamburg, 1976), pp. 165–167.

11. T. Struhsaker, "Auditory Communication among Vervet Monkeys (Cercopithecus aethiops)," in S. A. Altmann, ed. *Social Communication among Primates* (Chicago, 1967).

12. This too has an antecedent in ritual, defined as "action pre-done or re-done" by J. Harrison, *Epilegomena to the Study of Greek Religion* (Cambridge, 1921), xliii.

13. Cf. J. Assmann, *Das kulturelle Gedächtnis* (Munich, 1992).

14. Cf. Durkheim, 1912.

15. Cf. Ditfurth, p. 269.

16. Aesch. Hik. 479.

17. Cf. Burkert, *The Orientalizing Revolution* (Cambridge, MA, 1992).

From *New Woman and New Earth: Sexist Ideologies and Human Liberation*

ROSEMARY RADFORD RUETHER

SEXISM AND ECOLOGICAL DESTRUCTIVENESS are related in the symbolic patterns of patriarchal consciousness, but they also take intensive socioeconomic form in modern industrial society. Rapid industrialization went hand in hand with the depletion of the economic functions of women traditionally centered around the home. Industrialization also drew many poor women into the factory at exploitative wages, far below those even of the exploited male worker. But industrial society transformed the relationship of the home to economic production. The very word economy originally meant "functions of the home." Originally, except for a few luxury items, the basic economic processes of daily life, both of food growing and processing and of manufacture of tools and goods, went on in or contiguous with the home. Industrialization meant the progressive alienation of more and more productive processes from the home. Male work, once taking place in farms and shops in or around the home, became increasingly disconnected with the home and collectivized in a separate sphere. Women more and more lost their own productive work, as well as their integration with male work. The home was refashioned from a producer to a consumer unit in society, totally dependent upon a separate

Reprinted from New Woman and New Earth: Sexist Ideologies and Human Liberation *(New York: Seabury Press, 1975), pp. 196–211.*

work structure no longer under its control. The work of the home and hence of women became concentrated on intensive interpersonal emotionality, extended child nurture, and the primary physical support (eating, sleeping) of male work. A new type of family and a new definition of woman's "place" that had never existed before in so narrow a form came into being for the bourgeois woman. Having lost the productive functions that had been theirs in preindustrial society, they were confined exclusively to the spheres of reproduction, intensive child-rearing, emotional compensation, and the housekeeping functions (with the loss of servants) that free the bourgeois male for the industrial workday.

The confining of women to a home defined as the sphere of "love," child nurture, and housekeeping forced them into a new underdevelopment, in contrast to the nineteenth-century feminist quest for increased education and activity (indeed, becoming the contradiction that helped create this feminist demand). Women's careers became children. Population began to expand rapidly in the industrial era until it reached today's crisis proportions. Today an ecologically sound population policy would demand that most couples have two children and some have less, in order to reduce the population to safer levels. Yet the social ideology of woman's role continues to insist that women build their entire lives and identities (with an increasing life expectancy) around the nurture of less and less children. It is hardly surprising that modern women are afflicted by a desperate vacuity.

Victorian society attempted to pacify the contradiction between the growing woman's consciousness and the depleted functions of woman's "sphere" by the idealization of domesticity. But this was developed under the traditional Christian psychology of sexual repression. By the turn of the century the contradiction between intensified domesticity and sexual repression became so violent that the underside of Victorian society exploded in the Freudian

revolution. But Freudianism, as we have seen, was unwilling to criticize the socioeconomic basis of female "hysteria," and so its lifting of the skirts of sexual repression was fed back into a renewed intensification of female suppression. A greater recognition of sexuality was integrated into the psychology of the bourgeois family as an integral element of its maintenance. The eroticization of the private sector of life is deliberately stimulated in capitalist society to compensate for and pacify male alienation from, and loss of control over, the work and political processes and to intensify the compensatory role of women and the home. Women are trapped in the private sector to service these male compensatory needs. They become not only the full-time child nurturers, but also the ideal friend and the sexual playmate, creating for themselves an illusory sense of a multiplicity of important roles.[1] The eroticization of private life around the home also stimulates its function as the prime consumer unit in an economic system built on increasing consumption of products, most of which glut the appetites but distort basic needs. Through advertising, the imagination of society is invaded by artificial needs for products designed to decay and be replaced rapidly. Women become both the chief buyer and the sexual image through which the appetites of consumption are stimulated. Woman becomes a self-alienated "beautiful object" who sells her own quickly decaying façade to herself. Deprived of an integral existence, she exists to be seen and used by others, like eye makeup, which does not help a woman to see, but turns her eyes into objects to be seen. She is both the image and the manager of a home which is to be converted into a voracious mouth, stimulated by the sensual image of the female, to devour the products of consumer society. A continual stream of garbage flows forth in increasing quantity from this home, destroying the earth. Yet the home and women are not the originator but the victim of this system.[2]

As we have seen in earlier discussions, the split between the consumer home and alienated work was sanctified in Protestant theology, the theology of bourgeois society, in the form of the split between "moral man and immoral society." Reinhold Niebuhr became the chief formulator of this essential dichotomy in bourgeois culture between the home and public life.[3] With the secularization of society, religion and morality become feminized or privatized. Morality becomes appropriate only to the individual person-to-person relation exemplified by marriage. Love morality is "unrealistic" in the public sphere. Here the only possible morality is that of a "justice" defined as a balancing of competitive egoism. Women become pre-eminently the symbol of the private sphere of altruistic "morality." They are pre-eminently "moral man," while the male sphere of public life becomes rational in a way that is emptied of human values. Morality is privatized, sentimentalized, and identified with the "feminine" in a way that both conceals the essential immorality of sexism and rationalizes a value-free public world. A morality defined as "feminine" has no place in the "real world" of competitive male egoism and technological rationality.

The domestication of morality and religion in bourgeois culture also becomes a new "law" by which women are morally forbidden to "leave the home" and participate in the public world of men. It is now argued that this implies no inferiority in the view of women, but rather, a recognition of her "superior moral nature" which exists by virtue of her identification with the moral sphere of the "home." To step out of this sanctuary to enter the "dirty world" of business and politics would only lower woman's "nature" and prevent her from "elevating the world" through that "uplifting" influence that she exercises from the "home."[4] All this language, of course, totally mystifies the powerless, dependent status of women and the relation of the home to society. The emptying of the public realm of the humanistic values represented by personal morality also makes careers in politics, business, and technology uncongenial to the kinds of personalities developed in women.

Women's education is concentrated on the "humanities," and women are generally undereducated in scientific and technological knowledge. This reinforces their psychological aversion to the most critical areas where real power is exercised in society and their decision to confine themselves to the home or to seek careers only in those auxiliary spheres, such as nursing and social work, that extend the work of the home, but without challenging the antihuman values of the public realm.

Women should look with considerable suspicion upon the ecological band-aids presently being peddled by business and government to overcome the crisis of exploitative technology. The ideology which splits private morality from public business will try to put the burden of ecological morality on the private sector. To compensate for the follies of the system, the individual consumers will be asked to tighten their belts; the system itself will not be challenged to change. Changes in the consumption patterns of the home can only be tokenism, since ecological immorality belongs to the patterns of production and social exploitation that is systemic. The home is its victim and tool, but not the originator of these patterns. A society which makes the individual worker totally dependent on the private auto for transportation is not serious when it asks that private worker to change his or her patterns of gas consumption, since there is no alternative method by which the home can be linked to the worlds of work and shopping necessary for survival. The auto is not a private luxury, but a systemic element that links all the other elements of the system to the home. Reforms directed at the private sphere can only be tokenism. Women will naturally be pressed into becoming the self-help ecologists in band-aid remedies that increase the dissipation of their energies in trivia, but have minimal effects on the ecological imbalances.

Ecological morality aimed at the home must also turn ecological concern itself into a new consumer product for women's use. The ecological factor will be built into consumer products in some trivial way and then sold with much advertising to women as a luxury item tacked onto present consumer products to placate the conscience.

The actual patterns of rapid destruction of the raw materials necessary to maintain the existing level of industrial production is already creating a world crisis and will soon result in economic devolution and declining production worldwide, only temporarily staved off by intensified search for untapped raw materials and energy resources. Women are on the bottom of those groups who are "last hired and first fired." Women have been forced into production in large numbers only when war production artificially escalates the need for industrial workers, while draining off the males available for such work. Thus in any situation of declining production, working-class women will be the first to be laid off in industry and women in all professions marginalized in a shrinking job market. The demand of women for more jobs thus must inevitably meet with new strategies of domestication by male-dominated society. A failing affluence and productivity, structured on the present distribution of power, means that the present elites (male, white, upper class) will try to be the last to lose their affluence and high-consumption patterns. Upper-class Western white males will try to shift the burdens of a declining job market to those who are marginal and dependent, the groups who are regarded as surplus labor or sources for raw materials (women, the jobless poor, the third world). Thus the claim of a capitalist-oriented "development" to gradually overcome the present patterns of social injustice, through expansion of its present system of production, must be regarded as increasingly fallacious.

This does not mean that the resources of the earth were not originally and are perhaps not still now capable of supporting a postscarcity, ecologically balanced society, where everyone is given meaningful social activity. It simply means that this cannot happen by infinite expansion of the present patterns based on unjust social relations between the sexes, classes, and nations and a destructive relation to the earth. All dependent or impoverished groups must look to the disappointment of their hopes for inclusion in Western affluence through the expansion of this model of development. The Western pattern of industrialization cannot include traditionally dependent groups because it is based on the rape of the raw materials of the globe to feed an affluent elite. To expand this level of production worldwide for all would destroy the raw materials and poison the ecological systems of the entire world in a few decades. The earth cannot long support the maintenance of this style of industrialization, much less expand it in depth to the poor. What appears to be an internationalization of this system at present reflects only the neocolonialism of domination of world resources by an international cartel, not the spread of affluence downward to the masses.

Women too must recognize the fallacy of the claim to include them as active contributors in the present economic system by its infinite expansion. Only in the heroic age of rapid industrialization in the West, and in a similar period of rapid industrial revolution in communist countries, have women been invited to participate in industrial work in large numbers, although, even in Marxist countries, seldom on equal terms with male workers. Wartime also becomes a time when even fascist countries put aside their sexism to invite "Rosie the Riveter" to come into the factory to maintain the industry of the Fatherland, while the males hurl the fruits of her womb and her hands at each other. In wartime, too, women are encouraged to attend universities in greater numbers, to fill the places of absent males. This has no connection with translating their education into jobs, however, which must be reserved for returning males. Expanded job opportunities for women have happened when there is a great need for "hands" because of these kinds of special crises. But the overall pattern of industrial society has been one which marginalized women's participation in the economy and must be expected to do so more as this system begins to fail.

Finally women must look with suspicion on the symbolic role they will be asked to play in an ecological crisis analyzed within patriarchal culture. Any effort to reconcile such a male with "nature," which does not restructure the psychology and social patterns which make nature "alien," will tend to shape women, the patriarchal symbol of "nature," into romanticized servitude to a male-defined alienation. The concern with ecology could repeat the mistakes of nineteenth-century romanticism with its renewed emphasis on the opposite, "complementary natures" of men and women. Women will again be asked to be the "natural" wood-nymph and earth mother and to create places of escape from the destructive patterns of the dominant culture. Women will be told that their "highest calling" is to service this type of male need for sex, rest, emotionality, and escape from reality in a simulated grassy flower Eden. But the real power structures that are creating the crisis will be unaffected by such leisure-time games. Many women in the fundamentalist and communal movements have already been suckered into these roles based on romantic male escapism.[5] Women must recognize that they represent the oldest and ultimate ideology of patriarchal culture, who serve to maintain its patterns of male domination and world exploitation. Already aspects of the ecological, communal, and human potential movements are deeply infected by this type of romantic escapism which evades the real structure of the problem while recreating women's role as the symbol and servant of male self-alienation.

Women's Liberation, Ecology, and Social Revolution

Women must see that there can be no liberation for them and no solution to the ecological crisis within a society whose fundamental model of relationships continues to be one of domination. They must unite the demands of the women's movement with those of the ecological movement to envision a radical reshaping of the basic socioeconomic relations and the underlying values of this society. The concept of domination of nature has been based from the first on social domination between master and servant groups, starting with the basic relation between men and women. An ecological revolution must overthrow all the social structures of domination. This means transforming that world-view which underlies domination and replacing it with an alternative value system. It is here that the values and development learned in the patriarchal family and in the local community are of great importance. How do we change the self-concept of a society from the drives toward possession, conquest, and accumulation to the values of reciprocity and acceptance of mutual limitation? It is hard even to imagine a coherent alternative beyond the present horizons of crisis and impending disaster. Even when reasonable and possible alternatives can be sketched, the practical power to counteract the systems which perpetuate the world of global exploitation and war escape us. We seem to be awaiting a planetary rebirth which can come about only when massive catastrophe decisively discredits the present systems of power. We scarcely know whether either the physical or the spiritual resources exist to make such a creative leap beyond disaster. So it is with fear and trembling that we even try to dream of new things.[6] First of all, harmony between the human community and natural systems has nothing to do with anti-intellectual or anti-technological primitivism. The human capacity for technological rationality is itself the highest gift of nature. It needs to be freed from its captivity to ruling-class domination and not be regarded as inherently evil. Escapist, romantic primitivism tends to be the response of alienated children of the elite. It has little to offer those left out of the present affluence. What is needed is democratization of decision-making over technological development and equalization of its benefits. It must become impossible for a small ruling class to monopolize the wealth from world resources, while transferring the social costs to the people in the form of poisoned air, water, and soil. This also demands the development of new ecological technology oriented toward preservation of the earth.

Some obvious changes are necessary. High on the agenda is a total overhaul of the present method of transportation that is based on the private auto and the freeway system. The gasoline auto will have to be phased out, to be replaced by public mass transit between urban centers, and bicycles and electric cars and buses within local areas. Congested areas should be cleared of trucks or cars entirely, to allow only bicycles or pedestrians. We are fully capable of designing such an alternative, but lack of coordinated planning and commitment of politicians to the present automobile, trucking, and oil interests keeps us tied to a transportation system that is heading for disaster. There must be a general shift from energy sources which are polluting and limited to those which are nonpolluting and renewable, such as sun, wind, water, electricity, and perhaps nuclear energy, if ways can be found to handle its wastes. Clearly an ecological technology will demand great scientific imagination, but an imagination directed toward the common good of the entire world community and one which seeks to integrate the human sociosphere into the biosphere of nature in a positively reinforcing relationship.

It seems possible that, as disasters mount from the present unregulated system, there may come a time when the major systems of power in the United States, Russia, and perhaps even China would move together to create a global planned society. This will be called a "socialist revolution," and many well-meaning liberals will be convinced that democracy must be sacrificed for human survival. Even persons such as Henry Kissinger have been free to suggest that democracy's days are numbered.[7] One can well imagine a sudden unanimity about this among right-wing and left-wing world leaders, all of whom are basically fascists. Some unified management of world resources is needed, so that national rivalries cease to keep the planet in a permanent state of economic and military warfare. The destruction of our resources in war technology and its threat to survival must be ended. But if that government is to be other than totalitarian, managed for the benefit of a world ruling class, socialist communities must be built from the bottom up.

A democratic socialism has to be a communitarian socialism. This means the economic and political sectors of local communities are run on the principles of subsidiarity, self-ownership, and self-management. Planning, distribution, and enforcement of standards need to be ceded to larger units: metropolitan regions, states, nations, and international bodies. But these levels of government must be rooted in strong self-governing local communities, with representatives elected from the base. Only in this way can socialism be kept from becoming total alienation of the atomized individual in huge impersonal corporatisms. An urgent task for those concerned about the society of the future is the development of viable forms of local communalization on the level of residential groups, work places, and townships that can increase our control over the quality of our own lives.

It is on the level of the local community that socialism can change the dependency of women by transforming the relationship among power, work, and home. The nuclear family cannot overcome the caste status of women because it is the victim of a rigid complementarity of work-home, male-female dualities. As we saw earlier, Marxist or state socialism has tended to solve this by giving over female work to state agencies in order to integrate women into productive labor. The strategy of a communitarian socialist society is different. It would bring work back into an integrated relationship to self-governing living communities. Women's work is still communalized and professionalized, but control over these functions remains with families themselves who band together in groups on the level appropriate for particular functions. For example, a residential group would develop communal shopping, cooking, child care, cleaning, or gardening by collectivizing its own resources. The child is not taken out of the family into an impersonal state agency to free the mother for other activity. Rather, it gains a tribe while remaining rooted in the family.

Communalization of functions of local groups should not be confused with what is called a commune in contemporary America, i.e., eight or ten young adults in a house built for a nuclear family. This is an unstable unit at best. What we are talking about is the principle of the kibbutz, but applied in a diversity of forms to different living and working patterns. Communalized living requires a new architecture which balances private and corporate dimensions of life. It calls for new urban planning to integrate living with work. Clear, objective political forms that maximize personal participation need to be developed. Short-term committees with rotating membership who bring propositions before a direct primary assembly would be my own preference. Models for such communities are not beyond our reach. We have a long tradition of Christian communitarianism to draw from. Even residential colleges, although not fully democratic, are a well-accepted example of a self-governing community for work and living.

I will outline a few of the ways in which socialized local communities could greatly alter the traditional role of women. Communalization of child-raising in residential groups or even in work places could change the childbearing patterns in nuclear families. The isolated family tries to have several children in order to create a mini-community. In a communal family, children would grow up with a sense of a large group of "brothers and sisters." A bonding of children of a group of families would develop, extending the child's own peer group and also gaining relations with a large group of other adults who are personally concerned with her or him. The personal child-parent relationship would not be destroyed, but it would be supplemented by a larger group of siblings, mothers and fathers, and older brothers and sis-

ters, much as is the case today where the family is still rooted in clan and tribe. Adults who do not have their own children would also have an opportunity to nurture and develop the lives of children. Children would have a sense of a variety of other adults, older children and peers to whom they could turn for resources that might not exist in their immediate families. Fifty adults might have between them about twenty or twenty-five children, which would still afford a bountiful community of children, but rapidly return the population to a level which the earth would be better able to support.

The tasks of housekeeping, child-raising, food procurement and preparation would be communalized and spread between men and women. One sexual group would no longer be structured into exclusive responsibility for this type of work, isolated from each other and from the work places. Those who chose to be managers of these functions would be skilled professionals and suitably rewarded. Dimensions of private life and control over personal needs would still be retained, allowing for individual choice in relating private and communal aspects of life. The communalization of much of the equipment of daily life—such as communal kitchens, communally owned vehicles and tools signed out on need—could drastically reduce the present patterns of consumption, waste, and duplication of equipment in nuclear families. A decentralized economy would return much of the production to small factories, workshops, and farms owned and run by the local community. Materials would be made to be long-lasting. The shoddy goods made to decay and be replaced rapidly in the profit economy would lose their rationale. There would also return a pride in craftsmanship essential to the dealienation of labor. Home and work, production and consumption, field and factory would be related organically, making each human group aware of the ecological relations of its own material life with that of nature. Human society, patterned for a balance through diversity, would be consciously integrated into its environment.

The key to this integration is the use of wastes. In an ecologically balanced society, there should be no real "waste." In effect, the wastes of each system should become converted into being the fuel or food of another system in a recycling process that continually renews and beautifies the environment.

Since local communities would make many of the decisions that affect their immediate lives, self-government would counteract much of the present sense of alienation and powerlessness of the atomized individual. The interrelationship of home and work would allow men and women to take an equal hand in both nurturing and supportive roles and also in work and political life. The split between alienated work life and shrunken domesticity, which segregates women on one side of this divide, would be overcome by bridging the gap between the two, rather than by abolishing and devaluing the roles of family life. Not only would women be allowed the participation in the larger social processes that they have historically been denied, but men also would recover the affective and nurturing roles with children and other people historically denied them, which has repressed the gentle, humane side of males and shaped the male personality into that hyper-aggressivity and antagonistic combativeness that has been called "masculine." Without sex-role stereotyping, sex-personality stereotyping would disappear, allowing for genuine individuation of personality. Instead of being forced into a mold of masculine or feminine "types," each individual could shape a complex whole from the full range of human psychic potential for intellect and feeling, activity and receptivity. A richer pattern of friendship could also develop among adults, diffusing the often over-exclusivism of the nuclear marriage that makes two married adults each other's sole personal nurturers of personal intimacy over a lifetime.

The center of such a new society would have to be not just the appropriate new social form, but a new social vision, a new soul that would inspire the whole. Society would have to be transfigured by the glimpse of a new type of social personality, a "new humanity" appropriate to a "new earth." One might call this even a "new religion," if one understands by this the prophetic vision to shape a new world on earth, and not an alienated spirituality. A society no longer bent on "conquering the earth" might, however, also have more time for the cultivation of interiority, for contemplation, for artistic work that celebrated being for its own sake. But such interiority would not be cultivated at the expense of the community, as in monastic escape from "the world." It would be a cultivation of the self that would be at one with an affirmation of others, both our immediate neighbors and all humanity and the earth itself, as that "thou" with whom "I" am in a state of reciprocal interdependence.

Such solidarity is not utopian, but eminently practical, pointing to our actual solidarity with all others and with our mother, the earth, which is the actual ground of our being. Perhaps this also demands a letting-go of that self-infinitizing view of the self that culminates in the wish for personal immortality. One accepts the fact that it is the whole, not the individual, which is that "infinite" out of whose womb we arise at birth and into whose womb we are content to return at death, using the human capacity for consciousness, not to alienate ourselves from nature, but rather, to nurture, perfect, and renew her natural harmonies, so that earth might be fair, not only for us and our children, but for all generations of living things still to come.

NOTES

1. Barbara Welter, "The Cult of True Womanhood, 1820–1860," *American Quarterly* 18 (Summer 1966); Dorothy Bass Fraser, "The Feminine Mystique, 1989–1910," *Union Seminary Quarterly Review* (Summer 1972), pp. 225ff; R. Ruether, "The Cult of True Womanhood," *Commonweal* (Nov. 9, 1973), pp. 127–32.

2. Betty Friedan, *The Feminine Mystique* (New York: Norton, 1963), was the catalytic statement of the relationship between the ideology of femininity and the woman's

consumer role. H. Marcuse, *One Dimensional Man* (Boston: Beacon Press, 1964), pp. 71–78, has some pithy things to say about the use of the erotic image in modern consumer society.

3. Reinhold Niebuhr, *Moral Man and Immoral Society* (New York: Scribner's, 1932), pp. 257–58; also W. Rauschenbusch, *Christianity and Social Crisis* (New York: Macmillan, 1907), pp. 276–79.

4. R. Ruether, "Are Women's Colleges Obsolete?" in *The Critic* (1968), pp. 58–64.

5. Traditionalism toward women in religious communal groups is evident in the Brüderhof; see Benjamin Zablocki, *The Joyful Community* (Baltimore, MD: Penguin, 1972), pp. 117–22.

6. An effort to develop a strategy of change is found in George Lakey, *Strategy for a Living Revolution* (San Francisco: W. H. Freeman, 1973).

7. See Joseph Alsop, "Understanding Henry Kissinger," *The Washington Post*, Jan. 27, 1975 (editorial page, A section).

Sin, Nature, and Black Women's Bodies

DELORES S. WILLIAMS

As EARLY AS THE 1960s, people in the Western world were beginning to realize that technology was developing to the point of dismembering the natural environment, of rendering the planet uninhabitable. Many Americans were beginning to realize that the preservation of what was known as "The American Way of Life" (i.e., luxury and comfort, compared to poverty in the two-thirds world) was rapidly depleting the world's natural resources. Some scholars even contended that Christianity's encouragement of technological invention was, in part, responsible for the environmental crisis.[1]

However, very few people made the connection between America's contribution to the abuse and exploitation of the natural environment today with the dominating culture's historic abuse and exploitation of African-American women's bodies in the nineteenth century. Just as technology's rapid and often unchecked contribution to the destruction of nature is rationalized on the basis of technology providing greater profits, comfort, and leisure for more Americans, the exploitation of the

black woman's body was rationalized to the advantage of white slave owners. Female slaves were beaten, overworked, and made to experience excessive childbearing in order to provide income, comfort, and leisure for slave-owning families. Because, in the nineteenth century, slave owner consciousness imaged black people as belonging to a lower order of nature than white people, black people were to be controlled and tamed like the rest of the natural environment. Black women (and black men) were "viewed as beasts, as cattle, as 'articles' for sale."[2] The taming of these "lower orders of nature" would assure the well-being of both master and slave—so slave owner consciousness imagined. Put simply, the assault upon the natural environment today is but an extension of the assault upon black women's bodies in the nineteenth century.

Within the last ten years African-American women have begun developing Womanist Theology and have labeled this assault upon the environment and upon black women's bodies as sin. In some womanist theological quarters, this

Reprinted from Delores S. Williams, "Sin, Nature, and Black Women's Bodies," Ecofeminism and the Sacred, *ed. Carol J. Adams (New York: Continuum, 1999, pp. 24–29). Reprinted by permission of the Continuum International Publishing Company*

sin has been named "defilement." Different from the traditional theological understanding of sin as alienation or estrangement from God and humanity, the sin of defilement manifests itself in human attacks upon creation so as to ravish, violate, and destroy creation: to exploit and control the production and reproduction capacities of nature, to destroy the unity in nature's placements, to obliterate the spirit of the created.

Assuming a relation between the defilement of earth's body and the defilement of black women's bodies, this article will attempt one task. That is to show the correlations between the defilement of aspects of the natural environment today and the defilement of black women's bodies in the nineteenth century. Finally I suggest how American national consciousness has been shaped so that Christians do not readily see the manifestations of the sin of defilement in relation to black women's experience and to nature.

Strip-Mining and Breeder Women

As the environmental crisis became more obvious, strip-mining was recognized as a problem, as an assault upon the earth. Richard Cartwright Austin describes strip-mining as "Modern technology in the form of giant shovels, bulldozers, and other . . . equipment . . . at war with the earth to extract coal. The people who lived among these once-beautiful hills [of West Virginia] often became casualties along with the landscape."[3] Because of the use of explosives and heavy machinery, strip-mining on top of the earth's surface "helped" the mine owners realize faster and larger profits than could be realized with men furnishing the energy for releasing the coal from beneath the earth's surface. Austin testifies that "those with capital were dismembering the hills, using dynamite and bulldozers to harvest coal cheaply."[4] Strip-mining ultimately exhausts the earth's capacity to produce coal. The bottom line here is regular and consistent defilement and abuse of the

earth's body (the land) for the sake of economic profit—destroying the earth's production capacities for the benefit of a few people with money.

Just as strip-mining exhausts the earth's body, so did the practice of breeding female slaves exhaust black women's bodies. One slave woman tells of her aunt, who was a breeder woman during slavery and "brought in chillum ev'y twelve mont's jes lak a cow bringing in a calf."[5] This practice was continued until many of the breeder women were no longer able to have children. Breeding women with men one already owned was a much cheaper way of obtaining more slaves than buying them on the slave market. The violation of the land's production capacities in strip-mining is no more severe than the violation of black women's bodies and reproduction capacities during slavery. . . .

Just as the land is vulnerable to all kind of uses by those who own the means of production in our society, the nineteenth-century slave woman's body was equally as vulnerable. "Black women . . . were sexually available to any white man who cared to use them. . . . The sexual exploitation of black women by white men was so widespread as to be general."[6]

Destroying the Unity in Nature's Placements

Violation and exploitation of the land and of women's bodies is, in part, caused by widespread human disrespect for the unity of nature's placements. This disrespect has led to the destruction of natural processes in nature. . . .

This disrespect and destruction of nature's placements with regard to the land and its vegetation has a parallel in the disrespect seventeenth-, eighteenth- and nineteenth-century Western white men had for the natural location of the earth's peoples. Snatching African bodies, female and male, from their homeland in order to enslave them and make a profit, Western white males depleted the African continent's human resources that had been fundamental for institutional life in many African villages. These "body snatchers" not only captured ordinary Africans for slavery, they also snatched rulers, kings, and queens. In the middle passage, as these captured Africans were sailing to America, the black women's bodies, regardless of their former social status, were raped by crewmen. Thus many African women arrived on American shores pregnant.

Attack upon Nature's Spirit and the Human Spirit

There can be little doubt that this Western disrespect for the unity of nature's placements, for nature's own cycles of production and reproduction, has emerged with the growth and development of biblical monotheism. Lynn White, Jr., was correct when he said that the spread of this monotheism stamped out the animism present in the popular religious consciousness. Austin, reporting White's ideas, says common people believed "that spirits inhabited trees, springs, hills and other features of the landscape . . . [therefore] common people had traditionally empathized with their environment and had sought to placate it while they used it."[7] White says that "By destroying paganism, Christianity made it possible to exploit nature in a mood of indifference to the feelings of natural objects."[8] The present environmental crisis, perceived in the context of animistic faith, has resulted from Western assault upon the spirits of nature. (It is not uncharacteristic of some African-American and African-Christian faiths to believe that the spirit of God created nature and prevails in it. Therefore, the assault upon nature is an attack upon both the creation and the divine spirit.)

Many African-American slave narratives mention the work of men called "Negro breakers" or "Spirit breakers," who were hired by slave owners "to break" the spirit of slaves on the plantation who seemed to have too much self-esteem, too much sense of independence, who seemed to be "uppity." Often the slave master,

himself, broke the spirit of such slave women by constantly raping them. Ex-slave Solomon Northup told the story of the slave woman Patsey, who was "slim and straight. . . . There was an air of loftiness in her movement, that neither labor, nor weariness, nor punishment could destroy." Northup says Patsey was "naturally . . . a joyous creature, a laughing, light-hearted girl, rejoicing in the mere sense of existence." But Patsey suffered more than any of the other slave women, because "it had fallen her lot to be the slave of a licentious master and a jealous mistress. Finally, for a trifling offense, Patsey was given a savage whipping, while her mistress and the master's children watched with obvious satisfaction. She almost died." Northup says "From that time forward she was not what she had been . . . the bounding vigor, the sprightly . . . spirit . . . was gone."[9] In his narrative, the ex-slave Frederick Douglas told of the "Negro Breakers" whom slave owners hired to break the spirit of "uppity" slaves.

Breaking the spirit of nature today through rape and violence done to the earth, and breaking the spirit of nineteenth-century slave women through rape and violence, constitute crimes against nature and against the human spirit. Inasmuch as some Christianity has historically advocated that God gave man [sic] dominion over nature to use to his own advantage, it has not been difficult to create rationales to support this rape and violence. Christian slaveholders, believing they had ownership over the lower orders of nature (i.e., lower than themselves, who were the "highest" order of nature), assigned black men and women to the order of subhuman, on par with the lower animals. Thus these black people needed to be controlled.

Invisibilizing the Defilement of Black Women

American national consciousness has been structured so that the defilement of black women is invisible due to the kind of associations made with the color of their black skin. In North

America, popular culture, religion, science, and politics have worked together to assign permanent negative value to the color black. This has led to the formation of a national consciousness that considers black frightening, dangerous, repulsive, and a prime candidate for destruction. In this kind of consciousness, nothing black can be violated, because illegality and disaster are associated with blackness. For instance, blackmail and the black market are illegal. When the stock market fell in 1987, the day was referred to, in the media and elsewhere, as Black Monday. When the movie Ghost showed in American movie houses recently, whiteness was associated with heaven, while blackness was associated with hell. The hero in the movie died and ultimately walked into a bright, white light apparently leading to heaven. When the villains in the movie died, jet-black figures escorted them, apparently into hell.

Not only today, but also in earlier times, negative associations were made with the color black. The American economic crash of 1873 was referred to as Black September. In the early days of the Industrial Revolution in America, when the factory system was emerging, management circulated blacklists. On these lists were the names of workers whom management designated as troublemakers or undesirable for one reason or another. Antipathy toward blackness was expressed as early as the first century, in an early Christian document titled *The Epistle of Barnabas*. This document provided the following "portrait" of the devil:

> The way of the Black One [i.e., the devil] is crooked and full of cursing, for it is the way of death eternal with punishment, and in it are the things that destroy their soul: idolatry, forwardness, arrogance of power, hypocrisy, double-heartedness, adultery, murder, robbery, pride, transgression, fraud, malice, self-sufficiency, enchantments, magic, covetousness.[10]

In the nineteenth century, the newly developing science called physical anthropology went to great lengths to "prove" the intellectual and moral inferiority of black people, including black women.[11] Put all this structuring of the national consciousness about blackness with the structuring of the national consciousness to devalue black womanhood, and it is not difficult to understand why black women's defilement is invisible to mainstream America. Then put all of this together with the practice of controlling and using nature, which many Christians have believed to be their God-given right, and it is not difficult to understand why Westerners did not recognize in the early stages of technological development the defilement of nature that could and surely would occur.

This defilement of nature's body and of black women's bodies is sin, since its occurrence denies that black women and nature are made in the image of God. Its occurrence is an assault upon the spirit of creation in women and nature. Whereas theologians such as Paul Tillich spoke of sin as man's [sic] estrangement from God and from other humans, womanist theologians can claim that humanity in the Western world has fallen to deeper states of degradation and depravity. Western Christians, some of whom are the manipulators of technology and concepts of development, no longer have to struggle only with the despair of being alienated from God (or the ground of being). They must now struggle with the attack Western man has waged against creation itself. They must struggle against the sin of defilement (evidenced today in nature and in the history of black women) —the sin that now threatens to destroy all life on the planet.

NOTES

1. Lynn White, Jr. "The Historical Roots of Our Ecologic Crisis," *Science* 155, no. 3767 (March 10, 1967), p. 1205.

2. Charles Nichols, *Many Thousand Gone* (Leiden: E. J. Brill, 1963), p. 12.

3. Richard Cartwright Austin, *Hope for the Land: Nature in the Bible* (Atlanta: John Knox Press, 1988), p. 3.

4. Ibid., p. 4.

5. Wolfgang Lederer, *The Fear of Women* (New York: Harcourt Brace Jovanovich, 1968), p. 48.

6. Ibid., pp. 45–46.

7. Austin, p. 2.

8. Ibid.

9. Solomon Northup, *Narrative of Solomon Northrup, Twelve Years a Slave* (Auburn, NY: Derby and Miller, 1853), pp. 188–90, 198, 156–159.

10. Kirsopp Lake, trans. *The Apostolic Fathers,* 2 vols (New York: L. G. P. Putnam's Sons, 1919), 1: 407.

11. William Stanton, *The Leopard's Spots: Scientific Attitudes Toward Race in America, 1815–1859* (Chicago: University of Chicago Press, 1960).

Counterpoint:
Ecological Approaches to the Study of Religion

HERBERT BURHENN

Herbert Burhenn teaches at the University of Tennessee, Chattanooga.

. . . OVER THE PAST SEVERAL DECADES the concept of ecology, whose original home was in the biological sciences, has been appropriated by the social sciences. Tracing out the role of social institutions in permitting society to adapt to the non-human environment has proved a fruitful tactic in the hands of a number of anthropologists, beginning with the pioneering work of Julian Steward (1972). With a suitable time lag we are now beginning to see these same ecological concerns used to develop naturalistic explanations of religion.

The purpose of this article is to try to chart what has been achieved to date by ecological approaches in the study of religion. The efforts I examine here can be categorized under two broad headings—those which attempt to trace out mono-directional causation and those which attempt to show functional relationships with feedback loops. An examination of some of the representative practitioners of each approach will be elucidating.

. . . *Mono-Directional Theories*

The most prolific advocate of an ecological approach to the study of religion has been the Swedish anthropologist Åke Hultkrantz, whose own fieldwork has concentrated on North American Indians. In a series of articles spanning several decades Hultkrantz has touted the virtues and minimized the vices of appealing to ecological factors in trying to understand religion, and his recently published textbook on North American native religions contains some illustrations of such appeals.

Hultkrantz's methodological thesis is so simple that he allows it to emerge by implication: some features of religion can be explained as consequences of environmental factors or as adaptations to the natural environment. But to state his thesis so simply is, of course, to open it to all sorts of misinterpretation and to make it sound suspiciously similar to old-fashioned environmental determinism. Hultkrantz is fully

Reprinted from Herbert Burhenn, "Ecological Approaches to the Study of Religion." Method and Theory in the Study of Religion *9/2 (1997): 111–126.*

aware of this hazard and devotes virtually all of his methodological essays to guarding himself against it. His strategies are numerous. I shall try to describe the principal ones.

(1) Hultkrantz[1] repeatedly insists that ecology of religion is not deterministic. Environmental factors influence religion not directly but only through a "cultural filter." In some cases the influence may be very indirect, as when adaptation to the environment produces a particular kind of social structure and this in turn influences religious beliefs and rituals. Furthermore, we should think of the environment as stimulating cultural creativity rather than restricting what it is possible for a culture to achieve.[2]

(2) Ecology of religion, Hultkrantz maintains, is not reductionist. It attempts to explain the form of religion, but does not "touch the religious values as such."[3] These values, Hultkrantz asserts, are rooted "in the psychic equipment of man," though he offers no defense of this claim.[4] In any case the point of his protestations is clear: ecology of religion does not purport to explain why human beings are religious, but only the forms which their religious beliefs and practices happen to assume.

(3) Hultkrantz restricts the scope of ecology of religion to the study of primitive or tribal religions, those not affected by urbanization or industrialization, for he believes that their "cultures are most exposed to the forces of environment."[5] He recognizes that ecological considerations are not likely to illuminate the religions of more complex societies, except in so far as they include residual features left over from a time when they were more greatly exposed to environmental influence.[6]

So far I have made Hultkrantz's program seem entirely negative and defensive, but he clearly does have a positive goal—namely, to identify types of religion and arrange them into historical strata. Hultkrantz seeks to develop his notion of type of religion from Julian Steward's idea of cultural type. Steward proposes that we recognize that several geographically separated cultures may be of a common type (that is, share a common core though they may differ in historical particulars) because they have had to adapt to similar environments. If we are willing to recognize such common culture types arising in similar environments but with no possibility of diffusion, then we must also acknowledge a causal relationship between the environment and the cultural core. Similarly, Hultkrantz maintains, if we can recognize that several religions which are geographically separated but share similar environments are of a common type we can assume that this type (again, the core features rather than historical particulars) has arisen in response to the environment: ". . . the type of religion is in its essence timeless: in principle it should occur wherever ecological and technological conditions of a similar level and integration appear."[7]

We can see this approach exemplified in Hultkrantz's recent introductory text, *Native Religions of North America* (1987). The central fact about North America which must be reflected in an account of its native religion is that it was populated through a series of roughly datable human migrations. The migrants were hunting peoples who shared a "rather uniform circumpolar and circumboreal culture and religions which were centred about shamanism and animal ceremonialism."[8] As horticulture developed in the temperate and tropical areas of the New World, new religious practices and ideas emerged which bear striking resemblances to the agricultural religions of the Old World—permanent shrines, calendrical ritual, priests, fertility ceremonies, gods and goddesses. These parallels between geographically separated religions suggest that the agricultural way of life has exerted a similar causal influence in both the New and the Old Worlds. The diversity of Native American religions can thus be analyzed as historical variations of these basic hunting and horticultural types. Since we know that the hunting type and its variations preceded the agricultural type, we can arrange religious ideas and practices into a rough historical sequence and recognize in agricultural religions remnants and transformations of hunting religions.

In his book *Priests, Warriors, and Cattle* (1981), Bruce Lincoln explicitly adopts what he describes as Hultkrantz's "daring new means of attack on the problem of comparing religions rooted in similar cultures."[9] Lincoln chooses for his comparative study two religions rooted in cattle-raising cultures but totally separated from one another by both space and time. His one example is the religion and culture of contemporary Nilotes—principally the Nuer, the Dinka, and the Masai—who have been studied by several very distinguished ethnographers. His other example is the religion and culture of the proto-Indo-Iranians, who migrated southeastward from the south Russian steppes beginning in the third millennium B.C.E. Since we have no texts from the latter people (and of course no ethnographic studies of them!), Lincoln is dependent for his knowledge of them upon scholarly analyses of later texts, principally the *Rig Veda* and *Zend Avesta*, which attempt to identify common myths, rituals, names, and ideas that derive from the parent culture antecedent to both of these texts.[10] Recent archaeological investigations have also proved useful in reconstructing Indo-Iranian religion and culture.

The Nilotic and Indo-Iranian cultures are ecologically similar in respect to the two principal points of comparison which Hultkrantz stresses. Both have the same means of subsistence, the keeping of the cattle, and both have the same fundamental unit of social organization, the herding party. The two therefore provide us with "a perfect case for study," Lincoln concludes.[11]

In these ecologically similar cultures we find strikingly similar religious systems. Both can be analyzed in terms of one complex of practices and ideas (which Lincoln calls a cycle) associated with priests and a second complex associated with warriors. The priestly complex focuses on the ritual of sacrifice, for which cattle are the preferred, though not the only, victims.

Appropriately enough, the principal myth of the priestly complex is concerned with the first sacrifice, which becomes the model for future sacrifice. The priestly concept of the divine is associated with the sky. In both cultures there is an established social hierarchy which places priests above warriors. The warrior complex, in turn, focuses on the ritual of the cattle raid, idealized as an example of heroism and usually carried out with some priestly assistance. The principal myth is concerned with the first raid, which provides both the model and the justification for all future raids. Warriors are organized into groups by age and require initiation for group membership. In preparation for the cattle raid, meat-eating and intoxicants are used to increase strength and courage. The divine is conceptualized in terms of warrior gods, located in the atmosphere and sometimes associated with storms.[12]

The purpose of the priestly and warrior cycles is the same—to get more cattle—though the means (sacrifice versus raid) differ. Despite the agreement on ends, there is a conflict between priests and warriors inherent in both cultures. Priests have hierarchical superiority, but warriors clearly possess superior physical strength. The priest-warrior tension is manifested in numerous ways, but perhaps most explicitly in a fundamental disagreement over the slaughter of cattle: for the priests sacrifice is the only appropriate occasion for such slaughter, whereas warriors wish to slaughter cattle to provide meat for strengthening.

These, then, are the broad patterns of similarity between Nilotic and Indo-Iranian religion. As Hultkrantz's method would lead us to expect, there are numerous particulars on which the two religious systems differ. The chief one of these differences, according to Lincoln, has to do with the priestly conception of the divine. In the Nilotic system there is a single celestial sovereign who is thought of as responsible for the creation and maintenance of the world order. For Indo-Iranian priests, on the other hand, there are a number of celestial sovereigns, with varying attitudes toward humankind, and new ones replace older ones over a period of time.

Almost the entirety of Lincoln's book is devoted to establishing the agreement in type between Nilotic and Indo-Iranian religion. Only in the last few pages does he address the question of how such an agreement might have occurred. He answers this question by sketching out a mono-directional causal sequence. . . . Each of these practices, in turn, gives birth to a class of specialists. Each class develops "modes of valued conduct" and employs myths as sacred precedents for such conduct.[13] Priests and warriors present different answers to the question of how to obtain more cattle; therefore, some tension and rivalry between the classes is likewise to be expected. . . .

. . . Conclusions

We have looked now at a variety of explanatory approaches to religion which I hope have been intriguing and which should at least have expanded our notion of what might be possible in developing explanations. It should be obvious that all of these approaches are directed to explaining specific features of religious belief and practice rather than to explaining human religiosity as such, as the grand proposals of Durkheim or Freud purport to do. But we must not let such modesty deflect critical appraisal of what has been accomplished.

(1) This modesty may hide a bit of immodesty, specifically in Hultkrantz's use of the term "ecological." His work and that of Lincoln do not, in fact, deal with ecosystems described in any detail but only with the most general features of material life. While it may be helpful to correlate religious practices with the conditions of material life, much of what is purportedly explained by such correlations is hardly surprising. We should certainly expect people to draw elements from their environment as they develop religious beliefs and practices. The only point at which the work of Hultkrantz and Lincoln takes us significantly beyond

the obvious is through the old notion of survivals—specifically, the possibility that the religious beliefs and practices of agricultural peoples may retain elements from their hunter forebears.

(2) Ecology in its biological manifestation is a highly quantitative discipline. Clearly one of the elements missing from almost all of the explanations surveyed here is attention to quantitative measurement. . . .

(3) All of the explanations considered here force us to reflect on the well-worn emic/etic distinction. None of the explanations are concerned with societies which had access to contemporary ecological concepts, and so all of these explanations use etic terminology. But two partial exceptions are worth noting. . . . What makes the work of Hultkrantz and Lincoln considerably less satisfying is the paucity of etic concepts and their failure to draw on, in any technical way, ecological notions.

(4) Surveying these explanations should also reinforce in our thinking a principle which I should like to call explanatory pluralism. Numerous philosophers have noted that phenomena can be explained only after they have been described and that accordingly the proffered explanation explains the phenomenon only under that description.[14] Any religious phenomenon we might want to explain can be described in many ways and with varying degrees of specificity. Consequently, no explanation we offer will be exhaustive. With a functionalist ecological explanation, for example, a phenomenon can be explained only if it can be treated as an element in the ecosystem of which a particular society is a part. But treating the phenomenon in that way certainly leaves many of its dimensions untouched. . . .

(5) Keeping in mind the principle of explanatory pluralism should free us, finally, from the widely-voiced fear that ecological explanations might somehow be reductionistic. The concept of reduction has undergone a good bit of refinement in recent philosophy of science, and I shall try to distil from that discussion a formulation that might be appropriate for theories of religion. . . .

Despite Hultkrantz' assurances to the contrary, ecological theories of religion do purport to be reductionistic . . ., and that characteristic is precisely what makes them valuable. They challenge us to discover how much we can understand about a religious belief or practice by construing it as an element of an ecosystem. What makes the explanations we have surveyed here valuable is that they do in fact contribute to our understanding, especially of practices that might otherwise seem anomalous. Do they supersede other types of explanation? Unless we subscribe to the sort of explanatory monism that has determined what level of explanation is ultimately fundamental, the question of superseding other types of explanation must be decided on a case-by-case basis. An essential part of that decision involves determining whether an ecological explanation is concerned with the same phenomenon under a sufficiently similar description as another type of explanation might be. As long as we do not presume to know the answers to these questions in advance, we can acknowledge the contribution of ecological explanations without granting them the only or the last word.

NOTES

1. Åke Hultkrantz, "An Ecological Approach to Religion," *Ethnos* 31 (1966), p. 139.

2. "Ecology of Religion: Its Scope and Methodology," in Lauri Honko ed. *Science of Religion: Studies in Methodology* (The Hague: Mouton, 1979), p. 224.

3. Ibid., p. 226.

4. Ibid.

5. Ibid., pp. 224, 229.

6. Ibid., p. 224.

7. Idem, "An Ecological Approach," pp. 147–48.

8. Idem, *Native Religions of North America: The Power of Visions and Fertility* (San Francisco: Harper and Row, 1987), p. 12.

9. Bruce Lincoln, *Priests, Warriors and Cattle: A Study in the Ecology of Religions* (Berkeley: University of California Press, 1981), p. 9.

10. Ibid., p. 2.

11. Ibid., p. 10.

12. Ibid.

13. Ibid., p. 174.

14. Arthur Danto, *Analytical Philosophy of History* (Cambridge: Cambridge University Press, 1965), pp. 201–32.

Chapter 10

Feminist Perspectives on Religion

Feminist scholars have challenged the many different kinds of approaches to the study of religion that we have examined thus far in this anthology, because many of these approaches neglect the importance of how gender shapes a scholar's basic presuppositions, understanding of the subject, perception about what is important and what is superfluous to grasping the subject, and how gender affects one's participation in religion. Feminist scholars distinguish gender from sex because the latter represents a biologically inherited attribute, whereas gender refers to cultural expectations of what it means to be one sex or another, with particular cultural perceptions that differ from one culture to another. Even though feminist scholars agree that gender is socially constructed and possesses general importance for the study of religion, they represent wide, multidimensional, and complex views about various religious traditions and the role of women in those traditions. To reinterpret, retrieve, or transform their religious traditions, many feminists have addressed problems of sexism and patriarchal social structure in theological analysis. Yet, this anthology is committed to excluding theological approaches to the field of religion because of its parochial and apologetic features. We will also exclude theological approaches to issues on gender from a feminist perspective in this chapter to a large extent.

Even if we exclude feminist theological approaches to issues of gender, we find that feminists from nontheological perspectives are still attempting to counter similar obstacles that are often identified as patriarchy and sexism. By patriarchy, feminists usually understand a historical, social, cultural, and political institutionalization of male power that results in the domination, subordination, and marginalization of women. The all-embracing specter of patriarchy is supported by sexism that can be defined as the ideology of male supremacy. Within the all-encompassing matrix of patriarchy and male sexism, feminist theorists seek to retrieve from the history of various cultures the roles played by women, their place within different societies, the contributions that they have made to their religious cultures, and how and why women have been excluded from certain roles within cultures. Because the visions, voices, memories, and sources of and about women have often been lost or suppressed by various cultures, feminists find themselves with the task of reconstructing the past to the best of their ability. This implies that an individual female scholar not only considers the presence of women within a religious tradition, but she must also search for clues that inform her about the absence of women in certain aspects of a society. In some religious traditions, it is possible to hear the ancient voices of women, but there are also instances when feminist scholars encounter absolute silence. It is at such moments when they have to call upon their powers of imagination and discernment to construct a coherent view of women's contributions to a particular religious culture. Although this does not suggest that feminist scholarship lacks any objectivity, it does suggest that absence and silence can be informative in their own way and be used by insightful scholars.

Due to the transformative and historically revolutionary nature of their work in a male-dominated cultural context, feminists find themselves not only reconstructing the past of a religious tradition, but also looking for new paradigms for thinking, perceiving, and understanding. This can be found among female scholars like Christine Downing and Carol P. Christ who advocate the importance of the goddess. Instead of theology, Christ refers to her work as "thea-logy" to stress the importance of the goddess. By focusing on gender issues, feminists necessarily change the way data is collected, sifted, described, analyzed, and interpreted. This can open new windows on the subject of religion and broaden the understanding of the subject.

The feminist approach is unique in its fundamental challenge to the study of religion, which is deeply and historically grounded within an androcentric framework. It is exactly this androcentric framework that represents a prison from which feminists want to free everyone. This prison of patriarchy and androcentric domination is reflected in a politics of knowledge that male figures have constructed. To free oneself from such a prison, one must find new ways of knowing that will lead to a completely new and liberating paradigm shift in the field of religion. What might this new type of thinking be like? Based on current feminist trends, this new mode of thinking attempts to break free of standard rational and objectifying modes of thinking. Some feminists want to introduce a more emotional approach, envisioning people and historical events as more human, in contrast to strictly objective and scientific approaches. This is witnessed in Rita Gross's approach, emphasizing empathy. Whatever form is eventually assumed by the new paradigm(s) or mode(s) of thinking, feminists will base the changes in the experience of a generally shared perspective about the history of women as they search for new ways of thinking and living that will liberate everyone from hierarchical domination expressed in social and political structures, confining cultural norms, sexism, and elitism.

The vast majority of feminists perceive their work (or at least its goal) as transformative and liberating. Such efforts have been undertaken for several decades. Without attempting to be completely exhaustive, it is possible to review some trends in feminist scholarship. Within the Christian religious tradition, feminists have expended considerable effort. To present some of the approaches taken by feminist scholars within the western cultural context, we can look briefly at the efforts of Mary Daly. For instance, many feminists agree that the God symbolism is problematic, but they offer divergent solutions to the problem.

In her book *Beyond God the Father*, Mary Daly argues that masculine pronouns and titles like king, lord, son, and father indubitably imply that male power is divine. This basic point suggests that male power becomes legitimated at the expense of female power. Furthermore, female power is denigrated in comparison to the powerful male titles that suggest a masculine model that is synonymous with perfection. Thus feminists must reject sexist symbolism of domination.

Feminists propose different solutions to the problematic nature of masculine God symbolism. From one perspective, it is possible to reinterpret the religious tradition. It is also suggested that male sexist symbolism be rejected. Some feminists reject the biblical faiths like Judaism and Christianity because sexist symbolism and language are endemic to their essence. In the place of the biblical faiths, some feminists propose to introduce goddess symbolism, replace Judeo-Christian language and symbols with sexually neutral expressions, or use androgynous modes of expression. Still other feminists like Carol P. Christ and Naomi R. Goldenberg suggest embracing goddess devotion. In some instances, goddess worship is connected with the contemporary witchcraft movement that combines medieval witchcraft beliefs and practices with views about the meaning of goddess symbolism. Such goddess symbolism serves as a symbol of life, death, and rebirth for a feminist like Starhawk. It is also connected to the energy of nature and culture, and revitalized personal and communal modes of life.

From the perspective of black women like Delores Williams and Katie Cannon, it is impossible for a single feminist's perspective to encompass the religious experience of all women. These women argue that the experience of black women has been neglected or ignored by white, middle-class, feminine scholars. Williams argues, for example, that it is insufficient to discuss liberation from patriarchy when it is necessary to become liberated from class and race domination. The oppression of black women includes an attack on their ability to reproduce, an assault on their self-esteem, and a denial of their rights to meaningful relationships. Williams identifies the oppressors as white males and females along with black males. Black scholars like Williams and Cannon call their approach "womanist" to distinguish it from the various approaches of white feminists.

In contrast to the approaches of black feminists and Mary Daly's call in her later works for a women-centered world that is virtually exclusive of male intervention, another type of approach arises. Feminist thinkers like Anne Carr of the University of Chicago propose a more holistic and inclusive approach to the issue and problems associated with gender. Her approach seeks to overcome the fundamental polarization of male and female identities that remains in a position like the one advocated by Daly. Why does Carr advocate such an approach? Basically, the experience of women has always been a relational one because women have always been in relationship to men with particular social and cultural contextual wholes. Thus Carr wants to move toward something more inclusive in which the interrelatedness and interconnectedness between men and women assume a more central role in analysis.

Contrasting the perspective of Carr, Marsha Aileen Hewitt gives us a Marxist viewpoint. Because this chapter uses her critique of other feminist thinkers as a counterpoint in a couple of places and thus highlights her contribution to feminist theory, we would be remiss if we did not explain briefly the historical background of what Marsha Aileen Hewitt of Trinity College and the University of Toronto calls "critical theory" in her work. She identifies her approach with thinkers like Karl Marx, Max Horkheimer, Theodor W. Adorno, and more recently, Jürgen Habermas. These last three figures are associated with the so-called Frankfurt School of German philosophy, which traces its origin to the thought of Hegel and Marx, although it was systematized by Horkheimer and others.

But what is critical theory? It can be simply defined as a tool of reason that possesses the power to change society. By basing itself on a Hegelian-Marxist foundation and the Enlightenment assumption that rational reflection is emancipatory, critical theory reflects the philosophical conviction that when theory is connected with practical activity (*praxis*) it possesses the political goal of social transformation. Horkheimer perceived that social science had been imitating natural science with respect to its definition of theory. This finding, combined with the tendency of researchers to conform to generalizations that imitate ideas already present in their minds, posed a danger for theory. This mind-conforming type of theory was thus divorced from empirical experience. There was thus no connection between theoretical activity and actual life. To counteract this problem, it was incumbent upon a scholar to develop a critical theory. Horkheimer and Adorno discovered some help from Max Weber and his notion that reason could succeed against its falsifications or alienation, whereas Marx looked toward social action as the remedy for alienation. Weber envisioned reason becoming more secular and freed from mythic and religious associations and becoming more purposeful, calculating, useful, and more directed toward means rather than toward ends. What Weber called purposive rational action, Horkheimer designated as instrumental reason because he grasped reason as an overwhelming force for the purposes of social control. In contrast to Horkheimer, Habermas disagrees about the instrumental nature of reason, and he argues that rationality is helpless to regenerate itself once it is reduced to an instrumental basis. From Habermas's perspective, Weber, Horkheimer, and Adorno went astray because they perceived rationality in terms of dualistic or subject-object relations. By viewing the problem in this way, Habermas attempted to develop an alternative theory of rationality that he identified with his theory of communicative action, which is noninstrumental. Embodying within itself a claim to validity, the theory of communicative action leads to a progressive emancipation. Hewitt also utilizes the work of others who rest on the philosophical left wing, like Herbert Marcuse and Walter Benjamin.

In her book entitled *Critical Theory of Religion,* Hewitt assumes a courageous feminist position by attempting to stray from the thought of other feminists. She is critical of thought that lacks political power for change, social relevancy, and concrete social analysis. She stands opposed to injustice, making humans a means to some end rather than ends in themselves, authoritarian attitudes, ethical hierarchy, a dualism between males and females, and antidemocratic actions or sentiments. Hewitt's notion of liberation is universal because it includes not only women, but it also includes nature and the whole of humanity. She envisions a more humane and happier of "Hag-ocracy," a wild realm of hags and crones, that seek to break free from the language identified as "phallocracy."

Carol P. Christ, who was born on December 20, 1945 in Pasadena, California, advocates that women return to devotion of the goddess. For many years, Christ was professor of Women's Studies and Religious Studies at San Jose State University. She retired from teaching to devote her time to supervising tours of ancient sites connected to the goddess cult in Greece and the island of Crete, although she still continues to publish in the field. Besides editing a couple of very successful anthologies with Judith Plaskow, Christ published the following works on feminist issues and goddess devotion: *Diving Deep and Surfacing: Women Writers on Spiritual Quest* (1980), *Laughter of Aphrodite: Reflections on a Journey to the Goddess* (1987), *Odyssey With the Goddess: A Spiritual Quest in Crete* (1995), and *Rebirth of the Goddess: Finding Meaning in Feminist Spirituality* (1997). Some of these works reflect a perception of the hopelessness of transforming the Western religious tradition because of its dominance by the prevailing patriarchal culture. Christ thinks that it is possible for women to find an alternative form of spirituality that is more attuned to feminist concerns in ancient goddess devotion.

An excellent example of the feminist challenge to the androcentric way of studying religion is offered by Rita M. Gross who received her doctorate from the University of Chicago with a dissertation on the role of women in tribal Australian religion. She has taught at the University of Wisconsin–Eau Claire for many years, and she has been active in the dialogue between Buddhists and Christians. Besides numerous essays on the topic of women and religion, Gross edited (along with Nancy Auer Falk) a widely used book in courses on women and world religions entitled *Unspoken Worlds: Women's Religious Lives in Non-Western Cultures* (1980). Her most important book with respect to this anthology is *Feminism and Religion: An Introduction* (1996), a work that reflects her commitment to bringing a feminist perspective to the study of religion and her background in the history of religions. Her keen interest in Buddhism is evident in the following two books: *Buddhism After Patriarchy: A Feminist History, Analysis and Reconstruction of Buddhism* (1993) and *Soaring and Settling: Buddhist Perspectives on Contemporary Social and Religious Issues* (1998). Gross's history of religions approach and its Buddhist-influenced perspective stands in sharp contrast to the "womanist" approach of Williams, even though they share a feminist perspective.

Contrary to the white feminine viewpoint, Delores Williams provides a so-called "womanist" (black feminine) perspective. After completing her undergraduate studies at the University of Louisville, Williams earned a master's degree from Columbia University and a doctorate in 1991 from Union Theological Seminary where she teaches and holds an endowed chair called the Paul Tillich Professor of Theology and Culture Chair. In addition to numerous articles in scholarly journals and books, Williams is recognized as a black spokeswoman for publishing *Sisters in the Wilderness: The Challenge of Womanist God-Talk* (1993) and the *Daughters of Hagar: The Challenge of Womanist God-Talk* (2000). These works reflect her critical voice advocating issues of social and political justice for black women.

Womanist thinkers like Williams adopted the term "womanist" from the novelist Alice Walker, and adapted it for their own purposes. Walker had called attention to world in which to live that will enhance opportunities for humans to seek freedom and happiness. Finally, she wants to preserve a utopian hope for absolute justice and social reconciliation.

Although this introduction hardly does justice to the variety of feminist approaches, it should provide its sense of critical and transformative dimensions. It should emphasize that there is no monolithic feminist's position. Moreover, feminism represents a significant challenge to the historically androcentric approach to the study of religion. Male scholars of religion are challenged by feminists to reexamine their basic methodological presuppositions and to be more gender inclusive. This challenge is evident in the selections in this anthology.

Although this anthology will not present works specifically concerned with theology, we would be remiss to omit the perspective of Mary Daly because of her broad influence on both the theological and nontheological feminist issues. Important philosophical issues of her work are also germane to this anthology.

Among the radical feminine voices demanding justice, no voice is more prominent and pronounced than that of Mary Daly, who was born on October 16, 1928 in Schenectady, New York. She taught at Boston College for over 30 years until a controversy developed between her and the institution's administration over the issue of a male student's admittance into her course on feminist thought. Early in her scholarly career, Daly published a book on speculative theology and another on the problem of God in the philosophy of Jacques Maritain. She then turned her attention to feminist issues within the context of religion with books like the following: *Beyond God the Father: Toward a Philosophy of Women's Liberation* (1985), *The Church and the Second Sex* (1985), *Gyn/Ecology, the Metaethics of Radical Feminism* (1990), *Pure Lust: Elemental Feminist Philosophy* (1992), *Outercourse: The Bedazzling Voyage Containing Recollections from My Logbook of a Radical Feminist Philosopher* (1992), and *Quintessence: Realizing the Outrageous Contagious Courage of Women: A Radical Elemental Feminist Manifesto* (1998). These works reflect Daly's radical critique of the Western patriarchal culture and its domination, oppression, and subordination of women.

In her book *Beyond God the Father,* Daly challenges patriarchal religion and examines the potential of the women's revolution to transform human consciousness. To enhance this transformation, it is essential for women to reclaim their rights to name things, which involves a liberation of language that is connected to self-liberation. She refers to the necessity of castrating the language of a sexist world. This entails castrating the male arrogance associated with the myths of sin and salvation. Within her castration process, masculine symbols and images for the incarnation, for instance, lose their credibility and make way for an awareness of the power of being in everyone. She argues in part that Jesus embodied the qualities of the idealized victim and simply reinforces the scapegoat image for women, concluding that women cannot seek suitable models for liberation within Christianity. Is there another alternative? Daly thinks that one must live precariously on the boundary of patriarchal space to be free from the oppressiveness of the past and tradition. Daly advocates that women discover personal validity within their own experience. In her later work, *Gyn/Ecology,* Daly continues to advocate a process of self-discovery and renaming within a context of a web of interrelationships. This is described as a spinning process black women of the slave tradition that were mentally and emotionally strong. These black women were also self-determined, sassy, lovers, and caregivers to the black community. But most of all they were survivors. The term feminist cannot do justice to the experience of these black women. Therefore, womanist thought is a critique of the racism of white women and white men and sexism of all men. Such a critique is performed from within a context of a black woman's experience of racism, sexism, and classism. Besides using the history of black women to reveal their long-silent voices, womanist thinkers are concerned with issues of power that not only involve relations between women and men, but they are also concerned with the dehumanizing results of issues like abuse, exploitation, and oppression for African-American women. Thus womanist thought tends to be prophetic, political, and survivalist.

Guideline Questions

By inventing and using terms, what is Daly attempting to accomplish for feminism?

How do *eros*, empathy, and goddesses fit together for Christ, and how do they contribute to what she calls a "paradigm shift?"

How does empathy function in Gross's methodology and what advantages does her feminist approach to the study of religion offer in comparison to methods developed by men?

What does Williams discover about black women from slave narratives and how does her discovery shape her "womanist" perspective?

From *Gyn/Ecology:*
The Metaethics of Radical Feminism

MARY DALY

THIS BOOK IS ABOUT THE JOURNEY of women becoming, that is, radical feminism. The voyage is described and roughly charted here. I say "roughly" by way of understatement and pun. We do not know exactly what is on the Other Side until we arrive there—and the journey *is rough*. The charting done here is based on some knowledge from the past, upon present experience, and upon hopes for the future. These three sources are inseparable, intertwined. Radical feminist consciousness spirals in all directions, discovering the past, creating/disclosing the present/future.

The radical be-ing of women is very much an Otherworld Journey. It is both discovery and creation of a world other than patriarchy. Patriarchy appears to be "everywhere." Even outer space and the future have been colonized. As a rule, even the more imaginative science-fiction writers (allegedly the most foretelling futurists) cannot/will not create a space and time in which women get far beyond the role of space stewardess. Nor does this colonization exist simply "outside" women's minds, securely fastened into institutions we can physically leave behind. Rather, it is also internalized, festering inside women's heads, even feminist heads.

The Journey, then, involves exorcism of the internalized Godfather in his various manifestations (his name is legion). It involves dangerous encounters with these demons. Within the Christian tradition, particularly in medieval times, evil spirits have sometimes been associated with the "Seven Deadly Sins," both as personifications and as causes.[1] A standard listing of the Sins is the following: pride, avarice, anger, lust, gluttony, envy, and sloth. The feminist voyage discloses that these have all been radically misnamed, that is, inadequately and perversely "understood." They are particularized expressions of the overall use of "evil" to victimize women. Our journey involves confrontations with the demonic manifestations of evil. . . .

The Background into which feminist journeying spins is the wild realm of Hags and Crones. It is Hag-ocracy. The demons who attempt to block the gateways to the deep spaces of this realm often take ghostly/ghastly forms, comparable to noxious gases not noticeable by ordinary sense perception.[2] Each time we move into deeper space, these numbing ghostly gases work to paralyze us, to trap us, so that we will be unable to move further. Each time we succeed in overcoming their numbing effect, more dormant senses come alive. Our inner eyes open, our inner ears become unblocked. We are strengthened to move through the next gateway and the next. This movement inward/outward is be-ing. It is spinning cosmic tapestries. It is spinning and whirling into the Background.

The spinning process requires seeking out the sources of the ghostly gases that have seeped into the deep chambers of our minds. . . . Thus, for example, the word *spinster* is commonly used as a deprecating term, but it can only function this way when apprehended exclusively on a superficial (foreground) level. Its deep meaning, which

has receded into the Background so far that we have to spin deeply in order to retrieve it, is clear and strong: "a woman whose occupation is to spin." There is no reason to limit the meaning of this rich and cosmic verb. A woman whose occupation is to spin participates in the whirling movement of creation. She who has chosen her Self, who defines her Self, by choice, neither in relation to children nor to men, who is Self-identified, is a Spinster, a whirling dervish, spinning in a new time/space. . . .

Spinsters can find our way back to reality by destroying the false perceptions of it inflicted upon us by the language and myths of Babel. We must learn to dis-spell the language of phallocracy, which keeps us under the spell of brokenness. This spell splits our perceptions of our Selves and of the cosmos, overtly and subliminally. Journeying into our Background will mean recognizing that both the "spirit" and the "matter" presented to us in the fathers' foreground are reifications, condensations. . . .

The Journey is itself participation in Paradise. This word, which is said to be from the Iranian *pairi* (meaning around) and *daēza* (meaning wall), is commonly used to conjure an image of a walled-in pleasure garden. Patriarchal Paradise, as projected in Western and Eastern religious mythology, is imaged as a place or a state in which the souls of the righteous after death enjoy eternal bliss, that is, heaven. Despite theological attempts to make this seem lively, the image is one of stagnation (in a stag-nation) as suggested in the expression, "the Afterlife." In contrast to this, the Paradise which is cosmic spinning is not containment within walls. Rather, it is movement that is not containable, weaving around and past walls, leaving them in the past. It moves into the Background which is the moving center of the Self, enabling the Self to act "out-wardly" in the cosmos as she comes alive. This metapatriarchal movement is not Afterlife, but Living now, discovering Life.

A primary definition of *paradise* is "pleasure park." The walls of the Patriarchal Pleasure Park represent the condition of being perpetually parked, locked into the parking lot of the past. A basic meaning of *park* is a "game preserve." The fathers' foreground is precisely this: an arena where the wildness of nature and of women's Selves is domesticated, preserved. It is the place for the preservation of females who are the "fair game" of the fathers, that they may be served to these predatory Park Owners, and service them at their pleasure. Patriarchal Paradise is the arena of games, the place where the pleas of women are silenced, where the law is: Please the Patrons. Women who break through the imprisoning walls of the Playboys' Playground are entering the process which is our happening/happiness. This is Paradise beyond the boundaries of "paradise." Since our passage into this process requires making breaks in the walls, it means setting free the fair game, breaking the rules of the games, breaking the names of the games. Breaking through the foreground which is the Playboys' Playground means letting out the bunnies, the bitches, the beavers, the squirrels, the chicks, the pussycats, the cows, the nags, the foxy ladies, the old bats and biddies, so that they can at last begin naming themselves.

I have coined the term *metapatriarchal* to describe the journey, because the prefix *meta* has multiple meanings. It incorporates the idea of "postpatriarchal," for it means occurring later. It puts patriarchy in the past without denying that its walls/ruins and demons are still around. Since *meta* also means "situated behind," it suggests that the direction of the journey is into the Background. Another meaning of this prefix is "change in, transformation of." This, of course, suggests the transforming power of the journey. By this I do not mean that women's movement "reforms" patriarchy, but that it transforms our Selves. Since *meta* means "beyond, transcending," it contains a built-in corrective to reductive notions of mere reformism. . . .

The title of this book, *Gyn/Ecology,* says exactly what I mean it to say. "Ecology" is about the complex web of interrelationships between organisms and their environment. In her book, *Le Féminisme ou la mort,* Françoise

d'Eaubonne coins the expression "eco-feminisme."[3] She maintains that the fate of the human species and of the planet is at stake, and that no male-led "revolution" will counteract the horrors of overpopulation and destruction of natural resources. I share this basic premise, but my approach and emphasis are different. Although I am concerned with all forms of pollution in phallotechnic society, this book is primarily concerned with the mind/spirit/body pollution inflicted through patriarchal myth and language on all levels. . . .

The title *Gyn/Ecology* is a way of wrenching back some wordpower. The fact that most gynecologists are males is in itself a colossal comment on "our" society. It is a symptom and example of male control over women and over language, and a clue to the extent of this control. . . .

Hagiography is a term employed by Christians, and is defined as "the biography of saints; saints' lives; biography of an idealizing or idolizing character." Hagiology has a similar meaning; it is "a description of sacred writings or sacred persons." Both of these terms are from the Greek *hagios,* meaning holy. Surviving, moving women can hardly look to the masochistic martyrs of sadospiritual religion as models. Since most patriarchal writing that purports to deal with women is pornography or hagiography (which amount to the same thing), women in a world from which woman-identified writing has been eliminated are trying to break away from these moldy "models," both of writing and of living. Our foresisters were the Great Hags whom the institutionally powerful but privately impotent patriarchs found too threatening for coexistence, and whom historians erase. *Hag* is from an Old English word meaning harpy, witch. Webster's gives as the first and "archaic" meaning of *hag*: "a female demon: FURY, HARPY." It also formerly meant: "an evil or frightening spirit." . . . A third archaic definition of *hag* is "nightmare." . . . *Hag* is also defined as "an ugly or evil-looking old woman." But this, considering the source, may be considered a compliment. For the beauty of strong, creative women is "ugly" by misogynistic standards of "beauty." The look of female-identified women is "evil" to those who fear us. As for "old," ageism is a feature of phallic society. For women who have transvaluated this, a Crone is one who should be an example of strength, courage and wisdom.

For women who are on the journey of radical be-ing, the lives of the witches, of the Great Hags of our hidden history are deeply intertwined with our own process. As we write/live our own story, we are uncovering their history, creating Hagography and Hag-ology. Unlike the "saints" of Christianity, who must, by definition, be dead, Hags live. Women traveling into feminist time/space are creating Hag-ocracy, the place we govern. To govern is to steer, to pilot. We are learning individually and together to pilot the time/spaceships of our voyage. The vehicles of our voyage may be any creative enterprises that further women's process. The point is that they should be governed by the Witch within—the *Hag* within. . . .

Haggard writing is by and for haggard women, those who are intractable, willful, wanton, unchaste, and, especially, those who are reluctant to yield to wooing. It belongs to the tradition of those who refuse to assume the woes of wooed women, who cast off these woes as unworthy of Hags, of Harpies. Haggard women are not man-wooed. As Furies, women in the tradition of the Great Hags reject the curse of compromise.

The Great Hags of history, when their lives have not been prematurely terminated, have lived to be Crones. Crones are the long-lasting ones. They are the Survivors of the perpetual witchcraze of patriarchy, the Survivors of The Burning Times. In living/writing, feminists are recording and creating the history of Crones. Women who can identify with the Great Crones may wish to call our writing of women's history Croneography.

It is also appropriate to think of our writing in this tradition as Crone-ology. *Chronology,* generally speaking, means an arrangement (as of data, events) in order of time of occurrence or appearance. In a specific sense, however, it refers to "the classification of archeological sites or prehistoric periods of culture." Since the history of Hags and Crones is truly Prehistoric in relation to patriarchal history—being prior both in time and in importance—haggard women should consider that our Crone-ology is indeed our chronology. In writing/recording/creating Crone-ography and in studying our own Prehistoric chronology, we are unmasking deceptive patriarchal history, rendering it obsolete. Women who refuse to be wooed by patriarchal scholarship can conjure the chronicles of the Great Crones, foresisters of our present and future Selves. . . . As unwooed women unearth more of our tradition, we can begin to hear and understand.

Hag-ographers perceive the hilarious hypocrisy of "his" history. At first this may be difficult, for when the whole is hypocrisy, the parts may not initially appear untrue. To put it another way, when everything is bizarre, nothing seems bizarre. Hags are women who struggle to see connections. Hags risk a great deal—if necessary, everything—knowing that there is only Nothing to lose. Hags may rage and roar, but they do not titter. . . .

There is nothing like the sound of women really laughing. The roaring laughter of women is like the roaring of the eternal sea. Hags can cackle and roar at themselves, but more and more, one hears them roaring at the reversal that is patriarchy, that monstrous jock's joke, the Male Mothers Club that gives birth only to putrefaction and deception. One can hear pain and perhaps cynicism in the laughter of Hags who witness the spectacle of Male Mothers (Murderers) dismembering a planet they have already condemned to death. But this laughter is the one true hope, for as long as it is audible there is evidence that someone is seeing through the Dirty Joke. It is in this hope that this Hag-ography is written. . . .

In the course of The Second Passage, Crone-ographers who have survived discovering the various manifestations of Goddess-murder on this patriarchal planet have become aware of the deep and universal intent to destroy the divine spark in women. We have seen that the perpetrators of this planetary atrocity are acting out the deadly myths of patriarchy and that this ritual enactment of the sado-myths has become more refined with the "progress of civilization." This refinement includes an escalation of violence and visibility and at the same time a decrease of visibility to those mesmerized by the Processions of fathers, sons, and holy ghosts. . . .

Since we have come through the somber Passage of recognizing the alien/alienating environment in which woman-hating rituals vary from *suttee* to gynecological iatrogenesis, we can begin to tread/thread our way in new time/space. This knowing/acting/Self-centering Process is itself the creating of a new, woman-identified environment. It is the becoming of Gyn/Ecology. This involves the dis-spelling of the mind/spirit/body pollution that is produced out of man-made myths, language, ritual atrocities, and meta-rituals such as "scholarship," which erase our Selves. It also involves discovering the sources of the Self's original movement, hearing the moving of this movement. It involves speaking forth the New Words which correspond to this deep listening, speaking the words of our lives.

Breaking out of the patriarchal processions into our own Gyn/Ecological process is the specific theme of this, The Third Passage. In a general sense, our movement through the preceding Passages has all been and is Gyn/Ecological Journeying. Moreover, since our movement is not linear but rather resembles spiraling, we continue to re-member/re-call/reclaim the knowledge gained in the preceding Passages, assuming this into our present/future. Hence, there is no authentic way in which the preceding Passages can be dissociated from the Third. Thus, Gyn/Ecology is not the climax or linear end point in time of the Journey, but rather it is a defining theme/thread in our Labyrinthine Journey of the inner ear, in the course of which we constantly hear deeper and deeper reverberations from all of the Passages and learn to be attuned to echoes, subtleties, and distinctions not attended to before. Yet, Gyn/Ecology is the proper name for The Third Passage, for it names the patterns/designs of the moving Female-identified environment which can only be heard/seen after the Journeyer has been initiated through The First and The Second Passages.

As the Spinster spins into and through this Passage she is encouraged by her strengthened powers of hearing and seeing. By now she has begun to develop a kind of multidimensional/multiform power of sensing/understanding her environment. This is a Self-identified *synaesthesia:* it is woman-identified *gynaesthesia*. It is a complex way of perceiving the interrelatedness of seemingly disparate phenomena. It is also a pattern-detecting power which may be named positive paranoia. Far from being a debilitating "mental disease," this is strengthening and realistic dis-ease in a polluted and destructive environment. Derived from the Greek terms *para,* meaning beyond, outside of, and *nous,* meaning mind, the term *paranoia* is appropriate to describe movement beyond, outside of, the patriarchal mind-set. It is the State of Positively Revolting Hags.

Moving through all three Passages is moving from the state of anesthesia to empowering gynaesthesia, as dormant senses become awake and alive. Since, in The Second Passage, the Voyager became more aware not only of the blatancy and interconnectedness of phallocratic evil, but also of its reality, she is enabled to detect and name its implicit presence and therefore to overcome roadblocks in her discovery of be-ing. Empowered with positive paranoia she can move with increasing confidence.

We have seen that this is the age of holy ghosts, with particular reference to gynecology. It is an age of manipulation through/by invisible and *almost* insensible presences. Some of these might be called physical, such as radiation and "white noise." Others more properly may be said to belong to the realm of the spirit, of "ghost." We are dealing here with the realm of implicit or subliminal manipulation, of quiet, almost indiscernible, intent on the part of the manipulators and quiet, unacknowledged acceptance of their ghostly presences and messages by their victims. Hence, the first chapter of this Passage will be concerned with Spooking. The Haggard Journeyer will not be astonished to find that Spooking is multileveled. Women are spooked by patriarchal males in a variety of ways; for example, through implicit messages of their institutions, through body language, through the silences and deceptive devices of their media, their grammar, their education, their professions, their technology, their oppressive and confusing fashions, customs, etiquette, "humor," through their subliminal advertising and their "sublime" music (such as Christmas carols piped into supermarkets that seduce the listener into identifying with the tamed Goddess who abjectly adores her son).

Women are also spooked by other women who act as instrumental agents for patriarchal males, concurring, with varying degrees of conscious complicity, in all of the above tactics. To the extent that any woman acts—or nonacts when action is required—in such complicity, she functions as a double agent of spooking, for politically she *is and is not* functioning as a woman. Since Hags/Witches have expectations of her—righteous expectations which are almost impossible to discard without falling into total cynicism and despair—she spooks us doubly, particularly by her absences/silences/nonsupport. Finally, Spinsters are spooked by the alien presences that have been inspired (breathed into) our own spirits/minds. These involve fragments of the false self which are still acting/nonacting in complicity with the Possessors. They also take the shape of nameless fears, unbearable implanted guilt feelings for affirming our own being, fear of our newly discovered powers and of successful use of them, fear of dis-covering/releasing our own deep wells of anger, particularly fear of our anger against

other women and against ourselves for failing our Selves. Spinsters are spooked by fear of the Ultimate Irony, which would be to become a martyr/scapegoat for feminism, whose purpose is to release women from the role of martyr and scapegoat.

Faced with being spooked, Spinsters are learning to Spook/Speak back. This Spinster-Spooking is also re-calling/re-membering/re-claiming our Witches' power to cast spells, to charm, to overcome prestige with prestidigitation, to cast glamours, to employ occult grammar, to enthrall, to bewitch. Spinster-Spooking is both cognitive and tactical. Cognitively, it means pattern-detecting. It means understanding the time-warps through which women are divided from each other—since each woman comes to consciousness through the unique events of her own history. It means also seeing the problems caused through space-warps—since Hags and potential Hags are divided from each other in separate institutional settings, disabled from sharing survival tactics in our condition of common isolation, spooked by our apparent aloneness. Tactically, Spooking means learning to refuse the seductive summons by the Passive Voices that call us into the State of Animated Death. It means learning to hear and respond to the call of the wild, learning ways of encouraging and en-spiriting the Self and other Spinsters, learning con-questing, learning methods of dispossession, specifically of dispossessing the Self of possession by the past and possession by the future. It means a-mazing the modern witchcraze, developing skills for unpainting the Painted Birds possessed through the device of tokenism, exposing the Thoroughly Therapeutic Society.

Since Spooking cannot always be done alone, and since it is a primary but not complete expression of Gyn/Ecology, the second chapter of this Passage is concerned with Sparking. In order to move on the con-questing Voyage, Spinsters need fire. It is significant that witches and widows were burned alive, consumed by fire. For fire is source and symbol of energy, of gynergy. It is because women are known to be energy sources that patriarchal males seek to possess and consume us. This is done less dramatically in day-by-day draining of energy, in the slow and steady extinguishing of women's fire. Sparking is necessary to re-claim our fire. Sparking, like Spooking, is a form of Gyn/Ecology. Sparking is Speaking with tongues of fire. Sparking is igniting the divine Spark in women. Light and warmth, which are necessary for creating and moving, are results of Sparking. Sparking is creating a room of one's own, a moving time/spaceship of one's own, in which the Self can expand, in which the Self can join with other Self-centering Selves.

Sparking is making possible Female Friendship, which is totally Other from male comradeship. Hence, the Spinster will examine male comradeship/fraternity, in order to avoid the trap of confusing sisterhood with brotherhood, of thinking (even in some small dusty corner of the mind) of sisterhood as if it were simply a gender-correlative of brotherhood. She will come to see that the term *bonding*, as it applies to Hags/Harpies/Furies/Crones is as thoroughly Other from "male bonding" as Hags are the Other in relation to patriarchy. Male comradeship/bonding depends upon energy drained from women (its secret glue), since women are generators of energy. The bonding of Hags in friendship for women is not draining but rather energizing/gynergizing. It is the opposite of brotherhood, not essentially because Self-centering women oppose and fight patriarchy in a reactive way, but because we are/act for our Selves.

Sparking means building the fires of gynergetic communication and confidence. As a result, each Sparking Hag not only begins to live in a lighted and warm room of her own; she prepares a place for a loom of her own. In this space she can begin to weave the tapestries of her own creation. With her increasing fire and force, she can begin to Spin. As she and her sisters Spin together, we create The Network of our time/space.

Gyn/Ecological Spinning is essential for entry into our Otherworld. The Voyager who does not Spin is in mortal danger. She may become trapped in one of the blind alleys of the maze which has been uncovered in The Second Passage. That is, she may become fixated upon the atrocities of androcracy, "spinning her wheels" instead of spinning on her heel and facing in Other directions. Or the nonspinner may make the fatal mistake of trying to jump over the atrocities into pseudoecstasy. As a result of this escapism, this blind "leap of faith," she can only fall into a tailspin. . . .

We have seen that the Female Self is The Enemy targeted by the State of War. This Self becomes ultimately threatening when she bonds in networks with other Self-accepting Female Selves. Since we have been conditioned to think quantitatively, feminists often begin the Journey with the misconception that we require large numbers in order to have a realistic hope of victory. This mistake is rooted in a serious underestimation of the force/fire of female bonding. It occurs when Amazons fall into the trap of imagining that sisterhood is like male comradeship. Because of the inherent weakness of its cogs, the male machine does require large numbers of self-sacrificing comrades. Because of the inherent strength of a woman who is Friend to her Self, the force of female bonding does not require multitudes. . . .

Sisterhood has nothing to do with breaking down "the walls of self," but with burning/melting/vaporizing the constricting walls imposed upon the Self. Moreover, female friendship is not concerned with "expanding walls and keeping them intact," but with expanding energy, power, vision, psychic and physical space. Sisterhood and female friendship burn down the walls of male-defined categories and definitions. However, hagocratic separatism/separation is not essentially about walls at all. Rather, it is expanding room of our own, moving outside the realm of the War State, War Stare. . . .

It is Crone-logical to conclude that internal separation or separatism, that is, paring away, burning away the false selves encasing the Self, is the core of all authentic separations and thus is normative for all personal/political decisions about acts/forms of separatism. It is axiomatic for Amazons that all external/internalized influences, such as myths, names, ideologies, social structures, which cut off the flow of the Self's original movement should be pared away.

Since each Self is unique, since each woman has her own history, and since there are deep differences in temperament and abilities, Hags should acknowledge this variety in all discussions of separatism. While it is true that all women have had many similar experiences under patriarchy, it is also true that there have been wide variations on the theme of possession and in struggles for dispossession. To simplify differences would be to settle for a less than Dreadful judgment of the multiple horrors of gynocide. It would also impoverish our imaginations, limiting our vision of the Otherworld Journey's dimensions. Finally, minimizing the variety in Amazon Journeyers' experiences, temperaments, and talents would blind us to the necessity for separating at times even from sisters, in order to allow our Selves the freedom and space for our own unique discoveries. Acknowledging the deep differences among friends/sisters is one of the most difficult stages of the Journey and it is essential for those who are Sparking in free and independent friendship rather than merely melting into mass mergers. Recognizing the chasms of differences among sister Voyagers is coming to understand the terrifying terrain through which we must travel together and apart. At the same time, the spaces between us are encouraging signs of our immeasurable unique potentialities, which need free room of their own to grow in, to Spark in, to Blaze in. The greatness of our differences signals the immensity/intensity of the Fire that will flame from our combined creative Fury.

Whereas discussions of relations between men and women eulogize the so-called complementarity of opposites, an Amazonian analysis of female friendship/love discovers the fact that the basis of woman-identified relationships is neither biological differences nor socially constructed opposite roles. . . . Rather than relying upon stereotypic role relationships, Amazon friends/lovers/sisters cast our Selves into a creative variety of developing relationships with each other. Since there are no models, no roles, no institutionalized relationships to fall back upon, we move together and apart in ever-varying patterns of relating. As each friend moves more deeply into her own Background she becomes both her earlier and her present Self. At times this re-membered integrity makes her appear Strange to her friends, and since the latter are also remembering, the encounters of these older/younger Selves can be multiply Strange. This Dreadful Strangeness is part of the terrain of the Otherworld Journey. It is essential to the Amazon adventure.

Women who have the courage to travel can see the absence of standardized roles as an asset, for such roles inhibit our struggle for truthfulness and fidelity. Heterosexist society does not reward Lesbians for friendship and fidelity to each other. Therefore, the way is clear for honest Amazon bonding. Since we know that our friendships will not in the final analysis yield social approval, we are free to seek Self-approval. We are free to follow our passion for Self-centering. As de Beauvoir correctly points out, men and women are always playing a part before one another. In contrast to this, Lesbians need not pretend. As she observes: "They [these liaisons] are not sanctioned by an institution or by the mores, nor are they regulated by conventions; hence they are marked by especial sincerity."[4]

Such sincerity involves risks. Since woman-identified relationships are unrestrained by mystification over biological and role-defined differences, there is often great intensity and turbulence in be-ing together. It has been observed that sisterhood involves stages when one seems to be stepping off a cliff, and that, mysteriously, the ground rises under the

Journeyer's feet. That ground is the Self's own confrontation with her reality, her truth—a confrontation made possible and unavoidable by her unprotected situation. Having defied the patriarchal protection racket, she finds her Dreadless Self. . . .

Spanning requires spinning, in many senses of this term. Understood in a cosmic sense it describes the whirling movement of creation. According to Merriam-Webster, *spin* is connected in its origin to the Latin term *sponte*, meaning "of one's free will, voluntarily." Thus Spinning implies spontaneous movement, the free creativity that springs from integrity of be-ing. The first definition given in Merriam-Webster for the verb to *spin* is "to draw and twist thread: make yarn or thread from fiber." This immediately calls to mind the image of "spinning a yarn"—a creative enterprise of mind and imagination. Spin also means "to form a thread, web, or cocoon by extruding a viscous rapidly hardening fluid used of a spider or silkworm." Gyn/Ecological creativity is spinning in this sense, too—dis-covering the lost thread of connectedness within the cosmos, repairing this web as we create.

Spin means "to revolve or whirl rapidly: GYRATE, ROTATE." This comes even closer to naming Gyn/Ecological creating. Spinsters whirl and twirl the threads of life on the axis of our own be-ing. This be-ing is itself the spindle, the thread, the whirl. Spinning be-ing moves in many directions, with force and speed.

Spin means "to turn quickly on one's heel: face about in place." Women spinning counterclockwise counter the "wisdom" of Father Time with his time-killing time-clocks. Women whirling in be-ing shift the center of gravity. As vortices of thinking, imaging, feeling, we spin around, "face about in place." As the Masters' March of Time continues its monodirectional goose-stepping into oblivion, Spinsters are learning to re-direct energy. Turning quickly on our heels, facing many other directions, we spin away from the death march. As whirling dervishes we move backward, sideward, forward, upward, downward, outward, inward—transforming our time/space. . . .

Spin also means "to last out, extend." This names the tactic of biding one's time, that patient alertness which appears to be stillness but which comes from an inner movement that is so fast it is imperceptible to those who see only the "outsides" and cannot perceive inner reality. This enduring, easily mistaken by males for passivity, is an active power of secretly watching, planning, testing tactics for springing free. It is the inner whirl, gathering momentum to jet forth threads of gynergetic communication. . . .

Self-Centering Spinsters whirl around the axis of our own be-ing, and as we do so, matter/spirit becomes more subtle/supple. Adding that *vortex* also means "something resembling such rapid rotary motion," the same dictionary illustrates this definition with a sentence about looking forward to a time "when human beings shall have sloughed off the body and become vortices of thought." Spinsters need not "look forward" to sloughing off the body in order to become vortices. The whirling dance of be-ing is thinking/creating/transcending earlier movements of both mind and body.

NOTES

1. See Morton W. Bloomfield, *The Seven Deadly Sins: An Introduction to the History of a Religious Concept with Special Reference to Medieval English Literature* (Michigan State University Press, 1967), especially pp. 7–27.

2. See Mary Daly, "The Qualitative Leap Beyond Patriarchal Religion," *Quest: A Feminist Quarterly*, Vol. 1, No. 4 (Spring 1975), pp. 20–40.

3. Françoise d'Eaubonne, *Le Féminisme ou la mort* (Paris: Pierre Horay, 1974), pp. 213–52.

4. Marie Bonaparte, *Female Sexuality* (New York: International Universities Press, 1953), p. 204.

Counterpoint:
From *Critical Theory of Religion: A Feminist Analysis*

MARSHA AILEEN HEWITT

MARCUSE'S THESIS CONCERNING "natural" female specificity as an adequate basis for political praxis anticipates a theoretical expression in contemporary feminism that can be described most accurately as *gynocentrism*.[1] Although gynocentric feminism is differently nuanced in the work of various feminist authors, it can be described according to certain common features. In part, gynocentric feminism accounts for women's oppression in terms of the historical denial and exclusion of values and ways of thinking and relating that are traditionally defined as feminine. More significantly, gynocentric feminism presumes the existence of an ontological, metaphysical "stable subject of feminism"[2] who exists behind the sociocultural category of gender. The premise of an abstract, stable subject, woman, that grounds the characteristics and activities of individual women also provides the basis for the formulation of an equally abstract notion of "universal patriarchy"[3] that is the source and sustainer of women's oppression.

The notion of woman as the stable subject of feminine gender constructions functions as an underlying unity of all cultural, racial, class, and linguistic difference between women and in turn is seen as providing a basis for solidarity among women by virtue of their universal commonality. . . . Further, the presumption of a stable subject encourages the designation of a set of characteristics or attributes that are sex-specific, and natural, which can be used to provide the foundation of a corresponding female-centered ethics. According to this theory, patriarchal societies value and promote male-specific qualities such as aggressiveness, assertiveness, and control at the expense of female-associated values, which are their potential negation and must therefore be subjected to a sustained repression and repudiation.

One of the most important theorists of contemporary gynocentric feminism is Mary Daly. The influence of her thought, especially in her later work, extends beyond the field of feminist religious thought. Hers was not always a gynocentric feminist approach, however. Daly's first book, *The Church and the Second Sex* (1968), is a feminist critique of the treatment of women in the Catholic theological and ecclesiastical tradition. The tone of this book is strongly marked by the liberal spirit of the Second Vatican council, which Daly briefly attended. In this work, Daly seeks to reclaim and articulate the emancipatory elements in Christianity that could be appropriated as "sources of further development toward a more personalist conception of the man-woman relationship on all levels." . . .

In her next book, *Beyond God the Father*, Daly's religious vision began to embrace a Tillichian "theism above theism" or "ground of being" in a supersession of God reformulated as the "Verb of Verbs, Be-ing,"[4] including displacement of Jesus with the Goddess. Yet Daly still expressed the hope of human beings "becoming . . . androgynous human persons." In her later works, she repudiates her view of

Reprinted from *Marsha Aileen Hewitt*, Critical Theory of Religion: A Feminist Analysis (*Minneapolis: Fortress Press, 1995.*)

androgyny as an adequate model of human wholeness. . . . Even at the stage of *Beyond God the Father* her feminist critique and rejection of Christianity as one of the sources of the oppression of women had not yet taken the completely gynocentric turn that was to surface in *Gyn/Ecology and Pure Lust.* The perspective in these later works, although anticipated in the previous books, marks an extreme shift in Daly's thinking in her move toward an apparently militant gynocentric philosophy of women's liberation.

The feminist critical philosophy advanced in *Gyn/Ecology and Pure Lust* has its roots in the post-Enlightenment intellectual traditions of the West. It is perhaps better understood if read in the key of a Marcusean-Hegelian theme of being, negativity, and reconciliation. Daly's treatment of these themes bears a strong Hegelian influence (intended or not) that is largely modified by a Marcusean reading of Hegel. The kind of identification Marcuse made between negativity and the "feminine principle," or Eros, emerges as well in highly metaphoric fashion in Daly's later work. . . .

For Daly, Spirit is the Background of authentic female Being, toward which specific women move in a dynamic process of casting off the alienated forms of femininity constructed and imposed by patriarchy, forms with which women are compelled to conform. Daly's idealist philosophical vision postulates a world of alienation against which women struggle in order to realize their inner psychic and spiritual creativity and integrity, which she describes as a journey or quest toward "Elemental participation in Being. Our passion is for . . . recalling original wholeness."[5] . . .

Against the negative force of "Phallic lust" that spawns pseudo/ sado-societies whose aim is to contain and control women's striving for the abundance of Be-ing, Daly counterposes Elemental Female Lust, the negation of phallic negation, an "intense longing/craving for the cosmic concrescence that is creation."[6] Women who consciously embark on this quest are blaz-

ing pathways to a "Background/homeland" from which they have been cut off but which they dimly remember. In overcoming the alienation of forgetting the source and end of their Elemental Be-ing, women move or "race" toward an ontological state of reconciliation, where female inner essence finally comes into unity with its original integrity, or Self. In achieving this ultimate reconciliation, women negate those forces that negated their potentialities, thus overcoming the alienated state of life in the Foreground in order to come into their "truth," finding groundedness and oneness in "Metabeing."[7] The dialectic between Spirit and history is reconceived by Daly as the dialectic between Elemental, Cosmic Female Being and the struggles of women to break through the patriarchal alienation that permeates and structures the existential realm. She is quite clear that this dialectic does not include males.

Daly's discussion of the journey to the Background/homeland that leads away from the alienated Foreground to participation in Metabeing to some extent parallels Hegel's idea of the movement of Absolute Spirit toward unity with itself, after having overcome and negated all previous forms of alienation. . . .

Daly's dialectic of the "male-centered and monodimensional" world of alienation, or "foreground,"[8] must be negated, overcome, and superseded in the process of women's movement to the Background, the state of complete reconciliation of women's being with Elemental Be-ing. As Hegelian philosophy posits a universal structure of all being, so does Daly, but whereas with Hegel all forms of particularity will be reconciled into Absolute Spirit, for Daly female particularity attains an analogous ontological reconciliation through the negation and exclusion of male particularity in all its manifestations. In order to come into their ontological and existential truth in the fulfillment of their inner potentialities, women must exorcise the false male-identified characteristics within, such as "male approval desire

"(MAD)," as well as aspirations toward "femininity," a "man-made construct" and "quintessentially" male attribute.[9]

Daly's uncompromising analysis of atrocities enacted against women in history, such as Chinese foot-binding practices, the Indian rite of suttee or widow-burning, the horrors of the gynecological profession, and her somewhat inflated account of the burning of "hundreds of thousands—probably millions—of women"[10] in the European witch-hunts, is an attempt to demonstrate beyond all doubt the gynocidal intent of patriarchy. The murderous drive of patriarchal societies is directed at destroying the female power or "divine spark"[11] that resides in women and is reflected in the divine cosmic power of the Goddess. The concept of negativity functions in Daly's work much as it does in Marcuse and Hegel, as a means for uncovering the latent truth implicit in forms of determinate being that could then be released and actualized. With Daly this represents a movement of women to wholeness and authenticity that is contingent on the negation of the male both within the female self and in external phallicist social forms, described by Daly in terms such as "phallocracy," "cockocracy," "boreocracy," "sadosociety," "Vapor State," "jockdom," "Daddydom," and so on. Daly's conceptualization of reconciliation departs from Marcuse and Hegel in the significant respect that it is not inclusive of all humanity inasmuch as all authentic being, including Being,[12] is identified exclusively with the female element.

Despite the flamboyant and intensely metaphoric language Daly uses in her later work, her underlying philosophical theory is steeped in the Western intellectual tradition in which she was formed. In like fashion with Hegel and those elements of critical theory that address the woman question, Daly also reproduces and sustains reified, idealized concepts of "woman" that arise out of an identity logic that marks most of this philosophical tradition. The core structure of her feminist philosophy conceptualizes an authentic female Being to which all women ultimately correspond, but from which they have become alienated through the dominating and repressive practices of patriarchy. For Daly, the Goddess represents "the deep Source of creative integrity in women,"[13] which they may yet again uncover within themselves through recollection and the right form of consciousness. The Goddess symbolizes an ontological, metaphysical female identity that provides a unifying foundation or ground of the likeness of all women. Although Daly acknowledges differences between women, these differences are rooted in a deeper, "authentic likeness" that "Lesbians/Spinsters" share.[14]

She reinforces this philosophical view with historical claims about the existence of a universal matriarchal world that existed in prehistory, wherein Goddess religion prevailed prior to patriarchy. The origins of humanity were clearly gynocentric, with egalitarian and nonauthoritarian social structures; primary worship centered around a female deity. Although patriarchy has attempted to eradicate the Goddess in various forms of Goddess murder, She nonetheless lives on in a variety of manifestations yet is one cosmic substance.[15] Goddess murder occurs whenever the "divine life and creative integrity" of women are destroyed.[16] Daly formulates a correspondence between the divine feminine and an interior, authentic female nature that is contained in individual women. Thus with Daly, not women but "woman" functions as the underlying abstract subject or ontological principle to which individual women must correspond if they are to realize their Elemental Selves.

This is straight identity theorizing where unalienated, almost "pure" female-identified Being emerges as the standard or measure against which alienation on the particular level of concrete existence is defined. Her somewhat uncharitable discussion of the "painted bird,"[17] that cosmeticized token and totally unreal agent of patriarchy whose purpose is to undermine natural, authentic women, indicates a dubious politics that separates the real women from the "fembots" and "totalled women" who participate in maintaining their own servitude.[18] . . . Such women are cut off from their inner essence, an essence that can only be realized in the negative process of dissolving the patriarchy within. The painted birds of patriarchal distortion do not fit within Daly's identitary theory and have nothing to do with the "correspondence between the minds of Musing women and the intelligible structures of reality." These enemies of feminism and real womanhood are excluded from the "process of Realizing Elemental ontological reason" that can actualize the "natural, elemental relation between women's minds and the structures of our own reality."[19] In traditional theological terminology, it might be said that such women are damned, alienated from salvation, steeped in the sinfulness of collaborating with patriarchal evil. . . .

Daly expresses a . . . dualism in her dichotomy of Pure Lust and "Pure Thrust," the latter understood as "phallicism," or "phallocracy," "the basic structure underlying the various forms of oppression,"[20] in which all forms of domination are rooted. Daly cautions women not to forget that "racial and ethnic oppression, like the sexual oppression which is the primary and universal model of . . . victimization, is a male invention."[21]

Here we see a serious difficulty in Daly's thought, which claims reconciliation and participation in the flow of Being as its goal but which at the same time is rooted in the antagonistic dichotomy of woman against man that is both ontological and existential. This is a significant reversal of her earlier position of partnership and androgyny. For Daly, men have no place in the cosmic flow of creative Being; rather they represent its evil antithesis that seeks to destroy the female identified life force. Women have an opportunity to overcome the alienations of existence imposed on them by patriarchal domination. For men, there is no redemption. . . .

By replacing capitalism with sexism as the focus of critical social theory, however, Daly dangerously narrows the scope of domination and simplifies its dynamics, reducing it to a basic antagonism between male and female. In doing this she dismisses—without serious consideration—Marcuse's critical insights into the subtle and intangible workings of domination that have become so sophisticated in late twentieth-century industrial-technological societies as to be nearly invisible. Her critique of Marcuse's attempt at a comprehensive social theory tacitly repudiates the context of sexism in larger, more complex, and pervasive forms of domination. Sexism cannot be analyzed in isolation from other forms of oppression, but Daly appears uninterested in these if they do not directly focus on injustice to women. Her implication is that in eradicating male power over women, or at least rendering it ineffectual, women will have no problems whatsoever and will encounter no barriers on their journey to the Background/homeland of Elemental Be-ing. A comprehensive social theory of domination is irrelevant, as far as Daly is concerned, to understanding and addressing the subjugated condition of women.

Daly hardly addresses the question of the context of women's journey toward authenticity; where does it take place, in history or in some other realm to which only women have access? She writes of living "on the boundary," and of "creative boundary-living" that is "expressed and symbolized" by "whales and dolphins," the "tortoise," and "the hermit crab," whose main virtue is that she is "at home on the road."[22] Daly describes the hermit crab's "resourcefulness of . . . moving into the discarded shells of other animals . . . in which she comfortably travels while seeking larger shells to occupy as she increases in size." This is a loosely metaphoric expression of the Hegelian concept of negativity, where *Geist,* in the process of congealing into external forms that are momentarily adequate to its unfolding, must also continuously negate, discard, and finally supersede them.

Daly's theorizing is here similarly vulnerable to Marx's critique of Hegel, which objected that the moving, creative force of history was not Spirit but human beings in their concrete laboring activity. As Hegel displaced human beings as the subjects of history, Daly exhibits a tendency in the same direction as she ontologizes femaleness and thus objectifies and revifies it with the result that living individual women all but disappear. It is not the activities of struggling, laboring women that contribute to the movement of history, but an ontological female Spirit that animates the cosmic creative life forces that underlie the patriarchal distortion of the phenomenal world.

Concerning Daly's exhortation for boundary living, it must be said that most women already live on the boundary of social existence and do not find it a poetic experience. However heightened many women's ecological consciousness may have become, it is both sentimental and absurd to offer hermit crabs and tortoises as symbolic models for how women might live alternative lives away from patriarchal oppression. What Daly proposes here is little more than a form of romantic escapism by driving women's revolutionary energy for social and personal transformation into esoteric realms of privatized experience. Her extended essays and detailed passages outlining the specific atrocities committed against women in various cultures and historical periods are actually lists of horrors devoid of any social analysis beyond the theoretically inadequate assertions of male perversity, evil, and gynocidal intent. Daly's exposition of crimes against women tends far more toward accumulative classification of brutalities than analysis of their root causes and sustaining conditions.

For all his inadequacies concerning his portrayals of the "feminine" as a kind of redemptive, transformative power of history, the value of Marcuse's social theory is that it offers profound and relevant insights into the complex dynamics of domination by examining its social and psychological mediations. Moreover, Marcuse's vision of a liberated, transformed humanity is profoundly humanist and inclusive. Daly's religio-philosophical vision is exclusivist and *antihumanist*. Not only does her philosophy exclude all men, it suggests that heterosexual women—"fembots," "painted birds," "totalled women"—are stamped with the alienation of patriarchy and collude in preserving its interests.

Gynocentric feminism, as represented by Daly and as a general theory of women's liberation, is self-defeating in that it rests on an identitary logic that generates a regulatory fiction of what true femaleness is by imposing a compulsory correspondence between a transcendental female subject and individual women. Daly's Elemental, Lusty, Racing Race of Women, Crones, Hags, Archelogians, Hag-Gnostics, Spinners, and Websters say little to women who daily struggle against domination in its nearly infinite variety of forms. Daly's A-mazing Amazons are mythological figures with which no woman can identify in ways that can open insights into oppression that may further lead to practical, emancipatory action. Daly is spinning new reifications of female nature, and her exhortations for living on the boundary drive revolutionary activity into imaginary esoteric realms that are mostly severed from concrete reality. In this, she shares in Marcuse's failure adequately to address women's oppression and construct an effective theory and practice of liberation. But Marcuse at least connected feminism with socialism, recognizing the need for a comprehensive feminist social theory that directly addressed women's condition in a way that opened up emancipatory possibilities for all humanity. Daly simply dismisses socialism and "its by-product, 'socialist feminism,'" as nothing more than a "bombardment of verbiage which often replaces/displaces any signs or acts of genuine biophilic concern."[23]

Daly's feminist philosophy at best is capable of providing only an abstract unity *among* women at the expense of the concrete differences that exist *between* women. Efforts to promote an abstract unity dissipate and atrophy revolutionary energy that addresses itself to the transformation of concrete conditions. Moreover, they all too easily result in oppressive politics of regulatory practices that exclude difference in the name of an illusory reconciliation only possible in a mythic utopia.[24] Most disturbing of all, the political implications of Daly's theorizing are authoritarian and hierarchical; not only are males excluded from her unifying vision of reconciliation of existence and essence, but so, it appears, are those women who do not conform to her view of real womanhood, the criteria of which are defined by Daly alone. . . .

Although memory is an important dimension of Mary Daly's thought, she conceptualizes it as recollection of a female golden age that was overthrown but not totally destroyed by patriarchy. While she writes a great deal about an elemental, authentic background realm where women may rediscover their true selves, what the true female self is and how it is to reach its ground in elemental being remains extremely vague. It appears that Daly can only indicate what this metaphysical dimension is through a decisive separation from what it is absolutely not: maleness, and the patriarchal foreground. There is an elitist, antidemocratic strain to this line in her thinking that separates those women who are beginning to connect with their true selves from those women who seem irrevocably lost to patriarchal delusion; the former act as harbingers of a new age, while the latter are left to wallow in their demeaned state. Despite Daly's lengthy cataloging of the atrocities and brutalities committed by men against women throughout history, these memories of specific sufferings do not address the conditions and structures that continue to produce them. . . .

NOTES

1. For a clear, concise, and fairly accurate description of gynocentrism, along with examples of feminist writers who are identified with it, see Iris Marion Young, "Humanism, Gynocentrism and Feminist Politics," *Women's Studies International Forum* 8, no. 3 (1985): 173–83.

2. See Judith Butler, *Gender Trouble: Feminism and the Subversion of Identity* (New York: Routledge, 1990).

3. Ibid., 3.

4. Mary Daly, *Websters' First New Intergalactic Wickedary of the English Language* (London: The Women's Press Ltd., 1988), 64.

5. Idem, *Pure Lust: Elemental Feminist Philosophy* (Boston: Beacon Press, 1984), ix.

6. Ibid., 1, 3.

7. Ibid., 61.

8. Idem, *Wickedary*, 76.

9. Idem, *Gyn/Ecology*, 72, 68, 69.

10. Ibid., 208.

11. Ibid., 315.

12. Idem, *Pure Lust*, 138.

13. Ibid., 111.

14. Ibid., 382.

15. Ibid., 90.

16. Ibid., 130.

17. For a different critical perspective on the "painted bird" as metaphor in *Gyn/Ecology*, see Ann-Janine Morey-Gaines, "Metaphor and Radical Feminism: Some Cautionary Comments on Mary Daly's *Gyn/Ecology*," *Soundings* 65 (Fall 1982), 347–49.

18. Daly, *Wickedary*, 198, 232.

19. Idem, *Pure Lust*, 163, 165.

20. Ibid., 320.

21. Ibid., 381.

22. Idem, *Gyn/Ecology*, 394–95.

23. Idem, *Pure Lust*, 326.

24. For example, see Audre Lorde's "An Open Letter to Mary Daly," in *Sister Outsider* (New York: The Crossing Press, 1984), 66–71.

Toward a Paradigm Shift in the Academy and in Religious Studies

CAROL P. CHRIST

Carol P. Christ is a leading figure in the study of women and religion and the author of four books, including Rebirth of the Goddess, 1998.

. . . FEMINIST SCHOLARSHIP, as most of us who practice it are aware, requires a paradigm shift, a questioning of fundamental and unquestioned assumptions about canon, ideas, value, authority, and method that operate in the academy and in the disciplines. Feminist scholars have begun to name the implicit androcentric perspective that operates in every field to highlight the achievements and accomplishments of elite men and to screen out or obscure the achievements of all women and non-elite men. . . . In order to see through the androcentric veil, we must shift to another paradigm, a paradigm that begins with the assumption that all women (and non-elite men) are as intelligent and valuable as elite men and that our contributions to history must have been as significant as those of elite men. . . .

Lifting the Androcentric Veil

Feminist research in all fields, including religious studies, begins with a paradigm shift that lifts the androcentric veil. The feminist paradigm assumes the importance and value of women, and thus finds it necessary to criticize the implicit androcentric assumptions that have labeled us as "nondata" and our questions as "non-questions." The paradigm shift implicit in making us both questioner and data is profound. . . .

But the paradigm shift implicit in feminist scholarship applies not only to the content, but also to the *form* of our disciplines. We not only ask "nonquestions" about "non-data," but we

also use a "non-method" as Mary Daly has noted. We question the most unquestioned scholarly assumption of all, namely, the assumption that scholarship is objective.

Our work reveals that scholarship which has been presented to us as "objective," "rational," "analytical," "dispassionate," "disinterested," and "*true*" is in fact rooted in an irrational and distorted androcentric vision, and that its implicit passion and interest is the preservation of patriarchy, of elite male power. As feminists we know that the ethos of scholarly objectivity is in fact mythos. We know that there is no dispassionate, disinterested scholarship. We know that our scholarship is passionate, is interested, is aimed at transforming the world we have inherited. Therefore our first task as scholars is to deconstruct the *ethos of objectivity* that operates in the academy as a whole, and to offer a new construction or model of scholarship. This act of deconstruction and construction of *scholarly method* is one that concerns all feminist scholars, especially those of us who work in the humanities and humanistic social sciences.

Deconstructing the Ethos of Objectivity

. . . It is difficult for feminist scholars to deconstruct and disavow the ethos of objectivity for two reasons. One is economic and political, and has to do with the power structure in the university. The other has to do with the distortions of subjectivity and objectivity, reason and

Reprinted from Carol P. Christ, "Toward a Paradigm Shift in the Academy and in Religious Studies," The Impact of Feminist Research in the Academy, *ed. Christie Farnham (Bloomington: Indiana University Press, 1987): 53–76.*

emotion, that are rooted in the structure of our thought and language.

As feminist scholars we seek employment in the university. The first and easiest way to discredit our work is to call it personal or political, therefore not objective, therefore not scholarly, therefore no tenure. Because of the very real economic pressures we face, many of us have chosen to hide the personal and social relevance and meaning of our work behind the mask of a dispassionate, objective voice. "I'm not interested in finding the meaning of my life through my work, or in changing the world through it," we say. "I'm only interested in analyzing the meter and form of Sappho's poetry." Even as we adopt this strategy, we know that our work has the capacity to give meaning to our lives and to transform the world, but we hope that the powers of the academy will not notice this, or at least will not think us unscholarly because our work has this capacity. (Of course they do notice, and they do find our work threatening.)

The second reason many of us have used the forms of objective scholarship has to do with the way in which the ethos of objectivity has distorted both itself and the alternatives to it. If the alternative to objective scholarship is "non-scholarship" (to continue Daly's word game), then not all of us who have been trained as scholars will be comfortable embracing it. If the alternative is "irrationality . . . Nazi Germany," then we will call our scholarship objective. We need to deconstruct the ethos of objectivity in order to expose the distortions of thought and feeling, intellect and life which it enshrines, before we can construct alternative notions of scholarship.

The false dualism implicit in the notion of the ethos of objectivity is a dualism that posits rationality, objectivity, dispassion, and analysis on one side, and irrationality, subjectivity, passion, and chaos on the other. The origins of this sort of dualism can be traced back as far as the myths of the slaying of the primordial Goddesses such as Tiamat, Python, and Gorgon, by male Gods and heroes such as Marduk, Apollo, and Hercules in stories which define primordial female power as chaos.[1] Such thinking is also found in the philosophy of Plato, who identified the rational and the good with that which transcends the changeable, the personal, the finite, and the so-called "animal" passions. It can also be seen to be rooted in the Enlightenment notion that Reason is the key that will enable mankind [sic] to rise out of the chaos of Ignorance and Superstition.[2] The ethos of objectivity is of course found in the Scientific Method, in which the researcher aspires to dispassionate, disinterested, "scientific" analysis and control of data. . . .

If we continue to deconstruct the ethos of objectivity, we can see that it is rooted in what "object" relations theorists[3] (this terminology also needs to be deconstructed) would view as a masculine psychology that emphasizes the separation of subject and object rather than their connection. According to object relations theorists, our experiences as babies shape our habitual ways of perceiving the world. For the baby the first experience is one of connection to the mother. For the boy baby, the experience of separation is intensified as he realizes that he is not "like" his mother. For females, on the other hand, the experience of separation is softened as they realize that they are "like" their mothers. According to this theory, though we all continue to experience both separation and connection, males tend to focus more on and be more comfortable with a self that is clearly marked off from others, while females tend to be more comfortable when they can identify with and connect with others. The ethos of objectivity can be related to the male experience of separation and distance, while the ethos of eros and empathy that I will discuss . . . , and that I propose as an alternative model for scholarship, can be related to the female experience of connection. The ethos of eros and empathy can also be correlated with the ethic of caring which Carol Gilligan has named a distinctively (though not necessarily exclusively) female ethical style, while the ethos of objectivity can be related to the normative male ethics of principle, also discussed by Gilligan. My proposals concerning the ethos of eros and empathy as a model for scholarship do not depend upon object relations theory for their validity. But if object relations theory is correct, it helps us understand one of the reasons women scholars are challenging the ethos of objectivity in scholarship.

Constructing the Ethos of Eros and Empathy as a Model for Scholarship

The experience of connection suggests the ethos of eros and empathy as a model for scholarship. The ethos of eros and empathy reminds us that the root of our scholarship and research is eros, a passion to connect, the desire to understand the experience of another, the desire to deepen our understanding of ourselves and our world, the passion to transform or preserve the world as we understand it more deeply. At its best, scholarship becomes a way of loving ourselves, others, and our world more deeply. The ethos of eros and empathy reminds us that one of the goals of our scholarship is empathy, a form of understanding that reaches out to the otherness of the other, rooted in a desire to understand the world from a different point of view. Empathy is the ability to put ourselves in the other's place, to feel, to know, to experience the world from a standpoint other than our own. Empathy is possible because we have the capacity to make connections between our own experience and the experiences of others. Empathy means not simply recognizing the connections, but also the differences between persons, texts, cultures, whatever is being studied. . . .

Within the ethos of eros and empathy, the scholar remains firmly rooted in her or his own body, life experience, history, values, judgments, and interests. Rather than presuming to speak universally, objectively, or dispassionately, the scholar speaks out of a standpoint that is acknowledged to be finite and limited. In the first moment of scholarship, she or he names the eros, the passion, the desire—to understand, to connect, to preserve or change the world—that inspired her or his research. This does not mean

that the scholar's work is narrowly personal, solipsistic, or self-indulgent, terms taken from the ethos of objectivity. But it does mean that she or he names the interests that inspired and to some extent shape her research.

The second moment of scholarship is directed toward enlarging the scholar's perspective through understanding the experience presented in a text, in the lives of a group of people, in a historical time, etc. The ethos of eros and empathy posits that empathy, the ability to put oneself in another's place (in Novak's terms to "pass over" to the experience of another; in Buber's terms, to experience the other side "bodily"; in Lorde's terms to make an erotic connection through difference), is possible, and is the basis of understanding. Empathy flows from eros, the drive to connect, and is aided by imagination, which enables us to make connections between our own experiences and those of others. Imagination also enables us to see and understand difference, the otherness of the other. All the standard tools of scholarly research, including criticism, historical research, analysis, careful attention to data, statistical research, theory, concern for truth, etc., are brought to bear upon the task of understanding the subject matter in this second moment of disciplined research. In this second moment our work will not differ dramatically from what we have been trained to do under the standards of the ethos of objectivity. What will differ is that we keep in mind the limits of our ability to be objective, while at the same time keeping in mind that we can be far more than simply subjective. Moreover, in this second moment, the scholar does not lose sight of the eros and empathy, the drive to understand and connect that impelled the research in the first place. But in this moment, the goal remains to get as close to the intrinsic meaning of the text, group, historical time, etc., studied, and to a communally verifiable point of view, or truth, as possible.

The third moment of scholarship is judgment. After completing research and analysis, the scholar returns to her or his now expanded standpoint. In an act of judgment, she or he incorporates the insights gained from research and analysis into her or his expanded standpoint or perspective. The scholar acknowledges that the judgments she or he makes are finite, limited by the body, history, life experiences, values, and judgments of their author. But again this does not mean that judgments are narrowly personal, or merely polemical, as the ethos of objectivity would label them. Nor hopefully are they uncritically ethnocentric or imperialistic. Rather, the scholar recognizes that her or his standpoint has been enlarged by her or his research, by entering into the disciplined analysis of a text or historical period, etc. The scholar also recognizes her or his grounding in the *community* of scholars, a community of discourse, within which she or he shares and receives criticism on both the research and analysis and the judgments made. The scholar avoids solipsism and polemic not by attempting to become objective, but by ever expanding the range of her or his empathy, her or his grounding in an ever expanding community of knowledge and scholarship, which in turn expands her or his standpoint.

Though the ethos of eros and empathy contrasts sharply with the ethos of objectivity as a model for scholarship, it seems to me that the best scholarship has always derived from the ethos of eros and empathy. The best education, study, and research has always been erotic and empathetic because it enables us to see and feel the world differently, because it transforms us through enlarging our vision. It seems to me that not only feminists, but all scholars, would be much more true to the real aims and visions of scholarship if we framed our scholarship explicitly within an ethos that includes eros and empathy rather than within the ethos of objectivity as narrowly defined.

Toward a Paradigm Shift in Religious Studies

. . . During the past twenty-five years, religious studies as an academic discipline has separated itself from the denominational context. The argument was made that teaching "about" religion could be separated from the teaching "of" religion. Religious history could be studied as history; the Bible and other scriptures could be studied as history and literature; even theology and ethics could be studied as the history of ideas and values. The argument for the establishment of religious studies departments was stated in the language of the prevailing ethos of the university, the ethos of objectivity. In order to insure objectivity, it was argued that the study of religions other than Protestant Christianity, including Catholicism, Judaism, Hinduism, Buddhism, etc., would become integral parts of religious studies curricula. In practice, religious studies departments were usually formed around a core of scholars trained at seminaries in Protestant Christian theological and Biblical studies. Gradually specialists in Catholicism, Judaism, and non-Western religions (usually Hinduism or Buddhism, more rarely Islam or nonliterary religious traditions) were added to the departments. In the late 1960s and early 1970s religious studies departments burgeoned as the baby boom generation, an expanding economy, and abundant federal funding allowed the growth of universities. When this expansion came to a halt in the mid-1970s, religious studies departments were firmly entrenched in the universities, but their proposed (and needed) growth was curtailed.

Though there have been many attempts to forge a single methodology for religious studies, in practice the field is multi-disciplinary; some scholars focus on texts and translation; others employ historical, philosophical, literary, anthropological, psychological, sociological, and other methods. . . .

Though women scholars are a small minority in the field of religious studies, and feminist scholars an even smaller group, we have been very visible in recent years. Feminist studies in religion is flourishing and firmly established in the academy, if not in the hiring priorities of major religious studies departments. Feminist scholarship in religion is as diverse as the field itself. Feminist scholars in religion attempt to uncover the religious lives and experiences of women in all times and places, to reconstruct theology on the basis of women's experience, to construct theory with which to understand women's religious lives in patriarchal contexts, to discover whether women have ever named our own religious experience. We study history and prehistory; we study the texts of so-called "higher" religions; we study tribal and nonliterary traditions; we study women religious leaders; we study the effects of patriarchal religious symbolism on culture. Feminist scholarship in religion began with the naming and analyzing of obvious instances of sexism within religious traditions, such as the attribution of evil to Eve, the admonition that women keep silent in church, the symbol of God as Father. As we deepened our analysis, we began to understand that sexism is not peripheral but central in most religious traditions, that the so-called "higher" religions express deeply androcentric visions of God, humanity, and the cosmos. We also discovered that the academic study of religion is based upon implicitly androcentric presuppositions; that what we generally studied was the religious lives and visions of men. We began to insist that the religious lives and visions of women also be studied. Some of us wrote openly about the need to transform or move beyond Judaism and Christianity, while others began to search for times and places before, within, or in reaction to patriarchal religion where women may have been able to express our own religious insights. . . .

If religious studies, like other disciplines, is guided by implicit androcentric biases and prejudices, then not only the form, but also the content of what is researched and studied must change. To discuss all the various ways a field as diverse as religious studies will be transformed by feminist scholarship would require far more space than is available here. Therefore, I will limit my discussion of the paradigm shift in religious studies to a single area, which, however,

has broad implications for the field as a whole. This area is the study of the prehistoric Goddesses of Old Europe and the Near East. Many of the points I will make with regard to the study of the prehistoric Goddesses of Old Europe and the Near East may also apply to the study of prehistoric Goddesses in other cultures, and to the study of prehistoric and preliterate cultures more generally.

Prehistoric Goddesses and the Paradigm Shift in Religious Studies

The study of prehistoric religions of Old Europe and the Near East in which Goddess symbolism is prominent and in which there is no evidence of female subordination in religion and society, presents a profound challenge to the field of religious studies. The prehistoric Goddesses threaten the alleged truth of patriarchal religion that "in the beginning God created the heavens and the earth" (Gen. 1:1). They also challenge the implicit, unstated, and unexamined principle of patriarchal societies that men have always held the power in religion and society. Finally, they reveal how much the supposedly value-free discipline of religious studies remains shaped by implicit and largely uncriticized androcentric assumptions about God, time, and text which are derived from Biblical religion, and which are implicitly supportive of both patriarchal religions and patriarchal societies. A paradigm shift is required in relation to these assumptions. . . .

God, Time, and Text: The Prehistoric Goddesses and the Paradigm Shift in Religious Studies

The prehistory of the Goddesses provides one lens through which we may deconstruct assumptions about God, time, and text which continue to structure the field of religious studies. The notions of God, time, and text which shape the field of religious studies are very much intertwined, and all three can be shown to be related to Biblical and Christian theological categories. Feminist scholars are by no means the first to question the use of Biblical and theological categories to raise questions about and to interpret data from non-Biblical religions. Historians and anthropologists of religion have been raising similar sorts of questions for a long time. However, because of the origin of the field in Biblical and theological studies, and because habits of mind are very hard to break, Biblical and theological notions of God, time, and text continue to exert a very powerful influence on the field. Thus, for example, scholars of non-Western religions remain very much wedded to the analysis of text, and the prehistory of non-Western religions (where Goddesses were also more powerful and more prominent than in their patriarchal texts) is not studied sufficiently. And the scholarly study of the religions of nonliterary peoples remains peripheral in the field of religious studies. Thus it remains important to outline some of the ways in which feminist scholarship about the prehistoric Goddesses challenges the field of religious studies to change its central paradigms.

TIME

For those working in Western religions, and these are still the vast majority of scholars in religious studies, time generally begins with the *time of* the Hebrew patriarchs, with Abraham (c. 1800 B.C.E.) or with Moses (c. 1300–1200 B.C.E.). Time proceeds from Abraham and Moses, through the Davidic kingship (c. 1000 B.C.E.), to the time of the prophets, to the time of the origins of Christianity and Rabbinic Judaism in the first century C.E. If time before Abraham is mentioned, it is usually discussed within the framework provided by Samuel Noah Kramer's book, *History Begins at Sumer* as Anne Barstow has noted. The Babylonian creation epic, *The Enuma Elish,* which depicts the slaying of the primordial Goddess Tiamat and the *Epic of Gilgamesh* in which the Goddess Ishtar is

called an "old fat whore" may be discussed as providing evidence about the origins of religion in the Near East. Frequently even this material is discussed primarily as the backdrop which enables us to understand the distinctive (and superior) contributions of Hebrew religion.

From a feminist perspective on the prehistory of the Goddesses, it is clear that these texts derive from a time when patriarchy is already well established. If history begins with Sumer or with Israel, then history is patriarchal history. We may discover the roles of women within patriarchal history (and these may be substantial), but we do not have the history of a time when women's roles in religion and culture were central and unquestioned.

Feminist research on the prehistory of the Goddesses challenges the field of religious studies dramatically to expand its concept of time. The time of the Neolithic revolution (began c. 9000 B.C.E. in the Near East) is nearly 8000 years before the time of Moses and David, more than 5000 years before history was said to have begun at Sumer. The Paleolithic period in which religion originated is tens of thousands of years before the Neolithic revolution. Feminist research on the prehistoric Goddesses challenges the field of religious studies to do more than pay lip service to the time before Moses and Abraham, to the time before Sumer.

Anyone who studies prehistory (or any non-Christian religion, including Judaism), rapidly becomes aware that the Christian naming of time as "before" and "after" Christ distorts their research, making it difficult to grasp the relationships of time "before Christ" (it is counterintuitive to think of 457 B.C.E. as being after 579 B.C.E.), difficult to grasp the relationships of times before and after Christ (there was in fact no major break in history between 50 B.C.E. and 50 C.E.), and even more difficult to grasp the scope of history (the time of Moses is little more than 3000 years ago, while the time of the Neolithic revolution is more than 11,000 years ago). The naming we give to time is not a trivial or arbitrary matter, as Christian rulers recognized when they took control of it. It will be difficult for us to fully grasp and understand ancient prehistory as long as we are rooted by language and conceptuality in the Christian naming of time. (Anthropologists have recognized this and devised their own naming of time as "before present," or b.p.) From this point of view the suggestion made by Merlin Stone that we rename time from a feminist perspective—she suggested that we begin from the time when women invented agriculture—is by no means trivial.[4]

TEXT

To do more than pay lip service to the origins of religion in prehistory, the field of religious studies will also have to re-examine its *logos* orientation, its commitment to the written word, its commitment to text. "And God spoke, and said, 'Let there be light'" (Gen. 1: 1). "In the beginning was the Word, and the Word was with God, and the Word was God" (John 1:1). Scholars of course consider the complex meanings embedded in the notion of speech and in the word *logos* and recognize these two accounts of creation as myth, as historically and culturally grounded. But most scholars in the field of religious studies implicitly accept the deep message of these texts: their reverence for Word, for text. Though they know that nonliterary religions exist, most scholars in the field of religious studies focus on the interpretation of texts—whether those texts be the Hebrew and Christian or other scriptures, the writings of Jewish and Christian or other theologians or interpreters of scriptural texts, or the works of philosophers. The commitment to texts is also found in the field of history. One of the reasons history is said to have begun at Sumer is because writing was invented there in the fourth millennium. The field of history, like the field of religious studies, is deeply committed to the written word. The written word is said to provide the only reliable, "scientific" "evidence" about the past. The terms "history" and "prehistory" themselves reflect the bias in favor of the written word. Where there is no text, we have no

history, it is said, but a prelude to history, and history is where everything important happened. This naming serves to diminish the importance of prehistory, almost to render it non-data. New names must be developed. I suggest we abandon the term prehistory, and speak rather of early or ancient history, though I will continue to use the term "prehistory" in quotes in the last part of this article. The texts about Goddesses come from the times of "history" when patriarchy is already established. If texts provide the only reliable evidence, then we would perhaps be forced to conclude that Goddesses do not reflect autonomous female power. Almost all of these texts are written by men and almost all of them implicitly or explicitly support patriarchy. However if we expand our notion of history to include the study of cultures which left no written records, then we can begin to allow the data of "prehistory" and anthropology of religion to transform not only our understandings of Goddesses and women in religion, but also our notions about religious origins and our theories about the nature of religion.

The great historian of religion Mircea Eliade has been influential in the attempt to expand the parameters of the field of religious studies into the study of myth and ritual, including the study of nonliterary traditions. But ritual studies, which by some accounts of the nature of religion, might even *form* the core of the field, are still relegated to the periphery. More is at stake here than simple inherited prejudice toward the study of texts. Ritual embodies in a fuller way than text, the nonrational, the physical side of religion. Ritual puts us in the presence of body and blood, milk and honey and wine, song and dance, sexuality and ecstasy. Underlying the preference for texts in religious studies lies the fear of the nonrational and the physical, the fear of chaos, a fear which I discussed earlier in relation to the ethos of objectivity in scholarship.

Feminist scholarship on the "prehistoric" Goddesses, then, challenges the field of religious studies to abandon its nearly exclusive commitment to text. Feminist scholarship on the Goddesses requires us to accept physical evidence: paintings, sculptures, bones, pots, weavings, etc., as reliable data upon which to base theory. To do this religious studies would need to strengthen its connections with the fields of archaeology, art history, and anthropology. In a larger sense it means that not only do Neolithic and Paleolithic history need to become more central in shaping our conceptions of religious origins, but also that we need to devote more attention to the religious lives of nonliterary peoples in general, to tribal and folk religions, and to nonliterary expressions within the so-called "higher" religions.

GOD

Feminist study of the history of the Goddesses also challenges prevailing ideas about divinity. Most of us in the field of religious studies are far more influenced by Biblical notions of God than we care to reflect upon. The Goddesses are presented in the Bible as "abomination," and it is hard to shake the mindset that has encouraged us to think of Goddesses in relation to terms such as "idolatry," "fertility fetish," "nature religion," "orgiastic," "bloodthirsty," "cult prostitution."[5] All of these prejudices can be countered. An idol is another person's religious symbol. The Goddesses represented fertility and sexuality as cosmic power of transformation, not in a limited, certainly not in a negative sense. Sexual rituals associated with Goddess religions celebrated sexuality as transformative power.[6] Prostitution for money is the product of a patriarchal class-stratified society.[7]

Underlying scholars' prejudices about Goddess religion are several deeper issues that bear reflection. One is the notion that divinity represents rationality, order, and transcendence, as opposed to the alleged irrationality and chaos of the finite changeable world, the world we call nature. This notion is the basis of the (usually negative) comparison made between the gods [sic] of nature and the God of history and law, the God of Sinai. As discussed earlier, ancient Near Eastern and Greek mythology also records man's (here the generic seems appropriate) attempts to separate himself and his Gods from the forces of finitude and death (but in so doing also from life and renewal) which he labels chaotic and irrational. The attempt to sever divinity from the forces of so-called "chaos" is vividly depicted in the stories of the slaying of Tiamat by Marduk, Medusa by Perseus, and Python by Apollo, mentioned earlier. The deep structure of these and similar myths depicts female power (for each of these monsters is female) as chaos, as destructive, as associated with darkness and death. Each of these myths tells us that it is the task of the male hero or God to slay and dismember, to banish the forces of "chaos" from his world. By the time of the Genesis 1 creation story, the power of the female forces of chaos had been so diminished that God could subdue *tohu wabohu*, the formless and the void, and *tehom*, the great deep, simply by the power of his word, though the struggle with the chaos monster is reflected in Psalm 89 and in Job 9:8–13. The Hebrew God of the Genesis 1 creation story is identified with the powers of order and goodness; he declares everything he orders and separates "very good." "Chaos" remains to be projected upon the "abominations" worshipped by the indigenous Canaanites and many of the people of Israel and Judah.

Once again we come face to face with dualisms of thought and expression that are deeply embedded in the structure of our thought and language. If we are to grasp the meaning of the prepatriarchal Goddesses, then we must attempt to conceptualize divinity as embodying neither exclusively order, nor exclusively chaos, but as inclusive of both. For me the easiest way to think about this is to think of the prepatriarchal Goddesses as embodying the forces of life, death, and regeneration that occur in all natural and creative processes in the universe. The Goddesses embody the "chaos" of death and disintegration equally as they embody the forces of growth and renewal. These processes are chaotic when viewed from the standpoint of rational control, but they are not essentially chaotic. They have their own inner logic, they follow rhythmical patterns which are regular, though not entirely predictable or controllable. Everything changes, everything that is born will surely die, everything that is will transform. And as Margaret Atwood has written, "nothing has died, everything is alive, everything is waiting to become alive."[8] The "prehistoric" Goddesses are not difficult to understand, they are not chaos, but their relation to individual finite life and will remains a mystery. We can understand them only if we shed deeply held prejudices that divinity, and especially "higher" divinity, is associated with a rational order which is transcendent of change.

The "prehistoric" Goddesses also challenge us to transcend the philosophical tradition which tells us that divinity, humanity, and nature are three completely distinct categories. The categorical distinction between divinity, humanity, and nature (or as it is more commonly put, God, man, and nature—the status of women is sometimes a non-question, sometimes women are viewed as having the same rational essence as "man"; sometimes women are viewed as defective "men"), is embedded in the structure of our language and thinking and is reflected in philosophies and theologies. These categories reflect man's continuing attempt to ally himself with a principle, a transcendent and rational deity, that will enable him to escape finitude and mortality, which he then consigns to the realm of nature. According to most Western philosophies and theologies since Plato, God is identified with a timeless rational principle which transcends the changeable world of nature. Man is situated halfway between God and nature. With his rational mind man communes with timeless principles, while with his body he participates in a world of changeable nature. In this scheme, sexuality which is of the body is viewed as being of a "lower" order and in some sense threatening to man's "higher" nature.

In the absence of written language, we cannot know how Paleolithic and Neolithic peoples understood the images they created which we call "Goddesses." But we do know that in many American Indian and African groups, for example, the categorical distinctions we make between God, man, and nature are unknown. In many American Indian groups "divinity" is called "Grandmother" or "Grandfather" and it does not seem that a clear distinction is being made (as it is in Genesis 2–3) between the ancestors of the clan and the divinity. In thinking about the Goddesses of the Neolithic it seems to me that we are probably dealing with images which incorporate concepts of "awesome female sexual and lifegiving power," "ancestress," "powers of nature," "powers of transformation," "powers of birth, death, and renewal." The "prehistoric" Goddesses were probably not understood to be categorically distinct or separate from the powers of women who give birth, nurture, plant, weave, create pots, and enact roles in ritual, not distinct from the awesome powers of growth, death, and regeneration in nature. To understand them, then, we must develop different understandings of the relation of God, humanity, and nature than those we have inherited.

One aspect of the "prehistoric" Goddesses that has troubled many scholars is their awesome sexuality. Whether full or thin of body, they are often depicted unclothed, with prominent breasts and pubic triangles, to which they often point. Some are giving birth, or holding children, but many simply stand alone, self-confidently affirming their sexual power. Such images of "divinity" are quite alien to recent Western consciousness, because Western thinkers have considered the body and sexuality as "lower" than the rational mind which they associate with the divinity and with man's "higher" nature. Thus the "prehistoric" Goddesses are called mere "fertility fetishes," or "orgiastic images," and are said to reflect a "more primitive" or "lower" stage of consciousness. Only if we dispense with the Western preference for a rational divinity who is transcendent of this life and of change, can we begin to understand the "prehistoric" Goddesses as more than "fertility fetishes."

The "prehistoric" Goddesses, then, challenge us to rethink our concept of God. In order to understand the "prehistoric" Goddesses we must move beyond the notions of divinity as categorically distinct from humanity and nature, as asexual, and as set apart from change, from finitude, from that which has been called chaos.

Conclusion

This paper, which I originally had conceptualized as having two distinct parts, has come full circle. Now we can see that both the ethos of objectivity and the notions of God, time, and text, which continue to influence the field of religious studies are very much connected. The critical issue in both cases, it seems to me, is the erection of a rational structure against powers that are defined as chaos. But as we deconstruct the ethos of objectivity and the concepts of God, time, and text, we begin to see that the chaos feared by many is not chaos at all, but finitude, limitation, body, feeling, change, and

death. I believe that feminist thought calls us to embrace this finitude, rather than defend against it. But this takes us into the realm of feminist theology, which is not, strictly speaking, the subject of this paper.

NOTES

1. For the story of Marduk's slaying of Tiamat, see the Babylonian Creation Epic, "The Enuma Elish," in *Primal Myths,* Barbara C. Sproul ed. (New York: Harper and Row, 1979), 91–113.

2. See Zillah Eisenstein, *The Radical Future of Liberal Feminism* (New York: Longman, 1981).

3. See Nancy Chodorow, *The Reproduction of Mothering* (Berkeley: University of California Press, 1978).

4. Merlin Stone, "9978: Repairing the Time Warp and Other Related Realities," *Heresies* 5 (1978), 124–26.

5. See Barstow, "The Uses," 10, and Stone, *When God Was a Woman,* xvii–xviv, for citation and discussion of scholarly prejudice against Goddesses.

6. See Mircea Eliade, *A History of Religious Ideas,* Vol. I, Willard Trask, trans. (Chicago: University of Chicago Press, 1978), 283.

7. See Rohrlich, "State Formation," 91–92.

8. Margaret Atwood, *Surfacing* (New York: Simon and Schuster, 1972), 182.

Counterpoint:
Do Women Really Need a 'God/ess' to Save Them? An Inquiry into Notions of the Divine Feminine

MARSHA AILEEN HEWITT

1. God or God/ess: What is at stake?

Several years ago, the well-known feminist Rosemary Radford Ruether[1] posed the question as to whether a male savior could really save women. Although the question is primarily theological it nonetheless bears implications for a feminist critical approach to the study of religion,

Reprinted from Marsha Aileen Hewitt, "Do Women Really Need a 'God/ess' to Save Them? An Inquiry into Notions of the Divine Feminine," Method & Theory in the Study of Religion 10 *(1998): 149–156.*

as will become apparent later in this essay. Feminist Christian theologians, for more than three decades, have been actively engaged in a variety of reconstructive projects, the aim of which, in many respects, is twofold: to secure an equal place for women within the Christian theological and ecclesiastical traditions and to restore Christianity to what many believe is its "true" or "genuine" emancipatory and egalitarian impulse. For many Christian feminists, these aims, although distinct, are indivisible, motivated by both faith as well as a political commitment to the liberation of women. In terms of its overall theoretical and scholarly approach, Christian feminism derives much of its insight from nonreligious feminist theory.

Many feminists, both Christian and "post-Christian" are attempting to reconceive God in terms of femininity, sometimes replacing the exclusively male God of the Jewish and Christian religious traditions with a female Goddess. In fact, this has been and continues to be one of the major preoccupations of Christian feminism. In part, reconstructions of notions of divinity in terms of the feminine seeks to reverse the harmful psychological, social, and political effects such privileging of male divinity has exerted on women for centuries. The continuing critique of God as male within a religious paradigm is understood to serve women in their struggles against sexist domination and oppression in the sociological realm. For many women, the idea of female divinity, and worship practices focused upon a Goddess, is seen as a crucial element in the struggle against sexism in a variety of arenas. This essay will attempt a critical interrogation of this assumption through an initial discussion of the emancipatory themes of nonreligious feminist theory, while brief attention will be given to feminist religious thinkers. The discussion will then turn to an examination of the notion of the divine feminine in a non-theologian, Luce Irigaray, in order to raise questions about the contribution such a notion could make to a feminist theory of liberation.

2. Theorizing Freedom

Before proceeding with the critique of the notion of the divine feminine (however it appears either as Goddess spirituality or as a general psychological necessity) some preliminary points need to be made about feminist theory and feminist approaches to the study of religion. The critique of the divine feminine advanced here does not proceed from a theological point of view. Rather, the approach taken is situated within feminist critical theory which is then expanded to generate a feminist critique of developments within contemporary Christianity. Not only in religion, but in most disciplines, feminist scholarship understands itself as located within or related to a feminist movement. This does not privilege any particular concrete wing of a specific feminist movement, or a particular issue. The feminist movement to which I refer includes the vast number of activities both theoretical and practical which, in a variety of ways, and from a diversity of perspectives, address and expose the injustices and conditions that produce women as occupying a subordinate position in all aspects of life.

Feminist theory proceeds from an explicit and conscious solidarity with women; the theory not only discusses women's oppression, it strives to overcome and abolish it. Theorizing women's liberation is understood to be part of the emancipatory process. In this sense, feminist theory is driven by an emancipatory interest that seeks to transform the condition of women on the levels of thought and practice. As an explicitly emancipatory and partisan theory, feminism arises with modernity and largely derives, consciously or not, from Marxian social theory. . . .

Having said that feminist theory is both emancipatory and self-consciously partisan does not mean that it results inevitably in faulty scholarship and thought, although it can. So can—and do—those theories that consciously aspire to "value freedom," which for Marx was an element of ideology. Another way of expressing this is to say that feminism acknowledges the advocacy nature of its theoretical inquiries, while other theories perhaps do not, which is not to say that the latter are free of partisanship. Feminist criticism in all fields recognizes and exposes the ideological nature of value-free, objective (in an absolutist sense) theorizing, opting for a theoretical practice which specifically situates the theorist in a relationship of solidarity with women, whereby "the theoretician and his [/her] specific object are seen as forming a dynamic unity with the oppressed class. In this way, his[/her] presentation of societal contradictions is not merely an expression of the concrete historical situation but also a force within it to stimulate change."[2]

This understanding of the role of the theoretician may then become an antidote to the ideologizing tendencies within thought. Like many emancipatory theories, feminist religious thought is not always so successful in this task, as is evidenced by the turn to the Goddess which is becoming increasingly popular. In part, the failure of Goddess spirituality to adequately guard against reproducing different, although no less ideological, tendencies arises from the continuation of theology within feminist religious thought by other means. The fact that it offers an *alternative* theology does not solve the problem. A further related part of the problem involves the spinning of new ideologies and reifications of women, thereby contributing to their already entrenched inferior social position by providing illusory avenues of freedom. . . .

While there are a number of historical problems with the turn to the Goddess in contemporary Christian feminism, the more severe and troubling problems are theoretical. Although I have dealt with the historical and theoretical problems with reference to feminist religious thinkers elsewhere,[3] my concern here is to explore the theoretical difficulties of the notion of the divine feminine in Luce Irigaray, a major

feminist theorist who is not a theologian. An examination of her use of the concept helps uncover some of the elements at work in the powerful attraction of goddess spirituality.

3. Luce Irigaray

One of Irigaray's most important contributions to feminist theory is her critique of identitary thinking. Her exposure of domination inherent in the "logic of the Same" reveals the ways in which women are reduced to the status of subordinate and silenced shadows in the prison house of phallocentric rationality and discourse. The focus on non-identitary thinking in the work of Irigaray[4] and others continues to provide an important critical tool within feminist theory as it interrogates the notion of gender identity, which it attempts to subvert by focusing on the difference and diversity of female identities.

Non-identitary thinking or reason refuses to colonize others within predetermined concepts whose logic is to compel objects to conform to its pregiven idea. Identitary thinking, which seeks to capture the objects of its own inquiry, does violence to others, destroys difference, and expels that which it cannot fully absorb to the margins of theory and practice. Irigaray and other non-identitary theorists not only critique this mode of reason, they also expose the harmful effects that intellectual traditions structured in terms of identitary logic have had on women. Within the very rationality of feminist non-identitary thinking, the turn to the Goddess and notions of the divine feminine raise serious problems for feminist theory. The projection of an image or concept of a female deity can only occur with the mobilization of identitary reasoning, where the attributes of the Goddess are meant to mirror female attributes and potentialities back to individual women. Female divinity is "Woman," writ in cosmic letters, revealing to women not only *what* they are, however imperfect, but more importantly, what they might become (who apparently is not the correct interrogative pronoun). The question as to *who decides what* the valued characteristics of the divine feminine are and whence they originate is never answered. From the perspective of feminist religious thought articulated by such writers as Mary Daly[5] and Carol P. Christ,[6] the divine feminine represents a female centered ontology in which all women (at least potentially) have the power to participate by realizing their genuine selves. The construction of such images and divine categories with which women are somehow to identify can only, in the end, establish new regulatory mechanisms to which individual women will be pressured to conform.

Drawing heavily on the work of Ludwig Feuerbach, Luce Irigaray considers the creative function that a notion of female divinity might possess with regard to the formation of a non-phallocentric, specifically female subjectivity. Irigaray thinks that women need to believe in and identify with an ideal feminine divinity in order to develop a healthy subjectivity that is neither distorted nor crippled by the exclusive male deity of the Christian tradition. While Feuerbach was fully aware of the "anthropological" secret of religion, he was also critical of it on the grounds that it is an inhibiting factor to full human development, and that religious illusions are "profoundly injurious" in their effects on humanity. . . . Irigaray appropriates the logic of Feuerbach for the construction of a divine feminine, which she thinks is necessary for women's self-becoming since the psychological process he describes has been applied only to males. While she takes up his argument and refashions it for women, she does not address his criticism of the psychology of religious belief wherein "man" exists in a state of infantilism. According to Feuerbach, religion is harmful because it divests humanity of the full knowledge of its moral power and ethical qualities by locating them in God alone. Love, for example, is for Feuerbach[7] divine *in itself,* not because it is a "predicate" of God. Ethical relations for Feuerbach are as well religious *per se,*

and life "in its essential, substantive relations" is "of a divine nature." However, by allocating human possibility and achievement in God, humanity deprives itself of a "genuine sense of truth and virtue," and remains in an immature, humanly incomplete state. Yet Irigaray does not address any of this.[8] Instead, she embraces for women what Feuerbach rejects for humankind. Women need a God. . . . At best, Irigaray offers here a feminist corrective to a fundamentally questionable psychological process without interrogating the process itself. She appears unhesitatingly to accept the *homo religiosus* thesis about the nature of humanity, failing to consider that human subjectivity may not absolutely require religious symbols and myths in order to develop. This is a specific kind of assumption that is concluded from the knowledge that most known cultures have practiced some form of religion. This in itself does not logically lead to the belief that human beings must universally hold religious beliefs in order to achieve psychic wholeness. Surely it is possible for contemporary women to achieve a creative and positive sense of identity without adopting a notion of a feminine divinity. A feminist approach to the study of religion needs seriously to consider Feuerbach's criticism of the psychological process itself that requires illusions as a necessary and intrinsic stage in the maturation process of the human species and individuals. Feuerbach, like Sigmund Freud, attempts in his critique of religion to "educate human beings to reality." The point of both their critiques of the psychological dynamics of religion was to expose the ways in which ideas and beliefs function to enslave human beings, preventing them from achieving their full mature potential. Even if Feuerbach's psychological and anthropological critique of religion is open to question, feminism still must contend with the fact that in urging women to embrace a female divinity in any way is to suggest at least a partial abdication of their subjectivity and autonomy as fully active human agents of history, and in their own lives.

This poses a grave contradiction within feminist theory itself, one that threatens to undercut feminism's own explicit emancipatory interest by advocating regressive forms of praxis—no matter how inspiring they may be for many women.

One commentator defends Irigaray's notion of the divine feminine by focusing on its intended political implications which do not require "a religious conversion or a leap of faith. Rather, Irigaray's idea undergirds a political and textual strategy for the positive reinscription of women's bodies, identities, and futures in relation to and in exchange with the other sex."[9] While the emphasis in Irigaray's thinking may well be consciously emancipatory and thus consciously poetical, her theoretical strategy nevertheless runs counter to her intent. In whatever way a deity or divine image may contain the projected ideal attributes of humanity, the divinity remains an abstraction, no matter how conditioned by social, cultural and historical factors. As a posited abstraction that is meant to represent women in the ideal—and thus unreal form—the consequent danger lies in its becoming a reified category which, like all reified categories is non-human. It might well recoil back on the women its creation was intended to serve. What happens to women, and what are they to think of themselves if their self-image does not correspond to a divine feminine?

4. Conclusion

The projection of a feminine divinity as a necessary horizon whose function is to act as a kind of a psychological guarantee, protecting women from being forced to fashion their identities and subjectivities within male reflections, does not contribute to the establishment of women's autonomy and freedom, but rather works against it. Inevitably, notions of a divine feminine will erase the vast differences that exist among and between women. At this point one needs to take seriously Feuerbach's caution concerning religious illusions. As far as a feminist critique of religion that contains an emancipatory interest is concerned, it must be extremely careful that it does not collaborate in maintaining conditions of oppression that women will tolerate better if they can devise more efficient illusions.

NOTES

1. Rosemary Radford Ruether, "Christology and Feminism: Can a Male Savior Save Women?" *To Change the World: Christology and Cultural Criticism* (London: SCM, 1981), p. 45.

2. Max Horkheimer, *Critical Theory: Selected Essays,* trans. Matthen J. O'Connell (New York: Continuum, 1972), p. 215.

3. Marsha Aileen Hewitt, *Critical Theory of Religion: A Feminist Analysis* (Minneapolis: Fortress Press, 1995).

4. Luce Irigaray, *Speculum of the Other Woman,* trans. Gillian C. Gill (Ithaca: Cornell University Press, 1985) and *Divine Women,* trans. Stephen Muecke, Occasional paper 8 (Sydney: Local Consumption, 1986).

5. Mary Daly, *Gyn/Ecology: The Metaethics of Radical Feminism* (Boston: Beacon Press, 1978) and *Pure Lust: Elemental Feminist Philosophy* (Boston: Beacon Press, 1984).

6. Carol P. Christ, *Laughter of Aphrodite: Reflections on a Journey to the Goddess* (San Francisco: Harper and Row, 1987).

7. Ludwig Feuerbach, *The Essence of Christianity,* trans. George Eliot (New York: Harper and Row, 1957), p. 273.

8. Irigaray, *Divine Women,* p. 6.

9. Elizabeth Grosz, "Irigaray and the Divine," in *Transfigurations: Theology and the French Feminists,* eds. C. W. Maggie Kim, et al. (Minneapolis: Fortress Press, 1993), p. 214.

From *Feminism and Religion: An Introduction*

RITA GROSS

The Academic Study of Religion

Religion was the last of the controversial, passion-inspiring human pursuits—such as politics, economics, and ethics—to be accorded its own academic discipline in the neutral setting of research, debate, and free thinking that characterizes the university. As an undergraduate, I could not major in religious studies because the state university system in which I was educated did not believe it was possible for a public institution to teach religion without violating the separation of church and state. Eight years later, I returned to that same system to teach religious studies to undergraduates. What had changed in educational philosophy in the intervening years?

The single greatest change that enabled religious studies to emerge as an academic discipline was the recognition that one could *understand* a religious position without *adhering* to it. I believe that this recognition was made possible by the study of non-Western religions; more removed from sectarian battles within culturally familiar religious settings, scholars realized that they could understand and appreciate, with great empathy, a point of view that they did not share. Therefore, such understanding could also be taught to others, without the rancor, dogmatism, competitiveness, hostility, and suasion that typically characterize sectarian religious education. Knowing about and understanding a religion is quite different from believing in it. The academic study of religion depends on that distinction.

Another major factor in the development of religious studies was the recognition that since religion has been a major mover and motivator in human culture from time immemorial to the present, it is impossible to understand human history and culture while ignoring religion. Only an extremely artificial division of human life and culture could tolerate the teaching of history, art, or social custom without understanding their connection with religion. Those trained in these disciplines are not fully prepared to explicate the religious beliefs that inform their subject matter; scholars formally trained in religious studies could contribute greatly to the overall environment of inquiry and learning that characterize a university.

Finally, the new imperative to understand divergent cultures, worldviews, and value systems in our complex world has brought religious studies to the fore. Except for anthropology, no academic discipline is so thoroughly imbued with the mandate to study its matter cross-culturally as is religious studies. In fact this characteristic of religious studies was essential to its development; to justify themselves as practitioners of a genuine academic discipline rather than a sectarian recruiting exercise, professors of religious studies encouraged a cross-cultural, comparative dimension in the field from the beginning. "To know one religion is to know none" paraphrases a famous and widely circulated statement made by Max Müller (1823–1900),[1] often credited as the founder of comparative studies in religion.

What is the academic study of religion? At the most basic level it is a descriptive discipline that gathers and disseminates accurate information about the variety of religious beliefs and practices people have entertained and engaged in throughout time and space. The academic study of religion, I often say on the first day of class, takes controversial material about which people

Reprinted from Rita Gross, Feminism and Religion: An Introduction *(Boston: Beacon Press, 1996).*

care deeply and places it in the neutral setting of the academic classroom, so that we can examine it and learn about it. Personal agreement or disagreement with the symbols, rituals, and beliefs about which we are learning is largely irrelevant at this stage. Scholars may debate alternative hypotheses about the information being studied, but debating the truth or falsity of the religious ideas is irrelevant to the academic study of religion as a descriptive discipline. If one truly understands what the academic study of religion is about, it will not be problematic or stressful to learn that Hinduism and Christianity have very different ideas about deity, and to learn both sets of ideas. And it will not be too tempting to argue that the Christian, Hindu, or some other view of deity is "correct." . . .

Though professionals in the study of religion do not agree on a single definition of religion, it is clear that a nonethnocentric definition of religion would not focus on the *content* of belief systems. There are no universally held religious beliefs or symbols. But the various beliefs and symbols found in the world's religions do share a similar *function* in human life. Religious beliefs and behaviors typically answer people's questions regarding matters of significant, overriding importance to them. Thus, many widely used definitions of religion in the academic study of religion talk of religion as one's "ultimate concern" or what one regards as sacred. Central to any particular religion is its worldview, the basic, often unconscious presuppositions its followers hold about the nature of reality.

By this definition any belief that functions as the most significant arbiter for decisions and actions and any behaviors whose value is unlimited to the actor are religious beliefs and behaviors, whatever their content. This definition is both broad enough to avoid ethnocentrism and specific enough to distinguish religious phenomena from nonreligious phenomena. Things of limited importance or significance are not religious. This definition also allows one to study the "religious" dimensions of phenomena not usually classified as religion, such as political

allegiance and deeply held psychological orientations. This working definition of religion is especially helpful when considering the impact of feminism on religious studies.

Religion and Religious Studies

When discussing controversial subjects about which people already have strong opinions, employing empathy is the only pedagogically appropriate method. Without empathy, we cannot attain the accuracy that is so central to academic teaching and learning.

How does empathy work in the academic study of religion? I define empathy as a two-step process. First, it involves temporarily dropping, or "bracketing," one's own worldview, values, and preconceptions as much as possible while engaged in study. The subject matter should be approached with an open mind, which includes the possibility of leaving the learning situation changed by new knowledge. Second, empathy involves imaginatively entering into the milieu of the phenomenon being studied. One cannot *become* an insider, contrary to the expectations of some who want to appropriate completely the perceptions and views of the insider. But one can and should understand and appreciate why insiders feel compelled by their views and behaviors. Scholars of religion try to speak as if they participate in the point of view under discussion, though they well may not. For example, one of my all-time favorite teaching evaluations, meant as a criticism but taken as a compliment, read, "The problem with her is that she teaches all those religions as if they were true!"

To continue the example introduced earlier, the academic study of religion may seek to impart accurate information about Christian and Hindu concepts of deity, which are quite different from each other. Those involved in the learning enterprise should be able to explain and *understand* why a Hindu finds a plurality of divine images cogent with the same facility that they can explain and understand why a Christian finds monotheism compelling.

Without such empathy, one can be neither accurate nor informed about religion, nor can one acquire what limited ojectivity is possible in the study of religion. More dangerous, without such empathy, the acquisition of information may increase ethnocentrism, intolerance, and chauvinism. Someone who learns that Hinduism encourages multiple images of the divine and that such images are often venerated in their painted or sculpted forms, without learning to understand why such concepts and practices make sense to the Hindu, has not been helped by the academic study of religion. She may, in fact, be more dangerously ill informed than before, precisely because she has more facts at her disposal, but does not understand them accurately and empathically.

Thus, as empathic scholars, we come to the issue of the relationship between religious studies as a discipline and the personal practice of religion, an issue which should be faced head-on rather than skirted. Although religious studies is not instruction about what one should believe religiously, learning information about religious views and behaviors other than one's own can still be unnerving. Truly understanding religious data requires empathy, but empathy often changes the way we think about the world and our place in it. This is not to say that our religious affiliation will change when we study religion academically and empathically, but our *attitudes* about religion may well change. Some attitudes we had previously rejected may become more appealing, whereas others that had seemed obviously correct may become less tenable. Such changes are especially likely when studying feminism and religion together. To expect or advocate otherwise is to promote academic learning in the worst sense of the term *academic:* a collection of irrelevant information that does not affect its bearer in any way.

If the practice of empathy is so important to the academic study of religion, does that mean that one can never evaluate the religious beliefs and behaviors being studied? This question is quite important in the study of feminism and religion, since most feminists criticize religious patriarchy. The practice of empathy does not mean that one must agree with or approve of the point of view being studied; although empathy involves appreciatively entering into the spirit of that which is being studied, one could not agree with all the positions one understands empathically because many are mutually exclusive.

Some kinds of evaluation are not incompatible with empathic understanding, if a few basic ground rules are observed. First, an empathic understanding of the religion must *precede* evaluation. Before formulating suggestions or critiques, it is important to have some idea of the justifications for current beliefs and behaviors put forth by those who adhere to them. Otherwise the evaluation is likely to be extremely ethnocentric, a problem to which feminism is not immune. Second, the same evaluative standards must be applied to all traditions, whether familiar or foreign, whether one's own or that of another.

Most scholars of religious studies talk more about the importance of neutrality and objectivity than they do about empathy, and indeed certain commonsense meanings of neutrality and objectivity are appropriate for the academic study of religion. The academy is not the place for proselytizing for any specific religion or religious position. Full and fair presentation of the strengths and weaknesses of all positions studied can and should be expected. However, although students and teachers should exhibit neutrality concerning interreligious competition and rivalry, a completely value-free position is impossible. Being objective and neutral when discussing controversial issues does not mean being value-free. On closer inspection, "objectivity" often turns out to be nothing more than advocacy of the current conventions and not a neutral position at all. Some perceive feminist scholarship as adversarial because it challenges such conventions; still, feminist scholarship can claim to be more "objective" than male-centered scholarship, because it is more inclusive and therefore more accurate.

Looking more deeply into neutrality and objectivity as they pertain to the academic study of religion helps to fully clarify the relationship between religious studies and religion. Students of religion sometimes expect or even hope that academic neutrality means that what they learn about the variety of religious phenomena will not affect their beliefs in any way. But simply because the academic study of religion is neutral vis-à-vis competing religions' claims does not mean that it is value-free. The study of religion can never be value-free because the very existence of the discipline depends on this value: the development of a worldview that cherishes a neutral position vis-à-vis the various religions as well as an ability to see the internal coherence and logic that empowers each of them. This value is emphatically rejected by at least some segments of all major religions.

In other words, living with religious diversity and regarding it as an interesting resource, rather than an undesirable deviation from truth, are the values that dominate the academic study of religion. Information about unfamiliar perspectives on religion is meant to challenge monolithic or universalistic presuppositions about the world. One *should* feel that sexist, racist, ethnocentric, and religious chauvinisms, if present, are being threatened by the academic study of religion. Even neutral and objective information, if absorbed rather than merely memorized, can change the one who assimilates that information. It is rarely possible to conclude one's studies carrying the same opinions regarding religious, ethnic, class, gender, and cultural diversity with which one began.

The academic study of religion is radically deabsolutizing because accurate information about and empathy for the other is radically deabsolutizing. Once one really understands the point of view of "the other" or the foreign, claims that one's belief is the only truth are no longer as attractive or compelling. This is the most significant point of contact between the academic study of religion and the way in which religion is sometimes practiced as a personal faith perspective. If religion necessarily involves war among absolute truth claims, its subject matter would be too disruptive and counterproductive to the rational and dispassionate discourse favored in the academy. But the empathic understanding required in the academic of religion encourages one to separate the absolutism some religions claim for themselves from information about their beliefs and practices, resulting in deabsolutized understanding of all religions and deabsolutized appreciation of religious pluralism and diversity.

For some, the appreciation of religious diversity is difficult because it contradicts religious instruction they have received. It may be helpful for people experiencing this difficulty to realize that it is quite possible to appreciate one's own perspective without believing that all people everywhere should adopt it. Such appreciation is a *different*, not a *lesser*, valuing of one's own particularity. This distinction is often difficult to appreciate at first, but I believe that no other alternative is possible in the global village in which we live. No lesson learned from the academic study of religion could be more valuable.

Like neutrality, objectivity in the study of religion is more complex than it appears. Because religion is so controversial and engenders such passion, calls for objectivity—approaching the subject without a point of view—are frequent. But all scholars speak and write from a particular point of view whether or not they claim objectivity for themselves. Once scholars agree upon methodological rules that determine what data are relevant and what techniques of interpretation are standard, scholarship can, in fact, be relatively "objective" within the limits of that system. For example, male-centered scholarship agreed upon the rule that data about women did not need to be included. Scholars abiding by that rule can do "objective" scholarship that is not gender inclusive. But when other scholars challenge that rule by demonstrating that one should also include data about women, it becomes clear that male-centered scholarship was objective only in a limited sense.

Because academic fashions can become relatively entrenched and long lasting, methodologically less reflective scholars sometimes think that their work is genuinely objective. Nevertheless, their work does not transcend the worldview and the methodology within which they record and interpret. It is not objective in the sense of having no perspective or reflecting no interests and values. Claims of objectivity from a scholar who is relatively unaware of his biases and perspectives do not obviate or negate his actual standpoint.

This issue is especially important for feminist studies in religion, since feminist scholarship is often thought to be "biased" because it self-consciously and deliberately includes information about women, whereas conventional androcentric scholarship is not similarly regarded as biased because it includes more information about men. For example, some believe courses on women and religion or gender-balanced mainstream courses on religion to be biased because they present more information about women than other courses do. But these kinds of claims only mask a desire to hear familiar perspectives and emphases, a wish that assumptions that have been taken for granted should not be challenged. This mistaken perception of bias is intensified because feminist scholars usually make their methodological values explicit, whereas conventional androcentric scholars usually do not, thereby fostering the illusion that they are without any specific agenda. But first-generation feminist scholars such as myself, who were reared to regard the generic masculine as genuinely generic and inclusive but could not find ourselves and our sisters in the data we studied, will never again be naive enough to think scholarship can be value-free.

Instead, scholars need to practice intense methodological self-awareness and introspection, combined with honest self-disclosure. Once one recognizes one's own standpoint, one can then argue on its behalf, making the case openly that this specific standpoint is more adequate than the alternatives. For example, when teaching my course on world religions, I always explain that I teach from a perspective that values diversity because only that approach promotes harmony and well-being in the global village. I also explain that the course will be gender balanced, which, to those used to androcentrism, may give the false impression that the course focuses on women. Likewise, in my course on feminist theology, I explain that, by definition, this course is quite critical of conventional religious points of view. Furthermore, in a course on feminist theology, neutrality involves presenting the various options within feminist theology but does not include antifeminist arguments or conventional theology in addition.

I also state openly that in my *viewpoint,* scholarship that values pluralism and diversity is more moral and humane than scholarship that longs for universal agreement and unity, and that in my viewpoint, gender-balanced and gender-inclusive scholarship is far more objective than androcentric scholarship, simply because it is more complete. Having stated the values that guide my scholarship and teaching, I have achieved the level of objectivity that is possible. Everyone, including me, knows *why* I include the data that I include and why I prefer the interpretations that I prefer. I can argue cogently for those preferences. Other scholars may offer other points of view, but not greater objectivity.

Feminism as Academic Method and as Social Vision

Learning feminist perspectives is more likely to change one's personal point of view than the academic study of religion. But popular perceptions of feminism, many of which are negative, have little to do with feminism as it intersects with the academic study of religion. Because such different impressions of feminism are found in our culture, it is important to clarify what is meant by feminism in this book.

The most basic definition of *feminism* is the conviction that women really do inhabit the human realm and are not "other," not a separate species. Sometimes I wear a T-shirt that proclaims: "Feminism is the radical proposition that women are human beings." This proclamation seems so simple and obvious, but its implications are profound and radical because neither conventional scholarship nor lifestyles really take the humanity of women seriously. Fully internalizing that statement involves a subtle and profound change of consciousness for both men and women. Living it out definitely involves a change in lifestyle for most people.

This definition of *feminism* has implications for both the academic study of religion and for the personal practice of religion because feminism can be understood as both an academic method and as a social vision. Although these two forms of feminism are interdependent because both grow out of the paradigm shift that occurs with the realization that women are human beings, they are more easily understood if they are initially separated. I prefer to call feminism as academic method *women studies,* to highlight the fact that it has no political implications, or agenda (even though it arose out of one) and to differentiate women studies from *feminism,* by which I mean a critical and reconstructive stance vis-à-vis the institutions and values of one's own culture, religion, and academic environments.

Women Studies: Feminism as Academic Method

One can use feminism as an academic method without embracing feminism as a social vision. Scholars who are reluctant to change their lifestyle to transcend gender roles and stereotypes and otherwise accommodate the full humanity of women nevertheless should recognize the need to study women as thoroughly, as critically, and as empathically as men. To do less is to fail to understand the human. Women studies has irrevocably changed our information-gathering habits, so that we can never again be content to know only what men did or

thought, or to have a reading list that includes only male authors (unless men are the subject of the study). Every course in the religious studies curriculum would change if those who taught it and took it understood that women are human beings whose lives are not adequately covered and included by the "generic masculine."

The first challenge of women studies is to expose and critique the androcentrism that underlies most traditional scholarship. I will offer a simple example of this androcentrism in lieu of a definition. I have often heard or read the equivalent of the following statement: "The Egyptians allow (or don't allow) women to. . . ." The structure is so commonplace that even today many do not see what is wrong with it. But for both those who make such statements and for those who hear them without wincing, real Egyptians are men. Egyptian women are objects acted upon by real Egyptians, but are not themselves full Egyptians. What, in more analytical terms, is behind this long-standing habitual pattern of speech? The androcentric model of humanity has three central characteristics that, when stated bluntly, suffice to demonstrate both the nature and the inadequacy of androcentrism.

First, the male norm and the human norm are collapsed and seen as identical. Recognition that maleness is but one kind of human experience is minimal or nonexistent. . . . Thus in androcentric thinking, any awareness of a distinction between maleness and humanity is clouded over, and femaleness is viewed as an exception to the norm.

The second characteristic of androcentrism follows directly from the first. When I first questioned the completeness of androcentric accounts of religion, my mentors told me that the generic masculine includes the feminine, making it unnecessary to study women specifically. This is a logical implication of collapsing maleness with humanity, but the result is that research about religion actually deals mainly with the lives and thinking of males, whereas women's religious lives are treated much more peripherally, as a footnote or a short chapter toward the end of the book. The habit of thinking and doing research in the generic masculine is so ingrained that many scholars are genuinely unaware that the religious lives and thoughts of men are only part of a religious situation.

The third and most problematic aspect of androcentrism is its attempt to deal with the fact that, since men and women are taught to be different in all cultures, the generic masculine simply does not cover the feminine. The generic masculine would work only in religions or cultures that had no sex roles, but no such culture exists. Therefore, women must sometimes be mentioned in accounts of religion. At this point, adherents of the androcentric model of humanity reach a logical impasse. Their solution to this impasse is the most devastating component of the androcentric outlook. Because women inevitably deviate from male norms, androcentric thinking deals with them only as objects exterior to "mankind," needing to be explained and fitted in somewhere, having the same epistemological and ontological status as trees, unicorns, deities, and other objects that must be discussed to make experience intelligible. Therefore, in most accounts of religion, although males are presented as religious subjects and as namers of reality, females are presented only in relation to the males being studied, only as objects being named by the males being studied, only as they appear to the males being studied.

Nothing less than a paradigm shift in our model of humanity will remedy these problems. Instead of the current androcentric, "one-sexed" model of humanity, we need an androgynous, "two-sexed" or bisexual model of humanity. A more accurate model of humanity would compel recognition that humans come in two sexes and that both sexes are human. It would also recognize that in virtually every religion, culture, or society, gender roles and stereotypes intensify biological sexual differences. As a result, men's and women's lives are

more separate and different from each other's than is biologically dictated. An accurate model of humanity would also forbid placing one gender in the center and the other on the periphery. Androgyny as a two-sex model of humanity, as the conviction that despite gender and sexual differences, women and men are equally human, meets those requirements; both traditional androcentrism, which objecti[fies] women, and a sex-neutral model of humanity, which ignores the reality of culture-based gender roles, do not. . . .

When this model of humanity and these methodological guidelines are applied to virtually any subject in the humanities or social sciences, massive changes in scholarship result, affecting what one studies, how one studies it, what conclusions one draws from research data, the analyses one finds cogent, and the overarching theories that one accepts as good basic tools with which to understand the world. Furthermore, internalizing this model of humanity often results in a transformation of consciousness so profound that one's everyday habits of language and perception change as well. Once one makes the change from an androcentric to an androgynous model of humanity, other models seem completely inadquate.

It is important to recognize that feminist scholarship does not inherently make judgments about what women's position in society should be. It only entails a requirement to study women thoroughly and completely. To construct a feminist vision of society is a different task. Therefore, feminism, at least in the academic context, is first and foremost an academic method, not a socio-political perspective. The key issue is including information about women in all studies about any human phenomenon. The scholar's personal views are irrelevant to whether he has an academic obligation to teach a gender-balanced course: Even nonfeminists must include information about women in their scholarship if they want to claim that their scholarship is accurate.

Feminism as Social Vision

My claim that feminism is, *first,* an academic method is controversial because the emergence of the feminist method was inextricably linked with a movement of social protest and dissatisfaction. Indeed, the methodological demand to gather and include information about women could not have emerged and flourished apart from feminism as an alternative social vision, for it was protest against women's limited options in American society that first impelled feminist scholars to notice and name androcentricism and to create women studies methodology.

Feminism as social vision deals with views about ideal social arrangements and interactions between women and men. Therefore, almost by definition, all feminist perspectives are radically critical of current conventional norms and expectations and advocate some degree of change in social, academic, political, religious, and economic institutions to foster greater equity between men and women. Just as feminist scholarship finds androcentrism to be the basic problem with previous scholarship, so feminist social philosophy has focused on patriarchy as the fundamental obstacle to human well-being for women, as well as for men, to a lesser extent. Just as androcentrism regards men as normal and women as exceptions to the norm, so patriarchy regards men as rightful leaders and holders of all positions that society values, whereas women should be subservient and help men maintain their status. As such, the word *patriarchy* has become feminist shorthand for the anti-vision of female subservience and irrelevance that fueled much of society and religion for the past several thousand years and led to the mind-set in which the androcentric model of humanity not only found acceptance, but reigned without conceptual alternatives.

For more than twenty years, feminists have discussed the creation, outlines, and inadequacies of patriarchy and have formulated visions of a postpatriarchal world. Because women in a number of religious traditions are feminist and use feminist ideals to critique and reenvision their traditions, feminism as a social vision, although different from women studies, does in fact intersect with the academic study of religion. Feminists' use of feminism as a social vision in their reflections on their religions has become data for the academic study of religion. Therefore, the ways in which feminism as a social philosophy has affected, criticized, and changed the world's religions must be included in academic study of contemporary religion.

Feminism as social vision relies upon the results of feminist scholarship in history, sociology, and psychology, as well as religion. The most important conclusion of feminist scholarship is that patriarchy is the cultural creation of a certain epoch in human history, not an inevitable necessity of human biology.[2] The importance of this claim is that whatever is created within time is subject to decay and dissolutions a point commonplace in Buddhism among other major religions. This realization overcomes the advice given to generations of rebellious daughters: "You can't do anything about *that.*" One *can* do something about patriarchy, though the task is immense.

Well before feminists felt confident of the case that patriarchy emerged relatively late in human history, they were very clear in their critique of it. The early literature of feminism was an outcry of pain; from the nineteenth century on, feminists have claimed that patriarchy is "without redeeming social value," that it is dearly linked with the most destructive forces in human history, and that it harms all people, including men, though not as obviously, directly, or extremely as it harms women.

What about patriarchy makes it such an offensive system to its critics? The literal meaning of patriarchy—"rule by fathers"—provides two clues. First, patriarchy is a system, in which rulership, "power over," is quite central; second, by definition, men have power over women. The extent of men's power over women was the first element of the complex to be thoroughly recognized and described. Men monopolize or dominate all the roles and pursuits that society most values and rewards, such as religious leadership or economic power. Therefore, inequality became one of the first patriarchal demons to be named. Furthermore, men literally ruled over women, setting the rules and limits by which and within which they were expected to operate. Women who did not conform, and many who did, could be subjected to another form of male dominance—physical violence.

As the analysis of patriarchy deepened, many feminists focused not merely on the way in which men hold power over women, but also on the centrality of the concept of having power over others in patriarchal society. Many see male power over females as the basic model of all forms of social hierarchy and oppression. From this conclusion, many analysts move on to link patriarchy with militarism and with ecologically dangerous use of the environment. This conclusion is based on the fact that all these policies share an attitude of glorifying and approving the power of one group over another as inevitable and appropriate.

In my view, these typical feminist diagnoses are correct but incomplete because they do not sufficiently clarify the fundametal aspiration of modern feminism, which is far more important than equality or total lack of hierarchy: *freedom from gender roles.* I believe that gender roles are the source of the pain and suffering in current gender arrangements and that eliminating them is the most essential aspect of the program to overcome that pain. If people are forced to find their social place on the basis of their physiological sex, then there will be suffering and injustice even in a situation of "gender equality" —whatever that might mean.

The difference between freedom from gender roles and gender equality is profound. Any concept of gender equality presupposes the continued existence of gender roles and all the imprisoning implied in such conditions. Early liberal feminists usually envisioned equality as meaning that women should be able to do the things men had always done, and, sometimes, that men should be forced to do the things that women had always done. This definition depends on the fact that the male role (rather than men) is preferred to the female role. A frequently cited alternative meaning of equality is that what women do should be regarded as of *equal value* with what men do—a version of separate-but-equal thinking that is often advocated as a conservative alternative to patriarchy.

Neither of these visions of equality escapes the prison of gender roles. Claiming that the female role is distinctive, but of equal rather than of inferior value, still assumes that only women can fulfill the female role and that all women must conform to that female gender role. Giving women access to men's roles, which often requires an attempt to get men into women's roles as well, comes closer to conceptualizing the basic truth that gender roles are the problem to be overcome, but it still collapses sexual identity and social roles. Whenever sexual identity and social roles are conflated, even when the possibility of "cross-over" is acknowledged, the result is a kind of anatomy-is-destiny thinking, which allows no hope for postpatriarchal vision of life outside the prison of gender roles.

On the other hand, if we do not merely suggest or validate crossovers between sexual identity and social role but break the links between sexual identity and social roles altogether, then a social order beyond patriarchy becomes inevitable. Patriarchy depends, in the final analysis, on fixed gender roles. Without gender roles, no one will have automatic access to any role or automatic power over another because of her physiological sex.

Seeing the problem as gender roles and the vision as freedom from gender roles also puts the feminist critique of patriarchy as "power over" in another light. The abuse of power is certainly a major human problem, and patriarchy is rife with abuse of power. But one of the most abusive aspects of patriarchal power is men's automatic, rather than earned or deserved, power over women. Though we must guard against abuses of power, a totally egalitarian society in which no one has more influence, prestige, or wealth than anyone else seems quite impossible. Given that hierarchy is inevitable, therefore, the issue is establishing *proper hierarchy*. This complex and difficult topic cannot be fully explicated in this context, but I must clarify that proper hierarchy is not the same thing as what feminists mean by "domination" or "power over" in their critique of the patriarchal use of power. It connotes the proper use of power that has been properly earned, a topic not much explored in feminist thought. But if postpatriarchal vision is freedom from gender roles, men would no longer automatically receive any power, prestige, influence, or position simply because of their sex. Though following this guideline would not, by itself, guarantee proper hierarchy, it would abolish the worst abuses of patriarchal power.

My claim that the problem of patriarchy is the very existence of gender roles and that postpatriarchy is freedom from gender roles is both radical and controversial. Some may well feel that a world without gender roles is even more unlikely to develop than a world without relationships of domination and submission. Some may think that feminists' goal should be finding and institutionalizing more equitable and just gender roles, rather than abolishing them. It is clear, however, that virtually every feminist critique of patriarchy and every feminist agenda for the future really derives from an unstated assumption that sex is not a relevant criterion for awarding roles or value. Furthermore, any set of gender roles whatsoever will be a prison for those who do not readily fit them. Because the prison of gender roles has been one of the greatest sources of suffering in my life, I am reluctant to make any place for them in a visionary postpatriarchal future.

What might life free from gender roles be like? In some ways, one's sex is important and in other ways not at all. In some ways, it remains necessary to rely on traditional concepts of masculinity and femininity, at least in the short run,

and in other ways they are already irrelevant. I think of my own life as participating in a post-patriarchal mode of existence. I am a female; I do not fill the female gender role or the male gender role; I believe that my psychology and lifestyle are both traditionally feminine and traditionally masculine. Thus, my own experience provides me with some of the guidelines for a postpatriarchal future free of gender roles. Sexual identity remains clear. Sexual differentiation is so obvious and so basic that it seems impossible to ignore or deny one's sex. But one's sex implies nothing inevitable about one's reproductive decisions, one's economic and social roles, or even one's psychological traits and tendencies.

Would "masculinity" and "femininity" have any meaning in a world free from the prison of gender roles? On this question, there is no feminist consensus. My own views, largely derived from Tibetan Vajrayana Buddhist ideas about the masculine and the feminine, call for completely severing the idea that men should be masculine and that women should be feminine, while continuing to use the terms as symbols. Because the experience of paired entities is so common, we have inherited a whole repertoire of traits and qualities that are commonly labeled "masculine" and "feminine." That, in itself, is not problematic, so long as we remember that these labels are products of culture, not biology, and differ considerably from culture to culture. What imprisons is the expectation that women should be feminine and men should be masculine. But without the prison of gender roles, these expectations would not hold. Instead men and women would become whatever combination of "masculine" and "feminine" best suited them. In such a context, the symbols of femininity and masculinity might well become more finely tuned, not less.

However, a *society,* free from gender roles will be much more "feminine" than current patriarchal society. Why? Because in patriarchy, women must be feminine, which demands that they be silent, whereas men must be masculine and therefore can be articulate. As a result, in patriarchy, most public policy and most religious thought is "masculine" and quite incomplete. Some argue cogently that such partial views, although not wrong, are dangerous so long as they remain incomplete. When women become more articulate and women's experiences of femininity and masculinity become part of public discourse and public policy, society will become both more feminine and more androgynous. At that point individuals of both sexes will more easily become androgynous, whole Persons instead of "half-humans" trapped in female or male gender roles.

Conclusion

It is important to note what links these two arenas of feminist thought. Feminism as scholarly method is critical of the androcentric mind-set. Feminism as social vision is critical of patriarchal culture. Androcentrism and patriarchy share the same attitude toward women. In both cases, women are objectified as nonhuman, are spoken about as if they were objects but not subjects, and are manipulated by others. In both cases, the end result is silence about women and the silencing of women. Androcentric scholarship proceeds as if women do not exist, or as if they are objects rather than subjects. Patriarchal culture discourages women from naming reality, and patriarchal scholarship then ignores the namings of reality that women create nevertheless. But women studies scholarship takes seriously women's namings of reality, even in patriarchal contexts, and feminism as social philosophy encourages women's authentic, empowered namings of reality and demands that these namings be taken seriously by the whole society.

NOTES

1. William E. Paden, *Religious Worlds: The Comparative Study of Religion* (Boston: Beacon Press, 1988), p. 38.

2. Gerda Lerner, *The Creation of Patriarchy* (New York: Oxford University Press, 1986).

Counterpoint:
Having Your Cake and Eating It Too:
Feminism and Religion

KATHERINE K. YOUNG

Katherine K. Young is a professor of Hinduism in the Faculty of Religious Studies at McGill University, Montreal, Canada.

CHARACTERISTIC OF FEMINIST APPROACHES to religion is that of Rita Gross. In *Feminism and Religion* she offers basic definitions of technical terms, discusses the relation between descriptive and normative approaches to the study of religion, explores the historical interaction between

Reprinted from the Journal of the American Academy of Religion 67, 1 (1999): 167–184.

feminism and religion, and examines four specific problems (referring to the "exclusion" of women from discussions of religion, the "sexism" in world religions, whether the latter is primordial, and what form a new religion should take).

Like her feminist colleagues in the academic world, of course, Gross attacks male scholars. To her credit, she attacks some feminists as well (though more gently). The latter are ethnocentric, she argues, because they have not widened their scope beyond Christianity and Judaism to include the many other traditions studied by historians of religions. In any case, she succumbs to several rather serious fallacies. Some of these, after decades of feminist advocacy in the name of scholarship, had already become conventional wisdom long before this book was written. Others, though, appear for the first time in her attempt to integrate the methods of feminism and the history of religions.

Definitions

Politics and psychology over religion: Gross's definition of the word "religion" relies on both Paul Tillich's notion of "ultimate concern" and Mircea Eliade's notion of the "sacred." There is nothing new here for academics in the field of religious studies. But she gives the concept of ultimate concern her own gloss. It includes "religious dimensions of phenomena not usually classified as religion, such as political allegiance and deeply held psychological orientations. This working definition of religion is especially helpful when considering the impact of feminism on religious studies."[1] This builds a bridge between religion on the one side and politics and psychology on the other. Once built, though, the bridge disappears. Because religion is about ultimate concern and feminism is about ultimate concern, religion is feminism. This is the fallacy of the ambiguous middle: the middle term (ultimate concern) has a different meaning in each of the two premises. To put it another way, a term that belongs to one category (religion) is treated as if it belongs to another (secular politics and psychology). What makes this even more confusing is that feminists have created a religion of their own to foster this illusion. Even though explicitly religious phenomena appear (such as myths, rituals, and theologies), the implicit values that inform them are inherently secular (even though they have ultimate value for those concerned) and, therefore, have little to do with traditional forms of religions. I will return to this observation in due course and argue that the impact of feminism on the history of religions amounts to nothing more or less than the attempt to transform an academic discipline into a secular worldview in the guise of a religion (and thus to transform the university classroom into a mission field).

Feminism over women's studies: Useful, at first glance anyway, is Gross's distinction between women's studies (which not only documents the absence or marginalization of women in religion but also presents information about them, expressed whenever possible in their own "voices") and feminism (which attacks religions as patriarchal and often, after deconstructing them, tries to reconstruct them in what are considered more suitable forms). Although women's studies had its origin in feminism, observes Gross, it developed without "political implications or agenda."[2] Unfortunately, Gross herself does not maintain this distinction. "It is important to recognize," she writes, "that feminist scholarship does not inherently make judgments about what women's position in society should be. It only entails a requirement to study women thoroughly and completely. . . . Therefore, feminism, at least in the academic context, is first and foremost an academic method, not a socio-political perspective. The key issue is including information about women in all studies about any human phenomenon."[3]

By her own definition, "women's studies" clearly refers to scholarship. "Feminism" on the other hand, clearly refers to advocacy. The term "feminist scholarship," therefore, is an oxymoron. Why introduce the latter when the term "women's studies" would suffice? Gross's preference for the term "feminism" even in connection with scholarship indicates that her goal is not scholarship at all but what could be called informed advocacy—that is, feminist transformation of society and its religions. And yet, she hides this problem by paying lip service to the methods of the history of religions. She refers repeatedly to "accurate" information[4] and even to "objectivity" (both of which are suspect, to say the least, in feminism). So what is going on here?

Methods

Academic neutrality over parochialism: Gross begins by introducing the history of religions, a field in which she herself was trained at the University of Chicago. (Before proceeding, remember that this discipline was developed very self-consciously by its pioneers as a descriptive and interpretative discipline; theology and ethics were considered evaluative and normative ones.) At first she seems willing to accept its distinctive orientation. She writes, for instance, that it invites "a neutral position vis-à-vis the various religions as well as an ability to see the internal coherence and logic that empowers each of them."[5] Value neutrality is usually understood as a combination of *epoché* (trying to become as self-conscious as possible about our own presuppositions in order to set them aside temporarily and thus allow phenomena to be seen on their own terms) and *empathy* (imaginative entrance into the perspectives of insiders). These two principles lie at the heart of phenomenological description. Gross argues that description done with empathy must precede evaluation, because "otherwise the evaluation is likely to be extremely ethnocentric, a problem to which feminism is not immune."[6] In other words, the conflict between description and evaluation can be avoided by separating the two steps. But she herself does not hold to this distinction. In her word, description becomes the first step in transforming the world. . . .

Tolerance over neutrality: Next Gross argues that academic neutrality—value neutrality—is itself based on a value: tolerance. This should inform scholarship, she observes, making it more moral and humane. "I also state openly," writes Gross, "that in my *viewpoint,* scholarship that values pluralism and diversity is more moral and humane than scholarship that longs for universal agreement and unity."[7]

But value neutrality is not the same as tolerance. The latter means respecting (or at least enduring) the beliefs and practices of others. Mistaking an *is* (value neutrality) for an *ought* (the moral duty to be tolerant) creates a classic fallacy. Just because two cultures are different, moreover, does not mean that either one is ethical. Besides, valuing everything equally (even if that were humanly possible) would add up to nothing more than relativism. And what about all the resulting contradictions?

In any case, Gross is being somewhat disingenuous. Her interest in tolerance does not arise from the ethical position that virtue is an end in itself. Nor does it arise from the scholarly need to understand religions on their own terms. It arises from the political urge to destabilize religious worldviews—beginning with the western ones of her students—by showing how ignorant and biased they really are for holding "monolithic or universalistic presuppositions about the world."[8] . . .

Once tolerance is understood, Gross believes, people will support those who are demanding change. In her words, "[t]ruly understanding religious data requires empathy, but empathy often changes the way we think about the world and our place in it."[9] The ground for conversion, despite her disclaimer in the name of religion, has been prepared.

By focusing on the diversity of religions Gross establishes an important link with postmodernism. The latter is very fashionable in academic circles, of course. It is *de rigueur* in feminist circles, specifically, because its rhetoric is so heavily laden with words such as "pluralism," "inclusiveness," and "diversity" (words made necessary by the charge of African-American and Hispanic women that North American feminism is the product of a white, middle-class establishment). In Gross's words "to many, it seemed that white, middle-class, heterosexual, Christian feminists had assumed that they could speak for all women. During the 1980s, many diverse voices spoke much more loudly and clearly, sometimes with frank frustration, so that today feminist theology more accurately reflects the diversity of women."[10]

Like other feminists, though, Gross is *selective* in her use of postmodern rhetoric. She has no intention of accepting *everything*, after all, that the world's religions have to offer. So tolerance is by no means the *sine qua non* of pluralism. . . .

Gross argues first that to "truly understand" means to learn from everyone.[11] Then, however, she argues that to "truly understand" means to find some religions (or some aspects of religions) more appealing than others.[12] She begins with the model of equality, in other words but then replaces it with the model of hierarchy (superiority and inferiority). She tries to legitimate this measure in a way that could be rendered as the following syllogism: 1) Historians of religions acknowledge that each worldview considers itself superior in some way to the others. 2) Feminism is a worldview. 3) Ergo, historians of religions should acknowledge feminism's claim to superiority. I see no problem with the argument as it stands, as long as it is read very carefully. The three points should be understood as phenomenological descriptions of *how each views itself*. Problems arise only when these phenomenological descriptions of *emic* (insider) views are understood as statements of superiority evaluated according to some *etic* (outsider) criterion.

Gross's message of tolerance is directed not only to those who are religiously chauvinistic but also to western feminists. "Since my training is in the cross-cultural study of religion, and because I am personally involved in a major non-Western tradition, I constantly strive to redress the imbalance and Eurocentrism of current feminist and neofeminist perspectives on religion. In my view, the Western orientation of most feminist thinking about religion is a serious limitation. . . . Clearly, chief among my methodological biases is the conviction that relevant thinking can no longer afford the luxury of Eurocentrism."[13]

Advocacy over objectivity: Feminists often argue that the ideal of objectivity must be deconstructed because it does not take into account the inherent biases of readers or the inherent ambiguity of language itself. According to this approach, the whole notion of objectivity must be rejected. Gross tries to have it both ways. She wants to retain objectivity (as a historian of religions)[14] but only when it suits her. According to her, "being objective and neutral when discussing controversial issues does not mean being value-free. On closer inspection, 'objectivity' often turns out to be nothing more than advocacy of the current conventions and not a neutral position at all. Some perceive feminist scholarship as adversarial because it challenges such conventions; still, feminist scholarship can claim to be more 'objective' than male-centred scholarship, because it is more inclusive and therefore more accurate."[15]

What are these "conventions"? Gross does note that feminists challenge them. And her book is addressed to feminists. By "conventions," then, she obviously refers to those of *androcentric* worldviews, to those of *patriarchal* religions. She suggests that male scholars (and their supporters) consciously create the illusion of objectivity, because their real purpose is to *advocate* traditional religion (presumably because it "excludes" women and serves their interests). Even though "some" (presumably, these same men and their supporters) consider feminism adversarial because it attacks them and their religion, according to Gross, feminism is actually "more objective" simply because it pays more attention to women, even though it usually pays *exclusive* attention to women on the dubious grounds that just as women have been ignored in the past, now men can be ignored.

And all in the name of objectivity and inclusiveness! Gross admits that promoting values is not scholarly, whether it is done by men or women, yet she implies that doing so by men is somehow more wrong—even though that would be oxymoronic—than doing so by women. Those who take objectivity seriously are not only deluded, moreover, but wilfully deluded. Bias is universal, in other words, but "our" biases are better than "their" biases. Two wrongs, in short, make a right. Gross has succumbed, once again, to the fallacy of mistaking an "is" (bias in favor of men exists, presumably) for an "ought" (bias in favor of women should exist).

By now Gross has moved a long way from the notion that women's studies, like the history of religions, produces scholarship because it values objectivity. In fact, she suggests, there can be no objectivity at all on controversial topics. But advocacy is simply not the same as objectivity. It is true that unconscious biases can diminish the objectivity of scholarship. But that is no reason to abandon the search for it by adopting *conscious* biases. We can never have perfect democracy, after all. Does that mean we should abandon democracy? . . .

After decades of relentless feminist attacks on (patriarchal) scholarship and of scholarly reform, moreover, I wonder if it can be said that scholarship today is "*often*" tainted by patriarchal conventions. If anything, it seems to me, scholarship is now far more often tainted by feminist conventions. Returning over and over again to biases common in the past *as if* they were just as common in the present is tendentious. In fact, it is anachronistic to superimpose a feature of one historical period onto another. This is a feminist version of the fallacy known as *argumentum ad populum:* an opinion formed by "reading texts" not on their own terms but as mediated by ideas so taken for granted that they have become conventional wisdom. To avoid this problem, it would have to be demonstrated that *contemporary* (male) scholars often advocate the maintenance of conventions (patriarchal traditions). The fact that this is seldom documented suggests to me that many feminists ignore historical accuracy to gain political leverage by claiming their own moral superiority.

Objectivity must be assessed by specific criteria. Does a description present the true complexity or ambiguity of some historical situation? Does the evidence reveal anomalies? If so, how can these be explained? Could they be explained better by abandoning one hypothesis for another? Although complete objectivity is impossible—new information comes to light, new methods are developed, scholars point out mistakes, and so on—scholarship is designed to help us approach this goal. I believe that objectivity *should continue* to remain an ideal, because it demands *accountability* to something (text, context, ritual, formal logic, and so forth) and insists that generalizations be based on appropriate samples. . . . For her, objectivity now means nothing more than the disclosure of biases. But that makes no sense. Even though her conclusion follows from a premise, it must have some other support (empirical evidence, formal reasoning, and so forth). Failing to provide any, she succumbs to the fallacy of *petitio principii.*

It is certainly true that *epoché* implies an attempt to be conscious of our own biases. This does not mean that scholars always succeed, of course. Consequently, they must be evaluated independently by their peers (hence, the concept of "peer review"). Simply stating a proposition does not make it correct (even though doing so might help readers understand the author's self-understanding and intentionality). In other words, merely claiming an androgynous approach and opining that "an accurate model of humanity would also forbid placing one gender in the center and the other on the periphery"[16] hardly rules out the possibility of a gynocentric or androcentric one.

Stating our own biases can contribute, moreover, to scholarly laziness. In the past, students were trained to search for presuppositions, partial selection of data, and erroneous arguments. Today students are told simply to accept whatever authors say in their introductory paragraphs. This undermines their ability to learn through the dialectic of critique and response. The problem with Gross's approach, which is shared by many other feminists, becomes especially apparent when she argues that neutrality "involves presenting the various options within feminism, but does not include anti-feminist arguments or conventional theology in addition."[17] Here she alludes to the "pluralism" celebrated by postmodernism. Nevertheless, the only definition of plurality allowed is one defined by women and serving the interests of women. This makes me wonder, of course, what Gross can possibly mean by calling, as she does, for a new human vision.

And what if the conclusions of two or more scholars are different? Worse yet, what if they are contradictory? Assuming that both are "objective" (in that they both contain explicit statements of bias), according to Gross, both are equal. But would she tolerate a man stating his *androcentric* bias and then arguing that the latter is just as good as a gynocentric one? Not likely.

Must we assume that stating our presuppositions is a good idea? Not necessarily. It is a moot point. What counts, though, is that we become as self-conscious as possible about them and that we learn from multiple assessments of our presuppositions, selection of facts, logic, and so on. Nothing that detracts from vigilance in this academic exercise will serve the cause of good scholarship (let alone of social change). Once again, it is true that we can never be assured of having attained complete objectivity (and, indeed, perfection is impossible for finite beings). Nevertheless, methods designed to improve description and prevent fallacious arguments can move us toward this goal.

What about Gross's claim that greater objectivity is gained by the inclusion of women? One of her arguments, which I note here in syllogistic form, is this: 1) Scholars must include women for scholarship to provide an objective description of the human race; 2) Conventional (read: "patriarchal") scholars have excluded women but feminists have included them; 3) Ergo, feminists are more objective than the former. But this rationale is problematic for several reasons. Information about women is not always found in the historical record (except where women have lived at least partly in the public realm). Even with the best of intentions, therefore, this information is beyond recovery. In some cases, moreover, information about women is not even relevant to the topic at hand. For either reason, or both, it would be unfair to accuse modern historians of biases. My point is not that they should ignore the need to fill in lacunae by combing through existing records or searching for new types of record or raising new research questions. My point is merely that, at the end of the day, they cannot avoid the inherent limitations of the historical record.

A double standard is implicit in Gross's book. Bias is considered illegitimate when it comes from "sexist" authors but perfectly legitimate when it comes from feminist authors. She fails to acknowledge, moreover, that bias can be reduced considerably by adopting well-known methods such as *epoché* and empathy, even though she herself pays homage to these while establishing her credentials as a historian of religions at the beginning of her book. Consequences follow from shifting the emphasis from a phenomenon to the "reader" and from objectivity (and accountability) to subjectivity. For one thing, it appears to legitimate conscious and unconscious biases; that is cynicism. Even worse, it appears to legitimate political exploitation of these biases; that is opportunism. Bias becomes the basis for advocacy in the name of scholarship.

Next, once people are existentially engaged, Gross introduces the feminist critique of male hegemony—sometimes broadened to "sexist, racist, ethnocentric, and religious chauvinisms."[18] Because these are pervasive in existing religions, she believes, both conventional pluralism (the world's religions) and specific religions stand in need of radical change.

Visions

Androgyny over patriarchy. Gross calls for an androgynous approach in her words, a "two-sexed or bisexual model of humanity."[19] Unfortunately, once again she does not live up to her own standard. She offers descriptions of women and feminist critiques of men as patriarchal (and thus immoral). She assumes, moreover, that the experiences and "voices" of men are always included. . . .

False generalization about men is particularly significant when the topic is power. Gross, like other feminists, not only labels most interpretations of the past "patriarchal," she also condemns them as reflections of male "power over" women. This last phrase, made popular by Marilyn French in *Beyond Power,* sums up the feminist view of patriarchy. "Power over" is not merely regrettable but sinister as well. . . . In a brief disclaimer, Gross admits that all this can harm men too. And she chides Mary Daly for being deterministic on the topic of men's nature as "necrophilic patriarchs, by virtue of their male bodies."[20] Even so, she encourages readers to accept without question a highly negative stereotype of men as immoral (selfish, destructive, violent). Her own view is exposed when she comments "But Daly balances her condemnation of men with an ecstatic celebration of women's discovery of their own worth and power, a naming more joyful than many of the writings discussed in this book." Balance?

Nothing could be more gynocentric (and less "androgynous") than the theory that men are responsible, whether due to nature or culture, for all human problems. In fact, it is a gynocentric version of the Fall. The Christian story of the Fall has been turned on its head. At first, in the Bible, blame was laid on the man, the woman, and the serpent. As this story was interpreted later on, blame was laid primarily (but not exclusively) on the woman. Now, we have moved in the opposite direction: blame is laid, in effect, entirely on the man—that is, on men. History is interpreted as nothing less than a conspiracy of men to subordinate (or exploit, or punish) women. Having argued that men have stereotyped women as immoral, many feminists do precisely the same thing to men. They find it easy to ignore men's altruistic acts as providers for their families and protectors of their communities. One explanation for this tendency flies in the face of feminist orthodoxy (and, despite the rhetoric of "diversity" and "pluralism" and "multivocality," some feminist beliefs have become orthodox): it is politically expedient to proclaim women's victimhood, on the one hand, and their moral superiority, on the other (a strategy that has been popular since the nineteenth century).

On the surface it would seem that Gross has moved beyond both androcentric and gynocentric approaches by calling for an "androgynous" one. As I have said, though, she consciously or unconsciously loads the word "androgyny" with the content of gynocentrism. Is there a way out? One way, I suggest, is to adopt the metaphor of stereoscopic vision. The two eyes of humans and other primates are anatomically positioned to provide three-dimensional sight. Each eye sees the world from a slightly—not very, but slightly—different angle. Together the two perspectives are blended to provide a three-dimensional vision that would be impossible with either eye alone. Now apply this to the perspectives of men and women. By taking both seriously the result would be greatly improved phenomenology. This way we would learn about the effects of nature and culture on both women *and men*. We would be better able to understand differences between the sexes (and account for the needs and problems of *both* sexes before demanding social change) but also understand *the similarities* (what makes both sexes human). Being reductive neither to differences nor similarities, we could truly move beyond androcentric, gynocentric, and even universalistic views. Adopting this approach could shift, once again, our understanding of the past. The exclusion of women has not always been due to a conscious act of malice.

For example, very often it has been due to deeply engrained cultural norms accepted by both men *and women*. Today, of course, there is no excuse for the exclusion or marginalization of either sex (which is the situation of men in some forms of the "goddess" movement). The methods of *epoché* and empathy, if applied to men no less than to women, could destroy all gender stereotypes and help us develop a more nuanced view of both the past and the future, one that distinguishes between the types of power used (or abused) by both men *and women*.

From a feminist perspective, of course, all this will sound "revisionist," if not worse. Be that as it may, my perspective extends the fruitful methods developed by the phenomenology and history of religions. It is true that many of the pioneers in religious studies (all men) completely ignored women. Yes, they can be accused of using these methods selectively (though not always consciously). But neither of these facts means there was or is anything wrong with the methods themselves. They should be used now to study the distinctive religious experiences of both men and women. They should be applied to new sources of information, making the anthropology of religion and popular culture much more important complements to the history of religions than they have been. My point is that adequate descriptions of the lives of both women *and men* in other times and places will create the only enduring foundation for thinking about the direction of social change in our own.

But Gross presents an even more difficult problem. She moves beyond the call for "androgynous scholarship" to suggest that men and women, as such, should be androgynous. This can be achieved, she suggests, by breaking the link between sexual identity and social roles. . . . On the surface, this solution looks attractive. But, as I have discovered in the course of my research with Nathanson, there is much more to be said on this topic. By not examining the significance of both biology and culture, it

denies several deep asymmetries. Men cannot gestate or lactate. And male children must separate from their mothers in a far more radical way than girls to establish their identity as males. As Nathanson and I have found in our research, every society has had to address the problem of biological asymmetry; at least a few symbols (such as the blowpipe) or activities (such as hunting or wrestling) are exclusively reserved for men even in otherwise egalitarian societies. We suspect that this is a universal cultural adjustment to the power and exclusivity of women's reproductive capacity. Since the urban revolution, moreover, the male body has become less and less significant as a source of identity. Now that speed, size, and upper-body strength are more irrelevant than ever due to machines and computers, and now that women are participating fully in almost every sphere of activity, the problem of male identity has become extremely acute. . . .

By not coming to terms with these deep biological and cultural asymmetries, it is easy to foster the illusion of androgyny: that men and women are interchangeable. But this causes the fallacy of *ignoratio elenchi*: missing the point. The really difficult problem is how to *acknowledge* the differences on which gender roles have been based but *avoid* the problems created by those gender roles. This is not what Gross has in mind. By calling for androgyny she admits that her goal is to give women (but not necessarily men) *"freedom from gender roles."*[21] Given female biology and new freedoms, in short, women (but not necessarily men) can have it all and on their own terms.

New religions over old religions: Feminists demand that traditional worldviews be swept away; the latter, they say, are intolerable for *women.* (They often softpedal what amounts to a call for revolution, however, by using the word "reform.") The result of their radical critique, presumably, would be a religious tabula rasa. . . . . Despite that disclaimer Gross has already encouraged feminists to build new and superior religious visions in the ruins created by their deconstruction of patriarchal religions. They do not need to reinvent the wheel, she notes. They need only select those sources from various religions—especially goddess ones—that they find most useful. . . .

Gross's notion of progress is summed up in her account of returning to the small Wisconsin town where she grew up. There she found not only that her former church now had a female pastor but that the pastor "refused to use any generic masculine language for humanity or any specifically male pronouns or metaphors for deity."[22] Female metaphors apparently are okay for androgyny but not male ones. Without any sense of contradiction, she notes with approval the male horned god in Wicca. She sees no reason to avoid the pronoun "he." . . .

Because feminists are creating a new worldview, I suggest, their role is functionally equivalent to that of religious founders. And when feminists systematically explore their new worldview, they do so as the functional equivalents of theologians—which is why feminist "revisioning" or "re-imagining" (as in the "Goddess" and "Sophia" movements) have been called "thealogy" (*thea* referring to goddess, *theo* to god). But, as I observed at the beginning of this review, the new feminist religion is religious only on the surface. Lurking beneath it is an implicitly secular value system related to feminist politics and psychology.

Vajrayana Buddhism (reformed) over other religions: Gross's use of the word "reform" makes sense only for the religion she likes best: Vajrayana Buddhism. Drawing here from her earlier work, *Buddhism After Patriarchy* (1993), she shows that Buddhism's traditional teachings contain many of the same insights as those of feminism: impermanence (in the sense that patriarchy is a temporary construct), interdependence, and so forth). Vajrayana Buddhism, of course, is not yet completely free of "patriarchal" bias. Nevertheless, according to her, it is ahead of other religions. She believes that it could become a post-patriarchal religion of the future—if it heeds her admonition to undergo reforms so that women can become leaders, child care can be considered meditation, lay communities can be valued, immanence can be given its rightful place, and so on. . . .

At any rate, Gross stops short of claiming that Vajrayana Buddhism is superior to the new goddess "religions." I can think of three possible reasons for this. First, avoiding that claim allows her to preserve her stance as a pluralist and postmodernist by celebrating the diversity of feminism. In fact, her view of pluralism is even more expansive. . . . Second, she can preach to adherents of both: western feminists creating goddess religions should learn from Asian religions, and Asian religions should learn from feminists. Third, she can claim to be a pioneer in the development of a new western goddess religion.[23]

Conclusions

In the final analysis, Gross is a crusader for feminism in general and new feminist "religions" or a reformed Vajrayana Buddhism in particular. According to a generous interpretation of her approach, it is "informed advocacy." According to a less generous one, it is not even that well informed. After all, it does not apply the same standards of research to the lives of men as it does to those of women. This makes her view gynocentric, not "androgynous." Despite the rhetoric of sameness and equality, she encourages the view that women and men are different and unequal. By continually associating male scholars and men with patriarchal religions (even though countless women, I might add, have found truth in them), she gains the moral high road for female scholars and women at large. Gross does not follow the implications of her logic as far as other feminists do. She does not demand separate spheres for men and women. Nevertheless, she leaves the door open to that. To be blunt, she leaves the door open to the form of dualism that has characterized some schools of feminism: women are good but men (other than male converts to feminism) are bad.

So, what does all this mean for the academy? Conflating the history of religions and feminism could well encourage reductionism by conflating the boundaries between disciplines in the field of religious studies. There is a reason why scholars have clearly distinguished the history of religions from theology and ethics. By bracketing out questions of existence or nonexistence and truth or falsity, they have tried to avoid prefabricated interpretations and thus to see this or that phenomenon in its own right (including the categories offered by insiders). This does not rule out discussions of power relations or gender. Nor does it rule out the possibility of writing *additional* works on ethics or theology.

Gross has suggested that evaluation should *follow* description. In that case the two tasks will be differentiated adequately (even though she does not always take her own advice). At first I was attracted to this idea. As long as readers are warned of the transition, I thought, proper boundaries could be maintained. Then I thought of an academic description of Srivaisnava (Hindu) image worship being followed by a critique of it (Christian, Buddhist, Islamic, secular, or even that of another Hindu system of thought). If the description were followed by a critique in such close proximity, Srivaisnava theology would not be given room to create its own world of meaning. And that would pre-empt any possibility of understanding it.

Why maintain boundaries? Because doing so allows for distinctive insights. Phenomenological analysis is not the same as ethical analysis, though both help explain complexity or ambiguity. Collapsing the boundaries between disciplines and their methods leads to reductionism both of sight and insight. That creates the very monistic perspective ostensibly decried by feminists. Why then would feminists be attracted to this? Possibly because their *raison d' être,* power, really is monistic. Their penchant for power as the *sine qua non,* or ultimate concern, explains their penchant for expediency: paying lip service to objectivity while advocating bias, to reform while advocating revolution, and to androgyny (for Gross) while advocating gynocentrism. As a result of all these contradictions and fallacies, it is clear that their ultimate value is not scholarship but women's power.

When the classroom is used to promote this orientation (which is necessary given the political mission of feminism), the fine distinction that separates church and state (the custodian of the educational system) is breached. For those whose goal is revolution, of course, that is desirable. For others it should cause grave concern. One way out of this conflict is to maintain Gross's initial distinction of women's studies and feminism, viewing the former as a proper domain of the university and the latter of the public square.

NOTES

1. Rita M. Gross, *Feminism & Religion: An Introduction* (Boston: Beacon Press, 1996), p. 9.

2. Ibid., p. 17.

3. Ibid., p. 31.

4. Ibid., pp. 10, 71–72, 196.

5. Ibid., p. 13.

6. Ibid., p. 12.

7. Ibid., p. 16.

8. Ibid., p. 13.

9. Ibid., p. 11.

10. Ibid., p. 50.

11. Ibid., p. 8.

12. Ibid., p. 11.

13. Ibid., p. 3.

14. Ibid., p. 10.

15. Ibid., p. 12.

16. Ibid., p. 20.

17. Ibid., p. 16.

18. Ibid., p. 13.

19. Ibid., p. 20.

20. Ibid., p. 224.

21. Ibid., p. 24.

22. Ibid., p. 203.

23. Ibid., p. 225.

From *Sisters in the Wilderness:*
The Challenge of Womanist God-Talk

DELORES S. WILLIAMS

WHERE WOULD I BEGIN in order to construct Christian theology (or god-talk) from the point of view of African-American women? I pondered this question for over a year. Then one day my professor responded to my complaint about the absence of black women's experience from all Christian theology (black liberation and feminist theologies included). He suggested that my anxiety might lessen if my exploration of African-American cultural sources was consciously informed by the statement "I am a black WOMAN." He was right. I had not realized before that I read African-American sources from a black male perspective. I assumed black women were included. I had not noticed that what the sources presented as "black experience" was really black male experience. . . .

Nevertheless, when I began reading available black female and black male sources with my female identity fixed firmly in my consciousness, I made a startling discovery. I discovered that even though black liberation theologians used biblical paradigms supporting an androcentric bias in their theological statements, the African-American community had used the Bible quite differently. For over a hundred years, the community had appropriated the Bible in such a way that black women's experience figured just as eminently as black men's in the community's memory, in its self-understanding and in its understanding of God's relation to its life. As I read deeper in black American sources from my female perspective, I began to see that it was possible to identify at least two traditions of

African-American biblical appropriation that were useful for the construction of black theology in North America.

One of these traditions of biblical appropriation emphasized liberation of the oppressed and showed God relating to men in the liberation struggles. In some African-American spiritual songs, in slave narratives and in sermons by black preachers reference was made to biblical stories and personalities who were involved in liberation struggle. Moses, Jesus/God, Paul and Silas delivered from jail, Shadrak, Meshack and Abednego delivered from the fiery furnace and "My God delivered Daniel and why not every man"—all of these references appeared in the deposits of African-American culture. Black male theologians had reflected upon these sources and also had been inspired by the liberation emphasis in the 1960s black cultural and political revolution. So they produced black liberation theology. Their validating biblical paradigm in the Hebrew testament was the exodus event when God delivered the oppressed Hebrew slaves from their oppressors in Egypt. Their Christian testament paradigm was Luke 4, when Jesus described his mission and ministry in terms of liberation. Their normative claim for biblical interpretation was "God the liberator of the poor and oppressed." I reasoned that it is possible, then, to name this tradition the *liberation tradition of African-American biblical appropriation*.

My discovery of the second tradition of African-American biblical appropriation excited me greatly. This tradition emphasized female

Reprinted from Sisters in the Wilderness: The Challenge of Womanist God-Talk *(Maryknoll, NY: Orbis Books, 1993).*

activity and de-emphasized male authority. It lifted up from the Bible the story of a female slave of African descent who was forced to be a surrogate mother, reproducing a child by her slave master because the slave master's wife was barren. For more than a hundred years Hagar—the African slave of the Hebrew woman Sarah—has appeared in the deposits of African-American culture. Sculptors, writers, poets, scholars, preachers and just plain folks have passed along the biblical figure Hagar to generation after generation of black folks.

As I encountered Hagar again and again in African-American sources, I reread her story in the Hebrew testament and Paul's reference to her in the Christian testament. I slowly realized there were striking similarities between Hagar's story and the story of African-American women. Hagar's heritage was African as was black women's. Hagar was a slave. Black American women had emerged from a slave heritage and still lived in light of it. Hagar was brutalized by her slave owner, the Hebrew woman Sarah. The slave narratives of African-American women and some of the narratives of contemporary day-workers tell of the brutal or cruel treatment black women have received from the wives of slave masters and from contemporary white female employers. Hagar had no control over her body. It belonged to her slave owner, whose husband, Abraham, ravished Hagar. A child Ishmael was born; mother and child were eventually cast out of Abraham's and Sarah's home without resources for survival. The bodies of African-American slave women were owned by their masters. Time after time they were raped by their owners and bore children whom the masters seldom claimed—children who were slaves—children and their mothers whom slave-master fathers often cast out by selling them to other slave holders. Hagar resisted the brutalities of slavery by running away. Black American women have a long resistance history that includes running away from slavery in the antebellum era. Like Hagar and her child Ishmael, African-American female

slaves and their children, after slavery, were expelled from the homes of many slave holders and given no resources for survival. Hagar, like many women throughout African-American women's history, was a single parent. But she had serious personal and salvific encounters with God—encounters which aided Hagar in the survival struggle of herself and her son. Over and over again, black women in the churches have testified about their serious personal and salvific encounters with God, encounters that helped them and their families survive.

I realized I had stumbled upon the beginning of an answer to my question: Where was I to begin in my effort to construct theology from the point of view of black women's experience? I was to begin with the black community (composed of females and males) and its understanding of God's historic relation to black female life. And, inasmuch as Hagar's story had been appropriated so extensively and for such a long time by the African-American community, I reasoned that her story must be the community's analogue for African-American women's historic experience. My reasoning was supported, I thought, by the striking similarities between Hagar's story and African-American women's history in North America. But what would I name this Hagar-centered tradition of African-American biblical appropriation? I did not feel that it belonged to the liberation tradition of African-American biblical appropriation. My exposure to feminist studies had convinced me that women must claim their experience, which has for so long been submerged by the overlay of oppressive, patriarchal cultural forms. And one way to claim experience is to name it. Naming also establishes some permanence and visibility for women's experience in history.

At this point, my effort to name the women-centered tradition was facilitated by the work of anthropologist Lawrence Levine. He concluded that African Americans (especially during slavery) did not accommodate themselves to the Bible. Rather, they accommodated the Bible to the urgent necessities of their lives.[1] But in this business of accommodating the Bible to life, I knew that the black American religious community had not traditionally put final emphasis upon the hopelessness of the painful aspects of black history, whether paralleled in the Bible or not. Rather, black people used the Bible to put primary emphasis upon God's response to the community's situations of pain and bondage. So I asked myself. What was God's response to Hagar's predicament? Were her pain and God's response to it congruent with African-American women's predicament and their understanding of God's response to black women's suffering? Perhaps by answering these questions I could arrive at a name for this Hagar-centered tradition of African-American biblical appropriation.

A very superficial reading of Genesis 16:1–16 and 21:9–21 in the Hebrew testament revealed that Hagar's predicament involved slavery, poverty, ethnicity, sexual and economic exploitation, surrogacy, rape, domestic violence, homelessness, motherhood, single-parenting and radical encounters with God. Another aspect of Hagar's predicament was made clear in the Christian testament when Paul (Galatians 4:21–5:1) relegated her and her progeny to a position outside of and antagonistic to the great promise Paul says Christ brought to humankind. Thus in Paul's text Hagar bears only negative relation to the new creation Christ represents. In the Christian context of Paul, then, Hagar and her descendants represent the outsider position par excellence. So alienation is also part of the predicament of Hagar and her progeny.

God's response to Hagar's story in the Hebrew testament is not liberation. Rather, God participates in Hagar's and her child's survival on two occasions. When she was a runaway slave, God met her in the wilderness and told her to resubmit herself to her oppressor Sarah, that is, to return to bondage. Latin American biblical scholar Elsa Tamez may be correct when she interprets God's action here to be on behalf of the survival of Hagar and child. Hagar could not give birth in the wilderness.

Perhaps neither she nor the child could survive such an ordeal. Perhaps the best resources for assuring the life of mother and child were in the home of Abraham and Sarah. Then, when Hagar and her child were finally cast out of the home of their oppressors and were not given proper resources for survival, God provided Hagar with a resource. God gave her new vision to see survival resources where she had seen none before. Liberation in the Hagar stories is not given by God; it finds its source in human initiative. Finally, in Hagar's story there is the suggestion that God will be instrumental in the development of Ishmael's and Hagar's quality of life, for "God was with the boy. He grew up and made his home in the desert [wilderness], and he became an archer" (Genesis 21:20).

Thus it seemed to me that God's response to Hagar's (and her child's) situation was survival and involvement in their development of an appropriate quality of life, that is, appropriate to their situation and their heritage. Because they would finally live in the wilderness without the protection of a larger social unit, it was perhaps to their advantage that Ishmael be skillful with the bow. He could protect himself and his mother. The fact that Hagar took a wife for Ishmael "from the land of Egypt" suggests that Hagar wanted to perpetuate her own cultural heritage, which was Egyptian, and not that of her oppressors Abraham and Sarah.

Even today, most of Hagar's situation is congruent with many African-American women's predicament of poverty, sexual and economic exploitation, surrogacy, domestic violence, homelessness, rape, motherhood, single-parenting, ethnicity and meetings with God. Many black women have testified that "God helped them make a way out of no way." They believe God is involved not only in their survival struggle, but that God also supports their struggle for quality of life, which "making a way" suggests.

I concluded, then, that the female-centered tradition of African-American biblical appropriation could be named the *survival/quality-of-life tradition of African-American biblical appropriation*. This naming was consistent with the black American community's way of appropriating the Bible so that emphasis is put upon God's response to black people's situation rather than upon what would appear to be hopeless aspects of African-American people's existence in North America. In black consciousness, God's response of survival and quality of life to Hagar is God's response of survival and quality of life to African-American women and mothers of slave descent struggling to sustain their families with God's help. . . .

The slaves' effort to create an alternative value system represents a struggle to achieve a positive quality of life. With their syncretized African-American religion (syncretized by elements of African traditional religions) they believed in God's presence with them. This belief, connecting with the survival/quality-of-life struggle, gave hope to the slaves' daily lives of oppression and toil.

Affirming the similarities between Hagar's predicament and African-American women's historic predicament (as well as affirming the congruence of the two understandings of God's response to these situations), the survival/quality-of-life tradition of African-American biblical appropriation showed me more clearly what was involved in constructing womanist god-talk.

The first step was to provide black people with a deeper understanding of Hagar's story than the account in the Hebrew testament. This meant exploring social and cultural realities relevant to the biblical account. Thus Chapter I of *Sisters in the Wilderness*—entitled "Hagar's Story: A Route to Black Women's Issues"—rereads Hagar's story in the Hebrew testament taking seriously some of the Hebraic, Egyptian and nomadic social and cultural forces that could have had an impact upon Hagar's situation.

My rereading is a method of biblical interpretation shaped by the Latin American feminist way of viewing Hagar's story from the perspective of poor, oppressed women. What this means is attempting to see the Hagar-Sarah texts in the Bible from the position of the slave woman Hagar rather than from the perspective of slave owners (Abraham and Sarah) and their culture. For the purposes of *Sisters in the Wilderness* this method is suitable because the African-American community in North America has already appropriated the story with Hagar as the central human figure rather than Sarah or Abraham.

Tensions in Motherhood: From Slavery to Freedom

Like Hagar's story, African-American women's story has been closely associated with motherhood. Sociologists LaFrances Rogers Rose and Joyce Ladner claim that the social and economic significance of motherhood in Africa did not lose its importance when African women were brought to America and enslaved. The close bond between black women and children that existed in Africa was reinforced in the slavocracy. Many slave women were left alone to nurture their offspring because the fathers lived on other plantations or were used as "studs" to father a host of other children—or the father was the slave holder, who did not claim his black children. Slave mothers worked in the fields and were often hired out in other capacities if they were city slaves. Yet they often simultaneously nursed and nurtured their children. In parts of Africa mothers were market women, earning their own living and simultaneously nurturing their children. Thus many African women and African-American female slaves had a long heritage of public and private functions associated with motherhood. All of this African-derived female knowledge was useful in the slavocracy. Slave women could nurse and nurture their own children and also "mammy" the slave master's children.

One should not assume, however, that African-American women's history is an immediate and unaltered link with an African traditional past. From the beginning of her history in North America, the black woman was controlled by a host of alien social and political forces. Anglo-American social and family demands controlled her life during slavery. African-American social, political and family needs shaped her life after slavery into the present. Hence, in the course of her long history in America, the black woman has often found herself trapped in a mesh of cultural redefinitions, role exploitation and black male-female crises that have seriously affected her well-being. Whatever her role as mother and nurturer in Africa, the new world of American slavery adjusted it to meet American institutional needs at the time.

Yet there is no denying that black women's roles as mothers and nurturers have been important for the development of institutional life in both the Anglo and the African-American communities. Attempts to understand social life in the African-American community must take seriously the history of the black woman's motherhood roles, which were institutionalized in the slavocracy as "mammy" and were later redeemed from negative connotations and reinstitutionalized in some African-American denominational churches as "mothers of the church." Mammies had considerable authority in the context of white family life in the antebellum South. Mothers of the church were not only powerful figures in the church. They were also greatly respected and had considerable power in the communities in which they lived.

From antebellum time in North America until the present, African-American literary history has revealed the importance of black mothers for the development of community life. It has also shown how black mothers used religion to support themselves emotionally, psychologically and spiritually when they were exploited first by the white world and later by some members of the black community. After the Civil War, some African-American literary history began to suggest that certain religious customs practiced by black mothers and nurturers during slavery caused problems for the kind of social change necessary in the African-American community following emancipation.

But in the lyrics of some African-American spiritual songs created during slavery—women's roles are associated with birthing and nurturing functions in a positive way. One encounters lines celebrating "Mary had a baby," and that "Mary and Martha feed my lambs, feed my lambs." Of the one hundred and thirty spiritual songs in the Ballanta Taylor collection published in 1925, twenty-three songs contain positive references to mother. Five contain references to Mary "who had a baby" and to Mary and Martha. On the whole, then, spiritual songs project a positive image of women as helpful and caring mothers and nurturers. In these documents of slave culture there is no suggestion of conflict in the community about how black women's mothering and nurturing roles ought to function.

Like the spiritual songs, many slave narratives describe black mothers and nurturers burdened by a system of bondage. Unlike the spiritual songs, the narratives tell how the relation between slave owners and slave women was exploitative and affected the well-being of slave mothers. Linda Brent's slave narrative describes her Aunt Nancy, a slave woman, caught in the conflict between white and black demands upon her mothering and nurturing roles. The relation between the slave-owner's wife and the slave woman is, like Sarah's and Hagar's relation, built upon the exploitation of the slave woman's body and labor. . . . In another narrative an old slave woman tells of her aunt's exploitation as a "breeder woman" for a white slave owner. This breeder woman was forced to birth children for the slavocracy every twelve months.[2]

Yet slave mothers were dedicated to the care of their young ones. Even the labor practices of the slavocracy did not interfere with the mothering and nurturing functions of some antebellum black women. Charles Ball, a slave writing in 1836, tells of slave mothers nursing their babies as they worked in the fields. One slave woman fastened her child to her body in a crude knapsack as she worked in the fields. . . .

Apparently great strength was required of the slave mother. This strength was manifested not only by her ability to perform the difficult tasks associated with her mothering and nurturing roles. Strength was also manifested in her ability to endure and to gain victory over the suffering and pain often accompanying these tasks. That this endurance and victory were directly related to the mother's dependence upon God and religious faith is revealed in both spiritual songs and slave narratives. . . .

Linda Brent's narrative shows how the slave mother's religion shaped her relationships with her children and other people in the slavocracy. Brent tells of her grandmother's untiring efforts to purchase the freedom of her children and of the grandmother's belief that God supported her efforts.[3] She tells of her grandmother's ordeal of witnessing the death of her last surviving daughter and of the supportive role played by her religion and faith. . . .

Another slave describes a mother's use of religious ritual as she tries to rear him. He says that he and his mother were close. She taught him to pray and how to survive because she feared that he would be sold or that she would be sold. She spent much time in prayer and she always asked God to take care of him.[4] One of the most moving personal testimonies came from Sojourner Truth. At a women's rights convention in 1851, in Ohio, she told of her reliance upon Jesus to support her as she bore the pain connected with being a slave mother. . . .

Apparently the roles of slave mothers and nurturers were determined more by the institutions of slavery than by the internal demands of the slave community. Their roles were fixed. They were primarily to labor, reproduce and nurture. But mothering and nurturing tasks could range from birthing children to breast-feeding white children, to caring for the family needs of the master and his household, to tending to children as she worked in the fields, to protecting the lives of hundreds of slaves she helped escape from slavery to freedom (as did Harriet Tubman).

The American slavocracy was an all-compassing legal, political and economic system that affected every relationship in the slave community. Therefore the social process in the antebellum slave community turned black motherhood into something totally different from what was thought to be the model of motherhood in white society. The mothering and nurturing function of the African-American slave woman extended beyond the mere limits of female role activity into areas of control that should have belonged to the black man (according to American standards of male role functioning).

It was the black mother who often protected the children and family as far as they could be protected during slavery. It was a black female nurturer, called Moses by her people, who led regiments and scouted for the Union Army during the American Civil War.[5] Sometimes it was the slave mother who was given permission by the slave master to operate her own business and thereby provide economic security for her children. An ex-slave woman tells the story of her mother, whom her slave master allowed to go into business to support herself and her children. The slave mother had to give her slave master one half of what she earned working in the garrison of Fort Washington, Maryland. There, she "carried on a little business of selling pies, hot coffee, etc., to the marines and exchanging the same for rations." Within three years she was able to buy a horse and wagon to carry her goods to the fort. Her business continued to prosper until the poor white people "became jealous in a body and waited on the major and gave vent to their feelings."[6]

Incorporated, then, within the mothering and nurturing functions of slave women were often the tasks of protecting, providing for, resisting oppression and liberating. All of these tasks suggest strength. But it must be emphasized that strength is not necessarily synonymous with power, nor does it here imply an idea of black matriarchy. . . . The antebellum black mother had no real power. The power above her and her family was the white antebellum slave master and his family. But it is perhaps not too far-fetched to suggest that in their struggle to survive and nurture their own, many antebellum black mothers often had as their helpmate not the black man but black religion. The black male was the lowest in authority in the slave system. Hence black mothers and nurturers depended upon their religion for psychological and emotional support. And black Christian religion became, after the Civil War, greatly dependent upon these black women for its form and sustenance. . . .

But in terms of some slave mothers and religion, it also seems that an additional internalization process operated. God and religion fulfilled some very basic needs that could not be fulfilled by the slave community or the black man. Thus the slave narratives often portray black mothers exhibiting a vigorous spiritual self-confidence even though their sexuality has been completely brutalized and exploited by white men of every social class. Though they were continuously raped, used as breeder women and made accessible to the sexual appetite of all white males, many slave mothers endured with strength and dignity. . . .

Tensions in the Community over Motherhood

In some African-American literary history following the antebellum period, black writers infer that this kind of God-consciousness and God-dependence supporting black mothers is problematic. They suggest that for some black mothers, this consciousness and dependence created needs that could only be fulfilled within the limits of the black mother's religion. James Baldwin, an avid student of African-American religion, demonstrated this in a scene in his novel *If Beale Street Could Talk*. Here, a black Christian woman can only make love to her husband by psychologically substituting God for the husband. Thus the woman's pillow talk is also her god-talk, from which the husband is excluded.

Postbellum black writers were trying to present the black woman's mothering and nurturing roles in relation to the transformative social processes occurring in the black community after the Civil War. Especially important was the process of strengthening the black male's role as father and giving him uncontested authority over black family life. During slavery this control had been exercised first by the slave master and his family and next by the slave woman.

In the newly freed African-American community, this business of transferring authority to the black male represented a process of translating power in the ex-slave community into a more stable patriarchal model. There are indications that even before the Civil War the institutionalization of black religion into various forms like African Methodist Episcopal carried with it the subordination and oppression of women. The following testimonies of black mothering and nurturing figures Jarena Lee, Maria Stewart and Old Elizabeth show how sexism accompanied the practice and understanding of institutional religion in the black community during and directly after the antebellum period in North America. . . .

In the development of African-American musical and literary history, it is in blues art that the process of power transferal from female to male begins to show itself. Some blues artists, consciously or unconsciously, diminish the reflection of the black woman's God-consciousness and God-dependence in relation to her role as mother and nurturer. She is often pictured as completely dependent upon the quality of male-female relationships for the emotional and spiritual support she needs. Neither her religion nor her God is mentioned in a substantial way. And her mothering and nurturing function reflected in blues art had less to do with children and more to do with the care and love for black men.

"Mamma-Baby" in Blues Literature

Emerging shortly after the Civil War during the reconstruction period, the lyrics to many blues songs often present black women in conflicting roles as mamma and baby simultaneously. Reflecting an ambivalence about mothering roles, the blues lyrics diminish the independent strength of mothers and portray weakened female figures. . . .

Whereas the black woman in some blues art is still "mamma," she is no longer "mamma" like the Rock of Gibraltar. She is "mamma" with a certain dependency, like a baby. Though her suffering prevails, the black woman in blues art has not the uncanny spiritual and emotional endurance of her literary progenitor, the ante-bellum slave mother. The blues woman is only human, supported by neither God nor man. She merely "hangs her head and cries" in the face of trouble while her man may "take a train and ride" to escape it. The fact that most blues art does not associate the black woman's mothering and nurturing role with religion (as do some of the lyrics of the spiritual songs and many of the slave narratives) diminishes her characteristic strength, which she believed came from God through her religious faith. When blues artists de-emphasized religion, they not only lessened the importance of the mothering and nurturing function of the black woman, but they also directed attention away from the exploitation of these roles by forces inside and beyond the postbellum black communit[ies].

The works of some postbellum black protest novelists and dramatists advance the blues artists trend of casting aspersions on the effect of the black mother's religion upon the performance of her mothering and nurturing tasks. But contrary to the blues artists, some of the postbellum protest writers show black mothers depending very much upon the African-American denominational churches, the black preacher and black religion to support their mothering and nurturing roles. However, the protest writers criticize this relation. They question the compatibility of the black mother's religion with the demands a complex urban world makes upon her. Unlike the blues artists, writers James Baldwin and Richard Wright stage their protest about the relation of the black mother to religious phenomena on a much more sophisticated sociological level. Both men agree that the black mother's church religion (mediated by the black preacher) has made her oblivious to the real needs of black people and to the destructive nature of the social, political and legal forces governing black life in white America.

Black Mamma, Black Preacher, Black Protest

In his play *Amen Corner*, James Baldwin creates a black mother character who consciously rejects her black husband as she selects black religion to help her perform her mothering and nurturing tasks. The results are, of course, disastrous for the family. The father dies destitute and unhappy, having been deprived of his place in the family because of the mother's call to preach. The son goes out into the world as a musician to find his black manhood, which his mother had tried to smother in the obligation of a forced religious commitment. Baldwin believes black mothers hold fast to religion for psychological, emotional and physical security black men cannot or will not provide.[7] According to Baldwin, the instability of her family and socioeconomic condition, the corrupt elements in her black urban community and white oppression cause the black mother to develop an "unnatural" dependency upon religion. This dependency renders her extremely vulnerable before the religious authority in the black church or exalts her to a position of religious authority through which she exploits other people.

An important point to recognize about some protest writers' portrayal of the black mother in relation to religious phenomena is that Christian religion does not often play a supportive, productive role. In his novel *The Long Dream*, Richard Wright reveals the great degree to which a black preacher and his theology are indifferent to the suffering of black mothers.

First Wright presents a black mother questioning God following the lynching of her son Chris and the mutilation of his body by the white lynchers. . . .

In some of his fiction Richard Wright suggests the Christian religion has failed to meet the black mother's needs because it has confounded her understanding of black suffering and has caused her to accept untenable explanations for it. She, in turn, tries to pass these ineffective explanations to her children as tools for dealing with white oppression.

Richard Wright's major protest, then, is against the black mother's dependence upon Christian religion for support in her mothering and nurturing roles. He suggests that this religion exploits her intellect by stunting the growth of her critical faculties, thereby limiting the action she can choose to alter her family's oppression. The black preacher's contribution to all of this is that his theology bears a relationship with the social forces that oppress the black woman and the black community. This is clearly revealed in that section of Richard Wright's novel *Native Son* where the black preacher visits the main character, Bigger Thomas, who is in jail accused of murdering a young, rich, white woman. . . .

Wright and Baldwin, in part, build their images of the black mother upon the foundations laid by both antebellum and postbellum blues writers. The antebellum image of black motherhood yielded the "strong black mamma," capable of uncanny endurance and dignity because of her faith in the effectiveness of her religion. The postbellum blues artist presented an image of the black woman (without religious faith or involvement) that emphasized the dependency and weakness of the black mother vulnerable before a host of emotional, economic, domestic and social crises. Baldwin and Wright, on the other hand, merge the two images (antebellum and blues) into one—but with an important difference. Though their female characters are absorbed in their mothering and nurturing roles, though they are

dependent upon religion, they are exploited by this religion and by some black preachers. This experience makes these women inept in dealing with oppression. Richard Wright, more than Baldwin, raises serious theological questions about the Christian religion in relation to black mothers' and black people's experience of racial oppression in America. Wright raises the theodicy question of why a good God lets innocent people suffer along with the guilty.

Black Women Authors Differ

Some postbellum women writers provide images of black motherhood that are radically different from what their male counterparts (that is, Wright and Baldwin) have projected. Two examples are Margaret Walker and Alice Walker. Margaret Walker's novel *Jubilee* reinforces the image of the slave mother, but more detail is added. Alice Walker in her novel *The Color Purple* recasts the image of black motherhood, emphasizing the importance of the development of "SELF-consciousness" and a new spirituality on the part of black mothers. Neither of these two female writers criticizes the function of Christian religion in relation to black mothering and nurturing roles. However, other black women writers like Zora Hurston and Nella Larson (both part of the Harlem Renaissance movement in the 1920s) find fault with the effect some black preachers have upon the lives and roles of black mothers.

Margaret Walker, in *Jubilee*—set in the antebellum South—emphasizes the positive role religion plays in the development of what every African-American slave mother needed, that is, survival intelligence. The endurance of the protagonist Vyry is assured by the shrewd survival intelligence she developed under the tutelage of Mammy Sukey and Aunt Sally, both mothers and both religious women. One part of this survival intelligence had to do with plantation politics of learning how to be visible and accessible while simultaneously keeping out of the way of Big Missy, the slave-master's cruel wife. A second part had to do with learning how to survive physically on the basis of the correct knowledge of the effects of roots and herbs. The third part of survival intelligence had to do with developing a deep spirituality that provided psychological and emotional support in the time of trouble. The parts were held together by Vyry's God-consciousness and absolute dependence upon God, which allowed her at an early age to understand her life processes in a positive light even though she was a slave. Thus in *Jubilee* Margaret Walker emphasizes an important point about African-American mothers not considered by male blues and protest writers. The concern of many African-American mothers has been for the survival of their children, the family and the race. The economic, spiritual and physical assault upon black life in America by white people and white-controlled institutions has caused the African-American mother to try to develop survival strategies her family can use. She has not always been successful, but she has depended upon her religion to help her develop these strategies and to muster the courage to survive when survival gave no promise.

Often these survival strategies took the form of spiritual values. Black literary critic Mary Burgher describes this reality well when she says that spiritually, black mothers are usually the strongest in the community. They maintain and transmit values and ideas that support and enrich the black community "as a viable unit." Burgher describes these transmitted values as belief in a promised land beyond bondage and oppression; belief that black people have the natural "resourcefulness to find strength in . . . weakness, joy in sorrow and hope in what seems to be despair." . . .

Few black male writers have taken seriously the intensity of the black mother's commitment to the survival of her children and her willingness to do what is necessary (including being a mammy, a domestic or stealing food from the white folks) to maintain the life of her offspring. Therefore, some black male writers, such as Richard Wright, portray the black mother as an impediment to the black male's struggle for manhood in America.[8]

Margaret Walker's depiction of Vyry as the "strong black mamma" supported by her religious faith reiterates what slave women's narratives and what some other postbellum black female writers declare about the black mother. . . .

Yet, prior to Margaret Walker's time, some black female writers interpreted as problematic some black mothers' relation to black Christian preachers. Zora Hurston and Nella Larson criticized the emotional exploitation of black women by black preachers who hid their exploitative tactics in the submissive theology advocated in their sermons. While Hurston's book *Jonah's Gourd Vine* portrays an intelligent black mother emotionally bedazzled by her philandering preacher husband, Nella Larson in *Quicksand* portrays an octoroon woman rejected by (and rejecting) the values of white upper-class culture. Larson's character turns to the religious values of the black community modeled in the black preacher she ultimately marries. Zora Hurston's mother-character Lucy dies leaving a word of advice all black women would do well to heed: "Don't love nobody bettern' yo' self, do you'll be dying before your time is out." Lucy has loved her preacher husband best of all. Nella Larson's mother character, smothered by religion in the black community, dies burdened and oppressed by excessive childbearing.

Alice Walker represents one of the most able voices of a cadre of modern black women writers who are trying to recast the image of the black mother for the black community. Walker's novel *The Color Purple* does what black feminist literary critic Barbara Christian understands as finding a female voice for mothers so they can tell their own stories realistically.[9] Walker uses feminist issues to shape the situations in which her mother-characters find themselves. Their stories are about domestic violence, rape, racial oppression, the white male exploitation of nature, black sexism, consciousness-raising, sexuality, work, survival and liberation. Because she employs a feminist framework to present the image of African-American mothers, Alice Walker radically recasts both the image of black mothers and the nature of the religious perspectives black mothers need for self-realization. It is this radical recasting of images in a feminist mode that distinguishes Walker's work from that of the other writers considered in this study. . . .

Like the blues artists, Alice Walker does not emphasize women's roles as mothers and nurturers of children. Though every major female character in the book is a mother, none has the responsibility of rearing her biological offspring. Unlike blues artists, Alice Walker wants us to recognize that the inordinate demands men make upon the nurturing capacities of black mothers are destructive for women (for example, Mr. Albert's demands upon Celie, and Harpo's demands upon Sophia). Walker's work suggests that the exertion of male power to make sure women meet these demands constitutes sexism in the black community.

From the beginning of the novel this sexism is in place. The exploitation of black women's sexuality occurs throughout the book. The bodies of the mothers become targets for the gratification of male lust. Nettie's rape by her stepfather is prevented because Celie offers her own body instead; Mr. Albert, Celie's husband, expels Nettie from their house because she refuses his advances. Men have been so brutally intent upon their own gratification in their sexual relations with Celie that she does not discover her body's erotic zones until another woman points them out to her. The white prison warden rationalizes his abuse of the body of (the black woman) Mary Agnes on the grounds that he has indulged in a bit of fornication that "everybody is guilty of."[10]

Freeing the black mothers from debilitating impotence, Alice Walker presents an image of women emerging into self-awareness, power and autonomy. Consciousness-raising; new notions about female sexuality, about God, man and church; new notions about female bonding

and women's economic independence are the "tools" Walker uses to move Celie (the main mother-character) from impotence to empowerment. Celie's progress toward empowerment begins when she and the bisexual woman Shug bond in true friendship. Shug is the catalyst causing the changes in Celie's consciousness. She nurtures Celie through the transformations in thinking and action necessary for Celie to become an autonomous woman, taking full responsibility for her own life. Shug guides Celie through her struggle with self-hate and shame to the final realization of her independence as a self-confident lesbian woman.

Shug helps Celie to reexamine certain religious values Celie has held all her life—religious values supporting her bondage rather than her empowerment as a new, liberated woman. This reexamination centers on notions of God, man and church. This reflection shows Celie her image of God as man has limited her perception of the connectedness of all reality. Shug convinces Celie that church is not a place to find God. Rather, church is a place where people come to share God. . . .

Celie's change of consciousness about "God-as-man" frees her psychologically from the fear of her husband, who was as stern as any God she had imagined. After years of silently suffering, Celie "enters into creation."[11] Her revaluing and her departure from her husband's house with Shug liberate her for self-discovery. Shug helps her achieve economic independence. So when Celie returns to Georgia where her husband and his children reside, she is a new woman with a new morality, a new sense of herself and a new financial independence. She has moved from impotence to full autonomy, from self-abasement to self-confidence, from passivity to active responsibility.

Alice Walker's use of feminist issues to structure *The Color Purple* brings a "new word" to talk about black motherhood in African-American literature. Speaking to the community, Walker communicates an inclusive understanding of who is to provide the nurturing for children. Walker portrays mothers (Celie, Shug, Sophia, Mary Agnes) who are separated from their children. But these children are lovingly nurtured by family members and others beyond the family. Jack, Odessa, Harpo and Mary Agnes love and nurture Sophia's children as Sophia serves out her lengthy incarceration. Sophia and Harpo nurture Mary Agnes's child while she seeks a singing career. In the "redistribution" of children, Walker suggests that the nurturing of children is the task of the entire black community—male and female.

Walker also presents an image of black mothers nurturing one another in order to help each other develop self-love and self-esteem. Shug nurtures Celie into a fully responsible moral agent who can take control of her own life and destiny. In her recasting of the image of motherhood, Walker shows the redemptive character of lesbian relationships for some women's lives. Walker also depicts the heterosexual relation between Samuel and Nettie as loving and as productive for both people. Thus Walker suggests that there are loving and nurturing possibilities in both homosexual and heterosexual relationships.

Finally, Walker transforms the character of the religious perceptions the black mothers use to help them in their progress toward self-consciousness and freedom. At the beginning of *The Color Purple,* when Nettie tells Celie "I hate to leave you here with these rotten children [Mr. Albert's children]," Celie answers "Never mine, never mine, long as I can spell G-O-D I got somebody along."[12] Thus Celie continues her long painful correspondence with God whom she imagines to be old, white and a man. Celie maintains this image of God as long as she nurtures Mr. Albert and his children and works in his fields—as long as she denies herself and possesses a consciousness primarily occupied with self-sacrifice and with surviving the brutality men inflict upon her. As long as she lives in transcendent relation to her own experience, she is content to image God as male, old and white. But when Shug helps Celie begin her

process of self discovery, Celie starts to understand that her notion of God must change. . . . Thus Celie's God becomes an internal experience rather than a physical manifestation to be worshiped like the man Jesus. . . .

Unlike the protest writers Richard Wright and James Baldwin, Alice Walker portrays religion as a positive force supporting black mothers in their transformative processes. But she shows that the black mother's religion must move beyond male-female imagery in order to accommodate the black mother's realization of self-esteem, autonomy and liberation. The idea of the divine spirit working within humans is more efficacious for women's development of self-worth than notions of God in male or female form. Like Margaret Walker, Alice Walker does not project an image of a black male preacher exploiting the nurturing capacities of black women. . . .

Motherhood in a Context of Resistance

Through black mothering and nurturing depicted in the deposits of African-American culture we see social process in the black community (in both the antebellum and postbellum periods) affected by the God-consciousness and God-dependence of African-American women. Whether positively or negatively assessed by the various artists used in this study, the African-American mother's God-consciousness and absolute dependence upon God provided hope in personal and community relationships where hope seemed absurd. Therefore, systems of bondage like racism and sexism did not bring permanent lethargy to the community.

Black mothers often defied laws and custom in order to nurture black people with care and compassion. Sometimes they suffered severe consequences for this defiance. . . . For the slave mother, caring for slave children also meant telling the child who her father was even though there were laws against this. The octoroon slave Louisa Picquet shares an incident in which her mother received a penalty for this offense. . . .

Some scholars also make reference to a practice among free black communities during the antebellum period where "free colored men owned their women and children in order that the latter might escape the invidious law against Negroes recently emancipated." The same report tells of the practice among the free people of Northfolk, Virginia, where "several women owned their husbands."[13] Slave women did what they could to enhance relationships in the family and community, even if they had to assume what was customarily thought of as "male roles."

During the antebellum period, every person was affected by the laws, customs and economics of the slavocracy. The well-being of black mothers and nurturers was constantly threatened. But these women often built networks of female support and resistance to aid themselves in whatever tasks they were involved in. Jarena Lee and Old Elizabeth—in their nurturing tasks as preachers—tell of the women who readily opened their houses for women to preach when black male authorities in the churches denied them ordination or use of church buildings. Lee tells of the women who walked with her for ten or even twenty miles to her preaching engagements and to visit the sick. Historian Deborah Gray White, in her treatment of slave women's reality, also speaks of the female slave networks. She claims that adult female cooperation and interdependence was a fact of female slave life. . . .

Apparently this kind of networking extended to parenting in the black community during the antebellum era. Jarena Lee and Zilpha Elaw left their children with other women in the community for extended periods while they traveled through the country preaching the gospel. The children survived and thrived. In the postbellum period this female networking extended into the African-American denominational churches and possibly into later developments like the club movement among black women.

What all this suggests is that the modern phenomenon of black mothers like Rosa Parks acting as catalysts for social change stems from a long tradition of black mothers and nurturers who were catalysts for social change in and beyond the African-American community—even though some social processes in the community restricted black women's opportunities while expanding black men's opportunities. A case in point is the sexism that confronted black women in their effort to become ordained ministers and the lack of restrictions based on sex for black men seeking the same opportunity. This sexism exists today in both the African-American denominational churches and also exists in most of the male theology that issued from the churches after slavery and before the 1980s. . . .

NOTES

1. See Lawrence Levine, *Slave Culture and Slave Consciousness* (New York: Oxford University Press, 1977), pp. 23–38.

2. Gerda Lerner, *Black Women in White America* (New York: Pantheon Books, 1972), p. 152.

3. Linda Brent, *Incidents in the Life of a Slave Girl* (New York: Harcourt Brace Jovanovich, 1973), p. 36.

4. Lerner, p. 69.

5. See Sarah Bradford, ed. *Harriet Tubman: The "Moses" of Her People* (by the author, 1896; reprinted, New York, Corinth Books, 1961).

6. Lerner, pp. 34–35.

7. See James Baldwin, *Go Tell It on the Mountain* (New York: Alfred A. Knopf, 1953), p. 175.

8. See the discussion of this problem in Daryl C. Dance, "Black Eve or Madonna? A Study of the Antithetical Views of the Mother in Black American Literature," in Bell et al., *Sturdy Black Bridges,* pp. 123–32.

9. Barbara Christian, "An Angle of Seeing Motherhood," in *Black Feminist Criticism* (New York: Pergamon Press, 1985), pp. 211–52.

10. Alice Walker, *The Color Purple* (New York: Harcourt Brace Jovanovich, 1982), p. 84.

11. Ibid, p. 170.

12. Ibid., p. 18.

13. Benjamin Griffith Brawley, *A Social History of the American Negro* (New York: Macmillan Company, 1921), p. 245.

Counterpoint:
From Womanist Thought to Womanist Action

PETER J. PARIS

Peter J. Paris teaches at Princeton Theological Seminary in Princeton, New Jersey. Among his published works are the following books: *The Social Teachings of the Black Churches* and *Black Leaders in Conflict.*

THE RISE OF WOMANIST THOUGHT in religious scholarship marked the appearance of voices that were long excluded from the halls of academe. In contrast with the experiences of both white women and black men, the emergence of African American women in ranked-faculty positions in theological education began less than two decades ago. These academic pioneers were destined to be trailblazers in making the spiritual strivings of black women a subject for theological inquiry. Happily, a growing number of womanist thinkers have already made constructive contributions to theological scholarship and, on the whole, their mission has been strongly supported and encouraged by white feminist and black male theologians.

In my judgment, the ongoing constructive work in womanist thought must continue to be the special preserve of black women scholars because they alone have the experiential base. Being fully appreciative of womanist leadership and sincerely desirous of its effective dissemination both within and without the academy, I should like to focus attention in this essay on the practical implications of the womanist agenda. I am convinced that the time has come for womanist scholars in religion to concretize their theoretical analyses into deliberate strategies for social change in general and for ecclesiastical change in particular. Practical guidelines might help us discern appropriate action and avoid unnecessary ambiguity about effective means for attaining the practical end of womanist scholarship.

This essay is based on the assumption that social and ecclesiastical change constitutes the primary aim of womanist theology. Although womanist theologians long for justice they seem to have neglected the task of setting forth a political program. Here, bell hooks has been in the vanguard, repeatedly emphasizing the transformative goal of feminist thought in general and of black feminism in particular. . . .

Unfortunately, womanist theology has had greater difficulty in gaining the kind of legitimacy in the black community it both deserves and needs. On the one hand, this has been due to the apparent isolation of womanist theological scholarship from definite spheres of public praxis outside the academy, while, on the other hand, the alienation of the black community from the theological academy also constitutes a significant structural restraint. I contend, however, that a major alliance could occur between womanist scholars and the women's organizations in the black churches and that such an alliance would be mutually beneficial. Laywomen in the churches need the constructive thought of womanist scholars who, in turn, need the potential power of women's organizations in

Reprinted from Peter J. Paris, *"From Womanist Thought to Womanist Action,"* Journal of Feminist Studies in Religion 9 *(1993): 115–125.*

order to effect significant institutional reform in the churches. . . .

Clearly, the black male clergy constitutes a formidable force in opposition to an infinitesimal band of black womanist academics whose thought, more often than not is viewed as an alien force both within the black churches as a whole and among black male clergy in particular. Admittedly, the conversion of the mass of black male clergy is a frightful task for such a small band of womanist scholars to face. Yet such a struggle is not without precedent. African American woman's history offers many sources of encouragement and strength for those who press social criticism into the service of significant ecclesiastical reform.

We must not forget that many of our black foremothers seemed absurdly weak agents confronting immense powers. Nevertheless, they won victories over forces that seemed virtually invulnerable. Happily, long before Alice Walker coined the term *womanist,* numerous African American women had already gained notability for their remarkable public deeds and their courageous work as agents of social change. In spite of the immense odds against them they achieved many impressive results not only in the postbellum era but in the antebellum period as well. Many who were born and reared in slavery made unique and lasting contributions to the literary arts, educational leadership, evangelical preaching, abolitionist and feminist active. . . .

Like its counterparts, black liberation and white feminist theologies, womanist theology is thoroughly practical both in its subject matter (that is, the active life of black women) and its two-fold goal: (a) to liberate the world from the oppressive structures of racism, sexism and classism and (b) to help establish a new societal order of peace and justice for all peoples. Hence, like all liberation theologies, the starting point of womanist theology is critical multidimensional analyses rooted in the thought and practice of black women (past and present) and the quest for a constructive social practice that liberates not only black women but all people from every form of injustice. Thus womanist thought insists on a broad inclusive agenda that includes not only black women's liberation, but the liberation of all women and men alike from the evils of racism, sexism, and classism. This holistic methodological focus is a constitutive mark of womanist theology, only comprises one of its major strengths but also conceals a potential weakness.

In this respect, the strengths and weaknesses of womanist theology bear striking similarities to the strengths and weaknesses of the historic church tradition. A closer look at the latter may help us evaluate the practical implications of the former.

I contend that the holistic methodology of womanist theology has much in common with the holistic prophetic witness of the black Christian tradition. Katie Cannon recognized this fact when she argued that the thought of Howard Thurman and Martin Luther King, Jr. yields significant resources for a constructive womanist ethic in spite of the fact that neither thematized the plight of black womanhood.[1]

Throughout the nineteenth and twentieth centuries, the primary mission of the independent black churches was proclaiming the parenthood of God and the kinship of all peoples. In word and deed they sought the restoration of human community and the establishment of justice and peace for all citizens. Martin Luther King, Jr. has been acclaimed as this century's exemplar of that tradition.

The strength of the black church tradition lay in its theological and moral principles and the corresponding devotion of its people to commensurate practices. Thus, imbued with the courage of their convictions, blacks gradually institutionalized those principles within their churches and set themselves to the task of persuading the larger society to embrace them similarly in all dimensions of public life. Blacks felt compelled to condemn all contrary practices by using at first strategies of moral suasion and, subsequently, more aggressive methods of direct nonviolent resistance. The black Christian tradition affirmed the need to maximize the power necessary to effect the desired change: power that was regulated by love and directed toward the attainment of justice. However, the protests of black churches were aimed not at making enemies of their oppressors but rather, at redeeming them from the religious and moral consequences of their wrongdoing. These holistic goals made it difficult to concentrate on narrower racial objectives.

This weakness of the black church prophetic tradition is shared by the nascent womanist tradition. Both have difficulty in moving from the holism of interracial dialogue to the particular problems of the black community. The complexity of this issue is demonstrated in the internal conflict between Martin Luther King, Jr. and the black power movement in the late sixties. In brief, Dr. King's aim was to bring about healing for the whole of America while the black power movement was concerned solely with self-determination for black Americans. Then and now, the difficulty of conjoining holistic goals with the particular goals of racial communities is immense.

The quest for racial justice within the body politic comprises the essence of the black protest tradition. Representatives of this tradition have always thought that the desired goal of racial justice would benefit not blacks alone, but the nation as a whole. Consequently they have always found it difficult to justify interest-group politics which they feel contradicts the essence of the black Christian tradition which is to proclaim "good news" to the world at large and not just to their own race. Black churches have always viewed their struggle for racial liberation as contributing to the liberation of all people. Historically, the black churches have enriched the public realm time and again by keeping alive issues of social justice relative to public responsibility and citizenship rights. They have viewed themselves as advocates for social policies that they believed would have a positive effect on the nation as a whole. . . .

Now how can the black Christian tradition be helpful to womanist theology? In my judgment the women's organizations within the black churches constitute the single most important vehicle for the realization of the womanist goal of ecclesiastical transformation.

Interestingly, the recent emergence of womanist theology correlates with a significant increase in black women in theological education. Unhappily, though not surprisingly, Lincoln and Mamiya's survey data show deeply rooted negative attitudes among both black clergy and laity concerning the ordination of women. As a consequence, a growing number of theologically educated black women have been leaving black denominations and joining white denominations in their quest for positions in which to carry out their ministry.

However, it is a curious fact that while approximately seventy percent of the membership of the black churches is women, it is generally assumed that a large percentage of these have negative attitudes about clergywomen. Since men and women have been socialized similarly in our culture, one should not expect any great differences between them with respect to the predominant traditions, customs and values governing their lives. After many generations of socialization, human beings have the capacity to adapt themselves to their destiny, whether or not it be a tragic one. Was this not the case with the African American slaves? Many engaged in the dangerous activity of prophetic resistance, to be sure. But stories also abound of many; who delivered the prophets to their executioners, perhaps not so much because they loved their condition, but because they were unable to envision the possibility of significant change. As a consequence, they could only think that change would worsen their suffering as they could not imagine altering a system that seemed to them to be eternal. I submit that the majority of women in our churches think and act similarly. . . .

Clearly, we know little about effective strategies for eradicating such a pervasive phenomenon as sexism, which appears to be indelibly etched in the cultural roots of every society. Yet it is obvious that providing adequate analysis is the starting point for any such transformation. Womanist theologians have been deeply absorbed in this task for the past several years. Yet there remains the need for careful and deliberate inquiry into strategies for change since analysis must be in the service of its ultimate goal. . . .

I am confident that a ready audience exists in many women's organizations both within and without the churches to discuss these and related works. It appears to me, however, that insufficient work has been done in forging continued conversation between African American laywomen in the churches and those in theological education. Many womanist scholars have ready access to black church laywomen and their organizations. The significance of these associations should not be overlooked because they serve several important purposes, among which are the following: (a) bridging the gap between the academy and the women's organizations; (b) conscientizing churchwoman about their tradition; (c) expanding the horizons of all concerned with respect to ongoing problems and the need for their solution. This traffic should not flow in only one direction; churchwoman should be invited to the seminaries to make presentations on subjects of mutual concern. In short the conditions are rapidly developing for meaningful dialogue between the theological academy and the church organizations of African American women. Such dialogue initiated by womanist scholars could affect the common destiny of all concerned and clearly demonstrate more graphically than anything else the practical implications of womanist theology. More importantly, this strategic orientation is rooted in the presumption that structural injustices in society can be abolished only by political action. This implies the maximum development of adequate power through the building of a strong coalition between womanist scholars and African American laywomen. The effective transformation of misogyny within the black churches requires nothing less.

NOTES

1. Katie G. Cannon, *Black Womanist Ethics* (Atlanta: Scholars Press, 1988), chap. 6.

Chapter 11

Poststructural/Postmodern Approaches to Religion

Poststructuralism is best grasped within the context of French structuralism and the influence of the Swiss linguist Ferdinand de Saussure (1857–1913). In his work compiled by his students from course lectures entitled *Course in General Linguistics* (1916), de Saussure made four major distinctions that are helpful in understanding his overall theory of linguists. These four distinctions are between signifier and signified; *langue* and *parole;* syntagm and system; and diachrony and synchrony. For de Saussure, a sign is not merely a word; it is both a word and a concept that he called a signifier and signified. The word or signifier does the signifying, whereas the signified is the concept that is signified, which together constitute a binary pair called a sign. For a sign like the word tree to become a sign, it must distinguish itself from other signs like mountain, valley, or bird within the same language. Thus a sign is defined and recognized by its difference from all other signs in the sign system. Moreover, the relation between a signifier and a signified is entirely arbitrary. By his distinction between *langue* and *parole,* de Saussure wanted to stress a difference between another binary pair to clarify that language (*langue*) consists of elements that constitute a particular language, whereas *parole* refers to the actual speaking of that language within a particular context and at a given time. The third binary pair was represented by the distinction between syntagm and system (paradigm). If one acknowledges that a sentence is a sequence of signs, this means that the signs of a sentence follow a syntagmatic line. Consider the following sentence: "The mature oak tree provides considerable shade during the summer." As the signs of this sentence suggest, each sign is contiguous with the next sign. Furthermore, the sequence of each sign produces meaning. If one substitutes the terms in the sentence given, one can alter the sense of the sentence. The final binary opposition is that between diachrony and synchrony. The diachronic relates to the study of a sign over time in a chronological way. Because this approach tends to isolate a sign studied from its context and framework, one necessarily needs a synchronic approach, which is concerned with the set of relations among a whole complex of signs and elements that originates at the same time and in the same context. De Saussure wants then to compare the results of these two approaches to discern any similarities and differences.

Because de Saussure was primarily concerned with language, what was located outside of language was not relevant to his task. However, Lévi-Strauss adopted this linguistic model and extended it to the study of social groups. A poststructuralist like Michel Foucault extended it to history and culture while also rejecting the static internal relations of the structuralist model. Within the context of the signifier-signified distinction, a poststructuralist like Foucault is more interested in its multiple and dynamic possibilities. And in contrast to the notion of the subject as a self-contained *cogito* or consciousness like that found in phenomenology and existential philosophies, poststructural thinkers shared with structural thinkers a rejection of such a paradigm. Besides the lack of a present subject, poststructuralists perceived no centered place of origin and no unique place of focus. Although we will consider the implications for such tendencies for a thinker like Foucault a bit later, we will find that postmodern thinkers agree with some of the results of poststructuralism.

Due to the diverse opinions various writers have about the term *postmodernism*, it is difficult to define the term with any precision. Some scholars think that the term originated with changes in architectural design and art, whereas other thinkers identify it with a significant historical event like the explosion of the atom bomb in Hiroshima, Japan on August 6, 1945. Other thinkers view postmodernism as a crisis of narratives in which knowledge becomes a commodity to be produced and sold like any other industrial product, resulting in the loss of utility and value of knowledge. And still other thinkers refer to the loss of a sense of historical past and an inability to think historically. In response to those who deny these various scenarios or the advent of postmodernism itself, postmodern thinkers point to evidence in contemporary culture like the various changes in lifestyle with the disappearance of single career patterns, fragmented modes of existence, greater complexity of everyday life, the eclipse of authority, and the passing of former patterns of retirement. Other social evidence is manifested with the loss of traditional household structures characterized by the absence of a father figure, children being raised by gay couples, single working mothers raising children, or other nontraditional, fragmented, and diversified types of families. Due to the consequences of globalization, postmodernists point to the emergence of ethnic multiculturalism and cultural diversity as further evidence of a new era. Postmodernists call attention to developments like urbanization, advanced technology, impersonal rules, and growth of bureaucracy, humanism, liberal democracy and egalitarianism as further evidence of a postmodern era. Phenomena like global economic markets and labor, the Internet, and tourism are further evidence of globalization in an ever-changing postmodern world. For some postmodernists, favorite examples of artificial creations that are simulated to appear real are Las Vegas, Nevada and Disney World in Orlando, Florida.

According to some postmodern writers, postmodernity is not really connected to a temporal succession that implies that it comes after the modern. Rather the term *postmodern* is implied by the very term *modern* because the latter embodies an impulsion to exceed itself into another state. For such thinkers, postmodernity is more of an experiment, a matter of tone, style, and multiplicity. Rejecting staid academic styles of writing, postmodernists often experiment with different styles of writing that tend to be argumentative and self-referential, make extensive use of irony and parody, simulation, and randomness. Many postmodernists reject the authority of so-called high culture or elite intellectual traditions. Many of them also tend to mix together high and low culture. These tendencies can be grasped as attempts to reject all kinds of hierarchies. Many postmodern thinkers tend to stress fragmentation, complexity, artificiality, and difference. Instead of writing, some postmodernists emphasize rewriting to make modernity itself real, but it does not result in new knowledge of the past because it is more concerned with forgetfulness of the past. This type of rewriting experiment de-emphasizes the importance or desirability of grand theories. Such postmodern experiments reject all truth-claims, all standards of valid argumentation, or efforts to separate the real from fantasy.

From a more philosophical perspective, it is possible to view postmodernism as a reaction in part against the philosophy of the Enlightenment and its values like tolerance, individual freedom, reasonableness, and confidence in the inevitable nature of progress. This progress is due to scientific discoveries and rationality that served as the criterion of measurement for progress and as a reliable guide in a universe that could be gradually understood. People viewed the Enlightenment period in Europe as a time of learning the secrets of nature and the laws that govern the physical world and gaining control over nature to improve human life. At an elevated position in the center of the world stood the rational, self-determined, autonomous human being, reflecting an epistemological optimism and anthropocentrism that is anathema to many postmodernists.

Within the context of postmodern thought and in contrast to Enlightenment modes of thought, the self disappears to the margin of the world instead of occupying its center. Although there was a skeptical spirit in Enlightenment philosophy, especially with respect to metaphysics, postmodernists developed this trend even further by stressing that meaning and knowledge are uncertain and that one cannot rely on texts for certainty. For a poststructuralist/postmodern thinker like Michel Foucault, knowledge becomes an act of power. Because there is no longer any truth or certainty that can be established by a correspondence between people and objective reality, and because it is impossible to gain any vantage point outside of the world to conceive of a unified worldview, this mode of thought implies that not only is an all-encompassing worldview untenable, but it also suggests that we should give up the search for truth.

In contrast to the static world envisioned by Enlightenment figures like Immanuel Kant (1724–1804) and René Descartes (1596–1650), postmodernists emphasize becoming, contingency, relativity, and chance. This type of approach rejects imitating or conforming to models. It acknowledges that there is no place from which one can begin and no place at which one will arrive. Within the world of flux, there are no universal and timeless truths to be discovered because everything is relative and indeterminate, which suggests that our knowledge is always incomplete, fragmented, and historically and culturally conditioned. Therefore, there can be no foundation for philosophy or any theory, and it is wise to be suspicious of any universal claims to validity made by reason. Moreover, there is no center of the individual, society, culture, or history. There is instead an emphasis on pluralism, that is, for instance, expressed by artists deliberately juxtaposing different styles for diverse sources in the way that the *bricolage* reconfigures different objects or images. The use of irony exemplifies a preference for aesthetic categories and a different style of writing that attempts to extend itself to the very limits of human experience.

The postmodern era is characterized by discontinuity, irregularity, rupture, decenteredness, and lack of hope for any type of utopia. There is also no transhistorical value for many postmodernists because of the death of God, an example of the postmodern iconoclastic spirit. Even though there might not be any utopia or God to be discovered, a person can be a revolutionary because anyone who can write can play such a role. But writing involves a wandering, erring, marginal lifestyle in which one experiments with words and thoughts. The postmodern thinker Gilles Deleuze advocates, for instance, becoming a nomadic thinker without a past or future. Where does this wandering, nomadic, erring type of journey lead? According to some postmodern thinkers, the future destiny of modernity is decadence, which anticipates an unpredictable postmodernism.

Among the experiments conducted by postmodern thinkers are a series of experiments within time that emphasizes the present moment. Many postmodern thinkers tend to problematize time because they are uncomfortable with the past that tends to embody the roots of logocentrism, a metaphysics of presence, and other undesirable things like authority, the scientific worldview, hierarchy, hegemony, and grand narratives. Postmodernists stress the present over the past and future, reflecting their convictions that the future offers little hope for realizing utopian dreams and that the past is associated with authority, hegemony, and ideology. Postmodernists desire to be free of tradition to view indifferently the play of heterogeneous discourses.

The various facets of postmodern thought pose a challenge to different approaches to the study of religion contained in this anthology. The theory of evolution, for instance, presupposes a concept of time that is homogeneous, regular, and purposive. In contrast to those scholars of religion like Tylor, Frazer, Spencer, and Durkheim who were influenced by the theory of evolution, postmodernists reject such a chronological or linear view of time because it is too technical, rational, scientific, and hierarchical. These characteristics of linear time oppress and control individuals and their actions. Some postmodernists suggest replacing the linear understanding of time with one that is disparate, crisscrossed, anarchical, layered, disconnected, or misaligned. If the chronological concept of time is undermined, scholars in the social sciences like history, sociology, anthropology, or psychology will not be able to examine cause-and-effect relationships. They will also not be able to establish temporal priority or to construct theories about religion that are not effervescent and transient. Because such scholars depend on past evidence to understand the nature of religion, their scholarly work will prove to be impossible. From a postmodern perspective, you have been exposed to many conflicting theories about the nature of religion in this anthology, and this situation illustrates that theories conceal, distort, and obfuscate the truth about the subject rather than giving you any theoretical unity. Whether you are looking seriously at the theories of Frazer, Durkheim, Freud, or Eliade, you are exposed to a multitude of theories of which none can claim superiority over the others. Should you lament this situation? Several postmodernists respond that you must accept multiplicity, contradictoriness, and even inconsistency with respect to theories. In fact, these features are to be expected and even embraced. This suggests the postmodern emphasis on difference and the uniqueness of parts rather than sameness and the whole.

Besides striving to develop theories of religion and assuming a linear view of time, the scholars that you have read assume that it is possible to discover the intention of the author of a text. Many postmodernists claim that it is impossible to discern the intention of authors; authorship is ambiguous because it is difficult to distinguish the beliefs of authors about their work and basic intentions for the text. Moreover, there can be no primary author or original text because every text is a copy, a simulacrum. From the viewpoint of many postmodernists, authors lack authority and power, and thus their importance is diminished as composers of the texts. Some postmodernists even refer to the demise of authors as the causal agent of texts. By eclipsing the authority, accountability, causality, and responsibility of the author, a void is created that is filled by the twofold elevation of the texts and readers. Readers are not merely observers because they are also participants in the creation of the text being read. This suggests that readers possess the power to define and create textual meaning with every reading of a work, giving readers unprecedented autonomy because they can attribute meaning to a text. And because all readings are equal to each other, individual readers do not have to be concerned with ethical responsibility or the consequences of their reading. The autonomy experienced by readers is also shared by the text, which assumes an independent status from the author, is free of constraint, devoid of meaning, and unburdened of any objective content. Lacking a formal structure, there are no two identical texts and no two readings of a particular text that are ever identical because all texts are repetitions of other texts and each reader brings something different to each encounter with a text. What is important is the interaction between the reader and the text. It is within this ever unique and temporary interaction between the reader and text that meaning can be attributed to it by the reader, even though the text itself is devoid of tangible content. Postmodernists push the notion of the text even further by asserting that it is impermanent and open. This implies the plural nature of a text that possesses the potential to render many different interpretations just as it is possible to rewrite it with every reading. And because each particular text is related to every other text and is nothing more than a repetition of other texts, everything must be grasped as a play of intertextual relationships. Thus no text can stand alone because it is part of a web of intertextuality.

Within this web of intertextuality, we might suppose that the self stands in the role of author. We would assume incorrectly because many postmodernists think that the self is a fictitious construction, a mere linguistic convention. If the self is a result of our mode of thinking or language, the self lacks enduring presence. By examining the self within a system of difference, some postmodernists conclude that the self cannot be present as itself or render itself present to itself. Within the system of difference, the self is nothing more than a trace, which represents an erasure of the self and its presence. Moreover, because the self is radically temporal and an inseparable modality of each moment of time, it possesses a synthetic and not an enduring identity because difference is always associated with the identity of the self, representing a union of identity and difference and presence and absence. The interplay of identity and difference and presence and absence causes a disruption in the presence of the self and dislocation in its present modality of time, which suggests that the present is merely a trace and that time is forever a transition of moments. Once the self becomes aware of its condition, it discovers to its horror that its proper name is without meaning, it possesses no enduring identity, is decentered, marginal, and is without a definite presence. Not only does this scenario result in the absence of a permanent self, it also subverts the traditional understanding of an author of a text, which implies that an author is not the origin of a piece of writing or any other form of expression for that matter. The postmodern approach to the problem of the self, which is a free floating and groundless absence/presence, leaves the various disciplines reviewed thus far in this anthology without an enduring and permanent subject. Thus, social scientists, phenomenologists, and historians of religion do not have any subject to study. When such marginal, impermanent, and decentered scholars themselves attempt to study such an elusive subject, they can reach no certitude, make no rational arguments, or engage in an objective, empirical method. This represents a double subversion: scholar and object of study.

It is exactly this subject/object type of thinking and the representational mode of thinking that accompanies it that postmodernists are attempting to overcome. From a postmodern perspective, the representational mode of thinking assumes a correspondence between appearance and reality and is supported by a metaphysical edifice. Postmodernists insist that those using the representational mode of thinking assume the validity of the image created in the mind of the observer when it is only a copy of a copy. The representational mode of thinking also assumes that there is something true or valid external to the subject, assumes the identity of a concept with something possessing presence, assumes that it is possible to duplicate external reality, and assumes that it can represent it. All of the approaches to the study of religion that have been examined in this anthology cannot function without thinking in a representational manner, which implies forming an image in one's mind of that which one is studying or observing. By challenging and attempting to subvert the representational mode of thinking, postmodernists attempt to undermine using comparison and broad generalizations, identifying one religious phenomenon with another, or tracing the historical development of a phenomenon. For many postmodernists, the representational mode of thinking, which is always indeterminate from their viewpoint, cannot do justice to difference. Because postmodern thinking rejects the epistemological assumptions, methodological approaches, and knowledge claims used within various disciplines included in this anthology, it is possible to understand postmodernism as both revolutionary and a form of radical skepticism. Three representatives of the poststructural/postmodern approach included in this anthology are Georges Bataille, Michel Foucault, and Jacques Derrida.

Bataille was born in Puy-de-Dome in France in 1897 and died in 1962, and was destined to influence postmodern thinkers like Foucault and Derrida. Early in his life he converted to Catholicism, only to renounce his faith 6 years later after considering the priesthood as a possible vocation. He spent much of his adult life working as an archivist for the Bibliothéque Nationale in Paris. Between 1929 and 1930, Bataille was involved in the surrealist movement until he was expelled by André Breton for devoting too much attention to the vile and corrupt matters within the world. For instance, Breton thought that Bataille's novels bordered on pornography, and some of his essays addressed things that were embarrassing, ignoble, filthy, deformed, and idiotic, much like the work of his literary hero, the Marquis de Sade. During the 1930s and 1940s, Bataille joined, cofounded, or established a number of organizations that were often associated with Marxist philosophy. Bataille was connected to the Collège de Sociologie, which became a gathering place for avant-garde intellectuals and social scientists intent on replacing functionalist sociology with a discipline that would account for various kinds of expenditure. In 1946, Bataille founded the review *Critique,* and served as editor-in-chief until his death in 1962. His editorship of this journal secured his place in Parisian intellectual circles after World War II and placed him in opposition to the existential philosophy of Jean-Paul Sartre and his journal *Les Temps Modernes.* Besides his work with various journals and the publication of several novels, Bataille's collected works run to twelve volumes in French. His books that have been translated into English and pertain to the subject of religion include the following: *Inner Experience* (1988), *Death and Sensuality: A Study of Eroticism and the Taboo* (1984), and *Theory of Religion* (1989).

These works reflect a fascinating and controversial theory of religion and ritual. Bataille suggested that religion, which he identifies with the sacred, could best be understood by the interconnections and workings of eroticism, violence, and sacrifice. According to Bataille, a common feature of eroticism, sacrifice, and religion is violence that represents a danger to overflow at anytime. If eroticism opens the way to death, sacrifice effects it. Unable to reject violence, Bataille maintained that people practice both internal and external forms of violence in sacrifice. And because the love object of a sexual encounter and the victim of a sacrifice are stripped of their identity in these respective activities, there is an intimate connection between eroticism and sacrifice.

Unlike Bataille, Michel Foucault (1926–1984) never explored religion in a thorough and systematic manner during his career, although he did have some things to say about the subject and did influence subsequent scholars with his methodology and theory of power. Foucault was born into an economically prosperous family in Poitiers located in western France, studied at the prestigious École Normale Supérieure in Paris, held various academic positions in Europe and North Africa, was appointed chair of the History of Systems of Thought at the Collège de France in 1970, and finally died of AIDS after a very productive career. Foucault joined the Communist Party in 1950, only to leave it by 1953. He became an ardent anticommunist, although he did champion various left-wing causes and took his strong convictions to the streets to protest perceived social and political injustices. He also challenged post-World War II French thought that focused on Marxism, phenomenology, and existentialism. In contrast to these streams of thought, Foucault referred to himself as an experimenter rather than a theorist. The fruits of his experiments can be discovered in the following works translated into English: *Mental Illness and*

Psychology (1954), *Madness and Civilization: A History of Insanity in the Age of Reason* (1961), *The Birth of the Clinic: An Archaeology of Medical Perception* (1963), *The Order of Things: An Archaeology of the Human Sciences* (1966), *The Archaeology of Knowledge* (1969), *Discipline and Punish: The Birth of the Prison* (1975); and his three-volume work on the history of sexuality that was originally supposed to be a six-volume work. The entire six-volume project was never completed. The fourth volume was intended, for instance, to examine the role of Christianity in the development of sexuality.

Much like Freud, Foucault was an acknowledged atheist. This did not mean that he neglected religion, because he considered it, even though he did not study it systematically, as one aspect of a complex process that worked to shape Western knowledge. If Foucault was an avowed atheist, from what cultural situation did he discuss religion? He wrote about religion from the margins of Western culture, and his reflections on the subject radically challenged traditional religious modes of thinking. For instance, within the context of Christianity he examined phenomena like silence and confession, both mechanisms of power used by the church to manipulate, control, coerce, and oppress people. Having developed such practices from monastic models of ordered existence, Christianity is merely part of a much wider disciplinary apparatus used by cultures to control and manipulate its members. Confession and silence—examples of discipline and power—are also connected to uncovering laws that shape our knowledge, how it became formulated, how it came to control others, and how it excluded other possibilities. This train of scholarship suggests that Foucault wanted to expose the fundamental assumptions, ideological unity, and teleological expectations of Western culture by examining the disunities and discontinuities within its history.

According to Foucault, power and knowledge implied each other, and it was possible to expose their interrelationship by using adequate methodological tools. Foucault adopted a purely descriptive approach that he called archaeology to account for the discontinuity of history, its temporal ruptures, and factual gaps. To eliminate meaning from the concerns of the historian, Foucault emphasized identifying differences, dividing, increasing diversity, and blurring lines of established communication by finding multiple layers of events within discourse. And because history represented a series of reinterpretations in narrative form, it was only possible in the final analysis for the historian to compose fiction. In his later works, Foucault turned to his intellectual hero Nietzsche and his notion of genealogy to complement his earlier archaeological method. This helped him to develop a new theory of discourse in order to find a more adequate method for his purposes. Therefore, the descriptive approach of the archaeologist was complemented by the diagnostic method of the genealogist by focusing on the interrelations of power, knowledge, and the human body. The genealogist concentrated on scientific statements, philosophy, moral propositions, architecture, institutions, laws, and administrative practices and decisions. This heterogeneous ensemble helped the genealogist to discern the punctuating gaps of history in order to compose a history of the present, which was a history of the basic duality of Western consciousness. A history of the present could only be composed by being located within the web of power in the present moment and not outside of historical time and place and the interconnecting web of power relations.

This type of history was devoid of metaphysics, acknowledged no absolutes, did not claim to be objective, and was without constants. This radical type of history asserted no truth claims and recognized that all knowledge was relative.

This spirit of skepticism was also embodied in the thought of Jacques Derrida, born in El-Biar, Algeria in 1930. He studied philosophy at the École Normale Supérieure in Paris and later taught there from 1965 to 1984. In addition to teaching at the Sorbonne in Paris, Derrida has also taught at several universities in the United States. He is best known for advocating deconstruction, a strategy of textural analysis that was influential in subjects like literature, philosophy, law, architecture, and religion. Among his many publications translated into English, there are several prominent works: *Speech and Phenomena* (1973), *Glas* (1974), *Of Grammatology* (1976), *Writing and Difference* (1978), *The Post Card* (1980), *Positions* (1981), *Dissemination* (1981), *Of Spirit* (1989), *Signeponge* (1988), *Aporias* (1993), *Gift of Death* (1995), and *Religion* (1998). These various works reflect Derrida's use of irony and his tendency to play with language in very clever and creative ways. Like the pattern of Foucault's career, Derrida has turned more toward religious themes later in his scholarly career, although he does not deal extensively with the subject. Nonetheless, Derrida has deeply influenced those more deeply involved in the subject by shaping the viewpoint of some scholars and causing others to react critically to his perspective.

Like so many of Derrida's terms, deconstruction continues to remain elusive and difficult to define with absolute precision. Derrida admitted to be influenced by the term *Abbau* (dismantling) from Edmund Husserl, for whom it represented a nonreflective procedure that made it possible to regress to something that cannot in principle be given by the pre-given world. Derrida also acknowledged an intellectual debt to Martin Heidegger for his notion of *Destruktion* in his work entitled *Being and Time,* where he discussed the necessity of destroying the old philosophical traditions to allow Being to become concrete. Heidegger advocated a nonreflective movement of thought that was a nonobjective, calm surrender to Being, representing a nonrepresentational mode of thinking that stands opposed to ordinary consciousness. Derrida continued the work that Heidegger began and attempted to conclude it by striving to deconstruct the presence of the present moment. Acknowledging the ambiguity of the term *deconstruction,* Derrida intended to suggest the disarranging of the construction of terms in a sentence and disassembling the parts of a whole by turning, for instance, a document against itself. Therefore, deconstruction was about the deconstruction of texts that attempted to exceed the sphere of its conceptual totality. The overall goal of deconstruction was to locate an instance of otherness or difference within a text that reflected a metaphysical conceptuality from the standpoint of difference. This position of otherness or alterity was a form of writing that was accomplished on the margin of the text. When Derrida wrote that deconstruction was not a method, he intended to claim that it was not a method because it was not reductive like an ordinary method; it was also not a non-method because it did not advocate uncontrollable free play. For Derrida, deconstruction is like an inscription on the face of a coin or at the beginning of a book, suggesting the functions of making something evident, bringing forth, or displaying. Like an inscription, deconstruction possessed value only within a context or in a series of possible substitutions of inscriptions. By using deconstruction and turning a text against itself, Derrida claimed to find concepts, for instance, that were cracked and fissured by differences and contradictions. Moreover, deconstruction did not attempt to overcome these internal differences, but rather worked to maintain those differences. Therefore, deconstruction functioned in Derrida's works in a parasitic manner because it preyed on other readings or interpretations in an endless process. By using deconstruction, Derrida suggested subordinating rationality to spontaneity, and he attacked subjectivity because there was no central point of reference for any position to become permanent. As intellectual positions became established, they were immediately erased and subverted from the inside. This approach served to overturn hierarchies of all kinds. Thus we can also expect Derrida to subvert the notion of religion.

Guideline Questions

What role does the notion of excess play in Bataille's theory of religion?

In what way(s) is power connected to or reflected by the practice of chastity in Foucault's essay?

What evidence can you find of Derrida's deconstruction of the notion of religion?

From *Theory of Religion*

GEORGES BATAILLE

The Sacred

All peoples have doubtless conceived this supreme being, but the operation seems to have failed everywhere. The supreme being apparently did not have any prestige comparable to that which the God of the Jews, and later that of the Christians, was to obtain. As if the operation had taken place at a time when the sense of continuity was too strong, as if the animal or divine continuity of living beings with the world had at first seemed limited, impoverished by a first clumsy attempt at a reduction to an objective individuality. There is every indication that the first men were closer than we are to the animal world; they distinguished the animal from themselves perhaps, but not without a feeling of doubt mixed with terror and longing. The sense of continuity that we must attribute to animals no longer impressed itself on the mind unequivocally (the positing of distinct objects was in fact its negation). But it had derived a new significance from the contrast it formed to the world of things. This continuity, which for the animal could not be distinguished from anything else, which was in it and for it the only possible mode of being, offered man all the fascination of the sacred world, as against the poverty of the profane tool (of the discontinuous object).

The sense of the sacred obviously is not that of the animal lost in the mists of continuity

Reprinted from Georges Bataille, Theory of Religion, *trans. Robert Hurley (New York: Zone Books, 1989). Copyright © 1989 Urzone, Inc.*

where nothing is distinct. In the first place, while it is true that the confusion has not ceased in the world of mists, the latter do oppose an opaque aggregate to a clear world. This aggregate appears distinctly at the boundary of that which is clear: it is at least distinguishable, externally, from that which is clear. Moreover, the animal accepted the immanence that submerged it without apparent protest, whereas man feels a kind of impotent horror in the sense of the sacred. This horror is ambiguous. Undoubtedly, what is sacred attracts and possesses an incomparable value, but at the same time it appears vertiginously dangerous for that clear and profane world where mankind situates its privileged domain.

The Spirits and the Gods

The equality and inequality of these various existences, all opposed to the things that pure objects are, resolves into a hierarchy of spirits. Men and the supreme being, but also, in a first representation, animals, plants, meteors . . . are spirits. A scale is built into this conception: the supreme being is in a sense a pure spirit; similarly, the spirit of a dead man does not depend on a clear material reality like that of a living one; finally, the connection of the animal or plant spirit (or the like) with an individual animal or plant is very vague: such spirits are mythical independent of the given realities. Under these conditions, the hierarchy of spirits tends to be based on a fundamental distinction between spirits that depend on a body, like those of men, and the autonomous spirits of the supreme being, of animals, of dead people, and so on, which tend to form a homogeneous world, a mythical world, within which the hierarchical differences are usually slight. The supreme being, the sovereign deity, the god of heaven, is generally only a more powerful god of the same nature as the others.

The gods are simply mythical spirits, without any substratum of reality. The spirit that is not subordinated to the reality of a mortal body is a god, is purely divine (sacred). Insofar as he is himself a spirit, man is divine (sacred), but he is not supremely so, since he is real. . . .

The Eaten Animal, the Corpse, and the Thing

The definition of the animal as a thing has become a basic human given. The animal has lost its status as man's fellow creature, and man, perceiving the animality in himself, regards it as a defect. There is undoubtedly a measure of falsity in the fact of regarding the animal as a thing. An animal exists for itself and in order to be a thing it must be dead or domesticated. Thus the eaten animal can be posited as an object only provided it is eaten dead. Indeed it is fully a thing only in a roasted, grilled, or boiled form. Moreover, the preparation of meat is not primarily connected with a gastronomical pursuit: before that it has to do with the fact that man does not eat anything before he has made an object of it. At least in ordinary circumstances, man is an animal that does not have a part in that which he eats. But to kill the animal and alter it as one pleases is not merely to change into a thing that which doubtless was not a thing from the start; it is to define the animal as a thing beforehand. Concerning that which I kill, which I cut up, which I cook, I implicitly affirm that that has never been anything but a thing. To cut up, cook, and eat a man is on the contrary abominable. It does no harm to anyone; in fact it is often unreasonable not to do something with man. Yet the study of anatomy ceased to be scandalous only a short time ago. And despite appearances, even hardened materialists are still so religious that in their eyes it is always a crime to make a man into a thing—a roast, a stew. . . . In any case, the human attitude toward the body is formidably complex. Insofar as he is spirit, it is man's misfortune to have the body of an animal and thus to be like a thing, but it is the glory of the human body to be the substratum of a spirit. And the spirit is so closely linked to the body as a thing that the body never ceases to be haunted, is never a thing except virtually, so much so that if death reduces it to the condition of a thing, the spirit is more present than ever: the body that has betrayed it reveals it more clearly than when it served it. In a sense the corpse is the most complete affirmation of the spirit. What death's definitive impotence and absence reveals is the very essence of the spirit, just as the scream of the one that is killed is the supreme affirmation of life. Conversely, man's corpse reveals the complete reduction of the animal body, and therefore the living animal, to thinghood. In theory the body is a strictly subordinate element, which is of no consequence for itself—a utility of the same nature as canvas, iron, or lumber.

The Worker and the Tool

Generally speaking, the world of things is perceived as a fallen world. It entails the alienation of the one who created it. This is the basic principle: to subordinate is not only to alter the subordinated element but to be altered oneself. The tool changes nature and man at the same time: it subjugates nature to man, who makes and uses it, but it ties man to subjugated nature. Nature becomes man's property but it ceases to be immanent to him. It is his on condition that it is closed to him. If he places the world in his power, this is to the extent that he forgets that he is himself the world: he denies the world but it is himself that he denies. Everything in my power declares that I have compelled that which is equal to me no longer to exist for its own purpose but rather for a purpose that is alien to it. The purpose of a plow is alien to the reality that constitutes it; and with greater reason, the same is true of a grain of wheat or a calf. If I ate the wheat or the calf in an animal way, they would also be diverted from their own purpose, but they would be suddenly destroyed as wheat and as calf. At no time would the wheat and the calf be the things that they are from the start. The grain of wheat is a unit of agricultural produc-

tion; the cow is a head of livestock, and the one who cultivates the wheat is a farmer; the one who raises the steer is a stock raiser. Now, during the time when he is cultivating, the farmer's purpose is not his own purpose, and during the time when he is tending the stock, the purpose of the stock raiser is not his own purpose. The agricultural product and the livestock are things, and the farmer or the stock raiser, during the time they are working, are also things. All this is foreign to the immanent immensity, where there are neither separations nor limits. In the degree that he is the immanent immensity, that he is being, that he is of the world, man is a stranger for himself. The farmer is not a man: he is the plow of the one who eats the bread. At the limit, the act of the eater himself is already agricultural labor, to which he furnishes the energy.

The Need that is Met by Sacrifice and its Principle

The first fruits of the harvest or a head of livestock are sacrificed in order to remove the plant and the animal, together with the farmer and the stock raiser, from the world of things.

The principle of sacrifice is destruction, but though it sometimes goes so far as to destroy completely (as in a holocaust), the destruction that sacrifice is intended to bring about is not annihilation. The thing—only the thing—is what sacrifice means to destroy in the victim. Sacrifice destroys an object's real ties of subordination; it draws the victim out of the world of utility and restores it to that of unintelligible caprice. When the offered animal enters the circle in which the priest will immolate it, it passes from the world of things which are closed to man and are nothing to him, which he knows from the outside—to the world that is immanent to it, intimate, known as the wife is known in sexual consumption (*consumation charnelle*). This assumes that it has ceased to be separated from its own intimacy, as it is in the subordination of labor. The sacrificer's prior separation from the world of things is necessary for the return to intimacy, of immanence between man and the world, between the subject and the object. The sacrificer needs the sacrifice in order to separate himself from the world of things and the victim could not be separated from it in turn if the sacrificer was not already separated in advance. The sacrificer declares: "Intimately, I belong to the sovereign world of the gods and myths, to the world of violent and uncalculated generosity, just as my wife belongs to my desires. I withdraw you, victim, from the world in which you were and could only be reduced to the condition of a thing, having a meaning that was foreign to your intimate nature. I call you back to the intimacy of the divine world, of the profound immanence of all that is."

The Unreality of the Divine World

Of course this is a monologue and the victim can neither understand nor reply. Sacrifice essentially turns its back on real relations. If it took them into account, it would go against its own nature, which is precisely the opposite of that world of things on which distinct reality is founded. It could not destroy the animal as a thing without denying the animal's objective reality. This is what gives the world of sacrifice an appearance of puerile gratuitousness. But one cannot at the same time destroy the values that found reality and accept their limits. The return to immanent intimacy implies a beclouded consciousness: consciousness is tied to the positing of objects as such, grasped directly, apart from a vague perception, beyond the always unreal images of a thinking based on participation.

The Ordinary Association of Death and Sacrifice

The puerile unconsciousness of sacrifice even goes so far that killing appears as a way of redressing the wrong done to the animal, miserably reduced to the condition of a thing. As a

matter of fact, killing in the literal sense is not necessary. But the greatest negation of the real order is the one most favorable to the appearance of the mythical order. Moreover, sacrificial killing resolves the painful antinomy of life and death by means of a reversal. In fact death is nothing in immanence, but because it is nothing, a being is never truly separated from it. Because death has no meaning, because there is no difference between it and life, and there is no fear of it or defense against it, it invades everything without giving rise to any resistance. . . .

As a matter of fact, that is a superficial view. What has no place in the world of things, what is unreal in the real world is not exactly death. Death actually discloses the imposture of reality, not only in that the absence of duration gives the lie to it, but above all because death is the great affirmer, the wonder-struck cry of life. The real order does not so much reject the negation of life that is death as it reacts the affirmation of intimate life, whose measureless violence is a danger to the stability of things, an affirmation that is fully revealed only in death. The real order must annul—neutralize—that intimate life and replace it with the thing that the individual is in the society of labor. But it cannot prevent life's disappearance in death from revealing the invisible brilliance of life that is not a thing. The power of death signifies that this real world can only have a neutral image of life, that life's intimacy does not reveal its dazzling consumption until the moment it gives out. No one knew it was there when it was; it was overlooked in favor of real things: death was one real thing among others. But death suddenly shows that the real society was lying. Then it is not the loss of the thing, of the useful member, that is taken into consideration. What the real society has lost is not a member but rather its truth. That intimate life, which had lost the ability to fully reach me, which I regarded primarily as a thing, is fully restored to my sensibility through its absence. Death reveals life in its plenitude and dissolves the real order. Henceforth it matters very little that this real order is the need for the duration of that which no longer exists. When an element escapes its demands, what remains is not an entity that suffers bereavement; all at once that entity, the real order, has completely dissipated. There is no more question of it and what death brings in tears is the useless consumption of the intimate order. . . .

The Consummation of Sacrifice

The power that death generally has illuminates the meaning of sacrifice, which functions like death in that it restores a lost value through a relinquishment of that value. But death is not necessarily linked to it, and the most solemn sacrifice may not be bloody. To sacrifice is not to kill but to relinquish and to give. Killing is only the exhibition of a deep meaning. What is important is to pass from a lasting order, in which all consumption of resources is subordinated to the need for duration, to the violence of an unconditional consumption; what is important is to leave a world of real things, whose reality derives from a long term operation and never resides in the moment—a world that creates and preserves (that creates for the benefit of a lasting reality). Sacrifice is the antithesis of production, which is accomplished with a view to the future; it is consumption that is concerned only with the moment. This is the sense in which it is gift and relinquishment, but what is given cannot be an object of preservation for the receiver: the gift of an offering makes it pass precisely into the world of abrupt consumption.

This is the meaning of "sacrificing to the deity," whose sacred essence is comparable to a fire. To sacrifice is to give as one gives coal to the furnace. But the furnace ordinarily has an undeniable utility, to which the coal is subordinated, whereas in sacrifice the offering is rescued from all utility.

This is so clearly the precise meaning of sacrifice, that one sacrifices what is useful; one does not sacrifice luxurious objects. There could be no sacrifice if the offering were destroyed beforehand. Now, depriving the labor of manu-

facture of its usefulness at the outset, luxury has already destroyed that labor; it has dissipated it in vainglory; in the very moment, it has lost it for good. To sacrifice a luxury object would be to sacrifice the same object twice.

But neither could one sacrifice that which was not first withdrawn from immanence, that which, never having belonged to immanence, would not have been secondarily subjugated, domesticated, and reduced to being a thing. Sacrifice is made of objects that could have been spirits, such as animals or plant substances, but that have become things and that need to be restored to the immanence whence they come, to the vague sphere of lost intimacy.

The Individual, Anguish, and Sacrifice

Intimacy cannot be expressed discursively.

The swelling to the bursting point, the malice that breaks out with clenched teeth and weeps; the sinking feeling that doesn't know where it comes from or what it's about; the fear that sings its head off in the dark; the white-eyed pallor, the sweet sadness, the rage and the vomiting . . . are so many evasions.

What is intimate, in the strong sense, is what has the passion of an absence of individuality, the imperceptible sonority of a river, the empty limpidity of the sky: this is still a negative definition, from which the essential is missing.

These statements have the vague quality of inaccessible distances, but on the other hand articulated definitions substitute the tree for the forest, the distinct articulation for that which is articulated.

I will resort to articulation nevertheless.

Paradoxically, intimacy is violence, and it is destruction, because it is not compatible with the positing of the separate individual. If one describes the individual in the operation of sacrifice, he is defined by anguish. But if sacrifice is distressing, the reason is that the individual takes part in it. The individual identifies with the victim in the sudden movement that restores it to immanence (to intimacy), but the assimilation that is linked to the return to immanence is nonetheless based on the fact that the victim is the thing, just as the sacrificer is the individual. The separate individual is of the same nature as the thing, or rather the anxiousness to remain personally alive that establishes the person's individuality is linked to the integration of existence into the world of things. To put it differently, work and the fear of dying are interdependent; the former implies the thing and vice versa. In fact it is not even necessary to work in order to be the thing of fear: man is an individual to the extent that his apprehension ties him to the results of labor. But man is not, as one might think, a thing because he is afraid. He would have no anguish if he were not the individual (the thing), and it is essentially the fact of being an individual that fuels his anguish. It is in order to satisfy the demands of the thing, it is insofar as the world of things has posited his duration as the basic condition of his worth, that he learns anguish. He is afraid of death as soon as he enters the system of projects that is the order of things. Death disturbs the order of things and the order of things holds us. Man is afraid of the intimate order that is not reconcilable with the order of things. Otherwise there would be no sacrifice, and there would be no mankind either. The intimate order would not reveal itself in the destruction and the sacred anguish of the individual. Because man is not squarely within that order, but only partakes of it through a thing that is threatened in its nature (in the projects that constitute it), intimacy, in the trembling of the individual, is holy, sacred, and suffused with anguish.

The Festival

The sacred is that prodigious effervescence of life that, for the sake of duration, the order of things holds in check, and that this holding changes into a breaking loose, that is, into violence. It constantly threatens to break the dikes, to confront productive activity with the precipitate and contagious movement of a purely glo-

rious consumption. The sacred is exactly comparable to the flame that destroys the wood by consuming it. It is that opposite of a thing which an unlimited fire is; it spreads, it radiates heat and light, it suddenly inflames and blinds in turn. Sacrifice burns like the sun that slowly dies of the prodigious radiation whose brilliance our eyes cannot bear, but it is never isolated and, in a world of individuals, it calls for the general negation of individuals as such.

The divine world is contagious and its contagion is dangerous. In theory, what is started in the operation of sacrifice is like the action of lightning: in theory there is no limit to the conflagration. It favors human life and not animality; the resistance to immanence is what regulates its resurgence, so poignant in tears and so strong in the unavowable pleasure of anguish. But if man surrendered unreservedly to immanence, he would fall short of humanity; he would achieve it only to lose it and eventually life would return to the unconscious intimacy of animals. The constant problem posed by the impossibility of being human without being a thing and of escaping the limits of things without returning to animal slumber receives the limited solution of the festival.

The initial movement of the festival is given in elementary humanity, but it reaches the plenitude of an effusion only if the anguished concentration of sacrifice sets it loose. The festival assembles men whom the consumption of the contagious offering (communion) opens up to a conflagration, but one that is limited by a countervailing prudence: there is an aspiration for destruction that breaks out in the festival, but there is a conservative prudence that regulates and limits it. On the one hand, all the possibilities of consumption are brought together: dance and poetry, music and the different arts contribute to making the festival the place and the time of a spectacular letting loose. But consciousness, awake in anguish, is disposed, in a reversal commanded by an inability to go along with the letting loose, to subordinate it to the need that the order of things has—being fettered by nature and self-paralyzed—to receive an impetus from the outside. Thus the letting loose of the festival is finally, if not fettered, then at least confined to the limits of a reality of which it is the negation. The festival is tolerated to the extent that it reserves the necessities of the profane world.

Limitation, the Utilitarian Interpretation of the Festival, and the Positing of the Group

The festival is the fusion of human life. For the thing and the individual, it is the crucible where distinctions melt in the intense heat of intimate life. But its intimacy is dissolved in the real and individualized positing of the ensemble that is at stake in the rituals. For the sake of a real community, of a social fact that is given is a thing—of a common operation in view of a future time—the festival is limited: it is itself integrated as a link in the concatenation of useful works. As drunkenness, chaos, sexual orgy, that which it tends to be, it drowns everything in immanence in a sense; it then even exceeds the limits of the hybrid world of spirits, but its ritual movements slip into the world of immanence only through the mediation of spirits. To the spirits borne by the festival, to whom the sacrifice is offered, and to whose intimacy the victims are restored, an operative power is attributed in the same way it is attributed to things. In the end the festival itself is viewed as an operation and its effectiveness is not questioned. The possibility of producing, of fecundating the fields and the herds is given to rites whose least servile operative forms are aimed, through a concession, at cutting the losses from the dreadful violence of the divine world. In any case, positively in fecundation, negatively in propitiation, the community first appears in the festival as a thing, a definite individualization and a shared project with a view to duration. The festival is not a true return to immanence but rather an amicable reconciliation, full of anguish, between the incompatible necessities. . . .

Human Sacrifice

The sacrifices of slaves illustrate the principle according to which what is useful is destined for sacrifice. Sacrifice surrenders the slave, whose servitude accentuates the degradation of the human order, to the baleful intimacy of unfettered violence.

In general, human sacrifice is the acute stage of a dispute setting the movement of a measureless violence against the real order and duration. It is the most radical contestation of the primacy of utility. It is at the same time the highest degree of an unleashing of internal violence. The society in which this sacrifice rages mainly affirms the rejection of a disequilibrium of the two violences. He who unleashes his forces of destruction on the outside cannot be sparing of his resources. If he reduces the enemy to slavery, he must, in a spectacular fashion, make a glorious use of this new source of wealth. He must partly destroy these things that serve him, for there is nothing useful around him that can fail to satisfy, first of all, the mythical order's demand for consumption. Thus a continual surpassing toward destruction denies, at the same time that it affirms, the individual status of the group.

But this demand for consumption is brought to bear on the slave insofar as the latter is his property and his thing. It should not be confused with the movements of violence that have the outside, the enemy, as their object. In this respect the sacrifice of a slave is far from being pure. In a sense it is an extension of military combat, and internal violence, the essence of sacrifice, is not satisfied by it. Intense consumption requires victims at the top who are not only the useful wealth of a people, but this people itself; or at least, elements that signify it and that will be destined for sacrifice, this time not owing to an alienation from the sacred world—a fall—but, quite the contrary, owing to an exceptional proximity, such as the sovereign or the children (whose killing finally realizes the performance of a sacrifice twice over). . . .

Counterpoint:
Eroticism, Violence, and Sacrifice:
A Postmodern Theory of Religion and Ritual

CARL OLSON

Carl Olson teaches at Allegheny College in Meadville, Pennsylvania. He is the author of several books including the following: *The Theology and Philosophy of Eliade: A Search for the Centre* and *Zen and the Art of Postmodern Philosophy.*

Theory of Religion

Bataille develops his theory of religion through his unusual methodology. We are given a hint of the type of method that he prefers when he writes: "My method, or rather my absence of method, is my life."[1] This quotation is suggestive because it implies his dislike for any kind of systematic or all-encompassing method. Bataille's insistence on using life as a mode of hermeneutics sets a limit on interpretation, an approach that is consistent with his use of a heterological theory of knowledge. Due to the basic contradictions of life, a heterological method is an absolute necessity because it considers questions of heterogeneity and helps one deal with the contradictions of life that are beyond the view of scientific knowledge (which is only concerned with homogeneous elements) and the Hegelian dialectic (which tends to totalize everything or to give a homogeneous representation of the world). Instead of emphasizing sameness, then, heterology reverses the philosophical process and stresses differences. No longer an instrument of appropriation, philosophy must now serve excretion. Heterology leads to the possibility of excess by introducing a demand for material gratification in a violent manner.[2]

Heterology must not be confused with a science of the heterogeneous because scientific knowledge can only be applied to homogeneous elements. Not only is heterology opposed to any philosophical system, it actually reverses the philosophical process because it functions in an excessive manner and does not strive to appropriate anything.[3] Heterology is an excessive method because it is connected to violence, transgression of norms, and wastefulness. This method gives Bataille's work a revolutionary and radical character and impetus, which represents a "mode of non-dialectical materialism where the primary goal is not collective social revolution, but individual sovereignty."[4] By stressing difference, otherness, transgression, and excess, the heterological method shapes Bataille's understanding of the nature of religion as a fundamental distinction between sacred and profane, forming a kind of microcosm of the greater macrocosmic polarity between heterogeneity and homogeneity.

Bataille's method concentrates on heterological objects, which can take the form of excrement, tears, death, the cult of cadavers, religious ecstasy, and heedless expenditure. The continual expulsion of heterological objects by a person manifests an impossibility for a self to maintain its identity because its heterological nature is continuously transgressing the bodily barrier that separates and defines subjects and objects.[5]

Reprinted from Carl Olson, "Eroticism, Violence, and Sacrifice: A Postmodern Theory of Religion and Ritual," Method & Theory in the Study of Religion, *6/3 (1994): 231–250.*

This suggests that the self, which normally makes knowledge possible, is called into question by the otherness of the heterological object that is itself not an object of knowledge. This transgressive nature of heterological objects connected to the self is also evident in the sacred.

The social customs, laws, and mode of governance of a particular culture are characteristic of the homogeneity of profane human society. This profane realm is a genuine order in which discontinuity, a lucid differentiation between contrasting subjects and objects, is common. In sharp contrast to the homogeneity of the profane realm is the heterogeneity of the sacred, a world of madness, violence, and general excess. The otherness of the sacred as compared to the profane is characterized by its unproductive expenditure of energy, whereas the profane is the realm of work, productivity, and reason.[6] Within the profane world, excessive action is limited and desire is repressed because of its inherent tendency to exceed social limits. The sacred, which represents a realm of immanence in contrast to the profane, is a dangerous threat because it continually tends to irrupt into violence: "The sacred is exactly comparable to the flame that destroys the wood by consuming it."[7] The threat that the sacred will break out into violence reflects its contagious character that is envisioned as dangerous.[8]

Bataille's distinction and definition of the sacred and profane is an exact parallel to Nietzsche's contrast between Apollonian and Dionysian opposition. For Nietzsche, the Apollonian represents order, light, reason, limitation, and the perfection of dreamland, whereas the Dionysian aspect symbolizes a destructive force, chaos, fantasy, and limitlessness. The Apollonian element of Nietzsche becomes Bataille's profane world, whereas the sacred is equated with the Dionysian. In sharp contrast, the distinction between the sacred and profane in the theory of religion espoused by Mircea Eliade interprets this basic distinction in a totally opposite way. For Eliade, the sacred

represents order and the profane symbolizes chaos.[9] Bataille's work is, of course, influenced by the earlier distinction made by Emile Durkheim who argued that the division between the sacred and the profane was the most distinctive trait of religious thought and that their distinction was indicative of their absolute heterogeneity.[10] . . .

For Bataille, the dynamic and violent aspects of the sacred provoke a response of terror. Why is terror evoked in human beings by the sacred? The sacred, an effervescent aspect of life, is constantly threatening to overflow into violence.[11] There is the continual danger that human beings will be overwhelmed by the contagious violence of the sacred, a malefic force that destroys through contagion anything that comes close to it. For Bataille, this indicates that the sacred itself is divided: "the dark and malefic sacred is opposed to the white and beneficent sacred and the deities that partake of the one or the other are neither rational nor moral."[12] Although the sacred possesses value, it is also vertiginously dangerous. Moreover, Bataille's heterological approach, which is not a genuine or systematic method, enables him to see that the sacred is different within itself and not merely distinct from the profane. Even though the sacred is equivalent to religion for Bataille, this simple equation does not give us a complete view of the nature of religion, a perspective that can only come by examining the interrelations between eroticism, violence, and sacrifice.

Eroticism and Death

Without giving any historical proof for his position, Bataille asserts that the origin of eroticism can be traced prior to the division of humanity into those who were free and those who were slaves. Its origins can be found in prehistoric signs of erotic life embodied by figures with large breasts and erect penises, but its foundation is the sexual act itself.[13] The knowledge of death plays an important role in the origin of eroticism. Although his claim cannot be refuted or proven, Bataille asserts that prehistoric beings were aware of death, an awareness that gave rise to an awareness of eroticism. The knowledge of death is essential because it gives rise to a sensibility that in turn stimulates eroticism, an extreme emotion that separates the sexuality of humans from that of animals.[14] The difference between humans and animals is more precisely defined when he states that "eroticism differs from the animal sexual impulse in that it is, in principle, just as work is, the conscious searching for an end, for sensual pleasure."[15] There is also an anticipation by the participants in erotic play that it will culminate with sensual pleasure. In the pleasure of erotic play one does not gain anything or become enriched, unlike engaging in work, because eroticism is a realm of pure play, whose "essence is above all to obey seduction, to respond to passion."[16]

If humans are discontinuous beings who yearn for continuity, as Bataille claims, eroticism gives us a foretaste of continuity because it strikes at the centre of our being. . . . By participating in erotic activity, individual beings have their fundamental continuity revealed to them. In sharp contrast to discontinuous existence stands nakedness, a state of communication that reveals a search for a possible condition of existence beyond that of self-possession.[17] By stripping naked and standing in the open for anyone to see your flesh, the self becomes dispossessed by its nudity, which finds its consummation in a subsequent erotic act. Nakedness and the dispossession of the self are partially indicative of radical and anti-social aspects of eroticism that "entails a breaking down of established patterns . . . of the regulated social order basic to our discontinuous mode of existence as defined and separate individuals."[18] Eroticism is also anti-social by its very nature because it is a solitary activity done in secret that is outside the confines of everyday life.[19]

Eroticism must not be confused with an ordinary sexual act between two or more partners or with oneself. In other words, human sexuality is not by itself necessarily erotic.

Eroticism, an aspect of an individual's inner life, represents a disequilibrium that stimulates a person consciously to call his/her own being into question.[20] By stressing eroticism as a part of a person's inner nature and as disequilibrium, Bataille presents eroticism as an essential part of a person's inner or religious life and its ability to disrupt an individual. Calling attention to the erotic images carved in stone on Hindu temples, Bataille confirms the religious aspect of eroticism by stating that it is fundamentally divine.[21]

Eroticism must also not be confused with desire: "The object of desire is different from eroticism itself; it is not eroticism in its completeness, but eroticism working through it."[22] Desire suggests the transgressive nature of eroticism because within "eroticism is the desire that triumphs over the taboo."[23] The nature of desire and the impulse to transgression contribute to the apparent insane world of eroticism that render it unrecognizable by others. Transgression is violent and a principle that causes chaos, although it does help us to close the boundaries to a continuity of being, which Bataille equates with death.

It is death that represents the final sense of eroticism. According to Bataille, eroticism "opens the way to death. Death opens the way to the denial of our individual lives."[24] From our discontinuous way of life, death can return us to continuity by means of eroticism. Even though life and death are opposites, Bataille seems to suggest that they can be reconciled and combined into a holy alliance or *coincidentia oppositorum,* an event that occurs by means of eroticism. In his novel entitled *My Mother* and its central theme of incest, the son, for instance, finally engages in sexual intercourse with the corpse of his mother, representing a union of the erotic and death.

Violence and Sacrifice

According to Bataille, human beings have never been able to reject violence and utter a definitive no to it. The reason for this inability to discard violence is partially due to its origins in basic human emotions such as anger, fear, and desire. For Bataille, the acceptance of violence makes humans dizzy, nauseous, and pass through an experience of vertigo.[25] Although human beings accept violence in the depths of their being, they still try to reject it, but they are not wholly successful in controlling the excessive urges to commit violence. Unlike René Girard, who thinks that violence can be controlled by ritual, Bataille argues that nothing can control it. Violence is connected to animal or human flesh because it is the flesh that it transgresses and violates, a feature that suggests that sexual activity is a form of violence. Because, as Bataille maintains, violence is directly connected to the flesh, its relation to eroticism is also apparent: "In essence, the domain of eroticism is the domain of violence, of violation."[26] Moreover, the intimate connection between violence and sacrifice is even more apparent than that between violence and eroticism.

If violence reaches its culmination in the event of death, sacrifice is the ritual activity par excellence of destruction, its primary principle. However, this does not mean that the basic intent of sacrifice is annihilation. According to Bataille, "[t]he thing—only the thing—is what sacrifice means to destroy in the victim."[27] By means of the sacrifice, the victim is drawn out of the world of things into a realm that is immanent to the victim. Bataille argues that this separation from the world of things is also true for the sacrificer.[28] . . . Sacrifice, then, is an inward form of violence, whereas war represents an outwardly directed form of violence.

Even though violence is directed toward the victim, it is not necessary to destroy the victim except as a thing in order for the victim and the sacrificer to regain a lost intimacy, a realm that, for Bataille, is antithetical to the real world.[29] He refers to the victim as the "accursed share" that is destined for violent consumption, a mode of communication for separate beings. He also describes the victim as "a surplus taken from the mass of useful wealth."[30] This tends to suggest that the intention of sacrifice is not necessarily to kill the surplus victim but rather to give something. That which is given is ideally accomplished in a selfless spirit without any expectation of receiving an economic or personal benefit. The violence perpetrated upon the sacrificial victim calls attention to the violation of its flesh, which indicates a connection to the sexual act.

Both the sexual act and sacrifice are similar because they both reveal the flesh. By calling attention to the flesh, the external violence of the sacrifice becomes evident, and the internal violence of the subject is revealed. Bataille further argues that sacrifice and sexual/erotic intercourse also share violence in common.[31] . . . Thus, eroticism is like sacrifice because the female partner, either within or outside of marriage, plays the role of the victim, especially when she is a virgin whose blood flows, with the male assuming the part of the sacrificer, while both participants lose themselves in the continuity established by the violence. Therefore, Bataille suggests that the continuity of life is not affected by death, but is rather proven by death, a reflection of its ability to illuminate the meaning of sacrifice and life.[32] Therefore, death "reveals life in its plenitude and dissolves the real order."[33] This implies that the intimacy of life is not revealed until the last possible moment when death becomes a sign of life. In the final analysis, then, sacrifice brings life and death into harmony.

Bataille's theory enables us to see interconnections between religion, sacrifice, eroticism, violence, and death. By showing their intimate relations, Bataille is able to stress themes that are important to him, such as separation, difference, transgression, and excess. It is also important for Bataille to reintroduce eroticism into a theory of religion and ritual. His rationale is that "[i]n casting eroticism out of religion, men reduced religion to a utilitarian morality. Eroticism, having lost its sacred character, became unclean."[34] By nature of its connection with eroticism, violence, and death, sacrifice is excessive and creates differences; for, as Jonathan Z. Smith has put it, "[r]itual is, above all, an assertion of difference."[35] Its transgressive nature, which is grounded in eroticism and violence, necessarily means that sacrifice stands in sharp contrast to morality.

Bataille's Theory and the Sun Dance

Bataille failed to test his theory of sacrifice by applying it to actual examples of sacrifice in the religions of the world. Having defined the nature of sacrifice for Bataille, it is therefore necessary to compare it to an actual sacrifice. In order to demonstrate the shortcomings of Bataille's theory of sacrifice I have chosen to apply it to the Sun Dance of the Sioux. Following this example, I suggest that, contrary to Bataille's theory, a more reasonable interpretation of the Sun Dance can be attained by concentrating on its symbolism. This approach is suggested by the theoretical work of Clifford Geertz and Victor Turner, the latter of whom refers to a symbol as the smallest unit of ritual or as storage units of dynamic entities. My account of the Sun Dance relies on the work [of] James R. Walker[36] because his information was gathered from several different sources, and it represents the most authoritative account available to us of the rite in one period of its history. My approach presupposes that the rite and its meaning have continued to change in response to new circumstances for the Sioux. By selecting this rite, I am being eminently fair to Bataille, from one perspective, because the erotic and violent features of the Sun Dance could be used to prove the validity of his theory. . . .

The heterological method of Bataille is intended to alleviate the contradictions of life and free the individual from the homogeneity of the world. In contrast to Bataille's insistence on a search for radical difference, the worldview of the Sioux, embodied in the symbolic aspects of the Sun Dance conceived as an offering of body and soul to Wakan-Tanka (the Great Spirit),

suggests a homogeneous view of the cosmos. The universe, for instance, is represented by the round form of the ceremonial drum, whose steady beat is the throbbing at the centre of the cosmos.[37] Within the context of the Sun Dance, the cosmic pillar of the universe is represented by the cottonwood tree, which further represents the enemy who is symbolically killed and transported back to the centre of the camp by means of sticks because human hands are not allowed to touch the body. The ritual participants consecrate the tree with the stem of the sacred pipe, another symbol of the earth, the buffalo, and everything that lives and grows on the earth. Once the tree is trimmed of its branches and its sides and branch tips are painted red, the rawhide effigies of a man and a buffalo are suspended from the crosspiece of the sacred tree, which is then placed into a hole at the centre of the camp. The sacred tree not only suggests a universal pillar, but it also represents the way of the people.[38] Other cosmic symbols are the sun and earth signified by a red circle, symbolic of all that is sacred. In the centre of the circle representing the sun is a blue circle which suggests Wakan-Tanka, the centre of the cosmos and all existence. Moreover, the lodge of the Sun Dance is composed of twenty-eight poles, each signifying an object of creation, and staked in a circle that represents the entire created world.[39] It is difficult to find anything excessive or transgressive in these cosmic symbols of the Sioux that would support Bataille's position.

Rather than achieving the differentiation that Bataille's theory advocates, the sun dancer symbolically acquires the cosmos. According to the ethnological report of Walker,[40] the candidate who dances the most excruciatingly painful form of the dance with the intention of becoming a shaman is given a small hoop by his mentor. This hoop is symbolic of the sky, the four winds, time, all things that grow, and all circular things made by the tribe. After his successful completion of the dance, the sun dancer is allowed to place this symbol on his tipi. This privilege suggests that he attains all that the hoop symbolizes. Contrary to Bataille's theory, the highest aspiring sun dancer does not find that the cosmos becomes other for him, and he does not stand as an individual sovereign within the cosmos. He rather becomes part of the whole, and he acquires the cosmos.

Instead of perceiving the cosmic symbolism associated with the most painful performance of the rite, Bataille's writings suggest that he would stress its sadistic and masochistic aspects. Sadism, an excessive violation of modesty and a violent excretion, is not only an eruption of excremental forces, but it also forms a limitation by subjugating whatever is opposed to such an eruption.[41] If masochism is an enjoyment of pain, the violence exercised on the flesh of the sun dancers would be viewed by Bataille as a transgression and violation of the participant's flesh, which also calls attention to the flesh itself and connects it to the erotic. Bataille also maintains that violence against the flesh is an external manifestation of the internal violence of the sacrificial participant, which is perceived as a loss of blood and various forms of ejaculations.[42] Moreover, for Bataille the cutting of the flesh would be suggestive of the discontinuity of the self.

Unlike the solitary activity of eroticism for Bataille, the sun dancer of the Sioux rite does not distinguish or divorce himself from his society because he represents the people and suffers on their behalf during the rite. After purifying themselves, their clothing, and the equipment to be used in the rite, the participants cry at the centre of the camp and assume the suffering of the people, which enables other tribal members to gain understanding and strength.[43] If there is present the discontinuity characteristic of Bataille's profane human society among the Sioux, the Sun Dance bridges any social divisions by uniting the social bonds of a particular tribe and uniting them with different Indian tribes. By means of an invitation from the tribe initiating the rite prior to its beginning, other Indian tribes are invited to participate in the

rite, even though some of the visitors may be hereditary enemies.[44] This scenario enhances the social solidarity of the Indian nation and builds a closer relationship with the things of the universe; the sacred centre created by the dancers is alleged always to be with them throughout the remainder of their existence. There is no evidence of transgressive or excessive social behaviour by the sun dancers in Bataille's sense. Moreover, the dancers have acquired a sacred power during the rite that they may later share with other members of their society. According to Powers, the acquired power of the sun dancers may be invested in those who are sick by the placement of the dancers' hands on the less fortunate.[45] Thereby the sacred power is shared to cure the sick, and enter into communion with others. In comparison to Bataille's theory, the sun dancers do not differentiate themselves from their society. They share a sacred power that can benefit every member of the tribe. Bataille's heterological method and its stress on finding radical difference prevents him from seeing the socially unifying possibilities of a rite such as the Sun Dance.

According to Bataille, violence is inevitable because human beings cannot totally reject it. In contrast to Bataille's theory, the Sun Dance represents a threefold sacrifice of which the initial two sacrificial actions are symbolic: cutting down the cottonwood tree which is symbolic of the enemy; shooting at the effigies of a man and buffalo suspended from the crosspiece of the sacred tree, and the final action of the actual sacrifice of human flesh on the fourth day of the rite. The second symbolic killing of the effigies of a man and buffalo, amid much rejoicing by the participants, represents the hope for future success in hunting and victory in war.[46] These symbolic killings by the Sioux violate Bataille's assertion that violence cannot be controlled. Rather, the symbolic nature of the Sioux killings suggests a limiting and eventual termination of violence and not a promoting of any cycle of violence. Although Bataille is right to emphasize the importance of violence in sacrifice, there does not appear to be any danger that the contagious violence of the sacred will overflow and overwhelm the Sioux and other tribes. There are certainly martial features to the Sun Dance, but their symbolic nature suggests a containment of violence rather than any overflowing of it. Bataille's theory does make clear, however, that the Sioux accept violence, even though they try to reject or control it.

Within the drama of the Sun Dance, there is a hint of an inherent prestige associated with victims who choose to perform the sacrifice in the most painful and violent manner. The actual sacrificial victims, for instance, can choose to dance in any of four ways: gazing at the sun from dawn to dusk; having wooden skewers, tied to rawhide ropes secured about half way up the sacred pole, inserted into their breasts; having wooden skewers inserted into the breasts and then being suspended about one foot off the ground; or having wooden skewers inserted which then are attached with thongs to one or more buffalo skull(s) that must be dragged along the dance area.[47] The Sun Dance is not completed until the flesh of the victim has been torn through, representing the death and rebirth of the victim. It is permissible for others to assist by pulling on the ropes to end the victim's agony. As well, the multiple number of sun dancers contradicts Bataille's assertion that a victim represents a surplus of communal wealth and substitutes for other members of the community.[48] Neither is the victim an accursed share destined for violent destruction. Bataille is right, however, to emphasize the importance of death in sacrifice, which possesses the power to return one to continuity by means of eroticism. What he fails to see is the connection between death and spiritual rebirth. And due to his notion of eroticism, which represents a disequilibrium that stimulates a person consciously to call one's being into question, Bataille is not able to recognize that the sun dancer is actually able to find his identity.

Although Bataille's theory of sacrifice does not account for the Sun Dance in its entirety, the rite does adhere to his theory to some extent because it calls attention to the flesh and reveals external violence and the internal violence of the subject. The violation and breaking of the sun dancer's flesh does suggest the usefulness of Bataille's observation about the intimate connection between human flesh and violence. However, by giving pieces of their flesh, the sun dancers impugn Bataille's claim that the violation of the victim's flesh connotes a connection to a sexual act. At this point, Bataille's theory is problematic because it lacks consistent sense in the context of the Sun Dance. Bataille's need to reintroduce eroticism blinds him to the facts or drama of an actual sacrifice. The flesh of the sacrificial victim in the Sun Dance represents ignorance and not the dispossession of the self, an anti-social aspect of eroticism for Bataille. From an existential perspective, to be freed from the ropes tied to the skewers symbolizes freedom from the bonds of the flesh and not some erotic urge. The lack of an erotic emotion is evident in the symbolism of donning rabbit skins on the dancer's arms and legs. The rabbit is a symbol of humility, a virtue with which one must approach Wakan-Tanka. The victim is also equated symbolically with the sacred pipe that stretches from heaven to earth. In this context, the sacred pipe indicates the transcending of earthly flesh. The dancer becomes the centre of the world in which the four directions meet when he is tied at the centre of the four poles, so that the four directions converge in his body.[49]

Within the drama of the Sun Dance, elements of eroticism, violence, and death are evident. This does not mean, however, that these features of sacrifice necessarily involve stressing separation, difference, transgression, and excess. Although it is possible to find these features in the Sun Dance to some degree, the Sioux rite stresses finding one's identity within a religious and social tradition. By successfully completing the rite, a sun dancer does not separate himself from the group or become distinct from other things; rather, he often assumes a position of leadership within the tribe. And, as already noted, the sun dancer is intimately related to his mentor, ritual assistant or second, and other members of the tribe who play various roles in the rite. All this suggests the socially unifying nature of the rite. Moreover, within a tribal society such as the Sioux, the individual's identity is socially defined, even though one's visions and dreams help one to define oneself and one's place within a wider social context. . . .

Concluding Remarks

The significance of the Sun Dance enables us to see that there is an alternative interpretation to Bataille's theory that is more faithful to the actual evidence and is not simply imposed on the ritual activities by the creative imagination of a theorist. This interpretive analysis of the Sun Dance is suggested by the patterns exhibited by the rite itself and reflects more accurately the actual rite and its religious and symbolic context. Bataille, however, includes a personal agenda because he wants to re-introduce the erotic into religion. In other words, Bataille's theoretical speculation about eroticism shapes his theory of religion and sacrifice. Thus, his theoretical world-view takes precedence over the religious phenomena that he examines.

With his involvement in the Surrealist movement, his emphasis on embracing bodily waste, his anal and erotic obsessions, the role of the ambiguous pineal eye in his works, and composition of excessively obscene novels, all suggest an explicit advocacy of decadence by Bataille. In his work entitled *My Mother*, the socially excessive theme is incest. His novel *The Blue of Noon*, for instance, focuses on the nauseous and squalid aspects of human life where its characters are engaged in endless orgies, vomiting, and urinating. The erotic and death are continually united in his *Story of the Eye* when, for

example, the two leading libertines of the novel have sexual intercourse next to the cadaver of a young girl they have driven to death. Two further dramatic examples are the rape of a priest by the female protagonist and his death by strangulation and simultaneous sexual orgasm, and the death of the distracted matador gorged through his eye by the horn of a bull as he is distracted and blinded by the obscene antics of the female protagonist.

Bataille's hermeneutical method of heterology is designed to lead to excess and decadence. Trying to explain his *méthode de meditation* used in his book on religious experience, Bataille writes, "I think like a girl takes off her dress. At its most extreme point, thought is immodesty, obscenity itself."[50] This kind of statement seems to suggest de Sade or Mephistopheles becoming Faust. . . . And if, as suggested by Rosen, this decadence originates in political despair, Bataille's hermeneutical program is a political manifesto and not an apt tool for interpreting religious phenomena.

From a more positive perspective, Bataille's theory of religion does call attention to neglected elements in the study of religion in the form of bodily waste: excrement, saliva, tears, urine, mucus, dirt, skin, and so forth. Although his distinction between the sacred and the profane cannot be applied consistently as a useful hermeneutical device with the religious phenomena or world-view of Native American Indians, his emphasis on the difference within the sacred itself is suggestive. He is also right to stress the violent aspects of sacrifice and their sexual implications.

Although violence is certainly present in the Sun Dance, the Sioux rite appears to move in the direction of nonviolence—by symbolically killing an enemy represented by a tree, for instance—that undermines Bataille's opinion that violence cannot be contained. By offering his body and soul, the Sioux sun dancer points to a renewal and continuance of cosmic generative forces. The Sun Dance also joins Indian societies together and provides for social continuity by allowing others to share in the sacred power engendered by the rituals. Moreover, the rite enables the sun dancer to become ontologically transformed by being reborn and being set free of his mortal flesh. Although there is a sense in which the sun dancer is distinctive, the emphasis of the rite is unity with society and social well-being rather than stressing the differences between the sacrificial victim and society. . . .

NOTES

1. Georges Bataille, *Oeuvres complètes,* 12 vols. (Paris: Gallimard, 1970–1988), VI, 313.

2. Idem, *Visions of Excess: Selected Writings, 1927–1939,* Volume 14, Theory and History of Literature, trans. Allan Stoekl, Carl R. Lovitt, Donald M. Leslie, Jr. (Minneapolis: University of Minnesota Press, 1985), p. 97.

3. Ibid.

4. Allen S. Weiss, *The Aesthetics of Excess* (Albany, NY: State University of New York Press, 1989), p. 90.

5. Bataille, *Visions of Excess,* p. 95.

6. Idem, *Theory of Religion* (New York: Zone Books, 1989), pp. 27–33.

7. Ibid., p. 53.

8. Ibid.

9. Mircea Eliade, *The Sacred and the Profane: The Nature of Religion,* trans. Willard R. Trask (New York: Harcourt, Brace and Company, 1959), pp. 15–45.

10. Emile Durkheim, *The Elementary Forms of the Religious Life,* trans. Joseph Ward Swain (London: George Allen & Unwin, 1954), pp. 37–38.

11. Bataille, *Theory of Religion,* p. 52.

12. Ibid., p. 72.

13. Idem, *The Tears of Eros,* trans. Peter Connor (San Francisco: City Lights Books, 1989), p. 66.

14. Ibid., pp. 31–52.

15. Ibid., p. 44.

16. Ibid., p. 48.

17. Idem, *Death and Sensuality: A Study of Eroticism and the Taboo* (Salem, NH: Ayer, 1984), p. 17.

18. Ibid., p. 18.

19. Ibid., p. 52.

20. Ibid., pp. 29, 31.

21. Ibid., p. 139.

22. Ibid., p. 130.

23. Ibid., p. 256.

24. Ibid., p. 24.

25. Ibid., p. 69.

26. Ibid., p. 16.

27. Idem, *Theory of Religion,* p. 43.

28. Ibid., pp. 65–66.

29. Ibid., pp. 56–58.

30. Idem, *The Accursed Share: An Essay on General Economy,* Vol. I, trans. Robert Hurley (New York: Zone Books, 1988), p. 59.

31. Idem, *Death and Sensuality,* p. 90.

32. Ibid., p. 21.

33. Idem, *Theory of Religion,* p. 47.

34. Idem, *The Tears of Eros,* p. 74.

35. Jonathan Z. Smith, *To Take Place: Toward Theory in Ritual* (Chicago: University of Chicago Press, 1987), p. 109.

36. James R. Walker, *Lakota Belief and Ritual,* eds. Raymond J. De Mallie, Elaine A. Jahner (Lincoln: University of Nebraska Press, 1980).

37. Joseph Epes Brown ed., *The Sacred Pipe* (New York: Penguin Books, 1979), p. 69.

38. Ibid., pp. 69, 75–76.

39. Ibid., p. 80.

40. Walker, p. 114.

41. Bataille, *Oeuvres complètes,* II, 56.

42. Idem, *Death and Sensuality,* p. 91.

43. Brown, pp. 72, 78.

44. J. Owen Dorsey, *A Study of Siouan Cults,* Eleventh Annual Report of the Bureau of American Ethnology, (Washington, DC: Bureau of American Ethnology, 1894), p. 452.

45. William K. Powers, *Oglala Religion* (Lincoln: Univeristy of Nebraska Press, 1977), p. 100.

46. Ibid., p. 98.

47. Ibid., pp. 98–99.

48. Bataille, *The Accursed Share,* p. 59.

49. Brown, pp. 85, 95, 74.

50. George Bataille, *L' Expérience intérieure* (Paris: Gallimard, 1954), p. 216.

Nietzsche, Genealogy, History

MICHEL FOUCAULT

GENEALOGY IS GRAY, meticulous, and patiently documentary. It operates on a field of entangled and confused parchments, on documents that have been scratched over and recopied many times. . . .

Genealogy . . . requires patience and a knowledge of details, and it depends on a vast accumulation of source material. Its "cyclopean monuments"[1] are constructed from "discreet and apparently insignificant truths and according to a rigorous method"; they cannot be the product of "large and well-meaning errors."[2] In short, genealogy demands relentless erudition. Genealogy does not oppose itself to history as the lofty and profound gaze of the philosopher might compare to the molelike perspective of the scholar; on the contrary, it rejects the metahistorical deployment of ideal significations and indefinite teleologies. It opposes itself to the search for "origins."

In Nietzsche, we find two uses of the word *Ursprung*. The first is unstressed, and it is found alternately with other terms such as *Entstehung, Herkunft, Abkunft, Geburt*. . . .

The other use of the word is stressed. On occasion, Nietzsche places the term in opposition to another: in the first paragraph of *Human, All Too Human* the miraculous origin (*Wunderursprung*) sought by metaphysics is set against the analyses of historical philosophy, which poses questions *Über Herkunft und Anfang*. *Ursprung* is also used in an ironic and deceptive manner. In what, for instance, do we find the original basis (*Ursprung*) of morality, a foundation sought after since Plato? . . . It belongs, very simply, to an invention (*Erfindung*), a sleight-of-hand, an artifice (*Kunststück*), a secret formula,

in the rituals of black magic, in the work of the *Schwarzkünstler*.[3] . . .

Why does Nietzsche challenge the pursuit of the origin (*Ursprung*), at least on those occasions when he is truly a genealogist? First, because it is an attempt to capture the exact essence of things, their purest possibilities, and their carefully protected identifies; because this search assumes the existence of immobile forms that precede the external world of accident and succession. This search is directed to "that which was already there," the image of a primordial truth fully adequate to its nature, and it necessitates the removal of every mask to ultimately disclose an original identity. However, if the genealogist refuses to extend his faith in metaphysics, if he listens to history, he finds that there is "something altogether different" behind things: not a timeless and essential secret, but the secret that they have no essence or that their essence was fabricated in a piecemeal fashion from alien forms. Examining the history of reason, he learns that it was born in an altogether "reasonable" fashion—from chance;[4] devotion to truth and the precision of scientific methods arose from the passion of scholars, their reciprocal hatred, their fanatical and unending discussions, and their spirit of competition—the personal conflicts that slowly forged the weapons of reason.[5] Further, genealogical analysis shows that the concept of liberty is an "invention of the ruling classes"[6] and not fundamental to man's nature or at the root of his attachment to being and truth. What is found at the historical beginning of things is not the inviolable identity of their origin; it is the dissension of other things. It is disparity.[7]

Reprinted from Michel Foucault, "Nietzsche, Genealogy, History," Language, Counter-Memory, Practice: Selected Essays and Interviews, *trans. Donald F. Bouchard and Sherry Simon. Copyright* © *1977 Cornell Unversity. Used by permission of the publisher, Cornell University Press.*

History also teaches how to laugh at the solemnities of the origin. The lofty origin is no more than "a metaphysical extension which arises from the belief that things are most precious and essential at the moment of birth."[8] We tend to think that this is the moment of their greatest perfection, when they emerged dazzling from the hands of a creator or in the shadowless light of a first morning. The origin always precedes the Fall. It comes before the body, before the world and time; it is associated with the gods, and its story is always sung as a theogony. But historical beginnings are lowly: not in the sense of modest or discreet like the steps of a dove, but derisive and ironic, capable of undoing every infatuation. . . .

The final postulate of the origin is linked to the first two in being the site of truth. From the vantage point of an absolute distance, free from the restraints of positive knowledge, the origin makes possible a field of knowledge whose function is to recover it, but always in a false recognition due to the excesses of its own speech. The origin lies at a place of inevitable loss, the point where the truth of things corresponded to a truthful discourse, the site of a fleeting articulation that discourse has obscured and finally lost. It is a new cruelty of history that compels a reversal of this relationship and the abandonment of "adolescent" quests: behind the always recent, avaricious, and measured truth, it posits the ancient proliferation of errors. It is now impossible to believe that "in the rending of the veil, truth remains truthful; we have lived long enough not to be taken in."[9] Truth is undoubtedly the sort of error that cannot be refuted because it was hardened into an unalterable form in the long baking process of history.[10] Moreover, the very question of truth, the right it appropriates to refute error and oppose itself to appearance, the manner in which it developed (initially made available to the wise, then withdrawn by men of piety to an unattainable world where it was given the double role of consolation and imperative, finally rejected as a useless notion, superfluous and contradicted on

all sides)—does this not form a history, the history of an error we call truth? Truth, and its original reign, has had a history within history from which we are barely emerging "in the time of the shortest shadow," when light no longer seems to flow from the depths of the sky or to arise from the first moments of the day.[11]

A genealogy of values, morality, asceticism, and knowledge will never confuse itself with a quest for their "origins," will never neglect as inaccessible the vicissitudes of history. On the contrary, it will cultivate the details and accidents that accompany every beginning; it will be scrupulously attentive to their petty malice; it will await their emergence, once unmasked, as the face of the other. Wherever it is made to go, it will not be reticent—in "excavating the depths," in allowing time for these elements to escape from a labyrinth where no truth had ever detained them. The genealogist needs history to dispel the chimeras of the origin, somewhat in the manner of the pious philosopher who needs a doctor to exorcise the shadow of his soul. He must be able to recognize the events of history, its jolts, its surprises, its unsteady victories and unpalatable defeats—the basis of all beginnings, atavisms, and heredities. Similarly, he must be able to diagnose the illnesses of the body, its conditions of weakness and strength, its breakdowns and resistances, to be in a position to judge philosophical discourse. History is the concrete body of a development, with its moments of intensity, its lapses, its extended periods of feverish agitation, its fainting spells; and only a metaphysician would seek its soul in the distant ideality of the origin. . . .

The analysis of descent permits the dissociation of the self, its recognition and displacement as an empty synthesis, in liberating a profusion of lost events.

An examination of descent also permits the discovery, under the unique aspect of a trait or a concept, of the myriad events through which —thanks to which, against which—they were formed. Genealogy does not pretend to go back in time to restore an unbroken continuity that operates beyond the dispersion of forgotten things; its duty is not to demonstrate that the past actively exists in the present, that it continues secretly to animate the present, having imposed a predetermined form on all its vicissitudes. Genealogy does not resemble the evolution of a species and does not map the destiny of a people. On the contrary, to follow the complex course of descent is to maintain passing events in their proper dispersion; it is to identify the accidents, the minute deviations—or conversely, the complete reversals—the errors, the false appraisals, and the faulty calculations that gave birth to those things that continue to exist and have value for us; it is to discover that truth or being does not lie at the root of what we know and what we are, but the exteriority of accidents.[12] This is undoubtedly why every origin of morality from the moment it stops being pious—and *Herkunft* can never be—has value as a critique.[13]

. . . The search for descent is not the erecting of foundations: on the contrary, it disturbs what was previously considered immobile; it fragments what was thought unified; it shows the heterogeneity of what was imagined consistent with itself. What convictions and, far more decisively, what knowledge can resist it? If a genealogical analysis of a scholar were made—of one who collects facts and carefully accounts for them—his *Herkunft* would quickly divulge the official papers of the scribe and the pleadings of the lawyer—their father[14]—in their apparently disinterested attention, in the "pure" devotion to objectivity.

Finally, descent attaches itself to the body.[15] It inscribes itself in the nervous system, in temperament, in the digestive apparatus; it appears in faulty respiration, in improper diets, in the debilitated and prostrate bodies of those whose ancestors committed errors. . . .

The body is the inscribed surface of events (traced by language and dissolved by ideas), the locus of a dissociated self (adopting the illusion of a substantial unity), and a volume in perpetual disintegration. Genealogy, as an analysis of descent, is thus situated within the articulation of the body and history. Its task is to expose a body totally imprinted by history and the process of history's destruction of the body.

Entstehung designates *emergence*, the moment of arising. It stands as the principle and the singular law of an apparition. As it is wrong to search for descent in an uninterrupted continuity, we should avoid thinking of emergence as the final term of a historical development; the eye was not always intended for contemplation, and punishment has had other purposes than setting an example. These developments may appear as a culmination, but they are merely the current episodes in a series of subjugations: the eye initially responded to the requirements of hunting and warfare; and punishment has been subjected, throughout its history, to a variety of needs—revenge, excluding an aggressor, compensating a victim, creating fear. In placing present needs at the origin, the metaphysician would convince us of an obscure purpose that seeks its realization at the moment it arises. Genealogy, however, seeks to reestablish the various systems of subjection: not the anticipatory power of meaning, but the hazardous play of dominations. . . .

Emergence is thus the entry of forces; it is their eruption, the leap from the wings to center stage, each in its youthful strength. What Nietzsche calls the *Entstehungsherd*[16] of the concept of goodness is not specifically the energy of the strong or the reaction of the weak, but precisely this scene where they are displayed superimposed or face-to-face. It is nothing but the space that divides them, the void through which they exchange their threatening gestures and speeches. As descent qualifies the strength or weakness of an instinct and its inscription on a body, emergence designates a place of confrontation, but not as a closed field offering the spectacle of a struggle among equals. Rather, as Nietzsche demonstrates in his analysis of good and evil, it is a "non-place," a pure distance, which indicates that the adversaries do not belong to a common space. Consequently, no one is responsible for an emergence; no one can glory in it, since it always occurs in the interstice.

In a sense, only a single drama is ever staged in this "nonplace," the endlessly repeated play of dominations. The domination of certain men over others leads to the differentiation of values;[17] class domination generates the idea of liberty;[18] and the forceful appropriation of things necessary to survival and the imposition of a duration not intrinsic to them account for the origin of logic.[19] This relationship of domination is no more a "relationship" than the place where it occurs is a place; and, precisely for this reason, it is fixed, throughout its history, in rituals, in meticulous procedures that impose rights and obligations. It establishes marks of its power and engraves memories on things and even within bodies. It makes itself accountable for debts and gives rise to the universe of rules, which is by no means designed to temper violence, but rather to satisfy it. Following traditional beliefs, it would be false to think that total war exhausts itself in its own contradictions and ends by renouncing violence and submitting to civil laws. On the contrary, the law is a calculated and relentless pleasure, delight in the promised blood, which permits the perpetual instigation of new dominations and the staging of meticulously repeated scenes of violence. The desire for peace, the serenity of compromise, and the tacit acceptance of the law, far from representing a major moral conversion or a utilitarian calculation that gave rise to the law, are but its result and, in point of fact, its perversion: "guilt, conscience, and duty had their threshold of emergence in the right to secure obligations; and their inception, like that of any major event on earth, was saturated in blood."[20] Humanity does not gradually progress from combat to combat until it arrives at universal reciprocity, where the rule of law finally replaces warfare; humanity installs each of its violences in a system of rules and thus proceeds from domination to domination.

The nature of these rules allows violence to be inflicted on violence and the resurgence of new forces that are sufficiently strong to dominate those in power. Rules are empty in themselves, violent and unfinalized; they are impersonal and can be bent to any purpose. The successes of history belong to those who are capable of seizing these rules, to replace those who had used them, to disguise themselves so as to pervert them, invert their meaning, and redirect them against those who had initially imposed them; controlling this complex mechanism, they will make it function so as to overcome the rulers through their own rules.

The isolation of different points of emergence does not conform to the successive configurations of an identical meaning; rather, they result from substitutions, displacements, disguised conquests, and systematic reversals. If interpretation were the slow exposure of the meaning hidden in an origin, then only metaphysics could interpret the development of humanity. But if interpretation is the violent or surreptitious appropriation of a system of rules, which in itself has no essential meaning, in order to impose a direction, to bend it to a new will, to force its participation in a different game, and to subject it to secondary rules, then the development of humanity is a series of interpretations. The role of genealogy is to record its history: the history of morals, ideals, and metaphysical concepts, the history of the concept of liberty or of the ascetic life; as they stand for the emergence of different interpretations, they must be made to appear as events on the stage of historical process.

How can we define the relationship between genealogy, seen as the examination of *Herkunft* and *Entstehung,* and history in the traditional sense? We could, of course, examine Nietzsche's celebrated apostrophes against history, but we will put these aside for the moment and consider those instances when he conceives of genealogy as *wirkliche Historie,* or its more frequent characterization as historical "spirit" or "sense." In fact, Nietzsche's criticism, beginning with the second of the *Untimely Meditations,* always questioned the form of history that reintroduces (and always assumes) a suprahistorical perspective: a history whose function is to compose the finally reduced diversity of time into a totality fully closed upon itself; a history that always encourages subjective recognitions and attributes a form of reconciliation to all the displacements of the past; a history whose perspective on all that precedes it implies the end of time, a completed development. The historian's history finds its support outside of time and pretends to base its judgments on an apocalyptic objectivity. This is only possible, however, because the immortality of the soul, and the nature of consciousness [i]s always identical to itself. Once the historical sense is mastered by a suprahistorical perspective, metaphysics can bend it to its own purpose, and, by aligning it to the demands of objective science, it can impose its own "Egyptianism." On the other hand, the historical sense can evade metaphysics and become a privileged instrument of genealogy if it refuses the certainty of absolutes. Given this, it corresponds to the acuity of a glance that distinguishes, separates, and disperses; that is capable of liberating divergence and marginal elements—the kind of dissociating view that is capable of decomposing itself, capable of shattering the unity of man's being through which it was thought that he could extend his sovereignty to the events of his past.

Historical meaning becomes a dimension of *wirkliche Historie* to the extent that it places within a process of development everything considered immortal in man. We believe that feelings are immutable, but every sentiment, particularly the noblest and most disinterested, has a history. We believe in the dull constancy of instinctual life and imagine that it continues to exert its force indiscriminately in the present as it did in the past. But a knowledge of history easily disintegrates this unity, depicts its wavering course, locates its moments of strength and weakness, and defines its oscillating reign. It easily seizes the slow elaboration of instincts and those movements where, in turning upon themselves, they relentlessly set about their self-destruction.[21] We believe, in any event, that the body obeys the exclusive laws of physiology and that it escapes the influence of history, but this too is false. The body is molded by a great many distinct regimes; it is broken down by the rhythms of work, rest, and holidays; it is poisoned by food or values, through eating habits or moral laws; it constructs resistances.[22] "Effective" history differs from traditional history in being without constants. Nothing in man—not even his body—is sufficiently stable to serve as the basis for self-recognition or for understanding other men. The traditional devices for constructing a comprehensive view of history and for retracing the past as a patient and continuous development must be systematically dismantled. Necessarily, we must dismiss those tendencies that encourage the consoling play of recognitions. Knowledge, even under the banner of history, does not depend on "rediscovery," and it emphatically excludes the "rediscovery of ourselves." History becomes "effective" to the degree that it introduces discontinuity into our very being—as it divides our emotions, dramatizes our instincts, multiplies our body and sets it against itself. "Effective" history deprives the self of the reassuring stability of life and nature, and it will not permit itself to be transported by a voiceless obstinacy toward a millennial ending. It will uproot its traditional foundations and relentlessly disrupt its pretended continuity. This is because knowledge is not made for understanding; it is made for cutting.

From these observations, we can grasp the particular traits of historical meaning as Nietzsche understood it—the sense which opposes *wirkliche Historie* to traditional history. The former transposes the relationship ordinarily established between the eruption of an event and necessary continuity. An entire historical tradition (theological or rationalistic) aims at dissolving the singular event into an ideal continuity—as a teleological movement or a natural process. "Effective" history, however, deals with events in terms of their most unique characteristics, their most acute manifestations. An event, consequently, is not a decision, a treaty, a reign, or a battle, but the reversal of a relationship of forces, the usurpation of power, the appropriation of a vocabulary turned against those who had once used it, a feeble domination that poisons itself as it grows lax, the entry of a masked "other." The forces operating in history are not controlled by destiny or regulative mechanisms, but respond to haphazard conflicts.[23] They do not manifest the successive forms of a primordial intention and their attraction is not that of a conclusion, for they always appear through the singular randomness of events. The inverse of the Christian world, spun entirely by a divine spider, and different from the world of the Greeks, divided between the realm of will and the great cosmic folly, the world of effective history knows only one kingdom, without providence or final cause, where there is only "the iron hand of necessity shaking the dice-box of chance."[24] Chance is not simply the drawing of lots, but raising the stakes in every attempt to master chance through the will to power, and giving rise to the risk of an even greater chance.[25] The world we know is not this ultimately simple configuration where events are reduced to accentuate their essential traits, their final meaning, or their initial and final value. On the contrary, it is a profusion of entangled events. If it appears as a "marvelous motley, profound and totally meaningful," this is because it began and continues its secret existence through a "host of errors and phantasms."[26] We want historians to confirm our belief that the present rests upon profound intentions and immutable necessities. But the true historical sense confirms our existence among countless lost events, without a landmark or a point of reference.

Effective history can also invert the relationship that traditional history, in its dependence on metaphysics, establishes between proximity and distance. The latter is given to a contemplation of distances and heights: the noblest periods, the highest forms, the most abstract ideas, the purest individualities. It accomplishes this by getting as near as possible, placing itself at the foot of its mountain peaks, at the risk of adopting the famous perspective of frogs. Effective history, on the other hand, shortens its vision to those things nearest to it—the body, the nervous system, nutrition, digestion, and energies; it unearths the periods of decadence, and if it chances upon lofty epochs, it is with the suspi-

cion—not vindictive but joyous—of finding a barbarous and shameful confusion. It has no fear of looking down, so long as it is understood that it looks from above and descends to seize the various perspectives, to disclose dispersions and differences, to leave things undisturbed in their own dimension and intensity. It reverses the surreptitious practice of historians, their pretension to examine things furthest from themselves, the groveling manner in which they approach this promising distance (like the metaphysicians who proclaim the existence of an afterlife, situated at a distance from this world, as a promise of their reward). Effective history studies what is closest, but in an abrupt dispossession, so as to seize it at a distance (an approach similar to that of a doctor who looks closely, who plunges to make a diagnosis and to state its difference). Historical sense has more in common with medicine than philosophy; and it should not surprise us that Nietzsche occasionally employs the phrase "historically and physiologically,"[27] since among the philosopher's idiosyncrasies is a complete denial of the body. This includes, as well, "the absence of historical sense, a hatred for the idea of development, Egyptianism," the obstinate "placing of conclusions at the beginning," of "making last things first."[28] History has a more important task than to be a handmaiden to philosophy, to recount the necessary birth of truth and values; it should become a differential knowledge of energies and failings, heights and degenerations, poisons and antidotes. Its task is to become a curative science.[29]

The final trait of effective history is its affirmation of knowledge as perspective. Historians take unusual pains to erase the elements in their work which reveal their grounding in a particular time and place, their preferences in a controversy—the unavoidable obstacles of their passion. Nietzsche's version of historical sense is explicit in its perspective and acknowledges its system of injustice. Its perception is slanted, being a deliberate appraisal, affirmation, or negation; it reaches the lingering and poisonous traces in order to prescribe the best antidote. It is not given to a discreet effacement before the objects it observes and does not submit itself to their processes; nor does it seek laws, since it gives equal weight to its own sight and to its objects. Through this historical sense, knowledge is allowed to create its own genealogy in the act of cognition; and *wirkliche Historie* composes a genealogy of history as the vertical projection of its position. . . .

NOTES

1. F. W. Nietzsche, *The Gay Science* (1882), trans. Walter Kaufmann (New York: Random House, 1974), p. 7.

2. Idem, *Human, All Too Human* (1878) (New York: Gordon Press, 1974), p. 3.

3. Idem, *Gay Science*, pp. 151, 353.

4. Idem, *Dawn*, p. 123.

5. Idem, *Human, All To Human*, p. 34.

6. Idem, *The Wanderer and His Shadow* (1880) in *Complete Works* (New York: Gordon Press, 1974), p. 9.

7. Ed.: A wide range of key terms, found in Foucault's *The Archaeology of Knowledge,* are related to this theme of "disparity": the concepts of series, discontinuity, division, and difference. If the same is found in the realm and movement of the dialects, the disparate presents itself as an "event" in the world of chance.

8. Nietzsche, *Wanderer*, p. 3.

9. Idem, *Nietzsche contra Wagner* (1888), in *Portable Nietzsche*.

10. Idem, *Gay Science,* pp. 2110, 265.

11. Idem, "How the True World Finally Became a Fable," *Twilight of Idols.*

12. Idem, *Genealogy* III, sec. 17.

13. Idem, "'Reason' in Philosophy," *Twilight of Idols.*

14. Idem, *Gay Science,* pp. 348–9.

15. Ibid.

16. Idem, *Genealogy,* I, sec. 2.

17. Idem, *Beyond Good and Evil,* p. 260; see also *Genealogy,* II, sec. 12.

18. Idem, *Wanderer,* p. 9.

19. Idem, *Gay Science,* p. 111.

20. Idem, *Genealogy, II,* p. 6.

21. Idem, *Gay Science,* p. 7.

22. Ibid.

23. Idem, *Genealogy II,* sec. 12.

24. Idem, *Dawn,* p. 130.

25. Idem, *Genealogy,* II, sec. 12.

26. Idem, *Human, All Too Human,* p. 16.

27. Idem, *Twilight of Idols,* p. 44.

28. Idem, "'Reason' in Philosophy," *Twilight of Idols,* pp. 1, 4.

29. Idem, *Wanderer,* p. 188.

Counterpoint:
From *The Ascetic Imperative in Culture and Criticism*

GEOFFREY GALT HARPHAM

Geoffrey Galt Harpham is a professor of English at Tulane University and has published *On the Grotesque: Strategies of Contradiction in Art and Literature, Getting It Right: Language, Literature and Criticism, One of Us: The Mastery of Joseph Conrad,* and *Shadows of Ethics: Criticism and the Just Society.*

. . . FOUCAULT'S WORK has always seemed susceptible to a critique predicated on the imperative to resist temptation—to an ascetical critique. The responsibility for this surely lies with the various but often covert forms of asceticism in his work itself. Take as one example the neo-Nietzschean project of "archeology." As defined in *The Archeology of Knowledge* (1969) archeology interrogation of discursive practices is an attempt to uncover their regularities. All notions of expression, of historical or epistemological continuity, of presence, of "genius," of freedom, of formalism, of the "tender, consoling certainty of being able to change, if not the world, if not life, at least their 'meaning,' simply with a fresh word that can come only from" ourselves—all this is excluded from the outset as irrelevant, nonproductive, and illusionary. Language, as he says in "The Discourse on Language" (1970), appended to the English translation of *The Archeology of Knowledge,* is to be treated as a "system of exclusions" according to a radical textual materialism that excludes above all the "presence" of the creative, expressive authorspeaker whose intentions determine the text. What is sought instead of these pre-textual intentions is the "obscure set of anonymous rules" governing the discourses that govern us. The sovereign subject is revealed by archeology as subject to the discursive practices that establish only the death of the subject, not its fertile presence. Renouncing the Logos and all notions of proximity to the source of meaning, archeology seeks "to cleanse" the "history of thought" from all "transcendental narcissism," rigorously to remain within the discourses it interrogates, producing a "rewriting," a "regulated transformation of what has already been written." Archeology is thus undertaken in the spirit of Nietzsche's attack on the ascetic ideal. And like that attack, it is self-compromised: the archeologist seeks only "a pure description of discursive events"—an ascetic imitation, a humbling and depersonalizing submission to the Rule of Discourse.

Of course, such a project must be haunted at every moment by the unities, continuities, syntheses, and idealizations it banishes, for they, too, are discursive functions; they might even be glimpsed in the notion of a "series" linking discursive events, or in the "fellowships of discourse" described in "The Discourse on Language." These are temptations, threats to the archeologist's negative innocence, which is tenuously, and tenaciously, preserved at every moment through resistances to totalization, unity, and even what the vulgar may call coherence inscribed in the text itself. Such resistances appear not only on the thematic or statement level, but also in the stylistic aberrations and disruptions that constitute the "difficulty" of the Foucauldian text: definition by multiple negation (archeology is neither the history of ideas, nor intellectual history, nor the history of mind); the insistence on reversing the constant tendency of interpretation to eliminate doubt and produce certainty; and even his own pronounced disinclination to "idealizations" (interpretations, applications) of his work. The mighty disfiguring force of resistance to regularized or predictable meaning embedded in the style produces what Said, in a generous postmortem tribute, describes as "the almost terrifying stalemate one feels in his work between the anonymity of discourse and 'discursive regularity,' on [one] side, and on the other side, the pressures of 'infamous' egos, including Foucault's own, whose will to powerful knowledge challenges the formidable establishment of impersonal rules, authorless statements, disciplined enunciations." The idiosyncrasy of Foucault's writing is a resistance arising at the stylistic level to his own insistence on the mere contingency or even impossibility of a truly productive idiosyncrasy.

Some of the most powerful effects of Foucault's style arise through its insistence on its own eccentric and self-rewarding singularity. Hayden White has caught this feature well, describing Foucault's style as "a rhetoric apparently designed to frustrate summary, paraphrase, economical quotation for illustrative purposes, or translation into traditional critical terminology. . . . His interminable sentences, parentheses, repetitions, neologisms, paradoxes, oxymorons, alternation of analytical with lyrical passages, and his combination of scientist with mythic terminology—all this appears to be consciously designed to render his discourse impenetrable to any critical technique based on ideological principles other than his own. . . . Foucault's discourse is willfully superficial." Above all, for White, Foucault's discourse is willful, a pure product of the will to power-knowledge. Accepting White's characterization, we can begin to understand how complex are the implications of Foucauldian idiosyncrasy: as a resistance to the temptations of illusion and ideality, idiosyncrasy is an ethical gesture serving the interests of truth; while as a resistance to appropriation and an assertion of power, it is beyond good and evil, and beyond truth as well.

Even before he becomes a theoretician of resistance in the first volume of *The History of Sexuality,* then, Foucault is a practitioner of resistance. To insist on this point is to bring to light the network of avoidances and exclusions that runs through Foucault's work. But it is also necessarily to run against one tendency of Foucault's work by crediting it with a dimension of the "unexpressed," and therefore with the kind of "depth" that Foucault often seeks to discredit as a methodological perversion. Moreover, to read those resistances as specifically ascetic in character is to place his work in precisely the context he seeks to "rewrite." . . . Foucault himself accepts in principle a powerful, even coercive, practice of interpretation. Reading the resistances, we are only following a Nietzschean, and even a Foucauldian imperative.

Let us begin by positing two species of resistance, based on cenobitic and eremitic principles. The Rule of Discourse has a cenobitic emphasis: routine, anonymous, nontranscendent, "external." Within the Rule, all notions of consciousness are subjugated to a mortification. The Rule is most formulaically enunciated in the famous 1969 essay, "What Is an Author?" in which the classical conception of authorship is reduced to a discursive function in the service of nostalgic demands for unity and coherence: "the author" is not an expressive subject but a check on interpretation, a principle of thrift set against the possible proliferation of meaning; or, conversely, a fiction that fills up the interstices or gaps of signification with "meaning," a term for which Foucault reserves a special contempt. Arguing against the exegetical desire to reinscribe the "sacred origin" of the moment of creation through interpretation, Foucault insists that the "author-function" is an effect rather than a cause of the text. Writing "no longer" guarantees the immortality of the self, as the Greeks thought, but serves as an instrument of cenobitic ascesis. . . .

The 1971 essay on "Nietzsche, Genealogy, History" could be emblematically opposed to "What Is an Author?" in its daring abandonment of all the continuities and coherences associated with the author-function, its focus on "the singularity of events" as the subject of "genealogical" inquiry, and its positing of the body as the perpetually disintegrating but "inscribed surface of events." In this essay archeology gives way to genealogy, the text to the body, and rules to the eruption of conflicting, random forces. Here, too, the notion of the death of writing is supplanted by that of the "proper individuality" that stands opposed to the "faceless anonymity" of "the family of ascetics." But the case is not anti-ascetic; it is merely anticenobitic. In changing the direction of his work of the year before, Foucault did not discover a form of history without denial, but rather advanced a new mode of denial predicated not on "knowledge" but on "creativity," multiplicity of being, the body, and irregularity—in short, on eremitic asceticism. The saint in temptation epitomizes the multiplicity of being in the singularity of the event. . . .

So far I have been forcing, adjusting, omitting, abbreviating—perhaps even violently and surreptitiously appropriating—Foucault's work, reading it according to my own preoccupations. But Foucault takes a dramatic step closer to these preoccupations in *La Volonté de savior* (1976), translated as *The History of Sexuality* although it is the first volume of what Foucault projected as a six-volume series by that name.

Foucault immediately demonstrates in this most Nietzschean book that he has solved Nietzsche's most intractable problem, the reversibility of power-terms. The initial target is "the repressive hypothesis," according to which sexuality, the object of repression, is conceived as the reservoir of a secret or essential selfhood. This hypothesis holds that the forces responsible for repression had, in alliance with the rise of capitalism, enforced a ritual, and, since the seventeenth century, increasingly effective, denial of the body, a subjugation of everything incompatible with the work ethic. Moreover (according to this hypothesis) any truthful discourse—about sex, for example—resists established power, and the rise in the quantity of discourse about sex since the nineteenth century constitutes a massive and effective resistance. As an alternative to the repressive hypothesis Foucault proposes a new theory of the relation between power, truth, and the body, in which all power is a material force operating on the body, and yet producing knowledge, which in turn produces not resistances but only new forms of power. . . .

Foucault does what Nietzsche cannot: he avoids attributing knowledge to weakness and opposing knowledge to strength.

In fact, he avoids the notion of weakness altogether through an analysis of power as an omnipresent force issuing not from a central point but from innumerable points in a play of differential and mobile relations. Foucauldian power is "intentional and nonsubjective," a "moving substrate of force relations" operating locally and constantly in every relation. The nonsubjective character of Foucauldian power contrasts sharply not only with Nietzsche's power but with that of nearly all other analysts. . . .

Foucault avoids the difficulties connected with the strength of weakness by focusing not on the miserable and immutable character of the weak, but on the moment of reversal itself, when the weak have overcome their own weakness. Hence, in the essay on Nietzsche, the definition of "the event": "not a decision, a treaty, a reign, or a battle, but the reversal of a relationship of forces, the usurpation of power, the appropriation of a vocabulary turned against those who had once used it, a feeble domination that poisons itself as it grows lax, the entry of a masked 'other.'" Foucault claims Nietzschean authority for this definition, but a stronger case could be made that Nietzsche situated his critique in prehistory precisely in order to escape such a definition of the event. Speculating about prehistory, Nietzsche can imagine the dominance of strength in a "natural" setting, a world in which there should be no such "events," no reversals. What troubles the argument of the *Genealogy* is the intrusion of the events of history into the prehistoric, an intrusion that repeats the Fall. Foucault posits no such natural condition, but while he has thereby accommodated reversibility in his theory of power, he is still scandalized by another aspect of power—its pleasure. What reversibility is for Nietzsche, pleasure is for Foucault: an incomprehensible and regrettable accident of power. . . .

While Foucault understands in a fundamentally new way the relation between sexuality and discourse, and has gone a very long way toward the defetishization of sexuality, he is still capable of considering perverted the pleasure that attends the exercise of power, the sexuality of discourse, or, to put a finer point on it, the "sexuality of history." In other words, Foucault, apparently in full consciousness, replicates the strategy he analyzes and censures.

Why would Foucault so willingly participate in the activity he calls perverse? The answer may be provided by the section in which Foucault opposes the Western "*scientia sexualis*" which sustains the will to knowledge and truth primarily through the form of confession, to the "*ars erotica*" of certain non-Western societies. Such societies draw truth "from pleasure itself, understood as a practice and accumulated as experience," while the Western confessing cultures systematically violate the sanctity of silent practice. Perversely, this violation procures a new and intense form of pleasure. Nietzsche, it will be recalled, invoked science as the last possible resistance to asceticism only to conclude that it was in fact the greatest ascetical force in the modern world. Here Foucault does the opposite, assimilating the ascetical West to the liberated East, conceding at last that the will to controlling knowledge is only an exaggerated form of *ars erotica*. Western techniques of control, then, do not deny pleasure as much as they appropriate and complicate it. Within Western discourse, pleasure is pre-perverted.

The "event," in Foucault's definition, entails "the entry of a masked 'other,'" In this respect power is a true event, tolerable only on condition that it mask a substantial part of itself." What power masks is, however, not only its "mechanisms," as Foucault says, nor its indifference to Law, its capricious imposition of brute force; power masks its pleasure, the source of its perversion. Moreover, the proposition may be reversed. Pleasure itself, we could say, always masks an "other"—power—in order to please. . . .

Resisted power is doubled, mirrored, self-contradicted, self-confirmed—as multiple, relational, and unstable in its being as it is in its functioning. And yet only resistance can make power coherent. Without resistance power is omnipotent and infinitely efficient; without resistance power has no possible connection to pleasure because no domination or "friction"; without resistance power has no "other" and no need to conceal a part of itself; without resistance power is formless, theoretical, an impossible singularity on a denuded, radically simplified landscape—indeed, on no landscape at all. Without resistance, in short, power is inconceivable. Resistance is neither an addition to nor an aspect of power; it is the site and condition of power. We cannot, to retrieve a figure used earlier, think of power without

resistance any more than we can think of an electrical impulse without the circuit that provides its resistance. In this sense, all power is electrical. Even to speak of "power" and "resistance" as though they were independent terms may be a case of what Nietzsche calls language "doubling the deed," but we cannot correct language's error by resolving the two terms into one. Power-resistance condition(s) thought in the same way as "narrativity-closure," to seeing that one and two are not necessarily the only choices we have. There is, in addition, a figure of relation that is neither single nor double but both, a figure within which notions of single and double arise. Foucault's political "position" is complicated and somewhat softened by the fact that resistance to instituted power is necessary not so much on ideological or ethical grounds, but on a far more fundamental basis. Resistance can be desired, planned, and undertaken, but it does not originate with the conscious will of the intending subject, for the power-situation testifies to its presence from the first. People and groups can modify and direct resistance as a counter to power, just as they can modify and direct power as a counter to resistance; but they can neither invent nor fully control either power or resistance.

Man's life on earth is power. And with the belated introduction of resistance to the power-knowledge network, Foucault's work becomes assimilable—entering into explicit resistance—to the ascetic task of the management of desire. In fact, it complements it. Power-knowledge-pleasure; each providing the "unspoken" or "masked" resistance to the other two.

At the most revealing of his dialogic moments, Foucault accuses himself of suppressing sex itself. In his critique of "groundless effects, ramifications without roots," he has, his "other" insists, produced an account of sexuality without sex. . . . Accusing himself of asceticism—a charge he resists by saying that "I think we can reply in the negative" (who is "we"?)—he then repeats his contention that sex is "a problem of truth," "a complex idea that was formed inside the deployment of sexuality." With one voice arguing for sex and another constantly deflecting or transposing sex into the power-knowledge registers, the text itself is in resistance. The force of the final pages is that power produces sex, that sex has "an essential and positive relation to power," that sex is not simply that-which-is-dominated, not an autonomous agency, that "liberation" is not at issue here. To think so is to "evade what gives 'power' its power," namely, its complicity with desire. We have not, he insists, "broken free of a long period of harsh repression, a protracted Christian asceticism, greedily and fastidiously adapted to the imperatives of bourgeois economy." Freedom is not the point. Sex is a fraud, historically subordinate to a larger deployment of sexuality that interprets, controls, normalizes, and disciplines; resistance to this deployment now must rally around bodies and pleasures, not sex.

In this crucial but problematic formulation of a nonsexual economy of pleasure (why should bodies and pleasures be any more historically or conceptually substantial than sex?), Foucault conceives of a resistance to ascetic power-strategies in general. Having earlier urged a new conceptualzation of "sex without the law," he now sees that sex in any form will not serve, for it has been, "from the dawn of time, under the sway of law and right." The "austere monarchy of sex" is a "shadow" which we have forced to confess itself as though it were genuinely opposed to power and allied with truth. Having begun, then, by speaking for the simplicity of "pleasure itself" in the *ars erotica*, Foucault ends by renouncing "this idea of sex in itself" and indeed the idea of sex as anything other than an ideal, speculative entity created by power-mechanisms. The new species of pleasure will issue from such sources as writing about oneself. While the "Introduction of the individual into the realm of documentation" is described in *Discipline and Punish* (1975) as a coercive instrument of normalization, it is rehabilitated at the beginning of *The Use of Pleasure*, in which writing about the self is seen as a "kind of curiosity" that "enables one to get free of oneself." The philosophical essay, Foucault notes, may serve as a kind of confession. . . . It is tempting to think that the hinge for this sonnet-like turn in Foucault's thinking about writing occurred with the passage in *The History of Sexuality* in which resistance was for the first time situated within power. At that point, writing became conceivable as both an instrument of and an opposition to power—as a resistance, a means of self-immobilization and of liberation, figured now in terms of detachment rather than freedom. From this point on, writing's power is bound up with its capacity to remove the subject from the world and even from itself, to achieve an exhilarating weightlessness. . . .

Just as Nietzsche had begun by attacking the delusions of the ascetic ideal and ended by praising the honesty of that very ideal, so now Foucault, the most trenchant modern critic of the ascetic denial of body-pleasures, advances, in this text and in others more recent, ascetic practices precisely as means of securing a complex species of pleasure. Nietzsche resisted the consolations of ideality, and Foucault the control and normalization of the subject; but as resistances, both gestures were implicated in a larger ascesis, at which they both eventually arrived. They arrived not despite their resistances but through them, as a reward for their own rigor. The task "of our days," Foucault said in a late essay on "The Subject and Power," "is not to discover what we are but to refuse what we are." A task for all days, and yet a hopeless assignment; for on this "distinctively ascetic planet" (to recall Nietzsche's phrase), this refusal is what we are.

Letter to a Japanese Friend

JACQUES DERRIDA

Dear Professor Izutsu,

At our last meeting I promised you some schematic and preliminary reflections on the word "deconstruction." What we discussed were prolegomena to a possible translation of this word into Japanese, one which would at least try to avoid, if *possible,* a negative determination of its significations or connotations. The question would be therefore what deconstruction is not, or rather *ought* not to be.

I underline these words "possible" and "ought." For if the difficulties of translation can be anticipated (and the question of deconstruction is also through and through the question of translation, and of the language of concepts, of the conceptual corpus of so-called Western metaphysics), one should not begin by naively believing that the word "deconstruction" corresponds in French to some clear and univocal signification. . . .

When I choose this word, or when it imposed itself upon me—I think it was in *Of Grammatology*—I little thought it would be credited with such a central role in the discourse that interested me at the time. Among other things I wished to translate and adapt to my own ends the Heideggerian word *Destruktion* or *Abbau*. Each signified in this context an operation bearing on the structure or traditional architecture of the fundamental concepts of ontology or of Western metaphysics. But in French "destruction" too obviously implied an annihilation or a negative reduction much closer perhaps to Nietzschean "demolition" than to the Heideggerian interpretation or to the type of reading that I proposed. So I ruled that out. . . .

All the same, and in spite of appearances, deconstruction is neither an analysis nor a critique and its translation would have to take that into consideration. It is not an analysis in particular because the dismantling of a structure is not a regression toward a simple element, toward an indissoluble origin. These values, like that of analysis, are themselves philosophemes subject to deconstruction. No more is it a critique, in a general sense or in a Kantian sense. The instance of *krinein* or of *krisis* (decision, choice, judgment, discernment) is itself, as is all the apparatus of transcendental critique, one of the essential "themes" or "objects" of deconstruction.

I would say the same about method. Deconstruction is not a method and cannot be transformed into one. Especially if the technical and procedural significations of the words are stressed. It is true that in certain circles (university or cultural, especially in the United States) the technical and methodological "metaphor" that seems necessarily attached to the very word "deconstruction" has been able to seduce or lead astray. Hence the debate that has developed in these circles: Can deconstruction become a methodology for reading and for interpretation? Can it thus let itself be reappropriated and domesticated by academic institutions?

It is not enough to say that deconstruction could not be reduced to some methodological instrumentality or to a set of rules and transposable procedures. Nor will it do to claim that each deconstructive "event" remains singular or, in any case, as close as possible to something like an idiom or a signature. It must also be made clear that deconstruction is not even an

Reprinted from Jacques Derrida, "Letter to a Japanese Friend," A Derrida Reader: Between the Blinds, trans. David Wood and Andrew Benjamin (New York: Columbia University Press, 1998, pp. 270–276).

act or an operation. Not only because there would be something "patient" or "passive" about it (as Blanchot says, more passive than passivity, than the passivity that is opposed to activity). Not only because it does not return to an individual or collective subject who would take the initiative and apply it to an object, a text, a theme, etc. Deconstruction takes place, it is an event that does not await the deliberation, consciousness, or organization of a subject, or even of modernity. It *deconstructs it-self*. It can be deconstructed. . . . The "it" [ça] is not here an impersonal thing that is opposed to some egological subjectivity. . . .

If deconstruction takes place everywhere it [ça] takes place, where there is something (and is not therefore limited to meaning or to the text in the current and bookish sense of the word), we still have to think through what is happening in our world, in modernity, at the time when deconstruction is becoming a motif, with its word, its privileged themes, its mobile strategy, etc. I have no simple and formalizable response to this question. All my essays are attempts to have it out with this formidable question. They are modest symptoms of it, quite as much as tentative interpretations. I would not even dare to say, following a Heideggerian schema, that we are in an "epoch" of being-in-deconstruction, of a being-in-deconstruction that would manifest or dissimulate itself at one and the same time in other "epochs." This thought of "epochs" and especially that of a gathering of the destiny of being and of the unity of its destination or its dispersions (*Schicken, Geschick*) will never be very convincing.

To be very schematic I would say that the difficulty of defining and therefore also of translating the word "deconstruction" stems from the fact that all the predicates, all the defining concepts, all the lexical significations, and even the syntactic articulations, which seem at one moment to lend themselves to this definition or to that translation, are also deconstructed or

deconstructible, directly or otherwise, etc. And that goes for the word, the very unity of the word deconstruction, as for every word. *Of Grammatology* questioned the unity "word" and all the privileges with which it was credited, especially in its nominal form. It is therefore only a discourse or rather a writing that can make up for the incapacity of the word to be equal to a "thought." All sentences of the type "deconstruction is X" or "deconstruction is not X" *a priori* miss the point, which is to say that they are at least false. As you know, one of the principal things at stake in what is called in my texts "deconstruction" is precisely the delimiting of ontology and above all of the third person present indicative: S is P.

The word "deconstruction," like all other words, acquires its value only from its inscription in a chain of possible substitutions, in what is too blithely called a "context." For me, for what I have tried and still try to write, the word has interest only within a certain context, where it replaces and lets itself be determined by such other words as "écriture," "trace," "differance," "supplement," "hymen," "pharmakon," "marge," "entame," "parergon," etc. By definition, the list can never be closed, and I have cited only names, which is inadequate and done only for reasons of economy. In fact, I should have cited the sentences and the interlinking of sentences which in their turn determine these names in some of my texts.

What deconstruction is not? everything of course!

What is deconstruction? nothing of course!

I do not think, for all these reasons, that it is a good word [*un bon mot*]. It is certainly not elegant [*beau*]. It has definitely been of service in a highly determined situation. In order to know what has been imposed upon it in a chain of possible substitutions, despite its essential imperfection, this "highly determined situation" will need to be analyzed and deconstructed. This is difficult and I am not going to do it here.

From *Religion*

JACQUES DERRIDA

RELIGION, IN THE SINGULAR? Response: "Religion is the response." Is it not there, perhaps, that we must seek the beginning of a response? Assuming, that is, that one knows what responding means, and also responsibility. Assuming, that is, that one knows it—and believes in it. No response, indeed, without a principle of responsibility: one must respond to the other, before the other and for oneself. And no responsibility without a given word, a sworn faith <*foi jurée*>, without a pledge, without an oath, without some sacrament. . . . Before even envisaging the semantic history of testimony, of oaths, of the given word (a genealogy and interpretation that are indispensable to whomever hopes to think religion under its proper or secularized forms), before even recalling that some sort of "I promise the truth" is always at work, and some sort of "I make this commitment before the other from the moment that I address him, even and perhaps above all to commit perjury," we must formally take note of the fact that we are already speaking Latin. We make a point of this in order to recall that the world today speaks Latin (most often via Anglo-American) when it authorizes itself in the name of religion. Presupposed at the origin of all address, coming from the other *to whom it is also addressed,* the wager <*gageure*> of a sworn promise, taking immediately God as its witness, cannot not but have already, if one can put it this way, engendered God quasi-mechanically. *A priori* ineluctable, a descent of God *ex machina* would stage a transcendental addressing machine. One would thus have begun by posing, retrospectively, the absolute right of ante-

riority, the absolute "birthright" . . . of a One who is not born. For in taking God as witness, even when he is not named in the most "secular" <*laïque*> pledge of commitment, the oath cannot not produce, invoke or convoke him as already there, and therefore as unengendered and unengenderable, prior to being itself: unproducible. And absent in place. Production and reproduction of the unproducible absent in place. Everything begins with the presence of that absence. The "deaths of God," before Christianity, in it and beyond it, are only figures and episodes. The unengenderable thus re-engendered is the empty place. Without God, no absolute witness. No absolute witness to be taken as witness in testifying. But with God, a God that is present, the existence of a third (*terstis, testis*) that is absolute, all attestation becomes superfluous, insignificant or secondary. Testimony, which is to say, testament as well. In the irrepressible invoking of a witness, God would remain then one name of the witness, he would be called as witness, thus named, even if sometimes the named of this name remains unpronounceable, indeterminable, in short: unnameable in his very name; and even if he ought to remain absent, non-existent, and above all, in every sense of the word, unproducible. God: the witness as "nameable-unnameable," present-absent witness of every oath or of every possible pledge. As long as one supposes . . . that religion has the slightest relation to what we thus call God, it would pertain not only to the general history of nomination, but, more strictly here, under its name of religion to a history of the *sacramentum* and of the *testimonium*. It would be this history, it would merge with it. On the boat that brought us from Naples to Capri, I told myself that I would begin by recalling this sort of too luminous evidence, but I did not dare. I also told myself, silently, that one would blind oneself to the phenomenon called "of religion" or of the "return of the religious" today if one continued to oppose so naively Reason and Religion, Critique or Science and Religion, technoscientific Modernity and Religion. Supposing that what was at stake was to understand, would one understand anything about "what's-going-on-today-in-the-world-with-religion" (and why "in the world"? What is the "world"? What does such a presupposition involve? etc.) if one continues to believe in this opposition, even in this incompatibility, which is to say, if one remains within a certain tradition of the Enlightenment. . . . It would be necessary to demonstrate, which would not be simple, that religion and reason have the same source. . . . Religion and reason develop in tandem, drawing from this common resource: the testimonial pledge of every performative, committing it to respond as much before the other as for the high-performance performativity of technoscience. The same unique source divides itself mechanically, automatically, and sets itself reactively in opposition to itself: whence the two sources in one. This reactivity is a process of *sacrificial indemnification,* it strives to restore the unscathed (*heilig*) that it itself threatens. And it is also the possibility of the two, of n+1, the same possibility as that of the *testimonial deus ex machina.* As for the response, it is *either or. Either* it addresses the absolute other as such, with an address that is understood, heard, respected faithfully and responsibly; or it retorts, retaliates, compensates and *indemnifies itself* in the war of resentment and of reactivity. One of the two responses ought always to be able to contaminate the other. It will never be proven whether it is the one or the other, never in an act of determining, theoretical or cognitive judgement. This might be the place and the respon-

sibility of what is called belief, trustworthiness or fidelity, the fiduciary, "trust" <*la "fiance">* in general, the tribunal <*instance*> of faith.

But we are already speaking Latin. For the Capri meeting, the "theme" I believed myself constrained to propose, religion, was named in Latin, let us never forget it. Does not "the question of *religio,*" however, quite simply merge, one could say, with the question of Latin? By which should be understood, beyond a "question of language and of culture," the strange phenomenon of Latinity and of its globalization. We are not speaking here of universality, even of an idea of universality, only of a process of universalization that is finite but enigmatic. It is rarely investigated in its geopolitical and ethico-juridical scope, precisely where such a power finds itself overtaken, deployed, its paradoxical heritage revived by the global and still irresistible hegemony of a "language," which is to say, also of a culture that in part is not Latin but Anglo-American. For everything that touches religion in particular, for everything that speaks "religion," for whoever speaks religiously or about religion, Anglo-American remains Latin. Religion circulates in the world, one might say, like an English word . . . that has been to Rome and taken a detour to the United States. Well beyond its strictly capitalist or politico-military figures, a hyper-imperialist appropriation has been underway now for centuries. It imposes itself in a particularly palpable manner within the conceptual apparatus of international law and of global political rhetoric. Wherever this apparatus dominates, it articulates itself through a discourse on religion. From here on, the word "religion" is calmly (and violently) applied to things which have always been and remain foreign to what this word names and arrests in its history. The same remark could apply to many other words, for the entire "religious vocabulary" beginning with "cult," "faith," "belief," "sacred," "holy," "saved," "unscathed" (*heilig*). But by ineluctable contagion, no semantic cell can remain alien, I dare not say "safe and sound," "unscathed," in this apparently borderless process. *Globalatinization* (essentially Christian, to be sure), this word names a unique event to which a metalanguage seems incapable of acceding, although such a language remains, all the same, of the greatest necessity here. For at the same time that we no longer perceive its limits, we know that such globalization is finite and only projected. What is involved here is a Latinization and, rather than globality, a globalization that is running out of breath <*essoufflée*>, however irresistible and imperial it still may be. What are we to think of this running out of breath? Whether it holds a future or is held in store for it, we do not know and by definition cannot know. But at the bottom of such non-knowing, this expiring breath is blasting the ether of the world. Some breathe there better than others, some are stifled. The war of religions deploys itself there in its element, but also under a protective stratum that threatens to burst. The co-extensiveness of the two questions (religion and worldwide Latinization) marks the dimensions of what henceforth cannot be reduced to a question of language, culture, semantics, nor even, without doubt, to one of anthropology or of history. **And what if religio remained untranslatable?** No *religio* without *sacramentum*, without alliance and promise of testifying truthfully to the truth, which is to say, to speak the truth: that is to say, to begin with, no religion without the promise of keeping one's promise to tell the truth—and to have already told it!—in the very act of promising. To have already told it, *veritas*, in Latin, and thus to consider it told. The event to come has already taken place. The promise promises itself, it is already promised, that is the sworn faith, the given word, and hence the response. *Religio* would begin there. . . .

But religion does not follow the movement of faith any necessarily than the latter rushes towards faith in God. For if the concept of "religion" implies an institution that is separa-

ble, identifiable, circumscribable, tied through its letter to the Roman *ius,* its essential relation both to faith and to God is anything but self-evident. When we speak, **we Europeans,** so ordinarily and so confusedly today about a "return of the religious," what do we thereby name? To what do we refer? The "religious," the religiosity that is vaguely associated with the experience of the sacredness of the divine, of the holy, of the saved or of the unscathed (*heilig*)—is it religion? In what and to what extent does a "sworn faith," a belief have to be *committed* or *engaged*? Inversely, not every sworn faith, given word, trustworthiness, trust or confidence in general is necessarily inscribed in a "religion," even if the latter does mark the convergence of two experiences that are generally held to be equally religious:

1. the experience of belief, on the one hand (believing or credit, the fiduciary or the trustworthy in the act of faith, fidelity, the appeal to blind confidence, the testimonial that is always beyond proof, demonstrative reason, intuition); and

2. the experience of the unscathed, of *sacredness* or of *holiness*, on the other?

These two veins (or two strata or two sources) of the religious should be distinguished from one another. They can doubtless be associated with each other and certain of their possible co-implications analysed, but they should never be confused or reduced to one another as is almost always done. In principle, it is possible to sanctify, to sacralize the unscathed or to maintain oneself *in the presence* of the sacrosanct in various ways without bringing into play an act of belief, if at least belief, faith or fidelity signifies here acquiescing to the testimony of the other—of the *utterly other* who is inaccessible in its absolute source. And there where every other is utterly other. . . . Conversely, if it carries beyond the presence of what would offer itself to be seen, touched, proven, the acquiescence of trust still does not in itself necessarily involve the sacred. . . .

Religion today allies itself with tele-techno-science, to which it reacts with all its forces. It is, on the one hand, globalization; it produces, weds, exploits the capital and knowledge of tele-mediatization: neither the trips and global spectacularizing of the Pope, nor the interstate dimensions of the "Rushdie affair," nor planetary terrorism would otherwise be possible, at this rhythm and we could multiply such indications *ad infinitum*. But, *on the other hand,* it reacts immediately, *simultaneously,* declaring war against that which gives it this new power only at the cost of dislodging it from all its proper places, *in truth from place itself,* from the *taking-place* of its truth. It conducts a terrible war against that which protects it only by threatening it, according to this double and contradictory structure: immunitary and autoimmunitary. The relation between these two motions or these two sources is ineluctable, and therefore automatic and mechanical, between one which has the form of the machine (mechanization, automatization, machination or *mechane*), and the other, that of living spontaneity, of the *unscathed* property of life, that is to say, of another (claimed) self-determination. But the auto-immunitary haunts the community and its system of immunitary survival like the hyperbole of its own possibility. Nothing in *common,* nothing immune, safe and sound, *heilig* and holy, nothing unscathed in the most autonomous living present without a risk of auto-immunity. As always, the risk charges itself twice, the same finite risk. Two times rather than one: with a menace and with a chance. In two words, it must take charge of—one could also say: take in trust—the *possibility* of that radical evil without which good would be for nothing. . . .

Religion, as a response that is both ambiguous and ambivalent, . . . is thus an ellipsis: the ellipsis of sacrifice. Is a religion imaginable without sacrifice and without prayer? The sign through which Heidegger believes ontotheology can be recognized is when the relation to the absolute Being or to the supreme Cause has freed itself of both, thereby losing access to sacrificial offering no less than to prayer. But there as well, two sources: the divided law, the *double bind,* also the dual foci, the ellipsis or originary duplicity of religion, consists therein, that the law of the unscathed, the salvation of the safe, the humble respect of that which is sacrosanct (*heilig,* holy) *both requires and excludes sacrifice,* which is to say, the indemnification of the unscathed, the price of immunity. Hence: auto-immunization and the sacrifice of sacrifice. The latter always represents the same movement, the price to pay for not injuring or wronging the absolute other. **Violence** of sacrifice in the name of non-violence. Absolute respect enjoins first and foremost sacrifice of self, of one's most precious interest. If Kant speaks of the "holiness" of the moral law, it is while explicitly holding a discourse on "sacrifice," which is to say, on another instantiation of religion "within the limits of reason *alone*": the Christian religion as the only "moral" religion. Self-sacrifice thus sacrifices the most proper in the service of the most proper. As though *pure* reason, in a process of auto-immune indemnification, could only oppose religion as such to a religion or pure faith to this or that belief.

In our "wars of religion," violence has two ages. The one, already discussed above, appears "contemporary," in sync or in step with the hypersophistication of military tele-technology—of "digital" and cyberspaced culture. The other is a "new archaic violence," if one can put it that way. It counters the first and everything it represents. Revenge. Resorting, in fact, to the same resources of mediatic power, it *reverts* (according to the return, the resource, the repristination and the law of internal and auto-immune reactivity we are trying to formalize here) as closely as possible to the body proper and to the premachinal living being. In any case, to its desire and to its phantasm. Revenge is taken against the decorporalizing and expropriating machine by resorting—reverting—to bare hands, to the sexual organs or to primitive tools, often to weapons other than firearms (l' arme blanche'). What is referred to as "killings" and "atrocities"—words never used in "clean" or "proper" wars, where, precisely, the dead are no longer counted (guided or "intelligent" missiles directed at entire cities, for instance)—is here supplanted by tortures, beheadings and mutilations of all sorts. What is involved is always avowed vengeance, often declared as sexual revenge: rapes, mutilated genitals or severed hands, corpses exhibited, heads paraded, as not so long ago in France, impaled on the end of stakes (phallic processions of "natural religions"). This is the case, for example, but it is only an example, in Algeria today, in the name of Islam, invoked by both belligerent parties, each in its own way. These are also symptoms of a reactive and negative recourse, the vengeance of the body proper against an expropriatory and delocalizing tele-technoscience, identified with the globality of the market, with military-capitalistic hegemony, with the globalatinization of the European democratic model, in its double form: secular and religious. Whence—another figure of double origin the foreseeable alliance of the worst effects of fanaticism, dogmatism or irrationalist obscurantism with hypercritical acumen and incisive analysis of the hegemonies and the models of the adversary (globalatinization, religion that does not speak its name, ethnocentrism putting on, as always, a show of "universalism," market-driven science and technology, democratic rhetoric, "humanitarian" strategy or "keeping the peace" by means of peacekeeping forces, while never counting the dead of Rwanda, for instance, in the same manner as those of the United States of America or of Europe). This archaic and ostensibly more savage radicalization of "religious" violence claims, in the name

of "religion," to allow the living community to rediscover its roots, its place, its body and its idiom intact (unscathed, safe, pure, proper). It spreads death and unleashes self-destruction in a desperate (auto-immune) gesture that attacks the blood of its own body: as though thereby to eradicate uprootedness and reappropriate the sacredness of life safe and sound. Double root, double uprootedness, double eradication.

The possibility of **radical evil** both destroys and institutes the religious. Ontotheology does the same when it suspends sacrifice and prayer, the truth of this prayer that maintains itself, recalling Aristotle one more time, beyond the true and the false, beyond their opposition, in any case, according to a certain concept of truth or of judgement. Like benediction, prayer pertains to the originary regime of testimonial faith or of martyrdom that we are trying to think here in its most "critical" force. Ontotheology **encrypts** faith and destines it to the condition of a sort of Spanish Marrano who would have lost—in truth, dispersed, multiplied—everything up to and including the memory of his unique secret. Emblem of a still life: an opened pomegranate, one Passover evening, on a tray.

At the bottom without bottom of this **crypt,** the One + n incalculably engenders all these supplements. *It makes violence of itself, does violence to itself and keeps itself from the other.* The auto-immunity of religion can only indemnify itself without assignable end. On the bottom without bottom of an always virgin impassibility, *chora* of tomorrow in languages we no longer know or do not yet speak. This place is unique, it is the One without name. It *makes way, perhaps,* but without the slightest generosity, neither divine nor human. The dispersion of ashes is not even promised there, nor death given. . . .

Counterpoint:
From *Hermeneutics as Politics*

STANLEY ROSEN

Stanley Rosen is Professor of Philosophy at Boston University. He has published numerous books including the following: *Nihilism, Plato's Symposium, The Mask of Enlightenment, The Question of Being,* and *The Ancients and the Moderns.*

WHAT IS THE DIFFERENCE between speech and writing? This is the point of orientation for the extravagant discourse (spoken and written) of Jacques Derrida, the most prominent contemporary opponent of the Enlightenment. In his dispensation of darkness, Derrida is a paradigm for a multitude of lesser antiluminaries. One cannot quite say that they shine in his reflected brilliance without sacrificing what I believe is a valid metaphor. Perhaps it would be better to think of Derrida's disciples as consequences of what he himself calls "the trace." To quote the master: "the trace is in effect the absolute origin of sense in general. But this amounts to saying, once more, that there is no absolute origin of sense in general. The trace is the *différance* that opens appearance and signification."[1]

To say that sense originates in *différance* is still something of a euphemism, since what in fact originates is an endless sequence of signifiers. The trace, or *différance,* is a kind of postontological yet fecund *nihil,* or a posttheistic version of what Hegel called "the terrible labor of the negative." In a word, for Derrida, it is not God who illuminates the darkness, but the darkness that produces such light as there is. So too, at least in the United States, Derrida spawns his progeny, ostensibly opposed by the last vestiges of analytical philosophy, but at a deeper level strengthened by their common heritage in the conception of ontology as grammatology.

"Deconstruction" is then like calling to like, or a radical secularization of destiny. . . .

Socrates encourages the madness of a silent and direct approach to the Ideas; indeed, he refers to this erotic ascent as "divine madness." We shall look carefully at the details of this encouragement later; I hope thereby to show that Derrida's central insight into Plato is also a profound (and therefore fruitful) misunderstanding. Speech is a consequence of whatever success we may obtain through divine madness; it is not the medium of that success. To anticipate, Derrida is quite mistaken to associate speech in Plato with a metaphysics of presence and to infer from this association an ontological meaning in Socrates' criticism of writing. Speech, more specifically human, speech, is as much a mark of absence as is writing. Derrida fails to appreciate the significance of the fact that logos means neither speech nor writing in Plato's vocabulary and hence that it can be used in a secondary sense for either the one or the other. The distinction between speech and writing that Derrida finds in Plato (although, as we shall see, he also denies that it is there) is imposed onto the text by a contemporary or post-Kantian incapacity to detach oneself from language, from the sign as signifier, not of a being (to say nothing of Being), but of another signifier.

The man of religious faith regards it as madness to attempt to become a god. The pagan philosophers, especially those of the Socratic school, thought otherwise. To the Hebrew at least, speech (Torah) is the certain sign of the presence and absence of God, and hence of the difference between creator and created. It is this speech that enforces the distinction between writing (commentary on Torah) and scribbling (philosophy and postphilosophical deconstruction). To the pagan philosopher, certainly to the Socrates of Derrida's prooftext, the *Phaedrus,* the crucial difference between speech and writing is political, not ontological. Nevertheless, the distinction between speech and writing has something to do with the philosophical inversion of the religious interpretation of madness. At the risk of seeming to propound a paradox, I want to maintain that human speech is superior to human writing because it is closer to silence. (The reason for the qualifying "human" will appear shortly.) By this I mean two things. First, in addressing human beings, as Socrates points out in the *Phaedrus,* the speaker knows when to keep silent, whereas writings do not. Second, writing is "garrulous" precisely for the reason that Derrida prefers it to speech. Writing, as it were, cannot stop talking, because, as the "trace" of absence, it has no idea where it is, and in fact as detached from the guidance of speech, it is *nowhere*. But this is not to support the thesis that the excellence of speech is to keep talking in the illumination of the presence of Being. Speech is the living presence, not of Being, but of the speaker to himself, of intellect or *Geist,* not of form. And *Geist* is accessible to itself only as myth: so at least Socrates teaches us in the *Phaedrus*. If I, as the "receptivity" of form that must be formally indeterminate, am present to myself as speech, then speech is "formally" the presence of absence. . . .

To come back to Derrida after this necessary digression, that he is not a genuine Talmudist follows trivially from the fact that he is not a Jew, not in the sense of Levinas. For Derrida, the partisan of original finitude, of the origin as differentiation, hence of an infinite sequence of finite writings, it is indeed the case that nothing

has occurred before writing. There is no life antecedent to writing. As Derrida another text, "Life must be thought of as trace before Being may be determined as presence."[2] However, he is also not a genuine Socratic, not because he rejects or deconstructs Platonism, understood as the metaphysics of presence, but because he does not know that this has already been done by Plato, with the assistance of a Socrates grown young and beautiful.[3] And this in turn, I suspect, is because he has been prevented by the legacy of Nietzsche, Freud, and Heidegger from following the Socratic maxim: "know thyself." He has mistaken this maxim as an injunction to ontological epistemology, or the reification of being. Derrida, who apparently identifies the self with the modern doctrine of subjectivity, which he believes himself to have deconstructed, has on his account, no self. As a consequence, he has no knowledge. . . .

Derrida does not make these distinctions. Despite his often extraordinary eye for the significant detail, not to mention his exorbitant taste for the superfluous complexity, Derrida's deconstructive hermeneutics is not attentive to the written text in its own terms, largely because he denies the significance of the author's intention. Instead, he hurries to identify Thamus, "the king who speaks," with the (ontological) *father* who rejects his son, or the offering of his son; "the father suspects and always supervises writing."[4] From here it is an easy step "to the permanence of a Platonic scheme that assigns the origin and the power of speech [*parole*], and precisely of *logos,* to the paternal position." For Derrida, this is a "structural constraint" by which "platonism" (behind which hides Plato), "which imposes all of Western metaphysics in its conceptuality," has transmitted the ambiguous understanding of writing as a *pharmakon:* a remedy that is also a poison. . . .

It follows that the aforementioned reversal is not a self-contradiction but a signal of complexity. Using Derrida's own expression, but not his intention (and on Derridean grounds, his own intention is irrelevant), writing that takes place within a problematic of truth" is, when viewed from the exterior (from the prespective of a god), not, the writing-down of "truth" in the pejorative sense but poetic speech that provides an interpretation of the "everyday" or "pretheoretical" world, and so that constitutes the intelligible cosmos, but not, to repeat an earlier warning, in the sense of the Kantian transcendental ego. . . .

Talmudic hermeneutics is not philology. We shall state our conclusion in the middle, in good Talmudic form. What, then, is the difference between speech and writing? Answer: none, or in other words, silence.

Otherwise put, speech and writing differentiate silence: they are the origin of difference, and hence of *différance*. Derrida, of course, believes the contrary, because, like all linguistic (post-) ontologists, he takes language or writing to be its own origin. Posthuman writing originates in nothing: "if writing is secondary at this point, nothing, however, has occurred before it."[5] Divine writing of the Hebraic kind is the same as speech; it produces the world. Platonic writing interprets the world as a cosmos. . . .

Derrida does not understand that his own account of the "reversal" in the Socratic argument, together with the ensuing restriction of the criticism to didactic writing, limits the scope or significance of his own deconstruction of the ostensible Platonic preference for speech. He understands that speech is already a mark of absence but not that this is precisely why Socrates defines speech in terms of writing. Hence he does not understand (despite his evasive use of "platonism") that *there is no metaphysics of Presence in Plato*. In the alternative formulation, there is no ontology in Plato, because Plato regards ontology as impossible. What we find instead is a daydream, couched in a mixture of mathematical and poetic rhetoric, of ontology; better, we find a rhetorical praise of eidetic phenomenology. Let us see how this is done.

Derrida has two main theses. The first is that Plato prefers speech to writing. The second is that this preference is deconstructed by the exigency of *différance*. Derrida is presumably not especially impressed by the principle of noncontradiction. We philologists, nevertheless, must insist that the second thesis is contradicted by his admission that Plato does not criticize writing *tout court*, but a certain kind of writing. Now (sic) let us move backward to the first thesis, assisted by our interpretation of the second, which illuminates, rather than follows from or explains, the first.

According to the first thesis, writing, the favorite son of *différance*, is the hand of Esau within Jacob's coat. In Derrida's own terms, for Plato, speech is preferable to writing because it is fully alive, invigorated by the ontological sun, hence present to the truth as presence, as *eidos* or visible form. On the other hand, the dialogues show that "any *full, absolute* presence of what is . . . is impossible." Even further, the *Sophist* supports the conclusion that "if truth is the presence of the *eidos,* it must always, on pain of mortal blinding by the sun's fires, come to terms with relation, nonpresence, and thus nontruth."[6] Stated with maximum concision, Derrida holds that language dilutes or conceals presence with absence. The Platonic dialogues, thanks to "the absolute invisibility of the origin of the visible," are "a structure of replacements such that all presences will be supplements substituted for the absent origin."[7] . . .

In the *Phaedrus,* Socrates says that the soul is mantic, and prophecy is associated with Eros at the beginning of the Stesichorean myth.[8] But there is an ambiguity in the nature of prophecy that turns upon the relation of speech to silence, which becomes the fundamental opposition as soon as we grant the intrinsic sameness of writing and speech. Derrida never sees this, because for him, the primordial nature of writing makes silence impossible. And this is why there can be no difference in Derrida between writing and reading. Derrida cannot read at all, because reading requires a moment of silence in which we *see* the text. For Derrida, however, seeing is already writing; hence reading is a displacing or rendering absent of the text. It is the replacement of the absent original by another, different text, which is in its turn implicitly absent, implicitly replaceable, but *never legible*. Derridean writing thus becomes a satire on Eros, which is continuously changing its shape. Yet the Derridean soul, because of the absence of a divine gift, is neither erotic nor mantic. His madness (if that is the right term) is postmodern, hence neither divine nor human.

Prophetic or divine madness originates in vision and silence. This is why the soul is almost entirely silent in the ascent to the hyperuranian beings, and the exception proves the rule. Conversation occurs between the mythical parts of the soul only when they debate whether or not to have sexual intercourse with a beautiful youth.[9] At the same time, prophetic vision produces speech: the discourse of revelation, as spoken to us, via Phaedrus, by Socrates. The vision is instantaneous;[10] in the imagery of the *Phaedrus,* it punctuates the moments of the revolution of cosmic genesis. The speech, however, is temporal; perhaps one could say that it is human temporality as such. The Platonic dia-logues, then, are indeed "texts," that is, a web of speech and silence, but as speeches, they are artifactual phantasms of the truth, produced in the full seriousness of divine play and requiring "correction" by the reader through the use of the laws of psychic perspective, or in other words, through an erotic hermeneutic.

NOTES

1. *De la grammatologie* (Paris: Editions de Minuit, 1967), p. 95.

2. "Freud and the Scene of Writing," in *Writing and Difference,* p. 203.

3. *Epistolae* B, 314c1–3.

4. "Pharmacie," p. 86.

5. "Violence and Metaphysics: An Essay on Emmanuel Levinas," in *Writing and Difference,* tr. A. Bass (Chicago: Univeristy of Chicago Press, 1978), pp. 102–03.

6. "Pharmacie," p. 192.

7. Ibid., p. 193.

8. *Phaedrus,* 274c1, 244a–5ff.

9. Ibid., 254a–3ff.

10. *Symposium* 21oe3–5.

Index